No. 4.

PROFESSIONAL PAPERS

OF THE

CORPS OF TOPOGRAPHICAL ENGINEERS,

UNITED STATES ARMY.

PUBLISHED BY AUTHORITY OF THE WAR DEPARTMENT.

BUREAU OF TOPOGRAPHICAL ENGINEERS.

1861.

REPORT

UPON

THE PHYSICS AND HYDRAULICS

OF

THE MISSISSIPPI RIVER;

UPON THE

PROTECTION OF THE ALLUVIAL REGION AGAINST OVERFLOW;

AND UPON THE

DEEPENING OF THE MOUTHS:

BASED UPON

SURVEYS AND INVESTIGATIONS

MADE UNDER THE ACTS OF CONGRESS DIRECTING THE TOPOGRAPHICAL AND HYDROGRAPHICAL SURVEY OF THE DELTA OF THE MISSISSIPPI RIVER, WITH SUCH INVESTIGATIONS AS MIGHT LEAD TO DETERMINE THE MOST PRACTICABLE PLAN FOR SECURING IT FROM INUNDATION, AND THE BEST MODE OF DEEPENING THE CHANNELS AT THE MOUTHS OF THE RIVER.

Submitted to the Bureau of Topographical Engineers, War Department, 1861.

PREPARED BY

CAPTAIN A. A. HUMPHREYS

AND

LIEUT. H. L. ABBOT,

CORPS OF TOPOGRAPHICAL ENGINEERS, UNITED STATES ARMY.

CONTENTS.

CHAPTER I.

BASIN OF THE MISSISSIPPI RIVER.

CHAPTER II.

THE MISSISSIPPI RIVER BELOW THE JUNCTION OF THE MISSOURI.

CHAPTER III.

STATE OF THE SCIENCE OF HYDRAULICS AS APPLIED TO RIVERS.

CHAPTER IV.

METHOD OF GAUGING THE MISSISSIPPI, ITS TRIBUTARIES, AND ITS CREVASSES.

CHAPTER V.

EXPERIMENTAL THEORY OF WATER IN MOTION; NEW LAWS, FORMULÆ, ETC.

CHAPTER VI.

PROTECTION AGAINST THE FLOODS OF THE MISSISSIPPI.

CHAPTER VII.

DELTA OF THE MISSISSIPPI.

CHAPTER VIII.

MOUTHS OF THE MISSISSIPPI.

APPENDICES.

APPENDIX A.

SURVEY OF THE MOUTHS OF THE MISSISSIPPI BY CAPTAIN TALCOTT, IN 1838.

APPENDIX B.

DAILY GAUGE REGISTERS.

APPENDIX C.

CROSS-SECTIONS OF THE MISSISSIPPI AND OF ITS BRANCHES.

APPENDIX D.

CURRENT-MEASUREMENTS UPON THE MISSISSIPPI AND ITS BRANCHES.

APPENDIX E.

DAILY DISCHARGE AT VELOCITY STATIONS.

APPENDIX F.

SECTIONS OF MISSISSIPPI SWAMP LANDS.

APPENDIX G.

CURRENT-MEASUREMENTS AT THE SOUTHWEST PASS.

LIST OF PLATES.

LETTER OF CAPTAIN A. A. HUMPHREYS,

CORPS OF TOPOGRAPHICAL ENGINEERS,

TRANSMITTING THE

REPORT TO THE BUREAU OF TOPOGRAPHICAL ENGINEERS.

MAJOR HARTMAN BACHE,

CORPS OF TOPOGRAPHICAL ENGINEERS,

IN CHARGE OF BUREAU OF TOPOGRAPHICAL ENGINEERS,

WAR DEPARTMENT, WASHINGTON.

OFFICE OF THE MISSISSIPPI DELTA SURVEY,
WASHINGTON, *August* 5, 1861.

SIR:—

UNDER the act of Congress directing the Topographical and Hydrographical Survey of the Delta of the Mississippi river, with such Investigations as might lead to determine the most Practicable Plan for securing it from Inundation, a Board, consisting of Lieutenant-Colonel S. H. Long, Topographical Engineers, and myself, was organized in November, 1850, and directed to examine the river with a view to decide upon the character and extent of the surveys required. It was further ordered that, the duty of the Board being completed and a report thereon being made, I should take the direction of the work.

Preliminary Board.

In accordance with those instructions, the report of the Board was made from Napoleon, Arkansas, December 18, 1850. That report was communicated to Congress and printed in Senate Ex. Doc. No. 13, 31st Congress, 2d Session. The field of survey and investigation by measurement, as enlarged by authority of the Bureau of Topographical Engineers in the following spring, extended from the head of the alluvial region at Cape Girardeau to the gulf of Mexico. At a still later date, the investigations were authorized to include within their scope the best mode of deepening the channels at the mouths of the river, an object which had been likewise contemplated in the original appropriation act.

Three parties organized.

That act required a topographical and hydrographical survey of the delta of the Mississippi to be made in connection with the investigations; and in execution of the plan of operations laid down in the report of the Board of December 18, 1850, three parties were at once organized to determine the topography, hydrography, and hydrometry of the alluvial region. Fortunately for the objects of the Survey, the succeeding high water proved to be a flood of a peculiar character.

The topographical party.

The topographical party in charge of Mr. James K. Ford, assisted by Mr. Joseph Bennett, Mr. W. Thornton Thompson, Mr. George F. Fuller, and Mr. Samuel Hill, made a minute topographical survey of the Mississippi river, extending from one mile above Routh's point to one mile below the Barataria-canal locks, just above New Orleans, collecting at the same time information concerning the crevasses of former years, old flood-marks, the history of levee construction, the dimensions of levees, well authenticated changes in the banks of the river, etc. etc. Owing to the high stage of the river, and the consequent inaccessibility of the east bank between the foot of the Raccourci cut-off and a point one mile above Baton Rouge, that portion was omitted. The Survey included the mouth of Red river, the heads of bayous Atchafalaya, Plaquemine, and La Fourche, and numerous off-set lines—among them one from Carrollton to the mouth of the new Canal, lake Pontchartrain. It comprised carefully determined lines of level throughout. The maps of Captain Campbell Graham and of Captain G. W. Hughes, Topographical Engineers, accompanying their reports upon the Military Reconnoissance of the Approaches to New Orleans, and those of Captain A. Talcott of the Mouths and Passes of the River, afford sufficient data for any general purposes connected with the river for the remainder of its course from Carrollton to the gulf.

The hydrographical party.

The hydrographical party was placed in charge of Mr. G. Castor Smith, aided by Mr. James O'Rourke* and Mr. Otto Sackersdorff, and subsequently by Mr. Joseph Gorlinski. Its operations included the measurement of sets of cross-sections of the Mississippi at Routh's point, at Red-river landing, in the Raccourci cut-off, at Raccourci bend, at Baton Rouge, at site of Bonnet-Carré crevasse, at Carrollton and above and below that locality, and of sets of cross-sections of the mouth of Red-river, of Old-Red river bend, and of the heads of bayous Atchafalaya, Plaquemine, and La Fourche. In each set of cross-sections, the velocity of the current was measured—in some instances, with great elaboration. The nature of the material pushed along at the bottom of the river was examined from time to time. The operations of this party were greatly impeded and interrupted by the high water. It was intended that it should make an accurate, detailed hydrographic survey of the river from the mouth of Red river to New Orleans; but this—from the difficulties encountered in the strength of the current, the great depth of the river, and the cli-

* Mr. O'Rourke was, during the progress of the Survey, detached from this party, and, in connection with the topographical party, made the triangulations connecting the two banks of the river.

mate—was found to be impracticable without a greater expenditure of money than a proper regard for the other branches of the Survey would allow. A similar though much less elaborate survey of the bayous Atchafalaya and Plaquemine was likewise contemplated, but for a like reason was not executed.

Previous to commencing the hydrography, this party made a survey from McMaster's plantation on the Mississippi, eleven miles below New Orleans, to lake Borgne.

The topographical survey of the site of the Bonnet-Carré crevasse and vicinity, and of Carrollton and vicinity, and of the line to the mouth of the new Canal, lake Pontchartrain, were made by this party when temporarily under the charge of Lieutenant G. K. Warren, Topographical Engineers.

The hydrometrical party.

The hydrometrical party was placed in charge of Professor C. G. Forshey, assisted by Mr. William Sidney Smith and Mr. William Forshey, and—upon the cessation of the field duties of the topographical and hydrographical parties—by Mr. Thompson and Mr. O'Rourke* for brief periods. Subsequently, Mr. William H. Williams took the place of Mr. W. Forshey.

In connection with the operations of this party, gauge-rods were established in lakes Pontchartrain and Borgne, in the gulf bayou at Fort St. Philip, and—in the river—at Fort St. Philip, Carrollton, Donaldsonville, Baton Rouge, Red-river landing, Natchez, New Carthage, and Lake Providence. Most of these observations were continued for two years, and some of them longer. The gauge-observations made under the Navy Department at the Memphis Navy Yard were relied upon for that position, and private gauge-observations at Napoleon and Cairo for those localities. Temporary gauge-rods were likewise observed at Berwick's bay, at Field's Mills on bayou La Fourche, and at Indian Village on bayou Plaquemine.

The chief labor of the hydrometrical party, however, was directed to the constant measurement of the velocity of the current of the Mississippi in all parts of the width and depth of the Carrollton section, in order to obtain the volume of discharge in every condition of the river throughout the period of a river year; and with a view to determine the law of change of velocity from the surface to the bottom, and from side to side; including the effect of wind; and thus to furnish the hydrometrical data for completing the determination of the laws governing the flow of water in natural channels. During a portion of the periods of high and low water, similar measurements were made upon a section of the river at Baton Rouge, in which vicinity the course of the river is nearly straight for several miles.

In connection with these operations, the amount of sedimentary matter held in suspension by the river was measured daily for two years, together with the temperature

* Zeal for the public service led Mr. O'Rourke to volunteer for this duty. The exposure necessarily attendant upon its performance brought on sickness, which proved fatal to him very soon after he rejoined the topographical party at Louisville, Kentucky.

of the river-water, and the air, etc. The character of the material pushed along the bottom was likewise examined from time to time.

Detachments from this party measured the discharge of the crevasses in the vicinity of Carrollton, the cross-sections of Berwick's bay, and of the La Fourche, at Pain Court, Thibodeaux, and Field's Mills, and ran a line of levels from the high-water mark of the Mississippi, at McMaster's plantation, to the gauge-rod at Proctorsville on lake Borgne. Mr. Smith's lines of cross-section, at Carrollton, were likewise re-sounded by this party in low water, 1851.

It also made experiments upon the velocities of the current from the surface to the bottom at the mouths of the Mississippi, both in the high and low stages of the river, sounded the bars, and determined by measurement the advance of that of the Southwest pass.

Results of the operations of these parties.

The results of the labors of all these parties enter into the most important deductions of the Report; they will be found embodied in the chapters devoted to the subjects for which they were designed to furnish the data.

The original large-scale topographical and hydrographical maps, profiles, sections, and diagrams, and hydrometric plats and drawings, are, however, valuable for the information they convey in other connections than those they have with the problem of protection against overflow. They are therefore transmitted to the Bureau. A list of them will be found in a subsequent part of this letter.

Acknowledgments.

Professor Forshey is entitled to great credit for the zealous and intelligent manner in which he devoted himself, for many years previous to the organization of the Delta Survey, to observing and collecting facts relative to river phenomena, without aid from any source whatever; he thus accumulated a mass of valuable material, which has been available for the purposes of the Delta Survey. When it is considered how difficult and costly perfect observations are, of the character of some of those made by him as an amateur, it is a matter of surprise that so much should have been done by the unassisted enterprise of a private individual. His knowledge of the alluvial region afforded me valuable aid, and I esteemed myself fortunate in securing his services. The duties entrusted to him comprehended a great variety of subjects, some requiring the most delicately conducted experiments, and all exacting severe labor; the important results that have been deduced from these observations are evidences of the care with which they were made.

Lieutenant G. K. Warren, Topographical Engineers, established the river gauge-rods, made portions of the topographical and hydrographical surveys, prepared several of the topographical sheets, and aided in the general supervision and direction of the work, a duty which he performed in a highly intelligent manner, and which, acceptable to me at all times, was particularly so when I was almost entirely disabled by sickness.

To all the gentlemen composing the parties enumerated, acknowledgments are due for the faithful performance of difficult and arduous duties.

Interruption of the work.

While engaged in the field, in the summer of 1851, I was suddenly prostrated by sickness, which obliged me early in the following winter to relinquish the charge of the work to Lieutenant-Colonel Long, Topographical Engineers. The operations in the field were soon after entirely suspended, with the exception already stated in connection with the Carrollton work, and continued so until the fall of 1857, when, the charge of the work having been previously resumed by me, the surveys and investigations were again vigorously prosecuted.

Examination of European rivers.

During the interval, while they were in abeyance, the state of my health still rendering me unfit for duty, I sought and obtained authority to visit Europe, with instructions to examine its delta rivers, and ascertain what the experience of many centuries had really proved as to the ultimate as well as immediate effects of the different methods of protection against inundation. Such of the results of that visit as have immediate application to the Mississippi river are briefly embodied in the text of the Report.

Upon returning from Europe, in the summer of 1854, I was assigned to special service under the immediate orders of the War Department, and placed in charge of the Office organized in connection with the Explorations and Surveys, then in progress, for the Determination of the Most Practicable and Economical Route for a Railroad from the Mississippi river to the Pacific ocean. The duties thus devolved upon me prevented my giving sufficient attention to the Survey of the Delta of the Mississippi to admit of its active resumption until the autumn of 1857.

The investigations resumed.

At my request, Lieutenant Henry L. Abbot, Topographical Engineers, was then directed to report to me for duty on the Delta Survey. This request was made in order that Lieutenant Abbot might take the immediate charge of the parties of the Delta Survey under my direction, the office being established at this place. An arrangement of this kind was rendered absolutely necessary by the nature of the duties then imposed upon me. Having the general charge, under the direction of the Secretary of War, of the Explorations and Surveys for a Pacific Railroad Route, of Geographical Explorations, and of other operations in the field more or less directly connected with those, and being also a Member of the Light-house Board, I could not, with any effort, give that constant, daily, undivided attention to the Delta Survey required for its steady progress; and to remain long in the field was impossible. During the further progress of that work—in the field and office—I was besides appointed a Member of several temporary Commissions, the last of which was the Commission instituted by the 8th section of the Act of Congress of June 21, 1860, to examine into the Organization, System of Discipline, and Course of Instruction of the Military Academy.

Previous to the resumption of the field work of the Survey, Lieutenant Abbot recomputed the volumes of discharge at Carrollton from the original notes; Mr. James S. Williams, a civil engineer of high standing, carefully revised the level notes of the Survey, and deduced the results used in the Report; and Mr. George F. Fuller completed the drawing of the topographical sheets of the Survey.

Partial reduction of the results of the former field work.

As other important duties required my presence in Washington at that time, Lieutenant Abbot was directed by me in November, 1857, to proceed to the Mississippi river, organize the necessary parties, and prosecute the surveys and investigations. The completion of the Topographical and Hydrographical Survey of the Delta in the manner in which it was commenced in 1851 was not attempted; because the Investigations, the more important of the two classes of work called for by the appropriation acts, required the expenditure of the balance of the appropriation. It was extremely fortunate that they were resumed just at that time, for the flood of 1858 was one of a remarkable character, and furnished data which could not have been collected if the appropriation had been exhausted by the resumption of the Survey in a previous year, inasmuch as no Mississippi flood occurred between 1851 and 1858.

Field work resumed.

In compliance with these instructions, gauge-rods were established at Columbus, Kentucky; Memphis, Tennessee; Napoleon, Arkansas; Vicksburg, and Natchez, Mississippi; and Red-river landing and Carrollton, Louisiana. Donaldsonville, Louisiana, and Cairo, Illinois, were subsequently added to the list. A daily record of the height of the water upon the rod, the state of the weather, the direction and force of the wind, etc., was kept at these stations until January, 1859. The observations at Columbus, Memphis, and Vicksburg were continued until September, 1859, and those at Carrollton until April 30, 1861. From May 11, 1859, to June 5, 1860, a self-registering tide-gauge was maintained at the mouth of the Southwest pass, a portion of the corresponding Carrollton observations also being made with one of these instruments.

Gauge-rods.

A party in charge of Mr. Henry C. Fillebrown, assisted at first by Mr. W. E. Webster and subsequently by Mr. C. L. Jones, was established at Columbus, Kentucky, 20 miles below the mouth of the Ohio, which measured daily the velocity of the current from bank to bank, and occasionally from surface to bottom. To this duty were added the determination of the quantity of earthy matter held in suspension by the river-water, and a careful survey of the river above and below the base of current-observations, with lines of level to determine the slope of the river at high and low water. A survey across the low grounds between Cape Girardeau and the Commerce bluffs was likewise made by this party.

Discharge measurements at Columbus.

A party with similar duties, in charge of Lieutenant H. S. Putnam, Topographical

Engineers, assisted by Mr. J. T. Champneys, was stationed at Natchez, Mississippi; but was subsequently moved to Vicksburg, Mississippi, and placed in charge of Mr. Holmes A. Pattison, upon Lieutenant Putnam's being assigned to duty with the troops in Utah. In addition to its regular duty of current-measurements, this party made a careful survey of the river for about eight miles at Vicksburg, including the site of the velocity sections, with exceedingly accurate lines of level to determine the slope of the water surface at various stages between high and low water, entirely around the abrupt bend above Vicksburg. The discharge of the Yazoo river was also measured by this party, whenever it could be done without interfering with the regular progress of the work of the Vicksburg station. Subsequent to November 5, the gauging of the Mississippi at Vicksburg was conducted by Mr. J. J. Conway, assisted by Mr. J. M. Couper, Mr. Pattison's party having been detached to make an important survey through the Yazoo bottom, which could be best done in that month.

At Natchez and Vicksburg.

The observations at Columbus were continued until November 16, 1858, and those at Vicksburg until December 15, 1858. The summer of 1858 was remarkable for its intense heat and sickly character, notwithstanding which, the gentlemen composing these parties never relaxed their exertions.

Similar but much less elaborate observations were made by Mr. A. A. Edington, to ascertain the daily discharge of the Arkansas river at Napoleon. These commenced on January 1, and continued until November 30, 1858.

Discharge measurements upon the Arkansas.

Aided by Mr. Pattison, and, at times, by others of the assistants already named, Lieutenant Abbot, besides establishing the parties at Columbus and Natchez, measured accurate cross-sections with corresponding velocities, of the following streams, to determine approximately their discharge during the flood: the Ohio, the Hatchee, the St. Francis, the White, the Arkansas, the cut-off between the Arkansas and White rivers, the Yazoo, the Red, the Black, the Atchafalaya bayou, Old river above Red-river landing, and Grand river at Berwick's bay, Louisiana. In addition, accurate measurements of the high-water cross-sections of the Mississippi were made by him at Columbus, Kentucky; New Madrid, Missouri; a point two miles above Osceola, Arkansas; Randolph, Tennessee; Helena, Arkansas; Napoleon, Arkansas; Lake Providence, Louisiana; Vicksburg, Mississippi; New Carthage, Louisiana; Natchez, Mississippi; Baton Rouge, Louisiana; Bonnet Carré, Louisiana; and Fort St. Philip, Louisiana.

Upon other tributaries; with soundings in the Mississippi and bayous.

Mr. Pattison, assisted by Mr. J. D. Julian, measured in 1859 similar sections on the lines of survey of 1851 above and below the site of the Bonnet-Carré crevasse, and on two of those at Carrollton, Louisiana. He likewise re-sounded the bayous Plaquemine and La Fourche, on the lines of 1851, with some additions; and re-surveyed the heads of these bayous and of bayou Atchafalaya with a view to detect any changes which might have occurred since 1851.

Operations upon crevasses.

Aided by Mr. W. H. Williams, Lieutenant Abbot measured with great care the discharge of the Bell crevasse near New Orleans in May, 1858, and thus, in connection with the observations made by the parties in 1851, obtained the elements necessary to frame rules for ascertaining the discharge of crevasses. The locality of this crevasse and that of the La Branche were surveyed with minute accuracy by Mr. W. H. Williams during the following low water.

As soon as the flood of 1858 subsided, a party was organized under Mr. William Sidney Smith, which passed down the Mississippi, from Cairo to the mouth of Red river, in a yawl, measuring the dimensions of the various crevasses occasioned by that flood, and collecting all the information regarding date of occurrence, rate of increase, etc. This duty, an exceedingly difficult one, was performed in a highly satisfactory manner, notwithstanding the great exposure to sickness in a season remarkably unhealthy. To this gentleman the Survey is likewise indebted for communicating information useful in the work.

Section of the Yazoo bottom lands.

A line from the high lands east of the Yazoo bottom, *via* Greenwood and McNutt, to Prentiss on the Mississippi river, was accurately surveyed in 1859, by Mr. Pattison, assisted by Mr. Julian. It was the first survey made across that great swamp, and, besides affording the means of determining the average depth of overflow, furnished other valuable data.

Of the Tensas bottom lands.

A similar survey across the Tensas bottom was made by Mr. Pattison's party from Vidalia to Harrisonburg on the Washita.

After the termination of field labors, Mr. Pattison was employed, until April 30, 1861, in various kinds of office work, which he executed with the same fidelity and zeal that characterized his labors in the field.

Miscellaneous information collected.

Great care was taken to obtain from every available source correct information respecting the dimensions, condition, and extent of the levees throughout the alluvial region, the history of their progress, etc.; respecting the height and date of the floods throughout the same region; the depth of overflow in the swamps bordering the river, the nature of the growth upon them and their geological character; and the seasons and dates of the floods, the range, etc. of the tributaries of the Mississippi.

The intelligent and energetic labors of Lieutenant Abbot, faithfully aided by the gentlemen already named, accomplished a great amount of work.

Observations at the mouths of the river.

Series of detailed observations upon the currents at and near the bar of the Southwest pass, from the surface to the bottom, were made by Mr. C. A. Fuller, assisted by Mr. William Sidney Smith, in May, 1859, repeated by him in August, and with less elaboration at various times from that date to June, 1860. The services of Mr. Fuller were for the greater part of the time given without compensation. This valuable aid to the Survey was preceded by the voluntary contribution of gauge-rod observations at the head and foot of the Red-river raft.

Various circumstances successively delayed my intended inspection of the operations in progress on the Mississippi in 1858, and the examination of particular localities, until the month of May. A short time after my arrival in Louisiana, a return of my former illness, induced by the excessive heat of the climate, rendered me unable to perform, without great suffering, any duty for the remainder of the summer.

Upon a feeder of the Chesapeake and Ohio canal.

In the fall of 1859, measurements similar to those made at the permanent hydrometric stations of Carrollton, etc. were made upon a canal feeder of the Chesapeake and Ohio canal, at the Little Falls of the Potomac, by Lieutenant Abbot, assisted by Mr. Pattison and Mr. Vaughan, with a view to determine the laws governing variations in certain co-efficients entering the new formulæ derived from the Mississippi observations.

Data purchased by, or presented to the Survey.

To complete the Delta Survey, every source from which reliable information connected with the question of Mississippi floods could be collected was examined. Wherever a record of the rise and fall of the Mississippi and its tributaries had been made, it was secured if possible.

Gauge-records at Carrollton.

Thus the gauge-rod observations at Carrollton, or in that vicinity, having been continued by Professor Forshey after those of the Government ceased in 1853, the records up to May, 1855, were purchased from him at the same time with similar records at the same locality during 1848, 1849, and 1850. The purchase included notes upon the rise and fall of the river at Natchez, from 1817 to 1847, and a mass of information upon the high-water marks and dates of old floods in that vicinity, together with a cross-section of the Mississippi alluvion along the northern boundary of the State of Louisiana.

At Donaldsonville.

The gauge observations at Donaldsonville were continued by Mr. Gingry after those of the Government ceased in 1853, and in a spirit of great liberality copies of them, comprising the records for the years 1854–5–6–7–9, and part of 1860, were courteously placed at the disposal of the Delta Survey. These observations, it is believed, are still continued by Mr. Gingry, who will thus be enabled to contribute information that will be found highly valuable in testing the correctness of some of the conclusions found in the Delta Report, and in solving those questions connected with the river, the data for which rest upon long-continued, careful gauge-rod observations.

At Memphis.

The records of the gauge-rod observations at the Memphis Navy Yard, from August, 1848, to May, 1852, were courteously placed at the disposal of the Survey by the Chief of the Bureau of Yards and Docks. Similar records, filed at the United States Arsenal near St. Louis, Missouri, from May, 1843, to May, 1845, made under the direction of Captain T. J. Cram, Topographical Engineers, were furnished by the courtesy of Lieutenant Benét, U. S. Ordnance, and partial records of that character kept by Captain Richard Fatherly, Military Store-keeper at the United States Arsenal, at Little Rock, Arkansas, from January, 1858, to January, 1860, were kindly furnished to the Survey by him.

Railroad surveys.

For the fall of the Mississippi river above Natchez, use has been made of the surveys of various railroad routes mentioned in the Report. Similar surveys have likewise furnished cross-sections of the alluvial land, and depth of overflow, as follows:—

1. The survey of the Cairo and Fulton railroad company furnished a cross-section from Bird's landing, opposite Cairo, to the St. Francis river.

2. The survey of the Memphis and Little Rock railroad company furnished a cross-section from Memphis to Crowley's ridge.

3. The survey of the United States military road from Memphis to Little Rock furnished a similar cross-section.

4. The survey of the Gaines' landing and Fulton railroad company furnished a cross-section of the upper part of the Tensas bottom.

5. The survey of Professor Forshey, as already stated, furnished a cross-section on the northern boundary of Louisiana.

6. The railroad surveys of the Bureau of Topographical Engineers, War Department, furnished a cross-section from Lake Providence to Washita river.

7. The survey of the Vicksburg, Shreveport, and Texas railroad company furnished a cross-section from Vicksburg to Washita river.

Surveys by the State of Louisiana.

The surveys of the State of Louisiana afforded the means of compiling approximate cross-sections of the Atchafalaya basin.

8. From this source a profile of the Atchafalaya bayou was prepared.

9. Also a cross-section from Morganza on the Mississippi to Washington on the bayou Courtableau.

10. And a cross-section from Baton Rouge to Port Baré on the Courtableau.

11. The surveys of the New Orleans and Opelousas railroad company furnished an accurate profile from New Orleans to Berwick's bay across the La Fourche and Terre Bonne region.

To the Chief Engineers of the Railroad Companies referred to, and to the Officers of the Engineer Department of the State of Louisiana, acknowledgments are due for the liberal and polite manner in which all the information in their offices, applicable to the Survey of the Delta, was made available for it.

Acknowledgments.

The Survey is under especial obligation to Mr. G. W. R. Bayley, Chief Engineer of the New Orleans and Opelousas railroad company, for the obliging communication of valuable information. Also to Mr. M. Lynch, Chief Engineer of the Memphis and Little Rock railroad, for similar favors; to Major H. J. Ranney, of New Orleans, lessee of the new Canal, for copies of the gauge records kept at the mouth of the Canal, in lake Pontchartrain, from February, 1850, to July, 1859; to Colonel W. S. Campbell, for a profile from the Mississippi river at Carrollton to the mouth of the new Canal, lake Pontchartrain, and for information and assistance on various occasions; to Mr. Andrew Gingry, for a copy of the daily record of gauge-rod readings kept by him at Donaldsonville for more than five years, a highly valuable paper; to Mr. H. D. Mandeville, for a copy of gauge-rod observations upon bayou Tensas during the floods of 1844, 1849, 1850, and 1858; to Dr. N. B. Benedict, for a section of the artesian well in New Orleans; to Dr. R. W. Mitchell, for copies of meteorological observations at Memphis, Tennessee, during the year 1858; to Mr. Samuel Hollingsworth, for a detailed account of the occurrence and progress of the Bonnet-Carré crevasse of 1859.

To Professor Joseph Henry, Secretary of the Smithsonian Institution, the Survey is under obligation for the communication at different times of copies of meteorological observations.

To name all those who aided myself, the assistants, and numerous parties of the Survey, by the communication of information, would swell the list to an extent inadmissible in a paper intended to give merely a very brief account of the Delta Survey; yet it is difficult to decide where, precisely, to draw the line of distinction. Without exception, all of whom inquiries were made imparted whatever information they possessed, and facilitated our labors as far as it was in their power. It is hoped they will accept this general expression of the indebtedness of the Survey to them as an evidence of the appreciation of their kindness and liberality.

Large-scale maps and diagrams transmitted to the Bureau of Topographical Engineers.

The original large-scale maps and diagrams of this Survey, being useful in connection with other objects than those which form the subject of this Report, are herewith submitted. They comprise:

Topographical sheets, thirty in number, drawn upon a scale of 1 : 10,000, exhibiting in minute detail the topographical features from the mouth of Red river to New Orleans.

Hydrographical maps of the Mississippi river, at Carrollton (one sheet—scale 1 : 2000); at Baton Rouge (one sheet—scale 1 : 2000); at Vicksburg (one sheet—scale 1 : 7200); at Columbus (one sheet—scale 1 : 7200); of head of bayou Atchafalaya, in 1851 and 1858 (two sheets—scale 1 : 2400); of head of bayou Plaquemine, 1858 (one sheet—scale 1 : 1200); of head of bayou La Fourche, 1858 (one sheet—scale 1 : 1200).

Topographical maps of the survey through Yazoo bottom (two sheets—scale 1 : 50,000); of that through Tensas bottom (one sheet—scale 1 : 50,000); of Cape-

Girardeau inlet (one sheet—scale 1 : 60,000); and of the sites of the Bell and La Branche crevasses of 1858 (two sheets—scale 1 : 800).

A copy, by Mr. C. Ritter, of the Topographical and Hydrographical map of New Orleans and vicinity, comprised within 10 miles square, scale 1 : 12,000, from the surveys of Maurice Harrison, Esq., under the direction of the Commissioners appointed by the State of Louisiana, in 1845, to inquire into the most effectual means of protecting the city of New Orleans against inundation.

Twenty-one sheets of profiles of the alluvial region from original surveys, and twenty sheets purchased or presented.

Seventy-three sheets exhibiting cross-sections of the Mississippi river and of its branches.

The original field-note books, two hundred and fourteen in number, the plats of current measurements and of daily oscillations of the river and gulf, the sheets of analytical curves and of miscellaneous diagrams used in the preparation of the Report, numbering in all about six hundred sheets, together with the other records of the Survey, its collections and property, will be duly transmitted to the Bureau.

Office work of the Survey.

As the surveys and investigations progressed, the great labor commenced of reducing the observations, of assembling the results, of combining and digesting them, of the development of the laws governing all the phenomena that were subjects of examination, and, finally, of the application of these laws to the solution of the great problem which formed the object of the Delta Survey.

This work, which was in fact the preparation of the Report, was performed by myself and Lieutenant Abbot. It involved an amount of labor and study, which will not perhaps be fully appreciated even by professional persons. Devoted to the task, Lieutenant Abbot brought to its performance great industry, energy, sagacity, and skill in analysis, the fruits of which, to be found in every part of the Report, are particularly exhibited by the chapters in which the flow of water in natural channels is treated. But a perusal of the Report will convey a more forcible impression of the extent and value of Lieutenant Abbot's labors than any terms of acknowledgment that I can use. In the mass of exceedingly intricate calculation necessarily attendant upon such a work, Lieutenant Abbot has been aided by Mr. F. W. Vaughan, a skilful computer, whose zeal, unwearied care, and industry in the performance of the duties he was employed upon, entitle him to more than the ordinary terms of acknowledgment.

Remarks upon the problem to be solved by the operations of this Survey.

Some reference to the state of the question of protection against inundation, at the time when the Survey of the Mississippi Delta was begun, appears to be proper here, in order that the necessity of such extended and laborious investigations as were made may be appreciated, and that it may be understood how absolutely essential it was in every division of the subject to collect fact upon fact, until the assemblage of all revealed what were and what would be the true conditions of the river in every stage that it had passed through or could attain, and thus to substitute observed facts and the laws connecting them for assumed or imperfectly observed data and theoretical speculations.

A wide discretion was necessarily entrusted to the officer in charge of the Mississippi Delta Survey. I entered upon the execution of that duty with an apprehension that the laws of flowing water in natural channels, as enunciated in treatises upon the hydraulics of rivers, were not based upon sufficiently extended experiments upon natural streams, and, hence, that the formulæ found in them could not be relied upon for the solution of the questions upon which the plans of protection against inundation from overflow depended. The system of measurements and investigations carried on at Carrollton, Louisiana, Vicksburg, Mississippi, and Columbus, Kentucky, while it was intended to render the solution of the problem of the protection of the alluvial region of the Mississippi against inundation independent of the laws and formulæ of the books, was at the same time designed, in connection with other parts of the Survey, to afford the means of determining, by experiments on a far more extended scale than any ever before attempted, the laws governing the flow of water in natural channels, and of expressing them in formulæ that could be safely and readily used in practical applications. The success that has attended this part of the work has even exceeded my expectations. Laws have been revealed that were before unknown; new formulæ have been prepared, possessing far greater precision than the old; and improved methods of gauging streams have been devised.

The science of river hydraulics was in a very imperfect state.

But the imperfect state of the science of hydraulics as applied to rivers was not the only difficulty to be encountered in the execution of the duty imposed upon the officer in charge of this work. The much-agitated question of the best method of protection against inundation had been always discussed upon assumed data, and the truth of the very groundwork upon which these discussions rested had to be experimentally investigated by this Survey. For instance, the Mississippi had always been regarded as flowing through a channel excavated in the alluvial soil formed by the deposition of its own sedimentary matter. So important an assumption was inadmissible; and great pains were accordingly taken to collect specimens of the bed wherever soundings were made, and by every means to ascertain the depth of the alluvial soil from Cape Girardeau to the gulf. This investigation has resulted in proving that the bed of the Mississippi is not formed in alluvial soil, but in a stiff tenacious clay of an older geological formation than the alluvion, and that the sides of the channel do not consist of homogeneous material; facts that have an important bearing upon all plans of protection.

The most essential facts upon which protection against inundation depends were unknown.

Further, it was held by the advocates of the exclusive use of artificial embankments that the levees of Louisiana had already lowered the bed and floods of the Mississippi river, and that their extension throughout the alluvial region above would still further lower the floods by deepening the bed and reducing the slope of the river. The advocates of outlets, on the contrary, contended that the experience of many centuries, on the Po, proved that levees had raised the bed and floods of that river—to such an extent, indeed, that it was impracticable any longer to protect the country, except by opening new channels to the sea. This conclusion appeared to be sustained on the authority of two distinguished names, Cuvier and de Prony. While the investigations of the Delta Survey have rendered untenable that position of the advocates of the exclusive use of levees on the one hand, the investigations of the Chevalier Elia Lombardini have shown the supposed facts advanced by the latter class to be entirely erroneous, and their apprehensions to be unfounded.

The effects of levees were not understood.

The effects of cut-offs were likewise the subjects of controversy among engineers, a controversy which the measurements of the Delta Survey must set at rest, since they demonstrate that cut-offs raise the floods below them, a conclusion sustained by the well-established effects of such works upon the Po and Adige.

The effects of cut-offs were not known.

Outlets were advocated by some engineers because they were considered a ready and inexpensive means of reducing the floods. On the contrary, they were objected to by others because, as they claimed, outlets would raise the bed and floods of the river. The investigations of the Delta Survey prove that outlets, in the few localities where they are practicable, may be made to reduce the floods to any desired extent in certain divisions of the river; but that they would not be inexpensive, and would entail dangers and disasters which should not be risked. These conclusions, it is shown, are sanctioned by the experience of Europe, upon the Po, the Rhine, and the Vistula.

The effects of outlets had not been investigated.

The effect of a great swamp like that of the Yazoo upon the floods of the Mississippi, a subject that has formed the theme of speculation for at least thirty years, has also been established by the collection of facts; as likewise the law governing the rise, fall, and discharge of the river throughout the alluvial region; the manner in which the flood is propagated; the modifications introduced by tributaries; the succession of river stages; the drainage of its basin and that of its tributaries; the proportion of drainage to downfall; and the discharge of outlets: in fact, every river phenomenon has been experimentally investigated and elucidated.

The effect of a great swamp like that of the Yazoo was misapprehended, etc. etc. etc.

The problem of protection against overflow solved.

Thus every important fact connected with the various physical conditions of the river and the laws uniting them being ascertained, the great problem of protection against inundation was solved.

At the mouths of the river, a similar course has resulted in the development of the law under which the bars are formed, the depth upon them maintained, and the regular advance into the gulf continued; and, as a consequence, the principles upon which plans for deepening the channels over them should be based, and the best mode of applying them. The rate at which the river progresses into the gulf, and the extent, thickness, and relative level of the alluvial formation having been ascertained, its probable age has been estimated; and the ancient form of the coast, and the changes that have taken place in the present geological age, have been surmised.

The law regulating the depths at the mouths of the river deduced, etc. etc. etc.

The Report exhibits in detail the investigation of each of these subjects, and many others not enumerated in this letter. Based upon extended survey and investigation in the field, made at times under circumstances of great exposure, it contains the results of many years labor, comprising laborious office work, extended research, patient investigation, and exhaustive mental effort. The association of Lieutenant Abbot with me in this duty has been of such a character that the title of the Report should bear his name as well as mine. I beg leave therefore to submit it herewith, to the Bureau of Topographical Engineers, as our joint Report upon the Survey of the Delta of the Mississippi river.

The Report submitted.

Very respectfully, your obedient servant,

A. A. HUMPHREYS,

Captain Topographical Engineers, U. S. Army.

NOTE.

Throughout this Report and the Appendices, "Old Style" figures are employed to indicate interpolation.

REPORT

ON THE

MISSISSIPPI RIVER.

CHAPTER I.

BASIN OF THE MISSISSIPPI RIVER.

Natural subdivisions.—Red river basin.—Red river.—Its slope, dimensions of cross-section, range, navigation, succession of stages, and great floods.—Its tributary, Black river, with the principal branches, Washita river and bayou Tensas.—Basin of Arkansas and White rivers.—Arkansas river.—Its slope, dimensions of cross-section, range, annual succession of stages, and great floods.—Its tributaries, Canadian and White rivers.—St. Francis basin.—Boundaries and area.—Topography.—Geology of the bottom lands.—Their growth.—Their floods.—St. Francis river.—Mounds, etc.—Missouri basin.—Missouri river.—Its slope, range, width, and navigability.—Its tributaries, the Niobrara, the Platte, the Kansas.—Upper Mississippi basin.—Upper Mississippi river.—Its slope, range, and dimensions of cross-section.—Its tributaries.—Ohio basin.—Ohio river.—Its slope, range, dimensions of cross-section, discharge, annual succession of stages, and great floods.—Its tributaries.—Yazoo basin.—Boundaries and area.—Topography of the bottom lands.—Their geology.—Their growth.—Their floods.—Yazoo river.—Indian mounds, etc.—Basins of small direct tributaries.—The Maramee.—The Kaskaskia.—The Obion.—The Big Black.—Tabular summary of Mississippi basin.

Natural divisions of the Mississippi valley.

THE Mississippi drains the greater part of the territory of the United States lying between the Alleghany and the Rocky mountains. (See plate I.) Its basin, more than equal in area to the whole continent of Europe, exclusive of Russia, Norway, and Sweden, is greatly diversified in features, in soil, in climate, and in productions. A knowledge of the hydrographic relations of the different parts of this basin to the main river is essential to a full appreciation of all the elements of the problem the solution of which forms the subject of this report. The region is too vast and diversified to be treated under a single head, and some convenient and natural subdivision is therefore to be sought.

The true Mississippi river begins at the confluence of the Missouri and Upper Mississippi. It has eight principal tributaries, which, in the order of the magnitude of their basins, are the Missouri, the Ohio, the Upper Mississippi, the Arkansas, the Red, the White, the Yazoo, and the St. Francis. It may excite some surprise that the two latter are included in this category, but it will be hereafter seen that, although comparatively small streams, they are important from their position and volume of discharge. Just below the confluence of Red river is found the first of the bayous which, fed by the Mississippi, discharge into the gulf. Below this point, the Mississippi receives no appreciable increase from tributaries; it may, therefore, for these two reasons be considered the head of the delta.

The delta and the basins of the eight tributaries form natural subdivisions of the great basin. They include the whole area except the small basins of several comparatively unimportant branches, which may be classed together under one general heading. As it is proposed to state, in this chapter, such facts in relation to these several subdivisions as shall exhibit their hydrographic relations to the main river, it is, in some sort, an introduction to the report.

DELTA OF THE MISSISSIPPI.

There are many questions intimately connected with this division of the valley, which cannot be properly treated here, because they require a knowledge of facts and principles hereafter to be mentioned. For this reason, all remarks upon the delta of the Mississippi will be deferred for the present, and the subject be treated by itself in Chapter VII.

RED RIVER BASIN.

Its great diversity of character.

Few regions so limited in extent as this basin contain districts so entirely different in character. Its total area is only 97,000 square miles, yet it encloses large tracts of the richest Mississippi alluvion, a range of primitive mountains of considerable altitude, numerous lakes, a rolling and tolerably fertile prairie country, and an uncultivable tract of salt desert. The annual fall of rain varies from 15 inches in the western to 65 inches in the eastern portion; the climate is mild throughout the whole region. There is very great variety in the productions of the soil.

Extreme source.

Red river.—The sources of this river were first explored by Captain Marcy, U. S. A., in 1852. The river rises in the eastern rim of the vast and sterile desert plain called *el Llano Estacado*, at an elevation of about 2500 feet above the sea. Its extreme source, situated in a deep ravine, is thus described by Captain Marcy: "The gigantic escarpments of sandstone, rising to the giddy height of 800 feet upon each side, gradually closed in until they were only a few yards apart, and finally united overhead, leaving a long, narrow corridor beneath, at the base of which the head spring of the principal or main branch of Red river takes its rise. This spring bursts out from its cavernous reservoir, and, leaping down over the huge masses of rock below, here commences its long journey to unite with other tributaries in making the Mississippi the noblest river in the universe."

Its gorge through the Llano.

The ravine, some 60 miles in length, through which this stream escapes from the *Llano*, is described as follows: "Our course was very circuitous, from being obliged to follow the windings made by the numerous detours in the river. The lofty escarpments, which bounded the valley upon each side, rose precipitately from the banks of the river to the enormous height of from 500 to 800 feet; and in many places there was not room for a man to pass between the foot of the acclivities and the river. It was altogether impossible to travel upon either side of the river, so much broken and cut up was the ground; and the only place where a passage for a horse can be found is directly along the defile of the river bed. We found frequent small rivulets flowing into the river through the deep glens upon each side, but, most unfortunately for us, the water in them all was acid and nauseating." This latter peculiarity is characteristic of upper Red river. Except for the first two miles, the whole valley above the junction of the North fork, which enters some 150 miles below the source, is characterized by water "exceedingly unpalatable," producing "sickness at the stomach, attended with loss of appetite and a most raging and feverish thirst." This is attributed by Captain Marcy to its traversing a gypsum formation, and not to the presence of common salt in solution.

Its debouché from the Llano.

The following is Captain Marcy's description, when ascending the river, of the point where it debouches from the *Llano Estacado:* "After marching 8 miles over a succession of very rugged hills and valleys, which rise as they recede from the river, we reached the base of these towering and majestic cliffs, which rise almost perpendicularly from the undulating swells of prairie at the base, to the height of 800 feet, and terminate at the summit in a plateau almost as level as the sea, which spreads out to the south and west like the steppes of Central Asia, in an apparently illimitable desert.

"I supposed, from the appearance of the country at a distance, that I should be able to find a passage for the wagons along at the foot of these cliffs; but, upon a closer examination, find the ground between them and the river so much cut up by abrupt ridges and deep glens, that it is wholly impracticable to take our train any farther up this branch of the river. We have sought for a passage by which we might take the trains to the top of the bluffs, where, as they run nearly parallel to the course of the river, we might have continued on with the wagons; but, after making a careful examination, we have abandoned the idea, not being able to discover a place where we could even take our horses up the steep sides of the precipice.

"The geological formation of these bluffs is a red, indurated clay, resting upon a red sandstone, overlaid with a soft, dark-gray sandstone, and the whole capped with a white calcareous sandstone, the strata resting horizontally, and receding in terraces from the base to the summit."

The gypsum desert prairie.

About 8 miles below the edge of the cliffs the river is "nine hundred yards wide, flowing over a very sandy bed, with but little water in the channel, and is fortified upon each side by rugged hills and deep gullies, over which I think it will be impossible to take our train. The soil throughout this section is a light ferruginous clay, with no timber except a few hackberry and cottonwood trees upon the banks of the streams. There is but little water either in the river or in the creeks, and in a dry season I doubt if there would be any found here."

Below this point the bluffs were so near the bed of the stream that Captain Marcy was obliged to leave it and travel over the sterile prairie. He continued to do so for the rest of the route, and gives no further facts respecting the river. The first important tributary is the North fork, which enters on the western border of the Witchita mountains. This range lies upon the eastern boundary of the gypsum desert region, and a great change takes place in the character of the country.

The Witchita mountains.

Approaching them from the west, Captain Marcy states: "The mountains here appear to be in groups or clusters of detached peaks of a conical form, indicating a volcanic origin, with smooth, level glades intervening, and rising, as they do, perfectly isolated from all surrounding eminences upon the plateau of the great prairies, their rugged and precipitous granite sides almost denuded of vegetation, they present a very peculiar and imposing feature in the topographical aspect of the country. From the fact that the ground occupying the space between the mountains is a level, smooth surface, and exhibits no evidence of upheaval or distortion, may it not with propriety be inferred that the deposition here is of an origin subsequent to that of the upheaval of the mountains?" * * * * * * * * * * "We find the soil good at all places near the mountains, and the country well wooded and watered. The grass, consisting of several varieties of the grama, is of a superior quality and grows luxuriantly. The climate is salubrious; and the almost constant cool and bracing breezes of the summer months, with the entire absence of anything like marshes or stagnant water, remove all sources of noxious malaria, with its attendant evils of autumnal fevers." * * * * * * "Within a distance of six miles around our camp, I should estimate the amount of woodland at eight thousand acres. The grass is of the very best quality, and the soil cannot be surpassed for fertility. We are, at this place, directly at the base of one of the most lofty and rugged mountains of the range. Its bare and naked sides are almost destitute of anything in the shape of a tree or plant, and it is only here and there that a small patch of green can be discerned. Huge masses of flesh-colored granite, standing out in jagged crags upon the lofty acclivities, everywhere present themselves to the eye, and the scenery is most picturesque, grand, and imposing." * * * * * "Several gentlemen of the party ascended the mountain near our camp this evening, and obtained a fine view of the adjoining country. They discovered that there were three distinct ranges running from northeast to southwest; at this place they appear to be united in one chain, and there seems to be no pass practicable for wagons in this vicinity."

* * * "The most elevated mountain in the Witchita chain I have taken the liberty, in honor of our distinguished commanding general, to call 'Mount Scott.' This peak, towering as it does above all surrounding eminences, presents a very imposing feature in the landscape, and is a conspicuous land-mark for many miles around. The altitude above the base, as determined by triangulation with the sextant, is 1135 feet."

Of the eastern base of the chain, Captain Marcy states: "The more we have seen of the country about these mountains, the more pleased we have been with it. Indeed, I have never visited any country that, in my opinion, possessed greater natural local advantages for agriculture than this."

The Cross-timbers.

The next striking feature of the valley is the "Cross-timbers," lying between long. 98° and long. 97°. "This extensive belt of woodland, which forms one of the most prominent and anomalous features upon the face of the country, is from 5 to 30 miles wide, and extends from the Arkansas river, in a southwesterly direction, to the Brazos, some 400 miles. At six different points where I have passed through it, I have found it characterized by the same peculiarities—

the trees consisting principally of post-oak and black-jack, standing at such intervals that wagons can without difficulty pass between them in any direction. The soil is thin, sandy, and poorly watered." * * * * * * * * * "Upon the east side there are numerous spring-brooks, flowing over a highly prolific soil, with a superabundance of the best of timber and an exuberant vegetation, teeming with the delightful perfume of flowers of the most brilliant hues; here and there interspersed with verdant glades and small prairies, affording inexhaustible grazing, and the most beautiful natural meadows that can be imagined; while on the other side commence those barren and desolate wastes, where but few small streams greet the eye of the traveller, and these are soon swallowed up by the thirsty sands over which they flow. Here but little woodland is found except on the immediate borders of the water-courses."

The Red-river raft.

East of the "Cross-timbers" the False Washita unites with Red river, and the main stream flows, through rich and densely-wooded alluvial bottoms, to the head of the celebrated "raft." This raft is composed of an immense accumulation of drift-logs—some floating, and others so water-logged as to sink, and thus still more effectually block up the channel. From the rotting of the logs at the lower end, and the fresh accessions at the upper end, the raft gradually moves up stream. Its lower extremity was once at Natchitoches, if not, as many suppose, still farther down the stream. Large sums have been expended by the United States government in its removal. In 1854 it had advanced to a point 53 miles above Shreveport. Its length was then 13 miles, and it was forming at a rate of 1.5 to 2 miles per year. The following extracts from the report of the United States agent and engineer, Mr. C. A. Fuller, dated January 18, 1855, convey interesting information:—

"My survey was made during the low water of November ultimo, and embraced a region of country extending from the outlet of Red bayou to Shreveport—a distance of about 75 miles." * * * * "The total fall of the low-water surface of the river, from the head of Red bayou to Shreveport, is 36.60 feet. From Red bayou to the head of the present raft, a distance of 4½ miles, but little if any fall exists—the raft acting as a dam, and backing the water for some 20 or 30 miles above. The cross-section lines, run from the river, show that the surface of the country has a gradual fall from the river westwardly of about 5½ feet to the mile; while the difference of level of the water surfaces is about 3¾ feet on the same section—a little over 1 foot to the mile; consequently, at low water the river has a constant tendency to flow to the west through every natural outlet, deserting its old channel, which runs, as it were, upon a ridge, and seeking a lower level near the bluffs that border the western shores of the lakes; while at high water, the banks being submerged, the currents naturally follow the same direction. The obstruction of the raft has thrown a large proportion of the water of the river (about three-fourths) through two natural outlets (Dooley's and Red bayou) into Soda lake, affording a navigation around the raft [right bank], which is constantly improving as the action of the water widens and deepens these channels. The channel of Red river, from the head of the present raft to Shreveport, besides being thus elevated, exhibits such an entire deficiency of width, depth, and fall, that *up-stream* currents are found through more than one-half of its distance during every freshet. The bed is strewn with logs, stumps, etc. The stream is not only narrow, but very tortuous; and although a navigable channel might be opened through it, at great expense, for short periods only, its want of capacity for carrying raft would be a fatal objection to the permanency of its navigation."

* * * "This portion of Red river, therefore, having neither the capacity to carry raft, or capability of being made subservient to the purposes of navigation, forces us to look for other channels in the vicinity to attain our object. Of the natural outlets, Dooley's bayou appears most capable of improvement and best adapted to our purpose, being the shortest, widest, and deepest; its currents strongest, and its soil the lightest alluvial, and consequently the easiest washed. I propose, as will be hereafter explained, to open the navigation through this bayou into Shiftail lake (see map), thence through Stumpy bayou to Soda lake, and thence through Soda lake and Twelve-mile bayou to Shreveport, making a distance of about 40 miles, in which we will have the same fall as is found by the river in a distance of 70 miles, viz., 36.60 feet."

Lower Red river.

Below the raft, Red river traverses a fertile and populous country, of which no description is necessary here. The stream is interrupted by two small rapids just above Alexandria, where the bluffs leave the river and artificial embankments become necessary to protect the country from inundation during river floods. In 1858 the levees only extended to Dunn's bayou, about 25 miles below Alexandria, and were restricted to the right bank.

Slope of Red river.

The following table, exhibiting the slope of the Red river, has been compiled from the best available authorities. The elevation at Shreveport was determined by the levels of the Vicksburg and Shreveport railroad; the elevation of the head of the raft above that point, by Mr. Fuller's levels; the elevation at Fulton, by the levels of the St. Louis and Fulton, and Gaines' landing and Fulton railroads. The authorities for the data upon which the table is formed are stated, because they confirm the fact of the extraordinary reduction of slope above the raft, indicated by the table.

High-water slope of Red river.

Locality.	Distance above mouth.	Elevation above gulf level.	Fall per mile.	Authority.
	Miles.	*Feet.*	*Feet.*	
Source	1200	2450	0.00	Captain Marcy.
At Preston	820	641	4 80	Captain Pope.
At Fulton	595	242	1.80	Railroad levels.
At head of raft	405	207	0.20	Mr. C. A. Fuller.
At Shreveport	330	180	0.36	Railroad levels.
Mouth of Black river (high water 1828)	30	58	0.41	Delta Survey.
Mouth (high water 1828)	00	54	0.14	Delta Survey.

Its width.

The width of the Red river between its banks, eight miles below the point where it issues from the Llano Estacado, is 2700 feet; just below the mouth of North fork, 2000 feet; about 50 miles below the mouth of this tributary, 2100 feet; at the mouth of the Big Witchita, 600 feet; at Alexandria, 720 feet; at mouth of Black river, 785 feet; at mouth, 1800 feet. These numbers indicate the characteristic variation in width. While traversing the sandy desert, the river spreads out to a width greatly disproportionate to the depth; but when the more fertile and clayey soil is entered, it contracts to the normal dimensions corresponding to its discharge.

Its depth. The depth of Red river varies inversely as its width, being only 6 or 8 feet, even in floods, throughout the desert, while it is some 50 feet in the fertile region. In extreme low water a depth of 3 feet may be depended upon below Alexandria, about 4 feet thence to the head of the raft, and 1 foot thence to Fort Towson.

Navigation. Steamers of 4 feet draught can ascend to Shreveport at any time except in extreme low water, but to Fort Towson or even Fulton, for only about three months in the year, and frequently only run in one direction during a single rise. The river above the raft rises and falls more rapidly than the Arkansas, and thus is less favorable to navigation. The raft also is a serious obstacle, as it requires the boats to leave the channel and pass through lakes and bayous.

Its area. The high-water area of cross-section throughout the desert country is probably about 12,000 square feet, and in the cultivated region from 30,000 to 40,000.

Its range. The range of the river is greatly affected by the raft. Thus at Fort Towson it is some 45 feet, the maximum (January 27, 1843) being 51 feet; at Fulton it is 35 feet; at the head of the raft, 10 feet; at Shreveport, 25 feet; at Alexandria, 47 feet; at the mouth, 45 feet. These numbers illustrate the effect of lakes in moderating floods.

Its succession of stages. The raft also greatly modifies the normal succession of stages in the lower river, by equalizing the flow of the freshets, which are very sudden above the raft. They are mainly due to heavy rains in or east of the Witchita mountains. The following extract from Captain Marcy's report is interesting in this connection:—

"May 18 [1852]. * * * We encamped upon a small affluent of Cache creek, where, on our arrival, we found no water except in occasional pools along the bed; however, in the course of an hour, some of the men who had gone a short distance up the creek came running back into camp and crying at the top of their voices, 'Here comes a plenty of water for us, boys!' And, indeed, in a few minutes, much to our astonishment and delight (as we were doubtful about having a supply), a perfect torrent came rushing down the dry bed of the rivulet, filling it to the top of the banks, and continued running, turbid and covered with froth, as long as we remained."

These rains occur with great irregularity, but generally during the winter and spring. Modified by the lakes of the raft country, they usually serve to maintain the lower river in a good boating condition from December to June or July, the remainder of the year being the season of low water. The *floods* of the lower river have their immediate origin in the contributions of Rocky bayou, Cane river, Darrow bayou, and a host of other small streams, which rapidly collect any wide-spread and continuous rain in the region below the raft, and pour it at once into the channel of the main river, already well filled by the water draining from the lakes of the raft district. For this reason, the dates of the freshets of Red river are variable.

The moderating influence of the raft lakes upon the floods of the river is now used to its utmost capacity by the works nature herself has established. The moderating effect of the lakes below the raft might probably be rendered greater, but could hardly be relied upon to influence materially the floods of the Mississippi.

No complete records are to be had respecting the great floods of Red river; but the following facts have been collected from reliable sources. The highest water ever recorded at Fort Towson occurred on January 27, 1843. At Alexandria, the greatest flood on record was highest on August 15, 1849, the river then being 47 feet above its very lowest stage (attained in the summer of 1856, the autumn of 1855, and the autumn of 1851). The second greatest flood was highest on March 18, 1851, and was 1.1 feet below the high water of 1849. On April 22, 1858, the water was only 3 feet below the flood of 1849, and was about equal to the highest stand of the river in 1828 and in 1844. At the mouth of Black river, within the influence of the Mississippi, the highest flood on record is that of 1828, which was 5 feet above that of 1850, and 8 feet above that of 1844, these being the only floods since 1828 which have risen above the high natural banks at that locality.

Its great floods.

With reference to the origin of the peculiar red color which gives the name to this river, no very definite information has been obtained, but the color is probably derived from the red clay of the gypseous formation in which the upper course of the river lies. Captain Marcy states that the North fork, at the mouth of Otter creek, among the Witchita mountains, "is only 120 yards wide; the banks of red clay are from 3 to 8 feet high, the water extending entirely across the bed, and at this time (a high stage) about 6 feet deep in the channel, with a rapid current of 4 miles per hour, highly charged with a dull-red sedimentary matter, and slightly brackish to the taste." He states that this red clay is found in the bluffs of the Llano Estacado, and it is therefore probable that the river has its characteristic color throughout its whole extent.

The peculiar color of its water.

Tributaries.—The only tributary of Red river which requires particular notice, is Black river. The stream known by this name is formed by the junction of Washita (the Indian name for Black) river, Little river, and bayou Tensas, and is only 54 miles in length. It is a deep, navigable river throughout, with an extreme range of about 50 feet (high water of 1828 to low water of 1839 and 1850). From a point about 20 miles above its mouth, it is leveed continuously to the junction of the three rivers. It has an average width of about 800 feet, and an average area of cross-section of about 30,000 square feet.

Black river.

Of its three branches, Little river is a mere drain from Catahoula lake, and requires no especial notice.

Of Washita river, Darby states it "draws its source from the mountainous prairies between Red and Arkansas rivers, about 95° 30′ W. long., and 34° N. lat. From this elevated steep arise many other streams, which, winding over this broken region, at length unite above the Hot springs, and form the Ouachitta" [Washita].

Washita river.

"The mountains out of which the Ouachitta flows are composed of secondary materials, marine exuviæ are everywhere found mixed with the schistus, argillaceous earth, and other matters that compose the face and interior of those rugged mountains. The whole face of the country indicates marine submersion at some remote period.

"The Fourche au Cado, Little Missouri and Saline branches of Ouachitta, rise in the same ridge with the principal stream.

"The lands around the head of Ouachitta partake of the sterility of the great salt plains of Texas, which indeed they very much resemble. Southeast of the Maserne mountains, on the waters of Little Missouri, the soil becomes of better quality, and some tracts are extremely fertile. Indications of metals become more rare, timber is abundant, and the prairies imperceptibly disappear. Pine and that species of oak known by the appellation of upland black oak are frequently met with in large bodies. Ash, linden, dogwood, and other timber, the usual growth on good second-rate land, is likewise plentiful. The soil is adapted to the culture of small grain, to legumes, the potato, and almost every plant and herb suitable to the climate." * * *

"Few rivers differ more in the quantity of water at different seasons than the Ouachitta. Flowing from a hilly or mountainous tract, more constancy might be expected in the column of water; but though the places drained by the Little Missouri and Fourche au Cado are not deficient in springs, yet the extensive region toward the sources of Ouachitta has little water except what is supplied by rains in winter and spring. When the parching heat of summer has dried the country above the mouth of the Little Missouri, the Ouachitta becomes very low as far south as the head of Black river."

* * * "About 33° 10′ of north latitude, the Saline, a small river from the angle between Ouachitta and Arkansas, falls into the former river. The Saline rises 12 miles east of the Hot springs, and pursuing a course nearly parallel to Ouachitta river, about 120 miles of comparative length, is navigable 70 or 80 miles from its mouth with boats of considerable size in time of high water." * * * * *

"The river Barthelemy falls into Ouachitta three miles below the Derbane, but from the contrary side. The Barthelemy rises near the Arkansas, and has a course of upwards of 100 miles of comparative length. The banks are high and not subject to inundation, and are composed of second-rate land; some of the bottoms, however, are equal to any lands on Red river."

Bayou Tensas branch.

The third branch of Black river, bayou Tensas, is the chief drain of a large region bordering upon the Mississippi and subject to annual inundation by that river. The general characteristics of this region are the same as those of the Yazoo and St. Francis bottom lands, which will soon receive detailed notice. The boundaries of this region are laid down on plate II, and the general configuration of the country is well shown by plate IV. The bayou Tensas heads in lake Providence, and after being joined by a parallel stream, bayou Maçon, which heads above Gaines' landing, and by many other swamp-land drains, becomes a river some 600 feet in width and 16,000 square feet in cross-section in the high-water season of the year. The gradual extension of the levee system upon the banks of the Mississippi has deprived this net-work of bayous of their chief supply of water, and they now never rise to the level of their banks except upon the occurrence of many large crevasses in the Mississippi levees. Formerly, the whole region was deeply inundated in floods. In 1828, when the greatest inundation of which there is even a tradition occurred, the average depth of the water across the swamp on the Louisiana boundary line was 7.1 feet; and between Vidalia and Harrisonburg, 7.7 feet. The mean depth throughout the whole swamp was probably as much as 7 feet. This inundation, however, was fully 3 feet deeper than any other of which we have records.

A party of this Survey, in charge of Mr. H. A. Pattison, C. E., made a level and transit survey of the route from Vidalia to Harrisonburg in January, 1859. The following facts are taken from Mr. Pattison's report. To be fully understood, they require a reference to the description of the Yazoo swamp contained in a subsequent part of this chapter.

The soil is altogether similar to that between the Mississippi and Sunflower rivers in the Yazoo bottom. On the eastern bank of bayou Tensas, there are some light and sandy ridges; but to the westward, as far as the high bluffs near Harrisonburg, the soil is of tough, sticky clay, more or less impregnated with lime. Many wells have been dug near the line of survey, generally to a depth of 18 or 20 feet, penetrating strata of clay, sand, and gravel. Blue clay is frequently but not always found. Water reached in its immediate vicinity is invariably unhealthy. Water circulates through the sand strata, causing the wells near the banks of the Mississippi and bayou Tensas to oscillate with those streams.

The growth upon the route examined by Mr. Pattison was similar to that found near his line across the Yazoo bottom, but between the Mississippi and bayou Tensas was apparently older. West of the bayou, it was much younger. East of the Tensas, many large cypresses of immense age, probably the remains of cypress brakes, are found mingled with the other timber. The growth consists mainly of white, cow, Spanish, willow, black, and red oaks, sweet and black gum, holly, privet or elbow tree, swamp dogwood, red and black haw, elm, sassafras, papaw, pecan, hickory, very little walnut, willow, cottonwood, but only on the borders of large streams, hackberry, white ash, and tupelo gum. In low, flat, and swampy ground, spicewood, palmetto or palm, grape and muscadine vines grow to great size. Most of the underbrush peculiar to a rich soil is found in great profusion throughout the swamp.

Slope of Black river and its tributaries.

The following data have been collected respecting the slope of Black river and of its principal tributaries:—

High-water Slope of Washita and Black Rivers.

Locality.	Distance from mouth of Black river.	Elevation above gulf.	Fall per mile.	Authority.
	Miles.	*Feet.*	*Feet.*	
Extreme source of Washita river	550	2000 (?)	0.00	Lieutenant Whipple.
Arkadelphia	367	200	9.80	St. Louis and Fulton RR.
Near Camden	307	123	1.30	Gaines' landing & Fulton RR.
Mouth of bayou Bartholomew	194	93	0.27	Providence and Fulton RR.
Monroe	169	88	0.20	Vicksburg & Shreveport RR.
Harrisonburg (high water 1828)	69	67	0.20	Delta Survey.
Mouth Black river (high water 1828)	00	58	0.14	Delta Survey.

The elevation in the flood of 1828 of the water surface of bayou Tensas at the crossing of the Vidalia and Harrisonburg road was 68 feet above the gulf; that of lake Providence, its source, being about 122 feet above the same level. The natural bank of bayou Tensas was covered about 5 feet deep in that great flood.

The high-water elevations above the gulf of bayou Bartholomew and Saline river where crossed by the Gaines' landing and Fulton railroad, are 144 and 121 feet respectively, the ranges between low and high water being 19 and 25 feet respectively.

BASIN OF THE ARKANSAS AND WHITE RIVERS.

General character.

The western border of this region lies among the summits of the Rocky mountains. The middle portion comprises the great sterile plain which spreads between the mountains and the 97th meridian of longitude. The eastern part contains the rich alluvion of the Mississippi valley. Its total area is 189,000 square miles. Although great diversity of climate and production is found in this region, less than half its area is capable of supporting a civilized population, the greater part being adapted only to the wants of a nomadic race.

Extreme source.

Arkansas river.—The extreme sources of this river were first explored by Lieutenant Pike, U. S. A., in 1806. They lie among the mountains westward of the South Park, in lat. 39° 00′ and long. 106° 00′, at an elevation of about 10,000 feet above the level of the sea. The stream is at first a mountain torrent, losing about half of its elevation above the sea in the first 150 miles. The following description of the point where it issues from the mountains is taken from the report of Major Long, who visited this region in 1820:—

Point where it leaves the mountains.

"The river pours with great impetuosity and violence through a deep and narrow fissure in the gneiss rock, which rises so abruptly on both sides to such a height as to oppose an impassable barrier to all further progress. According to the delineation of Pike's route, upon the map which accompanies his work, he must have entered the mountains at this place; but no corroboration can be derived from his journal. It appears almost incredible that he should have passed by this route and have neglected to mention the extreme difficulty which must have attended the undertaking." For the next 30 miles the Arkansas "has an average breadth of about 60 yards, it is from 3 to 5 feet deep, and the current rapid. At the mountains the water was transparent and pure, but soon after entering the plains it becomes turbid and brackish."

Thence to the Big bend.

After leaving the mountains, the stream traverses a sterile, hilly region, sustaining considerable timber. The hills gradually diminish in size until they subside into the plain to the westward of Bent's Fort, near the meridian of 104°. Between that point and the great bend of the Arkansas, the country is sufficiently described in the following extracts from Major Emory's report upon General Kearny's route in 1846. Speaking of the river, he says: "Its bed is of sand, sometimes of rounded pebbles of the primitive rock. It is seldom more than 150 yards wide, and, but for the quicksands, is everywhere fordable. The bottom land, a few feet above the level of the water, varies in width from half a mile to two miles, and is generally covered with good, nutritious grass. Beyond this, the ground rises by gentle slopes into a wilderness of sand hills on the south, and into prairie on the north.

* * * * * * * * * * *

"The soil of the plains is a granitic sand, intermixed with the exuviæ of animals and vegetable matter, supporting a scanty vegetation. The eye wanders in vain over these immense wastes in search of trees. Not one is to be seen. * * *

"The narrow strip which I have described as the bottom land of the Arkansas, varying from half a mile to two or three miles wide, contains a luxuriant growth of grasses, which, by the judicious selection and distribution of the camps, sustained all the animals of the Army of the West while on the river. The only tree of any magnitude found on its course is the cottonwood (Populus Canadensis), and it frequently happens that not one of these is seen in a whole day's journey, and the buffalo dung and wild sage constitute the only fuel to be procured. About 35 miles before reaching [east of] Bent's Fort is found what is called the 'big timber.' Here the valley of the river widens, and the banks on either side fall toward it in gentle slopes. The 'big timber' is a thinly-scattered growth of large cottonwoods, not more than three-quarters of a mile wide, and three or four miles long."

The following facts respecting the Arkansas between the Big bend and Fort Smith are taken from the report of Captain Bell, who led a detachment of Major Long's party down the left bank of the Arkansas in 1820.

Thence to Fort Smith and the mouth.

The first timber was found in the valley of the Little Arkansas. It consisted partly of honey-locust and buttonwood, but chiefly of cottonwood, elm, and ash. A few miles farther on, the bluffs, hitherto remote from the bed of the river, approached so closely as to render it necessary to travel upon them. The plain became more densely covered with grass. Ravines were more abundant, and, together with the banks of the river itself, became well wooded. The water of the Arkansas, hitherto fresh, began to be slightly brackish from the contributions of saline creeks upon the right bank. Below what is now called Suicide creek, "the river bottom becoming very narrow obliged us to ascend upon the high grounds, which we found to be little less than mountainous, often rocky and steep, and, as usual, intersected by profound ravines." * * * "We were now traversing a high ridge of country, which at many points may be safely estimated at 500 feet above the surface of the river, and wooded to a great distance from the stream." * * * * * * * * * "In the course of a few miles we arrived at the edge of this forest, which here crowned a much elevated region. It was in fact higher, in proportion to the surface before us, than any other portion of the country we had seen on this side of the mountains. The eye from this height roved over a vast distance of prairie and comparatively low country." Below the Cimarron, "we were all immediately struck with the change in the appearance of the water of the river. No longer of that pale clay color to which we have been accustomed, it has now assumed a reddish hue hardly unlike that of the blood of the human arteries, and is still perfectly opaque from the quantity of an earthy substance of this tint, which it holds in suspension; its banks and bars are, from deposition, of the same color." A few miles farther on, he states: "The prairie is now very fertile, interspersed with pleasing groves of oak, and swelling on either hand and in the distance into remarkable pyramids and conical hills, of which the summits are rocky. The spice-wood (Laurus benzoin) and the pecan (Carya olivæformis) first occurred to-day." This character of country extends to Fort Gibson, which is situated at the head of navigation. The remaining 642 miles of the river traverses a fertile and settled region, of which nothing need be said here, except that it has been found necessary to levee both banks below Pine bluffs, in order to restrain the floods.

With reference to the river itself, Captain Bell states: "The Arkansa, below the

Great bend, becomes more serpentine than it is above, and very much obstructed by sandbars and islands, either naked or clothed with a recent vegetation; they are but little elevated above the water, and are covered to some depth during the prevalence of floods in the river. At Belle point (near Fort Smith) and some distance above, these islands almost wholly disappear, but the sandy shores still continue, and are, as above, alternately situated on either side of the river, as the stream approaches or recedes from the opposite river bottoms. The color of the water was now olive green. All the red coloring matter, with which it is sometimes imbued, is contributed by streams entering on the southern side. The current of the Arkansa is much less rapid than that of the Platte, but the character of these two rivers, in a great degree, corresponds in their widely spreading waters of but little depth, running over a bed of yielding sand."

Slope of the Arkansas.

The following table, exhibiting the slope of the Arkansas, has been compiled from the best available data. Although mainly derived from barometric levelling, it is sufficiently accurate for the object of its compilation.

High-water Slope of Arkansas River.

Locality.	Distance above mouth.	Elevation above sea level.	Fall per mile.	Authority.
	Miles.	*Feet.*	*Feet.*	
Source	1,514	10,000	0.00	Captain Fremont.
Mouth of Boiling-spring river	1,364	4,880	34.13	"
Mouth of Apishpa creek	1,323	4,371	12.41	Captain Gunnison.
Near Bent's fort	1,289	3,672	20.56	"
Near Fort Atkinson	1,095	2,331	6.91	"
Great bend	992	1,658	6.53	Major Emory.
Near Fort Gibson	642	560	3.14	
Near Fort Smith	522	418	1.18	Lieutenant Whipple.
Near Little Rock	250	252	0.61	Railroad levels.
Mouth	0	162	0.36	Railroad levels.

Its width.

The width of the Arkansas undergoes great variations. Near the mountains it does not exceed 150 feet. It gradually increases to about a mile, as it traverses the sandy desert. After entering the hilly and fertile region it varies from 1000 to 2000 feet.

Its depth.

The depth of the Arkansas also varies greatly in different parts of its course. Throughout the prairie region it averages about 2 or 3 feet, exclusive of shoals, but there are seasons when the water entirely disappears, being absorbed by the immense beds of sand in which its channel is formed. In the navigable part of the river the least depth found upon the bars in extreme low water, from the mouth to the Post of Arkansas, is from 2.5 to 3.0 feet; thence to Little Rock, 2 feet; thence to Fort Gibson, 1 foot.

Its range.

The range of the river between low and high water is about 45 feet at Napoleon; 40 feet at South bend; 35 feet at Little Rock; 25 feet at Fort Smith; 10 feet at Fort Gibson, and still less at points above. These numbers do not represent the *extreme* ranges, although they are much greater than those that usually occur.

Its annual succession of stages.

There are generally three annual rises in the Arkansas. As observed by Colonel Charles Thomas, U. S. Army, who served at Fort Gibson many years, they are as follows: One usually begins in February, owing to the winter rains, and lasts, on an average, about fifteen days. The next—

the principal rise in the year—is occasioned by the melting snows in the mountains and the late spring or early summer rains. It occurs in May and June, and continues into July, and sometimes into August. The river generally keeps up, between these two rises, some 1 or 2 feet above its lowest stage. The last rise is in November, produced by the late autumn rains, and lasts from ten to twenty days.

Steamboats from 3 to 4 feet draught can almost always reach a point some 40 miles above Little Rock, and during the floods can reach as far as Fort Smith and Fort Gibson, with a fair prospect of being able to return. Both the Canadian and Arkansas have been navigated with small steamers as far up as the wants of the military service have required. Steamers of 8 feet draught have reached Fort Smith, but their return during the same rise is not certain. The river is generally very low after the November rise. During the lowest stage it is difficult for boats of the lightest draught to reach Fort Smith.

Floods of the Arkansas.

The greatest flood of the Arkansas on record occurred in 1833. Authorities differ as to its relative height at Little Rock, but the evidence tends to the conclusion that it exceeded any subsequent flood by at least 2 feet. It was followed by nine years of low water. The next flood occurred in 1843, when, on January 24, the water stood 26 feet above low-water mark at Fort Smith. The following year the river rose still higher, being at Fort Smith 27.5 feet above low-water mark on May 25, and at Little Rock 2 feet below the high water of 1833. The next flood occurred in 1848, when on May 28 the river stood 20 feet above low-water mark at Fort Smith. The same stand was reached on June 7, 1853, and a point 2 feet higher on June 13, 1854. Freshets, whose heights were not recorded, occurred in 1851 and 1857. The next flood occurred in 1858. It was highest at Little Rock on March 22, being then 5 feet below high water of 1833. No flood in the river has occurred since that date up to the present time (1861). It should be added that back-water from the Mississippi and the construction of levees both have so much affected the relative heights of different floods at points below Little Rock, that they are not criterions by which to judge of the real floods of the Arkansas.

Tributaries.

Tributaries.—This great river has only two tributaries which require notice—the Canadian and the White.

Canadian river.

The former rises in the Raton pass, between Bent's Fort and Santa Fé, at an elevation of about 6000 feet above the level of the sea, and after traversing, in a course of about 1000 miles, the same barren region through which the Arkansas flows, discharges into the latter about midway between Fort Smith and Fort Gibson. The following extracts from the report of Major Long, who first explored this stream (1820), sufficiently describe its character:—

"This river has a broad valley, bounded by bluffs from 200 to 500 feet high, faced with rocky precipices near its source, and presenting abrupt declivities, intersected by numerous ravines lower down. It has a spacious bed, depressed but a few feet below the bottoms, and exhibiting one continued stratum of sand through the greater part of its length. It is the channel through which the water of a vast extent of country is carried off; yet, during most of the summer season, it is entirely destitute of running water throughout a large proportion of its extent—a circumstance in proof of the aridity of the region drained by it. Fifty miles above its mouth it receives at least two-thirds of its water from its principal tributary, denominated the North fork. This fork rises between the Arkansa and Canadian, and has a meandering course of about 700 miles. Six miles above the fork just mentioned, another tributary enters the Canadian, called the South fork, about half as large as the other. Notwithstanding the supplies afforded by these two tributaries, the Canadian has not a sufficiency of water in summer to render it navigable even to their mouths." * * * "The bottoms of the Canadian, in the neighborhood of its mouth, are possessed of a soil exceedingly prolific; but, like those of the other rivers of this region, the more remote their situation from the mouth of the river, the more sandy and sterile is their appearance. Its valley is plentifully supplied with timber of an excellent quality for a distance of about 200 miles on the lower part of the river; and the high lands, for nearly the same distance, are agreeably diversified with prairies and woodlands." * * * "Proceeding westward, a very gradual change is observable in the apparent fertility of the soil—the surface becoming more sandy and sterile, and the vegetation less vigorous and luxuriant. The bottoms appear to be composed in many places almost exclusively of loose sand." West of long. 96°, the waters "appear to hold in solution a greater or less proportion of common salt and sulphate of magnesia, which, in many instances, render them too brackish or bitter for use. Saline and nitrous efflorescences frequently occur upon the surface in various parts of the country, and incrustations of salt, of considerable thickness, are to be found in some few places south of the Arkansa river. As to the existence of rock salt in a mineral state, some doubts are to be entertained, if the decision is to rest upon the character of the specimens exhibited as proofs of the fact. The several examples of this formation that we have witnessed are evidently crystalline salt, deposited by a regular process of evaporation and crystallization, and formed into concrete masses or crusts upon the surface of the ground."

White river.

The second tributary of the Arkansas, White river, is of an entirely different character.* It drains the fertile region between the St. Francis bottom and the Ozark divide, which, after leaving the Mississippi near Cape Girardeau, crosses the Arkansas above Fort Gibson, as already described. For about 80 miles above the mouth the country is low and swampy, being liable to inundation from the floods of the river. Above that point the stream traverses a rolling prairie, gradually becoming hilly, and even mountainous near the sources.

For some 350 miles, up to the mouth of Black river (its principal tributary), White river is a deep, narrow, and sluggish stream, flowing, with a very crooked course, between banks composed of a clayey soil of sufficient consistence to prevent caving. The water is of a white color—very different from the red tint of the Arkansas near its mouth.

The freshets of White river are irregular, occurring as early as January and as late as June, but generally in March or April. The extreme range is about 35 feet at the mouth of Black river, and 45 feet near its own mouth.

---

* It is perhaps improper to class this river as a tributary of the Arkansas, since it has an independent channel to the Mississippi. The two streams, however, are connected by a large bayou 6 miles above the mouth of White river, through which the current moves sometimes in one direction and sometimes in the other, according to the relative stand of the rivers. In low stages, the greater part of the Arkansas water flows through this bayou, and it may therefore be considered in some sort as a double-mouthed stream, to which White river is a tributary. For convenience of description, this supposition has been adopted.

The flood surface of the river is, at the mouth, 168 feet, and at the mouth of Black river, 223 feet, above the level of the gulf. These points are about 350 miles apart, giving, for the slope of the river between them, 0.16 of a foot per mile. The sources of the stream are probably at about the same height as those of the St. Francis river, or 1200 feet above the gulf.

ST. FRANCIS BASIN.

St. Francis basin. The St. Francis basin consists of the St. Francis bottom and its water-shed.

By the former (see plate II) is understood the belt of swamp lands and low ridges lying between the Mississippi river and the line of high hills which extends almost continuously from Cape Girardeau to Helena. Some small portions of this area do not drain into the St. Francis river, but, being similar in character, the entire region is properly designated by a general name.

Its bottom lands.

Its water-shed. A portion of the southern slope of the Ozark mountains constitutes the chief water-shed of this region.

Sources of information in reference to these regions.

As the St. Francis bottom lands are the most northern of those regions which have been generally considered "vast reservoirs for the flood waters of the Mississippi," great efforts have been made to collect all possible information about their real character. Extended personal inquiries and measurements have been made in many different localities. The surveys of the military road from Memphis to the St. Francis river, made by Dr. William Howard, U. S. civil engineer, in 1833; those of the Memphis and Little Rock railroad company, made in 1854; those of the Fulton and Little Rock railroad company, made in 1855 (?); and those of the route from St. Louis to Fulton, made in 1850, under the direction of the Bureau of Topographical Engineers, War Department, by Joshua Barney, C. E., have all been carefully studied. Much assistance has also been derived from the admirable chapter upon the swamp lands of southeastern Missouri, contained in the report of Messrs. O'Sullivan and Morley, engineers of the St. Louis and Iron Mountain railroad company, and published with the second annual report of the board of directors of that road (St. Louis, 1854). Together with its accompanying maps, this work furnishes nearly all the general information which could be desired about the Missouri portion of these bottom lands.

Boundaries of the bottom lands.

Boundaries and area.—The St. Francis bottom is bounded as follows: Starting at Cape Girardeau, on the Mississippi river, the line runs a little south of west to the northwest corner of T. 29, R. 11, east; thence southwest to the St. Francis river, near the northeast corner of T. 26, R. 7, east; thence south along the St. Francis river* to the southeast corner of T. 22, R. 8, east; thence southwest to the northeast corner of T. 14, R. 4, east; thence nearly south to the middle of T. 3, R. 3, east; thence to Helena, and thence, following the Mississippi river, to Cape Girardeau. Within these limits there are many isolated ridges entirely above overflow.

* The St. Francis river, when in flood, loses some of its water in this vicinity by bayous connecting with Black river, a tributary of White river of Arkansas.

The limits of the water-shed of the St. Francis basin can be readily and exactly traced upon Hutawa's sectional map of Missouri, by following the divide which separates small streams running to and from the bottom lands. The Ozark slope constitutes fully two-thirds of the entire region.

Of the water-shed.

The following table has been carefully computed in accordance with the above boundary, and is believed to be quite accurate:—

Area of the basin.

	Square miles
Water-shed of St. Francis bottom lands	3,600
Ridges known to be above overflow in St. Francis bottom lands	600
Lands liable to be submerged in " " "	6,300
Total area of St. Francis basin	10,500

Topography.—The northern water-shed is a broken, hilly country, sloping very abruptly to the bottom lands. Its mean descent southward is about 1200 feet in 70 miles, or at a mean rate of about 17 feet per mile.

General topographical features.

The swamp region is, in general character, a great plain sloping from north to south at a mean rate of about 0.7 of a foot per mile, judging by the fall of the Mississippi between Cape Girardeau and Helena; and from east to west at a mean rate of about 0.5 of a foot per mile, judging by the levels of the Memphis and Little Rock railroad, which crossed the bottom near the middle line (plate IV). This country is separated from the rolling prairies west of it, which drain into White river, by a single narrow ridge averaging 300 feet in height.

The above is a fair general indication of the topography of the St. Francis basin, but further details are necessary to convey a really correct idea of the region.

The portion of the southern slope of the Ozark mountains which constitutes the northern water-shed is drained by three rivers: the St. Francis, the Castor, and the White (of Missouri). These streams have a fall of several feet per mile from their sources to the line of bottom lands; but, after passing it, their slope is greatly reduced, and general overflows of their banks during floods are the natural consequence. These overflows do not at once find free admittance to the great belt of swamp lands. The high range of hills pierced by the Mississippi at Commerce, after extending in a southwest direction for some 15 miles, is then broken by a gap some 10 or 12 miles in width at its narrowest place. Through this gap the waters of the White and Castor rivers, increased in great floods by much the greater part of the water which escapes from the Mississippi between Cape Girardeau and Commerce, enter the sunken lands west of New Madrid. After spreading out into a chain of lakes, they eventually drain by many bayous to the St. Francis river, debouching mainly between Randolph and Memphis.

The hill country and its system of drainage.

The continuation of Commerce bluffs west of the gap just mentioned is known by the name of Bloomfield ridge. It immediately forks. One branch extends westwardly to within 2.3 miles of the Ozark slope, where it terminates, leaving a narrow passage toward the west for the St. Francis; the other extends southwardly to Chalk bluffs, where this stream, after traversing a part of the bottom lands of Black river, turns again toward the east, and pierces the line of hills. Below Chalk bluffs the ridge extends southward to Helena, under the name of Crowley's ridge. This singular range of hills varies in height from 200 to 400 feet, with an average base not exceeding 6 or

8 miles. It is composed mainly of clay and gravel, often impregnated with saline matter. Its eastern base is washed by the St. Francis river. West of it lie the prairie lands of White river (of Arkansas). It is unbroken below Chalk bluffs, except by l'Anguille river, a small branch of the St. Francis.

The great swamp region and its subdivisions.

It would be a great mistake to suppose that, even after passing Crowley's ridge and its prolongations—Bloomfield ridge and Commerce bluffs—the three upland rivers enter a single vast swamp. There are many ridges—some wholly, and others mainly above overflow—which traverse it from north to south throughout its whole extent. One of these ridges separates for a time the St. Francis and Little rivers. Another, fully 20 feet above the highest overflow, extends, under the name of Big prairie, from New Madrid and Point Pleasant to Commerce bluffs, thus cutting off from the sunken lands west of New Madrid, and hence from the St. Francis river, all overflow from the Mississippi between Commerce and New Madrid, except what passes by one insignificant slough. The region east of Big prairie is in its turn traversed by a north and south ridge, called Matthews' prairie, which is nearly or quite above overflow. Doubtless further surveys would indicate other ridges. They are reported to exist in every part of the swamp. In the foregoing table, only those *known* to be entirely above overflow are included.

These north and south ridges, together with the southwest course of the Mississippi, cause several bayous to discharge their drainage, when the swamps are full during floods, directly into that river instead of into the St. Francis. Among such bayous may be named James bayou, near Island 8; bayou St. John, at New Madrid; Walker's bayou, near Island 15; Mill bayou, opposite Island 30; Wappenoky bayou, near Island 40; and a bayou near the head of Island 46. Some artificial system of drainage for the local basins of these bayous will have to be devised before the continuous chain of levees upon the bank of the Mississippi, so necessary to reclaim the swamp lands, is possible. In 1858 many levees, especially in the vicinity of the mouths of these bayous, were washed away by crevasse-water pouring back from the swamp into the Mississippi. It would seem that there must always be a risk of such accidents between Commerce and New Madrid. For the lower part of the bottom, less danger exists, since the drainage to the St. Francis is much less interrupted.

Surface soil.

Geology of the bottom lands.—The surface soil of the St. Francis bottom is a rich loam of exceeding fertility. It varies in different localities, being sometimes a heavy, black mould, and sometimes a light and sandy material. Gravel and small pebbles are occasionally found on the ridges, which are common throughout the whole region.

Sub-soil.

The following facts relative to the strata pierced in digging wells have been collected from authentic sources. Opposite Cairo, on the Mississippi bank, is a well 47 feet deep. The strata pierced are alternately clay and sand. The bottom of the well is sand. The wells in this part of the bottom are generally dug to sand before water is obtained. This is also the case near the latitude of Memphis, where the sand is reached after piercing clay strata some 15 or 20 feet in thickness. The depth of water in these wells varies with the stage of the Mississippi, even when several miles from its banks. Near Osceola, a well on the bank of the Mississippi was dug through sandy clay, some 23 feet, to black sand. This well oscillates with the Mississippi, but is never dry, even at low water, its supply then draining from the swamp. In the bottom, 18 miles farther west, the wells are some 15 to 20 feet deep, dug through clay to a beautiful white sand which supplies excellent water. On Frenchman's bayou, about 12 miles west of Randolph, a well was dug through more than 20 feet of hard, blue clay, before sand and water were reached. This well is on the prolongation of the ridge which separates the St. Francis and Little rivers. The land is entirely above overflow, and is probably not alluvial.

A sycamore log, buried 30 feet deep, was found about 4 miles from the Mississippi, in the bottom lands opposite Memphis, where the tree is now never found growing. A cypress log was found imbedded in sand, 30 feet below the surface, near Cairo.

Much of this region not Mississippi alluvion.

It is difficult to decide upon the geological character of the St. Francis bottom. It is well known that great changes occurred in the level of the northern part of the country during the earthquake in 1811, and that even now slight shocks are not unfrequently felt in the vicinity of New Madrid, indicating a probability of further changes. The bank, on which the town is built, unquestionably belongs to the same formation as the river bluffs, for it forms part of a ridge entirely above overflow, which extends southward from Commerce bluffs, and is pierced by the Mississippi at New Madrid. Its composition is quite different from the recent deposits of the Mississippi. Sir Charles Lyell, not being familiar with the country, conceived this to be the present Mississippi alluvion. Under this impression he states, in his "Second Visit to the United States" (page 174): "I examined the perpendicular face of the bank with some interest, as exemplifying the kind of deposits which the Mississippi throws down near its margin. They differ in no way from accumulations of sand and loam of high antiquity, with which the geologist is familiar; some beds are made up of horizontal layers; in others they are slanting, or in what is called cross-stratification. Some are white, others yellow, and here and there a seam of black carbonaceous matter, derived apparently from the destruction of older strata, is conspicuous."

A stronger confirmation of its ancient character could hardly be desired. The bank examined by him, although much lowered by the great earthquake, still remains entirely above overflow. A short distance to the west, however, the whole country for miles sank so as to be now submerged from 15 to 20 feet in floods.

It is apparent that it is impossible, where such changes are occurring, to decide with any exactness as to the real average depth of the Mississippi alluvion in this bottom. The facts above stated in relation to the wells, however, warrant the conclusion that the surface soil is underlain by a stratum of clay, a few feet in thickness, resting upon a stratum of sand, through which water passes freely back and forth, as the river changes its level. The shallow lakes of this country may be drained by boring through the clay to this stratum. It will be hereafter seen that there are good reasons for believing that this sand, in its turn, is underlain by a stratum of hard, drab-colored or blue clay, belonging to a geological formation long antecedent to the present. Indeed, it may be safely affirmed that the Mississippi alluvion has no great depth in these bottom lands, and that there are many ridges upon which it has no existence. Pebbles, characteristic of the river bluffs, are found on these ridges, and the two formations are doubtless identical in geological character.

Growth on the bottom lands.—On the high land, rarely, if ever, overflowed, the growth consists of sweet and black gum, walnut, hickory, box-elder, hackberry, ash, white oak, pecan, red elm, black and red haw, sassafras, and a little beech, maple, and dogwood. Heavy cane grows on the high banks of the rivers.

Forest growth on "high" land in swamp region.

On the "middle" land, liable—before levees were built—to annual overflow, the growth consists of sweet and black gum, hickory, hackberry, several kinds of oak, red elm, black and red haw, and cane.

On "middle" land.

On the lowest swamp lands the growth consists of cypress, water-oaks, swamp ash, elm, hickory, red elm, honey-tree, and willow.

On lowest land.

Floods in the bottom lands.—Three* cross-sections of the St. Francis bottom have been obtained (see plates II and IV). One, the profile of the Cairo and Fulton railroad, extending from Rodney's landing, near Cairo, to the St. Francis river (59.2 miles), furnished by Mr. J. S. Williams. The second, the profile of the military road between Memphis and Little Rock, made by Dr. William Howard, in 1833, under instructions from the U. S. Engineer Department. The third, the profile of the Memphis and Little Rock railroad, furnished by Mr. M. Lynch. These profiles are all somewhat indefinite in respect to the depth of overflow, since that was not the especial object of the engineers, and the dates of high water are not well determined. Still, they furnish the means of forming an approximate estimate of it. Including lands never submerged, crossed by the roads, the mean depth of overflow is 1.3, 1.6, and 5.2 feet, respectively. Exclusive of land above high-water mark, viz., 32.7 miles for the first, 17 miles for the second, and 3 miles for the third, the mean depths of overflow are, respectively, 2.9, 3.0, and 5.9 feet, the maximum being 10.0, 5.0, and 15.5 feet.

Average overflow of these bottom lands.

From these figures, it would seem that 3 feet may be considered the mean depth of overflow in great flood years throughout the entire submerged lands, exclusive of the ridges. This accords with the estimates of many gentlemen well acquainted with these lands, and is believed to be nearly correct.

It should be remarked that much of this water is due to rain, the fall of which is always excessive upon the bottom lands in great flood years. This was especially the case in 1828, 1850, and 1858. In 1858 the swamps were so full of rain-water before the April rise—the first which entered them to any considerable extent—that the St. Francis river was not backed up even for a day after the January rise. That its current should from the beginning resist such a Mississippi rise as that which occurred in March, shows that a sensible portion of the water in the swamps, when these great floods occur, is due to rain.

Effect of rain.

During ordinary years, the St. Francis bottom is now entirely protected from the Mississippi water by its levees, and is, consequently, only submerged in its lowest parts by rain-water, and by the floods of the St. Francis, Castor, and White rivers.

Effect of existing levees.

---

* Several sections of the swamp lands were made by Messrs. O'Sullivan and Morley. Their report to the Iron Mountain railroad company, however, does not furnish the means of estimating with any exactness the mean depth of overflow on these lines.

St. Francis river.—The St. Francis river heads among the Ozark mountains just west of Pilot Knob, at an elevation of 1150 feet above the gulf of Mexico. It flows toward the southeast, receiving many mountain tributaries, until, just before entering the swamp region, at a distance of 105 miles from its source, by its longest fork, it has reduced its high-water elevation above the gulf to 330 feet. Here its high-water cross-section is 9400 square feet. At Indian ford, where it first leaves the hills on its right bank, its high-water cross-section has been reduced to 5100 square feet by water lost into the Castor-river swamps. About 17 miles farther on, or 11 miles above Chalk bluffs, its high-water cross-section is only 2330 square feet. This reduction is due to the loss of water into the swamps of Black river, a tributary of White river of Arkansas. At its passage through the ridge at Chalk bluffs, its high-water elevation above the gulf is 280 feet. It immediately divides into a maze of channels, or rather lakes, which extend nearly to the latitude of Randolph. Here, beginning to receive by many bayous the united waters of Castor and White (of Missouri) rivers, it again becomes a river in the usual acceptation of the term. At the crossing of the Memphis and Little Rock railroad its high-water surface is 209 feet above the gulf, its cross-section being 21,000 feet. About 1 mile above its mouth, near Porter's Mill, its high-water cross-section is 37,000 square feet (see Appendix C), its high-water elevation above the gulf being about 200 feet.

Slope and cross-section of St. Francis river.

This river is navigable to Wittsburg, a distance of 80 miles, during about six months of the year, for boats drawing 3 feet water. Its mean width between banks in this distance is about 700 feet; its range from low to high water, about 40 feet; its fall per mile, about 0.2 of a foot; and its current usually sluggish.

The Mississippi levees, incomplete as they are, have still exerted a great influence upon the regimen of the St. Francis.

Before these levees were made, numerous bayous, whose beds were from 5 to 15 feet below the surface of the natural bank, gave free admission to the Mississippi water long before the top of the flood. The swamps, thus becoming gradually flooded, drained into the St. Francis river, or into the bayous which serve as their outlets. At the top of the Mississippi flood, therefore, these streams were also in full flood, returning vast quantities of water. This fact has been established by careful inquiries among those residing upon the spot, and personally cognizant of what they state. There has been but one answer to such inquiries—that there was *always* a very strong current discharging into the Mississippi at the top of a Mississippi flood. This was especially noticed at the mouth of the St. Francis, in the floods of 1844, 1849, and 1850. In the latter particularly, the current was powerful; but even with this great velocity, the water-way was not sufficient for the discharge. The flood poured over the country between Stirling and Helena, and discharged itself over the bank into the Mississippi. In 1858 this happened not only at the mouth, but in many other places, as will be fully shown in a subsequent chapter. There is, therefore, a manifest error in the assumption, which has been often made, that these great swamp regions served as non-returning "reservoirs" to diminish materially the discharge of the Mississippi below them at the date of highest water.

Its regimen before levees were made.

Its present regimen.

At present, the regimen of the river is greatly changed. During rapid rises of the Mississippi, the St. Francis is generally backed up, sometimes even as far as Wittsburg. Not unfrequently, there is a rapid current up stream at such times. This was the case in the January rise of 1858, when drift-wood was carried several miles up the river. It does not always occur, however; for, if the swamp be full of rain-water, the discharge may be maintained without receiving supplies from the Mississippi, even during quite rapid and high rises of that river. This was the case in the March rise of 1858.

The floods of the St. Francis, independently of Mississippi water, are trifling, never raising the river below Wittsburg to within several feet of high-water mark. They depend entirely upon local rain, and have, therefore, but little regularity.

Its annual discharge.

As nearly as can be ascertained, this river drains about 9700 square miles. The mean annual downfall in this region (see Chapter II) is about 41 inches. The ratio between downfall and drainage for this region (see Chapter IV) is shown by the operations of this Survey to be about 0.9, giving for the annual discharge of the St. Francis river, $9700 \times 5280^2 \times 3.4 \times 0.9 =$ 908,619,000,000 cubic feet, or about the twenty-first part of the mean annual discharge of the Mississippi itself.

Its levees.

There are no levees upon the banks of the St. Francis, as they are never flooded below Wittsburg, except when the Mississippi has access to the swamp.

Indian mounds belonging to Mr. Edmondson.

Mounds and Indian relics.—There are many Indian mounds in the St. Francis bottom, some of which are reported to be very large. A collection of them belonging to Mr. Edmondson, situated about 15 miles from Memphis, on the line of the Memphis and Little Rock railroad, was examined with a view to collecting facts which might determine the question of the depth of the alluvion in this region. Their situation is peculiar. A small bayou flows near the house and almost parallel to the railroad. The mounds are all upon its high northern bank, which is very undulating in its character—so much so, indeed, that it is difficult to determine how many of the swells are natural, and how many artificial. The soil of this ridge is quite different from that of the swamp around. It has a reddish color, and contains many small pebbles, some of which resemble those from the Memphis bluff. That the ridge is natural, with many natural inequalities upon it, is beyond a doubt. There are, however, three little swells, which seem to be artificial, from the fact that there are pits at the bottom of each, from which earth may have been taken. Mr. Edmondson's house is built on the largest of these three mounds, which is of a uniform shape, having a circular base and a rounded top. Its height above the ridge is about 15 feet, and its base is from 100 to 150 feet in diameter. The top is perhaps 50 feet in diameter and level. Its dimensions may have been materially altered by Mr. Edmondson in building his house. The other two mounds are smaller and are now under cultivation. Scattered over them are fragments of Indian pottery, red brick, flint, and rounded stones. Many Indian curiosities are turned up in ploughing These consist of jugs, often colored red or yellow, hatchets of flint or of hard slate, human bones, etc. These remains are generally found within 18 inches of the surface. A cistern 16 feet deep has been dug in the largest mound. The excavation was made through clay and sand irregularly stratified. A large charcoal log was found some 6 feet below the top of the mound, but no Indian remains except near the surface. The irregularity of the strata made the digging of the cistern quite difficult. The railroad passes through a small mound at a short distance from Mr. Edmondson's house. The cut was 3 feet deep, and a jug and other curiosities were obtained.

Mr. H. H. Brackenridge, in a letter to Thomas Jefferson, from Baton Rouge, July 25, 1813, on the Population and Tumuli of the Aborigines of America, states that there are several mounds near New Madrid, the largest being 350 feet in diameter at the base.

MISSOURI BASIN.

General character.

This is much the largest of any of the tributary basins of the Mississippi, and differs from all the rest in containing a large area covered by lofty mountain chains. The river issues from the Rocky mountains in many branches, which form a series of large rivers that flow through the great uncultivable plains. Comparatively little rain falls upon the mountains and the plains, and hence the size of the main river is disproportionately small, when the drainage area alone is considered. Its annual discharge is only about three-quarters of that of the Ohio, although its basin is nearly two and a half times as large. (See next chapter.) After passing the 98th meridian the banks of the river become more and more fertile, and the region through which it passes gradually changes from an uncultivated waste to a populous country. The total area of the basin, including the mountains, the plains, and the fertile region, is 518,000 square miles.

Sources of the river.

Missouri river.—Ascending the river, the Missouri is found to divide, at Fort Union, into two main branches of about equal size, the Yellowstone and the Upper Missouri. About 265 miles above its mouth the former again divides into two nearly equal branches, the Big Horn and the Upper Yellowstone. The Upper Missouri remains a single stream to within about 100 miles of its sources, where it divides into three forks, named Jefferson, Madison, and Gallatin. It was first explored to the sources of Jefferson fork by Captains Lewis and Clarke, U. S. A., in 1806. When returning, Captain Clarke followed up Gallatin's fork a short distance, crossed over to the Yellowstone near where it issues from Snow mountains, and passed down the river in canoes to its mouth. The next expedition was conducted in 1833 by Captain Bonneville, who then explored a portion of the Big-Horn river. The maps of this region made by these early explorers have been superseded by more accurate surveys, conducted chiefly upon the Upper-Missouri branch by detachments of Governor Stevens' Pacific Railroad party in 1853; but so far as a knowledge of the sources of the Missouri river are concerned, very little additional information had been acquired previous to the year 1859. At this date a party under Captain W. F. Raynolds, U. S. Topl. Engrs., was organized by the War Department, to explore the region. This party accurately mapped the Yellowstone from its mouth to the point where it issues from the Snow mountains; the Big Horn to its sources; the Madison fork to its sources; and acquired definite information respecting the Gallatin fork and the Upper Yellowstone. The report has not yet been published, but through the kindness of Captain Raynolds, with the sanction of the War Department, the following facts have been communicated.

Union Peak.

In lat. 43° 30′ and long. 110° 00′, a mountain rises to some 14,000 feet above the level of the sea. It is named by Captain Raynolds, Union Peak, because water trickling from its northern side flows into the Mississippi, from its southern side into the Great Colorado, and from its western side into the Columbia. Within one degree of longitude westward and about one degree of latitude northward from this peak are four of the sources of the Missouri, where the Big Horn, the Yellowstone, and the Madison and Gallatin forks take their rise.*

The Big-Horn branch.

The Big Horn (here called Wind river) flows southeastwardly to long. 108° 30′, through a narrow bottom land, varying from 1 to 3 miles in width, bounded on the south side by the impassable Wind-river chain, and on the north by an elevated prairie rising into mountains. It is then joined by the Popo Agie, and turning abruptly toward the north forces its way through the Big-Horn mountains, here forming a double chain, to the prairies bordering upon the Yellowstone.

The Upper-Missouri branch.

The Madison fork flows northward, chiefly through a rugged defile, to the junction of the three forks, where it is joined first by the Jefferson fork. This is rather the larger river of the two, and heads among beautiful Rocky-mountain valleys, about two degrees of longitude farther to the westward. Neither of these streams is fordable near its mouth. About half a mile below their junction, the Gallatin fork, smaller than either of the others, enters from the southeast. These three forks unite in an extensive plain surrounded by lofty mountains. The united waters soon enter, and for nearly a degree of latitude traverse, a succession of mountain valleys and enormous cañons, of which an idea may be formed from the following description, taken from Lewis and Clarke's travels:—

Its "Gate."

"A mile and a half beyond this creek the rocks approach the river on both sides, forming a most sublime and extraordinary spectacle. For five and three-quarter miles these rocks rise perpendicularly from the water's edge to the height of nearly 1200 feet. They are composed of a black granite near its base, but from its lighter color above, and from the fragments, we suppose the upper part to be flint of a yellowish brown and cream color. Nothing can be imagined more tremendous than the frowning darkness of these rocks, which project over the river and menace us with destruction. The river, of 350 yards in width, seems to have forced its channel down this solid mass, but so reluctantly has it given way that during the whole distance the water is very deep even at the edges, and for the first 3 miles there is not a spot, except one of a few yards, in which a man could stand between the water and the towering perpendicular of the mountain: the convulsion of the passage must have been terrible, since at its outlet there are vast columns of rock torn from the mountain, which are strewed on both sides of the river, the trophies, as it were, of the victory. Several fine springs burst out from the chasms of the rock, and contribute to

* Captain Raynolds' map not yet having been published, this section of country upon plate I has been delineated from the older maps, and does not exactly conform to this description. It is, however, sufficiently correct for all general purposes.

increase the river, which has now a strong current, but very fortunately we are able to overcome it with our oars, since it would be impossible to use either the cord or the pole. We were obliged to go on some time after dark, not being able to find a spot large enough to encamp on, but at length, about 2 miles above a small island in the middle of the river, we met with a spot on the left side, where we procured plenty of light wood and pitch-pine. This extraordinary range of rocks we called the Gates of the Rocky mountains."

Its Great falls.

About 35 miles above Fort Benton, the river pours over the Great Falls and becomes a navigable stream. The following description of those falls is from the report of Lieutenant Grover, U. S. A.:—

"There are five principal cascades. The first, about 3 miles below the mouth of the Sun river, falls about 25 feet. The second, nearly 3 miles below the first, is a small, crooked cascade, of 5 feet 11 inches pitch. Immediately below is the third. Here, between high banks, a ledge, nearly as straight as if formed by art, runs obliquely across the river, over which the waters fall 42 feet in one continuous sheet of 470 yards in width. At the foot of this cascade, so beautiful for its length and regularity, is a small island, covered with willow, cottonwood, and wild cherry. Half a mile below this, again, is the fourth—a small, irregular fall of about 12 feet descent. There is a small knot of an island near the middle, and between that and the right bank of the river the ledge of the fall is very crooked, and the water reaches the basin below in two pitches. But between the island and the left bank there is simply a succession of rapids; the stream then hurries on, lashed and churned by numerous rapids, about 5 miles farther, where it precipitates itself over a precipice of 76 feet in height. This is the fifth and 'Great Fall' of the Missouri. The banks are high and abrupt on both sides; and above and below, deep ravines with bare, steep sides extend out into the prairie from 1 to 2 miles. But opposite the fall, on the north side, a narrow tongue of waving prairie runs near to the river, and breaks off in terraces to a small bottom below the cascade. The lower plain, embracing 2 or 3 acres, is a rounded point of land, which, with a rock-bound shoulder, half encircles the basin of the cascade, and for a short distance below confines the water-course to half its usual width. Near its head a broken and disconnected ledge of rocks rises some 30 feet or more above the water; but lower down there is some soil and a few scattered cottonwood, willow, and cherry trees."

The Yellowstone branch.

Between the Big-Horn and Upper-Missouri branches, in long. 110° 30′ and lat. 44° 30′, the Upper Yellowstone has its source in a large lake, as yet only visited by trappers and Indians, whence it plunges through an impassable gorge to the highest point visited by Captain Raynolds' party. From this point, where it is 200 yards wide and 6 feet deep, it winds to the northeast, through a narrow valley, to the mouth of Clarke's fork. In this distance it is characterized by many islands, and by bold, sweeping curves, frequently impinging upon the hills. Between Clarke's fork and the mouth of the Big Horn, the river is from 500 to 600 yards in width, unobstructed by rapids, and flowing with a swift current of some 3 or 4 miles per hour.

Below Big-Horn river, to Powder river, the width increases to 800 or 900 yards, and the river becomes turbid, resembling the Missouri.

From Powder river to the Missouri the banks are low and caving, and the river assumes the characteristic appearance of the Missouri, containing numerous sand-bars, densely timbered islands, etc. There are also some rapids and shoals.

Captain Raynolds is of the opinion that the Yellowstone can be navigated with boats drawing 3 feet of water, up to the point where it issues from the mountains, from the middle of May to the first of August. The floods are neither sudden nor excessive, and the river is probably better adapted to steamboat navigation than the Missouri, although there are difficult rapids at the mouth of Powder river.

The Missouri below the head of navigation.

Having thus followed the principal branches of the Missouri out of the mountains, the main river will be described, from the head of navigation downward. The following extracts are from the report of Lieutenant Grover, U. S. A.:—

"The Missouri, from its falls for many miles on its way, traces its course at the bottom of a deep cañon worn by its waters. The faces of this cañon are generally very abrupt and bare, and approach quite close upon the water-course, at the same time determining only the general direction of the river, so that each detour of the stream leaves a small, rich interval in the bend, covered with luxuriant grass, and sometimes skirted with a few small cottonwood trees." As far as the mouth of Maria's river, the banks of the Missouri vary "from 100 to 160 feet in height; its bed has been very crooked, and composed entirely of loose gravel—the stream perfectly clear and transparent. The current flows with a tolerably uniform velocity of about 2.7 miles per hour except at some points where its unusual shallowness gives a slight increase of rate."

Below Maria's river the bluffs fall back with a gradual slope to the general prairie level, and the river flows with sweeping curves among beautiful islands. On reaching Bear-Paw mountains, the scenery assumes an entirely different phase. "The bluffs were now more abrupt, and crowded the river; colonnades and odd-detached pillars of partially cemented sand, capped with huge globes of light-brownish sandstone, tower up from their steep sides to the height of 100 feet or more above the water. Then the action of the weather upon the bluffs in the background has worn them into a thousand grotesque forms, while lower down their faces, seams of volcanic rock from 3 to 6 feet thick, with a dip nearly vertical and no uniform strike, beaten and cracked by the weather, rising from 6 to 8 feet above the surface, run up and down the steep faces and projecting shoulders of the cliffs—a most perfect imitation of dry-stone walls." Below these mountains the river resumes its former character, until the vicinity of Judith river is reached. There "we took leave for a while of many of the wild beauties of nature which lay scattered along the river in an ever-varying panorama, to take a view of the other side of the picture—of nature's wild deformities—a master-piece in its way. The 'Mauvaises Terres,' or Bad Lands, which this section is very appropriately called, is characterized by a total absence of anything which could by any possibility give pleasure to the eye or gratification to the mind by any associations of utility. Not an island, nor a shrub of any account—nothing but huge, bare piles of mud, towering up as high as they can stand, and crowding each other for room. The banks, varying from 200 to 300 feet in height, were of this nature on both sides of the river all day." They continued so on the following day. Then Lieutenant Grover writes: "We are rapidly approaching a more inhabitable country. The bluffs are less high and more sloping, and covered with grass. The bottoms along the river increase in width and richness of soil, and fields of rank grass alternate with thick groves of cottonwood, cherry, and willow." This character of country continues to the mouth of the Muscle-shell. Below this river there are very few places where a rocky bottom is found in the Missouri. About one day's travel below that point, Lieutenant Grover states: "The banks on the south side of the river are still quite high and much broken, and a few scrubby pines and dwarf cedars are to be seen near their tops. Incrustations of glauber salt whiten the banks in many places—a peculiarity by no means local, but, on the contrary, of very general occurrence all along the river. On landing, at noon, we picked up some more specimens of fossil shell-fish, also some conglomerated fossil marine shells, in which the cementing substance was carbonate of lime. This fossiliferous region appears pretty extensive." A few miles below, another strip of Mauvaise Terre was passed. Having now reached a point about midway between Fort Benton and the mouth of the Yellowstone, Lieutenant Grover writes: "The river has now become quite similar in every respect to the lower Missouri. It is nearly as wide; its bottom is sandy; and broad, shifting sand-bars render the channel about as uncertain. The adjacent bottoms increase in width, richness of soil, and density of growth. The bluffs on the north side have declined and receded very much, being now nothing more than the breaking down of the high, rolling prairie to the immediate valley of the river. But to the south they are still quite high and abrupt, but have more grass on them."

Between the mouth of Milk river and Fort Union, the Missouri is described by Mr. Lambert, Governor Stevens' topographer, as "a wide and turgid stream, with an ever-shifting channel, choked with sand-bars, which are influenced by every storm; its great volume of water, however, insuring a navigable channel on one side or other. It flows with a very sinuous course through an intervale of variable width, enclosed by the tall bluffs of the plateaux on either side, which sometimes project upon the bank, in some places leaving an intervale of 5 or 6 miles; it is generally deeply fringed with the cottonwood and its congeners, and occasionally a dense underbrush, affording a secure haunt to the fierce grizzly bear; good grazing occurs in spots, but is generally better among the bluffs and coulées than on the plain, where the soil is mostly hard and dusty, affording, it might be supposed, but a scanty sustenance even to the swarms of grasshoppers, which in certain conditions of the atmosphere take wing, and are seen drifting in a darkening cloud for hours before the wind. The bluffs are composed mainly of a soft, half-formed sandstone, which crumbles under a slight pressure, and is washed by the rains into the most fantastic shapes, resembling fortifications and ordinary buildings."

The following brief recapitulation of the character of the river, from the mountains to the Yellowstone, is from the report of Lieutenant Saxton:—

"The regimen of the river above the mouth of the Muscle-shell is fixed. The banks change very little, and there is very little timber. Should steamers run here eventually, there will be a scarcity of fuel; enough, however, can be collected for present purposes.

"The Mauvaises Terres lie directly above the Muscle-shell; through these the channel is very good. The worst bar in the river is above the Bad Lands, a few miles below Fort Benton, where there was but 15 inches of water.

"From the Muscle-shell downward toward the mouth of the Yellowstone, the river changes. The water gradually becomes muddy from the washing away of the banks; the channel is constantly shifting its position; the forests of cottonwood, with which the banks are lined, falling into the river, causes numerous snags and sawyers. Below the Yellowstone, the Missouri assumes the same character it maintains to the mouth. It becomes thick and muddy with the alluvial deposit it is ceaselessly bearing onward to the gulf of Mexico. The bed of the river is much broader; the waters separate into many different channels, forming numerous sand-islands, sometimes covered with forests of cottonwood."

Below the mouth of the Yellowstone, the character of the Missouri undergoes comparatively little variation, and is sufficiently described by the following extracts from Lieutenant Warren's report:—

"This great stream has generally a uniform width from the junction with the Yellowstone to its mouth, varying from one-third to half a mile when the banks are full. In low water, the width is much less, and dry bars of sand occupy portions of the bed, from which the water has withdrawn. In the upper part of the river, where the trees do not destroy the force of the wind, the sand is blown about in the most astonishing manner, and the clouds of sand can be seen for many miles. Sand-banks are thus formed, generally at the edges of the trees on the islands and points, and which are often many feet above the level of the highest floods." * * * * *

"Along the banks of the Missouri, the bluffs are generally clothed with various species of trees as far up as the mouth of the Platte; above this point, the timber is generally confined to the ravines and bottom lands. These bottom lands attain a width of from 10 to 15 miles, after we get above Council Bluffs, which is almost continuous to the mouth of James river. Throughout this section, the edges of the banks are lined with heavy cottonwood and other trees, and fuel for steamboats can now generally be found cut up and prepared for their use.

"At James river the bluffs close in so that the general width of the space between is only from 1 to 2 miles all the way to the upper Big bend, near the 48th parallel. Here, again, the bottom lands become wider, and continue at a width of from 3 to 6 miles to a point about 50 miles above the Yellowstone. In this last section there is also an abundance of large cottonwood timber, and the appearance of the river is quite similar to what it is at Sioux City."

"The bottom lands on the Missouri, along the western boundary of Iowa, as well as the prairie lands on either side, are very fertile. The valley of the Big Sioux, above its mouth, forms the continuation in direction of that of the Missouri below, and is said to be fertile. The Hupan-Kutey prairie, lying between this stream and the Vermilion, is low and fertile, and is about the last of the continuous fertile country as you advance up the Missouri, which here comes from the west. Above this [to the upper Big bend] the bottom lands of the Missouri are sometimes 1 and 2 miles wide, and will give but precarious support to an agricultural people; it is doubtful whether even this can be said of the high prairie lying back from the stream."

Its slope.

The following table has been carefully prepared to exhibit the slope of the Missouri. The distances below Fort Union are from Lieutenant Warren's reconnoissance; those above Fort Benton, from Captain Raynolds' original unpublished maps.

Low-water slope of the Missouri.

Locality.	Distance above the mouth.	Elevation above the gulf.	Fall per mile.	Authority.
Big-Horn Branch.	*Miles.*	*Feet.*	*Feet.*	
Source (Wind river)	2565	7527	0.00	Captain Raynolds.
Mouth of Popo Agie	2450	5347	18.96	"
Leaves Big-Horn mountains	2231	3534	8.22	"
Mouth of Big Horn	2159	2831	9.78	"
Yellowstone Branch.				
Source (lake)	2439	6500 (?)	0.00	"
Leaves Snow mountains	2345	4705	19.10	"
Mouth of Big Horn	2159	2831	10.08	"
Mouth of Yellowstone	1894	2188	2.43	"
Upper-Missouri Branch.				
Source of Madison fork	2908	6800 (?)	0.00	"
Three forks of Missouri	2824	4319	29.52	"
Mouth of Sun river	2689	3578	5.54	"
Foot of falls	2670	2964	31.59	"
At Fort Benton	2644	2845	4.56	"
At Fort Union	1894	2194	0.88	"
At Fort Pierre	1246	1475	1.10	Lieutenant Warren.
At Sioux City	842	1065	1.01	Railroad levels.
At St. Joseph, Missouri	484	756	0.86	Railroad levels.
At mouth	0	381	0.77	Railroad levels.

Its range.

With reference to the range of the Missouri between low and high water, but little can be said. It is about 35 feet at the mouth; 20 feet at St. Joseph, Missouri; and still less above, being at Fort Benton only about 6 feet. Ice dams in the spring sometimes occasion great local rises.

Its width.

Its high-water width, for so long a river, is remarkably uniform. In the vicinity of Fort Benton it varies from 500 to 1000 feet. Near the mouth of Milk river, it has increased to 1500 feet. Below the Yellowstone, it is about 2000 feet. From this vicinity the river gradually attains an average width of about 3000 feet, which it holds for some 600 miles to its mouth.

Its discharge.

Its annual discharge is about 4 trillions of cubic feet, or about one-fifth of that of the Mississippi. (See next chapter.)

Its navigability.

With reference to the navigability of the Missouri above Milk river, the following is the opinion of Lieutenant Grover, based upon information derived from members of the American Fur Company:—

"The fact of this part of the river lying near its sources in the Rocky mountains would naturally lead one to suppose that the changes in its volume of water from month to month would be nearly the same, for the same month, from year to year. This is found to be the case. As winter breaks up and warmer weather gradually comes on in the spring, the ice becomes rotten, and the river swollen by the melting of the snow in the valley; and as early as the first of May, the river is clear. Such is the great range of elevation, and consequently the great range of temperature, covered by this feeding reservoir of snow, that, instead of melting in the short space of a month and swelling the river to a torrent, the process of melting commences with the valleys in the early spring, and goes on gradually to higher elevations as the season advances, constantly diminishing, of course, till August, when all that has a sensible effect upon the river is expended, when it commences falling more rapidly till the latter part of September. The minimum additional depth of water above that of the latter part of September, according to the information above referred to, is as follows, viz.: For the first of June, 3 feet; first of July, 2½ feet; first of August, 2 feet; and first of September, 1 foot.

"It would then seem that, up to the first of August, there is water enough for navigation by boats of 3 feet draught loaded; and up to the first of September, for boats of 2 feet draught; and later than the twentieth of September, for boats not exceeding 18 inches in draught."

In the summer of 1859 a steamboat belonging to the North American Fur Company ascended the Missouri river to Fort Benton. In the summer of 1860 two steamboats of that company, carrying a detachment of 300 United States troops, ascended the river to the same point.

The navigation of the lower part of the river is thus described by Lieutenant Warren, in his report dated November 24, 1858:—

"The navigation is generally closed by ice at Sioux City by the tenth of November, and at Fort Leavenworth by the first of December. The rainy season of the spring and summer commences in different years between the fifteenth of May and the thirtieth of June (in the latitude of Kansas, Missouri, Iowa, and Southern Nebraska), and lasts about two months. During this period, the tributaries of the Missouri in these latitudes maintain this river in good boating stage. The floods produced by the melting snows in the mountains come from the Platte, the Big Shyenne, the Yellowstone, and the Missouri above the Yellowstone, and reach the lower river about the first part of July, and it is mainly to these that the navigator of the Missouri above the Niobrara depends. The length of time the flood lasts is in proportion to the quantity of snow in the mountains, which varies greatly in different years. On the average it may be said to last a month; but a steamer starting from St. Louis, on the first indication there of such a rise, would not generally reach the Yellowstone before it was nearly past this latter point. Rivers like this, whose navigation depends upon the temporary floods, are greatly inferior for ascending than descending boats. The rise at the Yellowstone would be about ten days reaching St. Louis, and any good system of telegraphing along the stream, which would apprise those below, would more than double the advantages to the upward navigation. If a miscalculation is made by taking a temporary rise for the main one, the boat has to lay by in the middle part of the river till the main rise comes." * * * * * * *

"The American Fur Company's boats are of the largest class of freight boats now navigating the Missouri. They are ably managed, and the company possesses information, by expresses sent from its trading posts near the mountains, as to the amount of snow that has fallen and the probable extent and time of the rise produced by its melting. The boats are loaded and time of starting fixed accordingly. Their boats carry from 150 to 200 tons to the Yellowstone, a distance of 1900 miles, drawing from 3 to 4½ feet of water, and make the passage up in from twenty-two to thirty-five days. Considerable freight is taken out for the post of Fort Union, and they generally ascend with that for Fort Benton to about 60 miles above the mouth of the Yellowstone, and have on one occasion gone to Milk river, 100 miles farther.

"The quantity of water is, on the average, about equal from the Yellowstone and Missouri at their junction, and above this point, steamboats venture with caution. The great risk in proceeding farther, of having the boat caught in the upper river during the winter, more than counterbalances the prospective gain."

"One of the greatest obstructions to the navigation of the Missouri consists in the great number of snags or trees, whose roots, imbedded in the channel by the caving of the banks, stand at various inclinations pointing down the stream. These obstructions are, comparatively, quite rare above the mouth of James river, but from this point down to the Mississippi, it is a wonder often how a steamboat can be navigated through them. As it is, they cause the boats to lie by during the night, and thus occasion a loss of nearly half of their running time. But this is not the only delay, for often on account of the wind the bends filled with snags cannot be passed, and the vessel is frequently detained for days on this account. This effect of the wind is much more seriously felt as you ascend above Council Bluffs, for the protection afforded by the trees on the banks is constantly diminishing."

Their distances apart.

Tributaries.—The following table exhibits the distances between several important points upon the Missouri, as determined by the reconnoissance of Lieutenant Warren:—

Distances upon the Missouri.

Locality.	Distance above mouth of Missouri.	Locality.	Distance above mouth of Missouri.
	Miles.		*Miles.*
Mouth of Osage river	132	Mouth of Big-Shyenne river	1300
Mouth of Kansas river	382	Mouth of Moreau river	1367
Northern boundary of Kansas	530	Mouth of Grand river	1391
Northern boundary of Missouri	617	Mouth of Cannon-Ball river	1479
Mouth of Platte river	640	Mouth of Heart river	1522
Mouth of Big-Sioux river	842	Fort Clarke	1584
Mouth of James river	976	Mouth of Knife river	1593
Mouth of Niobrara river	1026	Mouth of Little-Missouri river	1673
Mouth of White-Earth river	1136	Mouth of Yellowstone river	1888
Fort Pierre	1246	Fort Union	1894

The Niobrara.

The only tributaries of the Missouri below the Yellowstone, which require notice here, are the Niobrara, the Platte, and the Kansas. The first is thus described by Lieutenant Warren, Topographical Engineers, its first explorer:—

"This river is about 350 miles long. From its source to long. 103° 15′ it is a beautiful little stream of clear running water, of a width of from 10 to 15 feet, gradually widening as it descends. Its valley furnishes here very good grass, abounding in rushes or prele, but is for the most part destitute of wood, even for cooking. After flowing thus far, it rapidly widens till in long. 102° 30′ it attains a width of 60 to 80 yards; its valley is still quite open and easy to travel along, but destitute of wood, except occasional pines on the distant hills to the north. In long. 102° 30′ it enters between high, steep banks, which closely confine it, and for a long way it is a complete cañon; here, however, wood becomes more abundant, and pine is occasionally seen on the bluffs, while small clusters of cottonwood, elm, and ash occupy the narrow points left by its windings. In long. 101° 45′ the sand hills come, on the north side, close to the river, while, on the south side, they are at the distance of from 1 to 2 miles off, leaving a smooth road to travel on along the bluffs. The bluffs gradually appear higher and higher above the stream as it descends, until they reach the height of 300 feet. The sand mostly ceases on the north side in long. 100° 23′; but it lies close to the stream on the south side nearly all the way to the Wazi-honska. Throughout this section, lying between long. 102° 00′ and long. 99° 20′, a distance of 180 miles, the Niobrara is in every respect a peculiar stream, and there is none that I know of that it can be compared with. It flows here between high, rocky banks of soft, white and yellowish, calcareous and silicious sandstone, standing often in precipices at the water's edge, its verticality being preserved by a capping of hard grit. It is here impossible to travel any considerable distance along its immediate banks without having frequently to climb the ridges which rise sometimes perpendicularly from the stream. As you approach from the north or south, there are no indications of a river till you come within 2 or 3 miles of the banks, and then only by the trees whose tops occasionally rise above the ravines in which they grow, so completely is it walled in by the high bluffs which enclose its narrow valley. It seems as if it had resulted from a fissure in the earth's crust, and now flows at a depth of about 300 feet below the general level of the prairie. The soft rock which forms the bluffs is worn into the most intricate labyrinths by the little streams, all of which have their sources in beautiful, gushing springs of clear cold water. In these small, deep valleys the grass is luxuriant; pine, ash, and oak are abundant. To the agriculturist this section has, however, comparatively little attraction, and that between long. 99° 20′ and the mouth, an extent of about 90 miles, is perhaps far more valuable. Here the bottoms will probably average a width of a quarter of a mile, are susceptible of cultivation, and cottonwood, oak, walnut, and ash will furnish settlements with all the timber and fuel they will need. The river banks seem to present no good building stone, nor did we, though searching diligently, discover any signs of coal or other valuable minerals."

The Platte.

The Platte is thus concisely described by Lieutenant Warren:—

"The Platte river is the most important tributary of the Missouri in the region under consideration; its broad and grass-covered valley leading to the west furnishes one of the best wagon roads of its length in America. From its mouth to the forks, the bluffs are from 2 to 5 miles from the water, making an intermediate bottom valley of from 4 to 8 miles wide. From the forks to Fort Laramie, the bluffs occasionally come down to the water's edge, and the road has to cross the points of the ridges. From Ash Hollow to Fort Laramie, the road is sometimes heavy with sand. Fine cottonwood grows along the banks, and on the islands, from the mouth to Fort Kearny; from here up it is scarce and of small size. Cedar is found in the ravines of the bluffs, in the neighborhood of the forks, and above. The river is about a mile wide, and flows over a sandy bottom; when the banks are full, it is about 6 feet deep throughout, having a remarkably level bed; but it is of no use for navigation, as the bed is so broad that the water seldom attains sufficient depth, and then the rise is of short duration.

"The water is sometimes so low, as was the case last season [1855], that it can be crossed anywhere without difficulty, the only care requisite being to avoid quicksands.

"The manner in which this stream spreads out over its entire bed in low water is one of its most striking features, and it is peculiar to the rivers of the sandy region. A short distance above Fort Laramie, the Platte comes out from among the gorges and cañons, and its character there is that of a mountain stream."

The Kansas.

The Kansas river is a large and wide stream, which, heading in the barren plains, enters the fertile region in about long. 98°, and traverses a beautiful bottom land bounded by rolling hills, to the Missouri near Fort Leavenworth. In the uncultivable region, the character of the stream is similar to that of the Platte and Arkansas. In the fertile region, it is so well known as to require no description here.

UPPER-MISSISSIPPI BASIN.

Its general character.

The distinguishing characteristic of this portion of the Mississippi basin is the entire absence of mountains. Near the source of the river the country is only some 1600 feet above the level of the sea, and is covered with swamps and lakes, divided by hills of sand and boulders belonging to the drift epoch. The middle and southern portions of the basin consist of prairie land, and are rapidly becoming cultivated. The agricultural and mineral resources of this basin are great, the climate is salubrious, and the country must eventually sustain a large and wealthy population. Its total area is 169,000 square miles.

The river.

*Upper-Mississippi river.**—Although this tributary is neither the longest, nor the greatest contributor of drainage, nor the branch most like in character to the great Mississippi, it has its *name*, and thus has always been an object of especial interest to geographers. Few travellers have explored its remote sources, and few persons have more than a very general idea of their character. For these reasons the following somewhat detailed account has been compiled from the reports of the explorers.

Its source.

The source of the Mississippi, according to Mr. Schoolcraft, who, in the year 1832, in company with Lieutenant Allen, U. S. A., was the first to visit it, is a lake, named by them Itasca. This lake was called by the Chippeways Omoshkos Sagaigon, by the French traders Lac la Biche. It is a beautiful sheet of deep, transparent water, about 7 miles long, and from 1 to 3 miles broad, abounding in fish. It is adorned with one small island, 150 yards long by 50 yards broad, elevated 20 to 30 feet above the water. The irregular shores of the lake are skirted with bushes, behind which are pine-covered hills of moderate elevation rising, in places, abruptly from the water's edge. Boulders of primitive rock are scattered along the beach, but no rock in place is visible. Mr. Schoolcraft surmised that this lake was fed by invisible springs, but Mr. Nicollet, who visited it in 1836, and determined its geographical position and elevation as now laid down on the maps (lat. 47° 14′ N., long. 95° 02′ W. of Greenwich), considers this supposition unnecessary. He says:

* The following facts respecting this river have been mainly compiled by Lieutenant Warren, Corps of Topographical Engineers.

"There are five creeks that fall into it, formed by innumerable streamlets oozing from the clay beds at the bases of the hills, that consist of an accumulation of sand and clay, intermixed with erratic fragments, being a more prominent portion of the great erratic deposit, which here is known by the name of *Hauteurs des Terres*,—heights of land. These elevations are commonly flat at top, varying in height from 85 to 100 feet above the level of the surrounding waters. They are covered with thick forests, in which the coniferous plants predominate. South of Itasca lake, they form a semicircular region, with a boggy bottom, extending to the southwest a distance of several miles; thence these Hauteurs des Terres ascend to the northwest and north; and then, stretching to the northeast and east, through the zone between 47° and 48° of latitude, make the dividing ridge between waters that empty into Hudson bay and those which discharge themselves into the gulf of Mexico. The principal group of these Hauteurs des Terres is subdivided into several ramifications varying in extent, elevation, and course, so as to determine the hydrographical basins of all the innumerable lakes and rivers that so peculiarly characterize this region of country." * * * * * *

"Of the five creeks that empty into Itasca lake, one empties into the east bay of the lake, the four others into the west bay; and among the latter there is one remarkable above the others, inasmuch as its course is longer, and its waters more abundant, so that in obedience to the geographical rule, 'that the sources of a river are those which are most distant from its mouth,' this creek is truly the infant Mississippi; all others below it feeders and tributaries." Mr. Nicollet continues: "The day on which I explored this principal creek, August 29, 1836, I judged that at its entrance to Itasca lake its bed was from 15 to 20 feet wide, and the depth of water from 2 to 3 feet. We stemmed its pretty brisk current during ten or twenty minutes, but the obstructions occasioned by fallen trees compelled us to abandon the canoe and to seek its springs on foot along the hills. After a walk of 3 miles, during which we took care not to lose sight of the Mississippi, my guide informed me that it was better to descend into the trough of the valley; where accordingly we found numberless streamlets oozing from the bases of the hills. * * * They unite at a small distance from the hills whence they originate, and form a small lake, from which the Mississippi flows with a breadth of a foot and a half, and a depth of one foot." Mr. Nicollet gives 6 miles as the length of this source. The results of his *barometrical observations* place the summit of the Hauteurs des Terres 1680 feet, and Itasca lake 1575 feet, above the ocean level. Mr. Schoolcraft previously *estimated* this latter level to be 1500 feet.

Itasca lake to Lac Travers.

Mr. Schoolcraft says (July 13, 1832): "The outlet of Itasca lake is perhaps 10 or 12 feet broad, with an apparent depth of 12 to 18 inches. * * We soon felt our motion accelerated by a current, and began to glide with velocity down a clear stream with sandy and pebbly bottom, strewed with shells and overhung by foliage. Ten feet would in most places reach from bank to bank, and the depth would probably average over a foot. A strong current and winding channel made it a labor of active watchfulness for the canoe-men to keep our frail vessels from being dashed against boulders, or torn in pieces by fallen timber or overhanging trees. Chopping with the axe was frequently necessary to clear the passage, and no small labor was imposed by getting through the drift wood, piled up at almost every sudden bend. We were almost imperceptibly drawn into a series of rapids and pretty falls, where the stream was more compressed and the water deepened, but the danger rendered tenfold greater by boulders of blackened rocks, and furious jets of the stream. We were rather hurled than paddled through these rapid passes, which increased in frequency and fury as we advanced. After being driven down about 12 miles of this species of navigation, during which the turns are very abrupt, the river displays itself, so to say, in a savanna valley, where the channel is wider and deeper, but equally or more circuitous, and bordered with sedge and aquatic plants. This forms the first plateau. It extends 8 or 9 miles. The river then narrows and enters another defile beset with an almost continued series of rapids. The frowning rock often rears its dark head to dispute the passage, and calls for the exertion of every muscle to avoid by dexterity of movement a violent contact. Often it became necessary to step into the channel and lead down the canoes, where the violence of the eddies made it impracticable otherwise to guide them. At a place called 'Kakabikous,' or the Little falls, we made a slight portage. The second series of rapids was followed by a second level or plateau, in which the channel assumes a width nearly or quite double to that which it presents on the rapids. On this level the Canoe river comes in as a tributary on the right shore. The volume of the water is perceptibly increased by it. This plateau may extend 9 miles. It is succeeded by rapids of a milder character, below which the river again displays itself in savannas, with a comparatively wide, winding channel. These are finally terminated by short and easy rapids, which bring the river out of what we may designate as its Alpine passes. * * The Pinniddiwin, a tributary from the left, having its origin a lake," enters "the Mississippi amid an extensive marsh of rushes, which gives it rather the appearance of a marsh than a lake. It is, however, called Lac la Folle." About 18 miles below this point the river became "sufficiently broad, deep, and equable" to enable Mr. Schoolcraft to proceed during the night to Lac Travers.

Lac Travers.

This lake is the most northern point of the Mississippi. It is, according to Mr. Schoolcraft, a "magnificent sheet of water, from 10 to 12 miles long with a breadth of from 4 to 5, perfectly clear and without islands, the eye having a free command over gently swelling hills," and "beautiful vistas" of pine and hard-wood groves. Its transparent water leaves a beach of pure white sand. The Mississippi enters the south end of the lake, "flowing with a brisk and deep current, and exhibiting a width of perhaps 150 feet," and runs out at the east side not far from its entrance, leaving the great body of the lake on the north.

Thence to Cass lake.

For the first 25 miles below Lac Travers the river forms a series of strong rapids, of which there are ten principal ones. In these, however, there are no falls, and they are produced by granitic boulders, no rock being visible in place. The Mississippi has a width of about 40 or 50 yards, and depth from 2 to 6 feet, between Travers and Cass lakes (Lieutenant Allen, July 10, 1832). From the series of rapids to Cass lake is about 15 miles. Hills of sand covered with yellow pines here present themselves, and the river exhibits either a sand-bank or savanna border. In this space the stream has a sluggish current and twice expands into small lakes, and here the "Meadow lands begin."

Cass lake.

Cass lake has an area of probably 120 square miles. Its greatest expansion is north and south, and amounts to from 16 to 20 miles. Both the entrance and outlet of the Mississippi are on the northern part, and are about 8 miles apart. This lake embosoms four islands, the largest of which (Grand island) is nearly 8 miles long. The waters are deep and clear, and abound in excellent fish. Its shores are sandy, and strewn with primitive-rock boulders, and the banks are high and thickly wooded with pine, elm, and maple.

Thence to lake Winnipec.

The Mississippi flows out of it with a width of 172 feet and a depth of 8 feet (Mr. Schoolcraft, July 9, 1832). Between Cass and Winnipec lakes the river pursues a devious course in a savanna valley from 1 to 3 miles wide, the strong grass and reeds growing in the stream in a manner similar to that hereafter described between Leech river and the falls of Peckagama. The valley is bordered with sandy bluffs, clothed in many places with thick forests of large white and yellow pine.

Lakes Winnipec.

Upper lake Winnipec is about 14 miles long by 9 wide. Its water is deep and clear, containing no islands. Its immediate shores are low, covered for 200 yards out from the water's edge with rushes and wild oats. A short distance back are high hills, supporting oak, maple, poplar, birch, and pine. Ten miles farther down, the Mississippi passes through Little lake Winnipec. This is 5 miles long and 3 wide, with low and marshy shores, and wild rice in places extending entirely across it, giving it the appearance of a marsh.

Thence to the falls of Peckagama.

At a distance of 40 miles below Little lake Winnipec, the junction of Leech river takes place. Throughout this distance the Mississippi has, by Mr. Schoolcraft's estimate, a width of about 20 yards and a slope of 4 inches per mile (July 20, 1820). It winds in abrupt folds through a broad savanna, which continues all the way to the falls of Peckagama.

The Mississippi and Leech rivers at their junction are of nearly equal size. This affluent, 50 miles in length, has its source in Leech lake, and is very tortuous, winding through a broad savanna. Leech lake has a circumference of not less than 160 miles, and is the largest of the lakes forming the sources of the Mississippi.

Below the junction of Leech river the width and volume of the Mississippi is nearly doubled; and thence to the falls of Peckagama, Mr. Schoolcraft estimates its average slope at about 2 inches per mile, with a gentle current of about 1 mile per hour. The most perfect type of what are known in this region as savannas, is to be found in this intermediate distance. The following quotation is from Mr. Schoolcraft's narrative of his journey *up* the Mississippi, in 1820: "After passing the falls of Peckagama, a striking change is witnessed in the character of the country. We appear to have attained the summit level of waters. The forests of maple, elm, and oak cease, and the river winds in the most devious manner through an extensive prairie, covered with tall grass, wild rice, and rushes. This prairie has a mean width of 3 miles, and is bounded by ridges of dry sand, of moderate elevation, and covered sparingly with yellow pine. Sometimes the river washes close against one of these sand ridges, then turns into the centre of the prairie, or crosses to the opposite side; but nothing can equal its sinuosities,—we move toward all points of the compass in the same hour, and we appear to be winding about in an endless labyrinth, without approaching nearer to the object in view. While sitting in our canoes, in the centre of this prairie, the rank growth of grass, rushes, etc., completely hid the adjoining forests from view, and it appeared as if we were lost in a boundless field of waving grass." Lieutenant Allen says: "The whole country seemed covered with water, from 1 to 3 feet deep, but the grass rose several feet above the surface in the deepest parts, growing very thick, and possessing a strength so great that in many places, as in short bends, where the current washed against it with great velocity and force, it stood as erect, as green, and as healthy as that remote from the river. Having an Indian guide who knew the general course of the river, we were enabled to cut off many of its great bends by running directly through the peninsulas of grass; but, although the water was two or three times more than deep enough to float our canoes, such was the nature and growth of the grass that it required the united strength of the whole crew to force a canoe through it."

It will be seen from this description how uncertain must be the estimate given of the length of the Mississippi in this portion of its course.

Falls of Peckagama.

Mr. Schoolcraft thus describes the falls of Peckagama, July 19th, 1820: "At the falls of Peckagama the river has a descent of 20 feet in 300 yards. This forms an interruption to the navigation, and there is a portage around the falls of 275 yards. The Mississippi at this fall is compressed to 80 feet in width, and precipitated over a rugged bed of sandstone, highly inclined toward the northeast. There is no perpendicular pitch, but the river rushes down a rocky channel, inclined at an angle of from 35° to 40°. The view is wild and picturesque. Immediately at the head of the falls is the first island noticed in the river. It is small, rocky, covered with spruce and cedar, and divides the channel nearly in its centre, at the point where the fall commences."

Thence to the Little falls.

The Mississippi from the falls of Peckagama to Swan river is very serpentine, and the curves are short, seldom exceeding a mile. The width of the river may be computed to average 40 yards; the current is strong, computed by Captain Douglas at 2.4 miles per hour. No island or rock strata are seen, but detached stones of hornblende, sandstone, and granite appear upon the rapids, and occasionally along the shore. The banks are of the most recent kind of alluvion, containing very minute, shining particles of mica. A number of snags and drifts were encountered. In the upper portion are ridges of pine land, elevated 20 to 30 feet above the water, and Lieutenant Allen says these are composed of sand; some of them are 100 feet high, the river frequently washing them at the bends. The trees on the alluvial banks consist of elm, maple, oak, poplar, and ash, the first two predominating.

Between Swan river and Sandy-lake river there are six rapids, and the Mississippi receives no tributaries and contains no islands. The country is low and swampy a short distance from the river, and no hills were seen. The rapids are formed by boulders similar to those heretofore mentioned. Just above the mouth of Sandy river the Mississippi has a width of 60 yards, a strong current of reddish water a little turbid, and some snags and drift. The banks are alluvial and elevated from 4 to 8 feet, bearing a forest in which elm predominates; maple and oak are common, and pine, ash, and poplar sparing.

Lieutenant Allen says (July 5, 1832): "The river, though considered high, was generally 8 or 10 feet within its banks; the current was gentle, about 2 miles per hour, except around the bends, where it was frequently quite strong." "It winds deviously through a valley of low, rich, alluvial bottom, of the best quality of soil and beautifully timbered, but all subject to inundation." From this we should infer that the extreme rise and fall of the Mississippi in this portion was not less than 20 feet.

Sandy lake is only 1.5 miles, by the course of its outlet, from the Mississippi, and during floods the waters are over 15 feet, and the whole intermediate country is inundated. The lake varies much in size at different times, as do all the innumerable lakes of this region. Savanna river enters Sandy lake, and is the main canoe route between the Mississippi and lake Superior, via Fond du Lac river.

The following extracts are taken from Mr. Schoolcraft's narrative of his journey from Sandy lake to the mouth of the St. Peter's river in 1820:—

"July 25. * * The current of the river below the outlet of Sandy lake, and the natural appearances, are similar to what it exhibits for 100 miles above; the banks are alluvial, elevated from 6 to 10 feet; trees—elm, maple, pine, and birch. We descended 28 miles, and encamped on a high, sunny bank on the west shore. The river has several rapids in that distance, and some islands covered entirely with grass and small tufts of willows, with piles of driftwood collected at their heads. No rock strata appear, but loose stones of granite, hornblende, and red ferruginous quartz are seen in the bed of the stream in passing over the rapids, and in some places along the margin of the river. Among the forest trees, pine appears to predominate on the lands which lie a distance off the river, but elm is most abundant along the shore; maple and birch less so, and black walnut and oak sparing. The color of the water on looking into the river resembles that of chocolate, but on dipping up a cupful it appears colorless and clear."

Between this camp and Pine river—a distance of about 100 miles—Mr. Schoolcraft writes: "The river has presented several rapids, islands, and ripples. The fall of none of the rapids will exceed 6 feet in a distance of 300 yards. The islands are small and not well wooded, and are encumbered with piles of drifted trees, limbs, and leaves, which give them a novel appearance, and at the same time serve to convey an idea of the rise of the river, and of the force of its current during its semi-annual floods. Snags become more frequent in this part of the channel, and the river in several places undermines its banks, which are elevated from 10 to 20 feet, and bear a forest of elm, birch, pine, maple, black walnut and oak (Quercus nigra). Loose stones are found at all rapids; they are chiefly referable to the different varieties of granite, hornblende, slate, and sandstone."

"The pine lands which commenced at the junction of Pine river with the Mississippi continued to within a short distance of the mouth of the river De Corbeau (Crow-wing river). They are elevated from 60 to 100 feet, and lie in ridges. The principal timber is the yellow pine. Mixed with the sand, which is in some places naked and destitute of vegetation, are fragments of granite, hornblende, quartz, jasper, and cornelian. This strip of sandy country was denominated the *Dead Pines* by Pike."

"The river De Corbeau (Crow-wing river) is the largest tributary which the Mississippi receives above the falls of St. Anthony, being nearly of equal magnitude. The lands upon its banks are rich, and covered with a heavy growth of hard wood, chiefly elm, sugar-tree, black walnut, and oak. At the point of junction there is a large and well-wooded island, called the Isle de Corbeau, by which the river is hid from the view until you have nearly passed it, when, by turning the eye toward the south, you have a fine view of its broad and beautiful surface and the luxuriant foliage which overshadows its banks. The Mississippi assumes an increased width below, and is particularly characterized by numerous and heavy-timbered islands, all of which present immense drifts of flood-wood at their heads, and, by dividing the river into a number of channels, serve to increase its width and the difficulties of its navigation. Here, also, the Buffalo plains commence, and continue downward on both banks of the river to the falls of St. Anthony. These plains are elevated about 60 feet above the summer level of the water, and consist of a sandy alluvion covered with rank grass and occasional clumps of the dwarf black oak. They generally present steep, naked, and falling-in banks toward the river, and disclose innumerable small fragments of cornelian, agate, and jasper, along with masses of coarser rock, such as granite, hornblende, etc." * * *

The Little falls.

"The Little falls are four miles below the mouth of Elk river, where the Mississippi forces its way through a narrow defile of rocks which appear in rugged masses in the bed of the stream" (for the first time below the falls of Peckagama, according to Lieutenant Allen), "and attain an elevation of from 20 to 40 feet upon its banks. Passing with great velocity over the schute of the falls, it was difficult to ascertain the geological character of the rock, but it appeared to be granite, very much mixed and darkened with hornblende.* The river at this place is narrowed to half its usual width. The descent of water may be estimated at 10 feet in 150 yards.

Thence to the Big falls.

"Between Elk river and Little falls we pass the Painted Rock, standing upon the west bank of the river. It consists of a mass of granite and hornblende, upon which the Indians have drawn a number of hieroglyphics and rude designs."

About 6 miles above Sac river, on the east side of the river, "there is a bed of granite 250 feet in height. It is considerably mixed with hornblende. On ascending it, I found the most charming prospects in every direction. It commands a view of the prairies on both banks of the Mississippi, with the windings of the stream, and its islands and rapids for many miles above and below." * * * * *

The Big falls.

"The Big falls consist of a series of breaks and schutes extending about 800 yards, in which distance the river may be estimated to have an aggregate fall of 16 feet. The bed of the river at this fall is beset with sharp fragments of granite and hornblende rock, which also appear in rolled masses upon the shores.

Thence to the falls of St. Anthony.

"The next remarkable trait in the river is Prairie rapids, which are six in number, and have a mean descent of about 20 feet in 5 miles. At half-past four in the afternoon we passed the mouth of the river St. Francis, a large stream falling in on the east shore. For a great distance above its mouth it runs parallel with the Mississippi, which is the cause that so few tributaries enter the latter on the east shore after passing the mouth of the river De Corbeau

* Lieutenant Allen calls this a formation of talcose slate, and Mr. Lander, in his report to Governor Stevens, vol. i., Pacific Railroad Reports, confirms his opinion, stating: "At the island near Little falls is a very fine crossing of 325 feet. Four wing abutments and a slight increase of truss will be required, from the destructible nature of the ledge foundation, which is of slate rock strongly impregnated with iron, and affected by the atmosphere."

(Crow-wing river). Its principal fork is Muddy river. Here Carver terminated his travels up the Mississippi in the year 1765; and Father Hennepin in 1681. An island in the river opposite its mouth hides the view of it from those who descended by the west channel."

Between Elk and Crow rivers "the current has been unusually strong, with many rapids and ripples. Very few snags have been observed. A great many islands were passed in the afternoon, and some small sand bars, being the first noticed. Prairies continue on both banks, with occasional clumps of trees, and forests of 2 or 3 miles in extent. The growth of wood upon the islands is elm, black and white walnut, maple, oak, and ash; upon the prairies, dwarf black oak. Along the banks of the river pebbles of quartz, granite, hornblende, cornelian, and agate, are seen. In one instance I picked up a fine specimen of agatized wood, such as is common upon the lower Mississippi, and along the shores of the Missouri. The color of the water continues a light chocolate brown in the stream, but appears clear in small quantities. Pebbles at the bottom of the river can be plainly discerned through it at 4 or 5 feet depth. The quality of the soil of the prairies improves as we descend, and during the last 20 miles may be considered of the richest kind. The prairies are in fact covered with a stratum of the most recently deposited black, marly alluvion, which appears to be composed, in a great degree, of vegetable mould. It is entirely destitute of those rounded pebbles and stones which generally characterize upland soils, although bottomed upon a stratum of alluvion, in which they are abundantly disseminated. The whole, apparently, rests immediately upon granitic and hornblende rock, which occasionally rises through it in rugged peaks and beds."

Falls of St. Anthony.

At the falls of St. Anthony "the river has a perpendicular pitch of forty feet, with a formidable rapid above and below.* An island, at the brink of the falls, divides the current into two sheets, the largest of which passes on the west of the island. The rapid below the schute is filled with large fragments of rock, in the interstices of which some alluvial soil has accumulated, which nourishes a stinted growth of cedars. This rapid extends half a mile, in which distance the river may be estimated to have a descent of 15 feet. The rapid preceding the falls has a descent of about 10 feet in the distance of 300 yards, where the river runs with a swift but unruffled current over a smooth stratum of rock a little inclined toward the brink. The entire fall, therefore, in less than three-fourths of a mile, is 65 feet. The rock is a white sandstone, overlayed by secondary limestone. This formation is first seen half a mile above the falls, where it breaks out abruptly on the banks of the river." * * * * * * * *

"It is in fact the precise point of transition where the beautiful prairies of the Upper Mississippi are merged in the rugged limestone bluffs which skirt the banks of

* Lieutenant Allen states: "The falls have been described by Mr. Schoolcraft and other former travellers, who had more time to observe them than was allotted to me. I have only to correct an error in the height of the perpendicular fall. It was estimated by Lieutenant Pike, 16 feet, and by Mr. Schoolcraft, 40 feet. I was told by an officer at Fort Snelling that by actual measurement it was 18 feet precisely. Below the falls there is a considerable rapid, and the whole descent at this place, including also the rapid above, may be estimated at 80 feet. Between the falls and Fort Snelling, a distance of 9 miles, the channel is contracted in a deep ravine, and the river runs in a torrent all the way."

the river from that point downward. With this change of geological character, we perceive a corresponding one in the vegetable productions, and the eye embraces at one view the copses of oak upon the prairies, and the cedars and pines which characterize the calcareous bluffs. Nothing can exceed the beauty of the prairies which skirt both banks of the river above the falls. They do not, however, consist of an unbroken plain, but are diversified with gentle ascents and small ravines, covered with the most luxuriant growth of grass and heath-flowers, interspersed with groves of oak, which throw an air of the most picturesque beauty over the scene.

"The length of the portage around the falls, as measured by Lieutenant Pike in 1805, is 260 poles, but in high water is somewhat less. The width of the river on the brink of the fall is stated at 227 yards, but narrows to 209 yards a short distance below, where the river is compressed between opposing ledges of rock."

Thence to the mouth of the river Missouri.

Below the falls of St. Anthony the Mississippi is so well known as to require no detailed description here. About 55 miles below the mouth of St. Peter's, the river expands into lake Pepin, which is 2 or 3 miles broad and 27 miles long. About 270 miles farther down, Rock Island rapids are reached. They are covered by ledges of stratified limestone and sandstone, and extend down the river about 13 miles, with a fall at low water of 22 feet. About 115 miles farther on, Montrose, situated at the head of the Des Moines rapids, is reached. They extend 11 miles, with a fall at low water of 21 feet.

From lake Pepin to the junction of the Missouri, the Mississippi is characterized by almost innumerable wooded islands. The main volume of the stream is confined to one channel, but branches from it ramify in various directions, forming sloughs, as they are generally named, and making its water-course, with enclosed islands, seldom less than a mile in width.

Slope of the Upper Mississippi.

The following table has been carefully computed from the best authorities to exhibit the low-water slope of the Upper Mississippi. Above St. Paul, Mr. Nicollet is the only authority for elevation above the sea. Below that point the various railroad surveys furnish more exact determinations. Thus: From the report of Captain Meade, Topographical Engineers (Oct. 20, 1860), it appears that the approximate elevations above the sea, of lakes Superior and Michigan, are 600 and 576 feet respectively. Mr. D. C. Shephard, Chief Engineer Minnesota Pacific railroad, states that the ordinary level (range about 18 feet) of the Mississippi at St. Paul is 80 feet above lake Superior at Fond du Lac. Mr. E. Goodrate, Manager of the La Crosse and Milwaukee railroad, stated that the Mississippi at La Crosse (range 10 feet) is 63 feet above the level of lake Michigan. Mr. W. Jervis, Superintendent Milwaukee and Mississippi railroad, states that low water at Prairie du Chien is 24 feet above the level of lake Michigan. Mr. H. Farnum states that low water at Rock Island is 77 feet below the level of lake Michigan. The altitude of the mouth has been deduced by prolonging the measured slope between St. Louis and Cairo. The corresponding distances are taken with great care from the Land-office plats as far as the mouth of Crow-wing river. Above they are given as estimated by Mr. Nicollet.

Low-water slope of Upper Mississippi.

Locality.	Distance above mouth of Missouri.	Elevation above sea.	Fall per mile.	Authority.	Remarks.
	Miles.	*Feet.*	*Feet.*		
Utmost source	1330	1680	0.00	Mr. Nicollet.	
Itasca lake	1324	1575	17.50	"	
Entrance to Lac Travers	1284	1456	1.32	"	
Entrance to lake Cass	1189	1402	1.20	"	10 miles through lakes.
Mouth Leech-lake river	1109	1356	0.57	"	35 miles through lakes.
Head of falls of Peckagama	1061	1340	0.33	"	
Mouth Swan river	998	1290	0.73	"	Rapids intervening.
Mouth Sandy-lake river	960	1253	0.95	"	Rapids intervening.
Mouth Pine river	863	1176	0.79	"	Rapids intervening.
Mouth Crow-wing river	815	1130	0.95	"	Rapids intervening.
St. Paul	658	670	2.93	Railroad levels.	Sauk rapids, falls of St. Anthony, etc.
La Crosse	514	639	0.22	" "	
Prairie du Chien	458	600	0.64	" "	
Head Rock Island rapids	310	505	0.66	" "	
Foot " " "	295	483	1.47	" "	Rapids intervening.
Mouth	0	381	0.35	" "	Des Moines rapids intervening (low-water fall 21 feet).

These elevations refer to the low water of the Mississippi. The range between high and low water level is about 20 feet near Sandy-lake river; about 20 feet at St. Paul; about 10 feet (extreme, 14 feet) at La Crosse; about 12 feet (in 1858, 18.5 feet) at Prairie du Chien; about 16 feet at Rock Island; about 20 feet at Hannibal, and about 35 feet at the mouth. These ranges are much less than those of the Ohio, and, excepting the Missouri, of the other tributaries of the Mississippi, where they pass through the cultivable region. Their small extent is due to the generally flat character of the basin, from which the drainage is consequently slow; the existence upon it of numberless lakes; the great width of the river; the gradual change in season that takes place along its course; and the comparatively dry climate of the upper part of the basin.

Its range.

Its dimensions of cross-section.

The following facts respecting the dimensions of the Upper Mississippi have been collected.

At entrance to Itasca lake (Mr. Nicollet, August 29, 1836) "bed, 15 to 20 feet wide, water 2 to 3 deep."

The outlet from Itasca lake (Mr. Schoolcraft, July 13, 1832) 10 to 12 feet wide, 12 to 18 inches deep; (Lieutenant Allen, July 13, 1832) "channel 20 feet broad, 2 feet deep, current 2 miles per hour;" (Mr. Nicollet, August, 1836) "width 16 feet, depth 14 inches."

At entrance to Lac Travers (Mr. Schoolcraft, July 13, 1832) "brisk and deep current, width, perhaps 150 feet."

Between Lac Travers and Cass lake (Lieutenant Allen, July 10, 1832) "width 40 to 50 yards, depth 2 to 6 feet."

At outlet of Cass lake (Mr. Schoolcraft, July 9, 1832) "172 feet wide, depth 8 feet."

Between lake Winnepec and Leech-lake river (Mr. Schoolcraft, July 20, 1820) "width averages 20 yards and slope of surface 4 inches per mile."

Between Leech-lake river and falls of Peckagama (Mr. Schoolcraft, July, 1820) "average width about 120 feet, slope about 2 inches per mile, current about 1 mile per hour." Lieutenant Allen says the river was sometimes 300 yards broad.

Falls of Peckagama (Mr. Schoolcraft, July, 1820) "descent 20 feet in 300 yards, river 80 feet wide"; (Lieutenant Allen, July 6, 1832) "descent 20 to 30 feet in 100 yards."

Between falls of Peckagama and Swan river (Mr. Schoolcraft, July, 1820) "width averages about 40 yards, current 2.4 miles per hour."

Just above mouth of Sandy-lake river (Mr. Schoolcraft, July 17, 1820) "60 yards wide;" just below (Mr. Schoolcraft, July 4, 1832) "331 feet wide." Lieutenant Allen (July 4, 1832) says width just above is 75 yards; just below, 110 yards.

Between Sauk and Elk rivers the width averages 900 feet; thence to St. Francis, 300 or 400 yards; thence to Fort Snelling, 400 yards (Lieutenant Allen).

Beyond the gorge below Fort Snelling, the width of the Mississippi is 576 feet (Mr. Nicollet).

From lake Pepin to the mouth of the Missouri, the average width is about 1 mile.

Table of chief tributaries.

Tributaries.—The following table exhibits a correct list of the tributaries of the Mississippi. Below the mouth of Crow-wing river, the distances upon the Mississippi have been carefully measured on the plats of the Land-office surveys; below the St. Peter's river, the lengths of the tributaries are taken from G. W. Colton's guide map published in 1861. The other numbers are those estimated by Mr. Nicollet and are doubtless in excess:—

Tributaries of the Upper Mississippi.

Name.	Distance of mouth above mouth of Missouri.	Length of tributary.	Remarks.	Name.	Distance of mouth above mouth of Missouri.	Length of tributary.	Remarks.
	Miles.	*Miles.*			*Miles.*	*Miles.*	
Source branch...........	1824		Itasca lake.	Elk or St. Francis river	705	100	
Turtle river..............	1180	40	Cass lake.	Crow river..............	699		
Leech-lake river.........	1109	50		Rum river..............	690	150	
Mash-kudens river	1055			Rice river	683		
Swan river...............	998		Rapids intervening.	St. Peter's river........	663		
Sandy-lake river	960		"	St. Croix river	631	168	
Willow river.............	930			Vermilion river	630		
Pine river................	863	140	"	Cannon river	611	82	
Crow-wing river.........	815		"	Chippeway river.......	581	165	
Nokay river..............	806			Embarras river.........	562		
Belle Prairie creek......	796			White river.............	560		
Elk creek.................	782			Black and La Crosse rivers..................	516	128	Black river.
Pike creek	787			Root river	511	83	
Swan river...............	786			Upper Iowa river......	489		
Two rivers................	777			Wisconsin river........	448	338	
Spunk river..............	773			Turkey river............	425		
Platte river..............	771			Wabesipinnicon river	320	205	
Little Rock creek.......	760			Rock river.........	291	245	
Watab and Winnebago rivers.....................	757			Cedar river..............	245	255	
Lower Watab	754			Skunk river............	205		
Sauk river................	752		Rapids 1 mile.	Des Moines river......	165	402	
Nechoado river	744			Illinois river............	24	397	
Clear-water river	736			Missouri river..........	0		

Of these tributaries, St. Peter's river alone is at the same time comparatively unknown and of sufficient importance to require a description here. According to

St. Peter's river.

Mr. Nicollet it has its source among a magnificent group of lakes at the very head of the Coteau des prairies, the elevation above the sea being 1896 feet. It flows for a distance of about 50 miles in an easterly direction, when it expands into what is improperly called a lake—Big-Stone lake. At the point where it enters, it is, according to Mr. Keating, July, 1823, "less than 7 yards wide." Big-Stone lake has a width of about 2 miles, a length of 30 miles, and an elevation of 966 feet. Upon reaching a point 35 miles below the lake, the river expands again into what is known as Lac qui Parle, which is from 1 to 2 miles wide and extends 6 miles. In the intervening space it receives three tributaries, but Mr. Keating, July, 1823, describes it as "a mere rivulet 20 to 30 feet wide." Thence to Patterson's rapids the distance is 61 miles, and the river receives several tributaries of small size. Mr. Keating says, "in fact they are mere brooks conveying waters on the crest of the ridge" (of the Coteau); "but probably about the spring of the year they are much swollen by the thawing of the snow and ice upon the ridge; it is in this manner that we may account for the water-mark found along the bluffs which enclose their comparatively large valleys." Thus far the stream has nowhere a width of "more than 15 or 20 yards," and "is everywhere fordable." "The valley presents a fine rich soil, rather swampy in places, and is covered with high grass and wild rice; it is often woody. Wherever the primitive rocks are found, they are bare. The trees consist principally of cottonwood and ash." The Red-wood joins 5 miles below Patterson's rapids, and 62 miles farther on, the Big and Little Warajee are received. The Mankato (meaning Blue-earth) river enters 32 miles below. This latter stream is thus described by Mr. Nicollet:

"The Mankato becomes navigable with boats within a few miles of its sources. It is deep, with a moderate current along a great portion of its course, but becomes very rapid at its approach to the St. Peter's. Its bed is narrowly walled up by banks rising to an elevation of from 60 to 80 feet, and reaching up to the uplands through which the river flows. These banks are frequently cliffs or vertical escarpments. The breadth of the river is pretty uniformly from 80 to 120 feet wide; and the average breadth of the valley through which it flows, scarcely a quarter of a mile. The latter as well as the high grounds are well wooded; the timber beginning to spread out on both shores, especially since they have become less frequented by the Sioux hunters and are not so often fired."

"The great number of the navigable tributaries of the Mankato, spreading themselves out in the shape of a fan; the group of lakes surrounded by well-wooded hills; some wide-spreading prairies with a fertile soil; others apparently less favored but open to improvement; the whole together bestow upon the region a most picturesque appearance." Mr. Nicollet gave it "the name of Undine Region."

At the point where the Mankato joins St. Peter's river the latter turns its course at a right angle and flows northwest to the Mississippi, the intervening distance being 148 miles by the meanderings of the stream.

The Illinois river.

The following facts respecting the Illinois river are taken from the report of Captain Stansbury, Corps Topl. Engrs., U. S. A., dated in 1838. The river bottom lands are from 2 to 10 miles wide, and raised only a few feet above the usual level of the stream. They have a sandy and alluvial soil. The immediate banks are low alluvial swamps skirted by lagoons, most of them connected with the river and overflowed every freshet from 1 to 15 feet. The current is gentle and uniform up to Peru, some 250 miles above the mouth. Excepting for two summer months, the river admits of navigation as far as this town with boats of 3 feet draught. The only obstructions are bars, which are usually diagonal, and sometimes even parallel to the current. Their position is shown at low water by the weeds which cover them. The bars remain unaltered unless destroyed by ice. Sometimes they are mere lumps with deep water surrounding them.

OHIO BASIN.

Character of the basin.

The Ohio river drains the northeast portion of the Mississippi basin—a fertile and populous region throughout nearly its whole extent. The southern tributaries rise in the Alleghany mountains, and flow northward through an undulating and beautiful country to the main stream. The northern tributaries have their source in the crest of the level plateau which lies immediately south of the great lakes, at an elevation varying from 500 to 1000 feet above their water surfaces, and flow southward through a fertile prairie and undulating country to the Ohio. The boundaries of the basin are indicated on plate I, and its character is so well known as to require no description here. Its total area is 214,000 square miles.

Character of the river.

Ohio river.—The Ohio is formed by the junction of the Alleghany and Monongahela rivers. The former, which is the principal branch, rises in the mountains of Pennsylvania, the latter in those of Virginia. Throughout its whole length (975 miles) the river flows with a gentle current, uninterrupted by rapids except at the "falls of the Ohio" near Louisville, when it descends 26 feet in 3 miles. It traverses a beautiful valley and is constantly augmented by tributary streams.

The Ohio in low water is a succession of long pools and ripples, with a current alternately sluggish and rapid. The bars in the upper part of the river are mainly composed of gravel, and in the lower part, of shifting sand.

Of the Alleghany branch, nothing need be said except that near its sources it flows between hills, through a very narrow strip of fertile bottom land, and with a more uniform slope than near the mouth, where it traverses a rocky and precipitous ravine, with a bed composed mainly of sandstone or gravel-bars. [Captain Hughes, Topl. Engrs., U. S. A.]

Of the Monongahela branch, some curious facts stated by Dr. William Howard in 1833 merit attention. It rises in the Alleghany mountains and subordinate ranges in Virginia, and is formed by the junction of the East and West branches and Cheat river. The former streams head in Laurel ridge, and flow in rocky channels. The tributaries of Cheat river rise in the summit of the Alleghanies, and form mountain torrents until they unite in a river scarcely less wild than themselves. The Cheat forces its way through deep gorges with nearly perpendicular side-slopes to the Monongahela, falling 2400 feet in the last 80 miles. Below the junction the river is gentle in character. It winds with a serpentine course, without islands, through a terraced valley. Its slope here is *less than that of the Ohio*. Thus the fall from the mouth of Cheat river to Brownsville (35 miles) is 44 feet, or 1.26 feet per mile, and from Brownsville to Pittsburg (55 miles), only 31 feet, or 0.56 of a foot per mile; while the corresponding fall of the Ohio near Pittsburg is about 1 foot per mile. The fall of the Monongahela, above the junction of Cheat river, averages about 2 feet per mile for over 100 miles. The anomaly in slope near the mouth of this river is less in high than in low water, the usual range at Brownsville being 15 or 20 feet more than at Pittsburg. At low water the Monongahela is a succession of pools separated by bars composed of gravel and loose stones, not subject to sudden changes. Its water is quite free from sedimentary matter.

Its slope.

In a paper published by the Smithsonian Institution, in 1849, Mr. Ellet gives much statistical information relative to the slope of the Ohio and of its principal tributaries, mostly compiled from data furnished by the various railroad surveys, which have so thoroughly covered the region. The following table is extracted from this paper, the distances being added from an accompanying diagram:—

Low-water slope of the Ohio.

Locality.	Distance above mouth.	Elevation above tide.	Fall per mile.
	Miles.	*Feet.*	*Feet.*
Mouth of Ohio	0	275	0.00
Mouth of Wabash (approximately)	130	297	0.17
Evansville (approximately)	187	320	0.25
New Albany, below the falls	358	353	0.20
Louisville, above the falls	361	377	8.00
Cincinnati	515	432	0.36
Portsmouth	620	474	0.40
Mouth of Great Kanawha	714	522	0.51
Head of Le Tart's shoals	769	555	0.60
Marietta (mouth of Muskingum)	800	571	0.52
Wheeling	889	620	0.55
Pittsburg	975	699	0.92
Franklin	1105	960	2.00
Warren	1175	1187	3.24
Chautauque lake		1306	
Olean point	1225	1403	4.32
Mouth of Oswaya		1419	
Smithport		1480	
Coudersport	1265	1649	6.15
Surface of lake Erie		565	

Its range between low and high water.

It will be noticed that these elevations correspond to the low-water period. The range between extreme low and extreme high water seems to be about 45 feet throughout the entire river. Thus at Wheeling, it is 45 feet; at Louisville, 42 feet *on* the falls and 64 feet *below* them;* at Evansville, 40 feet; at Paducah, 51 feet; and at the mouth of the river, 51 feet. The usual range does not exceed 25 feet.

Its low-water depth.

The least low-water depth on the bars, from the mouth of the river to Paducah, is about 3.0 feet; thence to Louisville, 1.5 feet; thence to Cincinnati, 2.0 to 2.5 feet; thence to Wheeling, 1.0 foot.

From the maps of the United States surveys made by Mr. C. A. Fuller, under the direction of Captain J. Saunders, U. S. A., and now on file in the Bureau

* At a medium stage of water, a rise of 1 foot on the falls makes a rise of about 3 feet below them, until the water on the falls is about 5 feet deep. Subsequently the rate of rise below is rather less than 2 feet.

of Topographical Engineers, War Department, the mean width of the Ohio between Pittsburg and Point Pleasant (the upper third of the river) is 1000 feet at low water and 1200 feet at high water, the corresponding areas of cross-section being about 5000 and 50,000 square feet, respectively. These dimensions gradually increase until, near the mouth of the river, the widths become about 2500 feet and 3000 feet, and the areas 50,000 square feet and 150,000 square feet, respectively.

Its width and area of cross-section.

The Ohio river, as will appear in the next chapter, discharges annually about 5 trillions of cubic feet, or about one-quarter of the annual discharge of the Mississippi. Its flood discharge varies of course at different localities, and has not been well determined. At Wheeling, at the top of the flood of 1849 (May 8), when the river stood 29.0 feet above low-water mark, Mr. Ellet found the discharge to be about 200,000 cubic feet per second. In June, 1858, the discharge at the mouth could not have been less than 700,000 cubic feet per second, judging by the measurements conducted upon the Mississippi, at Columbus.

Its discharge.

The following information has been collected from reliable sources respecting the usual succession of stages of the Ohio. The first rise occurs when the snows melt and the winter breaks up. Generally, this occurs in February, but is sometimes later. This rise is generally 10 or 15 feet greater than any other at Louisville. The average spring rise is about 25 feet at the mouth of the Ohio, the river remaining high about six weeks, the tributaries discharging their floods very nearly at the same time. On Louisville falls, it is from 15 to 20 feet. This is the rise which occasions floods in the Ohio.

Its annual succession of stages.

The next rise usually occurs in May or June. This is due to the summer rains. It is usually the smallest of the three regular rises known in the Ohio. It lasts three or four weeks at Cairo and one or two at Louisville.

The next regular rise is in the autumn. In October the river is always low, but early in November, generally, it begins to rise and often continues to do so until the banks are full. This rise, however, is not to be depended upon. It is due to autumn rains, and sometimes occurs as late as Christmas.

The Ohio is generally lowest in August and September, when it is only navigable for boats of 18 inches draught.

It freezes generally about Christmas, and sometimes remains frozen for four weeks. In 1855 it was frozen at Louisville sixty-five days, the longest time ever known. The ice from Alleghany river is the most dangerous for boats, as it is heavier and thicker than that from any other tributary.

In fine, the usual succession of stages appears to be as follows: January, river frozen; February, breaking up and high; March, high; April, high; May, falls somewhat; June, rises again; July, falls and is low; August, very low; September, very low; October, very low; November, rises; December, well up.

At Louisville, the greatest flood ever recorded occurred on February 22, 1832. The water stood 42 feet above low-water mark at the head of the falls and 64 feet at their foot. The second flood at this city was highest on December 20, 1847, and stood 41.2 feet above low-water mark at the head of the falls, and 63.2 feet at their foot. In April (?), 1851, two great rises of equal

Its great floods.

height occurred, separated by a fall of some 10 or 12 feet. They attained a level 33.5 feet above low water on the falls. A destructive flood, which stood 34 feet on the falls, occurred in 1854. Another about 2 feet lower attained its height on February 24, 1859, followed by a second rise (May 2), which stood 27 feet on the falls, or only 5 feet below the level of the first rise.

Its tributaries.

Tributaries.—The principal tributary of the Ohio is the Tennessee. The true source of this stream (Holston river) rises in the Alleghany mountains, at an elevation of 2500 feet above the level of the sea. It is a rapid stream, some 400 feet in width, flowing through a narrow valley over a rocky bed. It doubles its size when joined by the French Broad, a river which heads in the Blue ridge and winds through a broader and more fertile valley than the Holston. Below the junction, the pools become from 20 to 40 feet in depth, and the shoals less frequent. Clinch river increases the volume of the Tennessee some 50 per cent. Islands become numerous. In four places the river is contracted by high promontories, and made very deep and rapid. Below these obstructions, the course is more direct and the current gentle and uniform to the Muscle shoals. These shoals extend 36.5 miles. They are composed of a stratum of compact limestone mixed with flint. The river flows over them with a rapid current and occasional deep pools. It is here from 0.5 to 1.5 miles wide, and has a minimum depth in low water of about 1 foot. The total fall from the head to the foot of the shoals is 164 feet, or at a mean rate of 4.4 feet per mile. [Surveys of board of U. S. engineers.] Below the shoals, the current is gentle and uniform. The extreme range between high and low water in both the Holston and French Broad is about 25 feet; just above Muscle shoals, 12 feet; on the shoals, 5 feet; at their foot, 20 feet; 28 miles below them, 30 feet; at the mouth of Tennessee river, about 50 feet. The elevation above the sea at the Seven-mile ford of the Holston in Virginia is, according to Mr. Ellet, 1914 feet; at Chattanooga, 643 feet; and at the mouth (low water), 286 feet. These numbers indicate the mean slope between these stations to be 2.5 and 0.6 feet, respectively.

The next tributary of the Ohio in importance is the Cumberland. This stream rises in the Cumberland mountains, and has a rapid descent to the plains. It then flows more gently to the falls, where it pours over a cliff of pudding-stone 56 feet in height. Below these falls it is enclosed between bluffs some 500 feet in height, and has a rapid current as far down as Laurel river. Here commences the coal region, which extends 13 miles down the stream. The principal obstruction to navigation below is the triple rapid, called Smith's shoals, where the river falls 54 feet in about 6 miles. The stream here expands from its usual width (375 feet) to about 600 feet. [Captain Stansbury, U. S. A.] The elevation above the sea, of the Cumberland at its mouth (low water), is, according to Mr. Ellet, 284 feet, and at Nashville, 388 feet, giving a mean slope in this part of its course of about 6.5 inches per mile.

The following extracts from the paper of Mr. Ellet, already mentioned, present data of interest respecting the slope of the other tributaries of the Ohio:—

"The Wabash, next in succession, but perhaps equal in volume to the Cumberland, is the largest of the tributaries of the Ohio which descend along its northern plane. The elevation of low water at the mouth of the Wabash is 297 feet above tide. In the first 91 miles, extending from its confluence with the Ohio to the mouth of White river, the fall is 57 feet, or 7½ inches per mile. * * * The total descent from the mouth of Little river to the Ohio, a distance computed at 370 miles, is 385 feet, or a small fraction over 12 inches per mile.

"Green river enters on the left border of the Ohio, from the State of Kentucky. The average inclination of this stream from Bowling Green, on Barren river, a tributary of Green river, to its mouth—a distance of 175 miles—is 4⅛ inches per mile. The actual fall in this distance is 60 feet, and the rate of inclination but one-third greater than that of the lower Ohio. * * * * * * * * *

"Kentucky river is the next important tributary which we find on ascending toward the north. The distance by the meanders of this stream from Three forks to its mouth is 257½ miles, and the total fall 216 feet, or 10 inches per mile.

* * * * * * * * * * * * *

"The Licking river from West Liberty to the Ohio, a distance of 231 miles, falls 316 feet, or 16½ inches per mile; while Guyandotte river, from Logan's court-house to the Ohio, a distance of 74 miles, falls 142 feet, or 23 inches per mile. * *

"The Great Kanawha, the next in succession, is a navigable river, and is correctly represented in the profile. From Loup-creek shoals to the mouth of the river is 89 miles, and the descent 86 feet, or very nearly 12 inches per mile. * * *

"The Little Kanawha, from Bulltown to Elizabethtown, 108½ miles, falls 181 feet; and from Elizabethtown to the Ohio, 27¼ miles, the fall is 28 feet, or 12⅓ inches per mile. * * * * * * * * * * * * *

"The Scioto is not navigable. The distance from Columbus to Portsmouth is about 100 miles by water, and the fall 302 feet.

"The Muskingum, from Zanesville to Marietta, about 60 miles, falls 104 feet."

With regard to the annual spring freshets of the tributaries, little definite information exists. The Cumberland and Tennessee usually send out their floods together and first. The Wabash follows. Lastly, the upper tributaries contribute their discharge. There is, however, very little difference in the times of these floods, and, for all practical purposes, they may be said to be coincident at the mouth of the Ohio.

The Tennessee and Cumberland are navigable for seven months in the year; the former to Muscle shoals, some 600 miles, and the latter to Burkesville, 370 miles. The Wabash is navigable to Lafayette, 335 miles, for about five months. The Kentucky and Green rivers and some of the smaller rivers have locks, which make them navigable for about ten months in ordinary years.

YAZOO BASIN.

Yazoo basin.

The Yazoo basin consists of the Yazoo bottom and its water-shed.

Boundaries and area.—The exterior limits of the Yazoo basin can be easily traced upon La Tourrette's map, which is drawn on so large a scale that the dividing ridge between small streams draining into and away from the bottom lands can be readily distinguished. Its total area is 13,850 square miles.

Yazoo bottom; its boundaries.

The Yazoo bottom is a tract of alluvial land of an oval shape, bordering upon the Mississippi between Memphis and Vicksburg, and constituting the western portion of the basin. (See plate II.)

In the preliminary report* of Mr. L. Harper, the State Geologist of Mississippi, the boundary of this region is defined as follows: Beginning at a point on the Tennessee State boundary, near the dividing line between R. 8, W. and R. 9, W., it extends southward to T. 4, R. 8, W., where it passes around a projection of the bottom lands of Coldwater river. From the division line of T.'s 4 and 5, R. 9, W., in De Soto county, it runs again in a southern direction to T. 29, R. 8, W., in Panola county, where it runs around a projection of the bottom lands of the Tallahatchee river. From T. 28, R. 8, W., in Panola county, it takes again a southern course toward Charleston, in Tallahatchee county, passes about a mile west of that town through T.'s 25, 24, 23, R. 2, E., and then runs around a projection of the alluvion of the Yallabusha river. From the line of Tallahatchee county, T. 22, R. 2, E., it turns again south, down R. 2, E., through the townships 21, 20, 19, 18, 17, in Carroll, and T.'s 16 and 15, in Holmes county. Thence it takes a southwest direction toward the southwest corner of T. 14, R. 1, E., in Holmes county; continues in that direction to Yazoo City, where the bluff comes within a very short distance of the Yazoo river; and then passes through ranges 8 and 7, E., townships 11 and 10, to a mile below Satartia. Thence it runs through T. 19, R. 6, W., in Yazoo county, and through T.'s 18 and 19, ranges 5 and 4, W., in Warren county, to Vicksburg. Thence the Mississippi forms its boundary northward to the Tennessee State line. The portion of the bottom which extends into the State of Tennessee is very trifling in extent.

Its area.

Mr. Harper estimates the area of the Yazoo bottom in Mississippi at 7092 square miles. By drawing on La Tourrette's map the boundary just given, and accurately computing the extent of the bottom, including the strip in Tennessee, the entire area was found to be 7110 square miles, thus confirming the accuracy of Mr. Harper's computation.

It is traversed by a line of high land.

This region is not entirely alluvial. The operations of this Survey, together with reliable information communicated by persons residing in the bottom lands, show that it is traversed by a line of high lands, some 2 to 6 miles in width, which are very rarely, if ever, overflowed. They extend from Honey island to Delta, on the Mississippi, separating the Yazoo and Tallahatchee rivers from the Sunflower. The soil is different from that of the rest of the bottom, and the ridge is believed, for many reasons, to be the true prolongation of Crowley's ridge, which has heretofore been supposed to terminate at Helena. The area of this belt of high land, as nearly as it can be estimated, is about 310 square miles.

Area of Yazoo basin classified.

The entire basin therefore consists of:

	Square miles.
Bottom lands liable to be submerged	6,800
Ridges in bottom lands	310
Lands draining into bottom	6,740
Total basin of Yazoo river	13,850

General topography of Yazoo bottom.

Topography of the bottom lands.—In its general features, this region is a vast, densely timbered plain, sloping from the Mississippi river toward the east, at a mean rate of about 0.4 of a foot per mile, according to the levels run by Mr. Pattison's party near its middle parallel (plate IV); and sloping from

* Preliminary Report on the Geology and Agriculture of the State of Mississippi. Jackson, 1857.

north to south, at a mean rate of about 0.6 of a foot per mile, as deduced from the fall of the Mississippi between Memphis and Vicksburg.

System of drainage.

The natural system of drainage of this region is very favorable to its protection against overflow and to the conversion of the swamp lands into cultivable ground. Parallel to the tertiary hills which form the eastern border of the bottom, and but a few miles distant from them, is found the main stream. It is known successively as the Cold-water river, as the Tallahatchee river, and, finally, as the Yazoo river, and is a large, navigable stream. It receives many tributaries from the hills, the principal being the Cold-water, the Tallahatchee, the Yock-na-pa-ta-fa, and the Yallabusha. Until very recently (1852?) it was connected with the Mississippi by the Yazoo pass, a large bayou, which left the river about 10 miles below Helena; but a levee is now built across this inlet. While the Yazoo flows nearly south, it receives comparatively little of the drainage of the swamp lands west of it; but when it bends toward the Mississippi, in the lower part of its course, its volume is soon augmented by the contribution of a system of large swamp drains or bayous. The principal of these are the Sunflower river, Deer creek, and Steele's bayou, but there are many others, which, under different names, connect the various cypress swamps and winter lakes of the interior. These channels, with the single exception of McKinney's bayou, which empties into the Mississippi just above Stirling, all drain away from the Mississippi to the Yazoo river with a general southerly course. They were formerly annually overflowed by water which left the Mississippi through innumerable bayous, whose beds varied from 15 to 5 feet below the level of the natural banks of that river. This water, in annually filling and spreading over the banks of the great swamp drains, deposited its sediment upon them, and thus formed a system of high banks or natural levees, extending in a general direction from north to south through the swamps. The annual supply of sediment-bearing water is now cut off by the Mississippi levees, except in great flood years, but the natural swamp levees remain and serve a useful end in restricting the limits of overflow when crevasses do occur.*

Its advantages in an economical point of view.

The natural advantages presented by this system of drainage for protecting the country from overflow are apparent. The whole region is supplied with natural drains having ample slope to carry off its downfall, provided the Mississippi water can be excluded. Since none of these drains discharge into the Mississippi, they do not prevent a continuous chain of levees upon its banks. Lastly, even if a few crevasses do occur, the water poured into the swamps is confined by natural levees to comparatively narrow belts of land, and large areas are thus left unflooded.

Geological data.

Geology of the bottom lands.—It is impossible to give detailed information respecting the character of the soil, etc. of the greater part of the Yazoo bottom, since the region has been very little explored, and what little information has been collected has not been published. The route from the hills east of Greenwood, via McNutt, to Prentiss, on the Mississippi river, has, however, been carefully examined by a party of this Survey in charge of Mr. H. A. Pattison. Besides running transit and level lines across the swamp, this party collected a great deal of information

* Thus in the April rise of 1858, the high banks of Deer creek almost entirely protected the swamps east of them from Mississippi water.

concerning it, which forms the basis of this account. The line surveyed crossed the bottom near its middle parallel of latitude, and probably gives a fair general idea of the whole.

Surface soil. From the tertiary hills to Yazoo river, near the route surveyed, the surface soil is dark alluvial earth, underlain by a stratum of gravel similar to that of the hills, but less coarse. The roads become so solid after a rain that the shoes of the horses hardly make any impression upon them. Between Yazoo river and McNutt, the character of the soil is identical with that just described. From McNutt to Sunflower river, underlying the vegetable mould and the alluvion is a stratum of dark heavy clay, which, when exposed, is called "buckshot" land by the settlers, from its fancied resemblance to leaden balls, when it has been baked and cracked by the sun. Strata of blue clay frequently crop out in low places. After passing Tompkins' bayou, the soil contains much lime; so much, indeed, as to whiten leaves lying upon it after a rain. The Sunflower river itself is very strongly impregnated with lime. At low water, it is of a dark-green color, and very transparent. It evidently receives its water in part from limestone or mineral springs, the latter of which abound on the eastern border of the bottom lands. From Sunflower river to Jones' bayou, the soil is generally similar to that between Sunflower and McNutt, but in some places it begins to resemble more nearly the deposit from Mississippi water. Between Jones' bayou and the Mississippi, the surface soil is composed of this deposit.

The surface soil in Bolivia and Washington counties is reported to be black mud with some calcareous marl. Limestone waters are unquestionably found in these counties.

Sub-soil. To ascertain the nature of the sub-soil, inquiries were made respecting the strata pierced in digging wells, etc. No great variation was found in different parts of the swamp. At Greenwood, many wells were examined. For 2 or 3 feet, a dark-colored alluvial stratum is penetrated; then a layer of heavy red and yellow clay, some 18 or 20 feet thick; then blue clay, from 2 to 4 feet thick; then coarse gravel, which is water-bearing. At McNutt, the upper stratum, some 2 or 3 feet thick, is the ordinary surface soil; next is a stratum of light-red sand and clay, some 20 or 30 feet thick. Frequently strata of blue clay, from 2 to 5 feet thick, are encountered 16 or 20 feet below the surface, and at this depth sticks and leaves are met with. At Sunflower river, the surface soil is about 10 feet thick; then comes a stratum of light-red clay, some 6 or 7 feet thick. At 32 feet below the surface, a stratum of clear white sand with water is found. At Bogue Falaya, wells are not used, and cisterns only have been dug. The soil is light and sandy for some 10 or 20 feet, and then blue mud is found. At Bluck's mill, near the mouth of Yazoo river, a well has been dug through a stratum of hard clay containing many sticks and leaves. At 40 feet below the surface, a layer of quicksand was reached, which rose several feet in the well and prevented farther progress. At Mr. Blake's plantation, 10 miles above the mouth of Yazoo river and bordering upon the hills, the strata pierced are surface soil, clay and sand, gravel—often containing large trees—and, lastly, blue clay, which is some 12 or 14 feet below the surface. This blue clay underlies all the hills. These hills contain much gravel and limestone, and often rest upon strata of sand. Near lake Washington, some 5 miles from the Mississippi, a sycamore tree, in a state of perfect preservation, is said to have been found at a depth of 40 feet below the surface.

The beds of Yazoo and Sunflower rivers are both composed of the same kind of blue clay as that which forms the bed of the Mississippi, and what is a singular and interesting fact, the bottoms of these three rivers are all upon the same absolute level, where crossed by the line of the survey.

Beds of swamp rivers.

The preceding facts seem to warrant the conclusion that the alluvial soil of the entire region, which is unsurpassed in fertility, is underlain by a stratum of clay, varying from 20 to 40 feet in thickness and resting upon a stratum of gravel or sand.

Growth on the bottom lands.—There are three classes of land in the Yazoo bottom: the "high" land, which is rarely overflowed; the "middle" land, which is overflowed during the wet season; and the low "cypress swamps," parts of which always contain water.

Forest growth.

The high land sustains a growth of heavy cane, gum, white oak, white, black, and red hickory, holly, spicewood, dogwood, sassafras, walnut, and pecan.

Upon high land.

The middle land is covered with ash, gum, over-cup oak, black oak, and hackberry.

Upon middle land.

The low swamps contain cypress, many varieties of water-oaks, privet, box-elder, hackberry, and swamp ash. The cypress swamps, which are found in all parts of Yazoo bottom, are from 2 to 10 feet deep at low water. The deepest parts, near the middle, are usually without timber. They are unquestionably the remains of lakes which have been annually filling up by deposit from the Mississippi river.

Upon low land.

The timber between Greenwood and McNutt, on the line of the survey, is rather small, owing probably to the stiff nature of the soil. From McNutt to Bogue Falaya the route traverses an almost unbroken cane-brake. Oak, hickory and other trees common to the swamp, are scattered through this cane, and, where the soil is especially rich, the growth is luxuriant, resembling tropical vegetation.

On the line surveyed.

The size of some of the swamp trees is enormous. One cypress log was rafted out, which was 84 feet long, and 5 feet 4 inches in diameter at the smaller end. Another was sawed at Mr. Bluck's mill, 60 feet long, and 5 feet 1 inch in diameter at the smallest place.

Size of the timber.

Floods in the bottom lands.—Full and exact information relative to overflow was collected on Mr. Pattison's transit and level survey through the Yazoo bottom. (See plate II.) In Appendix F will be found a table giving the depth at high water, 1858, at stations 1000 feet apart on this line, which extends entirely across the middle part of the region, from the hills to the Mississippi river, a distance of 72.5 miles. A profile of this line is also shown on plate IV. East of Bogue Falaya the line was run twice, as a check against errors, and tested thoroughly. The mean depth of overflow on this whole route at high water, 1858, was 2.35 feet. If about 12 miles, not overflowed, be deducted, the mean depth on the remaining part of the line, which, of course, includes all land actually submerged, was 3.08 feet. The deepest overflow was between Bogue Falaya and Jones' bayou, where the mean depth for the 10 miles was 5.5 feet, the maximum being 12.5 feet.

Depth of overflow in 1858.

This line was selected particularly with a view to determining as closely as possible the mean overflow of the entire swamp. The resulting mean depth accords with the estimates of many gentlemen well acquainted with the region. For instance, several months before Mr. Pattison's survey, Mr. John O'Malley, of Vicksburg, who has spent much of his life in the bottom, estimated the depth of overflow on a line between Greenville and McNutt, as follows:—

Confirmation of this result.

Estimated section of Yazoo bottom.

Locality.	Distance.	Mean overflow.
	Miles.	*Feet.*
Greenville to Deer creek	10	2
Deer creek to Bogue Falaya	5	2
Bogue Falaya to Indian bayou	12	4
Indian bayou to Sunflower	7	0
Sunflower to McNutt	25	4

Making a total distance of 59 miles, with a mean overflow, for the whole distance, of 3.01 feet; a singular accordance with the result of Mr. Pattison's subsequent survey over an entirely different route. This, with other verbal testimony to the same effect, induces the belief that about 3.0 feet is an accurate estimate of the mean depth of overflow in the submerged portion of Yazoo bottom at high water in 1858.

Mr. Pattison availed himself of every opportunity to compare exact high-water marks of the different great-flood years in the swamp. The following table exhibits the data thus collected. The datum-plane to which the figures in the table refer is the level of the high water of the Mississippi river in 1858 at Prentiss. They denote, therefore, the number of feet below that plane of the swamp high-water marks:—

Relative depth of overflow in former floods.

Flood-marks in Yazoo bottom.

Locality.	1828.		1844.		1849.		1850.		1851.		1858.	
	Feet.	Date.	Feet.	Date.	Feet.	Date.	Feet.	Date.	Feet.	Date.	Feet.	Date.
Greenwood	19.7	Aug. 15.	24.2	Aug. 21.	21.2		21.2	April 20.	21.1	April.	21.7	July 21.
8 miles above Greenwood									19.5		17.9	July 17.
McNutt	20.6	August.	27.6	Aug. 21.			24.4	May 1.	24.4	May.	23.6	July 18.
Sunflower river	15 0		17.2				15.2		15.2		14.8	July 12.
Bogue Falaya							15.7				14.8	July 10.
Clear creek							17.5				16.0	

In 1828 the depth of overflow exceeded that of any subsequent flood. It is probable that the entire region between Yazoo river and the Mississippi was overflowed, as, after the water fell, the Indian mounds were found covered with the remains of wild animals which had perished on them from starvation. This is said to have also occurred in the great flood of 1782. In 1828 the rains began early and continued until August, making the season an unusually

Facts respecting flood of 1828.

wet one. The tributaries of the Yazoo and Tallahatchee were flooded, and the swamp was impassable from rain-water before the overflow from the Mississippi entered.

Of 1844. In 1844, also, the swamps were full of rain-water before the rise in the Mississippi occurred. This flood was not equal to that of 1858.

Of 1850. In 1850 there were two distinct rises: one, the highest, in May; the other in June. Neither of them was equal to the highest rise in 1858.

Of 1851. In 1851 the flood was about equal to that of the preceding year.

Of 1858. In 1858 the swamps were impassable from rain-water before the Mississippi rose. Even on the first of January this was the case on the route between Prentiss and McNutt, and the survey of the line was for this reason deferred until low water. During the spring the Yazoo and its tributaries were within 5 feet of extreme high water. There were two distinct overflows in the swamp: one in April, of very short duration; the other in June and July. The latter was much the higher of the two, and covered on July 15, as already seen, 6800 square miles of the swamp to a mean depth of about 3.0 feet. It was probably the deepest overflow which has occurred since the flood of 1828, although not very different from those of 1850 and 1851.

Traditional flood-marks in swamp. There are in many parts of the swamp extraordinary high-water marks, which have given rise to much speculation, being too high to have been made by a general flood, unless by one which far exceeded any of those known to the present generation. One of these marks is 4.3 feet above the high-water level of 1858. It is distant about 2 miles from McNutt, in a lake, or rather a kind of drain from the swamp to the Tallahatchee river, which discharges much water when the swamps are flooded. There are also two large inlets to this drain from Tallahatchee river: one 10, and the other 20 miles above McNutt. This high-water mark was doubtless caused by the simultaneous occurrence of a large flood both in the swamp and in the Tallahatchee river, which filled the drain so rapidly that it became very unusually full of water. Another of these marks, situated near Porter's bayou, is some 3.0 feet above ordinary flood-marks at the same place, but is explained by similar local causes. Until one of these extraordinary marks is found so situated that it can only be accounted for upon the supposition of a *general overflow*, they cannot be accepted as evidences of the occurrence of a flood in former times greatly surpassing all those of which there is record or tradition.

Yazoo river; its character, slope, and cross-section. *Yazoo river.*—This river is in many respects a peculiar stream. It flows near the eastern part of the Yazoo bottom, from its northern to its southern extremity, being known as Cold-water river until joined by the Tallahatchee, and then as Tallahatchee river until joined by the Yallabusha. Below the latter junction it assumes its proper name—Yazoo river. The total length of this stream, from its proper source, Horn lake, to the Mississippi, is about 500 miles. At its high stage it is navigable for steamboats drawing 5 or 6 feet water, as far as Panola, on Tallahatchee river, and as far as Grenada, on Yallabusha river. It is navigable for boats drawing from 2 to 3 feet water, as far as Greenwood, a distance of 240 miles, at all seasons of the year. Its average high-water width below Greenwood is about 850 feet. Its high-water cross-section is, near Greenwood, 17,000 square feet, and just below the mouth of Steele's bayou, 50,000 square feet; the difference being mainly due to the swamp tributaries.* Its range at Greenwood is 36 feet; at Yazoo City, 35 feet; and at its mouth, 48 feet. Its total fall at high water, from Greenwood to its mouth, is shown by the levels of this Survey to be about 40 feet, giving a mean slope per mile, in this distance, of 0.16 of a foot. Its current is sluggish, rarely exceeding 3 miles per hour below Greenwood, even in the swiftest part of the stream.

Its annual discharge. The total annual discharge of the Yazoo river can be estimated in the following manner. The area of the entire Yazoo basin, as already seen, is 13,850 square miles. The mean annual downfall in this part of the Mississippi valley is (see Chapter II) about 46 inches. In 1858 it was 54 inches. By a process hereafter explained, it is demonstrated that 0.95 of the entire downfall in this basin in the year 1858 eventually drained into the Mississippi. It is safe, therefore, to assume 0.9 as the usual value of this ratio. This gives 1,350,000,000,000 cubic feet for the mean annual discharge of the Yazoo river; a quantity nearly one-fourteenth part of the mean annual discharge of the Mississippi.

Its floods. The floods of the Yazoo river proper, exclusive of the Mississippi water, are irregular in the time of their occurrence. There is generally, however, a flood in February and March, and often another in the autumn. The river is usually low from June to December.

The Mississippi levees have already effected a great change in the regimen of the river.

Its former regimen. Formerly, even as recently as 1850, the Mississippi began to pour into the swamp in large quantities when fully 10 feet below high water. This water filled up the bottom lands and passed through the innumerable drains to Yazoo river, causing it to *discharge uniformly a great volume of water back into the Mississippi, even at the top of the highest floods.* This fact is established by the direct evidence of many who speak from personal knowledge. It was particularly noted in 1828 and 1850, when the velocity of the current in Yazoo river is stated by eye-witnesses to have exceeded even that of the Mississippi itself. It may, therefore, be doubted whether these swamp lands reduced in the least the discharge at the top of the floods, at points below them, before the levees were made. Even in 1858, when the water was excluded until the river was very high (and when, therefore, the swamps should, if ever, have served as reservoirs), at the actual top of the flood, the Yazoo river, *by measurements,* returned 129,000 cubic feet per second at the date of highest water at Vicksburg (June 27) to the water-prism, which in passing the entire front of Yazoo bottom had lost only 124,000 cubic feet per second by crevasses. There is a grave error, therefore, in the following views: "The floods of the Mississippi are produced by water which does not go into the swamps at all, but which descends through the main channel of the river, aided by the discharge received from the tributaries on the way. The height of the flood at any point depends on the volume that is brought down by the river and its tributaries, and not by the discharge from the swamps. But, *after the*

* See Appendix C for detailed information respecting these sections and those of the tributaries crossed by Mr. Pattison's party.

river has attained its height, the supply is kept up, and the duration of the flood prolonged, by the subsequent discharge from the swamps."* This matter is fully discussed in Chapter VI, where it properly belongs. Here it is only incidentally noticed.

Its present regimen.

At present, as long as the Mississippi levees remain unbroken, the Yazoo is backed up so as to become dead water (sometimes even for 70 miles) during rapid rises of the Mississippi. If there happen, however, to be freshets in some of its tributaries, the Yazoo may maintain its discharge even in very rapid rises of this river, as, for instance, in the December rise of 1857, during the whole of which a moderate downward current was observed. Sometimes, but very rarely, there is an upward current of Mississippi water, which has been known to extend 40 miles up the river.

Change in color of the water.

It is stated that a marked change in the color of the water has occurred near the mouth of the Yazoo river, within the last eight or ten years. Formerly the floods were clear. Now they are becoming more and more muddy every year, probably from the increased cultivation of the banks of the river.

Yazoo levees.

No general system of leveeing has yet been adopted for this river, but several private levees have been made on its banks and on those of its bayous.

Yazoo river in 1858.

The following facts were collected relative to the Yazoo river during the flood of 1858. At Greenwood there was a great freshet in January; the river again rose, from rain-water alone, so as to be in April within 5 feet of extreme high water. It then fell rapidly some 20 feet. When the breaks in the Mississippi levees began to occur, it rose rapidly and steadily to a point 0.5 of a foot below the high water of 1850. At a place some 8 miles above Greenwood, however, it stood 0.7 of a foot above the high water of 1850. It only remained standing a single day (July 21), and then fell rapidly to comparatively low water. At its mouth, the river followed very closely the oscillations marked by the Vicksburg gauge. Exact measurements of discharge were made from time to time at this locality, so that the daily discharge during the flood is accurately known. (See Appendix E.)

Traces of a former race of inhabitants.

Indian mounds, etc.—Indian mounds are to be found throughout the entire bottom. They are evidently artificial, being composed of the ordinary swamp soil, and containing bones, articles of pottery, etc. These mounds are especially numerous near Sunflower river, as are also Indian burial places. In one locality the caving of the river bank has exposed many human bones and other relics of the former occupants of this region. The great age of these mounds may be inferred from the fact that some of the largest trees of the region are now growing upon them. On the banks of the Yazoo river many shell mounds exist. They are above overflow, and are made of the shells of fresh-water muscles, such as are now found in the river. No traditions relative to their origin are preserved among the Indian tribes of the present day. Old fortifications are also reported to exist in the swamps, but none were examined by the parties of this Survey.

* Report on the Overflow of the Delta of the Mississippi, by Charles Ellet, Jr., C. E.

BASINS OF SMALL DIRECT TRIBUTARIES.

The great divisions already described comprise nearly the whole of the basin of the Mississippi, but there are a few small streams which discharge directly into the main river below the junction of the Missouri and Upper Mississippi, and which are, therefore, not included. These will be briefly noticed under four heads: the Maramec, the Kaskaskia, the Obion, and the Big-Black basins.

Maramec basin.—The northern slope of the eastern portion of the Ozark mountains drains into the Maramec river, a stream which enters the Mississippi a few miles below St. Louis. This basin is hilly in character, containing no lands liable to inundation. Its area, taken from Hutawa's sectional map of Missouri, is 5470 square miles. This estimate includes all the country between the Missouri and Cape Girardeau, on the right bank, which drains directly into the Mississippi.

Kaskaskia basin.—Under this head is included all the region draining into the Mississippi on the left bank, between the mouth of the Missouri and the mouth of the Ohio. It is named from its principal stream, although there are others of considerable size—the Big Muddy, for instance. The country is mainly prairie, but, upon the immediate bank of the Mississippi, a considerable area is liable to inundation in great floods. The "American bottom," between the mouths of the Missouri and Kaskaskia rivers, contains the greater part of this swamp country, but there is another limited belt above Cairo. The area of the whole basin is about 9420 square miles.

The Kaskaskia river itself resembles the Illinois. It flows with a very crooked course through a heavily timbered alluvial bottom, liable to be overflowed to a depth of 8 or 10 feet in freshets. Its bed is almost dry in the summer, but, when high, the stream has a strong current.

Obion basin.—Between the Ohio river and the head of the Yazoo basin lies an extended tract of country, which, for want of a better name, has been designated the Obion basin. It is drained by four nearly parallel rivers: the Obion, the Forked-deer, the Hatchee, and the Wolf; the Hatchee alone being, properly speaking, a navigable stream. The area of the entire region is about 10,250 square miles.

This region is in the main an upland, hilly country, but, as shown on plate II, the Obion and Forked-deer rivers flow through somewhat extensive swamps near their mouths. It is generally believed that the great earthquake in 1811, which depressed so much country on the opposite bank, materially increased the area of these swamps.

The Hatchee river, before certain railroads were built, was an important avenue for transporting cotton from the interior to the Mississippi. It is navigable to Bolivar—some 150 miles—from four to six months in the year; its usual range between low and high water being about 15 feet at Bolivar and 30 feet at its mouth. Its average high-water width is about 350 feet, and its high-water cross-section about 8000 square feet.

Big-Black basin.—The region draining into the Mississippi between the mouth of the Yazoo river and the alluvial lands below Baton Rouge is classed under this general head. It is drained by many streams, the two principal being the Big Black, which enters the Mississippi just above Grand Gulf, and the Homo Chitto, which enters below Ellis cliffs. Excepting a narrow strip along the immediate bank of the Mississippi, this whole basin is made up of a rolling, hilly country, entirely above any danger of inundation. Its area is about 7260 square miles.

Summary.—These small basins compose all of the Mississippi valley not included in the preceding grand subdivisions. Their total area is as follows:—

	Square miles.
Maramee basin	5,470
Kaskaskia basin	9,420
Obion basin	10,250
Big-Black basin	7,260
Total	32,400

This country is situated in that portion of the Mississippi valley where the rain is greatest, and contributes a much larger proportion to the annual discharge of the river than is generally supposed. In other respects it possesses but little interest in the discussions of this report, a small portion of it, only, being subject to overflow.

TABULAR SUMMARY.

It is often convenient to be able to refer to a condensed tabular exhibit of the principal hydrographical features of the basin of a great river like the Mississippi. For this reason the following table has been prepared, partly from the preceding description of its several subdivisions, and partly from the next chapter, where the main river is treated. All the important direct tributaries may thus at a glance be compared in respect to their length, slope, dimensions of cross-section, discharge, area of basin, downfall of rain, and drainage.

The Mississippi and its tributaries.

River.	Distance from mouth.	Elevation above sea.	Fall per mile.	Width between banks.	Least low-water depth upon the bars.	Range between low and high water.	Area of cross-section at high water.	Remarks.
	Miles.	*Feet.* low water	*Feet.*	*Feet.*	*Feet.*	*Feet.*	*Sq. feet.*	
Ohio river.								Area of basin, 214,000 sq.m. Downfall of rain, 41.5 in. Annual discharge, 5,000,-000,000,000 cu. ft. Ratio between downfall and drainage, 0.24 Mean discharge per second, 158,000 cu. ft.
Coudersport	1265	1649						
Olean point	1225	1403	6.15					
Warren	1175	1187	4.32					
Franklin	1105	960	3.24					
Pittsburg	975	699	2.00					
Wheeling	889	620	0.92			45		
Marietta	800	571	0.55	1200			50,000	
Head Le Tart's shoals	769	555	0.52		1.0			
Mouth Great Kanawha.	714	522	0.60					
Portsmouth	620	474	0.51					
Cincinnati	515	432	0.40		2.0			
Above falls	361	377	0.36			42		
Below falls	358	353	8.00			64		
Evansville	187	320	0.20		1.5	40		
Mouth Wabash	130	297	0.25	3000			150,000	
Mouth	0	275	0.17		3.0	51		

River.	Distance from mouth.	Elevation above sea.	Fall per mile.	Width between banks.	Least low-water depth upon the bars.	Range between low and high water.	Area of cross-section at high water.	Remarks.
	Miles.	*Feet.*	*Feet.*	*Feet.*	*Feet.*	*Feet.*	*Sq. feet.*	
Upper Mississippi.		low water						Area of basin, 169,000 sq. m. Downfall of rain, 35.2 in. Annual discharge, 3,300,000,000,000 cu. ft. Ratio between downfall and drainage, 0.24. Mean discharge per second, 105,000 cu. ft.
Utmost source	1330	1680						
Itasca lake	1324	1575	17.50	15			50	
Entrance to Lac Travers	1234	1456	1.32	150				
Entrance to lake Cass	1189	1402	1.20	175			1,400	
Mouth Leech-lake river	1109	1356	0.57					
Head falls of Peckagama	1061	1340	0.33	120				
Mouth Swan river	998	1290	0.73					
Mouth Sandy-lake river	960	1253	0.95	300		20.0		
Mouth Pine river	863	1176	0.79					
Mouth Crow-wing river	815	1130	0.95	1200				
St. Paul	658	670	2.93			20.0		
La Crosse	514	639	0.22		2.0	14.0		
Prairie du Chien	453	600	0.64			18.5	100,000	
Head Rock-Isl'd rapids	310	505	0.66	5000		16.0		
Fort Rock-Isl'd rapids	295	483	1.47		2 0			
Mouth Missouri	0	381	0.35			35.0		
Missouri river.		low water						Area of basin. 518,000 sq m. Downfall of rain, 20.9 in. Annual discharge, 3,780-000,000,000 cu. ft. Ratio between downfall and drainage, 0.15. Mean discharge per second, 120,000 cu. ft.
Source Madison fork	2908	6800(?)						
Three forks Missouri	2824	4319	29.52					
Mouth Sun river	2689	3573	5.54					
Foot of falls	2670	2964	31.59					
At Fort Benton	2644	2845	4.56	1500		6		
At Fort Union	1894	2188	0.88					
At Fort Pierre	1246	1475	1.10	2500	1.0			
At Sioux City	842	1065	1.01					
At St. Joseph	484	756	0.86	3000		20	75,000	
At mouth	0	381	0.77			35		
Arkansas river.		high wat.						Area of basin (including White r.), 189,000 sq. m. Downfall of rain (including White r.), 29.3 in. Annual discharge (including White river), 2,000,000,000,000 cu. ft. Ratio between downfall and drainage, 0.15. Mean discharge per second (including White river), 63,000 cu. ft.
Source	1514	10000						
Mouth Boiling-spring r.	1364	4880	34.13	150				
Mouth Apishpa creek	1323	4371	12.41					
Near Bent's Fort	1289	3672	20.56					
Near Fort Atkinson	1095	2331	6.91	5000	0.0	6	30,000	
Great bend	992	1658	6.53					
Near Fort Gibson	642	560	8.14		1.0	10		
Near Fort Smith	522	418	1.18	1500		25	70,000	
Near Little Rock	250	252	0.61		2.0	35		
Mouth	0	162	0.36			45		
Red river.		high wat.						Area of basin, 97,000 sq. m. Downfall of rain, 39.0 in. Annual discharge, 1,800,000,000,000 cu. ft. Ratio between downfall and drainage, 0.20. Mean discharge per second, 57,000 cu. ft.
Source	1200	2450		2000		8	12,000	
At Preston	820	641	4.80			40		
At Fulton	595	242	1.80		1.0	35		
At head of raft	405	207	0.20			10		
At Shreveport	330	180	0.36	800	3.0	25	40,000	
Mouth Black river	30	58	0.41			45		
Mouth	0	54	0.14					
Yazoo river.		high wat.						Area of basin, 13,850 sq. m. Downfall of rain, 46.3 in. Annual discharge, 1,350,000,000,000 cu. ft. Ratio between downfall and drainage, 0.90. Mean discharge per second, 43,000 cu. ft.
Horn lake	500	210						
Greenwood	240	140	0.27	850	2.5	36	17,000	
Mouth	0	103	0.16			48	50,000	

River.	Distance from mouth.	Elevation above sea.	Fall per mile.	Width between banks.	Least low-water depth upon the bars.	Range between low and high water.	Area of cross-section at high water.	Remarks.
	Miles.	*Feet.*	*Feet.*	*Feet.*	*Feet.*	*Feet.*	*Sq. feet.*	
St. Francis river.		high wat.						Area of basin, 10,500 sq m.
Source	380	1150						Downfall of rain, 41.1 in.
Head swamp region	275	330	7.81				9,400	Annual discharge, 990,000,000,000 cu. ft.
Chalk bluffs	225	280	1.00				2,300	
M. and L. R. railroad	55	209	0.42	} 700		} 40	21,000	Ratio between downfall and drainage, 0.90.
Mouth	0	200	0.16				37,000	Mean discharge per second, 31,000 cu. ft.
Main Mississippi.		high wat.						Drainage area, 1,244,000 square miles.
Mouth of Missouri	1286	416.0						
St. Louis	1270	408 0	0.500		} 2.0	37.0		Downfall of rain, 30.4 in.
Cairo	1097	322.0	0.497			51.0		Annual discharge (including 3 outlet bayous), 21,300,000,000,000 cu. ft.
Columbus	1076	310.0	0.571	} 4470	} 5.0	47.0	} 191,000	
Memphis	872	221.0	0.486			40.0		
Gaines' landing	647	149.0	0.320					Ratio between downfall and drainage, 0.25.
Natchez	378	66.0	0 309	} 4080	} 6.0	51.0	} 199,000	
Red-river landing	316	49.5	0.266			44.3		Mean discharge per second, 675,000 cu. ft.
Baton Rouge	245	33.9	0.220	} 3000		31.1	} 200,000	
Donaldsonville	193	25.8	0 156			24.3		
Carrollton	121	15.2	0.147			14.4		
Fort St. Philip	37	5.2	0.119	} 2470		4 5	} 199,000	
Head of passes	17	2.9	0.115			2.3		
Gulf	0	0.0	0.171			0.0		

CHAPTER II.

THE MISSISSIPPI RIVER BELOW THE JUNCTION OF THE MISSOURI.

Geology of the river banks.—Geology of the channel.—Age of the blue clay.—Artesian well at New Orleans.—Growth upon the river banks.—Changes of the bed.—Oscillations of the gulf and their effects upon the lakes and river.—Tidal oscillations of the river.—Hurricanes and their effects.—Range of the Mississippi between low and high water.—Elevation above the gulf of the surface of the river.—Usual succession of stages.—Dimensions of cross-section.—Yearly amount of rain in the basin.—Annual discharge of the Mississippi and of its principal tributaries.—How the former may readily be measured.—Ratio between rain and drainage in the basin.—Sedimentary matter in Mississippi water.—Matter rolling along upon the bottom.—Temperature of the water.—History of the progress of levees in the Mississippi valley.—Levee organization in the different states.—Dimensions and cost of existing levees.—The earlier floods.—Those of 1828, 1844, 1849, 1850, 1851, 1858, and 1859.

Introductory remarks.

AT the mouth of the Missouri the Mississippi river first assumes its characteristic appearance of a turbid and boiling torrent, immense in volume and force. From that point, its waters pursue their devious course for 1300 miles, destroying banks and islands at one locality, reconstructing them at another, absorbing tributary after tributary, without visible increase of size, until at length it is in turn absorbed in the greater volume of the gulf. But a true conception of a river whose enormous volume and apparently irresistible power impart to it something of sublimity, cannot be formed from a written description of its magnitude and motion. Seemingly unrestrained, the Mississippi is really governed by laws, the development of which was the first object of these investigations. The present chapter, illustrated by plate II, is designed to give an introductory synopsis of the physical characteristics of the river.

TOPOGRAPHY.

Right bank between the Missouri and the Ohio.

Geology of the river banks.—After passing the bottom lands near the mouth of the Missouri, the right bank of the Mississippi is mainly composed of high limestone bluffs, which seldom recede more than a mile or two from the river, until Cape Girardeau is reached. Here there is a strip of low land, about 4 miles in length, which serves as an inlet to the St. Francis bottom. Commerce bluffs next border the river for a few miles. They are about 125 feet in height, and are composed partly of loam and clay, and partly of a flinty rock, too hard for profitable use in building. The clay is shipped in large quantities to various points on the Ohio river, to be used in the manufacture of pottery. From the lower end of the bluff to the mouth of the Ohio, the right bank is subject to overflow, except at a few points, where it consists of low, sandy ridges.

The left bank of the Mississippi, from the mouth of the Missouri to the mouth of the Kaskaskia, consists of a strip of low land, called the American bottom, which is subject to overflow in the highest floods. Thence to Commerce, the bank is formed of bluffs like those on the opposite side of the river. They frequently assume fantastic shapes, which are properly accounted great natural curiosities. From Commerce to Cairo, the left bank is liable to be overflowed in floods.

Left bank between the Missouri and the Ohio.

From the mouth of the Ohio, the river flows mainly through an alluvial region below the level of its floods. It first strikes high land at Columbus. The bluff is on the left bank, and is (by levels) 200 feet above the river at high water. Above the town it is called the "Iron banks," from containing large quantities of iron ore. It is composed of successive strata of coarse silicious sand, colored red or yellow, of coarse brown clay, of very fine bluish clay, delicately tinted with lake and yellow, of fine sand, colored purple, red, and white, and of coarse gravel, limestone, and a kind of pudding-stone cemented by clay and iron. Clay concretions, beautifully tinted, are common in the sand strata. Below the town, the bluff is called the "Chalk bank," from its pure white color.

Columbus bluffs.

The river next touches high land at Hickman, on the left bank, where the bluff is similar to that at Columbus, but less interesting in its structure.

Bluffs at Hickman.

Between New Madrid and Point Pleasant the Mississippi cuts through a low ridge, which is from 1 to 15 feet above overflow. This ridge extends southward from Commerce bluffs, and its soil is not Mississippi alluvion.

Prolongation of Commerce bluffs.

The river next touches land above overflow at the four Chickasaw bluffs on the left bank. The first lies between Islands 33 and 34; the second, between Hatchee river and Island 35; the third, opposite Island 36; and the fourth, between Wolf river and the foot of Island 46. Fulton is built upon the first, Randolph upon the second, and Memphis on the fourth of these noted bluffs. They average about 150 feet above the level of the river at high water. The Memphis bluff is composed of yellow loam, underlain near the high water level by a stratum of silicious sand. Two kinds, one white and the other yellow, are very fine and pure. They are, although rather too fine for that purpose, used for building. They rest upon blue clay.

The Chickasaw bluffs.

The river next approaches land secure from overflow on its right bank. The bluff is the southern extremity of Crowley's ridge, which apparently terminates a few hundred yards back of Helena. In reality, it reappears in Yazoo bottom, as has been already seen. This bluff is the last point near the river, on the right bank, which is above overflow.

Crowley's ridge.

The bank near Cypress creek, opposite Island 77, is quite low and composed of a red, tenacious clay. It is underlain by sand, and consequently caves badly. Its peculiar color is doubtless caused by sediment from water, which, escaping in floods from Arkansas river, enters the Mississippi by this creek. The first bend to the right, below Island 78, is called Yellow bend, from the peculiar color of the soil of the right bank. This soil is very tenacious clay, and does not cave.

Peculiar soil near Island 77 and 78.

Vicksburg bluffs and those below them on the left bank.

At Vicksburg, about 300 miles below Helena, the Mississippi again approaches on its left bank the bluffs, which it continues to wash at short intervals for 250 miles. The points at which it touches this formation are Vicksburg, Grand Gulf, Rodney, a point just below the mouth of Cole creek (bluff half a mile back from river), about 8 miles above Natchez, Ellis cliffs, Fort Adams, Bayou Sara, Port Hudson, and Baton Rouge. From the last-named point to the gulf, the banks are uniformly below the high-water level of the river. The geological formation of these bluffs is interesting. They are composed of loess, a post-pleiocene formation, similar to that of the Rhine, superposed upon eocene tertiary. That at Vicksburg, called the Walnut hills, is (by levels) 300 feet high, and underlain near low-water mark by a solid stratum of blue clay, containing carbonized wood. Above the latter is a stratum containing many marine shells and corals. Next are deposits of yellow loam and sand, containing vast numbers of fresh-water shells. The sand is occasionally solidified into sandstone, sufficiently firm for pavements, building purposes, etc. The bluff at Grand Gulf is similar in height and character. There is the same stratum of blue clay, the white, silicious sand and sandstone, and the yellow loam at top. The Natchez bluff is about 150 feet in height. The lower part is composed of gravel and sand, containing many corals and other fossils. Next comes a stratum of clay, rich in fossils of large extinct species of quadrupeds. The top is made up of yellow loam, sand, and clay, also fossiliferous. Curious clay and iron concretions, of a dirty rust color on the outside, but hollow and delicately tinted pink and red on the inside, are common. Springs, and occasionally the Mississippi itself, are gradually washing out the sandy strata in this bluff, and thus causing extensive land slips. The bluff at Port Hudson is about 100 feet high. It is mainly composed of the yellow loam and silicious sand, but is underlain near low-water mark by a stratum of vegetable mould, containing sticks, leaves, and the remains of a fossil forest, partly upright and partly horizontal.

Alluvial banks.

The banks of the river liable to overflow between Cape Girardeau and the gulf are alluvial, being composed of the sediment deposited by the river-water which flows over them in times of flood. It is hardly necessary to add that they are unsurpassed in fertility. The portion of this new-made land nearest the river is the highest, since there the deposit is greatest in amount and coarsest in material. For an average distance of about a mile the slope from the river is greatest. It then rapidly diminishes until the swamps, which are seldom more than 3, and often not more than 2 miles distant, are reached. The following table shows the average fall in the first mile.

Slope of the natural banks of the Mississippi.

Locality.	Bank.	Fall in first mile from river.	Authority.
		Feet.	
Near Cairo	Right.	4	Cairo and Fulton railroad company.
Near Memphis (measured from bank of Mill-seat lake)	Right.	6	Military road—Memphis to Little Rock.
Near Prentiss	Left.	7	Delta Survey (party of Mr. Pattison).
Near Gaines' landing	Right.	5	Gaines' landing and Fulton railroad company.
Northern boundary of Louisiana	Right.	8	Professor C. G. Forshey.
Near Lake Providence	Right.	8	Providence and Fulton railroad company.
Near Natchez; measured from bank of lake Concordia	Right.	8	Delta Survey (party of Mr. Pattison).
6.6 miles above Williamsport	Right.	7	Delta Survey (party of Mr. Ford).
1.3 miles above Williamsport	Right.	5	Delta Survey (party of Mr. Ford).
Below Williamsport, near Morgan's	Right.	9	Delta Survey (party of Mr. Ford).
New Texas road	Right.	10	Swamp-land commissioner's office, La.
11 miles above Point Coupée church	Right.	3	Delta Survey (party of Mr. Ford).
3 miles above Waterloo	Right.	12	Delta Survey (party of Mr. Ford).
4 miles below Port Hudson	Right.	9	Delta Survey (party of Mr. Ford).
7 miles below Lobdell's store	Right.	5	Delta Survey (party of Mr. Ford).
5 miles above Baton Rouge	Right.	3	Delta Survey (party of Mr. Ford).
Grosse Tête railroad	Right.	10	Dr. William Sidney Smith.
6 miles below Baton Rouge	Right.	13	Delta Survey (party of Mr. Ford).
7.5 miles below Baton Rouge	Right.	12	Delta Survey (party of Mr. Ford).
1.5 miles above bayou Manchac	Left.	6	Delta Survey (party of Mr. Ford).
Opposite bayou Manchac	Right.	11	Delta Survey (party of Mr. Ford).
4 miles above Bayou Goula	Right.	10	Delta Survey (party of Mr. Ford).
1.5 miles above Bayou Goula	Right.	6	Delta Survey (party of Mr. Ford).
8 miles below Bayou Goula	Right.	5	Delta Survey (party of Mr. Ford).
1 mile below Domenique's landing	Right.	6	Delta Survey (party of Mr. Ford).
3.5 miles above Donaldsonville	Right.	3	Delta Survey (party of Mr. Ford).
5 miles below Donaldsonville	Left.	5	Delta Survey (party of Mr. Ford).
10 miles below Donaldsonville	Left.	9	Delta Survey (party of Mr. Ford).
10 miles below Donaldsonville	Right.	6	Delta Survey (party of Mr. Ford).
20 miles below Donaldsonville	Left.	8	Delta Survey (party of Mr. Ford).
4 miles above Bonnet Carré church	Right.	7	Delta Survey (party of Mr. Ford).
Upper end Bonnet Carré crevasse	Left.	10	Delta Survey (party of Lieutenant Warren).
Lower end Bonnet Carré crevasse	Left.	3	Delta Survey (party of Lieutenant Warren).
Barataria canal	Right.	7	Surveys of canal company.
1 mile below Barataria canal	Right.	4	Delta Survey (party of Mr. Ford).
Near New Orleans	Right.	10	New Orleans and Opelousas railroad company.
Near New Orleans	Left.	10	Mr. G. W. R. Bailey
11 miles below New Orleans	Left.	8	Delta Survey (party of Mr. G. C. Smith).

Their formation.

The mean fall is about 7 feet. The variations shown in the table are explained by the fact that caving is effecting constant changes. Where levees do not exist, the slope of the bank should be greatest in a part of the river which has remained a long time unchanged. Indeed, it would seem that natural levees might eventually confine the stream in such places to its channel. This has actually occurred on the Colorado of the West. The conditions most favorable to such a result are: annual floods of nearly equal height; dense undergrowth on the banks; and sand drifting from the uncovered parts of the bed at low water. When, however, a bank of this character begins to cave, it loses its highest land, and if the change is rapid and continuous, the slope may temporarily become very much reduced. With levees this reduction becomes permanent. The new land added in the mean time to the opposite bank will also have a gentle slope, because it will be built up about to the uniform level of the old edge. Add to this normal cause of change in slope, the local effects of cut-offs, bayous leading from the river—whose banks of course follow the same law as those of the parent stream—etc., etc., and the variations from the mean fall in the first mile, that are shown in the table, are sufficiently explained.

It is evident that this natural form of the banks necessitates the construction of the levees *as near to the river as would be safe*, both to reduce their height and consequently their cost to the minimum amount, and also to secure for cultivation the highest and the best land of the valley. The flood depth near the edge of the natural banks, with the levees in their present condition, varies from 1 to 15 feet; the mean from Cape Girardeau to the gulf being probably about 4 feet.

Important consequence of their peculiar form.

Geology of the channel.—A knowledge of the character of the bed of the Mississippi river is of the highest practical importance, as will be hereafter seen, and great efforts have, accordingly, been made to acquire it.

Bed of the river.

The numerous soundings of the Survey, between the mouth of the Ohio and Fort St. Philip, were made with prepared leads, and the samples of the bottom were carefully preserved for examination and comparison. The details of these operations are explained in Chapter IV, and the results exhibited in Appendix C. It is here proposed to discuss the results obtained.

Samples collected.

The samples showed—what, indeed, is evident to the eye at low water—that immense beds of pure silicious sand, and fine gravel, entirely free from the muddy sedimentary matter with which the water is charged, exist in the channel-way. They are found below points, in island chutes, sometimes, though rarely, entirely across the bed, and, in general, wherever the water moves with a current too rapid to deposit its sediment, and yet not sufficiently strong to wash away all the sand transported to that place. The material of which these bars are composed grows finer the nearer the gulf is approached, a fact which accords with the well-known law of rivers that the particles of gravel and sand in the bed are not stationary, but gradually roll forward toward the mouth under the impulse communicated by the current.

Sand-bars.

Opposite caving bends, in the eddies below islands, and at other points where for any cause the current becomes nearly dead, the sediment transported by the river-water is deposited, forming gently-sloping, sandy, mud-banks, called willow battures (or, if on islands, tow-heads), from the growth of willows which soon makes its appearance upon them. This process of land-formation serves to fix a normal limit beyond which the river cannot increase its width by caving, but it cannot properly be said to affect the character of its true bottom.

Battures. Tow-heads.

What then constitutes the real bed of the river, upon which rest the moving sand-bars and the new willow-batture formations? From the mouth of the Ohio down, at least as far as Fort St. Philip, it seems to be composed of a single substance, a hard, blue or drab-colored clay. In the channel between the Ohio and Red rivers, this clay is not usually found much above low-water mark, but it sometimes appears at a higher level in the bottom lands remote from the river, as between McNutt and Jones' bayou, in Yazoo bottom, and between Washita river and Black bayou, opposite Natchez, where it occasionally crops out at the surface

Sub-stratum of blue clay.

in an impure form, constituting the "buckshot land." The formation seems to be widely distributed throughout the delta proper, where it often appears at a higher level than in the channel, as the following facts establish.

General distribution of this clay throughout the delta proper.

It is found at the head of bayou Plaquemine, 25 feet below high-water mark, or 5 feet above the mean level of the gulf. The soundings indicate that here it extends, without interruption, down into the Mississippi river to a depth of at least 153 feet below high-water mark, denoting a thickness of at least 128 feet. It must be remarked, however, that soundings cannot be entirely relied upon in a matter of this kind.

It is found in bayou La Fourche. At the head its top is 25 feet below high water, or at about the mean level of the gulf. At Thibodeaux its top is 25 feet below high water, or about at the mean level of the gulf. In the canal between Lockport and lake Field it is also found at about the same level.

Major Blanchard states that blue clay is found from 8 to 10 feet below the level of the gulf, on the prairies between the Mississippi and La Fourche, on the line of the Opelousas railroad surveyed by him.

It was repeatedly stated by gentlemen residing in the vicinity of Grand lake, that the bottom of that sheet of water is made up of a hard stratum of blue clay, where the current occasioned by the tides and by the discharge of the several bayous is sufficient to remove the soft mud. This lake is from 2 to 18 feet deep in low water, and the clay is, therefore, probably a few feet below the gulf level. None of it is found in lake Palourde.

Mr. Bayley states that a hard, blue clay is found from 1 to 3 feet below the surface, or at about the level of the gulf, in the Chacahoula swamp, west of the La Fourche, on the line of the Opelousas railroad, and that it is found at about the same depth in all the cypress swamps west of the Mississippi in this section of country. East of the Mississippi, the depth at which it is found is much greater, and varies from 5 to 40 feet below the surface of the ground.

The clays mentioned by Mr. Bayley and Major Blanchard, and those at the bottom of Grand lake, probably belong to the same geological age as the first bed of clay pierced by the artesian well at New Orleans, at the level of the gulf.

Inferences respecting this clay and facts bearing upon its probable age.

The facts mentioned are very important, for they prove either that the peculiar blue clay in the bed of the river is an alluvial deposit, or that the thickness of the alluvial stratum in the delta region has been greatly over-estimated, and that the river is flowing through it in a channel belonging to a geological epoch antecedent to the present. All facts bearing upon the *age* of this blue clay are, therefore, highly important. The following have been collected:—

Its physical characteristics.

1. The clay is quite different in appearance, color, etc., from any deposit now made by the river. As long as it remains wet, it seems nearly insoluble, resisting for years the strong current of the Mississippi. If it be thoroughly dried, however, and then again placed in water, it rapidly disintegrates into a powder. The clay itself has a somewhat gritty feel between the teeth and a peculiar taste. It effervesces less with acids than the present deposits of the river, judging by the samples of the latter collected by the Survey.

It underlies the Yazoo bottom.

2. It underlies the whole Yazoo bottom, below the great sand stratum, if we may judge from the fact that it constitutes the bottom of the bed of the Yazoo and Sunflower rivers, as well as that of the Mississippi, and that all three are on the same level.

It underlies the Vicksburg bluff, which is a tertiary formation.

3. In the bluff at Vicksburg, it underlies the stratum which contains marine shells, and which Sir Charles Lyell and Dr. Harper both pronounce eocene tertiary; that is, the oldest tertiary stratum. It would seem then to belong either to the eocene tertiary or to the cretaceous (upper secondary) below it. It undoubtedly underlies others of the river bluffs, but no examinations were made for it elsewhere at low water, when alone it would be visible.

It exists more than 600 feet below New Orleans.

4. It underlies New Orleans in strata alternating with sand and marine shells for at least 630 feet, as shown by the artesian well which was begun in that city in February, 1854, and carried to that depth before it was abandoned. Dr. N. B. Benedict, recording secretary of the New Orleans Academy of Sciences, in behalf of a committee of that body, of which he was a member, devoted himself to the study of this well, securing samples of every stratum pierced, and otherwise thoroughly investigating the subject. These observations have never been published in full, but Dr. Benedict very kindly exhibited his samples, presented the Survey with the following authentic list of strata, and supplied all needful information respecting the history of the well. The geological ages of the strata pierced are not well established, but it is evident that none below the depth of 41 feet from the surface (or about 37 feet below the level of the gulf) were deposited by the river. The same must be acknowledged in reference to the channel of the Mississippi itself, for it is identical in character with a sample of the very last stratum, which was presented for comparison by Dr. Benedict. The artesian water, which rose from the sand stratum 335 feet below the surface, was strongly alkaline and chalybeate, closely resembling the celebrated Bladon Springs of Alabama.

Section of artesian well at New Orleans, La.

Character of strata.	Thickness of stratum.	Top of stratum below surface.
No.	*Feet.*	*Feet.*
1 Heterogeneous matters—the common surface	2.0	0
2 Clay; blue, tenacious, uniform	15.0	2.0
3 " coal-black, containing woody matters, rootlets, etc	3.8	17.0
4 Sand and clay mixed; subtile, like annual deposits of Mississippi river	10.2	20.8
5 Clay; dark, semi-fluid, nearly destitute of grittiness	7.0	31.0
6 " same as No. 5, but becoming sandy	3.0	38.0
7 Sand, leaden-blue, coarse; many small shells; water abundant	0.7	41.0
8 Shells exclusively, great variety, very compacted	1.3	41.7
9 Sand, identical with No. 7	13.0	43.0
10 " clay and shells mixed, olive-colored, of consistency of "mortar"	10.0	56.0
11 " coarse, dark brown; small cypress roots and water-worn pebbles	4.0	66.0
12 " " light blue, destitute of shells	5.0	70.0
13 " blue, mixed with fragments of shells	1.0	75.0
14 Shells exclusively, compacted; a few water-worn pebbles in lowest part	6.5	76.0
15 Clay, olive-green, tenacious, like wax	2.5	82.5
16 Sand, nearly impalpable, so subtile that little could be brought up	3.0	85.0
17 Clay, like No. 15, but a section of it is a little mottled with yellow	1.0	88.0
18 Sand, gray or light-blue	1.0	89.0
19 Clay, blue as if half dried, with umber-colored masses, each enclosing a yellowish stone	1.0	90.0
20 Sand, " subtile, with a little clay	4.0	91.0
21 Sand and clay, identical with No. 4	3.0	95.0
22 Clay, identical with No. 19; stones contorted, fantastic forms, perforated, effervesce with acid	1.0	98.0
23 Sand, subtile, like German sand for grinding and fining glass, imported at 50 cts. an ounce	9.0	99.0
24 Clay, masses of two different colors, both very dark, tenacious and pure	1.0	108.0
25 " and sand, blue, soft; tools sink by their own weight	3.0	109.0
26 " dark drab, like tallow between teeth; effervesces by acid, leaving pores surrounded by dark line	34.0	112.0
27 Sand, clay, shells, and stones like indurated clay	3.0	146.0
28 Clay, blue, tenacious—a mere flake	0.2	149.0
29 Sand, etc. identical with No. 27	0.8	149.2
30 Clay, striated, changing to matter like vegetable mould	3.0	150.0
31 Wood, cedar log, sound, striated with thin plates of silicious matter	0.5	153.0
32 Vegetable mould, changing to striated clay, identical with No. 30 inverted; shells destitute of animal matter	1.0	153.5
33 Sand, greenish blue, tenacious from slight mixture of clay	2.0	154.5
34 Clay, pure; color identical with No. 33; tenacious	9.5	156.5
35 Sand, very subtile, rendered adhesive by a little clay	4.0	166.0
36 Clay, drab, tenacious, containing lumps exactly like pieces of chocolate	5.0	170.0
37 " umber-colored but darker, tenacious	1.0	175.0
38 Sand, green; a little clay which increases with the depth	4.0	176.0
39 Clay, color same as the sand of No. 38 (still a little sand)	2.0	180.0
40 Sand, like No. 38; color still the same green as No. 38	1.0	182.0
41 " coarse, whitish green; very variable as to clay mixture	13.0	183.0
42 Clay, leaden-blue, not gritty; effervesces with acid	32.5	196.0
43 Sand, " coarse; comminuted shells; a little clay	21.5	228.5
44 Mixed, like Nos. 30 and 32	2.0	250.0
45 Clay, pale lead or dirty white; tenacious, unctuous, like tallow between teeth, not gritty	39.0	252.0
46 " sand and shells; soft mass, but *looks* like common sandstone	2.0	291.0
47 Sand, unmixed	29.0	293.0
48 Clay, pale olive; very pure	4.0	322.0
49 Sand, like No. 47	6.0	326.0
50 Clay, like No. 48	3.0	332.0
51 Sand, ash-colored (pure white and black), coarse; (*artesian water.*)	95.0	335.0
52 " nearly black, subtile, a little clay (360 *gallons of water an hour*)	50.0	430.0
53 Clay, blue, tenacious, firm; little gritty; no more water	63.5	480.0
54 Sand; many minute shells and fragments	2.5	543.5
55 Clay, blue, firm, tenacious (containing a stratum of sand at 566 to 568½; no specimen obtained)	36.0	546.0
56 Sand and a little clay; hardness nearly stony (penetrated to 584 feet)		582.0
Total depth attained 630 feet.		

5. Mr. A. M. Lea, of Knoxville, Tennessee, an engineer of high scientific attainments, formerly of the army, states that this identical clay, with which he is familiar, crops out under calcareous sandstone at the depth of 24 feet below the level of the gulf at Aransas bay and Laguna Madre on the coast of Texas.

It crops out under sandstone on the coast of Texas.

6. In boring his artesian well on the Llano Estacado, near the intersection of the river Pecos and the 32d parallel, Captain John Pope, Topographical Engineers, pierced a stratum some 200 feet in thickness, which he describes* as "red and blue marly clay, with intercalations of soft red and yellow quartzose sandstone." He considers this to belong to the upper secondary formation. The close analogy between the physical characteristics of such a formation and that underlying the Vicksburg bluff, together with the similarity in their supposed geological ages, suggests that they may be identical. If so, the great antiquity of the bottom of the Mississippi is established. The surface of the ground at Captain Pope's well is some 3000 feet above the gulf, and the stratum in question was encountered at a depth of about 400 feet.

It possibly underlies the Llano Estacado.

7. Lieutenant G. K. Warren, Topographical Engineers, states that this peculiar blue clay very closely resembles a formation which covers a great area in the immediate valley of the Missouri, east of the Black hills. His geological assistant, Dr. Hayden, assigns a place to this formation near the middle of the cretaceous, and describes† it as follows: "Bluish and dark-gray plastic clays, containing *Nautilus DeKayi*, *Ammonites placenta*, *Baculites ovatus*, and *B. compressus*, with numerous other marine mollusca—remains of *Mosasauras*. Thickness 350 feet." Its upper surface is about 2000 feet above the sea.

It probably covers much country in the Missouri valley.

Although no one of these facts may be considered in itself conclusive, it must be allowed that, together, they afford good grounds for doubting the recent alluvial character of the *bed* of the Mississippi, even as far down as the head of the passes. Whether this clay stratum which composes it, and which seems to have so wide a distribution throughout the valley, belongs properly to the eocene or to the cretaceous formation—although a matter of much scientific interest—is of little practical importance to the discussions of this report. Whether it belongs to either one of those geological epochs or to the present, on the contrary, has a most important practical bearing, as will hereafter be seen. It is believed that the facts stated establish that its formation is long antecedent to the present epoch.

Necessary inference from these facts is that the bed of the Mississippi is not formed of recent deposit from its waters.

The correctness of this opinion is confirmed—it may almost be said demonstrated—by the form of the cross-section of the river. If the bottom were formed of alluvion, it would be comparatively smooth, like a sand-bar or willow batture. In reality, it is very rough, being in many places full of blue-clay ridges and lumps, some of them many feet in height, as in the Bonnet Carré and Natchez sections (plate X and Appendix C). Lest it be supposed that these irregularities are due to old logs or to errors in sounding, it is well to state that in three instances—once at Bonnet Carré, once at Natchez, and once at Randolph—the lead was lost while being drawn up after the sounding, by the chain striking one of these clay lumps as the boat drifted down stream. Large quantities of the clay

Further proofs of the correctness of this opinion.

* See diagram accompanying the annual report of the Office of Explorations and Surveys, War Department, for 1858. Ho. Ex. Doc. No. 2, 2d session 35th Congress.

† Preliminary report of Explorations in Nebraska and Dakota, 1855-6-7, by Lieutenant G. K. Warren, Topographical Engineers, accompanying the annual report of the Office of Explorations and Surveys, War Department 1858. Ho. Ex. Doc. No. 2, 2d session 35th Congress.

were found adhering to the broken end of the chain at a distance, in one case, of more than 30 feet above the lead. Further evidence is offered in Appendix C, where it will be seen that the maximum depth in the straight portion of the river in front of Carrollton varies fully 40 feet, even in a distance of a few thousand feet. Further, the boils and whirls, which cover the surface of the Mississippi, demonstrate the great irregularities of its bed, and hence its ancient origin.

Growth upon the river banks.—The staple productions of the regions immediately bordering the Mississippi river vary as the gulf is approached. From the mouth of the Missouri to the mouth of Hatchee river, near lat. 35° 30′, corn is the chief product. Thence to the mouth of Red river, in lat. 31°, cotton is the important staple. Thence to Point La Hache, near lat 29° 30′, sugar is mainly cultivated. Below Point La Hache there are many luxuriant orange groves upon the narrow belts of land between the river and the salt-marshes of the gulf.

Staple productions of the alluvial region.

Upon the forest growth, difference of latitude has less effect.

Forest growth.

From Cairo to Memphis it consists of cottonwood, willow, sycamore, white and swamp ash, hackberry, box-elder, cypress, red and slippery elm, black, sweet, and tupelo gum, white, red, black, Spanish, willow, over-cup, and swamp oak, with many other varieties, two varieties of maple, two varieties of mulberry, black, white, and honey locust, sassafras, black walnut, cane, many varieties of hickory, pecan, chincapin, papaw, persimmon, elder, dogwood, thorn, haw, privet, or elbow-tree, and many vines, creepers, etc.

From Memphis to Natchez the timber is the same, but the sycamore becomes more scarce, and the cypress, ash, and gum are more abundant. The Spanish moss, a characteristic feature of Louisiana forests, first makes its appearance near Island 82; where the palmetto also first begins to be seen in the swamps.

Below Natchez, in addition to the above forest-trees, are found the magnolia, or bay-tree, and the sweet bay (small).

From Baton Rouge to the Balize, and near the floating prairies or sea-marshes, the live-oak is occasionally seen.

The cottonwood and willow are almost universally found on the immediate bank of the river, on the islands, and on all new batture formations. On the latter they always constitute the first growth.

Changes historical and in progress in 1858.—The Mississippi river is constantly excavating its banks in bends, and forming new land on points, throughout the alluvial region. This action is progressing much more rapidly in the upper part of the river than in the lower, where it seems to have comparatively ceased.

Unstable character of the banks of the Mississippi.

It may reasonably be asked, how it is that the river can act so efficiently upon its banks when the soil is so tenacious as to be but slightly affected by crevasses, through which the water flows with equal or greater velocity? The answer is obvious. The river banks are underlain by strata of nearly pure sand throughout the whole region under consideration. A slight change of direction of the current in high water—produced by a new sand-bar, a new island, a new cut-off, or by any other cause—turns its force more directly against a certain portion of the

Its cause.

bank. The sand is washed out from under the tenacious soil. At first, the water supports the land, but, when the river subsides, the bank falls by its own weight, and being dissolved, is swept away by the current. These sand strata are often below low-water mark—an unfortunate circumstance, which renders the protection of the banks difficult if not impossible.

Origin of "cut-offs."

It occasionally happens that by this constant caving two bends approach each other, until the river cuts the narrow neck of land between them and forms a "cut-off," which suddenly and materially reduces its length. The increased slope of the water surface at once makes this new bed the main channel of the river. The upper and lower mouths of the "old river" are gradually silted up with sediment, drift-wood, etc., until, eventually, one of the crescent-shaped lakes so common in the alluvial region is formed.

Their recent history.

The dates of formation of many of these lakes are long antecedent to the discovery of the country, as is proved by numerous crescent lakes upon both banks of the Mississippi, mentioned as such by the earliest explorers of the Mississippi river.

These changes have been constantly going on since the settlement of the country, but the old maps and records are so defective that it is impossible to determine much about those which occurred prior to 1800. Since that date the following list is believed to be nearly, if not quite, complete. It will be seen that the total shortening of the river by these cut-offs is 80 miles. Many persons consider that this shortening is only apparent, being counterbalanced by increased caving and lengthening of the remaining bends.

Name.	Locality.	Date.	Length of bend.	Remarks.
			Miles.	
Bunch's	Between Islands 89 and 92	......	13	
Needham's	Between Islands 21 and 25	1821	11	
Shreve's	Just above Red-river landing	1831	18	Made by U. S. Engineer Dept.
Raccourci	Just below Red-river landing	1848	21	Made by the State of Louisiana.
Horse-shoe	Between Islands 60 and 61	1848	8	
American bend	Between Islands 84 and 86	1858	10	

Where now imminent.

The effect of cut-offs upon the high-water level above and below them will be discussed in a succeeding chapter. They are believed to be likely to occur before many years at the neck above Napoleon, which was only 1400 feet across in 1858, and caving above; at the neck (Terrapin) between Islands 98 and 101, then reported to be 1200 feet across, and caving badly above; at the neck between Islands 105 and 110 (Palmyra), said to have been 10,000 feet across in 1808, and to be only 2700 feet now, and caving above; and at the neck between Islands 113 and 114, caving badly above, and reported in 1858 to be only 2400 feet across. There are other narrow necks—as those near Vicksburg and Grand Gulf, for instance—but there seems to be no reason to anticipate the early occurrence of cut-offs at them. It is very difficult, however, to predict with certainty where cut-offs are to be expected, as caving which has been rapidly going on for years will sometimes suddenly stop from some change in the direction of the current. Careful surveys of several of these doubtful places would be of great value hereafter as a means of testing changes.

Upon the islands the action of the Mississippi is not less striking than upon the banks. They are constantly forming, disappearing, or becoming connected with the main land by the filling up of their chutes.* The process of formation and destruction is interesting. Drift-wood becomes lodged upon a sand-bar. Deposition of sediment follows. A willow growth succeeds. In high water more deposition is caused by the resistance thus presented to the current. In low water, the sand blown by the wind lodges among the bushes. An island thus rises gradually to the level of high water, and sometimes even above it, sustaining a dense growth of cottonwoods, willows, etc. By a similar process the island becomes connected with the main land; or, by a slight change of direction of the current, the underlying sand-bar is washed away, the new-made land caves into the river, and the island disappears.

Unstable character of the islands of the Mississippi.

Among islands which have disappeared during the present century, may be named one in Plumb-point bend, just above Osceola, where now a large sand-bar exists, and one just below the mouth of bayou Plaquemine, which has entirely disappeared.

Lost islands.

The following effects of the flood of 1858 are reported by Dr. William S. Smith, as observed by him during his low-water survey of the sites of the crevasses, and confirmed by reliable statements of residents. From Cairo to Memphis there was a sandy deposit upon the overflowed banks, varying from 6 inches to over 3 feet in depth. Below Memphis this deposit was much less in amount. Throughout the whole river channel, from Cairo to Red-river landing, there was a marked increase in the size of the sand-bars and in the caving of the banks. Below the recent American-bend cut-off, which occurred on April 15, 1858, a very decided change in the location, both of the sand-bars and of the caving, was produced by the change of direction of the current. The following island chutes were rapidly filling up by deposit: right side Island 6; right side Island 7; left side Island 15; left side Island 33 (once main channel); left side Island 46; left side Island 60; right side Island 62; right side Island 64; left side Island 83; left side Island 117.

Littoral effects of the flood of 1858.

SLOPE.

The slope of the Mississippi diminishes as it approaches the gulf. The oscillations caused by variation in discharge also gradually diminish from the vicinity of Natchez to the mouth of the river, while those corresponding to changes of level in the gulf become gradually more apparent and important. The mean level of the gulf is the proper datum-plane to which to refer the surface of the river. For these reasons, and to solve other questions within the scope of the Delta Survey, the subject of the lake and gulf oscillations, with the effects of the latter upon the Mississippi river, was investigated.

The gulf of Mexico exercises too important an influence upon the river slope to be neglected.

* *Chute.*—A name applied to that arm of the river opposite an island, having the lesser width.

Oscillations of the gulf and their effects upon the lakes and river.—For the purposes stated, gauge-rods were observed at the mouth of the new canal, in lake Pontchartrain; at Proctorsville, on lake Borgne; and at bayou St. Philip, a small inlet from the gulf near the fort of that name. Daily observations were continued at these three localities for ten, seven, and twelve months, respectively, in 1851–52, as may be seen by referring to Appendix B, where the data thus collected appear in detail.

Observations to determine the extent of gulf and lake oscillation.

A self-registering tide-gauge was established at the telegraph station near the mouth of the Southwest pass, and observations were made with it from May, 1859, to June, 1860. The detailed observations, together with those of a similar character upon the Mississippi river at Carrollton, will be found in Appendix B. The following table exhibits the results of all these observations:—

Oscillations of the lakes and gulf.

Locality.	Mean daily gauge-reading.			Difference, or mean tidal oscillation.	Highest observed stand.		Lowest observed stand.		Difference, or extreme range.	
	At high water.	At low water.	Mean.		Date.	Gauge-reading.	Date.	Gauge-reading.	Observ'd	Corrected for tidal oscillation.
	Feet.	*Feet.*	*Feet.*	*Feet.*		*Feet.*		*Feet.*	*Feet.*	*Feet.*
New canal; lake Pontchartrain	8.34	7.93	8.14	0.41	Nov. 13, '51	10.4	Feb. 6, '51.	6.8	3.6	3.2
Proctorsville, on lake Borgne..	4.30	3.10	3.70	1.20	Nov. 13, '51	6.5	July 31, Aug. 17, '51	2.0	4.5	3.0
Bayou St. Philip..................	3.60	2.40	3.00	1.20	Nov. 13, '51	5.3	Jan. 5, Jan. 9, Jan. 10, '52	1.2	4.1	2.6
Mouth Southwest pass..........	1.90	0.70	1.30	1.20	Nov. 11, '59	2.9	Dec. 10, '59.	—0.5	3.4	1.2

Tidal oscillations and their effect upon the river.

The tides at the mouths of the Mississippi are of the diurnal, or single-day type, there being generally but one high water and one low water in twenty-four hours: the rise and fall being greatest when the moon's declination is greatest. The character of the tides was made known by the observations of the Coast Survey.

To determine the tidal oscillations in the river, observations were made in 1851 at various points from Fort St. Philip to Red river, not only at high and low water, but in all the conditions of the river. It was intended to make observations with a self-registering tide-gauge at Carrollton in 1859 and 1860, simultaneously with those at the Southwest pass, but, owing to unavoidable delays, the instrument was not in operation until late in November, 1859. It was destroyed by a storm in the July following, up to which time it was used. The following table gives the results of these several observations. The tides are probably felt even at Red-river landing in low water, but the observations there were not sufficiently minute to detect them:—

Tidal oscillations of the Mississippi.

Locality.	Distance from gulf.	High stage of river.				Low stage of river.			
		Elevation above gulf.	Spring tide.	Neap tide.	Mean tide.	Elevation above gulf.	Spring tide.	Neap tide.	Mean tide.
	Miles.	*Feet.*	*Feet.*	*Feet.*	*Feet.*	*Feet.*	*Feet.*	*Feet.*	*Feet.*
Gulf	0	0	1.7	0.50	1.2	0	1.7	0.50	1.2
Fort St. Philip	36	5	0.6	0.15	0.4	0.7	1.4	0.40	1.0
Carrollton	120	15	0.3	0.10	0.2	0.8	1.1	0.30	0.8
Donaldsonville	192	26	None	detect	ed.	1.5	0.9	0.20	0.6
Baton Rouge	244	34	None	detect	ed.	3.0	0.4	0.15	0.2
Red-river landing	315	49	None	detect	ed.	5.0	None	detect	ed.

The difference in time between the tides at the mouth of the Southwest pass and those at Carrollton is the same in the high and low stages of the river, and is five hours and fifty minutes; the distance between the two points being 118 miles.*

Oscillations due to prevailing winds.

The changes in the level of the gulf caused by winds are much greater than those produced by the tides, as is shown by the table preceding the last. The duration of these oscillations varies from a day or less to several days, and in some years is of such extent as to affect materially the mean level of the gulf during a whole month, and even during a season. This subject is somewhat elaborately treated in Chapter VIII. It is there shown that the winds at the mouths of the Mississippi have in part the characteristics of the northeast trade-winds. Blowing chiefly between northeast and southeast, they veer toward the south as the summer approaches, and continue to blow from that quarter and from the east during the summer and early part of the autumn. Changing toward the north upon the approach of winter, they blow principally from that direction during the winter months. It is not intended here to decide upon the character of these winds, and to class them definitely among the trades, although the topographical features and physical conditions of the basin of the Mississippi, and its position relative to the great bodies of water lying south, must modify the character of the great normal winds described by Professor Henry in his papers upon meteorology, and perhaps produce along this portion of the gulf of Mexico a resemblance to the trade-winds.

The effect of such winds upon the level of the gulf was very marked in the winter of 1851–52. During January, 1852, the mean level of the gulf was 1.5 feet lower than during the month of September, 1851, and a foot lower than the mean monthly level of several other months of the year. The mean level during December and January was 0.6 of a foot lower than the mean yearly level of the gulf. In the summer months, the gulf remained at the mean yearly level. In the winter of 1859–60, the effect of these winds upon the level of the gulf was slight.

Their effect upon the river.

The mean level of the river when low conforms to these gulf oscillations, if they are of several days' duration. Thus the gauges indicate that an oscillation of this kind, of the magnitude of 2 feet, which occurred between the 10th and 18th of November, 1851 (when the river was very low),

* The difference in time between the tides at Cape May, Delaware bay, and those at Philadelphia is five hours and three minutes; the distance between the two places being about 100 miles.

was felt as far up as New Carthage, 460 miles from the gulf. At the mouth of Red river the oscillation was 1.5 feet.

To what extent the river at the top of the flood conforms to these gulf oscillations, the observations do not show. When their duration exceeds that of a tidal oscillation, the effect upon the river must likewise exceed the effect of a tide of equal rise or fall. The following facts have been collected respecting the effects of some of the extraordinary rises in the gulf.

The information collected by Mr. John Communy, or observations made by him, previous to 1851, show that strong easterly or southeasterly winds raised the surface of lake Pontchartrain, at the mouth of the new canal, above its mean level 3.3 feet. Hurricanes had raised it 4.3 feet.

Major M. M. Clark, Quartermaster U. S. Army, states that in August, 1831, a hurricane raised the gulf 2 feet above the top of the levee at Fort Jackson, where he was stationed. According to this statement, the gulf must have been raised at least 7 feet above its mean yearly level.

In the gale of August 11, 1860, when the gulf rose 4.25 feet at the mouths of the river, and lake Borgne rose 8.5 feet (or, according to the report of the Chief Engineer of the State of Louisiana, 11 feet), the river at Carrollton—which was 1.5 feet above extreme low water—rose 4.6 feet in two hours. At Donaldsonville it rose 2 feet. What the effect was farther up has not been ascertained. At Natchez there was no effect. The duration of the rise and fall of the gulf was less than that of a tidal oscillation, and the effect upon the river was proportionately less.

In the gale of September 15, 1860, the gulf rose 7 feet at the mouth of pass à l'Outre, and 3 feet at the mouth of the Southwest pass. The river at Carrollton rose 2.5 feet. At Donaldsonville it rose much less than on August 11. Above Donaldsonville its effects have not been traced. The duration of this rise and fall did not exceed that of a gulf tide.

In the gale of October 2, 1860, the gulf at the mouths of the passes rose 3 feet; lake Pontchartrain rose 5 feet; the river at Carrollton rose 3 feet, and at Donaldsonville 4.5 feet. Above Donaldsonville the effects of the storm have not been traced. At Natchez its effect upon the river was not perceived. The duration of the storm was greater than that of the others. The effect at Donaldsonville was in part local.

The disastrous effects of these extraordinary rises in the gulf would be still further aggravated in the present condition of the levees, if these oscillations were not produced by causes connected with those which occasion the low stages of the river. Crevasses along the river are not, therefore, occasioned by hurricanes. But a long continuance of southerly gales does sometimes occur at the period of highest water in the river, as in 1823, and may increase the height of the flood several inches at New Orleans.

Oscillations in the river due to variations in discharge.

The subject of gulf oscillations and their effect upon the river having been examined, the range of the river, that is, the amount of the oscillation between low and high water, will be next investigated.

Range of the Mississippi between low and high water.—It is very difficult to obtain exact verbal information upon this subject, because, when the river has once retired within its banks, it becomes harmless, and few persons care to record its changes until it again excites alarm by a new rise. Moreover, it seldom

Data collected.

remains stationary for more than a day or two at a time, even at low water, and a *series* of measurements is therefore necessary to determine which, among many oscillations, includes the lowest point attained in any given year. Add to this the practical difficulty of ascertaining, by any instrument at the command of the unprofessional observer, an absolute difference of level which often amounts to over 40 feet, and no surprise will be felt that few data other than the measurements of this Survey can be presented in reference to the range of the river. Some information upon this subject of a definite character, however, has been acquired from residents of certain localities. Together with that deduced from the daily gauge-records soon to be discussed, it is presented in the following table, which thus contains all known facts upon the subject. For convenience of reference, the low-water level is uniformly referred to the high water of 1858. To compare it with any other high water, the difference between the level of the high water of 1858 and that of the required year at the given locality, taken from the table under the head of "Great Floods," is to be applied with its proper sign.

Range of the Mississippi between low and high water.

Year.	Level of low water of Mississippi below high water of 1858.																
	St. Louis.	Cairo.	Columbus.	Memphis.	Helena.	Napoleon.	Gaines' landing.	Lake Providence.	Vicksburg.	New Carthage.	Natchez.	Red-river landing.	Baton Rouge.	Donaldsonville.	St. John's.	Carrollton.	Fort St. Philip.
	Feet.	*Feet.*	*Feet.*	*Feet.*	*Feet.*	*Feet.*	*Feet.*	*Feet.*	*Feet.*	*Feet.*	*Feet.*	*Feet.*	*Feet.*	*Feet.*	*Feet.*	*Feet.*	*Feet.*
Unknown.		47.0		36.1	42.5	45.0		39.0		48.0	47.5						7.0
1819.........											50.3						
1830.........											50.3						
1839.........											50.3						
1841.........															18.0		
1842.........					47.0												
1843.........	34.5																
1844.........	33.6																
1845.........				37.1							48.2						
1848.........				32.8												15.0	
1849.........				30.7												13.0	
1850.........				31.7												15.6	
1851.........				30.7				34.6		37.6	41.3	44.2	31.0	24.8		14.9	5.8
1852.........				31.1						41.1			30.4	24.0		13.1	
1853.........		48.4												25.0		13.9	
1854.........		46.0					44.0						34.3	27.0		14.8	
1855.........			46.6						48.3		51.5			25.8			
1856.........			43.7											27.0			
1857.........		44.7												26.8		14.9	
1858.........		41.8	37.8	31.3		40.8			39.7		42.1	39.6		26.0		14.7	
1859.........				30.2	40.6				43.6		43.0			26.5		15.5	
1860.........	36.5															15.8	

Above the mouth of Red river, this table exhibits the true range of the Mississippi, *i.e.* the extent of the oscillation due to the difference between the low-water and high-water discharges. Below Red river it does not, because this part of the river in low stages is within the influence of the gulf, not only for tidal oscillations, but also for those caused by wind. The flood of 1851 must therefore be adopted in fixing the normal range of the river below Red-river landing, since in no other year were these gulf oscillations measured. Red river proper reached its lowest recorded point in this year, and the range of the Mississippi below its mouth was probably as great as is ever known. The numerical value of this range of the several localities, together with the data from which it is derived, is given in the following table:—

Locality.	Highest stand of river, 1851.				Lowest stand of river, 1851.					Extreme range in 1851.	
	Date.	Observ'd gauge-reading.	River tide.	Corrected gauge-reading.	Date.	Observ'd gauge-reading.	River tide.	Gulf at mean tide above its mean level.	Corrected gauge-reading.	Observ'd	Corrected for oscillations.
		Feet.	*Feet.*	*Feet.*		*Feet.*	*Feet.*	*Feet.*	*Feet.*	*Feet.*	*Feet.*
Head of the passes				2.6					0.3	3.7	2.3
Fort St. Philip	April 7	8.3	0.4	8.1	Nov. 25–6.	2.5	1.5	—0.4	3.6	5.8	4.5
Carrollton	March 30	15.4		15.4	Nov. 25–6.	0.0	1.2	—0.4	1.0	15.4	14.4
Donaldsonville	March 30	30.3		30.3	Nov. 25–6.	5.2	0.9	—0.4	6.0	25.1	24.3
Baton Rouge	March 30	33.4		33.4	Nov. 24–5.	2.2	0.4	+0.1	2.3	31.2	31.1
Red-river landing	April 1	46.4		46.4	Nov. 24–5.	2.2		+0.1	2.1	44.2	44.3

Above Red-river landing, 1851 was not a low-water year; neither was 1858, in which more measurements were made than in any other. In the year 1855, however, the lowest level on record seems to have occurred. By the table it appears that in this year the river fell below the low-water level of 1858, at Columbus, Vicksburg, and Natchez, 8.8, 8.6, and 9.4 feet, respectively. The accordance between these numbers establishes that the extreme range at all points between the mouths of the Ohio and Red rivers may be found by adding about 9 feet to that noted in 1858. At St. Louis, in default of an exact measurement, the low water of 1860 is adopted as a corresponding level.

The numerical values of all these adopted ranges will be found in the next table, where the corresponding high-water and low-water elevations above the gulf—next to be noticed—will also appear.

Adopted mean level of the gulf.

Elevation above the gulf of the surface of the Mississippi.—The mean level of the gulf, the datum-plane to which the absolute level of the surface of the Mississippi throughout the alluvial region is to be referred, was determined, as before stated, by observations upon gauge-rods in lake Pontchartrain, lake Borgne, and bayou St. Philip. It was assumed that the mean level of those lakes is the mean level of the gulf, an assumption which was confirmed by the results of the observations; and hence the mean of the readings of any one of these gauges may be adopted as the datum-plane. That of the lake Pontchartrain gauge was selected and transferred to the river levels by the following process.

It is transferred to the river and reads 0.14 on the Carrollton gauge.

The result of a careful levelling between Carrollton and lake Pontchartrain shows that a certain bench-mark on the machine shop of the New Orleans and Carrollton railroad company, called Hampson's bench-mark, is 7.92 feet above the mean gauge-reading (8.14) in lake Pontchartrain. The result of a previous careful levelling by engineers employed upon the railroads in the vicinity of New Orleans, furnished the Survey by Colonel W. S. Campbell, gave 8.20 as the corresponding difference of level. Adopting the mean of the two, or 8.06, and deducting from it the carefully measured difference in level (7.92 feet) between Hampson's bench-mark and the zero of the Carrollton gauge, we find that the mean level of the gulf reads 0.14 on that gauge.

The surface of the Mississippi between Red river and New Orleans was referred to this datum-plane by connecting the following levelling operations of this Survey with the river gauge at Carrollton.

Surface of the Mississippi between Red river and New Orleans referred to this datum-plane.

A line was run with the greatest care from Routh's point, above Red-river landing, along the west bank of the river to the locks of the Barataria canal, below Carrollton. This line was connected with the mouth of Red river and the mouth of the Atchafalaya. It was extended down the Plaquemine to Indian village, where tidal observations were made at low water.

A line was also run along the east bank of the river from Baton Rouge to Carrollton. These two lines were connected with each other by transfer across the river at different points, and also with the river gauges. Both lines, below Baton Rouge, were revised in the field at the close of the season.

Below New Orleans.

Below Carrollton, only two determinations were made of the absolute elevation of the river surface above the mean level of the gulf. The first was made at Fort St. Philip, where, for purposes connected with the construction of that work, the gauge in the river was connected with that in bayou St. Philip by a careful levelling. The second was made at the head of the passes by measurements at low water upon a high-water mark of 1851, and by transferring the gulf level from the bayou St. Philip gauge. This transfer was made at the lowest stage of the river, by assuming the measured slope between Carrollton and Fort St. Philip to extend 20 miles farther to the head of the passes. The almost inappreciable slope of the river (0.28 of a foot fall in 84 miles) renders this a strictly accurate method.

The gauge in lake Borgne was connected by a careful levelling with a high-water mark of 1851 on the Mississippi river, near bayou Duprés; but this mark proved not to have been determined with sufficient accuracy for use in so delicate an operation, since it gave an excess in elevation to the high-water level of 0.6 of a foot. It was accordingly rejected.

Elevation of water surface at Natchez.

The high-water elevation in 1858, at Natchez, was determined by a party of this Survey, in charge of Dr. William Sidney Smith, in the following manner: A line of levels was run from the high-water mark of 1858, opposite Natchez, to a water-mark at the lower end of lake Concordia (3 miles distant), made just before the breaking of the Haggaman crevasse. Bayou Tensas, and Black river, excepting near its mouth, were securely leveed on the east bank previous to this flood, so that before the Haggaman crevasse occurred (June 17th), the only supply of water to lake Concordia was by backwater from Red river through Cocodrie bayou. The measured difference of level between the two water-marks above mentioned (14.3 feet) was, then, the fall at high water from the surface of the Mississippi at Natchez, to the mouth of Cocodrie bayou, 12 miles above the mouth of Red river. Allowing 2 feet for the fall between this point and Red-river landing (see approximate fall deduced from levelling between Natchez and Harrisonburg), we have 16.3 feet for the fall of the Mississippi between Natchez and Red-river landing at high water of 1858. This determination is, of course, only approximate, but it accords so well with the measured slopes above and below Natchez, that it cannot be sensibly erroneous.

Railroad surveys depended upon for elevation of water surface at points above Natchez.

For the data by which the elevation of the Mississippi at points above Natchez was determined, the Survey is indebted to the work of civil engineers engaged upon the railroads connected with the river. The data and the points determined are as follows:—

Gaines' landing.

The high-water elevation at Gaines' landing with respect to that at St. Louis, was deduced from the levels of the St. Louis and Fulton and the Gaines' landing and Fulton railroads, the former obtained from the Bureau of Topographical Engineers, War Department, and the latter from Mr. William H. Davidson, Principal Assistant Engineer of the road. They show that the high water of Red river, at the point of junction of the two roads near Fulton, is 170.1 feet below high water of 1844 at St. Louis, and 93.5 feet above high water of 1858 at Gaines' landing, making a difference of level between the high water of 1844 at St. Louis and that of 1858 at Gaines' landing of 263.6 feet.

Memphis.

The high-water elevation at Memphis was determined by the levels of the Memphis and Charleston and the Mobile and Ohio railroads. It was furnished by Mr. F. C. Arms, Engineer and General Superintendent of the first-named road, who states that the high-water level in 1844 at Memphis was 220.44 feet above tide-water in Mobile bay.

Columbus and Cairo.

The high-water elevations at Columbus and Cairo were determined by the levels of the Mobile and Ohio railroad. They were furnished by Mr. L. J. Fleming, Chief Engineer of the road, who states that the high-water level of 1849 at Columbus was 308.25 feet above tide-water at Mobile, and that the high-water level at Cairo (probably that of 1849) was 320 feet above the same plane of reference.

St. Louis.

The high-water elevation at St. Louis with respect to that at Cairo was determined by the levels of the Illinois Central and the Ohio and Mississippi railroads, furnished by Captain George B. McClellan, Vice-President of the first-named road. By this determination the high-water level of 1844 at St. Louis is 90.5 feet above high water (year not specified) at Cairo. The "St. Louis Directrix" (top of curbstone at corner of Market street and the levee), the general bench-mark of the city, is then, according to these levels and those of the Mobile and Ohio railroad, 405 feet above the gulf. This exactly accords with the result deduced by Dr. Engelmann from a long series of barometrical observations.

Table of results exhibiting corrected heights of water surface, slope, etc., of Mississippi.

Some of these determinations differ slightly from those heretofore announced upon the authority of other and less direct measurements, but they check each other, and are unquestionably very nearly, if not absolutely, correct. From them the following table has been constructed, the main features of which are represented by figure 1, plate IX. The mean bottom of the river in its deepest part is added to this diagram according to the data contained in the table on page 121.

Slope of the Mississippi river.

Locality.	Distance from head of passes, 1860.	Range of Mississippi.			Corresponding elevation above gulf.		Resulting fall per mile in water surface.			
		High water of	Low water of	Am'nt.	High water.	Low water.	To—	Dist'nce.	At high water.	At low water.
	Miles.	*Year.*	*Year.*	*Feet.*	*Feet.*	*Feet.*		*Miles.*	*Feet.*	*Feet.*
Head of passes	0	1851	1851	2.3	2.8	0.5	Gulf by S. W. pass	17	0.165	0.029
							Gulf by N. E. pass	16	0.175	0.031
							Gulf by pass à l'Outre	15	0.187	0.033
							Gulf by South pass	14	0.200	0.036
Fort St. Philip	20	1851	1851	4.5	5.1	0.6	Head of passes	20	0.115	0.005
Carrollton	104	1851	1851	14.4	15.3	0.9	Fort St. Philip	84	0.121	0.004
Donaldsonville	176	1851	1851	24.3	25.8	1.5	Carrollton	72	0.146	0.008
Baton Rouge	228	1851	1851	31.1	33.9	2.8	Donaldsonville	52	0.156	0.025
Red-river landing	299	1851	1851	44.3	49.5	5.2	Baton Rouge	71	0.220	0.034
Natchez	361	1858	1855	51.0	66.0	15.0	Red-river landing	62	0.266	0.158
Vicksburg	470	1858	1855	49.0						
Gaines' landing	630	1858	1855		149.0		Natchez	269	0.309	
Napoleon	672	1858	1855	50.0						
Memphis	855	1858	1855	40.0	221.0	181.0	Gaines' landing	225	0.320	
Columbus	1059	1858	1855	47.0	310.0	263.0	Memphis	204	0.436	0.402
Cairo	1080	1858	1855	51.0	322.0	271.0	Columbus	21	0.571	0.381
St. Louis	1253	1858	1860	37.0	408.0	371.0	Cairo	173	0.497	0.578

The usual succession of stages now to be considered.

Having thus determined the absolute elevation and the range of the river from St. Louis to the gulf, with the effects produced upon both by the oscillation of the gulf, the discussion of the slope of the Mississippi will be completed by considering the usual succession of stages of the river.

Mean annual succession of stages.—The lower Mississippi, as already seen, receives its water from many tributaries, whose basins differ from each other in position relatively to the great physical features of the continent, in geological character, in topographical features, in climate, soil, degree of cultivation, etc. The downfall of rain in these basins varying greatly, from year to year, both in time and in amount, produces corresponding variations in the floods of the rivers in respect both to date and to height. The lower Mississippi has not therefore a regular, uniform succession of stages. Nevertheless, as the great characteristic variations in the discharge and height of the river are dependent upon causes which, considered in reference to a series of years, act uniformly, long-continued observations will make known the general law governing these variations, although it may not include the minor oscillations. The nature and amount of the data collected in connection with this investigation, upon which much labor has been bestowed, will be seen from the following account of the daily measurements made of the stand of the river at various localities.

Different methods used in establishing river gauges.

Such measurements require the erection of permanent gauge-rods, which, in the case of the Mississippi, is rendered peculiarly difficult by the caving of its banks, by its great range, and by its accumulations of floating drift logs. Different plans for establishing the rods were adopted at different localities. Thus, at Carrollton and New Carthage, the rod was nailed in sections to short piles at different distances from the edge of the natural bank. At Donaldsonville, it was spiked to a wharf, where it yet remains uninjured. At Natchez, the rod was secured to Mr. Brown's breakwater. At Baton Rouge, at Red-river landing in 1858, at Lake Providence, and at Memphis, the upper part of the rod, several feet in length, was nailed to a tree standing upon the extreme edge of the vertical natural bank. When the river fell below the bottom of the rod, temporary pieces were planted and carefully referred to the main rod by means of a spirit level. At Red-river landing in 1851, and at Columbus, an upright to sustain the rod was planted at the foot of a steep bank, and securely braced at top by cross-pieces pinned to the ground. At Napoleon, where the shelving bank rendered this plan impracticable, a pile was sunk in the most secure place, and protected against drift by a floating framework of timber, in the form of the letter V, the vertex being directed toward the river, and the ends lashed to trees and braced against the edge of the bank. At Vicksburg, even this method was impracticable from the number of steamboats constantly arriving and departing. A series of benches was made upon stones planted at different distances down the slope, and the daily stand of the river was determined by referring the water surface to one of them with a spirit level. When the velocity observations terminated, a rod was established on the other bank of the river in the same manner as at Memphis.

Amount of data collected by this Survey.

Having, by means of the various plans enumerated, established a fixed scale of reference, the daily height of the river at each of the stations was observed and recorded, together with the state of the weather, the force and direction of the wind, etc. As already stated, at stations where tidal influence was suspected, additional readings were taken, or self-registering gauges were used; but for oscillations due to variations in discharge, a single observation per day is sufficient, and such only have been presented in No. 1, Appendix B, which contains all the details necessary to be known respecting these operations. Their extent is exhibited in the following table:—

Number of months, or parts of months, of daily gauge record. (*See Appendix B.*)

Locality.	1851.	1852.	1853.	1857.	1858.	1859.	1860.	1861.
Cairo					8			
Columbus				1	12	8		
Memphis				1	12	8		
Napoleon				1	12	1		
Lake Providence	10							
Vicksburg					11	9		
New Carthage	11	7	3					
Natchez	10				12	1		
Red-river landing	11	5			12	1		
Baton Rouge	11	12	2					
Donaldsonville	12	12	12		12			
Carrollton	12	12		2	12	12	12	3
Fort St. Philip	11	1						

Other data collected.

Besides these measurements made by the Survey, many other data relative to the subject have been presented in Appendix B.

At Donaldsonville.

Thus Mr. Andrew Gingry, who kept the record at Donaldsonville, continued the observations after those of the government ceased, and as stated in the letter transmitting this Report, presented to the Survey a transcript of his notes taken three times a day for the years 1854–55–56–57–59, and part of 1860. This record is especially valuable, because no accident has happened to the gauge-rod since it was first put up by Lieutenant Warren, in 1851. Its adjustment was found to have remained exact, when tested, in 1859, by the old bench-mark. The other rods were displaced several times, but were frequently tested, and the records are known to be correct. As, however, the relative heights of some of the high-water marks will excite surprise (judging from statements which have from time to time appeared over the signatures of distinguished engineers), it is satisfactory to be able to establish their accuracy by their accordance with this continuous record at Donaldsonville. This register is also especially valuable for supplying the break in the Carrollton record during the years 1855–56–57, and thus, as will be hereafter seen, aiding in discussing the annual discharge of the river.

At Memphis.

Appendix B also contains records kept at the Memphis navy yard, for 1848–49–50–51–52, and copied from the record books of the yard by permission of Commodore Joseph Smith, U. S. N., Chief of the Bureau of Yards and Docks, Navy Department.

At St. Louis.

It also contains records observed at the St. Louis arsenal (Captain W. H. Bell, U. S. Ordnance, Commanding), in 1843–44–45, under the direction of Captain T. J. Cram, U. S. Topographical Engineers.

At Carrollton.

It also contains records at Carrollton for the years 1848–49–50 and 1853–54–55, made under the direction of Professor Forshey.

Miscellaneous.

Approximate gauge-records at Helena and Providence for the flood months of 1858, and various approximate registers of the oscillations of the tributaries of the Mississippi—the latter mostly compiled from the daily newspapers—have also been added to this appendix.

At Natchez.

Plate VII has been prepared to exhibit the original data compiled by Professor Forshey from the records of Governor Winthrop Sargent, Mr. Samuel Davis, and himself at Vidalia opposite Natchez. As many references will be made to these data in the division of this chapter treating of "great floods," it is only necessary to state here that they are now made public for the first time in detail; although in Professor Forshey's "Memoir upon the Physics of the Mississippi," printed to accompany the report of the joint committee on levees of the legislature of Louisiana in 1850, there is a diagram which represents these data reduced to the range or oscillation at Carrollton, and combined in mean curves of ten years each.

These data represented by diagrams.

This completes the list of data available for determining the usual succession of stages of the Mississippi between St. Louis and the gulf. The most important portions for this purpose are presented in diagrams on plates V, VI, VII, VIII, and IX.

Classification of them for the present purpose.

Each of these annual gauge-records is, of course, an exact register of the variation in stage of the river at that place for that year. By comparing the plates which exhibit the oscillations at the same locality in different years, it will be seen, as already intimated, that the river varies greatly with respect both to the date and to the extent of its oscillations. Its mean or *usual* succession of stages then, can be determined only by combining several years' observations. It is, moreover, apparent that each tributary has a varying effect upon this mean law of the river, and, therefore, that somewhat different successions of stages are to be expected in different parts of its course. The information collected is not sufficient for the investigation of this subject above the mouth of the Ohio. Below that point, the river is divided by its tributaries into three sections: the first between the Ohio and the Arkansas, the second between the Arkansas and the Red, and the third below Red river. The records are, then, to be examined with reference to the mean yearly oscillations in each of these sections or divisions.

The Ohio to the Arkansas. Between the Ohio and Arkansas rivers, Memphis is the only place where gauge-records have been kept for a series of years. (See plate VIII.) By legitimate interpolation for missing observations, the register at that place can be made complete for five years, a period of time not so long as could be desired, but still sufficient to entitle the mean result to some confidence. The mean readings for each month during the five years are contained in the following table.

The Arkansas to the Red. Between the Arkansas and Red rivers, Natchez is the point selected, since Professor Forshey's compiled record at Vidalia, opposite the city, is available, in addition to the two years' observations of this Survey. (See plates V, VI, and VII.) Professor Forshey's records are incomplete, and the rigid rules of interpolation adopted in preparing this report admit of the use, for the present purpose, of only twenty-three of his curves. The several monthly means taken from the diagram will be found in the following table.

Below Red river. Below Red river, the data are more exact both at Donaldsonville and Carrollton. The yearly record is complete at Donaldsonville for the nine years, 1851–59, and at Carrollton for the twelve years, 1849–60, except for the years 1855–56–57. For these years it can be supplied from the Donaldsonville record by the following process. The mean high water, as determined by monthly means, reads on the Donaldsonville gauge 24.2, and on the Carrollton gauge, 12.2; the mean yearly range, as determined by monthly means, being 17.9 and 10.4 feet respectively. It is evident, since the range in this part of the river decreases uniformly as the gulf is approached, that any mean monthly reading may be quite accurately ascertained by subtracting from 12.2 the product obtained by multiplying $\frac{10.4}{17.9}=0.58$ by the difference between 24.2 and the mean reading for the month at Donaldsonville. A few trials will show that this process gives results which accord very closely with actual observations. Indeed the errors are absolutely inappreciable in this use of gauge-records.

General table and diagram of results. The following table exhibits the data just enumerated, the mean results of which are also presented in figures 3 and 4, plate IX.

Mean monthly gauge-rod readings.

Locality.	Year.	Jan.	Feb.	March.	April.	May.	June.	July.	August.	Sept.	October.	Nov.	Dec.
		Feet.	*Feet.*	*Feet.*	*Feet.*	*Feet.*	*Feet.*	*Feet.*	*Feet.*	*Feet.*	*Feet.*	*Feet.*	*Feet.*
Memphis	1849	27.1	29.3	27.0	27.6	23.0	21.8	19.5	13.9	8.0	7.6	8.1	18.6
	1850	26.0	31.3	32.0	30.3	33.9	17.2	15.1	13.2	11.0	5.6	5.4	16.5
	1851	12.9	16.9	33.0	27.0	17.0	28.5	31.0	23.0	11.5	8.4	7.0	7.9
	1858	19.6	15.8	22.3	29.0	32.5	34.9	26.5	19.8	10.6	5.1	9.5	15 3
	1859	23.6	23.6	34.7	34.6	33.7	23.9	18.3	11.8	5.0	6.0	7.0	19.0
Monthly	mean ..	21.8	23.4	29.8	29.7	28.0	25 3	22.1	16.2	9.2	6.5	7.4	15.4
Natchez....................	1819	16.5	23.0	28.5	35.5	46.0	45.5	36.0	24.5	13.5	5 5	2.5	3.0
	1822	23.5	32.5	34.5	35.5	45.5	46.5	48.0	36.5	18.5	10.5	29.5	41.5
	1823	43 5	45.0	43.5	50.0	52.5	51.5	48.5	42.5	30.5	16.5	8.5	5.5
	1824	21.0	38.5	42.0	49.5	51.0	49.5	47.0	36.0	19.5	12.5	12.5	28.0
	1825	38.5	18.5	27.0	41.5	49.5	47.0	36.5	23.5	14.0	9.5	6.0	4.5
	1828	42.5	48 5	51.5	51.0	50.5	49.0	46.0	41.0	30.5	20.5	16.5	23.5
	1829	26.5	18.0	24.5	38.0	41.5	28.0	17.5	13 0	10.0	14.0	25.5	37.0
	1830	41.0	29.5	33.5	48.0	48.0	46.5	40.5	25.0	9.5	3.5	2.5	12.5
	1831	24.5	28.0	38.0	44.5	49.0	44.0	35.0	25.0	15.0	12.0	13.0	8.0
	1834	42.0	44.0	43.0	45.0	33.0	20.0	34.0	39.5	29.5	19.5	17.0	17.0
	1835	17.5	30.5	34.5	39.0	41.0	43.5	35.5	25.5	20.5	19.5	31.5	34.5
	1836	30.5	34.0	38.5	49.5	50.5	48.5	38.5	24.5	13.5	8.0	9.5	25.5
	1837	33.5	24.5	33.0	46.0	41.0	27.5	21.0	16.0	13.0	12.0	18.0	23.0
	1838	24.5	27.5	37.5	46.5	38.5	27.5	21.0	15.5	10.5	8.5	14.0	15.0
	1839	16.5	27.0	29.5	36 0	27.5	21.5	13.5	8.5	5.0	2.5	2.5	7.5
	1840	14.0	24.0	48.5	46.5	50.5	49.5	41.0	26.5	15 5	20.5	26.5	33.0
	1841	46.0	47.0	48.0	47.0	49.0	48.0	24.5	16.0	12.0	10.0	13.0	17.0
	1844	41.5	44.5	46.5	49.5	51.5	52.5	52.5	48.5	35.5	28.5	27.5	31.0
	1845	29.5	39.0	47.0	44.5	37.5	26.5	39.0	24.5	11.5	13.5	12.0	7.0
	1846	7.0	25.5	36.0	43.0	44.5	42.5	28.5	15.5	14.5	7.5	10.7	35.5
	1847	40.0	41.5	47.0	51.5	42.3	36.0	35.5	25.5	21.5	19.0	19.0	23.0
	1851	26.0	26.0	49.9	51.6	39.7	43.1	46.1	37.4	21.8	12.5	11.6	12.5
	1858	43.9	41.7	39.5	49.9	51.8	52.6	51.9	44.6	23.2	12.9	20.6	27.8
Monthly	mean ..	30.0	33.0	38.8	45.2	44.9	40.9	36.2	27.6	17.8	13.0	15.2	20.6
Donaldsonville...	1851	9 8	16.3	28.8	29.3	23.9	23.9	25.3	21.0	11.4	6.8	6.4	6.6
	1852	10.7	12.9	24.6	26.8	27.6	27.7	20.2	9.6	7.2	7.0	10.4	18.0
	1853	25.5	24.1	27.0	26.0	27.1	26.3	19.0	11.4	7.8	6.8	5.8	6.3
	1854	5.9	20.2	21.6	26.0	25.3	24.0	18.1	7.9	6.4	6.3	4.9	4.4
	1855	7.0	6.3	7.6	13.9	10.3	10.7	10.0	9.2	10.0	9.7	10.1	12.9
	1856	12.6	6.7	22.3	20.2	23.7	20.8	8 5	5.6	4.8	4.1	4.2	12.3
	1857	10 2	14.4	24.7	18.7	20.8	19.5	14.8	7.2	4.8	3.9	5.2	14.6
	1858	25.0	24.0	23.6	28.1	29.4	29.1	28.9	25.9	12.3	7.0	6 6	12.8
	1859	23.5	20.4	26.8	29.0	29.2	26.3	19.8	8.0	3.9	5.6	4.3	14.0
Monthly	mean ..	14.5	16.1	23.0	24.2	24.1	23.1	18.2	11.7	7.6	6.3	6.4	11.3
Carrollton...................	1849	13.6	14.6	14.8	14.7	14.2	13.2	12.1	12.4	8 1	2.8	3.4	8.5
	1850	13 0	13.2	12.9	12.8	12.3	12.0	8.5	3.2	1.8	1.0	0.2	3.1
	1851	6.7	6.9	14.8	14.8	12.0	11.6	12.5	9.9	4.1	1.5	1.1	0.8
	1852	3.0	4.0	11.7	12.9	13.6	13.5	9.2	3.1	2.8	2.7	4.3	8.4
	1853	13.7	12.6	14.3	13.8	14.4	13.9	9.6	5.0	2.9	2.2	1.7	2.0
	1854	1.8	10.4	11.1	13.8	12.7	13.9	9.4	2.1	2.0	1.9	1.2	0.9
	1855	2.4	2.0	2.9	6.5	4.4	4.6	4.5	4.0	4.5	4.3	4.5	6.2
	1856	5.9	2.5	11.7	10.5	12.5	10.8	3.6	1.9	1.4	1.0	1.1	5.8
	1857	4.6	7.0	12.9	9.6	10.8	10.0	7.3	2.8	1.4	0.9	1.3	6.2
	1858	12.7	12.5	11.7	14.2	14.7	14.2	13.7	11.9	4.0	1.3	2.3	5.3
	1859	10.9	9.0	12.9	14.7	14.5	12.7	8.7	3.2	1.7	1.6	0.7	5.6
	1860	9.8	11.9	12.7	7.7	7.0	4.1	2.0	1.3	1.0	0.3	1.0	2.1
Monthly	mean ..	8.2	8.9	12.0	12.2	11.9	11.2	8.4	5.1	3.0	1.8	1.9	4.7

Analytical comparison of these results.

To render these mean results more directly comparable with each other, the following table has been prepared, exhibiting the mean monthly stand of the river, expressed in decimals of the total mean yearly range as determined by monthly means. That yearly range is 10.4 feet at Carrollton, 17.9 feet at Donaldsonville, 32.2 feet at Natchez, and 23.3 feet at Memphis; the corresponding mean high-water gauge-readings, as determined by monthly means, being 12.2, 24.2, 45.2, and 29.8. The table is computed by dividing by the yearly range the number of feet of each mean monthly reading below high water.

Mean stages of the Mississippi river.

Month.	Monthly stand of river below high water, in decimals of total mean yearly range.			
	Memphis. (5 years.)	Natchez. (23 years.)	Donaldsonville. (9 years.)	Carrollton. (12 years.)
January	0.34	0.47	0.54	0.38
February	0.27	0.38	0.45	0.32
March	0.00	0.20	0.07	0.02
April	0.00	0.00	0.00	0.00
May	0.08	0.01	0.00	0.03
June	0.19	0.13	0.07	0.10
July	0.33	0.28	0.34	0.37
August	0 58	0.55	0.70	0.68
September	0.88	0.85	0.93	0.88
October	1.00	1.00	1.00	1.00
November	0.96	0.93	0.99	0.99
December	0.62	0.76	0.72	0.72

General laws governing the stages of the river.

This table, except for Natchez, where the curve is less accurately determined than at the other localities, is illustrated by figure 3, plate IX. It is to be remarked that the oscillations at the flood stages are in some measure obscured at Memphis by the effect of the St. Francis swamp, at Natchez by that of the Tensas swamp, and at Donaldsonville and Carrollton by the combined effect of those swamps and of crevasses below Red river. It is then perceived from the mean curves: 1st. That the law which governs the mean annual rise and fall of the Mississippi varies but little from the Ohio to the gulf. 2d. That the rains which accompany the three great changes in season (to winter, spring, and summer) throughout the larger part of the Mississippi basin, produce three corresponding rises in the river (augmented in the spring by melting snow). 3d. That, above the mouth of the Arkansas, the rise occasioned by the rains and melting snow which attend the setting in of the southwest winds at the transition from winter to spring, in the northern and eastern part of the great valley, usually attains its highest point in the latter part of March. The river then subsides until the arrival (commonly in June) of the Rocky-mountain rise, swelled by the early summer rains of the lower Missouri, and by those of the eastern portion of the Mississippi basin.* It then falls rapidly until the latter

* The rainy season along the foot of the Rocky mountains in the region drained by the tributaries of the Missouri river, occurs in the latter half of spring. One-third of the yearly precipitation takes place at that time. It is attended by the melting of the snow in the mountains. The rise thus produced reaches that portion of the Missouri river east of the 98th meridian (Greenwich longitude) at the time of the early summer rains. The waters of the Missouri receive that peculiar color by which they are recognized even at New Orleans from the clays of the Mauvaises Terres, through which they pass.

The tributaries of the Arkansas that rise in the Rocky mountains have, in like manner, a late spring rise, which is joined by the summer rains of the lower part of the basin, but with less regularity than occurs in the junction of a similar character on the Missouri.

The Red river rises in the Llano Estacado, not in the Rocky mountains. Its summer rains are later than those of the Missouri, and its spring and summer rises occur at later periods than those of the upper tributaries of the Mississippi.

The Arkansas partakes somewhat of the character of the Red river.

part of October, when the lowest point is attained. After remaining at a stand for two or three weeks, it again rises—and more rapidly than at any other season—until checked by freezing and the diminution of rain (precipitation) in the basins of the upper rivers in January and February. 4th. Below Red river, the same general oscillations occur, but somewhat later in the season, the only modification being that the tributaries below the Ohio contribute their corresponding floods somewhat later, and thus maintain the stand of the river for a longer period. 5th. The river is above its mid-stage for seven months, from the latter part of December to the latter part of July, and below it for the rest of the year.

Caution.

What was said at the beginning of this discussion should, perhaps, be repeated here. Although the surface of the river follows in a general manner the succession of stages indicated, yet climatic variations produce each year oscillations differing from the mean and from those of each preceding year. Consequently, these mean curves, which exhibit so beautifully the existence of a law governing the general succession of stages of the river, do not furnish the means of predicting its stand at any given epoch.

CROSS-SECTION.

Introductory remarks.

It would be useless to attempt to discover the *exact* average width, depth, and area of cross-section, of a river like the Mississippi, without a vast expenditure of time and money in measurements. Neither the importance of the knowledge to be thus gained, nor the amount of the appropriation for the present survey has justified such extended operations, and they have not been attempted. Still, as it is essential to have the approximate value of these quantities, measurements were made, with a view to their determination, at numerous carefully-selected localities. The details of these operations will be found in the next chapter and in Appendix C. It is proposed in this place to discuss the results there recorded, and to derive from them as close an approximation as possible to the true dimensions of the cross-section of the river at high and at low water, below the mouth of the Ohio.

Classification of data.

High water.—The first point for consideration is the general grouping of the sections. Although the data are already meagre, yet it seems so probable that the contributions of the great tributaries affect the dimensions of the main river, that it is considered important to subdivide them. Four grand divisions will therefore be considered, namely: from the Ohio to the Arkansas; from the Arkansas to the Red; from the Red to bayou La Fourche; and from bayou La Fourche to the head of the passes. In each the same general plan of computation will be adopted.

Proper method of grouping the sections.

The next point which suggests itself is the proper weight to be given to the different sections in deducing a mean value for the river. It will be seen from Appendix C, that, at some localities, many cross-sections were made in the same immediate vicinity, and in others only one. Now, since the object is to determine a *mean* cross-section, it is evident that, if all the sections are allowed equal weight, the different localities, which all equally affect the true mean, will be very unfairly represented. In other words, the resulting mean will correspond not to the whole river, but to certain portions assumed to resemble most nearly this quantity. The *mean of all sections in the same vicinity* is, therefore, in all cases assumed to be the true section there, and only regarded as a single section in finding the grand mean.

Examination of published data.

The propriety of combining published data with those collected by the Survey next suggests itself. Very few of these data are to be found, but such as there are will be briefly noticed.

Lieut. Marr's.

The section at Memphis, made by Lieutenant Marr, U. S. N., is undoubtedly correct, and has been adopted.

Those of Senate committee of Louisiana.

The sections made by the Senate committee of the Louisiana legislature in 1850 were only designed for general purposes; the places of the different soundings not being fixed by triangulation, but being assumed to be equidistant. This kind of work, although valuable for the general purposes contemplated by the committee, does not possess the exactness requisite for the operations of this Survey, and no use has been made of it.

Mr. Ellet's.

The data presented by Mr. Ellet in his report upon the Mississippi in 1851 next claim attention. No opinion of the care with which the measurements were made or even of the method employed, can be formed from the published report. By examining the archives of the Bureau of Topographical Engineers, War Department, however, several of the original diagrams were found, and they show that the exactness of measurement deemed essential in the operations of this Survey was not attempted by Mr. Ellet. For instance, most of his sections of the Mississippi river on file were determined by *less than ten soundings*, and even these were so imperfectly distributed that very large intervals (one interval exceeding 1100 feet) were left on several of the sections. By comparing the areas of cross-section determined by Mr. Ellet with those given in this report, when the sections happen to be at the same place, it will be found that the two values sometimes agree closely, but that at other times they differ very much. Thus, just below the mouth of Red river, Mr. Ellet's section (high water of 1850) is 268,646 square feet. That found by this Survey for the same high water at the same locality (mean of two sections) is 269,500. This is a satisfactory agreement; but at Raccourci cut-off, only 3 miles below, Mr. Ellet gives 148,790 square feet for the area at high water, 1850; while the accurate determinations of this Survey, made about the same time and published in full in Appendix C, give (mean of two sections) for the same place and date 186,900 square feet, showing an error in Mr. Ellet's work of some 38,000 square feet. This particular instance is cited because it shows that Mr. Ellet's opinion is based upon erroneous measurements when he decides that "the area of the section of the Mississippi in high water through the Raccourci cut-off is but little more than two-thirds of the average area from Vicksburg to Bonnet Carré;" and that "the conclusions which will be drawn from this fact will be found of the highest importance in treating of the effect of cultivation, of cut-offs, and the extension of the levees, in fact in all measures tending to throw more water into any part of the channel in a given time." The truth is that, at the date of his field work, the area of cross-section at Raccourci cut-off had attained the normal dimensions for straight portions of the river in this part of its course—as, for instance, at Vicksburg or at Baton Rouge. But to return to the subject under discussion, Mr. Ellet's measurements of cross-section, being found to be less exact than those of this Survey, have not been used whenever operations were conducted by both parties in the same locality. As, however, they undoubtedly approximate to correctness, they have been used for general purposes where no corresponding measurements were made by this Survey. Due acknowledgment has been made for such as have been so used.

Tables exhibiting the mean high-water areas and mid-channel depth of the Mississippi.

It only remains to explain that the areas in the following table have been taken from the table in Appendix C, and reduced to the high water of 1858, when sensibly differing from that level, by means of the table of relative heights of different floods, given under the head of "Great Floods." For Mr. Ellet's sections, the high water of 1858 has been considered to be 2 feet higher than that of 1850 above the mouth of the Arkansas, and of equal height below. In two or three sections of the Survey, where large permanent eddies are known to exist, their measured area has been deducted.

By the maximum high-water depth is meant the mid-channel depth of the river at high water, and consequently, when several sections have been made at the same locality, the mean of their maximum depths, and not the greatest depth observed on any one of them, is entered in the table. They are all taken from Appendix C, for the sections made by this Survey.

In all other respects the tables explain themselves.

High-water areas and maximum depths of the Mississippi between banks.

Ohio river to Arkansas river.					Arkansas river to Red river.				
Locality.	No. of sections.	Max. depth, h. w. 1858.	Area for discharge, h. w. 1858.	Authority.*	Locality.	No. of sections.	Max. depth, h. w. 1858.	Area for discharge, h. w. 1858.	Authority.*
		Ft.	Sq. ft.				Ft.	Sq. ft.	
1 mile below Ohio.......	1	73	243,800	Mr. Ellet.	Below mouth of Ark.......	1	88	211,700	Delta Survey.
Columbus..................	4	96	166,200	Delta Survey.	0.75 m. below Arkansas...	1	81	196,400	Mr. Ellet.
New Madrid...............	1	96	209,600	" "	Upper side American bend	1	104	170,100	" "
Above Osceola............	1	89	198,900	" "	Lower " " "	1	79	187,200	" "
Below Randolph.........	1	119	171,200	" "	Lake Providence............	1	87	201,700	Delta Survey.
Memphis....................		83	176,000	Lieut. Marr.	Upper side Terrapin neck	1	88	178,200	Mr. Ellet.
Helena	1	71	205,800	Delta Survey.	Lower " " "	1	102	168,100	" "
Horse-shoe cut-off.......	1	75	167,000	Mr. Ellet.	7 miles above Vicksburg..	1	120	160,200	" "
0.75 m. above Ark.......	1	82	176,800	" "	Vicksburg......................	8	101	179,500	Delta Survey.
					Above Palmyra bend......	1	96	187,200	Mr. Ellet.
					New Carthage................	1	111	208,000	Delta Survey.
					Below Palmyra bend.......	1	91	256,800	Mr. Ellet.
					Above Grand Gulf..........	1	105	175,800	" "
					Below " "	1	76	264,800	" "
					Natchez.........................	2	118	221,600	Delta Survey.
					Above Red river............	1	84	209,600	" "
Mean—say........		87	191,000		Mean—say...........		96	199,000	

* As it sometimes happened that different employés of the Survey made sections at the same localities, it is impossible to give credit to individuals here. Exact information on this point may, however, be found in Appendix C.

Red river to bayou La Fourche.					Bayou La Fourche to head of passes.				
Locality.	No. of sections.	Max. depth, h. w. 1858.	Area for discharge, h. w. 1858.	Authority.*	Locality.	No. of sections.	Max. depth, h. w. 1858.	Area for discharge, h. w. 1858.	Authority.*
		Ft.	*Sq. ft.*				*Ft.*	*Sq. ft.*	
Red-river landing.......	2	126	240,000	Delta Survey.	0.5 m. bel. Donald'v'le.	1	103	214,600	Mr. Ellet.
Raccourci cut-off.........	2	107	187,600	" "	2.2 miles below Bonnet Carré church..........	1	180	202,100	Delta Survey.
Tunica bend.............	1	88	233,900	Mr. Ellet.	Ab. B. C. crevasse 1850	4	111	228,000	" "
1 mile ab. Baton Rouge	2	107	191,000	Delta Survey.	Bel. " " "	5	82	164,600	" "
Baton Rouge..............	3	103	181,000	" "	17 m. ab. New Orleans.	1	138	174,000	" "
1 m. bel. Baton Rouge.	2	118	189,000	" "	15 " " "	1	122	181,000	" "
1.5 m. ab. Plaquemine.	1	123	181,500	Mr. Ellet.	Bend ab. Carrollton.....	18	147	216,300	" "
1.5 m. bel. "	1	128	199,300	" "	In front of Carrollton..	20	137	184,700	" "
1 m. ab. Donaldsonville	1	118	200,200	" "	Barataria canal locks...	5	122	187,800	" "
					Fort St. Philip...........	1	151	231,300	" "
Mean—say.........		113	200,000		Mean—say.........		129	199,000	

Tables exhibiting the high-water width of the Mississippi.

The same principles apply to the determination of the high-water width as to that of the high-water area, but the exact topographical survey of both banks, made between Baton Rouge and Carrollton, in 1851, furnishes the means of determining it for the lower part of the river with greater precision. The width at equal intervals of about 4000 feet between these two places is given in the following table, and but one explanatory remark is required. Between Red river and Baton Rouge there are several islands, while between the latter place and bayou La Fourche only one exists. As islands materially increase the width of a river, it is evident that the table, containing, as it does, 68 widths below Baton Rouge and only 7 above this city—and most of these not taken in the vicinity of the islands—must give too small a mean width. The numerical mean of the column in the table is 2860, but 140 feet more have been allowed, to correct approximately for this cause of error, giving 3000 feet as adopted.

* As it sometimes happened that different employés of the Survey made sections at the same localities, it is impossible to give credit to individuals here. Exact information on this point may, however, be found in Appendix C.

High-water widths of the Mississippi between banks.

Ohio river to Arkansas river.

Locality.	High-water width between banks.	Party of
	Feet.	
1 mile below Ohio	4030	Mr. Ellet's report.
Near Island 4	6280	Mr. W. S. Smith.
Columbus	2240	Mr. H. C. Fillebrown.
Hickman	3600	Lt. Abbot.
Above New Madrid	6880	" "
3.5 miles below New Madrid	5800	Mr. W. S. Smith.
2 miles above Osceola	6080	Lt. Abbot.
1.5 miles below Osceola	7670	Mr. W. S. Smith.
Randolph	3410	Lt. Abbot.
0.5 m. below Randolph	2800	" "
Narrowest point—Randolph bluff.	2280	" "
Memphis, opposite Gayoso house	3360	Mr. W. S. Smith.
1 mile above Helena	4800	" " "
Helena	4080	Lt. Abbot.
10 miles below Helena	7080	Mr. W. S. Smith.
Friar's point	6500	Lt. Abbot.
Horse-shoe cut-off	2940	Mr. Ellet's report.
Foot of Island 68	4250	Lt. Abbot.
1 mile below Island 68	2460	Mr. W. S. Smith.
0.75 m. above Arkansas river	2810	Mr. Ellet's report.
Mean—say	4470	

Arkansas river to Red river.

Locality.	High-water width between banks.	Party of
	Feet.	
Below mouth of Arkansas	3220	Lt. Putnam.
0.75 m. below Arkansas	3730	Mr. Ellet's report.
Fort of Island 76	7800	Lt. Abbot.
Head of Island 83	5050	" "
Greenville	4700	" "
Upper side American bend	3360	Mr. Ellet's report.
Lower " " "	3290	" "
Lake Providence	3580	Lt. Abbot.
0.5 m. bel. lake Providence	3400	Mr. W. S. Smith.
2.5 " " " "	4670	Lt. Abbot.
3.5 " " " "	4940	Mr. W. S. Smith.
Head of Island 98	3350	Lt. Abbot.
Upper side Terrapin neck	3440	Mr. Ellet's report.
Lower " " "	3540	" "
7 miles above Vicksburg	3510	" "
Vicksburg	2660	Mr. H. A. Pattison.
4.5 miles below Vicksburg	4290	Mr. W. S. Smith.
Above Palmyra bend	4050	Mr. Ellet's report.
New Carthage	4300	Lt. Abbot.
Below Palmyra bend	5610	Mr. Ellet's report.
4 miles above Grand Gulf	3640	" "
3 miles below " "	5900	" "
Bruinsburg	4080	Mr. W. S. Smith.
Coal-creek point	2350	Lt. Abbot.
Natchez—at breakwater	4540	" "
Ellis cliffs	3250	Mr. W. S. Smith.
Routh's point	3880	Mr. G. C. Smith.
Mean—say	4080	

Red river to bayou La Fourche.

Locality.	High-water width between banks.	Party of
Mouth of Red river	3500	Mr. J. K. Ford.
4,000 feet below Red river	3600	" "
8,000 " " " "	3700	" "
12,000 " " " "	3000	" "
Raccourci cut-off—upper end	2400	" "
" " lower end	2400	" "
Tunica bend	3320	Mr. Ellet's report.
Baton Rouge—opposite arsenal	2900	Mr. J. K. Ford.
" " " State House.	2350	" "
4,000 feet below " "	2200	" "
8,000 " " " "	2650	" "
12,000 " " " "	3025	" "
16,000 " " " "	2400	" "
20,000 " " " "	3100	" "
24,000 " " " "	3400	" "
28,000 " " " "	3000	" "
32,000 " " " "	2650	" "
36,000 " " " "	3250	" "
40,000 " " " "	3400	" "
44,000 " " " "	2250	" "
48,000 " " " "	2250	" "
52,000 " " " "	2475	" "
56,000 " " " "	2550	" "
60,000 " " " "	2500	" "
64,000 " " " "	2450	" "
68,000 " " " "	3700	" "
Mouth of bayou Manchac	2950	" "
4,000 ft. bel. " "	2400	" "
8,000 " " " "	2800	" "
12,000 " " " "	2450	" "
16,000 " " " "	3250	" "
20,000 " " " "	2900	" "

Bayou La Fourche to head of passes.

Locality.	High-water width between banks.	Party of
Donaldsonville	3300	Mr. J. K. Ford.
4,000 ft. bel. Donaldsonville.	3175	" "
8,000 " " "	2700	" "
12,000 " " "	2450	" "
16,000 " " "	2350	" "
20,000 " " "	2350	" "
24,000 " " "	2300	" "
28,000 " " "	2150	" "
32,000 " " "	1950	" "
36,000 " " "	2150	" "
40,000 " " "	1950	" "
44,000 " " "	2050	" "
48,000 " " "	2200	" "
52,000 " " "	2500	" "
56,000 " " "	2200	" "
60,000 " " "	2200	" "
64,000 " " "	2100	" "
68,000 " " "	1900	" "
72,000 " " "	2400	" "
76,000 " " "	2400	" "
80,000 " " "	2150	" "
Convent	2450	" "
4,000 feet below convent	2350	" "
8,000 " " "	2400	" "
Jefferson College	3000	" "
4,000 ft. bel. Jefferson Coll.	2650	" "
8,000 " " " "	2750	" "
12,000 " " " "	2475	" "
16,000 " " " "	2850	" "
20,000 " " " "	2800	" "
24,000 " " " "	3300	" "
28,000 " " " "	2050	" "

Red river to bayou La Fourche.		
Locality.	High-water width between banks.	Party of
	Feet.	
24,000 ft. bel. bayou Manchac....	2400	Mr. J. K. Ford.
Just above mouth bayou Plaq'ne.	2700	" "
4,000 feet below " "	2750	" "
8,000 " " " "	2575	" "
12,000 " " " "	2930	" "
16,000 " " " "	2930	" "
20,000 " " " "	2930	" "
24,000 " " " "	4400	" "
28,000 " " " "	3500	" "
32,000 " " " "	2500	" "
36,000 " " " "	2400	" "
40,000 " " " "	2850	" "
44,000 " " " "	2700	" "
48,000 " " " "	2450	" "
52,000 " " " "	2450	" "
56,000 " " " "	2800	" "
Just above Bayou Goula............	3750	" "
4,000 ft. bel. " "	3250	" "
8,000 " " " "	2650	" "
12,000 " " " "	2650	" "
16,000 " " " "	2500	" "
20,000 " " " "	2250	" "
24,000 " " " "	2400	" "
28,000 " " " "	2500	" "
32,000 " " " "	3100	" "
36,000 " " " "	3500	" "
40,000 " " " "	3700	" "
Opposite Claiborne island	3400	" "
4,000 ft. bel. " "	2450	" "
8,000 " " " "	2800	" "
12,000 " " " "	3100	" "
16,000 " " " "	3000	" "
20,000 " " " "	2500	" "
D. F. Kenner's plant'n(Ashland)..	2550	" "
4,000 ft. bel. D. F. Kenner's pl'n.	3550	" "
8,000 " " " " "	3500	" "
12,000 " " " " "	3000	" "
16,000 " " " " "	3000	" "
20,000 " " " " "	2450	" "
24,000 " " " " "	2600	" "
28,000 " " " " "	2700	" "
32,000 " " " " "	2600	" "
Just above Donaldsonville.........	3050	" "
Mean—say..................	3000	

Bayou La Fourche to head of passes.		
Locality.	High-water width between banks.	Party of
	Feet.	
32,000 ft. bel. Jefferson Coll.	2000	Mr. J. K. Ford.
36,000 " " " "	2200	" "
40,000 " " " "	2300	" "
44,000 " " " "	2250	" "
48,000 " " " "	2150	" "
52,000 " " " "	2200	" "
56,000 " " " "	2500	" "
60,000 " " " "	2400	" "
64,000 " " " "	2800	" "
68,000 " " " "	2700	" "
72,000 " " " "	2250	" "
76,000 " " " "	2300	" "
Barker's plantation............	2400	" "
4,000 ft. bel. Barker's plt'n.	2100	" "
8,000 " " " "	2400	" "
12,000 " " " "	2000	" "
Bonnet Carré church..........	2000	" "
4,000 ft. bel. B. C. church..	1800	" "
8,000 " " " "	1950	" "
12,000 " " " "	2400	" "
16,000 " " " "	4950	" "
St. John's Post-office..........	4800	" "
4,000 ft. bel. St. John's P.O.	3300	" "
8,000 " " " " "	4200	" "
12,000 " " " " "	3200	" "
16,000 " " " " "	2350	" "
20,000 " " " " "	2200	" "
24,000 " " " " "	2350	" "
28,000 " " " " "	2150	" "
32,000 " " " " "	2100	" "
36,000 " " " " "	2100	" "
40,000 " " " " "	2300	" "
44,000 " " " " "	2150	" "
48,000 " " " " "	3350	" "
52,000 " " " " "	2900	" "
56,000 " " " " "	2700	" "
60,000 " " " " "	2250	" "
Red church.......................	2400	" "
4,000 ft. below Red church.	2200	" "
8,000 " " " "	1950	" "
12,000 " " " "	2100	" "
16,000 " " " "	2300	" "
20,000 " " " "	2500	" "
La Branche's plantation......	2400	" "
4,000 ft. bel. La Branche's p.	2600	" "
8,000 " " " " "	2900	" "
12,000 " " " " "	2350	" "
16,000 " " " " "	2050	" "
20,000 " " " " "	2150	" "
Sauvé crevasse..................	2200	" "
4,000 ft. bel. Sauvé crevasse.	2250	" "
Fortier crevasse................	2100	" "
4,000 ft. bel. Fortier crevasse.	2000	" "
8,000 " " " "	2000	" "
12,000 " " " "	2650	" "
16,000 " " " "	2950	" "
20,000 " " " "	2550	" "
24,000 " " " "	2550	" "
28,000 " " " "	2875	" "
32,000 " " " "	2700	" "
36,000 " " " "	2500	" "
40,000 " " " "	2700	" "
Barataria canal locks.........	2300	" "
11 miles below New Orleans.	2430	Mr. Ellet's report
Fort St. Philip..................	2400	Lt. Abbot.
Mean—say............	2470	

Low water.—The mean low-water dimensions of the Mississippi river are more difficult to determine than those at the high-water stage, partly because there is a much greater relative change in the different parts of the river, and partly because the data are more meagre. It should be remembered, however, that when the mean low-water width is fixed, and the mean range known, the mean low-water area can be found by subtracting from the mean high-water area the area of a trapezoid whose parallel sides are respectively equal to the high-water and low-water widths, and whose altitude is equal to the mean range in the part of the river considered. Also that the low-water mid-channel depth is equal to the same quantity at high water, minus the mean range. The range of the river below Red river, in 1851, and between the Ohio and Red rivers, in 1858, is well fixed by the observations of the Survey. It is only necessary, therefore, to find the *mean low-water widths*, for the four grand divisions already considered, in order to fix all the mean low-water dimensions from Cairo to the gulf.

Outline of plan adopted for determining low-water dimensions.

Low-water widths are only known where the cross-section and range have been determined. Mr. Ellet does not give the quantity for any of his sections. The only existing exact data are, therefore, the widths taken from the cross-sections made by this Survey. Below the mouth of Red river there are very few islands and sand-bars, and the mean range is comparatively small. It is therefore probable that a tolerably uniform ratio exists between the high-water and low-water widths. If so, it may be deduced even from a comparatively small number of measurements. The following table exhibits all the data available for this part of the river:—

The low-water width below Red river.

Locality.	Number of sections.	Width.	
		At high water, between banks.	At low water.
		Feet.	*Feet.*
Red-river landing	2	3620	2650
Raccourci cut-off	2	2330	2090
1 mile above Baton Rouge	2	2800	2590
Baton Rouge	3	2560	2370
1 mile below Baton Rouge	2	2190	2000
2.2 miles below Bonnet Carré church	1	1900	1650
Above Bonnet Carré crevasse	4	3080	2960
Below " " "	5	3170	2690
17 miles above New Orleans	1	2200	2130
15 " " "	1	2200	2070
Bend above Carrollton	18	2637	2448
In front of Carrollton	20	2384	2281
Barataria canal locks	5	2575	2490
Fort St. Philip	1	2360	2335
Mean	....	2572	2340

The ratio between the mean high-water and low-water widths given by this table is 0.91, and it has been adopted, giving, for the mean low-water width between Red river and bayou La Fourche, 2750 feet, and for that below bayou La Fourche, 2250 feet.

Above the mouth of Red river, the channel of the Mississippi is entirely different in character. The range between high and low water is great; many islands exist, and large sand-bars are found opposite the

Low-water width above Red river.

fundus of almost every bend. The variation in width at high and low water is therefore very irregular, in some places being very small, as at Columbus and Vicksburg, and at others very great, as at New Madrid, Natchez (at Mr. Brown's breakwater), etc. To arrive at a correct mean value for a ratio which undergoes so great variations, from the few measurements of this Survey (eleven low-water widths in a distance of nearly 800 miles), could hardly be expected, nor was it necessary to depend upon them. A careful reconnoissance of the river at its low-water stage, from St. Louis to New Orleans, was made in the months of October, November, and December, 1821, by Captain Young, Captain Poussin, and Lieutenant Tuttle, of the U. S. Army, under the direction of the Board of Engineers. They prepared a series of maps (scale, 1 inch per mile for lengths and 2 inches per mile for widths) exhibiting the islands, the sand-bars, the worst collections of snags, the course of the main channel, etc., etc. These maps accompanied the report upon the Ohio and Mississippi rivers, addressed by the board (General Bernard and Lieutenant-Colonel Totten) to the Colonel commanding U. S. Engineers, dated December 22, 1822, and published by order of the U. S. House of Representatives in 1823. The maps were not published, but are now on file in the Bureau of Topographical Engineers, War Department. They exhibit much detail in the location and relative dimensions of the bars, islands, etc., and although the survey was not of a sufficiently exact character to furnish a reliable estimate of the absolute widths, a close approximation to the ratio between these quantities at high and low water may be drawn from it. This ratio for the river between the Ohio and the Arkansas, determined by seventy-seven equidistant measurements on the map, was 0.72, and between the Arkansas and Red river, determined by sixty-one equidistant measurements, was 0.74. It is, therefore, evident that, for the portion of the Mississippi lying between the mouths of the Ohio and Red rivers, the low-water width may fairly be assumed at three-quarters of the high-water width, or at 3400 feet between the Ohio and the Arkansas, and at 3060 between the Arkansas and Red rivers.

Mean range of river; 1851 and 1858.

The mean observed range in 1851 below bayou La Fourche (mean between the range at Donaldsonville and that at Fort St. Philip) was $\frac{25.1+5.8}{2}=15.4$. Between bayou La Fourche and Red river in the same year (mean of observed ranges at Donaldsonville and Red-river landing) it was $\frac{25.1+44.2}{2}=34.7$. Between Red river and the Arkansas in 1858 (mean of ranges at Red river, Natchez, Vicksburg, and Napoleon) it was $\frac{39.6+42.1+39.7+40.8}{4}=40.5$. Between the Arkansas and the Ohio (mean of ranges at Napoleon, Memphis, and Cairo) it was $\frac{40.8+31.3+41.8}{3}=38.0$.

Mean low-water areas.

The mean low-water area is, therefore, equal to the high-water area, minus the following areas, viz:—

Below bayou La Fourche.............................. $2250\times15.4+(2470-2250)\frac{15.4}{2}=$ say 36,000.

Bayou La Fourche to Red river...................... $2750\times34.7+(3000-2750)\frac{34.7}{2}=$ say 100,000.

Red river to Arkansas river.......................... $3060\times40.5+(4080-3060)\frac{40.5}{2}=$ say 145,000.

Arkansas river to Ohio river.......................... $3400\times38.0+(4470-3400)\frac{38.0}{2}=$ say 150,000.

Mean low-water mid-channel depths.

The low-water maximum depths result from subtracting the mean ranges in the four divisions from the corresponding high-water maximum depths.

The following table exhibits the mean values of the dimensions just deduced for high and low water, it being remembered that the usual and not the extreme low water is considered.

General table of resulting mean dimensions.

Mean dimensions of cross-section of the Mississippi river.

Locality.	High water.			Low water.		
	Area.	Width.	Maxm. depth.	Area.	Width.	Maxm. depth.
	Sq. feet.	*Feet.*	*Feet.*	*Sq. feet.*	*Feet.*	*Feet.*
Ohio river to Arkansas river	191,000	4470	87	45,000	3400	49
Arkansas river to Red river	199,000	4080	96	54,000	3060	56
Red river to bayou La Fourche	200,000	3000	113	100,000	2750	78
Bayou La Fourche to head of passes	199,000	2470	129	163,000	2250	114

As stated at the beginning of this discussion, it is not claimed that the existing data are more than sufficient to determine approximately the mean dimensions of the Mississippi river, but it is certain that the mean values of the different quantities exhibited by the above table are deduced in a legitimate manner from all known existing data. When the results are compared, the changes in the values of the different quantities from Cairo to the gulf exhibit so much the appearance of some governing law, that the probability of the accuracy of the determination is increased. At both high and low water the width diminishes, and the depth increases, as the gulf is approached, facts long suspected, but never before reduced to figures. The water added by the successive tributaries increases the high-water area of cross-section. The Atchafalaya nearly prevents Red river from exerting any such influence. The water discharged by bayous Plaquemine and La Fourche diminishes the area. These are the results to be anticipated, and these are the results indicated by the above figures. Add to these reasons for believing in the general accuracy of the determination, the fact fully set forth in Chapter V, that the values accord very closely with those given by the best river formulæ, and it is believed that their adoption will not be objected to, at least until further, more extended measurements indicate the necessity of correcting them.

Remarks upon this table.

Plate X has been prepared to exhibit the characteristic variations in form to which the cross-section of the river is liable, as well as to show its relative dimensions as compared with those of the principal tributaries below the head of the alluvial region. The normal effect of a bend upon the local form of cross-section is indicated by a small diagram upon plate XII.

DRAINAGE.

To comprehend fully the character of a river, the relations existing in its basin between the quantity of rain and the drainage should be known. This subject will therefore be next considered.

Yearly amount of rain.—To determine with precision the quantity of rain that falls in a region of such vast extent and such diversity of climate as the basin of the Mississippi river, would involve much more labor than has been expended upon the problem up to the present time. Still it must not be inferred that little has been done toward its solution. An extended system of observations has been carried on continuously since the year 1836, at the military posts, by the Medical Department of the United States Army. Another, established under the auspices of the Smithsonian Institution in 1849, has been the means of accumulating a mass of material throughout the settled portion of the valley. Learned societies, colleges, and individual observers have contributed to the general fund. By the use of these observations an approximation to the truth may be made, that will be sufficiently accurate for any general purpose contemplated in this report.

Data collected respecting downfall in the Mississippi basin.

The first set of charts ever published exhibiting the distribution of rain in the Mississippi basin was that illustrating the Army Meteorological Register (fourth in the series), which was published in 1855. These charts are arranged to exhibit the mean downfall in each of the four seasons as well as in the entire year. By transferring the boundaries of the different rain-districts, as there laid down, to the more recent maps constructed upon a much larger scale, the downfall in the basin of each of the main tributaries has been computed with all the accuracy possible. The results will be found in a following table.

Army charts.

In 1858 Mr. Lorin Blodget published his "Climatology of the United States," which was illustrated by a series of rain-charts similar to that just mentioned. Mr. Blodget had been engaged, as assistant to Dr. R. H. Coolidge, U. S. A., in the preparation of the Army charts. In reconstructing them for his own work, he modified them in some respects by adding such other reliable data as he could obtain. Computations similar to those detailed above have therefore been based upon his charts. The results will be found in a following table.

Mr. Blodget's charts.

In 1860 a new Army Meteorological Register (fifth in the series) was published by the Medical Department of the Army. This volume contains no rain-charts. The additional observations, however, are too valuable to be neglected, and they have been united with those published in 1855; with those in Mr. Blodget's work; and with such private observations as have been available to the Survey, with a view to exhausting the subject up to the present date. The results, which thus include all available information relative to the downfall in the Mississippi basin up to the year 1860, are presented in the following table:—

New Army data, etc.

Observations upon yearly amount of rain.

Station.	Years and months.		Downfall of rain in inches.				
	Y.	*M.*	Spring.	Summer.	Autumn.	Winter.	Year.
Atkinson, Fort	2	1	12.2	20.4	4.8	2.8	39.7
Arbuckle, "	8	0	8.0	10.6	9.0	5.2	32.8
Ann Arbor, Michigan	3	0	7.3	11.2	7.0	3.1	28.6
Athens, Illinois	10	0	12.2	13.3	9.2	7.1	41.8
Buffalo barracks	3	1	8.5	9.2	13 5	7.5	38.8
Brady, Fort	17	7	5.8	9.6	10.5	5.0	30.8
Benton, Fort			4.9	1.0(?)	2.1(?)	5.1	13.1
Burgwin, Camp	2	11	3.5	3.4	8.8	2 8	20.5
Baton Rouge barracks	15	0	13.5	18.4	12.2	15.0	60.4
Belknap, Fort	6	4	5.7	8.7	5.2	3.0	22.5
Battle Creek, Michigan	3	6	7.5	11.2	7.1	6.8	32.7
Beloit College, Wisconsin	4	0	13.2	18.1	10.4	6.4	48.1
Crawford, Fort	9	3	7.6	11.9	7.9	4.0	31.4
Chadbourne, Fort	8	2	6.4	6.6	7.7	3.6	24.3
Croghan, "	4	3	11.6	7.8	8.3	8.9	36.6
Church Hill, Mississippi	4	6	11.4	12.0	8.1	17.0	49.5
Cincinnati, Ohio	20	0	12.1	13.7	9.9	11.4	47.1
Dodge, Fort	1	10	7.9	8.1	8.2	3.1	27.3
Detroit arsenal	12	4	8.5	9.3	7.4	4.9	31.1
Graham, Fort	3	6	12.0	6.0	9.8	11.9	40.6
Gratiot, "	10	10	8.0	10.0	8.9	5.7	32.6
Gibson, "	20	5	9.2	9.4	9.3	6.4	34.3
Germantown, Ohio	5	0	10.7	10.1	8.6	9.5	38.9
Howard, Fort	7	6	9.0	14.4	7.8	3.4	34.6
Huntsville, Alabama	12	0	14.9	14.6	10 0	15.4	54.9
Hudson, Ohio	9	0	10.0	9.4	7.5	7.6	33.6
Jefferson barracks	18	6	9.9	13.3	9 6	6.6	39.4
Jesup, Fort	9	11	13.7	10.9	9.7	11.5	45.8
Jackson, Mississippi	3	6	10.9	14.2	9.5	18.4	53.0
Kearny, Fort	11	3	9.4	11.3	4.7	1.6	26.6
Leavenworth, Fort	24	2	8.1	13.5	7.8	3.2	32.3
Laramie, "	10	8	7.0	5.2	3.1	1.3	16.6
Mackinac, "	12	4	4.5	9.0	7.0	3.3	23.7
Mt. Vernon arsenal	17	5	13.3	17.6	13.7	16.0	59.6
McKavett, Fort	7	2	4.5	5.3	7.5	3.7	21.3
Mobile, Alabama	2	0	14.2	18.0	13.9	18.3	64.4
Monroeville, Alabama	4	0	19.2	21.4	8.7	16.2	65.5
Memphis, Tennessee	3	0	11.0	7.8	7.9	15.0	41.8
Marietta, Ohio	28	0	10.0	12.8	9.2	9.6	41.6
Milwaukee, Wisconsin	9	0	7.1	9.4	7.1	4.2	27.8
Muscatine, Iowa	10	0	11.2	15.1	10.3	6.7	44.3
Madison, Fort	4	0	15.3	15 9	14.5	4.7	50.4
Niagara, "	10	0	6.9	9.8	8.7	6.4	31.7
Natchez, Mississippi	13	0	13.0	11.7	11.6	14.9	51.2
Nashville, Tennessee	12	6	14.4	13.8	13.5	12.2	53.9
Newport, Kentucky	5	0	12.5	12.9	10.4	10.1	45.9
New Harmony, Indiana	2	0	10.5	12.8	7.3	12.2	42.8
New Orleans, Louisiana	24	0	11.1	16.6	11.8	12.0	51.5
Pittsburg, Pennsylvania	22	7	8.7	9.7	9.0	7.4	34.8
Phantom Hill, Texas	1	6	3.8	4.1	7.3	2.0	17.2
Plaquemine, Louisiana	6	0	15.9	26.3	9.4	15.7	66.3
Portsmouth, Ohio	15	0	10.0	11.6	8.1	8.5	38.2
Pierre, Fort	1	11	4.6	3.3	3.8	2.1	13.8
Ripley, "	10	1	6.2	11.1	7.2	2.2	26.8
Rapides, Louisiana	3	0	13.4	21.0	12.3	19.7	68.4
Ridgely, Fort	5	0	8.4	9.6	5.9	6.5	30.4
Snelling, "	22	2	6.4	9.9	6.3	2.3	24.9
St. Louis arsenal	18	8	12.8	13.8	8.8	6.2	41.6
Scott, Fort	10	3	12.6	16.3	8.4	4.8	42.1
Smith, "	19	5	11.5	12.4	10.0	7.2	41.0
San Antonio, Texas	3	2	8.6	10.2	7.6	7.3	33.8
St. Francisville, Louisiana	5	0	16.5	13.1	12.0	13.6	55.2
Springdale, Kentucky	11	0	12.1	14.8	9.0	12.2	48.1
Steubenville, Ohio	19	0	10.4	10.9	9.0	6.9	37.3
Towson, Fort	15	9	15.5	14.4	12.2	8.9	51.0
Union, "	9	10	2.4	10.6	5.2	1.9	19.2
Vicksburg, Mississippi	14	6	11.7	11.2	10.9	15.0	48.9
Washita, Fort	15	1	11.5	10.2	10.0	6.4	38.1
Worth, Fort	3	9	14.5	8.8	9.5	8.0	40.8
West Feliciana, Louisiana	13	0	20.0	14.8	10.5	18.1	63.4
West Salem, Illinois	1	0	11.9	17.3	12.2	9.5	50.9
Winnebago, Fort	9	0	5.6	11.5	7.6	2.8	27.5

Analysis of these data.

The mean annual downfall in inches at each of these localities has been placed upon plate I, which thus becomes a more complete rain-chart of the Mississippi basin than any yet published. It exhibits not only what is actually known, but how much more the system of observation must be extended before the boundaries of the different rain-districts can be accurately laid down. It has not been deemed advisable to attempt, at present, to mark these boundaries; and the mean downfall in the basin of each of the principal tributaries has, therefore, been deduced in the manner indicated in the following table. The grouping of the different stations has been adjusted with a view to represent, as nearly as possible, equal areas.

Classification of downfall in the Mississippi basin.

Basin.	Locality.	Downfall of rain in inches.				
		Spring.	Summer.	Autumn.	Winter.	Year.
Delta of the Mississippi	Rapides West Feliciana St. Francisville Baton Rouge Plaquemine New Orleans	13.1	15.6	9.4	13.6	60.9
	Mean	13.1	15.6	9.4	13.6	60.9
Of the Red river	Fort Union Fort Belknap	4.0	9.6	5.2	2.5	20.8
	Fort Arbuckle Fort Washita Fort Worth Fort Towson	12.4	11.0	10.1	6.8	40.7
	Fort Jesup Rapides Church Hill Natchez West Feliciana St. Francisville	14.6	17.3	11.0	15.8	55.6
	Mean	10.3	12.6	8.7	8.3	39.0
Of the Arkansas and White rivers	Fort Union	2.4	10.6	5.2	1.9	19.2
	Fort Gibson Fort Scott Fort Smith Memphis	11.1	12.7	9.2	6.1	39.5
	Mean	6.8	11.6	7.2	4.0	29.3
Of the St. Francis river	Memphis	11.0	7.8	7.9	15.0	41.8
	St. Louis Jefferson	11.3	13.5	9.2	6.4	40.5
	Mean	11.1	10.6	8.5	10.7	41.1
Of the Missouri river	Fort Scott Fort Dodge Fort Leavenworth	9·5	12.6	8.1	3.7	33.9
	Fort Kearny Fort Pierre	7.0	7.3	4.3	1.8	20.2
	Fort Laramie	7.0	5.2	3.1	1.3	13.1
	Fort Benton	4.9	1.0	2.1	5.1	16.6
	Mean	7.1	6.5	4.4	2.7	20.9

Basin.	Locality.	Downfall of rain in inches.				
		Spring.	Summer.	Autumn.	Winter.	Year.
Of the Upper Mississippi....	Fort Ripley, Fort Snelling, Fort Ridgely	7.0	10.2	6.5	3.6	27.3
	Fort Dodge, Muscatine, Fort Atkinson, Fort Crawford, Fort Winnebago, Fort Howard, Milwaukee, Beloit	9.2	13.6	8.0	4.2	35.0
	Fort Madison, Athens, St. Louis, Jefferson barracks	12.5	14.1	10.5	6.2	43.3
	Mean	9.9	12.6	8.3	4.7	35.2
Of the Ohio river	Huntsville, Nashville	14.6	14.2	11.7	13.8	54.2
	New Harmony, Springdale, Germantown, Cincinnati, Newport	11.6	12.8	9.0	11.0	44.5
	Battle Creek, Ann Arbor, Detroit	7.8	10.5	7.2	4.9	30.8
	Portsmouth, Marietta, Steubenville, Hudson, Pittsburg, Buffalo, Fort Niagara	9.2	10.5	9.3	7.7	36.5
	Mean	10.8	12.0	9.3	9.3	41.5
Of the Yazoo river	Memphis	11.0	7.8	7.9	15.0	41.8
	Vicksburg, Jackson	11.3	12.7	10.2	16.7	50.9
	Mean	11.1	10.2	9.0	15.8	46.3
Of the small tributaries	St. Louis, Jefferson barracks, West Salem	11.5	14.8	10.2	7.4	43.9
	West Salem, Memphis	11.4	12.5	10.0	12.2	46.3
	Vicksburg, Jackson	11.3	12.7	10.2	16.7	50.9
	Church Hill, Natchez	12.2	11.8	9.8	15.9	50.3
	Mean	11.6	12.9	10.0	13.0	47.8

Annual downfall in the basins of the several tributaries.

The following table presents the annual downfall in each of the subdivisions of the Mississippi basin, that marked "Delta-Survey map" having been deduced by multiplying the areas of the several basins by the mean annual downfall indicated in the above table. The three different determinations evidently accord well with each other, and thus show that the "adopted" results must be sensibly correct.

Yearly amount of rain in the basin of the Mississippi.

Basin.		Army map.	Blodget's map.	Delta-Survey map.	Value adopted.
Name.	Area.				
	Sq. miles.	*Cubic feet.*	*Cubic feet.*	*Cubic feet.*	*Cubic feet.*
Delta	12 300	1 509 000 000 000	1 577 000 000 000	1 749 000 000 000	1 700 000 000 000
Red river	97 000	9 069 000 000 000	8 717 000 000 000	8 810 000 000 000	8 800 000 000 000
Arkansas and White rivers	189 000	13 770 000 000 000	12 941 000 000 000	12 951 000 000 000	13 000 000 000 000
St. Francis	10 500	1 220 000 000 000	1 265 000 000 000	1 054 000 000 000	1 100 000 000 000
Missouri	518 000	26 460 000 000 000	26 156 000 000 000	25 156 000 000 000	25 200 000 000 000
Upper Mississippi	169 000	13 276 000 000 000	12 840 000 000 000	13 819 000 000 000	13 800 000 000 000
Ohio	214 000	21 088 000 000 000	22 750 000 000 000	20 684 000 000 000	20 700 000 000 000
Yazoo	13 850	1 610 000 000 000	1 841 000 000 000	1 493 000 000 000	1 500 000 000 000
Small tributaries	32 400	3 670 000 000 000	3 869 000 000 000	3 598 000 000 000	3 600 000 000 000
Total	1 256 050	91 672 000 000 000	91 956 000 000 000	89 314 000 000 000	89 400 000 000 000

Drainage of the basin.

The next subject for consideration is the annual discharge of the Mississippi river and of the several tributaries. It is not proposed to give any account of the *manner* in which the discharge has been determined, since this subject will be fully elaborated in Chapter IV. The object here is merely to state certain results, and to draw certain general conclusions from them.

Tables of discharge corresponding to the different stages of the river.

Annual discharge.—Upon plate XIV is represented the measured daily discharge of the Mississippi at Carrollton for an entire year, plotted with respect to the daily stand of the river. It is evident that the condition of the river, whether rising or falling, makes a great difference in discharge at any given stand; but it is equally evident that a mean line between these two extremes can be drawn that shall form the basis of a table by which the *annual* discharge can be deduced from the recorded gauge-readings. For any given day, its indication will be erroneous, but for the entire year, which includes both the rising and the falling branches of the curve, it will be sufficiently accurate. Such a table has been prepared for Carrollton from this diagram; for Donaldsonville, from a similar one, constructed by transferring these discharges to that place by a process hereafter to be explained; and for Natchez, from the measurements made there or transferred thither from Vicksburg in 1858 (see plate XV). These three localities have been selected, because the long-continued series of gauge-readings at them can thus be made the basis of an accurate estimate of the annual discharge of the Mississippi for a series of years. From the data published in this report it will be easy, with the aid of the principles laid down in Chapter IV, to construct similar tables for any locality below Helena. It is thus placed in the power of any one residing upon the Mississippi below Helena, to measure accurately the amount of water annually passing his residence, by keeping a daily record of the stand of the river. The computation involved in preparing the table and in computing the discharge from it will be trifling, while the results obtained will possess much value. The following is the table above mentioned. For the list of bench-marks, etc., see Appendix B.

Table exhibiting the discharge of the Mississippi at different stages.

Carrollton.		Donaldsonville.		Natchez.	
Gauge.	Discharge per second.	Gauge.	Discharge per second.	Gauge.	Discharge per second.
Feet.	*Cubic feet.*	*Feet.*	*Cubic feet.*	*Feet.*	*Cubic feet.*
16 0	1 210 000	31.0	1 220 000	54.0	1 285 000
15.5	1 160 000	30.0	1 150 000	52.0	1 200 000
15.0	1 110 000	29.0	1 085 000	50.0	1 115 000
14.5	1 065 000	28.0	1 030 000	48.0	1 038 000
14.0	1 020 000	27.0	980 000	46.0	968 000
13.5	975 000	26.0	930 000	44.0	904 000
13.0	930 000	25.0	885 000	42.0	844 000
12.5	900 000	24.0	845 000	40.0	788 000
12.0	860 000	23.0	805 000	38.0	736 000
11.5	825 000	22.0	765 000	36.0	686 000
11.0	790 000	21.0	730 000	34.0	638 000
10.5	755 000	20.0	695 000	32.0	592 000
10.0	720 000	19.0	660 000	30.0	550 000
9.5	685 000	18.0	625 000	28.0	510 000
9.0	650 000	17.0	590 000	26.0	472 000
8.5	620 000	16.0	555 000	24.0	436 000
8.0	590 000	15.0	525 000	22.0	402 000
7.5	560 000	14.0	495 000	20.0	370 000
7.0	530 000	13.0	465 000	18.0	340 000
6.5	505 000	12.0	435 000	16.0	312 000
6 0	480 000	11.0	405 000	14.0	286 000
5.5	455 000	10.0	375 000	12.0	262 000
5.0	430 000	9.0	345 000	10.0	240 000
4.5	405 000	8.0	315 000	8.0	220 000
4.0	380 000	7.0	290 000	6.0	202 000
3.5	360 000	6.0	265 000	4.0	186 000
3.0	340 000	5.0	240 000	2.0	172 000
2.5	320 000	4.0	220 000	0.0	160 000
2.0	300 000	3.0	200 000		
1.5	285 000	2.0			
1.0	270 000	1.0			
0.5	260 000	0.0			
0.0	250 000				

The method of applying this table to determining the annual discharge is very simple. The discharges taken from the table corresponding to the twelve mean monthly gauge-readings of the river year (November 1st to October 31st) are added together, and their sum is multiplied by one-twelfth of the number of seconds in a year. By taking the sum of the discharges corresponding to the recorded daily gauge-reading and correcting the result for the odd hours, minutes, and seconds of the year, a more mathematically exact determination may be made; but the small difference in the results will be of no practical importance. The first three columns* of the following table exhibit the results obtained by applying the former process to the mean monthly gauge-readings.

Method of applying them.

The next question is how to determine the *true discharge of the river* from these three columns. Natchez is situated below all the tributaries except Red river. Donaldsonville and Carrollton are situated below the three bayous which derive their supply from the Mississippi. Supposing no

Corrections for anomalous influences.

* The gauge-records at Carrollton for 1853 and 1854 were obtained from Professor Forshey. They were not all kept at the same locality, and they are less exact than the rest. This is indicated by the table. For the years 1851, 1852, 1858, and 1859, when the gauge was regularly kept, the discharges computed at Donaldsonville and at Carrollton accord very closely. For the years 1853 and 1854 a marked discrepancy is observable. For this reason it is concluded that the Donaldsonville work for those years is the more correct of the two. For the year 1858, as will be hereafter fully explained, an anomalous influence affected the discharge curve both at Donaldsonville and at Carrollton.

crevasses to occur between Natchez and Carrollton, then the difference between the discharge at Natchez and that at the two other localities measures the difference between the contributions of Red river and the amount lost through bayous Atchafalaya, Plaquemine, and La Fourche. But this latter difference is insignificant, and may be neglected, as the grand mean discharge at the three localities indicates, as well as that in 1851. If then the discharges at Donaldsonville and Carrollton be increased by the amount of crevasse water lost below Natchez, the results will be directly comparable with those determined for former years at Natchez. They truly represent the quantity which it is the object of this discussion to deduce, *i.e.* the discharge of the Mississippi below all its tributaries; the Red river not being considered one of these, but as emptying into the gulf through the bayous Atchafalaya, Plaquemine, and La Fourche. The data for determining the needful crevasse discharge, as will hereafter appear, were secured by this Survey with all the accuracy requisite for the present purpose. The last column of the table exhibits the final results of the computation.

Annual discharge of the Mississippi river.

Year.	At Carrollton.	At Donaldsonville.	At Natchez.	True discharge.
	Cubic feet.	*Cubic feet.*	*Cubic feet.*	*Cubic feet.*
Nov. 1818 to Oct. 1819......			15 438 000 000 000	15 400 000 000 000
Jan. 1822 to Dec. 1822......			20 528 000 000 000	20 500 000 000 000
Nov. 1822 to Oct. 1823......			27 266 000 000 000	27 300 000 000 000
Nov. 1823 to Oct. 1824......			21 168 000 000 000	21 200 000 000 000
Nov. 1824 to Oct. 1825......			18 206 000 000 000	18 200 000 000 000
Nov. 1827 to Oct. 1828......			26 402 000 000 000	26 400 000 000 000
Nov. 1828 to Oct. 1829......			13 698 000 000 000	13 700 000 000 000
Nov. 1829 to Oct. 1830......			20 701 000 000 000	20 700 000 000 000
Nov. 1830 to Oct. 1831......			17 605 000 000 000	17 600 000 000 000
Nov. 1833 to Oct. 1834......			20 344 000 000 000	20 300 000 000 000
Nov. 1834 to Oct. 1835......			17 156 000 000 000	17 200 000 000 000
Nov. 1835 to Oct. 1836......			21 409 000 000 000	21 400 000 000 000
Nov. 1836 to Oct. 1837......			15 485 000 000 000	15 500 000 000 000
Nov. 1837 to Oct. 1838......			15 278 000 000 000	15 300 000 000 000
Nov. 1838 to Oct. 1839......			11 515 000 000 000	11 500 000 000 000
Nov. 1839 to Oct. 1840......			18 885 000 000 000	18 900 000 000 000
Nov. 1840 to Oct. 1841......			21 386 000 000 000	21 400 000 000 000
Nov. 1843 to Oct. 1844......			29 281 000 000 000	29 300 000 000 000
Nov. 1844 to Oct. 1845......			18 998 000 000 000	19 000 000 000 000
Nov. 1845 to Oct. 1846......			15 265 000 000 000	15 300 000 000 000
Nov. 1846 to Oct. 1847......			21 328 000 000 000	21 300 000 000 000
Nov. 1848 to Oct. 1849......	25 904 000 000 000			27 000 000 000 000
Nov. 1849 to Oct. 1850......	20 916 000 000 000			24 000 000 000 000
Nov. 1850 to Oct. 1851......	20 457 000 000 000	20 140 000 000 000	20 452 000 000 000	20 600 000 000 000
Nov. 1851 to Oct. 1852......	17 445 000 000 000	18 174 000 000 000		17 800 000 000 000
Nov. 1852 to Oct. 1853......	23 062 000 000 000	21 724 000 000 000		22 000 000 000 000
Nov. 1853 to Oct. 1854......	18 193 000 000 000	16 810 000 000 000		17 000 000 000 000
Nov. 1854 to Oct. 1855......	11 534 000 000 000	10 684 000 000 000		11 000 000 000 000
Nov. 1855 to Oct. 1856......		14 832 000 000 000		14 800 000 000 000
Nov. 1856 to Oct. 1857......		15 076 000 000 000		15 100 000 000 000
Nov. 1857 to Oct. 1858......	23 834 000 000 000	24 379 000 000 000	25 607 000 000 000	26 000 000 000 000
Nov. 1858 to Oct. 1859......	20 289 000 000 000	20 588 000 000 000		21 000 000 000 000
Nov. 1859 to Oct. 1860......	15 183 000 000 000			15 200 000 000 000
Mean..................	19 682 000 000 000	18 045 000 000 000	19 713 000 000 000	19 400 000 000 000

Several interesting results are exhibited by this table.

Remarks upon this table.

The annual discharge of the river, although subject to great variations, averages about 19½ trillions of cubic feet. There appear to be three well-defined classes of years: the extreme low-water years, as 1839 and 1855, when the discharge is only about 11 trillions of cubic feet; the ordinary years, when it is about 19½ trillions; and the great-flood years, as 1823, 1828, 1844, 1849, and 1858, when it averages about 27 trillions.* The differences between these quantities necessarily imply corresponding variations in the yearly amount of rain in the basin, and are perhaps due to the same general physical causes that occasion the secular oscillations of the great northern lakes.

Without being sufficiently complete to be decisive upon the subject, this table is certainly calculated to inspire the belief that the changes which cultivation has effected in the valley since 1819, have produced no appreciable effect upon the annual discharge of the river. Thus:—

	Cubic feet.
For the 8 measured years prior to 1830, the mean annual discharge is	20 400 000 000 000
" 8 " " between 1830 and 1840, the mean annual discharge is	17 200 000 000 000
" 7 " " " 1840 " 1850, " " "	22 500 000 000 000
" 10 " " " 1850 " 1860, " " "	18 000 000 000 000

In order to be decisive, the discharge of *every* year ought to be determined; a condition which the defective state of the gauge-records renders it impossible to fulfil.

Mean ratio for the entire basin.

Ratio between the yearly amount of rain and drainage in the basin.—Adopting the mean yearly amount of rain already determined, and remembering that the annual discharge of the Mississippi fixed by the preceding analysis is exclusive of any contribution from Red river, the discharge of that stream being carried off by bayous Atchafalaya, Plaquemine, and La Fourche, the mean ratio between rain and drainage in the Mississippi basin is $\frac{19\ 500\ 000\ 000\ 000}{78\ 900\ 000\ 000\ 000}=0.25$.

Ratio in the swamp country.

This ratio varies greatly, however, in different parts of the basin. In Chapter IV it will be proved that, for the basins of the St. Francis and Yazoo rivers, and of some of the smaller tributaries, its value is about 0.9; and also that the Arkansas and White rivers discharge about 2 trillions of cubic feet per annum. These numbers furnish a clue to the approximate determination of the ratio in question for the basin of each of the great tributaries, and hence fix the mean annual discharge of each of those rivers.

Ratio for the Arkansas, White, and Missouri, and for the Upper Mississippi and Ohio basins.

Thus the ratio for the basin of the Arkansas and White rivers is $\frac{2\ 000\ 000\ 000\ 000}{13\ 000\ 000\ 000\ 000}=0.15$. But this basin is entirely similar—so far as downfall and drainage are concerned—to that of the Missouri. Hence the annual discharge of the latter is $25\ 200\ 000\ 000\ 000\times0.15=3\ 780\ 000\ 000\ 000$ cubic feet. The ratio being 0.9 for the Yazoo, St. Francis, and smaller tributary basins, the discharge of those streams is $1\ 500\ 000\ 000\ 000\times0.9=$ $1\ 350\ 000\ 000\ 000$ cubic feet, $1\ 100\ 000\ 000\ 000\times0.9=990\ 000$-$000\ 000$ cubic feet, and $3\ 600\ 000\ 000\ 000\times0.9=3\ 240\ 000\ 000\ 000$ cubic feet, respectively. But if the total discharge from these five basins be deducted from 19½ trillions of cubic feet, the result will be the annual discharge from the only two remaining basins—those of the Upper Mississippi and the Ohio. It is 8 140 000 000 000 cubic feet. These basins are so similar in physical characteristics that the same ratio may be assumed for both. This ratio is, therefore, $\frac{8\ 140\ 000\ 000\ 000}{13\ 800\ 000\ 000\ 000+20\ 700\ 000\ 000\ 000}=$ 0.24, giving for the annual discharge of the Upper Mississippi $13\ 800\ 000\ 000\ 000\times$

* To prevent misconception, it should be remarked that the total annual discharge is no fair standard by which to compare the different great floods of the river. It is the *maximum* discharge during a flood which determines its height and destructive character, and which therefore furnishes the proper standard.

0.24=3 300 000 000 000, and for that of the Ohio 20 700 000 000 000×0.24= 5 000 000 000 000 cubic feet.

Ratio for Red-river basin.

It being assumed that the annual discharge of the Red river is equal to that of the three bayous, the ratio between downfall and drainage in that basin also may be deduced. Thus the mean annual stand of the river below high water, 1851 (transferred from Natchez, Donaldsonville, and Carrollton) being—at the upper mouths of bayous Atchafalaya, Plaquemine, and La Fourche—23.5, 14.0, and 8.0 feet respectively, and the corresponding discharges per second of the bayous about 50,000, 5,000 and 2,000 cubic feet respectively (see Chapter IV), the mean discharge of Red river is 57,000 cubic feet per second, or about 1 800 000 000 000 cubic feet per annum. The ratio is then $\frac{1\ 800\ 000\ 000\ 000}{8\ 800\ 000\ 000\ 000}=0.20$. As this basin has proportionally less of the dry plateau formation than that of the Arkansas, and more than that of the Ohio and Upper Mississippi, this value of the ratio corresponds well with those deduced for those basins. It cannot therefore vary much from exactness.

General table of results of downfall and drainage measurements.

The following table has been prepared to exhibit in a convenient form a recapitulation of these several determinations, the names of the tributaries being arranged in the order of their annual discharge.

Annual downfall and drainage.

Basin.		Annual downfall.	Annual drainage.	Ratio.
Name.	Area.			
	Square miles.	*Cubic feet.*	*Cubic feet.*	
Ohio river	214 000	20 700 000 000 000	5 000 000 000 000	0.24
Missouri river	518 000	25 200 000 000 000	3 780 000 000 000	0.15
Upper Mississippi	169 000	13 800 000 000 000	3 300 000 000 000	0.24
Small tributaries	32 400	3 600 000 000 000	3 240 000 000 000	0.90
Arkansas and White rivers	189 000	13 000 000 000 000	2 000 000 000 000	0.15
Red river	97 000	8 800 000 000 000	1 800 000 000 000	0.20
Yazoo river	13 850	1 500 000 000 000	1 350 000 000 000	0.90
St. Francis river	10 500	1 100 000 000 000	9 990 000 000 000	0.90
Entire Mississippi exclusive of Red river	1 147 000	78 900 000 000 000	19 500 000 000 000	0.25

This table, taken in connection with a map of the region, shows that neither the size of its basin nor the length of its course is any criterion of the hydrographic importance of a tributary stream.

SEDIMENT.

Introductory remarks.

Measurements by the Delta Survey.—A knowledge of the amount of sedimentary matter held in suspension by the Mississippi at its different stages, and, in general, of the laws which govern the formation of the alluvial delta of this river, is of high practical importance. With a view to investigate thoroughly one branch of the subject, Professor Forshey in 1851, in addition to his current-measurements at Carrollton, was charged with the duty of collecting, daily, samples of water from different parts of the river at that station, so as to present a fair average of the whole, and of carefully weighing and preserving the sediment.

The stations were selected opposite the velocity base; one about 300 feet from the east bank, the next in the middle of the river, and the other about 400 feet from the west bank. The high-water depths at these stations were 100, 100, and 40 feet respectively. Samples of water were collected daily (Sundays excepted) at surface, mid-depth, and bottom at the first two stations; and at surface and bottom at the third. The samples below the surface were secured by a small keg, heavily weighted at the bottom and provided at each of its heads with a large valve, opening upward. These valves allowed a free passage to the water while the keg was sinking to the required depth, but prevented its escape while being drawn up. When the keg reached the surface, the water contained in it was thoroughly stirred, and a bottle filled from it. On returning to the office, 100 grammes of water were accurately measured from each of the eight samples, and each parcel was separately preserved in a precipitating bottle. After receiving six days' contributions, these bottles were set aside for two weeks to settle. The greater part of the water, then perfectly clear, was removed by a syphon. The remainder, after thorough shaking, was poured upon a double filter composed of two pieces of filtering paper of exactly equal weight. The bottle was then rinsed with clear water and again emptied upon the filter, so as to secure all the sediment. After becoming quite dry, the two papers were separated and placed—one containing all the sediment of the 600 grammes of river-water, and the other perfectly pure—in opposite sides of a very delicate balance (correct to a milligramme). The difference of weight, which was, of course, the exact weight of the sediment, was then accurately ascertained.

Details of the measurements at Carrollton.

These elaborate measurements were begun on February 17, 1851, and continued fifty-two weeks. During the next year it was not deemed necessary to make the operation so laborious, since the ratio between the sediment contained in the water at any one of the positions, and that contained in the whole river, might fairly be considered to be determined by the first year's observations. For the second year, therefore, only one sample daily was obtained. It was taken from the surface at the position 300 feet from the east bank.

The following table exhibits the results of these two years' measurements at Carrollton. The figures denote the number of grammes of dry sediment contained in 600 grammes of river-water. The observations of the first year are represented by a diagram upon plate XII.

Table of results.

Sediment contained in Mississippi water at Carrollton.

Number of week.	First year, 1851-52.								Second year, 1852-53.		
	First position.			Second position.			Third position.		First position.		
	Surface.	Mid-depth.	Bottom.	Surface.	Mid-depth.	Bottom.	Surface.	Bottom.	Surface.	Mid-depth.	Bottom.
	Gram.	*Gram.*	*Gram.*	*Gram.*	*Gram.*	*Gram.*	*Gram.*	*Gram.*	*Gram.*	*Gram.*	*Gram.*
3d in February	0.320	0.260	0.306	0.310	0.305	0.326	0.318	0.318	0.297		
4th "	0.506	0.558	0.571	0.551	0.628	0.653	0.640	0.805	0.715		
1st in March	0.521	0.530	0.548	0.570	0.617	0.638	0.563	0.771	0.636		
2d "	0.393	0.406	0.396	0.373	0.480	0.504	0.418	0.568	0.482		
3d "	0.294	0.337	0.323	0.350	0.359	0.357	0.289	0.456	0.481		
4th "	0.228	0.207	0.259	0.233	0.310	0.310	0.255	0.368	0.548		
1st in April	0.207	0.237	0.245	0.235	0.253	0.270	0.210	0.273	0.428		
2d "	0.158	0.201	0.205	0.192	0.211	0.225	0.215	0.232	0.370		
3d "	0.190	0.190	0.195	0.186	0.191	0.214	0.172	0.237	0.320		
4th "	0.265	0.250	0.272	0.265	0.303	0.306	0.264	0.284	0.840		
1st in May	0.210	0.259	0.236	0.208	0.253	0.252	0.223	0.262	0.590		
2d "	0.188	0.210	0.205	0.199	0.225	0.252	0.181	0.237	0.440		
3d "	0.150	0.177	0.183	0.158	0.185	0.184	0.144	0.178	0.465		
4th "	0.130	0.147	0.144	0.149	0.142	0.160	0.095	0.162	0.402		
5th "	0.117	0.139	0.132	0.118	0.134	0.150	0.105	0.152	0.377		
1st in June	0.345	0.407	0.187	0.365	0.415	0.410	0.285	0.390	0.364		
2d "	0.456	0.507	0.510	0.477	0.515	0.517	0.365	0.457	0.442		
3d "	0.917	0.960	0.940	0.731	0.981	1.105	0.666	1.046	0.447		
4th "	0.498	0.570	0.557	0.528	0.597	0.601	0.427	0.536	0.452		
1st in July	0.407	0.456	0.459	0.395	0.457	0.482	0.462	0.425	0.599		
2d "	0.422	0.492	0.511	0.441	0.516	0.435	0.390	0.467	0.684		
3d "	0.501	0.542	0.570	0.528	0.576	0.582	0.475	0.572	0.664		
4th "	0.613	0.638	0.648	0.612	0.672	0.675	0.674	0.612	0.596		
1st in August	0.536	0.587	0.621	0.627	0.660	0.637	0.501	0.625	0.470		
2d "	0.617	0.678	0.697	0.638	0.719	0.728	0.517	0.711	0.490		
3d "	0.512	0.620	0.637	0.440	0.718	0.702	0.361	0.741	0.332		
4th "	0.652	0.716	0.738	0.583	0.780	0.819	0.460	0.788	0.300		
5th "	0.456	0.560	0.572	0.452	0.590	0.598	0.372	0.561	0.205		
1st in September	0.423	0.500	0.535	0.393	0.564	0.562	0.256	0.559	0.190		
2d "	0.310	0.450	0.444	0.277	0.485	0.535	0.278	0.540	0.112		
3d "	0.292	0.395	0.418	0.214	0.428	0.460	0.283	0.511	0.152		
4th "	0.183	0.258	0.310	0.173	0.317	0.348	0.158	0.382	0.100		
1st in October	0.137	0.187	0.220	0.125	0.215	0.235	0.096	0.265	0.170		
2d "	0.120	0.169	0.170	0.109	0.193	0.220	0.107	0.235	0.092		
3d "	0.100	0.132	0.136	0.097	0.146	0.159	0.084	0.195	0.071		
4th "	0.068	0.096	0.106	0.054	0.115	0.116	0.061	0.136	0.081		
1st in November	0.090	0.140	0.127	0.100	0.143	0.146	0.080	0.175	0.141		
2d "	0.120	0.151	0.152	0.115	0.167	0.173	0.111	0.207	0.068		
3d "	0.115	0.130	0.141	0.109	0.151	0.146	0.108	0.218	0.056		
4th "	0.117	0.152	0.165	0.117	0.167	0.166	0.102	0.202	0.225		
5th "	0.109	0.107	0.119	0.106	0.132	0.139	0.110	0.151	0.402		
1st in December	0.204	0.204	0.222	0.180	0.225	0.242	0.155	0.160	0.800		
2d "	0.168	0.235	0.246	0.197	0.251	0.267	0.180	0.329	0.315		
3d "	0.234	0.294	0.295	0.207	0.333	0.345	0.200	0.346	0.325		
4th "	0.160	0.215	0.240	0.160	0.205	0.245	0.150	0.260	0.342		
1st in January	0.160	0.207	0.190	0.190	0.200	0.196	0.128	0.200	0.255		
2d "	0.144	0.193	0.195	0.135	0.210	0.215	0.130	0.248	0.503		
3d "	0.470	0.533	0.535	0.450	0.560	0.550	0.406	0.605	0.520		
4th "	0.471	0.531	0.610	0.416	0.551	0.574	0.386	0.543	0.370		
5th "	0.137	0.216	0.223	0.161	0.206	0.201	0.171	0.221	0.332		
1st in February	0.079	0.106	0.099	0.081	0.106	0.101	0.097	0.065	0.308		
2d "	0.082	0.115	0.115	0.081	0.115	0.105	0.071	0.094	0.234		
Total	15.302	17.552	17.880	15.156	18.977	19.538	13.845	20.070	19.100		

This table is fruitful in results. It establishes that the Mississippi water is not charged to its maximum capacity with sediment; because the distribution of the material is different from that which must have place were this the case. Dupuit demonstrates (Chapter V, "Etudes Theoriques et Pratiques sur le Mouvement des Eaux Courantes") that the power of suspension is due to the fact that the different layers of water are actuated by different velocities, and thus exert different pressures upon the different sides of the suspended atoms. Hence, the greater the difference in the velocity of consecutive layers, the greater will be the power of suspension. Now it is conclusively proved in Chapter IV that the change of velocity from layer to layer is, in horizontal planes, the greatest near the banks, and the least near the thread of the current; and in vertical planes parallel to the current, the greatest near the bottom and surface, and the least at a point about 0.3 of the depth below the surface, where the absolute velocity has its maximum value. If, then, the water be either charged to its maximum capacity or overcharged with sediment, we must find the greatest amount near the banks and near the surface and bottom, and the least amount near the thread of the current and near the layer 0.3 of the depth below the surface. If the water be undercharged, on the contrary, the distribution of sediment will follow no law, the amount at any point being fixed by the accidental circumstances of whirls, boils, etc., although, of course, there will be an accumulation of the material near the bottom, where the suspending power is very much greater than elsewhere. Bearing these well-established principles in mind, an inspection of the preceding table must convince any one that the Mississippi water is undercharged with sediment, even in the low-water stage. A most important practical deduction may be drawn from this fact, namely, the error of the popular idea that a slight artificial retardation of the current, that caused by a crevasse, for instance, must produce a deposit in the channel of the river below it. The error of this theory is fully exposed in Chapter VI, where the subject is so thoroughly discussed that it does not require notice here.

Mississippi water undercharged with sediment. Important practical deduction.

This table also shows that, for the year 1851–52, the river-water (mean of the three positions) contained the greatest amount of sediment in the third week of June, when the weight of this matter constituted $\frac{1}{681}$ of the weight of the river-water; that the minimum amount was found in the fourth week of October, when the above fraction was only $\frac{1}{6383}$; and that the mean value for the year was $\frac{1}{1808}$.

Maximum and minimum amounts of sediment in 1851.

The observations of the second year show what caution should be observed in attempting to generalize upon the proportion of sediment contained in the Mississippi water, even when the observations extend over long periods. If it be allowable to assume the same ratio to exist as in 1851–52, between the amount of sediment in the entire river and that at the surface of the first division, we have—for the maximum, minimum, and mean proportions of sediment to water, by weight, during the second year—the fractions $\frac{1}{572}$ (fourth week of April), $\frac{1}{8584}$ (third

In 1852.

week of November), and $\frac{1}{1449}$; which differ materially from the above values for the previous year.*

Further data upon this subject.

Before drawing any general conclusion, therefore, as to the amount of sedimentary matter annually discharged by the Mississippi into the gulf, it is well to examine all other data upon the subject. The observations of this Survey at Columbus in 1858 are the first in order.

Observations of the Survey at Columbus.

These observations were undertaken voluntarily by Mr. Fillebrown's assistant, Mr. Webster, and continued until he left the party, in June. From that date they were made by Mr. Fillebrown. These observations are especially interesting in one respect. They demonstrate that the Mississippi and the Ohio waters do not mingle until after passing Columbus, which is fully 20 miles below the junction of these rivers. Where the waters do become completely blended is not known, but they are very distinct at Columbus, as the following table shows.

Details of these observations.

The method of observing differed from that adopted at Carrollton. Mr. Webster took daily one "measure" of Ohio and one of Mississippi water at points about midway between the banks and the dividing line, which could be distinguished by the eye. Mr. Fillebrown took two "measures" of each, one near the shore, and the other near the dividing line. Prior to May 1st, the "measure" contained 54 cubic inches. Subsequent to that date, one was used containing 70.5 cubic inches. Surface water only was collected. The samples of the two waters were filtered separately every day with great care, and the weight of the sediment contained in each was determined. The results are presented in the following table. To avoid the confusion arising from different amounts of water being collected at different dates, the table has been modified so as to exhibit in all cases the number of grains Troy of sediment contained in one cubic foot of water. The column headed "mean of river" has been computed by multiplying the numerical mean of the other two columns by 1.2, the ratio between the surface and the true mean at all depths, derived from the Carrollton observations.

---

* Specimens of the characteristic varieties of the sedimentary matter taken from the river at Carrollton in 1851 have been placed in the hands of Mr. de Pourtales, of the U. S. Coast Survey, for microscopic and chemical examination. The same disposition has been made of characteristic specimens of the bed and banks of the river, and of the surface of the bar of the Southwest pass, and of portions of the alluvial lands.

Sediment contained in Mississippi water at Columbus.

Day of the month.	March, 1858.			April, 1858.			May, 1858.			June, 1858.			July, 1858.		
	Ohio water.	Miss. water.	Mean of river.	Ohio water.	Miss. water.	Mean of river.	Ohio water.	Miss. water.	Mean of river.	Ohio water.	Miss. water.	Mean of river.	Ohio water.	Miss. water.	Mean of river.
	Grains	*Grains*	*Grains*	*Grains*	*Grains*	*Grains*	*Grains*	*Grains*	*Grains*	*Grains*	*Grains*	*Grains*	*Grains*	*Grains*	*Grains*
1......													394	504	539
2......				96	320	288					343		418	640	635
3......															
4......				96	320	288	147	245	235				355	590	567
5......							171	294	279				344	541	531
6......										135	343	286	418	455	524
7......													541	467	605
8......													553	516	641
9......				128	320	269	245	318	238				541	455	598
10......				96	384	288							357	541	539
11......													529	406	561
12......							147	343	294				517	504	613
13......				64	288	211							443	664	664
14......				160	320	280				147	392	323	554	541	657
15......	128	320	269	304	512	490	110	220	198						
16......													615	467	648
17......	128	336	378	352	576	557							455	615	642
18......	160	416	346	288	608	538	171	171	206				455	615	642
19......	128	416	326	320	480	480	147	147	176				418	357	465
20......	128	320	269				122	122	147				394	283	406
21......				368	528	538							615	615	738
22......				384	400	470							701	627	797
23......	128	320	269												
24......	128	384	307	240	352	355							529	664	716
25......							147	245	235						
26......							196	441	382	172	258	258	553	504	634
27......										123	258	229	307	258	339
28......	96	256	211				208	404	367	61	197	155	184	369	332
29......	128	320	269								246				
30......				112	352	278	110	343	272	74	258	199			
31......	128	320	269												
Mean..	128.0	340.8	293.3	214.9	411.4	380.7	160.1	274.4	260.7	118.7	284.3	241.7	466.2	508.2	584.7

	August, 1858.			September, 1858.			October, 1858.			November, 1858.		
1......	172	128	177				123	148	162	541	86	376
2......	123	111	140	455	689	686	160	160	192			
3......				246	541	472	74			209	381	354
4......	234	209	266	307	394	420					443	
5......	234	271	303	148	246	236	135	123	155	448	393	502
6......	258	209	280	209	123	199					529	
7......	320	332	391									
8......							123	148	163	492	135	376
9......	344	246	354	184	160	206	98	135	140		307	
10......	332	369	421									
11......	357	455	487	221	184	243	135	86	133	320	209	317
12......	443	480	554	148	123	163	135	135	162	295	283	347
13......	603	443	628	148	111	155	111	86	118	332	381	428
14......	357	480	502	160	246	244						
15......							148	111	155	271	246	310
16......	344	394	443	197	271	281	87	61	59			
17......	344	295	383									
18......	307	396	422	135	258	236		74				
19......	504	418	553	246	160	243	49	25	44			
20......	455						25	111	82			
21......	406	529	561	184	246	258	86	37	74			
22......				135	184	191	61	61	73			
23......	406	492	539	98	123	133	98	25	74			
24......	332	664	598	135	123	154	49	94	86			
25......				98	111	125	86	135	133			
26......				86	184	162	98	111	125			
27......	566	456	613									
28......							98	148	148			
29......	332	578	546	184	184	221	98	172	162			
30......	639	541	708	184	160	206						
31......												
Mean..	361.7	385.9	448.6	186.1	229.6	249.2	97.6	105.6	122.0	362 9	264.2	376.2

To represent these "mean-of-river" results properly, they have been plotted on a large scale and interpolations made for lacking days. The mean weekly amount of sediment per cubic foot of water thus calculated (table in Chapter VI) is shown on plate XIII. This curve confirms the inference drawn from the Carrollton work, that no artificial diminution of the high water of the river can produce a deposit in the channel.

Diagram to represent them.

From the above table, it can readily be computed that the maximum, the minimum, and the grand mean proportions, by weight, of the sediment to the river-water (considering 1 cubic foot of this water to weigh 436,247 grains Troy) are $\frac{1}{670}$, $\frac{1}{7152}$, and $\frac{1}{1321}$, respectively; the date of the maximum proportion being the third week in July, and of the minimum the third week in October. This result, when compared with those deduced from the Carrollton observations, indicates the variable nature of these ratios.

Resulting maximum and minimum proportions of sedimentary matter.

These three results will now be compared with those obtained by former observers. A great difficulty is encountered at the outset. It has sometimes been the custom to measure not the *weight of sediment* in a given weight or volume of water, but the *volume of sediment* in a given *volume of water*. This method is considered to be objectionable, inasmuch as the *volume* of the sediment depends upon its density, which may vary with the manner of deposition. A series of experiments was made to test this question.

Defect in some former measurements of this character.

Professor Forshey was provided with a glass tube of uniform bore, 29 inches long and 1 inch in diameter. Into this, fixed permanently in a vertical position, he poured 6 grammes of river-water from each of the eight bottles collected daily during the year 1851–52. This water was introduced near the bottom of the tube by a second funnel-mouthed tube, which, being smaller than the first, could readily be inserted. The main tube contained about four days' collections, and the water near the top thus had time to become perfectly clear before it was forced out by new contributions. At the end of the year he thus secured the sediment from 14,976 grammes of river-water, which, with the diameter of his tube, would have made a column about 186 feet in height.

Test measurements to determine the density of sediment artificially deposited in the usual manner.

The following extract from his manuscript report contains interesting details:—

Observed phenomena.

"A severe frost in January froze the water and cracked the tube, but it lost only some clear water near the top. The mud in the bottom was curdled into rolls and no longer lay compactly. It was 2.5 inches to the top of the curdled mass.

"Fungi grew in the water and along the walls of the tube during the summer, but decayed and disappeared in the winter.

"Leaving the tube full of the last water contributed, I reached with a small wire and sponge the mass of alluvium, and stirred it completely, and then washed down the walls of the tube and left it to settle. At the end of three months the height of the alluvial column was 2 inches.

"I found by inserting a wire that one inch was tolerably solid alluvium, while the other was soft, blackish slime, probably decayed fungi and algæ and other carbonaceous matters.

"I then left the cork out, and, in the course of a year, the entire column of water, say 15 inches, up to the crack made by the frost in the tube, had evaporated, and left a mass of blackish matter, contracted so as to leave the walls on all sides near 1½ inches high."

Analysis of results.

He proceeds to state that this deposit was 1 inch in height solid matter, and hence that the volume of the deposit was $\frac{1}{2232}$ of the volume of the turbid water.

This result demonstrates that the specific gravity of this solid matter was much less than that of the ordinary depositions of the Mississippi, or, in other words, that the conditions under which the deposit was made affected its density, as it had been suspected would be the case. This is evident from the following considerations.

The river-water placed in the tube was taken from the identical collection, of which sedimentary matter was shown to constitute $\frac{1}{1808}$ part, by weight. This matter, as deposited in the tube, constituted $\frac{1}{2232}$ part, by volume. Its specific gravity was, then, $\frac{2232}{1808}=1.23$.* The specific gravity of common earth is usually considered to be 1.5; that of sand, 1.8; that of clay, 1.93. Professor Forshey found the specific gravity of three samples of the bank of the river, at Carrollton, to be 1.91, 1.93, and 1.96. Two samples of the deposit made by the Mississippi, upon the bank opposite Vicksburg, in the flood of 1858, gave 1.92 and 1.93, respectively, for this quantity. (At the gulf the material deposited is still more dense. Thus, of samples collected by this Survey at the mouth of the Southwest pass, in 20 feet water inside the bar, on the bar, and in 30 and 40 feet water outside the bar, the specific gravity was uniformly 2.6. In 20 feet water outside the bar, it was 2.8.) It is evident, then, that the density of the solid in Professor Forshey's tube was materially less than if it had been deposited naturally upon the river bank.

Resulting proof of the error in an old method of observing.

The error of noting only the *volume* of the sediment is then demonstrated, since the result, being dependent upon the peculiar manipulations adopted by the observer, is not determinate. Discrepancies in measurements, when only the volume has been considered, should therefore be expected.

Former measurements of the sedimentary matter contained in Mississippi water. Captain Talcott.

Measurements upon the Mississippi by other parties.—Mr. Meade and Mr. Sidell, assistants of Captain Talcott in his survey of the mouths of the Mississippi, in 1838, measured the amount of sedimentary matter contained in the water. The former, from observations made in April and May, considers the quantity to be the $\frac{1}{1256}$ part, by weight. The latter adopts $\frac{1}{1724}$ for this ratio. Further details of these observations are presented in Appendix A of this report.

The only experiments which are known to have been published are those of Professor J. L. Riddell, published in 1846, in De Bow's Commercial Review; those of Mr. Andrew Brown, published in the proceedings of the American Association for the Advancement of Science for the year 1848; those of Lieutenant R. A. Marr, U. S. N., published in the

* Professor Forshey did not check this determination by actual measurement.

proceedings of the same association for the year 1849; and those of the same officer, published in 1853 in the Washington Astronomical Observations, vol. III. These labors will be noticed in turn.

Those of Professor Riddell.

Professor Riddell's first experiments upon the amount of sediment contained in Mississippi water are reported in a letter addressed to Sir Charles Lyell, on March 5, 1846. The following is an extract from this letter:—

"In July, 1843, I made some careful experiments to determine the amount of sedimentary matter in the Mississippi water, which then possessed about an average degree of turbidness. For each experiment I used near a pint of water, 475.85 grammes (Fr.) actual weight. The sediment was allowed near ten days for natural subsidence; it was then carefully collected, allowed to dry spontaneously, and when effectually dry was carefully weighed.

	Sediment in grammes.	Ratio by weight to the whole.
No. 1.—Procured from opposite Randolph, by Dr. Drake, in June, 1843..............	0.40	1–1190
No. 2.—Opposite Carthage, in June, Dr. Drake..	0.38	1–1250
No. 3.—Opposite New Orleans, June, Dr. Drake..	0.35	1–1350
No. 4.—Opposite New Orleans, July 6th, 1843..	0.40	1–1190

"Average ratio of dry sedimentary matter in numbers 1, 2, 3, 4, to the weight of water and sediment, = near 1–1245." He adds that by volume, the ratio is near $\frac{1}{3000}$.

Second series.

Professor Riddell's second experiments were made when a member of a committee appointed by the Association of American Geologists and Naturalists to ascertain the amount of sediment carried into the sea by the Mississippi river. His report was read at the meeting of this body in 1846. The following extracts sufficiently explain his labors:—

"The following table embraces the results of experiments upon Mississippi water, taken at intervals of three days, extending from May 21 to August 13, 1846. The water was drawn up in a pail from a wharf near the mint, where there is considerable current. Its temperature was observed at the time, and the height of the river determined. Some minutes afterward the pail of water was agitated, and two samples of one pint each measured out. The glass pint measure was graduated by weighing into it, at 60° Fahr., 7295.581 grains of distilled water, and marking the height with a diamond.

"From the pint samples of water, after standing a day or two, most of the matter mechanically suspended would subside to the bottom of the containing vessels. Near two-thirds of the clear supernatant liquid was next decanted, while the remaining water, along with the sediment, was, in each instance, poured upon a double filter, the two parts of which had been previously adjusted to be of equal weight. The filters were numbered and laid aside, and ultimately dried in the sunshine under like circumstances, in two parcels, one embracing the experiments from May 21st to July 15th; the other from July 17th to August 13th. The difference in weight between the two parts of each double filter was then carefully ascertained, and as to the inner filter alone the sediment was attached, its excess of weight indicated the amount of sediment. I employed Mr. John Chandler, a skilful manipulator, to assist me in all these operations.

Date of experiment.	Height of river above low water.		Tempera-ture.	Grains sediment in pint water.		Date of experiment.	Height of river above low water.		Tempera-ture.	Grains sediment in pint water.	
1846.	*Ft.*	*In.*	°	A.	B.	1846.	*Ft.*	*In.*	°	A.	B.
May 21	10	11	72	6.66	7.00	July 3	7	2	79.5	9.63	10.00
" 25	10	11	73	9.08	9.12	" 6	6	2	81	8.20	7.57
" 27	10	10	73	7.80	9.00	" 8	6	0	81	7.30	6.96
" 29	11	0	74	7.30	8.10	" 10	6	1	81	6.12	6.28
June 2	11	1	75	4.80	5.45	" 13	5	9	82	7.72	7.30
" 4	11	1	75	7.87	6.10	" 15	5	10	82	6.67	6.80
" 6	11	4	75	4.60	4.90	" 17	5	10	82	4.65	4.57
" 8	11	4	75.5	5.48	5.60	" 20	5	4	82	6.07	5.75
" 10	10	4	76	6.70	6.80	" 24	3	10	84	5.76	5.72
" 12	10	8	76	6.50	6.30	" 27	3	1	84	4.77	4.60
" 14	10	5	76.5	6.00	6.00	" 29	3	11	84.5	4.28	4.13
" 16	10	4	76.5	6.47	6.15	Aug. 1	2	6	85	4.40	4.44
" 20	10	4	77	7.08	7.40	" 3	2	0	84	3.18	3.34
" 22	10	2	77	9.88	9.00	" 5	1	9	83	3.56	3.40
" 24	9	8	77	8.40	8.48	" 7	1	5	83	2.85	2.85
" 26	8	9	77.5	8.25	8.78	" 10	1	6	83	3.08	2.92
" 28	8	0	79	9.10	9.58	" 13	2	3	84	2.97	3.00
July 1	7	2	79.5	9.15	9.25						

The mean average of column A. is.......6.32 grains
" " " " " B. is.......6.30 "

"By repeated trials in the first week in July, by direct and careful comparison with distilled water, the specific gravity of the filtered river-water was found to be 1.000 25; consequently a pint of such water at 60° weighs 7297.404 grains. Thence by weight, the ratio of the sediment to the water is as 1 to 1158.3."

Mr. Brown made a series of measurements between the dates July 1, 1846, and June 30, 1848, upon the sedimentary matter transported by the Mississippi. The following extracts from his printed report exhibit the results of his labors:—

Those of Mr. Andrew Brown.

"A series of glass vessels of a cylindrical form were procured, to one end of which (that being the section of a cylinder) there was attached a tin tube of the same cylindrical diameter as that of the glass vessel to which it was attached; in this tin tube, immediately above its junction with the glass cylinder, there was inserted a small brass cock, by which the tin tube could be conveniently discharged of its contents at pleasure, without causing any disturbance to the contents of the glass vessel below; this attached tin tube was in length, above its lower opening, 48 inches.

"This tube was charged with water from the Mississippi river, and that water allowed time to deposit its contents into the glass vessel below; that being accomplished, the water was drawn off, and the tube recharged by more water from the river, each particular charge being carefully noted; this process was successively repeated for the different conditions and stages of the river's height and velocity, which very materially affected the quantity in suspension. Thus, by a succession of such chargings and dischargings of the tin tube, amounting in all to four hundred and eighty-four times, or, in the aggregate, to a column of water of 1936 feet, there was deposited a column of sediment or solid matter of 46½ inches (such column of sediment herein submitted), inclosed in three of the respective glass cylinders above named, and in which the same was deposited from the water in the attached tin tube. But this sediment still seems to evince some slight disposition for further settlement, and, with a knowledge of its former habits, we would say that it would be unsafe to decide on its final quantity being more than 44 inches; greater certainty would have been obtained by giving it another year; but, as the most of it has been long collected, it cannot now, we think, shrink to less than 44 inches. Assuming that, therefore, to be the true quantity, and the product of a column of river-water of 23,232 inches, it necessarily follows, that as 44 is to 23,232, so is the quantity of solid or sedimentary matter contained in the water to the volume of the river; or, in words and figures, the mean proportional quantity of sediment to the river is as 1 to 528."

* * * * * * * * *

"In collecting the test water from which the above 44 inches of sediment was obtained, much care was taken to procure it from that part of the current where it was sufficiently agitated to prevent, in any measure, a subsidence of such matter as should he held in suspension. It was fully decided, after many trials, that there was no sensible difference of quantity contained in any part of the water throughout its whole depth, or from the top to the bottom of the river, provided it was in the main current; for where agitation was equal and effective, there also the suspension of sedimentary matter was found to be equal.

"There can be no question but that much matter in the character of coarse sand and gravel is transported by the river current; of the quantity of this your committee could have no possible opportunity of estimating the value, or even ascertaining its existence, only that the many sand and gravel bars visible at low-water stages of the river are composed, to a considerable extent, of such matter, and they are subject to a perpetual change of position, and consequent tendency of their matter to the river's mouth."

* * * * * * * * *

"We found, in the incipient stages of the depositing process, a very decided want of uniformity to take place in the deposition of the sedimentary matter in the glass tube, which, in place of settling level, was, on the contrary, found to be settling in such a manner as to give it a very inclined upper surface. The cause of this unexpected peculiarity was inquired into, and at once suspected to proceed from the unequal distribution or action of light; one side of the tube being more disposed to that influence than the other. To verify this conjecture, the tube was turned round in an opposite direction to that influence, when the low side not only recovered itself, but very soon had an inclination upward; and, as often as the turning round was resorted to, the same effect was produced; for most sediment would persist in settling on the dark side of the tube, that being least agitated by the action of light. To render the cause of this phenomenon a fact no longer to be doubted, a slip of black paper was procured, in width about half the circumference of the glass cylinder, and to one side of which it was applied in order to exclude the light from that side, while it had free access to the other; the result was as anticipated, for it caused a very much increased deposit on the sides shaded by the paper.

"This variation, or inclined settling, progressively decreased as the lighter part of the tube, through which the particles had to fall, became shortened by its filling up with sediment."

These interesting observations as to the effect of light upon the deposition of sediment are certainly confirmatory of the conclusion already arrived at—that the density of the deposit from the same sample of river-water may vary materially, according to the circumstances under which it is deposited.

Lieutenant Marr's first sediment observations were continued during the months of April, May, and June, and a part of July, 1849. He thus reports the results:—

Those of Lieutenant Marr.

"The quantity of silt has been ascertained by daily placing a known quantity of river-water in a box, drawing off the water as it becomes clear, and weighing (when dried) the earth thus deposited. The average quantity of earth contained in 100 cubic feet of river-water is twelve and seven-tenths pounds."

The fraction representing the proportion, by weight, of the sediment to the water is $\frac{1}{596}$. This is certainly too large for a true yearly mean, on account of the turbid rise in the Missouri, which always occurs about this date. In 1856 the value for these months at Columbus was $\frac{1}{1266}$, while for the whole period of the observations, it was only $\frac{1}{1321}$. Had not a very unusual flood of comparatively pure water from the Ohio occurred, the difference between these fractions would have been much greater. (See preceding table of sediment at Columbus.)

Lieutenant Marr's second series of observations upon Mississippi sediment were continued from March 1, 1850, to March 1, 1851. The following extract from his report explains his method of taking them:—

Second series.

"A quantity of water has been daily obtained from the middle of the surface of the river, and two quarts of it placed in a barrel to settle. In bulk, the sediment thus obtained has been found to be in proportion to the water by which it was deposited as 1 to 2950."

The preceding observations are all that have been collected from which the proportion of sediment contained in Mississippi water may be determined. The following facts relative to European rivers are of value as affording a means of comparison.

Observations upon other rivers.

Measurements upon European and other rivers.—In the report of M. A. Surell upon the Improvement of the Mouths of the Rhone, it is stated that from the experiments made by a commission at Lyons in 1844, the quantity of earthy matter held in suspension by the Rhone at that point was, by weight, $\frac{1}{17000}$. From similar experiments made at Arles, the head of the delta of the Rhone, during four months in 1808 and 1809, by Messrs. Gorsse and Subours, the quantity of sedimentary matter held by the Rhone at that place was, by weight, $\frac{1}{7000}$ in the low stage of the river, and $\frac{1}{280}$ for the maximum in the floods, and $\frac{1}{2000}$ in the mean condition of the river. According to M. Surell's own researches, the quantity of earthy matter suspended by the waters of the Rhone, in its course through the delta, increases from the surface to the bottom, the proportions between the two being as 100 to 188.

The Rhone.

In certain circumstances (not mentioned) the proportionate quantity of earthy matter is not the same from the head of the delta to the mouths of the river.

The greatest floods do not contain the greatest quantities of earthy matter; the maximums observed in several periods corresponded to a mean stage of the river.

The greatest quantity ever observed was, by weight, $\frac{1}{45}$. It was found when the river was two-thirds up with a mean velocity of probably about 8 feet per second.

The mean was, by weight, $\frac{1}{2500}$, which, he states, should be regarded as a minimum.

The Po.

The Chevalier Lombardini, in his papers upon the Po, uses $\frac{1}{300}$ for the proportion by volume of earthy matter held in suspension by the Po; the determination of this proportion he credits to Tadini.

The Vistula.

M. Spittel states that in the Vistula the quantity of sedimentary matter is greatest just after the passage of the ice, when it is $\frac{1}{48}$ by volume, the mean velocity being about 10 feet per second. It is stated that the velocity in the thread of the current, at the height of the flood, is 20 feet per second in that part of the river just above the point of separation of the Nogat. Experiments to determine the mean amount have not been made—at least not published.

The Rhine.

The sedimentary matter carried by the Rhine in Holland during the flood, according to Hartsoeker, is by volume $\frac{1}{100}$.

According to experiments made by M. Leonard Horner at Bonn, the Rhine at that place, more than 100 miles above the head of the delta, carries $\frac{1}{16000}$ of its volume of sedimentary matter.

The Ganges.

Mr. Everest, who made a series of experiments upon the Ganges at Ghazipur, Bengal, found that the mean annual proportion of sedimentary matter transported by that river was about $\frac{1}{510}$ by weight, or $\frac{1}{1021}$ by volume, of that of the water. In the four flood months these numbers were $\frac{1}{428}$ and $\frac{1}{856}$ respectively.

Summary of results.—For convenience of reference, the different results above mentioned are recapitulated in the following table, the denominator of the fraction whose numerator is unity being given.

Proportion of sediment in river-water.

River.	Authority.	Water to sediment.		Measurements made.
		By weight.	By bulk.	
Mississippi at Carrollton	Mississippi Delta Survey	1,808	3,435*	For 12 months, 1851–52.
" Carrollton	Mississippi Delta Survey	1,449	2,753*	For 12 months, 1852–53.
" Columbus	Mississippi Delta Survey	1,321	2,510*	For 9 months, 1858.
" the mouths	Mr. Meade	1,256	2,386*	For 2 months, 1838.
" "	Mr. Sidell	1,724	3,276*	1838.
" various places	Professor Riddell	1,245	2,366*	For 14 days, summer 1843.
" New Orleans	Professor Riddell	1,155	3,000	For 35 days, summer 1846.
" Natchez	Mr. Brown	....	528	At irregular dates, 1846–48.
" Memphis	Lieutenant Marr	596	1,132*	For 3.5 flood-months, 1849.
" Memphis	Lieutenant Marr	....	2,950	For 12 months, 1850–51.
Rhone at Lyons	M. Surell	17,000		1844.
" Arles	MM. Gorsse and Subours	2,000		For 4 months, 1808–9.
" in delta	M. Surell	2,500		
Po	M. Tadini	....	300	
Ganges	Mr. Everest	510	1,021	For 12 months.

Conclusions respecting proportion of sedimentary matter.

A comparison of these different results leads to the belief that no material error will result from assuming that the sediment of the Mississippi is to the water, by weight, nearly as 1 to 1500, and by bulk, nearly as 1 to 2900; provided long periods of time be considered.

* Computed by assuming the specific gravity to be 1.9, which, as already shown, is nearly that of the natural deposits of the Mississippi river.

If this be so, and if the mean annual discharge of the Mississippi be correctly assumed at 19 500 000 000 000 cubic feet, it follows that 812 500 000 000 pounds of sedimentary matter, constituting one square mile of deposit 241 feet in depth, are yearly transported in a state of suspension into the gulf.

Annual amount transported to the gulf.

When the Mississippi swamp lands are securely protected against overflow, the earthy matter, which, in their original condition, was annually deposited upon them, will be carried to the gulf, and the yearly depositions in it will be thus increased. The amount of this increase can be approximately estimated by the aid of certain numbers deduced in a subsequent part of this report. Thus, the discharge into any one of the great swamps, the Yazoo for example, during the mean annual flood, may be taken at 100,000 cubic feet per second during a period of one month. As there are four of these great swamps, a simple calculation gives for the additional amount of sedimentary matter that will be carried to the gulf, one-eighteenth of that transported to it before the construction of levees.

Besides the amount held in suspension, the Mississippi pushes along into the gulf large quantities of earthy matter.

Observations upon material rolling along the bottom of the river.

The well-known fact that rivers in their upper courses transport gravel and sand, and the experiments of Dubuat upon the velocities required to move various materials composing the beds of rivers, and the rate at which fine sand was pushed along the bed of the river Hayne, together with some experiments by Mr. George G. Meade, now Captain Topographical Engineers, on the bar of the Southwest pass in 1838, to ascertain the nature of the earthy matter suspended by the river near the bottom, led to the attempt in 1851 to ascertain by experiment whether any material was pushed along the bottom of the Mississippi in its lower trunk, and what the nature of that material was. The first experiment was made near the mouth of Red river, and the facts elicited by it induced the direction to the Carrollton party to include these experiments in its regular duty, and, subsequently, to comprise this subject among those to be investigated at the mouth of the river. A keg similar to that used in collecting water below the surface was sunk to the bottom of the river. The current immediately overturned it, and the valves opening allowed the water to pass freely through. After remaining a few minutes it was drawn suddenly up, and was invariably found to contain material such as gravel, sand, and earthy matter. These experiments were made at various stations from Red-river landing to Carrollton. At Red-river landing the material was chiefly small gravel and coarse sand. At Morganza coarse sand and small balls of blue clay. At Fausse Rivière (Waterloo) coarse sand. At Carrollton these experiments were frequently repeated at all stages of the river, and always with the same result, chiefly sand and earthy matter being collected.

No exact measurement of the amount of the annual contributions to the gulf from this source can be made, but from the yearly rate of progress of the bars into the gulf (see Chapter VIII), it appears to be about 750,000,000 cubic feet, which would cover a square mile about 27 feet deep.

Total annual contributions of the river to the gulf.

The total yearly contributions from the river to the gulf amount then to a prism 268 feet in height, with a base of one square mile.

To determine the age of the delta from such data, the extent of the area upon which the sedimentary matter is deposited, and the depth below the surface of the former bottom of the gulf, must be known. Neither has been ascertained with sufficient accuracy to make the computation of any value.

TEMPERATURE.

Measurements.

Measurements to ascertain the relative temperature (Fahr.) of the air and water were conducted daily for two years at Carrollton. The air temperature has been determined by taking a mean of observations made at 6 A.M., 3 P.M., and 9 P.M., which very nearly represents the mean for the twenty-four hours.

Air and water temperature at Carrollton.

Week.	1851.		1852.		Week.	1851–52.		1852–53.	
	Air.	Water.	Air.	Water.		Air.	Water.	Air.	Water.
	°	°	°	°		°	°	°	°
3d in February	62	44	62	44	4th in August	81	85	82	84
4th "	63	45	63	45	5th "	80	83	82	84
1st in March	66	48	66	48	1st in September	81	82	80	83
2d "	69	48	65	50	2d "	78	82	78	83
3d "	69	51	57	51	3d "	76	82	78	82
4th "	69	56	71	54	4th "	73	81	80	81
1st in April	70	59	66	55	1st in October	75	78	77	79
2d "	69	62	67	57	2d "	70	75	75	78
3d "	68	64	65	58	3d "	62	72	72	75
4th "	65	63	65	56	4th "	64	69	74	73
1st in May	72	63	74	58	1st in November	66	65	68	70
2d "	74	64	72	61	2d "	55	62	70	68
3d "	81	67	76	65	3d "	62	59	62	63
4th "	79	72	78	68	4th "	56	57	58	65
5th "	78	76	76	72	5th "	51	54	59	51
1st in June	79	79	78	73	1st in December	50	51	61	49
2d "	81	79	77	75	2d "	60	48	59	48
3d "	77	79	81	77	3d "	41	45	64	48
4th "	79	78	82	79	4th "	58	43	67	49
1st in July	81	79	82	80	1st in January	54	44	54	48
2d "	85	80	82	81	2d "	47	46	56	46
3d "	84	80	79	83	3d "	39	42	50	45
4th "	81	81	80	84	4th "	37	37	49	43
1st in August	82	83	84	86	5th "	52	35	52	43
2d "	80	82	82	86	1st in February	57	38	56	44
3d "	83	84	79	85	2d "	52	43	57	43

Results.

From this table it appears that the mean annual temperature of the river-water for the first and second years was 63.9° and 64.3° Fahr., the corresponding air temperatures being 67.6° and 69.8°. That is, the mean temperature of the river-water at this point of its course is about 4.5 degrees colder than that of the atmosphere. To illustrate the relative changes of temperature in air and water at different seasons of the year, a small diagram has been added to plate XII. The curves represent the mean of the two years' observations given in the above table. They show that the changes of temperature in the water are much more uniform and gradual than the corresponding changes in the atmosphere, and also that they occur later. The water is warmest in the latter part of August, and coldest in the latter part of January, the difference between these extremes of mean weekly temperature being 46 degrees. The corresponding difference in air temperature is only about 40 degrees, the mean weekly temperature of the water reaching greater extremes, both of heat and of cold, than that of the air.

These observations being rather of scientific interest than of practical value, were not repeated when field work was resumed in 1857, lest they might interfere with more important duties. A similar series was conducted, however, by Lieutenant Marr, U. S. N., at Memphis, between March 1, 1850, and February 28, 1851, with the following results: "The mean temperature of the river is 60.95°; that of the atmosphere, 60.44°. I expected to find the former the lower, as the river flows from more northern latitudes. Wolf river, which runs along the same parallel of latitude, and enters the Mississippi at this place, has a greater temperature than the Mississippi. From this it seems that the mean temperature of each of these rivers is greater than that of the atmosphere about them. The gradual manner in which the temperature of the Mississippi river is affected by local changes in the temperature of the atmosphere, suggests the idea that it may be regarded as an index of the mean temperature of the climates through which the river flows. The difference between the temperature of the water at the surface and at the bottom of the river is usually so slight as not to be observable with the common thermometer. Occasionally I have found a difference of a small fraction of a degree."

Lieut. Marr's observations.

These measurements, in connection with those of this Survey, indicate that the mean temperature of the Mississippi water increases 3° Fahrenheit in traversing the 750 miles of river channel between Memphis and Carrollton. The corresponding difference of mean annual temperature of the atmosphere is about 8° Fahrenheit.

General deductions.

LEVEES.

It is designed to limit the discussion of this subject in this chapter to the history of the progress of the levees in the Mississippi valley; the present general organizations for the maintenance of the levee system in the different States; and, lastly, the dimensions and cost of the existing levees. In Chapter VI the subject will be continued, and the dimensions required to effectually protect the country, the dangers of the system, etc. will be fully considered.

Scope of the present discussion.

History of the progress of the levees in the Mississippi valley.—As already seen, by far the greater and more fertile portion of the natural banks of the Mississippi river between Cape Girardeau and the gulf is below the level of the floods. Since this condition has existed from a period long anterior to the discovery of the country, the first object of the settler has always been to secure himself from inundation during the high stages of the river. Throughout the entire region the levee system has been adopted for this purpose, to the exclusion of every other except that of cut-offs, which has been partially tried in a very few instances for local objects. The history of the levees is, therefore, intimately connected with that of the settlement of the country.

Levee system coextensive with civilization below the mouth of the Ohio.

First settlements of the country.

The first permanent settlements by Europeans in the valley of the lower Mississippi were made at Natchez and at the present site of New Orleans. At Natchez the bluffs were occupied, but at New Orleans precautions had to be at once taken to protect the colony from inundation.

Levees in 1717.

According to Dumont, De la Tour, the engineer who laid out the city of New Orleans in 1717, directed "a dyke or levee to be raised in front, the more effectually to preserve the city from overflow." Although this work was so early contemplated, it was not completed until November, 1727, when Governor Perrier announced that the New Orleans levee was finished, it being 5400 feet in length, and 18 feet wide on the top. He added that within a year a levee would be constructed for 18 miles above and below the city, which, though not so strong as that at the city, "would answer the purpose of preventing overflows."

In 1723.

In the mean time, colonists continued to arrive slowly and occupy the land along the river banks, so that in 1723, according to Francios Xavier Martin, "the only settlements then began below the Natchez were those of St. Reine and Madame de Mezieres, a little below Point Coupée—that of Diron d'Artaguette, at Baton Rouge—that of Paris, near bayou Manchac—that of the Marquis d'Anconio, below Lafourche—that of the Marquis d'Artagnac, at *Cannes Brulées*—that of de Meuse, a little below, and a plantation of three brothers of the name of Chauvin, lately from Canada, at the Tchapitoulas."

In 1728.

In 1728 Dumont says there were five colonies "extending for 30 miles above New Orleans, who were obliged to construct levees of earth for their protection." The expense of constructing these embankments was borne by the planters, each building a levee the length of his river front.

In 1735.

In 1731 the Mississippi company gave up the colony to the French crown. In 1735 Du Pratz states that "the levees extended from English bend, 12 miles below, to 30 miles above and on both sides of the river." The same year, the insufficiency of the works was demonstrated, as "the water was very high, and the levee broke in many places." It is certain that this difficulty continued to be felt, for in 1743, according to Gayarré, "an ordinance was promulgated requiring the inhabitants to complete their levees by the 1st of January, 1744, under a penalty of forfeiture of their lands to the crown."

In 1752.

According to Monette, in 1752 the plantations extended "20 miles below, and 30 miles above New Orleans," and in that distance "nearly the whole coast was in a high state of cultivation, and securely protected from floods."

In 1770.

Captain Philip Pittman, who published a work in 1770, defines the settlements at that date as extending only "30 miles above, and 20 miles below New Orleans." In other words, the inhabitants for twenty years had been devoting themselves to the cultivation and improvement of those districts already partially reclaimed, instead of trying to extend the levees farther along the bank. The wars between England and France, the cession by the latter power of all her territory on the Mississippi to Spain in 1763, and the impolitic course pursued by the Spanish governors, doubtless contributed to retard the growth of the colony at that epoch. It also appears to have been supposed that the settlements could not be extended farther down the river, "on account of the immense expense attending the levees necessary to protect the fields from the inundations of sea and land floods," which would render it advisable to defer the settlement of that section of the country "until the land shall be raised by the accession of soil." (Francios Xavier Martin.)

In the year 1800 the territory was ceded back to France, Napoleon being then First Consul. In 1803 it was ceded to the United States. Its condition may be inferred from the following extracts from the Abstract of Documents of the State Department and of the Treasury, 1802–5:— **In 1805.**

"The principal settlements in Louisiana are on the Mississippi river, which begins to be cultivated about twenty (20) leagues from the sea. Ascending, you see them improve on each side till you reach the city [New Orleans]. Except on the point just below Iberville, the country from New Orleans is settled the whole way."

"Above Baton Rouge, at the distance of 50 leagues from New Orleans and on the west side of the Mississippi, is Pointe Coupée, a populous and rich settlement, extending 8 leagues along the river. Behind it, on an old bed of the river now a lake whose outlets are closed up, is the settlement of Fausse Rivière."

"There is no other settlement on the Mississippi except the small one called Concord, opposite Natchez, till you come to the Arkansas river, 250 leagues above New Orleans. Here is a small settlement. There is no other settlement from this place to New Madrid."

"On both banks of this creek [bayou La Fourche] there are settlements one plantation deep for near 15 leagues."

"Bayou Plaquemine, 32 leagues above New Orleans, is the principal and swiftest communication to the rich and populous settlement of Atacapas and Opelousas."

Louisiana was admitted to the Federal Union in 1812. Stoddard, in his history of Louisiana, published in that year, states: "These banks [levees] extend on both sides of the river, from the lowest settlements to Point Coupée on one side, and to the neighborhood of Baton Rouge on the other, except where the country remains unoccupied." **In 1812.**

"Few settlements are formed on the west bank of the Mississippi between the Red and Arkansas rivers. They are thinly scattered along from Red river to the mouth of the Yazoo."

Brackenridge states: "From Pointe Coupée to La Fourche, two-thirds of the banks are perfectly cleared, and from thence to New Orleans the settlements continue without interruption on both sides, and present the appearance of a continued village."

In 1828 the levees were continuous from New Orleans nearly to Red-river landing, excepting above Baton Rouge on the left bank, where the bluffs rendered them unnecessary. Above Red river they were in a very disconnected and unfinished state on the right bank as far as Napoleon. Elsewhere in the alluvial region their extent was so limited as to make it unnecessary to mention them. **In 1828.**

In 1844 the levees had been made nearly continuous from New Orleans to Napoleon on the right bank, and many isolated levees existed along the lower part of the Yazoo front. Above Napoleon, few or none had yet been attempted. **In 1844.**

In September, 1850, a great impulse was given to the work of reclaiming the allu-

Donation by the Federal Government in 1850. vial region below the mouth of the Ohio by the Federal Government, which, by an act approved September 28, 1850, granted to the several States all swamp and overflowed lands within their limits remaining unsold, in order to provide a fund to reclaim the districts liable to inundation. The States of Louisiana, Mississippi, Arkansas, and Missouri soon organized offices for the sale of the swamp lands, and appointed commissioners for the location and construction of the levees. The systems adopted were generally faulty, and have undergone many modifications. Those now in force will be explained under the next subdivision of this subject.

Condition of levees in 1858. Careful examinations and inquiries made by parties of the Delta Survey, in the autumn of 1857 and the winter of 1858, resulted in the following exhibit of the actual condition of the levees at that date. Each bank of the river will be noticed in turn.

On the right bank. Beginning at the head of the alluvial region, on the right bank the inlet between Cape Girardeau and Commerce bluffs was closed by a macadamized road, some 4 feet high, which crossed the low ground about 2.5 miles from the river bank. From Commerce bluffs to a sandy ridge above overflow near Dog-tooth bend, the levees were nearly completed. Thence, they were finished to a point 6 miles below Cairo. Here was a gap of 3 miles, but upon land so elevated as to be overflowed only in the highest floods. Next was a strip of high land above overflow, 3 miles in extent. Next came 8.5 miles of completed levee; next 0.5 of a mile of high land above overflow. This point is about 5 miles above Hickman. Thence to bayou St. John, there was a continuous levee. Thence to Point Pleasant, the land is entirely above overflow. Thence to the northern boundary of Arkansas, the levees were nearly completed. Between the northern boundary of Arkansas and Osceola, there were about 2.5 miles of unfinished levees. In the bend below Osceola was a gap, 1.5 miles long. Opposite Island 34 was another, 1.5 miles long. Between Islands 36 and 37 was another, 2.5 miles long. At foot of Island 37 was another, 4 miles long. At foot of Island 39 was another, 1.5 miles long. At foot of Island 41 was another, 0.3 of a mile long. Six miles below Memphis was another, 1.5 miles long. In Council bend, near Island 53, was another, 3 miles long. In Walnut bend, near Island 56, was another, 1 mile long. The above list includes the whole St. Francis bottom. By summing up the different gaps, it will be found that they were about 25 miles in length. It would be a great error to imagine that the bottom was securely leveed with the exception of these breaks. The levees had all been made since the flood of 1851, and consequently had never been tested. They were much too low, hardly averaging 3 feet in height, although some of them, across old bayous, were of enormous size, as, for instance, a short one near the northern boundary of Crittenden county, which was reported to be 40 feet high, 40 feet wide at top and 320 feet wide at bottom. Generally their cross-section was much too small, and, upon the whole, they were quite inadequate to effect the object for which they were intended.

From the mouth of St. Francis river to Old Town, the levees were complete. Between this place and Scrub-grass bayou, there were several gaps, amounting to about 14 miles. Thence to Napoleon there were no levees. Between Napoleon and the high land, south of Cypress creek, there were only about 3 miles of levee. Thence nearly to Point La Hache, below New Orleans, the embankments were completed.

On the left bank, excepting a few unimportant private levees, there were no artificial embankments between the mouth of the Ohio and the southern boundary of Tennessee. The near approach of the hills to the river, throughout the greater part of this region, has the effect of flooding by hill drainage the narrow belts of swamp land, and there is no immediate prospect of any attempt to reclaim them. Whether leveed or not, they are too trifling in extent to have any sensible influence upon the high-water level of the Mississippi river.

On the left bank.

The Yazoo bottom below the Mississippi State boundary was considered to be well protected by levees. They, however, averaged only about 4 feet in height, and, having been mainly constructed since 1853, had never been tested by a great flood. They were much too low and too narrow, as the flood of 1858 proved. The levee which closed the Yazoo pass was an enormous embankment across an old lake. It was 1152 feet long, and 28 feet high, with a base spread out to the width of 300 feet. About 10 miles of gaps in Coahoma and Tunica counties (between Islands 51 and 67) had been closed in the winter of 1858, and consequently the levees had not had time to settle properly before the occurrence of the high water. There was only one open gap. It was nearly opposite Helena, and had been caused by a caving bank.

Between Vicksburg and Baton Rouge, on the left bank, the levees were complete where there was any occasion for them. The hills approach so near to the river in this part of its course, that the bottom lands are limited in extent, and hence somewhat liable to injury from sudden upland drainage.

From Baton Rouge nearly to Point La Hache, the whole river-coast was leveed.

Levee organization in the different States.—It is important that it should be understood, that much of the want of success attending the efforts to secure the alluvial lands from overflow has arisen not from inherent difficulties in the construction of works of protection, but from the adoption of systems which have allowed one district to be submerged in consequence of the insufficient character or faulty execution of the laws of another, or left it to be protected by taxes levied upon another. For this reason a general outline of the existing levee organization in the different States will be given.

Reason for treating of this subject.

The laws regulating the maintenance of the levees in Louisiana mark the gradual progress of the system. They are involved, and very unlike in different parts of the State. Premising that the "Police Jury" of each parish is an elective body, which has the general control of the affairs of that parish, the following extracts from the Revised Statutes (1856) exhibit the most important features of the complex levee organization of the State.

Levee laws of Louisiana.

"SECTION 1. The Police Juries of all the parishes of this State are authorized to pass all such ordinances as they may deem necessary, relative to roads and levees, bridges and ditches; and to impose such fines and penalties to enforce the same as they may judge proper and expedient, to be recovered and enforced by indictment or information."

General laws.

"SEC. 5. Throughout all that portion of the State, watered by the Mississippi and

Laws applicable to all of the parishes except Concordia, Washita, Pointe Coupee, West Baton Rouge, Iberville, Plaquemines, and St. Bernard.

the bayous running to and from the same, which are settled, where levees are necessary to confine the waters, and to protect the inhabitants against inundation, the said levees shall be made by the riparian proprietors, in the proportions and at the time hereinafter prescribed."

"SEC. 18. The Police Jury of every parish of this State where levees are necessary to protect the inhabitants against inundations, shall meet once in every year, for the purpose of proceeding to the appointment by ballot of such number of Inspectors as shall be deemed necessary, in such a manner, however, that no Inspector shall be charged with the inspection of the roads and levees to a greater extent than three leagues."

"SEC. 20. It shall be the duty of the Inspector to make every week, at least during high water, one inspection of the roads and levees subject to his inspection, and to ascertain whether the obligations imposed upon the riparian proprietors have been complied with. * * * * * * * *

"SEC. 21. * * * * * * * *

"The Inspector shall provide all the means which he shall deem expedient, in order that the repairs be made in time; and for that purpose he shall be authorized to furnish the proprietors, on urgent necessity, with any number of slaves he may deem necessary, not only from his own section, but also from the other sections of the parish situate on the same side of the river. * * * * * * *

"SEC. 22. The Road and Levee Inspectors are hereby empowered within the several parishes to call out to work on the levees therein, in case of a crevasse or threatened crevasse, all the male slaves above the age of fifteen years and under sixty, or so many thereof as may be deemed necessary, whose owners reside on the same side of the river or bayou within seven miles of the threatened danger; except persons on high lands, that is, lands not alluvial."

* * * * * * * *

"SEC. 27. If any Inspector of Roads and Levees shall not cause the levees in his district to be repaired or made anew by the first of November of each year, it shall be the duty of the other Inspectors appointed for the same parish and on the same side of the river, to cause the repairs or new levees to be made; and for these purposes they are invested with all the powers vested in the Inspector of the respective districts, and subjected to the same penalties for omissions. If there are no other Inspectors in the parish, on the same side of the river, or if they are absent, or do not act, any planter of the parish, on the same side of the river, may notify the President of the Police Jury that he undertakes to act as Inspector; and by the fact of giving such notice, he shall be invested with all the powers vested in Inspectors of Roads and Levees."

"SEC. 29. Every proprietor whose levee has been broken by his own neglect, shall be liable for all damages and losses caused thereby, agreeably to articles two thousand two hundred and ninety-four and two thousand two hundred and ninety-five of the Civil Code."

"SEC. 43. Where there exist levees, the making and repairs of which devolve upon the parishes, all the Inspectors of such parishes shall join to cause the same to be made or repaired by proportional requisition of slaves, on the proprietors within their respective sections."

"SEC. 50. The alluvial lands of the parishes of Carroll, Madison, and Catahoula shall be constituted a levee district."

Laws constituting a levee district of three parishes.

"SEC. 51. For the purpose of building or making and repairing all levees in the said levee district, an annual tax of 300 per cent. on the State mill tax, shall be levied in the parishes of Madison and Carroll, according to the State assessment roll of each year. No tax for that purpose shall be levied in the parish of Catahoula."

"SEC. 56. The levee tax shall be a common levee fund, to be applied to making and repairing all levees in the levee district."

"SEC. 57. There shall be elected in each of said parishes, by the qualified voters of said levee district, three Commissioners, who shall be styled and shall constitute a 'Board of Levee Commissioners.'

"SEC. 58. The first election of Commissioners shall be held on the first Monday in November, 1855, and biennially thereafter."

"SEC. 61. No person shall vote in the election of said Commissioners who is not a qualified voter under the Constitution and Laws of the State, and who does not reside on the alluvial lands in the said levee district: *Provided*, no person shall be denied the privilege of voting who may live on the hill lands but cultivate alluvial lands."

"SEC. 62. The Board of Commissioners shall be sole judges of the election and qualifications of its members, and shall have power to prescribe all rules and regulations necessary for determining the same."

"SEC. 63. They shall have power and authority to select their Treasurer, their several Inspectors, Engineer, and all other officers appointed by them; to fix the time for which they shall be appointed or elected, the causes of removal, the amount of the bonds to be given, and all other acts necessary to carry into effect the provisions of this law."

"SEC. 69. It shall be their duty to lay off levee wards on the Mississippi river, or any other river or bayou in said levee district; to appoint Levee Inspectors for each of said wards; to prescribe their duties, and the penalties for neglect thereof; and they are further empowered to employ an Engineer for said levee district, if deemed necessary."

"SEC. 72. It shall be their duty, at their meetings on the first Monday of May of each year, to order the levees at the most important points in each of said parishes of Madison and Carroll, to be repaired or built."

"SEC. 75. It shall be the duty of each of the Inspectors to let out, to the lowest bidder, the building or repairing of the levees in their respective wards, after public notice thereof having been given, by publication in some newspaper published in the parish in which the levee shall be built or repaired, for thirty days."

"SEC. 77. They shall always require the levees to be completed by the first day of February in each year."

"SEC. 79. They shall have full authority, within their respective wards, to call out to work on the levees, during high water, all the male slaves above the age of fifteen and under sixty, or so many thereof as may be deemed necessary." * *

"SEC. 84. The Police Jury of the parish of Tensas shall divide the parish into five

Parish of Tensas. districts, to be called levee wards, giving the metes and bounds of each, and shall cause a map or plat of the same to be made and kept in the Police Clerk's office, as the property of the parish, for reference."

"SEC. 85. They shall annually appoint a Levee Inspector or Engineer for the parish, to continue in office until a successor be appointed." * * * *

"SEC. 86. They shall annually appoint, in each levee ward, two Commissioners, whose duty it shall be to act in conjunction with the Inspector, in laying off new levees in their respective wards, and to assist him at other times, when he may deem it necessary; in case of absence or resignation of the Inspector, they shall perform all the duties belonging to the Inspector, until a successor be appointed, or until the Inspector shall return to the performance of his duties."

"SEC. 87. It shall be the duty of the Levee Inspector or Engineer to direct and superintend the construction and repairs of all levees in the parish in accordance with the requisition of the Police Jury." * * * * * *

"SEC. 90. The Police Jury are authorized to levy and collect, in the same manner that the State and parish taxes are now collected, an annual tax upon the assessed value of real estate as returned by the Assessors of State taxes. Said tax, when collected, shall form a special fund for levee purposes alone."

"SEC. 107. The Police Jury of the parish of Rapides are authorized to lay off their parish into levee districts; and with the consent of a majority of the inhabitants of said districts owning lands therein, to lay a tax upon all lands within the several districts which were overflowed in the year eighteen hundred and forty-nine, for the purpose of making levees on Red river, within the parish, and constructing such embankments as they may consider necessary across all bayous connecting with the river; and for the purpose also of creating and maintaining the permanent levee fund hereinafter mentioned.

Parish of Rapides.

"The Police Jury, in levying said tax, shall discriminate equitably between the front and back lands, so that they may be taxed as nearly as possible in proportion to the benefit to be derived by them respectively from levees, the tax so levied by the Police Jury on the front and back lands to be binding on both.

"SEC. 108. The Police Jury shall appoint annually on the first Monday of June, three Levee Commissioners for each district, whose duty it shall be to locate the levees and embankments within their respective districts, and to let out contracts for constructing the same; which contracts shall be let out to the lowest bidder. * *

"SEC. 109. The Police Jury shall also appoint annually at the same time one or more Levee Syndics in each district, whose duty it shall be to cause to be made all needful repairs or additions to the levees within their respective districts." * *

Parish of Catahoula.

"SEC. 115. The Police Jury of the parish of Catahoula shall have full and unlimited power to establish levee wards within its limits, and enforce the construction of levees therein."

"SEC. 116. They shall have power to cause, with a previous notice of thirty days, the election in each levee ward by the qualified voters thereof, of three Levee Commissioners, who shall choose one Inspector; the term of office, duties and qualifications of the Commissioners and Inspector to be prescribed by the Police Jury.

"SEC. 117. They shall have power also to levy and enforce the collection of such taxes as may be deemed necessary in any ward, for the construction of levees therein; the fund so raised to be expended upon the levees in the ward wherein the same is collected."

"SEC. 118. The Police Juries of the parishes of Concordia and Ouachita shall have plenary and unlimited power to make such enactments with regard to roads and levees within their respective limits as may be deemed necessary and proper by those bodies, including the power to authorize the assessment and collection of any taxes which they may deem necessary on the private land claims within any levee district established by them, to cover the expenses of leveeing any public land included in such district or other necessary work or expense authorized by any ordinance of said juries respectively."

Parishes of Concordia and Washita.

"SEC. 127. It shall be the study of the Police Jury of the parish of Pointe Coupée to levy an annual tax, not to exceed the one-half of a mill on a dollar on the estimated value of all the property subject to taxation not otherwise hereinafter provided for in said parish, which tax shall be collected by the Collector of the Parish Taxes in the same manner and form that the parish tax is now collected; and shall form a special and distinct fund in the parish treasury for the repairs or making of roads and levees; and the Parish Treasurer shall keep a separate and distinct account of all taxes so collected."

Parish of Pointe Coupée.

The fund derived from the sales of land granted by Congress for aiding in constructing the levees and drains necessary to reclaim the swamp land is subject to an especial set of State laws, independent of parish organization. Since the Revised Statutes were published in 1856, a change in the organization for controlling this fund has been made by abolishing the "Board of Swamp-land Commissioners," and replacing it by the "Board of Public Works," which now has charge of all the public works of the State. The law relating to the swamp-land fund declares that it shall not be employed in the reconstruction or repair of levees now existing, it being the intention to expend the money in supplying the deficiencies in the present system. If, however, a levee shall be destroyed by the action of the current, one-half the cost of repairing it shall be paid from the fund; the other half being borne by the riparian proprietors.

Disposition of the swamp-land fund received from Congress.

The present levee organization in the State of Mississippi is based upon a law passed by the legislature in November, 1858. It went into practical execution in June, 1859. The following extracts from the law sufficiently explain the general system; it being understood that a "Board of Police" is an elective body which controls the affairs of a county:—

Levee laws of the State of Mississippi.

"SEC. 8. *Be it further enacted*, That it shall be the duty of the Board of Police of the several counties of De Soto, Tunica, Coahoma, Bolivar, Washington, Issaquena, Yazoo, Sunflower, Tallahatchie, and Panola, to meet at the Court-house of their respective counties on the first Monday in February, 1859, and then and there to elect a citizen of their respective counties to serve as a Levee Commissioner for three years from that time."

Board of Levee Commissioners—their powers and duties.

* * * * * * * * * *

"SEC. 9. *Be it further enacted*, That it shall be the duty of such persons so elected Levee Commissioners for said counties, to assemble together, on or before the first Monday in March thereafter, in the town of Prentiss, in the county of Bolivar, in this State, and when assembled, to elect one of their number, or some freeholder in the district, as President of said body; said President and said Levee Commissioners shall be a body politic, to be styled the Levee Commissioners, and in that name may sue and be sued, contract and be contracted with. The President of said board shall keep his office in the said town of Prentiss, and service of process on the President shall be notice sufficient to bring the corporation into court. Should said board elect one of their own members President, then the Board of Police of the proper county shall fill the vacancy occasioned by said election, by a special election, made at such time as they may see proper."

"SEC. 12. *Be it further enacted,* That said Board of Levee Commissioners shall hold their regular meetings at the town of Prentiss on the second Mondays of April and October, of each year, and at such other times as they may appoint, and as often as they may be called together by the President on ten days' notice of the time of meeting." * * * * * * * * * * * *

"SEC. 13. *Be it further enacted,* That it shall be the duty of the Board of Levee Commissioners to expend all moneys they may receive as general funds, under this or any other act, in re-building, strengthening, or elevating the old levee, or in making new embankments, when they may regard such to be necessary, through the counties fronting the Mississippi river and within their district. * * * * * * Said Board of Levee Commissioners shall have all the power of a body corporate to carry out the objects of its creation. They shall have power to pass all necessary by-laws and ordinances as they may regard proper for their own government or for the government of the work under their charge, as well as for the protection of the same. They shall have power to employ all engineers or agents necessary to the work, and do all other acts not inconsistent with this law, nor in violation of the laws of this State. They shall determine the base, height, slope and elevation of the levee—may abandon any portion of the old levee that they may regard as unsafe or improperly built, and may build new works, and repair old on such ground as they may select, and make all needful regulations necessary in their opinion to secure the counties under their charge from overflow by the Mississippi river."

Additional tax.

"SEC. 21. *Be it further enacted,* That in addition to the levee tax assessed in the first section of this act, the Boards of Police in the counties of Tunica, Coahoma, Bolivar, Washington, and Issaquena, shall have power to assess a tax, annually, on all the lands within their respective counties, subject to tax, under the provisions of this act, not exceeding twenty-five cents per acre, to be used under the direction of such persons as said Board of Police may respectively appoint, for re-building old, or erecting new levees; said tax to be assessed and collected after the form now provided in the local laws of such counties, and the same shall not become a portion of the general fund, nor be subject to the control of the General Board, further than the Boards of Police for the counties respectively shall allow, but shall be a specific fund for the use of the county in which the same shall be collected."

By-laws of the Board of Levee Commissioners.

The following extracts from the by-laws of the Board of Levee Commissioners are sufficient to indicate the practical system of constructing and protecting the levees adopted by them:—

"An Engineer in Chief shall be elected by the Board on nomination by the President, and in case of a vacancy during a recess of the Board, the President may appoint a successor *ad interim*. Upon a failure or refusal of the Board to confirm the nomination of Chief Engineer by the President, any member of the Board may nominate."

Chief Engineer; his duties.

"During the recess extending from April to October, 1859, the Chief Engineer shall appoint his own assistants, the number to be determined by the President; but at the regular meeting in October, 1859, and at every regular meeting thereafter, the Board shall elect Assistant Engineers on nomination by the Chief Engineer."

"He shall make such surveys on the line of work, with such plans and specifications, maps and reports connected therewith, as the President shall require of him, and shall keep a record-copy of the same as the property of his department."

"Besides the report and chart of his general survey, he shall make a report to the President, to be by him laid before the Board at each regular meeting, showing the number and extent of his local surveys and all other operations of his department during the current recess, and shall make such recommendations as he may deem important and within the scope of the duties of his department."

"Instruments, stationery, and camp equipage required for the use of his department, together with the wages of chainmen, rodmen, and laborers necessary to the field service shall be charged to the Board, and paid for by the Treasurer on the order of the President, accompanied by the accounts with his approval endorsed thereon."

"The Chief Engineer may be removed at any regular or called meeting of the Board, on motion, two-thirds of the members present concurring."

"Each river county shall be divided into Inspectors' Districts, to wit: one in De Soto, three in Tunica, three in Coahoma, four in Bolivar, four in Washington, and three in Issaquena, and an Inspector for each district shall be elected by the Board on nomination by the Commissioners of the front counties—each of said Commissioners nominating the Inspectors for his own county."

Inspectors; their duties.

"It shall be the duty of every Inspector to make immediate report to the President of all instances falling within his knowledge or belief of wilful damage to the levee, or other violation of the Levee Laws; and once in every week he shall inspect all the levee work going on in his district, and report the progress of the same to the County Commissioner, to be by the latter reported when necessary to the President."

"Each Inspector shall also be charged with the general supervision of the permanent laborers employed on the levee in his district, and shall report to the President all instances of misbehavior or neglect of duty on their part, without additional charge on the levee fund."

In Arkansas, immediately after the passage by Congress in 1850 of the law donating the swamp-land to the State, an act was passed organizing a "board of Swamp-land Commissioners" to fix the price of the overflowed lands, to district the State, to determine upon the necessary levees and drains, and to let out the contracts to the lowest and best bidders. This board was abolished in December, 1856. The following extracts from an act approved in January, 1857, exhibit the present system. There are seven swamp-land districts.

Levee laws of the State of Arkansas.

"SECTION 1. *Be it enacted by the General Assembly of the State of Arkansas,* That in order to close up the gaps in levees on the rivers Mississippi, and so much of the Arkansas as is embraced in the Helena district, as established by the act to which this is supplemental, it shall be lawful for any engineer, under instructions from the Governor, to let out contracts for the construction of such levees to close up such gaps: *Provided,* that each contract which shall be made for the performance of any of such work, shall expressly state that the work will only be paid for in specie, which shall be obtained by the sales of swamp and overflowed lands, situated within the limits of the district in which said work is required." *

Mississippi and Arkansas rivers, how to be leveed.

"SEC. 4. That the Governor be and he is hereby authorized to appoint, from time to time, a swamp-land secretary, who shall hold his office during the pleasure of the Governor, not to exceed a term of two years, or until his successor shall be qualified.

Swamp-land secretary; his duties.

* * * * * * * * * *

"SEC. 5. That said Secretary shall have charge of all the books, maps, records, papers, contracts, and all the furniture and property, of every description or nature which appertains to the office of the former swamp-land commissioners, or to the office of the secretary of such commissioners, as well as other papers which may be filed with him, which may relate to the swamp-lands or contracts for work under the swamp-land laws, and shall be responsible for the preservation of the same in his office, and shall investigate, and ascertain, and report to the Governor, whether any of the work which shall be reported for payment by any engineer, has already been in part or wholly paid for or not, so that the same work may not be twice paid for." * * *

"SEC. 10. That in order to prevent a useless accumulation of specie in the State treasury from the sales of swamp and overflowed lands, whenever there shall be in the State treasury as much as five thousand dollars in specie, obtained from the sales of such lands, situated in any district as established by the act to which this is a supplement, it shall be lawful for any engineer, under directions of the Governor, to let out contracts for making levees, ditching, draining, and reclaiming swamp and overflowed lands situated in the district, by the sales of lands in which district the specie in the State treasury shall have been obtained." * *

General levees and drains in the swamp region.

New system inaugurated.

The Helena district, embracing the counties along the Mississippi river, has already expended its quota of swamp-lands; and some of the counties are therefore making their own levee laws.

Levee laws of Missouri, Kentucky, and Tennessee.

The proportional amount of alluvial land liable to inundation in the State of Missouri is so small that no detailed notice of its levee laws is required. In Kentucky and Tennessee none have been enacted.

Louisiana statutes for construction and dimensions of levees.

Dimensions and cost of existing levees.—The following extracts from the laws of Louisiana exhibit the statute requirements in that State:—

"SEC. 6. Every levee which shall contain one perpendicular foot of water, and not above three feet, shall have at least five feet base for each and every foot in height.

"Every levee which shall contain more than three perpendicular feet of water, and not above five feet, shall have at least six feet base for each and every foot in height.

"Every levee which shall contain more than five perpendicular feet of water, and not above six feet, shall have at least seven feet base for each and every foot in height.

"Every levee which shall contain above six perpendicular feet of water, shall have at least eight feet base for each and every foot in height.

"The summit of every levee shall be of the breadth of one-third of its base; and, finally, every levee shall be of such height that, after the sinking of the earth, it be still raised one foot above the level of the water when highest. * * *

"SEC. 7. Every new levee shall be constructed, in places where the bank is caving, at the distance of at least one arpent [about 192 feet] from the water's edge, and in places where the bank does not cave, at the distance of at least sixty feet; in both cases the distance shall be measured from the summit of the bank of the river, under the penalty prescribed in the prescribing section."

"SEC. 9. The earth which shall be employed for the repairs and construction of a levee shall be taken at the distance of at least twenty feet from the base of the levee on the side next the river, under the penalty prescribed in the sixth section.

"SEC. 10. Every new levee, or every portion of a levee which shall be made anew, shall be fascined on the river side, either with palmetto or otherwise with pickets, under the penalty prescribed in the sixth section.

"SEC. 11. All new or old levees on the unsettled and uncultivated lands, situated on the river or on the bayous running to and from the same, or other waters connected therewith, shall be constantly fascined or palisaded." * * * *

"SEC. 16. It shall be the duty of every riparian owner of lands, in places where levees are necessary to confine the waters, to cause attentively and carefully to be dug and filled up every year the holes which crawfish, muskrats, or other animals, may have made in the said levees, and to adopt constantly all the necessary means to prevent the progress of those which happen during the high water as soon as they shall be apprised of it." * * * * * * * * *

"SEC. 41. In future no bayou, which receives the waters of the Mississippi, when that river is high, and which then affords an outlet to the said waters, shall, under any pretence, be shut up without a special law." * * * * *

Provisions in the Carroll, Madison, and Catahoula levee district.

"SEC. 81. All levees shall be made as follows: All trees, stumps, and logs shall be removed from the foundation of the levees, a ditch, at least three feet wide and three feet deep, shall be cut in the centre of the foundation; and the levees shall be made at least three feet above the highest water, and shall have six feet base for every foot in height, and shall have such width on top as the Inspector shall think necessary."

Actual dimensions of levees in Louisiana between Red-river landing and Carrollton.

The actual dimensions of the levees fall far short of those required by these statutes. The transit and level survey of the right bank from Red-river landing to Carrollton, and of the left bank from Baton Rouge to Carrollton, has supplied the following data by which the average dimensions of the levees between those points, in 1851, may be accurately judged. So far as known, no change in these mean dimensions has been made since that survey.

Dimensions of levees in Louisiana.

Locality on right bank.	Width.		Level of top.	
	At top.	At base.	Above ground.	Above h.w. 1851.
	Feet.	*Feet.*	*Feet.*	*Feet.*
Raccourci bend	11.0	17.6	6.2	2.0
Raccourci bend	11.0	19.0	8.0	2.0
Raccourci bend	2.0	15.6	3.1	2.0
Raccourci bend	2.0	8.8	3.4	2.0
Raccourci bayou	6.0	12.0	4.2	2.0
Raccourci bayou	6.0	12.0	4.8	2.0
Raccourci bayou	6.0	17.3	7.5	2.0
2 miles above Morganza	4.0	13.0	4.0	2.0
1 mile above Morganza	5.0	25.0	6.8	2.0
3.5 miles below Port Hudson	2.0	18.6	4.0	2.0
5.5 miles above Baton Rouge	6.0	18.0	5.1	1.0
Near Baton Rouge	4.0	13.5	4.5	1.0
Near Baton Rouge	3.5	11.5	3.6	1.0
Near Baton Rouge	6.0	13.5	4.5	1.0
11 miles above Plaquemine	7.0	32.0	7.8	1.0
8 miles above Plaquemine	3.5	8.0	2.6	1.0
1 mile above Plaquemine	4.0	8.0	4.0	1.0
6 miles below Plaquemine	4.0	7.0	3.0	1.0
8 miles below Plaquemine	4.0	8.5	3.5	1.0
4 miles below Bayou Goula	4.0	......	.....	1.0
2 miles below Bayou Goula	4.0	......	.....	1.0
2 miles above Claiborne island	4.0	9.0	4.0	1.0
3 miles below Claiborne island	3.5	9.0	4.3	2.6
6 miles below Claiborne island	4.0	13.0	5.0	1.0
9 miles below Claiborne island	3.5	9.0	4.0	0.0
2 miles below Donaldsonville	5.0	15.0	4.5	2.0
4.5 miles above Jefferson College	4.0	16.0	4.2	1.0
0.75 of a mile below Jefferson College.	8.0	24.0	6.0	1.0
4.5 miles below Jefferson College	3.5	20.0	5.6	1.0
6 miles above Bonnet Carré church	4.0	18.0	4.5	2.0
3 miles above Bonnet Carré church	3.0	22.0	4.0	1.0
1.75 miles above Bonnet Carré church.	5.0	15.0	5.0	1.0
0.75 of a mile below Bonnet Carré church	3.5	9.0	3.9	1.0
2.75 miles below Bonnet Carré church.	4.0	18.0	7.2	2.0
4.75 miles below Bonnet Carré church.	4.0	10.0	4.0	1.0
2 miles below Bonnet Carré crevasse	4.0	12.0	6.7	1.0
5.5 miles above Red church	4.0	10.0	4.0	1.0
7.5 miles below Red church	6.0	19.0	4.0	1.0
Mean	4.7	14.6	4.7	1.4

Locality on left bank.	Width.		Level of top.	
	At top.	At base.	Above ground.	Above h.w. 1851.
	Feet.	*Feet.*	*Feet.*	*Feet.*
Near Baton Rouge	3.5	8.0	3.0	1.0
Near Baton Rouge	3.5	10.0	2.5	1.0
6 miles above Plaquemine	5.7	14.0	4.5	2.0
6 miles below Plaquemine	3.5	9.0	4.0	2.0
2.5 miles above Bayou Goula	4.0	11.0	5.5	1.0
3.25 miles below Bayou Goula	5.0	13.0	6.0	1.0
1 mile below Bayou Goula	6.0	......	.....	1.0
2 miles above Claiborne island	4.0	......	.....	1.0
2 miles below Claiborne island	4.0	......	.....	1.0
10 miles below Claiborne island	4.0	9.0	4.0	1.0
2.5 miles below Donaldsonville	4.0	12.0	4.5	1.0
4.75 miles above Jefferson College	4.0	8.0	1.8	1.0
2 miles below Jefferson College	4.0	0	4.3	1.0
14.5 miles above Bonnet Carré church.	4.0	10.0	6.4	1.0
11.75 miles above Bonnet Carré church.	4.0	8.0	2.5	1.0
6 miles above Bonnet Carré church	4.0	12.0	5.5	1.0
0.5 of a mile above Bonnet Carré church	4.0	10.0	5.3	1.0
Bonnet Carré church	4.0	12.0	4.9	1.0
1.25 miles below Bonnet Carré church.	4.0	10.0	4.0	1.0
4.25 miles below Bonnet Carré crevasse.	3.5	10.0	3.6	1.0
7 miles below Red church	4.0	13.0	6.0	1.0
Mean	4.0	1.05	4.3	1.0

Regulations in the State of Mississippi respecting the construction and dimensions of levees.

In the State of Mississippi, the new levees are constructed according to the following specifications, but these are not always adhered to in repairing old levees:—

"3. The levee will be graded 5 feet wide on top, except where otherwise directed by the Chief Engineer, with side slopes of such inclination as the Chief Engineer in each case shall designate (usually 6 to 1 on the river side, and 2½ to 1 on the other side) and in conformity to such heights of filling as may have been, or may hereafter be, determined upon* by the Chief Engineer."

* According to the information obtained, all new levees are now (since 1860) constructed in accordance with the following regulation:—

In De Soto and Tunica counties	4 feet above the highest known flood.
" Coahoma county	4.5 feet " " " " "
" Bolivar and Washington counties	5.0 " " " " " "
" Issaquena county	5.4 " " " " " "

This makes the average height of the new levees along the entire front of the Yazoo bottom about 10 feet, the cubical contents per mile being about 1,000,000 cubic yards, and the cost about $20,000.

"4. The ground to be occupied by the levee must first be cleared of trees, stumps, logs, trash, weeds and all perishable matter, the trees and stumps being cut up by the roots, at least 1 foot below the suface of the ground. The entire surface must then be thoroughly broken with a spade or plough, in order to form a bond with the earth deposited. Then a muck ditch must be cut, 6 feet wide at top, and 3 feet at bottom, and 4 feet deep; all stumps and roots crossing it being carefully taken out and removed beyond the base of the levee. The muck ditch must be cut 10 feet from the centre-line of the levee (great care being exercised not to displace any of the stakes of the centre-line) on that side next to the river, the earth from it being thrown entirely on that side of the ditch next to the river. As each section of a mile in length is thus cleared, broken and muck ditch cut, the contractor must notify the engineer in charge of the fact, when he will * * * * set stakes each side of the centre at the proper distance for the base of the levee. * * * * As soon as the work is staked, the muck ditch must be filled in again with buckshot earth or clay obtained from without the base of the levee, and the earth tramped in by horses or mules ridden rapidly back and forward constantly while the earth is being put in; at least one horse to every eight wheelbarrows being thus employed. This filling and tramping to be kept 1 mile in advance of the embankment. The surface of all old levees must be well broken. In cases where the chief constituent of the levee is sand or other porous material, the Chief Engineer may require a wall of buckshot or clay, 5 feet thick, to be continued up from the muck ditch to the top of the levee, the earth being tramped in by horses in the same manner as the muck ditch, as the levee is built up on each side of it, the object being to obtain a stratum through the levee impervious to sipe-water. * * * * * * * *

"5. When the ground is prepared, as required by article 4, the embankment will be commenced, and must be formed in uniform layers, not exceeding 1 foot in thickness; a sufficient number of dumping men being continually kept on the levee to spread the earth as it is wheeled or carted in. The slopes shall in every case be commenced FULL OUT TO THE SIDE STAKES, and carried regularly up as the embankment progresses. * * * * * * * * *

"6. Material taken from ditches or drains (except when otherwise directed by the engineer in charge) shall be deposited in the adjacent levee, the cost of removing which, when the haul is not more than 300 feet, will be included in the price paid for excavation. In procuring material for the levee, the place will be designated by the engineer in charge (always on the river side, unless otherwise directed), and in excavating and removing it, care must be taken to injure or disfigure the land as little as possible. In no case must it be obtained within 20 feet of the base of the levee on the river side, and the slope of the pit next to the embankment must not be less than 2 to 1. If, from unavoidable causes, it becomes necessary to procure material on the inside of the levee, it must not be taken within 60 feet of the base. But is not to be taken from the inside at all, unless forced by high water, or some insuperable difficulty. Any encroachment upon the limits either side must be measured by the engineer in charge, and deducted from the amount of the final estimate. At intervals of 100 feet, bermes must be left across the barrow-pits, to prevent the flow of a current along the levee. In procuring material for the embankment, if the place designated by the engineer in charge exceed 300 feet from the centre-line of the levee, three-fourths of a cent per cubic yard will be paid in addition to the contract price, for every 100 feet of average haul exceeding 300 feet that said material may be transported. All levees shall be estimated in embankment and not in excavation, and be paid for by the cubic yard.

"7. All earth designed for embankment must be *entirely* divested of roots, trash and all other perishable matter before being thrown into the carts or wheelbarrows.

"8. After an embankment shall have been raised 3 feet, the sides must be trimmed with slope-boards, and any irregularities appearing on the slope must be corrected at once; this trimming must steadily progress as the embankment increases in height.

"9. In cutting drains or new channels for streams, they shall be cut at such distance from the levee as the Chief Engineer may require; the materials deposited in the adjacent embankment, and paid for as specified in article 6 of these specifications.

"10. The Chief Engineer may, whenever he deems it necessary, require a double course of sheet-piling, breaking joints, to be driven at the centre or either side of the levee, 5 feet below the surface of ground, and extending up within 6 inches of grade; the plank to be of heart red gum, white oak or cypress, or such other timber as the Chief Engineer may select, and of such dimensions as he may determine; the material and labor to be paid for by the thousand feet, board measure. All piling must be driven in advance of the levee, and the embankment constructed on both sides of the piling simultaneously. The Chief Engineer may also, whenever he deems it necessary, require a breakwater to be constructed on the river slope of the levee, of post and plank fence, properly braced, and filled in behind with earth, according to detailed plan and specifications in the office; the material and labor to be paid for by the thousand feet, board measure, and the filling at the contract price per cubic yard, stipulated for embankment."

"14. The ends of all levees shall be protected from flood by a double course of sheet-piling closely driven and securely braced, extending across the base and around each side, not less than 100 feet. This protection always to be put up on the completion of the levee, unless otherwise directed by the engineer in charge, and also during the progress of the work in anticipation of destructive floods. The Chief Engineer may also require the base of the levee to be covered with a causeway of timber, whenever necessary to support the embankment, for which an extra compensation, to be determined in each case, will be made."

* * * * * * * * * *

In Arkansas, the levees are constructed in accordance with the following specifications:—

Arkansas regulations for the construction and dimensions of levees.

"The levee or embankment shall be entirely of earth; and should any tree, log, chunk, wood, brushwood, cane, or other perishable material be imbedded in the levee, the party of the first part [the contractors] in addition to forfeiting all right to any compensation whatever for any and all work done, or which shall be done under this contract, shall also forfeit the full amount of the bond annexed thereto."

"All trees, brushwood, logs, and other perishable materials, shall be removed from off the surface of the ground to be occupied by the embankment or levee, so as not to injure the adjoining land. All stumps shall be cut off close to the ground. The clearing shall be sufficiently wide on either side of the centre-line of location to clear the berme banks."

"The embankment or levee shall have the following dimensions, viz.: For every foot in height, 1 foot wide on top, and, in addition, 7 feet base. The embankment shall be at least 30 inches above overflow. A berme bank, 6 feet wide on either side of the base of the embankment, shall in all cases be preserved; and the berme bank slope shall be cut conformable with the slope of the embankment. Earth benches, each 100 feet apart, on the river side of the embankment, shall be left standing, at right angles with the centre-line of location, connecting with the berme bank, to prevent the abrasure of the embankment, by the flow of water, at times of flood."

"All material which will when rotted leave conduit pipes, or which retain water, or upon which frost acts, by heaving, shall be removed from the base."

"Where the levee crosses county or neighborhood roads, a crossing shall be made of earth 15 feet wide on top, sloping uniformly at right angles from the centre of the levee, on either side, a distance seven times greater than the height of the levee; which crossing shall be so elevated in the centre that water falling upon it will run off on either side; and said crossing shall have uniform side slopes extending out on each side 1 foot for each foot in height; and the same shall be paid for at the regular contract price."

Cost of levees per cubic yard in the several States.

Careful inquiries were made with a view to ascertain the usual cost of levees. The contractor's price for the Ohio levee at Cairo, the finest on the river, was 35 cents per cubic yard. It is an enormous embankment, having a wide street and a railroad track upon the top. Its river slope is covered 1 foot thick with broken stone, costing $2.00 per cubic yard. It is also protected at the edge by a rip-rap wall. It is fully 15 feet high, its top being above the level of the flood of 1858. In the State of Mississippi, the contractor's price of levees is from 18 to 20 cents per cubic yard. In Arkansas, it averages about 20 cents. In Louisiana, it averages about 15 cents in open ground and 23 cents in forest regions, where the trees are to be cut down and a "muck ditch" is to be dug through their roots.

GREAT FLOODS.

General character of the histories of the great floods.

Such historical notices of the great floods as can be prepared from existing records are added to this chapter. The analytical comparison of the floods cannot be attempted here, for the reason that the system upon which it is based yet remains to be explained. A general statement, however, of what tributaries produced those destructive overflows; at what dates they occurred; and what damage they occasioned in the different parts of the great alluvial region, forms a fitting conclusion to the present chapter, besides precluding the necessity of hereafter interrupting trains of reasoning in themselves sufficiently involved.

Earlier records.

In preparing these histories, great care has been taken to collect information from all reliable sources. For the more recent floods, this has been comparatively easy, but, for those of former times, it has been found impossible to determine even the most essential particulars. The list of floods, however, is complete for the present century; for in 1798 a regular record was begun at Natchez by Governor Winthrop Sargent, and continued by him until 1819. From that date until 1841, observations at the same place were made by Mr. Samuel Davis. They were continued by Professor Forshey, until 1848, when he removed to Carrollton and began a new series there. The latter, together with the records kept at the Memphis navy yard, render the information complete up to the date of the commencement of the present Survey in 1851. From these old papers Professor Forshey has compiled (see plate VII) a set of gauge-curves to represent the oscillations of the river at Natchez from 1817 to 1847. The scale of high waters at Natchez (figure 2, plate IX) is also mainly constructed from these records.

Prior to 1798, we have only occasional notes preserved among the papers of the colonies. Governor Sargent, however, states that according to tradition there was no very high water between 1750 and 1770, and that from 1770 to 1798, there was no general overflow. The latter statement is contradicted by the records respecting the flood of 1782, as will soon be seen.

Flood of 1718.—"An extraordinary rise of the Mississippi this year. Bienville had selected a site for a city, but the colony not having means to build dykes or levees, the idea was for the present abandoned." (Francios Xavier Martin.)

Flood of 1735.—Gayarré states that in this year the waters were so high that many levees were broken, and much damage was done. New Orleans itself was inundated. The flood continued from the latter part of December to the latter part of June. When the river fell, it reached a lower point than ever before noted, the range at New Orleans being 15 feet.

Flood of 1770.—A great flood, according to the tradition recorded by Governor Sargent, but the published statements concerning it are so ambiguous as to render it uncertain whether this flood was equal to that of 1811, or a foot higher, at Natchez.

Flood of 1782.—"This year the Mississippi rose to a greater height than was remembered by the oldest inhabitants. In the Attakapas and Opelousas, the inundation was extreme. The few spots which the water did not reach were covered with deer." (Francios Xavier Martin.) "1782 was l'annee des eaux." (Brackenridge.)

Flood of 1785.—A great flood at St. Louis, in April, said to have been equal to that of 1844. Professor J. L. Riddell, of New Orleans, states on the authority of the l'Amie des Lois and Evening Journal, May 25, 1816, that New Orleans was flooded by crevasses.

Flood of 1791.—Same remarks at New Orleans as for the flood of 1785.

Flood of 1796.—The Teche overflowed its banks for some 60 miles above New Iberia, and poured into Grand lake in a smooth sheet of water. The lake at this date attained the highest level on record, being 2.5 feet higher than in 1828, 6.8 feet higher than in 1850, and 14 feet higher than the ordinary gulf level. (Verbal statement of Mr. —— Fuller, upon the authority of a creole resident.)

Flood of 1799.—Same remarks at New Orleans as for the flood of 1785.

Flood of 1809.—A disastrous flood, which, according to Governor Sargent's notes, inundated all the plantations near Natchez, and destroyed the crops. It was imagined by the sufferers that the northern lakes had found a channel to the river. At Natchez, this flood was 1.6 feet below that of 1815, and 2.1 feet below that of 1859, the highest ever known in that vicinity. The date of highest water was May 4.

Flood of 1811.—"There was a great flood this year." (Brackenridge.) "During the great floods of 1811 and 1813, much damage was done by the water rushing through the rents in the levees." (Darby.) Governor Sargent places this flood at Natchez 1.5 feet below the high water of 1815, or 2.0 feet below the high water of 1859, the date of highest water being June 4.

Flood of 1813.—"Was 6 to 8 inches higher than 1811." (Brackenridge.) This writer also states that a rise "within 2 or 3 feet of high water" occurred in December of the preceding year. "In 1813, when the Point Coupée levee was broken, the water" (in lower part of Atchafalaya basin—Grand lake) "rose 4 or 5 feet above any elevation it had attained since 1780. During the month of June of that year, which is ordinarily the season of greatest rise, the level of the general body of water, from the efflux of Atchafalaya, could not have augmented in height more than 4 feet without having thrown the water of the inundation into the Teche in almost its whole length above the town of St. Martin." (Darby.) Governor Sargent's notes at Natchez place this flood 0.3 of a foot below the high water of 1815 or 0.8 of a foot below the high water of 1859, the date being June 8.

Flood of 1815.—A very great flood. At the mouth of the Ohio it attained the highest point ever recorded, *i.e.* 2 feet above the high water of 1858. The highest water there occurred on April 9. (Verbal statement of Mr. John Bird from his own observations.) It was due to a general coincidence of freshets in the Ohio, the Upper Mississippi, the Missouri, the Cumberland, and the Tennessee. (Letter of Mr. T. B. Martin, accompanying the report of the Secretary of the Treasury upon the levees of the Mississippi river, December 9, 1835.) At Natchez, Governor Sargent's notes state that it was highest on June 22, when it was 2 inches higher than any flood of which we have records, except that of 1859. Red river must have been low enough to allow bayou Atchafalaya to do good service as an outlet, for, at Morganza, the flood was 0.6 of a foot lower than that of 1828 (Colonel Morgan's manuscript journal), and no damage below Red-river landing is recorded.

Flood of 1816.—Same remarks at New Orleans as for the flood of 1785.

Flood of 1823.—This was a great flood, which was highest at Napoleon, on June 1, and at Natchez, on May 23. It was caused by a flood in the Arkansas, which occurred when the Mississippi was high. Between the Arkansas and Red rivers, this flood rose generally a little higher than that of 1828, but probably not quite so high as that of 1815. Mr. Samuel Davis' notes place it 0.2 of a foot below high water of 1815, or 0.7 of a foot below high water of 1859. A great number of crevasses occurred below Red river on both banks of the river.

Flood of 1824.—This flood was 0.7 of a foot below the high water of 1815, or 1.2 feet below that of 1859, at Natchez, according to the notes of Mr. Samuel Davis. It was highest on May 6.

The more recent floods.

Between 1824 and 1860, the only great flood years were 1828, 1844, 1849, 1850, 1851, 1858, and 1859. It is true that the river was quite high at certain localities in some of the intermediate years, as in 1832, 1836, and 1847, but the floods were of so secondary a character in a general point of view, that they do not require discussion. Before proceeding to the more detailed history of these seven comparatively well-known floods, the following table exhibiting their relative heights will be given. It should be remembered that it presents only a general comparison of them, since the extension of the levees, the formation of cut-offs, the location of crevasses, etc. materially modify the local heights attained in different years even when the volume of discharge is the same.

Their comparative heights.

The plane of reference adopted in the table is the flood level in 1858. The sign + denotes that the flood in question exceeded the height attained in 1858; and the sign —, that it fell short of this height. The numbers following the signs denote the difference in the height attained in the two floods. Great care has been taken to insure accuracy throughout this table; but as some of the numbers are better determined than others, a distinction has been drawn between them. Wherever a careful mark was made at the date of the flood, and the exactness of the determination therefore admits of no question, the number in the table is not marked by an asterisk; otherwise it is, however good the authority for the height of the flood may be.

Comparative heights of the modern floods of the Mississippi.

Locality.	1828.		1844.		1849.		1850.		1851.		1859.	
	Diff.	Date.	Diff.	Date.	Diff.	Date.	Diff.	Date.	Diff.	Date.	Diff.	Date.
	Feet.		*Feet.*		*Feet.*		*Feet.*		*Feet.*		*Feet.*	
St. Louis	—0.7*		+4.3	June 28.					—0.4	June 11.		
Cape Girardeau	—4.3*		+3.7				—6.3*		+0.4			
Cairo, Illinois				July 4.								
Norfolk, Missouri			—4.4*		—2.5*							
Opposite Island 4			—2.5*		—1.6*							
Columbus			—0.9	July 4.	—1.6*		—2.7*		—5.0*	(?)	—2.1	May 8.
Hickman			—0.5*		—1.0*							
Mouth James bayou			—2.5*									
Opposite Island 10			—2.5*									
" " 15			—2.5*		—2.5*							
" " 16			—1.5									
First Chickasaw bluff			—1.5*									
1.5 miles below Randolph	—0.8		—0.7									
Opposite Island 35			—0.7*									
" " 38			—0.6*						—0.6*			
Memphis	—1.3		—1.0	July.	—3.3	Feb. 8 & 16.	—0.6	May 14–21.	—1.0	March 11.	—0.1	May 12–13.
Opposite Island 49			—0.9									
" " 51			—1.0*									
" " 56	—0.6*											
Helena	—1.5		—2.4*		—1.8*		—1.8	May 1 and 20.	—4.8*		—1.0	March 22.
Opposite Island 68	+0.4*		—2.0*									
" " 74	—0.7		—1.5									
Napoleon			—1.7	June 5.			—2.4		—2.9	April 10.	+0.3*	March.
Near Island 78			—1.2*									
" " 80			—1.0*									
Greenville			—1.2									
Near Island 88			—1.5*				—1.2*					
Providence							—2.6		—2.1	March 10.	+0.8	April 25–28.
Near Island 100			—0.7*				—0.4*					
Vicksburg	—0.6*		—0.8	June 28.	—0.6	April 26.	+0.1	June 4.		April 3.	+1.3	April 21–30.
4 miles below Vicksburg			—0.6*				+0.3*					
New Carthage			—1.7*	June.	—1.0*		—0.5	May.	—1.5	Mar. 31–Apl. 2.		
Natchez	+0.7*	March 26.	+0.1	July 16.	—0.3*		—0.5		—0.7	April 1–5.	+1.2	May 2.
Near Island 116	+1.7		+0.4				+0.2					
Routh's Point (ab. Red-river landing)	+5.3		+2.9				+1.9					
Head bayou Atchafalaya	+3.9						+1.9		+0.7			
Red-river landing							+1.8		+0.7	April 1–3.		
Just ab. Raccourci cut-off			+1.5		—1.3							
Just below " "	—0.3*		—3.0		—1.6							
Bayou Sara		March 14.		July 11.		March 2.		March 15.				
Baton Rouge	+0.2		—0.6		+0.4		0.0	March 15.	0.0	Mar. 29–Apl. 1.	+0.5	May 6.
Plaquemine	+0.3		—0.9		0.0		—0.6		+0.1			
5 miles below Plaquemine	+0.1		—0.7		0.0		—0.4					
Donaldsonville					+0.1		—1.2		+0.3	March 27–31.	+0.5	May 6.
Bonnet Carré point					0.0				+0.2		+0.4	May 3.
Carrollton	+0.1	April 1.	—0.6		+0.1	March 11–15.	—1.3	Jan. 28–Feb. 2.	+0.3	March 27–30.	+0.4	May 6.

Some uncertainty about this flood.

Flood of 1828.—This flood occurred before the country above Red-river landing was much settled, and it is probable that its marks have been confounded with those of 1815 in many localities; because, while we have the direct testimony of Mr. John Bird, who has resided at the mouth of the Ohio for over a half a century, that at that point the flood of 1828 was fully 4 feet lower than that of 1815, the former is almost universally claimed to have been the greatest flood of the present century in every one of the great swamp regions below the Ohio. These statements can only be reconciled by supposing a great difference in the duration of these two floods, but respecting this it has been impossible to obtain any information.

Its height throughout the alluvial region.

At the mouth of the Ohio, there were three rises in this flood, two in the winter and one in the spring, all equal in height and fully 2 feet below the high water of 1858.

At Randolph, at Memphis, at Helena, and opposite Island 74, this flood was, by exact measurement, between 1 and 2 feet below that of 1858.

At Natchez, Professor Forshey's compiled gauge-record (plate VII) places it 0.7 of a foot above the high water of 1858. This may be due to the effect of the Red-river and Raccourci cut-offs, both of which were made subsequently to 1828. Their effect in the vicinity of Red-river landing is strikingly shown by the table just given.

Below the influence of these cut-offs, the floods of 1828 and 1858 were sensibly equal in height.

Action of the tributaries.

No records of the history of the different tributaries in this flood have been preserved, but it is known that a Red-river flood, which, according to Professor Forshey's papers, was highest in June, was at Alexandria at least 2.5 feet lower than in 1849, and at the mouth of Black river, 5.0 feet higher than in 1850.

Flood in the northern swamps.

The St. Francis and Yazoo bottoms were deeply inundated, being entirely unprotected by levees.

In the Tensas bottom.

The following facts have been collected relative to this flood in the Tensas bottom, where it was the highest of which we have even traditions. The whole region was under water. The mean depth of overflow on the Louisiana line was 7.1 feet, or 4.0 feet greater than in 1850. Between Vidalia and Harrisonburg, this quantity was 7.7 feet, or 3.0 feet greater than in 1850. At the mouth of Black river, the water stood 5.0 feet above the flood level of 1850 and 7.5 feet above that of 1844.

In the Atchafalaya bottom.

In the western part of the Atchafalaya basin the flood was the greatest of which we have record, for, there being no levees for several miles below the mouth of Red river, and Shreve's cut-off not yet having been made, the water from the Tensas bottom poured over the banks in immense quantities. At the upper mouth of bayou Atchafalaya it was 2.0 feet above the ground and the flood level of 1850; at the mouth of bayou de Glaize it was 4.5 feet above the ground and the flood level of 1850; at the mouth of bayou Courtableau it was 4.0 feet above the ground and 3.0 feet above the flood level of 1850; at the head of Grand lake it was 4.3 feet above the flood level of 1850; and at Brashear City, 3.0 feet above the same level. The overflow extended to the extreme western limit of the alluvial formation, instead of only 6 or 8 miles from bayou Atchafalaya, as in ordinary floods. The Courtableau at Washita was at least 10 feet higher than in 1850. The plantations along the upper part of the Teche were not flooded, but the crops were lost on those within the influence of the backwater from the Atchafalaya overflow. At St. Martinsville the bayou was some 15 or 20 feet above low water, the usual range being only 3 or 4 feet.

In the lower country.

The eastern part of the Atchafalaya basin, indeed the whole region bordering upon the Mississippi below the head of this basin, seems to have nearly escaped damage; the only exception being the Grosse Tête region, which was deeply flooded by backwater from the Atchafalaya overflow, and by a break in the grand levee of the parish of Pointe Coupée near Morganza.

Character of information respecting this flood.

Flood of 1844.—The information collected respecting this flood is meagre, but still sufficient to establish its general history. (See plate VII.)

First rise.

A considerable rise occurred in April, from a freshet in Arkansas river, which poured into the Mississippi when that stream was already high from rains prevailing in the valleys of its upper tributaries. This rise below Napoleon only attained a level of from 1 to 2 feet above the natural bank, and consequently did very little damage.

Second rise.

In May, however, before the lower river had subsided, another and much greater flood in the Arkansas river occurred. It was second only to the flood of 1833, and was highest at Fort Smith on May 25. A corresponding rise, doubtless due to the same general causes, attained its height at St. Louis on May 22, and did much damage above the mouth of the Ohio. Simultaneous rises occurred in bayou Maçon and bayou Tensas, but they were not of sufficient height to injure the valleys of those streams. In the region bordering upon the Mississippi itself, however, the effect of this combination of floods was serious. Above the mouth of Red river the country was more or less flooded, but Red river being fortunately low, the Atchafalaya carried off enough water to protect the plantations below the mouth of that stream from serious damage.

Third rise.

This was the condition of the river in June, when the great combined flood of the Upper Mississippi and the Missouri, which has rendered this year memorable in river annals, occurred. At St. Louis it exceeded the preceding rise by more than 8 feet, and all other floods of which we have records by more than 4 feet. The daily gauge-record at St. Louis, given in Appendix B, furnishes all necessary details for that vicinity. Throughout the whole alluvial region, except between Napoleon and New Carthage, where the local effect of the preceding flood in the Arkansas was predominant, this Upper Mississippi and Missouri flood produced the highest water of the year.

Ravages of the flood.

The country above the mouth of Red river was generally flooded. The St. Francis and Yazoo bottoms were nearly unprotected by levees, and the water had, of course, free entrance. The Tensas bottom was badly inundated through breaks in the levees. The gauge kept by Mr. Mandeville (see Appendix B) shows that, at his plantation, situated where the Vidalia and Harrisonburg road crosses bayou Tensas, the water was at its greatest height from July 18 to July 21, and that it was then 1.5 feet higher than it has ever been since, except in the flood of 1850. Below Red-river landing the country escaped with but little injury, owing to the very low stage of Red river, which allowed the Atchafalaya to carry off the greater part of the surplus discharge of the Mississippi.

Flood of 1849.—The only gauge-records kept during this flood are those at Memphis (plate VIII) and at Carrollton (plate IX). The former indicates that the river was undergoing constant oscillations, but without attaining its great flood level. Its highest stand occurred about the middle of February, when it was 3.3 feet below the high water of 1858. In the latter part of March it again reached nearly the same level. At these dates it was fully 3 feet higher than at any other period of the year. According to Lieutenant Marr's gaugings, the discharge at no time exceeded 900,000 cubic feet per second. By referring to the table just given, showing the relative heights of the floods, however, it is evident that the gauge at Memphis does not present a fair view of this flood in the upper river. At points near the mouth of the Ohio and at Helena it lacked only 1 or 2 feet of the level attained in 1858, a fact which indicates that much water must have passed Memphis through the St. Francis bottom and returned again at Stirling to swell the flood below. Such was really the case, as stated by residents near the mouth of the St. Francis river.

Observations made during this flood.

The gauge at Carrollton indicates that the river rose nearly to high-water mark in the latter part of January, and remained there, with occasional oscillations, until the middle of May. It then gradually declined until the latter part of July, when a second rise of short duration and of much less height occurred. The water then fell with unusual rapidity to its lowest stage for the year.

Unfortunately, the history of the condition of the different tributaries during this flood is so defective, that it is impossible to trace the sources of this flood. It is known that there was a flood in the Arkansas, which was highest at Fort Smith on June 9; and a very great flood in Red river, the highest, indeed, of which we have records, which came to a stand 4 feet above the natural bank at Alexandria about the middle of August. It is evident, however, that other floods must have occurred in the lower tributaries, for upon no other supposition can the Memphis and Carrollton gauges be reconciled.

Action of the tributaries.

Above Red-river landing the ravages occasioned by this flood were comparatively slight. Mr. Mandeville's gauge on bayou Tensas shows that the water there when highest (May 10) was 1.4 feet below the flood of 1844, and 3.0 feet below that of 1850, and exactly equal with that of 1858, and that it rapidly subsided after May 21. The St. Francis and Yazoo bottom lands were inundated, but to an extent not unusual for great flood years.

Ravages of this flood.

Below Red-river landing the injury done was so immense that the flood is justly classed among the most destructive ever known. The first great crevasse occurred in March, a few miles below Red-river landing, on the right bank. Soon after, several more broke on the same side of the river, between Port Hudson and Donaldsonville. These breaks remained open until low water, and submerged much of the Atchafalaya basin. At Brashear City the water was over the banks for eight days, and only lacked 0.3 of a foot of attaining the same level as in 1850. On April 7 another crevasse broke, also on the west bank, about 15 miles above New Orleans, at Fortier's plantation. This flooded the country between the Mississippi and bayou La Fourche to a depth of about 4 feet, and thus submerged the rear of many rich sugar plantations. The effect of this crevasse upon the bed of the river has been much discussed. On the left bank, a crevasse occurred on May 3 at Sauvé's plantation, 17 miles above New Orleans, by which that city was inundated. The break remained open forty-eight days, and did an immense amount of damage. Many interesting details relative to these several crevasses, and to the flood generally, are given by Professor Forshey in an article which appeared in vol. I, Southern Medical Reports, edited by Dr. Fenner, of New Orleans, in 1849.

Observations made during this flood.

Flood of 1850.—Only two complete records of the oscillations of the river in this flood have been preserved. One was kept at Memphis, and the other at Carrollton. Both are contained in Appendix B, and are exhibited on plates VIII and IX.

By the Memphis record, it appears that there were four principal rises, of which the first and second produced very little if any damage. The third was highest in the latter part of March, and the fourth in the middle of May. The maximum discharge at Memphis in each of the last two rises was about 1,050,000 cubic feet per second, according to Lieutenant Marr's corrected gaugings. After the middle of May, the flood in the upper river rapidly subsided, the regular June rise being hardly perceptible.

Action of the tributaries.

The records do not show what tributaries caused this flood at the head of the alluvial region, but mention is made of a great flood in the Upper Mississippi, which was the highest on record at St. Paul. In the lower river the flood began earlier than at Memphis, being high even on January 1. This was caused by heavy rains, which produced freshets successively in the Arkansas, Red and Black rivers, and thus flooded the whole region below Napoleon. The water did not subside until the middle of June.

Ravages above Red-river landing.

The damage occasioned by this flood was immense. The St. Francis and Yazoo bottoms were not protected by levees, and were both deeply flooded. The Tensas bottom was submerged more effectually than in any year subsequent to 1828. This was in some degree due to the heavy rains already mentioned, which filled the swamp-drains before the crevasses occurred, and thus retarded the escape of the Mississippi water. The principal breaks were several above the Louisiana line, which flooded bayou Maçon; that at Point Lookout, just below Lake Providence, which was 1.5 miles wide and from 5 to 8 feet deep; that near Island 102, which was 1 mile wide and 7 feet deep; that between Lake Providence and New Carthage (gap in levee), 10 miles wide and about 3 feet deep; that just below Rodney, which was 1300 feet wide; and that opposite Ellis cliffs, which was 3000 feet wide. These dimensions are only approximate, as no survey of the breaks was made. The history of the flood in this bottom is well exhibited by Mr. Mandeville's gauge-record (Appendix B), kept on bayou Tensas at the crossing of the Vidalia and Harrisonburg road. The water rose steadily until March 15, then declined slowly until early in April, then rose again until the middle of May, when it attained its highest point, and then rapidly subsided. The flood was 1.6 feet higher than in 1844, and 3.0 feet higher than in 1849 and 1858 at this locality. At Trinity (marks of Major Liddell) the water was 1.8 feet higher than in 1844; 3.0 feet higher than in 1849; and 3.8 feet lower than in 1828. At the mouth of Black river, this flood was 3.0 feet above that of 1844, and 5.0 feet below that of 1828. After these figures, it is needless to add that nearly the whole region was submerged and the crops destroyed.

Below Red-river landing the country fared but little better. The water pouring from Red river exceeded the discharging capacity of bayou Atchafalaya, and the surplus forced its way into the Mississippi by both of the mouths of Old river. The flood from above, augmented by this new supply, maintained an elevation sufficient to keep the numerous crevasses below Red-river landing actively discharging for more than four months. As a detailed computation of the quantity of water thus taken from the river will be given in Chapter VI, the effects of the overflow alone will be referred to here. The Atchafalaya basin was more deeply flooded than in any other year since 1828. At Brashear City, the water began to rise rapidly on May 10, and continued to do so until June 20. It then stood at a level about 3 feet lower than the highest point attained in 1828 until July 4, when it began falling so rapidly that the land was uncovered in 4 days. The basin between bayou La Fourche and the Mississippi escaped nearly uninjured. The crops upon the left bank, above New Orleans, were much injured by the celebrated Bonnet Carré crevasse, which attained a width of nearly 7000 feet, and continued flowing for more than six months.

Ravages below Red-river landing.

Flood of 1851.—Plate V illustrates this flood. There were three principal rises at the head of the alluvial region. The first occurred in December, 1850. It nowhere attained to the level of the natural banks; and as several weeks intervened between it and the second rise, the water nearly drained from the channel before the occurrence of the latter. The first rise, therefore, exercised very little, if any, influence upon the succeeding overflow.

First rise of this flood.

The second rise, so far as can be ascertained, was caused mainly by the Ohio. At Columbus it attained a point about 5 feet below the high water of 1858. At Memphis it was highest on March 11, being then only 1 foot below the level of the same flood. This relative difference in height is explained by the greater amount of water which escaped into the St. Francis bottom lands between the two places in 1858. This rise was characterized, at least at Memphis, by the extraordinary rapidity with which it attained its height. From February 10 to February 21, inclusive, the river at that city rose 21.7 feet, or at a mean rate of 1.8 feet in 24 hours, the maximum in this time being 3.3 feet. The total rise amounted to 28 feet. At Helena the highest stand was 4.8 feet below the high water of 1858, an apparent anomaly, which is explained by the fact that, at the date of high water in 1858, a large volume of water escaped into the St. Francis bottom above Memphis, passed through the swamp, and returned to the river just above Helena, whereas, as just seen, in 1851 but little water escaped from the river above Memphis, and consequently but little returned to it near Helena. At Napoleon the height of the rise was modified by a freshet in the Arkansas, which, pouring out just after the maximum discharge from above had passed, produced, on April 10, the highest water of the year in the immediate vicinity. Its height was 2.9 feet below the high water of 1858. At Lake Providence the effect of a very large crevasse at Point Lookout, just below the town, was evident. The break occurred on March 10, when the water stood 2.1 feet below the high water of 1858. A gradual fall in the river at Lake Providence began at that date, precisely as occurred from a similar cause in 1858. On April 10 (the date of high water at Napoleon) this fall amounted to 2.6 feet. All of this fall should not be considered the effect of the Lookout crevasse, since there were others between the two places,

Second rise.

especially on the left bank; but its influence was predominant. At New Carthage the river was at its highest point from March 31 to April 2, inclusive, when it stood 1.5 feet below the high water of 1858. The difference in date and in relative height of the flood at this place and at Lake Providence is attributable partly to water which returned to the Mississippi from the Yazoo bottom by way of the Yazoo river, where the current was credibly reported to be very strong, and partly to the local effect of the crevasses near Lake Providence. At Red-river landing, the flood was at its height from April 1 to April 3, when it stood 0.7 of a foot *above* the high water of 1858. The reasons for the anomaly in the height of the two floods at this place and at points below, as compared with points above, have been fully developed by the operations of the Survey. They are too involved for discussion in this preliminary synopsis, but in Chapter VI they are treated at length. Here it is sufficient to state in general terms that the combined influence of a great flood in Red river, and of some crevasses above and below the mouth of Red river, produced all the apparent contradictions. The last table, on page 171, exhibits the heights and dates of the highest water in this rise at points below Red-river landing.

Third rise.

The third rise of the flood of 1851 was caused by a combination of great floods in the Upper Mississippi and Missouri. The rapid rise at St. Louis began in the latter part of May, the river being, on May 31, 15.7 feet below the high water of 1844. On June 6 it was 10.1 feet; on June 7, 8.5 feet; on June 8, 6.8 feet; and on June 11, 4.8 feet, below this level. The latter stand was the highest attained during the flood. A gradual decline, amounting by June 19 to about 1.1 feet, took place, but at this date the river again began to rise, and continued to do so until June 23, when it stood 5.3 feet below the high water of 1844, or 0.5 of a foot below the preceding rise. Subsequent to June 23 it gradually declined. Excepting the floods of 1844 and of 1858, this was the greatest flood at St. Louis of which we have records. The flood of 1858 was 0.4 of a foot above that of 1851. At Cape Girardeau the flood of 1851 exceeded the flood of 1858, being 0.4 of a foot higher. Fortunately for the alluvial region, however, the Ohio river and the main tributaries below it were low at this period, and the flood passed onward to the gulf without attaining the level of the preceding rise at any point below the mouth of the Ohio. The following table exhibits the relative heights of these two rises:—

Locality.	Date of high water in June rise.	June rise below March rise.	Remarks.
		Feet.	
Memphis	June 28	0.3	See gauge-records in Appendices for further details.
Lake Providence	July 16	3.3	
Vicksburg	July 10–25	3.5	
New Carthage	July 18–25	2.2	
Natchez	July 19–20	5.4	
Red-river landing	July 25–30	7.5	
Baton Rouge	July 25–26	5.7	
Donaldsonville	July 23–26	4.6	
Carrollton	July 25	2.4	

Ravages of the flood.

The Yazoo bottom was partially flooded by the second rise, and the St. Francis by both the second and third rises of this flood. The Tensas bottom escaped with little injury, the natural drains being sufficient to carry off the crevasse water. Below Red-river landing there were several crevasses, a list of which is given in Chapter VI. The damage occasioned by them was local. The Atchafalaya basin escaped unharmed.

In conclusion, it may be said that this was a very unusual flood in the Mississippi above the mouth of the Ohio and below the mouth of Red river; but that between those points it cannot be so classed. So far as Louisiana is concerned, it is fully discussed in Chapter VI.

Flood of 1858.—By reference to plate VI, it will be seen that in the flood of 1858 there were four great rises, besides several minor oscillations, at the head of the alluvial region. The first rise, caused mainly by a flood in the Ohio, occurred in December, 1857. It filled the Mississippi to about the top of the banks, but no water escaped over them into the swamps. The maximum discharge at Columbus was 1,190,000 cubic feet per second. In passing down the river, this rise received considerable contributions from the Arkansas, Yazoo, and Red rivers, which were all high at the time, and thus raised the water at Donaldsonville from a comparatively low stage to within 5 feet of high-water mark. The St. Francis and White rivers were low and were backed up. It was stated upon good authority that heavy drift-wood passed from the Mississippi several miles up both those rivers.

First rise of this flood.

The second rise occurred in the latter part of March and first part of April, 1858, and was caused by a general swelling of the lower tributaries of the Missouri, of the Upper Mississippi, and of the lower tributaries of the Ohio. The Illinois and Wabash rivers were especially high. The maximum discharge at Columbus was 1,130,000 cubic feet per second, and no water escaped to the bottom lands above the town. Between Columbus and Helena, the swamps on the left bank received a little water, but as the levees along the St. Francis bottom remained unbroken, and as the river rapidly subsided within its banks, the quantity was quite inconsiderable. This rise was higher than the first, although the discharge was less; the reason being that the rise in December was consumed in filling the channel of the lower river, which contained comparatively little water when it occurred. In passing St. Francis river, the March rise was augmented by a discharge of more than 30,000 cubic feet per second—that stream being high from rain in the swamps and from hill drainage. At the mouths of the White and Arkansas rivers, it encountered great floods in both streams, which produced the highest water of the season in that immediate vicinity. The Yazoo river, also, was high from a flood in the Yallabusha and other hill tributaries, and thus contributed its quota—some 70,000 cubic feet per second—to increase the Mississippi discharge. The Red river was rather low and added nothing, but it prevented the Atchafalaya from reducing the flood. During this rise considerable water escaped, through gaps in the levees and crevasses, into the White river and Yazoo bottoms, a little into the Tensas swamp, but none below, except a trifling amount which passed through the Bell crevasse, near New Orleans, after April 11, the date of its breaking. The American-bend cut-off occurred in this rise (April 5).

Second rise.

The third great rise in the upper river occurred in the latter part of April, and was caused by heavy rains which flooded the lower tribu-

Third rise.

taries of the Missouri, of the Ohio, and of the Upper Mississippi. The Tennessee river was unusually high. The maximum discharge at Columbus was 1,260,000 cubic feet per second, and as the overflow into the bottom lands above the town was small, this quantity truly measures the flood which entered the alluvial region. It received considerable contributions in passing each of the main tributaries, although all of them except the Red river were comparatively low. Their supply came from the swamp drainage proper and the crevasse water which had escaped during the preceding rise, and which returned just in time to swell the present one. If this rise had occurred two weeks sooner, it would have encountered a great flood from the Red river, and its effects in the actual condition of the levees would probably have been disastrous in the region below Red-river landing. As it was, the rise proved unfortunate for the region above this point. The channel being nearly filled by the remains of the preceding rise, and the draining of crevasse water from the swamps, the increase of the discharge caused by the flood mostly poured into the St. Francis and White-river basins. Although comparatively little of this flood entered the Yazoo and Tensas bottoms, yet the rise prevented many of the breaks in the levees from being closed, and thus indirectly augmented the ruinous effect of the next rise.

Fourth and memorable rise.

The last and greatest rise in the flood of 1858 occurred at the head of the alluvial region in the month of June. About the middle of May extensive rains prevailed in the Ohio valley, and occasioned much damage by flooding the small streams. They also prevailed west of the Ohio basin and caused a rapid rise in the lower tributaries of the Upper Mississippi and Missouri. These rains continued, especially in the States of Ohio, Indiana, Illinois, and Missouri, raised the Miami, Wabash, and Illinois rivers to unprecedented heights, and filled all the lower tributaries of the Missouri. The usual June rise of the latter river, occasioned by the melting of snow in the Rocky mountains, and the spring and early summer rains along its course, arrived just in time to contribute its waters to the general flood. With the Ohio and Mississippi both in full flood, the torrent which poured into the alluvial region by the river itself and through the swamps above Columbus, was immensely greater than in any of the earlier rises of the year, and second to none of which we have records. For seven days (June 16–22) it amounted to 1,475,000 cubic feet per second. It inundated the city of Cairo. It washed away miles of the insignificant levees along the St. Francis front, and poured rapidly into the bottom lands of that river, which were already deeply overflowed from heavy rains and from the crevasses of the April rise. So small was the actual reservoir capacity of that region that the channels of the six large bayous and of the St. Francis itself were insufficient to give water-way to the flood, returning to the Mississippi. For miles above Stirling, it poured over the banks themselves, washing the remains of the levees into the river. It passed like a great wave through the swamp, causing the deepest overflow ever known. Collecting again, in this manner, at Helena, in about two weeks after it entered the alluvial region, it poured with renewed force upon the lower country. In the White-river swamps, the same conditions existed as in the St. Francis bottom. The Yazoo and Tensas bottoms, on the contrary, were comparatively empty, owing to the general resistance of their levees in the former rises, and served in some degree as reservoirs to diminish the height of the flood below. The former was deeply inundated, although the Yazoo river was returning more than 125,000 cubic feet per second during the whole rise. The latter escaped almost entirely, its bayous being sufficient to carry off the limited amount of crevasse water, and discharge it into Black river, whence it passed down bayou Atchafalaya. Below Red-river landing, the levees remained unbroken, except at the Bell and La Branche crevasses, which submerged the country between the Mississippi and bayou La Fourche. Fortunately the upland tributaries below the Ohio were all low during this great rise, for to this circumstance alone is due the escape of the lower country from general overflow.

Termination of the flood.

The June rise terminated the flood. At the head of the alluvial region, the river fell rapidly to low-water mark, being only retarded by a slight rise which occurred in July. The water that drained from the great St. Francis and Yazoo bottoms maintained the flood discharge at points below them for about six weeks; after which the lower river also subsided rapidly to its lowest stage for the year.

First rise of this flood.

Flood of 1859.—By reference to plate VI, it will be seen that this flood was characterized by two principal rises at the head of the alluvial region. The first, which occurred in December, 1858, was due entirely to a general swelling of the tributaries of the Ohio. In passing down the Mississippi, it received important accessions from the Arkansas and Red rivers, which were both high; but it nowhere attained the level of the natural banks, and consequently produced no direct injury to the country. By filling the channel of the lower river, however, it exerted an important influence upon the succeeding rise. Its height and date were as follows:—

First rise in the flood of 1859.

Locality.	Date.	Stand below h. w. of 1858.
		Feet.
Columbus	December 27–28, 1858.	11.4
Memphis	January 1, 1859.	4.5
Napoleon	December 23, 1858.	8.7
Vicksburg	January 5–7, 1859.	6.7
Natchez	January 7, 1859.	7.8
Red-river landing	January 7–10, 1859.	8.9
Donaldsonville	January 12, 1859.	5.2
Carrollton	January 12–13, 1859.	3.3

Second rise.

The second and great rise at the head of the alluvial region occurred earlier, and remained at its height much longer, than is usual. It consisted of three successive swells, which followed in such rapid succession as to prevent any material fall of the river between them. The first of these swells was occasioned by great freshets in the southern tributaries of the Ohio, which produced a flood in that river. At Louisville, the rapid rise began on February 15. After an actual rise of 37.5 feet at the foot of the falls, the river reached, on February 24, a point above any flood subsequent to 1854, and only 2 feet below the great flood in March of that year. It stood 32 feet on the falls at Louisville, or 10 feet below the highest water ever known. The Missouri, the Upper Mississippi and the northern tributaries of the Ohio were in excellent boating condition, but not, properly speaking, in flood. This swell in the Mississippi at Columbus was highest on March 7, when it was 2.9 feet below the high water of 1858. After a gradual subsidence of 4.3 feet, the river at this point again rose under the combined influence of a series of freshets in the lower tributaries of the Upper Mississippi and Ohio, until, on April 1, it attained a point only 0.6 of a foot below the former swell. It then again gradually receded until, on April 25, it had fallen 4.0 feet. It at once began to swell again, however, from a general flood in the Ohio valley, which attained its height at Louisville (5 feet below the February rise) on May 2. This produced the highest water of the season at Columbus, where, on May 8, the river stood only 2.1 feet below high water of 1858. It fell immediately about 9 feet, when a sudden freshet in the Missouri and Upper Mississippi brought it to a stand, but only for about two weeks. It then again rapidly and finally subsided, being only checked about three weeks, in the latter part of June and first part of July, by the mountain rise of the Missouri, aided by a great freshet in the Upper Mississippi.

Explanatory remarks upon this flood, above the Ohio.

Such is the general history of this flood at the head of the alluvial region. Only a small quantity of water escaped from the river into the St. Francis bottom above Columbus. The highest point attained there was more than 2 feet below the level of the flood of 1858, and the maximum discharge into the alluvial region was at least 200,000 cubic feet per second less than in that great flood. (See Chapter VI.)

At Memphis.

By reference to plate VI, it will be seen that the three swells, which constituted the great rise at Columbus, became blended into one at Memphis, and thus caused the river to remain for *eighty consecutive days* within about a foot of high-water mark. This anomaly was due partly to the reservoir action on the channel between these two places, and partly to the loss of the water which escaped into the St. Francis bottom at the top of the swells, and thus passed Memphis, not in the river-bed but in the swamps. The highest point attained in 1859 was 0.1 of a foot below the high water of 1858, a difference doubtless accidental. The *duration* of the high stand, however, so far from the gulf, was unprecedented; and it explains many apparent contradictions in the history of this peculiar flood. *For about eighty consecutive days, as much water entered the delta region as could pass Memphis in the channel of the river in the present condition of the levees.* Consequently, freshets in the lower tributaries, which, under the usual varying condition of the upper river, might pour into the Mississppi and pass off unnoticed, must have exercised a most important influence upon local high-water marks in this *continuous* flood of the upper river. Such was actually the case. To exhibit the anomalous character of this long duration of extreme high water at Memphis, the following table has been prepared from Appendix B:—

Stand of the river at Memphis in different floods.

River stood at Memphis	1849.	1850.	1851.	1858.	1859.	Remarks.
	Days.	*Days.*	*Days.*	*Days.*	*Days.*	
Within 1 foot of highest water................	0	33	0	37	69	Highest water-mark (1858) reads 35.3 on gauge.
" 2 feet " "	0	55	28 ?	52	84	
" 3 feet " "	0	66	42 ?	70	91	

At Helena.

At Helena the river was highest on March 22, when it attained a level 1 foot below the high water of 1858. It then gradually declined with gentle oscillations, being, on April 2, 2.1 feet, and on May 14, 3.1 feet, and on May 26, 2.8 feet below the high water of 1858. This early date of high water at Helena was caused by a freshet in the St. Francis river. The heavy rains, which, as already seen, produced the first swell of the great rise by filling the southern tributaries of the Ohio, extended over the basins of the St. Francis and White rivers, and caused floods in both these streams. The former stream was so full that the rapid rise of the Mississippi at its mouth did not back it up even for a day. In the latter part of March, its current was credibly reported to exceed 6 feet per second, which would give a discharge of 200,000 cubic feet per second. Much of this was doubtless returning Mississippi water that had escaped below Columbus, at which town the discharge at this date (plate XVII) was about 250,000 cubic feet per second less than at high water in 1858. Much of the St. Francis discharge, however, was undoubtedly legitimate drainage from the basin. The subsequent gradual fall of the Mississippi at Helena was due partly to the failure of this supply and partly to the increasing dimensions of the crevasses below the town.

Between the St. Francis and Arkansas rivers.

Between Helena and Napoleon, the crevasses were less disastrous than in 1858. The Yazoo-pass levee resisted the flood in 1859, and the breaks which did occur were much fewer in number than in the preceding year. The effect of this was to increase relatively the height of the flood in 1859 at Napoleon. This result was still further promoted by the condition of the White and Arkansas rivers, the former of which was in flood and the latter in good boating condition in March, at the precise date when the freshet in the St. Francis river was producing the maximum discharge in the year at its mouth. White river was very high, being on March 24 about half a foot higher at Indian-bay landing than at any time in 1858. This coincidence of the maximum discharge from above with the freshet in White river, produced the highest water of the year at Napoleon, where, in the latter part of March, the river stood 0.3 of a foot above the high water of 1858.

Between Napoleon and Lake Providence.

Between Napoleon and Lake Providence, the number of crevasses was about the same as in 1858, but the influence of the American-bend cut-off, in depressing the flood level immediately above and elevating it immediately below, was indicated by the general exemption from breaks in the levees above, and by the large number of them which occurred in the bends just below its site. At Lake Providence the river attained its highest stand (0.8 of a foot above the high water of 1858) about April 25–28, the date being doubtless affected by backwater from the mouth of Yazoo river.

Between Lake Providence and New Orleans.

Between Napoleon and Vicksburg, the crevasses in 1858 and 1859 were about equal, and we accordingly find that, at the date of high water at Napoleon in 1859, the river had about the same relative stand (0.3 of a foot above the high water of 1858) at the two places. This date, however, was not that of highest water at Vicksburg and points below. The Yazoo river caused this apparent anomaly. As already stated, the Yazoo-pass levee remained unbroken, and the number of crevasses in the *upper part of the bottom* (which alone drain past Yazoo City in Yazoo river) was materially less in 1859 than in 1858. Yet we find that at Yazoo City, on March 17, the river was rapidly rising; on March 25, it lacked only 4 feet of the high water of 1858, heavy rains in northern Mississippi, with freshets in Yallabusha and Tallahatchee rivers, being also reported; on April 3, the flood was equal to that of 1858, and, on April 15, with far less water from the Mississippi, it was *half a foot above that level.* By May 20, the river had fallen 0.9 of a foot at Yazoo City, and from that date it continued to recede slowly. *This rain-water freshet* in the Yazoo river, encountering the *continuous* maximum channel discharge from the head of the alluvial region, produced at Vicksburg, and many points below, the highest flood level ever yet recorded. High water occurred at Vicksburg on April 21, continuing to April 30, and was 1.3 feet above the high water of 1858; at Natchez, on May 2, and was 1.2 feet above the high water of 1858; at Baton Rouge, on May 6, and was 0.5 of a foot above the high water of 1858; at Donaldsonville, on May 6, and was 0.5 of a foot above the high water of 1858; and at Carrollton, on May 6, and was 0.4 of a foot above the high water of 1858. Red river was low during this entire flood, and it is probable that bayou Atchafalaya, besides carrying off the river and crevasse drainage from the Tensas bottom lands, relieved the Mississippi by the channel of Old river of some part of its surplus discharge. Owing to the absence of the gentleman who had formerly kept the gauge at Red river, however, no definite information as to this flood at that point has been collected.

Crevasses in this flood.

No reconnoissance of the crevasses of this year was made, and the information collected respecting them is, consequently, somewhat vague. Especial attention, however, has been bestowed upon collecting all available data, and the following list is believed to be tolerably exact, and—for the region below Napoleon at least—nearly complete:—

Crevasses in the flood of 1859.

Locality.	Bank.	Date of breaking.	Remarks.
Opposite mouth of St. Francis river	Left.	Prior to March 25.	
Opposite Helena	Left.	Prior to March 25.	
Near Friar's point	Left.	Prior to March 25.	
Near Island 66	Left.	Prior to March 30.	Bad break.
Below Island 68	Right.	March 20.	
Below Island 74	Left.	Prior to March 25.	
At Prentiss	Left.	March 17.	900 feet wide; much excavation.
Near Island 78	Left.	Prior to March 25.	
Below Greenville	Left.	Prior to March 31.	
In Old river; American bend	Left.	Prior to March 31.	
In Kentucky bend	Left.	In March.	Several breaks.
Above Island 88	Right.	Prior to March 18.	
Below Island 89	Left.	Prior to March 25.	
Below Tallula	Left.	March 14.	Maximum width, 3000 ft.; depth, 3 ft.
Opposite Island 100	Left.	March 10.	Closed May 21.
Below Island 102	Right.	April 17.	
Bend above Vicksburg	Right.	March 24.	Maximum width, 1000 feet.
Opposite Vicksburg	Right.	March 9.	
Near Warrenton	Right.	April 20.	
Near Warrenton	Right.	March 30.	
Near Warrenton	Right.	April 10.	
Opposite Island 104	Right.	March 31.	
Above Island 106	Left.	April 9.	
Below New Carthage	Right.	Prior to April 25.	
Above Island 110	Right.	May 1.	
Above Grand Gulf	Right.	April 9.	
Near Island 115	Right.	April 5.	
Above Ellis cliffs	Right.	April 20.	
Above Port Adams	Right.	April 25.	
Below Red-river landing	Right.	April 14.	
10 miles above Baton Rouge	Right.	Prior to May 5.	
In Bonnet Carré bend	Left.	April 19.	Max. depth, 9 ft.; max. width, 4000 ft

It will be seen, by referring to plate VI, that the river subsided unusually early, a fortunate circumstance, which enabled many planters to raise fair crops even in the inundated districts. The general ravages of the flood may be summed up as follows: The St. Francis bottom was overflowed, but to a much less extent than in 1858. Above the mouth of White river, the Yazoo bottom escaped with comparatively trifling damage, but below that point it was deeply flooded. The White-river bottom lands were submerged. The Tensas bottom lands above Columbia escaped uninjured, but below that town they were badly overflowed. Below Red-river landing no serious damage was done, except on the left bank in the vicinity of Bonnet Carré, where the country was flooded by a crevasse which occurred at the lower end of the site of the celebrated break of 1850.

Ravages of this flood.

In conclusion, it may be said that the flood of 1859 was peculiar in many respects, and that many erroneous deductions have been made from it by those possessed of only a limited knowledge of the important facts bearing upon the subject. The preceding statement of the actual condition of the river and of its tributaries is authentic, and, as will appear in Chapter VI, it explains perfectly all the apparent anomalies presented by the flood.

Concluding remarks.

CHAPTER III.

STATE OF THE SCIENCE OF HYDRAULICS AS APPLIED TO RIVERS.

Early history of hydraulics.—Epoch of Guglielmini.—Era of modern experimental investigation.—New system of notation.—Various methods of measuring the velocity of rivers.—Velocity below the surface in any given vertical plane.—Horizontal curves of velocity.—True mean velocity.—Chezy formula.—Dubuat formula.—Girard formula.—De Prony formula.—Eytelwein formula.—Young formula.—Local formulæ of Lombardini.—Weisbach formula.—Baumgarten formula.—Dupuit formula.—Local formula of Ellet.—Taylor formula.—Saint Venant formula.—Ellet formula.—Stevenson formula.

Scope of this chapter.

THE solution of that great problem, the best method of preventing the overflows of the Mississippi, exacted difficult measurements and extremely intricate computations. In connection with it, a careful examination of all writings upon hydraulics that were within reach was made, to ascertain precisely the present state of that science; a list of the principal publications upon the subject, with a brief synopsis of those parts of their contents that are connected with the present problem, has been prepared for future reference. It will be found from this that the laws which govern the flow of water in natural channels were only partially and imperfectly developed; but, as a knowledge of those laws was essential to the determination of the plans of protecting the Mississippi valley from inundation, the investigations of the Delta Survey, conducted with that object, in accomplishing it, have necessarily contributed to the advancement of the science of hydraulics. An account of these investigations will be presented in full detail in the two following chapters. This chapter is devoted to a brief notice of published works, which is partly original and partly compiled from similar notices by Rennie, Lombardini, Storrow, and others, and from the various encyclopædias.

OUTLINE OF THE HISTORY OF HYDRAULICS APPLIED TO RIVERS.

Early history of the science of hydraulics.

Earlier history.—Practical acquaintance with the general laws of flowing water preceded any knowledge of hydraulics as a science, and, even after some of its fundamental principles had been discovered by Archimedes, the progress of the science was almost imperceptible for ages. It is probably because the complicated nature of its problems renders an extensive knowledge of the mechanics of solids essential before their solution can be attempted, that no abstract discussion of the subject in the writings of the early engineers is found, even when describing hydraulic works, which, like the Roman aqueducts, remain to this day unsurpassed in extent and magnificence. Although Rome in A.D. 98 was supplied with water by nine aqueducts whose aggregate length amounted to 250 miles, and whose discharge was 27,000,000 cubic feet per day, still hydraulics was not considered entitled to the rank of a science until about the fourteenth century. At this time the difficulty of navigating the mountain streams of Italy, the devastating effects of their floods, and the continual litigation arising from the precautionary measures adopted to restrain them, drew the attention of philosophers to the subject. The invention of the canal lock was the result of their labors, and marked a new era in hydraulic engineering.* Several canals were constructed, and many more projected. In fact, the new invention for a season withdrew attention from rivers and concentrated it upon canals.

In the seventeenth century the science of hydraulics began to assume a rapidly progressive character, a change attributed to the influence of Galileo, although he personally contributed little to the subject.

In 1628 a valuable treatise upon rivers was published by Castelli, a disciple of this great master, who investigated the subject by direction of Pope Urban VIII. He first introduced the velocity as an element in estimating the discharge of a river.

Torricelli's theory.

In 1643 another pupil of Galileo, the celebrated Torricelli, discovered that, abstracting all resistances, the velocities of fluid veins flowing freely from small orifices in a reservoir are equal to those of heavy bodies which have fallen *in vacuo*, distances equal to the depths of the orifices below the water surface; that is, they are proportional to the square roots of these depths, whence he deduced his fundamental theorem, destined to become the basis of a general theory of hydraulics, that, neglecting resistances, the velocities of fluids in motion are in the subduplicate ratio of the pressures. He also endeavored to trace an analogy between such spouting fluids and rivers, and argued that the acceleration of the currents of the latter is due to the slope of their surfaces.

Several contributions to the science were made by Pascal, in his works published between the years 1646 and 1663.

In 1665 contests among the inhabitants of the Chiana valley induced the governments of Rome and Florence to assemble a scientific congress to report upon the best method of disposing of the water of the stream which occasioned the disputes. Many theoretical essays upon river improvements were the result, but little of value was added to the science.

In 1684 the great work† of Mariotte appeared. It was published after the death of the author. Adopting Torricelli's parabolic theory of flowing water, he discussed many problems in a masterly manner, but the chief benefit which he conferred upon the science was to point out by his numerous experiments the only true method of investigating the subject.

Guglielmini.

Epoch of Guglielmini.—The works of Guglielmini, the great master of the Italian school, appeared near the close of the seventeenth century. Adopting the theorem of Torricelli, he perfected the celebrated parabolic theory

* The lock was first applied to the canal leading from the Ticino to Milan, upon which the stone for the construction of the cathedral, which has been nearly five centuries in process of erection, was transported. In that city the first lock was built, and it remains at the present day unimpaired by time. To it Leonardo da Vinci, one of the many architects employed upon the cathedral, made the first application of his invention of the mitre-sill gate in the last decade of the fifteenth, or the first of the sixteenth century. (Lombardini.)

† Traité du Mouvement des Eaux.

of rivers, which may be briefly stated as follows: Any particle x feet below the surface of a fluid mass will have a tendency to move with the same velocity with which it would issue from an orifice in the side of a reservoir, x feet below the surface of the fluid contained in it: that is, with the velocity it would acquire in falling x feet *in vacuo*, a velocity given by the formula $V = (2gx)^{1/2}$. Hence if a vertical line is drawn through the point and made the axis of a parabola whose vertex is at the water surface and whose parameter is equal to four times the distance through which a heavy body will pass in the first second of its fall, the velocity with which the particle has a tendency to move will be shown by its ordinate.

According to this theory the velocity of any particle of water in a river will be equal to that acquired by a heavy body which has fallen from a state of rest through a distance equal to the distance of the particle below the plane of the surface of its source, produced.

The legitimate consequences which result from this theory are all contrary to observation, and the fact that it was adopted by so many eminent writers shows how entirely the science was separated from observation at this period of its history. Guglielmini was sensible of the great discrepancies between his theoretical and the practical laws of rivers, and endeavored to explain them. His works have given him the chief place among the Italian hydraulic engineers of his time.

Newton, in his Principia, discussed the friction of fluids on solids, and the discharge through orifices in reservoirs. Some of the conclusions at which he arrived were shown to be erroneous, and he materially, although not sufficiently, modified them in the edition of 1714. His contributions to hydraulics, although important, were much less valuable than those to other departments of science.

The Marquis Poleni published a work* in 1718 upon the discharge of fluids from orifices, which was based upon numerous experiments. He was the first to discover that the discharge through an orifice in a thin plate may be increased by adapting to it a small cylindrical tube.

In 1725 Varignon published his ingenious work on hydraulics, in which he reduced the opinions of Guglielmini to algebraic formulæ, but added no new ideas of consequence to the science.

Error of the adopted theory demonstrated by observations with Pitot's tube.

Several papers upon hydraulics were submitted to the French Academy, by Pitot, between the years 1730 and 1738, in one of which, published in 1732, he detailed the results of a series of experiments upon velocities at different depths, made by means of the tube which bears his name, experiments which demonstrate the fallacy of the parabolic theory of flowing water.

The results of a noted series of experiments by Couplet, upon the discharge of the water-pipes at Versailles, were published in the Memoirs of the French Academy in 1732. About this time the works of many Italian writers of celebrity appeared. Among these may be enumerated Grandi, Manfredi, Zendrini, Frisi,† Zanotti, Gennette, etc.

---

* De Castellis per quæ Derivantur Fluviorum Aquæ.

† On Rivers and Torrents, translated by General Garstin. London, 1818.

Bernouilli school.

In 1738 the work* of Daniel Bernouilli appeared. In it he applied the principle of living force to the motion of fluids, and thus originated one of the schools of hydraulics.

In 1742 the work of John Bernouilli appeared, containing an exposition of his theory of flowing water, upon the study of which he had been long engaged. His results did not differ materially from those of his son, although deduced in a different way.

The celebrated writings of d'Alembert appeared between 1743 and 1752, works which have been considered of value to the theoretical science of hydraulics.

Lecchi, an engineer of celebrity, published, in 1765, a very complete work at Milan, in which he discussed the various theories of flowing water.

Profound theoretical papers by Euler, upon the motion of fluids, may be found in the Memoirs of the Academy of St. Petersburg, for the years 1768, 1769, 1770, 1771, but they have little practical value, as he assumes a mathematical fluidity as the basis of his system.

Commencement of the era of experimental investigation.

Era of experimental investigation.—It was reserved for Professor Michelotti, of Turin, and the Abbé Bossut, of Paris, to inaugurate a new era in hydraulics, by establishing, as a fundamental principle, that formulæ must be deduced from experiment, and not from abstract reasoning. The former, in 1764, undertook an extensive series of experiments, under the patronage of the king of Sardinia. The results were published,† in detail, in 1774. The latter, under the patronage of the French government, made numerous experiments on a less scale than his rival, but better adapted to solve practical questions. The results were published from 1771 to 1778, and have been of very great value to later writers in deducing constants, and testing formulæ.

From this epoch may be dated the origin of the modern school of hydraulics. Earlier writings now possess comparatively little importance to the practical engineer.

First formula for mean velocity in terms of the slope and dimensions of cross-section.

In 1775 M. Chezy, a celebrated French engineer, first attempted to express by an algebraic formula the laws of water in motion, taking into account the effect of the retarding forces.

In 1782 Belidor published his voluminous work‡ on hydraulics.

In 1784 two papers, on the expenditure of water through large orifices, and on the junction and separation of rivers, were published in the Memoirs of the Academy of Science, at Toulouse, by M. l'Espinasse.

Dubuat's great work.

In 1779 appeared the preliminary edition, and in 1786, the completed work§ of M. Dubuat, upon which he had expended the labor of ten years. Starting with the law that, when water flows uniformly in any channel, the forces which keep it in motion are equal to the sum of all the resistances, Dubuat reasoned that the true method of deducing a formula to express the laws of water in uniform motion was to find by experiment algebraic expressions for these two

* Hydrodynamica seu de Viribus et Motibus Fluidorum Commentarii. Strasburg.

† Sperienze Idrauliche.

‡ Architecture Hydraulique. Paris.

§ Principes d'Hydraulique Vérifiés par un Grand Nombre d'Expériences, faites par Ordre de Gouvernement. An enlarged edition, called Principes d'Hydraulique et de Pyrodynamique, appeared in 1816.

equal and contrary forces and equate them. This he did in a manner that beautifully illustrates Daniel Bernouilli's empirical method of generalizing natural phenomena. He established the principles that the motive force of each particle of water in a river is due entirely to the surface slope, and that the resistances are due to viscosity and the friction upon the bed. First proving that a close analogy can be traced between the motion of water in pipes and in rivers, he proceeded, by many ingenious experiments upon pipes, and logical deductions therefrom, to determine values for these various quantities, until finally he produced a formula, which, although complicated, is applicable to most problems of water in uniform motion. In his treatise he fully illustrated the manner of its practical application, discussed the general questions interesting to the hydraulic engineer, and, in fine, produced a work which is still of standard authority in the science.

In 1787 a valuable work* on hydraulics, by Bernard, appeared; based in part upon the theories of Dubuat, Bossut, d'Alembert, and Bernouilli.

In 1789 and 1790 Brünings† made some important experiments upon velocity at different depths.

A work‡ upon hydraulics, in four volumes, by Woltmann, appeared at Göttingen between the years of 1791 and 1799.

In 1797 Fabre published a work§ on torrents.

Venturi published a memoir, in 1798, giving the results of a series of experiments upon the contraction of the fluid vein, in which, among other questions, he discusses the effect of eddies in rivers, and shows that they are a cause of retardation to the current. This paper was translated by William Nicholson in 1799, and published by Thomas Tredgold in his "Tracts on Hydraulics."

Coulomb's law.

In 1800 Coulomb published a paper,‖ in which, after an elaborate investigation of the laws of friction between fluids and solids, he shows, besides other results, that the resistances may be represented by a function consisting only of two terms, one containing the first, and the other the second, power of the velocity. He did not, however, apply this most valuable discovery to equations representing the movement of flowing water.

In 1801 M. Eytelwein published a large work¶ on hydraulics, which has been translated by Nicholson, besides receiving a detailed notice from Dr. Young in the Journal of the Royal Institution. The writer followed the methods of Dubuat in discussing the motion of water in open channels.

It is applied to water flowing in open channels.

In 1803 M. Girard** first applied the law of Coulomb to the motion of water flowing in open channels, deducing a formula much more simple than that of Dubuat. He wrote several other articles upon hydraulics, more especially treating of canals, and made many valuable experiments.

---

* Nouveaux Principes d'Hydraulique.

† Sur la Communication Latéral du Mouvements des Fluides.

‡ Beiträge zur Hydraulischen Architektur.

§ Théorie des Torrents et Rivières. Paris, 1797.

‖ Expériences destinées à Determiner la Cohérence des Fluides et les Lois de leurs Resistances dans les Mouvements tres Lentes.

¶ Handbuch der Mechanik und der Hydraulik.

** Rapport sur le Projet Général du Canal de l'Ourcq.

The next writer of note upon the subject was M. de Prony. His first work* contained nothing relating to rivers. His second work† upon hydraulics appeared in 1802. In this he discussed the methods of gauging by weirs, reservoirs, etc., and determined valuable formulæ for the discharge through vertical and horizontal orifices. It is, however, his third work,‡ published in 1804, that has placed him among the chief writers upon river hydraulics. In this work he begins by discussing the laws which govern a system of heavy bodies moving in circumstances similar to those of fluids in uniform motion. He then modifies his results by introducing the condition of fluidity. He next shows, by discussing experiments, that as indicated by Coulomb, the resistances may in practice be represented by an expression involving only two terms, one containing the first, and the other the second, power of the mean velocity; but that, contrary to the results of both Coulomb and Girard, these terms should be affected by independent coefficients and not by a common one. He then proceeds to discuss various careful observations of Dubuat and others, and to deduce from them the values of these coefficients for pipes and for canals, and for either indiscriminately. This he does by employing two methods given by La Place in his Mécanique Céleste, and, finally, by a general equalization of disturbing causes. He explains how to simplify the calculus of La Place, in deducing these values, by some ingenious diagrams; discusses Dubuat's formula for obtaining the mean velocity, etc., from that at the surface; advances a new formula of his own for this purpose, etc., etc. This work must always remain a standard authority upon the uniform motion of water in pipes and open channels, and it is much to be regretted that it is now entirely out of print.

De Prony's writings.

Another paper§ upon the subject was published by M. de Prony, in 1825, giving methods of simplifying computations by his formulæ, etc.

In 1804 Lecreulx published a work|| upon the formation of the beds of streams.

In the Memoirs of the Italian Society, 1807, a paper by Focacci appeared, detailing the results of certain measurements of velocity below the surface.

In the Philosophical Transactions of the Royal Society for 1808, a paper by Dr. Thomas Young was published, giving new formulæ for flowing water.

In 1808–9 a work¶ upon hydraulic architecture, by Fünk, appeared.

In 1809 experiments were made by MM. Mallet and Vici, upon the discharge of water-pipes.

In 1813 M. Kraÿenhoff presented a very full collection of tables of observations** upon the topography and hydrography of Holland, a work whose value will be only increased by time. He made a few detailed measurements of discharge, slope of surface, etc., determining the velocity at various distances from the banks by noting the time of transit past a base line, of vertical float-poles extending from the surface nearly to the bottom. This work contains extensive tables of the slopes of the rivers in Holland, records of gauge observations

Kraÿenhoff's observations upon the rivers of Holland.

* Nouvelle Architecture Hydraulique (first volume published in 1790, and second in 1796).

† Sur le Jaugeage des Eaux Courantes.

‡ Recherches Physico-mathématiques sur la Théorie des Eaux Courantes.

§ Recueil de Cinq Tables pour Faciliter et Abréger les Calculs des Formules Relatifs au Mouvement des Eaux, etc.

|| Recherches sur la Formation et l'Existence des Ruisseaux, Rivières et Torrents. Paris, 1804.

¶ Beiträge zur allgemeinen Wasserbaukunst.

** Recueil des Observations Hydrauliques et Topographiques faites en Hollande, 1835.

upon them referred to a common datum-plane, etc. A similar work upon the Mississippi, bearing the same date, would now be of very great value.

In the Memoirs of the Academy of Berlin, 1814, 1815, articles by M. Eytelwein appeared, giving his celebrated new values to the constants in de Prony's formulæ, etc.

In two memoirs, presented to the Académie Royale des Sciences, in 1815 and 1816, M. Hachette treated of the form of fluid veins.

In 1816 Girard read before the French Academy an elaborate work* upon the Nile.

Girard upon the Nile.

This paper was accompanied by a diagram showing the readings of a daily gauge kept for the years 1799, 1800, and 1801; being the first graphic representation of the kind on record.

In 1820 a second work was published by Fünk,† upon the hydraulics of rivers.

In 1821 Escher de la Linth read a paper‡ before the Helvetic Society of Natural Sciences in Basle upon the upper Rhine. Modifying the discharge given by Eytelwein's formula by a few measurements of surface velocity, he prepared a scale of discharge adapted to a daily gauge-record, and thence deduced the annual discharge from 1809 to 1821 at Basle.

In 1822 Brewster published a large collection of philosophical writings§ by Robison, which contains (in vol. II) papers upon the resistances of fluids, rivers, etc. The article upon rivers chiefly consists, after a brief historical notice of the subject, of an extended synopsis of Dubuat's great work, whose views Robison in the main adopts.

In 1822 de Prony published his well-known work‖ on the Pontine Marshes.

In 1822 General Bernard and Lieutenant-Colonel Totten, then constituting a Board

Report upon the Ohio and Mississippi rivers.

of Engineers, submitted a report upon the Ohio and Mississippi rivers to the Colonel Commandant of the U. S. Engineers. This report was transmitted to Congress and printed,¶ but without the accompanying maps. It contains much definite information about the falls of the Ohio and about the bars below them, of which there were then twenty-one. The remarks upon the Mississippi are in less detail, but the accompanying series of manuscript maps made by Captain Young, Captain Poussin, and Lieutenant Tuttle, furnishes an admirable model for a river reconnoissance. They are now on file in the Bureau of Topographical Engineers.

In 1823 a valuable collection of Italian papers upon hydraulics was published at Bologna. It was a continuation of the Italian collection noticed by Abbé Mann in the Philosophical Transactions, 1779.

In 1824 M. Bidone presented a paper** upon the flow of water over weirs.

Raucourt upon the Neva.

In 1824–26 M. Raucourt made his celebrated experiments upon the Neva when frozen and when open. These were partially tested by MM. Destrem and Henry.††

* Observations sur la Vallée d'Egypte et sur Exhaussement Séculaire du Sol qui la Recouvre. Mém. de l'Acad. des Sci. 1817. Paris, 1819.

† Von der Bewegung des Wassers in Strom- und Flussbetten. Berlin, 1824. 4to.

‡ For an extract, see Biblioteca Universale di Ginevra, 1821.

§ System of Mechanical Philosophy by John Robison, with notes by David Brewster; in four volumes and a volume of plates. Edinburgh, 1822.

‖ Description Hydrographique et Historique des Marais Pontins. Paris, 1822.

¶ Report of the Board of Engineers on the Ohio and Mississippi rivers, from an Examination made in the months of September, October, November, and December, 1821. Washington, 1823.

** Mémoires de l'Académie des Sciences de Turin.

†† Journal des Voies de Communication, 1826. St. Petersbourg.

Theory of "permanent motion" introduced.

M. Poncelet published, in 1828, a work* treating of water in permanent motion, that is, while moving with an established regimen through a canal whose area and slope vary within limits.

In the same year M. Belanger published his noted work† upon water in permanent motion, containing an original formula based upon assumptions more nearly analogous to the condition of water flowing in rivers than any which had preceded it.

In 1829 M. Genieys published a practical treatise‡ upon water-works, in which he treated of various questions interesting to the hydraulic engineer.

In 1826 and 1827 a series of experiments upon discharge through various kinds of orifices was made by M. Bidone, and in 1829 he read two papers—the first giving the results of the experiments, and the second, the theoretical deduction from them—to the Academy of Sciences at Turin.

In 1831 Girard published an elaborate report§ upon the Canal de l'Ourcq, which had been under his direction. In this report he treats theoretically of the movements of flowing water.

In 1831 Laval submitted a project for the improvement of the navigation of the river Midouze, based upon the principle of deepening the channel by confining the current between artificial banks of a peculiar kind. This paper is to be found in the Annales des Ponts et Chaussées, 1831. Its author gives the data collected when gauging the river during a flood in 1826, but without any satisfactory details.

The Poncelet and Lesbros experiments.

In 1827 experiments were begun at Metz upon a large scale to establish the principles of, and fix the values of the constants in, the formulæ for water flowing through orifices. The work was performed under the patronage of the French government, by MM. Poncelet and Lesbros. A paper upon the subject was read before the Académie des Sciences in 1829. The report|| was published in 1832.

In the Journal of the Asiatic Society, 1832, appeared a paper by Everest, upon the earthy matter and volume of water brought down by the Ganges at Ghazipur, Bengal. He considered the annual discharge to be about 6½ trillions of cubic feet, the contributions of sedimentary matter being about 6 billions of cubic feet.

Defontaine upon the Rhine.

In 1820 M. Defontaine began a series of observations upon the Rhine and its tributaries, the results of which were published¶ in 1833. These are among the most valuable contributions of modern times, from the number of experiments and the detailed information upon the different methods in use for conducting works of river improvement. The object of these works was to protect the banks from caving, and the surrounding country from overflow during floods. They were of two classes, temporary and permanent. The former consisted of works to close chutes by inducing deposits of sediment, etc., which, being of no service after their object was accomplished, were made of perishable materials. The latter consisted

* Cours de Mécanique fait a l'École d'Artillerie de Metz.

† Essai sur la Solution Numérique de quelques Problêmes relatifs au Mouvement Permanent des Eaux Courantes.

‡ Essai sur les moyens de Conduire, d'Élever, et de Distribuer les Eaux. Paris.

§ Mémoires sur le Canal de l'Ourcq. Paris.

|| Expériences sur les Lois d'Écoulement de l'Eau à les Orifices Rectangulaires Verticaux en Minces Parois Planes. Paris, 1832. Also continued by Lesbros. Paris, 1851.

¶ Travaux du Rhin. See also Annales des Ponts et Chaussées. Mém. 1833.

of levees and either solid revetements or breakwaters, to secure the banks when exposed to caving. The details of the construction of these different classes of works are very fully set forth in the memoir, together with a mass of exact information about the Rhine itself. The dimensions of the levees are far greater than those of the Mississippi levees, being about 10 feet thick at top, with a slope of one upon two toward the river, and one upon one and a half toward the land. The top is made with a very gentle transverse slope, so as to drain inland the rain which falls upon it. The heights of the levees are calculated so as to be a foot and a half above the highest floods. Even those large levees are not considered sufficient. Strips of grass-land are left on both sides, 6½ feet wide on the outside and 3½ on the inside, reckoning from the foot of the slope of the levee. Willows and poplars are planted at the outside edges of these strips of grass-land. When the levees are more than about 7 feet high, a substantial inner and outer banquette is added to guard against filtration. Where the current of the river would be liable to act upon the levees, its force is broken by large and strong traverses, placed from 600 to 1000 feet apart, and guarded, if need be, with fascines. Defontaine made a few careful measurements of discharge, with a view to test the various formulæ for mean velocity, but he did not publish his results in this memoir, except to state in a general way that the usual formulæ for deducing the mean from the surface velocity gave too small a discharge. His experiments upon velocity below the surface will be mentioned elsewhere. He advocates, for improving the Rhine, first, the closing of all chutes, so as to confine the river to a single channel; and second, the reduction of all straight lines in the river's course to curved. The reason for the latter recommendation is that in a bend the caving is limited to one bank, and it can therefore be more cheaply prevented than when a double line of defensive works is necessary.

The Reports of the British Association for 1833 and 1834 contain two interesting articles by Mr. Rennie, upon the progress of the science. He also details some experiments of his own, upon the friction of fluids upon solids.

Papers treating of water in permanent motion were published by de Saint-Guilhem in the Memoirs of the Academy of Toulouse, 1834 and 1836.

In 1834 a general treatise* upon hydraulics was published by D'Aubuisson de Voisins. A second edition appeared in 1840. A translation of the work, by Mr. J. C. Bennett, was published in Boston in 1852, all the formulæ being adapted to English units of length. This admirable treatise is well known to engineers.

In 1834 M. Deschamps published a memoir† relative to the improvement of navigation on the rivers in the southwest of France, especially on the Garonne. Two years later, he added a supplement,‡ devoted exclusively to the navigation of the Garonne. These works treat especially of canalization, low-water dams, etc., etc.

Destrem upon the Neva.

In 1835 M. Destrem published a collection of memoirs§ on various subjects, some of which had already appeared in the Journal des Voies de Communication. One of them treated of a careful gauging of the Neva river and of its various branches, conducted by himself.

---

* Traité d'Hydraulique à l'usage des Ingénieurs. Strasbourg et Paris.

† Recherches et Considérations sur les Canaux et les Rivières. Paris, 1834.

‡ Supplément aux Recherches et Considérations sur les Canaux et les Rivières. Paris, 1836.

§ Mémoires sur Divers Objets relatifs à la Science de l'Ingénieur. St. Petersbourg, 1835.

In 1835 a work* was published by Mr. Charles S. Storrow, containing a short historical sketch of the progress of hydraulics, with demonstrations of various formulæ proposed by different writers, their practical applications in the construction of water-works, etc. etc.

In the Annales des Ponts et Chaussées, 1836, appeared a memoir by M. Borrel upon the improvement of the navigation of the Garonne and other rivers which flow over gravel beds through alternate rapids and pools.

In the same volume is a long and detailed article upon the theory of water in permanent motion, with several practical applications, by Vauthier.

In the same volume, M. de Coriolis treats of the same subject.

In the publications of the Academy of Sciences of Bologna in 1836 are three memoirs by M. Venturoli, giving a discussion of a daily gauge-record of the Tiber, kept by himself at Rome, for eleven years, together with corresponding discharges computed with Eytelwein's formulæ, assuming the slope to remain constant.

In 1836 Tredgold published, with notes, a collection† of short papers on hydraulics, viz.: Smeaton's experimental papers on the power of water and wind to turn mills; Venturi's experiments on the motion of fluids (1798); and Dr. Young's summary of practical hydraulics, chiefly from the German of Eytelwein. (The latter first appeared in the Journal of the Royal Institute, 1802.)

A series of careful experiments upon flowing water was made at Toulouse in 1835, by Castel, and published in the Annales de Chimie et de Physique, vol. LXII. Paris, 1836. Also in Mémoires de l'Académie des Sciences de Toulouse, t. IV, 1837.

M. Hennocque made a series of measurements and observations upon the Rhine, near Strasburg, in 1839.

M. Baumgarten did the same upon the Garonne between the years 1837 and 1846.

In 1840 M. Dausse obtained the Monthyon premium for a paper inserted in the Comptes Rendus de l'Académie des Sciences, 1840. It was chiefly a discussion of a large collection of statistics of the principal rivers of France, collected with a view to throw light upon the best methods of improving their navigation.

Lombardini's works.

In 1840 Lombardini prepared a treatise‡ upon the basin of the Po, which was published in the third volume of the Politecnico di Milano.

In 1843 a second article§ appeared in the sixth volume of the same publication. Other papers from the pen of this distinguished hydraulic engineer have, from time to time, appeared in the Journal of the I. R. Istituto Lombardo di Scienze, Lettere ed Arti. Among these are, in 1846, two memoirs, one|| upon the importance of the study of the statistics of rivers, containing a brief notice of the labors of various hydraulic engineers; the other¶ upon the effect of lakes in moderating the inundations of rivers. In 1852 a paper** upon the changes in the hydraulic condition of the river Po in the territory of Ferrara, in which he demonstrates that levees have not raised the bed of

* A Treatise on Water-works. Boston, 1835.

† Tracts on Hydraulics. Second edition. London, 1836.

‡ Intorno al Sistema Idraulico del Po.

§ Altre Osservazioni sul Po.

|| Importanza degli Studj sulla Statistica dei Fiumi.

¶ Della Natura dei Laghi.

** Dei Cangiamenti cui Soggiacque l'Idraulica Condizione del Po, nel Territorio di Ferrara.

the Po, although the gradual perfection of their construction and maintenance within the last century and a half has increased the height of the floods by retaining within the banks the water which before escaped through crevasses; and this height has been still further increased, he thinks, by the more rapid flow caused by clearing the sides of the mountains of their forests. This conclusion had been already announced in his earlier works. In 1853 a paper* upon freeing Mantua from the inundations of the Po, in which he proposes, as a part of the plan, to cut off the discharge of the Mincio, during floods in the Po, by a dam with gates at the efflux of lake Garda; the surplus water thus collected to be used to increase the deficient discharge of the river Mincio at low water. This writer, who is well known as one of the first hydraulic engineers of the age, also prepared Chapters IV and V of the first volume of the "Notizie Naturali e Civili su la Lombardia. Milano, 1844." They treat of the natural and artificial hydraulic condition of Lombardy, and are replete with information statistical and scientific. Among other tables are two containing the monthly discharges of the Adda and the Po for many years, computed from known gauge-readings by original formulæ, which will soon receive further attention. This paper, together with those already named, published in 1840 and 1843, were reproduced in a condensed form by M. Baumgarten in the Annales des Ponts et Chaussées, 1847.

In 1841 a work† was published by Mr. W. A. Brooks, treating chiefly of bars and other obstructions to river navigation. In the appendix the author published a report, prepared by Murray in 1833, upon the improvements in the river Clyde.

In the Annales des Ponts et Chaussées, 1841, may be found an article by M. Laval upon a great freshet in the river Saone, which occurred in the preceding year. It is complete and interesting, especially for showing the very sensible effect of bridges in increasing the height of the flood.

In 1841 M. Surell published a paper‡ upon the torrents of the Alps, in which, among other things, he demonstrates that forests exercise a very important moderating effect, and advises the cultivation of growth on the mountains for this purpose.

In 1842 M. Vallée published a memoir§ upon converting lake Geneva into an artificial reservoir for the surplus flood waters of the Rhone, and eventually using them to improve navigation in the river in seasons of low water.

In the Annales des Ponts et Chaussées for 1842 appeared an elaborate paper by Dausse upon downfall of rain and the influences of forests upon rivers.

In 1843 M. de Buffon published a very complete work|| upon irrigation, in three volumes, the first being historical and descriptive in character; the second treating of practical questions of distribution, construction, etc.; and the third discussing the administration, etc., of irrigating canals. Chapters XIV and XV (contained in vol. II) especially treat of the gauging of streams. In the former the writer, after a cursory notice of the forces acting upon water in motion, and of the great difficulties to be encountered in deducing a correct formula for the mean velocity, refers to the formulæ

---

* Della Sistemazione dei Laghi di Mantova.

† Treatise on the Improvement of the Navigation of Rivers. London, 1841.

‡ Etude sur les Torrents des Hautes Alpes. Paris, 1841.

§ Du Rhône et du Lac de Genève. Paris, 1842.

|| Traité Théorique et Pratique des Irrigations. Paris.

proposed by Chezy, Dubuat, and de Prony. He finally adopts de Prony's formula with Eytelwein's coefficients as the most accurate known, and proceeds to indicate the method of applying it to a few practical problems. In Chapter XV he treats of methods of actually measuring the discharge. He mentions several of the ordinary instruments for determining the velocity, but expresses the opinion that the float, from its simplicity, is superior to them all. After explaining the methods in common use for gauging very small streams, he proceeds to give, in great detail, a statement of the method adopted in gauging the Tiber at Rome on June 19, 1821; considering that in every respect a model to be imitated. The method was, in effect, that adopted by Kraÿenhoff, but carried out with greater exactness both in the field work and in the computation.

In 1845 M. Bourriceau published a work* upon the prevention of obstructions to navigation at the mouths of rivers, in which he advocates the use of diverging walls.

M. M. Sonnet published a work† on hydraulics in 1845.

M. Weisbach, in a work on mechanics, published at Freiberg in 1846, treats very fully of hydraulics; a subject which he had made an especial study. This work was translated‡ in 1848 by Mr. W. R. Johnson.

Surell upon the mouths of the Rhone.

In 1847 M. Surell published an elaborate work§ upon the improvement of the mouths of the Rhone, giving an historical sketch of previous works, a discussion of the feasibility, expense, and advantages of deepening the channel at the mouth by closing all but one of the branches, and a project for a canal to admit vessels to the river, independently of the natural entrances.

Dupuit's work.

M. Dupuit published in 1848 a treatise‖ giving the results of an original and profound theoretical study of the laws of flowing water. This important work appears to be very little known in this country. It treats fully of the laws of water in uniform and permanent motion and contains a discussion of the regimen of rivers well worthy of study.

In the Annales des Ponts et Chaussées for 1848 will be found a summary of the results of a series of experiments made at Roanne to test the truth of some curious indications of the formulæ for water in permanent motion. The experiments were conducted and the article prepared by MM. P. Vauthier and L. L. Vauthier.

Baumgarten on the Garonne.

The Annales des Ponts et Chaussées for 1848 contain a long and exceedingly interesting memoir by M. Baumgarten upon a portion of the Garonne, with an historical notice of the various works of improvement executed upon the river and a discussion of their effects. The writer treats of the topography, geology, and meteorology of the valley; the character of the bed of the river; the movement of its gravel, sand, etc.; its sediment; the slope of surface, both local and general; the duration of the different stages of the river; the temperature of the water; the discharge; the navigability, etc., etc. He reports some interesting and unique measurements upon the transverse section of the water surface at a nearly straight portion of

* Etude de la Navigation des Rivières à Marèe. Paris, 1845.

† Recherches sur le Mouvement des Eaux dans les Tuyaux de Conduite et les Canaux Découverts. Paris.

‡ Weisbach's Mechanics and Engineering. Philadelphia.

§ Mémoire sur l'Amélioration des Embouchures du Rhône. Nîmes, 1847.

‖ Etude Théorique et Pratique sur le Mouvement des Eaux Courantes. Paris.

the river (width about 600 feet), both when the water was rising and falling. When rising, at the rate of about 5 feet in twenty-four hours, with a maximum velocity of about 7 feet per second, he found the water in the middle to be about 0.4 of a foot above that on the right bank, and 0.1 above that on the left. When falling, at the rate of about 8 feet in twenty-four hours, with a maximum velocity of about 7.5 feet per second, the water surface was sensibly a plane, being at the right bank a little less than 0.1 of a foot above its level at the opposite side of the river. The velocities at the banks are unfortunately not given in either case.

In the proceedings of the American Association for the Advancement of Science, for 1848, may be found an interesting paper by Mr. Andrew Brown, detailing the results of a series of discharge and sediment measurements conducted by himself upon the Mississippi river at Natchez. A supplemental paper appeared in the same proceedings in 1853.

Marr upon the Mississippi: first series.

In the proceedings* of the American Association for the Advancement of Science, 1849, is contained a report by Lieutenant Marr, U. S. N., upon certain observations upon the Mississippi river, conducted by himself, at Memphis, Tennessee, during the months of April, May, June, and July, 1849. This report was presented by Lieutenant Maury, U. S. N., at whose instance the observations were directed by the Secretary of the Navy. It contains tables giving the daily gauge-reading, daily discharge, daily mean temperature, weekly evaporation, and daily rain from April 1 to July 15, 1848. For a part of the time the temperature of the river-water at surface and bottom is added. To determine these discharges a cross-section of the river was made, and subdivided into three partial areas. The surface velocity in each of these areas was measured by anchoring the boat and using a "chip" and line. During calm weather the relative velocity near the bottom was also measured by comparing the velocities of a surface float and a double float whose lower portion, composed of a tin vessel, was sunk nearly to the bottom. The discharge was found by taking the sum of the products of the partial areas by the "average" velocities in them. The temperature of the water at the bottom was found to be the same as at the surface. The velocity near the bottom was to that at the surface in the ratio of 268 to 300. The average downfall was 0.11 inches and the average evaporation from the surface of water of considerable depth, 0.13 inches daily.

Ellet upon the Ohio.

In 1849 Mr. Ellet submitted to the Smithsonian Institution a memoir containing some valuable statistical information relative to the physical geography of the Mississippi valley, together with an argument in favor of applying the reservoir system to the improvement of the navigation of the Ohio and other rivers.†

In 1849 appeared the second edition of a collection of tables‡ by M. Claudel; which, among the formulæ, etc., relating to hydraulics, contains some brief extracts from Dupuit's work upon the laws of flowing water.

In Dr. Fenner's Southern Medical Reports, vols. I and II (1849 and 1850, pub-

---

* Published at Boston, Mass., 1850.

† Smithsonian Contributions to Knowledge. Vol. II, Art. 4.

‡ Formules, Tables et Renseignements Pratiques. Paris.

lished in New York and New Orleans) will be found articles written by Professor Forshey which contain interesting facts relative to the floods of the Mississippi river in 1849 and 1850.

Forshey upon the Mississippi.

In 1844 the French government authorized M. Boileau to make a very extended series of hydraulic experiments, at Metz. The results of the experiments upon discharge by weirs and orifices were published in the Journal de l'École Polytechnique, in 1850. The detailed report,* giving the results of seven or eight years of labor, appeared in 1854. It contains many original formulæ, and is a work of much value to the science.

Boileau's extended experiments.

In 1850 a report to the legislature of Louisiana was made by a joint committee on levees. This document was published, and contains valuable information. Among the papers accompanying it is a "Memoir upon the Physics of the Mississippi River," by Professor Forshey, illustrated by several diagrams. Many other valuable papers upon the Mississippi river are to be found among the public documents of Louisiana.

In 1851 Mr. Ellet submitted a report to the Bureau of Topographical Engineers, War Department, upon a survey made by himself under its direction to determine the best method of preventing the overflows of the delta of the Mississippi. This paper constitutes part of Ex. Doc. 20, 1st Session, 32d Congress. Occasional references to it will be found in different parts of this report.

Ellet upon the Mississippi.

In 1851 was published a work† by Mr. T. J. Taylor, upon the laws governing the action of rivers, with an especial application of them to the Tyne. A discussion of the effect of the running water upon the bed itself constitutes the greater part of this book. The writer deduces, without naming the originators, Dubuat's formula for the velocity at the bottom in terms of that at the surface, and Chezy's formula for the mean velocity, adopting 100 for the experimental coefficient. He subsequently proposes an original formula for the mean velocity, which will be given in the proper place. He advocates for the improvement of the Tyne a prolongation of the banks by means of two piers to be carried out upon the bar to the point where the along-shore tidal currents are decidedly felt; and the closing, by a solid quay, of Yarrow Slake and the Coble Dean Indentations, tracts of low land, which serve as reservoirs at high tide. By these means he expects to increase the velocity sufficiently to deepen the bed in the lower portion of the river at least 5 feet.

In 1851 M. de Saint Venant published a work‡ on hydraulics, containing original views and formulæ.

A second series of observations upon the Mississippi river was made by Lieutenant Marr in 1850–51, in accordance with instructions from the Secretary of the Navy. His report constitutes Appendix B of the third volume of the Washington Astronomical Observations.§ The system adopted for measuring the discharge was identical with that already described in noticing his earlier labors. From a limited series of rough observations upon the relative velocity of sur-

Marr upon the Mississippi: second series.

---

* Traité de la Mesure des Eaux Courantes. Paris.

† An Inquiry into the Operation of Running Streams and Tidal Waters, with a View to Determine their Principles of Action, and an Application of those Principles to the Improvement of the River Tyne. London.

‡ Formules et Tables Nouvelles pour la Solution des Problèmes Relatifs aux Eaux Courantes. Paris.

§ Published at Washington, D. C., 1853.

face floats and double floats whose lower parts were sunk nearly to the bottom, Mr. Marr decided to deduct in all cases a little more than one-tenth from the discharge computed from the surface velocity alone. The investigations made by the present Survey indicate that this method of computation must give materially too small a discharge, and that the results obtained by using the surface velocity uncorrected are much nearer the truth. One-ninth should therefore be added to each of the tabulated discharges. The measurements were made daily from March 1, 1850, to February 28, 1851, and the results presented in a table giving for each day the gauge-reading, discharge, temperature of the air, temperature of the river-water, evaporation from bodies of water of considerable depth, and amount of rain. The annual discharge (corrected by adding a little less than one-ninth to that reported by Mr. Marr) was 15 000 000 000 000 cubic feet. The annual evaporation was 43.37 inches and the annual rain 49.47 inches. The mean temperature of the air was 60°.44, while that of the river was 60°.95. Mr. Marr preserved the sediment contained in two quarts of water taken daily from the central part of the river surface. At the end of the year he found the bulk of this sediment was to that of the water from which it was taken as 1 to 2950. Although the two series of observations conducted by Mr. Marr were made in addition to his duties as Acting Master of the Memphis navy yard, they probably constituted, at their date, the most extended series of actual measurements ever made upon any river. Although made in a somewhat rough manner, and exhibiting considerable discrepancies when closely analyzed, yet they answer well the general purposes for which they were designed.

In 1851 a report upon the subject of deepening the channel at the mouths of the Mississippi, made by Mr. C. Ellet, Jr., to the Bureau of Topographical Engineers, War Department, was published by Congress.*

Mr. Francis published a work† in 1855, giving the results of some extensive experiments upon the flow of water over weirs and through short, rectangular canals, together with trials of certain hydraulic motors. The experiments were made at Lowell, Massachusetts, at the expense of the manufacturing companies of that city. The velocity of the water through the canals was determined by Baron Kraÿenhoff's method, namely, by noting the time of transit over a given distance, and the paths, of long tubes so adjusted that they floated upright, with their lower ends very near the bottom, and their upper ends above the surface. From these data, Mr. Francis deduced the mean velocity, and hence the discharge, since the area of the section was known. A careful comparison of this method with that by weirs gave a small excess in favor of the former; but the experiments were not sufficiently numerous to give a reliable coefficient of comparison. He subsequently determined this coefficient by a very extended comparison of experiments, and has kindly communicated it, although yet unpublished, to the Delta Survey. It will appear in discussing the observations of M. de Buffon upon the Tiber, in Chapter V. This method was tested even when the discharge amounted to over 1000 cubic feet per second. To test M. de Prony's formula for the relation between surface and mean velocities, the surface velocity was measured

* Ex. Doc. No. 17, 31st Congress, 2d Session [Senate].

† Lowell Hydraulic Experiments. Boston.

by floating balls of wax, two inches in diameter, and the mean velocity determined from the discharge given by a weir measurement. The formula was found to give a result materially too small.

In 1855 Mr. Herman Haupt published a pamphlet upon the improvement of the Ohio river, advocating a low dam and chute plan.

In the Annales des Ponts et Chaussées for 1857 is to be found an article by Gras upon the torrents of the Alps.

The same volume contains a record of some gaugings of the Arve and Rhone by Chaix. The slope of the water surface, unfortunately, was not noted.

In the Journal of the Franklin Institute (1857) there are papers upon the improvement of the navigation of the Ohio river, by Mr. Elwood Morris, and Mr. Milnor Roberts.

In 1858 Lombardini published a memoir upon the recent inundations in France and the means proposed to remedy the evils thereof.

In 1858 Dupuit published a small work* upon floods, which contains an able argument in favor of the levee system. A note upon the flood of the Loire in 1846 by Boulangé, which originally appeared in the Annales des Ponts et Chaussées, 1848, is added as an appendix, after receiving a somewhat severe criticism from Dupuit.

In 1858 Mr. Charles Ellet, Jr., submitted to the James river and Kanawha company a report upon a survey made by himself to determine the feasibility of improving the navigation of the Kanawha river by artificial lakes. This report was published.† Attached to the appendix are to be found the details of an accurate gauging of the Ohio at Point Pleasant, just above the mouth of the Kanawha river, on November 20, 1858.

In 1858 Mr. David Stevenson published, as a separate treatise,‡ an article prepared by himself for the eighth edition of the Encyclopædia Britannica, upon "Inland Navigation." In this he treats at some length of canals, rivers, the effects of tides upon the latter, works of river improvement, the formation and reclamation of land, etc. In the chapter devoted to the physical characteristics of rivers, the writer gives a comparison of the accuracy of certain formulæ for mean velocity, determined by applying them to very careful measurements made by himself upon a small stream, and by Dr. Anderson upon the Tay. The formulæ selected were Dubuat's (erroneously called Robison's), Chezy's, with two new coefficients, proposed respectively by Leslie and Beardmore (erroneously called Leslie's and Beardmore's formulæ), Ellet's Mississippi formula, and Dubuat's formula for deducing the true mean from the maximum central surface velocity. The conclusion derived by Stevenson from this comparison and others, is that none of the formulæ are "*generally* applicable," and he adds (page 44), "We have seen that the formula applied to the Mississippi by Mr. Ellet does not apply to such rivers as the Tay, or to smaller water-courses; and until the result which he has given has been compared with the discharge obtained by actual measurement of the velocities at different parts of the cross-section, we do not think that the discharge of the Missis-

* Des Inondations. Examen des Moyens Proposés pour en Prévenir le Retour. Paris, 1858.

† Report on the Improvement of the Kanawha, and incidentally of the Ohio River, by means of Artificial Lakes. Philadelphia, 1858.

‡ Canal and River Engineering. Edinburgh, 1858.

sippi, which has been calculated by Mr. Ellet, can be relied on as very accurate." He proceeds to propose a formula which will be noticed in the proper place.

In 1860 M. Thomassy published a work* upon the geology of Louisiana, in which he gives an account of the various charts of the mouths of the Mississippi, many historical and geological facts and other interesting matter connected with the river.

In his annual report for 1860, Mr. J. K. Duncan, Chief Engineer of the Board of Public Works of the State of Louisiana, presented the results of certain surveys made in connection with projects for improving the low-water navigation of Old-Red river. The paper was illustrated by sketch maps.

In a periodical entitled De Bow's Review, published in New Orleans and Washington, many interesting papers upon the Mississippi river have appeared from time to time within the past twelve or fifteen years.

A detailed reference is not made here to the published reports of the officers of the Corps of Engineers and of the Corps of Topographical Engineers, upon river and harbor improvements, because of their great number. They contain a large amount of valuable information as nearly connected with the present subject as some of the writings named in this list. They will be found in the Executive and other official documents published by Congress.

METHODS, FORMULÆ, ETC., IN USE FOR GAUGING RIVERS.

Information derived from the preceding works now to be given.

Some of the works mentioned in the foregoing division of this chapter have not been consulted, because they were not attainable; but most of them have been, and whatever related to the practical gauging of streams or to the laws governing water moving in open channels, has been carefully examined. This article is devoted to a brief synopsis of the results of this examination, which, it is believed, presents a tolerably complete statement of the present condition of the subject. In order to prevent confusion, all comments are postponed; and it is, therefore, to be borne in mind that the views here stated are simply those of the authors of the works referred to.

New system of notation adopted.

New system of notation adopted.— In works treating of this subject, ambiguities arising from imperfect notation are frequently to be found. The number of quantities considered is so great that, unless especial care is taken, this fault is inevitable. For this reason, the following general system of notation has been devised and uniformly employed. Unless expressly stated to the contrary, the unit is always the English foot.

l = Length of a limited portion of the river.

$h = h_{,} + h_{,,}$ = Difference of level of the water surface at the two extremities of the distance l.

$h_{,}$ = The part of h consumed in overcoming the resistances of the channel supposed to be straight and of nearly uniform cross-section.

---

* Géologie Pratique de la Louisiane. Paris.

h_{ii} = The part of h consumed in overcoming the resistances of bends and important irregularities of cross-section.

$s = \frac{h_i}{l}$ = The sine of the slope; or the fall of the water surface in one English foot considering the channel straight and nearly uniform.

H = Fall in water surface in one English mile.

a = Area of cross-section.

p = Length of wetted perimeter.

$r = \frac{a}{p}$ = Mean radius, or hydraulic mean depth.

$r_i = \frac{a}{p + W}$ = Mean radius prime.

Q = Discharge in cubic feet per second.

$v = \frac{Q}{a}$ = The mean velocity of the river in feet per second.

D = Depth of the river at any given point of the surface.

d = Distance below the surface, of any given point.

d_i = Distance below the surface, of the fillet moving with the maximum velocity in the assumed vertical plane parallel to the current.

m = Distance below the surface, of the fillet moving with a velocity equal to the mean of the velocities of all fillets in the assumed vertical plane parallel to the current.

Δ = Maximum or mid-channel depth.

W = Width of the river surface at any given locality.

w = Perpendicular distance from the base-line to any point of the water surface.

w_i = Perpendicular distance from the base-line to the surface fillet moving with the maximum velocity.

V = Velocity in feet per second at any point in any vertical plane parallel to the current. When any particular plane is considered, its perpendicular distance from the base-line is placed below and to the left of V. Thus ${}_{500}V$ denotes the velocity at any depth below the surface in the vertical plane 500 feet from the base-line; ${}_{w_i}V$ denotes the same quantity in the vertical plane containing the maximum surface velocity, etc., etc. If the velocity at any particular depth is considered, it is designated by placing the perpendicular distance from the water surface below and to the right of the letter V. Thus, V_0, V_5, $V_{\frac{1}{2}D}$, V_D, V_{d_i}, V_m, denote, respectively, the velocity at the surface, that at a point 5 feet below it, that at mid-depth, that at the bottom, the maximum and the mean of the entire curve in any vertical plane parallel to the current. This system renders it easy to designate exactly the velocity at any point of the river cross-section. Thus, ${}_{100}V_{20}$ is the velocity 20 feet below a point on the surface at a perpendicular distance of 100 feet from the base-line.

U = Velocity in feet per second at any point in the mean of all vertical planes parallel to the current. The system for designating the depth below the surface is the same as that just described for V. Thus U_m signifies the grand mean of the mean velocities in all vertical planes parallel to the current between the river banks; U_r signifies the mean of the bottom velocities of all vertical planes, etc.

f = The number denoting the force of the wind; a calm or a wind blowing at right angles to the current being considered zero and a hurricane ten. Its essential sign is negative for a wind blowing down stream, and positive for a wind blowing up stream.

$\hat{a}$ = Angle of incidence of the water in passing round a bend. It is always assumed about equal to 30°, and the effect of the bend estimated by determining the number of such deflections necessary to pass round it.

G = Density of the river-water.

g = The velocity acquired in falling for one second. It is uniformly assumed at 32.138 feet, its value at the level of the sea in lat. 35°.

Methods of gauging rivers.

The discharge of a stream is usually estimated by the number of cubic feet of water which passes through its channel in a given time, as, for instance, one second. This quantity is equal to the sum of the products of each of the elementary areas of the cross-section by the velocity with which the water flows through it, or to the product of the total area of cross-section by the *mean velocity*, as a mean of all these elementary velocities is called. There are three methods in common use for determining the discharge, when, as is the case with most rivers, a dam measurement—the most accurate of any—is impracticable. In each of them a knowledge of the area of the cross-section of the stream is obtained by careful soundings, or, if desirable, by other more accurate means. The methods, therefore, differ only in the manner of determining the *mean velocity*. Each method will be noticed in the order of its accuracy.

Direct measurement of the mean velocity.

Method by actual measurement.—By this method, the velocity in all parts of the cross-section is actually measured, and a mean of the results taken for the mean velocity. If the cross-section is irregular in form, the only accurate manner of computation is to divide it into partial areas so small that the velocity throughout each may be considered unvarying. The discharge is then equal to the sum of the products of these partial areas by their velocities. The different means used to measure the velocity are:—

Method by floats.

1. By noting the time of transit of floating bodies over known distances. Small bodies, too light to be sensibly affected by the component of gravity parallel to the surface, must be selected. Bits of solid wood, and bottles filled with water until nearly submerged, have often been used for surface floats. Boileau proposes balls of soft wax on account of their adhesive properties. Dubuat used gooseberries for velocities near the bottom. Double floats for measuring the velocity below the surface were first used by da Vinci. They are of various kinds, usually consisting of small surface floats, of minimum size, supporting by cords larger submerged bodies. Krayenhoff used rods loaded at one end, and supported by a light float at the other, so as to assume a vertical position. They were made to extend from the surface nearly to the bottom, in order to obtain as closely as possible the mean velocity of all the fillets in the vertical plane. This method, with slight modifications, has been adopted by de Buffon, Destrem, Francis, and others. In small canals, Hirn

used light, covered frames, so arranged that they would assume a vertical position at right angles to the thread of the current, and nearly fill the whole cross-section. He thus measured, approximately, the mean velocity of the whole stream at once. Raucourt used a kind of ship's log for some of his experiments upon the Neva, a method adopted by Lieutenant Marr in his observations on the Mississippi at Memphis.

2. By noting the time of transit of a globule of air through a given portion of a glass tube immersed and held parallel to the current. The velocity of passage can be made as small as desirable by fitting a conical mouth-piece to the upper end of the tube. The expression for the ratio between this velocity and the true velocity of the current can be readily deduced by actual experiments with floats. (Boileau.)

By a modified air float.

3. By a light paddle-wheel with slight friction upon its axis, so placed that the paddles are submerged. The velocity of their centre of percussion, which can be deduced by noting the number of rotations in a given time, is nearly that of the water. This instrument, of course, only measures velocities very near the surface.

By revolutions of a wheel.

4. By different kinds of self-recording meters (Woltmann's, Brewster's, Laignel's, Saxton's, and others), to which motion is communicated by the water, which strikes fans like those of a windmill. The velocity is deduced from the number of rotations of the axle. These instruments can be used at any depth.

By self-recording meters.

5. By a box with a small hole in the up-stream side, which is sunk to the desired depth and withdrawn in a given time. The velocity is computed from the quantity of water found in the box. (Grandi.)

By a box.

6. By a glass tube bent at the lower end. Its lower orifice is directed against the current at any desired depth, and the velocity deduced from the difference of level between the water in the tube and that in the river. (Pitot.)

By Pitot's tube.

7. By means of a quadrant, to the centre of whose graduated arc a string supporting a ball is attached. The ball is immersed in the stream and the angular change induced by the current measures the velocity, which, for the same ball, is equal to the product of a constant coefficient by the square root of the tangent of this angular change. (Castelli.)

By a quadrant.

8. By measuring with a delicate balance the pressure of the current upon a ball immersed in the stream and attached to the balance by a wire. (Saint Venant.)

By a balance and submerged ball.

9. By means of a small plate connected by a system of pulleys and braces with a balance. The instrument is held firmly at the desired depth, so that the plate is directly opposed to the current. The balance indicates the pressure, and the velocity results from it by computation. Brünings' tachometer is constructed upon this principle.

By a balance and machinery.

10. By bringing a delicate thermometer to a fixed temperature and then noting the different rates of cooling, in and out of the current. (Leslie.)

By a thermometer.

Method by partial measurement.—By this method the velocity in one or more places

Usual theory to account for resistances encountered by water moving in a natural channel.

is measured by any of the above plans, and the mean velocity of the stream deduced by calculation. This method requires a knowledge of the relation between the velocities in different parts of the cross-section of streams, a relation which has not yet been discovered, although it has formed the subject of careful study. The theory adopted by most modern writers is the following: The movement being caused solely by the slope of the surface, the velocity would be equal in all parts of a river section were it not for the retarding influence of the bed. The layer of elementary particles next to the bed adheres firmly to it by virtue of the force of adhesion. The next layer is retarded partly by the cohesion existing between it and the first, partly by friction, and partly by the loss of living force arising from constant collision with the irregularities which, of course, correspond to those of the bed. The next layer is retarded in the same manner but in a less degree. Thus the effect of the resistances is diminished as the distance from the bed is increased. According to this theory, assuming, as is generally done, that no sensible resistance is experienced from the air, the maximum velocity should be found in the surface fillet situated at the greatest mean distance from the bed. Many experiments have been made to determine the actual variation in velocity at different depths, and, upon the surface, at different distances from the banks. Great diversity exists among the results obtained, as will be seen from the following synopsis. It shows that no mathematical relation, of sufficiently general application to constitute a practical law, has been hitherto discovered.

Velocity in any given vertical plane parallel to the current.

The velocity below the surface in any given vertical plane parallel to the current will first be considered.

Tadini (Italian collection, 1823) states that generally the velocity at the surface is to that at the bottom as 1 is to 0.0016; but that in parts of the Po where the current and slope are gentle and the surface parallel to the bed, the two are nearly equal.

Dubuat found, by forty-eight experiments upon a small canal less than 1 foot deep, that the difference between the surface and bottom velocities *in the thread of the current* was greater as the velocity was less. He thought the ratio was independent of the mean radius and nature of the bottom. His formula for the bottom velocity is—

$$_{w,}V_{D} = ({}_{w,}V_{0}^{1/2} - 0.29)^{2}.$$

He found the position of the fillet of mean velocity to be from ⅓ to ⅕ of the total depth of the water above the bottom, but he did not consider his experiments decisive upon this point.

Focacci found that, in a canal 5 feet deep, the maximum velocity was from 2 to 2.5 feet below the surface.

Gerstner considers the vertical law to be given by the ordinates of an ellipse.

Brünings found that the mean of the whole vertical curve varied from 0.89 to 0.96 of the velocity at the surface, or rather 1 foot below it, for velocities between 2 and 5 feet per second, in canals from 5 to 14 feet deep.

Woltmann states that the velocity diminishes from the surface downward in the ratio of the ordinates of a parabola whose axis is vertical and whose vertex is a certain distance below the bottom of the river.

Ximenes found the mean velocity in a vertical plane in the Arno, where it was 15 feet deep and had a surface velocity of 3 feet, to be 0.92 of that at the surface.

Eytelwein found no fixed law to exist, but finally admitted a decrease in an arithmetical progression, amounting to $\frac{1}{40}$ of the superficial velocity for each metre in depth. In other words, the law is shown by the ordinates of an inclined right line.

Fünk considers the law of diminution to be shown by a logarithmic curve.

Young considers $\frac{9}{10}$ of the superficial velocity sufficient for the mean of the vertical curve.

Defontaine states that in calm weather the velocity of the Rhine is greatest at the surface. It decreases insensibly at first as the depth is increased, but the change becomes quite rapid near the bottom. The law is given by the ordinates of two right lines forming an angle with each other. The mean velocity of the whole line varies from 0.85 to 0.89 of the maximum; its position is generally at about $\frac{3}{5}$ of the depth below the surface.

Raucourt made experiments upon the Neva where it is 900 feet wide and of regular section, the maximum depth being 63 feet. When the river was frozen over, the maximum velocity (2 feet 7 inches per second) was found a little below the middle of the deepest vertical. It was somewhat less than double that at the surface and bottom, which were nearly equal to each other. In summer he found the maximum velocity was near the surface in calm weather; but the wind had great effect, reducing the surface velocity when a strong wind was blowing up stream, so that it hardly exceeded that at the bottom. He considers the law of diminution to be given by the ordinates of an ellipse whose vertex is a little below the bottom, and whose lesser axis is a little below the surface.

Hennocque found the maximum velocity in the Rhine to be, in calm weather or with a light wind, $\frac{1}{5}$ of the depth below the surface; in a strong wind up stream, it was a little below mid-depth; in a strong wind down stream, it was at the surface.

Baumgarten found in the Garonne that the maximum velocity was generally at the surface, but that in one section (about 325 feet in width) it was always below; and in another it was below for a certain portion of the width (about $\frac{1}{3}$) and not so for the rest. Often, when the maximum velocity was below, and sometimes when it was at the surface, the curve of change was nearly a straight line; generally, however, there was a slight elbow, the upper part being vertical or inclining down or up stream. In the latter case the curve resembled a very open hyperbola whose vertex was at the point of maximum velocity. The direction and force of wind were not recorded in those experiments. In the Canal du Rhône au Rhin (45 feet wide) the maximum velocity was uniformly from $\frac{1}{3}$ to $\frac{1}{5}$ of the depth below the surface, except for about 3 feet in the middle, where it was at the surface. The point of maximum velocity was relatively higher as the depth was greater. The velocity below the point of maximum generally decreased according to the parabolic law.

D'Aubuisson considers that the velocity diminishes slowly at first, as the depth increases, but that near the bottom the change is more rapid. The bottom velocity is, however, always more than half that of the surface.

Boileau found, by experiment in a small canal, that the maximum velocity was $\frac{1}{4}$ to $\frac{1}{5}$ of the depth below the surface. Below this point the velocity diminished rapidly and nearly in the ratio of the ordinates of a parabola whose axis was at the surface. Above, he considered that the change followed no law, but was much affected by wind. He decided, from a discussion of the experiments of Defontaine, Hennocque, and Baumgarten, that in large rivers the mean velocity in a vertical plane is generally a very little more than 0.9 of the maximum in that plane, which is by no means always at the surface; also that no relation exists between the surface and mean velocities in a vertical plane; and that the velocity varies more on the same vertical as the velocity is increased and less as the depth is increased.

Horizontal curves of velocity.

The velocity at different points of the surface will next be considered. The form of the cross-section and the set of the current have such an effect upon the velocity at the surface, at different distances from the banks, that no definite law of change exists. There is generally an increase of velocity, as the distance from the banks is increased, until the maximum point is reached. Boileau, from discussing some observations made by himself upon a small wooden canal, and the observations of Defontaine and Baumgarten on the Rhine, considers that this decrease follows the parabolic law except for points very near the banks. He concludes that the velocity from point to point varies more in great than in small velocities and less in wide than in narrow rivers.

It is generally conceded that the variation in curves of surface velocity is too great to justify any attempt to deduce numerical relations, but, in practice, many engineers assume the same ratio between the mean and maximum velocities upon the surface that exists between the same quantities in a vertical plane.

True mean velocity of the stream by simple measurement.

The mean velocity of the stream comes next in order. This velocity is equal to the quotient arising from dividing the discharge in the unit of time by the area of cross-section. The ratio between it and the maximum surface velocity has formed the subject of much careful investigation.

Dubuat, from several experiments upon small wooden canals, has deduced the following formulæ:—

$$v = \frac{{}_{w,}V_0 + {}_{w,}V_D}{2},$$

$${}_{w,}V_0 = ({}_{w,}V_D^{1/2} + 0.299)^2,$$

$${}_{w,}V_D = ({}_{w,}V_0^{1/2} - 0.299)^2.$$

De Prony criticises these formulæ because v does not become zero when ${}_{w,}V_0 = 0$, which it should do to conform to nature. He deduces the following formula from Dubuat's experiments:—

$$v = {}_{w,}V_0 \frac{{}_{w,}V_0 + 7.78188}{{}_{w,}V_0 + 10.34508}.$$

He considers the formula—

$$v = 0.816458\ {}_{w,}V_0$$

to be sufficiently accurate in practice.

Young proposes the formula—

$$v = {}_{w,}V_0 + \frac{1}{2} - \left({}_{w,}V_0 + \frac{1}{4}\right)^{1/2}.$$

Most writers have been satisfied with deducing a simple numerical ratio between the mean velocity and the maximum surface velocity. The following are some of these ratios:—

Brünings adopts 0.85, varying between 0.72 and 0.98.

Dubuat, for small canals about 1 foot deep, proposes 0.71 to 0.96.

Destrem and de Prony consider, from observations upon the Neva, that the mean velocity of that river is $\frac{7}{9}$ of that at the surface.

Boileau found that no constant ratio could be deduced from his own and published experiments, and therefore considers it necessary to measure the mean velocity in a number of vertical planes sufficient to give a well-determined horizontal curve; and then to take a mean of this horizontal curve to obtain the mean velocity of the section. He considers 0.82 an approximate ratio for canals.

Baumgarten found, by his observations on the Garonne, that de Prony's formula, with a coefficient of 0.8, gave fair results.

Dupuit, from theoretical considerations, believes the ratio to vary between 0.67 and 1.00.

By formulæ in terms of dimensions of cross-section and slope. Two classes of such formulæ.

Method by formulæ.—By this method the mean velocity is computed from certain measured quantities of which it is a function. Many practical formulæ have been proposed for this purpose by hydraulic engineers. Some of these are based upon the supposition of "uniform," and others upon that of "permanent," motion. The former requires that the cross-section of the channel shall be invariable and the slope of the fluid-surface constant. In other words, if the stream be divided into straight filaments, parallel to the direction of its motion, the velocity may vary for different filaments, but not at different points of the same filament. The condition of permanent motion is essentially different. The cross-section and slope of the water-surface may undergo changes—provided, however, there be no sudden bends to produce eddies or undulation—but the discharge through the different cross-sections must be identical. In other words, the stream may be considered to be composed of filaments parallel to the general direction of motion, varying from point to point in diameter, and hence in velocity, but unvarying in discharge.

The latter supposition evidently corresponds to the more general case, and more nearly conforms to the actual condition of rivers, but the formulæ based upon it differ only from those for uniform motion in containing an expression which takes into account the changes of living force produced by changes of cross-section at different localities. If, therefore, the variations in the cross-section of the stream throughout the distance considered are unknown, the only distinctive terms between the two formulæ disappear. This is, in general, the case where a formula is required in the discussions contained in this report. For this reason, the formulæ proposed for water in *uniform motion* will alone be noticed.

That of Chezy.

1. M. Chezy considered that, from the manner in which the friction of the bed exerts its influence, the resistances encountered by water in uniform motion are directly proportional to the length of the wetted perimeter and to the length of the channel. He also, upon the supposition of a layer of immovable liquid particles lining the channel, considered the resistances to be proportional to the square of the mean velocity; since, by an increase of velocity, a proportionally greater number of particles are separated in a proportionally less time. That is, the resistances may be considered to be equal to $A\,v^2\,l\,p$. Placing this expression equal to

$a\,g\,h_{,}$, a product proportional to the effective component of the weight, which in uniform motion is entirely consumed in overcoming the resistances, and solving the equation with respect to v, he deduced the formula—

$$v = \left(\frac{g\,h_{,}\,a}{A\,l\,p}\right)^{1/2} = B\,(r s)^{1/2}.$$

When B has been determined by experiment, this formula gives the mean velocity by a very simple calculation. It is singular that this, the first practical formula ever proposed for the uniform motion of water in open channels, should be the one now generally adopted for large bodies of water in rapid motion. The number adopted for B by Chezy is not given in any of the papers met with which contain his formula, but several different values have been proposed by subsequent engineers. Thus Young, for large streams, adopts 84.3. Eytelwein uses 93.4. D'Aubuisson, for velocities over 2 feet, uses 95.6. Downings and Taylor, for large and rapid rivers, adopt 100. Leslie, for small streams, uses 68, and for large streams, 100. Beardmore adopts 94.2. Neville, for straight rapid rivers with a velocity of 1.5 feet, uses 92.3, and for greater velocities, 93.3. Stevenson, for small streams, adopts 69, and for large streams, 96, etc., etc.

That of Dubuat.

2. Dubuat exhibited great ingenuity in deducing his celebrated formula. To follow him through his theoretical analysis would extend this article beyond its proper limits, and, therefore, only a brief notice of the principal steps can be attempted.

He began by showing first, that the slope of the surface alone causes motion; and second, that in uniform motion the resistances are equal to the accelerating forces. He then demonstrated that a close analogy exists between the motion of water in pipes and in open channels, and thus inferred that theories for the movement of water in the latter may be tested by the more accurate experiments which can be made upon the former.

Considering reason and experiment both to indicate that the resistances increase as v^2, he assumed them to be proportional to $\frac{v^2}{A}$. The accelerating forces are proportional to $\frac{g\,h_{,}}{l}$. Hence, for a preliminary equation he deduced $\frac{v^2}{A} = \frac{g\,h_{,}}{l}$, or $v\left(\frac{l}{h_{,}}\right)^{1/2} = (g\,A)^{1/2}$, in which the second number is a constant quantity. On testing this formula by many experiments, he found that $v\left(\frac{l}{h_{,}}\right)^{1/2}$, even in the same channel, is not constant, but that it increases slightly as v increases. That is, in order to have A a constant, some function of the coefficient of v, which will increase less rapidly than the quantity itself, must be substituted. Denoting this function by x, the formula became—

$$v\,x = (g\,A)^{1/2}.$$

Experiment showed that, when the slope is very small, x is nearly equal to $\left(\frac{l}{h_{,}}\right)^{1/2}$, but that as it augments, x must become considerably less than $\left(\frac{l}{h_{,}}\right)^{1/2}$ and that $\frac{\left(\frac{l}{h_{,}}\right)^{1/2}}{x}$ must increase as $\left(\frac{l}{h_{,}}\right)^{1/2}$ diminishes. Many functions of $\left(\frac{l}{h_{,}}\right)^{1/2}$ were tried, and much reasoning upon the effect of variation in slopes was employed before Dubuat finally found that these conditions are numerically fulfilled in a satisfactory manner by the following expression, in which L is the hyperbolic logarithm:—

$$x = \left(\frac{l}{h_{\prime}}\right)^{\frac{1}{2}} - L\left(\frac{l}{h_{\prime}} + 1.6\right)^{\frac{1}{2}}.$$

Substituting this value for x, the formula became—

$$v\left(\left(\frac{l}{h_{\prime}}\right)^{\frac{1}{2}} - L\left(\frac{l}{h_{\prime}} + 1.6\right)^{\frac{1}{2}}\right) = (g\,A)^{\frac{1}{2}}.$$

Although this value of x made $v\,x$ constant for all cases where the slope alone varied, experiment showed that, where different beds were used, the expression again became a variable, being greater as the perimeter became greater with respect to the area. This is evidently to be expected, since the same amount of friction must become less effective as the number of particles upon which it acts is increased. Hence A cannot be a constant except for the same bed, as it must vary with the mean radius. Dubuat first tried a simple ratio, assuming—

$$v\,x = \left(\frac{g\,A}{r}\right)^{\frac{1}{2}}.$$

This modification did not quite agree with experiment, as $r^{\frac{1}{2}}$ increased rather more rapidly than $v\,x$. He then tried $r^{\frac{1}{2}} - 0.03$, and found it to make the first member sensibly constant for small pipes, where the viscidity produces little effect. The formula therefore became—

$$v\,x = \frac{(g\,A)^{\frac{1}{2}}}{r^{\frac{1}{2}} - 0.03},$$

in which the second member, being constant for small pipes, may be placed equal to B. Hence—

$$A = \frac{B^2}{g}\,(r^{\frac{1}{2}} - 0.03)^2.$$

That is, A, instead of being a constant, as was at first assumed, is in reality equal to a constant $\frac{B^2}{g}$ multiplied by a variable. Placing $\frac{B^2}{g} = C$, substituting the value of x and reducing, the general formula became—

$$v = \frac{(C\,g)^{\frac{1}{2}}\,(r^{\frac{1}{2}} - 0.03)}{\left(\frac{l}{h_{\prime}}\right)^{\frac{1}{2}} - L\left(\frac{l}{h_{\prime}} + 1.6\right)^{\frac{1}{2}}}.$$

This formula, when applied to large pipes or canals, was found to give results slightly in excess, the error increasing with the mean radius. This Dubuat attributed to viscidity, or the cohesion of the particles of water to each other. Since the difference of velocity of the adjacent particles alone brings this force into action, it must be very small. A certain portion of the slope, which otherwise would produce velocity, may be considered as constantly exerted in overcoming this force. Calling $\frac{h'_{\prime}}{l}$ this slope, the velocity due to it, or v', will be given by the formula—

$$v' = \frac{(C\,g)^{\frac{1}{2}}\,(r^{\frac{1}{2}} - 0.03)}{\left(\frac{l}{h'_{\prime}}\right)^{\frac{1}{2}} - L\left(\frac{l}{h'_{\prime}} + 1.6\right)^{\frac{1}{2}}}.$$

Since $h'_{\prime}$ is always very small, the second member becomes practically equal to $D\,(r^{\frac{1}{2}} - 0.03)$. But $\frac{h'_{\prime}}{l}$ is a portion of the slope which would cause velocity were not its effect absorbed by the viscidity. This value of v' must therefore be subtracted from the expression for v in order to obtain a true equation. With this correction the formula became—

$$v = \frac{(C\, g)^{\frac{1}{2}}\, (r^{\frac{1}{2}} - 0.03)}{\left(\frac{l}{h_,}\right)^{\frac{1}{2}} - L \left(\frac{l}{h_,} + 1.6\right)^{\frac{1}{2}}} - D\, (r^{\frac{1}{2}} - 0.03).$$

Substituting the numerical values of the constants deduced by Dubuat, and reducing to English feet, it finally takes the form—

$$v = \frac{88.49\, (r^{\frac{1}{2}} - 0.03)}{\left(\frac{l}{h_,}\right)^{\frac{1}{2}} - L \left(\frac{l}{h_,} + 1.6\right)^{\frac{1}{2}}} - 0.086\, (r^{\frac{1}{2}} - 0.03),$$

in which L, the hyperbolic logarithm, is equal to the corresponding common logarithm multiplied by 2.302585.

That of Girard.

3. Girard was the first to apply Coulomb's experimental laws for the friction of fluids upon solids, to deducing a formula for water flowing uniformly. These laws are that, in small velocities, the friction is nearly proportional to the square of the velocity, and to the area of the wetted surface; and entirely independent of the pressure and of the nature of the surface. Considering the viscidity proportional to the velocity, the resistances being proportional to the sum of the friction and viscidity, may be represented by $A\, l\, p\, (v + v^2)$. Placing this expression equal to $g\, h_,\, a$, an expression proportional to the accelerating force, and solving the equation with respect to v, he deduced the formula—

$$v = 0.5 + \left(0.25 + \frac{g\, h_,\, a}{A\, l\, p}\right)^{\frac{1}{2}}.$$

Considering that in canals, for which he especially deduced this formula, the velocity would be affected by the aquatic plants growing upon the sides, Girard assumed the effective perimeter to be equal to 1.7 p. He deduced the value of A from twelve experiments of Dubuat and Chezy, the maximum velocity being about 2.5 feet, and the maximum area 96 square feet. Substituting these values and reducing, the formula becomes in English feet:—

$$v = (2.69 + 26384\, r\, s)^{\frac{1}{2}} - 1.64.$$

That of de Prony.

4. De Prony, adopting the supposition of an immovable liquid layer lining the channel, placed Chezy's expression $\frac{g\, h_,\, a}{l\, p}$ equal to a function of the form $C + A\, v + B\, v^2 + D\, v^3 +$ etc., and proceeded to determine by experiment the values of C, A, B, D, etc. for water in uniform motion. He argued that since the value of C depends upon the values of a and $h_,$ when they allow the water to be on the point of moving but still to have no actual motion, it must be so small as to be safely neglected in practice. He also found that, for all practical purposes, terms involving v to higher powers than the second might be neglected. His formula therefore became—

$$g\, r\, s = A\, v + B\, v^2.$$

He then selected ten of Dubuat's and two of Chezy's experiments, and deduced from them, by La Place's methods for correcting anomalies, the values of A and B. Finding the formula gave satisfactory results, he instituted new and very careful experiments, and deduced by the same process from twenty-three of them, and eight of Dubuat's, still more accurate values. The maximum velocity in these experiments was about 3 feet, and the maximum area of cross-section 96 square feet. Substituting the values of A and B last determined and reducing, with the adopted value for g, the formula becomes in English feet—

$$v = (0.0556 + 10593\ r\ s)^{\frac{1}{2}} - 0.2357.$$

De Prony then deduced new values of A and B from fifty-one experiments upon pipes and thirty-one upon open channels, in order to frame a formula applicable to both kinds of discharge. The resulting formula is—

$$v = (0.0237 + 9966\ r\ s)^{\frac{1}{2}} - 0.1542.$$

Eytelwein proposed new values for A and B in de Prony's formula, deduced by himself from ninety-one observations on canals and rivers, where the velocity varied from 0.4 of a foot to 8 feet, and the cross-section from 0.2 of a square foot to 28020 square feet. The formula thus becomes—

$$v = (0.0119 + 8963\ r\ s)^{\frac{1}{2}} - 0.1089.$$

That of Eytelwein.

5. Eytelwein deduced a formula for water in uniform motion by the following train of reasoning. When water is moving uniformly, the whole component of gravity which causes the motion is employed in overcoming the friction. This component varies as the fall in a given distance. Hence the friction varies as this fall. But the velocity varies as the square root of the friction, since a proportionally greater number of particles are separated in a proportionally less time. Hence the velocity varies as the square root of the fall in a given distance. The friction also varies with the mean radius. Hence the velocity varies with the square root of this quantity. But, if the velocity varies with the square root of the fall in a given distance and with the square root of the mean radius, it must vary as the product of the square roots of those two quantities. Adopting 2 English miles as the length in which to estimate the fall, Eytelwein found the experimental coefficient to be $\frac{10}{11}$. His formula therefore took the form—

$$v = 0.9091\ (2\ H\ r)^{\frac{1}{2}},$$

in which H is the fall in one English mile. This is evidently a simple reproduction of the Chezy formula, since by reduction it can be put under the form—

$$v = 93.4\ (r\ s)^{\frac{1}{2}}.$$

That of Young.

6. Dr. Thomas Young, in some investigations relating to the circulation of the blood, had occasion to use formulæ for the flow of fluids through pipes. Being dissatisfied with those already existing, he undertook to deduce original ones from various published tables of experiments by Dubuat and others. He found that the friction could not be represented by any simple power of v, although it frequently varies with $v^{1.8}$. It could be represented by a function of v and v^2. The coefficients of these powers, however, must vary in pipes of different diameters; that of v being in very large pipes or rivers less, and in minute tubes greater, than that of v^2; while that of v^2 must be greater for a given area of the surface of the pipe as the diameter diminishes.

Now dividing the total head into two parts, one may be considered as employed entirely in overcoming friction. Calling this $h_{,}$, the diameter of the pipe D, its length l, and the mean velocity v, we may assume $h_{,} = A \frac{l}{D} v^2 + 2 B \frac{l}{D} v$, since friction is directly proportional to l and inversely to D. But $h_{,}$ he found from the experiments to be given by $h_{,} = h - \frac{v^2}{550}$, in which h is the total head, and the French inch the unit. Substituting this value, and deducing numerical expressions for A and B, he found, for the case of rivers, formulæ which, when reduced to English feet, become—

$$v = \left(\frac{r s}{3 A} + \frac{B^2}{144 A^2}\right)^{\frac{1}{2}} - \frac{B}{12 A},$$

in which A and B are variables depending upon r. He deduced the following values for them from published experiments:—

$$A = 0.0000001 \left(413 + \frac{1.5625}{r} - \frac{90}{3 r + 8} - \frac{15}{4 r + 0.0296}\right);$$

$$B = 0.0000001 \left(\frac{900 r^2}{r^2 + 0.5} + \frac{1}{(3 r)^{\frac{1}{2}}}\left(271.25 + \frac{6.88}{r} + \frac{0.0001146}{r^2}\right)\right).$$

For most rivers, as already stated in discussing the Chezy formula, he adopts $v = 84.3 (r s)^{\frac{1}{2}}$. Dr. Young gave tables of the values of A and B computed for various small values of r, both for French and English inches, in Philosophical Transactions, 1808. Mr. Storrow introduced these formulæ in his treatise on water-works, with the constants adapted to *French inches*, and by some oversight added the table of values for A and B computed for *English inches*.

Local formulæ of Lombardini.

7. Lombardini does not give the details from which he deduced his formulæ for computing the discharges of the Adda and the Po. He assumed Chezy's general equation for the mean velocity of water in uniform motion, viz:—

$$v = A (r s)^{\frac{1}{2}}.$$

Substituting D for r, and multiplying both members of the equation by a, it becomes

$$a v = Q = A a (D s)^{\frac{1}{2}} = AWD (D s)^{\frac{1}{2}} = AWD^{\frac{3}{2}} s^{\frac{1}{2}}.$$

Assuming the bed of the river and W to remain unchanged for all stages of water, he derived from a few actual measurements of discharge the values of A and s, the former proving to be a constant and the latter a function of D. The resulting formulæ, giving the discharge per second in cubic metres, are—

For the Adda . . . . . $Q = 100 D^{\frac{3}{2}} (1 - 0.032 D) = 100 D^{\frac{3}{2}} - 3.2 D^{\frac{5}{2}}$.

For the Po . . . . $Q = 767 D^{\frac{3}{2}} (0.115 - 0.00069 D^2)^{\frac{1}{2}}$.

These empirical formulæ are convenient for the purpose for which they were deduced,—namely, a rough computation of the discharge for a given gauge-reading, but being strictly local in character, no application of them to other rivers is possible. A glance at the measurements of the discharge of the Mississippi river, which will soon be stated in detail, will show that such formulæ can only be employed for the most general purposes.

That of Weisbach.

8. Weisbach, adopting Dubuat's theorem, that in uniform motion all the fall is consumed in overcoming friction, deduces a formula by placing the total fall in a given distance equal to the height due to the resistances of

friction, which, following the usual course of reasoning, he represents by $A \frac{l\,p}{a} \frac{v^2}{2\,g}$. Hence—

$$v = \left(\frac{2\,g}{a}\,r\,s\right)^{\frac{1}{2}}.$$

He considers that the quantity A, which he terms the "coefficient of the resistances," increases for small, and diminishes for great velocities, and adopts Lahmeyer's value, or:

$$A = 0.007409 \left(1 + \frac{0.0308}{v}\right).$$

He gives a table containing the values of A for different values of v, and advises a system of computation by successive approximations. This is needless labor, for, by a simple process of algebraic reduction, the formula becomes (for latitude 35°)—

$$v = (0.00024 + 8675\,r\,s)^{\frac{1}{2}} - 0.0154.$$

This is only a reproduction of de Prony's formula, the only change being in the numerical value of the coefficients. It will therefore be so classed when tested in Chapter V.

For floods, Weisbach considers the relative change of velocity to be one-half, and the relative change in the discharge three-halves, of the relative change in the depth of the water.

Local formula of Baumgarten.

9. Baumgarten gauged the Garonne twenty-five times between the years 1837 and 1847, at stages varying nearly from low to high water. From the data thus collected (which are not published in detail), he framed an empirical formula, adopting the general form of that proposed by Lombardini for the Po and Adda. It accords, within about five per cent., with the measured discharges. The unit being the metre, it is—

$$Q = 125\,D^2\,(0.201\,D - 0.044\,D^2 + 0.003\,D^3 - 0.094)^{\frac{1}{2}},$$

in which Q represents the discharge, and D the mean depth, at Tonneins. This formula is evidently entirely local, and liable to the objections raised against Lombardini's.

That of Dupuit.

10. Dupuit's formulæ are based upon assumptions which differ materially from those of most engineers. He proves, by an analytical demonstration, that the supposition of an immovable layer of liquid lining the channel, and thus reducing the friction from that of a liquid upon a solid to that of a liquid upon a liquid, is inadmissible, and that the cohesion between the different particles is very much greater than their adhesion to the solids on which they flow. He considers the resistances of adhesion and cohesion to have the common properties of being directly proportional to the surfaces in contact, and of being entirely independent of pressure; but that, while the former increases with the absolute velocity of the stream, and may be directly compared to the friction of solids, the latter is properly a kind of chemical affinity, which is proportional to the relative velocity of the contiguous molecules.

These ideas relative to the resistances acting upon water in motion suggest equations of equilibrium for a fluid mass flowing in any channel with any velocity whatever. For simplicity, he supposes the water to be flowing uniformly through a rectangular cross-section of indefinite width, so that no resistance is experienced from the sides. The motion in all vertical planes parallel to the current is here the same, and the attention may be confined to any one of them. The surface fillet in the selected plane is in the condition of a solid gliding over an inclined plane. The accelerating force of gravity acts on it proportionally to its weight and to the sine of the angle of inclination. Designating the velocities of the surface fillet and of the fillets below it, successively, by V_0, V_i, V_{ii}, etc. etc., the retarding force which holds the surface fillet in equilibrium is evidently a function of $(V_0 - V_i)$, otherwise the motion could not be uniform. The equation of equilibrium for the upper fillet is, therefore—

$$G g s \delta d = \varphi (V_0 - V_i).$$

Or, dividing both members by $G g$:—

$$s \delta d = \varphi (V_0 - V_i).$$

Each fillet below, except the bottom one, is urged forward by its weight and by its cohesion to the more rapidly moving fillet above, and is retarded by its cohesion to the slower fillet below. The bottom fillet is retarded by its adhesion to the bed. The following equations of equilibrium can therefore be written, in which the velocities of the bottom fillet and of the fillets above it, successively, are designated by V_D, V_{D-i}, V_{D-ii}, etc.:—

Surface fillet . . . . . $s \delta d = \varphi (V_0 - V_i)$
Next fillet . . . . . . $s \delta d = \varphi (V_i - V_{ii}) - \varphi (V_0 - V_i)$
* * * *
* * * *
Last fillet but one . $s \delta d = \varphi (V_{D-ii} - V_{D-i}) - \varphi (V_{D-iii} - V_{D-ii})$
Bottom fillet . . . . $s \delta d = \varphi (V_D) - \varphi (V_{D-ii} - V_{D-i})$.

Taking the sum of these equations, member by member, the following very important expression results:—

$$s D = \varphi (V_D).$$

The velocities at the bottom in all the vertical planes having been assumed equal, this may be put under the form:—

$$s a = p \varphi (U_D), \text{ or } r s = \varphi (U_D) = A U_D + B U_D^2 + \ldots .$$

This equation is analogous to the usual expression $r s = \varphi (v)$; but the difference is evidently a radical one. The needs of the science, however, require a formula for the *mean velocity*, and unless some algebraic relation between U_D and v can be established, this discussion amounts to little more than a barren demonstration of error in existing formulæ. The relation existing between U_D and v depends directly upon the law governing the action of cohesion, and is deduced by Dupuit by the following simple and ingenious train of reasoning. Since the force of cohesion is proportional to the infinitely small difference of velocity between contiguous molecules, it can only be expressed in finite quantities by adopting for the unit an infinitely small quantity, such as the distance between the elementary layers of the fluid. The algebraic expression for the resistance of cohesion between two layers becomes, therefore, $\varphi \left(\frac{\delta V}{\delta d}\right)$ in which δV is the infinitely small difference of velocity between the two layers, and δd the infinitely small distance between them. Substituting this expression for the difference of the velocities of the elementary fillets heretofore used, in the equations for the equilibrium of the fluid mass, and taking the sum of the equations, member by member, from the surface down to any assumed depth, d, the expression becomes—

$$s d = \varphi \left(\frac{V_d - V_{d-i}}{\delta d}\right) = \varphi \left(-\frac{\delta V}{\delta d}\right)$$

Dupuit proceeds to show that, in the development of this function, all terms but the first may be neglected, without sensible error, giving—

$$s\,d = -E\,\frac{\delta V}{\delta d}.$$

Integrating this equation, it becomes—

$$V = C - \frac{s}{2E}\,d^2.$$

Since the velocity at the bottom in all vertical planes is assumed to be equal, the constant C may be determined by the condition that, when $d = D$, V shall become equal to the value of U_D given by the equation $r\,s = A\,U_D + B\,U_D^2$. Hence the following equation results:—

$$V = U_D + \frac{s}{2E}\,(D^2 - d^2).$$

This is the equation of a parabola whose axis is at, and parallel to the plane of, the water surface, and whose parameter varies directly with the slope.* The velocity at the surface is evidently given by the equation—

$$V_0 = U_D + \frac{s\,D^2}{2\,E}.$$

The mean of the curve is readily computed by the aid of the well-known expression for the area bounded by the curve and its co-ordinates. It is—

$$V_m = U_D + \frac{2}{3}\,(V_0 - U_D) = U_D + \frac{D^2\,s}{3\,E}.$$

These equations evidently furnish a complete solution of the problem for the simplest case, that of a rectangular cross-section of indefinite width. Dupuit proceeds to apply the same principles to different forms of cross-section, and then to the general case, but the limits of this article, and the difficulty of rendering the processes clear without transcribing his diagrams, render it unadvisable to continue following him step by step. Suffice it to say that, for the general case, where the cross-section approximates to a circular form, he proposes the following formulæ as sufficiently accurate for practical purposes:—

$$r\,s = A\,U_r + B\,U_r^2,$$

$${}_{w_i}V_0 = U_r + \frac{s\,r\,a}{2\,E\,W},$$

$$v = \frac{{}_{w_i}V_0 + U_r}{2} = U_r + \frac{s\,r\,a}{4\,E\,W}.$$

These formulæ contain only three numerical coefficients, A, B and E. Dupuit concludes that new experiments are required to fix the proper values of these coefficients, and explains how they should be conducted. In default of such experiments, he proposes for A and B values a little larger than those proposed by de Prony; viz. (formula in English feet), 0.000018 and 0.000110. For E he suggests no numerical value,

* It should be stated that, although the brief extracts from the work of M. Dupuit contained in the Tables of Claudel had been examined at an early day, yet the work itself was consulted for the first time when imported from Paris in June, 1859. At that date, the experimental study of the change of velocity below the surface in the Mississippi river, which will be fully detailed in the next chapter, had been completed. Although the formula thereby deduced differs radically from that of M. Dupuit in some respects, its general resemblance is striking.

only remarking that 0.001025, the value proposed by Sonnet (formula reduced to English feet) is, in his opinion, much too small.

It is evident that without numerical values for A, B and E, no direct practical test can be applied to Dupuit's formulæ. His theoretical method of treating the subject is more exact than that of any writer who has preceded him, and elaborate measurements to fix the values of the three coefficients would have been undertaken, had not the observations of this Survey shown that the position of the fillet endowed with the maximum velocity, far from being always at the surface as Dupuit assumes, in truth varies in position in accordance with certain laws. His formulæ are therefore necessarily inexact, and no attempt has been made to deduce their coefficients. If, however, as Dupuit seems disposed to allow, these coefficients are constant for any given fluid, he has in effect by assigning values to A and B, furnished the means of deducing E from any accurate measurement of the mean velocity corresponding to a given slope, area, mean radius and width, since by combining his three general equations and eliminating $_{w,}V_0$ and U_r, the following value of this coefficient results:—

$$E = \frac{s\,r\,a}{4\,W\,(v + 0.082 - (0.0067 + 9114\,r\,s)^{\frac{1}{2}})}.$$

The numerical value of E for each of the thirty test observations given in Chapter V was computed by this formula. The values differed considerably among themselves. Their mean, allowing the proper weight to the different observations, is about 0.02 (formula in English feet), and this value has accordingly been adopted. With it and the values of A and B chosen by Dupuit, his three formulæ, reduced to English feet and consolidated into one, become—

$$v = \frac{s\,r\,a}{0.08\,W} - 0.082 + (0.0067 + 9114\,r\,s)^{\frac{1}{2}}.$$

In this form it has been subjected to the same tests as those of other engineers.

Local formula of Mr. Ellet.

11. From nineteen rough measurements of discharge made in 1849 at Wheeling, Mr. Ellet framed an empirical formula for the discharge of the Ohio at that point. He offers no demonstration or indication of the process by which he arrived at the form of the equation, but the expression is almost identical with that used by Lombardini for the Adda, a manner of deducing which has been already given. Denoting by Q the discharge per hour, and by D the "reduced depth" (probably the mean depth), this formula is, in English feet—

$$Q = 1083000\,D^2 - 10000\,D^3.$$

For remarks upon this expression, see those upon Lombardini's formula.

Taylor's formula.

12. Taylor deduces a formula for mean velocity by a train of reasoning which is in substance as follows: In rivers which are continuous, that is, not broken into rapids and pools, the resistance to the flow of the water must be considered as a whole. In this class of streams, the slope of the bed is so adjusted as just to allow the water in the lowest stages to pass off. When the discharge is increased, the height of the rise at any point increases proportionally to its distance from the sea (since the total resistance at any point is proportional to this distance) until a cascade or rapid is reached, which constitutes what is called the "equivalent origin" of the river. Below such "origin," therefore, the motive force at any point may

be assumed proportional to the mean depth there. But the resistances are directly proportional to the surface exposed to their action or to the mean perimeter below the given point multiplied by the distance to the outlet. They are also directly proportional to the *square* of the mean velocity, since a greater velocity implies both a greater force of impact and a greater number of impinging particles. They are inversely proportional to the mean area of cross-section below the given point, since their effect may be assumed to be divided equally among all the particles of the fluid. Equating the expressions for the motive forces and the resistances, and assuming a simple ratio to exist between them, the following expression results:—

$$D_{,} = C\frac{v^2 l p_{,}}{a_{,}},$$

in which $D_{,}$ is the depth of water at the locality considered; $a_{,}$ is the mean area of cross-section thence to the mouth; and $p_{,}$ is the corresponding mean perimeter. From certain "data of the Nile" (authority not stated), Taylor determines a value for C, which, when substituted, gives the following equation for the mean velocity:—

$$v = 384\left(\frac{D_{,}\, a_{,}}{l\, p_{,}}\right)^{\frac{1}{2}}.$$

This formula, from the peculiar quantities which enter it, seldom, if ever, admits of practical tests or applications, and it is therefore only given here in order to make the list complete.

13. In Boileau's treatise, the following formula is mentioned as proposed by Saint Venant, but without indicating his method of deducing it. The original work in which it was proposed could not be obtained in Paris in 1859. It is a very simple formula, and readily solved by logarithms. As quoted by Boileau, in metres, it is—

That of Saint Venant.

$$r s = 0.0004\, v^{\frac{21}{11}}.$$

Reduced to English feet, and solved with respect to v, it becomes—

$$v = 106.068\, (r s)^{\frac{11}{21}}.$$

14. The next formula to be considered is that proposed by Mr. Ellet in his "Report on the Overflows of the Delta of the Mississippi." This formula was deduced to solve certain problems of the highest practical importance in the work of protecting the Mississippi valley from overflow. Mr. Ellet fully appreciated the necessity for accuracy, for he writes: "It is important to ascertain what volume of water escaped through all the crevasses below Red river at the top of the flood of 1851; and also, approximately, some method to determine the volume of water that will be needed to raise the surface of the river, when in flood, any given height. These questions involve the unknown relations of depths, slope, and velocity of rivers; questions which have been discussed by several able and distinguished writers, but which, nevertheless, must receive a further examination here.

That of Mr. Ellet.

* * * * * * * * * *

"Several foreign writers on hydrauliques have published formulæ derived from experiments to exhibit the relations between the depths, slopes, and velocities of running streams. But their various equations are almost all derived from each other, or built upon the same observations; while these observations, limited in number, have been made on streams of very small dimensions. Where they are applied to great rivers, like the Mississippi or Ohio, they fail to give results in close agreement with the recognized facts. It has therefore been deemed advisable, indeed necessary, to derive new and better formulæ from a wider range of experiments—embracing great rivers of gentle slope in full flood, and passing from those to smaller streams of abrupt descent, and in various conditions of their channels. But great difficulties were encountered in the attempt to frame such a formula from observations on the flow of the Mississippi. The movements of this great river are remarkable, and need to be carefully studied before the resulting law can be confidently applied. The river descends on an average slope of about three and a quarter inches per mile, and the mean velocity of its current is, of course, due to that slope. Yet it not unfrequently happens, that while the mass of the water which its channel bears is sweeping to the *south* at a speed of four or five miles per hour, the water next the shore is running *to the north* at a speed of one or two miles per hour.

"It is no unusual thing to find a swift current and a corresponding fall on one shore toward the south, and on the opposite shore a visible current and an appreciable slope toward the north. In other words, the water is often running rapidly *up stream* on one side of the river, while sweeping with equal or much greater rapidity down stream on the opposite side.

"It is obvious, therefore, that no single or merely local observation on the rate of descent of the stream can be depended on for the determination of that element of an equation. The apparent slope is at every point affected by the bends of the river, and the centrifugal force acquired by the water in sweeping round the curves, and by the eddies which form on the opposite side, under the salient angles.

"The surface of the river is not, therefore, *a plane,* but a peculiarly complicated warped surface, varying from point to point, and inclining alternately from side to side.

"To neutralize in some degree the effect of such variations on the littoral measurements of the slope, levels and soundings were taken at different points along the shore, not very remote from each other, and mean slopes, depths, and velocities derived from many observations. As a check to the results, and a guard against material error, the average slope, depth, and velocity was obtained for considerable distances, embracing many bends of the river. And as a further check, the slopes, depths, areas, and velocities of the tributaries and outlets of the Mississippi, and of various small mountain streams, were collected and compared. A formula was then sought which should express the maxima or central velocities, in terms of the slope and maxima depths of each of these various streams."

"The equation produced by these investigations is here submitted, with the observations from which it was derived, and its application to each set of observations.

"Let d represent the maximum depth of the river, in feet, at the place of observation; f, the slope of the surface, in feet, per mile; v, the velocity of the central surface current, in feet, per second; then the formula proposed is—

$$v = 0.8\,(d\,f)^{\frac{1}{2}} + \frac{d\,f}{20}.$$

The application of this formula to many of the observations, with the amount of discrepancy in each case, will be found in note C.

"It was further ascertained from numerous observations conducted with much care, that the *mean velocity* of a great river, in a straight channel, is about eighty per cent. of its maximum velocity, as has been obtained by De Prony and others, for smaller streams. This proportion is close enough for any practical application needed in this paper; it is, probably, as close a general approximation as can be made in the premises."

On turning to note C, to examine the observations and the application of the formula to them, we read :—

"It was the intention of the writer to discuss this formula, in some detail, in a note to the text. But being under the necessity of submitting this report hastily, and wishing to test the formula on shallow mountain streams, he is compelled to reserve this discussion, which will form part of a supplemental paper."

No such paper has, so far as it is known, been yet published. When reduced to a single equation, with symbols corresponding to those adopted for this report, Mr. Ellet's formula becomes—

$$v = 0.64\ (\Delta\ \mathrm{H})^{\frac{1}{2}} + 0.04\ \Delta\ \mathrm{H}.$$

By this expression Mr. Ellet calculates the discharge of the Mississippi river, the discharge of *crevasses*, and, in fine, demonstrates the *impracticability of the levee system for the lower parts of the Mississippi river*. The task of criticism is always ungrateful, and if this formula had been proposed by an obscure writer, it would have remained unnoticed. Coming, however, from a civil engineer so well known as Mr. Ellet, and furnishing, as it does, the basis upon which rest practical conclusions believed to be most erroneous and most mischievous, it cannot be passed by in silence. The objections to it will be stated in the inverse order of their importance.

I. Mr. Ellet furnishes no demonstration for his formula, and publishes none of the data from which its constants were derived, thus rendering his personal accuracy and thoroughness its only guarantees.

II. While the form of the equation proves that it is based upon the supposition of uniform motion, Mr. Ellet shows that he does not understand the essential requirements of this condition by his remarks upon the slope of the surface of the river. No formula of this character can apply even approximately to such a river as he describes. There are very many places on the Mississippi where the current flows through a nearly straight and regular cross-section, and where the requisite approximation to uniformity for short distances may properly be considered to exist. To such places only can a simple formula like his apply. Observations which should be rejected have, therefore, probably been admitted among those from which its constants have been derived.

III. It does not bear the test of practical application. Stevenson reports its failure when applied to British streams. The observations of this Survey—and even the nice measurements made by Mr. Ellet himself upon the Ohio at Point Pleasant, in 1858, and reported in his pamphlet upon the Kanawha-river improvement—show that it is the worst ever suggested. Its enormous discrepancies, when applied to the Mississippi, will receive a further notice in Chapter V. Mr. Ellet himself seems to have discovered its errors since the publication of his report, for in his pamphlet on the Kanawha-river improvement, published in 1858, he does not refer to it, but uses "the hydraulic formula on which engineers rely for determining the flow of water."

IV. It is theoretically inexact—far more so than any of the others. No formula can be correct which does not contain all the essential variables upon which the solution of the problem depends. All writers of note upon the laws of flowing water agree that the area of cross-section and the perimeter are such variables; the ratio between them, denominated the mean radius, being the usual form under which they are introduced. No such variables are to be found in Mr. Ellet's formula. Their place is supplied by the *maximum depth*, a quantity which for good and sufficient reasons has never been introduced into any general equation heretofore proposed. Without further discussion, which will hardly be deemed necessary by those acquainted with the subject, it may be added that, according to Mr. Ellet's formula, the mean velocity would remain the same whether the stream were a few feet or a mile in width, the maximum depth and the slope continuing unchanged. Also that the mean velocity would be unchanged in a section containing a deep hole like that at Natchez (plate X), if the whole channel were to be excavated to a uniform depth equal to the maximum. If this formula were proposed for certain localities on a certain river, it might be supposed that Mr. Ellet had found no essential error to arise from assuming the ratio between the mean radius and the maximum depth to be constant, but being designed to embrace "great rivers of gentle slope in full flood, and passing from those to smaller streams of abrupt descent and in various conditions of their channels," the assumption is untenable, as a very cursory inspection of published cross-sections of rivers will show. To illustrate how entirely Mr. Ellet trusted to the exactness of this formula, it may be added that he actually considered it to be applicable to the involved and complex conditions governing the flow of water through crevasses. No further comments are needful to prepare one to learn that most of the practical conclusions of Mr. Ellet in reference to protection against the inundations of the Mississippi have been proved to be erroneous by the actual measurements of this Survey.

That of Stevenson.

15. Stevenson's formulæ are offered without any demonstration, and are as follows:—

$$x = y\,(r\,\mathrm{H})^{\frac{1}{2}}.$$

$$z = \frac{5280\,x}{60}.$$

$$\mathrm{Q} = a\,z.$$

Here x is the true mean velocity, in miles, per hour; z, the same quantity, in feet, per minute; H, the fall of the surface, in feet, per mile; and y, "a quantity which is found to vary from 0.65 for small streams under 2000 cubic feet per minute to 0.9 for large rivers such as the Clyde or the Tay."

A simple process of algebraic reduction resolves these equations into the Chezy formula, with a numerical coefficient equal to 106.6 y. Hence, as no equation for y was proposed by Mr. Stevenson, the result of his discussion of the subject might have been more simply stated by presenting Chezy's formula with a coefficient varying from 69 "for small streams under 2000 cubic feet per minute" to 96 "for large rivers such as the Clyde or the Tay." That is—

For small streams: $v = 69\,(r\,s)^{\frac{1}{2}}$.

For large streams: $v = 96\,(r\,s)^{\frac{1}{2}}$.

CHAPTER IV.

METHOD OF GAUGING THE MISSISSIPPI, ITS TRIBUTARIES AND ITS CREVASSES.

General scope of field operations. — Method of determining dimensions of cross-section. — Method of conducting velocity measurements.—Computation of discharge, neglecting change of velocity below the surface.—Investigation of the sub-surface curve of velocity.—Same of the horizontal curve.—Parameter law deduced.—It applies to sub-surface curves, with a modification for small streams.—Equation for mean of whole vertical curve.—Locus of maximum velocity below the surface, including effect of wind.—Preliminary computation of discharge corrected for change of velocity below the surface.—System for interpolating discharges.—Method of transferring measured discharges. — Phenomena attendant upon crevasses. — Measurements of velocity and resulting formula.—Depth.—Width.—Practical coefficient for exceptional case of crevasses.—Incidental computation of ratio between rain and drainage in Yazoo basin.

An extended system of measurements essential to the investigations of the present Survey.

THE preceding chapter exhibits the imperfect condition of river hydraulics. Discordant statements and theories are found in the works of the most eminent writers, and it is apparent that the laws enunciated rest upon hypothesis and imperfect data rather than upon principles established by extended and thorough experimental investigation.

This condition of the science of river hydraulics has been very unfortunate for the Mississippi valley, since it has prevented any satisfactory discussion of the best method of guarding against its inundations. The wild speculations and impracticable plans of security offered, even by writers of ability, are the necessary result of the want of knowledge, both of essential facts and of the principles upon which deductions should be drawn from such as are known.

The first object of the Survey was the establishment of a system of observation, by which a mass of facts would be collected to form the foundation of correct theories, and thus become the basis of an intelligent investigation of the subject. The nature of the practical requirements of the problem will be understood by a glance at one of the characteristic features of the alluvial lands of the Mississippi. The river below Cape Girardeau flows through immense swamps, which, from time immemorial, have received a portion of the flood waters. The extension and perfection of the levee system will result in shutting out this water from these swamps, and confining it to the river. Neglecting, for the present, the consideration of the effect which this will have in changing the abrading power of the stream, two great and equally important questions suggest themselves: first, how much water will thus be added to the present high-water discharge at any given point; and, second, what will be its effect in changing the local high-water mark? The object of the present chapter is to explain the method employed in collecting and reducing the data necessary to answer the first of these questions.

General scope of the field operations.

The general plan of operations was to determine, as accurately as possible, the discharge of the river in its different stages at all points from Cairo to New Orleans; the quantity added by the tributaries below the Ohio, and the quantity escaping during flood into the different swamps. The following is a synopsis of the field work performed:—

A series of daily measurements of discharge was made at Carrollton, Louisiana (plate III), from February 15, 1851, to February 18, 1852. When field work was resumed in 1857, similar series were made at Columbus, Kentucky (plate III), from December 11, 1857, to November 16, 1858; at Natchez, Mississippi, from January 8, to February 20, 1858; and at Vicksburg, Mississippi (plate III), from February 24, to December 15, 1858; together with corresponding observations upon the Arkansas river, at Napoleon, from December 29, 1857, to November 30, 1858. Besides these continuous series, many measurements of width, depth, area of cross-section, discharge, etc., were made both upon the Mississippi and upon its tributaries and bayous from the Ohio to the gulf.

Various gaugings were made of crevasses both large and small, and all facts essential to an approximate computation of the discharge of those which occurred between Red river and New Orleans, in 1851, and between Cape Girardeau and New Orleans, in 1858, were collected. As a check upon these measurements, which, from their nature, were liable to some inaccuracy, various cross-sections of the swamp lands were made, and others obtained from sources already named, with a view to determine as closely as possible the capacity of these swamps as reservoirs for the flood waters escaping through or over the river banks, and thus to collect the data for a double computation of the amount of water actually subtracted from the river.

Full details respecting field and office work essential.

The method of conducting the field work and of computing the results will be explained in great detail, in order that it may be seen what degree of confidence the conclusions hereafter to be drawn from this material are entitled to.

FIELD OPERATIONS FOR GAUGING THE MISSISSIPPI RIVER AND TRIBUTARIES.

Accurate measurements for determining the discharge of a river involve an exact determination of the cross-section at the locality chosen, and of the velocity of the water in passing through all portions of it. These two subjects will be treated in turn.

Practical method adopted for determining the dimensions of cross-section of the river.

Area of cross-section.—The strength of the current, the depth and width of the river, and the floating drift-wood, all combine to render an accurate measurement of this quantity a difficult operation on the Mississippi. After various experiments, the following system was adopted, by which accurate work may be done even in the highest stages of the river. The middle stages were usually selected for the purpose; being preferable to the low stages, during which there would be exposure to oppressive heat and disease, and more favorable than the high stages, when the difficulties attending accurate measurement are greatest.

Preparatory to making a cross-section of the river, whether for general purposes of comparison or for determining the discharge, a base-line, varying in length from 400 to

1000 feet, was measured along the bank near the water's edge. An observer, with a theodolite, was stationed at each extremity of this line. The one directed the telescope of his instrument across the river so as to command the line on which the soundings were to be made; the other prepared to follow the boat with his telescope in order to measure its angular distance from the base-line when each sounding was taken. The boat, a light, six-oared skiff, contained a man provided with a sounding-chain, a recorder with a flag, and three oarsmen. The strongest kind of welded jack-chain was employed, to which bits of buckskin were attached at intervals of 5 feet; smaller divisions being measured with a rod in the boat. The sinker, varying from ten to twenty pounds in weight, according to the force of the current, was a leaden bar whose bottom was hollowed out and armed with grease in order to bring up specimens of the bed of the river. The patent lead was also used for the latter purpose. The boat was rowed some little distance above the proposed section-line, and allowed to drift down with the current, the sounding-lead being lowered nearly to the bottom. By this precaution, the deflection of the line by the force of the current was prevented. When the first observer, stationed on the proposed section-line, saw that the boat had nearly reached it, he waved a flag as a signal to take a sounding, and then carefully turned his instrument so as to keep the vertical hair of his telescope upon the point where the chain crossed the gunwale of the boat. The recorder in the boat, seeing the signal, waved his flag to the second engineer to follow the boat carefully with his telescope. The man with the sounding-chain allowed it to slip rapidly through his hands until the lead struck the bottom, when he grasped the chain at the water surface and instantly rose to a standing position. This motion was the signal for arresting the movement of each telescope and recording the angles. The recorder in the boat noted the depth of the water, and the nature of the bottom adhering to the lead. By the angles measured at the base-line, the exact position of the sounding, which was never more than a few feet above or below the proposed section-line, was ascertained. The process was repeated until soundings enough had been taken to give an accurate cross-section of the river. Careful lines of level were then run up each bank from the water's surface to points above the level of the highest floods, when such points existed. Generally, the triangles were computed, and the work was plotted, before leaving the place, in order to fill, by additional soundings, any gaps which might appear on the diagram.

Additional precautions at permanent velocity stations.

Where a series of daily observations for discharge was to be made, two independent sections, 200 feet apart, were sounded with the greatest care. Soundings repeated from time to time upon these lines uniformly showed that no sensible changes took place in the bed of the river. The mean of all such sections, when reduced to the same stage of the river, was accordingly always taken for the true cross-section at the locality. The change in area produced by any change of level in water surface can be readily computed from the plotted section. To determine the daily changes of this level, a gauge-rod, graduated to feet and tenths, was observed daily; its correctness of adjustment being frequently tested by comparison with secure bench-marks. An accurate knowledge of the area of the cross-section of the river on any given day was thus obtained.

The detailed measurements of all the sounding operations are given in Appendix C, and a few of the characteristic sections exhibited on plate X.

Velocity of the current.—Narrow and straight portions of the river, where the form of its cross-section approximated most nearly to that of a canal, where the waters of the highest floods were confined to the channel by natural banks or by levees, and where the river at all stages was free from eddies, were selected for the permanent velocity stations.

Different instruments used for determining the velocity of the current.

The depth of the river and the violence of its current rendered the measurement of the velocity, especially below the surface, exceedingly difficult. Of all the methods known for determining this quantity, that by double floats was found to give the best results. A few measurements of the velocity of tributary streams, where both banks were submerged, were made with a ship's log; and some few observations were taken at the mouth of the river with Saxton's current-meter; but for all other velocity observations, the double float was exclusively used. Various kinds were tested. Solid cubes of wood about 1 foot on the edge were first tried. They were loaded with lead, so as to sink, and suspended by cords from surface floats of cork, bearing small flags. They proved to be too heavy for convenience. Bottles, partly filled with water and suspended in the same manner, were tested, but they did not present sufficient surface to the current to be adopted. Kegs without bottom or top, ballasted with strips of lead so as to sink and remain upright, were next tried for the lower floats. A rope handle was secured to the upper end of each, and connected by a cord with a surface float made either of light pine or cork, or hollow tin. A small flag was attached to a wire about a foot in length rising from the top of the surface float in order to make it visible. The dimensions of the floats were as follows: For the work in 1851, kegs 15 inches in height by 10 inches in diameter; cord two-tenths of an inch in diameter; surface float of cork about 8 inches square by 3 inches thick, submerged an inch and a half: for the work in 1858, kegs (paint kegs) about 9 inches in height by 6 inches in diameter; cord one-tenth of an inch in diameter; surface floats,—when of light pine, 5.5 by 5.5 by 0.5 inches,—when of tin, of an ellipsoidal form, the axes being 5.5 and 1.5 inches. For velocity observations more than 5 feet below the surface in 1851, no change was made, but in 1858 the kegs were made larger, being 12 inches in height by 8 inches in diameter, with a cord rather less than two-tenths of an inch in diameter. By varying the length of the cord, the keg could be made to sink to any required depth, and its size was so much greater than that of the surface float that the latter did not sensibly affect the rate of movement. This assumption was tested by placing the apparatus in still water during a high wind, and also by noticing the direction of the paths of the floats during a gale blowing directly across the river. No wind effect of consequence could be detected in either case. Hence by causing the keg to pass through the different parts of the cross-section of the river, the velocity at all points could be measured. The method of conducting these observations was the following:—

Method of conducting velocity measurements.

Two parallel cross-sections of the river having been made as already explained, 200 feet apart, a base-line of the same length was laid off upon the bank from one to the other, being of course perpendicular to both. This length was sufficient to insure accuracy without being too great either for convenience in communicating, or for observing many floats in a day, or for avoiding local changes in velocity. An observer with a theodolite was stationed at each extremity of the base-line. It is evident that when the telescopes were directed upon the river with their axes set at right angles to the base-line, the vertical cross-hairs marked out the lines of sounding upon the water surface, and that the time of passage of a float between these lines was that consumed in passing 200 feet. Also, that if the angular distance of a float from the base-line when crossing each line of sounding was measured, its distance in feet from the former could readily be computed and its path fixed.

Upon these principles, the observations were conducted. Two skiffs were stationed on the river, one considerably above the upper, and the other below the lower, section-line; the former boat being provided with several keg-floats. At a signal from the engineer at the upper station, whose telescope was set upon the upper section-line, a float was placed in the river. The keg immediately sank to the depth allowed by its cord, and the whole float moved down toward the upper line. The observer at the lower station followed its motion, keeping the cross-hair of his telescope directed constantly upon the flag. At the word "Mark!" uttered by his companion when the float crossed the upper line, he recorded the angle shown by his instrument, and then setting his telescope upon the lower line, watched for the arrival of the float. In the mean time the observer at the upper station, whose theodolite supported a watch with a large second-hand, recorded the time of transit of the float across the upper line, and then followed the flag with his telescope. At the word "Mark!" given by his assistant when the flag crossed the lower line, he recorded the time and angular distance from the base-line. The float was picked up by the lower boat. By this method the exact point of crossing each section-line and the time of transit were ascertained. When the velocity was not too great, the time was noted by the engineer at the lower station also, to guard against error. A stop-watch was sometimes used.

Difference in the systems adopted in 1851 and 1858.

This system was adopted for the observations both of 1851 and of 1858, with an important difference, however, in the depth of the floats. It is evidently impossible to observe floats daily in all parts of the cross-section. The best practical method, therefore, is to adopt a uniform depth for all the floats, distribute them equally across the entire river, and multiply the resulting discharge by the ratio of the velocity at the assumed depth to the mean velocity of the whole vertical curve. But this ratio was unknown in 1851, the practical law of change of velocity in a vertical plane parallel to the current having thus far baffled all efforts of hydraulic engineers for its elucidation. It was, therefore, deemed unsafe to depend upon this method at the outset, and Professor Forshey's party were instructed temporarily to distribute the floats as uniformly as possible, at all depths and at all distances from the banks, in measuring the discharge; while at the same time especial experiments were made to determine the law of change of velocity below the surface.

Observations for the determination of the law regulating the change of velocity from surface to bottom.

Various methods of observing for the latter purpose were resorted to. Saxton's current-meter was tried, but proved to be unsuited to measurements in a river of such great depth and violence of current. Only double floats were found to give reliable results. The observations were made at different distances from the banks, the boat being anchored considerably above the upper line. Many series of floats were thus observed at each station, the kegs passing at all depths from the surface nearly to the bottom. Discrepancies being manifest in the results, every care was taken to avoid causes of error, by changing the order of depth; sometimes observing a large number at the same depth consecutively, and at other times passing rapidly from the surface to the bottom of the river, observing a single float at each depth. Experiments were thus made at high and low water at various points near Carrollton and Baton Rouge. When field work was resumed in 1857, a uniform depth of 5 feet below the surface was taken for all floats, a few especial observations being however made upon the velocity at different depths in the same vertical plane. A full discussion of the law of change in velocity below the surface will be given in the next division of this chapter.

PRELIMINARY COMPUTATION OF DISCHARGE, NEGLECTING CHANGES IN VELOCITY BELOW THE SURFACE.

Method of plotting velocity measurements.

Mississippi river.—A separate plot of each day's velocity observations was made in the following manner: Lines were drawn upon section-paper to represent the section-lines, the base-line, and the water edges. The distances from the base-line to the points where each float crossed the section-lines were then computed by a table of natural tangents, and the points laid down upon the plot. Straight lines connecting the two corresponding points indicated the paths of the floats, which were, of course, nearly perpendicular to the section-lines. The number of seconds of transit and the depth of the float being inscribed upon these plotted paths, the resulting diagram afforded the means of conveniently comparing the velocities in different parts of the section.

System of grouping the floats.

Deferring for the present the discussion of the analytical relations shown to exist between these velocities, it is sufficient to state that the velocity increased gradually and quite uniformly with the distance from the banks until the thread of the current was reached. Conceiving the cross-section of the river to be divided by a system of vertical lines 200 feet apart, the velocity was found to vary but slightly throughout the spaces limited by these vertical lines, except in the immediate vicinity of the banks. The first step, therefore, was to divide the daily velocity plots by parallel lines 200 feet apart, the first being the base-line, and to take a mean of the seconds of transit of all floats in each of these *divisions*, so called. The corresponding velocity, taken from a table constructed for the purpose, was considered to be the mean velocity of the division—absolute for the observations of 1851, and relative for those of 1858. For the shore divisions, unless the floats happened to be well distributed through them, the mean velocity was assumed to be eight-tenths of that at the outer edge, a rule deduced from a subdivision and study of the velocity, when thoroughly measured in these divisions.

Method of checking; and, when necessary, of interpolating.

To guard against errors, the day's work was next plotted in a curve, whose ordinates were the mean velocities of the different divisions, and whose abscissæ were the distances of their middle points from the base-line. When observations on any day were wanting in a division, these curves afforded the best possible means for interpolation. When observations in several divisions were wanting, the following plan was adopted: A simple inspection of the daily curves showed a change in form corresponding to a change in mean velocity of the river. Deferring for the present the theoretical discussion of this change, it is sufficient to state that the form was found to remain sensibly the same for variations of a foot in this mean velocity. The complete or nearly complete daily observations were therefore computed, and the mean velocity of the river determined in the manner soon to be detailed. The daily curves were then grouped and mean curves computed and plotted for each even foot of these mean velocities. The defective sets of observations were next plotted, and the velocities of the wanting divisions interpolated from a comparison with the form of the mean curve of corresponding stage. These mean curves also served to correct errors in the work of 1851, arising from a deficiency in the number of the floats or from their imperfect distribution. They are represented on plate XI. The exact data for Carrollton are given in the following table:—

Locality.	Division.	Mean division velocity in feet per second for—						
		$v = 1.7269$	$v = 2.5250$	$v = 3.4930$	$v = 4.4539$	$v = 5.6767$	$v = 6.1399$	Grand mean. $v = 4.0026$
Carrollton..	I	1.2712	1.9800	2.8738	3.6661	4.6071	5.0522	3.2417
"	II	1.8504	2.7908	3.7419	4.7658	5.9876	6.5122	4.2748
"	III	1.9068	2.8183	3.9652	5.0475	6.2824	6.7644	4.4641
"	IV	1.9052	2.7467	3.9076	5.0004	6.1810	6.7178	4.4098
"	V	1.8648	2.6600	3.7971	4.8319	6.0114	6.4800	4.2742
"	VI	1.7988	2.5225	3.6567	4.6775	5.8586	6.3356	4.1416
"	VII	1.7108	2.4375	3.4486	4.4242	5.6395	6.0900	3.9584
"	VIII	1.5760	2.3233	3.1533	4.0989	5.4162	5.9022	3.7450
"	IX	1.4244	2.0883	2.8552	3.7619	5.1586	5.6322	3.4868
"	X	1.2468	1.8717	2 4671	3.3239	4.7252	5.3756	3.1684
"	XI	0.9916	1.5058	1.9952	2.6808	4.1695	4.4344	2.6296
"	XII	0.7780	1.1825	1.5957	2.1175	3.2495	3.6133	2.0894

The data for Natchez are presented in the following table, and for Columbus and Vicksburg in those on pages 240 and 242.

Locality, Natchez.	Mean velocity, in feet per second, five feet below the surface, in divisions—																					
	I	II	III	IV	V	VI	VII	VIII	IX	X	XI	XII	XIII	XIV	XV	XVI	XVII	XVIII	XIX	XX	XXI	XXII
27 days' observations......	0	3.53	4.72	5.57	5.77	5.17	4.79	4.52	4.49	4.46	4.46	4.41	4.34	4.36	4.32	4.29	4.18	4.09	3.90	3.64	3.32	1.93
Approximate mean velocity of river.................................... 4.2962 feet.																						

Method of computing the discharge.

In the tables in Appendix D, the mean velocity of every division for all discharge measurements made upon the Survey is given; "old style" figures being employed to distinguish interpolations from observations. Unless stated to the contrary, the width of the divisions is uniformly 200 feet. It is evident that, if the areas of all the divisions were equal, the discharge would be the product of the total area of cross-section by the mean of the velocities of all the divisions. This is, however, never the case for natural channels. Neither is the ratio of these areas constant for the different stages of the river. The only accurate method of computation, therefore, is to multiply each division area by its velocity, and take the sum of the products for the discharge. This sum, divided by the total area of cross-section, is the approximate mean velocity of the river. This method, although very laborious, was adopted for this Survey. As already intimated, a mean of the low-water areas on all the plots of both lines of soundings was taken for the true low-water area of each division. For the shore divisions, the areas at the other stages of the river were computed in the same way, but for the intermediate divisions, since they were all 200 feet in width, an addition to the low-water area of 200 × 0.1 = 20 square feet was made for each tenth of foot of rise in the river.

To simplify the computation, tables were prepared giving the velocity and its logarithm for all observed seconds of transit past a base-line of 200 feet, and the area of each division with its logarithm for every reading of the gauge corresponding to velocity observations. The sum of the two proper logarithms from those tables for any day was the logarithm of the discharge of the division in cubic feet per second, and the sum of these discharges for all the divisions was the total discharge of the river. When floats were observed at all depths, as at Carrollton in 1851, this discharge is as absolutely correct as can be deduced from the observations. When the floats were all at a fixed depth below the surface, as in the observations of 1857–58, this discharge is only approximate, and is to be multiplied by the ratio of the velocity at this depth to the mean of the whole vertical curve. In the latter case it is named "approximate dis charge" in the tables. The method of deducing the ratio for correction will receive a full discussion in the next division of this chapter.

Only exceptions to this method.

The method above detailed was used in computing all discharges of the Mississippi river, except those near Red river, on March 12 and 19, 1851. On these days, as only a few floats were observed, and as the curve of velocity in the different divisions was not sufficiently determined for accurate interpolation, it was thought better to assume that the discharge bore the same ratio to that on other days when it was accurately measured, as the mean velocity of all the floats observed bore to the mean of floats passing over the same paths on those other days.

More simple method of computing the discharge adopted for tributary streams.

Tributaries.—The labor which it exacts prevented the adoption of the partial-area system of computation for the tributaries and bayous. It was considered sufficiently accurate for those streams to deduce a discharge, called "approximate discharge" in the tables, by multiplying the area of cross-section by the mean of the velocities of all the divisions, the floats in each division being plotted and grouped as described for the Mississippi itself. To correct the result for the errors arising from difference in the area of different divisions and from change of velocity below the surface, this approximate discharge was multiplied by a ratio obtained by dividing the true mean velocity of the Mississippi by the corresponding mean velocity 5 feet below the surface. The following table exhibits these ratios for Columbus, Vicksburg, and Natchez:—

Locality.	Wind down stream.		Calm.		Wind up stream.	
	No. of days observed.	Ratio $\frac{v}{U_5}$.	No. of days observed.	Ratio $\frac{v}{U_5}$.	No. of days observed.	Ratio $\frac{v}{U_5}$.
Columbus	64	1.0641	24	1.0735	109	1.1149
Vicksburg	42	1.0174	88	1.0415	80	1.0522
Natchez	12	1.0547	5	1.0643	10	1.0922
Mean		1.0454		1.0598		1.0864

The three mean ratios were adopted for computing the discharge of all the tributaries and bayous except that of bayou Plaquemine and bayou La Fourche, where, as a very exact determination was required, the partial-area system was used; the sum of the approximate discharges of all the divisions being multiplied by a ratio between the velocity at the observed depth and the mean velocity of the whole vertical curve, deduced from especial observations upon the bayous themselves.

The change of velocity below the surface is a subject to be discussed, in order to explain the manner of deducing the ratios used in computing the revised discharges of the Mississippi, when all the observations were made at a fixed depth. For convenience it will be treated in an independent division of this chapter.

An important digression now necessary.

VELOCITY IN DIFFERENT PARTS OF THE CROSS-SECTION.

Before entering into this somewhat long and intricate discussion, the general principle upon which it has been conducted will be enunciated. The preceding chapter shows that two radically different methods have been heretofore used in such investigations. Some writers, adopting a system of laws based upon theoretical inferences, have proceeded to deduce corresponding formulæ. Others, of whom Michelotte and Dubuat are the chief, have limited their endeavors to generalizing by their formulæ the truths revealed by their observations. The latter method has been exclusively followed in this investigation of the true ratio between the velocity 5 feet below the surface in any vertical plane parallel to the current and the mean of all the velocities in this plane. New laws of great practical value have been developed, some theoretical use of which will be made in the next chapter, but here theories are only admitted when established by observations.

No theorizing admissible in investigating the laws governing the action of cohesion.

The list on pages 200, 201 and 202, which explains in full the rather peculiar system of notation rendered necessary by the unusual number of quantities to be considered, should be carefully examined.

List of symbols.

Velocity below the surface.—As already stated, very elaborate series of observations, to determine the law governing the change of velocity from surface to bottom, were conducted in 1851 at Carrollton (plate III) and Baton Rouge, from boats anchored at different distances from the banks, besides many isolated experiments while observing for discharge. To counteract, as far as possible, any effect of change in velocity during the observations, the order of observing at different depths was constantly varied. Sometimes the series of observations consisted of one at each depth from surface to bot-

Care taken to avoid sources of error in conducting the field work.

tom or bottom to surface. Sometimes many observations were made consecutively at each depth. Sometimes floats were started near the surface and near the bottom, and the distances from these planes were successively increased until the mid-depth was reached. In fine, every effort was made to avoid and eliminate error. The first steps toward deducing the law from the observations were, therefore, very simple.

Classification and primary combination of observations.

As floats are compelled to pass through nearly the same paths when starting from a fixed station, and are, consequently, unaffected by the change in velocity due to difference in distance from the banks, the principle was adopted of depending entirely upon the elaborated sets of observations from anchored boats. All the observations of each set being thus confined to nearly the same vertical plane, one great cause of error was practically eliminated. From the position of the boat, found by triangulation, the recorded gauge-reading, and the known depths of the different parts of the river section, the depth of water in each vertical plane of passage was readily determined. The velocity of each float was deduced from the recorded seconds of transit past the base-line, and a mean taken of all the observations at each depth for the true velocity at that depth. The curves resulting from applying this process to all the different sets of observations were next plotted upon section-paper on a large scale, the depths of the floats forming the ordinates, and their velocities the corresponding abscissæ. A general difference of form in the curve at high and at low stages of the river was manifest, although irregularities were sufficiently apparent, as may be seen by reference to the following tables. It was evident that some combination of curves was necessary to reconcile discrepancies of observations.

The first method adopted was to combine all curves of observation where neither the depth of water nor the velocity of the river varied materially. This was done by taking a mean of the velocities of all the floats at each depth, each set of observations thus receiving a weight proportioned to its number of observations at each point. When observations were wanting at any depth, careful interpolations were made from the plotted curve. The resulting mean curves are exhibited on plate XI, figures 1, 3, 10, 2, 4, 9, the numbers being shown in the following tables:—

Sub-surface velocity observations at high stages of the river, the water being about 110 *feet deep.*

Station at Carrollton.	Date.	Gauge.	Mean velocity of the river.	Wind.	Distance from base.	Depth.	No. of obs. at each point.	Velocity in feet per second at various depths below water surface.								
								Surface.	½ fath.	1 fath.	3 fath.	6 fath.	9 fath.	12 fath.	15 fath.	17 fath.
	1851.	*Feet.*	*Feet.*		*Feet.*	*Ft.*										
Prime base	Mar. 8	13.7	5.8151	Down 2	350	110	1	6.6666	6.6666	6.6666	6.6666	6.6666	6.4516	6.2500	5.8823	5.2631
" "	May 26	9.4	3.8157	Up 2	430	110	2	3.9215	4.2553	4.1666	4.2553	4.3478	4.3478	4.2553	4.0816	3.8461
" "	" 26	9.4	3.8157	Up 2	920	110	2	3.6363	3.7087	3.7735	3.8461	3.8461	3.8461	3.7735	3.7087	3.4482
" "	" 27	9.4	3.7703	0	1000	110	10	3.6633	3.7456	3.7526	3.8913	3 8537	3.7456	3 6108	3.6633	3.7246
" "	" 28	9.5	3.8919	0	350	110	6	4.0735	4.1666	4.1496	4.0816	4.0653	4.2553	4.1241	3.7526	3.4482
Race-course base..	June 3	10.6	4.1580	Up 2	430	105	2	4.4400	4.3500	4.7600	4.7600	4.7600	4.6500	4.5500	4.6500	4.4400
" "	" 3	10.6	4.1580	Up 2	840	105	2	4.5500	4.5500	4.7600	4.7600	4.6500	4.5500	4.3500	4.1700	4.0000
Locks base	" 4	10.7	3.6420	Up 3	960	105	2	3.7000	3.9200	4.0000	3.7700	3.8500	3.7700	3.7000	3.5700	3.5100
Prime base	" 6	10.7	4.0932	Up 3	300	110	9	4.5666	4.5666	4.4251	4.5877	4.8548	4.7176	4.5151	4.4444	4.1666
" "	" 11	10.8	4.2503	Up 1	300	110	16	4.2738	3.9529	4.1755	4.1241	4.1241	4.0082	3.8025	3.6298	3.5087
" "	" 12	11.0	4.3079	Down 1	900	110	16	4.3961	4.3671	4.3961	4.4848	4.5151	4.4747	4.4347	4.3864	4.4646
" "	" 25	11.6	4.2343	Up 2	200	110	2	4.1666	4.0816	4.0000	4.2553	4.2553	4.2553	4.1666	4.0816	4.0000
" "	" 25	11.6	4.2343	Up 2	800	110	2	4.5454	4.5454	4.5454	4.5454	5.0000	4.6511	5.1282	5.0000	4.6511
True mean.......			4.1216	Up 0.8					4.2801		4.2984	4.3463	4.2745	4.1580	4.0528	3.9481

Sub-surface velocity observations at high stages of the river, the water being about 70 *feet deep.*

Station at Carrollton.	Date.	Gauge.	Mean velocity of the river.	Wind.	Distance from base.	Depth.	No. of obs. at each point.	Velocity in ft. per sec. at various depths below water surface.						
								Surface.	½ fath.	1 fath.	3 fath.	6 fath.	9 fath.	11 fath.
	1851.	*Ft.*	*Feet.*		*Feet.*	*Ft.*								
Prime base	May 26	9.4	3.8157	Up 2	1400	65	2	3.1250	3.0769	3.1746	3.2786	3.4482	3.3333	3.2239
" "	" 29	9.7	3.8913	0	1600	65	8	2.8902	2.9155	3.0961	3.0536	3.1300	3.1448	3.1548
Race-course base	June 3	10.6	4.1580	Up 2	1360	70	2	4.4400	4.5500	4.6500	4.4400	4.0800	4.0000	3.8500
Locks base	" 4	10.7	3.6420	Up 3	1700	70	2	3.8600	4.6511	4.3500	4.2600	4.3500	4.3500	4.1700
" "	" 4	10.7	3.6420	Up 3	2070	70	2	4.3500	4.5500	4.6500	4.5500	4.5500	4.1700	3.8500
Prime base	" 9	10.8	4.1271	Down 1	1720	65	8	3.2628	3.4724	3.6430	3.7107	3.7037	3.5589	3.4724
" "	" 13	11.1	4.3773	Down 1	1620	65	16	3.5338	3.4845	3.6700	3.6363	3.7316	3.5651	3.4845
" "	" 26	11.6	4.3051	0	1500	65	2	3.8461	3.8461	3.9215	4.0816	4.0816	4.0816	3.8461
True mean			4.1279	Down 0.1				3.5503			3.6551	3.6999	3.5843	3.4917

Sub-surface velocity observations at high stages of the river, the water being about 55 *feet deep.*

Station at Carrollton.	Date.	Gauge.	Mean velocity of the river.	Wind.	Distance from base.	Depth.	No. of obs. at each point.	Vel. in ft. per sec. at various depths bel. water surface.					
								Surface.	½ fath.	1 fath.	3 fath.	5 fath.	6 fath.
	1851.	*Ft.*	*Feet.*		*Feet.*	*Ft.*							
Race-course base	June 3	10.6	4.1580	Up 2	1970	50	2	3.9215	3.6363	3.8461	3.8461	3.7062	3.6363
Prime base	" 9	10.8	4.1271	Down 1	1900	55	8	2.9631	2.8290	2.8944	3.0629	3.1696	2.9895
" "	" 14	11.2	4.4240	0	1850	55	16	2.6774	2.1811	2.6213	2.5642	2.6110	2.6042
" "	" 26	11.6	4.3051	0	1900	55	2	3.1250	3.1250	3.1746	3.1746	3.2786	2.9850
True mean			4.3117	Down 0.1				2.7623		2.8263	2.8311	2.8965	2.8152

Sub-surface velocity observations at low stages of the river, the water being about 100 *feet deep.*

Station at Carrollton.	Date.	Gauge.	Mean vel. of the river.	Wind.	Distance from base.	Depth.	No. of obs. at each point.	Velocity in feet per second at various depths below water surface.														
								Surface.	1 fathom.	2 fathoms	3 fathoms	4 fathoms	5 fathoms	6 fathoms	7 fathoms	8 fathoms	9 fathoms	10 fathoms	11 fathoms	12 fathoms	13 fathoms	14 fathoms
	1851.	*Ft.*	*Feet.*		*Ft.*	*Ft.*																
Prime base	Sept. 24	1.8	1.9428	Down 2	425	100	4	2.2222	2.2297	2.1575	2.1459	2.0264	2.0513	2.0471	2.0081	1.9286	1.9881	1.9139	1.9120	1.8416	1.8656	1.8467
" "	" 25	1.8	1.9045	" 2	900	100	4	2.2222	2.2962	2.3753	2.3809	2.3809	2.3202	2.2753	2.2002	2.2447	2.2372	2.2422	2.1716	2.1276	2.1074	2.1299
" "	Oct. 13	1.1	1.6577	" 3	400	100	4	1.3422	1.3746	1.3404	1.3513	1.3495	1.3140	1.3227	1.3315	1.3029	1.3157	1.3012	1.2886	1.2970	1.2484	1.2000
" "	" 14	1.0	1.6552	" 3	850	100	4	2.1276	2.1231	2.1231	2.1119	2.1119	2.0618	2.0471	2.0408	2.0305	2.0000	2.0020	2.0640	2.0000	1.9417	1.8518
" "	Nov. 20	0.9	1.5975	" 3	300	95	8	1.8518	1.7437	1.8333	1.9230	1.8840	1.8450	1.8667	1.8885	1.8484	1.8083	1.7444	1.6806	1.5832	1.4858	1.3614
True mean.			1.7250	" 2.7				1.9362	1.9185	1.9438	1.9727	1.9394	1.9062	1.9043	1.8929	1.8672	1.8596	1.8247	1.7996	1.7388	1.6891	1.6390

Sub-surface velocity observations at low stages of the river, the water being about 80 *feet deep.*

Station.	Date.	Gauge.	Mean vel. of the river.	Wind.	Distance from base.	Depth.	No. of obs. at each point.	Velocity in feet per second at various depths below water surface.												
								Surface.	1 fathom.	2 fathoms	3 fathoms	4 fathoms	5 fathoms	6 fathoms	7 fathoms	8 fathoms	9 fathoms	10 fathoms	11 fathoms	12 fathoms
	1851.	*Ft.*	*Ft.*		*Ft.*	*Ft.*														
Carrollton—prime base	Oct. 15	1.0	1.6610	Down 2	1250	80	4	1.9357	1.9596	1.9342	1.9089	1.8707	1.8628	1.8961	1.8961	1.8311	1.8281	1.7726	1.7178	1.5850
Baton Rouge—lower base	" 30	4.9	2.1603	0	1100	75	8	2.7200	2.7500	2.7200	2.6991	2.6585	2.6179	2.5605	2.5032	2.4846	2.4661	2.4221	2.3781	2.1930
Baton Rouge—lower base	" 31	4.8	2.2377	0	1550	80	8	2.3000	2.3300	2.3000	2.2805	2.2792	2.2779	2.2295	2.1811	2.1716	2.1622	2.1174	2.0726	2.0597
True mean			2.0914	Down 0.4				2.3951	2.4239	2.3998	2.3738	2.3492	2.3134	2.2952	2.2530	2.2287	2.2170	2.1703	2.1240	2.0181

Sub-surface velocity observations at low stages of the river, the water being about 60 *feet deep.*

Station.	Date.	Gauge.	Mean vel. of the river.	Wind.	Distance from base.	Depth.	No. of obs. at each point.	Velocity in feet per second at various depths below water surface.									
								Surface.	1 fathom.	2 fathoms	3 fathoms	4 fathoms	5 fathoms	6 fathoms	7 fathoms	8 fathoms	9 fathoms.
	1851.	*Ft.*	*Ft.*		*Ft.*	*Ft.*											
Carrollton—prime base	Sept. 26	1.5	1.8832	0	1500	55	4	2.1716	2.1599	2.1575	2.1119	2.1835	2.1308	2.1074	2.0534	1.9665	
Carrollton—prime base	" 26	1.5	1.8832	0	1800	55	4	1.9398	1.9065	1.8034	1.7746	1.7731	1.6694	1.6488	1.5898	1.5308	1.5662
Carrollton—prime base	Oct. 15	1.0	1.6610	Down 2	1600	55	4	1.6806	1.6849	1.6708	1.6597	1.6434	1.5786	1.5209	1.4630	1.4051	
Baton Rouge—upper base	" 30	4.9	2.4664	0	2050	65	8	2.8085	2.8571	2.7895	2.7855	2.8012	2.8091	2.7855	2.8290	2.7816	2.6631
Baton Rouge—lower base	" 30	4.9	2.1603	Down 1	600	60	8	2.9368	2.9674	2.9205	2.8737	2.7792	2.6847	2.6669	2.6491	2.5561	2.4631
Baton Rouge—lower base	" 31	4.8	2.4664	0	1900	55	8	2.2051	2.2962	2.3458	2.3053	2.3880	2.3474	2.2463	2.1119	2.0837	2.0555
True mean			2.1285	Down 0.4				2.3804	2.3910	2.3887	2.3504	2.3404	2.2929	2.2434	2.1088	2.1379	2.0628

General results.

These curves at once indicate the existence of law, although the discrepancies are too great to permit the deduction of any algebraic expression for it. It is evident, however, that the velocity differs very little at different depths; that it at first increases and then decreases as the depth is increased; that the point of maximum velocity is found at a very variable depth below the surface; and that the degree of curvature of the curve varies with the stage of the river.

Further combination of curves by proportional depths necessary.

It is manifest that some further combination is necessary in order to eliminate the effect of disturbing causes. Since the absolute depths differ, this can only be done by combining the velocities at proportional depths, leaving the correctness of this principle of combination to be eventually tested by the application to each individual curve of the laws thus deduced. The method adopted for this combination was to plot the mean curves on a scale so distorted that thousandths of a foot of velocity were readily distinguished. The entire depth was then divided into ten equal parts. Horizontal lines were drawn and the velocities at their points of cutting the curves noted. These numbers were the most correct interpolations that could be made for the velocity at each *tenth of depth,* and they were next combined in the ratio of the number of observations at each point of the original curves of observations. The points inclosed by circles in figure 16, plate XI, exhibit the mean points thus determined, the grand mean of all the observations from anchored boats. They are plotted from the first column of the next table. Each point is fixed by 222 observations; enough, as the result proves, to eliminate irregularities and to reveal the law governing the transmission of resistances through the fluid.

Algebraic analysis of resulting grand-mean curve.

The curve formed by connecting these points is evidently symmetrical, having a horizontal axis whose depth below the surface is about three-tenths of the total depth of the river. The peculiar form suggests that it may be one of the conic sections. To decide which one it must be, if either of them, the general equation of these curves is assumed referred to rectangular co-ordinate axes, the origin being at the vertex, and the axis of X being the axis of the curve.* The curve can be passed through any two points, $y, x,$ and $y_{\prime\prime}\ x_{\prime\prime},$ by assigning the following values to R^2 and $2\ P$, viz.:—

* $y^2 = R^2 x^2 + 2 P x.$

$$R^2 = \frac{y_{\prime\prime}^2 x_\prime - x_{\prime\prime} y_\prime^2}{x_{\prime\prime}^2 x_\prime - x_\prime^2 x_{\prime\prime}}.$$

$$2\,P = \frac{y_\prime^2 - R^2 x_\prime^2}{x_\prime}.$$

By a well-known law of the conic sections, when $R^2 = 0$, the curve is a parabola; when $R^2 < 0$, an ellipse; when $R^2 > 0$, an hyperbola. If, then, the known point of the curve most distant from the axis be assumed for $x_\prime$ $y_\prime$, and the intermediate points successively for $x_{\prime\prime}$ $y_{\prime\prime}$, the corresponding values of R^2 will decide which, if either, of these curves represents the law of change of velocity below the surface. It should be added that, as a mathematically regular curve never results from actual observations, it is not to be expected that R^2 shall become absolutely zero, even if the law be parabolic, but only that its different values shall be very small and of different signs. The first four columns of the next table exhibit the details of the application of this process to the curve in question. The values of $x_{\prime\prime}$ represent the differences between the maximum velocity (3.2611) and that at the depth considered. The values of $y_{\prime\prime}$ denote the distances from the axis (assumed at 0.3 of the depth below the surface) of the given points; the entire depth being considered unity.* The values of $x_\prime$ $y_\prime$ correspond to a depth of 0.9 D, viz., $x_\prime = 0.2852$; $y_\prime = 0.6$. The values of R^2 in the fourth column of this table prove conclusively that, if the curve which reveals the law of transmission of resistances through the fluid be either of the conic sections, it must be considered a parabola; for the term $R^2 x^2$ varies in sign, and has, uniformly, too small a numerical value to be of any importance. Whether it is this curve or not, must be decided by the degree of coincidence between the observations and the corresponding points of that parabola which gives the minimum mean difference. The next step, then, is to deduce the equation of this parabola.

The most rapid and convenient method in practice is the following, in which much calculation is saved by the eye, and all requisite accuracy attained. The equation of a common parabola, referred to rectangular co-ordinate axes (the axis of X being the axis of the curve), with the condition imposed of passing through two points, the co-ordinates of one of which are denoted by $x_\prime$ and 0, is—

$$x = \frac{x_{\prime\prime} - x_\prime}{y_{\prime\prime}^2}\, y^2 + x_\prime\,.$$

The axis of the curve of observations is approximately constructed, and assumed as the axis of X. It cuts the curve at the point $x_\prime$ 0, and thus fixes the value of $x_\prime$. The known point most distant from the axis of X is assumed for the point $x_{\prime\prime}$ $y_{\prime\prime}$. The constants of the equation being thus known, the values of x for all the depths at which observations have been made are computed. To make the parabola accord as closely as possible with the observations, the difference between the sum of these values of x and the sum of the observed velocities, divided by the number of points determined, is then applied as a correction to the arbitrary constant and to each computed value of x; a positive sign being used when the sum of the observed velocities is the greater, and a negative, when this sum is the less. Computing other points, if desirable, this

* This peculiar unit of depth was adopted for convenience, since it abridges the labor of computation. The final formulæ, in which depths are expressed in feet below the surface, are arranged to adjust themselves to this unit without a change of constants.

parabola is now plotted on the same scale as the curve of observations. When a copy on semi-transparent tracing-paper is placed upon the curve of observations, the eye at once detects if a closer approximation can be made by slightly changing the depth of the axis, or the position of the point $x_{\prime\prime}$ $y_{\prime\prime}$. After a little experience it is seldom necessary to make more than one or two trials. By this process, the following equation was deduced for the parabola corresponding to the grand-mean curve of observations:—

$$V = - 0.79222\ d_{\prime\prime}^2 + 3.2611,$$

in which V, taking the place of x, is the velocity in feet, and $d_{\prime\prime}$, taking the place of y, is the distance from the axis, in fractional parts of the whole depth, considered unity. The last columns of the following table exhibit the comparison between the observations and the parabola.

Depth of float below surface.	$x_{\prime\prime}$	$y_{\prime\prime}$	R^2	Velocity by observation.	Velocity by above equation.	Difference.	Remarks.
				Feet.	*Feet.*	*Feet.*	
Surface......	0.0661	+ 0.3	— 0.45	3.1950	3.1901	+ 0.0049	Grand mean of all observations taken from anchored boats, combined in ratio of number of observations at each determined point. They were taken at Carrollton and Baton Rouge in 1851. Each point is fixed by 222 observations. Mean maximum velocity, which is 0.297 D below the surface, is 3.2611 feet. Mean depth is 82 feet. Mean wind is down force 0.2. Mean velocity of river is 3.3814 feet per second.
0.1 D.........	0.0312	+ 0.2	— 0.08	3.2299	3.2293	+ 0.0006	
0.2 D.........	0.0079	+ 0.1	— 0.01	3.2532	3.2525	+ 0.0007	
0.3 D.........	0.0000	0.0	———	3.2611	3.2600	+ 0.0011	
0.4 D.........	0.0095	— 0.1	+ 0.73	3.2516	3.2525	— 0.0009	
0.5 D.........	0.0329	— 0.2	+ 0.18	3.2282	3.2274	+ 0.0008	
0.6 D.........	0.0804	— 0.3	+ 0.70	3.1807	3.1873	— 0.0066	
0.7 D.........	0.1345	— 0.4	+ 0.48	3.1266	3.1313	— 0.0047	
0.8 D.........	0.2017	— 0.5	+ 0 27	3.0594	3 0596	— 0.0002	
0.9 D.........				2.9759	2.9719	+ 0.0040	
Bottom......					2.8685		
Sum of common points.........................				31.7616	31.7619	0.0245	
Mean of common points.........................				3.1762	3.1762	0.0024	

It proves to be a parabola whose axis is parallel to and below the water surface.

The two curves, represented by figure 16, plate XI, almost coincide, and it is therefore claimed that experiment demonstrates that *the velocities at different depths below the surface, in a vertical plane, vary as the abscissæ of a parabola, whose axis is the axis of* X *and parallel to the water surface;* also that the axis of the curve *may be* considerably below the surface.

A further analysis of the data shows that the parameter and depth of axis both vary.

The next step in the investigation was to determine whether the parabola retained an unchanging parameter and a uniform position of axis. To solve these questions, a separate combination of all high-water and all low-water curves, reduced to tenths of depth, was made, each curve having a weight proportional to its number of observations at each point. Figures 15 and 14, plate XI, exhibit the two resulting curves. The mean high-water curve (the mean of all observations made at high stages of the river) is evidently parabolic in form, with the axis horizontal and about 0.350 of the depth below the surface. The mean low-water curve exhibits greater irregularities, but is still parabolic, with its axis about 0.150 of the depth below the surface. By further subdivision of the data, other mean curves were obtained, corresponding to intermediate stages, but the number of observations at each point was so limited that the errors of observation concealed the distinctive form of the curve. This was to be expected, since, in experiments of such delicacy, these errors can only be eliminated by the mutual obliteration resulting from a combination of many observations. By the process already detailed, the equations of parabolas which should coincide as nearly as possible with these high-water and low-water mean curves of observations, were deduced. The parameter (the constant which fixes the degree of curvature of the parabola) was found to vary materially in the high-water, the low-water, and the grand-mean curves. The position of the axis, as already seen, was also different in each of these curves.

The practical importance of this investigation, in deducing the absolute daily discharge of the river at Columbus, Vicksburg, and other places, rendered imperatively necessary a study of the laws by which these quantities varied, although the subject was rather unpromising in appearance.

Investigation of the law governing the change in the parameter.

Neglecting for the time the position of the axis, the law of change in the parameter (and, consequently, in the form of the curve) was first investigated. To this end a new curve had to be determined, which should exhibit the law of change in the parameter. The data, as already seen, consisted of the parameters of the grand mean, of the high-water mean and of the low-water mean curves; the first known accurately, the second quite closely, and the third only approximately, in consequence of discrepancies of observation having partially vitiated the form of the curves of observations, from which it was deduced. The reciprocals of these quantities were taken as the abscissæ in the parameter curve. The first question which arose was, what are the corresponding ordinates? that is, with what do the reciprocals of the parameters vary? with any particular velocity or with the mean velocity of the curves themselves? or with the mean velocity of the river? That they should vary with the velocity at any particular point of the curves themselves seemed highly improbable, since, in that case, they must be functions of the position of the axis, which, as will soon be seen, is liable to constant change. It remained, then, to consider whether they varied with the means of the abscissæ of the velocity curves themselves or with the mean velocity of the river. A little reflection shows that, in either case, the important inference may be drawn, that if either of those quantities becomes zero, the velocity curve becomes a right line, coinciding with the axis of Y. This requires the parameter of the velocity curve to become infinite, which makes its reciprocals zero, and thus adds a fourth to the known abscissæ of the parameter curve.

Plotting these four abscissæ of the parameter curve with the mean of the abscissæ of the corresponding velocity curves as ordinates, a laborious but unsuccessful effort was made to discover an equation by the curve thus formed, which should reveal any reasonable law. The mean velocities of the river were next tried as ordinates for the parameter curve, being computed by dividing, by the total number of observations at each point, the sum of the products of the number of observations at each point upon each day by the corresponding mean velocity of the river. It seemed more natural that this should be the velocity upon which the form of the curve depends, because this form in any vertical plane must be governed to some extent by that in adjacent planes, and hence be affected by any change in the mean velocity of the river. Although it became apparent that some law existed connecting the reciprocals of the four parameters and the corresponding grand-mean velocities of the river, yet the slight difference in the latter quantities and the somewhat uncertain determination of the parameter of the low-water curve rendered the result of the investigation unsatisfactory. It was found impossible to deduce sufficient proof to establish the existence of any mathematical law.

Baffled by the curves of sub-surface velocities themselves, a clue to the law was to

The result being unsatisfactory, a further clue is sought in the curves of surface velocities.

be sought for elsewhere. It was reasoned, since the form of these curves depends upon the general law of transmission of resistance to separation through the fluid, that the same law must govern the form of the curve of velocities from one bank to the other in a horizontal plane. Hence the desired clue might be found by a study of the curves of surface velocities, which were well determined at all stages of the river, both at Columbus and at Vicksburg. This subject, therefore, was examined at this stage of the discussion of sub-surface velocities.

Columbus curves selected for study.

Velocities near the surface at various distances from the banks.—In the series of observations at Columbus, Vicksburg, and Natchez (plate III), recorded in full detail in Appendix D, the uniform depth of 5 feet below the surface was adopted for all floats. At the first-named stations many observations were taken at every stage of the river at every point between the banks; but at Natchez the work was discontinued too soon to obtain a full series. At Carrollton, the only other permanent velocity station, the floats were observed at different depths, and were, consequently, variously affected by the resistances transmitted from the bottom. The use of those at the surface or at the same depth, would afford few observations compared with those at Columbus and Vicksburg, and although the curve would not probably be materially affected by the source of error stated—since the variation in velocity from bank to bank is very great, while that from surface to bottom is very small—still, as the Columbus and Vicksburg series were not liable to that objection, they alone were used in studying the law of change at different distances from the banks. An inspection of the plotted curves of velocities near the surface, in the different divisions at Columbus, at once showed that the entire curve, from one bank to the other, differed but slightly from a parabola; while that at Vicksburg was so modified by change of depth and by direction of the current, that it did not, as a whole, approximate to any known curve. The accidental regularity of the Columbus curve was a great advantage in the investigation, and it was accordingly selected for study.

Algebraic analysis of them.

In deducing the approximate discharge of the river, the daily velocities in each division of 200 feet in width, given in Appendix D, had been already carefully computed, and plotted in curves, whose ordinates were the velocities, and whose abscissæ were the corresponding distances from the base-line. These daily curves were first grouped according to each even foot of the approximate mean velocity of the river, obtained by dividing the approximate discharge by the total area of cross-section. Eight mean curves were thus obtained from the year's series of observations, every point being a mean of many days' observations. These curves are indicated on figure 19, plate XI, by the points inclosed by circles. The law already discovered to hold below the surface, that the less the approximate mean velocity the flatter the curve, was at once apparent to the eye in these curves, while their number and regularity promised success in deducing an analytical expression for the law of change. The first step was to deduce a grand-mean curve of all the observations, and to determine whether, as was hoped, it was a conic section. This was done by combining the eight mean curves, giving each, for simplicity of computation, equal weight (since each was evidently well determined), and then following the process already explained for deducing the equation of the sub-surface velocity curves. The grand-mean curve was found to differ but slightly from a parabola whose equation is—

$$V_5 = 6.6528 - 17.0665\, w_{\prime\prime}^2,$$

in which $w_{\prime\prime}$ is the distance of the point whose velocity is V_5 from the axis, expressed in decimals, the width of the river, from the middle of division I to the middle of division XI, being unity. Since this width is 2000 feet, each division of 200 feet becomes 0.1. This scale is convenient, as it renders the parameters of surface and sub-surface velocity curves directly comparable. The following table exhibits the comparison of the parabola with the curve of observations, a comparison also shown by figure 22, plate XI.

Grand-mean surface curve of velocity at Columbus.

Division.	Velocity 5 feet below surface.		Difference.	Remarks.
	By observation.	By formula.		
	Feet.	*Feet.*	*Feet.*	
I	2.8860	2.8828	+0.0032	Grand mean of 197 days' observations. Approximate mean velocity of river 5.3494 feet per second.
II	4.1697	4.3164	−0.1467	
III	5.2473	5.4087	−0.1614	
IV	6.3017	6.1596	+0.1421	
V	6.7187	6.5692	+0.1495	
VI	6.6559	6.6374	+0.0185	
VII	6.2472	6.3644	−0.1172	
VIII	5.5835	5.7500	−0.1665	
IX	4.7471	4.7943	−0.0472	
X	3.5743	3.4972	+0.0771	
XI	2.1074	1.8588	+0.2486	
Sum	54.2388	54.2388	1.2780	
Mean	4.9308	4.9308	0.1162	

Fortunately they prove to be parabolas.

This mean difference of only about 2 per cent. proves that the entire curve of surface velocities at the Columbus base sensibly forms part of one and the same parabola, thus making these observations especially valuable in studying the change in form produced by a change in velocity. When the cross-section is of a regular, elliptical form, and the direction of the current parallel to straight banks, this might be anticipated from the law already deduced by means of the sub-surface observations. In nature, these conditions are rarely, if ever, fulfilled.

At Columbus, a nearer approximation to them is made than at any other station where observations were made on the Mississippi river. It not unfrequently happens, that two half parabolas may be nearly adapted to a surface curve, the double axis lying at the thread of the current. In general, however, the form of the curve is so modified by the varying depth and the set of the current, that any general equation would necessarily contain functions of these quantities. It was remarkably fortunate for this investigation that these functions disappeared from the Columbus equation.

Their parameters vary with the reciprocals of the square roots of the mean velocities of the river.

It having been established that the curves of surface velocities at Columbus were parabolas, the next step was to endeavor to deduce the law by which their parameters varied. By the process already detailed (page 233) the equations of parabolas were deduced, which should coincide as nearly as possible with the eight mean curves of observations. The reciprocals of the parameters of these parabolas were then plotted as abscissæ, the corresponding approximate mean velocities of the river being the ordinates, it being remembered also that the reciprocal of infinity, or zero, corresponds to a mean velocity of zero. The curve formed by connecting these points could evidently be very nearly represented by a parabola, whose axis was the axis of Y. In other words, *the reciprocals of the parameters of the surface-velocity curves were proportional to the square roots of the corresponding mean velocities of the river.* This, then, appeared to be the desired law governing the change of form. The equation expressing it, being that of a parabola referred to its axis and the tangent at the vertex, becomes known when any point of the curve is known. The point to be selected, because best determined, is evidently that whose co-ordinates correspond to the grand-mean curve of all the observations. The reciprocal of the parameter of the parabola most nearly agreeing with the grand-mean yearly curve, as already stated, is 17.0665. The corresponding approximate mean velocity of the river, giving each of the curves equal weight, is 5.3494. The co-ordinates of the point are therefore 17.0665 and 5.3494; and the equation is—

$$y = \frac{5.3494}{(17.0665)^2} x^2.$$

In this equation, x is the reciprocal of the parameter of the surface curve which corresponds to a mean velocity y of the river. Substituting $\frac{1}{2\,P}$ for x, and v for y, and reducing, the following general parameter equation for all surface curves at the Columbus base results:—

$$\frac{1}{2\,P} = (54.4482\;v)^{\frac{1}{2}}.$$

Method of testing this law by the observations.

The parameter given by this equation for each of the eight curves of surface velocities differed but slightly from that already found for each by experiment, the accordance between the curves of observation and the resulting parabolas being rather *more close* than that given by the parabolas first constructed, thus confirming the law deduced. Its accuracy is now to be tested by basing upon it a general formula for velocity 5 feet below the surface at the Columbus base, and then noting the accordance between this formula and the actual measurements.

If the above general expression for $\frac{1}{2\,P}$ be substituted in the general parabola equation, $V_5 = {}_{w_{\prime}}V_5 - \frac{1}{2\,P}\,w_{\prime\prime}^2$, we have the equation—

$$V_5 = {}_{w_{\prime}}V_5 - (54.4482\;v)^{\frac{1}{2}}\,w_{\prime\prime}^2,$$

in which V_5 is the velocity 5 feet below the surface at any point of the velocity section at Columbus; ${}_{w_{\prime}}V_5$, the maximum velocity at the same depth; v, the corresponding mean velocity of the river; and $w_{\prime\prime}$, the distance from the axis (or line of maximum velocity) to the point whose velocity is V_5, expressed in fractional parts of the width of the river less 200 feet.* This quantity, $w_{\prime\prime}$, being expressed in a unit practically inconvenient, it became desirable to substitute for it an equivalent expression, in which the variable should be the distance in feet from the base-line to the desired point. Denoting this variable by w, and the distance in feet from the base-line to the axis or line of maximum velocity by $w_{\prime}$, the difference between these quantities, or $w - w_{\prime}$, is the distance in feet between the axis and the desired point. The essential sign of this expression is unimportant, since its square alone enters the formula. To reduce this to

* As the middle of each division is the point whose velocity is known, a diminution in width, of 100 feet at each bank, results.

decimals of the width, divide by W — 200, in which W is the total width. The resulting expression $\left(\frac{w - w_{\prime}}{W - 200}\right)^2$ is evidently equivalent to $w_{\prime\prime}^2$. Substituting it, placing for W its numerical value, 2200, and reducing, the equation becomes—

(1) $$V_5 = {}_{w_\prime}V_5 - (54.4482\ v)^{\frac{1}{2}}\ (0.0005\ [w - w_\prime])^2.$$

This general equation, being now in a convenient form, was tested by applying it to the eight curves of observation. The values adopted for $w_\prime$ and ${}_{w_\prime}V_5$ require explanation. The former was readily determined by inspecting the plotted curve, which must, of course, be symmetrical with respect to its axis. Its different values, given below in a note to the text, show that it varies but slightly, doubtless proportionally to the varying force of the wind blowing across the river. At any rate, no normal change due to a change of mean velocity can be detected. The quantity ${}_{w_\prime}V_5$ was at first assumed in each curve to be the maximum observed velocity. When the curve had been computed, a correction for this value was deduced by dividing the difference between the sum of all the observed division velocities and their corresponding computed values by the number of divisions. The effect of this correction, when applied with its proper sign, was to make the sum of the computed velocities equal to that of the corresponding observed, thus equalizing discrepancies. The corrected values thus found are given in the note below.*

The formula accords with the observations, and thus establishes the truth of the parameter law for Columbus.

The following table exhibits the result of the test, which is also graphically represented by figure 19, plate XI. The slight numerical values of the differences are within the limits of errors of observation, effect of wind, etc., and thus by demonstrating that the formula is correct, establish that at Columbus the parameters of the curves of velocities 5 feet below the surface vary proportionally to the square root of the mean velocity of the river.

* Although of no especial practical importance, it may be remarked that they are directly proportional to the mean velocity of the river, being very closely given by the equation—

$${}_{w_\prime}V_5 = \frac{(1.1699\ v + 0.3533)\ v}{v + 0.0001},$$

as will be seen by the following comparison :—

v	$w_\prime$	${}_{w_\prime}V_5$ Corrected mean.	${}_{w_\prime}V_5$ By formula given above.	Difference.	Remarks.
Feet.	*Feet.*	*Feet.*	*Feet.*	*Feet.*	
1.8199	1100	2.4782	2.4825	−0.0043	
2.7587	1100	3.5971	3.5676	+0.0295	
3.9532	1060	5.0226	4.9783	+0.0443	
4.8803	1020	6.1110	6.0630	+0.0480	
5.3494	1040	6.6528	6.6119	+0.0409	Grand mean.
5.9745	1020	7.2847	7.3432	−0.0585	
7.0861	1020	8.5771	8.6437	−0.0666	
7.8209	1060	9.4843	9.5034	−0.0191	
8.5069	1060	10.3017	10.3160	−0.0143	
Sum..........	9480	59.5095	59.5096	0.3255	
Mean.........	1053			0.0362	

This table plainly shows that $w_\prime$ and ${}_{w_\prime}V_5$, except in the case of high winds, disappear as independent variables from equation (1) which thus becomes—

$$V_5 = \frac{(1.1699\ v + 0.3533)\ v}{v + 0.0001} - (54.4482\ v)^{\frac{1}{2}}\ (0.0005\ [w - 1053]\ )^2.$$

It is believed that in calm weather this equation will give with accuracy the velocity 5 feet below the surface at the Columbus base at any stage of the river.

Mean surface curves of velocity at Columbus, Ky.

Division.	Velocity 5 ft. below surface.		Difference.	Remarks.	Division.	Velocity 5 ft. below surface.		Difference.	Remarks.
	By observation.	By formula (1.)				By observation.	By formula (1.)		
	Feet.	*Feet.*	*Feet.*			*Feet.*	*Feet.*	*Feet.*	
I......	0.6500	−0.0104	+0.6604	30 days' observations. Approximate mean velocity of river, 1.8199 feet.	I......	3.2698	3.4683	−0.1990	15 days' observations. Approximate mean velocity of river, 5.9745 feet.
II......	1.1113	0.8855	+0.2258		II......	4.6633	4.9472	−0.2839	
III......	1.5577	1.5823	−0.0246		III......	6.0160	6.0655	−0.0495	
IV......	1.9247	2.0800	−0.1553		IV......	7.0920	6.8230	+0.2690	
V......	2.1297	2.3787	−0.2490		V......	7.5840	7.2198	+0.3642	
VI......	2.2653	2.4782	−0.2129		VI......	7.5513	7.2558	−0.2955	
VII......	2.2530	2.3787	−0.1257		VII......	6.9893	6.9312	+0.0581	
VIII......	2.0543	2.0800	−0.0257		VIII......	6.0593	6.2458	−0.1865	
IX......	1.5193	1.5823	−0.0630		IX......	4.9733	5.1997	−0.2264	
X......	0.7953	0.8855	−0.0902		X......	3.5840	3.8001	−0.2161	
XI......	0.0500	−0.0104	+0.0604		XI......	2.2000	2.0254	+0.1746	
Sum...	16.3106	16.3104	1.8930		Sum....	59.9818	59.9818	2 3228	
Mean..	1.4828	1.4826	0.1721		Mean..	5.4529	5.4529	0.2112	
I......	0.8500	0.5359	+0.3141	26 days' observations. Approximate mean velocity of river, 2.7537 feet.	I......	4.2383	4.3127	−0.0744	23 days' observations. Approximate mean velocity of river, 7.0861 feet.
II......	1.6331	1.6379	−0.0048		II......	5.8513	6.0256	−0.1743	
III......	2.4108	2.4951	−0.0843		III......	7.1643	7.2462	−0.0819	
IV......	3.0108	3.1073	−0.0965		IV......	8.5000	8.0731	+0.4269	
V......	3.4504	3.4747	−0.0243		V......	8.7226	8.5062	+0.2164	
VI......	3.6146	3.5971	+0 0175		VI......	8.5439	8.5456	+0.0017	
VII......	3.5369	3.4747	+0.0622		VII......	8.0139	8.1912	−0.1773	
VIII......	3.1285	3.1073	+0.0212		VIII......	7.2100	7.4391	−0.2291	
IX......	2.4642	2 4951	−0.0309		IX......	6.3009	6.3012	−0.0003	
X......	1.4154	1.6379	−0.2225		X......	4.7404	4.7734	−0.0330	
XI......	0.5838	0.5359	+0.0479		XI......	2.9652	2.8362	+0.1290	
Sum....	26.0985	26.0989	0.9262		Sum...	72.2508	72.2505	1.5443	
Mean..	2.3726	2.3726	0.0842		Mean..	6.5683	6.5682	0.1495	
I......	1.7059	1.6424	+0.0635	44 days' observations. Approximate mean velocity of river, 3.9532 feet.	I......	4.7561	4.7298	+0.0263	23 days' observations. Approximate mean velocity of river, 7.8209 feet.
II......	2.7534	2.9041	−0.1507		II......	6.6723	6.5045	+0.1678	
III......	3.7393	3.8724	−0.1331		III......	8.1843	7.8666	−0.3177	
IV......	4.6039	4.5473	+0.0566		IV......	9.3509	8.8157	+0.5352	
V......	5.4102	4.9287	+0.4815		V......	9.5430	9.3522	+0.1908	
VI......	5.2977	5.0167	+0.2810		VI......	9.3278	9.4760	−0.1482	
VII......	4.7280	4.8113	−0.0833		VII......	8.7874	9.1871	−0.3997	
VIII......	4.1764	4.3125	−0.1361		VIII......	8.0804	8.4855	−0.4051	
IX......	3.2530	3.5203	−0.2673		IX......	7.2465	7.3712	−0.1247	
X......	2.2573	2.4346	−0.1773		X......	5.0900	5.8442	+0.2458	
XI......	1.1211	1.0555	+0.0656		XI......	3.4983	3.9044	−0.4061	
Sum....	39.0462	39.0458	1.8960		Sum...	81.5370	81.5372	2.9674	
Mean..	3 5497	3 5496	0.1724		Mean..	7.4125	7.4125	0,2698	
I......	2,6186	2.6617	−0.0431	35 days' observations. Approximate mean velocity of river, 4.8803 feet.	I......	5.0000	5.3431	−0.3431	1 day's observations. Approximate mean velocity of river, 8.5069 feet.
II......	3.7726	3.9984	−0.2258		II......	6.9000	7.1941	−0.2941	
III......	4.9060	5.0091	−0.1031		III.....	8.0000	8.6144	−0.6144	
IV......	5.9814	5.6937	+0.2877		IV......	10.0000	9.6044	+0.3956	
V......	6.3800	6.0523	+0.3277		V......	10.5300	10.1640	+0.3660	
VI......	6.1169	6.0849	+0.0320		VI......	10.5300	10.2931	+0.2369	
VII......	5.6691	5.7915	−0.1224		VII......	10.0000	9.9918	+0.0082	
VIII......	4.8689	5.1721	−0.3032		VIII......	9.0900	9.2600	−0.1700	
IX......	3.8894	4.2266	−0.3372		IX......	8.3300	8.0979	+0.2321	
X......	3.0417	2 9616	+0.0801		X......	6.6700	6.5053	+0.1647	
XI......	1.8151	1.3576	+0.4575		XI......	4.5000	4.4822	+0.0178	
Sum....	49.0097	49.0095	2.2698		Sum ..	89.5500	89.5503	2.8429	
Mean..	4.4554	4.4554	0.2063		Mean..	8.1409	8.1409	0.2584	

The parameter law further tested by an analysis of the Vicksburg surface curves.

In order to decide whether the parameter law deduced from the preceding observations is merely local, it was tested by the Vicksburg observations. It is seen by an inspection of the five curves (figure 20, plate XI) that here the whole curve is not regular. For the four divisions nearest the Vicksburg shore, however, the form is evidently parabolic, thus admitting of a test of the law of change in the parameter. The processes already detailed for the Columbus observations were adopted for this purpose. The equation of the parabola most nearly agreeing with the grand-mean curve deduced by combining the five curves—giving each equal weight—was found to be—

$$V_5 = 5.7991 - 31.5744\, w_{\prime\prime}^2,$$

the corresponding approximate mean velocity of the river being 4.8487.

The parameter equation deduced by passing a parabola, referred to its axis and the tangent at its vertex, through the point whose co-ordinates are 31.5744 and 5.7991, the axis of Y being the axis of the curve, is—

$$\frac{1}{2P} = (205.6103\, v)^{\frac{1}{2}}.$$

The general equation is, therefore—

$$V_5 = {}_{w_\prime}V_5 - (205.6103\, v)^{\frac{1}{2}} (0.0005\, [w - w_\prime])^2.$$

The values of ${}_{w_\prime}V_5$ and $w_\prime$ corresponding to the different values of v were determined in the manner already explained for the Columbus observations.* The following table exhibits the result of the test, which is also graphically represented in figure 20, plate XI.

* It will be seen that $w_\prime$ is a constant, and that ${}_{w_\prime}V_5$ follows the law already deduced from the Columbus observations, being directly proportioned to v. Its equation is very nearly—

$${}_{w_\prime}V_5 = \frac{(1.0445\, v + 0.7786)\, v}{v + 0.0001},$$

as shown by the column of differences.

v	$w_\prime$	${}_{w_\prime}V_5$ Corrected mean.	${}_{w_\prime}V_5$ By formula given above.	Difference.	Remarks.
Feet.	*Feet.*	*Feet.*	*Feet.*	*Feet.*	
3.1734	1820	4.0933	4.0416	+0.0517	
3.8425	1820	4.6474	4.7405	−0.0931	
4.6905	1820	5.5003	5.6262	−0.1259	
4.8487	1820	5.7991	5.7914	+0.0077	Grand mean.
5.7718	1820	6.8632	6.7556	+0.1076	
6.7653	1820	7.8451	7.7934	+0.0517	
Sum...........	....	34.7484	34.7487	0.4377	
Mean........	....	....	....	0.0729	

It will be hereafter demonstrated that, to be absolutely correct, this expression should involve functions of the depth of the stream and of the distance of the point of maximum velocity below the surface. As, however, the former does not exert much influence, and as the latter is nearly constant in all rivers for calm weather, it often happens that these approximate expressions give results differing but little from perfect accuracy. This is strikingly shown

Mean surface curves of velocity at Vicksburg.

Division.	Velocity 5 feet below surface.		Difference.	Remarks.	Division.	Velocity 5 feet below surface.		Difference.	Remarks.
	By observation.	By formula.				By observation.	By formula.		
	Feet.	*Feet.*	*Feet.*			*Feet.*	*Feet.*	*Feet.*	
I........	1.7143			7 days' observations. Approximate mean velocity of river, 3.1734 feet.	I........	3.8060			30 days' observations. Approximate mean velocity of river, 5.7718 feet.
II........	2.0171				II........	4.9940			
III........	1.8957				III........	5.2610			
IV........	2.3543				IV........	5.4243			
V........	2.8557				V........	5.7347			
VI........	3.3543				VI........	5.9370			
VII........	3.5771				VII........	6.1566			
VIII........	3.7314				VIII........	6.3030			
IX........	4.0857				IX........	6.5463			
X........	4.0400	4.0510	—0.0110		X........	6.7257	6.8081	—0.0824	
XI........	3.3957	3.5747	—0.1790		XI........	6.3433	6.1880	+0.1553	
XII........	2.5657	2.5693	+0.0036		XII........	4.8517	4.8789	—0.0272	
XIII........	1.2286	1.0348	+0.1938		XIII........	2.8353	2.8809	—0.0456	
Sum.....	11.2300	11.2298	0.3874		Sum.....	20.7560	20.7559	0.3105	
Mean...	2.8075	2.8075	0.0969		Mean...	5.1890	5.1890	0.0776	
I........	2.3621			36 days' observations. Approximate mean velocity of river, 3.8425 feet.	I........	4.4804			114 days' observations. Approximate mean velocity of river, 6.7653 feet.
II........	3.0500				II........	6.1373			
III........	3.3208				III........	6.4868			
IV........	3.3086				IV........	6.7553			
V........	3.6978				V........	6.9800			
VI........	4.0856				VI........	7.2259			
VII........	4.3233				VII........	7.4847			
VIII........	4.5994				VIII........	7.7635			
IX........	4.8336				IX........	7.9799			
X........	4.7408	4.6024	+0.1384		X........	7.8842	7.7854	+0.0988	
XI........	4.0511	4.0965	—0.0454		XI........	7.2183	7.1141	+0.1042	
XII........	2.7397	3.0284	—0.2887		XII........	5.8056	5.6968	+0.1088	
XIII........	1.5939	1.3981	+0.1958		XIII........	3.2219	3.5336	—0.3117	
Sum.....	13.1255	13.1254	0.6683		Sum.....	24.1300	24.1299	0.6235	
Mean...	3.2814	3.2814	0.1671		Mean...	6.0325	6.0325	0.1559	
I........	3.2032			22 days' observations. Approximate mean velocity of river, 4.6905 feet.	I........	3.1132			209 days' observations. Grand yearly mean. Approximate mean velocity of river, 4.8487 feet.
II........	4.3068				II........	4.1010			
III........	4.1614				III........	4.2251			
IV........	4.3455				IV........	4.4376			
V........	4.6323				V........	4.7801			
VI........	4.9609				VI........	5.1127			
VII........	5.2259				VII........	5.3478			
VIII........	5.4859				VIII........	5.5766			
IX........	5.5595				IX........	5.8010			
X........	5.6277	5.4506	+0.1771		X........	5.8036	5.7486	+0.0550	
XI........	4.9318	4.8916	+0.0402		XI........	5.1880	5.1802	+0.0078	
XII........	3.4909	3.7115	—0.2206		XII........	3.8907	3.9804	—0.0897	
XIII........	1.9014	1.8979	+0.0035		XIII........	2.1762	2.1491	+0.0271	
Sum.....	15.9518	15.9516	0.4414		Sum.....	17.0585	17.0583	0.1796	
Mean...	3.9879	3.9879	0.1104		Mean...	4.2646	4.2646	0.0449	

It holds good there also, and thus is general for surface curves.

These slight differences conclusively prove that the parameter law deduced from the Columbus observations holds good at Vicksburg. It may, therefore, be assumed that the object of this discussion of the surface velocity curves, namely, a determination of the law governing the change of form corresponding to a change in mean velocity, has been

by some observations made upon a small feeder of the Chesapeake and Ohio canal in 1859, of which the details will soon be given. The following table exhibits the observed maximum surface velocity and that computed by the attained. *The parameter of the curve of velocities 5 feet below the surface at any stage is proportional to the square root of the corresponding mean velocity of the river.*

The existence of this law in this class of curves justifies the assumption that it also holds good in sub-surface velocities. It is not necessary, however, to depend upon analogy, since the curves of observation below the surface, although not sufficient for the deduction of a law, are numerous enough to confirm or disprove one whose existence is suspected. This discussion will, therefore, be now resumed.

It can be tested for sub-surface curves by the observations.

Parameter changes in sub-surface curves.—The same process of reasoning was followed in applying the above law to sub-surface curves in a vertical plane as had been employed in the case of the Vicksburg horizontal curves near the surface. If the law hold good, the equation of the parameter curve must be that of a parabola referred to its axis and the tangent at its vertex, the axis of Y, or of mean velocities, being the axis of the curve. The best determined point from which to fix the parameter is that whose abscissa and ordinate are the reciprocal of the parameter and the mean velocity of the river corresponding to the grand-mean curve, or 0.79222 and 3.3814, respectively. The equation of this parabola is—

For this purpose it is introduced into the general formula for velocity below the surface.

$$y = \frac{3.3814}{(0.79222)^2} x^2.$$

Substituting $\frac{1}{2\text{P}}$ for x, and v for y, and reducing, this becomes—

$$\frac{1}{2\text{P}} = (0.1856\, v)^{\frac{1}{2}}.$$

Substituting this general value of $\frac{1}{2\text{P}}$ in the general equation for a sub-surface curve, $\text{V} = \text{V}_{d_{,}} - \frac{1}{2\text{P}} d_{,,}^2$, we have—

$$\text{V} = \text{V}_{d_{,}} - (0.1856\, v)^{\frac{1}{2}} d_{,,}^2,$$

in which v is the mean velocity of the river; $\text{V}_{d_{,}}$, the maximum or axis velocity in the vertical plane considered; V, the velocity at any point in this plane; and $d_{,,}$, the distance of the point whose velocity is V from the axis, expressed in decimals, the total depth of the river being unity. This unit for $d_{,,}^2$ is not convenient in a general formula,

expressions just deduced for ${}_{w_{,}}\text{V}_5$ at Columbus and Vicksburg, a velocity which, for the great depth of the Mississippi, is equivalent to that at the surface in small streams.

Date.	D	W	v	Observed ${}_{w_{,}}\text{V}_0$.	${}_{w_{,}}\text{V}_0$ as computed by		Mean difference.
					Columbus eq.	Vicksburg eq.	
	Feet.	*Feet.*	*Feet.*	*Feet.*	*Feet.*	*Feet.*	*Feet.*
November 26, 1859	7.2	23	2.4785	3.3840	3.2530	3.3674	0.0738
November 28, 1859	7.1	23	2.2202	3.0198	2.9508	3.0896	0.0002

A general equation for divisions 10, 11, 12, and 13 at the Vicksburg base can evidently be deduced by substituting 1820 for $w_{,}$ and the value just tested for ${}_{w_{,}}\text{V}_5$ in the above formula for V_5. It is—

$$\text{V}_5 = \frac{(1.0445\, v + 0.7786)\, v}{v + 0.0001} - (205.6103\, v)^{\frac{1}{2}} (0.0005\, [w - 1820]\,)^2.$$

and the equivalent expression $\left(\frac{d-d_{,}}{D}\right)^2$ is therefore substituted for it, in which d is the distance below the surface, in feet, of the point whose velocity is V; $d_{,}$, the distance below the surface, in feet, of the axis or line of maximum velocity; and D, the total depth of the water, in feet. The formula thus becomes—

$$(2) \qquad V = V_{d_{,}} - (0.1856\,v)^{\frac{1}{2}} \left(\frac{d-d_{,}}{D}\right)^2.$$

Some data not yet mentioned are available for the test of this formula.

This general formula is now to be tested as rigidly as possible by all the observations taken upon the Survey. Besides the measurements from anchored boats, some additional data were collected, which, although less exact in character, and therefore not admitted into the grand-mean curve, are for that very reason especially valuable for this purpose; the constants of the formula being deduced independently of them. Agreement with such independent observations furnishes the highest proof of general applicability. The nature and amount of these additional data will be described before proceeding to test the formula.

Observations upon bayou Plaquemine.

Observations were made on April 11, 1851, upon bayou Plaquemine, about 800 feet below the upper mouth or point of efflux from the river. The day was calm and favorable, the bayou being at a stand near high-water mark. The form of the cross-section was semi-elliptical and quite regular, the width being about 300 feet, and the area of cross-section, 5875 square feet. For 150 feet near the middle of the bayou, the depth was uniformly about 27 feet. The observations were conducted in the usual manner, the base-line being 400 feet in length. The floats were cylindrical blocks of green sweet-gum wood, 6.5 inches in diameter by 6 inches in height. They were slightly loaded with lead and supported by surface floats of white pine, 7 inches square by 0.75 of an inch thick. The flags were 3 inches square. The velocity was measured at the surface, and at 10, 15, and 20 feet below it, throughout the central portion, where the depth was uniform; and the results were plotted as usual. To reduce the observations to the same vertical plane, for the purpose of comparing the velocities at different depths, it was assumed that the change of velocity from bank to bank, in horizontal planes at the different depths at which floats were observed, was the same. This assumption was necessary, since there was not a sufficient number of observations at each depth to form a horizontal curve for each plane. The surface curve was very well determined. It was divided into six divisions, each 25 feet in width, and a scale of correction constructed, by which the velocity of any float could be reduced to that of a float passing at the same depth in the vertical plane selected, which was placed where the greatest number of floats at all depths had passed. The proper correction from this table was applied to each float, thus reducing them all to the same vertical plane. A mean of the velocities of all the floats at each depth was then taken, and the results were plotted in the manner already described. These data are given in the following table, and represented by figure 7, plate XI.

Observations upon bayou La Fourche.

Similar observations were made on bayou La Fourche, on April 19, 1851, about 2500 feet below the upper mouth or point of efflux from the river. The day was favorable. The bayou was at a stand near high-water mark; the cross-section regular and semi-elliptical; the uniform average depth, for about 150 feet near the middle, 27 feet; the total width, about 225 feet; the area of cross-section, 3630 square feet. The velocity was measured as on bayou Plaquemine, the length of base-line, the kind of floats, and their depths being the same. The same method was also used in deducing the curve of velocity below the surface, which is shown in figure 6, plate XI, and given in the following table.

Observations upon the Mississippi at Columbus.

Similar observations were made upon the Mississippi river at Columbus, Kentucky, at various times during the discharge measurements conducted there in 1858. Through a misapprehension of his instructions, the engineer in charge of this party observed no floats at a greater depth than 50 feet. This was, however, sufficiently near to the bottom to serve most of the purposes of the observations. It was designed that a series of floats should pass at every 10 feet of depth in several different vertical planes, but the impossibility of holding the boat by oars in a fixed position long enough for this purpose unavoidably caused the floats to be somewhat distributed. Corrections, to reduce the observations to their respective planes, were deduced and applied in the manner described for the Plaquemine observations. The results of these measurements will be found in the following table, and are represented by figure 11, plate XI.

Observations upon the Mississippi at Vicksburg.

Some observations of this kind were made at Vicksburg, Mississippi, in the year 1858, by the party stationed there. They were conducted and computed by the methods employed at Columbus. A few of the observations were made at nearly the high-water stage, when the mean velocity of the river was much greater than during similar measurements elsewhere upon the river, and—although too meagre to result in a smooth, well-determined curve—were of great value as affording a confirmation of the law. The principal curve is shown in figure 8, plate XI, and all the data are given in the following table.

Tables exhibiting these additional data.

Some observations of this class were made at Carrollton in 1851, but the floats were too much distributed to furnish data available for the present purpose. The careful observations from anchored boats were, therefore, alone depended upon for the law at this place.

The following tables exhibit the additional data just described:—

Sub-surface velocity observations upon the bayous.

Locality.	Distance below upper mouth.	Date.	Stage below h. w. of 1851.	Approx. mean velocity of bayou.	Wind.	Distance from base.	Depth.	Number of floats.	Velocity in feet per second at				
									Surface.	5 feet deep.	10 feet deep.	15 feet deep.	20 feet deep.
	Feet.		*Ft.*	*Feet.*		*Feet.*	*Ft.*						
Bayou Plaquemine...	800	April 11, 1851	0.6	5.41	Down 2	150	27	8	6.50	6.52	6.35	6.30	6.02
Bayou La Fourche....	2500	April 19, 1851	1.3	2.73	Up 0.7	100	27	6	3.16	3.23	3.25	3.22	3.15

Sub-surface velocity observations upon the Mississippi at medium stages, the depth being about 65 feet.

Locality.	Date.	Gauge	Approx. mean velocity of river.	Wind.	Distance from base.	Depth.	No. of obs. at each point.	Velocity in ft. per sec. at various depths below water surface.					
								Surface.	10 feet.	20 feet.	30 feet.	40 feet.	50 feet.
	1858.	*Feet.*	*Feet.*		*Ft.*	*Ft.*							
Columbus, Kentucky.	Jan. 30	17.7	4.6679	Down 1	900	70	3	7.6923	6.2500	6.0606	6.0606	6.2500	6.2500
" "	July 5	26.0	4.7183	Down 3	700	75	1	6.4516	7.1429	7.1429	8.0000	7.1429	6.8965
" "	" 8	22.8	4.2758	Down 1	900	75	3	6.4516	6.4516	6.6666	6.0606	6.4516	6.2500
" "	" 14	20.4	3.9733	Up 3	900	70	3	5.0000	5.1282	5.4054	5.4054	5.5555	6.0606
" "	" 22	23.7	4.7011	Up 2	500	75	3	4.2553	4.6511	4.7619	4.8780	4.8780	5.0000
" "	" 28	26.2	5.0164	Up 1	500	75	3	5.0000	5.0000	5.4054	5.1282	5.0000	5.1282
" "	Aug. 4	21.2	4.0716	Up 2	700	70	3	4.6511	4.8780	5.1282	5.1282	5.1282	4.8780
" "	" 11	20.9	4.1013	0	700	70	3	4.7619	5.2631	5.0000	5.1282	5.1282	5.1282
" "	" 18	18.3	3.4344	Down 2	500	70	3	3.7735	3.6363	3.6363	3.7037	3.7037	3.7037
" "	" 25	14.7	3.0722	Down 1	700	65	3	3.7037	3.9215	3.7735	3.8461	3.9215	3.9215
" "	Sept. 4	11.9	2.5908	Up 3	700	60	3	2.8571	2.7027	3.1250	3.1746	3.1250	3.0769
" "	" 9	9.5	2.4391	Up 4	900	60	3	2.6666	2.9850	2.8985	2.9411	2.9850	2.9411
" "	" 17	11.5	2.5141	Down 2	700	60	3	3.2258	2.9850	3.2258	3.3898	3.2258	3.2786
" "	" 30	6.5	2.1269	Up 4	700	55	3	2.0618	2.1978	2.2472	2.4096	2.3529	2.4096
" "	Oct. 12	4.0	1.7464	Up 3	900	55	3	1.9417	2.0833	2.0833	2.0833	2.1978	2.1276
" "	" 23	3.2	1.5214	Up 2	900	55	3	1.7094	2.0618	2.0618	2.0408	2.0618	1.9801
" "	Nov. 5	11.8	3.5003	Up 1	700	60	3	3.1746	4.0000	4.0000	4.1666	4.3478	4.1666
" "	" 12	15.0	3.7290	Up 3	800	65	3	4.2553	4.2553	4.3478	4.4444	4.1666	4.6511
True mean.........			3.4070	Up 1.2				3.9826	4.0864	4.1659	4.1917	4.1843	4.1875

Sub-surface velocity observations upon the Mississippi at its highest stage; the depth being about 75 feet.

Locality.	Date.	Gauge	Approx. mean velocity of river.	Wind.	Distance from base.	Depth.	No. of obs. at each point.	Velocity in ft. per sec. at various depths below water surface.				
								Surface.	40 feet.	50 feet.	60 feet.	70 feet.
	1858.	*Feet.*	*Feet.*		*Ft.*	*Ft.*						
Vicksburg, Miss......	May 13	47.4	6.9886	Up 2	1600	75	1	7.69	8.33	8.00	9.09	8.70
" "	Aug. 7	44.6	6.4445	0	1700	75	2	7.41	7.14	6.90	6.45	5.88
True mean.........			6.6092	Up 0.7				7.50	7.54	7.27	7.33	6.82

Sub-surface velocity observations upon the Mississippi at a medium stage; the depth being about 55 feet.

Locality.	Date.	Gauge	Approx. mean velocity of river.	Wind.	Distance from base.	Depth.	No. of obs. at each point.	Velocity in ft. per sec. at various depths below water surface.					
								Surface.	10 feet.	20 feet.	30 feet.	40 feet.	50 feet.
	1858.	*Feet.*	*Feet.*		*Ft.*	*Ft.*							
Vicksburg, Miss.......	Sept. 21	17.8	4.0894	Down 1	1900	55	2	4.88	4.88	5.00	4.76	4.44	5.00
" "	" 28	17.7	3.9181	Down 1	1800	55	3	4.76	4.82	4.88	4.88	4.55	4.35
" "	" 28	17.7	3.9181	Down 1	2200	65	2	4.76	4.76	4.76	4.00	3.17	2.34
" "	" 28	17.7	3.9181	Down 1	1300	45	1	4 76	4.26	3.35	3.23	3.11	2.99
" "	" 29	17.3	3.8652	0	2200	65	2	4.17	3.97	3.77	3.51	3.92	4.00
" "	" 29	17.3	3.8652	0	2000	60	2	5.00	4.83	4.65	4.55	4.08	3.51
" "	" 29	17.3	3.8652	0	1900	65	2	4.55	4.28	4.00	4.44	4.26	4.00
" "	Nov. 18	24.5	4.7366	Down 2	1900	65	2	4.94	5.41	5.88	5.56	5.88	6.25
" "	" 18	24.5	4.7366	Down 2	600	45	2	3.13	3.45	3.77	3.64	3.28	2.92
" "	" 18	24.5	4.7366	Down 2	1100	45	2	4 86	4.76	4.55	4.55	4.44	4.15
True mean.........			4.1599	Down 1				4.5810	4 5700	4.5375	4.3945	4.1850	4.0190

Formula first tested by the four mean curves. Tables of results.

The formula was first applied to the mean curves in which the observations had been combined by tenths of depth in the manner already explained. These curves were four in number, namely: the high-water mean and low-water mean curves deduced from the observations from anchored boats in 1851; the mean Columbus curve; and the mean middle-stage Vicksburg curve. The corresponding approximate mean velocity of the river was carefully deduced for these curves, the mean velocity on each day entering in proportion to the number of observations on that day. The corresponding mean depth was found in the same manner. The value $d_{,}$ was taken from the plot. $V_{d_{,}}$ was at first assumed equal to the maximum velocity, and afterward corrected so that the sum of the velocities of all the observed points and the sum of the corresponding computed values should be equal. The following tables exhibit the results of this comparison, which are also shown by the dotted lines on figures 15, 14, 12, and 13, plate XI.

Mean high-water sub-surface velocity curve at Carrollton.

Depth of float below surface.	Velocity in feet per second.					Differences.	Remarks.
	D = 110 ft.	D = 70 ft.	D = 55 ft.	True mean.	By formula.	*Feet.*	
Surface	4.2180	3.5300	2.7600	3.7270	3.7295	−0.0025	Observations (142 at each point) made from an anchored boat. Mean velocity of river 4.1605 feet. Mean depth 86 feet. Maximum velocity 3.8371 feet (at 0.35 D). Mean wind up 0.3.
0.1 D	4.2650	3.5800	2.8100	3.7755	3.7822	−0.0067	
0.2 D	4.3150	3.6300	2.8280	3.8192	3.8173	+0.0019	
0.3 D	4.3450	3.6750	2.8320	3.8485	3.8349	+0.0136	
0.4 D	4.3200	3.6900	2.8510	3.8440	3.8349	+0.0091	
0.5 D	4.2750	3.6999	2.8790	3.8296	3.8173	+0.0123	
0.6 D	4.2050	3.6600	2.8610	3.7789	3.7822	−0.0033	
0.7 D	4.1370	3.6100	2.8000	3.7175	3.7295	−0.0120	
0.8 D	4.0750	3.5580	2.7000	3.6510	3.6592	−0.0082	
0.9 D	3.9900	3.5010	2.5800	3.5673	3.5713	−0.0040	
Bottom					3.4658		
Sum of common points				37.5585	37.5583	0.0736	
Mean of common points				3.7558	3.7558	0.0074	

Mean low-water sub-surface velocity curve at Carrollton and Baton Rouge.

Depth of float below surface.	Velocity in feet per second.					Differences.	Remarks.
	D = 100 ft.	D = 80 ft.	D = 60 ft.	True mean.	By formula.	*Feet.*	
Surface	1.9362	2.3951	2.3804	2.2508	2.2386	+0.0122	Observations (80 at each point) made from an anchored boat. Mean velocity of river 1.9984 feet. Mean depth 75 feet. Maximum velocity 2.2523 feet (at 0.15 D). Mean wind down 1.1.
0.1 D	1.9380	2.4160	2.3910	2.2614	2.2508	+0.0106	
0.2 D	1.9680	2.3830	2.3887	2.2486	2.2508	−0.0022	
0.3 D	1.9110	2.3500	2.3504	2.2185	2.2386	−0.0201	
0.4 D	1.8980	2.3100	2.3404	2.2001	2.2142	−0.0141	
0.5 D	1.8672	2.2750	2.2929	2.1607	2.1777	−0.0170	
0.6 D	1.8390	2.2320	2.2434	2.1192	2.1290	−0.0098	
0.7 D	1.7860	2.2100	2.1988	2.0778	2.0681	+0.0097	
0.8 D	1.6980	2.1520	2.1379	2.0095	1.9950	+0.0145	
0.9 D	1.6180	2.0500	2.0628	1.9262	1.9097	+0.0165	
Bottom					1.8123		
Sum of common points				21.4728	21.4725	0.1267	
Mean of common points				2.1473	2.1473	0.0127	

Mean medium-stage sub-surface velocity curves at Columbus and Vicksburg.

Depth of float below surface.	Columbus, Ky.			Vicksburg, Miss.			Remarks.
	Velocity by observation.	Velocity by formula.	Difference.	Velocity by observation.	Velocity by formula.	Difference.	
	Feet.	*Feet.*	*Feet.*	*Feet.*	*Feet.*	*Feet.*	*Columbus curve.*
Surface	3.9826	3.9808	+0.0016	4.5810	4.5621	+0.0189	52 obs. at each point.
0.1 D.	4.0500	5.0555	—0.0055	4.5750	4.5709	+0.0041	Mean depth 65 ft. Max.
0.2 D.	4.1100	4.1144	—0.0044	4.5680	4.5621	+0.0059	velocity 4.1958 ft. (at
0.3 D.	4.1620	4.1573	+0.0047	4.5490	4.5358	+0.0132	0.52 D). Mean wind up
0.4 D.	4.1830	4.1843	—0.0013	4.5080	4.4918	+0.0162	1.2. Approx. mean ve-
0.5 D.	4.1900	4.1955	—0.0055	4.4300	4.4303	—0.0003	locity of river 3.4070 ft.
0.6 D.	4.1850	4.1907	—0.0057	4.3310	4.3512	—0.0202	
0.7 D.	4.1860	4.1700	+0.0160	4.2180	4.2546	—0.0366	*Vicksburg curve.*
0.8 D.		4.1835		4.1200	4.1403	—0.0203	20 obs. at each point.
0.9 D.		4.0810		4.0280	4.0085	+0.0195	Mean depth 55 ft. Max.
Bottom		4.0126			3.8592		velocity 4.5709 ft. (at
							0.1 D). Mean wind down
Sum of common points.	33.0485	33.0486	0.0447	43.9080	43.9076	0.1552	1. Approx. mean ve-
Mean of common points	4.1311	4.1311	0.0056	4.3908	4.3908	0.0155	locity of river 4.1599 ft.

Formula next tested by actual curves of observation. Tables of results. Although the principle upon which the curves of different depths were combined is believed to be sound, it may, perhaps, be called in question. The general equation has, therefore, been applied to all the original curves of observation, as first deduced by combining all observations where the depth was the same. The following tables exhibit the results, which, excepting the Vicksburg high-water curve, are also shown in figures 1, 3, 10, 2, 4, 9, 11, 8, 7, and 6, plate XI.

Mean high-water sub-surface velocity curves at Carrollton.

Depth of float below surface.	High water; depth 110 feet.			High water; depth 70 feet.			High water; depth 55 feet.		
	Velocity by observation.	Velocity by formula.	Difference.	Velocity by observation.	Velocity by formula.	Difference.	Velocity by observation.	Velocity by formula.	Difference.
	Feet.	*Feet.*	*Feet.*	*Feet.*	*Feet.*	*Feet.*	*Feet.*	*Feet.*	*Feet.*
1.5 *feet*							2.7623	2.7583	+0.0040
6 "	4.2301	4.2365	—0.0064	3.5503	3.5445	+0.0058			
3 "							2.8263	2.8069	+0.0194
18 "	4.2984	4.2853	+0.0131	3.6551	3.6587	—0.0036	2.8311	2.8779	—0.0468
30 "							2.8965	2.8637	+0.0328
36 "	4.3463	4.3009	+0.0454	3.6999	3.6895	+0.0104	2.8152	2.8246	—0.0094
54 "	4.2745	4.2697	+0.0048	3.5843	3.6047	—0.0204			
66 "				3.4917	3.4838	+0.0079			
72 "	4.1580	4.1917	—0.0337						
90 "	4.0528	4.0667	—0.0139						
102 "	3.9481	3.9575	—0.0094						
Point of max. velocity		4.3016	(depth 33 feet.)		3.6927	(depth 31.8 ft.)		2.8826	(depth 22 ft.)
Bottom		3.8730			3.4320			2.5605	
Sum of common points.	29.3082	29.3083	0.1267	17.9813	17.9812	0.0481	14.1314	14.1314	0.1124
Mean of common points.	4.1869	4.1869	0.0181	3.5962	3.5962	0.0096	2.8263	2.8263	0.0225

Mean low-water sub-surface velocity curves at Carrollton and Baton Rouge.

Depth of float below surface.	Low water; depth 100 feet.			Low water; depth 80 feet.			Low water; depth 60 feet.		
	Velocity by observation.	Velocity by formula.	Difference.	Velocity by observation.	Velocity by formula.	Difference.	Velocity by observation.	Velocity by formula.	Difference.
	Feet.	*Feet.*	*Feet.*	*Feet.*	*Feet.*	*Feet.*	*Feet.*	*Feet.*	*Feet.*
Surface	1.9362	1.9362	0.0000	2.3951	2.3819	+ 0.0132	2.3804	2.3674	+ 0.0130
6 *feet*	1.9185	1.9424	— 0.0239	2.4239	2.3896	+ 0.0343	2.3910	2.3811	+ 0.0099
12 "	1.9438	1.9444	— 0.0006	2.3998	2.3903	+ 0.0095	2.3887	2.3824	+ 0.0063
18 "	1.9727	1.9424	+ 0.0303	2.3738	2.3840	— 0.0102	2.3504	2.3711	— 0.0207
24 "	1.9394	1.9362	+ 0.0032	2.3492	2.3707	— 0.0215	2.3404	2.3472	— 0.0068
30 "	1.9062	1.9261	— 0.0199	2.3134	2.3504	— 0.0370	2.2929	2.3107	— 0.0178
36 "	1.9043	1.9218	— 0.0075	2.2952	2.3231	— 0.0279	2.2434	2.2617	— 0.0183
42 "	1.8929	1.8935	— 0.0006	2.2530	2.2887	— 0.0357	2.1988	2.2001	— 0.0013
48 "	1.8672	1.8710	— 0.0038	2.2287	2.2474	— 0.0187	2.1379	2.1259	+ 0.0120
54 "	1.8596	1.8446	+ 0.0150	2.2170	2.1990	+ 0.0180	2.0628	2.0392	+ 0.0236
60 "	1.8247	1.8140	+ 0.0107	2.1703	2.1436	+ 0.0267			
66 "	1.7996	1.7794	+ 0.0202	2.1240	2.0812	+ 0.0428			
72 "	1.7388	1.7406	— 0.0018	2.0181	2.0118	+ 0.0063			
78 "	1.6891	1.6978	— 0.0087						
84 "	1.6390	1.6510	— 0.0120						
Point of max. velocity		1.9444	(depth 12 feet.)		2.3909	(depth 9.6 ft.)		2.3834	(depth 9.6 ft.)
Bottom		1.5061			1.9084			1.9399	
Sum of common points	27.8320	27.8314	0.1582	29.5615	29.5617	0.3018	22.7867	22.7868	0.1297
Mean of common points	1.8555	1.8554	0.0105	2.2740	2.2740	0.0232	2.2787	2.2787	0.0130

Mean medium-stage sub-surface velocity curves at Columbus and Vicksburg.

Depth of float below surface.	Columbus; depth 65 feet.			Vicksburg; depth 75 feet.			Vicksburg; depth 55 feet.		
	Velocity by observation.	Velocity by formula.	Difference.	Velocity by observation.	Velocity by formula.	Difference.	Velocity by observation.	Velocity by formula.	Difference.
	Feet.	*Feet.*	*Feet.*	*Feet.*	*Feet.*	*Feet.*	*Feet.*	*Feet.*	*Feet.*
Surface	3.9826	3.9875	— 0.0049	7.5000	7.5339	— 0.0339	4.5810	4.5676	+ 0.0134
10 *feet*	4.0864	4.0959	— 0.0095		7.5733		4.5700	4.5705	— 0.0005
20 "	4.1659	4.1667	— 0.0008		7.5733		4.5375	4.5153	+ 0.0222
30 "	4.1917	4.1998	— 0.0081		7.5339		4.3945	4.4020	— 0.0075
40 "	4.1843	4.1953	— 0.0110	7.5400	7.4551	+ 0.0849	4.1850	4.2307	— 0.0457
50 "	4.1875	4.1531	+ 0.0344	7.2700	7.3370	— 0.0670	4.0190	4.0012	+ 0.0178
60 "		4.0733		7.3300	7.1795	+ 0.1505			
70 "				6.8200	6.9545	— 0.1345			
Point of max. velocity		4.2025	(depth 33.8 ft.)		7.5782	(depth 15 feet.)		4.5764	(depth 5.5 ft.)
Bottom		4.0193			6.8694			3.8657	
Sum of common points	24.7984	24.7983	0.0687	36.4600	36.4600	0.4708	26.2870	26.2873	0.1171
Mean of common points	4.1331	4.1331	0.0114	7.2920	7.2920	0.0942	4.3812	4.3812	0.0195

Mean sub-surface velocity curves in the bayous.

Depth of float below surface.	Bayou Plaquemine; depth 27 feet.			Bayou La Fourche; depth 27 feet.		
	Velocity by observation.	Velocity by formula.	Difference.	Velocity by observation.	Velocity by formula.	Difference.
	Feet.	*Feet.*	*Feet.*	*Feet.*	*Feet.*	*Feet.*
Surface	6.500	6.485	+ 0.015	3.160	3.163	— 0.003
5 *feet*	6.520	6.480	+ 0.040	3.230	3.231	— 0.001
10 "	6.350	6.406	— 0.056	3.250	3.249	+ 0.001
15 "	6.300	6.267	+ 0.033	3.220	3.221	— 0.001
20 "	6.020	6.054	— 0.034	3.150	3.141	+ 0.009
Point of maximum velocity		6.491	(depth 2.2 ft.)		3.250	(depth 9.5 ft.)
Bottom		5.644			2.950	
Sum of common points	31.690	31.692	0.178	16.010	16.005	0.015
Mean of common points	6.338	6.338	0.036	3.202	3.201	0.003

The result entirely satisfactory.

This weight of evidence in favor of the truth of the formula and of the accuracy of the reasoning by which it has been deduced is thought to be irresistible. When it is remembered that the forms of all these curves are fixed by one and the same equation, it must be admitted that so close an accordance with observations in localities and circumstances so different cannot be accidental.

Investigation of the parameter law further extended by applying the general formula to smaller streams.

That the numerical coefficient of $v^{\frac{1}{2}}$ should remain constant for so great changes in cross-section was a matter of surprise, and the question arose whether, for still smaller streams, it might not vary. Boileau's admirable observations on his wooden canals afforded a means of testing the matter.

Analysis of Captain Boileau's observations.

As stated in the last chapter, Captain Boileau considers his observations to indicate that the vertical curve below the point of maximum velocity is a parabola whose axis is at the surface, while the curve above the point of maximum velocity follows no discovered law. The first set of experiments was made in a wooden canal or trough about 2 feet wide and 1 foot deep. The observations near and below the point of maximum velocity were made partly with a new kind of hydrometric tube and partly with a current-meter. Above the vicinity of the point of maximum velocity, Boileau depended on floats which were observed only at the surface, thus leaving a relatively wide gap in the curve undetermined by measurement. Now it is evident that the difference between the surface velocity and that near the point of maximum must be affected by any error in the constants of the formulæ for computing the velocity from the tube and current-meter observations, and also by the retarding effect of the side-resistances, if the floats deviated ever so slightly from the exact plane of the rest of the observations. If the surface velocity was diminished by these causes of error to an amount equal to 0.077 of a foot per second, the entire curve agrees very well with a parabola whose vertex is at the point of maximum velocity, 0.178 of the depth below the surface. Boileau's second series of experiments, made when the depth was reduced to 0.67 of a foot, fully confirms this opinion, as this curve is evidently one and the same parabola both above and below the point of maximum velocity, which is about 0.237 of the depth below the surface. The two lower observations should probably be rejected, as they differ enough from the law of the others to suggest some anomalous influence of the bottom upon the current-meter. The following table exhibits a comparison between these curves of observation and the parabolas given by the formulæ—

$$V = 2.8254 - 1.5206 \left(\frac{d - 0.2034}{1.1418}\right)^2$$

$$V = 2.0079 - 1.2683 \left(\frac{d - 0.16}{0.676}\right)^2.$$

The axes are placed 0.178 and 0.237 of the depth below the surface, respectively, and the parabolas adjusted so that the mean of all the observations shall determine the mean of the corresponding points of the parabolas, disregarding, in the first case, the observation at the surface, and, in the second, the two observations nearest the bottom. The means of course include these observations.

Sub-surface velocity curves from Captain Boileau's experiments.

First experiment.				Second experiment.			
Depth.	Observed velocity.	Computed velocity.	Difference.	Depth.	Observed velocity.	Computed velocity.	Difference.
Feet.	*Feet.*	*Feet.*	*Feet.*	*Feet.*	*Feet.*	*Feet.*	*Feet.*
0.0000	2.7002	2.7771	— 0.0769	0.000	1.9420	1.9368	+ 0.0052
0.1706	2.8544	2.8241	+ 0.0303	0.045	1.9680	1.9713	— 0.0033
0.2034	2.8577	2.8254	+ 0.0323	0.078	1.9810	1.9892	— 0.0082
0 2362	2.8544	2.8241	+ 0.0303	0.111	2.0040	2.0009	+ 0.0031
0.2690	2.8478	2.8204	+ 0.0274	0.144	2.0170	2.0068	+ 0.0102
0.3016	2.8380	2.8142	+ 0.0238	0.177	2.0170	2.0070	+ 0.0100
0.3346	2.8281	2.8053	+ 0.0228	0.200	2.0040	2.0034	+ 0.0006
0.4659	2.7527	2.7432	+ 0.0095	0.229	1.9880	1.9957	— 0.0077
0.5653	2.6411	2.6726	— 0.0315	0.262	1.9680	1.9802	— 0.0122
0.6299	2.5624	5.6132	— 0.0408	0.328	1.9120	1.9295	— 0.0175
0.7940	2.3590	2.4186	— 0.0596	0.492	1.7250	1.7059	+ 0.0191
0.8924	2.2348	2 2727	— 0.0484	0.557	1.6660	1.5705	+ 0.0955
0.9580	2.1359	2.1612	— 0.0253	0.623	1.5370	1.4133	+ 0.1237
1.0236	2.0374	2.0408	— 0.0034				
1.0893	1.9423	1.9100	+ 0.0323				
Sum..........	38.4457	38.5229	0.4946	Sum..........	24.7290	24.5105	0.3163
Mean.........	2.5630	2.5682	0.0330	Mean.........	1.9022	1.8854	0.0243

They indicate a modification of the law for small streams.

The columns of differences, it is considered, justify the assumption that the law already proved to exist in the Mississippi river holds good in this little experimental canal. If so, the coefficient of $v^{1/2}$ in the parameter equation for a very small stream at once results. Boileau does not give the mean velocity of the canal, but, since the observations were in the thread of the current, it may be determined with approximate accuracy by taking 0.8 of that observed at the surface. This gives 2.1 and 1.5 feet for the mean velocity corresponding to the first and second series of experiments respectively. Hence, designating by $b^{1/2}$ the coefficient of the square root of the mean velocity, the following values of b result:—

$$b = \frac{(1.5206)^2}{2.1} = 1.10$$

$$b = \frac{(1.2683)^2}{1.5} = 1.07.$$

These results, although rendered somewhat uncertain by the necessity of approximating to the mean velocity, indicate a material change from 0.1856, the value of b already found for large rivers.

Further observations to test the matter.

The law of this change was considered an important object for investigation, but the existing data were insufficient until, when studying the effect of change in slope upon discharge, in the autumn of 1859, it became highly desirable to test certain formulæ by actual observations upon a small stream. A feeder of the Chesapeake and Ohio canal at the Little Falls of the Potomac, near Georgetown, D. C., was selected, and incidentally another value of b was determined. The details of these experiments, so far as they relate to sub-surface velocities, will now be given before finishing the discussion of b.

The observations were made by Lieutenant Abbot, on December 2, 1859, a calm and pleasant day. The clear water-way of the feeder, at the point selected, was 17 feet in width and 7.1 feet in depth, with a nearly rectangular, masonry cross-section. The total width of the feeder was 23 feet, but in this vicinity one bank had partially caved in, thus obstructing the channel and more or less disturbing the water for about 6 feet from one edge. Throughout the remaining 17 feet, the current flowed with uncommon regularity from surface to bottom, thus affording an advantageous location for the experiments. Every care was taken to obviate errors of observation. An examination of many published experiments had led to the belief that the subject, sufficiently difficult in itself, had been greatly complicated by the use of instruments whose intricate machinery introduced so many errors as to conceal the true form of the curve. Oftentimes, different instruments had been used at different depths, almost necessarily introducing relative errors. The double float had been generally rejected—apparently without sufficient grounds—and it was therefore decided to give this method a fair trial.

The lower float was made by bending in the middle two strips of sheet tin, 8 inches long by 2 inches wide, and then soldering the bent edges together, all the angles included between the four fans thus made being right angles. This sub-float, itself 2 inches in height, was supported by two pieces of cork, each 2 inches in diameter by half an inch in height. One piece was secured permanently to the top of the tin, thus increasing by its own area the area of the lower float. The other, forming the surface float, was attached by a very fine iron wire. It was submerged only about an eighth of an inch, and, therefore, exercised no appreciable effect upon the rate of movement of the lower float. By varying the length of the wire, the velocity at any depth could be measured, especial care being taken to place the centre of figure of the lower float at the exact depth required, a very important matter, especially for observations at considerable distances from the point of maximum velocity.

The vertical plane in which to measure the sub-surface velocities was carefully selected so as to be as nearly as possible that of the thread of the current, because the flatness of the horizontal curve in this vicinity would give to slight deviations of the floats from the exact vertical plane their minimum effect in inducing errors.

The velocity was determined by noting the times of transit of the floats between two cords 51 feet apart, stretched across the feeder just above the water surface. A chronometer was used with all the care employed in nice astronomical observations.

The floats were placed in the water sufficiently far above the upper line for the lower float to sink and attain the uniform velocity of the water at the desired depth before reaching the cord. Twelve series of observations were made in succession. The following table exhibits the data in full with a comparison of the grand-mean curve with the parabola whose equation is—

$$V = 2.5216 - 1.1 \left(\frac{d - 1.65}{7.1}\right)^2.$$

Sub-surface velocity observations upon a feeder of the Chesapeake and Ohio canal.

Series.	Velocities, in feet per second, of floats at various depths.									
	V_0	V_1	V_2	V_3	$V_{\frac{1}{3}D}$	V_4	V_5	$V_{6.1}$	$V_{7.1} = V_D$	V_m by eq. (5)
First	2.2787	2.4366	2.5590	2 4998		2.6154	2 3182	1.9285		
Second	2.3302	2.5580	2.4968	2.4998		2.4878	2.2667	1.9299		
Third	2.4406	2.5580	2.6244	2.5620		1.8889	2 3182	1.9814		
Fourth	2.2787	2.5580	2.3811	2.4406		2.3182	2.3182	2.0040		
Fifth	2.2294	2.5580	2.4376	2.4406		2.4286	2.3182	1.9655		
Sixth	2.3841	2 4366	2.6244	2.5620		2.4878	1.8889	1.9315		
Seventh	2.3841	2.3801	2.4968	2.4998		2.2174	2.1250	1.8585		
Eighth	2 3841	2.5580	2.4968	2.4406		2.4878	2.3721	2.0440		
Ninth	2.3841	2.5580	2.5590	2.3841		2.4878	2 3182	1.8254		
Tenth	2.2787	2.4958	2.5590	2.4998		2.4286	2.1702	1.7328		
Eleventh	2.3841	2.5580	2.6932	2.4998		2.4286	2.4878	2.0856		
Twelfth	2 2787	2.5580	2.2757	2.5620		2.4878	2.3182	2.2707		
Mean	2.3363	2.5178	2.5170	2.4909		2.3971	2.2683	1.9632		
Parabola	2.4626	2.5124	2.5190	2.4818	2.4428	2.4010	2.2767	2.0895	1.8725	2.3509
Difference.	−0.1263	+0.0054	−0.0020	+0.0091		−0.0039	−0.0084	−0.1263		

The small amount of these differences proves that the curve is a parabola whose axis is parallel to the water surface and 0.232 of the depth below it, a result satisfactory both as confirmatory of the Mississippi work and as indicating that even a few observations, carefully taken in a favorable locality with double floats, may reveal the form of the curve exhibiting the change of velocity below the surface. The mean velocity was carefully deduced from a set of observations taken across the feeder at a uniform depth, by multiplying the mean of this horizontal curve by the ratio between the velocity at its depth and the mean of the whole vertical curve. It was found to be 2.0830 feet per second. From this the following value of b results:—

Analysis of them.

$$b = \frac{(1.1)^2}{2.0830} = 0.58.$$

This new value of b confirmed the inference drawn from Boileau's observations, that the quantity varied inversely with the depth, and justified an attempt to deduce its equation. The observations upon the Mississippi show that b must remain nearly equal to 0.186 for depths varying between 110 and 55 feet, and—if the somewhat less exact measurements made upon bayous Plaquemine and La Fourche are to be relied upon in so delicate a matter—for depths even as small as 27 feet. When, however, the depth becomes 7.1 feet, a sensible increase is noticed, the quantity becoming 0.58, and when a further reduction to 0.9 of a foot is made, the quantity

They confirm the modification of the parameter law for small streams, and suggest an equation to represent it.

slightly exceeds unity, its value being about 1.1 (mean of Boileau's two results). The following expression fulfils these conditions with all needful accuracy, as is shown by the table of values:—

$$(3) \qquad b = \frac{1.69}{(D + 1.5)^{\frac{1}{2}}}.$$

Values of D, in feet	110	82	55	27	7.1	1.1	0.7
Values of *b* by equation (3)	0.161	0.186	0.225	0.317	0.58	1.04	1.14

Resulting equation for velocity below the surface.

Since the rivers discussed in this report are usually deep, b will be generally taken at 0.1856. If small streams are to be considered, the above value should be substituted in equation (2) making it—

$$(4) \qquad V = V_{d_{\prime}} - \left(\frac{1.69\,v}{(D + 1.5)^{\frac{1}{2}}}\right)^{\frac{1}{2}} \left(\frac{d - d_{\prime}}{D}\right)^2.$$

Its general applicability.

This is in truth a general equation. Whether applied to the Mississippi river, pouring its flood of waters with boils and whirls through a channel 200,000 square feet in cross-section and more than 100 feet in depth, or to the bayou La Fourche, flowing as smoothly as a canal through a narrow channel less than one-fortieth of the size, or even to the experimental canal, the result accords closely with the observations.

Retrospect.

Formula for the mean of the whole vertical curve.—This is a favorable place to consider both what has been already deduced and what more is required before the original problem—the general ratio of the velocity 5 feet below the surface to the mean of the whole vertical curve—can be solved. By experimentally establishing the correctness of the formula—

$$(4) \qquad V = V_{d_{\prime}} - \left(\frac{1.69\,v}{(D + 1.5)^{\frac{1}{2}}}\right)^{\frac{1}{2}} \left(\frac{d - d_{\prime}}{D}\right)^2,$$

it has been proved that the curve exhibiting the change of velocity in a vertical plane is a parabola, of which the ordinates are the depths, and the abscissæ the corresponding velocities; that the axis is parallel to, and, at times at least, below the plane of, the water surface; and that the parameter varies in a deduced ratio with the square root of the mean velocity of the river. Also that this ratio is such, for large streams, that a slight error in mean velocity may be made without materially affecting the form of the curve—a fortunate circumstance, since this quantity is only approximately determined by the preliminary computations. Equations for the mean velocity of the whole vertical curve and for one of the two remaining variables ($V_{d_{\prime}}$ and $d_{\prime}$) in general equation (4) are yet essential to complete the discussion.

Exact equation for mean of whole vertical curve of velocity below the surface.

A mathematically exact expression for the mean velocity of the whole curve at once results from what has already been established and from the well-known property of the parabola, that the area of the segment included between the co-ordinates of any point is equal to two-thirds of the rectangle constructed upon those co-ordinates. Indicating by V_m the mean of the whole vertical curve, the following equation results, each member being an expression for the area on figure 5, plate XI:—

$$V_m D = \frac{2}{3}(V_{d_{\prime}} - V_0)\, d_{\prime} + V_0 d_{\prime} + \frac{2}{3}(V_{d_{\prime}} - V_D)\,(D - d_{\prime}) + V_D\,(D - d_{\prime}).$$

By reduction it can be brought into the following convenient form for use:—

$$(5) \qquad V_m = \frac{2}{3} V_{d_{\prime}} + \frac{1}{3} V_D + \frac{d_{\prime}}{D}\left(\frac{1}{3} V_0 - \frac{1}{3} V_D\right).$$

Locus of maximum velocity in vertical curve to be investigated.

It only remains to deduce an equation for one of the two variables in equation (4). For several reasons, not necessary to mention, $d_{\prime}$ was selected for study in preference to $V_{d_{\prime}}$.

Observed facts and general inferences from them.

Position of axis or locus of maximum velocity.—For this investigation, it is evident that only the five combined mean curves can be used, since in these alone are the observations sufficiently numerous to insure the close agreement with the parabolic form which is necessary to an exact determination of the position of the axis. These five curves (figures 12, 13, 14, 15, and 16, plate XI) indicate that this position varies from near the surface to below mid-depth. The fallacy of the prevailing idea, that the maximum velocity is necessarily at or very near the surface, is apparent from these diagrams. As theory has been carefully avoided in discussing this subject, the object being to state correctly the facts expressed by the observations themselves, no attempt will be made in this place to explain the *cause* of this submersion of the axis. The fact itself, however, with the consequent inference that there is a well-marked, strong resistance at the surface, is established. As the distance from the surface increases, the effect of this resistance diminishes until it becomes equal to that of the resistance propagated by the same law from the bottom. This point of equal effective resistance from surface and bottom is the locus of the maximum velocity, or in other words, the vertex of the parabola; its depth below the surface being $d_{\prime}$. Since $d_{\prime}$ evidently varies, the relative resistance at the surface and bottom must vary. But the resistance at the bottom at any given point can change only with the velocity, a cause of variation which must similarly affect the surface resistance. The surface resistance, however, in addition to this cause of variation, must be affected by every varying wind. Here, then, is a cause which ought to make the axis change its position. Its effect must, therefore, be first eliminated from the five curves of observation, assuming, for the time, that a change in velocity of the river affects the surface and bottom resistances proportionally, and hence has no influence upon the position of the axis.

Determination of the effective force of wind acting upon the five mean curves of observations.

Full notes were made of the force and direction of the wind at the time of all the observations, as may be seen by reference to the preceding tables. The scale of notation was that usually adopted, a calm being denoted by force 0, and a hurricane by force 10. The highest wind at which velocity observations were possible was found to be force 4. The following process was adopted in determining the effective force of wind acting upon each of the five mean curves. The observations were separated into three classes: those taken when the wind blew up stream; those taken when it blew down stream; and those taken in a calm, or when the wind blew directly across the river, and hence produced no effect. For the first two classes, the sum of the products of the number of observations at each point by the numbers designating the corresponding forces of the wind was found. The difference between these two sums was divided by the total number of observations at all the points of the curve. The result was the effective force of the wind, which blew up or down stream, as the sum of the products of the first or second class predominated. The following table exhibits in full the data for the axis determination:—

Curve.	No. of obs. at each point.	Force of wind.	$\frac{d_{\prime}}{D}$	Approx. mean velocity of river.
				Feet.
Grand mean—Carrollton	222	Down 0.2	0.297	3.3814
High-water mean—Carrollton	142	Up 0.3	0.350	4.1605
Low-water mean—Carrollton	80	Down 1.1	0.150	1.9984
Mean—Columbus	52	Up 1.2	0.520	3.4070
Mean—Vicksburg	20	Down 1.0	0.100	4.1599

Its effects analyzed and eliminated.

As already stated, the first step was to eliminate the effect of wind, and thus determine what the mean position of the axis would have been, had all the observations been made during a calm. Since the mean effective wind acting upon the curves was very slight, its influence was assumed to be directly proportional to its force, whether blowing up or down stream—a law which was subsequently demonstrated to be true even for high winds. It is also evident that the effect of an up-stream wind will be to lower the axis, since it increases the resistance at the surface, while a down-stream wind must have a contrary effect. Making, therefore, $x =$ depth of axis in calm, expressed in decimals of depth of river, and $y =$ effect of wind force 1 in raising or lowering the axis, expressed in the same unit, it is evident that $\frac{d_{\prime}}{D}$ must be equal to x increased or diminished by the product of the number indicating the force of the wind by y, according as the wind blows up or down stream. Applying these principles to the five mean curves, and giving each curve a weight proportional to its number of observations at each point, the following equation results:—

$$\left.\begin{array}{r} 222\ (x - 0.2\,y) \\ +\ 142\ (x + 0.3\,y) \\ +\ 80\ (x - 1.1\,y) \\ +\ 52\ (x + 1.2\,y) \\ +\ 20\ (x - 1.0\,y) \end{array}\right\} = \left\{\begin{array}{l} 222 \times 0.297 \\ +\ 142 \times 0.350 \\ +\ 80 \times 0.150 \\ +\ 52 \times 0.520 \\ +\ 20 \times 0.100 \end{array}\right.$$

By reduction this becomes—

$$x = 0.3036 + 0.092\,y.$$

It is also evident that the difference between $\frac{d_{\prime}}{D}$ and x is equal to y multiplied by the number indicating the force of the wind. Hence the following equation results:—

$$\left.\begin{array}{r} 222\ (x - 0.297) \\ +\ 142\ (0.350 - x) \\ +\ 80\ (x - 0.150) \\ +\ 52\ (0.520 - x) \\ +\ 20\ (x - 0.100) \end{array}\right\} = \left\{\begin{array}{l} 222 \times 0.2\,y \\ +\ 142 \times 0.3\,y \\ +\ 80 \times 1.1\,y \\ +\ 52 \times 1.2\,y \\ +\ 20 \times 1.0\,y \end{array}\right.$$

By reduction this becomes—

$$x = 0.025 + 2.011\,y.$$

Combining and reducing these two equations, the following values of x and y result:—

$$x = 0.3170.$$
$$y = 0.1452.$$

The next step is to apply these values to the five curves and then to seek, in the resulting differences, the effect upon the axis of a change in velocity in the river.

The following table explains itself:—

Curve.	Force of wind.	Observed $\frac{d_{,}}{D}$	Observed $\frac{d_{,}}{D}$ reduced to calm.	Mean $\frac{d_{,}}{D}$	Difference.	Number of observations.
Grand mean—Carrollton	Down 0.2	0.297	$0.297 + 0.2 \times 0.1452 = 0.326$	0.317	-0.009	222
High-water mean—Carrollton..	Up 0.3	0.350	$0.350 - 0.3 \times 0.1452 = 0.306$	0.317	$+0.011$	142
Low-water mean—Carrollton...	Down 1.1	0.150	$0.150 + 1.1 \times 0.1452 = 0.310$	0.317	$+0.007$	80
Mean—Columbus	Up 1.2	0.520	$0.520 - 1.2 \times 0.1452 = 0.346$	0.317	-0.029	52
Mean—Vicksburg..................	Down 1.0	0.100	$0.100 + 1.0 \times 0.1452 = 0.245$	0.317	$+0.072$	20

Resulting law for the locus of the maximum velocity in calm weather.

By the process employed in deducing the values of x and y, each curve has a weight proportional to its number of observations at each point; and the resulting differences, when regard is had to sign and to the number of observations, very nearly balance each other. It is apparent that these differences are very slight, and nearly inversely proportional to the number of observations. The legitimate inference is that they are due to errors of observation, and hence *that the position of the axis in calm weather is about three-tenths of the depth below the surface, whatever be the mean velocity of the river.* This is a great point gained, since it renders it possible, by a process hereafter to be detailed, to deduce accurately the desired ratio between the velocity observed at 5 feet below the surface and the true mean of the vertical curve, for *calm days at all stages of the river.*

Difficulty of analyzing the effect of wind upon the locus of the maximum velocity.

The next step, namely, a study of the effect, in raising or lowering the axis, of winds of different forces, led to difficulties apparently insurmountable. The five mean curves were but slightly affected by wind, and afforded no data for judging of the effect of a strong wind. But few observations for velocity below the surface were made when the force of the wind was greater than 1; and, when grouped in up-stream and down-stream classes and combined, each set was found to be insufficient in number to eliminate errors of observation, so as to give a parabolic curve whose depth of axis could be accurately determined. Even if this had been possible, it would have been a wide generalization to assume that the mean effect upon the axis at all points of the river surface was the same as at isolated points generally located near the thread of the current. Here, then, the discussion must have closed, had all the data upon the subject consisted of the actual sub-surface observations. Fortunately, this was not the case.

Errors attributable to the effect of wind perceptible in the approximate computations of discharge at the velocity stations.

As already described, an approximate discharge per second had been computed for each day's observations at Columbus, Vicksburg, and Natchez, by taking the sum of the products of the areas of each division by the velocity observed in it 5 feet below the surface. These discharges were plotted in curves whose abscissæ were dates and whose ordinates were the discharges per second. Any one, desirous of studying these curves for himself, can easily do so by plotting them on plate XIII from the column marked "approximate discharge" in Appendix D. The printed curves on this diagram exhibit the "revised discharge." It is evident that such curves ought to be smooth, without such irregularities as produce a serrated appearance, provided the discharge be accurately known. Irregularities were, however, found to exist. A reference to the wind-record for the days in question accounted for them. The depressions, indicating too small discharges, were found to occur with remarkable uniformity when, according to the record, the wind had blown up stream; the sharp elevations, indicating excessive discharges, on the contrary, corresponded to down-stream winds. Not only was this true, but the great irregularities corresponded to winds of great force, while gentle breezes produced less effect. This is precisely the result which the laws of change of velocity in a vertical plane, already deduced, would lead one to expect. An up-stream wind increases the surface resistance, depresses the axis, and therefore moves farther from the vertex the point of the curve 5 feet below the surface. The ratio of the observed velocity to the mean of the curve is therefore greater, and the discharge, as yet uncorrected by this ratio, must be too small. With a down-stream wind, the effect is exactly the reverse.

Empirical correction deduced therefor.

This evident relation, existing between the irregularities and the recorded force of the wind, suggested the feasibility of deducing an empirical correction for wind-effect. The Columbus observations were selected for the trial, and the curve and wind-record carefully studied together. It is evident that, where the curve is nearly parallel to the axis of Y, a slight error in the ordinates—in other words, in the discharges per second—cannot be detected. Such portions of the curve were therefore neglected. For the other portions, the following system was adopted. A table was formed, containing columns for wind force 1, force 2, force 3, and force 4, both up stream and down stream. The curve was examined at each daily point, and the estimated correction in cubic feet per second which would remove its serrated appearance, was written in the column corresponding to the recorded wind force for that day. When the whole curve had been thus revised, a mean of each column was taken. One result, not altogether unexpected, was evident. Up-stream and down-stream winds of any given force produced about equal effects upon the discharge, the signs of course being different; in other words, they lowered or raised the axis by nearly equal amounts. There are some theoretical reasons for a tendency toward this result, but an absolute equality of effect could hardly be anticipated. A down-stream wind acts upon the water first by relieving it from the resistance of the calm atmosphere, so that its whole force is effective in raising the axis from the position it occupies in a calm, and is equal in amount to that of an up-stream wind of the same force. The effects of the two winds in creating waves, however, are different; that of the down-stream wind being proportional to the difference between its own and the river's velocity, while that of the up-stream wind is proportional to its whole force. The force of the wind is more effectively exerted when the waves are large than when they are small.*

Although, as just remarked, no perceptible difference could be detected in the

* Enough has now been learned to justify the remark that the resistance at the surface in calm weather can be only partly due to the friction against the air, otherwise a down-stream wind, moving with equal velocity with the water, must reduce it to zero and raise the axis to the surface—a result contrary to the observations. It occasions no surprise, however, to one familiar to the boils and whirls of the Mississippi, that they should cause a great loss of living force at the surface, and consequently a great retardation of the surface current.

amount of the irregularities in the curve of discharge caused by up-stream and down-stream winds, great differences were evident in the effects of winds of different force. The following is the numerical result of the study of the Columbus observations:—

	Cubic feet per second.
Up stream or down-stream wind, force 1, diminishes or increases the computed discharge	7,000
" " " " 2, " " " "	12,000
" " " " 3, " " " "	19,000
" " " " 4, " " " "	33,000

Its applicability is limited.

This empirical table of correction was applied to the Columbus, Vicksburg, and Natchez curves of discharge. It was found to diminish their serrated appearance greatly, but the correction was evidently too great for the low and too small for the high stages of the river. It was merely an empirical rule, and *each correction could properly be applied only in that stage of the river for which it was deduced, that is, when the mean velocity was about the same as the mean of the mean velocities of the days from whose observations it was deduced.*

It is made the basis of an analytical investigation of the effect of wind upon the locus of the maximum velocity in the mean vertical plane.

This idea appeared to furnish a clue to the solution of the problem analytically. The effect upon the discharge of a certain mean day for each of the four desired forces of the wind might fairly be considered to be known. If it were possible from this to deduce the amount which the axis of each of the mean sub-surface velocity curves of those four days must have moved from its calm position to produce this observed effect upon the computed discharge, data would be deduced from which it might be possible to discover the law governing the effect of the wind upon the axis. An effort to accomplish this object formed the next step in this investigation.

Numerical values of the quantities entering the computation.

The process was identical for each of the four forces under consideration, although the data were, of course, entirely distinct for each. A list of the days from which the empirical correction had been deduced was made. There were, then, computed for these days a mean approximate discharge, a mean approximate mean velocity of the river, a mean gauge-reading—and from this the corresponding mean radius of the river—an unneutralized effect of wind, found by dividing the number of days on which the wind was blowing in one direction more than in the other by the total number of days,—and, lastly, a mean velocity 5 feet below the surface. The latter was found by taking a mean of all the tabulated velocities for all the divisions on the specified days. These mean quantities, together with the deduced empirical correction for the force under consideration, constituted the only data necessary for solving the problem. The following table exhibits these data for each of the four forces of the wind, together with some quantities deduced therefrom in a manner subsequently to be explained:—

Wind.	Empirical correction.	Approx. v	Approx. discharge per second.	Unneutralized wind-effect.		r	Observed U_5	Wind-effect neutralized.						U''_5		$\frac{d_{\prime}}{r}$	
				Up.	Down			U'_5	$\frac{d_{\prime}}{r}$	$U'_{d_{\prime}}$	U'_0	U'_r	U_m	Wind up.	Wind down.	Wind up.	Wind down.
	C. ft.	*Ft.*	*C. ft*			*Ft.*	*Ft.*	*Ft.*		*Ft.*	*Ft.*	*Ft.*	*Ft.*	*Ft.*	*Ft.*		
Force 1	7000	5.2211	712220	0.38		58.91	4.7139	4.7314	0.317	4.7844	4.6855	4.3252	4.6694	4.6851	4.7777	0.374	0.260
Force 2	12000	3.8606	511473	0.22		53.76	3.6298	3.6399	0.317	3.6824	3.5973	3 2875	3.5835	3.5631	3.7335	0.441	0.193
Force 3	19000	4.2211	534790	0.44		54.52	3.7526	3.8109	0.317	3.8558	3.7669	3.4451	3.7529	3.6776	3.9442	0.505	0.130
Force 4	33000	5.9435	839886	0.13		61.87	5.4111	5.4377	0.317	5.4963	5.3908	5.0063	5.3736	5.2251	5 6503	0.560	0.080

Assuming equations (2) and (5), and substituting for V, $V_{d_,}$, D, V_m, V_D, and V_0, respectively, U, $U_{d_,}$, r, U_m, U_r, and U_0, the following general formulæ for large streams, applicable to the mean of all vertical curves, result—

The unneutralized effect of wind upon the observations eliminated.

(6) $$U = U_{d_,} - (0.1856\ v)^{\frac{1}{2}} \left(\frac{d - d_,}{r}\right)^2.$$

(7) $$U_m = \frac{2}{3} U_{d_,} + \frac{1}{3} U_r + \frac{d_,}{r} \left(\frac{1}{3} U_0 - \frac{1}{3} U_r\right).$$

If now, in equation (6), the tabulated values corresponding to the wind-force under consideration be substituted for U, v, and r, together with the corresponding value for d, namely, 5, it is evident that the formula contains only two unknown quantities, $U_{d_,}$ and $d_,$, and that if the corresponding value of either of these quantities can be determined, the other can be computed. The mean calm value of $d_,$, namely, 0.317 r, cannot be assumed, since the curve is still acted on by a certain fractional wind-force. This force is, however, known (see above table), and, from the given data, it is possible to compute what U_5 would have been had there been no wind; in other words, to compute a new value for U_5, which shall correspond to the known calm value of $d_,$. The effective force of the wind in each case is so small that no corresponding effect will be made upon v, which will sensibly change the small function of it that enters the formula. The new value of U_5, corresponding to a calm, is deduced from the following considerations. For small changes, the mean velocity 5 feet below the surface may be assumed to be directly proportional to the mean velocity of the river. But the latter is directly proportional to the discharge, when, as in this case, the area of cross-section remains the same. Hence U_5, in the above expression, is, for slight changes, directly proportional to the discharge. But the effect of the wind upon the computed discharge can be readily deduced, since the direction of blowing determines its sign, and the product of the fraction showing the effective force, by the empirical correction, its amount. Designating, therefore, by U'_5 the value U_5 would have had, if no wind had been blowing, the following proportion and resulting equation are deduced:—

Approximate discharge as computed : Approximate discharge, had it been calm : : $U_5 : U'_5$.

$$U'_5 = U_5 \frac{\text{Approximate discharge, had it been calm}}{\text{Approximate discharge as computed}}.$$

By this formula, the values given in the preceding table, in the column headed "U'_5", are deduced. Using these values for U, and 0.317 r for $d_,$, the other quantities remaining as before, equation (6) can now be solved, and the value of $U_{d_,}$ deduced. These values are given in the preceding table, in the column headed "$U'_{d_,}$". Substituting these values for $U_{d_,}$ in equation (6), with the tabulated values of v and r and the mean calm value of $d_,$, 0.317, and then making $d = 0$ and $d = r$, the values of the velocity at the surface and at the bottom, contained in the column headed "U'_0" and "U'_r", are deduced. All the quantities contained in the second member of equation (7) being now known, the values contained in the column headed "U_m" are computed.

What the approximate discharge and the curve of velocities in the mean vertical plane would have been on each of the four mean days, had no wind been blowing, has now been legitimately deduced. Moreover, the absolute discharge per second must be unaffected by any wind of uniform force. This reduces the problem to the question how much the axis

Analysis of the problem: What is the effect of wind upon the locus of

must be raised or lowered from its calm position, in order to make the product of the approximate discharge corrected for wind, plus or minus each of the empirical corrections in turn, by $\frac{U_m}{U''_5}$ equal to the product of the approximate discharge corrected for wind by $\frac{U_m}{U'_5}$, the quantity U''_5 being the mean of the velocities 5 feet below the surface corresponding to the particular wind-force under consideration. To answer this question, reference must again be had to equations (6) and (7), and values for the constants must be deduced, adapted to a curve acted upon by the several wind-forces in turn.

the maximum velocity in the mean vertical plane?

The same course of reasoning as that followed in deducing U'_5 will lead to the following expression for U''_5, in which only known quantities enter the second member. The computed values are entered in the preceding table, in the columns headed "Wind up U''_5" and "Wind down U''_5".

$$U''_5 = U'_5 \frac{\text{Approximate discharge corrected for wind} \pm \text{wind correction for force under consideration}}{\text{Approximate discharge corrected for wind}}.$$

For v, the approximate mean velocity of the river in the above table may be used without sensible error.

For d, use 5.

For r, use the mean radius given in the above table.

For U_m, use the value in the above table already computed, since it is evident from the following considerations that this quantity is unaffected by wind. Whatever be the uniform force or direction of the wind, the true discharge, and hence the true mean velocity, remain the same. But for a uniform rectangular cross-section, $U_m = v$. The difference between these quantities, being solely due to the form of cross-section, must be independent of wind except for its inappreciable effect upon the level of the surface, and hence upon the form of cross-section.

For U''_0 and U''_r, the following formulæ result by assigning the proper values to d in equation (6), — the quantities v and r for each wind-force having the numerical values just named.

$$U''_0 = U''_{d_,} - (0.1856\ v)^{\frac{1}{2}} \left(\frac{d_,}{r}\right)^2.$$

$$U''_r = U''_{d_,} - (0.1856\ v)^{\frac{1}{2}} \left(\frac{r - d_,}{r}\right)^2.$$

If this set of values be substituted in the two general formulæ (6) and (7), it will be found that only two quantities remain unknown, namely, $U''_{d_,}$ and $d_,$, the numerical values of which may therefore be computed. By a somewhat tedious process of combining these equations, eliminating $U''_{d_,}$, and reducing, the following value of $d_,$, in terms of known quantities, results:—

$$d_, = \frac{(0.1856\ v)^{\frac{1}{2}}\ (5\ r - \frac{1}{3}r^2 - 25) + r^2\ (U_5'' - U_m)}{(0.1856\ v)^{\frac{1}{2}}\ (10 - r)} + 5.$$

The resulting values of $d_,$, in decimals of the total depth, are given in the columns headed "Wind up $\frac{d_,}{r}$" and "Wind down $\frac{d_,}{r}$". These values of $\frac{d_,}{r}$, it will be remembered, are the numbers for which this laborious investigation was undertaken, and by which it was hoped that the law governing the action of the wind upon the axis of the mean sub-surface curve might be revealed. The following table exhibits an analysis of these values:—

Wind.	$\frac{d_{,}}{r}$	Successive differences.	Mean differences.	Differences bet. mean and successive differences.
Down—force 4	0.080	0.050	0.060	+ 0.010
Down—force 3	0.130	0.063	0.060	— 0.003
Down—force 2	0.193	0.067	0.060	— 0.007
Down—force 1	0.260	0.057	0.060	+ 0.003
0	0.317	0.057	0.060	+ 0.003
Up— force 1	0.374	0.067	0.060	— 0.007
Up— force 2	0.441	0.064	0.060	— 0.004
Up— force 3	0.505	0.055	0.060	+ 0.005
Up— force 4	0.560			
Sum		0.480	0.480	0.042

Resulting law, and general equation for the locus of the maximum velocity in the mean vertical plane.

No clearer revelation of law could be desired. *The effect of the wind, whether blowing up or down stream, is directly proportional to its force, in the former case lowering, and in the latter, raising the axis. Also, the amount of such lowering or raising is independent of the mean velocity of the river.* When it is remembered that every part of the data for detecting the effect of each wind-force is entirely independent of that for the other three forces, the slight amount of the differences in the last column of the above table is no less surprising than satisfactory. It is evident that $d_{,}$ is no longer an unknown quantity in equation (6). Its equation, which will receive a short discussion in the next chapter, is—

$$d_{,} = (0.317 + 0.06 f)\, r, \qquad (8)$$

in which f is the number indicating the force of the wind; a calm, or a wind blowing at right angles to the current, being denoted by 0, and a hurricane by 10. Its *essential sign* is *positive* when the wind blows up stream, and *negative* when down stream.

Explanation of discharge computations can now be resumed where it was left on page 229.

The especial object of this investigation of the laws governing the change of velocity below the surface is at length attained, since the complicated and varying ratio, necessary to correct the work of the year 1858, can now be readily deduced.

FINAL DETERMINATION OF DAILY DISCHARGE AT VELOCITY-STATIONS AND ELSEWHERE.

Method of correcting discharge measurements for changes of velocity below the surface.—

An equation for $\frac{U_m}{U_5}$ necessary to complete these equations.

It will be remembered that the method of determining the discharge from the velocity measurements has been already fully explained, upon the supposition that the velocity in any vertical plane parallel to the current is the same at all depths. The principles and equations just deduced render it possible to correct these approximate discharges for the error introduced by this assumption. This can evidently be done by multiplying them by the ratio $\frac{U_m}{U_5}$. It only remains, therefore, to deduce an analytical expression for this ratio, and to explain how it has been practically applied.

It is deduced.

Substituting in equation (7) for U_0 and U_r the following values (deduced from equation (6) by substituting the proper values of d), viz.:—

$$(9) \qquad U_0 = U_{d_{\prime}} - (b\,v)^{\frac{1}{2}} \left(\frac{d_{\prime}}{r}\right)^2,$$

$$(10) \qquad U_r = U_{d_{\prime}} - (b\,v)^{\frac{1}{2}} \left(\frac{r - d_{\prime}}{r}\right)^2,$$

and reducing, the following value of $U_{d_{\prime}}$ may be obtained:—

$$(11) \qquad U_{d_{\prime}} = U_m + (b\,v)^{\frac{1}{2}} \left(\frac{1}{3} + \frac{d_{\prime}\,(d_{\prime} - r)}{r^2}\right).$$

Substituting this value of $U_{d_{\prime}}$ in equation (6), giving $d_{\prime}$ its value in equation (8), making $d = 5$, and dividing the expression $U_m = U_m$, member by member, by the resulting equation, the following analytical expression for the desired ratio results:—

$$(12) \qquad \frac{U_m}{U_5} = \frac{U_m}{U_m + \left(\frac{1}{3} + \frac{(0.317 + 0.06\,f)\,(10\,r - r^2) - 25}{r^2}\right)\,\left(b\,v\right)^{\frac{1}{2}}}.$$

Manner of determining the numerical values of the quantities entering the second member of this equation; with table of resulting values of the ratio for Columbus, Vicksburg, and Natchez.

The numerical values of this expression were computed and tabulated for each velocity-base by the following process. The days on which observations were made were grouped according to even feet of the approximate mean velocities already computed, it being assumed that the effect upon the desired ratio, produced by changes in mean velocity of less than one foot, might be neglected. Each group was then examined in connection with the wind-record, and days were rejected until only calm days, or those on which the wind blew directly across stream, or those on which, when combined, the wind-effects balanced each other, were left. The resulting mean day in each group was equivalent to a calm day, so far as wind-effect was concerned. The following mean quantities were then deduced for each mean day by dividing the sum of the quantities by the number of days going to make up the mean day, viz.: an approximate mean velocity of the river, a gauge-reading—and hence a mean radius—and a mean velocity 5 feet below the surface (found by taking a mean of the tabulated velocities of all the different divisions). Substituting in equation (6) these mean values for v, r, and U, giving d its corresponding value, 5, and making $d_{\prime} = 0.317\,r$, and $b = 0.1856$, only $U_{d_{\prime}}$ remained unknown. Its numerical value was therefore computed and substituted, with the same values for v, $d_{\prime}$, and r, in equation (6), which now contained only two variables, d and U. By making $d = 0$, and $d = r$, and deducing the corresponding values of U, the velocity at the surface and bottom became known. Substituting in equation (7) these values, together with those computed for $U_{d_{\prime}}$, $d_{\prime}$, and r, the value of U_m resulted. Substituting in equation (12) these values of U_m, with those already deduced for v and r, and making $b = 0.1856$, f alone remained unknown. By giving it successively its value for each of the various forces and directions of the wind, the following table has been computed. It will be noticed that eight ratios were deduced for Columbus, five for Vicksburg, and one for Natchez; and that they differ very slightly at the different stations.

Table of ratios for correcting the "approximate" discharges of the Mississippi.

Locality.	Approx. mean veloc. of river.	Wind down 4.	Wind down 3.	Wind down 2.	Wind down 1.	Calm.	Wind up 1.	Wind up 2.	Wind up 3.	Wind up 4.
	Feet.									
Columbus, Kentucky.	1.6826	0.90759	0.92250	0.93791	0.95390	0.97040	0.98750	1.00521	1.02357	1.04262
	2.4440	0.92202	0.93519	0.94874	0.96273	0.97737	0.99192	1.00721	1.02294	1.03923
	3.6548	0.93719	0.94826	0.95917	0.97118	0.98302	0.99521	1.00767	1.02048	1.03359
	4.5097	0.94400	0.95407	0.96428	0.97463	0.98546	0.99641	1.00760	1.01903	1.03058
	4.3426	0.94908	0.95829	0.96809	0.97741	0.98723	0.99727	1.00689	1.01793	1.02858
	6.6496	0.95406	0.96261	0.97131	0.98016	0.98918	0.99837	1.00773	1.01727	1.02697
	7.4282	0.95751	0.96550	0.97365	0.98193	0.99035	0.99891	1.00762	1.01648	1.02551
	8.3162	0.95983	0.96747	0.97523	0.98311	0.99112	0.99927	1.00756	1.01598	1.02453
Vicksburg, Mississippi	3.6038	0.93881	0.94854	0.95846	0.96863	0.97895	0.98956	1.00037	1.01142	1.02271
	4.4110	0.94544	0.95458	0.96423	0.97340	0.98310	0.99300	1.00307	1.01337	1.02389
	5.5571	0.95161	0.96017	0.96895	0.97783	0.98693	0.99613	1.00557	1.01518	1.02494
	6.7363	0.95631	0.96440	0.97264	0.98103	0.98952	0.99823	1.00706	1.01604	1.02519
	7.0529					0.99006				
Natchez, Mississippi....	4.6901	0.94566	0.95501	0.96454	0.97428	0.98420	0.99433	1.00466	1.01522	1.02602

Application of this table to the final computation of the discharge.

The practical application of these ratios, so laboriously deduced, was very simple. The approximate discharge for each day at Columbus, Vicksburg, and Natchez was multiplied by the ratio, in the above table, most nearly corresponding to its approximate mean velocity, reference being had to the recorded force and direction of wind. A wind blowing directly across the river was considered calm. These discharges were then divided by the corresponding areas of cross-section, to determine the true mean velocity. The results of these operations are given in Appendix D, in the columns headed "Discharge" and "Mean velocity." The same operation was performed upon the following observations in 1851, in which all the floats passed near the surface, viz.:—

Routh's point..February 25.
Red-river landing..March 16.
Raccourci cut-off..March 19.
Baton Rouge..April 1 and April 26.
Bonnet Carré..May 20.

Internal evidence of accuracy.

These corrected values are plotted on plates XV, XVI, and XIII. On the two former, the ordinates are the daily gauge-readings, and the abscissæ the corresponding discharges per second. On the other, the ordinates are the daily discharges per second, and the abscissæ the corresponding dates. Many references will be hereafter made to these diagrams. At present, they are mentioned only to call attention to the evident smoothness and regularity of the curves. This is a severe test of the accuracy of the work, as the scale is sufficiently large to reveal readily by a serrated form any irregularities from day to day. To avoid complicating these diagrams, the "approximate discharge" has been omitted, but the curve can easily be added from the tabulated values in Appendix D, if it be desired. It will show that much of the freedom from irregularities is due to the application of the correction-ratios given in the last table. Indeed, it may reasonably be claimed, since this table is affected by every principle thus far enunciated in this discussion, that the effect of the deduced corrections upon the curves of approximate discharge would be a sufficient guarantee of the truth of the whole new theory for velocity below the surface, even if it rested upon abstract reasoning alone instead of upon observations.

The *corrected* values are of course used in all the discussions of this report. To guard against any cavillings which may be directed against a process so long and intricate as that by which these ratios have been deduced, all the data have been presented, necessary to enable any person to correct the approximate discharge, by any other desired process, for the difference between the velocity 5 feet below the surface and the mean of the whole vertical curve. It fortunately happens that the deduced correction-ratios differ so slightly from unity, that no general opinion can be based upon the revised result, which might not with equal propriety be drawn from the first approximation, wholly uncorrected.

Concluding remarks.

Interpolations of daily discharge at velocity-stations.—One uniform system was adopted at the several velocity-stations for determining the discharge on those days on which no current-observations were made. The discharges actually measured were plotted both with respect to time, as on plate XIII, and with respect to the stage of the river, as on plate XV. The determined points on one of the diagrams were then connected so as to make as smooth a curve as possible. The interpolations indicated by this curve were next tested and corrected by plotting them on the other diagram. A few trials will convince any one that, where observations are as numerous and exact as on this Survey, such interpolations are entitled to the same confidence as actual observations. They in fact amount to the same thing. For the tributary streams, the following explanations are required.

General system of interpolating the discharge when no measurements were made.—Mississippi river.

The measurements upon the Arkansas, at Napoleon, were sufficiently numerous to allow the system of interpolation just described to be employed for that river. A correction was necessary for a few days when the river was highest, in order to allow for some water which poured across the bend just above Napoleon. The amount of this correction from day to day was carefully estimated from reliable notes and records, and may be easily determined by comparing the discharges given in Appendices D and E.

Arkansas river.

The discharge of White river has been assumed the same as that of the Arkansas, at Napoleon; partly because the measured areas of cross-section of the streams near their mouths are about the same, and partly because the large connecting bayou or cut-off has the effect of equalizing the discharge through the two channels below it, no matter from which river the water originally comes.

White river.

In addition to his measurements upon the Mississippi river, in 1858, Mr. Pattison was charged with occasionally gauging the Yazoo river, and with fully informing himself, from the regular packets plying between Vicksburg and Yazoo City, of its daily condition. During high water, these measurements could be readily made, since he could pass in his skiff through the swamps, and return the same day. After the river fell, the work could not be prosecuted without interfering with the operations upon the Mississippi, and it was accordingly discontinued. Exact memoranda obtained from gentlemen residing upon the river, together with the measurements and notes of Mr. Pattison, furnish the means of accurately fixing the daily

Yazoo river.

discharge from December, 1857, up to the last gauging on July 23, 1858. Subsequent to that date, it is not attempted.

Red river. The contributions of Red river, during the flood-period of 1858, were determined with much accuracy by a general system of checks. Through the kindness of Mr. Thomas K. Smith, at Alexandria, the information needful for a knowledge of the daily stage of Red river at that point, was secured. The gauge of Mr. H. D. Mandeville, at the crossing of the Vidalia and Harrisonburg road, supplied all desired information relative to bayou Tensas. Besides the gauge-register at Red-river landing, Mr. Torras kept a daily record of the direction and force of the current in Old river. The gaugings of Red river, bayou Atchafalaya and Old river, made in 1851 by Mr. G. C. Smith's party, and repeated in 1858 by that of Lieutenant Abbot, afforded a definite idea of the capacity of these rivers for discharge. The measurements at Vicksburg, transferred down the river in the manner soon to be explained, fully checked and established the accuracy of the discharges estimated by discussing and studying these various records. It fortunately happened that, during the critical period of high water, Red river was low, and the Atchafalaya carried off the crevasse-water which drained through Black river. The water in Old river thus remained stationary, or nearly so, at this most important time, and no error of any practical importance can exist, therefore, in the estimated contributions of Red river to the Mississippi during the flood.

Bayous Plaquemine and La Fourche. Bayous Plaquemine and La Fourche so much resemble waste-weirs, that the amount received for any given stand of the Mississippi must be a nearly unvarying quantity.* By the aid of this principle, the measurements of the Survey afford all needful facilities for determining accurately the daily discharge during the flood-period, when a gauge-record has been kept. The following table has been computed for this purpose from the data contained in Appendix D. :—

* Bayou Atchafalaya belongs to this class of streams, but, owing to its peculiar situation, it is exposed to certain anomalous influences, which may produce an important effect upon its discharge. For this reason, no scale is constructed, although the following data are sufficient to furnish a closely approximate idea of the discharge at any given stand :—

Authority.	Date.	Stand below high water, 1851.	Discharge per second.
		Feet.	*Cubic feet.*
Mr. G. C. Smith's party	March 9, 1851.	4.2	105,000
Mr. G. C. Smith's party	March 8, 1851.	4.4	98,000
Lieutenant Abbot's party	Feb. 11, 1858.	8.3	77,000
Mr. Duncan, State Engineer of Louisiana.	July 1–9, 1860.	36.0 ±	29,000

Scale of discharge for the bayous.

Mississippi below high water, 1851, at upper mouth of bayou.	Discharge per second in cubic feet.	
	Bayou Plaquemine.	Bayou La Fourche.
Feet.		
0	35,000	11,500
1	32,000	10,500
2	29,000	9,600
3	26,000	8,800
4	23,000	7,900
5	21,000	7,100
6	18,000	6,300
7	15,000	5,400
8	12,000	4,600

A very satisfactory test of the exactness of this table is furnished by the result of the measurements of the discharge of bayou Plaquemine, made by Mr. Charles Ritter, at the date of high water, 1853, and kindly communicated by Mr. Louis Hèbert, State Engineer of Louisiana. The bayou stood about 2 feet below high water of 1851, and the discharge per second by the above table would therefore have been 29,000 cubic feet. Mr. Ritter found it to be 29,869 cubic feet—a difference of only about three per cent.

Outline of the process adopted for transferring measured discharges.

Transfer of measured discharge.—There is yet to be explained the general method of computing—from the tabular exhibit of the daily discharge per second at the velocity-stations and the daily loss per second by crevasses (assumed for the present to be known), together with the corresponding gauge-records at different points of the river—the daily discharge per second at various important points selected for study. One uniform system has been adopted for all such transfers of measured discharges. The mean rate of movement of the water having been computed by dividing the approximate discharge by the approximate mean area of the river between the points considered, the water-prism measured at the velocity-base is traced to the point where the discharge is required, and corrected for the losses by crevasses, and for the contributions from tributaries, shown by the measurements to have occurred at the dates of its passage. This is all that is needful, provided the river is at a stand while this prism is passing, which it is always at the top of the flood, when exact accuracy is most important. If, however, it be rising or falling, the prism is affected thereby; and a correction, found by multiplying the mean area of river surface between the stations by the mean rise or fall per second while the prism is passing, is to be applied with its proper sign. A single example will show the practical application of this process.

Example.

Let it be required to find the discharge per second at Helena on July 15, 1858. When the Mississippi is at high-water mark, its mean area of cross-section from Columbus to Vicksburg is about 194,000 square feet, and its discharge per second about 1,200,000 cubic feet. This gives for the rate of movement of the water about 100 miles in twenty-four hours. This rate may be assumed without sensible error for the flood period. The distance from Helena to Napoleon is 102 miles; thence to Providence, 132 miles; thence to Vicksburg, 70 miles; making a total distance of 304 miles from Helena to Vicksburg. It may, therefore, be assumed that the water-prism which, moving at the rate of 100 miles per day, passed Helena between sunset on July 14 and sunset on July 15, passed Napoleon between sunset on July 15 and sunset on July 16; passed Providence between sunset on July 16 and sunset on July 17; and passed Vicksburg, *where it was measured*, between sunset on July 17 and sunset on July 18. Corrections are, therefore, to be taken from the tabular exhibit in Appendix E, and the tables of crevasse discharge given in Chapter VI, to correspond to those dates, thus:—

	Cubic feet per second.
Measured discharge at Vicksburg, July 18	1,225,000
Deduct discharge Yazoo river, July 18	137,000
	1,088,000
Add crevasses, Providence to Vicksburg, July 18 { right bank	37,000
{ left bank	24,000
Approximate discharge at Providence, July 17	1,149,000
Add crevasses, Napoleon to Providence, July 17 { right bank	2,000
{ left bank	8,000
Approximate discharge at Napoleon, July 16	1,159,000
Deduct discharge Arkansas and White rivers, July 16	160,000
	999,000
Add crevasses, Helena to Napoleon, July 16 { right bank	16,000
{ left bank	63,000
Approximate discharge at Helena, July 15	1,078,000

This computation shows that, if the river had been at a stand during the passage of this prism of water, the discharge at Helena on July 15 would have been 1,078,000 cubic feet per second. By reference to the gauge-records at Helena, Napoleon, Providence and Vicksburg, however, it is seen that the river was falling during this period, and that, consequently, the discharge at Vicksburg was greater than that at Helena by the amount of water draining out of the channel between Helena and Vicksburg. The amount per second of this supply must, therefore, be deducted from 1,078,000, in order to find the true discharge per second at Helena. The gauge-records show that the river fell—

	Feet.
At Helena, July 14 to July 15	0.8
At Napoleon, July 15 to July 16	0.5
At Providence, July 16 to July 17	0.7
At Vicksburg, July 17 to July 18	0.0

Since the river fell 0.8 of a foot while the water-prism was passing Helena, and 0.5 of a foot while it was passing Napoleon, it fell $\frac{0.8 + 0.5}{2} = 0.65$ of a foot while passing through the channel between those two places. In like manner, the river fell 0.60 of a foot in passing between Napoleon and Providence, and 0.35 of a foot in passing between Providence and Vicksburg. Since these places are nearly equidistant, the entire amount of water which was added to the discharge at Vicksburg on July 18 by the draining of water from the channel between Helena and Vicksburg, can be obtained by multiplying the area of water surface between those places in square feet ($304 \times 5280 \times 4300$) by $\frac{0.65 + 0.60 + 0.35}{3}$, which gives 3,681,100,000 cubic feet. Dividing this amount by 86,400 (the number of seconds in 24 hours), we have 43,000 cubic feet for the amount thus added per second. Subtracting this amount from 1,078,000, we have 1,035,000 cubic feet for the required discharge per second at Helena on July 15.

Simpler method of computation.

In practical application, this process can be somewhat simplified by stating it in the form of an equation, and reducing the numerical coefficients. Thus, in the example just given, the process is represented by the following expression:—

$$\text{Channel correction} = \frac{304 \times 5280 \times 4300}{86,400} \times \frac{1}{6} \left\{ \begin{array}{ll} \text{Rise at Helena} \ldots\ldots & \text{July 14–15} \\ + \text{Twice rise at Napoleon} \ldots\ldots & \text{July 15–16} \\ + \text{Twice rise at Providence} \ldots\ldots & \text{July 16–17} \\ + \text{Rise at Vicksburg} \ldots\ldots & \text{July 17–18} \end{array} \right\}$$

By reduction the coefficient becomes, say 13,000. The method of computing the daily discharge at Helena, during a flood stage of the river, may then be indicated by the following expression:—

$$\left.\begin{array}{l}\text{Discharge per second} \\ \text{at Helena, July 15}\end{array}\right\} = \left\{ \begin{array}{ll} \text{Discharge per second at Vicksburg} \ldots\ldots & \text{July 18} \\ - \text{Discharge per second of Yazoo river} \ldots\ldots & \text{July 18} \\ + \text{Discharge per second of crevasses, Providence to Vicksburg} \ldots\ldots & \text{July 18} \\ + \text{Discharge per second of crevasses, Napoleon to Providence} \ldots\ldots & \text{July 17} \\ - \text{Discharge per second of Arkansas and White rivers} \ldots\ldots & \text{July 16} \\ + \text{Discharge per second of crevasses, Helena to Napoleon} \ldots\ldots & \text{July 16} \\ + 13,000 \left\{ \begin{array}{ll} \text{Rise at Helena} \ldots\ldots & \text{July 14–15} \\ + \text{Twice rise at Napoleon} \ldots\ldots & \text{July 15–16} \\ + \text{Twice rise at Providence} \ldots\ldots & \text{July 16–17} \\ + \text{Rise at Vicksburg} \ldots\ldots & \text{July 17–18} \end{array} \right\} & \end{array} \right\}$$

This method of computation has been applied, without exception, to all cases where local discharges have been determined from those measured at the velocity-bases. It is evidently a strictly mathematical process, allowing no latitude in its application.

Concluding remarks.

No further explanation is believed to be necessary to give an exact idea of the manner of determining all the discharges of the Mississippi river and of its tributaries, which enter into the discussions of this report. It may seem that an unnecessary degree of detail has been attempted, but, since practical conclusions of great importance are based upon these numbers, it is essential to demonstrate fully that they are worthy of confidence.

FIELD OPERATIONS UPON CREVASSES.—RESULTING FORMULÆ, ETC.

General phenomena attendant upon the flow of water through crevasses.

The requirements of the Survey made it imperative to undertake the measurement of the discharge of water through crevasses, or breaks in the levees, at seasons of high water, although the operation is so exceedingly difficult that it has rarely, if ever, been heretofore attempted. Several careful observations upon crevasses were accordingly made during the progress of the field work, and the results, although necessarily less accurate than the gaugings of the river itself or of its tributaries, yet seem, so far as they can be tested, to be worthy of confidence.

Before proceeding to detail these observations, a few preliminary remarks upon the general phenomena attendant upon the flow of water through crevasses may not be out of place. It is true of every crevasse, great or small, that its effect upon the currents of the river extends only a short distance from the bank. This was the case even with the Bell crevasse, when, on May 13, 1858, it was 327 feet in width, and, probably, about 15 feet deep along the line of levee. Even with these dimensions, no sensible influence was produced upon the line of motion of floating bodies passing at about 200 feet from the edge of the natural bank (or 300 feet from the break in the levee). The day was calm, and no known anomalous influence existed. Between the crevasse and this outer limit of its influence, there is always a movement of water toward the break from all points—below as well as above. This movement gradually increases in velocity until it passes the break and reaches the level of the ground in rear of the levee, when it rapidly diminishes; the water spreading in all directions, but mostly flowing toward the swamps. There is a sensible slope from the outer line of crevasse influence to the line of levee, where there is oftentimes a kind of cascade. In passing the break, whether by a cascade or not, the water is higher in the middle of the opening than at either side. These conditions are evident to the eye in large crevasses, unless, as may happen, the wind or a peculiar situation of the break with respect to the current of the river modifies the flow of the water. It may, therefore, be inferred that they exist in small crevasses also.

Difficulty of gauging a crevasse.

The difficulty of measuring the discharge of a crevasse can now be appreciated. The rush of the torrent through a break generally renders the use of a boat impracticable. The area of cross-section is constantly enlarged by the caving of the levee and washing of the natural bank, and can rarely be accurately determined. The swelling already mentioned, due to the excessive velocity in the middle of the break, besides drawing the floats from the sides to a narrow path near the thread of the current, prevents any very accurate measurement of the slope of the water surface. The constant change in velocity, from the outer line of crevasse influence to the point of spreading out over the ground back of the levee, renders the method of gauging by floats objectionable, but the almost irresistible force of the current and the great slope of the water surface make any other plan impracticable. From these considerations it is evident that strict accuracy cannot be expected; but the close agreement of several experiments, conducted by different individuals upon varied plans at different crevasses, induces the belief that a knowledge of the laws of discharge has been attained.

Rough measurements of velocity.

Observations upon the velocity of crevasses detailed and discussed.—On several occasions, the velocity of the thread of the current of different crevasses was roughly measured by timing floats past base-lines of different lengths, extending from the levee toward the swamp. The following table exhibits these results:—

Crevasse.	Date.	Length of base-line.	Observed central surface velocity.	Depth on line of levee. (Approximate.)	Width.	Party of—
		Feet.	*Feet per sec.*	*Feet.*	*Feet.*	
Doyal	April 24, 1851.	160	7	3	220	Mr. G. C. Smith.
Gardanne	March 22, 1851.	200	7	6	90	Prof. C. G. Forshey.
Gardanne	March 29, 1851.	200	8	6	130	Prof. C. G. Forshey.
Millandon	April 19, 1851.	250	8	3.5	100	Prof. C. G. Forshey.
Hesperia	May 22, 1858.	20	8	10 (?)	135	Mr. H. A. Pattison.
La Branche	June 2, 1858.	104	10	7	307	Mr. W. H. Williams.

In each of these cases, except at the Hesperia crevasse, the base-line was so long that the water must have undergone many and great changes of velocity, rendering it impossible to deduce from the observations that velocity with which it passed the line of levee—the only line upon which the area of cross-section of the stream can be determined even approximately. Moreover, the relation between the slope and the generated velocity not being noted, these observations cannot be used in deducing a general rule for discharge; nevertheless, they are of value because they show how much the popular idea respecting the velocity of crevasses is exaggerated.

Detailed measurements.

In addition to the above, three sets of observations were made with all possible exactness and with great care to obviate causes of error and arrive at practically useful results. They will be noticed in turn.

Fausse Rivière crevasse.

Observations upon the crevasse at *Fausse Rivière* were made by Mr. G. C. Smith's party, on March 28, 1851. This crevasse occurred where the levee was about 6 feet in height, with the water about 4.5 feet against it on March 28. The water, after rushing through a break 700 feet in width, passed into Fausse Rivière, and, being restrained by the banks, flowed for a time in the old bed. The measurement for discharge was made in this channel, where the stream had apparently attained a nearly uniform velocity, the surface being 3.2 feet below the river surface. The area of cross-section was 3420 square feet; the maximum central surface velocity, 6.5 feet. The ratio between the maximum surface velocity and the true mean velocity of a stream of about those dimensions may be assumed at 0.85, as will be hereafter seen. Hence the discharge per second of this crevasse was $3420 \times 6.5 \times 0.85 = 18{,}900$ cubic feet. By the usual formula for discharge through weirs, with Castel's coefficient for reduction in the case of a canal through a dike,* we have the discharge equal to $0.527 \times 5.348 \times 700 \times (4.5)^{\frac{3}{2}} = 18{,}830$ cubic feet. This coefficient (0.527) was deduced by Castel with great care from experiments upon a weir about 0.7 of a foot wide, with a canal 0.7 of a foot long, whose slope was 10 upon 133, and with a head varying from 0.16 to 0.36 of a foot. The closeness of the agreement of this formula with the observation is certainly satisfactory.

Gardanne crevasse.

Observations upon the *Gardanne crevasse* were made by Prof. Forshey's party, on April 19, 1851. The crevasse was 350 feet in width, the levee being 7 feet high, with the water about 5 feet against it on April 19. A pile-driving boat, about 80 feet in length, was moored in the crevasse, and the measurements were made from it. The velocity of the water in passing its entire length was 8 feet per second. Where it passed the line of levee, falling 2.5 feet in 10 feet, the velocity acquired at the latter part of this distance was 15 feet. The floats passed in the line of maximum velocity. Adopting the above ratio, the mean velocity is $15 \times 0.85 = 12.75$ feet. Hence the discharge is equal to $12.75 \times 350 \times (5 - 2.5) = 11{,}156$ cubic feet. The discharge determined by the weir formula with Castel's dike coefficient is equal to $0.527 \times 5.348 \times 350 \times 5^{\frac{3}{2}} = 11{,}025$ cubic feet—again in close accordance with the observations.

---

* $Q = 0.527\ (5.348\ W H^{\frac{3}{2}})$; in which Q = discharge, W = width of the weir, and H = the head of the lower edge of the weir.

Bell crevasse. Its depth.

Observations upon the *Bell crevasse* were made by Lieutenant Abbot, assisted by Mr. W. H. Williams, on May 13, 1858, the crevasse being 237 feet in width. The levee was generally about 7 feet high in the vicinity, but at the crevasse it varied greatly, being, at some places, 2 feet above the water surface, and, at others, so low that a row of gunny bags filled with earth, upon the top, was necessary to prevent the water from flowing over. This crevasse differed from the others upon which measurements were taken, by the water's having rapidly excavated a channel below the natural surface of the ground. The actual mean depth, on May 13, cannot be absolutely ascertained, but an approximation to it may be made by two distinct processes. Mr. G. W. R. Bayley, when attempting to close it, found a depth of 22 feet at the lower end, near the spot where he was driving piles on May 4. The water stood about 6 feet deep on the natural bank (see the Carrollton gauge), showing a local excavation at that time of 16 feet. A detailed survey of the site was made at low water (see figure 5, plate III), and an excavation of 40 feet found in the same hole, although the mean excavation in the part of the crevasse open on May 4 was only 25 feet. Hence, assuming the mean depths to be proportional to the depths in this hole, we have 40 : 16 : : 25 : 8, giving 8 feet for the mean excavation across the whole crevasse on May 4. The second process of approximation is as follows: At low water the width of the crevasse was 731 feet, an increase of 400 feet having been made at the lower end of the break since May 13. On this 400 feet a mean depth of 15 feet below the natural surface had been excavated by the water. Assuming the rate of excavation to be uniform, it is evident that the abrasion made previous to May 13 over the space of 327 feet must have subsequently increased 15 feet in depth. But, as already stated, the mean depth of excavation found at low water on this 237 feet of the crevasse was 25 feet. Hence the mean excavation of the crevasse on the line of levee on May 13 was 25 — 15 = 10 feet. These two independent computations agree so well, giving 8 feet for the mean depth of excavation on May 4, and 10 feet on May 13, that no material error need be apprehended in adopting the latter for the true mean depth excavated on the line of levee on May 13. On the natural bank, outside the levee, the abrasion was much less. By the survey at low water a mean excavation of only 14 feet was found on this line in front of the break made previous to May 13, while on the line of levee, as already stated, a mean depth of 25 feet had been excavated. Hence, allowing the rate of excavation on these two lines to be proportional, we have 25 : 10 : : 14 : 5.6, giving 5.6 feet for the depth excavated on the natural bank in front of the levee on May 13. Adding 5 feet for depth of water above natural surface, we have 10.6 feet for the mean depth of water on this line, and 15 feet for that on the line of levee on May 13.

Its velocity.

The excavation, although with a much less mean depth, extended some hundreds of feet back from the levee. Consequently, it modified the ordinary condition found at crevasses, where there is usually a well defined and sudden fall in water surface at the line of levee. The current moved smoothly from the outer edge of the crevasse influence with a rapidly accelerated velocity through the break, and for perhaps 100 feet beyond, when it broke into violent boils, undoubtedly due to the irregularities of the bottom, and then spread outward in all directions. The land was of course flooded, but a small spot remained uncovered, 66 feet back from the levee at the upper end of the crevasse. One instrument was placed on this island, and the other on the levee, and the time of floats in passing the distance between them noted. A mean of thirteen surface floats, tolerably well distributed across the crevasse, gave a mean velocity of 10 feet per second for the current from the line of levee back 66 feet. Mr. Bayley, while driving piles to close the crevasse on May 1, found exactly the same velocity by noting the transit of two or three floats past his boat, which was 60 feet in length.

The measurements of May 13 will be discussed with a view to deducing the discharge of the crevasse on that date. As already stated, the velocity of the current, in passing from the line of levee rearward 66 feet, was found to be 10 feet per second. As during the whole period of this transit it was apparently undergoing a uniform acceleration, this velocity may be assumed as that of the current at a point 33 feet back from the line of levee.

The water surface at the lower velocity-station was found by careful levelling to be 3.2 feet below that of the river outside the crevasse influence; assuming the nearly stationary water surface 200 feet above the crevasse to be uninfluenced by the break. As already remarked, the water surface in the middle of the torrent rushing through the crevasse was considerably above that at the edges, estimated on the spot at half a foot. Hence, assuming for reference a horizontal datum-plane passing through the water surface at the lower velocity-station, the height of the water surface where the floats passed, near the middle of the crevasse, 66 feet back from the levee, would be + 0.5, and that of the river surface + 3.2 feet. At the middle of the torrent, opposite the upper velocity-station, the depression of the surface below that of the river was estimated as closely as possible, by sighting through the level, at from 0.5 to 1 foot. Assuming it at 0.7 of a foot, the reference of this point above the datum-plane is $3.2 - 0.7 = 2.5$ feet. Considering the slope uniform between the two velocity-stations, the reference above the datum-plane of the point midway between them, where the velocity was 10 feet per second, is, then, $\frac{0.5 + 2.5}{2} = 1.5$ feet. But at the outer edge of crevasse influence, the crevasse velocity was zero, since the direction of the river current was parallel to the break in the levee. Therefore a fall of $3.2 - 1.5 = 1.7$ feet generated a velocity of 10 feet per second. But the general expression for the discharge on the line of levee is WDv, in which W is the width of the break, D its depth (which may be estimated with sufficient accuracy from the plane of the river surface), and v the mean velocity on the line of levee. The width of the current, 33 feet in rear of the levee, may be assumed to be the same as that at the break; the depth, considering the ground horizontal between the two lines, is $D - 1.7$; the velocity 10 feet. The discharge on this line, 33 feet in rear of the levee, is, therefore, $W \times (D - 1.7) \times 10$. Since the discharge on the two lines is equal, the equation results—

$$WDv = W \times (D - 1.7) \times 10.$$

By simple algebraic reduction, the following value for the velocity on the line of levee can be deduced :—

$$(13) \qquad v = 10 - \frac{17}{D}.$$

The next question which presents itself is important. Did the deep hole excavated on the line of levee increase the discharge of the Bell crevasse over what it would have been, had the depth there been the same as on the

Effect upon the discharge ex-

erted by holes in the bed of a crevasse.

natural bank between the levee and the river? In other words, is D equal to 15 or 10.6 in the above expression and in the expression for the area of cross-section WD? It is thought that it can be conclusively shown that the deep hole *did not increase*, but rather tended to *diminish* the discharge, and consequently that D cannot be greater than 10.6 in these expressions. In support of this opinion, it is claimed to be a well-established principle of hydraulics, that a limited hole in the bed of any stream, even if large enough to increase materially the local area of cross-section, has no accelerating, but rather a retarding effect upon the velocity of the current. This is probably due to the vertical eddies and boils which it occasions; but whether this be the true solution or not, the *fact* can hardly be disputed since the publication of Venturi's well-known experiments. To test the matter, he caused water to flow from a reservoir through a pipe whose diameter was alternately enlarged and then contracted to its original dimensions. These enlargements uniformly *lessened the discharge.* A pipe, 36 inches long and 9 lines in diameter, *discharged nearly double the amount of a pipe of the same dimensions, but enlarged in five places to a diameter of* 24 *lines.*

Although these experiments are very valuable for establishing the general principle in question, they are not necessary to prove that, for this particular case, the hole on the line of levee should not be allowed to increase the value of D in the formula. This can be proved by simple computation from the data just given. The area of cross-section on the line of levee, as already seen, was $327 \times 15 = 4905$ square feet. But the area of cross-section on the line *a*, *b*, *c*, *d* (figure 5, plate III), was equal to $10.6 (142 + 127 + 142) = 4357$ square feet, or 548 square feet smaller. The discharge on these two lines was of course equal. It follows, therefore, that the velocity on the line *a b*, *c*, *d* must have been greater than that on the line of levee. But this is manifestly absurd, since, both according to observation and to the general laws governing the flow of all crevasses, the rate of movement of the water underwent a constant acceleration between these lines and even for some distance after passing the levee. The absurdity arises from using too large a value for D, and the conclusion to be drawn from it is in perfect accordance with Venturi's experiments.

Discharge of the Bell crevasse when gauged on May 13.

With the depth on the natural bank in front of the crevasse, the discharge on May 13 becomes $327 \times 10.6 \times (10 - \frac{17}{10.6}) = 29{,}100$ cubic feet per second. The same values in the weir formula with Castel's coefficient make the discharge $0.527 \left(5.348 \times 327 \times (10.6)^{\frac{3}{2}}\right) = 31{,}806$ cubic feet. The near accordance of these two values leads to the belief that 30,000 cubic feet per second, although probably somewhat excessive, is as close an approximation to the discharge of the Bell crevasse on May 13 as can be made. It will be noticed that it is nearly three times the maximum discharge of bayou La Fourche, and five-sixths of the maximum discharge of bayou Plaquemine!

This concludes the discussion of all the observations made upon crevasses, but there are to be derived from them some general practical rules for computing the discharge, when, as was generally the case, no direct observations were made. Expressions for the velocity and the dimensions of cross-section are necessary. The former will be first considered.

Formulæ for velocity of crevasses.—The preceding tests of the weir formula with Castel's dike coefficient go far to establish its applicability to crevasses. Dividing both members by WD, the following expression for the mean velocity results:—

General rule for velocity of crevasses.

$$v = 0.527 \times 5.348\ D^{1/2} = 2.818\ D^{1/2}.$$

Before adopting this formula, however, it is well to examine the general expression already deduced for the mean velocity of the Bell crevasse, viz.:—

$$(13) \qquad v = 10 - \frac{17}{D}.$$

From the manner in which it was deduced, it ought, if the discharge of this crevasse was governed by the usual laws, to apply to all crevasses of similar depth, although from its form, it evidently cannot be used when D is less than 3 or 4 feet, since v becomes zero when D = 1.7. To test its general applicability to deep crevasses, it will be applied to the observations on those of Fausse Rivière and Gardanne. For the former it gives—

$$Q = 700 \times 4.5 \left(10 - \frac{17}{4.5}\right) = 19{,}530.$$

For the Gardanne crevasse, it gives—

$$Q = 350 \times 5 \left(10 - \frac{17}{5}\right) = 11{,}550.$$

The following table exhibits a comparison of these results with the measured discharges and with those given by the weir formula with Castel's dike coefficient:—

Crevasse.	Discharge per second in cubic feet.				
	Measured.	By weir formula.	Error.	By new formula.	Error.
Fausse Rivière	18,900	18,830	+ 70	19,530	—630
Gardanne	11,156	11,025	+131	11,550	—394

It is evident that both formulæ give nearly the same discharges, but as the new formula errs on the safe side for these two observations, while the weir formula probably gives a little too small results, and, as the new formula, being especially deduced from observations on a large crevasse, may be supposed to accord more nearly with this particular class, it has been adopted for depths greater than 3 feet. For depths less than 4 feet, the weir formula with Castel's coefficient is used. The following table exhibits the velocities computed by the two formulæ in the manner just explained:—

Scale of velocity for crevasses.

Values of D. in feet	1.0	2.0	3.0	4.0	5.0	6.0	7.0	8.0	9.0
Values of v in feet	2.8	4.0	4.9	5.8	6.6	7.2	7.6	7.9	8.1

This table has been uniformly employed in computing the discharge of crevasses. The manner of determining the value of D will next be explained.

Depth of crevasses.—In most crevasses, no excavation of importance is made, the

General rule for depth of crevasses.

depth varying with the rising or falling of the river. From the high-water depth on the line of levee, found by measurement after the river had fallen; from numerous river gauges observed daily at different points; and oftentimes from full local information from reliable sources, the daily depth of each crevasse, both in 1851 and in 1858, has been estimated with much certainty.

For the rare and particular case of excavating crevasses, it has been laid down as an invariable rule that the *mean depth of the water flowing over the natural bank* must be used for D, and that the *rate of excavation is proportional to the duration of the flowing of the crevasse.*

Test of the exactness of the method adopted for computing the discharge of crevasses, the width being known.

As an illustration of the exactness of this method of computation, even in extreme cases, the following check upon the accuracy of the computed discharge of the Bell and La Branche crevasses is given. The area of the basin into which they flowed was say $20 \times 50 = 1000$ square miles. By records furnished through the courtesy of the officers of the Opelousas railroad company, it appears that the depth of water in this basin continued to increase until July 29 when it came to a stand; and that on September 14 the flow of the crevasse ceased, the water in the basin having fallen 7.4 feet. These facts establish that on July 29 the discharge of the crevasse became equal to the amount which was draining from the basin into the gulf; and also that in the forty-eight days subsequent to that date, a volume of water 1000 square miles in area by 7.4 feet deep, plus the total amount received from the crevasses in those days, drained into the gulf. The character of the outlets through which this water drained renders it fair to assume that the discharge from the basin on July 29 was sensibly equal to the mean discharge from it in the forty-eight days under consideration. But the latter quantity was $\frac{(5280)^2 \times 1000 \times 7.4}{60 \times 60 \times 24 \times 48} =$ say 50,000 cubic feet per second, increased by the mean discharge per second of the crevasses. The latter quantity (see Chapter VI) was 107,000 cubic feet per second. Hence the approximate mean discharge from the basin in the forty-eight days—or its equivalent, the discharge of the two crevasses on July 29—was $50,000 + 107,000 = 157,000$ cubic feet per second. By the formula it was 144,000 cubic feet per second, giving a difference of only 13,000 cubic feet, which may be accounted for by rain-water draining from the basin. This accordance leaves no doubt as to the exactness of the computations.

General rule for determining the width of crevasses.

Width of crevasses.—The rate at which a crevasse increases in width depends upon so many fortuitous circumstances, that it is, in the nature of the case, impossible to frame any rule of universal application. Still, as some approximation to this constantly varying quantity must be attempted in computing the daily amount of water taken from the river by the different crevasses, the subject has received attention. The following list exhibits the only known series of accurately determined widths of the same crevasse at different dates. Although much shorter than could be desired, it will be seen that it includes both great and small crevasses.

Crevasse.	Date of breaking.	Width.		Width.		Width.		Width.	
		Date.	Feet.	Date.	Feet.	Date.	Feet.	Date.	Feet.
Gardanne......	March 18, '51	March 22	90	March 29	130	April 19	350		
La Branche...	May 3, '58	May 9	75	May 13	130	June 3	307	About Aug. 27	1050
Bell.............	April 11, '58	April 17	125	April 20	175	May 13	327	About Aug. 29	731
Bonnet Carré..	April 19, '59	April 20	150	June 1	2700	June 23	3700	July 27	4000

When these measurements are plotted in the form of curves, several curious results are apparent. First, the rate of increase of the Gardanne, La Branche, and Bell crevasses is nearly the same, although the two latter, especially the Bell crevasse, excavated deep holes, while the Gardanne crevasse abraded the surface but little. Second, the Bonnet Carré crevasse of 1859 increased in width seven or eight times as rapidly as the others, a result probably due to the fact that the soil of which the levee was made contained much sand. Third, the law of increase in width which might be anticipated is apparent in all the crevasses. It is that, when the break is first made, it increases rapidly until a considerable width, say about 100 feet, is attained. Afterward the width increases at a uniform but slower rate, until the river has fallen considerably below high-water mark. Doubtless, if the river were to fall very gradually, the caving of the levee would partially cease before the water returned to its banks, but it almost always happens that, after the first two or three feet of fall, which do not seem to affect the caving much, the river subsides very rapidly.

The last-named result of the study of these observations is important, as it affords a rule for approximating to the width of a crevasse whose date of breaking and maximum width are known, facts which can generally be ascertained. For simplicity of statement, the rule may be put in the form of an equation whose second member shall consist of two terms; the first being the width of the crevasse for each of the first five days of flow (assumed uniformly at 100 feet), and the second the product of the number of subsequent days by the mean rate of increase after that time. This equation is—

$$W = 100 + (n - 4)\left(\frac{W_{,} - 100}{N - 5}\right), \qquad (14)$$

in which W represents the width on any desired day; $W_{,}$, the width after the water has ceased to flow; n, the number of days of discharge which have preceded the given day; and N, the total number of days of discharge. When n is less than 4, the width is uniformly assumed at 100 feet, as a sufficiently close approximation.

Synopsis of manner of computing crevasse discharges.—To prevent all ambiguity, a brief synopsis of the manner of computing the discharge of a crevasse for a given day will be presented. Knowing, from the measurements made after the cessation of the flow, the high-water depth of the given crevasse,—estimated on the line of levee, if no material excavation was made there, and on the batture in front of the levee, if holes were dug on the line of the break,—the depth on the given day was found by subtracting for this high-water depth the stand of the river below high-water mark, a quantity which was always known either from local information or from a comparison of the nearest river-gauges. Entering the table on page 275 with this depth, the velocity of the crevasse

Recapitulation of general method of computing crevasse discharges.

was found. Knowing the date of breaking, and of ceasing to flow, from exact information, and the maximum width from measurement, the width on the day in question was computed by the expression just given. The product of this width by the depth multiplied into the velocity gives the required discharge per second. The whole operation can be represented by a formula,—equation (15) being used if D exceeds 3 feet, and equation (16), if it is less than 4 feet.

$$(15) \qquad Q = \left(100 + (n - 4)\left(\frac{W_{,} - 100}{N - 5}\right)\right) D \left(10 - \frac{17}{D}\right).$$

$$(16) \qquad Q = \left(100 + (n - 4)\left(\frac{W_{,} - 100}{N - 5}\right)\right) D \left(2.818\, D^{\frac{1}{2}}\right).$$

This process was applied to all the crevasses below the mouth of Red river, whose discharges are estimated in this report. In discussing the flood of 1858 in the great region above the mouth of Red river, as yet comparatively uncultivated, a coefficient of correction was evidently required, since the conditions governing the flow of the water where these formulæ were deduced were materially modified in that region. In many cases, the levee was so far distant from the river that the depth at the edge of the natural bank was much less than that at the base of the levee, a cause which diminished the actual discharge, although not allowed for by the formula. Oftentimes, trees, a dense growth of saplings, or other obstacles to the free flow of the water, existed in front or in rear of the break, and greatly reduced the discharge. The reported depth of the crevasses generally included whatever excavation existed on the line of levee, and thus both the velocity and the area of cross-section were unduly increased. Add to these sources of error the natural exaggeration which must exist in much of the information upon which the calculations are based, and we are prepared to find a much too large result for the discharge of the crevasses in this part of the Mississippi valley. The next point to be considered, then, is a method for deducing a practical coefficient of correction for general applications of the formula to crevasses in this upper part of the river.

Exception to the general rule.

Coefficient of correction for exceptional case of crevasses.—The daily measurements of the discharge of the river and its main tributaries, the tolerably exact information relative to all the crevasses which discharged into the Yazoo bottom, the determination of the amount of water actually in this swamp at the date of high water in 1858, and the Smithsonian records of rain-gauges, received from Professor Henry, render it possible to determine this coefficient with considerable accuracy.

Outline of process for determining a practical coefficient of correction for this exceptional case.

It has been seen that the area of the Yazoo bottom liable to be submerged is 6800 square miles; that, on December 1, 1857, this area was dry; that, at high water in 1858 (July 15), this area was submerged to a mean depth of 3.08 feet, and consequently, that this reservoir received between those dates $6800 \times (5280)^2 \times 3.08 = 583,885,209,600$ cubic feet of water more than was discharged by the channel of Yazoo river, its sole outlet. The total discharge of this outlet, from December 1 to July 14 inclusive, was —by the measurements of this Survey—1,408,665,600,000 cubic feet. Assuming, then, in order to be on the safe side, that all the water in the swamp on July 15 eventually found its way into the Mississippi, we have $583,885,209,600 + 1,408,665,600,000 = 1,992,550,809,600$ cubic feet for the total volume of water which, entering the Yazoo basin between the dates considered, eventually passed through it to the gulf. But water enters this reservoir only by direct fall of rain upon the bottom lands and upon the bounding water-shed, and through the Mississippi crevasses. If, then, it be possible to determine what amount of rain, falling in the hydrographic basin of Yazoo river in the period considered, eventually drained off into the Mississippi river, it is evident that the total discharge of the crevasses into the bottom, up to the date of high water there, may be determined, and the results given by the crevasse formula thus be checked and corrected, by subtracting the amount of this rain-water from 1,992,550,809,600. The operations of the Survey render this computation possible.

Fall of rain in Yazoo basin in period considered.

The first step in the process is to determine the total fall of rain in the hydrographic basin of Yazoo river between December 1, 1857, and July 15, 1858. This quantity is equal to the product of the area of the basin by the depth of downfall in it. The area of the basin (see page 82) is 13,850 square miles. The depth of downfall during the time considered is found by taking a mean between the quantity of rain at Memphis and that at Jackson, where accurate observations were made by Dr. Mitchell and Mr. Hatch respectively, the former observing for the Smithsonian Institution, and the latter as an amateur. The quantity at the two places was 3.19 feet and 4.08 feet respectively, giving for the required mean downfall in the basin of the Yazoo river, which lies between those two places, 3.64 feet. The total fall of rain in this basin is, then, $13,850 \times (5280)^2 \times 3.64 = 1,405,461,657,600$ cubic feet.

Ratio between rain and drainage in Yazoo basin. General views upon the subject.

The next point for consideration is what proportion of this eventually drains off into the Mississippi river. This question of the ratio between downfall and drainage, which has already been treated in a general manner in Chapter II, has been much discussed by engineers charged with constructing various civil works, such as canals, reservoirs for water-works, etc.; and many direct observations and measurements have been made to solve the problem. It has been satisfactorily shown that the ratio is very variable, depending upon the local conditions which govern the amount of evaporation and infiltration. The following table exhibits the results of many measurements, and establishes the fact that, in certain localities, by far the greater part of the rain-water passes away in the channels of the draining streams. It has been mainly taken from a pamphlet by Mr. Morris upon the improvement of the Ohio river, but is slightly corrected in a few instances by reference to the English authorities.

Ratio between downfall and drainage.

Locality.	Character of basin.	Drainage area.	Annual downfall.	Annual drainage.	Ratio of downfall and drainage.	Authority.
		Sq. miles.	*Inches.*	*Inches.*		
Bann reservoirs	Moorland.	5.15	72	48	0.67	Beardmore and Hughes.
Greenock	Flat moor.	7.88	60	41	0.68	" " "
Bute	Low country.	7.80	45	24	0.53	" " "
Belmont, 1843	Moorland.	2 81	63	51	0.81	" " "
", 1844	"	2.81	50	33	0.66	" " "
" 1845	"	2 81	55	41	0.75	" " "
" 1846	"	2.81	50	33	0.66	" " "
Rivington pike	"	16.25	55	24	0.44	" " "
" "	"	16.25	64	40	0.63	Hughes.
		3.18	46	41	0.89	" } (Turton and
		3.18	48	39	0.81	" } Entwistle).
Ashton		0.59	40	16	0.40	"
Paisley water-works			54	36	0.67	Stirratt.
Glasgow "			50	30	0.60	C. E. and A. Journal.
Greenock			65	42	0.65	Stirratt.
Peak Forest Summit			33	24	0.73	Homersham.
Longendale			60	40	0.67	Bateman.
Schuylkill Nav. Res.			36	18	0.50	Morris and Smith.
Eaton brook			34	23	0.68	McAlpine.
Madison brook			35	18	0.51	"
Patroon's creek			46	25	0.53	"
" "			42	18	0.43	"
Long Pond			40	18	0.45	Boston Water Commissioners.
West Fork Res.			36	14	0.39	Roberts.
Entire Mississippi valley	See Chapter I.	1,244,000.00	30 +	8 —	0.25	Mississippi Delta Survey.
Ohio and Upper Miss. valleys	"	383,000.00	39 —	8 —	0.24	" " "
Mo., Ark., and White-riv. val's.	"	707,000.00	23 +	3 —	0.15	" " "
Red-river valley	"	97,000.00	39 +	8 +	0.20	" " "

From this table it appears that, when the basin is well protected against evaporation and infiltration, some 0.8 or 0.9 of the total downfall *may be* carried off by its streams. It would be difficult to find a region better guarded against these causes of loss than the Yazoo basin. The hilly border of the swamp lands is narrow, and abrupt in slope. The rain which falls upon the steep clayey hill-sides runs rapidly to the channels of the streams, and is by them discharged into the great swamp reservoir, and thus added to the volume resulting from direct downfall there. This swamp region is a flat country, underlain by an impervious clay stratum, and shaded from the evaporating influence of the sun's rays by dense foliage. The water is in a *cistern*, and can only escape by the channels of the draining bayous into the Yazoo river, and by that into the Mississippi.

Especial computation of the ratio between rain and drainage in the alluvial region of the Mississippi. Outline of the process.

Guided by the preceding table of published observations, we may therefore assume that some 0.8 or 0.9 of the total downfall in this region eventually reaches the Mississippi. This assumption is not, however, necessary. The observations of the Survey enable us to *measure* the mean ratio for the bottom lands between Vicksburg and Cape Girardeau, including the Yazoo, St. Francis, and Kentucky and Tennessee bottoms, which are all similar in character, and which doubtless have sensibly the same ratio. The process by which this common ratio may be computed is as follows:—

In the low stage of the Mississippi river, the great swamp lands between Cape Girardeau and Vicksburg are dry; that is, the bayous carry off the rain-water and the drainage from the hills as fast as it is received. During floods, however, these regions are submerged by water coming partly from the Mississippi river, partly from the streams draining the surrounding water-sheds, and partly from direct rain. If, therefore, an entire flood, reckoned from one low stage to the following, be considered, the loss of water into the swamps by overflow does not diminish the total discharge of the Mississippi at points below them, since the water which enters the swamp during the flood is drained out again into the Mississippi when the river falls. Hence, if the total quantity of water passing the latitudes of Columbus and of Vicksburg be known for this river year, the difference between them, diminished by the discharge of the Arkansas and White rivers, and corrected for the difference between the quantity of water in the channel of the Mississippi at the end and that at the beginning of the year, will be the true drainage from the basins above named. The quotient of this drainage by the total downfall, as measured by rain-gauges, will be the mean ratio sought.

Before proceeding to reduce this process of reasoning to figures, it will be well to explain that, as the discharge of a few crevasses enters into the numerical value of the ratio sought, the final expression for it must involve, besides known terms, the as-yet-unknown coefficient of correction for the crevasse formula. This causes no difficulty in the process already indicated for deducing the numerical value of this coefficient, since, being the only unknown quantity, it matters not in how many terms it appears in the equation. In order to simplify the *explanation* of the process, however, this algebraic work will be avoided by using the *corrected* crevasse discharges in deducing the numerical value of the downfall and drainage ratio.

Total discharge past latitude of Columbus during the year.

To find the numerical values of the quantities which enter into this ratio is the next step of the process. The water which passed the latitude of Columbus, from December 1, 1857, to November 30, 1858, inclusive, was equal to the discharge measured at Columbus, increased by the water which passed into the St. Francis bottom through the Cape Girardeau inlet, and through the crevasses and gaps between Commerce bluffs and Columbus.

The discharge at Columbus during the river year was, by exact measurement, 19,470,858,278,000 cubic feet.

An accurate survey of the Cape Girardeau inlet was made in November, 1858. The high land which forms the west bank of the Mississippi river is here for the first time interrupted. The gap is about 3 miles in width, and conducts to the upper part of the great St. Francis bottom. At a distance of 2.5 miles from the river bank a macadamized road, raised to an average height of about 4 feet, has been built across the swamp, forming a kind of levee. During the high water of 1858, a portion of the northern part of this road, 10,500 feet in length, was submerged during nineteen days (June 9 to June 27, inclusive). The high-water depth was 3.7 feet, but the mean depth for the whole nineteen days was about 1.2 feet less, or 2.5 feet (see Cairo gauge), giving 26,000 square feet for the mean sectional area of discharge for the whole time. The velocity of the current through this break was estimated by an intelligent gentleman residing in the vicinity at about one-third of the low-water velocity of the Mississippi river in this part of its course. This is equivalent to a velocity of about one foot per second, and is probably excessive, since the dense forest on each side of the road must have greatly retarded the flow of the water, and the narrow branch of the swamp into which it first spread must have soon become choked. To guard against any under-estimate, however, this velocity has been adopted. The total quantity of water which passed through this outlet during the year is then equal to 26,000 × 1 × 86,400 × 19 = 42,681,600,000 cubic feet.

Below this gap, the Commerce bluffs border the river for a few miles. From the point where they terminate to Columbus, the swamps were protected against all but the June* rise by levees or high natural banks. During this rise, water entered the swamps by many small crevasses and by flowing over the tops of the levees. The average high-water depth over the natural bank, where these crevasses occurred, was about 5 feet. The discharge through them began about June 9, and continued for some twenty days. (See Cairo gauge.) From Mr. Smith's reconnoissance, from the observations of Mr. Fillebrown's party and from definite information obtained from well-informed residents, it is concluded that these numerous breaks may be assimilated to a single crevasse, 1000 feet wide on June 9, and 10,500 on June 28, with a daily depth given by the Cairo gauge, and a velocity given by the corrected crevasse formula. This gives a total discharge, during the twenty days, of 70,367,040,000 cubic feet. As this quantity is sufficient to flood the whole New Madrid swamp, into which it entered, to a mean depth of over 3 feet, and as the actual mean depth in this receptacle, including rain-water and the discharge of all the numerous crevasses below Columbus, was estimated by old residents at only about 5 feet, it is believed that this amount cannot differ materially from the truth. At any rate, no error can exist large enough to affect sensibly the final result of the computation.

The total quantity of water which passed the latitude of Columbus from December 1, 1857, to November 30, 1858, inclusive, was, therefore, 19,470,858,278,000 + 42,681,600,000 + 70,367,040,000 = 19,583,906,918,000 cubic feet.

Total discharge past latitude of Vicksburg during the year.

The next step is to ascertain how much passed the latitude of Vicksburg during the year. This quantity is equal to the discharge at Vicksburg, corrected for the difference between the quantity of water in the channel at the beginning and that at the end of the year, plus the amount which escaped through crevasses below Napoleon and flowed through the swamps west of Vicksburg.

The water which passed Columbus during the year from December 1, 1857, to November 30, 1858, inclusive, passed Vicksburg during the year from December 10, 1857, to December 9, 1858, inclusive; since the mean rate of movement at the low stage is about 3 miles per hour, and the distance between these two places is 589 miles. The total discharge at Vicksburg from December 10, 1857, to December 9, 1858, inclusive, is, therefore, what is required by the problem. The exact discharge at Vicksburg from January 1 to February 18, 1858, inclusive, results from the measurements at Natchez; the discharge from February 19 to December 9, 1858, inclusive, from the measurements at Vicksburg. The discharge from December 10 to December 31, 1857, inclusive, was not directly measured; but, since the river was within banks, it can be quite accurately estimated by adding to the measured discharge at Columbus from December 1 to December 22, 1857, inclusive, the contributions it received from the successive tributaries on its way to Vicksburg, and deducting the amount which remained in the channel to produce the rise that took place in this period. The dis-

* A very little water entered at the top of the April rise, through a few small breaks, but it was so small a quantity that it need not be estimated.

charge at Columbus from December 1 to December 22, inclusive, was 1,346,215,680,000 cubic feet. Full information was obtained respecting the state of the tributaries, and all needful measurements were made. The St. Francis and White rivers were backed up, and contributed nothing. The Arkansas added about 95,817,600,000 cubic feet, and the Yazoo about 73,180,800,000 cubic feet. In the 589 miles of river channel between Columbus and Vicksburg, the records of the Survey show a mean rise of about 18 feet in the twenty-two days. The mean width of the river in this distance is 4300 feet. There remained therefore in the channel 589 × 5280 × 4300 × 18 = 240,707,808,000 cubic feet of water. The total discharge for the twenty-two required days at Vicksburg was then 1,346,215,680,000 + 95,817,600,000 + 73,180,800,000 − 240,707,808,000 = 1,274,506,472,000 cubic feet. Hence we have for the total discharge at Vicksburg during the year the following value:—

	Cubic feet.
Discharge December 10–31, 1857, transferred from Columbus	1,274,506,472,000
Discharge January 1 to February 18, 1858, transferred from Natchez	4,465,815,552,000
Discharge February 19 to December 9, 1858, measured at Vicksburg	20,257,698,240,000
Discharge at Vicksburg, December 10, 1857, to December, 9, 1858	25,998,020,264,000

The total quantity of water which escaped through crevasses between Napoleon and Vicksburg on the right bank was 296,092,800,000 cubic feet.

Hence the total quantity of water which passed the latitude of Vicksburg from December 10, 1857, to December 9, 1858, was 25,998,020,264,000 + 296,092,800,000 = 26,294,113,064,000 cubic feet.

Discharge of Arkansas and White rivers during the year.

The total measured discharge of the Arkansas and White rivers, during the year considered, which, for Napoleon, extended from December 7, 1857, to December 6, 1858, inclusive, was 2,935,089,388,800 cubic feet. Of this, 597,456,000,000 cubic feet—the amount which, according to the measurements of the Survey, escaped from the Mississippi river into the White-river swamps—was no part of the real discharge of the Arkansas and White rivers. This real discharge was, therefore, 2,935,089,388,800 − 597,456,000,000 = 2,337,633,388,800 cubic feet.

Channel drainage between beginning and end of the year.

There is yet to be determined the difference in the amount of water in the channel of the river between Columbus and Vicksburg, on the first and last days of the year. The records show that the river was lower at the end of this period than at the beginning by a mean difference of 6.8 feet. The mean width between Columbus and Vicksburg at this low stage is 3300 feet. The water which passed Vicksburg from the draining of the channel was then 589 × 5280 × 3300 × 6.8 = 69,786,604,800 cubic feet.

Rain drainage during the year from the basins considered.

The total drainage for the year from the Yazoo, St. Francis, Tennessee and Kentucky bottom lands, exclusive of the crevasse water, results from the numbers just deduced, by the following process:—

	Cubic feet.
Water passing latitude of Vicksburg	26,294,113,064,000
Water passing latitude of Columbus	19,583,906,918,000
Difference	6,710,206,146,000
Deduct discharge Arkansas and White rivers	2,337,633,388,800
	4,372,572,757,200
Deduct for channel drainage	69,786,604,800
Rain drainage from the basins	4,302,786,152,400

Area of the basins considered.

The next point to determine is the area of the bottom lands in question and of their water-sheds. The extent of the Yazoo basin has been already given. That of the St. Francis basin and of the Tennessee and Kentucky basin, which includes the region lying between Memphis and Cairo, and draining directly into the Mississippi by various small streams, has been computed with great care from the best maps extant, as explained in Chapter I. The determination is believed to be accurate.

	Square miles.
Yazoo bottom	7,110
Yazoo water-shed	6,740
St. Francis bottom	6,900
St. Francis water-shed	3,600
Tennessee and Kentucky bottom lands	750
Tennessee and Kentucky water-shed	9,500
Total	34,600

Mean fall of rain during the year in the basins considered.

The mean fall of rain in this region, during the year considered, must now be determined. With the exception of the record at Jackson, by Mr. Hatch, the only available data are those furnished by the Smithsonian Institution. By these records it appears that the total precipitation from December, 1857, to November, 1858, inclusive, was—

	Feet.
At New Harmony, Indiana	3.92
At West Salem, Illinois	4.02
At St. Louis, Missouri	5.18
Mean downfall at head of region	4.38
At Memphis = downfall at middle of region	4.42
At Jackson = downfall at foot of region	4.99
Mean = mean downfall in region considered	4.60

The total downfall in the basins of the Yazoo and St. Francis rivers and in the Tennessee and Kentucky bottom lands and their water-sheds, during the year considered, was, therefore, $34,600 \times (5280)^2 \times 4.6 = 4,437,126,144,000$ cubic feet.

Deduced ratio between downfall and drainage in the alluvial region of the Mississippi.

For the desired ratio between the downfall and drainage, we have, therefore, $\frac{4,302,786,152,400}{4,437,126,144,000} =$ say 0.96. This value fully confirms the inference drawn from the preceding table of published results. From the vast extent of the region considered, and from the grand scale on which the observations were conducted, absolute exactness of determination can hardly be claimed; but the result, that nearly the whole of the great downfall in the basins below the mouth of the Ohio eventually passes into the Mississippi, cannot be questioned. The practical importance of this new proposition will be discussed elsewhere. Here it is a subordinate matter.

Deduced value of practical coefficient for exceptional case in applying crevasse formulæ.

The value for this ratio having been deduced, the computation of the practical coefficient of the crevasse formulæ may be resumed from page 279. The total amount of rain which fell in the basin of the Yazoo river between December 1, 1857, and July 15, 1858, was there shown to be 1,405,461,657,600 cubic feet. Of this amount, ninety-six hundredths, or 1,349,243,191,300 cubic feet, eventually drained off into the Mississippi. The difference between the latter quantity and

1,992,550,809,600 (the total water which, entering the Yazoo basin between the dates considered, eventually drained off into the Mississippi) is 643,307,618,300 cubic feet. This is the total amount of overflow from the Mississippi river into the Yazoo basin up to July 15, the date of high water in the swamp. This quantity, as computed by the uncorrected crevasse formula, is 1,758,153,600,000 cubic feet. The desired coefficient of correction for the formula is, therefore—

$$\frac{643,307,618,300}{1,758,153,600,000} = \text{say } \frac{1}{3}.$$

This closes the subject. It was shown at the outset, from considerations there adduced, that when the crevasse formula, deduced from observations in the open, cultivated region of lower Louisiana, where all the conditions were accurately ascertained, was applied to the comparatively unsettled country above the mouth of Red river, a very material reduction in the computed discharge would be required. The measurements of the Survey confirmed the inference; for, at the date of highest flood, the crevasse discharge below Helena, as computed by the uncorrected formula, would of itself have consumed the whole Columbus discharge, and drained the Mississippi at Vicksburg. The above close analysis of the measurements has resulted in a coefficient for practical correction. In the discussion of the flood of 1858, in reference to local high-water marks, it will be seen that the measurements reduced by the corrected formula accord perfectly with each other and with the Mississippi observations, and bear the severest tests. This coefficient may therefore be relied upon for the kind of crevasse for which it has been deduced.

CHAPTER V.

EXPERIMENTAL THEORY OF WATER IN MOTION; NEW LAWS, FORMULÆ, ETC.

Laws governing the action of cohesion.—Locus of the maximum velocity in the mean vertical plane.—Ratios heretofore proposed for gauging rivers, of but little practical utility.—Relation between the mean of all vertical curves of velocity and the mean velocity of the river.—The ratio of the mid-depth velocity to the mean velocity in any vertical plane discovered to be a sensibly constant quantity, unaffected by wind.—Practical advantages resulting from this discovery.—List of new formulæ for velocities in vertical planes.—A new formula for the mean velocity of rivers, in terms of the dimensions of cross-section and slope of water surface, deduced upon the supposition of modified uniform motion.—Observations to determine its constants.—Analysis of this new formula.—Formula for the effect of bends in retarding the flow of rivers.—List of all the old formulæ for mean velocity.—Table exhibiting their relative accuracy as compared with the new formula.—Double test of mean-velocity and bend formulæ.—Problem of the effect exerted upon the surface level of a river by increasing the discharge a given amount, solved upon the supposition that the new slope is known.—Discussion of changes in local slope.—Resulting general equations.—Combined test of all the new formulæ for computing the increased height to be apprehended in the floods of the Mississippi, the increase in discharge being known.—Concluding remarks.

The science of river hydraulics to be fully considered.

WHEN, in the last chapter, the subject of change of velocity below the surface was discussed, the especial object of deducing a ratio between the surface and the mean velocities of the entire vertical curve in any given plane was kept steadily in view, and no general use was made of the principles deduced. It is now proposed to consider the subject more fully, and to endeavor by the aid of these new principles to simplify the different methods of gauging rivers. For the signification of the symbols employed, reference should be made to page 200.

APPLICATION OF THE NEW LAWS TO THE GAUGING OF RIVERS BY MEASUREMENT.

Law governing the action of the force of cohesion.

New experimental theory for change of velocity below the surface.—The observations already detailed prove that even in a perfectly calm day there is a strong resistance to the motion of the water at the surface as well as at the bottom, and—as will soon be seen—that it is not wholly or even mainly caused by friction against the air. One important cause of this resistance is believed to be the loss of living force, arising from upward currents or transmitted motion occasioned by irregularities at the bottom. This loss is greater at the surface than near it. The experiment of transmitted motion through a series of ivory balls illustrates this effect. It is likewise illustrated on a large scale by the collision of two trains of cars on a railway, in which case it has been observed that the cars at the head of the train are the most injured and thrown the farthest from the track; those at the end of the train are next in order of injury and disturbance; while those in the middle of the train are but little injured or disturbed. Other causes may and probably do exist, but their investigation has, fortunately, more of scientific interest than practical value. For all general purposes, it may be assumed that there is a resistance at the surface, of the same order or nature as that which exists at the bottom. As the distance from the loci of these two resistances is increased, their effect, propagated by the cohesion of the different particles of water to each other, is diminished. Where these diminished resistances become equal, the current acquires its maximum velocity. Let this point in any vertical plane parallel to the current be considered the vertex of a parabola whose axis is parallel to the water surface, and the velocity at any depth in this plane will be given by the abscissa of the curve, the axis of the curve being considered the axis of X, and the origin of co-ordinates being taken at a distance from the vertex equal to the maximum velocity. The parameter of this curve, or in other words its curvature, varies with a known function of the depth and mean velocity of the river. The depth of the axis varies in direct proportion to the force of the wind, increasing for up-stream, and diminishing for down-stream breezes, but without producing any effect upon the form of the curve. The mean and maximum velocities of the curve are so related to each other that when either, with the depth of the axis, is known, the other and the curve itself may be determined. It may be added, that the difference between the greatest and least velocities is always a very small fraction of the mean of the curve.

Diagrams to illustrate this law.

To illustrate this experimental theory, figures 17 and 18, plate XI, have been prepared. The former represents the mean sub-surface curves at Columbus in calm weather, corresponding to those near the surface shown by figure 19 of the same plate. The change of form due to the combined influence of variations in mean velocity and depth in passing from low to high water, and the relations existing between the velocity measured at a point 5 feet below the surface and the rest of the curve, are both represented by this diagram. Figure 18 illustrates the extreme effect of wind upon the high-water curve at Columbus, when velocity observations were practicable, *i.e.* when the wind was blowing up stream with force 4 and down stream with force 4, respectively. The extreme variation produced in surface velocity is evidently about 0.6 of a foot.

It reveals the difficulties of its own discovery.

The above experimental theory suggests reasons why the problem has heretofore defied all efforts for its solution, and why its study has given rise to such incongruous results. Besides the great difficulty of taking the observations with sufficient nicety to detect the very slight difference of velocity at the different depths, there is a second cause of failure, namely, an almost constant relative change of velocity at the different depths. The axis can rarely be at rest; every varying breeze, however gentle, must affect its delicate adjustment, while the stronger pulsations of a high wind must produce an oscillatory movement even greater than that in the tops of the tallest trees. Different floats, therefore, although they may pass *at the same depths below the surface,* may yet pass at *very different distances from the axis,* and thus measure the velocity at very different points of the curve. This idea may explain in part a phenomenon noticed by the observers, and recorded in the note-books of the Survey as a pulse in the river, owing to which there seemed to be a regular increase and then decrease in the velocity of different floats observed consecutively at the same depth.* But there are other sources of variation in the velocity. The eddies to be found in every reach of the river change their magnitude and position at each instant, and must produce corresponding oscillations in the velocity of the river at any given point. Wind magnifies the pulsations of the eddies, and thus produces a double effect upon the variation in the velocity of the given point. As an instance of the force thus exerted by the wind, it may be mentioned that a southeast storm created an eddy just above Red-river landing, more than half a mile in length, with a width nearly half that of the river, and with an up-stream current exceeding 7 miles per hour.† It is manifest from these considerations, that no certainty of deducing the law experimentally can be had without taking a vast number of exceedingly accurate observations, and even then it seems remarkable that great discrepancies should not remain uneliminated.

It suggests a common cause for the different erroneous theories heretofore promulgated.

This variation of axis may also account for the different forms heretofore assigned to the curve. If the observations be taken when an up-stream wind forces the axis nearly to the mid depth, the observer may well mistake the curve for an ellipse. If a down-stream wind raises the axis above the surface, the curve closely approximates to a right line. If the axis be at the surface, a slightly defective set of observations may cause it to resemble a broken right line; or this accidental circumstance may be assumed to be a general law, and the curve considered to be a parabola or hyperbola whose axis is always at the surface. All these forms have been assigned to the curve by different observers.

Discussion of the locus of the maximum velocity of all vertical curves.

The preceding general remarks apply to the velocity below the surface in any vertical plane in any part of the river cross-section. It is now proposed to consider the grand mean of all such curves. An algebraic expression for the position of the axis of this mean curve has been already deduced and explained, but it will require some further notice here. It is—

$$d_{,} = (0.317 + 0.06\,f)\,r, \qquad (8)$$

in which f is the number denoting the force of the wind, a calm being represented by 0, and a hurricane by 10. Its essential sign is negative for a down-stream, and positive for an up-stream wind. It is evident from the formula, that a hurricane will depress the axis to a position only one-tenth of the depth above the bottom, if blowing up stream, and raise it to a position three-tenths of the depth above the surface, if blowing down stream. Also, that a down-stream wind, force 5, will place the axis very near the surface. As wind, force 1, is generally considered to move at a rate about

* It may also account in part for the oscillations of "sawyers," as the snags which are lightly secured by one end to the bottom are called. These logs, even at points far removed from any eddy, are constantly raising their upper ends above the water surface and then subsiding entirely out of sight below it. If the maximum force of the current is successively applied to points at different distances from the bottom, as would be the case should the axis change its position, this phenomenon, which is otherwise sufficiently perplexing, may be readily explained.

† The small diagram on plate XII, which indicates the normal effect of a bend upon the local form of cross-section, also shows the changes of direction that occur in the surface and bottom currents. Floats were placed in the river in juxtaposition, on section 50—one at the surface, the other at the bottom. New floats were put in the river on section 80, and again between sections 90 and 92. The paths of these floats indicate that the surface and bottom currents which correspond above a bend separate widely in passing it, but resume their original relative positions at the termination of the next bend, if the two bends are of equal curvature.

equal to the average velocity of the current, it is evident that the effect of friction against the air in calm weather depresses the axis 0.06 r, leaving $(0.317 - 0.06)\, r = 0.257\, r$ for the effect of other causes in placing the mean calm position of the axis below the surface. Whether these causes are common to, and have equal weight upon, all streams, cannot be decided from any existing data; but the fact that exact observations during calm weather—like those of Boileau, those upon the Little-Falls feeder, etc.—place the maximum velocity considerably below the surface, appears to indicate that this is the case.

But one other remark about $d_{,}$ seems required. It is in reference to the two distinct values deduced from the experiments for the coefficient of f, when f is unity. The first of these values was deduced by comparing the observed depths of axis of the different curves of sub-surface observations, and computing the mean wind-correction which would best eliminate the irregularities due to this cause. The value thus found, when $f = 1$, was 0.145. The second value of this coefficient was deduced by computing how much the axis of the mean vertical curve must move from its calm position in order to affect the computed discharge by the amount of the empirical correction for eliminating wind-effect, taken from the plotted curve of discharge. By this process, the mean coefficient for force 1 was found to be 0.060. It should be remembered that there is uncertainty in the determination of the force of the wind, that the two values were deduced by entirely different processes from entirely different sets of observations, and that the values are not directly comparable, since one applies to the mean of the curves in certain vertical planes of the river-section, while the other applies to the mean of the curves in all these vertical planes. Still, the difference between them has a very slight effect upon the absolute value of $d_{,}$. For a depth of 60 feet, which is about that for which both corrections were deduced, this difference in the computed values of $d_{,}$ amounts to only about 5 feet. For less depths, it is of course proportionally less.

Discussion of the different methods in use for gauging rivers by partial measurements.—The ratio which has been most sought for practical use in gauging streams is that between the maximum surface and true mean velocities, it being, in general, erroneously assumed that the surface velocity is the maximum velocity in any vertical plane. The equations deduced by this discussion render it easy to show that even with large streams, where b is a constant, the ratios $\frac{v}{{}_{w,}V_0}$ and $\frac{v}{{}_{w,}V_{d_,}}$, and even $\frac{v}{{}_{w,}U_0}$ and $\frac{v}{{}_{w,}U_{d_,}}$, vary with so many different quantities as to be of no practical utility when great accuracy is desired,—a result which might almost have been anticipated from the great difference in the numerical values deduced by different engineers.

Analysis of the different ratios heretofore proposed for practical use in gauging rivers.

Confining the attention first to the vertical plane containing the maximum surface velocity, the expressions for the surface and true maximum velocities derived from equation (2) are as follows:—

Ratio of maximum to mean velocity of rivers is too variable to be of practical use.

$$(17) \qquad {}_{w,}V_0 = {}_{w,}V_{d_,} - (0.1856\, v)^{1/2} \left(\frac{d_,}{D}\right)^2.$$

$$(18) \qquad {}_{w,}V_{d_,} = {}_{w,}V_D + (0.1856\, v)^{1/2} \left(1 - \frac{d_,}{D}\right)^2.$$

Since these two equations involve three variables, ${}_{w,}V_0$, ${}_{w,}V_{d_,}$, and ${}_{w,}V_D$, no general numerical values can be deduced for the ratios in question; but it is evident that they must vary with the mean velocity, the depth of the stream and the depth of the axis. In other words, no numerical values of general applicability, as proposed by many hydraulic engineers, can exist. Moreover, the simple formulæ proposed by Dubuat, de Prony, and Young, for the ratio $\frac{v}{{}_{w,}V_0}$ are evidently erroneous, as has been suspected by engineers, since they do not contain these variables. Indeed, it is now manifest that no reliable formula can be derived for either of these ratios until the laws connecting the velocity in consecutive vertical planes parallel to the current be known.

To show how great are the practical variations to which this maximum surface and true mean velocity ratio is liable, the following table has been constructed from the measurements of the Survey detailed in the Appendices; assuming, for the Mississippi observations, that the velocity measured 5 feet below the surface is in effect the same as that at the surface. The ratios are computed by dividing the corrected grand-mean velocity on all the days on which v varied between the limits indicated in the first column by the maximum velocity of the corresponding mean curve of velocities near the surface. For single days the ratios varied still more, as should be expected.

Ratio between true mean and maximum surface velocities.

Mean velocity of stream.	Mississippi river at			Ohio river.	Hatchee river.	St. Francis river.	White river.	Yazoo river.	Red river.	Black river.	Bayou Atchafalaya.	Bayou Plaquemine.	Bayou La Fourche.	Berwick's Bay.	C. and O. canal feeder.
	Columbus.	Vicksburg.	Natchez.												
Feet.															
1.0 to 1.9	0.767					0.726		0.660	0.825				0.793	0.845	
2.0 to 2.9	0.738	0.759		0.776	0.899		0.686	0.836		0.753			0.860		0.734
3.0 to 3.9	0.722	0.779		0.803					0.858		0.753				
4.0 to 4.9	0.753	0.821	0.799								1.000	0.826			
5.0 to 5.9	0.780	0.846										0.848			
6.0 to 6.9	0.805	0.841													
7.0 to 7.9	0.814														
8.0 to 8.9	0.804														
Mean yearly curve	0.787	0.823	0.799												

Having thus shown that the numerical value of the ratios $\frac{v}{{}_{w,}V_0}$ and $\frac{v}{{}_{w,}V_{d,}}$ cannot be computed, the next step, as already stated, is to show the same to be practically true for the corresponding points in the mean vertical plane. To do this, it is necessary to establish algebraic relations between U_m and v, which can evidently be done, since these quantities vary only with each other for the same cross-section.

Algebraic relation between the mean of all vertical curves of velocity and the mean velocity of the river must be investigated in order to continue the discussion.

Assuming the general equation $U_m = \varphi(v)$, it is evident that $\varphi(v)$ can contain no absolute term, since, when v is zero, U_m is also zero. Moreover, for a rectangular cross-section U_m is equal to v, and $\varphi(v)$ must reduce to v. The only direct data available for determining an expression for $\varphi(v)$, which, besides fulfilling these conditions, shall accord with actual observations, are the values of U_m and v corresponding to the Columbus and Vicksburg mean curves. These values are repeated in the following table, the true mean velocity, or v, being deduced from the approximate mean velocity by multiplying it by the proper ratio taken from the table in the last chapter. A study of the curve formed by plotting these values respectively as abscissæ and ordinates showed that a simple function of v, of the form $A\,v$, would fulfil the desired conditions. In this expression, A is a variable depending upon the form of cross-section, being unity when this is rectangular. Its law of change cannot be deduced from any observations now available, but its value, which is constant for the above-mentioned observations, is 0.93, giving the equation—

$$(19) \qquad U_m = 0.93\, v.$$

The true values of U_m, those given by this equation, and their differences are contained in the following table:—

Locality.	v	U_m	U_m by equation (19).	Difference.
	Feet.	*Feet.*	*Feet.*	*Feet.*
Columbus	1.6328	1.4289	1.5185	—0.0896
"	2.3875	2.0821	2.2204	—0.1383
"	3.5927	3.2185	3.3412	—0.1227
"	4.4441	4.0441	4.1330	—0.0889
"	5.2744	4.8648	4.9052	—0.0404
"	6.5776	6.0512	6.1172	—0.0660
"	7.3582	6.9385	6.8431	+0.0954
"	8.2424	7.7833	7.6654	+0.1179
Vicksburg	3.5278	3.2421	3.2806	—0.0385
"	4.3365	4.0840	4.0329	+0.0511
"	5.4845	5.2311	5.1006	+0.1305
"	6.6657	6.4177	6.1991	+0.2186
"	6.9828	6.7415	6.4940	+0.2475
Natchez	4.6160	4.2430	4.2929	—0.0499
Sum	71.1230	66.3708	66.1441	1.4953
Mean	5.0802	4.7408	4.7246	0.1068

This slight difference of only about two per cent. can leave no doubt that the true expression for U_m has been deduced. It is also evident that the law of change in A is, for rivers, practically unimportant, since the great differences in the form of cross-section at Columbus, Vicksburg, and Natchez (see plate X) do not cause a sensible variation.

For rivers a constant ratio exists between these quantities.

Returning, after this digression, to the ratios under consideration, the following values of U_0 and U_{d_i} are deduced by substituting in equations (9) and (11) the values of d_i and U_m for the mean plane, namely, $d_i = (0.317 + 0.06\,f)\,r$, and $U_m = 0.93\,v$, and reducing:—

The ratios $\frac{v}{U_0}$ and $\frac{v}{U_{d_i}}$ both vary too much to be of practical use.

$$(20) \quad U_0 = 0.93\,v + [0.333 - (0.317 + 0.06\,f)]\,(0.1856\,v)^{\frac{1}{2}}.$$

$$(21) \quad U_{d_i} = 0.93\,v + [(0.317 + 0.06\,f)^2 - (0.317 + 0.06\,f) + 0.333]\,(0.1856\,v)^{\frac{1}{2}}.$$

It is evident, from an inspection of these expressions, that $\frac{v}{U_0}$ and $\frac{v}{U_{d_i}}$, although independent of the depth of the river, are yet functions of the depth of the axis below the surface expressed in decimals of the total depth. In other words, they vary with every varying wind, and probably with the degree of smoothness of the bottom, and are therefore of little practical utility. Boileau based his practical rule for gauging streams on the supposition that $\frac{v}{U_{d_i}}$ is unchangeable or nearly so. This rule is evidently a theoretical improvement upon those advanced by Dubuat, de Prony, and Young, since one variable, the depth of the stream, is thereby eliminated from the correction ratio. It is also evident that, if he had adopted the plan of observing floats at the surface, the labor of the field work would have been greatly diminished without materially affecting the accuracy of the computed result, since the expressions for the ratios only differ by involving the first power of $\frac{d_{,}}{r}$, and the difference between the first and second powers of this quantity.

It may then be considered as fully proved by this discussion, that no numerical value for the ratio between v and either ${}_{w,}\mathrm{V}_0$ or ${}_{w,}\mathrm{V}_{d,}$ or U_0 or $\mathrm{U}_{d,}$ can be established, which will be of practical use when exactness is required.

All simple methods heretofore proposed for gauging large rivers are then defective.

Thus far, the new formulæ have only served to show the inaccuracy of all previously received simple methods of gauging rivers, and to exhibit more clearly the difficulties to be met in making such measurements accurately. It will now be determined whether they furnish the means of overcoming these difficulties in a less laborious manner than that used on this Survey.

The greatest practical simplification which can be reasonably sought.

New method proposed for gauging rivers by measurement.—If the ratio of the velocity at any given point in any given vertical plane to the true mean velocity of the river could be shown to be constant or nearly so, the greatest simplification of which the subject admits would be made. This result, however, cannot reasonably be expected in the present state of our knowledge, since no general formulæ are known, connecting the velocities in the different vertical planes with each other or with the mean velocity of the river. Such formulæ must, of necessity, be exceedingly complex, making it improbable that any simple relation, of the nature sought, exists. It seems, therefore, that efforts should be directed to simplifying the determination of the mean of all the velocities *in any vertical plane.* If the ratio between the velocity at any given depth and the mean of the vertical curve is independent of any of the variables in the general formula for velocity below the surface, this object may be accomplished.

Algebraic analysis of the problem.

To determine whether this is the case, let the following general equations be assumed, the second being deduced from equation (5) by a process similar to that used in deducing equation (11) from equation (7):

$$\text{(4)} \qquad \mathrm{V} = \mathrm{V}_{d,} - (b\,v)^{\frac{1}{2}} \left(\frac{d - d_{,}}{\mathrm{D}}\right)^2.$$

$$\text{(22)} \qquad \mathrm{V}_{d,} = \mathrm{V}_m + (b\,v)^{\frac{1}{2}} \left(\frac{1}{3} + \frac{d_{,}\,(d_{,} - \mathrm{D})}{\mathrm{D}^2}\right).$$

By combining these equations and reducing, the following expression results:—

$$\text{(23)} \qquad \mathrm{V} = \mathrm{V}_m + (b\,v)^{\frac{1}{2}} \left(\frac{\mathrm{D}^2 \wedge 3\,d_{,}\,\mathrm{D} - 3\,d^2 + 6\,d\,d_{,}}{3\,\mathrm{D}^2}\right).$$

If the expression $\mathrm{V}_m = \mathrm{V}_m$ be divided, member by member, by this equation, we have for a general equation of the ratio in question—

$$\frac{\mathrm{V}_m}{\mathrm{V}} = \frac{\mathrm{V}_m}{\mathrm{V}_m + (b\,v)^{\frac{1}{2}} \left(\frac{\mathrm{D}^2 - 3\,d_{,}\,\mathrm{D} - 3\,d^2 + 6\,d\,d_{,}}{3\,\mathrm{D}^2}\right)}.$$

Now it is evident that no value can be assigned to d which will reduce the fraction in the denominator of the second member to zero, and that the variables $b^{\frac{1}{2}}$ and $v^{\frac{1}{2}}$ must therefore remain in the ratio. If, however, d be made $\frac{1}{2}$ D, this fraction reduces to $\frac{1}{12}$, and both of the other variables, D and $d_{,}$, disappear, the equation becoming—

$$(24) \qquad \frac{V_m}{V_{\frac{1}{2}D}} = \frac{V_m}{V_m + \frac{1}{12}(b\,v)^{\frac{1}{2}}}.$$

This equation reveals a fact of great practical importance in gauging rivers, namely, that the ratio of the mid-depth velocity to the mean velocity in any vertical plane is independent of the width and depth of the stream,—except for their almost inappreciable effect upon b,—absolutely independent of the depth of the axis, and, from the small numerical value of $\frac{1}{12}b^{\frac{1}{2}}$, nearly independent of the mean velocity. But this is not all. From the form of the second member of equation (24), it is evident that changes in V_m, except when it is very small, will not sensibly affect the numerical value of the ratio. If, then, for V_m, its value in the mean vertical curve, $0.93\,v$, be substituted, it will be possible to predict from the resulting expression, viz., $\frac{0.93\,v}{0.93\,v + \frac{1}{12}(b\,v)^{\frac{1}{2}}}$, the absolute numerical value of the ratio for any curve of actual observations, provided the corresponding mean velocity of the river be approximately known.

The ratio of the mid-depth velocity to the mean velocity in any vertical plane is sensibly constant.

Neglecting, for the time, its importance in gauging streams, this discovery suggests a method by which the new theory of velocity below the surface can be subjected to the severest possible test, not only by the observations of this Survey, but also by all available published experiments, even when too imperfect to show a parabolic form in the curve. To aid in this comparison, the following table has been constructed, containing the values of the above expression for the different values of v usual in rivers, the quantity b being assumed 0.1856.

Severe test of the whole theory furnished by this discovery.

v	1 foot.	2 feet.	3 feet.	4 feet.	5 feet.	6 feet.	7 feet.	8 feet.
Ratio	0.9628	0.9734	0.9782	0.9811	0.9830	0.9845	0.9856	0.9865

The following table exhibits the data for the experimental test of the theory. The first five columns are given to show the amount of the variation in the quantities therein contained. The values of V_m and $V_{\frac{1}{2}D}$ for the experimental ratios of the sixth column, so far as the observations of this Survey are concerned, are taken from the *parabolas* adapted to the curves of observation contained in the tables already given, and exhibited on figures 16, 15, 14, 12, 13, 7, and 6, plate XI. The reasons for this are evident. The observed velocities differ very slightly from the corresponding points of the parabolas, and the mean of these velocities is always the same as that of the corresponding points of the parabolas. Good reasons certainly exist for believing that these parabolas give the actual law of the curve. If so, mathematically corresponding values of V_m and $V_{\frac{1}{2}D}$ can be obtained by the parabolas, while by any arbitrary system for the necessary interpolation in finding V_m, this correspondence will not be secured. For the observations of other surveys, this method has not been practicable, as the form of the curve is generally obscured by discrepancies of observation. For these, V_m has been uniformly deduced by taking a mean of all the observed velocities, including that at the bottom, found by rectilinear interpolation, provided the observations were made at equidistant depths. If the depths were variable, the curves have been plotted on a large scale,—the observed velocities connected by right lines,—and V_m considered equal to the mean of a series of ten or fifteen equidistant velocities, including surface and bottom, taken from the resulting curve. The mid-depth velocity, if not directly observed, has been found by interpolating in the same way. The theoretical values in the last column are computed by the expression $\frac{0.93\,v}{0.93\,v + \frac{1}{12}(b\,v)^{\frac{1}{2}}}$, remembering that, for the Little-Falls feeder and for Boileau's canal, it becomes $\frac{v}{v + \frac{1}{12}(b\,v)^{\frac{1}{2}}}$, since in these the cross-section is sensibly rectangular.

Curve.	Observer.	Wind.	$\frac{d_{\prime}}{D}$	D	W	v	Observed $\frac{V_m}{V_{\frac{1}{2}D}}$	Theoretical $\frac{V_m}{V_{\frac{1}{2}D}}$	Difference.
				Feet.	*Feet.*	*Feet.*			
Gr. mean—anch'd boats.	Prof. Forshey.	Down 0.2	0.297	82.000	2800.0	3.3814	0.9798	0.9798	0.0005
H.w. mean— " "	" "	Up 0.3	0.350	86.000	2500.0	4.1605	0.9808	0.9814	0.0006
L.w. mean— " "	" "	Down 1.1	0.150	75.000	2200.0	1.9984	0.9767	0.9734	0.0033
Mean—Columbus.........	Mr. Fillebrown.	Up 1.2	0.520	65.000	2200.0	3.4070	0.9845	0.9794	0.0051
Mean—Vicksburg........	Mr. Pattison.	Down 1.0	0.100	55.000	2600.0	4.1599	0.9835	0.9814	0.0021
Bayou Plaquemine.......	Mr. G. C. Smith.	Down 2.0	0.080	27.000	300.0	5.4100	0.9868	0.9836	0.0032
Bayou La Fourche.......	" " "	Up 0.7	0.350	27.000	225.0	2.7300	0.9817	0.9769	0.0048
C. and O. canal feeder..	Lieutenant Abbot.		0.232	7.100	17.0	2.0830	0.9624	0.9580	0.0044
Experimental canal......	M. Boileau.		0.178	1.100	2.2	2.1000*	0.9417	0.9444	0.0027
Experimental canal......	" "		0.238	0.676	2.2	1.5000*	0.9640	0.9321	0.0319
Rhine......................	M. Hennocque.†		0.225	8.100		1.8000*	0.0322	0.9530	0.0208
Rhine......................	M. Defontaine (fig. 5)		0.000	4.000		2.6800	0.9569	0.9556	0.0013
Rhine......................	" (fig. 6)		0.000	4.900		2.6800	0.9344	0.9572	0.0228
Rhine......................	" (fig. 7)		0.000	4.900		2.6800	0.9331	0.9572	0.0241
Rhine......................	" (fig. 8)		0.000	4.300		2.6800	0.9413	0.9562	0.0149

Every available observation confirms the truth of the discovery, and hence of the theory by aid of which it was made.

The exceedingly slight discrepancies between the theoretical ratios and those deduced from the actual observations, shown in the last column of this table, confirm what the analysis has demonstrated, namely, that the ratio of the mid-depth velocity to the mean velocity in any vertical plane is practically independent of the depth and the width of the stream, of the mean velocity of the river, of the mean velocity of the vertical curve, and of the locus of its maximum velocity. In other words, it is a sensibly constant quantity for practical purposes. This result, which must now be admitted to be as well demonstrated as most laws of hydraulics, is a beautiful example of the value of analysis when applied to natural phenomena. The solution of the problem of a constant ratio between an observable velocity and the mean of all the velocities in the vertical plane, so long sought in vain by hydraulic engineers, results as a simple consequence of transformation and reduction of equations, when the relations existing between those velocities are expressed in the language of analysis.

The discovery proves that the velocity at mid-depth is absolutely unaffected by wind.

The constancy of this ratio necessarily implies that the velocity of the mid-depth layer of water in a river is not affected by any changes that take place in the direction and force of the wind, whatever their extent may be, even from a calm to a hurricane. (See figure 18, plate XI.)

This conclusion may be equally derived from a consideration of the observed effects

* Deduced by 0.8 rule. † Reported by Boileau.

of the wind and the manner in which it acts. An up-stream wind, for instance, at first diminishes the velocity at the surface a certain amount, which diminution extends with a constantly decreasing effect to the bottom. During a brief period, the volume of discharge is diminished and an accumulation takes place in the bend above. (A corresponding depletion takes place in the bend below.) The slope, and therefore the velocity, is thus increased until the original volume of discharge is restored, since it has been observed that the level of the surface in the reach is not appreciably affected by wind. It is to be remarked that the new surface velocity cannot be equal to the original surface velocity, for in that case the volume of discharge would be increased. As this remains the same, the new slope adds as much velocity to the river as the wind consumes, and this effective increase of velocity must be greatest at the bottom, since the wind retardation is least there. It diminishes in proportion to the distance from the bottom. The resulting effective decrease in velocity is greatest at the surface and diminishes in proportion to the distance from the surface. As the effective increase of velocity and the effective decrease of velocity are equal to each other—the one greatest at the bottom, the other at the surface—the velocity of the mid-depth layer of the fluid mass must remain unaffected.

The same conclusion reached in another manner.

This being established, it follows that the mid-depth velocity is independent of the position of the axis, and therefore is not affected by irregularities of the bottom. As it is always greater than the mean of the velocities in the vertical plane, and as that mean must be less, in rivers of the same dimensions and slope, in proportion as the inequalities of the bed are greater, the ratio of the mean and mid-depth will be less in that proportion. Again, as the mean of the velocities in the vertical plane increases as the depth increases, the ratio of the mean to the mid-depth must be greater in large and deep rivers, than in small and shallow rivers. These conclusions are supported by the last table. From the nature of this ratio it is evident that its variations must be small; their actual extent is exhibited in the table just referred to.

Deductions.

To those who are practically familiar with the liability to inaccuracy and the laboriousness of the methods used for gauging large rivers, the discovery of this ratio will seem most valuable. It at once suggests several methods of determining with great nicety the mean velocity, and hence the discharge, of a river. The field operations will vary according to the accuracy demanded. If the stream be small, and considerable exactness be required, the boat should be anchored at various equidistant stations, the banks being considered two of them, and the actual mid-depth velocity be measured by any of the known methods. The number of these stations should be large enough to prevent any material change of velocity between consecutive stations. In the case of a large river, where this method is not convenient, if the depth is tolerably uniform, sufficient accuracy may be attained by observing, in the manner adopted on this Survey, a number of double floats well distributed across the river-section, the keg being uniformly sunk beneath the surface to a depth equal to half the mean radius of the river—a depth which can be readily computed from the plot of the cross-section by dividing the total area by twice the perimeter. The paths of the floats should then be plotted and grouped by divisions of equal width, and the mean of all floats in each division taken. By the former of these methods, the measured velocity

Field operations for gauging small streams and large rivers based upon the discovery.

will be absolutely, and by the latter nearly, unaffected by the wind, no matter what its direction or force may be.

Three methods of computation, the one to be selected depending upon the degree of accuracy required.

The method of computing the discharge from these observations will vary according to the accuracy required. A close approximate result may be obtained by taking a mean of all the different station or division mid-depth velocities. In this method, there are two causes of error which very nearly balance each other, namely, the inequality in area of the different divisions, and the difference between the mid-depth and mean velocities in any vertical plane. If greater precision be required, the mean of the different division mid-depth velocities may be substituted for $U_{\frac{1}{2}r}$ in the following formula, whose second member thus becomes known:—

$$(25) \qquad v = \left([1.08\ U_{\frac{1}{2}r} + 0.002\ b]^{\frac{1}{2}} - 0.045\ b^{\frac{1}{2}}\right)^2.$$

This formula is deduced by substituting for U_m, in the general expression $U_{\frac{1}{2}r} = U_m + \frac{1}{12}(b\,v)^{\frac{1}{2}}$, its value deduced from equation (19), and reducing the resulting equation. As has been already stated, when the mean radius exceeds about 12 feet, b may be assumed to be 0.1856. The formula would be exact, were it not for the error arising from variations in the quantity represented by A in the expression for U_m. It has been already seen that, for the Mississippi river, this quantity is constant, and, as it depends on the deviation of the form of cross-section from a rectangle, it is quite possible that nearly the same value may apply to all rivers. Should, however, so great nicety be demanded as to forbid this assumption, it may be avoided, and accuracy, affected only by instrumental errors of observation, be secured, by substituting the different station or division mid-depth velocities successively for $V_{\frac{1}{2}D}$ in the formula—

$$(26) \qquad V_m = V_{\frac{1}{2}D} - \frac{1}{12}(b\,v)^{\frac{1}{2}}.$$

The resulting values will be expressions for the mean velocities of the different divisions in terms of $v^{\frac{1}{2}}$ and known quantities. The sum of the products of these expressions by the corresponding division areas should then be placed equal to the product of v by the total area of cross-section. The resulting equation, involving only v and $v^{\frac{1}{2}}$ and known terms, may be readily solved and the values of v determined. There will be two such values, both positive: one, the lesser, corresponding to the actual case in nature, when the velocity at the axis is the greatest of any; the other, the greater, corresponding to the hypothetical condition that this velocity shall be the least. It need hardly be added that the former is the true mean velocity of the river. It is believed that the latter process of computation, applied to careful observations taken in the manner already detailed, will furnish the most accurate determination of the discharge of a large stream which can possibly be obtained. It is, however, laborious, and the other methods, which are very simple, will probably furnish results in which the inaccuracies of the computation will be less than those arising from unavoidable instrumental errors of observation.

Recapitulation of new formulæ for velocity below the surface.

Recapitulation of the most important new formulæ for velocity below the surface.—Before bringing this section to a close, the most important of the new general formulæ for velocities below the surface, will be repeated, the form of some of them being slightly modified for convenience in computation. The signification of the symbols is explained on page 200. For velocity in any plane, these formulæ are as follows—number (29) being deduced by combining (4) and (22) and reducing. It will be remembered that for all values of D greater than about 30 feet, b is sensibly 0.1856. For less values, if great exactness is required, it must be especially computed by its equation, viz.: $b = \frac{1.69}{(D + 1.5)^{\frac{1}{2}}}$. For the mean of all vertical planes, D becomes r in this expression.

(4) $$V = V_{d_{\prime}} - (b\,v)^{\frac{1}{2}} \left(\frac{d - d_{\prime}}{D}\right)^2.$$

(27) $$V_0 = V_{d_{\prime}} - (b\,v)^{\frac{1}{2}} \left(\frac{d_{\prime}}{D}\right)^2.$$

(28) $$V_D = V_{d_{\prime}} - (b\,v)^{\frac{1}{2}} \left(1 - \frac{d_{\prime}}{D}\right)^2.$$

(5) $$V_m = \frac{2}{3} V_{d_{\prime}} + \frac{1}{3} V_D + \frac{d_{\prime}}{D} \left(\frac{1}{3} V_0 - \frac{1}{3} V_D\right).$$

(26) $$V_{\frac{1}{2}D} = V_m + \frac{1}{12} (b\,v)^{\frac{1}{2}}.$$

(22) $$V_{d_{\prime}} = V_m + (b\,v)^{\frac{1}{2}} \left(\frac{1}{3} + \frac{d_{\prime}\,(d_{\prime} - D)}{D^2}\right).$$

(29) $$V = V_m + (b\,v)^{\frac{1}{2}} \left(\frac{D\,(\frac{1}{3} D - d_{\prime}) + d\,(2\,d_{\prime} - d)}{D^2}\right).$$

For velocity in the mean of all vertical planes, the following formulæ have been deduced. Equation (8) can probably be made applicable, without material error, to the velocity in any plane by substituting D for r.

(8) $$d_{\prime} = (0.317 + 0.06\,f)\,r.$$

(19) $$U_m = 0.93\,v.$$

(30) $$U = 0.93\,v + \left(\frac{d\,r\,(0.634 + 0.12\,f) - d^2}{r^2} - 0.06\,f + 0.016\right) (b\,v)^{\frac{1}{2}}.$$

(20) $$U_0 = 0.93\,v + (0.016 - 0.06\,f)\ (b\,v)^{\frac{1}{2}}.$$

(31) $$U_r = 0.93\,v + (0.06\,f - 0.350)\ (b\,v)^{\frac{1}{2}}.$$

(21) $$U_{d_{\prime}} = 0.93\,v + \left([0.317 + 0.06\,f]^2 - 0.06\,f + 0.016\right) (b\,v)^{\frac{1}{2}}.$$

(25) $$v = \left([1.08\,U_{\frac{1}{2}r} + 0.002\,b]^{\frac{1}{2}} - 0.045\,b^{\frac{1}{2}}\right)^2.$$

APPLICATION OF THE NEW LAWS TO THE GAUGING OF RIVERS BY FORMULÆ.

Thus far, in this investigation, the object has been, first, to determine the true method of computing the discharge from the data collected in the field, and second, to simplify the process of gauging streams by the application of the newly-discovered laws. There remains still another problem, much more difficult than either of these, whose solution is no less essential for the purposes of this Survey. It is the mathematical determination of the relations existing between the cross-section, the slope, and the mean

The objects of this Survey demand an exact formula expressing algebraically the relations existing between the dimensions of

cross-section, the slope of water surface, and the mean velocity of rivers.

velocity. A knowledge of these relations is necessary in order to determine the amount by which the surface-level of the river will be raised by the volume of water confined to the channel by levees. It is true that the most obvious and apparently direct method of solving this important practical question is to measure the quantity of water passing at the different stages of the river, and thus determine how much additional water passes for each additional foot of rise. This, as already seen, was done; but, as anticipated, it was found that the increase of water for a unit of rise varied greatly in different localities and at different stages of the river. Reasoning based entirely upon such proportional increase of rise must therefore be liable to the objections which can always be urged against the assumption of certain values for variables whose laws of variation are not known. It was therefore deemed necessary to find a general formula which, by a close agreement with actual observations, should inspire confidence in the accuracy of its predictions in cases where direct observations were impossible.

None of the old formulæ proving to be exact, a new one is to be deduced.

The first step taken was to collect and apply to certain observations, made especially for the purpose or published in standard works, all formulæ ever proposed for the mean velocity of water flowing in open channels of known dimensions and slope. These formulæ, with a sketch of the manner in which they were deduced, have already been given in Chapter III. The result of the comparison was not satisfactory, as may be seen by referring to a table in the latter part of this chapter. The development of the laws governing the change of velocity below the surface, and the possession of new and exact data, afforded the means of applying the principles of hydraulics to the deduction of a new formula, which should at least be free from certain theoretical errors believed to exist in all those already proposed. The following train of reasoning was pursued.

Of the two classes, that based upon the supposition of uniform motion is adopted.

Principles which determine the form of the new formula.—In Chapter III it has been shown that there are two classes of formulæ applicable to water moving in open channels: those based upon the supposition of "uniform" motion, and those based upon the supposition of "permanent" motion. It has also been shown that the only difference between these two classes is that the one has not, while the other has, a term which takes into account the changes in living force produced by gradual changes in cross-section. It was evident that such a term as this would be of no practical utility for the purposes of this Survey, because it would imply a more extended system of soundings than the limits of the appropriation would allow, and a greater degree of refinement in the computations than the exactness of any determination of the amount of water to be added could justify. The supposition of "uniform" motion was therefore adopted. The condition of this motion—that each particle of the fluid shall pass through the corresponding points of the several elementary cross-sections of the channel with equal velocity—can never be strictly fulfilled in a natural channel; but, by selecting stations where the bed is most regular, a certain approximation to this condition may be obtained. The difference between this practical approximate and the theoretical absolute uniformity of motion, the numerical values of the constants ought to correct; provided the observations from which they are deduced are properly conducted. The precautions necessary to be observed to this end will be noticed hereafter. At present, the *form* only of an equation based upon the supposition of perfect uniformity of motion is under consideration.

The truth of Dubuat's two theorems: that, when water is moving uniformly, the total accelerating force is equal to the total resistance; and that, for all open channels, the accelerating force arises solely from the slope of the water-surface,—is considered undeniable. The first indicates the most simple way of deducing such a formula, namely, to equate expressions for the accelerating and retarding forces. The second suggests an expression for the former, namely, the product of the weight of the water by the sine of the slope of its surface, a quantity which may in practice be assumed to be equal to the fall in a limited distance divided by this distance. The accelerating forces are therefore represented (for nomenclature see page 200) by $G\,g\,a\,l\,\frac{h_{\prime}}{l}$. An expression for the resistances must be deduced.

Formula to be framed by equating expressions for accelerating and retarding forces. Algebraic value of the former.

The water of a river may be considered to flow through a natural pipe, whose inner surface is formed by the bottom and sides of the channel and by the atmosphere. It has been demonstrated by experiment in the preceding chapter, first, that there is a strong resistance to the movement of the water, applied where it comes in contact with the air; and second, that this resistance, whatever its cause may be, is of the same order or nature as that at the bottom and sides of the channel, since the law of transmission through the fluid is the same in each case. One resistance to the flow of the water may therefore be compared to the friction arising from the forcing of a solid body through a pipe. Its locus is the entire outer elementary layer of the fluid, and, for want of a better name, it may be called the resistance due to the adhesion of this layer to the foreign bodies forming the inner surface of the great natural pipe. It retards the velocity of this outer elementary layer, but directly affects no other. The velocity of every other particle is diminished in accordance with the laws of an entirely different resistance, namely, that of the cohesion of the different particles to each other. This is properly a secondary resistance, being that which regulates the distribution of the effects of the primary resistance of adhesion among the different interior particles of the moving mass. The force of cohesion is of an entirely different order or nature from that of adhesion, and of far greater intensity. It admits of only a very slight difference of velocity between the different consecutive elementary layers of the fluid, while that of adhesion allows a velocity, often amounting to several feet, to exist in the outer layer of the fluid.

Retarding forces. Distinction between adhesion and cohesion.

These views concerning the nature of resistances to the movement of flowing water are, in some respects, different from those advanced by any writer upon the subject whose works have been consulted. The admission of a resistance at the surface, of the same order as that at the bottom, is entirely novel; but the results of this Survey, already detailed, and an examination of those of other surveys, with the clue afforded by the former, renders it absolutely necessary. The distinction drawn between the resistances of adhesion and cohesion is not admitted by most writers, although it has its advocates, among whom M. Dupuit is conspicuous. Writers in general consider the resistance of adhesion to be infinite, thus causing the layer in contact with the bed to remain stationary, and reducing the effective resistances to the friction of a liquid moving upon a stationary liquid layer, or, in other words, to the friction arising from cohesion. The reasons which have led them to adopt this assumption have been twofold: first, because experiments seem to indicate that the resistances are independent of the nature of the surface of the channel; and second, because an ignorance of the laws by which cohesion acts has rendered it impossible, without this assumption, to deduce any formula for the mean velocity. The reasoning which has led to the rejection of this hypothesis in framing the new formula is briefly this. The developments detailed in the last chapter, relative to the change of velocity below the surface, have made known the laws governing the action of cohesion, and shown that the change of velocity between the consecutive layers of the liquid is very slight, and in accordance with the parabolic law (see figure 18, plate XI). If, then, the velocity of the bottom layer were zero, that of the next layer would be infinitely small, and the successive increase from layer to layer, up to the point of maximum velocity, would be regular, being shown by the arc of a parabola having a horizontal axis, the vertex being at the point of maximum velocity. The measured velocity near the bottom would, therefore, always be very small compared with the maximum. But all experiments upon streams have shown that this is not so. Upon the Mississippi river, for instance, the velocity, as near the bottom as a float could be made to pass, was often as great as 5 or 6 feet per second, the difference between it and the maximum velocity rarely, if ever, exceeding half a foot. The supposition of this stationary layer is, therefore, clearly inadmissible. The question has been ably argued by M. Dupuit, who has arrived, from purely theoretical considerations, at this same result, which he has illustrated by reference to well-known physical facts. Should the correctness of the conclusion be doubted, it is hoped that a reference to his work, or to a synopsis of his reasoning on this point, contained in Chapter III of this report, will be made for a more elaborate demonstration.

Algebraic expression for retarding forces.

The deduction of an expression for the retarding forces, based upon the views already stated, is very simple. It is evident that the accelerating forces are primarily consumed in overcoming the resistances of *adhesion*, cohesion acting merely to govern the transmission of the effects of those resistances through the fluid. But the absolute resistances of adhesion are directly proportioned to the length of channel considered, multiplied by the circumference of the fluid, or $l\ (p + W)$, and to some function of the mean of the velocities of all the elements of the outer layer of the liquid. But U_0 is the mean of all the surface velocities, and U_r that of all the bottom and side velocities. Hence the expression for the mean of the velocities of all the elements of the outermost layer of the fluid is $\frac{U_0 W + U_r p}{W + p}$. The resistances of adhesion are therefore proportional to—

$$l\ (p + W)\ \varphi \left(\frac{U_0 W + U_r p}{W + p}\right).$$

New general formula.

By equating this expression with that already deduced for the accelerating forces, the following general formula results:—

$$G\ g\ a\ l\ \frac{h_{\prime}}{l} = l\ (p + W)\ \varphi \left(\frac{U_0 W + U_r p}{W + p}\right).$$

Dividing both members of the equation by $G\ g\ l$—since, for formulæ applying to water, $G\ g$ may be assumed constant for any moderate change of latitude—and substituting for $\frac{h_{\prime}}{l}$ its value, s, and for U_0 and U_r their values for ordinary river cross-sections, given by formulæ (20) and (31), remembering that $0.317 + 0.06 f = \frac{d_{\prime}}{r}$, this expression by reduction becomes—

$$(32) \qquad \frac{a\,s}{W + p} = \varphi \left\{ 0.93\, v + (b\, v)^{\frac{1}{2}} \left(\frac{W\left(0.333 - \frac{d_{\prime}}{r}\right) + p\left(\frac{d_{\prime}}{r} - 0.667\right)}{W + p} \right) \right\}.$$

This is the expression corresponding to the almost universally adopted formula:—

$$\frac{a\,s}{p} = \varphi\ (v).$$

It is believed to be theoretically far more accurate, while its absolute practical difference, as will soon be seen, is so slight as to account for the general accordance between the old formulæ and the published experiments upon small streams; an accordance which could hardly exist if M. Dupuit's expression, $\frac{a\,s}{p} = \varphi\ (U_r)$, were correct. Since the resistances at the surface are overlooked by this writer, it is evident that his expression cannot be considered theoretically exact.

Practical simplifications.

Substituting $q\,p$ for W in the fraction of the last term of the second member of equation (32), it becomes—

$$\frac{0.333\, q - \frac{d_{\prime}}{r}\, q + \frac{d_{\prime}}{r} - 0.667}{q + 1}.$$

But for rivers, q is never quite—although always very nearly—equal to unity. For the Mississippi, its mean value is about 0.99. No sensible error can, therefore, arise from assuming it equal to unity in the above fraction, which thus becomes — 0.167. The sign of this quantity must be changed, since, in the ultimate expression for v, which is a root of an equation of the second degree, the difference between the radical and the other term is the root of the equation corresponding to the true mean velocity. Without this change of sign, the deduced value of the numerical coefficient will correspond to the other root of the equation, which is the wrong one, since it does not become zero when the slope is zero. Substituting, then, the value + 0.167 for the fraction in the second member, equation (32) becomes—

$$(33) \qquad \frac{a\,s}{W + p} = \varphi\ (0.93\, v + 0.167\, b^{\frac{1}{2}}\, v^{\frac{1}{2}}) = \varphi\ (z).$$

Constants of the new formula must be determined from observations.

Thus far in the investigation, the views adopted respecting the forces in question indicate every step of the process with mathematical precision. This is no longer the case, since the form of the function composing the second member of this equation can only be determined by the study of observations. A somewhat extended discussion of the conditions which such observations should fulfil, seems to be required, as extraordinary errors have at times been made by hydraulic engineers of standing, both in conducting such measurements and in applying the various formulæ for mean velocity to particular cases.

Observations for deducing the constants of the new formula.—It is plain that, in such

Fall of rivers consumed in overcoming three distinct classes of resistances, which must be expressed by two distinct formulæ, whose constants cannot be determined from observations upon pipes and troughs.

observations, all the variables in equation (33) must be accurately measured. The manner of performing the necessary field work for measuring all except the slope has been detailed at the beginning of the last chapter, and no further comments are required. The determination of *the true s* suggests many important considerations. This quantity, for rivers, is usually stated to be equal to the quotient resulting from the division of the fall of the water's surface in a given distance by this distance. This is inaccurate language, and has led to many errors in applying the formulæ. The fall of any natural stream in any considerable distance is consumed in overcoming three entirely distinct resistances: first, that already described as due to the joint action of adhesion and cohesion; second, that arising from the loss of living force when the stream is deflected by bends; and, third, that arising from the loss of living force caused by changes in width and depth. The first, only, of these is taken into account by formulæ whose constants are derived from observations in which the condition of uniform motion is perfectly fulfilled. If, therefore, such formulæ are applied to rivers, the mean area, width, and perimeter between the upper and lower points considered must be used with a slope computed by dividing the actually observed fall between those points, *diminished by that expended in overcoming the other two resistances*, by the total distance. For the portion of the fall consumed in overcoming the resistances of bends, a formula will be hereafter discussed. For that consumed in overcoming the resistances due to changes in cross-section, it is clear that no practical equation can be framed, if for no other reason than that the requisite knowledge of the exact form of cross-section cannot be obtained in practice. Formulæ whose constants correspond to perfect uniformity of motion, then, cannot be applied to rivers. Hence, the constants of river formulæ must be deduced from observations upon *natural channels*, not, as generally heretofore, upon *pipes* and *troughs*.

Effect of changes in cross-section to be allowed for by modifying the constants of the two formulæ.

An extended examination of rivers with moderate slope (to which alone formulæ are usually applied) will show that, in general, where the stream flows with a straight course, the changes of cross-section are gradual; while, in bends, they are abrupt, giving rise to violent eddies and boils. This fact suggests the proper method of allowing for their effect. The constants of equation (33) should be adjusted to correct for the effect of ordinary, slight changes, while those of the bend formula should take into account the abrupt and violent changes.

Hence certain conditions must be fulfilled by observations from which the constants of the mean velocity formula are to be determined.

The above considerations indicate that three conditions should be fulfilled by observations conducted for the purpose of deducing the form of the function composing the second member of equation (33). First, they should be made upon a natural channel. Second, the bed must be straight at the locality, in order to avoid the effect of bends upon the slope. Third, the cross-section must be sensibly uniform, in order to avoid the effect of sudden variations upon the slope. To these it may be added, that the distance must be considerable—as great as possible, in fact—in order to reduce to a minimum the percentage of instrumental error in measuring the slope.

Even in a locality fulfilling all these conditions, the measurement is an operation of exceeding delicacy. The water surface, even then, is by no means a plane. The different velocities at different distances from the banks destroy any such character, since water in motion exerts less pressure than when at rest. This causes the level of the surface near the thread of the current to rise, in order to maintain the equilibrium.* The difference of height due to this cause is usually estimated by the formula:† $h = \frac{V_{\prime}^2 - V_{\prime\prime}^2}{2g}$. Thus the difference of level between the water moving near the bank with a velocity of 1 foot per second and that in the thread of the current, moving at the rate of 8 feet per second, is $\frac{8^2 - 1^2}{2g} = 0.98$ of a foot, or more than 11 inches. If, therefore, the water move with different velocities at the two level-stations, error will result. The air, also, is seldom entirely still, and even a gentle wind, besides producing oscillations in the surface, may sensibly affect the relative level at the two stations. The almost constant rising or falling of the river greatly increases the liability to error. Add to these and to local causes of variation—such as eddies and boils—the exceedingly small numerical value of the slope for most natural channels, and an idea can be formed of the difficulty of its determination at any particular locality.

Difficulty of measuring the fall of water surface.

This measurement was attempted at Vicksburg, Columbus, and Carrollton, in connection with observations for discharge. The locality of Vicksburg being especially favorable for the purpose, several observations were made to determine the slope at different stages of the river. An exceedingly careful transit and level survey was made by Mr. Pattison, between benches established at E and G, figure 4, plate III, the line of levels being run five times with an accurate instrument, and finally testing to within a very small fraction of an inch. When the slope was to be measured, graduated stakes were planted in the water opposite the bench-marks, and carefully referred to them by means of the levelling instrument. Accurate observations of the height of the water surface upon the stakes were then made simultaneously by different observers. Between these two stations, the current flows nearly parallel to the Louisiana shore, the cross-section is regular, and the difference of level of the water surface divided by the distance between the stations gives a result as near to the true slope as can possibly be obtained by measurement on the Mississippi river. The operation was performed five times in 1858. The corresponding area, width, and perimeter were found by taking a mean of all the sections indicated on figure 4, plate III, including as one section a mean of those at the velocity-base. The mean velocity of observation was obtained by dividing the discharge found at the velocity-base by this mean area.

Details of this operation at Vicksburg.

At Columbus peculiar difficulties existed, as may be seen by reference to figure 3, plate III. The eddy and bend above, the island below, and the rapid changes of width in the cross-section rendered it nearly impossible to measure properly the slope affecting the discharge at the velocity-base, where alone the dimensions of the cross-section were determined. The fall in water surface

At Columbus.

---

* See some interesting measurements to test this matter, by M. Baumgarten, detailed in Chapter III.

† Weisbach.

between the stations at G and A, on figure 3, plate III, was measured by Mr. Fillebrown, and in default of a better determination, the result is admitted, although probably somewhat inexact from instrumental errors, which the shortness of the line rendered very important.

At Carrollton.

At Carrollton the locality was tolerably favorable, the chief objection being the small numerical value of the slope, which rendered its measurement difficult. This was performed by the levelling party in charge of Mr. Ford. The upper station was in all cases at station A. (See figure 2, plate III.) The lower was, for observations No. 1 and No. 3, at station B; for observations No. 2 and No. 4, at station C. The area, width, and perimeter used in each case were found by taking a mean of those quantities on all sections indicated on the diagram lying between the stations. The mean velocity of observation was found by dividing the measured discharge by the mean area.

Observations upon bayou La Fourche.

The slope of the water surface of bayou La Fourche was measured within about 5 miles of the head, on May 6, 7, and 8, 1851, by the levelling party of the Survey. On May 6, the fall in a mile was found to be 0.239 of a foot. By the bend formula, soon to be explained, 0.042 of a foot of this were computed to be due to bends ($\sin.^2 \acute{a}$, measured on the transit-sheets of the Survey, being 0.689). On May 7, the fall in 1 mile, and on May 8, that in about 2 miles, were accurately determined in two different localities, where there were no sensible bends. The gauge-readings on those dates being known, the corresponding areas, widths, and perimeters were computed by taking a mean between the mean of the three sections at the mouth and that at Pain Court, distant about 9 miles from this point. The discharge was not measured, but was accurately determined by an interpolation between the quantities found by measurement when the water at Donaldsonville stood 1.2 and 7.3 feet below the high water of 1851 (being 10,250 and 5150 cubic feet per second at these two stands, respectively). Since the discharge depends directly upon the stand of the bayou at Donaldsonville, this must give a very close determination. The party also determined, by water-marks on trees, the total fall in the first 5 miles (less a few feet) at the high water of 1851. It was 1.231 feet. By the bend formula, 0.105 of a foot of this were found to be due to bends ($\sin.^2 \acute{a}$, measured on transit-sheets of the Survey, being 1.485). Deducting this quantity, the slope to be used with the formula was deduced. The area, width, perimeter, and discharge were found in the same manner as for May 7 and 8.

Upon bayou Plaquemine.

On January 16, 1859, Mr. Pattison measured the discharge and corresponding slope of bayou Plaquemine at its upper mouth. This slope, which was measured between A and B, figure 7, plate III, was evidently affected by bends and marked irregularities in cross-section. The total observed fall was 1.03 feet. By the bend formula the effect of these resistances was computed to be equal to 0.408 of a foot, leaving 0.62 of a foot for the fall to be used with the formula. The corresponding area, width, and perimeter were found by taking a mean between a mean of the three sections near the mouth and that near the mouth of bayou Jacob.

The field work of the Survey had been already brought to a close before this stage of

Upon Little-Falls feeder, near Georgetown, D. C.

the office investigations was reached. As the importance of further observations upon very small streams became apparent in the course of the investigation, the Little-Falls feeder of the Chesapeake and Ohio canal, near Georgetown, D. C., was selected for this purpose. The observations were made on November 26 and November 28, 1859, near where the feeder leaves the Potomac river at the Little Falls. At the spot selected, the feeder, for a distance of about 350 feet, has a straight course, and uniform, nearly rectangular cross-section, the bed being lined with stone masonry both on the sides and bottom. Above, the channel gradually enlarges to receive the water from the river, and below, it expands into a small basin. The banks are several feet above the water surface, and, in a few places, the sides have partially caved in, thus creating local eddies. Apart from this, the place is very favorable for such experiments. To measure the slope of the water surface, two benches, 335 feet apart, were established, one near the upper and the other near the lower end of the place above described. The difference of level between these benches was determined with great care by five successive levellings, giving the following results for the height of the upper bench above the lower: 0.247, 0.249, 0.248, 0.252, and 0.251 of a foot. The mean, or 0.249 of a foot, was adopted as the true difference of level. The benches were about a foot above the water surface, and by measuring this distance exactly, the fall in 335 feet, and hence the slope, could readily be found whenever desired. To determine the cross-section, a cord, graduated by bits of red tape to lengths of 2 feet, was stretched across the channel where no caving had occurred, and the depth measured with an ordinary lead and line at every bit of tape. The resulting area was that used in determining the discharge, as the floats were observed through a clear part of the channel. The area to correspond to the measured slope was found by deducting from the water-prism—computed by multiplying this area by the distance between the level-stations—the cubic contents of the small portions of the wall which had caved in. To measure the velocity, the tin double-floats, described on page 252, were used. The lower float was uniformly sunk to the mid-depth. The floats were made to pass at different distances from the banks, their velocities and paths being fixed by noting the times and points of crossing two graduated cords stretched across the feeder, 100 feet apart. A very slight down-stream wind was blowing on both days, but, as already demonstrated, it could exercise no influence upon the mid-depth velocity. The method of computation was the following: As the cross-section was nearly rectangular in form, it was considered unnecessary to subdivide it into partial areas for computing the mean velocity; this quantity being sensibly equal to the product of the mean of all the velocities in the horizontal plane at mid-depth by the ratio between the mid-depth and mean velocities in a vertical plane. To determine the mean velocity in the mid-depth horizontal plane, the paths of the floats were plotted and grouped, and the resulting velocities at different distances from the banks plotted in the form of a curve. It was evidently one and the same parabola on both days, being nearly given by the following equations, which only differ in the values of ${}_{w,}V_{\frac{1}{2}D}$:—

(Nov. 26) $$V_{\frac{1}{2}D} = 3.3642 - 8.78\left(\frac{w}{22} - 0.58\right)^2.$$

(Nov. 28) $$V_{\frac{1}{2}D} = 3.0000 - 8.78\left(\frac{w}{22} - 0.58\right)^2.$$

The following table exhibits a comparison between the observations and the velocities given by these formulæ:—

Measurements upon the Chesapeake and Ohio canal feeder.

November 26.				November 28.			
Distance from right bank.	Velocity at mid-depth.		Difference.	Distance from right bank.	Velocity at mid-depth.		Difference.
	Observed.	Computed.			Observed.	Computed.	
Feet.	*Feet.*	*Feet.*	*Feet.*	*Feet.*	*Feet.*	*Feet.*	*Feet.*
5.0	2.4400	2.2742	+ 0.1658	7.0	2.4188	2.4000	+ 0.0188
9.0	3.0500	3.1090	— 0.0590	8.5	2.5631	2.6722	— 0.1091
10.0	3.2105	3.2270	— 0.0165	10.0	2.8902	2.8628	+ 0.0274
12.0	3.3889	3.3540	+ 0.0349	12.0	3.0882	2.9898	+ 0.0984
14.0	3.2105	3.3358	— 0.1253	14.5	2.9167	2.9444	— 0.0277
				16.0	2.8005	2.8083	— 0.0078
Sum...........	15.2999	15.3000	0.4015	Sum.........	16.6775	16.6775	0.2892
Mean..........	3.0600	3.0600	0.0808	Mean........	2.7796	2.7796	0.0482

Since this comparison leaves no doubt that the actual curve was nearly that given by the above equations, the mean velocity in the entire plane from bank to bank was computed by equation (5), substituting ${}_{0}V_{\frac{1}{2}D}$, ${}_{w_{/}}V_{\frac{1}{2}D}$, and ${}_{W}V_{\frac{1}{2}D}$, respectively, for V_0, $V_{d_{/}}$, and V_D. This quantity, for November 26, was 2.5754, and for November 28, 2.3070. Multiplying these velocities by 0.9624, the ratio taken from the sub-surface curve of observation given on page 294, the following mean velocities resulted: November 26, 2.4785 feet; November 28, 2.2202 feet; giving for the discharge 367 and 324 cubic feet per second respectively. The mean velocity corresponding to the slope was the quotient of the discharge by the area corrected, as already explained, for the caving.

Character of such data given in published works.

All the original data of this Survey have now been enumerated. In relation to those found in published works, strange as it may seem, there is a very great scarcity of such observations upon natural channels, although there are many upon pipes and troughs. The measurements of the discharge and corresponding slope of a river are such delicate operations that a full statement both of the mode of conducting the observations and of the method of computation is essential in order to inspire confidence in the accuracy of the work. When this is not given, but little weight can be properly allowed to the data; for such detailed statements have generally revealed errors in some part of the process, even in experiments conducted by engineers of ability, as the following criticisms show.

Dubuat's observations.

Dubuat's six observations upon the Canal du Jard, a very small draining-canal, and four upon the river Haine, comprise all made by him upon natural channels. The *width* of these streams is not recorded. For the Haine, this may be deduced by subtracting from the perimeter half the mean radius—the usual rule for rivers; but for canals, no such relation exists, and errors, which the small size of the Canal du Jard would render important, would probably result from any such assumption for that stream. Moreover, in neither case did

Dubuat *measure* the mean velocity, but trusted to deducing it from the observed central surface velocity by his empirical formula. For these two reasons, the observations upon the Canal du Jard have been rejected. Two of the four observations upon the Haine were made when a lock interrupted its flow and reduced it to a kind of elongated basin, with an almost inappreciable slope. It cannot be assumed that this anomalous condition of the stream produced no effect upon the ordinary ratio between the central surface and true mean velocities, and these observations are, therefore, also rejected. The other two observations upon the river were made with great nicety under favorable circumstances, and have been admitted.

Kraÿenhoff's observations.

Kraÿenhoff made five careful measurements of the discharge, slope, etc. of certain rivers of Holland in 1812. The slope as measured requires some correction; for, since the level-stations were several miles apart, the observed fall must have been affected by bends and inequalities of cross-section. By the bend formula, soon to be discussed, the reductions on this account are computed as given in the fourth column of the following table, sin.^{2} δ being 0.75 per mile:—

River.	Distance between level-stations.	Observed fall in water surface.	Part of fall consumed in overcoming bends, etc.	Difference; or part of fall consumed in overcoming adhesion and cohesion.
	Feet.	*Feet.*	*Feet.*	*Feet.*
The Rhine at Byland	60,553	6.7	0.8	5.9
The Rhine at Pannerden	60,553	6.7	0.7	6.0
The Waal at upper mouth	62,111	7.1	0.6	6.5
The Rhine below the Yssel	44,496	5.6	0.4	5.2
The Yssel at upper mouth	5,190	0.6	0.0	0.6

The mean velocity was measured by means of vertical floating rods extending from the surface nearly to the bottom. The error arising from the rods not extending quite to the bottom was probably counterbalanced by Kraÿenhoff's method of computation, in which the mean velocity was considered a mean of the different division velocities without regarding difference of area.

Watt's observations.

Robison incidentally records the result of a gauging of a small canal by Watt, but without giving any of the details of the measurement. The great reputation of the engineer and the scarcity of published observations of this kind, have induced the use of this observation. The mean velocity is computed from the observed central surface velocity by de Prony's eight-tenths rule.

Destrem's observations.

In Destrem's operations upon the Neva, the velocity was measured by surface floats, from twelve to twenty-three being observed, according to the width of the stream. The discharge was computed by taking the sum of the discharges of the several partial areas into which the cross-section was divided. The mean velocity of each partial area was computed from the surface velocity observed in its central portion, by de Prony's formula for the mean velocity in terms of the central surface velocity. With a view to test the correctness of this novel use of the formula, which certainly was never contemplated by de Prony, a very few observations were made upon the relative velocity, in passing over the same path, of a surface float and one composed of a series of jointed rods so loaded with lead as to remain vertical and extend from the surface nearly to the bottom of the river. Although the observed ratios varied greatly among themselves, Destrem decided that they justified this use of the formula. If so, the formula is greatly in error, for neither de Prony nor Dubuat, of whose original formula this is a modification, designed any *subdivision of the cross-section.* As they proposed the formula, the mean velocity thus found would be—not that of the stream itself—but that of the stream subdivided into as many different streams as there are divisions; a process which would greatly diminish the velocity by the increase of friction. The observations of the Delta Survey prove that Destrem—not de Prony and Dubuat—must be in error in this matter, and a recomputation of all his discharges seems therefore necessary. This would not disturb their close accordance among themselves, as computed by him, while they would all be materially increased. The admirable manner in which they are reported renders their recomputation easy, and it has been undertaken in the two instances (Neva river, Table 2, and Great Nevka river, Table 6) in which the slope was measured. The sum of the products of the observed surface velocities in the different divisions by the areas of their respective divisions, divided by the total area of cross-section, is computed for an approximate mean velocity. The ratio between this and the true mean velocity is then deduced by the new process, fully explained in the last chapter. This ratio is respectively 0.9946 and 0.9922 for these two measurements; giving mean velocities of 3.2296 and 2.0486 feet, instead of 2.6441 and 1.6415 feet, as computed by Destrem. By de Prony's formula, applied *as he designed it,* these mean velocities are 3.2834 and 1.8074 feet, respectively; showing that Destrem's own measurements do not justify his novel application of it. For the purpose of testing de Prony's general formula for discharge, Destrem measured the fall in these two cases for about 3 and 5 miles respectively, immediately below his sections. In this operation, also, he was unfortunate. The detailed map accompanying his report shows that in neither case did the measured slope correspond to the flow at his section. In the first case, a large bend, a new tributary and a great increase in width are noticeable between the upper and lower level-stations. In the second, after passing the upper level-station, the stream bends gradually to a kind of delta, where it divides into a maze of channels forming large islands, on one of which the lower level-station was placed. It is evident that no formula based upon the supposition of uniform motion can accord with these observations, as they are stated, without thereby establishing its own inaccuracy. In default of a better method, the observed slope has been corrected by the formula already mentioned; the values of $\sin.^2 \mathring{a}$, measured on Destrem's map, being 1.44 and 2.17 respectively. The slopes as corrected become 0.00001389 and 0.00001487 in the place of 0.00002665 and 0.00002040. No great weight can be attached to these measurements, but, as observations upon the discharge of rivers, possessing such a degree of exactness, are very rare, it would hardly be justifiable to reject them, when thus corrected. They serve as approximate tests of the different formulæ.

Buffon's observations.

The gauging of the Tiber, including the slope measurement, detailed by Buffon, is superior in exactness to any already noticed. The velocity was measured by long floats, consisting of small bundles of rods, so loaded at one end as to float almost vertically, and extending from the surface nearly to the bottom. The time occupied in passing a distance of about 200 feet was noted for twelve floats well distributed in different parts of the stream. The area of cross-section was carefully measured by sounding, and the discharge computed by taking the sum of the products of several partial areas by the mean of the velocities observed in them. The measurement of the slope was unexceptionable. The admirable method used in reporting the data collected has afforded the means of making two slight corrections in the mean velocity as computed by Buffon. The first error arises from his assuming the velocity at the bank to be the same as that of the float nearest it. This is manifestly erroneous, and a new value has been deduced by assuming the same rate of increase of velocity between the bank and nearest float as between this float and the next. A simple diagram at once shows the necessity for this change. The second correction is for an error fully appreciated by M. Buffon, but which he had no data for eliminating. It is the excess in the measured velocity due to the fact that the rods were unaffected by the water between their lower ends and the bottom of the river. Very careful and extended experiments have been made by Mr. Francis at Lowell, Massachusetts, to determine the error arising from this cause, and the following unpublished formula for the coefficient of correction has been kindly furnished by him as the result deduced:—

$$\text{Coefficient} = 1.000 - 0.116 \left(\left[\frac{D - D_{\prime}}{D} \right]^{\frac{1}{2}} - 0.1 \right).$$

In this formula, D denotes the depth of the water, and $D_{\prime}$ the length of the immersed part of the rod. The mean velocity computed by Buffon is 3.6582 feet. The first correction reduced it 0.0925 of a foot, and the second 0.1525 of a foot, making the true mean velocity 3.4132 feet. This is believed to be still a little excessive, as the measured velocity of some of the floats (of float No. 3, for instance) is evidently too great; but, on the whole, it is considered a very reliable experiment.

Ellet's observations upon bayou Plaquemine.

On March 12, 1851, Mr. Ellet measured the slope of the water surface for several miles down bayou Plaquemine, at stations 1 mile apart. The details of this measurement were not published, but the original diagram is on file in the Bureau of Topographical Engineers, at Washington. The fall in the first mile was 1.45 feet, the Mississippi at Plaquemine being 2.1 feet below the high-water level of 1851. The discharge was not measured; but, as this quantity was accurately determined by the Delta Survey when the Mississippi stood 6.3 and 0.6 feet below the high-water level of 1851 (being 16,900 and 33,390 cubic feet per second, respectively, for those stands), the discharge on March 12 may be deduced by interpolation. This determination must be quite exact, as the quantity of water passing down the bayou depends entirely upon the stand of the Mississippi, and, for any given stand, can undergo but slight variations. The area, width, and perimeter were readily computed from the cross-sections made by the Survey, the stand of the river being given by Mr. Ellet. As the bayou winds considerably in the distance in which the fall was measured, the correction for bend-effect, hereafter to be explained, must be applied to the observed fall. $\text{Sin.}^2\,\delta$, measured on the transit-sheet of this Survey, was found to be 1.746, giving by the bend formula 0.36 of a foot for the fall due to bends and other resistances. This leaves a fall of 1.09 feet per mile for the true slope.

Mr. Ellet's gauging of the Ohio in 1858, including the measurement of the slope,

Ellet's observations upon the Ohio.

was admirably executed, as far as the field work was concerned, and equally well reported; but exception must be taken to the method of computation. The velocity was measured by surface floats well distributed across the river, and the discharge computed by taking eight-tenths of the sum of the products of the several subdivisions of the cross-section by the velocity observed in them. The correction-ratio, eight-tenths, is certainly not allowed by the best authorities. It seems to be a repetition of Destrem's misapplication of de Prony's rule. By applying the process deduced from the observations of this Survey—already fully explained—the true value of this ratio is found to be for this case 0.96, giving a mean velocity of 2.5152 instead of 2.1, as computed by Mr. Ellet. To prevent errors in testing this result, it may be added, that the "mean surface velocity" (a quantity which enters the formulæ) is not, as considered by Mr. Ellet, the quotient of the approximate discharge by the area of the cross-section, but the sum of the products of the widths of the different subdivisions by the mean surface velocity in them, divided by the total width of the river. In other words, it is in this case 2.50 instead of 2.62.

No more data available; but those collected sufficient for all the practical purposes of the Survey.

The above summary includes all observations upon water flowing in natural channels, published in sufficient detail to be entitled to confidence, that could be collected after diligent search. It is to be regretted that the works of Eytelwein and Fünk, which contain reports of such measurements, have not been accessible in the present investigations. It may, however, be doubted whether the operations therein detailed were conducted with the requisite accuracy. A new and extended series of such observations upon rivers of great slopes is absolutely necessary to the entire determination of the form of the function composing the second member of equation (33). The data above mentioned, however, which are all contained in the table on page 316, are sufficient to determine it for natural channels with slopes less than 0.0008 and cross-sections larger than 100 square feet,—limits amply sufficient for the practical requirements of the present Survey. The process used in determining the form of the function remains to be explained.

System adopted for the algebraic analysis of these data.

Determination of the constants of the new formula.—Since the enunciation of Coulomb's law, it has been the general custom to assume $\varphi\,(v)$ —which, as already explained, corresponds with most writers to $\varphi\,(z)$ in the new formula—to be equal to an expression of the form $B\,v + C\,v^2$, and then to find values for the coefficients B and C which would make the formula accord with experiment. De Prony alone (excepting Eytelwein, who followed his method) has exactly defined the process adopted in finding such values. He employed La Place's two methods, the one giving the minimum value for the maximum error, and the other the minimum value for the sum of the errors,—the curve whose co-ordinates are $\frac{r\,s}{v}$ and v (in this case $\frac{r_{,}\,s}{z}$ and z) being a *right line*. As the expression represented by z contains v and $v^{1/2}$, if terms involving its first and second powers are allowed to enter the formula, the final expression for v will be very complex. Moreover, a trial of this process proved that a right line would not conform with sufficient exactness to the data collected. For these reasons, it was necessary to try a new method. The expression $\varphi\,(z)$ in equation (33) was placed equal to the expression $C\,z^2$, giving by reduction the following equation:—

(34) $$C = \frac{a\, s}{(p + W)\, z^2}.$$

The second member containing only known terms, its numerical value was computed for the different observations already described, and it was at once evident that C could not be assumed to be constant. To detect its law of variation, the different values were plotted as ordinates to the corresponding values of $\frac{a}{p + W}$, v, and s, successively, as abscissæ. While serrated curves, following no apparent law, resulted when C was plotted with $\frac{a}{p + W}$ or v, a quite uniform result was obtained by using s. It was then reasonable to conclude that C was some function of this quantity. Much labor was expended before an equation representing this function was found. At first only the data obtained on the regular field work of the Survey were used; then, in succession, the data described above for the higher slopes were added. The successive additions modified the results already obtained, by requiring a change in the curve for these higher slopes. To give a detailed account of these trials would extend the discussion beyond its proper limits without answering any useful purpose. Suffice it to say that few classes of continuous curves for which equations of conditions for passing through two, three, or even four points can be conveniently computed, were left untried. There seemed to be some fatality from which there uniformly resulted either large discrepancies for some of the observations; or an absurd result when the quantity s approached its maximum real value, unity; or an expression so complex that it produced an equation of the third degree or higher, when solved with respect to s; or the necessity of leaving the curve and following a tangent, for slopes above a certain limit. At length it was discovered that the very simple curve—

$$C = \frac{s^{\frac{1}{2}}}{195}$$

would fulfil certain necessary conditions, which could not be forced upon curves whose equations are of a much higher degree. It was accordingly adopted. When this value for C is substituted in equation (34), it can be put under the form—

(35) $$z = \left(\frac{195\, a\, s^{\frac{1}{2}}}{p + W}\right)^{\frac{1}{2}}.$$

This is a general equation, from which the value of any one of the five variables may be deduced when the other four are known. It should be remarked, however, that W and p are hardly independent variables, as a knowledge of one often implies a knowledge of the other. Even when this is not the case, it will be found, for ordinary natural channels, that only a small percentage of error will arise from assuming $p = 1.015$ W. This reduces the variables to four: a, $(p + W)$, s and z. The last-named quantity is strictly a function of v and r, but the coefficient of r is so small that it may be neglected, and z be considered, for all practical purposes, a simple function of v. The following equations exhibit the value of each variable in terms of the other three:—

Algebraic values of each of the four variables in the resulting general formula.

(35) $$z = \left(\frac{195\, a\, s^{\frac{1}{2}}}{p + W}\right)^{\frac{1}{2}},$$

(36) $$s = \left(\frac{(p + W)\, z^2}{195\, a}\right)^2,$$

(37) $$a = \frac{(p + W)\, z^2}{195\, s^{1/2}},$$

(38) $$p + W = \frac{195\, a\, s^{1/2}}{z^2}.$$

It will be remembered that z is a variable of which only two absolute values are known, namely, that for a rectangular cross-section and that for an ordinary river cross-section. These are respectively—

$$z = v + 0.167\, b^{1/2}\, v^{1/2},$$

$$z = 0.93\, v + 0.167\, b^{1/2}\, v^{1/2}.$$

Substituting these values in equation (35), and solving with respect to v, we have the two equations—

(39) $$v = \left(\sqrt{0.0064\, b + (195\, r_{,}\, s^{1/2})^{1/2}} - 0.08\, b^{1/2}\right)^2,$$

(40) $$v = \left(\sqrt{0.0081\, b + (225\, r_{,}\, s^{1/2})^{1/2}} - 0.09\, b^{1/2}\right)^2.$$

As equation (39) is only applicable to a very limited class of streams flowing in artificial beds, it will receive no further notice. It is of exactly the same form as equation (40), and susceptible of the same simplifications for practical use.

Simplifications in these formulæ for large streams.

For small streams, b, as already shown, varies with r, being given by the equation: $b = \frac{1.69}{(r + 1.5)^{1/2}}$, but for rivers, whose mean radius exceeds 12 or 15 feet, the condition of most streams discussed in this report, b may be assumed to be 0.1856. This makes the numerical value of the term involving b so small that, for any but theoretically small velocities, it may be neglected, thus reducing equation (40) to—

(41) $$v = \left([225\, r_{,}\, s^{1/2}]^{1/4} - 0.0388\right)^2,$$

which is an approximate formula applicable to rivers as large as, or larger than, bayou Plaquemine. From this equation the two following formulæ may be deduced, which are sometimes convenient in finding approximate values of the quantities in question.

(42) $$r_{,} = \frac{(v^{1/2} + 0.0388)^4}{225\, s^{1/2}}.$$

(43) $$s = \left(\frac{(v^{1/2} + 0.0388)^4}{225\, r_{,}}\right)^2.$$

Solution when the discharge and two of the four variables are known.

It may happen that the discharge and two of the four variables in equation (35) are known. In this case, both the others may be computed, provided a and v are not the two known variables. This can be done by eliminating the unknown variable in the second member of that one of the above equations whose first member is the variable sought, by substituting for it its value deduced from the equation—

(44) $$v = \frac{Q}{a}.$$

No difficulty will be found in performing the operation except when s and $(p + W)$ are the two known variables. An equation of a higher degree than the second cannot in this case be avoided, and the following method of computation by successive approximations will be found convenient. Let a value of a be assumed, and the corresponding value of v be computed both by equation (40)—or (39) if the cross-section be rectangular —and by equation (44). If these values are identical, the assumed value of a and the corresponding computed value of v are correct. If these values differ, a slight change in the assumed value of a should be made and the operation repeated until any desirable degree of accordance be obtained. If the stream be large, this process may be greatly simplified by using equation (41) instead of (40) and putting it under the form—

$$v = \left(a^{\frac{1}{4}} \left(\frac{225\, s^{\frac{1}{2}}}{p + W}\right)^{\frac{1}{4}} - 0.0388\right)^2.$$

Tests of these new formulæ temporarily deferred.

Before proceeding to detail the numerous tests which have been applied to these formulæ, the various resistances opposed by bends to the flow of water will be discussed, inasmuch as some of the tests involve the use of the formula adopted for eliminating the effect of that class of resistances.

Bends in a river analogous to dams.

Effect of bends, abrupt inequalities of section, etc. upon the fall of rivers.—When water, moving uniformly in a straight channel, encounters a bend, the additional power required to make the change of direction can only be obtained by an increase of slope, and the water is backed up until this increase is attained. The fall in the reach above is adjusted to the level at the head of the bend, for a short distance above which the slope is less than in the straight reach, owing to the accumulation of water. On leaving the bend the water resumes its normal condition. The effect of every bend is, therefore, like that of a dam, to elevate permanently the plane of the water surface above it without affecting that a short distance below. The changes in the depth, the enlargement of the channel and the eddies usually noticeable at bends tend to increase this effect, since they increase still more the resistances in the bend.

Dubuat's empirical bend formula for pipes.

As already seen, it is an important practical matter to determine how much of the actual fall of a river is consumed in overcoming the increased resistances met in passing round bends. The exceedingly complex nature of the movement of the different fillets of water renders any summation of the resistances encountered by them impossible; but it is not to be inferred that no empirical expression can be found which shall satisfy the practical requirements of the hydraulic engineer. A very simple formula of this kind has been proposed by Dubuat in his great work. His reasoning was, briefly, as follows: If $h_{\prime\prime}$ denote the fall required to overcome the increased resistance, it is evident that it must be proportional to the number of bends, to some function of the mean velocity and to some function of the angle of incidence. Denoting by $\acute{a}$ this angle of incidence, which must not exceed a certain value, say from 36 to 40 degrees, and by ε a constant, he assumed for trial the expression—

$$h_{\prime\prime} = \frac{v^2 \sin.^2 \acute{a}}{\varepsilon}.$$

He found by many careful experiments upon pipes of various dimensions that, with ε equal to 2998.5 French inches, $h_{\prime\prime}$ and v being also expressed in this unit, this formula accorded well with the observations. When reduced to English feet it becomes—

$$h_{\prime\prime} = \frac{v^2 \sin.^2 \hat{a}}{266.3}.$$

Observations for determining a coefficient to adapt this formula to rivers.

It is evident that, being deduced entirely from observations upon small pipes, the numerical value of the constant cannot include the effect of the abrupt changes in cross-section always noticeable in river bends. A new value must therefore be deduced for natural channels. Measurements for this purpose were made at various bends between Baton Rouge and Carrollton during the progress of the level-survey between those points in 1851; and, with still greater nicety, at Vicksburg during the progress of the discharge measurements there in 1858. At the latter station, the work was imposed in addition to the usual onerous labors of the party, and the exertions of Mr. Pattison to accomplish it without allowing any interruption of the daily velocity observations, will be appreciated from the following statement. He made an exceedingly careful transit and level survey between permanent benches at the points marked A, E, and G, on figure 4, plate III, a distance of about *eight miles*, running the levels *five times* and making the work test to within a small fraction of an inch. He established graduated rods in the water opposite the three benches, and accurately determined their reference to the common datum-plane. Selecting times when no wind was blowing, the height of the water on these rods was observed simultaneously by different observers, and the true fall in water surface between them thus determined.

Discussion of the observations.

The method of deducing the effect of the bend upon the fall of the river from these observations is simple. If the bend had not existed, the slope measured in the straight portion of the river, multiplied by the distance between the extreme stations, would give the fall between them. The difference between this quantity and the observed fall is $h_{\prime\prime}$, the fall expended in overcoming the additional resistances occasioned by the bend. The corresponding value of $\hat{a}$ was found by plotting a line, containing angles of incidence of about 30°, upon the transit-sheets of the Survey, near the mid-channel. The sum of the squares of the natural sines of these angles gave the numerical value of $\sin.^2 \hat{a}$. For the Vicksburg observations, v was directly measured. For the bends between Baton Rouge and Carrollton, the discharge could be readily computed from the daily measurements at Carrollton and the known distance and rate of movement of the water. The corresponding areas of cross-section were not measured, for the reasons stated in the letter transmitting the report. The widths, however, were known from the transit-sheets, and the corresponding perimeters were found with sufficient accuracy by the rule above given. Knowing these two quantities, together with the discharge and the slope in the straight portion of the river, the corresponding value of a was computed by the general formula in the manner already explained.

New coefficient, and its tests by the observations.

When Dubuat's formula is applied to these data, it gives too small values for $h_{\prime\prime}$, which—as has been shown—ought to be the case for rivers; but with the new value 134 for ε, it agrees closely with the observations. The formula, for English feet, thus becomes—

$$h_{\prime\prime} = \frac{v^2 \sin.^2 \hat{a}}{134}. \tag{45}$$

The following table exhibits the data above described, together with a comparison between the values of $h_{\prime\prime}$ deduced from the measurements and those computed by formula (45):—

Bend.	Date.	Sin.$^2 \hat{a}$	Discharge.	Area of cross-section.	v	Observed slope in straight channel.	Distance between extreme stations.	Fall between extreme stations.		Difference, or $h_{\prime\prime}$.		Difference.
								Computed by slope.	Observed.	By measurement.	By formula.	
		Feet.	Cu. ft.	Sq. ft.	Feet.	Feet.	Feet	Feet.	Feet.	Feet.	Feet.	Feet.
Jefferson College............	May 14–16, 1851	0.989	780,000	143,250	5.44	$\frac{0.403}{19300}$	27,700	0.578	0.905	0.327	0.219	+0.108
43 miles above N. O........	May 20–21, 1851	0.519	710,000	129,100	5.50	$\frac{0.418}{21000}$	38,900	0.774	0.846	0.132	0.117	+0.015
Above Plàquemine..........	June 19–20, 1851	1.168	815,500	157,800	5.17	$\frac{0.170}{11320}$	45,280	0.680	0.954	0.274	0.233	+0.041
Bayou Goula.................	June 23–24, 1851	1.287	767,000	157,700	4.86	$\frac{0.053}{4400}$	38,800	0.467	0.633	0.166	0.227	—0.061
Above Vicksburg............	High water, '58	1.927	1,225,000	179,500	6.82	$\frac{0.490}{11225}$	43,525	1.900	2.650	0.550	0.670	—0.120
Above Vicksburg............	Dec. 18, 1858	1.927	750,000	134,940	5.56	$\frac{0.340}{11225}$	43,525	1.318	1.880	0.562	0.444	+0.118

Considering the great difficulties to be encountered in measuring such a quantity, the amount of the differences in the last column is surprisingly small. It is not upon this alone, however, that the proof of the applicability of the formula to rivers depends. It will soon be subjected to a further test, which is thought to establish its correctness.

The subject which was deferred for this discussion of bend resistances will now be resumed, and a detailed account given of the tests which have been applied to the various formulæ, new and old, designed to express mathematically the relations existing between the cross-section, the slope, and the mean velocity of water flowing in natural channels.

Table of data for testing mean velocity formulæ for rivers.

Tests of formulæ for velocity, slope, etc. of rivers.—The most obvious test, and that first applied, was to compare the results of the various formulæ with the direct measurements contained in the following table, which has been already fully discussed when explaining the manner of determining the form of the function that constitutes the second member of equation (33):—

Measurements of cross-section, slope, and resulting mean velocity of rivers.

Number of observation.	Stream.	Locality.	Date.	Dimensions of cross-section.				Mean velocity	Slope.	Authority.
				Area.	Width.	Perimeter.	Max. depth.			
				Sq. ft.	*Feet.*	*Feet.*	*Feet.*	*Feet.*		
1	Mississippi river....	Carrollton.	High w. 1851	193,968	2653	2693	136	5.9288	0.00002051	Delta Survey.
2	" "	"	" "	195,349	2656	2696	136	5.8869	0.00001713	" "
3	" "	"	May 31, 1851	180,968	2421	2461	131	4.0338	0.00000342	" "
4	" "	"	June 3, 1851	183,663	2429	2469	132	3.9775	0.00000384	" "
5	" "	Columbus.	May 15 1858	148,042	2214	2247	88	6.9575	0.00006800	" "
6	" "	Vicksburg.	June 7, 1858	178,137	2729	2779	100	6.9496	0.00006379	" "
7	" "	"	H. w. 1858	179,502	2732	2782	101	6.8245	0.00004365	" "
8	" "	"	Nov. 6, 1858	78,828	2507	2530	63	3.5234	0.00002227	" "
9	" "	"	Dec. 18, 1858	134,942	2556	2589	83	5.5580	0.00003029	" "
10	" "	"	Dec. 24, 1858	150,354	2580	2621	90	6.3186	0.00004811	" "
11	Bayou Plaquemine..	Near upper mouth.	Mar. 12, 1851	5,560	292	303	28	5.1979	0.00020644	Mr. C. Ellet.
12	" "	" " "	Jan. 16, 1859	4,259	268	278	24	3.9589	0.00014372	Delta Survey.
13	" La Fourche..	" " "	H. w. 1851	3,738	223	238	27	3.0765	0.00004468	" "
14	" "	" " "	May 6, 1851	3,025	223	232	24	2.8430	0.00003731	" "
15	" "	" " "	May 7, 1851	2,957	223	231	24	2.8069	0.00003655	" "
16	" "	" " "	May 8, 1851	2,868	223	230	23	2.7894	0.00004384	" "
17	C. & O. canal feeder	Near Georget'n, D. C.	Nov. 26, 1859	121	23	32.7	7.6	3.0323	0.00069851	" "
18	" "	" " "	Nov. 28, 1859	119	23	32.5	7.5	2.7227	0.00069851	" "
19	Ohio river............	Point Pleasant.	Nov. 20, 1858	7,218	1073	1074	8	2.5152	0.00009334	Mr. C. Ellet.
20	River Haine..........	France.	—— 1782	248.5	48	50.5	8 ?	2.4947	0.00016534	M. Dubuat.
21	" "	"	—— 1782	306.4	50.5	53.4	9 ?	2.5579	0.00015598	" "
22	Canal	England.		50	18	20.6	4	1.1336	0.00006313	Mr. Watt.
23	River Rhine..........	Byland.	June— 1812	19,135	1155	1163	20	3.5749	0.00009769	M. Kraÿenhoff
24	" "	Pannerden.	" "	6,304	557	563	17 ?	3.2766	0.00009986	" "
25	" Waal..........	Upper mouth.	" "	14,782	1328	1334	17 ?	3.1648	0.00010438	" "
26	" Rhine..........	Below the Yssel.	" "	5,341	700	704	12 ?	2.9167	0.00011744	" "
27	" Yssel	Upper mouth.	" "	1,930	321	324	9 ?	2.7727	0.00011657	" "
28	" Tiber	Rome.	June— 1821	2,355	243	249	15	3.4132	0.00013061	M. Buffon.
29	" Neva..........	Russia.	June— 18—	43,461	1218	1227	50	3.2296	0.00001389	M. Destrem.
30	" Great Nevka..	"	June— 18—	15,554	881	893	21	2.0486	0.00001487	" "

List of the old formulæ for the mean velocity of rivers, and table exhibiting their accuracy as compared with that of the new formula.

For convenience of reference, a complete list of the old formulæ (see Chapter III) is here repeated. The following table exhibits the result of the test. The figures denote the amount of the *discrepancies*, and the signs denote the manner in which they are to be applied to the computed mean velocities in order to reduce them to those given in the preceding table. Thus, under the first observation, the error by the Dubuat formula being + 3.1820 feet, the computed mean velocity is 2.7468 feet, since 2.7468 + 3.1820 = 5.9288 feet, the measured mean velocity.

Chezy . . . . .
(Young's coefficient) . . . . . $v = 84.3\,(r\,s)^{\frac{1}{2}}$.
(Eytelwein's coefficient) . . . . $v = 93.4\,(r\,s)^{\frac{1}{2}}$.
(Downing's and others' coefficient) . $v = 100.0\,(r\,s)^{\frac{1}{2}}$.

Dubuat. . . . . $$v = \frac{88.49\,(r^{\frac{1}{2}} - 0.03)}{\left(\frac{1}{s}\right)^{\frac{1}{2}} - \mathrm{L}\left(\frac{1}{s} + 1.6\right)^{\frac{1}{2}}} - 0.086\,(r^{\frac{1}{2}} - 0.03).$$

In which L = common logarithm multiplied by 2.302585.

Girard . . . . . $v = (2.69 + 26384\,r\,s)^{\frac{1}{2}} - 1.64$.

De Prony . . . (For canals) . . . . $v = (0.0556 + 10593\ r\ s)^{1/2} - 0.2357.$
(For canals and pipes) $v = (0.0237 + 9966\ r\ s)^{1/2} - 0.1542.$
(Eytelwein's coefficient) $v = (0.0119 + 8963\ r\ s)^{1/2} - 0.1089.$
(Weisbach's coefficient) $v = (0.00024 + 8675\ r\ s)^{1/2} - 0.0154.$

Young. . . . . $v = \left(\frac{r\ s}{3\ A} + \left(\frac{B}{12\ A}\right)^2\right)^{1/2} - \frac{B}{12\ A}.$

In which $A = 0.0000001 \left(413 + \frac{1.5625}{r} - \frac{90}{3\ r + 8} - \frac{15}{4\ r + 0.0296}\right),$

$B = 0.0000001 \left(\frac{900\ r^2}{r^2 + 0.5} + \frac{1}{(3\ r)^{1/2}} \left(271.25 + \frac{6.88}{r} + \frac{0.0001146}{r^2}\right)\right).$

Dupuit . . . . $v = \frac{s\ r\ a}{0.08\ W} + (0.0067 + 9114\ r\ s)^{1/2} - 0.082.$

St. Venant . . $v = 106.068\ (r\ s)^{\frac{11}{21}}.$

Ellet. . . . . . $v = 0.64\ (\Delta\ H)^{1/2} + 0.04\ \Delta\ H.$

In which Δ denotes the maximum depth of the stream, and H the fall in water surface in 1 English mile.

Tests of the several formulæ for mean velocity.

Number of observations.	Chezy's formula with coefficient of			Dubuat's formula.	Girard's formula.	De Prony's formula with coefficients				Young's formula.	Dupuit's formula.	St. Venant's formula.	Ellet's formula.	New formula.
	Young.	Eytelwein.	Downing and others.			For canals.	For pipes and canals.	By Eytelwein.	By Weisbach.					
	Feet.	*Feet.*	*Feet.*	*Feet.*	*Feet.*	*Feet.*	*Feet.*	*Feet.*	*Feet.*	*Feet.*	*Feet.*	*Feet.*	*Feet.*	*Feet.*
1	+ 2.6888	+ 2.3390	+ 2.0854	+ 3.1820	+ 1.1140	+ 2.2017	+ 2.2430	+ 2.3974	+ 2.3644	+ 2.6547	+ 1.0536	+ 2.4381	+ 2.8837	+ 0.0385
2	+ 2.9167	+ 2.5961	+ 2.3636	+ 3.4374	+ 1.5736	+ 2.4887	+ 2.5204	+ 2.6584	+ 2.6206	+ 2.9000	+ 1.4629	+ 2.7002	+ 3.1500	+ 0.2425
3	+ 2.6973	+ 2.5530	+ 2.4484	+ 3.3542	+ 2.6207	+ 2.6208	+ 2.5978	+ 2.6378	+ 2.5725	+ 2.7822	+ 2.3651	+ 2.6534	+ 2.9552	+ 0.2593
4	+ 2.5522	+ 2.3984	+ 2.2868	+ 3.2073	+ 2.4188	+ 2.4572	+ 2.4369	+ 2.4820	+ 2.4182	+ 2.6320	+ 2.1732	+ 2.5009	+ 2.8230	+ 0.0658
5	+ 1.3152	+ 0.7061	+ 0.2643	+ 1.5090	− 2.3975	+ 0.3004	+ 0.4281	+ 0.7288	+ 0.7388	+ 1.1238	− 3.0950	+ 0.7159	+ 2.0962	− 0.8093
6	+ 1.5591	+ 0.9772	+ 0.5552	+ 2.7722	− 1.9246	+ 0.5998	+ 0.7184	+ 1.0038	+ 1.0091	+ 1.3844	− 0.0904	+ 0.9996	+ 1.8883	− 0.4602
7	+ 2.3506	+ 1.8677	+ 1.5174	+ 2.6733	− 0.3106	+ 1.5929	+ 1.6784	+ 1.9078	+ 1.8968	+ 2.2359	− 0.4739	+ 1.9298	+ 2.8054	+ 0.0713
8	+ 1.3028	+ 1.0631	+ 0.8893	+ 1.6224	+ 0.5812	+ 1.0377	+ 1.0434	+ 1.1361	+ 1.0853	+ 1.3343	+ 0.8166	+ 1.1737	+ 1.4852	− 0.3978
9	+ 2.2085	+ 1.8469	+ 1.5847	+ 2.5718	+ 0.5389	+ 1.6975	+ 1.7427	+ 1.9037	+ 1.8726	+ 2.1690	+ 0.8041	+ 1.9437	+ 2.6953	+ 0.0430
10	+ 1.8902	+ 1.4121	+ 1.0654	+ 2.1721	− 0.7304	+ 1.1425	+ 1.2263	+ 1.4530	+ 1.4411	+ 1.7785	− 0.6254	+ 2.0143	+ 2.3442	− 0.1982
11	+ 0.0094	− 0.5507	− 0.9569	− 0.1965	− 3.2932	− 0.9055	− 0.7942	− 0.5211	− 0.5194	− 0.1556	− 1.4981	− 0.5187	+ 0.4408	− 0.0448
12	+ 0.0033	− 0.4238	− 0.7334	− 0.0583	− 2.1974	− 0.6407	− 0.5738	− 0.3760	− 0.3963	− 0.0801	− 0.8769	− 0.3435	+ 0.4993	− 0.3871
13	+ 0.8434	+ 0.6023	+ 0.4275	+ 1.0077	+ 0.1116	+ 0.5756	+ 0.5817	+ 0.6751	+ 0.6245	+ 0.8751	+ 0.4812	+ 0.7129	+ 1.2065	− 0.2076
14	+ 0.9837	+ 0.7829	+ 0.6374	+ 1.1533	+ 0.5428	+ 0.7964	+ 0.7900	+ 0.8069	+ 0.8040	+ 1.0392	+ 0.7353	+ 0.8921	+ 1.2623	+ 0.0213
15	+ 0.9835	+ 0.7866	+ 0.6439	+ 1.1535	+ 0.5695	+ 0.8039	+ 0.7963	+ 0.8651	+ 0.8076	+ 1.0613	+ 0.7447	+ 0.8954	+ 1.2442	+ 0.0304
16	+ 0.8184	+ 0.6056	+ 0.4513	+ 0.9686	+ 0.2926	+ 0.6072	+ 0.6044	+ 0.6821	+ 0.7270	+ 0.8657	+ 0.5499	+ 0.7156	+ 1.0997	− 0.0768
17	− 1.2535	− 1.7162	− 2.0517	− 1.7040	− 3.7470	− 1.9699	− 1.8912	− 1.6733	− 1.6876	− 1.3746	− 1.9100	− 1.6470	− 1.4773	− 0.0709
18	− 1.5406	− 2.0008	− 2.3346	− 1.9857	− 4.0141	− 2.2520	− 2.1741	− 1.9576	− 1.9723	− 1.6603	− 2.1895	− 1.8953	− 1.7497	− 0.3594
19	+ 0.4038	+ 0.1759	+ 0.0106	+ 0.6998	− 0.2313	+ 0.1623	+ 0.1643	+ 0.2504	+ 0.1977	+ 0.4406	+ 0.1520	+ 0.2864	+ 1.0867	+ 0.0298
20	+ 0.0901	− 0.1694	− 0.3577	+ 0.0453	− 0.7802	− 0.2148	− 0.2028	− 0.0990	− 0.1467	+ 0.1054	− 0.2003	− 0.0593	+ 0.5240	+ 0.0257
21	+ 0.0364	− 0.2358	− 0.4333	− 0.0038	− 0.9301	− 0.2940	− 0.2779	− 0.1671	− 0.2128	+ 0.0447	− 0.2847	− 0.1265	+ 0.5194	− 0.0886
22	+ 0.0901	− 0.0226	− 0.1043	+ 0.1478	+ 0.1788	+ 0.0737	+ 0.0425	+ 0.0655	− 0.0040	+ 0.1871	+ 0.0257	+ 0.0684	+ 0.3413	− 0.1965
23	+ 0.1952	− 0.1696	− 0.4342	+ 0.2315	− 1.5005	− 0.3224	− 0.2761	− 0.1133	− 0.1439	+ 0.1506	− 0.5043	− 0.0736	+ 1.1067	− 0.4809
24	+ 0.4577	+ 0.1534	− 0.0673	+ 0.4877	− 0.7571	+ 0.0627	+ 0.0891	+ 0.2179	+ 0.1774	+ 0.4492	+ 0.0070	+ 0.2597	+ 1.0020	− 0.0544
25	+ 0.2978	− 0.0117	− 0.2361	− 0.2478	− 0.9577	− 0.1078	− 0.0797	+ 0.0520	+ 0.0125	+ 0.2862	− 0.1620	+ 0.2895	+ 0.8310	− 0.1808
26	+ 0.4004	+ 0.1288	− 0.0682	+ 0.4037	− 0.5617	+ 0.0712	+ 0.0871	+ 0.1976	+ 0.1518	+ 0.4107	+ 0.0629	+ 0.2382	+ 0.8733	+ 0.0973
27	+ 0.5513	+ 0.3115	+ 0.1376	+ 0.5584	− 0.1711	+ 0.2860	+ 0.2918	+ 0.3845	+ 0.3337	+ 0.5803	+ 0.2855	+ 0.4221	+ 1.0048	+ 0.2993
28	+ 0.4503	+ 0.1305	− 0.1015	+ 0.4294	− 0.8867	+ 0.0238	+ 0.0553	+ 0.1928	+ 0.1587	+ 0.4315	− 0.0107	+ 0.2347	+ 0.9410	+ 0.1378
29	+ 1.3598	+ 1.1579	+ 1.0115	+ 1.4974	+ 0.9109	+ 1.1702	+ 1.1641	+ 1.2357	+ 1.1790	+ 1.4133	+ 0.9731	+ 1.2671	+ 1.8573	− 0.4976
30	+ 0.6919	+ 0.5455	+ 0.4393	+ 0.9601	+ 0.6026	+ 0.6112	+ 0.5888	+ 0.6300	+ 0.5649	+ 0.7771	+ 0.5348	+ 0.6463	+ 1.1609	− 0.5191
Sum	32.9420	28.4411	26.6988	40.4417	37.4472	28.0905	28.1506	29.5258	28.8412	33.3834	25.1488	30.6619	45.3547	6.3920

The discrepancies of the old formulæ have in general the wrong sign.

The great superiority of the new formula, for natural channels, is evident from this table. Moreover, erroneous as the old formulæ are made to appear, they are—with the exception of the Prony-Eytelwein and Ellet formulæ—in reality too favorably represented by these columns of differences. This is plain when it is remembered that their constants were almost exclusively deduced from observations where nearly absolute uniformity of motion existed; and that, therefore, when applied to natural channels, where a certain part of the actual slope is consumed in overcoming the resistances opposed by the inequalities of cross-section, they *ought* to give *too large* a mean velocity. Exactly the reverse is in general shown by the above table, and the formulæ, therefore, give results not only erroneous in *amount*, but also in *sign*. They ought to give too large, and they really give too small, a mean velocity.

This idea confirmed by applying the new formula to Dubuat's observations on a wooden trough.

If this is true, the converse is also true; that is, a correct *river* formula, when applied to observations made upon water flowing with perfect uniformity, ought to give too *small* a mean velocity. To test this question—and incidentally the new formula—it has been applied to Dubuat's observations upon his small wooden trough, where by ingenious contrivances he succeeded in securing perfect uniformity of motion. The result was in accordance with these views. Moreover, the deficiency followed a definite law for nearly all the observations, requiring the addition of a function of the true mean velocity, given by the expression: $0.66 \ (v - 0.4)$. The large numerical value of this correction was not anticipated. It may possibly be in part due to water having a less adhesion to smooth wood than to earth. For a long time after Coulomb's experiments, this question was believed to be decisively settled in the negative; but later writers, among whom may be named Dupuit, whose works place him in the first rank of those who have treated of hydraulic science, consider it to be still a subject for experimental investigation. The following table exhibits the results of the computations. It should be added, that it would doubtless be easy to deduce a new value of C, which would make the formula, without any empirical addition, accord closely with these observations, but not being required for any practical purpose, this has not been attempted.

New formula applied to Dubuat's observations on his trough.

Observation.	Dimensions of cross-section.			Mean radius.	Slope.	Mean velocity.			Difference.
	Area.	Width.	Perimeter.			Observed.	Computed.	Corrected as above.	
	Sq. feet.	*Feet.*	*Feet.*	*Feet.*		*Feet.*	*Feet.*	*Feet.*	*Feet.*
A.	0.1486	1.034	1.160	0.128	0.00471698	2.4433	0.8383	2.1869	+0.2564
B.	0.3991	1.526	2.620	0.152	0.00471698	2.5686	1.0120	2.4437	+0.1249
C.	0.6581	1.959	2.309	0.285	0.00242718	2.4105	1.0952	2.4221	−0.0116
D.	0.2146	1.195	1.360	0.158	0.00234192	1,6236	0.8606	1.6682	−0.0446
E.	0.3105	1.396	1.610	0.193	0.00234192	1.8030	0.8692	1.7952	+0.0078
F.	0.3979	1.557	1.809	0.220	0.00234192	1.9868	0.9367	1.9840	+0.0028
G.	0.4451	1.637	1.910	0.233	0.00234192	2.0907	0.9683	2.0841	+0.0066
H.	0.7947	2.141	2.534	0.314	0.00231482	2.5330	1.1418	2.5491	−0.0161
I.	0.9433	2.322	2.759	0.342	0.00231482	2.6787	1.1979	2.7018	−0.0231
K.	1.0310	2.422	2.884	0.358	0.00231482	2.8324	1.2286	2.8340	−0.0016
L.	1.0675	2.462	2.934	0.364	0.00231482	2.8883	1.2403	2.8826	+0.0057
M.	0.1643	1.074	1.210	0.136	0.00057870	0.7940	0.4806	0.7407	+0.0533
N.	0.2711	1.315	1.510	0.180	0.00057870	0.8624	0.5660	0.8712	−0.0088
O.	0.3314	1.436	1.660	0.200	0.00057870	1.0960	0.6021	1.0615	+0.0345
P.	0.2721	1.532	1.887	0.144	0.00218341	1.7976	0.6981	1.6205	+0.1771
Q.	0.6803	1.532	2.420	0.281	0.00218341	2.5126	1.0868	2.4811	+0.0315
R.	0.2721	1.532	1.887	0.144	0.00107643	1.2043	0.5744	1.1052	+0.0991
S.	0.2778	1.532	1.894	0.147	0.00070822	0.8162	0.5167	0.7914	+0.0248
T.	0.4082	1.532	2.065	0.198	0.00070822	1.0747	0.6235	1.0688	+0.0059
V.	0.6010	1.532	2.316	0.259	0.00070822	1.2585	0.7444	1.3110	−0.0525
X.	0.8107	1.532	2.591	0.313	0.00070822	1.3811	0.8453	1.4928	−0.1117
Y.	0.5443	1.532	2.243	0.243	0.00010767	0.4077	0.4226	0.4297	−0.0220
Z.	1.2246	1.532	3.131	0.391	0.00010767	0.5062	0.5925	0.6626	−0.1564
					Sum.	39.5702		39.1882	1.2788

But to return to the discussion of the errors of the several formulæ, as shown by the table preçeding the last. Of all these formulæ, Mr. Ellet's alone was deduced especially for rivers. For all except his, therefore, the excessive errors exhibited by this table are considered conclusive as to their non-applicability to water flowing in natural channels. The theoretical errors in Mr. Ellet's formula, exposed in Chapter III; its non-accordance with careful observations on small streams, as reported by Mr. Stevenson; and, above all, its non-accordance with the above observations upon the very river for which it was deduced, would seem to justify its rejection without further trial. This has not been deemed proper, however, because the rejection of this formula necessarily destroys the basis of some of the most important practical conclusions of Mr. Ellet's report. It has, therefore, been decided to apply to it, as well as to the new formula, the other, severer tests, which are considered essential before trusting to any formula where interests involving so many millions of dollars are concerned.

All the old formulæ except Mr. Ellet's, are to be rejected without further trial. Reason for excepting his.

The second test is very severe and applies equally to the mean-velocity and bend formulæ. It consists in computing, by equations (36) and (45), the fall in water surface between those points on the Mississippi and its tributary streams for which the necessary data and the real difference of level are known. These data are the mean dimensions of cross-section, the discharge corresponding to the known fall in water surface and the value of sin.^{2} δ for the distance considered.

Mean-velocity and bend formulæ both to be tested by computing the mean slope of the water surface in the Mississippi river and in certain of its tributaries.

For the Mississippi river below the mouth of the Ohio, the first two of these quantities have been determined with tolerable exactness, at

Data for the Mississippi river. Law respecting the quantity sin.^{2} $\acute{a}$.

both high and low water, by the operations conducted during the years 1851 and 1858. The method of computation by which they are derived from the observations, as well as a full discussion of the corresponding slopes of the water surface, will be found under the proper headings in Chapter II and Chapter VI. The values of sin.^{2} $\acute{a}$ have been carefully deduced from the best maps extant, viz.: from Fort St. Philip to New Orleans, on Captain Hughes' map; thence to Red river, on the original large-scale maps of the Delta Survey; thence to the northern boundary of Mississippi, on La Tourrette's map; thence to the northern boundary of Arkansas, on Langtree's sectional map; thence to the mouth of the Ohio, on Hutawa's State map of Missouri. As a rough test of the accuracy of these measurements, which are somewhat delicate, it was reasoned that, as the value of the sin.^{2} $\acute{a}$ depends upon the number of bends between the points considered, it should be approximately proportional to the excess of distance by the river over that by an air-line. Denoting this quantity expressed in miles by M, it was found that with a coefficient of 0.34, giving the equation—

$$\text{Sin.}^2\ \acute{a} = 0.34\ \text{M},$$

a much closer accordance with the measurements was secured than had been anticipated. It is very probable that a still more accurate formula might be deduced of the form sin. $\acute{a} = \varphi$ (M), but as the subject has little practical importance it was not pursued. The following table, comparing the measured values of sin.^{2} $\acute{a}$ with those computed by the above expression, is given as an illustration that, so far from being, as often declared in popular writings, a river without rule or beyond the restraint of law, the Mississippi is in reality controlled by laws that can be expressed in simple algebraic formulæ.

Curvature of the Mississippi.

Locality.	M.	Observed sin.^{2} a.	Computed sin.^{2} a.	Difference.
	Miles.			
Cairo to Columbus	3	2.04	1.02	+1.02
Columbus to Memphis	83	23.77	28.22	—4.45
Memphis to Helena	29	9.60	9.86	—0.26
Helena to Napoleon	44	11.92	14.96	—3.04
Napoleon to Lake Providence	63	19.79	21.42	—1.63
Lake Providence to Vicksburg	37	11.95	12.58	—0.63
Vicksburg to New Carthage	6	3.47	2.04	+1.43
New Carthage to Natchez	35	12.08	11.90	+0.18
Natchez to Red river	17	9.20	5.78	+3.42
Red river to Baton Rouge	26	7.17	8.84	—1.67
Baton Rouge to Donaldsonville	24	8.22	8.16	+0.06
Donaldsonville to Carrollton	22	12.30	7.48	+4.82
Carrollton to Fort St. Philip	28	9.30	9.52	—0.22
Sum		140.81	141.78	22.83

Besides the data for the Mississippi river just indicated, the operations of the Survey furnish the means of extending the test to bayou La Fourche and bayou Plaquemine in the manner now to be explained.

Data for bayou La Fourche.

The total fall of bayou La Fourche from Donaldsonville to Lockport, at the high water of 1851, was determined with accuracy. A close approximation to the corresponding mean area, width, and perimeter of the bayou was had by taking a mean of the sections made in 1851, at Lockport, Thibodeaux, Pain Court, and Donaldsonville. The high-water discharge is about 11,500 cubic feet per second, as shown by the measurements at Donaldsonville so often mentioned. The distance and sin.^{2} $\acute{d}$ were taken from Powell's map of La Fourche Interior, drawn on the scale of 1 inch to the mile, which is sufficiently large to insure all needful accuracy.

The comparative level of the high waters at Donaldsonville and Lockport for the years 1851 and 1858 was also found by exact marks; but a crevasse which occurred a short distance above Lockport on April 11, 1858, so lowered the water at that place that it did not subsequently attain the level of April 11, although the bayou at Donaldsonville rose 1.6 feet between that date and May 10–11, when it stood at its highest point for the year. The actual fall on April 11 was 8 feet; being equal to 11.9 (the fall in 1851), less 1.9 (the high water of 1858 being 0.3 below the high water of 1851 at Donaldsonville), less 2 feet (the elevation of the water on April 11, 1858, above the high-water level of 1851 at Lockport). As the cross-sections at Donaldsonville and Lockport are the only ones known on April 11, a mean between them is taken, in determining the area, width, and perimeter, to correspond to this fall. The values of the sin.^{2} $\acute{d}$ and the discharge are found as just explained for 1851.

Data for bayou Plaquemine.

The fall of bayou Plaquemine at high water in 1850 and 1851, between Plaquemine and Indian Village, was determined by this Survey by careful levelling between accurate marks at the two localities. The corresponding discharge of the bayou results by interpolation from the measurements made when the bayou was 0.6 and 6.3 feet below the high water of 1851. The distance and sin.^{2} $\acute{d}$ have been exactly measured on the transit-sheets of the Survey. To find the mean area of cross-section is a more uncertain matter, since no sections were made except near the mouth. As an approximation which is, probably, sufficiently exact, it has been assumed that the same ratio exists between this measured area at the mouth and the true mean of the bayou as between the corresponding quantities in bayou La Fourche. This gives, for the high-water area in 1851, 5700 square feet instead of 6175 as measured at the mouth. On March 12, 1851, Mr. Ellet measured the slope of the water surface from Plaquemine to a point just above Indian Village (exact distance 8 miles). These data, which were not published, may be found on file in the Bureau of Topographical Engineers, War Department. The levelling was apparently done with care, checks on the water surface being made every mile; and it has been accordingly used as a test of the formula, the values of the different variables being found in precisely the same manner as for the fall at the high water of 1850 and 1851, just detailed.

Application of this test to Mr. Ellet's formula.

As already explained, this test has been applied to the new formula and to that proposed by Mr. Ellet. As he intimates that he allowed for bend-effect in deducing his coefficients, no separate computation on that account is required with his formula. By it the value of h is—

$$h = \frac{l}{5280}\left(\left[\frac{64 + 25\,v}{\Delta}\right]^{\frac{1}{2}} - \frac{8}{\Delta^{\frac{1}{2}}}\right)^2.$$

The following table exhibits the data and the results of the test. Its severity is

Result of the test. Its severity and true significance.

evident when it is remembered that the formulæ give *the fall per foot*, and that, consequently, the discrepancies shown in the columns of errors are really the products of the errors by the number of feet between the level-stations. It must also be borne in mind that the formulæ do not require a change of level in the surface of the river, independently of the bottom, equal to the amount of the discrepancies, but only that the whole river, surface and bottom, shall be raised or lowered so as to affect the total fall by the amount of the discrepancy, without at all changing the present dimensions of cross-section.

Tests of the formulæ for slope.

Stream.	Level-stations.	Date.	Area.	Width.	Perimeter.	Maximum depth.	Discharge.	Measured between level-stations.			Ellet's formula.		New formula.			
								Sin.² $\acute{a}$.	Distance.	Fall.	Computed fall.	Error.	$h_{,}$	$h_{,,}$	Computed fall, or $h_{,}+h_{,,}$	Error.
			Sq. ft.	*Ft.*	*Ft.*	*Ft.*	*Cu. ft.*		*Miles.*	*Ft.*	*Ft.*	*Ft.*	*Ft.*	*Ft.*	*Ft.*	*Ft.*
Mississippi R...	Ft. St. Philip and B. La Fourche.	H. w. 1851	199,000	2,470	2,510	129	1,150,000	21.60	156.00	20.7	50.9	— 30.2	12.9	5.4	18.3	+ 2.4
" "	" " " " "	L. w. "	163,000	2,250	2,290	114	250,000	21.60	156.00	0.9	6.2	— 5.3	0.1	0.4	0.5	+ 0.4
" "	B. La Fourche and Red river.	H. w. "	200,000	3,000	3,035	113	1,200,000	15.39	122.60	23.7	47.7	— 24.0	17.0	4.1	21.1	+ 2.6
" "	" " " " "	L. w. "	100,000	2,750	2,770	78	250,000	15.39	122.60	3.7	16.6	— 12.9	1.8	0.7	2.5	+ 1.2
" "	Red river and Arkansas river.	H. w. 1858	199,000	4,080	4,115	96	1,200,000	56.50	373.00	112.0	172.1	— 60.1	98.4	15.3	113.7	— 1.7
" "	" " " " "	L. w. "	54,000	3,060	3,070	56	200,000	56.50	373.00	114.0	92.4	+ 21.6	117.7	5.8	123.5	— 9.5
" "	Arkansas river and Ohio river.	H. w. "	191,000	4,470	4,510	87	1,175,000	47.33	408.00	160.0	214.2	— 54.2	151.7	13.4	165.1	— 5.1
" "	" " " " "	L. w. "	45,000	3,400	3,410	49	150,000	47.33	408.00	159.0	121.2	+ 37.8	141.1	3.8	144.9	+ 14.1
B. Plaquemine.	Plaquemine and Indian Village.	H. w. 1850	5,500	300	318	31	33,500	8.63	8.33	20.0	12.1	+ 7.9	18.0	2.4	20.4	— 0.4
" "	" " " "	March 12, '51	5,120	300	315	30	29,000	8.63	8.00	17.9	10.7	+ 7.2	14.9	2.1	17.0	+ 0.9
" "	" " " "	H. w. "	5,700	300	320	32	35,000	8.63	8.33	20.0	11.9	+ 8.1	17.4	2.4	19.8	+ 0.2
B. La Fourche..	Donaldsonville and Lockport.	" " "	3,640	230	245	25	11,500	11.77	55.50	11.9	27.7	— 15.8	12.6	0.9	13.5	— 1.6
" "	" " "	April 11, '58	3,567	221	237	26	9,700	11.77	55.50	8.0	25.7	— 17.7	6.8	0.7	7.5	+ 0.5
Sum..........										671.8	809.4	302.8			667.8	40.6

The discrepancies of the new formulæ, small as they are, are not necessarily errors.

While it is conceded that some uncertainty exists as to the degree of exactness with which a few of the values in the above table of data have been determined, yet, taken as a whole, the test must have great weight even with the most sceptical. While it indicates that no confidence whatever can be placed in the results given by Mr. Ellet's formula, it confirms in a surprising manner the exactness of the new formulæ for this class of streams. The errors of the latter, small as they are, can in some cases be explained. Thus the real fall between Donaldsonville and Lockport at high water, 1851, which the new formulæ make 1.6 feet greater than was observed, was affected by certain small crevasses between those localities, and probably to about this amount. That is, if they had not occurred, the increased area of cross-section would have made the indication of the formulæ approximate more nearly to the real slope. The discrepancy in the fall at low water between the Ohio and Arkansas rivers may be due to the effect of the sand-bars. But a discussion of so small errors is needless.

The third and last test.

The third and last test consists in applying the formula in certain cases, where all the quantities involved have been measured, to the solution of the grand problem for which it was especially deduced, namely, to determine how much the surface of a river will be raised at a given locality, where the cross-section and discharge are known, by the addition of a given quantity of water. This problem, from its importance, requires a separate division of the chapter.

Effect produced upon the surface level of a river by variation in discharge.—This subject is very simple, as treated by Dubuat and most other writers, because they assume the slope to remain unchanged. It will soon be seen that this assumption is inadmissible, and that the question becomes, in consequence, a very involved one. But, waiving for the present the question what the new slope is, or rather assuming for the time that the new slope is known, the remaining part of the computation will be explained.

New solution of the problem, supposing the new slope to be known.

The following method is considered an improvement upon any heretofore suggested. It consists in deducing algebraic expressions for the new area, width, and perimeter in terms of known quantities, and of the rise or fall in feet produced by the change in the discharge. This rise or fall in feet will be called x. Designate by $a_{,}$, $p_{,}$, $W_{,}$, $Q_{,}$, and $v_{,}$, the given area, perimeter, width, discharge, and mean velocity (the latter being the quotient of $Q_{,}$ by $a_{,}$), and by $a_{,,}$, $p_{,,}$, $W_{,,}$, $Q_{,,}$, and $v_{,,}$, these quantities after the change in the discharge. Let $s_{,}$ be the primitive slope, computed from the given data, and $s_{,,}$ be the new slope, supposed for the time to be a known function of $s_{,}$ and x. On figure 8, plate III, let E D B F denote the curve of intersection of the natural bank and the plane containing the soundings, G B being the water surface before, and H D the same after, a certain increase in the discharge. It is evident that a straight line A B can always be drawn, which shall coincide sufficiently for all practical purposes with E D B F within the limits considered. The line B C represents x. Denoting by ϑ the angle C B D and by $\vartheta_{,}$ the corresponding angle at the other bank of the river, the following expressions can be readily deduced from the trapezoid representing the increase of area due to the rise:—

$$(46) \qquad \frac{a_{,,}}{p_{,,} + W_{,,}} = \frac{a_{,} + x\,(W_{,} + \frac{1}{2}\,x\,[\tan.\,\vartheta + \tan.\,\vartheta_{,}])}{p_{,} + W_{,} + x\left(\tan.\,\vartheta + \tan.\,\vartheta_{,} + \dfrac{1}{\cos.\,\vartheta} + \dfrac{1}{\cos.\,\vartheta_{,}}\right)},$$

$$(47) \qquad x = -\frac{W_{,}}{\tan.\,\vartheta + \tan.\,\vartheta_{,}} + \left(\left[\frac{W_{,}}{\tan.\,\vartheta + \tan.\,\vartheta_{,}}\right]^2 + \frac{2\,(Q_{,,} - v_{,,}\,a_{,})}{v_{,,}\,(\tan.\,\vartheta + \tan.\,\vartheta_{,})}\right)^{\frac{1}{2}}.$$

In general, unless a very great change in the discharge occurs, the banks may be assumed, without sensible error, to be vertical, in which case the above expressions become—

$$(48) \qquad \frac{a_{,,}}{p_{,,} + W_{,,}} = \frac{a_{,} + W_{,}\,x}{p_{,} + W_{,} + 2\,x},$$

$$(49) \qquad x = \frac{Q_{,,} - a_{,}\,v_{,,}}{W_{,}\,v_{,,}}.$$

By the aid of these equations, the method of successive approximations, which is necessary to avoid an equation of a higher degree than the second in solving the problem, becomes very simple. Let a value of x be assumed, and $\frac{a_{,,}}{p_{,,} + W_{,,}}$, in equation (46) or (48), be computed. With the value thus found, and $s_{,,}$, $v_{,,}$ can be deduced by equation (41); or, if the stream be small, by equation (40) or (39). With this value of $v_{,,}$, let x be computed by equation (47) or (49). If the value thus found is the same as that assumed, no change is required. If it differs, the operation should be repeated, assuming new values of x, until a sufficiently close approximation is made.

Discussion of the new slope. Its value cannot be deduced for any particular locality by noting the change in the mean slope for long distances.

The new slope ($s_{\prime\prime}$) is now to be discussed. It must evidently be a function of the primitive slope ($s_{\prime}$) and of the change (x) in surface level produced by the change in the discharge. The subject would be comparatively simple, so far as the practical problem is concerned, if the slope in long distances only was to be considered. But even then it is evident, from the following considerations, that different rules would be required for different parts of the Mississippi river.

While the level of the gulf is not sensibly affected by a flood of the Mississippi, the level of the water surface in the channel of that river is raised by an amount which increases nearly proportionally with the distance from the gulf until a point near Natchez is reached, where the range from extreme low to extreme high water exceeds 50 feet. For any point in this part of the river, therefore, the new mean slope is evidently equal to the primitive mean slope increased by the fraction—

$$\frac{x}{\text{Distance in feet to unchanging water level}}.$$

Between Natchez and the mouth of the Ohio, however, totally different conditions exist. The extreme range at these two localities is about equal, and there is, therefore, no sensible difference between the mean slope of this portion of the river at high and that at low water. If intermediate points are considered, however, even this rule fails, since the range, affected by local causes, is not uniform; and hence, for some long portions of the river between these localities, the mean slope at high water is greater than at low water, while, for others, directly the reverse is the case. No general rule, therefore, can apply to this part of the river.

Even if a general rule, governing changes in mean slope for long distances, could be deduced, it would have little practical value in discussing the levee question, because the variation in the quantity of water added at different parts of the river is so great, that a knowledge of the mean elevation of high-water mark in long distances would not be sufficient to solve the problem. It is apparent, therefore, that the laws governing *local* changes of slope must be ascertained, in order to fulfil the practical requirements of the Survey.

Some important information respecting changes of local slope may be derived from an inspection of plates XIV, XV, XVI, and XVII. For a given stand of the river, variations in discharge can only be produced by variations in slope, since all other quantities which influence the flow of the water remain unchanged. The practical effect of variations in the slope upon the discharge, amounting at Columbus, for some stands of the river, to 400,000 *cubic feet per second*, or about one-third of the usual flood discharge of the river, is apparent to the eye. By critically studying these three diagrams, the following general laws are perceived: First, the absolute value of the slope at any given stand of the river may be very different for different rises. This is especially true when the river is above mid-stage. The variation is much greater in the upper than in the lower

Local slope. Experimental laws which govern its variations.

part of the river. Second, the slope increases during a rise. The rate of this increase does not differ very much for different rises, but is generally more rapid, the higher the stage attained. Third, during any given oscillation, the slope is much greater when the river is rising than when it is falling, but the two parts of the curve formed by plotting this slope with respect to gaugé-reading are nearly parallel. Fourth, the maximum discharge for any given rise usually occurs when the river is a little below the highest point attained during that rise.

Explanation of them.

The explanation of these facts readily suggests itself. When a tributary discharges a sudden flood into the Mississippi, producing a rise, the water thus added moves toward the gulf in an immense wave, whose convexity depends upon the amount of water added per second, and upon the stage of the Mississippi above and below the mouth of the tributary. When this wave is passing a given locality, the local slope will be determined by this convexity. As long as the river is rising, the top of the wave has not yet arrived, and the slope, and hence the discharge, at any given stage of the river will have its maximum value for that oscillation. When the river reaches its highest point, the top of the wave is passing, and, the slope being less than before, the discharge must diminish. When the river is falling, the rear of the wave is passing, and the slope, and hence the discharge, at any given stage, will have its minimum value for that oscillation. Since the wave (see the gauge curves on plates V, VI, VII, VIII, and IX) has a tolerably regular form, the daily change of slope in rising and falling will be similar for any given stand of the gauge, and the two parts of the slope and gauge curve will thus be parallel. Lastly, since the channel of the Mississippi is a vast reservoir, the wave gradually loses its convex form by diffusion throughout that channel. The slope in the lower parts of the river is, therefore, liable to comparatively little fluctuation, being governed by the gradual filling and emptying of a reservoir, rather than by a succession of waves.

Algebraic analysis of variation in local slope, and resulting equation for Columbus.

This experimental theory to account for change of local slope suggests the proper method of treating the subject algebraically. It is evident that, when an expression for the increase of slope between the foot and the top of a rise has been found, it may be applied without sensible error to any part of that rise except near the top and near the bottom, since the rising and falling branches of the curve are nearly parallel. Near the top and bottom, the branches of the curve turn to unite, and the change of slope becomes too involved for algebraic analysis. If, then, a general expression for the increase of slope between the foot and top of rises at all stages of the river can be deduced for any given locality, the problem is solved for that locality. There were six well-defined rises at Columbus during the continuance of the discharge measurements; and, as that station is situated where the "wave" system is in full force, the general algebraic laws governing the change of slope can be more readily deduced for that locality than for places lower down the river, where the problem, although really much simpler, does not admit of so close an analysis. Columbus, therefore, was first selected for study. The data furnished by the six rises will be found in the following table:—

Variation in local slope at Columbus.

	Rise.	Gauge.	a	W	p	Q	s, computed by equation (36).	Increase in slope.
		Feet.	*Square feet.*	*Feet.*	*Feet.*	*Cubic feet.*		
1	December 3, 1857	7.0	92,730	2102	2115	220,000	0 000001568	0.000075334
	December 21, "	32.3	147,520	2212	2255	1,160,000	0.000076902	
2	March 17, 1858	19.7	119,780	2157	2200	590,000	0.000017575	0.000036913
	March 28, "	34.7	152,700	2214	2251	1,120,000	0.000054488	
3	April 11, "	18.7	117,680	2157	2200	570,000	0.000017087	0.000053357
	April 26, "	37.4	158,260	2220	2256	1,260,000	0.000070444	
4	May 7, "	26.3	134,180	2199	2242	776,550	0.000027442	0.000049130
	June 22, "	40.9	166,530	2237	2280	1,383,080	0.000076572	
5	July 17, "	19.6	119,580	2157	2200	424,530	0.000004874	0.000010217
	July 27, "	26.2	133,960	2199	2242	665,430	0.000015091	
6	October 30, "	4.1	86,670	2073	2086	143,710	0.000000432	0.000008063
	November 8, "	16.0	111,820	2157	2200	441,990	0.000008495	

A diagram was first made by plotting the slopes as abscissæ, and the gauge-readings as ordinates, and connecting the points indicating the top and bottom of each of the different rises, respectively, by a right line. These lines were not parallel, showing that the rate of increase of slope varied for the different rises. To ascertain whether this variation was normal, six lines were drawn through the origin of co-ordinates parallel to those just named. The acute angles which these lines made with the axis of X were found to be less for rises in high than in low stages of the river, indicating that the rate of increase of slope was greater for rises in high than in low stages of the river. To determine whether this variation followed any algebraic law, a curve was constructed, whose ordinates were the elevations of water surface above dead low water (gauge-reading minus 5.7 feet), at the top of the different rises, and whose abscissæ were the corresponding values of $\frac{s_{\prime\prime} - s_{\prime}}{x}$, the natural cotangent of the acute angle which the line denoting the increase of slope makes with the axis of X. The curve resulting from connecting these points must evidently pass through the origin of co-ordinates, a condition which adds another to the known points, besides simplifying the equation. This curve was found to be smooth and regular, being very nearly a parabola whose equation is—

$$\frac{s_{\prime\prime} - s_{\prime}}{x} = \frac{1}{2\,\mathrm{P}} (e + x)^2,$$

in which 2 P is a constant and in which e denotes the elevation above extreme low-water mark of the primitive surface of the river. By reduction, this equation can be put under the form—

$$(50) \qquad s_{\prime\prime} = s_{\prime} + \frac{1}{2\,\mathrm{P}} (e + x)^2\, x.$$

This equation is general. Method of deducing the numerical value of 2 P for any particular local-

Since this equation is nothing but an algebraic enunciation of the general laws revealed by plates XIV, XV and XVI, 2 P may reasonably be supposed to be a function of the range of the river, of the dimensions of cross-section, and of the convexity of the flood "waves." If this be so, the equation is general and can be made applicable to any particular locality where e is known, by substituting the local value for 2 P. The data collected at Vicksburg and Carrollton demonstrate the correctness of this inference, as will soon be seen, and thus establish that one general law governs the variation in local slope throughout the whole river. The numerical value of 2 P for any particular locality can be readily computed, provided e, the gauge-reading, the cross-section, and the discharge at the foot and top of any given rise be known; or (since the rising and falling portions of the slope and gauge curves are parallel to each other and hence to their mean line) provided the above quantities be known at any two times between which the river is either rising or falling *uniformly*. In either case, the reciprocal of 2 P is equal to the quotient arising from dividing the difference between the two computed slopes by $x\,(e + x)^2$. For Columbus, its value proved to be 0.0000000015; for Vicksburg, 0.0000000012; and for Carrollton, 0.000000015.

ity. Its value for Columbus, Vicksburg, and Carrollton.

It is needless to give separate tables exhibiting the tests of equation (50) with these several values, because its accuracy is necessarily proved by the satisfactory result of the final test which is now to be applied to the new velocity formula. Should it be desired, however, to discuss the subject more fully, the preceding and following tables of data and the Appendices afford ready means of so doing.

The data are furnished for the further prosecution of this investigation if desired.

As this third test of the formulæ involves identically the same computation as that which will hereafter be applied to solving the great practical problem of how much the high-water surface of the Mississippi will be raised by perfecting the levee system, the process will be recapitulated in detail.

Recapitulation of the new method of solving the problem.

For the new formulæ, $s_{,}$ is computed from the given data by the following equation, in which $z_{,} = 0.93\, v_{,} + 0.072\, v_{,}^{1/2}$:—

With new formulæ.

$$(36) \qquad s_{,} = \left(\frac{(p_{,} + W_{,})\, z_{,}^2}{195\, a_{,}}\right)^2.$$

A value of x is next assumed, and the numerical values of the first members of the two following equations are deduced, 2 P having its proper local value:—

$$(48) \qquad \frac{a_{,,}}{p_{,,} + W_{,,}} = \frac{a_{,} + W_{,}\, x}{p_{,} + W_{,} + 2\,x},$$

$$(50) \qquad s_{,,} = s_{,} + \frac{1}{2\,P}\,(e + x)^2\, x.$$

With these values, $v_{,,}$ is computed by the following equation:—

$$(41) \qquad v_{,,} = \left(\left[225\, s_{,,}^{1/2}\, \frac{a_{,,}}{p_{,,} + W_{,,}}\right]^{1/4} - 0.0388\right)^2.$$

With this value of $v_{,,}$, the value of x is computed by the following equation:—

$$(49) \qquad x = \frac{Q_{,,} - a_{,}\, v_{,,}}{W_{,}\, v_{,,}}.$$

If this value is identical with that assumed, it is the true value sought; if not, the process is to be repeated until such accordance is obtained. The true value of x is always intermediate between that first assumed and that first computed, and a few approximations will give the result with any desired accuracy.

With Mr. Ellet's formulæ.

In applying this test to Mr. Ellet's formula, a difficulty has arisen in respect to the value to be adopted for the new slope. He gives no rule whatever, but, in a practical example to illustrate his method of computation, increases the fall per mile by an amount equal to the quotient of the increased elevation of water surface by the distance to the gulf. Equation (50) cannot, without a change of constants, be used with his formula, and it has therefore been thought best to adopt the plan indicated in the example given in his report. The process of computation, then, is this. From the given data, $H_{,}$ is computed by his equation—

$$H_{,} = \left(\left[\frac{64 + 25\, v_{,}}{\Delta_{,}}\right]^{\frac{1}{2}} - \frac{8}{\Delta_{,}^{\frac{1}{2}}}\right)^{2}.$$

A value of x is next assumed, and the numerical value of the first members of the two following equations deduced; L representing the distance in miles from the given locality to the gulf:—

$$H_{,,} = H_{,} + \frac{x}{L},$$

$$\Delta_{,,} = \Delta_{,} + x.$$

With these values, $v_{,,}$ is computed by his equation—

$$v_{,,} = 0.64\ (\Delta_{,,}\ H_{,,})^{\frac{1}{2}} + 0.04\ \Delta_{,,}\ H_{,,}.$$

With this value of $v_{,,}$, the value of x is computed by the same general equation as with the new formulæ (equation 49). If the resulting value of x is identical with that assumed, it is the true one. If not, the process is to be repeated with new values of x until such accordance is obtained.

Data for the third test. Result for the new formulæ and for those of Mr. Ellet.

The following table of data has been selected from the Appendices for this test. It will be seen that every well-marked rise is included, reckoning from its day of lowest to its day of highest gauge-reading. The other data, which can be increased at will from the Appendices, have been taken at random, when the river was *rising or falling at a tolerably uniform rate.* Near the top or the foot of rises, as already intimated, the change of slope is so irregular that it can hardly be computed.

Tests for the formulæ for oscillation caused by variation in discharge.

Locality.	Date.	e	$\Delta_{,}$	L	$a_{,}$	$W_{,}$	$p_{,}$	$Q_{,}$	$Q_{,,} - Q_{,}$	True oscillation.		Computed oscillation.			
												Ellet's formula.		New formula.	
										Kind.	Am't.	x	Error.	x	Error.
		Feet	*Feet*	*Miles.*	*Sq. feet*	*Feet*	*Feet*	*Cu. feet.*	*Cubic feet.*		*Feet.*	*Feet.*	*Feet.*	*Feet.*	*Feet.*
Columbus....................	Dec. 3 to Dec. 21, 1857	12.7	62	1076	92,730	2102	2115	220,000	+ 940,000	Rise.	25.3	72.9	— 47.6	27.0	— 1.7
	Dec. 11 to Dec. 16, "	25.8	75	1076	120,660	2160	2204	691,630	+ 445,970	Rise.	12.2	20.8	— 8.6	13.8	— 1.6
	Mar. 17 to Mar. 28, 1858	25.4	75	1076	119,780	2157	2200	590,000	+ 530,000	Rise.	15.0	27.6	— 12.6	15.0	0.0
	April 11 to April 26, "	24.4	74	1076	117,630	2157	2200	570,000	+ 690,000	Rise.	18.7	35.1	— 16.4	18.7	0.0
	May 7 to June 22, "	32.0	81	1076	134,180	2199	2242	776,550	+ 606,530	Rise.	14.6	26.6	— 12.0	14.7	— 0.1
	June 3 to June 22, "	42.3	92	1076	156,500	2218	2252	1,160,970	+ 222,110	Rise.	4.3	8.2	— 3.9	5.2	— 0.9
	July 17 to July 27, "	25.3	75	1076	119,580	2157	2200	424,530	+ 240,900	Rise.	6.6	17.9	— 11.3	6.6	0.0
	Oct. 30 to Nov. 8, "	9.8	59	1076	86,670	2073	2086	143,710	+ 298,280	Rise.	11.9	37.8	— 25.9	11.6	+ 0.3
Vicksburg....................	March 6 to March 30, "	29.1	82	487	127,630	2522	2545	670,550	+ 438,880	Rise.	13.8	18.8	— 5.0	13.3	+ 0.5
	Mar. 10 to Mar. 23, "	30.9	84	487	132,200	2535	2560	748,200	+ 199,260	Rise.	6.1	8.5	— 2.4	6.3	— 0.2
	Mar. 20 to Mar. 30, "	34.5	87	487	141,350	2558	2585	841,570	+ 267,860	Rise.	8.4	10.5	— 2.1	7.4	+ 1.0
	April 19 to June 26, "	45.4	98	487	169,500	2660	2698	1,105,000	+ 125,900	Rise.	2.9	4.4	— 1.5	2.8	+ 0.1
	Aug. 6 to Aug. 26, "	45.0	98	487	168,600	2658	2698	1,086,400	— 372,340	Fall.	11.6	15.0	— 3.4	11.2	+ 0.4
	Aug. 26 to Sept. 1, "	33.4	86	487	138,530	2550	2575	714,060	— 173,140	Fall.	6.7	8.9	— 2.2	6.7	0.0
	Nov. 3 to Nov. 15, "	8.7	61	487	77,360	2420	2430	236,000	+ 359,000	Rise.	16.8	25.7	— 8.9	17.6	— 0.8
	Dec. 10 to Dec. 13, "	17.0	70	487	97,580	2455	2475	399,920	+ 117,700	Rise.	5.6	7.3	— 1.7	5.9	— 0.3
Carrollton....................	Feb. 17 to Feb. 23, 1851	6.3	128	121	164,170	2324	2355	534,780	+ 335,220	Rise.	5.2	9.8	— 4.6	4.5	+ 0.7
	Feb. 19 to March 1, "	8.2	130	121	168,840	2338	2368	630,000	+ 382,570	Rise.	5.2	11.0	— 5.8	4.7	+ 0.5
	Feb. 20 to Feb. 25, "	9.0	131	121	170,800	2344	2374	670,770	+ 239,130	Rise.	3.0	7.0	— 4.0	3.1	— 0.1
	Feb. 25 to March 21, "	12.0	134	121	177,900	2364	2398	909,900	+ 229,800	Rise.	3.1	6.2	— 3.1	3.0	+ 0.1
	April 17 to May 9, "	14.8	136	121	183,800	2378	2416	1,065,000	— 181,000	Fall.	1.8	5.1	— 3.3	3.2	— 1.4
	May 27 to July 25, "	9.9	132	121	173,000	2350	2380	652,330	+ 222,670	Rise.	3.0	6.5	— 3.5	2.5	+ 0.5
	July 31 to Aug. 15, "	12.4	134	121	178,810	2367	2401	845,000	— 175,610	Fall.	2.6	5.3	— 2.7	2.9	— 0.3
	Jan. 7, to Jan. 17, 1852	0.8	122	121	152,000	2287	2312	310,000	+ 220,000	Rise.	4.3	7.2	— 2.9	4.4	-- 0.1
										Sum..	208.7	404.1	195.4	212.1	11.6

This table furnishes the crowning proof of the exactness of the new formulæ as applied to water moving in natural channels. Joined to the two preceding tests, it establishes beyond reasonable doubt, first, that the same laws govern the flow of water in the largest rivers and in the smallest streams; second, that the new formulæ truly express those laws; and, third, that the formulæ heretofore proposed do not express them even approximately.

Concluding remarks.

The connection of the subject with such vast interests as those involved in the protection of the alluvial region of the Mississippi from inundation, has exacted the utmost care in its treatment. The measurements have been made with the greatest exactitude; experiment has been multiplied; the most rigid scrutiny has been exercised in the application of mechanical principles and algebraic analysis to the phenomena, and the newly developed laws are thus accompanied by a weight of evidence that establishes their truth. The formulæ by which they are expressed are therefore entitled to the confidence of practical men.

CHAPTER VI.

PROTECTION AGAINST THE FLOODS OF THE MISSISSIPPI.

Plan adopted for measuring the effect of the swamp lands upon the maximum discharge of the river.—Daily discharge of the tributaries, of the crevasses, and of the Mississippi itself, throughout the alluvial region in the flood of 1858.—Test of the exactness of the determination.—Effect of the swamps upon the discharge of the tributary streams.—Reservoir influence of the channel.—What would have been the maximum discharge throughout the alluvial region in 1858, had the levees been perfected.—Effect of the swamps upon the river floods in their present, their former, and their effectually leveed conditions.—Comparative analysis of the flood of 1858 with the floods of 1859, 1851, 1850, and 1828.—Flood of 1858 a safe standard for estimating the proper extent, and comparing the relative advantages, of the different protective measures.—Cut-offs pernicious in the Mississippi valley.—Plan of diverting tributaries impracticable for the Missouri, the Arkansas, the Red, or other branches.—Plan of artificial reservoirs chimerical, so far as restraining floods is concerned.—Outlets highly efficacious in reducing the river floods, but, except to a very limited extent, destructive to the great interests of Louisiana.—Plan of levees the most practicable, economical, and safe that can be adopted, both for the present time and hereafter.—Recommendations.—Proposed local heights and cross-sections to be given to the levees.—Suggestion relative to an outlet near Lake Providence.—Cost of a perfected levee system.—Importance of a systematic and continuous series of observations.

The problem of protection against inundation required, for a double reason, a very extended system of field operations.

ENTERTAINING the opinion that a long series of observations must be made before the various phenomena of the Mississippi could be subjected to accurate calculation, a plan of investigation was adopted far more extended than any previously attempted upon any river. It was, in brief, to measure daily with accuracy the discharge of the Mississippi, and of its important tributaries, throughout the alluvial region; to ascertain precisely how much water escaped in time of flood from the channel, and at what points; and thus to determine for any locality the increased discharge at high water which would have resulted had the river been confined to the channel. The operations necessary to carry out this plan, it was conceived, must furnish the mass of material essential to establish the fundamental principles of the science of river hydraulics. After accomplishing this, and deducing the increased high-water discharge to be guarded against, the problem of the best method of preventing inundations could be subjected to the exact reasoning of algebraic analysis, and thus be definitely solved.

One reason has been already elaborated and the results of the investigation announced.

The contributions to the science of river hydraulics, resulting from the application of this system, have been elaborately stated in the preceding chapter, where it is demonstrated that all knowledge requisite to accomplish the objects of the present investigation has been secured.

The other is now to be considered.

The maximum flood discharge which would occur at any point below Cape Girardeau, were the river confined to the channel, is now to be determined. The mechanical operations in the field, and the reduction of the data collected, have both been described in detail in Chapter IV.

All data necessary to an entire recomputation of the work have been presented either there or in the Appendices. Here, then, the attention will be restricted to the final results of operations and computations, which involve an amount of labor that few but those engaged upon the work will appreciate.

EFFECT PRODUCED UPON THE MAXIMUM DISCHARGE OF THE MISSISSIPPI BY RECLAIMING ITS SWAMP LANDS.

Outline of the steps proposed for the investigation.

It has been already stated that extensive gaugings of the river were made in 1851 and 1858, both of which, fortunately, were great flood years. In the histories of the floods contained in Chapter II, it is shown that in 1858 much the more general and extensive inundation occurred, and, moreover, that in that year the system of measurements extended over the whole alluvial region of the Mississippi, while in 1851 it was not carried out above the mouth of Red river. The operations of 1858, then, form the basis of the discussion of what would have been the maximum discharge at the different localities below Cape Girardeau, had no water escaped from the channel of the river. Having settled this important question for the flood of 1858, the other great floods (where the data admit of it) will be subjected, in turn, to a comparative analysis, in order to decide what may safely be adopted as the increase in maximum discharge to be guarded against when the whole river is confined to the channel. This quantity will then form the touchstone by which the different plans for protection will be tried and their merits ascertained.

Fortunate commencement of field work in 1857.

Analysis of the flood of 1858.—The plan of operating from the head of the alluvial region downward was matured in the autumn of 1857. The parties were organized in December, under the immediate direction of Lieutenant Abbot, and were soon established at their several posts. It was fortunate for the objects of the Survey, that one of the greatest floods ever known in the river was thus subjected to exact observation from its beginning to its end.

River gauges.

Daily gauge-readings were recorded at Cairo, Columbus, Memphis, Helena, Napoleon, Providence, Vicksburg, Natchez, Red-river landing, Donaldsonville, and Carrollton. (See Appendix B.)

Discharge measurements upon the Mississippi.

The daily discharge of the Mississippi, at Columbus and at Vicksburg, was measured with all possible exactness. (See Appendix E.)

Upon tributaries and bayous; with table of results.

During the flood-period, the daily contributions of the Arkansas, White, Red, and Yazoo rivers, and the daily loss by bayous Plaquemine and La Fourche, were determined with all requisite exactness, as explained in Chapter IV. They are exhibited in the following table. Full verbal information of the action of the St. Francis river was also secured, as will be hereafter explained.

Discharge per second of tributaries and bayous.

Date.		Arkansas and White rivers.	Red river.	Yazoo river.	Bayou Plaquemine.	Bayou La Fourche.
1858.		*Cubic feet.*	*Cubic feet.*	*Cubic feet.*	*Cubic feet.*	*Cubic feet.*
March	20	120,000	85,000	46,000	15,000	6,000
	21	125,000	80,000	46,000	14,000	6,000
	22	128,000	75,000	47,000	14,000	6,000
	23	132,000	70,000	48,000	15,000	6,000
	24	134,000	65,000	49,000	15,000	6,000
	25	138,000	60,000	50,000	16,000	6,000
	26	140,000	50,000	52,000	17,000	7,000
	27	142,000	40,000	54,000	19,000	7,000
	28	144,000	30,000	56,000	20,000	7,000
	29	148,000	20,000	58,000	21,000	8,000
	30	150,000	10,000	60,000	21,000	8,000
	31	152,000	— 5,000	62,000	21,000	8,000
April	1	154,000	—20,000	64,000	21,000	8,000
	2	156,000	—25,000	65,000	22,000	8,000
	3	158,000	—20,000	66,000	23,000	8,000
	4	158,000	—10,000	67,000	24,000	8,000
	5	160,000	— 5,000	68,000	25,000	9,000
	6	160,000	— 1,000	69,000	26,000	9,000
	7	160,000	0	69,000	27,000	9,000
	8	160,000	0	70,000	27,000	9,000
	9	158,000	0	70,000	28,000	9,000
	10	156,000	0	71,000	28,000	9,000
	11	154,000	0	71,000	29,000	10,000
	12	152,000	0	71,000	28,000	10,000
	13	148,000	1,000	72,000	28,000	10,000
	14	146,000	2,000	72,000	28,000	10,000
	15	142,000	7,000	73,000	28,000	10,000
	16	134,000	10,000	73,000	29,000	10,000
	17	131,000	15,000	74,000	29,000	10,000
	18	128,000	20,000	75,000	29,000	10,000
	19	128,000	30,000	75,000	30,000	10,000
	20	126,000	45,000	76,000	30,000	10,000
	21	126,000	55,000	77,000	30,000	10,000
	22	128,000	60,000	78,000	30,000	10,000
	23	128,000	60,000	79,000	30,000	10,000
	24	130,000	70,000	80,000	30,000	10,000
	25	132,000	70,000	81,000	31,000	10,000
	26	132,000	70,000	82,000	31,000	10,000
	27	132,000	68,000	83,000	32,000	10,000
	28	132,000	66,000	84,000	31,000	10,000
	29	130,000	64,000	86,000	31,000	10,000
	30	128,000	62,000	87,000	31,000	10,000
May	1	126,000	60,000	88,000	31,000	10,000
	2	126,000	58,000	90,000	31,000	10,000
	3	126,000	56,000	91,000	32,000	11,000
	4	128,000	54,000	92,000	32,000	11,000
	5	128,000	53,000	94,000	32,000	11,000
	6	130,000	52,000	95,000	33,000	11,000
	7	134,000	48,000	96,000	33,000	11,000
	8	132,000	45,000	97,000	34,000	11,000
	9	134,000	35,000	98,000	34,000	11,000
	10	136,000	30,000	99,000	34,000	11,000
	11	126,000	20,000	100,000	34,000	11,000
	12	136,000	15,000	100,000	33,000	11,000
	13	120,000	9,000	101,000	34,000	11,000
	14	126,000	5,000	102,000	33,000	11,000
	15	132,000	2,000	103,000	33,000	11,000
	16	134,000	1,000	103,000	33,000	11,000
	17	136,000	0	104,000	32,000	11,000
	18	138,000	0	105,000	32,000	11,000
	19	140,000	0	106,000	32,000	10,000
	20	142,000	0	106,000	32,000	10,000
	21	142,000	0	107,000	32,000	10,000
	22	144,000	0	108,000	31,000	10,000
	23	144,000	0	108,000	31,000	10,000
	24	144,000	1,000	109,000	31,000	10,000
	25	146,000	5,000	110,000	31,000	10,000
	26	146,000	11,000	110,000	31,000	10,000
	27	146,000	18,000	111,000	31,000	10,000

Discharge per second of tributaries and bayous—Continued.

Date.		Arkansas and White rivers.	Red river.	Yazoo river.	Bayou Plaquemine.	Bayou La Fourche.
1858.		*Cubic feet.*	*Cubic feet.*	*Cubic feet.*	*Cubic feet.*	*Cubic feet.*
May	28	144,000	20,000	112,000	31,000	10,000
	29	136,000	20,000	112,000	31,000	10,000
	30	138,000	15,000	113,000	31,000	10,000
	31	132,000	9,000	113,000	31,000	10,000
June	1	130,000	5,000	114,000	31,000	10,000
	2	140,000	1,000	115,000	31,000	10,000
	3	138,000	0	115,000	31,000	10,000
	4	146,000	0	116,000	31,000	10,000
	5	156,000	0	117,000	31,000	10,000
	6	142,000	0	117,000	31,000	10,000
	7	144,000	0	118,000	31,000	10,000
	8	146,000	0	118,000	31,000	10,000
	9	150,000	0	119,000	31,000	10,000
	10	150,000	0	119,000	31,000	10,000
	11	150,000	0	119,000	31,000	10,000
	12	148,000	0	120,000	32,000	11,000
	13	146,000	0	121,000	32,000	10,000
	14	144,000	0	122,000	32,000	11,000
	15	144,000	0	122,000	32,000	11,000
	16	146,000	0	123,000	32,000	10,000
	17	148,000	0	123,000	31,000	10,000
	18	148,000	0	124,000	31,000	10,000
	19	148,000	0	125,000	31,000	10,000
	20	146,000	0	125,000	31,000	10,000
	21	142,000	0	126,000	31,000	10,000
	22	140,000	0	126,000	31,000	10,000
	23	138,000	0	127,000	31,000	10,000
	24	136,000	0	127,000	31,000	10,000
	25	136,000	0	128,000	31,000	10,000
	26	134,000	0	128,000	31,000	10,000
	27	134,000	0	129,000	31,000	10,000
	28	134,000	0	129,000	31,000	10,000
	29	134,000	0	130,000	31,000	10,000
	30	134,000	0	130,000	31,000	10,000
July	1	134,000	0	131,000	31,000	10,000
	2	136,000	0	131,000	31,000	10,000
	3	138,000	0	132,000	31,000	10,000
	4	140,000	0	132,000	31,000	10,000
	5	142,000	0	132,000	31,000	10,000
	6	144,000	0	133,000	31,000	10,000
	7	148,000	0	133,000	31,000	10,000
	8	152,000	0	133,000	31,000	10,000
	9	156,000	0	134,000	31,000	10,000
	10	158,000	0	134,000	31,000	10,000
	11	160,000	0	135,000	31,000	10,000
	12	160,000	0	135,000	31,000	10,000
	13	162,000	0	135,000	31,000	10,000
	14	154,000	0	136,000	31,000	10,000
	15	172,000	0	136,000	31,000	10,000
	16	160,000	0	137,000	31,000	10,000
	17	164,000	0	137,000	31,000	10,000
	18	162,000	0	137,000	31,000	10,000
	19	162,000	0	138,000	31,000	10,000
	20	162,000	0	138,000	31,000	10,000
	21	163,000	0	138,000	31,000	10,000
	22	160,000	0	139,000	31,000	10,000
	23	158,000	0	139,000	31,000	10,000
	24	154,000	0	139,000	31,000	10,000
	25	150,000	0		30,000	10,000
	26	149,000	0		30,000	10,000
	27	148,000	0		30,000	10,000
	28	148,000	0		30,000	10,000
	29	148,000	0		30,000	10,000
	30	146,000	1,000		30,000	10,000
	31	146,000	1,000		30,000	10,000
August	1	145,000	2,000		29,000	10,000
	2	120,000	2,000		29,000	10,000
	3	110,000	2,000		28,000	10,000
	4	102,000	3,000		28,000	10,000

Discharge per second of tributaries and bayous—Continued.

Date.	Arkansas and White rivers.	Red river.	Yazoo river.	Bayou Plaquemine.	Bayou La Fourche.
1858.	*Cubic feet.*	*Cubic feet.*	*Cubic feet.*	*Cubic feet.*	*Cubic feet.*
August 5	94,000	3,000		28,000	9,000
6	84,000	3,000		27,000	9,000
7	72,000	4,000		27,000	9,000
8	67,000	4,000		26,000	9,000
9	67,000	4,000		26,000	9,000
10	64,000	5,000		25,000	9,000
11	59,000	5,000		25,000	9,000
12	56,000	5,000		24,000	9,000
13	54,000	6,000		24,000	8,000
14	52,000	6,000		24,000	8,000
15	52,000	6,000		24,000	8,000
16	52,000	7,000		23,000	8,000
17	49,000	7,000		23,000	8,000
18	49,000	8,000		22,000	8,000
19	48,000	8,000		22,000	8,000
20	46,000	9,000		21,000	8,000
21	43,000	9,000		20,000	7,000
22	33,000	9,000		19,000	7,000

Reconnoissance of crevasses; classification of results.

After the river fell, a careful and laborious reconnoissance was made between Cape Girardeau and New Orleans, with a view to collect the data for computing the daily discharge of the various crevasses between those places. For the St. Francis bottom, the information thus collected, although sufficient for all general purposes, as will be hereafter seen, was too vague to be reduced to figures; partly, because the levees had been so slightly constructed that the crevasses were too extensive for measurement, and partly, because the system of swamp ridges diverted much water back into the Mississippi at various places, thus greatly complicating the discussion. For all parts of the river below the St. Francis bottom lands, reliable information and measurements were obtained; and the daily discharge of the crevasses may be considered well determined. This difference in the exactness of the data collected renders it necessary to discuss the flood in different parts of the river upon somewhat different principles. That portion lying between the head of the Yazoo bottom and New Orleans will therefore be first considered; and subsequently the region between Cape Girardeau and the mouth of St. Francis river.

Data for computing the discharge of the crevasses below the mouth of St. Francis river.

The following table exhibits the most essential part of the data from which the daily discharge of crevasses has been computed. It should be stated that there were several breaks in the levee upon the left bank of the Mississippi, between the head of the Yazoo bottom and Helena, but the greater part of the water which entered by them was turned back into the river by swamp ridges, partly through McKinney's bayou and partly over the banks. The amount which eventually reached the great Yazoo bottom from these banks was balanced by that part of the discharge of crevasse No. 1 which returned to the Mississippi, from the same cause, in the bend below. This crevasse may then be considered, for all practical purposes, to be the first which discharged into the Yazoo bottom.

List of crevasses in flood of 1858.

No. of crevasse.	Locality.	Bank of river.	Date of Beginning to discharge.	Date of Ceasing to discharge.	Maximum width.	Mean depth at high water.	Remarks.
			1858.	1858.	*Feet.*	*Feet.*	
1	Just above Helena	Left	March 27	July 19	2,900	8	Two breaks. Bottom much and unevenly washed.
2	10 miles below Helena	Left	June 25	July 14	3,050	5	Eight breaks, separated by remains of levee.
3	Just below No. 3	Left	June 25	July 19	1,900	8	Two breaks. Bottom much washed.
4	Just below No. 4	Left	June 25	....	225	25	Old bayou.
5	Just above Delta	Left	June 23	July 12	1,000	4	
6	Between Delta and Friar's Point	Left	June 18	July 10	7,000	3	Many small breaks.
7	In Horse-shoe bend	Left	June 20	July 11	1,000	4	
8	Opposite foot of Island 63	Left	June 25	July 13	1,000	5	Caused by fall of a tree.
9	Opposite Island 64	Left	April 23	July 13	200	5	Supposed to be cut.
10	Opposite Island 66	Left	April 30	July 24	4,000	6	Supposed to be cut. Much damage.
11	Near foot of Island 66	Left	June 17	July 22	1,900	4	Three breaks.
12	Opposite Island 68	Left	June 17	July 22	1,000	4	Many small breaks.
13	Near Concordia	Left	June 10	July 28	512	9	Two breaks; one in an old bayou.
14	Opposite foot of Island 74	Left	June 8	July 22	1,030	5	Supposed to be cut.
15	1 mile below Helena	Right	July 1	July 17	900	7	Flooded Helena.
16*	Between No. 15 and Old Town	Right	....	July 16	20,000	6	Many small breaks and gaps.
17	Opposite Island 68	Right	April 4	July 17	420	6	
18	1 mile below No. 17	Right	June 27	July 19	940	7	Three breaks caused by old logs in levee.
19†	1 mile below No. 18	Right	April 4	July 17	730	6	Three breaks caused by crawfish.
20	5 miles below Bolivar	Left	March 28	April 10	1,500	5	Closed after April rise.
21	Opposite Island 78	Left	April 5	April 15	1,000	5	Closed after April rise.
22	Opposite Island 80	Left	April 2	April 15	300	4	Closed after April rise.
23	Below foot of Island 84	Left	April 5	April 17	2,180	3	Three breaks. Closed after April rise.
24	American-bend crevasses	Left	April 4	July 19	3,410	5	Seven breaks.
25	Opposite Islands 86 and 87	Left	June 25	July 19	3,475	4	Caused by bank caving. No excavation.
26	Opposite foot of Grand Lake	Left	May 10	July 14	360	3	Three small breaks.
27‡	Just above Island 82	Right	April 2	April 15	120	4	Closed after April rise.
28	2 miles above Columbia	Right	April 3	April 15	600	4	Closed after April rise.
29	Above American-bend cut-off	Right	April 5	July 20	350	6	
30	4 miles below Island 86	Right	April 5	July 17	150	4	
31	1 mile above Louisiana line	Right	April 4	July 28	300	5	Much excavation.
32	Above Tallula	Left	June 15	July 28	80	5	Two breaks.
33	Above Brunswick	Left	April 10	July 28	500	4	Much excavation.
34§	Near Island 100	Left	March 28	July 23	10,000	2	Caused by log in levee.
35	Below Lake Providence	Right	June 17	Aug. 10	400	8	Hole 23 ft. deep, nearly whole width of break, and excavated from bank rearward several hundred feet.
36	4 miles below Lake Providence	Right	April 30	Aug. 8	3,435	7	No serious excavation.
37‖	Near Warrenton	Left	June —	Aug. 1	7,500	4	Water returned at once through Big Black R.
38	4 miles below Baton Rouge	Left	April 11	April 19	210	6	Closed by Mr. Louis Hèbert, State Engineer, La.
39	4 miles below Vicksburg	Right	May 22	Aug. 10	152	6	Width May 24, 27, June 12, and Aug. 10, was 152, 135, 35, and 152 ft. respectively. Much excavation.
40	Just above Ellis's cliffs	Right	May 6	Aug. 9	300	5	Supposed to be cut.
41	1 mile below No. 40	Right	May 6	July 31	2,500	3	Caused by caving.
42	Near Island 116	Right	May 10	Aug. 15	150	4	Water returned through Red R.
43	Near Island 116	Right	June 1	Aug. 17	860	5	Three breaks. Water returned through Red R.
44	Near Red Church	Right	May 3	Sept. 5	1,050	11	Width May 9 was 75 ft. (See figure 6, plate III.)
45	0.5 of a mile above upper boundary of New Orleans	Right	April 11	Sept. 12	730	20	(See figure 5, plate III.)

* Below No. 16, between Old Town and the head of Island 68, there were numerous small breaks on the right bank. Many of these, however, only served as outlets for the swamp water to return to the Mississippi, as, for instance, those near the foot of Island 62 and near the head of Island 68. The information collected about them is sufficient to establish that these outlets returned fully as much water as was received by the rest of the breaks, and the whole series is accordingly neglected in the computation. Any error arising from this cause will be counterbalanced by the computations based upon the size of No. 16, which is probably somewhat exaggerated.

† From Island 69 to Island 71, there were only a few detached levees. Thence to Napoleon there were none. As much water returned to the river as left it in this distance, and no detailed estimate is, therefore, attempted of the different outlets and inlets. It depended upon the situation of the locality with respect to the bends, whether the water flowed to or from the river.

‡ From Napoleon to the high bank about 1.5 miles below Cypress slough (6 miles above head of Island 78), there are only about 3 miles of levee. All the water which enters this region is turned back by the high ridge, and is discharged back into the Mississippi in Cypress bend.

§ This crevasse is near the end of continuous levees on this bank. Between it and Vicksburg, no water of consequence drained into the Yazoo bottom, since whatever passed over the bank was immediately returned by Old river.

‖ From Big-Black river to Baton Rouge, the hills border the river so closely that no important quantity of water escapes.

Result of the computations.

Since the water lost through crevasse No. 37 returned almost immediately to the river, it had only a local effect and has not been computed. No. 38 was closed so soon that it had no sensible influence upon the river. The daily discharges of the others, arranged in convenient groups for discussing the flood, are given in the following table. The computations have been made with great care, in accordance with the principles laid down in Chapter IV. Much assistance has been derived from local information respecting the daily stand of the water at localities intermediate between the regular gauges, and it is believed that this table does not contain any material error.

Discharge per second of crevasses.

Date.	Helena to Napoleon.		Napoleon to Lake Providence.		Lake Providence to Vicksburg.		Vicksburg to Natchez.	Natchez to Red river.	Red river to Carrollton.	Opp. New Orleans (No. 45).
	Right bank	Left bank.	Right bank	Left bank.	Right bank	Left bank.	Right bank	Right bank	Right bank	Right bank
1858.	*Cu. feet.*	*Cu. feet.*	*Cu. feet.*	*Cu. feet.*	*Cu. feet.*	*Cu. feet.*	*Cu. feet.*	*Cu. feet.*	*Cu. feet.*	*Cu. feet.*
March 30	20,000	1,000	0	0	0	0	0	0	0	0
31	39,000	1,000	0	0	0	0	0	0	0	0
April 1	45,000	2,000	0	1,000	0	0	0	0	0	0
2	49,000	2,000	0	3,000	0	0	0	0	0	0
3	50,000	2,000	1,000	4,000	0	5,000	0	0	0	0
4	50,000	2,000	2,000	6,000	0	10,000	0	0	0	0
5	48,000	2,000	4,000	8,000	0	14,000	0	0	0	0
6	45,000	2,000	5,000	10,000	0	19,000	0	0	0	0
7	42,000	1,000	5,000	10,000	0	20,000	0	0	0	0
8	35,000	1,000	5,000	10,000	0	20,000	0	0	0	0
9	22,000	0	5,000	9,000	0	20,000	0	0	0	0
10	10,000	0	4,000	7,000	0	19,000	0	0	0	0
11	0	0	4,000	7,000	0	18,000	0	0	0	1,000
12	0	0	3,000	6,000	0	16,000	0	0	0	2,000
13	0	0	3,000	5,000	0	15,000	0	0	0	3,000
14	0	0	2,000	4,000	0	14,000	0	0	0	3,000
15	0	0	2,000	3,000	0	12,000	0	0	0	4,000
16	0	0	1,000	2,000	0	9,000	0	0	0	5,000
17	0	0	1,000	2,000	0	7,000	0	0	0	5,000
18	0	0	0	1,000	0	5,000	0	0	0	6,000
19	0	0	0	0	0	5,000	0	0	0	7,000
20	0	0	0	0	0	5,000	0	0	0	7,000
21	0	0	0	0	0	8,000	0	0	0	8,000
22	0	0	1,000	1,000	0	11,000	0	0	0	9,000
23	10,000	1,000	1,000	2,000	0	13,000	0	0	0	10,000
24	19,000	1,000	1,000	2,000	0	15,000	0	0	0	11,000
25	28,000	2,000	2,000	4,000	0	19,000	0	0	0	11,000
26	37,000	3,000	2,000	4,000	0	22,000	0	0	0	12,000
27	45,000	4,000	2,000	4,000	0	26,000	0	0	0	13,000
28	52,000	5,000	2,000	5,000	0	27,000	0	0	0	13,000
29	59,000	6,000	2,000	5,000	0	27,000	0	0	0	14,000
30	64,000	8,000	2,000	5,000	1,000	27,000	0	0	0	15,000
May 1	68,000	8,000	2,000	5,000	1,000	26,000	0	0	0	15,000
2	71,000	9,000	3,000	5,000	1,000	24,000	0	0	0	16,000
3	74,000	9,000	3,000	6,000	2,000	22,000	0	0	1,000	17,000
4	76,000	9,000	3,000	6,000	2,000	20,000	0	0	2,000	18,000
5	78,000	9,000	3,000	6,000	3,000	20,000	0	0	2,000	19,000
6	80,000	8,000	3,000	7,000	3,000	19,000	0	1,000	2,000	20,000
7	81,000	6,000	3,000	7,000	4,000	19,000	0	1,000	3,000	21,000
8	81,000	4,000	3,000	7,000	4,000	19,000	0	1,000	3,000	23,000
9	81,000	2,000	3,000	7,000	5,000	19,000	0	2,000	3,000	25,000
10	80,000	1,000	3,000	8,000	5,000	19,000	0	2,000	4,000	27,000
11	79,000	0	3,000	8,000	6,000	19,000	0	2,000	4,000	28,000
12	76,000	0	3,000	9,000	7,000	19,000	0	2,000	4,000	29,000
13	72,000	0	3,000	9,000	7,000	18,000	0	2,000	4,000	30,000
14	67,000	0	3,000	9,000	8,000	18,000	0	3,000	5,000	30,000
15	54,000	0	3,000	9,000	8,000	18,000	0	3,000	5,000	30,000
16	49,000	0	3,000	10,000	9,000	18,000	0	3,000	5,000	30,000
17	46,000	0	3,000	10,000	10,000	18,000	0	3,000	6,000	30,000
18	44,000	0	3,000	10,000	10,000	18,000	0	3,000	6,000	31,000

Discharge per second of crevasses—Continued.

Date.		Helena to Napoleon.		Napoleon to Lake Providence.		Lake Providence to Vicksburg.		Vicksburg to Natchez.	Natchez to Red river.	Red river to Carrollton.	Opp. New Orleans (No. 45).
		Right bank	Left bank.	Right bank	Left bank.	Right bank	Left bank.	Right bank	Right bank	Right bank	Right bank
	1858.	*Cu. feet.*	*Cu. feet.*	*Cu. feet.*	*Cu. feet.*	*Cu. feet.*	*Cu. feet.*	*Cu. feet.*	*Cu. feet.*	*Cu. feet.*	*Cu. feet.*
May	19	42,000	0	3,000	11,000	11,000	18,000	0	4,000	7,000	31,000
	20	41,000	1,000	3,000	11,000	12,000	18,000	0	4,000	7,000	31,000
	21	40,000	1,000	3,000	11,000	13,000	18,000	0	4,000	8,000	31,000
	22	40,000	2,000	3,000	11,000	14,000	18,000	4,000	4,000	8,000	31,000
	23	40,000	2,000	4,000	12,000	15,000	19,000	5,000	5,000	8,000	32,000
	24	41,000	2,000	4,000	12,000	16,000	19,000	7,000	5,000	9,000	32,000
	25	42,000	3,000	4,000	12,000	17,000	19,000	6,000	5,000	9,000	32,000
	26	43,000	3,000	4,000	13,000	18,000	19,000	6,000	6,000	10,000	32,000
	27	44,000	3,000	4,000	13,000	19,000	19,000	6,000	6,000	10,000	32,000
	28	46,000	4,000	4,000	14,000	19,000	19,000	6,000	6,000	10,000	33,000
	29	48,000	4,000	4,000	14,000	20,000	19,000	5,000	6,000	11,000	33,000
	30	51,000	4,000	4,000	15,000	20,000	20,000	5,000	7,000	11,000	33,000
	31	54,000	4,000	4,000	15,000	20,000	20,000	5,000	7,000	12,000	33,000
June	1	57,000	5,000	4,000	16,000	21,000	20,000	5,000	7,000	12,000	33,000
	2	61,000	5,000	4,000	16,000	21,000	20,000	4,000	8,000	13,000	34,000
	3	66,000	6,000	4,000	16,000	21,000	20,000	4,000	8,000	13,000	34,000
	4	69,000	6,000	4,000	17,000	22,000	21,000	4,000	8,000	14,000	35,000
	5	72,000	7,000	4,000	17,000	22,000	21,000	3,000	9,000	15,000	36,000
	6	75,000	8,000	4,000	18,000	22,000	21,000	3,000	9,000	16,000	37,000
	7	78,000	9,000	4,000	18,000	23,000	21,000	3,000	9,000	16,000	38,000
	8	81,000	10,000	4,000	19,000	23,000	21,000	3,000	10,000	17,000	38,000
	9	84,000	11,000	4,000	19,000	23,000	22,000	2,000	10,000	18,000	39,000
	10	87,000	12,000	4,000	20,000	24,000	22,000	2,000	11,000	19,000	40,000
	11	89,000	13,000	4,000	20,000	24,000	22,000	2,000	11,000	20,000	41,000
	12	91,000	14,000	5,000	21,000	24,000	22,000	2,000	12,000	21,000	42,000
	13	93,000	16,000	5,000	22,000	25,000	23,000	2,000	12,000	22,000	42,000
	14	95,000	18,000	5,000	22,000	25,000	23,000	2,000	13,000	22,000	43,000
	15	97,000	20,000	5,000	23,000	25,000	23,000	2,000	13,000	23,000	43,000
	16	99,000	22,000	5,000	24,000	26,000	23,000	2,000	13,000	24,000	44,000
	17	101,000	26,000	5,000	24,000	32,000	23,000	2,000	14,000	24,000	44,000
	18	103,000	32,000	5,000	25,000	33,000	23,000	3,000	14,000	25,000	45,000
	19	105,000	38,000	5,000	26,000	34,000	24,000	3,000	15,000	26,000	45,000
	20	107,000	43,000	5,000	27,000	35,000	24,000	3,000	15,000	26,000	46,000
	21	109,000	47,000	5,000	28,000	36,000	24,000	3,000	16,000	27,000	46,000
	22	110,000	52,000	5,000	28,000	37,000	24,000	4,000	16,000	28,000	47,000
	23	111,000	58,000	5,000	29,000	38,000	25,000	4,000	17,000	29,000	47,000
	24	112,000	63,000	5,000	29,000	40,000	25,000	4,000	17,000	30,000	48,000
	25	112,000	68,000	5,000	30,000	42,000	25,000	5,000	18,000	30,000	49,000
	26	113,000	75,000	5,000	30,000	44,000	26,000	5,000	19,000	31,000	49,000
	27	114,000	87,000	5,000	31,000	46,000	26,000	5,000	19,000	32,000	50,000
	28	114,000	98,000	5,000	31,000	48,000	26,000	4,000	20,000	32,000	51,000
	29	115,000	112,000	5,000	31,000	49,000	27,000	4,000	20,000	33,000	51,000
	30	115,000	124,000	5,000	32,000	50,000	27,000	5,000	21,000	34,000	52,000
July	1	116,000	136,000	5,000	32,000	50,000	27,000	5,000	21,000	35,000	53,000
	2	116,000	144,000	5,000	32,000	51,000	27,000	5,000	22,000	36,000	54,000
	3	116,000	150,000	5,000	32,000	52,000	27,000	5,000	22,000	37,000	55,000
	4	115,000	152,000	5,000	32,000	53,000	27,000	5,000	22,000	38,000	56,000
	5	115,000	154,000	5,000	32,000	53,000	27,000	5,000	23,000	39,000	57,000
	6	114,000	155,000	5,000	32,000	54,000	27,000	6,000	23,000	41,000	58,000
	7	113,000	155,000	5,000	31,000	55,000	27,000	6,000	23,000	42,000	58,000
	8	111,000	153,000	5,000	31,000	55,000	27,000	6,000	24,000	43,000	59,000
	9	108,000	148,000	5,000	30,000	55,000	27,000	6,000	24,000	44,000	60,000
	10	105,000	140,000	5,000	29,000	56,000	28,000	6,000	24,000	46,000	61,000
	11	97,000	123,000	4,000	27,000	56,000	28,000	6,000	24,000	47,000	62,000
	12	83,000	105,000	4,000	24,000	56,000	28,000	6,000	25,000	48,000	63,000
	13	67,000	97,000	4,000	21,000	56,000	28,000	6,000	25,000	50,000	64,000
	14	44,000	85,000	4,000	18,000	56,000	28,000	6,000	25,000	51,000	65,000
	15	35,000	72,000	3,000	15,000	56,000	28,000	6,000	25,000	52,000	66,000
	16	16,000	63,000	3,000	11,000	57,000	27,000	6,000	25,000	53,000	67,000
	17	8,000	53,000	2,000	8,000	57,000	26,000	6,000	25,000	55,000	68,000
	18	2,000	42,000	2,000	6,000	57,000	24,000	6,000	25,000	56,000	69,000
	19	1,000	32,000	1,000	5,000	57,000	18,000	6,000	25,000	57,000	70,000
	20	0	22,000	1,000	4,000	57,000	15,000	6,000	25,000	58,000	71,000
	21	0	16,000	0	3,000	58,000	10,000	6,000	25,000	59,000	72,000
	22	0	12,000	0	2,000	58,000	8,000	6,000	25,000	60,000	73,000
	23	0	9,000	0	1,000	58,000	6,000	6,000	25,000	61,000	74,000

Discharge per second of crevasses—Continued.

Date.	Helena to Napoleon.		Napoleon to Lake Providence.		Lake Providence to Vicksburg.		Vicksburg to Natchez.	Natchez to Red river.	Red river to Carrollton.	Opp. New Orleans (No. 45).
	Right bank	Left bank.	Right bank	Left bank.	Right bank	Left bank.	Right bank	Right bank	Right bank	Right bank
1858.	*Cu. feet.*	*Cu. feet.*	*Cu. feet.*	*Cu. feet.*	*Cu feet.*	*Cu. feet.*	*Cu. feet.*	*Cu. feet.*	*Cu. feet.*	*Cu. feet.*
July 24	0	6,000	0	0	59,000	8,000	6,000	25,000	62,000	74,000
25	0	4,000	0	0	57,000	2,000	6,000	25,000	63,000	75,000
26	0	3,000	0	0	55,000	1,000	6,000	24,000	64,000	76,000
27	0	2.000	0	0	51,000	0	6,000	24,000	64,000	77,000
28	0	1,000	0	0	47,000	0	5,000	23,000	65,000	78,000
29	0	0	0	0	45,000	0	5,000	23,000	66,000	78,000
30	0	0	0	0	39,000	0	5,000	22,000	67,000	79,000
31	0	0	0	0	35,000	0	5,000	22,000	68,000	79,000
August 1	0	0	0	0	31,000	0	5,000	21.000	69,000	80,000
2	0	0	0	0	27,000	0	5,000	20,000	69,000	80,000
3	0	0	0	0	22,000	0	3,000.	19,000	70,000	80,000
4	0	0	0	0	19,000	0	3,000	18,000	70,000	81,000
5	0	0	0	0	13,000	0	3,000	17,000	71,000	81,000
6	0	0	0	0	10,000	0	3,000	16,000	71,000	81,000
7	0	0	0	0	7,000	0	2,000	15,000	71,000	81,000
8	0	0	0	0	5,000	0	2,000	14,000	71,000	81,000
9	0	0	0	0	3,000	0	1,000	13.000	71,000	81,000
10	0	0	0	0	1,000	0	0	12,000	71,000	81,000
11	0	0	0	0	0	0	0	11,000	71,000	81,000
12	0	0	0	0	0	0	0	9,000	71,000	81,000
13	0	0	0	0	0	0	0	8,000	71,000	81,000
14	0	0	0	0	0	0	0	6,000	70,000	81,000
15	0	0	0	0	0	0	0	4,000	70,000	81,000
16	0	0	0	0	0	0	0	2,000	69,000	80,000
17	0	0	0	0	0	0	0	0	68,000	80,000
18	0	0	0	0	0	0	0	0	67,000	79,000
19	0	0	0	0	0	0	0	0	66,000	79,000
20	0	0	0	0	0	0	0	0	65,000	78,000
21	0	0	0	0	0	0	0	0	64,000	77,000
22	0	0	0	0	0	0	0	0	62,000	75,000
23	0	0	0	0	0	0	0	0	60,000	74,000
24	0	0	0	0	0	0	0	0	57,000	72,000
25	0	0	0	0	0	0	0	0	55,000	71,000
26	0	0	0	0	0	0	0	0	52,000	69,000
27	0	0	0	0	0	0	0	0	49,000	66,000
28	0	0	0	0	0	0	0	0	45,000	64,000
29	0	0	0	0	0	0	0	0	41,000	62,000
30	0	0	0	0	0	0	0	0	37,000	59,000
31	0	0	0	0	0	0	0	0	32,000	56,000
Sept. 1	0	0	0	0	0	0	0	0	28,000	52,000
2	0	0	0	0	0	0	0	0	24,000	49,000
3	0	0	0	0	0	0	0	0	17,000	45,000
4	0	0	0	0	0	0	0	0	9,000	40,000
5	0	0	0	0	0	0	0	0	0	36,000
6	0	0	0	0	0	0	0	0	0	31,000
7	0	0	0	0	0	0	0	0	0	26,000
8	0	0	0	0	0	0	0	0	0	20,000
9	0	0	0	0	0	0	0	0	0	15,000
10	0	0	0	0	0	0	0	0	0	9,000
11	0	0	0	0	0	0	0	0	0	4,000

Transfer of the discharge measured daily at Vicksburg to the points selected for study.

The next step is to determine, in accordance with the principles laid down in Chapter IV, what the actual daily discharge during the flood period was at the following localities, selected as being nearly equidistant and sufficient in number to answer all practical purposes: Helena, Napoleon, Lake Providence, Vicksburg, Natchez, Red-river landing, Donaldsonville, and Carrollton. The measurements at Columbus are evidently not available for this purpose, since the daily loss between that place and Helena, by gaps in the levee and by crevasses, could not be determined. Even if this quantity had been known, it would have been a very delicate operation to transfer discharges in this part of the valley, because the continual and excessive oscillations of the river—involving changes of level amounting sometimes even to 3 feet in a day—would have made the amount of the channel correction enormous and very difficult to estimate, especially as the mean width of the river is here so great. Vicksburg, therefore, is the important position from which the measured daily discharge is to be transferred both up and down the river. The following expressions, deduced in the manner described in Chapter IV, exhibit the rules for ascertaining all such discharges in the high stages of the river, the unit being the cubic foot:—

Discharge per second, Helena, July 15 =

Discharge per second at Vicksburg .... July 18
— Discharge per second of Yazoo river .... July 18
+ Discharge per second of crevasses, Lake Providence to Vicksburg .... July 18
+ Discharge per second of crevasses, Napoleon to Lake Providence .... July 17
— Discharge per second of Arkansas and White rivers .... July 16
+ Discharge per second of crevasses, Helena to Napoleon .... July 16
+ 13,000 {
    Rise, Helena .... July 14–15
    + Twice rise, Napoleon .... July 15–16
    + Twice rise, Lake Providence .... July 16–17
    + Rise, Vicksburg .... July 17–18 }

Discharge per second, Napoleon, July 16 =

Discharge per second at Vicksburg .... July 18
— Discharge per second of Yazoo river .... July 18
+ Discharge per second of crevasses, Lake Providence to Vicksburg .... July 18
+ Discharge per second of crevasses, Napoleon to Lake Providence .... July 17
+ 13,000 {
    Rise, Napoleon .... July 15–16
    + Twice rise, Lake Providence .... July 16–17
    + Rise, Vicksburg .... July 17–18 }

Discharge per second, Lake Providence, July 17 =

Discharge per second at Vicksburg .... July 18
— Discharge per second of Yazoo river .... July 18
+ Discharge per second of crevasses, Lake Providence to Vicksburg .... July 18
+ 10,000 {
    Rise, Lake Providence .... July 16–17
    + Rise, Vicksburg .... July 17–18 }

Discharge per second, Natchez, July 19 =

Discharge per second at Vicksburg .... July 18
— Discharge per second of crevasses, Vicksburg to Natchez .... July 18
+ 13,000 {
    Fall, Vicksburg .... July 17–18
    + Fall, Natchez .... July 18–19 }

Discharge per second, Red-river landing, July 20 =

Discharge per second at Vicksburg .... July 18
— Discharge per second of crevasses, Vicksburg to Natchez .... July 18
— Discharge per second of crevasses, Natchez to Red river .... July 20
+ Discharge per second from Red river .... July 20
+ 10,000 {
    Fall, Vicksburg .... July 17–18
    + Twice fall, Natchez .... July 18–19
    + Fall, Red-river landing .... July 19–20 }

Discharge per second, Donaldsonville, July 21 =

Discharge per second at Vicksburg .... July 18
— Discharge per second of crevasses, Vicksburg to Natchez .... July 18
— Discharge per second of crevasses, Natchez to Red river .... July 20
+ Discharge per second from Red river .... July 20
— Discharge per second of bayou Plaquemine .... July 21
— Discharge per second of bayou La Fourche .... July 21
+ 11,000 {
    Fall, Vicksburg .... July 17–18
    + Twice fall, Natchez .... July 18–19
    + Twice fall, Red-river landing .... July 19–20
    + Fall, Donaldsonville .... July 20–21 }

Discharge per second, Carrollton, July 22 =

Discharge per second at Vicksburg ....July 18
— Discharge per second of crevasses, Vicksburg to Natchez........................July 18
— Discharge per second of crevasses, Natchez to Red river........................July 20
+ Discharge per second from Red river ....July 20
— Discharge per second of bayou Plaquemine..July 21
— Discharge per second of bayou La Fourche ....July 21
— Discharge per second of crevasses, Red river to Carrollton........................July 22
+ 10,000 (
Fall, Vicksburg..July 17–18
+ Twice fall, Natchez..July 18–19
+ Twice fall, Red-river landing..July 19–20
+ Twice fall, Donaldsonville..July 20–21
+ Fall, Carrollton..July 21–22)

Table of results. The following table exhibits the results obtained by applying this process to the data given above or contained in Appendices B and E:—

Discharge per second of the Mississippi river.

Date.	Columbus.	Helena.	Napoleon.	Lake Providence.	Vicksburg.	Natchez.	Red-river landing.	Donaldson-ville.	Carrollton.
1858.	*Cubic feet.*	*Cubic feet.*	*Cubic feet.*	*Cubic feet.*	*Cubic feet.*	*Cubic feet.*	*Cubic feet.*	*Cubic feet.*	*Cubic feet.*
March 20......	740,000				842,000		930,000	901,000	891,000
21......	870,000				870,000		917,000	912,000	902,000
22......	981,000	892,000			910,000		909,000	897,000	914,000
23......	1,059,000	923,000	990,000		947,000		919,000	883,000	898,000
24......	1,098,000	938,000	1,021,000	960,000	961,000		951,000	890,000	880,000
25......	1,106,000	968,000	1,041,000	985,000	990,000	939,000	976,000	920,000	889,000
26......	1,130,000	963,000	1,070,000	1,007,000	1,017,000	967,000	981,000	940,000	918,000
27......	1,130,000	975,000	1,076,000	1,033,000	1,042,000	995,000	996,000	942,000	939,000
28......	1,120,000	985,000	1,085,000	1,049,000	1,070,000	1,019,000	1,017,000	953,000	939,000
29......	1,105,000	1,006,000	1,111,000	1,065,000	1,091,000	1,049,000	1,030,000	975,000	953,000
30......	1,090,000	997,000	1,112,000	1,077,000	1,109,000	1,078,000	1,052,000	990,000	972,000
31......	1,075,000	1,013,000	1,094,000	1,082,000	1,122,000	1,091,000	1,069,000	1,015,000	994,000
April 1......	1,059,000	1,020,000	1,108,000	1,076,000	1,129,000	1,105,000	1,063,000	1,035,000	1,016,000
2......	990,000	1,008,000	1,113,000	1,089,000	1,131,000	1,112,000	1,077,000	1,024,000	1,036,000
3......	947,000	1,015,000	1,111,000	1,093,000	1,139,000	1,118,000	1,086,000	1,036,000	1,025,000
4......	855,000	999,000	1,120,000	1,095,000	1,142,000	1,129,000	1,105,000	1,044,000	1,035,000
5......	778,000	996,000	1,111,000	1,103,000	1,144,000	1,133,000	1,120,000	1,061,000	1,043,000
6......	710,000	988,000	1,112,000	1,093,000	1,149,000	1,140,000	1,127,000	1,078,000	1,057,000
7......	623,000	960,000	1,112,000	1,094,000	1,140,000	1,144,000	1,136,000	1,084,000	1,078,000
8......	585,000	945,000	1,096,000	1,095,000	1,141,000	1,136,000	1,141,000	1,095,000	1,083,000
9......	568,000	931,000	1,095,000	1,087,000	1,143,000	1,136,000	1,132,000	1,099,000	1,092,000
10......	565,000	924,000	1,092,000	1,091,000	1,139,000	1,139,000	1,133,000	1,090,000	1,098,000
11......	570,000	899,000	1,090,000	1,098,000	1,145,000	1,135,000	1,135,000	1,088,000	1,085,000
12......	595,000	889,000	1,081,000	1,093,000	1,152,000	1,144,000	1,133,000	1,095,000	1,091,000
13......	625,000	873,000	1,063,000	1,090,000	1,154,000	1,151,000	1,144,000	1,093,000	1,098,000
14......	682,000	867,000	1,052,000	1,079,000	1,154,000	1,155,000	1,151,000	1,105,000	1,094,000
15......	800,000	886,000	1,039,000	1,067,000	1,147,000	1,157,000	1,163,000	1,111,000	1,105,000
16......	860,000	895,000	1,033,000	1,056,000	1,138,000	1,150,000	1,165,000	1,121,000	1,110,000
17......	900,000	918,000	1,031,000	1,037,000	1,129,000	1,143,000	1,163,000	1,126,000	1,119,000
18......	950,000	927,000	1,040,000	1,034,000	1,110,000	1,133,000	1,163,000	1,123,000	1,126,000
19......	1,000,000	945,000	1,038,000	1,037,000	1,105,000	1,111,000	1,162,000	1,114,000	1,124,000
20......	1,031,000	960,000	1,053,000	1,030,000	1,103,000	1,104,000	1,154,000	1,120,000	1,121,000
21......	1,086,000	974,000	1,069,000	1,047,000	1,099,000	1,098,000	1,155,000	1,111,000	1,121,000
22......	1,120,000	996,000	1,080,000	1,060,000	1,111,000	1,096,000	1,159,000	1,113,000	1,108,000
23......	1,210,000	1,006,000	1,095,000	1,069,000	1,123,000	1,110,000	1,161,000	1,119,000	1,114,000
24......	1,261,000	1,023,000	1,100,000	1,082,000	1,130,000	1,122,000	1,180,000	1,120,000	1,119,000
25......	1,265,000	1,021,000	1,107,000	1,088,000	1,140,000	1,127,000	1,191,000	1,137,000	1,119,000
26......	1,260,000	1,031,000	1,102,000	1,092,000	1,144,000	1,136,000	1,196,000	1,148,000	1,135,000
27......	1,237,000	1,041,000	1,103,000	1,089,000	1,146,000	1,138,000	1,203,000	1,150,000	1,146,000
28......	1,210,000	1,058,000	1,104,000	1,087,000	1,141,000	1,145,000	1,203,000	1,163,000	1,149,000
29......	1,170,000	1,053,000	1,114,000	1,089,000	1,141,000	1,135,000	1,208,000	1,162,000	1,164,000
30......	1,113,000	1,061,000	1,106,000	1,100,000	1,143,000	1,136,000	1,199,000	1,166,000	1,166,000
May 1......	1,050,000	1,067,000	1,107,000	1,097,000	1,160,000	1,138,000	1,193,000	1,157,000	1,164,000
2......	980,000	1,062,000	1,108,000	1,097,000	1,161,000	1,159,000	1,194,000	1,148,000	1,156,000
3......	890,000	1,077,000	1,104,000	1,095,000	1,162,000	1,156,000	1,210,000	1,145,000	1,145,000
4......	803,000	1,067,000	1,117,000	1,096,000	1,165,000	1,158,000	1,207,000	1,163,000	1,142,000
5......	787,000	1,072,000	1,108,000	1,105,000	1,167,000	1,164,000	1,210,000	1,161,000	1,163,000
6......	779,000	1,075,000	1,117,000	1,100,000	1,178,000	1,166,000	1,213,000	1,163,000	1,159,000
7......	777,000	1,083,000	1,125,000	1,106,000	1,174,000	1,178,000	1,213,000	1,165,000	1,160,000
8......	787,000	1,089,000	1,134,000	1,116,000	1,181,000	1,174,000	1,221,000	1,167,000	1,160,000

Discharge per second of the Mississippi river—Continued.

Date.	Columbus.	Helena.	Napoleon.	Lake Providence.	Vicksburg.	Natchez.	Red-river landing.	Donaldson-ville.	Carrollton.
1858.	*Cubic feet.*	*Cubic feet.*	*Cubic feet.*	*Cubic feet.*	*Cubic feet.*	*Cubic feet.*	*Cubic feet.*	*Cubic feet.*	*Cubic feet.*
May 9......	800,000	1,073,000	1,145,000	1,125,000	1,190,000	1,181,000	1,207,000	1,175,000	1,163,000
10......	820,000	1,096,000	1,130,000	1,134,000	1,200,000	1,187,000	1,207,000	1,161,000	1,169,000
11......	889,000	1,068,000	1,146,000	1,121,000	1,209,000	1,199,000	1,205,000	1,160,000	1,157,000
12......	955,000	1,097,000	1,135,000	1,134,000	1,200,000	1,209,000	1,212,000	1,163,000	1,155,000
13......	970,000	1,092,000	1,149,000	1,127,000	1,211,000	1,200,000	1,216,000	1,166,000	1,162,000
14......	1,005,000	1,083,000	1,152,000	1,140,000	1,204,000	1,214,000	1,202,000	1,174,000	1,163,000
15......	1,030,000	1,076,000	1,161,000	1,142,000	1,218,000	1,204,000	1,213,000	1,159,000	1,170,000
16......	1,030,000	1,076,000	1,161,000	1,147,000	1,220,000	1,219,000	1,203,000	1,170,000	1,156,000
17......	1,011,000	1,068,000	1,166,000	1,148,000	1,223,000	1,221,000	1,217,000	1,162,000	1,165,000
18......	1,008,000	1,071,000	1,162,000	1,153,000	1,224,000	1,224,000	1,218,000	1,174,000	1,156,000
19......	1,005,000	1,070,000	1,165,000	1,149,000	1,230,000	1,223,000	1,221,000	1,177,000	1,168,000
20......	990,000	1,074,000	1,170,000	1,147,000	1,225,000	1,229,000	1,219,000	1,179,000	1,172,000
21......	982,000	1,075,000	1,174,000	1,156,000	1,223,000	1,224,000	1,224,000	1,177,000	1,171,000
22......	985,000	1,074,000	1,177,000	1,160,000	1,232,000	1,223,000	1,221,000	1,184,000	1,169,000
23......	1,010,000	1,066,000	1,174,000	1,161,000	1,234,000	1,228,000	1,219,000	1,182,000	1,177,000
24......	1,045,000	1,075,000	1,169,000	1,160,000	1,235,000	1,229,000	1,224,000	1,179,000	1,168,000
25......	1,078,000	1,082,000	1,174,000	1,154,000	1,235,000	1,228,000	1,229,000	1,183,000	1,170,000
26......	1,114,000	1,075,000	1,180,000	1,155,000	1,227,000	1,228,000	1,233,000	1,188,000	1,173,000
27......	1,133,000	1,080,000	1,174,000	1,162,000	1,227,000	1,221,000	1,238,000	1,192,000	1,179,000
28......	1,137,000	1,096,000	1,174,000	1,159,000	1,236,000	1,220,000	1,235,000	1,197,000	1,182,000
29......	1,140,000	1,100,000	1,178,000	1,157,000	1,233,000	1,230,000	1,234,000	1,194,000	1,188,000
30......	1,140,000	1,116,000	1,180,000	1,158,000	1,230,000	1,229,000	1,238,000	1,193,000	1,183,000
31......	1,142,000	1,118,000	1,189,000	1,160,000	1,230,000	1,224,000	1,233,000	1,197,000	1,181,000
June 1......	1,143,000	1,117,000	1,184,000	1,169,000	1,232,000	1,225,000	1,221,000	1,194,000	1,186,000
2......	1,151,000	1,125,000	1,191,000	1,162,000	1,241,000	1,227,000	1,218,000	1,180,000	1,181,000
3......	1,161,000	1,122,000	1,192,000	1,171,000	1,233,000	1,237,000	1,219,000	1,177,000	1,168,000
4......	1,175,000	1,117,000	1,191,000	1,171,000	1,241,000	1,226,000	1,229,000	1,178,000	1,163,000
5......	1,185,000	1,114,000	1,192,000	1,169,000	1,242,000	1,236,000	1,217,000	1,188,000	1,163,000
6......	1,195,000	1,116,000	1,180,000	1,168,000	1,240,000	1,239,000	1,226,000	1,176,000	1,171,000
7......	1,206,000	1,126,000	1,169,000	1,157,000	1,238,000	1,236,000	1,230,000	1,183,000	1,160,000
8......	1,222,000	1,132,000	1,178,000	1,145,000	1,227,000	1,234,000	1,225,000	1,189,000	1,166,000
9......	1,241,000	1,141,000	1,185,000	1,152,000	1,214,000	1,223,000	1,224,000	1,184,000	1,171,000
10......	1,255,000	1,136,000	1,190,000	1,159,000	1,220,000	1,212,000	1,211,000	1,183,000	1,164,000
11......	1,270,000	1,137,000	1,183,000	1,164,000	1,225,000	1,218,000	1,201,000	1,169,000	1,163,000
12......	1,281,000	1,147,000	1,179,000	1,157,000	1,229,000	1,219,000	1,205,000	1,156,000	1,148,000
13......	1,300,000	1,150,000	1,183,000	1,152,000	1,222,000	1,224,000	1,206,000	1,163,000	1,133,000
14......	1,318,000	1,159,000	1,178,000	1,156,000	1,216,000	1,221,000	1,211,000	1,161,000	1,141,000
15......	1,349,000	1,167,000	1,185,000	1,149,000	1,219,000	1,214,000	1,209,000	1,168,000	1,139,000
16......	1,388,000	1,169,000	1,189,000	1,160,000	1,212,000	1,216,000	1,201,000	1,168,000	1,144,000
17......	1,403,000	1,185,000	1,187,000	1,160,000	1,218,000	1,210,000	1,201,000	1,161,000	1,146,000
18......	1,408,000	1,197,000	1,197,000	1,157,000	1,222,000	1,217,000	1,196,000	1,161,000	1,136,000
19......	1,400,000	1,217,000	1,200,000	1,166,000	1,218,000	1,219,000	1,203,000	1,155,000	1,137,000
20......	1,398,000	1,226,000	1,212,000	1,170,000	1,226,000	1,215,000	1,204,000	1,162,000	1,129,000
21......	1,395,000	1,244,000	1,209,000	1,180,000	1,231,000	1,223,000	1,199,000	1,164,000	1,135,000
22......	1,383,000	1,251,000	1,221,000	1,176,000	1,238,000	1,228,000	1,207,000	1,158,000	1,137,000
23......	1,360,000	1,250,000	1,219,000	1,188,000	1,234,000	1,233,000	1,211,000	1,166,000	1,129,000
24......	1,330,000	1,246,000	1,210,000	1,185,000	1,245,000	1,230,000	1,216,000	1,169,000	1,136,000
25......	1,286,000	1,245,000	1,199,000	1,176,000	1,242,000	1,239,000	1,212,000	1,175,000	1,137,000
26......	1,259,000	1,259,000	1,189,000	1,164,000	1,231,000	1,237,000	1,220,000	1,171,000	1,144,000
27......	1,220,000	1,268,000	1,189,000	1,153,000	1,220,000	1,225,000	1,218,000	1,179,000	1,140,000
28......	1,157,000	1,291,000	1,188,000	1,153,000	1,209,000	1,215,000	1,207,000	1,178,000	1,147,000
29......	1,090,000	1,309,000	1,196,000	1,153,000	1,207,000	1,206,000	1,195,000	1,165,000	1,146,000
30......	997,000	1,324,000	1,202,000	1,161,000	1,206,000	1,203,000	1,185,000	1,155,000	1,131,000
July 1......	841,000	1,327,000	1,203,000	1,166,000	1,216,000	1,201,000	1,183,000	1,144,000	1,122,000
2......	740,000	1,332,000	1,202,000	1,166,000	1,219,000	1,214,000	1,180,000	1,142,000	1,108,000
3......	671,000	1,323,000	1,201,000	1,166,000	1,219,000	1,214,000	1,194,000	1,139,000	1,106,000
4......	640,000	1,325,000	1,196,000	1,163,000	1,218,000	1,215,000	1,194,000	1,153,000	1,101,000
5......	619,000	1,334,000	1,198,000	1,159,000	1,215,000	1,214,000	1,195,000	1,153,000	1,114,000
6......	602,000	1,328,000	1,208,000	1,161,000	1,212,000	1,210,000	1,194,000	1,154,000	1,112,000
7......	568,000	1,309,000	1,208,000	1,170,000	1,212,000	1,207,000	1,189,000	1,152,000	1,112,000
8......	533,000	1,305,000	1,210,000	1,172,000	1,220,000	1,206,000	1,186,000	1,146,000	1,107,000
9......	500,000	1,275,000	1,206,000	1,176,000	1,224,000	1,213,000	1,186,000	1,146,000	1,101,000
10......	490,000	1,242,000	1,194,000	1,172,000	1,226,000	1,218,000	1,193,000	1,145,000	1,103,000
11......	485,000	1,190,000	1,188,000	1,167,000	1,223,000	1,220,000	1,198,000	1,152,000	1,098,000
12......	477,000	1,162,000	1,175,000	1,164,000	1,220,000	1,217,000	1,200,000	1,157,000	1,104,000
13......	464,000	1,123,000	1,172,000	1,163,000	1,218,000	1,214,000	1,196,000	1,159,000	1,108,000
14......	466,000	1,075,000	1,161,000	1,164,000	1,222,000	1,211,000	1,195,000	1,154,000	1,108,000
15......	460,000	1,036,000	1,155,000	1,163,000	1,220,000	1,217,000	1,191,000	1,155,000	1,103,000
16......	443,000	989,000	1,134,000	1,169,000	1,221,000	1,214,000	1,199,000	1,150,000	1,102,000
17......	425,000	963,000	1,112,000	1,162,000	1,229,000	1,215,000	1,195,000	1,158,000	1,095,000

Discharge per second of the Mississippi river—Continued.

Date.	Columbus.	Helena.	Napoleon.	Lake Providence.	Vicksburg.	Natchez.	Red-river landing.	Donaldson-ville.	Carrollton.
1858.	*Cubic feet.*	*Cubic feet.*	*Cubic feet.*	*Cubic feet.*	*Cubic feet.*	*Cubic feet.*	*Cubic feet.*	*Cubic feet.*	*Cubic feet.*
July 18......	425,000	944,000	1,098,000	1,143,000	1,225,000	1,224,000	1,197,000	1,155,000	1,101,000
19......	445,000	931,000	1,086,000	1,138,000	1,220,000	1,219,000	1,207,000	1,155,000	1,096,000
20......	493,000		1,086,000	1,136,000	1,218,000	1,215,000	1,202,000	1,166,000	1,099,000
21	521,000			1,139,000	1,216,000	1,212,000	1,199,000	1,161,000	1,107,000
22......	596,000				1,218,000	1,214,000	1,196,000	1,159,000	1,102,000
23......	620,000				1,210,000	1,214,000	1,198,000	1,155,000	1,098,000
24......	639,000				1,189,000	1,207,000	1,200,000	1,158,000	1,094,000
25......	660,000				1,180,000	1,186,000	1,193,000	1,163,000	1,096,000
26......	665,000				1,170,000	1,178,000	1,172,000	1,156,000	1,100,000
27......	665,000				1,155,000	1,169,000	1,164,000	1,132,000	1,091,000
28......	664,000				1,158,000	1,152,000	1,159,000	1,124,000	1,067,000
29......	662,000				1,155,000	1,157,000	1,141,000	1,122,000	1,059,000
30......	614,000				1,148,000	1,153,000	1,147,000	1,102,000	1,056,000
31......	589,000				1,147,000	1,146,000	1,144,000	1,109,000	1,034,000
Aug. 1......	560,000				1,140,000	1,147,000	1,138,000	1,108,000	1,040,000
2......	532,000				1,137,000	1,139,000	1,142,000	1,102,000	1,039,000
3......	514,000				1,117,000	1,137,000	1,134,000	1,107,000	1,032,000
4......	493,000				1,104,000	1,117,000	1,135,000	1,099,000	1,037,000
5......	480,000				1,098,000	1,106,000	1,116,000	1,102,000	1,028,000
6......	479,000				1,086,000	1,101,000	1,108,000	1,084,000	1,033,000
7......	480,000				1,067,000	1,092,000	1,106,000	1,074,000	1,014,000
8......	490,000				1,050,000	1,074,000	1,099.000	1,077,000	1,003,000
9......	496,000				1,026,000	1,057,000	1,083,000	1,068,000	1,008,000
10......	496,000				1,010,000	1,038,000	1,069,000	1,055,000	998,000
11......	495,000				993,000	1,029,000	1,049,000	1,040,000	986,000
12......	480,000				982,000	1,007,000	1,051,000	1,021,000	968,000
13......	468,000				951,000	992,000	1,029,000	1,027,000	949,000
14......	467,000				935,000	967,000	1,019,000	1,003,000	955,000
15......	450,000				920,000	948,000	993,000	994,000	933,000
16......	432,000				909,000	938,000	979,000	965,000	925,000
17......	411,000				904,000	918,000	972,000	952,000	897,000
18......	391,000				882,000	914,000	953,000	946,000	885,000
19......	385,000				873,000	895,000	954,000	927,000	880,000
20......	388,000				860,000	887,000	936,000	934,000	865,000
21......	369,000				832,000	879,000	930,000	920,000	872,000
22......	365,000				812,000	850,000	924,000	915,000	859,000
23......	364,000				791,000	829,000	895,000	912,000	863,000
24......	340,000				768,000		879,000	883,000	855,000
25......	333,000				749,000			871,000	830,000
26......	300,000				714,000				821,000

Conclusive proof of the exactness of the measurements of the Survey furnished by these tables and certain other transferred discharges.

On page 359 a table precisely similar to this exhibits the daily discharge at certain points below Red-river landing in the flood of 1851. Before proceeding with the discussion of the flood of 1858, these tables will be critically examined, with a view to test the exactness of this system for the transfer of discharge by determining whether the discharges and the corresponding stands of the river, at the several localities, as shown by the gauge-records, conform to the laws already deduced in Chapter V from the observations at the permanent velocity-stations. This, however, is not the only criterion by which the accuracy of the system can be judged. The actual measurements of discharge at certain dates at temporary stations above Carrollton, in 1851, furnish the severest possible test of the work. Long before the system in question was applied, all the computations of discharge had been made from the measurements, and the results appear in this report exactly as they were then prepared, without any change or modification whatever. The system of transferring discharge, as already explained, is a purely mathematical one, allowing no latitude in its application. The direct comparison by transfer of these results is thus a complete test of the exactness of the entire system of measurements and computations.

This test of the character of the work is represented by plate XVII. Excepting the curves for 1858 at Providence, Donaldsonville, and Carrollton, where large crevasses just below the towns modified the usual form, all of these curves accord with the laws laid down in Chapter V. To this presumptive evidence of their accuracy is added the remarkable agreement between the operations of the two years. At Red-river landing—and at Donaldsonville and Carrollton, prior to the breaking of the crevasses—the two curves are nearly coincident, and it will soon be seen that whatever differences do exist are explained by known differences in the conditions governing the discharges. The great test, however, as already intimated, is the comparison between the results obtained in 1851 by actually gauging the river, and those obtained by transferring the discharge measured at Carrollton up to the same point. Eight of these actual measurements were made at Baton Rouge or Red-river landing, and they are all represented on this plate. The gaugings were conducted at points more than 100 miles apart, between which the river was changing its stage, and discharging its surplus water through two large bayous and several crevasses. *When corrected for these causes of variation and transferred to the same point, the two independent results uniformly accord so closely with each other, that even a slight variation in the force or direction of the wind, if neglected, would have produced errors in either of the discharges greater in amount than the actual differences between the two.* No further demonstration of the exactness of the work can be required to entitle it to confidence.

Effect of the crevasses below Helena upon the discharge at points below that town, to be first investigated.

We are now ready to proceed with the analysis of the flood of 1858. Neglecting, for the time, the modification which would have been produced upon the reservoir action of the channel by confining the flood between its banks—a very important matter, as will be hereafter seen—the first step is to ascertain the amount by which the high-water discharges at the several localities under consideration were diminished by crevasses, supposing the river above Helena to have remained in its actual condition.

This requires a knowledge of the contributions proper of the several tributaries.

Below Red river this can be done by tracing each day's discharge down stream and adding to it the discharge of the different crevasses during its passage past them. Above Red-river landing, the question is more complicated, since the actual discharge of the different tributaries was greatly augmented by the return of crevasse-water through their channels. The allowance to be made for this augmentation will be considered for each tributary separately.

That of the Arkansas and White rivers.

The swamps near the mouths of Arkansas and White rivers are comparatively small, as may be seen by reference to plate II. They were open to the Mississippi for several miles near the mouth of White river in 1858, and were thus gradually filled as the Mississippi rose. White river itself also discharged much water into them during its great rise in March and April. They are not, therefore, to be regarded as reservoirs at the top of the flood in July, since they were already full of water, and whatever entered by crevasses and gaps at that time must have forced out a nearly equivalent amount through the two channels into the

Mississippi. The measurements of the Survey demonstrate the correctness of this opinion, as will now be shown. Definite information relative to the condition of the Arkansas and White rivers during the flood period was obtained. There was but one important rise in each river. In the Arkansas this occurred in March, being at its height at Little Rock on March 22, when it was only 3 feet below the great flood of 1844. The White river flood occurred early in April, being at its height at Des Arck about April 10, when it was only 1 foot below the flood of 1844. After the month of April, both rivers remained low, with occasional, unimportant rises, during the entire flood period. Let us now examine the discharge measurements at Napoleon, given in a preceding table. At the height of the combined flood, which occurred between April 5 and April 8, the two rivers were forcing about 160,000 cubic feet of water per second into the Mississippi, notwithstanding a large rise in that river, then passing Napoleon. As already stated, Arkansas and White rivers fell to an ordinary stage by the end of April. The measured discharge through their channels to the Mississippi, however, remained without any important diminution until August. From what source was the water derived which thus maintained the discharge after the supply above had failed? Evidently from the Mississippi itself, which poured through the crevasses and the gaps near the mouth of White river a large volume of water which returned immediately by the channels of the two rivers. What proportion of their discharge was upland drainage can be approximately determined in two ways. By the above tables the total discharge of the Arkansas and White rivers between April 23 and July 19, inclusive—the period during which the last great rise of the Mississippi was forcing water into their swamps—was 1,072,396,800,000 cubic feet. The total crevasse discharge into their bottom lands during this time was 558,144,000,000 cubic feet. On July 19 no more water remained in the swamps than was in them on April 23. The difference between these total discharges (514,252,800,000 cubic feet) is, then, the amount which Arkansas and White rivers proper contributed to the Mississippi in the eighty-seven days under consideration. This is at the mean rate of 63,000 cubic feet per second for the whole time. The second method of approximating to the daily discharge of the two rivers during the great rise is as follows: By August 6, the river at Napoleon had fallen over 11 feet, and all the water had drained from the White river and Arkansas swamps. During the succeeding fifteen days, when (according to the facts gathered concerning the condition of those rivers at points above the influence of the Mississippi river) the supply from above continued to be about the same as during the great rise of the Mississippi, the average discharge of these two rivers was 54,000 cubic feet per second. This quantity differs so little from the result of the former process, that no material error can arise from assuming that the Arkansas and White rivers together discharged about 60,000 cubic feet per second of drainage proper into the Mississippi during the last great rise. This estimate is sufficiently large, and is therefore safe. During the rise of the Mississippi in March, these swamps were doubtless reservoirs, which received and retained the water lost through the crevasses. They, however, partially returned it as the river fell between the two rises.

That of the Yazoo river.

The information collected respecting the condition of the Yazoo river during the flood was equally exact and decisive. Two rises of importance, independent of Mississippi water, occurred. One took place in January and the other in April. Subsequent to the latter, the river fell rapidly, and would have remained low for the rest of the season, had it not been for crevasses, which admitted water from the Mississippi. The contributions of the Yazoo at the height of its April rise (April 10) amounted to about 70,000 cubic feet per second. From that date they diminished, until, by the latter part of June, they could not have exceeded 30,000 cubic feet. To estimate that the latter discharge, independent of crevasse-water, continued during the flood is safe, because it is probably slightly in excess.

That of Red river, as modified by bayou Atchafalaya.

To determine what would have been the condition at Red-river landing, had no crevasses, draining into the Tensas and Black-river swamps, occurred, is a more complex problem. Old river, situated just above the landing, is a former bend of the Mississippi, which Shreve's cut-off transformed into a kind of lake. Its level depends directly upon that of the Mississippi, with which it is still connected. It receives the water of Red river, and is drained by bayou Atchafalaya, a species of immense waste-weir, which, for any given stand of Old river, must discharge a nearly unvarying amount of water. The direction and force of the current in the mouth of Old river thus depend directly upon the relative discharge of Red river and Atchafalaya bayou. When the former stream discharges more water than the Atchafalaya can carry off, its surplus empties into the Mississippi; and when, on the contrary, its supply is insufficient to maintain the discharge of that bayou, the deficiency is made up from the Mississippi. By reference to the table on page 333, it will be seen that for nearly the whole of the flood period in 1858 there was no sensible current in the mouth of Old river. Consequently, during this time the discharge of Red river into Old river was just sufficient to maintain the normal discharge of bayou Atchafalaya. In order to determine, therefore, what would have been the condition at Red-river landing, had the Mississippi been confined to its channel during the flood, the facts respecting Red river itself must be ascertained; for the Atchafalaya would have drawn from the Mississippi at that point precisely the amount which was actually contributed by the Mississippi crevasses to increase the normal discharge of Red river.

About 25 miles above its mouth, Red river receives the waters of Black river, an important tributary, which drains the whole swamp country west of the Mississippi between Cypress creek and Natchez, into which, in 1858, many crevasses were discharging. For this reason, the condition of Red river proper must be determined from observations above the mouth of Black river. At Alexandria the following facts relative to it were observed.

The first rise of Red river occurred in January. It was highest on January 12, when it was 7 feet below high water of 1849, the greatest recorded flood in the river. This rise was the highest which had occurred since 1851, when it stood, on March 20, 1 foot below the high water of 1849. By the last of January, 1858, the river had fallen about 4 feet, and then again began to rise. On February 1, it was 9.6 feet below high water of 1849, and was discharging 82,000 cubic feet per second. On February 2 it had risen 0.3 of a foot, and was discharging 90,000 cubic feet per second. It continued to rise until February 23, when it was only 3.9 feet below high water of 1849. It then fell, at first gradually, and then rapidly, until about the middle of March, when it was 19 feet below high water of 1849. It then began to rise, until on April 22 it had attained its highest point for the year, being only 3.0 feet below high water of

44

1849. It then gradually subsided to low-water mark. On June 24 it was exactly 23 feet below high water of 1849, and discharging very little water. It should be added that the extreme range of the river at Alexandria is 47 feet. The months of May, June, and July being those of highest water at Red-river landing, it is evident that Red river proper had no sensible effect upon the flood, and that the water which entered Old river through its channel, and supplied the whole of the discharge of Atchafalaya, came from Black river and the swamp bayous below it. Black river, then, is next to be examined, to ascertain what was its real discharge, independently of Mississippi crevasse-water.

This river is formed by the junction of three streams, the Washita and Little rivers, and bayou Tensas. The latter drains the Mississippi swamp lands, and the two former the hilly country to the west of them. There was no great flood in 1858 in either of these two streams, independent of the backing up occasioned by Mississippi water. They must have been quite low during the three flood months (May, June, and July), since this was the condition of both the Arkansas and Red rivers, which drain the country just north and south of their water-shed. With respect to bayou Tensas, more definite information was obtained. Mr. Mandeville, who resides at Westwood, near where Mr. Pattison's line of levels crosses the stream, has for many years kept a record of the oscillations of the bayou during floods, a copy of which he kindly presented to the Survey. These notes will be found in Appendix B. They show that in 1858 the bayou rose very slowly until August 5, when it was at its height. Its cross-section was then 16,000 square feet. (See Appendix C.) Its velocity during the flood period was estimated by Mr. Mandeville to vary from 4.5 to 5.0 feet per second. Assuming the latter rate for high water, we have for the discharge 16,000 × 5 = 80,000 cubic feet per second, of which much the greater part was Mississippi crevasse-water. Add to this the hill drainage and the contributions through Cocodrie bayou and through the swamps themselves, and it is evident that Black river must have discharged over 100,000 cubic feet per second into Red river, and, by its channel, to Old river, from which, as already seen, it all passed into bayou Atchafalaya. The discharge of this bayou is next to be considered. It was gauged three times during the Survey.

	Cubic feet.
On February 11, 1858, it was 7.6 feet below high water of 1858, and discharged	77,000
On March 8, 1851, " 3.7 " " " " "	98,000
On March 9, 1851, " 3.5 " " " " "	105,000

From May 2 to August 3, 1858, it was never more than one foot, and averaged only some 4 or 5 inches, below high water of 1858. During this period, then, it must have discharged 120,000 cubic feet per second, which accords closely with the amount just indicated above as its probable supply.

Having thus demonstrated that bayou Atchafalaya discharged some 120,000 cubic feet of water per second during the flood, that this amount was necessarily derived entirely from the channel of Red river, that all the hill tributaries of this river were low, and, lastly, that the swamp tributaries were flooded by Mississippi crevasse-water, the conclusion is inevitable, that, had the Mississippi levees remained unbroken, bayou Atchafalaya would have served as an outlet to reduce materially the quantity of water passing Red-river landing. In May, judging from the comparatively high stage of Red river proper, and from the small amount of water actually passing through the crevasses, this diminution would probably have been trifling, but at the height of the flood, in the latter part of June and in July, it could not have been less than 90,000 cubic feet per second, unless Red river be allowed more drainage from its basin than was discharged by either the Arkansas, the White, or the Yazoo rivers at that time.

Resulting rule for determining what would have been the discharge at points below Helena, had no crevasses occurred below that town; neglecting reservoir influence of channel.

Having thus analyzed the actual effect of the Mississippi crevasse-water upon the several tributary streams below Helena during the flood in 1858, we are prepared to decide how much the crevasses diminished the maximum discharge at the several stations selected; bearing in mind, however, that the results are still to be corrected for the reservoir influence of the channel. The system of computation is general. The actual discharge at each locality for each day during the flood period is to be increased by the amount of water lost in passing the crevasses above it, and to be diminished by the difference between the actual discharge of any tributary passed and its true discharge independent of crevasse-water. Thus, for example, we have for the discharge at Carrollton, at the height of the flood, the following expression:—

Discharge per second, Carrollton, July 8 } = {
Actual discharge per second, Carrollton....July 8
+ Discharge per second of crevasses, Helena to Napoleon....July 2
+ Discharge per second of crevasses, Napoleon to Lake Providence....July 3
+ Discharge per second of crevasses, Lake Providence to Vicksburg....July 4
+ Discharge per second of crevasses, Vicksburg to Natchez....July 4
+ Discharge per second of crevasses, Natchez to Red river....July 6
+ Discharge per second of crevasses, Red river to Carrollton....July 8
— Discharge per second of Arkansas and White rivers on....July 2 — 60,000
— Discharge per second of Yazoo river on....July 4 — 30,000
— 90,000 (for Atchafalaya) }

Maximum discharges computed by this rule, with explanatory remarks.

The dotted lines on plate XVIII indicate the approximate discharges at the several localities, computed by this process. The following table gives the grand results:—

First approximate maximum discharge per second, with levees perfected.

Locality.	Date.	Amount.	Remarks.
	1858.	*Cubic feet.*	
Helena	July 5	1,334,000	Upon the supposition that there were no crevasses below Helena, and no reduction by channel filling.
Napoleon	July 6	1,393,000	
Lake Providence	July 7	1,391,000	
Vicksburg	July 8	1,420,000	
Natchez	July 9	1,419,000	
Red-river landing	July 10	1,333,000	
Baton Rouge	July 11	1,333,000	
Donaldsonville	July 11	1,292,000	
Carrollton	July 12	1,292,000	

This discussion and resulting table present the subject under the most unfavorable conditions possible. It assumes the Arkansas, White, Yazoo, and Red rivers to have been securely leveed, so that they could not have been backed up enough, during the great rise which would have occurred in July, to diminish perceptibly their drainage-discharge into the Mississippi. All the swamps below Helena being thus protected are supposed to remain absolutely dry; the greater part of their rain-water even being poured into the Mississippi by the four rivers just named. The discharge of bayous Atchafalaya, Plaquemine, and La Fourche is supposed to remain unaffected by the increased height of the Mississippi at their upper mouths, or points of efflux. In a word, every minor circumstance tending to diminish the volume of the flood is neglected, in order to guard against all possibility of an under-estimate.

Effect of the bottom lands above Helena upon the maximum discharge below that town; still neglecting the reservoir influence of the channel.

Before proceeding to determine the effect of the great channel reservoir in diminishing the maximum discharges indicated by the above discussion and table, the effect exerted by the bottom lands above Helena upon the discharge at that point and below it, will be considered. This effect may be estimated quite closely, although, as already stated, the data for tracing out the local effect between the head of the alluvial region and Helena are somewhat defective. The history of the flood of 1858, already given in Chapter II, should be consulted for details bearing upon this subject.

The greatest discharge at Columbus occurred between June 16 and June 22, inclusive, when it was about 1,400,000 cubic feet per second. According to the notes of the Survey, about 35,000 cubic feet per second were entering the swamp through the Cape Girardeau inlet, and about 40,000 through the breaks between Commerce and Columbus. The total amount of water entering the head of the alluvial region was then about 1,475,000 cubic feet per second at the height of this flood. At Helena, the flood was highest between June 30 and July 6, inclusive, the discharge being about 1,330,000 cubic feet per second. Thus the rise was fourteen days later in date, and the discharge 145,000 cubic feet per second less in amount at Helena than at the head of the alluvial region. But the discharge at Helena contains the drainage proper of the St. Francis bottom, estimated, as we have already seen, at 30,000 cubic feet per second; and this quantity must be subtracted from the discharge at Helena before the full reservoir effect of the St. Francis bottom at the top of the flood of 1858 is obtained. Thus deduced, it is 175,000 cubic feet per second.

This general conclusion as to the effect—uncorrected for the reservoir influence of the channel—exerted by the St. Francis bottom upon the high-water discharge at Helena, will be compared with the corresponding effect of the Yazoo swamp upon the discharge at Vicksburg, which, as already seen, was accurately determined. These two swamps are similar in dimensions, and, usually, in depth of overflow; and general conclusions based upon the analogy existing between them are entitled to some confidence.

As already seen, the top of the flood passed Helena between June 30 and July 6, inclusive. By reference to the table of crevasse discharges given above, it will be seen that this prism of water lost 208,000 cubic feet per second into the Yazoo swamp. It passed the mouth of Yazoo river between July 3 and 9, inclusive, and received from that tributary (table on page 333) 133,000 cubic feet per second, which was 103,000 cubic feet more than it would have received if no crevasse had occurred. The difference (105,000 cubic feet per second) is then the amount by which the Yazoo bottom diminished the discharge past Vicksburg at the date when the highest flood would have occurred at that place, had the levees remained unbroken below Helena, and had the channel exerted no moderating influence.

It must be borne in mind that the St. Francis bottom was much less protected against the flood than the Yazoo bottom, and that the depth of overflow in the former was reported to be much greater than was ever before known. It is evident that 175,000 cubic feet per second must be added to each of the differences in the last table before they can be considered to include the influence of all the swamps below Cape Girardeau.

Moderating influence exerted by the great channel reservoir upon the maximum discharge in floods.

The next step in the analysis is to determine the effect which, under the new conditions indicated by this table, would have been exerted upon the maximum discharge by the moderating reservoir influence of the channel. As heretofore, the river is made to speak for itself.

Its effect upon the rise in December, 1857.

The rise in December, 1857, admirably illustrates this influence, since the water was then entirely confined to the channel, and the effect of crevasses is thus eliminated from the problem. This rise was at its height (8.5 feet below high water of 1858) at Columbus on December 21, the maximum discharge being 1,190,000 cubic feet per second. The St. Francis river was backed up, and contributed nothing. At Napoleon, the rise attained its highest point (7.1 feet below high water of 1858) on December 28. On December 29, the measured discharge of Arkansas river was 65,000 cubic feet per second. On January 1, the river had fallen 2.2 feet at Napoleon, and the measured discharge of Arkansas river was 59,000, and of White river 48,000 cubic feet per second. It is evident, then, that these two rivers must have added at least 100,000 cubic feet per second to the top of the flood wave, as it passed. At Yazoo river, according to accurate data, it received 45,000 cubic feet per second more. At the top of the flood at Natchez, which was 8.3 feet below high water, 1858, the discharge then should have been 1,190,000 + 100,000 + 45,000 = 1,335,000 cubic feet per second. It was measured on January 8, when the river had fallen 1.6 feet, and was found to be 845,000 cubic feet per second. Allowing a very liberal estimate for diminution of discharge at this date, the rise when highest could not have carried past Natchez more than 935,000 cubic feet per second. How, then, is this enormous difference of 400,000 cubic feet per second to be accounted for? Only in one way. The reservoir furnished by 550 square miles of channel between Columbus and Natchez absorbed it all. This is an extreme case, because such a rise at so low a stage is almost unprecedented, but it plainly shows that so important an element cannot be neglected in discussing the subject of river floods.

Its effect upon the rise in March, 1858.

The only other rise in the flood of 1858 which produced a sensible oscillation in the lower river was that which occurred near the end of March. This then was the only other rise sensibly modified by the reservoir influence of the channel. It was highest at Columbus on March 28–9, when it was 6.1 feet below high water of 1858; at Memphis, on April 2, when it was 1.8 feet below the same flood; and at Helena, on April 4, when it was 3.8 feet below the same flood. It was of very short duration, and did not break the levees of the St. Francis bottom. Very little water entered these swamps, and its volume was counterbalanced by the excess of the discharge of the St. Francis over 30,000 cubic feet per second. This river was pouring out a flood of rain-water from upland as well as swamp drainage. The maximum discharge at Columbus in this rise was 1,130,000 cubic feet per second. It was increased 30,000 cubic feet per second by the St. Francis river, and should therefore have been 1,160,000 cubic feet per second at Helena. The actual discharge at Helena was 1,020,000 cubic feet per second. The difference between those two quantities, 140,000 cubic feet per second, is the measure of the reservoir influence of the 250 square miles of channel between those two places.

Let us trace this rise still farther down the river. On arriving at Vicksburg, it had lost 75,000 cubic feet per second by crevasses and received 225,000 cubic feet per second from Arkansas, White, and Yazoo rivers. It should then have amounted to 1,170,000 cubic feet per second. It was measured, and really amounted to 1,145,000 cubic feet per second; the difference, due to the reservoir influence of the channel, being 25,000 cubic feet per second. The comparatively small amount of this effect in this part of the river is explained by the comparatively small and gradual oscillation of the river's surface, so clearly shown by plate XIII. Below Vicksburg, this influence upon the maximum discharge became practically unimportant, amounting only to some 5000 cubic feet per second at Red-river landing.

Other proofs of its importance.

The above are all the data collected by the Survey from which we may estimate the numerical value of this important influence which the channel exerts in moderating the maximum discharge in floods. They are by no means all that establish its existence. A single glance at plate XIII is conclusive upon this point. The enormous and evidently normal differences constantly exhibited between the discharges measured at Columbus and at Vicksburg are susceptible of explanation in no other way. The channel is evidently an immense reservoir, into which the floods of the tributaries are successively poured. In the upper river, this produces the constant oscillation which every gauge-record of the Survey exhibits. In the lower river, the channel becomes a simple drain from a lake, the supply of which is maintained by the successive contributions of the tributaries in all parts of the valley.

Its probable effect upon the maximum discharge in 1858 if no water had escaped from the river channel.

The question now to be considered is how much this moderating influence may be safely counted upon for reducing the maximum discharge in the great rise which would have occurred in June and July, 1858, had the river been confined to its channel. An inspection of the diagram will show that the huge wave must have produced a far greater oscillation in the channel between Columbus and Helena than the very considerable one which actually occurred, and that its rate of oscillation must have been at least equal to that of the March rise. Its effect may then be safely assimilated to that measured in the March rise; that is, it may be estimated at 140,000 cubic feet per second. Below Helena, it is apparent from plate XVIII, that the river would have been lower when the rise occurred, and much higher at the top of the flood, than was actually the case. The oscillation would probably have exceeded that at the height of the flood in March, and the influence in question have been correspondingly greater. Nevertheless, to guard against underrating the practical difficulties to be overcome in protecting these swamps from overflow, the measured influence of the March rise only is allowed to enter the estimate.

Final determination of the in-

To determine, then, what would have been the maximum discharge at the several localities considered, in the flood of 1858, if the swamp lands from Cape Girardeau down had all been effectually protected, we are to add to the maximum discharges per second given in the last table 175,000 cubic feet, minus, for Helena, 140,000 cubic feet;* for Napoleon, 150,000 cubic feet; for Lake Providence, 160,000 cubic feet; for Vicksburg, 165,000 cubic feet; and for Natchez and all points below, 170,000 cubic feet. This process is equivalent to deducting from the total volume that enters the head of the alluvial region, the channel effect at each point, after having added to the first the successive contributions of the tributaries. The following table exhibits the final results; that at Memphis being deduced by deducting from the discharge at Columbus the proportional part of the channel correction between Columbus and Helena, considering it to be proportional to the distance between those places:—

crease in the maximum discharge in this flood, which would have resulted from protecting all the swamp land below Cape Girardeau.

Flood of 1858.

Locality.	Actual maximum discharge per second.		Maximum discharge, had swamps below Cape Girardeau been reclaimed.		Difference, or reduction of discharge by swamps below Cape Girardeau.
	Date.	Amount.	Date.	Amount.	
		Cubic feet.		*Cubic feet.*	*Cubic feet.*
Columbus	June 18.	1,403,000	June 18.	1,478,000	75,000
Memphis				1,380,000	
Helena	July 5.	1,334,000	June 22?	1,369,000	35,000
Napoleon	June 22.	1,221,000	June 23?	1,418,000	197,000
Lake Providence	June 23.	1,188,000	June 24?	1,406,000	218,000
Vicksburg	June 24.	1,245,000	June 25?	1,430,000	185,000
Natchez	June 25.	1,239,000	June 26?	1,424,000	185,000
Red-river landing	May 30.	1,238,000	June 27?	1,338,000	100,000
Baton Rouge	May 31.	1,238,000	June 28?	1,338,000	100,000
Donaldsonville	May 31.	1,197,000	June 28?	1,297,000	100,000
Carrollton	May 29.	1,188,000	June 29?	1,297,000	109,000

This table, the most important which has thus far appeared in the report, gives a definite answer to the first part of the first question to be considered in solving the problem of the best method of protecting the bottom lands below Cape Girardeau from overflow; namely, *what was their actual effect upon the maximum discharge of the river in the flood of* 1858. It exhibits the results of years of patient labor and research. Every successive step of the analysis is based upon direct measurements, the accuracy of which has been demonstrated by numerous and constantly recurring checks. The final result, then, exhibited by this table is believed to be entitled to confidence even where such immense interests are at stake.

Its accurate character.

The next point for consideration is whether the flood of 1858 may be safely adopted as the standard, in estimating the extent of the artificial works required to protect the country from overflow in the future. Before entering upon this subject, however, a question which has an important bearing upon the discussion of the floods of 1828 and 1850 must be

Is the flood of 1858 a standard for estimating the proper

* This estimate allows about the usual amount of rain-water drainage to have been discharged by the St. Francis river, 30,000 cubic feet per second.

measures for protection?

considered. That question relates to the effect the great swamp regions above Red river produced upon a flood in the Mississippi, before levees were built.

General topography of these great bottom lands.

The so-called reservoir influence of the bottom lands.—The topographical features of the three great swamps, the St. Francis, the Yazoo, and the Tensas, are described in detail in Chapter I, and it is only necessary here to recapitulate their general characteristic features. Each great bottom is a flat plain, sloping from north to south at about 0.6 of a foot per mile, and from the Mississippi toward the bordering uplands, at a mean rate considerably less. Their systems of drainage are identical in character. On the outer border of the Yazoo and Tensas bottoms there is a river, which, rising in the uplands, collects in its course nearly the entire swamp drainage and pours it into the Mississippi* at the southern boundary of the region. The same general system exists in the St. Francis bottom, although modified by several limited basins, which drain directly into the Mississippi—not into the St. Francis river. This modification complicates the local problem of protecting the swamp against overflow, but does not affect the general problem now under discussion, inasmuch as each of these basins, being but a type of the larger swamp country, produces a similar effect upon a flood in the Mississippi.

Their legitimate downfall of rain.

By reference to plate I, it will be seen that these bottom lands are situated in that part of the great basin of the Mississippi where the precipitation of rain is nearly at its maximum, the average annual downfall being about 45 inches. It has already been shown in Chapter IV that their substratum of clay and thick growth of forests render both absorption and evaporation very slight, and that by far the greater part of their rain-water is therefore discharged into the Mississippi. The presence of this rain-water in the swamps in the spring of the year constitutes an important element in their action upon the floods.

Their influence upon the Mississippi in former times to be deduced from the measurements and facts collected by this Survey.

In their former condition, these regions were always more or less flooded in the spring by Mississippi water which escaped into them through many bayous, both large and small, and over the natural banks. At present, levees to exclude this water are under construction, and are already sufficiently advanced to modify materially the action of the swamps. Their effect upon the flood of 1858 was accurately measured, and it is proposed, first, to analyze this effect, and, second, to endeavor to deduce from it and from such other facts as can now be ascertained, the influence exerted by these so-called reservoirs upon the great floods of former times, when the natural condition of the country remained undisturbed. The Yazoo bottom is selected for this investigation.

Measured discharge to and

The tables of discharge of the crevasses into the Yazoo swamp, and of the Yazoo river into the Mississippi in 1858, already given, show that during the last great rise of that year the discharge of the crevasses, from having

* This remark needs some qualification for the Tensas bottom, there being no upland on the right bank of Red river for nearly 100 miles from its mouth. Thus, whenever there was a coincidence in the floods of that stream and of the Mississippi, a part of the water from the Tensas swamp did not return by Red river, but poured over its banks into Atchafalaya basin, and eventually discharged into the gulf through the draining bayous of that region.

been much less than the discharge of the Yazoo river, suddenly increased greatly, through the occurrence of many new breaks in the upper half of the swamp front, so that on June 28–29 it became equal to the Yazoo river discharge, or 130,000 cubic feet per second. During the six days from July 6 to July 11, when the volume entering the swamps through the crevasses was at its maximum, or 212,000 cubic feet per second, it exceeded the discharge of the Yazoo river by 80,000 cubic feet per second. By July 16, the crevasse and river discharges became again equal, being about 137,000 cubic feet per second. After that time, the crevasse discharge continued decreasing rapidly, so that by July 28 it was only 3000 cubic feet per second, while the Yazoo river discharge was 140,000 cubic feet per second.

from the Yazoo bottom in flood of 1858.

The water in the swamp began to rise in the latter part of June, and reached the highest mark along the mid-length of the swamp at dates nearly corresponding to the beginning of the decrease in supply from the river, showing that the changes in the swamp were rapid, and that the water, pouring through constantly enlarging inlets into a nearly empty swamp, passed through it like a wave. For these reasons the Yazoo bottom must have served as a reservoir in this flood. The extent to which it thus acted may be computed in the following manner.

It has already been explained in this chapter that, of the volume discharged by the Yazoo river during the period now considered, 30,000 cubic feet per second was its own rain drainage, leaving 103,000 cubic feet per second for the amount of crevasse-water returned to the Mississippi at the period of maximum crevasse discharge, when the swamp was receiving from that river 212,000 cubic feet per second. The difference between the two, or 109,000 cubic feet per second, was then the quantity held back by the swamp.

Let us now endeavor to determine what would have taken place, if the river had not been leveed. In former times the effect of the river upon the swamps began when the rising water surface attained the level of the beds of the connecting bayous, that is, when it rose to within some 10 or 15 feet of the top of the natural banks. The first effect was to stop the discharge of these bayous, and thus to accumulate the rain-water in the swamps. Even the Yazoo river itself, at this phase of the flood, was sometimes backed up so as to discharge no water into the Mississippi. In general, however, the amount of rain-water in the swamps was so large that the discharge of this stream into the Mississippi continued without any cessation from the beginning of the rise. The Mississippi continuing to rise, the water poured into the bottom lands through the numerous bayous and finally over the natural banks. It is a well-ascertained fact, attested by those familiar, from personal observation, with those great bottom lands, that the water in the swamps *continued to rise as long as the river rose, reached its highest level at the same time with the river, and began to fall when the river began to fall.* This fact leads to the solution of the problem of the general effect of those swamps upon the floods of the river; for the water in the swamp being always several feet below the high-water surface of the Mississippi, the existence of such conditions as those just described can only be accounted for by supposing the discharge from the swamp back to that river by the great swamp drain to have gone on increasing,

Well-established facts relative to the floods in these bottom lands before levees were constructed.

as the water in the swamp increased, until at the top of the flood it was equal to the discharge from the Mississippi.

This necessary inference from one observed fact is confirmed by another. It is the testimony of every intelligent resident upon the main draining rivers of these bottom lands, that in the great floods, before levees were constructed, there was *always a powerful current pouring into the Mississippi at the top of the flood.* Many assert that the current exceeded in velocity that of the Mississippi itself. This was particularly noticed at the mouth of Yazoo river in the floods of 1828 and 1850, and at the mouth of the St. Francis river in those of 1844, 1849, and 1850.

Necessary inference, that in their unleveed condition they did not act as reservoirs at the date of high water.

From these two well-established facts, each independent of and perfectly consistent with the other, it must be inferred that in great flood-years, before levees were made, the flood-wave received about as much water at the foot of each of these great swamp regions as it had lost in passing along their fronts; and hence that they exerted no sensible influence upon the maximum discharge at points below them.

This idea to be tested by the measurements made in 1858.

Let us now see how these conclusions accord with the numerical data collected respecting the flood of 1858 in the Yazoo bottom.

Probable discharge into the swamp, had no levees existed.

We must first ascertain what would have been the discharge into the swamp, had no levees existed. The high-water mark was about 4 feet above the bank along the Yazoo front. From April 23 to July 20, the river surface along that front was not at any time less than 3 feet above the bank. The river would then have been discharging a large volume into the swamps for a period of two months previous to the arrival of the great June flood. What the amount of that discharge would have been, cannot be computed with exactness; but the volume actually discharged through the crevasses on both banks from the head to the foot of the Yazoo swamp during that time (50,000 to 60,000 cubic feet per second), and the amount of the reduction of the river discharge required to sink its surface to the level of the bank, and the proportional effect of the swamps on either bank,* indicate that it would have been not less than 110,000 cubic feet per second into the Yazoo swamp, and 55,000 cubic feet per second into the Tensas swamp, making a total of 165,000 cubic feet per second. What would have been discharged into those two swamps at the top of the flood may be estimated in a similar manner. It would probably have been for the Yazoo swamp 270,000 cubic feet per second, instead of 212,000, and for the Tensas as far as Vicksburg, 140,000 cubic feet per second, instead of 60,000.

This value requires the escape of much water from the swamp in order to accord with

The next points to be considered are the probable depth of overflow in the Yazoo swamp which would have been caused by this discharge, and the consequent probable amount of the discharge back to the river. The history of the actual overflow in 1858 has already been detailed in Chapter I, and it is only necessary here to recall to mind that there was very little Mississippi overflow in that swamp—though much rain-water of

* The Tensas swamp was comparatively well protected against the flood of 1858. If there had been no levees, the discharge into the two swamps would have been distributed between them in proportion to the extent of their fronts, that is, in the proportion of 2 to 1.

its own downfall—when the top of the June flood came down, and, breaking the levees, raised the swamp water in twenty days to the level of the flood of 1828 in the Bogue Falaya, and even as far as the Sunflower river, which is about midway between the Mississippi and the hills. Near the eastern border of the swamp, however—at McNutt and Greenwood—where the general level is several feet below that near the Sunflower, the overflow in 1828 was 2 feet deeper than that of 1858. Now, knowing the area of this swamp (Chapter I), it is easy to compute that if—with the supposed discharge into it corresponding to its unleveed condition—the discharge of the Yazoo river in May, June, and July, 1858, had been equal to that actually measured during that time, the overflow from the Mississippi would have raised the surface of the water throughout the entire region to the level of that of 1828 by the 1st of June, a foot above that level toward the latter part of that month, and a foot and a half above it by the 8th or 10th of July. But there are many considerations* which lead to the conclusion that the depth of overflow would not have differed greatly from that in 1828. Hence the supposed discharge back to the Mississippi used in this computation was much too small. The swamp could not have acted as a non-returning reservoir, even to that extent, but must have discharged a much larger volume back to the Mississippi.

the probable depth of overflow.

We are now to see what relation the probable discharge of Yazoo river bears to the discharge into the swamp at the top of the flood. As the depth of the overflow in the swamp and the duration of the flood would not have been materially different from these quantities in 1828, the discharge back into the Mississippi would have been nearly the same as in that flood. But, as already stated, the strength of the current at the top of that flood was estimated, by those who observed it, to be even greater than that of the Mississippi. Now the mean velocity of the Mississippi, from the mouth of the Ohio to the gulf, at the top of such a flood as that of 1858, is 6.0 feet per second.† It may, then, be assumed that the mean velocity of the Yazoo river at its mouth, at the top of the flood in 1858, would have been 6.0 feet per second, had no levees been constructed. Since the area of cross-section was 50,000 square feet, this gives a discharge of 300,000 cubic feet per second. This quantity is identical with the probable discharge from the Mississippi into the swamp (270,000 cubic feet per second), allowing 30,000 cubic feet per second for the proper drainage of the Yazoo basin. Hence the proposition that the swamp could not have acted as a reservoir at the top of the flood is perfectly consistent with the other probable conditions.

The probable discharge of Yazoo river indicates that, at high water, as much water escaped from the swamp as entered it.

It is not claimed that the preceding figures are minutely accurate, but they are sufficiently so to demonstrate, first, that the great Yazoo swamp, even when unleveed, cannot have acted as a receiving, non-returning re-

Preceding analysis demon-

* Near the head of the Yazoo swamp, the Mississippi was about 1.5 feet higher in 1858 than in 1828, while at the foot it was about 0.6 of a foot lower. At Natchez, in 1828, the river stood during two months within a foot of the top of the flood, and during four and a half months, within 4 feet of that mark. In 1858, the river there stood for nearly three months (two months and three weeks) within a foot of the top of the flood, and for more than four months within four feet of that mark.

† At Columbus it was 8.5 feet per second, and at Vicksburg 7.1 feet per second. But these were narrow places, with smaller areas of cross-section than the mean. At Carrollton, where the area of cross-section is a mean of that part of the river, the velocity was 6.2 feet per second.

strates that these bottom lands, even when unleveed, could not have been reservoirs at date of high water.

servoir, inasmuch as the water marks now existing are much too low to admit the possibility of such action; and, second, that the conclusion logically derived from the reiterated statements of actual witnesses of the old inundations, namely, that the discharge from the swamp to the river at the top of the flood was equal to that from the river to the swamp, is perfectly consistent with the probable numerical values of these quantities resulting from the operations of 1858, as well as with the actual depth of overflow in the swamps themselves.

Conclusions respecting the effect of these swamp lands upon the floods of the Mississippi.

The following final conclusions respecting these swamp regions in their unleveed condition must therefore be considered established. First, they produced no effect whatever upon the volume of the maximum discharge of the Mississippi, above or below them, in great flood years. Second, they did reduce this volume along their fronts, and by an amount which increased from their upper to their lower limits.* Third, they retarded both the rising and the falling of the river at all points below them. Fourth, they tended to increase the duration of the floods throughout the alluvial region.

It may be added that, in their present semi-reclaimed condition, they do serve as reservoirs, inasmuch as the levees keep the swamps comparatively empty until near the top of the flood, when they break and relieve the river of a part of its excessive volume.

The extent of this comparison.

Analytical comparison of great floods.—The foregoing conclusions having been reached, we may proceed with the discussion whether the flood of 1858 may be safely adopted as the standard in estimating the extent of the artificial works required to protect the country from overflow in the future. This can only be determined by comparing it with the other great floods, whose histories, so far as they can now be learned, have already been given in Chapter II. It is there shown that the data in relation to those prior to the year 1828 are of too vague and general a character to be used for the present purpose; that none of those subsequent to 1828 were equal to that of 1858 at the head of the alluvial region, and hence that the latter is a fair standard for all points above the mouth of the Arkansas; and lastly, that the floods of 1844 and 1849 below that point were similar to and manifestly less than that of 1850, and hence that an especial study of them is unnecessary. These facts reduce the present discussion to an analytical comparison of the floods of 1828, 1850, 1851, and 1859, with that of 1858. They will be treated successively in an inverse order of date.

Analysis of the flood of 1859.

1. The flood of 1859 has already been so elaborately described and discussed in Chapter II, as to render a detailed notice of it unnecessary here. The full information collected respecting it, together with the known relations between the stand of the river and the discharge at the several localities named in the following table (subject to the modifications soon to be noted in this chapter in discussing the height required for the new levees), renders it easy to apply an approximate analysis similar to that adopted for the flood of 1858. The following table exhibits the result:—

---

* It must not be inferred that they diminished the *height of the flood* in precisely this manner, since the backwater occasioned by the returning volume must have been felt for a considerable distance above the foot of the swamp. The effect of the return of water at the foot of a great swamp in anomalously raising the river surface will be fully illustrated in discussing the flood of 1851 at the mouth of Red river.

Flood of 1859 *compared with that of* 1858.

Locality.	Actual maximum discharge per second.			Maximum discharge per second; levees perfected.		
	Flood of 1858.	Flood of 1859.	Difference.	Flood of 1858.	Flood of 1859.	Difference.
	Cubic feet.	*Cubic feet.*	*Cubic feet.*	*Cubic feet.*	*Cubic feet.*	*Cubic feet.*
Columbus	1,403,000	1,275,000	+ 128,000	1,478,000	1,275,000	+ 203,000
Helena	1,334,000	1,080,000	+ 254,000	1,369,000	1,200,000	+ 169,000
Napoleon	1,221,000	1,230,000	+ 9,000	1,418,000	1,320,000	+ 98,000
Vicksburg and points below.	1,245,000	1,285,000	— 40,000	1,430,000	1,350,000	+ 80,000

This table, while it shows conclusively that, had the levees been perfected in the two floods, that of 1858 would have risen much higher than that of 1859, and hence that any measures calculated to restrain the former would have been ample to secure the valley against the ravages of the latter, also furnishes the true explanation of the apparent anomalies between the high-water marks of the two years, viz., that at some localities the actual discharge in 1858 was larger than in 1859, while at others the reverse was the case.

It was a less flood than that of 1858.

2. The flood of 1851 below Red-river landing was subjected to exact measurement, and will therefore be discussed in detail. Above that point a part of the information collected was lost, and the existing data cannot be safely reduced to figures. The history of the flood, already given in Chapter II, however, plainly shows that throughout that region the maximum discharge must have been far less than in the flood of 1858, had the levees been perfected in both years. Indeed, it was the flood in Red river alone which made this a flood year in the lower country, and an analysis above Red-river landing would therefore have comparatively little interest.

Limited character of the flood of 1851.

Daily gauge-registers of the stand of the river were kept at Lake Providence, New Carthage, Natchez, Red-river landing, Baton Rouge, Donaldsonville, Carrollton, and Fort St. Philip. Similar daily records of the changes of level in the gulf were kept at lakes Pontchartrain and Borgne, and at bayou St. Philip, a small inlet near Fort St. Philip, to which the gulf has free access. From Red-river landing to the gulf, all gauge-rods were referred by accurate levels to one and the same datum-plane, thus making those records a complete measure of changes in the slope of the Mississippi between the stations. For these records see Appendix B.

Data collected for its discussion.

Daily measurements of the discharge of the river were made at Carrollton, checked by various similar operations at other stations above that place. (See Appendices D and E.)

Since bayous Plaquemine and La Fourche are simply waste-weirs, their discharge for any given stand of the Mississippi can vary but little. By making use of this principle, sufficient measurements were made upon these bayous to determine from the known gauge-reading at their upper mouths their daily discharge during the flood, as given in the next table. (See Chapter IV.)

All crevasses occurring between Red-river landing and New Orleans were accurately surveyed, and all data necessary to determine their daily discharge secured. There were eight of these crevasses, of which two, Nos. 7 and 8, were below the velocity-base at Carrollton. The following table exhibits all the elements which (exclusive of the daily gauge-record) are essential to a computation of the discharge of these crevasses by the formulæ already explained:—

Crevasses in flood of 1851.

Crevasse.	Locality.	Bank of river.	Date of— Beginning to discharge.	Date of— Ceasing to discharge.	Max. width.	Depth at high water.	Remarks.
			1851.	1851.	*Feet.*	*Feet.*	
1	Lower mouth Fausse Rivière......	Right	March 16	May 8	700	5	Measured discharge March 28, 18,000 cubic feet per second.
2	Opposite Island 124..................	Right	" 31	" 12	620	7	
3	2 miles above Plaquemine..........	Right	" 31	" 3	350	3	
4	2 miles below Plaquemine..........	Left	" 30	April 22	200	2	
5	6 miles below Plaquemine..........	Left	" 27	May 8	650	4	Four breaks near each other.
6	9 miles above Donaldsonville......	Left	" 23	" 5	440	3	Reopened by a raft.
7	Bend below Carrollton...............	Right	April 17	" 12	330	3	
8	Bend below Carrollton...............	Right	March 18	" 24	700(?)	6	Width March 22 was 90 feet. " " 29 " 130 " " April 19 " 350 "

Equations for transferring discharge. In accordance with the principles already laid down for transferring measured discharges, the daily discharge per second at Red-river landing, Baton Rouge, and Donaldsonville has been deduced. The following expressions sufficiently indicate the processes for each place, for high stages of the river; the unit being, of course, the cubic foot:—

Discharge per sec. Red R. landing, April 3 = {
Discharge per second at Carrollton.................................April 5
+ Discharge per second of bayou La Fourche.......................April 5
+ Discharge per second of bayou Plaquemine.......................April 4
+ Discharge per second of crevasses 1, 2, 3, 4, 5, 6..............April 4
+ 8,000 { Rise Red-river landing.....................April 2–3
+ Rise Baton Rouge...........................April 3–4
+ Rise Donaldsonville.........................April 3–4
+ Rise Carrollton..............................April 4–5 } }

Discharge per second Baton Rouge, April 4 = {
Discharge per second at Carrollton.................................April 5
+ Discharge per second of bayou La Fourche.......................April 5
+ Discharge per second of bayou Plaquemine.......................April 4
+ Discharge per second of crevasses 3, 4, 5, 6......................April 4
+ 10,000 { Rise Baton Rouge...............................April 3–4
+ Rise Carrollton...............................April 4–5 } }

Discharge per second Donaldsonville, April 4 = {
Discharge per second at Carrollton.................................April 5
+ 6,000 { Rise Donaldsonville...............................April 3–4
+ Rise Carrollton...............................April 4–5 } }

Table exhibiting daily discharges below Red-river landing. The following table—a complete exhibit of the flood of 1851 between Red-river landing and New Orleans—contains the daily discharge at these three places, computed as just explained. For convenience of comparison, that measured at Carrollton is added, together with the discharges of the crevasses and of the two bayous.

Discharge per second in 1851.

Date.	Mississippi river at—				Crevasses.		Bayous.	
	Red-river landing.	Baton Rouge.	Donaldsonville.	Carrollton.	Nos. 1 and 2.	Nos. 3, 4, 5, and 6.	Plaquemine.	La Fourche.
1851.	*Cubic feet.*	*Cubic feet.*	*Cubic feet.*	*Cubic feet.*	*Cubic feet.*	*Cubic feet.*	*Cubic feet.*	*Cubic feet.*
Feb. 24......	984,000	940,000	914,000	894,000	0	0	15,000	6,000
25......	993,000	970,000	944,000	910,000	0	0	16,000	6,000
26......	1,038,000	988,000	960,000	939,000	0	0	18,000	7,000
27......	1,057,000	1,031,000	1,000,000	955,000	0	0	19,000	7,000
28......	1,059,000	1,051,000	1,018,000	995,000	0	0	21,000	8,000
March 1......	1,057,000	1,051,000	1,021,000	1,013,000	0	0	21,000	8,000
2......	1,088,000	1,057,000	1,023,000	1,020,000	0	0	23,000	8,000
3......	1,089,000	1,078,000	1,044,000	1,020,000	0	0	23,000	8,000
4......	1,092,000	1,086,000	1,052,000	1,042,000	0	0	24,000	9,000
5......	1,100,000	1,089,000	1,052,000	1,050,000	0	0	25,000	9,000
6......	1,108,000	1,095,000	1,061,000	1,048,000	0	0	25,000	9,000
7......	1,115,000	1,105,000	1,068,000	1,060,000	0	0	26,000	9,000
8......	1,121,000	1,113,000	1,076,000	1,068,000	0	0	26,000	9,000
9......	1,142,000	1,118,000	1,079,000	1,075,000	0	0	27,000	9,000
10......	1,122,000	1,139,000	1,100,000	1,077,000	0	0	28,000	10,000
11......	1,141,000	1,118,000	1,079,000	1,098,000	0	0	28,000	10,000
12......	1,161,000	1,138,000	1,096,000	1,078,000	0	0	29,000	10,000
13......	1,181,000	1,160,000	1,118,000	1,094,000	0	0	30,000	10,000
14......	1,192,000	1,177,000	1,136,000	1,116,000	0	0	30,000	10,000
15......	1,202,000	1,190,000	1,147,000	1,135,000	0	0	31,000	10,000
16......	1,200,000	1,196,000	1,155,000	1,145,000	2,000	0	31,000	10,000
17......	1,189,000	1,194,000	1,151,000	1,153,000	4,000	0	31,000	10,000
18......	1,202,000	1,182,000	1,138,000	1,150,000	6,000	0	32,000	11,000
19......	1,199,000	1,192,000	1,149,000	1,137,000	8,000	0	32,000	11,000
20......	1,180,000	1,188,000	1,142,000	1,149,000	9,000	0	33,000	11,000
21......	1,190,000	1,168,000	1,124,000	1,140,000	10,000	0	33,000	11,000
22......	1,189,000	1,177,000	1,131,000	1,122,000	11,000	0	33,000	11,000
23......	1,160,000	1,176,000	1,128,000	1,130,000	12,000	1,000	34,000	11,000
24......	1,168,000	1,146,000	1,099,000	1,129,000	14,000	2,000	34,000	11,000
25......	1,181,000	1,150,000	1,101,000	1,099,000	16,000	3,000	34,000	11,000
26......	1,188,000	1,162,000	1,112,000	1,100,000	18,000	4,000	34,000	11,000
27......	1,187,000	1,164,000	1,114,000	1,110,000	20,000	4,000	34,000	11,000
28......	1,192,000	1,164,000	1,110,000	1,113,000	22,000	8,000	35,000	11,000
29......	1,199,000	1,166,000	1,110,000	1,110,000	25,000	9,000	35,000	11,000
30......	1,204,000	1,169,000	1,112,000	1,110,000	27,000	11,000	35,000	11,000
31......	1,206,000	1,173,000	1,115,000	1,113,000	29,000	12,000	35,000	11,000
April 1......	1,193,000	1,175,000	1,117,000	1,115,000	31,000	11,000	35,000	11,000
2......	1,192,000	1,160,000	1,106,000	1,118,000	33,000	10,000	34,000	11,000
3......	1,195,000	1,157,000	1,104,000	1,107,000	35,000	9,000	34,000	11,000
4......	1,192,000	1,159,000	1,106,000	1,105,000	36,000	8,000	34,000	11,000
5......	1,192,000	1,156,000	1,104,000	1,105,000	37,000	7,000	34,000	11,000
6......	1,188,000	1,157,000	1,104,000	1,105,000	37,000	7,000	34,000	11,000
7......	1,181,000	1,151,000	1,100,000	1,105,000	37,000	7,000	34,000	11,000
8......	1,152,000	1,145,000	1,094,000	1,100,000	36,000	7,000	34,000	11,000
9......	1,133,000	1,117,000	1,064,000	1,095,000	36,000	7,000	34,000	11,000
10......	1,133,000	1,097,000	1,047,000	1,064,000	35,000	8,000	33,000	11,000
11......	1,138,000	1,100,000	1,048,000	1,048,000	35,000	7,000	33,000	11,000
12......	1,142,000	1,105,000	1,054,000	1,048,000	34,000	8,000	33,000	11,000
13......	1,151,000	1,110,000	1,059,000	1,055,000	33,000	8,000	33,000	11,000
14......	1,152,000	1,120,000	1,069,000	1,060,000	32,000	9,000	33,000	11,000
15......	1,144,000	1,122,000	1,071,000	1,070,000	32,000	8,000	32,000	10,000
16......	1,135,000	1,114,000	1,064,000	1,072,000	31,000	9,000	32,000	10,000
17......	1,118,000	1,106,000	1,055,000	1,065,000	30,000	9,000	32,000	10,000
18......	1,115,000	1,088,000	1,040,000	1,056,000	30,000	9,000	31,000	10,000
19......	1,108,000	1,088,000	1,039,000	1,040,000	29,000	9,000	31,000	10,000
20......	1,104,000	1,081,000	1,031,000	1,040,000	29,000	9,000	31,000	10,000
21......	1,105,000	1,075,000	1,026,000	1,030,000	29,000	8,000	31,000	10,000
22......	1,099,000	1,079,000	1,029,000	1,026,000	28,000	8,000	31,000	10,000
23......	1,098,000	1,071,000	1,024,000	1,030,000	28,000	8,000	30,000	10,000
24......	1,097,000	1,073,000	1,025,000	1,025,000	27,000	8,000	30,000	10,000
25......	1,087,000	1,072,000	1,024,000	1,025,000	26,000	9,000	30,000	10,000
26......	1,084,000	1,062,000	1,015,000	1,025,000	26,000	8,000	30,000	10,000
27......	1,078,000	1,061,000	1,013,000	1,015,000	25,000	8,000	30,000	10,000
28......	1,062,000	1,054,000	1,009,000	1,015,000	25,000	7,000	29,000	10,000
29......	1,052,000	1,039,000	994,000	1,010,000	24,000	7,000	29,000	10,000
30......	1,047,000	1,030,000	985,000	995,000	23,000	7,000	29,000	10,000

Discharge per second in 1851—Continued.

Date.	Mississippi river at—				Crevasses.		Bayous.	
	Red-river landing.	Baton Rouge.	Donaldsonville.	Carrollton.	Nos. 1 and 2.	Nos. 3, 4, 5, and 6.	Plaquemine.	La Fourche.
1851.	*Cubic feet.*	*Cubic feet.*	*Cubic feet.*	*Cubic feet.*	*Cubic feet.*	*Cubic feet.*	*Cubic feet.*	*Cubic feet.*
May 1......	1,034,000	1,026,000	984,000	985,000	23,000	6,000	28,000	10,000
2......	1,013,000	1,014,000	973,000	985,000	22,000	5,000	28,000	9,000
3......	982,000	996,000	958,000	975,000	21,000	3,000	27,000	9,000
4......	964,000	967,000	929,000	960,000	18,000	4,000	27,000	9,000
5......	945,000	950,000	916,000	932,000	16,000	3,000	26,000	9,000
6......	923,000	938,000	906,000	920,000	13,000	2,000	24,000	9,000
7......	912,000	916,000	887,000	908,000	11,000	1,000	23,000	8,000
8......	897,000	909,000	880,000	890,000	8,000	1,000	22,000	8,000
9......	879,000	897,000	872,000	884,000	6,000	0	21,000	8,000
10......	865,000	880,000	857,000	875,000	4,000	0	20,000	7,000
11......	851,000	871,000	845,000	860,000	2,000	0	19,000	7,000
12......	823,000	857,000	836,000	849,000	1,000	0	18,000	7,000

Maximum discharges compared with those in 1858.

Since the modifying influence of the channel may be neglected below Red-river landing, the daily discharge per second at each of the four localities in this table, if no breaks in the levee had occurred, may be obtained by adding to the actual discharges the corresponding crevasse discharges, in the manner already indicated in the analysis of the flood of 1858. The daily modification in discharge effected by the crevasses is exhibited by plate XVIII. The actual and the modified maximum discharges are compared with the same quantities in 1858, in the following table:—

Flood of 1851 *compared with that of* 1858.

Locality.	Actual maximum discharge.			Maximum discharge; levees perfected.		
	Flood of 1851.	Flood of 1858.	Difference.	Flood of 1851 (below Red-river landing).	Flood of 1858 (below Cape Girardeau).	Difference.
	Cubic feet.	*Cubic feet.*	*Cubic feet.*	*Cubic feet.*	*Cubic feet.*	*Cubic feet.*
Red-river landing	1,206,000	1,238,000	32,000	1,206,000	1,338,000	132,000
Baton Rouge	1,196,000	1,238,000	42,000	1,206,000	1,338,000	132,000
Donaldsonville	1,155,000	1,197,000	42,000	1,158,000	1,297,000	139,000
Carrollton	1,153,000	1,188,000	35,000	1,159,000	1,297,000	138,000

First and most important result of this analysis is that this flood was much smaller than that of 1858.

Since the flood of 1851 was comparatively small above Red-river landing, this table establishes two important facts. First, that if the river had been confined to its channel, the maximum discharge in the flood of 1851 at all points below Red-river landing must have been some 100,000 cubic feet per second less than in 1858 under similar circumstances, and hence that any measure calculated to restrain the latter would have been amply sufficient to restrain the former. This is all that it is essential to determine, in order to serve the purposes of the present analysis; but the practical importance of the second fact justifies a short digression for the purpose of discussing it.

This second fact is that the crevasses in 1851 had scarcely any influence upon

Second result shows that Mr. Ellet's conclusions respecting this flood are entirely erroneous.

the actual maximum discharge in that year, and hence that they did not materially modify the high-water mark. This result is very different from that arrived at by Mr. Charles Ellet, Jr., who conducted, under the authority of the United States Government, a system of measurements in 1851, simultaneous with those of the present Survey. He reported that "if it be determined hereafter to rely exclusively on levees, and prevent the occurrence of crevasses altogether, these levees, to sustain a flood like that of 1851, must be made from Red river to New Orleans, competent to resist an increase of ten per cent. in the volume discharged by the river; or, in the view of the writer, at least 2 feet higher than the present banks. This condition, it is apparent, would involve the entire reconstruction of the embankments on both sides of the river; and hence, *in order to retain merely the crevasse-water of this year*, the levees must be entirely reconstructed, and made 2 feet higher; or new outlets must be opened competent to vent 100,000 cubic feet per second—which is more than the volume now drawn from the Mississippi at high water by the Atchafalaya itself."

Such contradictory conclusions as these, in regard to matters of so great practical importance, seem to demand some inquiry as to the causes of discordance. The data and the reasoning of Mr. Ellet will therefore be briefly examined.

Errors in the data upon which his opinion is based.

His opinion that "in order to retain merely the crevasse-water of this year, the levees must be entirely reconstructed and made 2 feet higher," is founded solely upon his belief respecting the amount taken from the river by crevasses at the date of actual high water. This quantity he computed to be 100,000 cubic feet per second by the following process.

On April 26, when the river had fallen 2.3 feet, he gauged the Mississippi below the mouth of Red river, and found the actual discharge per second to be 1,054,000 cubic feet. By his formula, whose errors have already been illustrated in Chapters III and V, he computed that at high water the discharge per second must have been 80,500 cubic feet more. Hence he inferred that at the date of high water the discharge per second at Red-river landing was 1,134,500 cubic feet. Plate XVII exhibits the relation of his single observation (there indicated) to the true maximum discharge; and hence the radical errors of any such method of determination. If he had happened to make his measurement on March 17, the date when the rising river had attained to the same stage as that of April 26, he must, by the same process of reasoning, have inferred that the discharge at the date of high water was 100,000 cubic feet per second more than his actual result; hence that the crevasses discharged double what he actually computed, and hence that the levees from Red river to New Orleans ought to be raised *four* feet instead of *two*, in order to restrain this flood. It is plain that a series of daily measurements alone can be depended upon for settling so important an element of the computation. This plan, as already seen, was carried out by this Survey, and the result (see last table but one) shows that the actual discharge per second at Red-river landing at the date of high water was 1,196,000 cubic feet, or 61,500 cubic feet more than Mr. Ellet computed.

Mr. Ellet next computed the high-water discharge of the Mississippi below New Orleans at the top of the flood by precisely the same process. He gauged the river at a point 11 miles below the city on April 16, when the water had subsided 0.5 of a foot, and found the discharge per second to be 979,240 cubic feet. Adding 15,760 cubic feet, the amount indicated by his formula, as the diminution caused by the subsidence, he inferred that the discharge per second at high water was 995,000 cubic feet. Professor Forshey's actual measurements at Carrollton (see last table but one) show that at that point this quantity was 1,111,000 cubic feet. Only one crevasse (No. 8), between Carrollton and the point where Mr. Ellet made his gauging, was flowing at the date of high water (March 27–30). On March 29, by actual measurement, this break was 130 feet wide by 6 feet deep, and its discharge per second was therefore 6000 cubic feet. Deducting this amount from the measured high-water discharge per second at Carrollton, we have for the true high-water discharge per second at the site of Mr. Ellet's gauging 1,105,000 cubic feet, or 110,000 cubic feet more than he computed.

Mr. Ellet's next step was to determine the discharge of bayous Plaquemine and La Fourche. He does not mention the dates at which he gauged these bayous, but states their high-water discharge per second to be respectively 28,500 cubic feet and 10,200 cubic feet, giving 38,700 cubic feet for the discharge per second of the two. The detailed operations of this Survey (see Appendix D) show that these quantities should be 35,000 cubic feet, 11,500 cubic feet, and 46,500 cubic feet, respectively. Mr. Ellet's discrepancy here, then, is comparatively small, being only 7800 cubic feet.

These three quantities form the basis of Mr. Ellet's determination of the discharge of the crevasses at the date of high water, 1851; for he argues that they must have discharged the quantity found by subtracting the discharge of the two bayous from the difference between the actual discharge below Red river and that below New Orleans. The following is the computation:—

At date of high water, 1851.	Quantities as computed by Mr. Ellet.	Quantities as measured by the Delta Survey.
	Cubic feet.	*Cubic feet.*
Discharge per second below Red-river landing	1,134,500	1,196,000
Discharge per second below New Orleans	995,000	1,105,000
Difference	139,500	91,000
Discharge per second of the bayous	38,700	46,000
Difference, or crevasse discharge per second	100,800	45,000

They account for one half of his error.

This table shows that, granting Mr. Ellet's reasoning to be correct, he was led to apprehend more than double the real difficulty in restraining this flood, by the errors he made in determining the numerical values of the quantities which enter his computation. The computed discharge per second of the crevasses at the date of high water, which he made 100,000 cubic feet, should have been only 45,000 cubic feet.

The other half was occasioned by his illogical reasoning.

The next point to be illustrated is that the foregoing train of reasoning, upon which Mr. Ellet bases his estimate of what is necessary to restrain the flood, is essentially erroneous. His method of computation is based upon two assumptions: first, that whether the levees are broken or not, the *date* of actual maximum discharge at any locality remains unchanged, and hence that what this discharge would be with levees perfected may be computed by adding to the discharge at actual high water the quantity then escaping by crevasses; and second, that the dates of maximum discharge and of highest water are necessarily identical. Neither of these suppositions is admissible. The first is clearly shown to be erroneous by the curves of daily discharge with and without crevasses, in the floods of 1851 and 1858, exhibited by plate XVIII. It is evident from this diagram that, had no crevasses been discharging below Red-river landing at the date of actual high water (about April 1), the discharge would not have been sensibly greater than that which was actually passing prior to the occurrence of any break in the levee, say about March 15. Hence, if Mr. Ellet's second supposition were correct, the high-water mark was absolutely unaffected by crevasses in this flood, instead of being lowered 2 feet as he supposed. In other words, his reasoning, applied to the actual conditions existing during this flood, leads logically to the conclusion that the levees, as then made, were of sufficient height to protect the country from overflow.

Correct explanation of the complex phenomena presented by this flood in Louisiana.

Mr. Ellet's second supposition, however, is erroneous, as has already been fully shown in discussing the subject of local slope in the last chapter. The flood of 1851 at Red-river landing illustrates this subject very prettily, as may be seen by inspecting plate XVII. From March 15 to March 19, the discharge per second remained uniformly about 1,200,000 cubic feet. At this time, Red river was pouring out a flood sufficient to supply the entire discharge of bayou Atchafalaya, and to contribute besides nearly 100,000 cubic feet per second to the Mississippi through the channel of Old river. (See Appendix D for details of measurements.) Floods from Red river, however, are of short duration, and this was the case in the present instance. By March 23, the supply had diminished somewhat more than 40,000 cubic feet per second, and the rate of rise at Red-river landing began to be retarded, as usual when the river is about to fall. But at this date the water from the Lookout crevasse (see Chapter II) began to pour in large quantities from the Tensas bottom lands into Red river, and, joining through Old river the gradually increasing discharge of the Mississippi from above, produced a second gradual increase in discharge at Red-river landing, until on March 29–31 it became sensibly equal to what it had been on March 15–19. The stand of the river, though, was 2 *feet higher than at that date.* This result, apparently so anomalous, is really perfectly in accordance with the principles which govern the changes in local slope. The diminution in the supply diminished the local slope, and, had it continued, would soon have produced a fall in the river. This was not actually the case, because a second increase in the supply took place, occasioning a new increase in local slope. But this new increase in slope was added to a *primitive slope smaller than it would have been had no diminution in supply previously occurred. Hence a higher stand of the river was necessary to carry off the increased discharge.* This important fact is well illustrated by the diagram (plate XVII). When the discharge began to decrease, the gauge read about 44.5. If the increase of about 40,000 cubic feet per second, which actually occurred between March 23 and March 30, had occurred at this time, the curve shows that—*as actually was the case in* 1858—the river would have risen about 1 foot higher, or to about 45.5 on the gauge, and would at that stand—which was 1 foot lower than the actual height attained—have discharged 40,000 cubic feet per second more than its actual maximum discharge in 1851. Hence it is clear that the Lookout crevasse, so far from lowering the high-water level at Red-river landing in that year, actually raised it nearly 1 foot by its mischievous influence upon the local slope.

Probable height of this flood under certain modified conditions.

What the height of the flood of 1851 would have been at points below Red-river landing, considering the crevasses above that point to have occurred as they did occur, and those below it to have been prevented by better constructed levees, can be easily estimated from the discharge of the crevasses given in the table before the last. Thus at Baton Rouge, at Donaldsonville, and at Carrollton, these quantities being on April 1 about 30,000, 40,000, and 40,000 cubic feet respectively, the increased height of the flood would have been about 0.7, 0.7, and 0.5 of a foot respectively. If there had been no crevasses above or below Red river, the flood at Carrollton would have risen 0.3 of a foot higher than the height actually attained.

Flood of 1850 in the upper river.

3. For the flood of 1850, the data are too meagre to admit of the close analysis which has been applied to the floods of 1859 and 1851. Indeed, for the region above the mouth of Red river, none can be attempted. It is certain, however, from a comparison of the high-water marks of the two years in the river itself and in the great swamps, that the flood of 1858 was the greater of the two in the upper river. If we bear in mind the principles already laid down relative to the action of these swamps, the following computations—based upon the surveys made below Red-river landing by the field parties in 1851, and upon the facts collected by them or derived from published documents of the State of Louisiana—render this equally certain for the lower river.

Data for computing the discharge of the crevasses below Red-river landing.

The dimensions of all the crevasses between Red-river landing and New Orleans were measured by the parties of this Survey, and all facts bearing upon their discharge determined. The following table exhibits the data collected. The bank in front of crevasse No. 1 was caving badly, and it is probable that from this cause the width of the crevasse as measured at low water was greater than when it was discharging. Crevasse No. 2 occurred where the levee crosses a neck of land, and where the supply of water was therefore indirect. Both of these crevasses, as well as No. 6, where the levee was several hundred feet from the edge of the bank, occurred where a dense growth of timber prevented the free flow of the water. These facts indicate that their discharge as computed by the usual formulæ should be corrected by the coefficient deduced for the breaks into the Yazoo swamp in the flood of 1858. The exact date of occurrence of several of these crevasses is somewhat uncertain, but no material error in this respect can have been made.

Crevasses in the flood of 1850.

Crevasse.	Locality.	Bank of river.	Date of— Beginning to discharge.	Date of— Ceasing to discharge.	Max. width.	Depth at high water.	Remarks.
				1850.	*Feet.*	*Feet.*	The crevasse at Bonnet Carré (No. 8) on Dec. 30, Jan. 20, Feb. 5, and July 1 was respectively 1200, 2500, 3500, and 5300 feet in width. At the last date, the break in the levee was 6900 feet long, but 1600 feet were obstructed by drift so as to prevent the flow of the water.
1	1 mile below Red-river landing...	Right	Feb. 15, 1850	July 5	3700	2.7	
2	20 miles below Red-river landing	Right	Feb. 10, "	July 5	1160	4.5	
3	25 miles below Red-river landing	Right	Feb. 15, "	July 5	2100	4.7	
4	28 miles below Red-river landing	Right	June 9, "	July 5	460	6.0	
5	47 miles below Red-river landing	Right	Feb. 15, "	June 20	4100	3.5	
6	50 miles below Red-river landing	Right	Feb. 15, "	June 20	9300	3.5	
7	53 miles below Red-river landing	Right	Feb. 15, "	June 20	2600	2.7	
8	Bonnet-Carré bend..................	Left	Dec. 29, 1849	July 13	6900	5.5	

Method of determining their discharge; with table exhibiting results.

The mean monthly discharge of these crevasses was computed by the usual method. No especial explanations are required except in reference to the manner of determining the depth at the different dates. The Carrollton gauge kept by Professor Forshey (see Appendix B) furnishes the basis of this determination. The mean depth of water surface below the high-water mark of 1850, during any given month at Carrollton, multiplied by the ratio between the total ranges of the river at that place and at Bonnet Carré $\left(\frac{18.3}{14.1}\right)$, was deducted from 5.5 feet for the mean depth of the Bonnet-Carré crevasse during that month. For crevasses 5, 6, and 7, which were all near together, and about 20 miles above Baton Rouge, the following process was adopted. Knowing the mean gauge-reading during any month at Carrollton, and the corresponding discharge of the Bonnet-Carré crevasse, it is easy to determine, from plate XIV, how much higher the river would have stood in that month, if this crevasse had not occurred; and hence, how much the water surface would have been below the high-water level of 1851. Multiplying this number by the ratio of the total ranges of the river at a point 20 miles above Baton Rouge and at Carrollton $\left(\frac{33.4}{14.1}\right)$, the depth below high water of 1851 at the three crevasses is determined. Deducting 0.4 of a foot for the recorded height of this flood above that of 1850 at this locality, we have a set of relatively correct depths below the high water of 1850 at the three crevasses. But the recorded date of this high water was March. Hence, the difference between the depths computed for this month and for any one of the rest, deducted from the maximum depth given in the above table, leaves the true depth of the crevasse in that month. At Red-river landing, the flood began to subside on June 11. There were oscillations prior to this date, but, as no record of them was kept, the river has been assumed, in the computation of the discharge of crevasse No. 1, to remain at high-water mark. Crevasses 2, 3, and 4 were midway between Red-river landing and crevasses 5, 6, and 7. Hence, for their depth in any month, one-half of the depth of water surface below high water of 1850 at the latter was subtracted from the maximum depth given in the above table. The following table exhibits the result of the computations:—

Mean discharge per second of crevasses in flood of 1850.

Date.	Right bank of the river.								Left bank.	Total both banks.
	No. 1.	No. 2.	No. 3.	No. 4.	No. 5.	No. 6.	No. 7.	Total.	Bonnet Carré.	
1850.	*Cu. feet.*	*Cu. feet.*	*Cu. feet.*	*Cu. feet.*	*Cu. feet.*	*Cu. feet.*	*Cu. feet.*	*Cu. feet.*	*Cu. feet.*	*Cu. feet.*
January									61,000	61,000
February									114,000	114,000
March	8,000	3,000	16,000		21,000	15,000	9,000	67,000	107,000	174,000
April	7,000	5,000	28,000		36,000	27,000	15,000	118,000	114,000	232,000
May	10,000	6,000	33,000		27,000	20,000	8,000	104,000	98,000	202,000
June 1–15	13,000	7,000	39,000	6,000	29,000	22,000	8,000	124,000	99,000	223,000
June 16–30	3,000	4,000	24,000	7,000	15,000	11,000	2,000	66,000	85,000	151,000

Test of the accuracy of this determination.

The exactness of the determination of the maximum discharge over the right bank may be tested in the following manner. The Atchafalaya river discharges not only the legitimate drainage of its basin, but also all the water which escapes from the Mississippi river by bayou Atchafalaya, by bayou Plaquemine, and by any crevasses on the right bank which may occur between Red river and bayou La Fourche. This whole volume of water is practically gathered at Brashear City into one channel called Berwick's bay.* Hence the difference in the maximum discharge through Berwick's bay, for any two floods, measures the sum of the corresponding differences in the rain drainage, the bayou contributions, and the crevasse discharges in the two years. No actual measurements of the maximum discharge at Berwick's bay in a great flood have ever been made, but the difference in this quantity in the floods of 1850 and 1851 may be computed by the new formulæ, since all the quantities upon which it depends were measured. The corresponding difference in rain drainage may be determined from the observations made by the Medical Department of the United States Army. The corresponding differences in the bayou contributions result from the measurements of this Survey. The discharge of the crevasses in 1851 has been already given. These quantities all being known, the exactness of the last table evidently admits of a direct test. The numerical value of each of the quantities which enter the computation will now be considered.

Difference in maximum discharge of Berwick's bay in 1850 and 1851.

The high-water dimensions of cross-section, and the elevation of water surface above the gulf, at Brashear City, were determined for the floods of 1850 and 1851. The distance from Brashear City to the gulf level is about 15 miles. The channel in this distance undergoes great changes, so that the *mean* dimensions of cross-section which correspond to the known fall of water surface cannot be inferred from the known cross-section at Brashear City. The *absolute* maximum discharge in neither of the floods, then, can be computed. This is not true for the *relative* discharge, however, since the variations in the cross-section and slope at Berwick's bay are both known. The difference in the maximum discharge in the two floods, as just seen, is all that the present problem

* One small draining bayou from Grand lake, named Bœuf, enters the Atchafalaya river just below Berwick's bay, but as its cross-section, even in the flood of 1828, was only about 12,000 square feet, it may be safely neglected, especially as the operations in 1851 at the upper mouth of bayou Atchafalaya indicate that under such circumstances the effect of the tributary upon the slope of the main stream diminishes the discharge by an amount nearly or quite equal to its entire contribution.

requires. The following are the data for its determination, and the result of the computation:—

Year.	Area.	Width.	Perimeter.	Slope.	Difference in discharge per second computed by equation (40.)
	Square feet.	*Feet.*	*Feet.*	*Feet.*	*Cubic feet.*
1850	93,000	1750	1783	$\frac{3}{79,200}$	132,000
1851	90,000	1750	1780	$\frac{1.5}{79,200}$	

By the army meteorological records kept at New Orleans and Baton Rouge, it appears that the downfall of rain in this basin in May, 1850, was 0.3 of a foot more than in March, 1851. The area of the Atchafalaya basin is 4610 square miles. The excess of drainage of rain-water in 1850 over that in 1851, at date of highest water at Brashear City, was then $\frac{(5280)^2 \times 4610 \times 0.3}{31 \times 24 \times 60 \times 60}$ = say 15,000 cubic feet per second.

Difference in corresponding downfall.

Bayou Atchafalaya, at its upper mouth, being 1.2 feet higher on June 1–15, 1850, than in April, 1851, discharged 10,000 cubic feet per second more. Bayou Plaquemine, being about 2 feet lower, discharged 6000 cubic feet per second less. The quantity entering the Atchafalaya basin in 1850 by these bayous was then 10,000 — 6000 = 4000 cubic feet per second more than in 1851.

Difference in corresponding bayou discharges.

From the table before the last it appears that the discharge of the crevasses in 1850, when the water was highest at Brashear City (June 1–15), was 124,000 cubic feet per second. By the table on page 359 it appears that in 1851 the corresponding discharge (April) was 30,000. The difference, 94,000 cubic feet per second, was then the difference of crevasse discharge in the two years.

Difference in computed crevasse discharges.

Hence the difference in discharge at Brashear City in the two years, if the computations of the crevasse discharges in 1850 are right, was 15,000 + 4000 + 94,000 = 113,000 cubic feet per second. The computation of this difference by the general formula gives, as just seen, 132,000 cubic feet per second. A discrepancy of only 19,000 cubic feet confirms the exactness of the determination of the quantities entering both computations, especially as it may be accounted for by the fact that Red river was over its banks at the mouth of Black river, and hence that there was probably some overflow into Atchafalaya basin in that vicinity.

Result of the test.

What would have been the maximum discharge below Red-river landing in 1850, provided none of the levees below that point had broken, may now be ascertained. The actual discharge per second at Carrollton may be closely determined for any day on which the gauge-reading is known, by means of the curve on plate XIV. Adding to this quantity the corresponding discharge of the crevasses given in the table preceding the last, we have the following result:—

Flood compared with that of 1858.

Discharge at Carrollton in flood of 1850.

Date.	Highest gauge-reading.	Actual discharge per second. (See plate XIV.)	Discharge per second with levees perfected.
1850.	*Feet.*	*Cubic feet.*	*Cubic feet.*
January	13.8	1,050,000	1,111,000
February	13.8	1,050,000	1,164,000
March	13.1	970,000	1,144,000
April	12.9	960,000	1,192,000
May	12.9	960,000	1,162,000
June 1–15	12.3	900,000	1,123,000
June 16–30	12.8	900,000	1,051,000

It proves to have been much smaller.

It will be remembered that in the flood of 1858 the maximum discharge at Carrollton with perfected levees would have been 1,297,000 cubic feet per second. This quantity is greater than the maximum discharge contained in the above table by more than 100,000 cubic feet per second. Any measures calculated to restrain a flood like that of 1858 must then be ample to restrain a flood like that of 1850.

Analysis of flood of 1828 less exact than those which have preceded it.

4. The flood of 1828 occurred so many years ago, and under conditions so different from those now existing, both in respect to levees and cut-offs, that it ought perhaps to be classed with the traditional floods, which cannot now be satisfactorily analyzed, because we cannot be sure of the essential facts upon which their discussion depends. This view would be taken, were it not for the extravagant ideas prevalent respecting the flood, which render some general discussion of it advisable, if for no other reason than to fix an approximate limit beyond which it would be idle to entertain fears of inundation. It is therefore to be borne in mind that this analysis is of a different character from those which have preceded it, being offered with no pretence to the same accuracy. Grounded, however, upon all the recorded facts which a diligent search has brought to light, and conducted upon the principles which actual observations have indicated to be true, it is considered to be as complete and exact a discussion of this greatest of all recorded overflows as can now be made.

The northern bottom lands may be disregarded in discussing this flood for Louisiana.

The St. Francis, Yazoo, and White river swamps were entirely unprotected by levees. Therefore, as already explained on pages 353–4, they produced no effect upon the high-water level below Vicksburg, and may be neglected in discussing the flood for Louisiana.

Synopsis of the flood in Louisiana.

The Tensas bottom was flooded to such an extent that, opposite Natchez, the water level in the swamp was nearly the same as in the river. Escaping in vast quantities at the southern border of this region, the water encountered a great flood in Red river. No natural channels existed for the discharge of such an immense accumulation. The result was an overflow of the entire southern bank of Red river from Alexandria to its mouth (excepting the Avoyelles prairie), and of the bank of the Mississippi from the mouth of Red river to the head of the levees, which then extended nearly up to Red-river landing. This great waste-weir saved the region bordering upon the Mississippi below the head of the levees from inundation, only one serious break — that near Morganza — occurring below that point.

These recorded facts show that the analysis of the flood is really more simple than that of any of those already discussed; since it is only necessary to determine how much water escaped through this natural waste-weir, the bayous and the crevasse, in order to determine what the maximum discharge would have been, had the levees been perfected.

Plan of the analysis.

The object, then, is to ascertain how much water would have been flowing in the Mississippi just below the mouth of Red river, in the flood of 1828, if all the river-water discharged into the Tensas swamp had been returned to the Mississippi at that point (or, what is the same thing, if the overflow of that swamp had been retained in the river), and if all the water discharged into the Mississippi by Red river had been retained. This quantity is equal to the actual discharge of the Mississippi below Plaquemine, plus the volume lost into the Atchafalaya basin by Red river and the Mississippi.

The actual discharge of the Mississippi below the last point where any overflow occurred.

The first step is to ascertain the actual high-water discharge of the river below Plaquemine, from which point to the gulf there was no lateral discharge excepting through bayou La Fourche. The gauge-records at Natchez for 1828 indicate that the river remained at the full-flood stage near the gulf for a considerable period. Its elevation at Carrollton during that period having been noted, the discharge can be closely estimated. (See plate XIV.) It is to be observed that, when the river at Carrollton is within 3 or 4 feet of the flood height, the difference between the rising and falling discharge at the same gauge-reading is 90,000 cubic feet per second, and between those conditions and a stand of the river at the same height, the difference in discharge is one-half that quantity. Hence the discharge below Plaquemine at the highest stage of the river in 1828 (gauge 15.2) was, according to the diagram, 1,110,000 cubic feet per second.

Volume lost into Atchafalaya basin next to be considered.

The next step is to determine the volume discharged into the Atchafalaya basin at the top of the flood, from Red river and from the Mississippi.

It can be deduced from the measurements at Berwick's bay.

In the analysis of the flood of 1850, it was shown that the Atchafalaya basin drained into the sea through Berwick's bay, and that the difference in discharge at this point between two floods can be computed by the general formula (equation 40), the cross-sections and elevations above the gulf being known. These quantities were measured* for the floods of

* In assuming that the greatest discharge through Berwick's bay took place at the top of the flood in 1828, the most unfavorable case is taken. The assumption is probably correct for that flood, since the discharge from Red river and from the Mississippi was almost entirely over banks and through bayous, and only to a small amount through crevasses.

If it be objected that the area of the channel at Berwick's bay has been diminished by the deposit of sedimentary matter since 1828, it may be replied that the soundings of the Survey in 1858, and those of Mr. Bayley, Chief Engineer of the Opelousas railroad, in 1853 (see Appendix C), were made upon exactly the same line, and that no change whatever occurred between those dates. The location of the soundings made by Professor Forshey, in 1851, could not be determined with sufficient precision in 1858 to admit of remeasurement, and none was therefore attempted. So far as actual soundings are concerned, then, there is no reason for supposing any diminution of area since 1828. The same conclusion is suggested by the following general considerations: the average number of days in a year during which water was flowing over the banks into the Atchafalaya basin at the epoch of 1828 was small; crevasses draining to that basin have generally occurred in the great floods since 1828; the bayous discharge certainly as much now as they did formerly; there is, then, no reason for supposing that the scouring power has materially diminished

1851 and 1828. The following table exhibits these data and the results of the computations:—

Year.	Area.	Width.	Perimeter.	Slope.	Difference in discharge per second, computed by equation (40).
	Square feet.	*Feet.*	*Feet.*	*Feet.*	*Cubic feet.*
1828	98,000	1,750	1,788	$\frac{6}{79200}$	268,000
1851	90,000	1,750	1,780	$\frac{1.5}{79200}$	

If, now, the excess of the rain drainage of the Atchafalaya basin at the flood of 1828 over that at the flood of 1851 be subtracted from the difference in discharge given in this table, the remainder will be the excess of the discharge from Red river and the Mississippi into the Atchafalaya basin at the flood of 1828 over that from those rivers at the flood of 1851. If to this latter quantity be added the actual discharge into the Atchafalaya basin from Red river and from the Mississippi at the flood in 1851, the result will be the discharge into the Atchafalaya basin from those rivers at the top of the flood in 1828.

Meteorological tables for the basin of the Atchafalaya in 1828 could not be found.

Comparative amount of rain in the Atchafalaya basin in 1828 and 1851.

In the discussion of the flood of 1850, it has been shown that the excess of rain drainage of that basin at the top of the flood over that of 1851 was not less than 15,000 cubic feet per second. The army meteorological observations show that in some years the rain at New Orleans and Baton Rouge (which may be taken as the measure of that upon the Atchafalaya basin) is 12 inches per month, during the winter and spring months, exceeding by 0.8 of a foot per month that which fell in 1851. It appears to be probable, from the statements made respecting the amount of rain in other parts of the alluvial region in 1828, that during the winter and spring months of that year such an excessive fall of rain took place in the Atchafalaya basin. In confirmation of this opinion, it may be added that the discharge of the Teche and the Courtableau together was not less than 50,000 cubic feet per second at that time, while at the flood of 1851 it was scarcely appreciable. These streams, however, were connected with Red river in 1828, and probably a large part of their water was received from that river, while in 1851 this connection was cut off by levees. Adopting this estimate of excess of rain (0.8 of a foot per month), 40,000 cubic feet per second is the volume by which the rain drainage of the Atchafalaya basin during the flood in 1828 exceeded that of 1851.

since 1828. Moreover, the maintenance of the depth of the channel is not in reality dependent upon the strength of the current during river floods, but upon the almost entire absence of sedimentary matter transported by the water. This is evident from the following considerations: the Atchafalaya river flows from a lake; the bayous that supply that lake, deposit at their mouths most of the matter they transport; hence whatever deposit the Atchafalaya river makes in its bed must take place chiefly if not entirely at the time of the annual change from high to low water in the Mississippi river, and that deposit must be mainly at its efflux and its mouth. Such a deposit must be removed by the usual southeasterly storms during the low-water period, which often raise Grand lake several feet and cause a rapid current from the gulf to the lake and the lake to the gulf. The supposition of the silting up of the channel is therefore untenable. (For further ideas upon this subject, see concluding remarks upon levees in this chapter.)

The next quantity to be considered is the actual discharge from Red river and the Mississippi into the Atchafalaya basin at the flood of 1851. The discharge from Red river below Alexandria through bayous to the Atchafalaya basin may be neglected.* The discharge per second of the bayou Atchafalaya at its efflux, in the flood of 1851, was 120,000 cubic feet per second. The discharge per second of the crevasses between Red-river landing and bayou Plaquemine at that period was 30,000 cubic feet. The discharge per second of bayou Plaquemine during the same time was 36,000. Hence the total discharge per second into the Atchafalaya basin from Red river and the Mississippi was 120,000 + 30,000 + 36,000 = 186,000 cubic feet.

Actual discharge from Red river and the Mississippi in flood of 1851.

The numerical values of the several quantities which determine the discharge from Red river and the Mississippi into the Atchafalaya basin at the flood of 1828 having been thus ascertained, the following computation gives the final result.

Resulting volume lost into the Atchafalaya basin in flood of 1828.

	Cubic feet per second.
Computed difference of discharge at Berwick's bay	268,600
Deduct excess of rain drainage	40,000
	228,000
Add the discharge into Atchafalaya basin in 1851	186,000
Discharge into Atchafalaya basin in 1828 =	414,000

This volume, added to the 1,110,000 cubic feet per second, discharged by the river below Plaquemine, gives for the result desired (namely, the discharge per second of the Mississippi just below the mouth of Red river in 1828, if all the overflow into the Tensas swamp and all the discharge of Red river had been retained in the river channel) 1,524,000 cubic feet per second.

Resulting discharge just below Red river in 1828, if levees had been perfected.

The Red-river cut-off, completed in 1831, has modified the condition of the Mississippi at this point; and in the discussion of the floods of 1858 and other years, Red-river landing, situated below the efflux of Atchafalaya, has been the point, in this section of the river, to which the analysis has been applied. For that reason, the discharge just obtained for the flood of 1828 at the mouth of Red river will be transferred to Red-river landing. As the object of this discussion is to determine the effect of the recurrence of such a flood as that of 1828, the discharging capacity of the bayou Atchafalaya will be taken to be that of its present cross-section, with the surface at the actual elevation of 1828. Under those conditions it would be 150,000 cubic feet per second, making the discharge per second of the Mississippi at Red-river landing 1,374,000 cubic feet. But, as already seen, this quantity in 1858 would have been 1,338,000 cubic feet, giving an excess in 1828 of 36,000 cubic feet.

Result transferred to Red-river landing and compared with the flood of 1858.

* It has been already remarked, that the volume received from Red river by the Courtableau and Teche through bayou Bœuf was exceedingly small in 1851. That portion of its volume sent off through Choctaw bayou which emptied into the Atchafalaya through bayou Rouge may be omitted, since it is to be presumed that those bayous will be always kept open, and that that portion of Red-river discharge which is now carried off by them will always continue to be discharged in that manner without reaching the Mississippi river. That portion of the Red-river volume which passes into the Atchafalaya by the bayou de Glaize is taken into account in the discharge of the bayou Atchafalaya at its efflux, for reasons elsewhere given.

With reference to a flood similar to that of 1828, it should be further remarked that the banks of Old river, west of the Atchafalaya, as well as the western bank of Red river for many miles above its mouth, are without levees; and that the discharge into the Atchafalaya basin through this natural waste-weir would reduce the volume of the river below to such a degree that the discharge at points between Red-river landing and the gulf would not exceed that determined for 1858. The volume thus poured into the Atchafalaya basin would not raise the surface of Grand lake as high as it was in 1850, even under the supposition of the simultaneous occurrence of the excessive downfall of rain adopted in discussing the flood of 1828. Indeed, the discharge into that basin, exclusive of that of bayou Plaquemine, would not exceed the volume of Red river itself in its flood state. Assuming, then, that this strip of low land is to remain unleveed, which appears to be probable, such a flood as that of 1828 would not produce a greater maximum discharge below Red-river landing than that which would have occurred in 1858.

The preceding analyses establish that the flood of 1858 is a safe standard by which to estimate the necessary measures for protection against overflow.

This completes the analyses of all the great floods for which the necessary data exist. The investigation establishes that, supposing the levees below Cape Girardeau to have been perfected, the maximum discharge in the June and July rise of 1858 would have exceeded the maximum discharge in any of the other floods at all points above the mouth of Red river; and, excepting in 1828, at all points below that locality; also that if the strip of low land above and near the mouth of Red river remain unleveed, the last exception need not be made. This flood, then, is a safe standard by which to judge of the merits of the different methods of protection, and it has accordingly been adopted for that purpose. For convenience of reference, the table exhibiting the actual maximum discharge, and the maximum discharge with levees perfected, is here repeated:—

Flood of 1858.

Locality.	Actual maximum discharge per second.		Maximum discharge, had swamps below Cape Girardeau been reclaimed.		Difference = reduction of discharge by swamps below Cape Girardeau.
	Date.	Amount.	Date.	Amount.	
		Cubic feet.		*Cubic feet.*	*Cubic feet.*
Columbus	June 18.	1,403,000	June 18.	1,478,000	75,000
Memphis				1,400,000	
Helena	July 5.	1,334,000	June 22 (?)	1,369,000	35,000
Napoleon	June 22.	1,221,000	" 23 (?)	1,418,000	197,000
Lake Providence	" 23.	1,188,000	" 24 (?)	1,406,000	218,000
Vicksburg	" 24.	1,245,000	" 25 (?)	1,430,000	185,000
Natchez	" 25.	1,239,000	" 26 (?)	1,424,000	185,000
Red-river landing	May 30.	1,238,000	" 27 (?)	1,338,000	100,000
Baton Rouge	" 31.	1,238,000	" 28 (?)	1,338,000	100,000
Donaldsonville	" 31.	1,197,000	" 28 (?)	1,297,000	100,000
Carrollton	" 29.	1,188,000	" 29 (?)	1,297,000	109,000

ANALYSIS OF PLANS FOR PROTECTION.

General classification of plans for protection.

Three distinct systems have been proposed for the protection of the bottom lands against overflow. These are: First, to modify the actual relations existing between the accelerating and retarding forces in the channel, in such a manner as to enable the former to carry off the surplus flood-water without so great a rise in the surface as they now require. To this system belong cut-offs. Second, to reduce the maximum discharge of the river. To this system belong diversion of tributaries, artificial reservoirs, and artificial outlets. Third, to confine the water to the channel, and allow it to regulate its own discharge. To this system belong levees, or artificial embankments. Each of these systems has its advantages and its disadvantages. Before deciding, then, upon the best practical system of protection from the floods of the Mississippi, each system must be examined in respect to its feasibility, its dangers and its cost, as applied to that river. This will be done separately for each plan in turn.

System of cutting off bends, to lower the water surface.

Cut-offs.—The system of diminishing the natural resistances opposed to the flow of the water, by cutting off the bends of a river and thus lowering the surface, has often been advocated for restraining the floods of the Mississippi river, and has even been partially applied under the authority of the General Government and of State legislation. It should therefore be fully discussed.

It is not applicable, as proposed by hydraulic writers, to large rivers like the Mississippi.

It is an essential part of the system of cut-offs, as proposed by writers on hydraulics, that the cuts shall be made continuously from the mouth of the river to that portion where it is proposed to reduce the height of the floods. This is urged upon the ground that the greater velocity of the water in the part where the slope has been increased by a cut, will bring a larger volume in floods to the portion below the cut, where the slope *has not been* increased, and where, consequently, the water will rise higher than before. A second cut must therefore be made below the first, and so on to the mouth. This reasoning may be sound when applied to the small streams had in view by the writers, where a few hours make a material change in the flood, but evidently it is not applicable to the Mississippi, where the water often remains for weeks at flood height. Moreover, such extended operations are manifestly impracticable, and, therefore, need not be considered.

Its effects, when applied to a single bend of that river, have been accurately measured.

The practical effect of cutting off a single bend of the Mississippi can be determined with much certainty from the measurements made upon the Red-river and Raccourci cut-offs, and this will first receive attention.

Effect above the cut by measurement.

It is well known that the Red-river and Raccourci cut-offs are in close proximity to each other. The first was made in 1831, and shortened the river 18 miles; the second was made in 1848 and 1849, and shortened the river 21 miles. The flood of 1851 was as high as that of 1828 at points 100 miles above and below the mouth of Red river, and the accessions received from Red river were the same in each flood. It is concluded, therefore, that the river would have been as high at Routh's point in 1851 as in 1828 but for the cut-offs.

The flood of 1851 was, however, 4.6 feet below that of 1828. This, then, is the effect of the two cut-offs in lowering the flood level just above their site.

By computation.

It is conceded that little confidence should be placed, in such a discussion as this, upon results computed by formulæ. Still, when careful observation has indicated that certain effects are produced, additional weight is given to such conclusions, if it can be shown that they accord with the general laws of flowing water as expressed by reliable formulæ. The following analytical discussion of the subject, based upon observed facts, is therefore added.

Let it be proposed to compute how much the high-water level in 1851 was lowered at Routh's point by the two cut-offs, assuming that they produced only a local effect upon the bed of the river. This problem will be solved in two ways, by discussing, first, the effect produced upon the river above, and second, the effect produced upon the river below, Routh's point.

The preceding comparison of the high-water level of the different floods has indicated that no sensible effect was produced by the cut-offs at a distance of about 100 miles above Routh's point. The first object then is to compute h'; that is, the fall of water surface in this distance, if the cut-offs had not existed. For mean dimensions in this part of the river we have the following:—

a' =	mean high-water area . . . . =	199,000 sq. ft.
W' =	proportional between mean widths above and below Red river =	3,450 feet,
p' =	width increased by about half mean radius . . . . . =	3,480 feet,
Q' =	discharge by Delta-Survey measurements . . . . . =	1,150,000 cu. ft.
$\text{Sin.}^2\,\delta'$ =	value measured on La Tourrette's map . . . . . . =	14,
l' =	distance considered . . . . =	528,000 feet.

Applying equations (36), (44), and (45) to these data, we find $h_{\prime}' = 15.95$, and $h'_{\prime\prime} = 3.49$, giving $h' = 19.44$ feet. If, now, x denotes the lowering effect of the cut-offs upon the water surface at Routh's point, expressed in feet, it is evident that the actual fall in the distance considered, at high water in 1851, denoted by h'', will be equal to $h' + x$; that the actual mean area (a'') will be equal to $a' - \frac{W'\,x}{2}$, and that the actual perimeter (p'') will be equal to $p' - x$, all the other quantities remaining unchanged. Computing the value of x by the method of successive approximations, we find that when $x = 4.4$, the analytical conditions are very nearly satisfied; that is, we have $h_{\prime}'' = 20.06$ and $h_{\prime\prime}'' = 3.77$, and hence $h'' = h_{\prime}'' + h_{\prime\prime}'' = 23.83$ feet, which very nearly accords with the value given above, viz.: $h'' = h' + x = 23.84$ feet. The effect of the cut-offs is, then, by this computation, to lower the level of the water surface at Routh's point at high water in 1851, 4.4 feet.

By a second computation.

The problem will next be solved by computing the effect of the cut-offs upon the river below Routh's point, assuming what the water marks establish, that no sensible effect was produced at Donaldsonville, and that, although there was an actual increase of mean area between the lower end of Raccourci cut-off and Donaldsonville, the change in direction of the currents produced such an increase of resistance as to be equivalent to a diminution of mean area.

Since the mean dimensions of cross-section between Red river and Donaldsonville, already deduced, correspond to the actual high water of 1851, we have the following numerical values for this flood:—

$$\begin{aligned} a'' &= 200{,}000 \text{ square feet,} \\ W'' &= 3{,}000 \text{ feet,} \\ p'' &= 3{,}035 \text{ feet,} \\ Q'' &= 1{,}200{,}000 \text{ cubic feet,} \\ \text{Sin.}^2\, \acute{d}'' &= 15.39, \\ l'' &= 647{,}330 \text{ feet.} \end{aligned}$$

Applying equations (36), (44), and (45) to these data, we find $h_{\prime}'' = 17.0$ and $h_{\prime\prime}'' = 4.1$, giving $h'' = 21.1$ feet. This quantity, as actually measured by the level parties of this Survey, was 22.8 feet, and, consequently, the final result of this computation must be increased in the ratio of 22.8 to 21.1. If, now, the cut-offs had not existed in 1851, we should have had—

$$\begin{aligned} h' &= h'' + x, \\ a' &= a'' + \frac{W''\,x}{2}, \\ p' &= p'' + x, \\ \text{Sin.}^2\, \acute{d}' &= 23.19 \text{ (from map),} \\ l' &= 858{,}530 \quad \text{“} \quad \text{“} \\ Q' &= Q'' = 1{,}200{,}000, \\ W' &= W'' = 3000. \end{aligned}$$

Computing the value of x by successive approximations, we find it to be about 3.9 feet, since with this value we have $h' = h'' + x = 25.00$ feet, and $h' = h_{\prime}' + h_{\prime\prime}' = 19.05 + 5.88 = 24.93$ feet. Increasing h' and $h_{\prime}'$ and $h_{\prime\prime}'$ in the ratio of 22.8 to 21.1, as already explained, we have for the final result of the computation, $h' = 20.6 + 6.4 = 27.0$ feet, and hence $x = 27.0 - 22.8 = 4.2$ feet.

Conclusion relative to the effect above the cut.

The result of these two computations may be stated as follows. By discussing analytically the lowering effect of the cut-offs upon the level of the top of the flood of 1851 at Routh's point, we find that the effect was equal to 4.4 feet, if we consider the river above this locality, and that it was 4.2 feet, if we consider the river below this locality. By comparing the high-water marks of different years, we have already decided that this effect was about 4.6 feet. It is hardly possible that these coincidences are accidental, and it must therefore be conceded that they demonstrate the actual effects produced by cut-offs above their sites.

Effect below the cut, by measurement.

It remains to determine this effect just below their site. At Baton Rouge the floods of 1828 and 1851 were practically of the same height, and the latter flood at this point was therefore unaffected by the cut-offs. The total measured fall between Routh's point and Baton Rouge in 1851 and 1828 was 16.24 and 20.84 feet respectively, the slope per mile being 0.222 and 0.188 of a foot respectively. Assuming the slope uniform between these two places, the river at the foot of the Raccourci bend in 1828 was 12.33 feet above the river at Baton Rouge, and in 1851 14.7 feet above the same level. But it was ascertained by careful measurement that in the flood of 1851 (and also in that of 1858) the fall per mile through the Raccourci cut-off was 0.56 of a foot, which would reduce the elevation at the foot of the Raccourci bend in 1851, as computed by the general slope, to 14.3 feet. The difference between the two elevations (1828 and 1851) was, then, 2.0 feet. It measures exactly the amount by which the water has been raised at the foot of the two cut-offs by those works.

Second measurement with same result.

The same result is deduced by another process. By measurement in March, 1851, when the river was rising and within 5 feet of the top of the flood at Red-river landing, the fall from Routh's point to the foot of the Raccourci cut-off was found to be 1.8 feet. The fall at the top of the flood was not materially different. Hence the river at the foot of the Raccourci cut-off at the flood of 1851 was 6.4 feet below the high-water mark of 1828 at Routh's point. At the top of the flood of 1828, the river at the foot of the Raccourci cut-off was, by levels, 8.4 feet below the surface at Routh's point, giving the same number as before (2 feet) for the increase in height of the flood below the site of these cut-offs.

Final conclusions respecting the effect of cut-offs.

We may, then, decide that the high-water mark of 1851 at Routh's point was 4.6 feet lower, and at the foot of Raccourci cut-off 2.0 feet higher, than it would have been if the cut-offs had not been made.

The elevation of the river's surface at the head of a bend, necessary to overcome the excess of resistance in a bend over that in a straight part of the river, will disappear when the cut-off is made, and the surface at the head will be lowered by this quantity. This effect in the two bends under consideration is 1.8 feet by equation (45). In 1828 the fall of a straight part of the river in 39 miles (the length of the two bends less the length of the two cuts) was 5.5 feet, or 0.14 of a foot per mile. One-half of this quantity, increased by 1.8 feet for the bend-effect, gives 4.55 feet, precisely the amount found as the actual depression of the high water of 1851 at Routh's point, the head of the Red-river cut-off. By comparing the flood of 1858 with that of 1828 at Routh's point, the difference in the conditions of Red river in the two floods being taken into account, the same result is obtained; and it must, therefore, be concluded that the river at the head of a cut-off will be depressed by the whole amount of the elevation at the head of the bend due to the bend's resistance, and by one-half of the fall in a straight part of the river equal in length to the shortening of the river.* Let us now determine how this conclusion accords with the facts observed at other cut-offs.

---

* The high-water marks of 1828 and 1844 at the head of the Red-river cut-off and at points 100 miles above and below have been adduced as evidence that the effect of a cut-off was to depress the surface of the river at the head of the cut-off more than the whole fall in the bend so cut off, and to depress the surface of the river at points below the cut-off, instead of elevating it. This conclusion is evidently contradicted by the facts above cited. The only new force which would diminish the slope below the cut-off would be the impulse derived from the increased velocity of the river in falling through the cut. This would be exhausted in a short distance. It is stated that 100 miles above the Red-river cut-off, the flood of 1844 was equal to that of 1828; that it was below that mark at Natchez, 0.6 of a foot; at the head of the cut-off, 2.4 feet; at Morganza, 1.7 feet; at Baton Rouge, 0.8 of a foot; and at Carrollton, 0.7 of a foot. Now it is to be remarked that all the facts relating to the flood of 1844 are not known. Among the items of information gathered by this Survey is a statement made at Waterloo, that there was a crevasse in the vicinity of Morganza in 1844. This would have depressed the flood at that place. But the great cause of the depression of the flood in 1844 at points below the mouth of Red river was the fact that Red river was low during the flood of that year, and that, consequently, between 50,000 and 100,000 cubic feet per second of Mississippi water was discharged through the Atchafalaya. In 1828 and 1851, on the contrary, the Red-river and Mississippi-river floods were nearly coincident. In the great flood of 1850, the Mississippi at points 100 miles above the Red-river cut-off was as high as in the flood of 1828, while at Routh's point it was 1 foot below the high water of 1844, and at least 1.3 feet *above it* below the Raccourci cut-off, notwithstanding the numerous and large crevasses of that year between Red river and New Orleans.

It is stated that the Fausse Rivière cut-off was made in 1722, when there were no levees. It shortened the river 20 miles, and must have depressed it at flood not less than 2.4 feet at Waterloo, the head of the cut-off. In 1851 a small levee, 18 inches high, was thrown up there for the first time, the high water being above the bank, an evidence that, from some cause, the surface of the river in that vicinity had been raised.

Tested by cut-off at Fausse Riviere.

The American-bend cut-off, 90 miles below Napoleon, occurred on April 15, 1858. On the 9th of May, when examined in connection with this Survey, the following conditions existed. The cut-off shortened the river 7.0 miles. Just above the cut-off the river was 2.3 feet below the highest point attained previous to that date. At Grand lake, just below the cut-off, the river was 0.25 of a foot below the highest point previously attained. From a scrutiny of the gauge-records at Napoleon and Vicksburg, the cut-off being midway between them, it appears that if no crevasses had existed at that time between those places, and if no other disturbing causes existed between them, the river at the cut-off ought to have been 0.2 of a foot below the highest point it had reached early in April of that year. The crevasses existing between Napoleon and Vicksburg at that time were sufficiently large to depress the river's surface about 0.8 of a foot. The bend-effect (equation (45)) was equal to 0.5 of a foot. The fall of the river in that part of its course, irrespective of bend-effect, is 0.26 of a foot per mile, and in 7 miles is 1.8 feet. The following result, then, is to be anticipated, if the laws above deduced are correct. The river at the American bend on May 11, without cut-off or crevasses, would have been 0.2 of a foot below the height it reached early in April. But 0.8 of a foot depression at American bend from crevasses; 0.5 of a foot depression at head of cut-off from bend-effect; and 0.9 of a foot, effect of shortening the river 7 miles, give at the head of the cut-off a total depression of 2.4 feet, which corresponds nearly to that observed. At the foot of the cut-off, the river, if undisturbed by cut-off or crevasses, would also have been 0.2 of a foot below the height it reached early in April. The elevation from shortening the river 7 miles was 0.9 of a foot; the depression from crevasses was 0.8 of a foot. These two effects nearly balancing each other, the level of the river should have been on May 11 about the same as it was early in April. It was found to be 0.25 of a foot below that stand; a sufficiently close approximation, when the somewhat uncertain nature of the data is considered.

By American-bend cut-off.

The laws indicated by the Red-river and Raccourci cut-offs apply to the Po. Thus it was stated in 1854 by M. Cattaneo, Engineer in charge of the Hydraulic Works in the district of Rovigo, that rectifications had been made in recent years upon the Adige, for the purpose of protecting the banks from erosion; that such a rectification was made in 1854 at Boara, about 10 miles from Rovigo (plate XIX), in which the cut was one-half the length of the bend; that the effect upon the surface of the river in floods, as noticed since that time, was to depress the surface at the head of the cut 0.8 of a foot, and to elevate it at the foot 0.4 of a foot.

By those upon the river Po.

The investigations of the Chevalier Elia Lombardini, Director-General of Public Works in the province of Milan, have brought to light the following interesting particulars. About midway between Pavia and Piacenza, the course of the Po is straight for many miles. This straight part extends from Albera to Monticelli. Above and below, the course is winding. Along the east bank of the straight part, the marks of former bends are still visible. On the west bank, all traces of those shown on the old maps are obliterated by the deposits of gravel and other heavy material brought down in large quantities by the short streams from the Apennines. The longer streams from the Alps, on the east side, bring a comparatively small quantity of light material. All the bends in this part of the river were cut off in the fourteenth century. At Port Albera, the head of these numerous cut-offs, the levees are only a few feet high; at Monticelli, the foot of the cut-offs, they are 16 feet high. The slope of the Po between Pavia and Piacenza is not less than 1.5 feet per mile; its bed not being in alluvial soil in this part of its course.

A theoretical objection to the above conclusions, met.

So far as observations are concerned, then, it must be admitted that the foregoing conclusions, based upon the observations on the Red-river and Raccourci cut-offs, are general. If it be objected upon theoretical grounds that the elevation of the river surface below the cut would give an increased slope and an increased cross-section to the river there, and thus cause an increased discharge, while in reality the discharge of the river remains constant, the reply is obvious. If the river were not leveed, the cut-off would really increase the discharge above, through and below the cut-off in floods; because, its surface being depressed above the cut, it would carry off through its channel what it before shed over its banks. But when the river is leveed, it sheds no water over its banks, and of course the discharge cannot be increased by the cut-off in the manner before described. How, then, in this case, can the increased cross-section and increased slope below the cut-off be reconciled with the fact that the discharge is not increased? The cross-section and velocities measured at Routh's point give the clue to the explanation. The greatest velocities in that part of the river *are not in the deepest water*. No cut-off upon any river has been made so as to introduce the current from the cut to the reach below in the same direction that it had before the cut was made. As a consequence, the swiftest current does not run in the deepest part as it did before; the resistances which it encounters are therefore greater than before; and in order to carry off the same discharge the surface must rise, and thus increase the slope and area of cross-section; unless, indeed, the power of the current is sufficient to excavate the bed at once. This, as will hereafter be seen, is not the case with the Mississippi, whose bed is not in alluvial soil but in an older geological formation of hard clay, which yields so slowly to the current that it may be considered almost permanent. The condition of the river for many miles below is thus changed by the cut-off. That the bed will gradually wear until the swiftest current flows in the deepest part of the channel, in those portions where the relations of the two were disturbed, is probable; but the process will be so gradual that the injurious effect of the cut-off in raising the surface of the river below may for all practical purposes be considered permanent. It should, however, be remarked that this elevation is comparatively local. In the two cases of the Red-river and Raccourci cut-offs, it did not reach below Baton Rouge, but its precise extent could not be ascertained. It is apparent that the current must tend more and more to resume its old direction, the greater the distance from the cut. The depression above the cut-off extends to a much greater distance, certainly not less than 100 miles.

It has been shown by the preceding discussion that a cut-off raises the surface of the river at the foot of the cut nearly as much as it depresses it at the head. The country above the cut is therefore relieved from the floods only at the expense of the country below. Moreover, if a series of cut-offs were to be made extending to the mouth of the river, the principles educed show that the heights of the floods would be regularly decreased from a point near midway of the series to the upper end, and regularly increased from the same point to the lower end. The system, therefore, is entirely inapplicable to the Mississippi river, in whole or in part.

The system as a measure of protection for the Mississippi valley is then pernicious.

Diverting tributaries.—It has been proposed to protect the lower Mississippi valley from overflow by diverting the course of certain main tributaries, and thus diminishing the discharge in floods. The general principle already enunciated, upon which this plan is based, is unquestionably correct; and we have only to determine whether the practical application of it would produce results commensurate with the requisite expenditure.

Plan of diverting tributaries.

Beginning in the northern part of the basin, the first proposed application is upon the Upper Missouri, which, it is suggested, might be turned into the Red river of the North. The cut would have to be made through the belt of prairie land lying between the "great bend" and Mouse river, a distance of 40 miles in the narrowest place. The following facts, taken from the report of Governor I. I. Stevens contained in vol. I Pacific Railroad Reports, are sufficient to show that the project is so costly as to be utterly impracticable.

The Missouri river.

Mouse river in this vicinity is 120 feet wide and 7 feet deep. It flows in a narrow valley varying from half a mile to 2 miles in width and bounded by bluffs some 200 feet in height. Massive sandstone rocks are occasionally seen in these bluffs. Between this valley and the Missouri, there is a plateau, averaging some 600 feet in height. In general, the substratum is a clayey loam, but boulders and stones are often mingled with the soil. The general level of the Missouri and Mouse-river valleys is about the same, but the information upon this subject is not sufficiently definite to decide which is the higher.

Even if this project were feasible at a moderate cost, its practical utility for the purpose contemplated would be more than doubtful; for floods in this part of the Missouri are to be little feared below the Ohio. It is the sudden rises in the lower tributaries which work the ruin below. Floods in these upper branches are nearly expended in the vast reservoir of the channel, and have but little influence upon the oscillations at St. Louis. Lastly, such a work would interfere with the navigation above the point of diversion, which extends for several hundred miles, and is every year becoming more important to the country.

The next tributary for which this plan presents any appearance of feasibility is the Arkansas. It has been proposed to turn the floods of this stream into the bayou Bartholomew or bayou Maçon. The practicability of this undertaking cannot be decided without a careful survey; but, as the plan must include the permanent protection of the banks of the bayous from over-

The Arkansas river.

flow, its execution would necessarily be costly. It is stated that the bayou Maçon rises within two or three miles of the Arkansas river, and that the intervening soil is light. No exact information respecting the cross-section of this bayou near its head, or respecting that of the bayou Bartholomew, has been collected, but they are believed to be too small to give much encouragement to the project. Assuming, however, that it is feasible, the plan has its advantages and disadvantages.

The floods of the Arkansas are particularly disastrous to the lower Mississippi. The operations of the Survey establish the fact that a given quantity of water introduced into the channel at the head of the alluvial region produces a less rise in the lower river than the same quantity added by one of the lower tributaries. This effect is due partly to the reservoir influence of the channel above the tributary; partly to the damming effect of conflicting currents near the mouth of the tributary; and, partly, as at the mouth of Red river, in the flood of 1851, to interference with the normal changes in local slope at points below the tributary. The observed fact accords perfectly with the views of planters residing upon the Mississippi below Arkansas and Red rivers, who have frequently stated that they dread the rises of these streams far more than those of the Ohio or of the Missouri. Keeping the Arkansas floods out of the Mississippi must, therefore, have a peculiarly beneficial effect from Napoleon down to Red-river landing, where the water would, of course, again make its appearance through the Red-river channel. Above Napoleon the effects would be but little felt. Below Red river they would be in some measure injurious, as just indicated. The plan must, therefore, be considered purely local—applicable, however, to the very part of the river where the difficulties to be overcome in restraining the floods are the greatest.

The objections to the scheme, supposing it to be feasible at a moderate cost, arise chiefly from the difficulty of preventing injurious effects upon the navigability of the Arkansas river; but it may also be objected that it would only furnish protection against *certain classes* of floods; for it often happens that the Arkansas is low, when the flood from above is passing its mouth. This was the case in the great July flood of 1858, which has been adopted as the basis of this discussion. As already seen, provision for a discharge some 200,000 cubic feet per second greater than that which actually passed at the height of this flood, was necessary to protect the country between Napoleon and Red-river landing from overflow; while the diversion of the entire waters of the Arkansas would only have relieved the river of 30,000. The works necessary to guard against this flood of 1858 would, so far as it is possible to foresee, be sufficient to restrain any probable combination of floods in the two rivers. The union of the greatest floods in both rivers is of course *possible,* but so highly improbable as to amount to a practical impossibility.

The Red river.

The next and only remaining tributary, to which this system might be applied, is Red river. It has been suggested, first, to turn the surplus waters of this stream into the channels draining to bayou Teche; or, second, to compel the Atchafalaya to carry off its entire discharge by closing Old river, above Red-river landing.

To the first of these projects, the remarks just made respecting the Arkansas river apply, excepting that the advantages to be derived are materially less, and the practical difficulties to be encountered even greater. The latter fact is evident from the following considerations. The shortest air-line distance between Red river and the Teche is fully 40 miles. These streams were formerly connected by a chain of bayous, 90 miles in length, but their communication with Red river has been cut off for the security of the plantations upon their banks. The chief link, bayou Bœuf, is only some 60 or 100 feet wide, and its cross-section does not probably exceed 2500 square feet. From the description of the Teche itself,* it is, doubtless, a partially deserted channel, with a cross-section capable of discharging about 10,000 cubic feet per second more than now passes through it. The bayou Courtableau, also, which forms, for a few miles, part of the chain connecting Red river and the Teche, and discharges into the Atchafalaya, might carry off the same additional volume. But it will be perceived that, even if it were important to draw off so small a quantity as 20,000 cubic feet per second, the works to effect it must be enormously costly.

The second project—to close Old river—would, if executed, entail disastrous consequences. Undoubtedly the Red river at times pours its flood into the Mississippi when that stream is so high as, in the defective condition of the levees, to render the effects dangerous to the lower country. This occurred in 1828 and 1851, but usually the floods of Red river do not raise the surface of the Mississippi to a dangerous height. Generally the Atchafalaya serves, directly or indirectly,† as an efficient outlet for the floods of the Mississippi. Such an outlet should not be sacrificed merely to guard against the contingency of a coincidence of floods, the worst effects of which, so far as indicated by the past (see discussion of the flood of 1828), will be provided against in the plans for protection based upon the standard flood of 1858.

But this is not the only evil that would follow the execution of the plan. The discharge of Red river at its mouth, in floods caused by its own drainage, is 225,000 cubic feet per second. The discharge of the Atchafalaya at full banks is only 130,000 cubic feet per second. If, therefore, the entrance of Red river to the Mississippi should be closed, the Red-river valley, the settlements along the bayou de Glaize and the Atchafalaya basin would all be deeply inundated at the recurrence of every Red-river flood.

The plan of reservoirs.

Reservoirs.—This plan is to hold back, in the flood season, by systems of artificial lakes upon the tributaries of the Mississippi, such a volume of water as may be requisite to reduce within banks the floods of that river. The volume thus held back is to be retained for improving low-water navigation. The discharge of each tributary is thus to be more nearly equalized throughout the year, and a double advantage secured.

Its antiquity.

The plan, in theory, is admirable, and has long been a subject of discussion among European engineers. Artificial lakes for protection against floods were constructed as early as 1711 upon the upper Loire, and they have since been advocated, both for improving navigation and for restraining floods, by

* For more than 100 miles above its mouth, the area of its cross-section exceeds 4500 square feet, and its slope is at least 0.16 of a foot per mile.

† When this action is indirect, it is obscured by the existence of dead water in Old river. Thus at the top of the flood in 1858, the bayou, although apparently inoperative as an outlet, carried off 90,000 cubic feet per second of Mississippi water which drained to it through the Tensas bottom. (See pages 345–7.) If the levees of the Tensas swamp had remained unbroken in that flood, the bayou would have drawn off the same amount through Old river, and its beneficial action would thus have been unmistakable.

eminent writers, among whom may be cited M. Polenceau, M. Lombardini, M. Boulangé, and M. Valleé.*

This equalizing tendency of lakes was pointed out in the first report upon the improvement of the navigation of the Ohio river [Report of the Board of Engineers on the Ohio and Mississippi rivers, by S. Bernard, Brigadier-General, and Joseph G. Totten, Major Engineers, and Brevet Lieutenant-Colonel—New York, December 22, 1822] not as a means to be resorted to for that object, but as exhibiting the condition of other rivers, the Rhine for instance, in contrast with that of the Ohio.†

American advocates.

Among American engineers who have advocated the application of a system of

* In July, 1847, M. Boulangé, Engineer in Chief of Bridges and Roads, in a brief notice of the inundations of the Loire in 1846, described the works on that river just referred to, and indicated where others of a similar character should be placed to prevent the inundations altogether, or restrain them within harmless bounds. (See Annales des Ponts et Chaussées, 1848.)

Previous to this, M. Polenceau had proposed a somewhat similar system for the rivers of France, with the same object.

In 1842, M. Valleé, Inspector of Bridges and Roads, Chief Engineer of the Canal that unites the Rhone and the Rhine, proposed to convert the lake of Geneva into an artificial reservoir, by constructing certain works at the efflux of the lake, with a view to keep back the floods of the Rhone and to improve the navigation of that river in low water, by supplying it in greater abundance than the natural flow from the lake at those periods.

For these objects he contemplated holding in reserve about 30,000,000,000 cubic feet of water, to be supplied to the river at Lyons (135 miles distant) during the periods of low water (the mean duration of which is stated to be forty-three days annually), in quantities varying from 6 to 40 millions cubic feet per hour, which, in addition to the natural flow there, would give a depth suitable to the navigation. By holding back 35,000 cubic feet per second from the discharge, M. Valleé expected to reduce the height of the flood nearly 5 feet at Lyons, and 2.5 feet at Avignon.

The obstacle to the execution of this project has been of a political rather than a physical character. France possesses no portion of the shores of lake Leman (Geneva), which lie within the territories of two Swiss cantons and Sardinia.

Among those who were of opinion that the advantages anticipated during the low water of the Rhone would be obtained by the execution of such a project, was M. Elia Lombardini, Director-General of Public Works in the province of Milan, one of the ablest and most learned hydraulic engineers living, if, indeed, he may not more properly be classed as the first hydraulic engineer of the age.

In a paper upon the nature of lakes, and of the works required to regulate their efflux, read before the Imperial Royal Institute of Lombardy, in August, 1845, and published at Milan in 1846, M. Lombardini dwells upon the beneficial influence of the lakes of Italy in regulating the flow of the waters of the Po, in restraining its floods by diminishing the volumes of its great tributaries to one-half and one-third of what they would be but for the interposition of these lakes (which at such times discharge so much less water than they receive), and in preventing excessive low water in that river by increasing the flow at that time, thus tending to equalize the volume of water at all seasons.

This moderating influence of the lakes had been previously pointed out by M. Lombardini, in detail, in a paper published in 1843.

At his suggestion, artificial works have been successfully resorted to at the outlet of one of these Italian lakes, to prevent, in conjunction with other works, inundations on the river issuing from it, in the country below.

† The Report states: "A geographical circumstance of great importance as regards the supply of rivers is the situation of large lakes at or near their sources. These, by retaining the waters, are so many reservoirs, regulating the expense of water in seasons of floods, and supplying an equivalent to this expense long after the causes of floods have ceased." As an instance in point it cites the Rhine, which rises in the Alps, where the melting of the snows is successive, and prolonged even to July. "In its upper part it traverses lakes, which economize the water and serve as reservoirs for seasons of scarcity." From the varied aspects of the different parts of the basin, winds from different directions blow at the same time in different parts of the same general valley; consequently the rains are not simultaneous over that valley, and the tributaries bring their floods in succession. The floods in the Rhine are not, therefore, great. On the contrary, the winds blow at the same time from the same direction in the whole basin of the Ohio, and the rains are simultaneous throughout the whole general valley. The mountains in the southern half of the basin are low, and the snows are melted rapidly and nearly simultaneously by the warm southerly winds and rains. The tributaries contribute their floods nearly at the same time, and the floods of the Ohio are therefore of great height.

artificial lakes to our western rivers are Mr. Charles Ellet and Mr. Elwood Morris. The former, in a paper published by the Smithsonian Institution in 1849, and the latter, in a series of articles which appeared in the Journal of the Franklin Institute subsequent to that date, have urged its adoption for the improvement of the navigation of the Ohio. Mr. Ellet has also, since the publication of his first paper, repeatedly recommended the system for restraining the floods of the Mississippi, even in the delta.

Its double character. Its applicability to restraining floods only to be considered here.

It will be noticed that two distinct advantages are claimed for this system. One is the improvement of navigation in low water; the other, protection against floods. The former is foreign to the purpose of this report, and it is not intended to discuss it, especially as the requisite data have never been collected for the Mississippi or for any of its main tributaries. It seems possible by establishing a system of dams in the mountains upon many tributaries, accumulating the rain which falls during many months in the year, and pouring it into the channel of the river in its lowest stage, to effect a marked improvement in the low-water navigation even of the Mississippi itself. To what extent this system is practicable, and what would be its probable cost, can only be decided by careful and extended investigation and survey. As already stated, it is a subject with which this report has no connection. The second advantage claimed for the plan, however, is very different. It is proposed by it "to protect the whole delta and the borders of every stream in it, primary or tributary, from overflow."* This branch of the subject, therefore, will be carefully examined.

General considerations are sufficient to show that it is inapplicable to restraining the floods of the Mississippi.

Little consideration is necessary to make it apparent that this system is not applicable to restraining the floods of all rivers. Certain topographical conditions are essential to its success. The valley must be of such a character that dams of reasonable dimensions can be constructed, which shall keep back *the identical water which otherwise would make up the flood.* It is not sufficient for this purpose, as for improving navigation, that a large volume of water may be collected by the accumulations of months. The floods of great rivers are torrents, caused by rapidly melting snows and by widely extended and heavy rains. The greater part of this water does not drain from the remote mountain sides, and issue from the distant mountain gorges. It falls in the valley itself; and the nearer to the main river, the more sudden and disastrous will be its effects; partly from the more rapid accumulation in the main stream of the contributions of the tributaries, and partly from the absence of the natural reservoir furnished by the various channels, which must be filled before a freshet originating near the sources can reach the lower part of a river. To control such floods with certainty and economy by artificial reservoirs, it is, therefore, essential that certain important tributaries which drain relatively large portions of the basin shall debouch near their mouths from narrower gorges, where dams can be constructed at reasonable cost, and where artificial lakes can be formed without injury to other interests.

But these essential conditions are the very reverse of those existing upon the lower

* Report of Mr. Ellet, 1851.

Mississippi. It is emphatically a river which drains a plain. The area of the narrow border of mountains around it is insignificant, when compared with the great extent of its basin. Moreover, the downfall of rain upon these mountains is but little more than half of that which falls upon the same area near the great artery itself; for, as already seen, it derives by far the greater part of its annual and of its flood discharge from the central and nearly flat portion of its valley. If we add to these peculiarities the fact that its main tributaries are all navigable rivers, which are too valuable, as routes of communication, to be interfered with by dams, even if the system were otherwise practicable, it is evident that reservoirs can be located only in the narrow belt of mountains upon the borders of the basin, where, as already seen, they can have but little effect upon the floods.

This can also be established by computations based upon the data collected in 1858.

In order to give a more definite character to these conclusions, they will be reduced to figures by aid of the data collected respecting the great June flood of 1858, by which the merits of all these different plans of protection are to be tested.

Quantity of water which reservoirs must have held back, to be successful, in the June flood of 1858.

To have protected "the whole delta and the borders of every stream in it, primary or tributary," against this flood, not more than 1,050,000 cubic feet per second could have been allowed to enter the head of the alluvial region.* Even this quantity would have submerged much of the lower country, had not the tributaries below the Ohio been so very low that their united contributions, joined to this amount, would only have been sufficient to maintain the river at full banks. The conditions of this flood were then the most favorable possible for the reservoir system.

During the thirty-six days in 1858 from May 25 to June 29, inclusive, the total amount of water passing the latitude of Columbus exceeded by 648,172,800,000 cubic feet that which would have resulted from a discharge per second of 1,050,000 cubic feet. Reservoirs situated above the mouth of the Ohio, and sufficient to have kept back *in a single month* fully 600,000,000,000 cubic feet of water, would, therefore, have been essential to the security of the delta, if this system had been depended upon for restraining this flood.

Where these reservoirs must be placed is the first question which presents itself.

Where the reservoirs must be placed.

The character of the basins of the Upper Mississippi and lower Missouri is such that the system is impracticable in them. (See Chapter I.) It is, then, in the Ohio basin that their locus must be sought. The northern slope of this basin presents few or no advantageous sites. The southern slope, on the contrary, is mountainous near the head-waters of the tributaries, and it is there, if anywhere, that reservoirs can be constructed.

Downfall of rain in this region at this epoch.

The downfall of rain in this region is next to be considered. The extended system of meteorological observations conducted under the auspices of the Smithsonian Institution has rendered it possible to

* If it be objected that, in the December rise of 1857, nearly 1,200,000 cubic feet per second entered the head of the alluvial region, and passed down without raising the river above the level of the banks, the reply is obvious. The river at the commencement of this rise was low, and the water was expended during the brief rise in filling the comparatively empty channel,—a condition which, producing a great local slope, also materially depresses the water surface. (See page 349.) In the flood season of the year, the river is always so nearly at the level of its banks that no such enormous reservoir exists.

trace, with great precision, the rains which occasioned this flood. They occurred in the month of May, and were heaviest *north* of the Ohio river. Thus the downfall in that month varied, through the States of Ohio, Indiana, and Illinois, from 7 to 12 inches, the mean from observations at nineteen well distributed stations being 9 inches. None of these stations were upon the immediate banks of the Ohio, where local influences could be suspected; and this is doubtless a correct estimate of the mean precipitation over the whole of this area, as well as over much of the basins of the Upper Mississippi and of the lower tributaries of the Missouri, to which these rains also extended. But since none of this vast region is adapted to the reservoir system, a knowledge of the downfall *in the mountainous part of the valleys of the southern tributaries of the Ohio* is demanded by the present investigation. The following table exhibits all the data available for this purpose, grouped in such a manner (plate I) as to represent truly the mean downfall throughout the entire region in question.

Locality.	Latitude.	Longitude.	Rain in May, 1858.	
			Observed.	Grouped to represent true mean.
	° ′	° ′	*Inches.*	*Inches.*
Murraysville, Pennsylvania	40 28	79 35	5.6	7.1
Cannonsburg, Pennsylvania	40 15	80 10	7.5	
Somerset, Pennsylvania	40 02	79 02	8.8	
Kanawha, Virginia	38 25	81 48	3.3	3.0
Poplar Grove, Virginia	38 20	81 21	2.8	
Millersburg, Kentucky	38 20	84 10	4.5	4.9
Paris, Kentucky	38 10	84 16	5.4	
Glenwood Cottage, Tennessee	36 28	87 18	4.5	4.5
Jackson, Mississippi	32 20	90 11	3.0	2.9
Green Springs, Alabama	32 50	87 46	2.8	
Mean				4.5

Amount which might have been collected.

For May, then, the average downfall in this mountain region was 4.5 inches. Adopting Mr. Ellet's estimate, which is certainly ample, 65 per cent. of this might have been collected; that is, 0.24 of a foot.

Drainage area required was far greater than the topography of the country would allow.

Having thus determined the total quantity of water to be collected, and the mean depth of the available downfall, we can determine what area in the mountains it would have been necessary to drain into reservoirs, in order to protect the delta from overflow. It is $\frac{600,000,000,000}{0.24 \times (5280)^2} = 90,000$ square miles, *an area much larger than the whole mountain region drained by the Ohio.**

* It may be objected to these conclusions, that the observations upon the fall of rain did not extend sufficiently into and over the mountain region, and hence that the effect of the Alleghany range in increasing the amount of rain is not taken into account. Observation has not yet determined the effect of this mountain system upon the fall of rain, nor has the general law of increase produced by mountains been ascertained with sufficient precision to admit of its numerical application to the Alleghany range. Nevertheless, an approximation to the effect may be made. The mountains upon the west coast of England increase the downfall of 40 inches at their foot-slopes to 57 inches at about their mean elevation, thus adding between one-third and one-half. If it be assumed, then, that the effect of the

The impracticability of the scheme requires no further demonstration, since this flood was of the character which the reservoir system is best adapted to controlling; that is, it was a flood of the upper tributaries of the Mississippi, all those below the Ohio being at a low stage.

Its probable cost, supposing the basin highly favorable.

It would be a work of supererogation to discuss questions of cost, now that the *physical impossibility* of protecting the alluvial region from overflow by this system has been made so evident; but to give some idea of the enormous expense which would attend its application, even if the topography of the Mississippi basin were favorable to the scheme, reference will be made to the data collected by Mr. Ellet in 1858, in a survey for a site of an artificial lake upon a branch of the Kanawha river. The character of the work is sufficiently explained in the note below.* Mr. Ellet's estimate of cost is as follows:—

Total estimated damages	$154,200
Estimated cost of dam	215,500
Estimated cost of preparing channel of Kanawha river for increased discharge	125,000
Total	$494,700

This site is doubtless one of the most favorable which could be selected in that region for constructing an artificial lake; but if, for the sake of argument, we admit it to be a fair standard, we see that, according to Mr. Ellet's estimate, an outlay of about half a million of dollars must be made in order to collect the drainage of 210 square miles. To have protected the alluvial region against the June flood of 1858, by this system, would then have required an estimated expenditure of about $215,000,000; and to have guaranteed "the whole delta, and the borders of every stream in it, primary or tributary," against inundation by floods from *any* of the great tributaries, the amount required would have been much greater.

Concluding remarks.

To guard against misconception, it may be well to repeat that the advantages of a reservoir system upon certain western rivers, for certain objects, are not questioned. By it, the low-water navigation of important streams flowing into the Ohio—perhaps of that river itself, and possibly even of the Mississippi—may be improved. The data for deciding whether the advantages

---

Alleghany range is to increase the rain near the foot of its slopes to a mean rain one-half greater over the whole area of its declivities, an assumption highly favorable to the reservoir project, the above estimate of downfall would only be increased one-sixth, since these mountain declivities do not occupy *more* than a third part of that portion of the basin of the Ohio south of the river. Upon this supposition, the area of drainage required for the reservoirs would be 75,700 square miles instead of 90,000 square miles, and the above remarks as to the entire impracticability of the scheme would still apply with equal force.

* The following extracts are taken from Mr. Ellet's report:—

"I propose to convert this entire area into an artificial lake by forming a mound of earth or a stone dam across its outlet. This dam will be 68 feet high from the low-water surface of the river to the bottom of the waste for the discharge of the surplus water.

"The length of the mound will be 140 feet at bottom, where the banks of the river draw near together, and 875 feet at the surface of the lake, 68 feet above the river.

"The length of the lake thus formed will be 21.4 miles. It will cover an area of 10,800 acres, or 16.9 square miles. * * * * * * * * * * * * *

"This great basin will hold no less than 13,587,815,000 cubic feet of water. It will receive the drainage from 209.2 square miles of territory, the whole of which, exclusive of the meadows which will form the bottom of the lake, is composed of steep, and, to a considerable extent, very elevated mountains, from the slopes of which the rains and melted snows will descend rapidly into the reservoir."

accruing from such works would be commensurate with the expense of constructing them have not yet been collected. But the idea that the *Mississippi delta may be economically secured against inundation* by such dams has been conclusively proved by the operations of this Survey to be in the highest degree chimerical.

Outlets.—This plan consists in reducing the flood discharge by waste-weirs, and conveying the surplus water to the gulf by channels other than that of the main river. From its nature, it is only applicable below the Arkansas river.

Plan of outlets.

The advantages of this system have been stoutly contested by many writers, on the ground that reducing the discharge of the Mississippi will occasion deposits in its channel, and eventually elevate rather than depress the surface level of the river. In support of this opinion, they have urged, first, that actual measurements upon the river at certain crevasses prove that deposits are made when the velocity is thus checked; and, second, that theoretical reasoning indicates that such deposits ought to be anticipated.

Arguments adduced against this plan.

Certain operations of this Survey were conducted with especial reference to determining the effects of outlets, and they demonstrate, with a degree of certainty rarely to be attained in such investigations, that the opinions advanced by these writers are totally erroneous. Their various arguments will be answered in detail.

If actual measurements establish that crevasses—which, so far as they affect the river, are outlets under another name—do produce deposits in the channel below them, the injurious effects of the system are proved. That measurements do establish this fact has been repeatedly asserted, and appears to be generally believed.

Direct measurements do not show that deposits occur in the river channel below crevasses.

The direct evidence adduced in support of these assertions, so far as can be ascertained, consists solely of certain soundings made above and below two crevasses—the Fortier crevasse of 1849 and the Bonnet-Carré crevasse of 1850—*after they had ceased to flow.* Because, in each of these cases, the cross-section of the river proved to be smaller below than above the crevasse, it was *assumed* that the difference was due to deposit caused by the diminution of velocity which the crevasse occasioned. If these lines had been sounded before the crevasses occurred, and the cross-sections had been found to be equal; and if the operation had been repeated after the crevasses had ceased to flow, and the cross-sections had been found to differ as stated; then it would have been a legitimate inference that the change had been produced by the crevasses. As it is, no such inference can be drawn. It will be seen by a glance at Appendix C, that such differences in cross-section are *usually* found when several sections are made at short distances apart. Unless the soundings have been made previous to the occurrence of a crevasse, the only possible mode of demonstrating that it has occasioned a deposit in the bed of the river below it, is to prove both that a bar does exist below the crevasse when it is closed, and that this bar is washed out by succeeding floods. This has not been done in either of the above cases, as will be shown for each in turn.

What such measurements must show, in order to prove that deposits have occurred in consequence of the crevasse.

The Fortier crevasse occurred in April, 1849, on the right bank of the Mississippi,

They do not show this for the Fortier crevasse.

about 13.5 miles above New Orleans. In August, 1850, the engineers and surveyors accompanying the Senate Committee of Louisiana made twelve soundings on a line 400 feet below the site of the crevasse, and fifteen soundings on a line half a mile above the site, with a view to determine the area of cross-section on each of these lines. The degree of exactness which is claimed for these measurements is shown by the following extract from their report: "These [soundings] were taken with lead and line from the deck of the steamer, in crossing between the points indicated on shore. The distances apart of the soundings are as nearly equal as the depth would admit. To enable us to treat these soundings as equidistant, the committee have added ten per centum to the arithmetical mean depth as derived from the soundings. This mean depth was then added to the height of the adjacent adopted water mark, above the present surface, and the whole depth thus obtained multiplied into the high-water width, for the high-water sectional area. The result is presented only as an approximation, the best we could expeditiously obtain."

The "approximate" areas of high-water cross-section thus determined are 183,000 square feet below the crevasse, and 228,500 square feet above it—difference, 45,500 square feet. In October, 1851, Professor Forshey, then an assistant on this Survey, re-sounded the lower of these lines with greater exactness, and found the high-water area of cross-section to be 174,700 square feet, thus showing this area to be 8300 square feet *less* than the approximate area determined by the Senate Committee. This difference only serves to confirm the want of exactness in the first measurement, so freely admitted by the engineers.

So far, then, as any conclusions can be derived from these facts, they are that the bar was *not washed out by the succeeding floods of* 1850 *and* 1851, *and hence that it probably existed before the breaking of the crevasse.* The details of Professor Forshey's measurement having never before been published, the survey of this crevasse has been frequently adduced as proving that crevasses do occasion deposits in the bed of the river below them, whereas it evidently indicates directly the reverse.

They do not show this for the Bonnet-Carre crevasse, but directly the reverse.

The great Bonnet-Carré crevasse of 1850 occurred in December, 1849, on the left bank of the Mississippi, about 5 miles below Bonnet-Carré church. Subsequent to the date when it ceased to flow, soundings, the results of which are given in the following table, were made above and below its site by several engineers. Those of Professor Forshey in 1850 were made before his connection with the Delta Survey. At the time of his measurements the water stood 10 feet below high water of 1849. The exact area between that stage and high-water mark was only approximately determined, but subsequent measurements in the vicinity by parties of this Survey have shown that 30,500 and 31,800 square feet, respectively, should be added to his upper and lower sections, as sounded, to reduce them to high water of 1849. These numbers do not differ materially from those of his estimate, in which the increased width at high water was disregarded. Mr. Ellet's sections were made in February, 1851. His published high-water areas refer to "between banks." In order to compare them with the others, they have been brought to "between levees," by adding 1266 and 1567 square feet, respectively, to his upper and lower sections—numbers found by comparing his high-water widths "between banks" with those measured by this Survey "between levees." Mr. Smith's and Mr. Pattison's sections (see Appendix C) are reduced to high water of 1849, by applying the correction given in the table in Chapter II.

At the Bonnet-Carré crevasse of 1850.

Authority.	Date.	Above crevasse.		Below crevasse.	
		High-water area, 1849.	Number of soundings.	High-water area, 1849.	Number of soundings.
		Square feet.		*Square feet.*	
Professor Forshey	July, 1850	216,300	26	147,500	17
Mr. Ellet	Feb. 1851	200,000	17*	154,000	28*
Mr. G. C. Smith	June, 1851	207,400	23	167,000	20
Mr. Pattison	Feb. 1859	207,500	30	151,200	34
Mean—say		208,000		155,000	

These sections were made on nearly the same lines—just above and just below the site of the crevasse—but being made by different parties without the use of common station marks, their exact location must vary somewhat, and absolute accordance in resulting area is, therefore, not to be anticipated. This being understood, the evidence they furnish, that no sensible change has taken place in the channel of the river at those two localities since the date of the crevasse, is too strong to be resisted. The succeeding floods have not washed out this so-called bar. Hence the persistent assumption, that it was caused by the crevasse, is unfounded.

Moreover, the small cross-section below this crevasse was required by a general law of the river.

But this is not all. The so-called bar undoubtedly existed before that crevasse occurred. Indeed, by one acquainted with the locality, its existence might have been predicted before the soundings were made. The crevasse occurred just below a bend. The upper section is near enough for its area to be increased in accordance with the usual effect of bends; while the lower section, being about 7000 feet farther down the river, is in a straight portion, and, consequently, ought to be smaller. To illustrate this fact, reference is made to the map of Carrollton bend on figure 2, plate III. The two Bonnet-Carré section-lines are shown by the transit work of this Survey to be situated, with respect to the bend, almost precisely as sections 66 and 90 on this map. The area of section 66 is 214,000 square feet; that of section 90 is 185,500 square feet. The difference is 28,500 square feet, which is less than that existing between the two Bonnet-Carré sections, but still large enough to lead to the inference that those two sections were not equal in area.

It is therefore an error to suppose that measurements prove out-

It is therefore evident that, so far from indicating a deposit in the channel, the measurements made upon the Fortier and Bonnet Carré crevasses—the only measurements adduced—prove that no change of this kind occurred. The claim that *actual measurements* confirm the

* From plot in Topographical Bureau of the War Department.

lets to be disadvantageous to the river.

opinion that outlets must occasion deposits in the channel thus falls to the ground, and the theoretical reasoning alone remains to be considered.

Theoretical reasoning upon which this opinion is based.

The arguments in favor of the hypothesis can hardly be better stated than in the following extract from the writings of Major J. G. Barnard, Corps of Engineers, United States Army, one of the ablest of the engineers who have treated of the Mississippi river:* "It is pretty well established, that certain relations exist between the configuration of the bed of a stream and the velocity of its current. This relation is the most clearly discernible, and capable of being subjected to calculation, in rivers (like the lower Mississippi) whose beds have been formed of materials brought down by their own currents; in other words, which have *made and shaped their own beds.*

"I find this principle laid down in the work of Frisi 'On Rivers and Torrents,' which was placed in my hands by W. S. Campbell. He quotes and confirms the rules established by another engineer, Guglielmini, which are, that 'the greater the quantity of water a river carries, *the less will be its fall,*' and 'the greater the force of the stream, the less will be the slope of its bed.' And, again, 'the slope of the bottom in rivers will diminish in the same proportion in which the body of water is increased,' and *vice versâ.* These rules have their explanation in the facts, that the beds of rivers, of the character above mentioned, are capable of resisting, unchanged, only a certain velocity of current; and, on the other hand, that the sedimentary matter, contained in the river-water, requires a certain degree of velocity to keep it in suspension. From the counteracting tendencies of the above two causes, a mean becomes established, at which the current ceases to deposit its sediment, and the bottom ceases to be abraded; in other words, the bottom becomes permanent. But if, from any cause, such as throwing off a portion of the water through a waste-weir, the velocity of the current is diminished, it is no longer able to maintain its sediment in suspension, but will continue to deposit in its bed, until, through the elevation of the bed, its velocity again becomes, what it was before it was disturbed, sufficient to maintain its sediment in permanent suspension."

Two assumptions upon which this reasoning is based.

It will be noticed that two important assumptions are necessary to support this reasoning: First, *that the bottom of the Mississippi is composed of its own alluvion, which can be readily acted upon by the current;* and, second, that its water is *always charged with sediment to the maximum capacity allowed by its velocity.* The first of these assumptions seems to have been universally adopted, at least for the lower river. The second, while it has been adopted by some without due consideration, has been clearly perceived by others to be essential to the argument.

Thus Major Barnard proceeds to state: "Paradoxical as it may appear, then, it is a certain result of the foregoing principles, that, the more water we throw off by waste-weirs, *after we have passed that limit at which the velocity is just sufficient to keep the bed clear,* the higher will the surface ultimately become. What that limit is, I do not pretend to decide. If we assume that the present velocity is necessary for that purpose,

* De Bow's Review of the Southern and Southwestern States, August, 1850.

and that any diminution will cause a deposit in the bottom, then we cannot throw off a single cubic foot of the water now necessary to maintain this velocity, without causing an ultimate rise both in the bed and surface." *Upon this assumption*, he computes by Dubuat's formula the ultimate rise in the bed at Carrollton which would follow certain reductions of the high-water discharge.*

An extended series of measurements has been conducted with especial reference to testing the correctness of the two important assumptions upon which is based the conclusion that outlets will raise the mean level of the bed of the Mississippi. They have demonstrated both to be erroneous.

One has been already proved to be erroneous.

The character of the channel of the river has already received a full discussion in Chapter II. Here, it is sufficient to recall to mind that, throughout the whole distance from Cairo to Fort St. Philip, the true bed consists of a tenacious clay, which is unlike the alluvial soil, wears slowly under the strongest currents, and is proved, by conclusive evidence, to belong to a geological formation antecedent to the present. This disposes of the first assumption.

The second assumption—that the water is always charged to its maximum capacity with sediment.

We come, then, to the second assumption, viz.: that the water is at all times charged with sediment to the maximum capacity allowed by its velocity. If this be so, the amount of sediment at different stages must vary proportionally with the mean velocity.† To determine this question, an extended series of elaborate daily measurements was made. These experiments have been fully detailed in Chapter II. From the table there given, the mean number of grains troy in a cubic foot of water has been computed for each week during the continuance of the velocity measurements both at Carrollton and at Columbus. The corresponding mean velocities are taken from Appendix D. The following table exhibits the results which are represented on plates XII and XIII:—

* Although Major Barnard guarded himself so carefully against misconception, he has been misunderstood and quoted as deducing from his computations (supposing the values of the variables in the formula to be correctly assumed) that the ultimate effect of an outlet, of the dimensions of the Bonnet-Carré crevasse of 1850, would be an elevation of the bed of the Mississippi at Carrollton, amounting to 18.5 feet. Evidently he did not present this as *his opinion*, but as the result which would take place *supposing the water to be charged to its utmost capacity with sediment*, a question which he "did not pretend to decide."

† According to Dupuit's theory, the power of a river to hold sedimentary matter in suspension is proportional to the difference in the velocity of the consecutive filaments of the water. This, however, does not militate in the least against the above proposition, for, as has already been seen, this difference, depending upon the parameters of the curves of vertical and horizontal velocity, varies with a function of the mean velocity.

Weekly sediment and velocity of the Mississippi river.

Number of week.	Carrollton, 1851–2.		Columbus, 1858.		Number of week.	Carrollton, 1851–2.		Columbus, 1858.	
	Mean velocity of river.	Sediment per cubic foot of water.	Mean velocity of river.	Sediment per cubic foot of water.		Mean velocity of river.	Sediment per cubic foot of water.	Mean velocity of river.	Sediment per cubic foot of water.
	Feet.	*Grains.*	*Feet.*	*Grains.*		*Feet.*	*Grains.*	*Feet.*	*Grains.*
3d in February....	3.94	224			4th in August......	3.68	503	2.97	585
4th "	5.31	447			5th "	3.38	378	2.57	608
1st in March.......	5.70	432			1st in September..	3.16	345	2.28	216
2d "	5.96	321	5.08	313	2d " ...	2.93	301	2.34	232
3d "	6.16	252	7.18	272	3d " ...	2.44	268	2.31	193
4th "	5.91	197	7.02	268	4th " ...	1.95	193	1.91	197
1st in April.........	5.90	175	5.28	276	1st in October.....	1.65	135	1.67	160
2d "	5.68	149	5.85	370	2d "	1.70	120	1.58	125
3d "	5.58	143	7.37	468	3d "	1.65	95	1.56	61
4th "	5.53	201	7.53	295	4th "	1.72	68	1.59	138
1st in May	5.32	172	5.78	286	1st in November..	1.78	91	3.05	396
2d "	4.93	154	6.47	274	2d " ...	1.71	109	3.77	366
3d "	4.44	123	6.73	175	3d " ...	1.75	101		
4th "	4.01	103	7.08	284	4th " ...	1.56	108		
5th "	3.51	95	7.63	271	5th " ...	1.64	89		
1st in June.........	4.04	255	7.95	306	1st in December..	1.78	145		
2d "	4.26	346	8.27	320	2d " ...	1.92	166		
3d "	4.41	641	8.07	290	3d " ...	1.88	205		
4th "	4.31	392	6.22	363	4th " ...	2.00	148		
1st in July.........	4.51	322	4.35	569	1st in January....	2.14	134		
2d "	4.75	334	3.78	634	2d "	2.00	134		
3d "	4.76	395	4.22	651	3d "	2.45	374		
4th "	4.85	468	4.84	406	4th "	2.89	371		
1st in August......	4.71	436	4.09	243	5th "	2.25	140		
2d "	4.70	482	3.98	465	1st in February....	1.87	67		
3d "	4.05	430	3.50	485	2d "	2.25	71		

The measurements of this Survey prove this assumption to be entirely erroneous.

A glance at the two diagrams is sufficient to demonstrate the falsity of the assumption, that Mississippi water is always charged with sediment to the maximum capacity allowed by its velocity. At the date of highest water, both in 1851 and in 1858, the river held in suspension but little more sediment* per cubic foot than at dead low water, when the soundings of the Survey proved that the river made no deposit in its channel. Moreover, it will be seen, by referring to Chapter II, that an analysis of the distribution of the sedimentary matter held in suspension leads to the same conclusion by establishing that the river is never charged to its maximum capacity of suspension. Hence, if enough water had been taken from the river at the date of those floods to reduce its velocity nearly to that of the lowest stage, no deposit in the channel could have occurred. These observations demonstrate beyond question *that no practicable high-water outlet or waste-weir can occasion any filling of the channel by deposition of sedimentary matter held in suspension by the water.* The second assumption is, then, as untenable as the first.

The observations of the Survey, however, in establishing the fact that the current

* The proportion of sediment contained in the river at any given time depends upon the source from which the water is derived; whether from the great sediment-bearing tributaries, the Red, the Arkansas, and the Missouri, or from those comparatively clear, like the Upper Mississippi, the Ohio, the Yazoo, the White and the Black; for it will be seen that the dates of greatest proportion of sediment correspond to those of the rises in the former streams. The caving of the banks, which takes place chiefly while the river is falling, appears also to affect the amount sensibly.

is rolling along upon the bottom of the river a certain quantity of earthy matter, suggests a new subject of inquiry. May not an outlet so diminish the velocity of the river below it, as to cause an accumulation of this material, and thus partially fill up the channel? To decide this question, it is necessary first to form a definite idea of the retarding effect that will be produced upon the velocity at the bottom by any outlet likely to be made; and, second, to determine whether this reduction of velocity will cause an accumulation of the earthy matter.

They however suggest a new subject for inquiry.

The data necessary for the first part of the discussion have been obtained by measurements at the site of the great Bonnet-Carré crevasse of 1850, where it has often been proposed to form a permanent outlet. They appear in the preceding analysis of the flood of 1850, or in the tables on pages 366, 368, and 389. When the discharge at the crevasse was at its maximum, or 114,000 cubic feet per second (February–April), the river was 2 feet below the high water of 1849; and its area of cross-section was 202,000 square feet above, and 148,000 square feet below, the site of the break. The discharge above the crevasse was 1,100,000 cubic feet per second. The mean velocity of the river was then $\frac{1,100,000}{202,000} = 5.45$ feet per second above, and $\frac{986,000}{148,000} = 6.66$ below, the crevasse; the corresponding velocity at the bottom being (equation 31) 4.72 and 5.80 feet respectively.

Difference existing in the velocity above and below the Bonnet-Carre crevasse.

The prevalent error of supposing that the "bar" below this crevasse was occasioned by the accumulation of material, from any source, collected in consequence of a diminution of velocity, is thus exposed. *The velocity at the bottom immediately below the break was more than a foot per second greater than that above*, and the problem should rather be to ascertain why the bar was not washed away in the flood. Its composition furnishes the solution. The soundings of this Survey show that the bar is composed of the *hard blue clay* so often mentioned, which the Mississippi currents wear so slowly as seemingly to produce no effect, unless the surface is occasionally exposed to the air. To this natural ridge might with some plausibility be ascribed the *cause* of the crevasse, especially as a second break occurred at the same place in 1859.

Why the so-called bar was not washed away, the real problem.

Since this crevasse was situated above a natural contraction in the channel, it cannot be inferred, from the facts connected with it, that an outlet *may* not occasion a serious reduction of velocity below its site. Hence, to determine the effect of an outlet upon the *mean* river, the great Bell crevasse of 1858 (No. 45) will be considered, and the cross-section assumed to be equal above and below the break.

General investigation as to the actual retardation in velocity at the bottom caused by an outlet.

The amount by which the depression of the water surface, due to the crevasse, diminished the area of the river section is first to be determined. It is evident, since the slope is here at the rate of only about one inch per mile, that the depression of water surface just below the break must be sensibly equal to that just above. But the depression above can be exactly estimated by referring to the Carrollton curve on plate XIV, which shows that when the crevasse was discharging most (August 1–17), the river surface was 1.5 feet lower than when, in 1851, the river at a similar stage was discharging the same amount (990,000 cubic feet per second). This difference of 1.5 feet, then, measures the maximum effect produced upon the river surface by the Bell crevasse. Hence the high-water area (gauge 15.4) being say 185,000 square feet, and the width say 2500 feet, the actual area of cross-section on August 1–17 (mean gauge 12.8) was 185,000 — 2500 (15.4 — 12.8) = 178,500 square feet; while, if the break had not occurred, the area (gauge 14.3) would have been 185,000—2500 (15.4—14.3)=182,300 square feet. But the actual mean discharge per second below the break was 910,000, when, but for the break, it would have been 990,000 cubic feet. Hence the actual mean velocity below the break was $\frac{910,000}{178,500} = 5.10$ feet per second, when, but for the break, it would have been $\frac{990,000}{182,300} = 5.43$ feet per second. This gives for the mean bottom velocity (equation 31) 4.40 and 4.70 feet respectively; difference, 0.3 of a foot, or about six per cent. We may therefore infer that the actual reduction of velocity, to be apprehended from an outlet, is very slight.

So small a reduction of velocity will cause no accumulation of material rolling upon the bottom of the river.

We now come to the second division of the subject. Will such reduction of velocity cause a deposition of any part of the material moving along the bottom?

To this question it may be replied that even moderate winds often occasion much larger reductions of the bottom velocity; while local variations in the area of cross-section are everywhere effecting similar changes, some of which exceed a foot per second, or nearly twenty per cent. in amount. This fact in reality decides the question in the negative upon general considerations; for, if the river were always rolling along upon the bottom the maximum amount of earthy matter of which its velocity was capable, deposits would be made in the large sections; and the area of cross-section would thus become uniform throughout. Since actual observations prove that great variations in the cross-section exist everywhere, it is evident that the maximum transporting power of the current is not called into requisition; and hence that no accumulations are to be apprehended from so small reductions of velocity as will be occasioned by outlets,—which, after all, are only designed to reduce the river to its normal condition before levees were made. If measurements of the quantity of the material transported along the bottom had been practicable, as it was in the case of the sedimentary matter, this conclusion would doubtless have been confirmed by direct observations; for the quantity collected at any one time was always small.

Outlets are then of great utility, so far as the river is concerned; but they are virtually impracticable from the difficulty of disposing of the water.

The facts above cited establish that there is no evidence that any filling up of the bed ever did occur in consequence of a high-water outlet; and, moreover, that it is impossible that it ever should occur, either from the deposition of sedimentary matter held in suspension, or from the accumulation of material drifting along the bottom. The conclusion is then inevitable, that *so far as the river itself is concerned, they are of great utility*. Few practical problems admit of so positive a solution. Unfortunately, however, *the relief of the river itself is only half of the difficulty*. The water taken from it still remains to be disposed of. Crevasses solve the problem by discharging this water into the swamps. The natural drains there, however, are insufficient, and the backwater gradually rises until the plantations upon the river banks are submerged, and ruin is thus spread far and wide. *A channel to conduct the water to the gulf must then be prepared.* Here lies the great practical difficulty which renders the system of comparatively little avail for protecting Louisiana against overflow. This will be apparent when an attempt is made to select an advantageous location for the works.

An outlet between the Arkansas and Red rivers possibly advantageous to a limited district.

As already intimated, no outlet is possible above the Arkansas river. Between that stream and the Yazoo river, where the difficulty of restraining the floods is greater than in any other part of the alluvial region, it is probable that a useful purpose may be served by drawing off a part of the surplus water and discharging it into bayou Tensas. This plan, which will be fully discussed in the next division of this chapter, would evidently be of no service to the region below Red-river landing; since the water taken from the Mississippi would pass through the Red-river channel to bayou Atchafalaya, and exclude a corresponding amount of Mississippi water which otherwise would enter through Old river. The plan is, therefore, purely local, and of no possible utility to lower Louisiana.

No artificial outlets practicable on the right bank below Red river.

Below Red-river landing, on the right bank, three natural outlets—bayous Atchafalaya, Plaquemine, and La Fourche—already exist; and, owing to the character of the delta, new outlets cannot be opened on that bank at a sufficient distance from the gulf to be of practical utility. The cost of so enlarging the channels of the three bayous as to enable them to carry off a volume sufficiently large to depress the floods materially, would be so great that the project is virtually impracticable.

On the left bank three localities have been suggested.

On the left bank, three localities have been suggested as peculiarly advantageous sites for outlets.

Old bayou Manchac.

The first is the old channel of bayou Manchac, a former outlet to the Amite river, and thence to lake Pontchartrain. Its dimensions were always insignificant. Du Pratz, writing about a century ago, calls it a "*chenal*," or natural canal. The following extracts from the report of Mr. A. D. Wooldridge, State Engineer, submitted to the Senate of Louisiana in 1852, demonstrate the disadvantages of reopening this bayou:—

"The bayou Manchac is the first of the natural outlets of the Mississippi on its eastern side, and is situated at the distance of fourteen miles from the *terminus* of the high lands below Baton Rouge. In periods of high water, it formerly connected the Mississippi with the gulf of Mexico by way of the Amite, lake Maurepas, and lake Pontchartrain. The distance from the head of the bayou, by its meanderings, to the Amite, is about 22 miles, and the whole distance of the water communication with lake Borgne is about 100. During the last war with England it was greatly obstructed to prevent the British from reaching the interior by that route, and in 1826 it was closed by a substantial dike to prevent its water from overflowing the settlements upon its banks and in its vicinity.

"In descending the bayou, its first tributary is the bayou Crocodile, on its southern bank, which drains Spanish lake and its inlets into the Manchac. The junction is 9 miles from its head. About half a mile below, it receives the bayou Fountaine on its northern bank, and a few miles below, Ward's creek on the same side.

"At its head, it is about 90 feet by a depth of 12, and its elevation above the lowest water of the Mississippi, 20 feet, the greatest rise of the river here being 32 feet. Consequently, it is necessary for the river to be 20 feet above low water before its waters can escape by the bayou. From its head to its junction with bayou Crocodile, it is usually a dry bayou and very tortuous in its course. It diminishes very rapidly in size as you descend from the river, and at a distance but little over a mile from its source, it has only a width of 44 feet from bank to bank, a depth of 10 feet, and a width at bottom of 15 feet. It is but little larger than at this point till it reaches the Crocodile. Below its junction with the Crocodile and Fountaine, it is 100 feet wide by a depth of 15, at the water surface being 70 feet. This may be considered as the very highest point of navigation in its present condition. The banks of the bayou are very low nearly all the way on its southern bank from its source to the Crocodile, and on the north to the bayou Fountaine. From these points to the Amite there is tolerably high land on both sides. The overflow for some miles, in case of crevasses, above the Crocodile and Fountaine, is from 8 to 15 feet.

"By taking cross-sections at the end of every mile from the head to the Crocodile, it is found that the average channel of discharge is 300 feet."

* * * * * * * * *

"As a depleting outlet, therefore, of the river, the bayou Manchac is utterly insignificant, and as its bed is composed of a close, stiff clay, it is unreasonable to suppose its importance would ever be materially augmented."

* * * * * * * * *

"If the bayou were opened, as an inevitable consequence, a large portion of the parishes of Ascension and Baton Rouge would be overflowed. Several hundred thousand acres of land, much of it highly improved, would have to be abandoned. The losses would have to be counted by millions of dollars. Suppose this could be prevented by leveeing the banks of the bayou, still the expense would be very great. Levees would have to be built of miles in length, from 12 to 15 feet in height to sustain the backwater from the Amite, as well as that coming down from the Mississippi. But, even with this, the country could not be protected."

* * * * * * * * *

"In view of the calamities that would be inflicted upon a worthy people, who have settled and improved, in good faith, and without expectation of change in the State policy, an important and fertile portion of the State, if the bayou were simply opened without steps being taken for their security, and of the vast cost of protecting them, and of its insignificance as an outlet of the river, I would respectfully recommend that the bayou Manchac be permitted to remain in its present condition.

"Circumstances of a peculiar character, in the early history of our State, gave an undue importance to the bayou Manchac or the famous river Iberville, and this importance has been awarded to it to the present day, probably from the fact of its being closed up from observation. Its ancient fame and reputation abroad soon vanish when it is seen."

Proposed outlet in Bonnet-Carre bend.

The next locality on the left bank suggested for an outlet is at the site of the great crevasses of 1850 and 1859, in the bend below Bonnet-Carré church. The distance between the bank of the Mississippi and lake Pontchartrain is here only 6 miles. The fall in water surface between the river and the mean level of the lake is at high water (1851) 19.6 feet. There can therefore be no doubt that by making two levees from the river to the lake and cutting the Mississippi levee between them, a high-water outlet of any dimensions can be made. Such an outlet would be of utility in reducing the height of floods for many miles above and below, but its construction would be followed by consequences disastrous to Louisiana. The following discussion of the subject will show that the works must be difficult and costly; that the navigation of the lake will be rapidly destroyed; and that there is danger that eventually the outlet will become a main branch of the river, and the navigation at the present mouths be thus seriously impaired.

Extent and costly character of the work.

With reference to the extent and cost of the works, it is apparent that a channel must be prepared for the outlet entirely through the swamp to the lake, so as to give a free discharge to its waters; for, if they were merely conducted to the swamp, the thick growth would so impede their flow that enormous levees would be required for many miles above and below the outlet, in order to protect the rear of the plantations from overflow.

The first question that presents itself is the discharging capacity that should be given to the outlet. To reduce the maximum discharge of the flood of 1858 to that of 1851 would require the abstraction from the river of 150,000 cubic feet per second. Applying the new formulæ to the data already given, the computed width of an outlet of that capacity would be 9000 feet, and the mean velocity about 3 feet per second. This discharge would raise the surface of the lake 2.0 feet,* and in this condition the occurrence of storms—the effect of which is shown in Chapter II—would flood the rear of plantations, which at the edge of the swamp are now but 1 or 2 feet above the lake. Levees must therefore be built along the edge of the swamp. Thus an outlet of a capacity only sufficient to reduce the flood of 1858 to that of 1851 must occasion large expenditures for levees both to form its channel and to prevent the lake from partially overflowing cultivated land.

But the flood of 1851 caused several crevasses; and the discharge of the river must be reduced still more, if outlets are to be relied upon as a sure means of protection. When we consider the cost of opening, to lake Pontchartrain, a stream a mile and a half in width, and the great inconveniences which would result, we must conclude that the outlet should be of a capacity sufficient to reduce to almost nothing the yearly expense of maintaining the river levees along the extent to be protected by the outlet; that is, in such a flood as that of 1858 it should depress the surface of the river at all points below it to the mean level of the banks, or to 3.3 feet below the flood of 1851. (See page 164.) The reduction of discharge necessary to this depression of the river surface is 300,000 cubic feet per second, and that must be the capacity of the out-

* The reading of the mean level of the lake during February, March, April, May, and June, 1850, while it received the discharge of the Bonnet-Carré crevasse, was 9.7 feet. The river began to fall rapidly about July 1, and by the middle of that month no longer discharged through the crevasse. The mean reading of the lake gauge during July, August, and September (the only months of the remaining part of the year of which there are records) was 8.0 feet. The reading of the mean level of the lake during February, March, April, May, and June, 1851, the season of the year during which, in 1850, the lake was elevated by the crevasse, was 8.0 feet. These facts show conclusively that the mean discharge through the Bonnet-Carré crevasse (105,000 cubic feet per second) elevated the level of the lake 1.7 feet. By a comparison with the mean yearly level of the lake, the same result is obtained. The greatest discharge of the crevasse into the lake was during February, the mean level then reading 10.2 feet. Thus the greatest elevation of the lake by the Bonnet-Carré crevasse was 2.2 feet.

let. By the formulæ and data before mentioned, its width would be 18,400 feet and its mean velocity 3.0 feet per second. In order to determine accurately how much such a discharge would raise the surface of the lake, the elevation of the shores, over which it would empty into the gulf, must be known. This information has not been collected, nor is it essential to the general discussion of the subject. It has been assumed to be 4 feet in the outlet mouth.

Would the outlet retain its primitive dimensions?

The next question is whether this outlet would be closed by its own depositions and the rapid growth upon it of willows, cottonwood, etc., such as usually springs up upon the alluvial depositions after the subsidence of a flood; or whether it would excavate its bed; and if the latter, to what extent.

It would not close itself.

Wherever there was a continued current inside the levees from the Bonnet-Carré crevasse of 1850, there was no deposit and no growth whatever. There is, therefore, no reason to anticipate that there would be any in the bed of the outlet. The cessation of the flow of water through it would be sudden, and the current would be of nearly equal rapidity as long as there was any discharge. It would be fortunate if a growth of willows did spring up every year in the channel-way; for the annual cutting of such a growth would cost comparatively little, and the stubble and roots would protect the bed from the wearing which is to be apprehended. By referring to Chapter VII, it will be seen that a stream situated like this would not be closed by the bar which would form around its mouth. It does not appear probable, then, that the outlet would be closed from any natural cause. We have next to see whether it would not excavate its bed.

It would excavate its bed.

From all the information collected, it appears that on the bank of the river in this vicinity the soil, to the depth of the mean level of the gulf, is composed of alluvial deposit, and that pure clay is met with for the first time at about that depth. At what depth it will be encountered on the lake shore is not positively ascertained. In the low ground, west of the river, it is found in some places at or near the level of the gulf, in others several feet below the gulf. Mr. Bayley, formerly State Engineer, who is familiar with all parts of the alluvial region of Louisiana, states that in the swamps on the east side of the river the first bed of clay lies at a much greater depth than on the west side. It will, therefore, be assumed that on the lake shore it will be met with at the mean depth of the lake (13 feet), since the bottom of the lake is chiefly clay. Now, although the alluvial surface soil along the river has considerable tenacity, yet it is unable to resist a current of 3 feet per second, a velocity which the currents that began to wear the Plaquemine efflux could not have exceeded. The bed of the outlet would therefore be cut down to the clay stratum, and the outlet would become an immense bayou or branch of the river, and, like the Atchafalaya, the Plaquemine, and the La Fourche, would advance a delta regularly into the receptacle of its discharge. That discharge would become enormous; indeed, the outlet would be the main river at high water, even if the deepening should cease at the first bed of clay. The injurious consequences that would follow from the discharge into lake Pontchartrain, of an outlet having the original capacity of that described (300,000 cubic feet per second), would of course be aggravated in proportion to the increase of that volume. One of two courses must therefore be adopted; either the bed of the outlet must be protected against the wearing of the current, at an immense cost, or the outlet must be made originally of such dimensions that, when the current has excavated the bed to the clay stratum, the maximum discharging capacity shall be equal to 300,000 cubic feet per second. A proposition to protect the bed of the outlet no one will seriously consider. The consequences flowing from the second proposition must be traced to their end.

Dangers of permitting this to occur.

An outlet to discharge 300,000 cubic feet per second, when excavated to the clay bed, must be 3200 feet wide. Its original maximum discharge would then be 56,000 cubic feet per second, and its velocity 3.2 feet per second. When the clay bed is reached, the mean flood velocity would be 5.5 feet per second; the mean annual velocity 3.8 feet per second. The thickness of that first stratum of clay is not known. Before undertaking the construction of the outlet, the nature of the strata forming the channel of the river in that locality, and those underlying to a considerable depth the proposed bed of the outlet, should be carefully ascertained by boring. In Chapter II, on page 101, under the head of geology of the banks of the river, the character of the various strata pierced in the boring of the Artesian well at New Orleans, to the depth of 580 feet below the surface of the gulf, is given. At the level of the gulf, a clay stratum begins, which is 19 feet thick. It is followed in the next 20 feet by various strata of little coherence. At that depth the marine strata begin, or those belonging to an earlier geological age than the present, or at least to a period before the material, brought down by the Mississippi river as now existing, began to accumulate in this locality. For the next 71 feet these strata consist chiefly of different kinds of sand, separated by thin layers of clay or compacted shells, the thickest of which is 6 feet in thickness. At this depth, 110 feet below the gulf level, a yellow-clay bed 34 feet thick begins, followed in the next 50 feet by alternate strata of sand and clay, the thickest of the latter being 9 feet through. At the end of this series, 194 feet below the gulf, a blue-clay bed 32 feet thick is found, followed by one of sand 23 feet thick, which is succeeded by another clay bed 39 feet thick, and so on. The strata at the site of the proposed outlet are undoubtedly of the same general character as these, although probably not precisely of the same thickness. The bottom of the Mississippi is always found in one of those thick beds of clay. When it has worn through one, it at once passes through the layers of sand to the next clay bed. What length of time would elapse before the outlet would wear through the first stratum of clay, which may be supposed to be 18 or 20 feet thick, of course cannot be predicted; but that, with its great annual velocity and volume, it would finally, though doubtless at a remote day, wear through that stratum and greatly deepen its channel, and thus become permanently a low-water as well as high-water branch of the Mississippi, seems to be probable. The consequent reduction of volume in the main river would lessen the depths upon the bars at its mouths, besides impairing the navigability. Constant examination would therefore be required to ascertain whether such changes were taking place, which, if detected, could be arrested only by closing the outlet.

These views are not speculative. There are well-authenticated instances of the Po and the Rhine, under circumstances somewhat similar to those attending the existence of the supposed outlet, having opened new channels to the sea, which are now either the main stream or principal branches of the rivers.*

* *Changes in the Po.*—The researches of the Chevalier Elia Lombardini, Director-General of Public Works in Lombardy [Hydraulic system of the Po, etc., etc., Milan, 1840 and 1852] establish that, previous to the year 1150, the Po ran in a single stem to Ferrara (plate XIX), where it was divided into two branches—the Po di Volano and the Po di Primaro—the mean distance to the sea from this point being 54 miles. In 1150 a crevasse occurred on the left bank of the Po at Ficarolo, near Stellata, 16 miles above Ferrara, the discharge through which was carried to the lagoon of Adria by a natural depression. Thus a new branch of the Po was formed, called the River of the Ficarolo crevasse, which finally became the sole channel, and is now known as the Po di Grande. [It has been supposed that this depression was a former bed of the Po, but this opinion is inconsistent with the authorities quoted by Lombardini.] The increase of the Po di Grande or Venetian Po was gradual. Before 1600 it had become the chief branch, and about that time the Ferrara branch was closed by dikes. In a short time after the crevasse at Ficarolo, the Po di Grande filled up the lagoon of Adria, and advanced beyond the *cordon littoral* into the sea, having a length from Stellata to its mouth of 51 miles. In 1604 it had advanced nearly 7 miles farther into the sea, and the mouths being directed toward the entrances of the lagoon of Venice, it was feared that their navigation would be impaired by the depositions of the Po. For this reason, its course was turned from that direction by a cut, which shortened the course to the sea. At the present time, the distance from Stellata to the two principal mouths of the Po is 64 miles, which is less than it was in 1150, when it reached the sea through the two branches of Volano and Primaro. Other instances of the formation of new branches of the Po by cuts and crevasses are cited, and similar changes in the Adige are related.

Changes in the Rhine.—The Rhine [Leçons de Géologie Pratique, par L. Elie de Beaumont; Paris, 1845] in the time of Cæsar had two branches (plate XIX); the right, called the Rhine, emptying into the sea at or near Katwyk, with a length of 96 miles; the left, the Waal, the larger of the two, which, after a course of about 70 miles, joined its estuary at a distance of 30 or 40 miles from the sea. The Yssel was then a small stream rising in the sand and gravel hills of Holland, and running parallel to the Rhine for the space of 20 or 30 miles above the point of bifurcation of that river. At the distance of about 6 miles below that point, the Yssel turned at right angles to the Rhine, and, running between two ranges of sand and gravel hills, emptied into Lake Flevo, now the Zuyder Zee. The ground where this change of direction took place was low; the distance between the two streams about 8 or 10 miles. The Romans then occupied Holland (Batavia), and at the beginning of the Christian era, Drusus connected the Rhine and Yssel by a cut in the locality just described. The increased volume of water thus introduced greatly enlarged the channel of the Yssel, which after a time became a principal branch of the Rhine. Its length to the Zuyder Zee was and is about 70 miles. Thirty miles below the point of separation of the Yssel, on the right bank of the Rhine, near the foot of the last line of sand-hills, was a Roman camp. The opposite bank was low and defended from the overflows of the river by a heavy dike, built by the Romans. The surface of both banks is at present composed of alluvial deposit. In the first century, the Batavians, retreating before the Romans, cut this dike, the river being at flood. The crevasse thus made finally became the arm of the Rhine known as the Leck. The length to its estuary was probably at that time what it is now, about 40 miles. The estuary is at the present time about 23 miles long. The corresponding length of the Old Rhine was and is about 70 miles.

The Waal branch carries off two-thirds of the volume of the main stem. This distribution of the waters is carefully preserved. The banks are revetted and each year soundings are made to ascertain whether any changes have taken place. Of the remaining one-third which passes down the Rhine branch, the Yssel carries off one-third, and the remainder goes to the sea by the Leck, the old Rhine having been entirely closed by dikes.

Changes in the Vistula.—[M. Spittel, Engineer in Charge of the Works for the division of the Vistula.—Pamphlet of M. J. W. Pfeffer, Inspector of Harbor Improvements, upon the hydrographic relations of the Vistula and the Nogat. Dantzic, 1849.] The Vistula divides into two branches (plate XIX) at Montauer Spitze (Montau Point). The right, called the Nogat, after a course of 30 miles empties into the Frische Haff, an arm of the Baltic sea. Previous to 1840, the left branch, called the Vistula, upon which Dantzic is situated, emptied into the Baltic at a distance of 45 miles from Montauer Spitze, sending off a small sub-branch, called Elbing-Vistula, to the Frische Haff at a point 18 miles above the mouth in the Baltic. In 1840, the ice brought down by a January flood gorged at a point about 9 miles from the mouth of the Vistula and cut a channel through the sand-hills to the sea. This is now the mouth of the Vistula, that passing Dantzic having been closed by a dike.

The area between the Vistula and the Nogat is protected against floods by levees from 20 to 25 feet high.

The Nogat was not originally a branch of the Vistula, but a small river, holding relations and position toward the Vistula similar to those of the old Yssel to the Rhine. A communication between the two existed during the floods of the Vistula at a point a few miles below the locality now called Montauer Spitze. A dense oak forest protected the Nogat from the floating ice of the Vistula, and prevented the complete union of the two streams. To improve the low-water navigation of the Nogat, the half-formed channel between them was perfected in 1552, and the oak forest in the vicinity was cut away. This uniting channel, however, soon began to enlarge, and the floating ice,

But another important change, the filling of lake Pontchartrain, would certainly follow upon the opening of a great outlet at this site. Supposing the wide outlet to be used with a protected bed, the mean annual duration of its discharge would be about equal to the mean number of days the river is above the natural bank at Carrollton, that is, one hundred and twenty-seven days. Its mean discharge during that time would be 154,000 cubic feet per second, and the volume of sedimentary matter carried from the river would cover a square mile to a depth of 21 feet. (See Chapter II.) The lake has an area of 600 square miles, and a mean depth of 13 feet. According to these data, the outlet would, in three hundred and seventy-five years, discharge into lake Pontchartrain earthy matter sufficient to fill it. It is true that this earthy matter would not all be deposited in the lake, but a large portion of it would be.

Serious injury which must follow the opening of any great outlet at this site.

Supposing that the outlet 3200 feet wide were used and its bed were allowed to reach the first clay stratum, near the level of the gulf; its mean discharge during the year being 128,000 cubic feet per second, the volume of earthy matter annually carried by it from the river would cover a square mile to a depth of 50 feet, and in one hundred and fifty-six years would be sufficient to fill lake Pontchartrain. The navigation of the lake would be obstructed long before the termination of these periods. With such indications as these before us, it is unnecessary to attempt to follow the precise progress of the mouth or mouths of the outlet through the lake.

If the project were tried by the conditions existing at the only other locality where it has been proposed to apply it, similar results would be found to attend its execution. This locality is where the Mississippi most nearly approaches lake Borgne—about 11 miles below New Orleans. The distance from the stream to the lake is about 5.5 miles. The fall of the ground from the bank of the river to the edge of the swamp (a distance of about 3000 feet) is 8 feet. From that point to the lake, the country is nearly flat, being for 2.5 miles a dense swamp, and for the rest of the distance a prairie or marsh, liable to be overflowed by the lake when the gulf is unusually high. The fall between the river surface at high water and the mean level of the lake is 13 feet. The velocity of the current would undoubtedly be sufficient to open the channel to the first clay bed at whatever depth that might be found. The area of lake Borgne being about one-third that of lake Pontchartrain, and the mean depth about the same, it would be filled in a proportionately shorter time; and at the end of that period the entrance to lake Pontchartrain would be nearly closed, as

Proposed outlet to lake Borgne.

---

which now passed into the Nogat, gorged at the narrow places (the river being very irregular in width), and caused disastrous crevasses. Attempts were soon made to arrest the enlargement of the channel, and for three centuries the proper division of the discharge of the main stream between the two branches has entailed great labor and expense. In 1840 the point of separation was from 2 to 3 miles above the original site. The opening of the Nogat branch, being deeper than the Vistula branch and more nearly in the direction of the upper river, carried off two-thirds of the volume in low water, and a constantly increasing quantity during floods, though less at such periods than the Vistula branch. Too large a proportion of floating ice also passed down the Nogat. To remedy these evils, and apportion the flow of water in each branch so that at all times the Vistula branch should carry off two-thirds of the whole river, and the Nogat one-third, immense works were begun in 1848. In 1853 the Nogat was closed at Montauer Spitze, and a new bed prepared for it some 2 or 3 miles below, at the site of the channel excavated in 1552. Some idea of the magnitude of the works may be formed from their cost, 2,000,000 Prussian dollars. The cost of similar works in this country would be at least the same number of American dollars.

the channel from it to the gulf would be merely sufficient for the discharge of its drainage. If outlets are to be used, however, this is the locality for their trial, since the results would be less injurious here than at lake Pontchartrain.

Outlets are not advisable.

Enough has been said to demonstrate, with all the certainty of which the subject is capable, the disastrous consequences that must follow the resort to this means of protection.

This most important measure of protection, to be treated under two headings—its extent and its possible dangers.

Levees.—In Chapter II, a brief account has been given of the progress and of the present condition of the artificial embankments or levees now in use for protecting the alluvial region of the Mississippi valley from overflow. It is there shown that the system is far from complete; and that it has never yet been fully tested, inasmuch as crevasses have always relieved the river of large volumes of water in the great flood years, and have thus materially reduced the high-water level. Great practical good, however, has resulted even from the imperfect application of the system; for without it the greater part of the alluvial region below the mouth of the Ohio would be an uninhabitable swamp in the high-water months of the year. There is no doubt that the plan will continue to be universally practised throughout the valley to the almost entire exclusion of all others, and it is therefore entitled to a most careful and thorough analysis. This includes: First, a discussion of the extent to which the system must be carried in order to afford present protection against river floods to all the alluvial region below Cape Girardeau; and, second, a discussion of the dangers which may ultimately arise from confining the flood waters to the channel of the river. These divisions of the subject will be treated in turn.

Plan for determining the extent necessary to be given to the system in order to insure protection.

1. To judge of the extent to which the levee system must be carried in order to afford present protection to the valley, it is only necessary to determine the amount by which the high-water level of the river would have been raised, had the water been confined to its channel in 1858; because, as already proved, the maximum discharge under such conditions would probably never have been greater than in this flood. The table on page 351 exhibits the amount by which the maximum discharge at several nearly equidistant points of the river would have been increased, had no water escaped into the swamp lands below Cape Girardeau. In Appendix C, the dimensions of cross-section at these localities are given, and on page 109 will be found the corresponding range of oscillation between high-water and low-water mark. These data, together with the gauge-records in Appendix B, and the table of discharges on page 340, render it easy, in accordance with the principles laid down in Chapter V, to determine exactly how much higher the water would have risen at each of these localities, had the increased volumes, indicated in the table on page 351, been confined to the channel of the river.

Values deduced for $\frac{1}{2P}$ at the several localities.

The first step in the computation is to deduce the numerical values of $\frac{1}{2P}$ for the several localities. This has been done precisely as described in the last chapter, and no explanations are needed except in the case of Memphis. At this city, as no discharge measurements were made by the Survey, and as the method of transferring the measured discharge from Columbus or Vicksburg could not be applied, owing to the general breaking of the levees of the St. Francis bottom, it became necessary to make use of the observations conducted by Lieutenant Marr, U. S. N., under direction of the Secretary of the Navy (Bureau of Ordnance and Hydrography) in 1850–51. An account of these operations has been given in Chapter III. The surface velocity only was measured, and Lieutenant Marr deducted one-tenth to correct for supposed retardation below. It has been already seen that the velocity at the surface is sometimes greater and sometimes less than the mean of all the velocities in the same vertical plane parallel to the current, but that it never differs materially from this quantity. The reduction by Lieutenant Marr, therefore, was erroneous, and it has been corrected by adding one-ninth to the discharge as computed by him. When the measurements, thus corrected, are plotted in a manner similar to that shown on plates XII to XVII, it is manifest from the serrated form of the curves that the observations were less exact than those conducted by this Survey; as indeed must have been the case from the comparatively rough manner of operating. By drawing a smooth line through the serrated parts of the curve, however, it is easy to correct approximately for these errors, and thus to derive tolerable data for determining the numerical value of $\frac{1}{2\,\mathrm{P}}$ at Memphis. The following table exhibits such data, together with those derived from the observations of this Survey for the other localities under consideration. The degree of exactness of the several values deduced for $\frac{1}{2\,\mathrm{P}}$ is shown by the last columns of this table.

Values of $\frac{1}{2\,\mathrm{P}}$ at various localities.

Locality.	Date.	$e_{\prime}$	$a_{\prime}$	$\mathrm{W}_{\prime}$	$p_{\prime}$	$\mathrm{Q}_{\prime}$	$\mathrm{Q}_{\prime\prime} - \mathrm{Q}_{\prime}$	Deduced $\frac{1}{2\,\mathrm{P}}$	Value of x		Difference.
									Observed	Computed	
		Feet.	*Sq. feet.*	*Feet.*	*Feet.*	*Cubic feet.*	*Cubic feet.*		*Feet.*	*Feet.*	*Feet.*
Columbus*								0.0000000150			
Memphis	April 4 to April 18, 1850	36.2	173,150	3160	3185	950,000	−350,000	0.0000000160	11.2	10.7	+0.5
"	April 18 to April 30, "	25.0	138,400	2875	2900	600,000	+400,000	"	10.9	10.1	+0.8
"	Nov. 26 to Dec. 18, "	7.5	88,500	2695	2715	200,000	+370,000	"	15.7	15.3	+0.4
"	Feb. 8 to Feb. 28, 1851	8.3	90,680	2700	2720	220,000	+930,000	"	26.9	27.4	−0.5
Helena	Feb. 26 to May 3, 1858	23.7	111,000	3980	3995	450,000	+627,000	0.0000000020	19.8	20.2	−0.4
"	April 27 to May 3, "	42.5	187,440	4080	4115	1,041,000	+ 36,000	"	1.0	1.0	0.0
Napoleon	April 17 to May 8, "	39.1	192,970	3220	3288	1,031,000	+103,000	0.0000000000	4.6	4.0	+0.6
"	May 13 to June 16, "	43.4	206,820	3220	3297	1,149,000	+ 40,000	"	1.5	1.5	0.0
Lake Providence	Feb. 24 to April 8, "	28.5	146,130	3540	3620	685,000	+410,000	0.0000000000	15.5	18.0	−2.5
"	April 17 to April 30, "	41.0	191,260	3580	3654	1,037,000	+ 63,000	"	2.5	2.2	+0.3
Vicksburg*								0.0000000120			
Natchez	March 25 to March 31 "	41.7	182,510	4540	4570	939,000	+152,000	0.00000000006	4.3	4.2	+0.1
"	Aug. 6 to Aug. 17, "	49.0	215,650	4540	4585	1,101,000	−183,000	"	5.1	5.2	−0.1
Red-river landing	March 22 to April 28, "	32.8	202,690	3616	3634	909,000	+294,000	0.0000000020	9.0	8.9	+0.1
"	Aug. 15 to Aug. 24, "	40.0	227,340	3616	3647	993,000	−114,000	"	3.6	3.6	0.0
Baton Rouge	Feb. 24 to March 16, 1851	26.8	170,000	2800	2810	940,000	+256,000	0.0000000190	5.9	5.8	+0.1
"	April 21 to May 12, "	32.9	187,080	2800	2822	1,075,000	−218,000	"	5.0	5.6	−0.6
Donaldsonville	Feb. 24 to March 15, "	20.8	180,780	3100	3118	914,000	+233,000	0.0000000300	4.9	4.8	+0.1
"	April 20 to May 12, "	25.7	195,970	3100	3127	1,031,000	−195,000	"	4.0	4.2	−0.2
Carrollton*								0.0000001500			

The next and final step is the practical application of the formulæ to the great problem—how much higher the flood of 1858 would have risen at these several localities, had the river been securely leveed. The method of computation is, obviously, to adopt for the primitive stand of the river at each locality the conditions existing there on the day of maximum

Outline of the computation for all but exceptional localities.

* See table on page 329.

discharge; and to compute, by the process explained in Chapter V, the value of x corresponding to the maximum discharge which would have occurred, had no water escaped from the river. These values of x denote the exact increase of height to which the flood would have attained at the several localities; inasmuch as any observed increase of height, subsequent to the day of actual maximum discharge, would doubtless have also occurred with a perfected condition of the levees. For Columbus, Napoleon, Vicksburg, Natchez, Red-river landing, and Baton Rouge, the application of this process requires no especial explanation. For the other localities the computations are more involved, and will therefore be noticed separately.

The computation for Memphis.

At Memphis, as already explained, the daily discharge during the flood of 1858 could not be deduced from the operations conducted either at Columbus or at Vicksburg. The actual maximum discharge at this locality, therefore, could not be determined. It is necessary, then, in order to solve the problem, to select, for the primitive stage, that existing at some other date, when the discharge and dimensions of cross-section are known. This selection may be made from the observations both of Lieutenant Marr and of this Survey. Thus Lieutenant Marr's measurements fix the values of these quantities on April 18, 1850; and the table just given establishes that the formulæ accord well with the rise actually observed at this period, due to a measured increase of 400,000 cubic feet per second in the discharge. Applying the formulæ then to this case, we find that if the discharge at the top of the rise had been 1,380,000 cubic feet per second (the maximum discharge with perfected levees) instead of 1,000,000, the rise would have been 17.0 instead of 10.1 feet. But on April 18, 1850, the river stood 12.1 feet below the actual high-water level attained in 1858. Hence a discharge of 1,380,000 cubic feet per second would raise the river $17.0 - 12.1 = 4.9$ feet above the high water of 1858. Adding 0.3 of a foot for the usual rise after the discharge begins to diminish, we have 5.2 feet for the computed increase in height of the flood of 1858, had the levee system been perfected. Again, as already stated, the computation may be based upon the Columbus measurements of 1858. By reference to plate XIII, it will be seen that about May 17, 1858, the discharge at Columbus underwent but very slight variations for several days, and that, in consequence, the stand of the river both at Columbus and Memphis remained nearly constant, and at too low a level to allow of any escape of water into the swamps. It may, then, be assumed that the discharge at Memphis on May 19, 1858, was the same as at Columbus, or about 1,010,000 cubic feet per second. The dimensions of cross-section at this date are known from the gauge-reading and Lieutenant Marr's tables. Applying the formulæ to this condition of the river we find that if the discharge had been increased to 1,380,000 cubic feet per second, the river would have risen 7.9 feet. But on May 19 the river was 2.9 feet below high water of 1858. For the rise above the latter level, then, we have $7.9 - 2.9 = 5.0$ feet. Adding the 0.3 of a foot, we have 5.3 feet for the computed height which the flood would have attained above the actual high-water level of 1858, had no water escaped to the swamps. This result, it will be noticed, differs only 0.1 of a foot from that deduced from Lieutenant Marr's data. So very close an agreement is doubtless accidental; but it is evident that no serious error can exist in the determination.

This result is confirmed by an analysis of an entirely different character. No tri-

Result checked by another totally different method.

butary worthy of the name enters the Mississippi between Columbus and Memphis (Hatchee river having a high-water section of only 8000 square feet; see Appendix C). When the river is below the level of the natural banks, then, the water which passes Memphis is sensibly the same as that which passes Columbus. Hence by comparing the actual oscillations at these two localities, shown by the gauge-records, we may ascertain the law which connects them, and thus infer from the Columbus gauge the effect produced by the swamp lands upon the Memphis gauge, when the river is above the natural banks. It is clear that such a comparison can only be made at the tops and bottoms of rises, because at other stages it is impossible to determine what gauge-readings at the two localities correspond. The only existing data for the comparison are those furnished by the gauge-records for 1857–59 contained in Appendix B. The following table exhibits an analysis of these records:—

Comparison of rises at Columbus and Memphis.

Columbus.					Memphis.					Difference in oscillation
Top of rise.		Bottom of rise.		Oscillation.	Top of rise.		Bottom of rise.		Oscillation.	
Date.	Gauge.	Date.	Gauge.		Date.	Gauge.	Date.	Gauge.		
	Feet.		*Feet.*	*Feet.*		*Feet.*		*Feet.*	*Feet.*	*Feet.*
Dec. 21, 1857...	32 8	Dec. 30, 1857...	20.8	12.0	Dec. 24, 1857..	31.2	Jan. 2, 1858...	20.9	10 8	+ 1.7
Jan. 8, 1858...	26.1	Jan. 16, 1858...	20.6	5.5	Jan. 11, 1858..	25.9	Jan. 18, "	22.0	3.9	+ 1.6
Jan. 20, " ...	22.3	Feb. 15, " ...	14.2	8.1	Jan. 22, " ..	22.6	Feb. 17, " ...	14.3	8.3	— 0.2
Feb. 19, " ...	16.4	Feb. 26, " ...	13.6	2.8	Feb. 23, " ..	16.1	March 1, "	14.1	2.0	+ 0.8
March 5, "	18.8	March 10, " ...	18.0	0.8	March 7, " ..	19.6	March 13 " ...	18.4	1.2	— 0.4
July 28, " ...	26.2	Aug. 7, " ...	20.3	5.9	July 30, " ..	26.6	Aug. 8, "	20.7	5.9	0.0
Aug. 10, " ...	21 1	Sept. 12, " ...	8.8	12.3	Aug. 12, " ..	21.4	Sept. 14, " ...	9.0	12.4	— 0.1
Sept. 18, "	11.2	Oct. 20, " ...	3.1	8.1	Sept. 20, " ..	12.2	Oct. 25, "	4.0	8.2	— 0.1
Dec. 27, " ...	29.5	Jan. 17, 1859...	17.6	11.9	Jan. 1, 1859...	30.8	Jan. 20, 1859..	19.0	11.8	+ 0.1
Jan. 30, 1859....	21.6	Feb. 9, " ...	17.2	4.4	Jan. 27, "	23.3	Feb. 11, " ..	17.7	5.6	— 1.2
June 26, " ...	23.7	Aug. 6, " ...	11.7	12.0	June 29, "	24.9	Aug. 9, " ..	12.8	12.1	— 0.1
			Sum....	83.8				Sum...	81.7	6.3

It is evident that there is no material difference between the oscillations at the two localities, that at Memphis being $\frac{81.7}{83.8} = 0.97$ of that at Columbus. But the oscillation at Columbus from high to low water in 1858 was 37.8 feet. Had the levee system been perfected, it would have been 1.8 feet greater, or 39.6 feet. The oscillation at Memphis under these conditions ought then to be $39.6 \times 0.97 = 38.4$ feet. That which actually occurred was 31.3 feet. The increase in the height of this flood, which a perfected levee system would have caused, is then $38.4 - 31.3 = 7.1$ feet. Two computations so entirely different in principle, the one giving 5.3 feet and the other 7.1 feet for this quantity, can leave no reasonable doubt that the mean—say 6.5 feet above the high water of 1858—is the height this flood would have attained at Memphis.

Helena is the next point for consideration. By reference to plate XVII, it will be

The computation for Helena.

seen that the increase of discharge, as compared with the rise in the gauge, is very much greater in the June rise than in either of the preceding rises. This is an anomalous effect, due to an exceptional increase in the local slope. It was caused partly by the depression of water surface between Helena and the mouth of White river, occasioned by very large crevasse discharges in that vicinity (more than 250,000 cubic feet per second), and partly by the elevation of the water surface just above Helena, occasioned by a flood of water returning to the river from the St. Francis bottom. In a perfected state of the levees, neither of these conditions would exist, and their effect must therefore be eliminated. This can be done by selecting for the primitive stand in the computation that existing at the top of the May rise (May 3). Applying the formulæ to these data, we find that to discharge 1,334,000 cubic feet per second (the actual maximum discharge), the river must rise 6.7 feet; and to discharge 1,369,000 cubic feet per second (the maximum discharge with perfected levees), it must rise 7.4 feet. But on May 3 the river stood 3.5 feet below high water of 1858. Hence, without the anomalous influence acting upon the slope, the river would have risen 6.7 — 3.5 = 3.2 feet higher than it actually rose, in order to carry off the maximum discharge; and 7.4 — 3.5 = 3.9 feet higher than it actually rose, in order to carry off the maximum discharge which would have occurred had the levees been in a perfected condition.

The computation for Lake Providence.

At Lake Providence, also, the normal condition of the river was affected by the large crevasses below the town, as shown by plate XVII. The Point Lookout crevasse occurred on April 30. The river, which had been steadily rising for several days, soon began to decline, although the discharge continued to increase. On June 23, the date of the actual maximum discharge, it had fallen 1.3 feet. To avoid the anomalous effect of these crevasses, a date prior to their exercising any perceptible influence, for instance April 30, ought to be selected for the primitive stage in the computation. Applying the formulæ to this stage, we find that, to discharge 1,188,000 cubic feet per second (the actual maximum discharge), the river must rise 3.0 feet; and to discharge 1,406,000 cubic feet per second (the maximum discharge with perfected levees), it must rise 10.0 feet. But on April 30 the river stood 0.5 of a foot below the highest point attained in 1858 (April 8). Deducting this amount, and adding 0.3 of a foot for estimated rise subsequent to date of maximum discharge, we have for the elevation above high water of 1858, due to the actual discharge unaffected by the local crevasses, 2.8 feet; and for that due to the discharge which would have occurred with a perfected levee system, 9.8 feet.

The computation for Donaldsonville.

Donaldsonville is the next point for consideration. Plate XVII indicates that the two crevasses below the town (Nos. 44 and 45) increased the slope of the river, and materially lowered the surface. To avoid this anomalous influence, it is necessary to select for the primitive stage a date prior to its existence, say May 2. At this time the river was 0.9 of a foot below high water of 1858, and the discharge was identical with that at the same stand in 1851. Applying the formulæ, we find that to discharge 1,197,000 cubic feet per second (actual maximum discharge), the river must rise 1.0 foot; and to discharge 1,297,000 cubic feet per second (maximum discharge with perfected levees), it must rise 2.8 feet. Adding 0.3 of a foot for probable rise subsequent to the date of maximum discharge, and deducting 0.9

of a foot for the depression of the primitive stand below high water of 1858, we have 0.4 and 2.2 feet for the respective heights which the river would have attained above the actual high-water level of 1858, supposing these discharges to have been unaffected by the local influence of the two crevasses. The former number fixes the amount by which the river was lowered at the date of maximum discharge (May 31) by the influence of these two crevasses; since, instead of being 0.4 of a foot above the actual high water of 1858, it was at this date 0.9 of a foot below it. Hence the influence in question amounted to 0.4 + 0.9 = 1.3 feet.

The computation for Carrollton.

At Carrollton the usual law of discharge of the river was affected far more than at Donaldsonville, as may be seen by inspecting plate XVII. The town is situated between the sites of the two crevasses, and only a few thousand feet above that of the larger (Bell's). To the influence of this crevasse alone, then, is to be attributed the anomaly of a greater discharge when the river was falling than when it was rising. In order to eliminate all errors, a date before the crevasses exercised any perceptible influence, and when the river discharge accorded with that at the same stand in 1851, is to be selected for the primitive stage. April 15 fulfils these conditions. The formulæ indicate that, to carry off 1,188,000 cubic feet per second (actual maximum discharge), the river must rise 1.2 feet; and to carry off 1,297,000 cubic feet per second (maximum discharge with perfected levees), it must rise 2.6 feet. Adding 0.3 of a foot for probable rise subsequent to date of maximum discharge, and deducting 0.5 of a foot (stand of river on April 15 below actual high water of 1858), we have, for the increase in height above the actual high-water level of 1858, in the two cases, 1.0 and 2.4 feet respectively. The depression occasioned by the crevasse at the date of maximum discharge in the river (May 29) is equal to the former number increased by the actual stand of the river at that date below high water of 1858, *i.e.* to 1.0 + 0.7 = 1.7 feet.

Results of the several computations, with data.

The following table exhibits the data above indicated for all the localities under consideration, and the results of the computations based upon them :—

Effect that would have been produced upon the flood of 1858 *if the levee system had been perfected.*

Locality.	Primitive stand of river.							Maximum discharge with levees perfected (flood of 1858).	Computed x	Increased height above actual h. w. of 1858 with levees perfected.
	Date.	Below high water 1858.	e	$a_{\prime}$	$W_{\prime}$	$p_{\prime}$	$Q_{\prime}$			
		Feet.	*Feet.*	*Sq. feet.*	*Feet.*	*Feet.*	*Cu. feet.*	*Cu. feet.*	*Feet.*	*Feet.*
Columbus	June 18, 1858	0.2	46.4	166,000	2237	2280	1,403,000	1,478,000	1.8	1.8
Memphis	April 18, 1850	12.1	25.0	138,400	2875	2900	600,000	1,380,000	17.0	6.5
"	May 19, 1858	2.9	34.2	166,860	3110	3135	1,010,000	1,380,000	7.9	
Helena	May 3, 1858	3.5	43.5	191,520	4080	4117	1,077,000	1,369,000	7.4	3.9
Napoleon	June 22, 1858	0.3	44.7	211,000	3220	3300	1,221,000	1,418,000	6.9	6.9
Lake Providence	April 30, 1858	0.5	43.5	200,210	3580	3659	1,100,000	1,406,000	10.0	9.8
Vicksburg	June 24, 1858	0.1	48.2	177,000	2700	2740	1,245,000	1,430,000	3.8	3.8
Natchez	June 25, 1858	0.0	51.5	227,000	4540	4590	1,239,000	1,424,000	4.6	4.6
Red-river landing	May 22, 1858	0.3	43.2	239,000	3616	3654	1,221,000	1,338,000	3.2	3.2
Baton Rouge	May 17, 1858	0.2	34.1	190,440	2800	2824	1,203,000	1,338,000	2.7	2.7
Donaldsonville	May 2, 1858	0.9	25.8	196,280	3100	3127	1,148,000	1,297,000	2.8	2.2
Carrollton	April 15, 1858	0.6	14.5	183,090	2378	2415	1,105,000	1,297,000	2.6	2.4

These results to be tested.

The last column of this table shows the increase in height to which the flood of 1858 would have gained, if the river below Cape Girardeau had been confined to its proper channel. As already seen, each number in it is the result of a careful analysis of the local problem. The investigation, however, is too important to be brought to a close without exhausting every possible check upon the accuracy of the determinations. One further test can be applied.

Outline of this test.

The second test of the new formulæ (see Chapter V) establishes that their indications accord perfectly with the actual flood conditions existing in the four grand divisions of the lower Mississippi; namely, that between the Ohio and the Arkansas; that between the Arkansas and the Red; that between the Red and bayou La Fourche; and that between bayou La Fourche and Fort St. Philip. The increase in flood height given in the last table determines the new mean dimensions of cross-section, and the new mean slope in each of these divisions. These quantities being known, the new maximum discharge can be computed by the formulæ. If this quantity accords with that derived from the new maximum discharges at the several localities, the exactness of the local determinations of the new flood heights will receive the strongest possible confirmation; since the new condition of the river will thus be shown to harmonize with the laws which govern it in its present condition.

Numerical values of the quantities entering the computation, and its results.

The application of this test is simple. The increase in the area is found by multiplying the width between banks by the mean increase in flood height. The latter quantity is found by dividing, by the total distance included in the division under consideration, the sum of the products of the mean increase of height between consecutive stations into the distance between them. The width, of course, undergoes no variation. The perimeter is assumed to remain unchanged, in order to allow, approximately, for the inconsiderable discharge which takes place between the edge of the natural bank and the levee. The $\sin.^2 \acute{a}$ is a constant quantity for each division. The new fall in water surface to be used in computing the new mean velocity is found by deducting the effect of bends from the present fall, increased by the new rise at the upper extremity of the division under consideration, and diminished by that at the lower. The real mean discharge to be compared with that computed by these data is derived from the new maximum discharge at each station, in the manner just described for deducing the mean increase in flood height in the several divisions.

The only explanations required for the local application of this general process are the following: The distance from Columbus to Memphis is 225 miles, or about double that between the other stations. Most of the surplus discharge in floods escapes into the swamps above a point midway between these two localities. The increase in flood height at this point, produced by confining the entire discharge to the channel, must then be about the same as at Memphis, *i.e.* 6.5 feet. Again, midway between Helena and Napoleon, the increased height of the flood level must be greater than at the latter of these places, on account of the influence exerted by the White-river bottom lands. A comparison of the amount of crevasse-water which escaped into these swamps, with that which returned by the White and Arkansas rivers in 1858, indicates that this increase is about 2 feet greater than at Napoleon, *i.e.* about 9 feet. These numbers have been used in computing the mean increased height of the flood level between the Ohio and Arkansas rivers. In computing the new mean discharge below Red river, bayou Plaquemine has been assumed to discharge 10,000, and bayou La Fourche 3000, cubic feet per second more than in the flood of 1858, on account of the increased rise of the Mississippi at their upper mouths. The following table exhibits these data and the results of the computations:—

Division of river.	Distance	Sin.^{2} $\acute{a}$	High water of 1858 with perfected levees.						Discharge computed by new formula.	Difference between real and computed discharges.
			Increased height of the flood.	Area.	Width.	Perimeter.	Total fall in water surface.	Discharge per second.		
	Miles.		*Feet.*	*Sq. feet.*	*Feet.*	*Feet*	*Feet.*	*Cubic feet.*	*Cubic feet.*	*Cubic feet.*
Ohio to Arkansas.....	408.0	47.33	5.7	217,000	4470	4510	156.9	1,409.000	1,399,000	+ 10,000
Arkansas to Red.....	373.0	56.50	6.1	224,000	4080	4115	115.7	1,420,000	1,434,000	— 14,000
Red to La Fourche...	122.6	15.39	2.9	209,000	3000	3035	23.8	1,327,000	1,321,000	+ 6,000
La F. to Ft. St. Philip	156.0	21.60	1.8	204,000	2470	2510	22.7	1,284,000	1,269,000	+ 15,000

The differences in the last column are so small as to render it certain that the great problem of protection against inundation has been solved. The increased height to which this standard flood would have risen, had the levee system been perfected, has been fixed by the local analysis at so many points as to furnish all the practical information needed for adjusting the proper local heights of the levees. The new dimensions and slope thus determined for the river prove to be almost identically those required to carry off the increased discharge. For this flood, then, the question is settled. But it has also been shown that the maximum discharge with perfected levees would have been as great in this flood as in any preceding one of which we have records. The true heights which ought to be given to the levees, in order to insure the present protection of the whole alluvial valley of the Mississippi, are thus established.

Fulness and truth of this determination of the proper heights for the levees.

2. Having thus disposed of the first division of this analysis of the levee system, we are now to consider the agencies which may hereafter affect its practical working. Three of a general character have been suggested. They are: First, the prolongation of the delta into the gulf, which must elevate the water surface near the mouth of the river; second, the increased cultivation of the valley, which may affect the discharge of the various tributaries, and, hence, that of the Mississippi itself; and, third, the increased velocity of the current, which, by causing an excavation of the channel, may reduce the new high-water level. These agencies will be noticed in turn.

Three general agencies which may hereafter affect the levee system.

The subject of the prolongation of the delta belongs properly to the next chapter, where it will be fully treated. Here it is sufficient to state that its rate of progress is so slow as to render its effect upon the level of the water surface of the river inappreciable, unless very long periods of time are considered. (See figure 1, plate IX.) It may, therefore, be neglected in estimating the heights now to be given to the levees.

The prolongation of the delta need not be dreaded.

The effects of cultivation are in a measure compensatory.

Effects of cultivation are in a measure compensatory.

On forest ground, the effect is to drain lakes, ponds, marshes, bogs, and meadows, which served as reservoirs; to render the surface smoother;

and thus to increase the rapidity of drainage and the heights of freshets. On the contrary, the removal of the matted undergrowth, and the softening of the earth, cause a greater quantity of rain to be absorbed; and the exposure of the surface to the sun increases evaporation. Snow, however, will be melted much more rapidly in the spring. The removal of forests on mountains will tend to increase the amount of rain by creating heated upward currents. In a prairie country, cultivation, by rendering the surface smoother and removing matted grass and roots, will increase the rapidity of drainage, and absorption, and also of evaporation, because the soil will be more exposed to the sun, and earth is a better conductor of heat than vegetable matter is. The growth of trees which cultivation produces on prairies will tend to increase the amount of rain by increasing the inequalities of the face of the country and of the temperature in air.

Thus in forest, mountain, and prairie countries cultivation brings into existence causes which tend some to increase and some to decrease the floods. It appears to be probable that the former will be the more powerful, and that the effect of cultivation will therefore be to render the floods greater and the low waters lower.

As the progress of cultivation over the basins of the great tributaries of the Mississippi, however, is not made at uniform rates, its relative effects on the floods of those tributaries will be unequal,* and may tend either to increase or to decrease the floods of

* The following table gives approximately the number of acres of cultivated land in the Mississippi basin, together with the approximate population, at intervals of ten years, commencing with 1800. This cultivated land lies east of the 98th meridian west from Greenwich, and the area of that portion of the basin of the Mississippi which comprises it is 700,000 square miles, or 448,000,000 acres. The annual downfall within those limits varies from 25 to 65 inches, the mean being about 40 inches. The larger portion of the increase of cultivation has taken place in the prairie regions. The dense forests on the most fertile parts of the southern portion of the basin render the opening of cultivation there more difficult and expensive, and its rate of progress consequently slower:—

Table showing the population and number of acres of improved or cultivated land in the Mississippi valley from 1800 *to* 1860.

State or Territory.	1800.		1810.		1820.		1830.		1840.		1850.		1860.	
	Population.	Improved land.	Population.	Improved land.	Population.	Improved land.	Population.	Improved land.	Population.	Improved land.	Population.	Improved land.	Population.	Improved land.
		Acres.		*Acres.*		*Acres.*		*Acres.*		*Acres.*		*Acres.*		*Acres.*
Pennsylvania	200,787	749,391	270,030	1,007,805	349,819	1,305,604	416,074	1,553,005	574,344	2,123,605	770,595	2,876,206	974,833	3,638,310
Virginia	330,075	2,405,330	365,484	2,663,370	399,516	2,911,370	454,275	3,310,410	464,922	3,888,000	533,121	3,885,051	597,449	4,353,760
Kentucky	220,955	1,342,350	406,511	2,469,620	564,317	3,428,310	687,917	4,179,200	779,828	4,737,520	982,405	5,968,270	1,159,609	7,044,880
Tennessee	105,602	545,028	261,727	1,350,810	422,813	2,182,200	681,904	3,519,410	829,210	4,279,675	1,002,717	5,175,173	1,146,640	5,917,985
Ohio	36,292	180,540	184,608	918,364	465,148	2,313,957	750,320	3,732,600	1,215,572	6,047,060	1,584,264	7,881,192	1,902,252	9,463,076
Indiana	4,875	24,890	24,530	125,530	147,178	751,445	343,031	1,751,409	685,866	3,485,729	988,416	5,046,543	1,370,802	6,998,898
Mississippi	4,425	25,128	20,176	114,576	37,724	213,981	68,310	387,920	187,825	1,066,630	303,263	1,722,179	443,579	2,519,008
Illinois			12,282	72,692	55,211	325,272	157,445	931,860	476,183	2,818,373	851,470	5,039,545	1,687,404	9,987,128
Louisiana			36,778	112,943	76,203	234,016	107,869	356,460	176,205	541,117	258,881	795,012	333,215	1,023,289
Missouri			20,845	89,805	66,586	286,870	140,455	605,117	383,702	1,653,001	682,044	2,938,425	1,201,209	5,175,125
Arkansas					14,273	53,142	30,388	113,144	97,574	363,298	209,897	781,530	440,775	1,641,143
Iowa									43,112	184,969	192,214	824,682	682,002	2,926,086
Wisconsin									25,785	88,275	254,490	871,245	640,404	2,192,442
Minnesota											6,077	5,035	172,793	143,161
Kansas													143,642	119,009
Nebraska													28,893	23,938
Total	903,011	5,272,657	1,602,971	8,925,515	2,598,788	14,006,167	3,837,988	20,440,535	5,940,128	31,297,258	8,619,854	33,810,088	12,925,501	63,167,238

The table was prepared in the following manner: The population and number of acres of cultivated land in all the States and Territories lying wholly within the Mississippi basin were obtained from the census tables of 1850. It was estimated that one-third of Pennsylvania, four-fifths of Ohio, three-eighths of Virginia, and one-half the States of Mississippi and Louisiana were included within the basin. These proportions of the population and cultivated land of the Mississippi, according as the contributions are thus made more or less coincident. Very careful observations through the whole period of progress could alone furnish the means of detecting such changes. It cannot be said that any, until recently, have even been attempted. The laws deduced from the operations of this Survey have placed it in the power of any one to determine the influence of this disturbing agency in the future, by keeping correct records of the oscillations of the river, year after year, and computing from them the mean annual and the flood discharges through long continuous periods of time. (See Chapter II.)

Effect of the increased velocity of the river.

Lastly, the effect produced upon the bed by the increased velocity due to the levees is to be considered. Several points require examination.

The increased velocity is of short duration.

1. Levees can, of course, exert no influence except during the period when the river is above the level of its natural banks. With a view to give a general idea as to the duration of this period in different parts of the river, the following table has been prepared from the gauge-records in Appendix B:—

Duration of Mississippi high water.

Locality.	Natural bank; reading on gauge.	Water surface above level of natural bank.											
		1849. (Flood year.)	1850. (Flood year.)	1851. (Flood year.)	1852.	1853.	1854.	1855.	1856.	1857.	1858. (Flood year.)	1859. (Flood year.)	1860.
	Feet.	*Days.*	*Days.*	*Days.*	*Days.*	*Days.*	*Days.*	*Days.*	*Days.*	*Days.*	*Days.*	*Days.*	*Days.*
Columbus	37.0										24	27	
Memphis	31.3	84	75								87	95	
Napoleon	41.4										100		
Lake Providence	41.6			97									
Vicksburg	44.3										129	103	
New Carthage	40.0			104									
Natchez	48.5			55							129		
Red-river landing	43.0			50							118		
Baton Rouge	30.0			57	31								
Donaldsonville	27.0			63	68	43	2	0	0	0	129	123	2
Carrollton	12.0	220	172	125	108	170	111	0			199	114	49

This table gives an exaggerated idea of the mean duration of the period during which the river is over its banks, since the records, excepting those of Donaldsonville and Carrollton, are mainly those of great flood years.

The increased velocity is partially balanced by the shorter duration of the flood period.

2. The effects of levees are compensatory, for, while they increase the *heights* of floods, they diminish their *duration*, as may be seen by examining plate XVIII. It is, then, possible that the system may not increase the absolute excavating power exerted by the river upon its bed during the flood period; since the increase of force may be balanced by the diminution in its period of operation.

these States were tabulated with the population and cultivated land of those States and Territories lying wholly in the basin. In the same manner the population of the basin was found for every ten years from 1800 to 1860, inclusive. The number of acres of improved land in any State at any time was found by multiplying its population at that time by the ratio of its population to the number of acres of improved land in 1850. Although the table is not strictly correct, yet it is the best that can be had without a very elaborate examination, which the use to be made of the table did not justify. It is sufficiently accurate for the subject it is intended to illustrate.

The bed is composed of too hard a material to be rapidly abraded.

3. The hard and permanent character of the bed of the river, already so often mentioned, demonstrates that none but very gradual changes can occur in its level. If, then, the flood velocity is increased by the levees sufficiently to enable the river to enlarge its channel, this enlargement must be chiefly at the expense of the comparatively soft alluvial banks. The width, not the depth, will be increased.* It may be added, that wherever soundings have been made by the Delta Survey, at different times on the same lines, no change of area attributable to a change of level of the bottom has ever been detected.

The absolute increase of velocity is slight.

4. The increase in velocity, which will result from the extension of the levees, is not alarming, when compared with that which has already occurred. This is shown by the following table, which is based upon computations already made :—

Division of river.	Mean velocity per second of Mississippi river in greatest floods.		
	Unleveed condition.	Present condition.	Levees perfected.
	Feet.	*Feet.*	*Feet.*
Ohio to Arkansas	6.07	6.15	6.49
Arkansas to Red	5.73	6.03	6.34
Red to La Fourche	5.58	6.00	6.36
La Fourche to head of passes	5.55	5.78	6.29

From this table, it appears that the mean velocity when greatest will only be about six per cent. greater than at present. The duration of the increase will be very brief.

Arguments favoring the theory of a change of bed to be now noticed.

These considerations lead to the conclusion that, in constructing the levees of the present day, no allowance should be made for any influence to be exerted by them upon the bed of the river. Before closing the subject, however, it may be well to notice certain arguments which suggest a different conclusion.

General misapprehension respecting the effect of levees upon the Po.

The first is based upon an error of fact, which has been very generally propagated upon the authority of a distinguished name, that of M. de Prony. This error is that the levees of the Po have raised the bed, and hence the surface, of that river to an alarming extent. The statements made by M. de Prony respecting the Po at Ferrara (plate XIX), upon information collected by him in a brief visit to Italy, have been shown to be entirely erroneous, by the Chevalier Lombardini, in his memoir† upon the Changes in the Hydraulic Condition of the Po, published at Milan in 1852. An exact translation

* To prove that the Mississippi has not increased its width since the construction of levees, Mr. Bayley, in a published letter addressed to three members of the Senate of Louisiana, March 8, 1858, adduces the mean widths of lakes St. John and Concordia, near Natchez, as measured by Mr. William G. Waller (localities of measurements not stated), and compares them with the mean width of the Mississippi below Red river (2513 feet), as measured by the Senate Committee in 1850. These lakes were formerly channels of the river, but had ceased to be such before the discovery of Louisiana. Their widths are respectively 2640 feet and 3250 feet. The mean is 2945 feet. The measurements of this Survey show that the mean width between the Red and Arkansas rivers (the division which formerly included these lakes) is now 4080 feet. It is to be remarked, however, that no inferences can be drawn from comparisons of this kind, until much more elaborate measurements have been made than any now existing.

† Dei Cangiamenti cui Soggiacque l'Idraulica Condizione del Po, nel Territorio di Ferrara.

of the language of this writer will be used wherever it can be conveniently quoted. He says, speaking of Cuvier:—

"In his celebrated discourse on the revolutions of the surface of the globe,* he expresses himself in the following manner: 'Every one can see in Holland and in Italy, with what rapidity the Rhine, the Po, and the Arno, now that they are inclosed by levees, elevate their beds; to what extent their mouths advance into the sea, forming long promontories on the coasts; and can judge from these facts how few centuries it has required for these streams to deposit the low plains through which they flow at the present time.' * * * * * * *

"'My learned associate at the Institute, M. de Prony, Inspector-General of Roads and Bridges, has communicated to me information exceedingly valuable as explaining the changes that have taken place in the shores of the Adriatic.† Having been commissioned by the government to ascertain what remedies should be applied to prevent the devastations caused by the floods of the Po, he states that this river, since the construction of the dikes, has elevated its bed to such a degree that *the surface of the river is now higher than the roofs of the houses in Ferrara*, while, at the same time, its alluvion has advanced into the sea with such rapidity that, on comparing the ancient charts with the present, it is found that the river has gained more than 6000 toises since 1604; which is equal to 150 or 180 feet, and in some places 200 feet (French measure), per year. *Both the Adige and the Po are at this day higher than all the country which lies between them;* and it is only by opening new beds for them in the soil which they formerly deposited, that the disasters which are now threatened can be averted.'

"Most of the books which have been published on the other side of the mountains, on physical geography, geology, hydrography, and hydraulics, have repeated the same statements with regard to the Po; and, when discussing projects for embanking rivers, have pointed to the solitary example of this river to warn others from following the same plan.

* * * * * * * * * *

"In some of my works I have confirmed the observations of de Prony touching the advancement of the alluvion of the Po into the sea, but at the same time have succeeded in showing the errors of his statements with regard to the rising of the bed of the Po, both in respect to its progress and its elevation compared with that of the adjacent country. But in his report, the Po and the Adige are represented to be in nearly the same condition, and the evil is asserted to be so far advanced as to leave no remedy but that of excavating new channels.

"The engineer Baumgarten, who was charged with the direction of the improvements of the river Rhine on the French frontier, passing through Milan in 1844, requested me to communicate to him some facts which should demonstrate the errors of de Prony, at least as far as they were stated by Cuvier. I sent them to him in a letter, which he published in connection with an extract from my writings on the rivers of Lombardy, in vol. XIII (1847) of the Annales des Ponts et Chaussées of France. In that letter I promised to submit to him some other facts concerning the territory

---

* Paris, 1830; page 150.

† In a note from the Extract from the Researches of M. de Prony on the hydraulic system of Italy.

and city of Ferrara, which I have not been able to do, owing to the cares of my official duties. Since then, there having been forwarded to me a letter from M. Minard,* Inspector-General and Professor of Construction in the School of the Corps of Ponts et Chaussées of France, one whom I hold in high esteem, wherein I have been asked to furnish the information I had promised touching a subject which they wish to examine thoroughly, and upon which they entertain some differences of opinion, I have prepared myself, not only by a collection of the facts, but by an examination of them, accompanied by reasonings which were necessary in order to demonstrate the truth."

M. Lombardini then demonstrates, by reference to historical records and ancient maps, that the distance to the sea (plate XIX) from Stellata—the ancient point of bifurcation, 16 miles above Ferrara—by the present course of the river is 6 miles shorter than it was in 1152, as stated in the reference to his works in that part of this chapter in which outlets are treated; and, consequently, that the surface of the river at that point could not have been elevated since that day by the prolongation of the Po. Next, he proves, by references to the foundations of flood-gates; that the extreme low-water surface of the river has not changed sensibly in more than two centuries, and, consequently, that the bottom of the river has not been elevated during that time, although local changes in the bottom have taken place. Then, by means of careful levellings, he shows that the high-water mark of 1839 (the greatest flood known), if transferred by the measured slope, from Ponte Lagoscuro—on the bank of the Po, 3 miles east of Ferrara—to Stellata, and thence to Ferrara by the old course of the river, will be 3 feet below the surface of the ancient embankment of the Po, and 5 feet above the ancient natural bank. The palace in Ferrara is about 1000 feet distant from the edge of the natural bank, and the ground there is lower than on the river shore. Referred to this locality, the flood of 1839 is 10 feet above the pavement, and 2.5 feet lower than the actual high-water line at Ponte Lagoscuro. An hydrometer is erected near that locality, with the high-water marks of several years upon it. At Ponte Lagoscuro, the levees are nearly 30 feet high. Before the crevasse of Ficarolo, this locality formed part of a great swamp or lake, and the lowest part of the ground back from the river is but 2 feet above the low-water line of the river. The name Lagoscuro (dark lake) refers to its ancient condition. The range of the Po at this point is about 28 feet; its mean depth at low water is 3 feet.

M. Lombardini also establishes that the regular increase of height (3.3 feet) that has taken place in the floods during the last century and a half has been caused by the gradual perfection of the levee system, by which crevasses have been constantly diminished in number, the country has been more and more effectually protected against overflow, and the volume of the river in floods has been constantly increased. The prolongation of the Po, as ascertained by M. de Prony, was from A.D. 1200 to A.D. 1600 at the rate of 81.5 feet per year; from A.D. 1600 to the present century, at the rate of 227 feet per year. But this is likewise shown by M. Lombardini to be erroneous,

* Elsewhere M. Lombardini says: "In the letter of M. Minard, he speaks of the *first floor*, and not of the *roofs* of the houses in Ferrara. It would seem that the exaggeration is due rather to Cuvier, and was not to be found in the text of de Prony, with which I am unacquainted, and from which the former published a solitary fragment."

The memoir of M. de Prony is not to be found in the Library of the British Museum nor in the Bibliothéque Française, Paris; probably it was never published.

and to have arisen from the conclusion of M. de Prony that, in a century after the occurrence of the crevasse of Ficarolo, the Ferrarese branch of the Po was entirely closed, and that the Grande was the sole channel. This really did not occur until A.D. 1600 instead of A.D. 1300; and the rate of progress from A.D. 1600 to the present day is merely one-fifth greater than formerly. This increased rate of prolongation is attributed to the greater volume which now reaches the sea, owing to the improved condition of the levees, and to the greater quantity of earthy matter brought down from the mountain sides since the forests have been cut down. An additional cause has been also suggested, namely, that this denudation of the mountains has likewise sensibly changed the meteorological conditions of the basin of the Po.

M. Lombardini further shows that the bed of the Po is nowhere above the level of the adjacent country, although it passes through and adjacent to low grounds, formerly swamps, and lakes which are now wholly or partially drained.

The slope of the Adige in its lower trunk is three times greater than that of the Po. In prolonging itself through these swamps and lakes, its bed was formed in its own deposit, just as the passes of the Mississippi are now formed in the deposit of that river. The bottom of these swamps and lakes is now dry ground, and is in some places lower than the deposit formed upon it, in which the bed of the Adige lies.

It is hoped that these researches of M. Lombardini will remove the apprehensions that may have been excited by M. de Prony respecting the injurious consequences of levees.

Same upon the Rhine.

Upon the Rhine the subject has been less elaborately examined; but in 1850 the observations upon the hydrometers at Keulan, Emmerich, Doornenburg (near the first division of the river), and Arnheim, extending over a period of eighty years, from 1772 to 1849, were published under the authority of the government. The tables and notes, or memoir, accompanying them were prepared for publication by M. I. G. W. Fijnje, hydraulic engineer, in the service of the government. These observations prove that there has been no change at the localities of the hydrometers in that period in the level either of the flood, or of the low water, or of the mean yearly stand of the river.

Fallacy of the argument based upon comparing high-water marks.

The second argument in support of the theory that levees affect the bed of the river is advanced by Professor Forshey in a memoir upon the Physics of the Mississippi, published in 1850. It is based upon a comparison of the mean high waters at Carrollton (transferred from Vidalia) during periods of ten years each, from 1817 to 1846. The resulting mean of the second decennial period being 4 inches lower than the mean of the first period, and that of the third 6 inches less than that of the first, Professor Forshey attributed these results to the levees, which he states did not exist to any considerable extent above Vidalia previous to 1827, but were in full operation for a long distance above and below that point after 1837. To show that this result was accidental, the following table of high waters at Carrollton (those previous to 1847 being deduced from the observations at Vidalia, used by Professor Forshey), for every year from 1811 to 1860, arranged in series of ten years each, has been prepared:—

Comparison of different high-water marks at Carrollton.

Year.	High-water reading on gauge.	Year.	High-water reading on gauge.	Year.	High-water reading on gauge.	Year.	High-water reading on gauge.	Year.	High-water reading on gauge.
	Feet.		*Feet.*		*Feet.*		*Feet.*		*Feet.*
1811	14.87	1821	14.72	1831	14.57	1841	14.47	1851	15.40
1812	14.22	1822	14.62	1832	14.55	1842	14.57	1852	14.10
1813	15.22	1823	15.26	1833	13.80	1843	14.76	1853	15.00
1814	14.50	1824	15.12	1834	13.64	1844	15.05	1854	14.70
1815	15.30	1825	14.80	1835	14.12	1845	14.86	1855	9.50
1816	14.53	1826	14.64	1836	15.05	1846	14.86	1856	12.80
1817	14.58	1827	14.05	1837	14.47	1847	15.05	1857	13.10
1818	14.26	1828	15.26	1838	14.00	1848	15.10	1858	15.10
1819	14 80	1829	13.20	1839	12.14	1849	15.21	1859	15.60
1820	14.22	1830	14.66	1840	15.03	1850	13.80	1860	13.40
Mean....	14.65		14.63		14.13		14 73		13.87
	Leaving out 1855, mean..............								14.20

By comparing the means of the periods, we see that the greatest was that from 1840 to 1850, or *after* the levees were "in full operation a long distance above and below Vidalia," and the least that from 1850 to 1860. But the decennial period from 1850 to 1860 is remarkable for three years of very low water; the high water of 1855 being nearly 25 per cent. lower than the lowest high water during the fifty years considered. This obviously exerts an undue influence on the mean result. Omitting that year, we find that the period of lowest high water is from 1830 to 1840, *before* the levees were "in full operation a long distance above and below Vidalia."

Again, if the high waters are arranged in sets of ten years, beginning with 1815 and extending to 1855, we have four complete decades. By this arrangement, the period of highest water is from 1845 to 1855, or after the levees were "in full operation;" and the lowest high water is from 1825 to 1835, or before they were "in full operation;" results indicating an effect precisely contrary to that attributed to the levees by Professor Forshey.

The fact is, that to determine the question whether levees elevate or depress the surface of the river by comparing the high waters of several years, it must first be ascertained that *the quantity of water passing in each year was the same.* This quantity may be affected in two ways. First, the quantity passing down the whole river may be less. Second, local causes may depress the surface in one year, when the supply at the point of observation is the same. Such local causes are cut-offs, crevasses, and the varying condition of natural outlets and affluents below the point of observation. All variations due to these sources must be eliminated before the table is in proper condition for use.

Many of the high waters in the preceding table are largely affected by crevasses. The data for their correction exist in some cases, but not in all. The corrections have not, therefore, been made, nor can any reliable conclusions be drawn from such observations, until all errors have been eliminated.

Moreover, it is a fundamental principle in observations of a series of facts from which laws are to be deduced or mean final results obtained, to continue the observations until the mean is not affected by any single observation, however largely differing from the mean. Since the omission of 1855 changes materially the mean of the period from 1850 to 1860, it is evident that periods of ten years are not sufficiently long to give a proper mean, even if all errors are eliminated and the high-water marks of equal discharges alone used.

Fallacy of the argument based upon the existence of high natural banks in the delta.

Another argument to prove that in floods the surface of the Mississippi does not rise any higher now than it did before levees were built, is based upon the statement that there are points where the natural banks have never been overflowed, within the recollection of any one living. The natural bank at Algiers has been referred to as a well-known instance, and will be taken as a type of these cases. It was visited by the parties of this Survey in 1858—on one occasion on May 15th. At that date, earth had been shovelled up at the highest point, opposite the Belleville foundery, for the space of 100 feet, to prevent overflow. The ground along the river front in this vicinity had evidently been disturbed at different times. It is used for ship yards. According to the levellings of the Delta Survey, the ground, where apparently undisturbed, was 0.3 of a foot below the high water of 1858. This shows the natural bank there to be nearly on the level of the highest floods. But it is a sufficient answer to the conclusions that have been based upon that fact, to state that there never has been a flood since levees were built, without the occurrence of a large number of crevasses below Red river, and, consequently, that the full volume of a flood has never yet passed New Orleans. These crevasses may reduce the surface of the river as low as, if not lower than, it would have been if the natural banks existed in their original, unleveed condition; for the mean level of the natural bank, where the levee system has been in operation for many years, must from constant caving be lower than it was originally. It may also be added that the enlargement of the bayous Atchafalaya and Plaquemine, since the construction of levees, is a well-established fact. This enlargement has contributed to depress the floods at New Orleans.

The agencies enumerated are practically unimportant in estimating the height of the levees.

These various considerations show that by none of the agencies enumerated will the heights of the floods be affected to such a degree as to be of practical importance in estimating the dimensions to be given to the levees of the present day.

RECOMMENDATIONS.

An organized levee system must be depended upon for protection against floods in the Mississippi valley.

The preceding discussion of the different plans of protection has been so elaborate and the conclusions adopted have been so well established, that little remains to be said under the head of recommendations. It has been *demonstrated* that no advantage can be derived either from diverting tributaries or constructing reservoirs, and that the plans of cut-offs, and of new or enlarged outlets to the gulf, are too costly and too dangerous to be attempted. The plan of levees, on the contrary, which has always recommended itself by its simplicity and its direct repayment of investments, may be relied upon for protecting all the alluvial bottom lands liable to inundation below Cape Girardeau. The works, it is true, will be extensive and costly, and will exact much more unity of action than has thus far been attained. The recent legislation of Mississippi in organizing a judicious State system of operations, however, shows that the necessity of more concert is beginning to be understood. When each of the other States adopts a similar plan, and all unite in a general system so far as may be requisite for the perfection of each part, the alluvial valley of the Mississippi may be protected against inundation.

Proper heights to be given to the levees.

To secure this end in the most economical manner, the operations of this Survey indicate that levees should be constructed. Near the mouth of the Ohio, they should be made about 3 feet above the actual high-water level of 1858, which has been selected as the plane of reference, because more unvarying than the surface of the ground. The height above this level should be gradually increased to about 7 feet at Osceola. Thence to Helena, the latter height should be maintained. Thence to Island 71, the height should be gradually increased to 10 feet. Thence to the vicinity of Napoleon, it may be gradually reduced to 8 feet. Thence to Lake Providence, it must be gradually increased to 11 feet. Thence to the mouth of the Yazoo, it may be gradually reduced to about 6 feet, and should be thus maintained to Red-river landing. Between that locality and Baton Rouge, it should be kept uniformly about 4 feet, and below Baton Rouge about 3 feet. If the water-mark of 1858 be unknown at any locality, it may be reduced to any well-determined local mark by the table in Chapter II. The above estimate is exclusive of settling, and allows about a foot for possible rise above the height necessary for restraining the flood of 1858.

It should be remarked that these heights are based upon the supposition of *absolute security*, so far as its conditions can be ascertained. In building the levees, it may be more economical to incur certain risks of inundation than to expend so large an amount at once in the construction of levees. Thus for the region above the mouth of the St. Francis river the flood of 1858 far exceeded any other of which we have records, except that of 1815. The data presented and the principles so fully elaborated in this report will render it easy for the engineers in charge of the work of construction to decide what degree of protection it is economical to secure. It should be remarked, however, that below the upper limit of the influence of the Arkansas and White rivers, it will be unsafe to make any material reduction in the above heights of the levees, computed with reference to restraining the flood of 1858.

An outlet near Lake Providence may be advisable.

It will be noticed that near Lake Providence the levees must be constructed of enormous height to restrain the floods. It may, therefore, be well to reduce them by constructing, near that town, an outlet leading to bayou Tensas and Black river. Its capacity should not exceed 100,000 cubic feet per second, a volume which might be made to pass off through the natural drains of the Tensas swamp without producing serious inundation. Those drains have always discharged a large amount of crevasse-water in the great flood years, and may be depended upon for sensibly relieving the river in that vicinity. Abstracting 100,000 cubic feet per second at that point would reduce the river flood three feet throughout that part of the region between Napoleon and Vicksburg which it is most difficult to protect, and would thus materially reduce the cost of the levees and the danger of crevasses. Before undertaking the project, however, extensive borings should be made to ascertain the character of the substrata. Unless a solid bed of clay should be found at a moderate depth, the outlet should not be undertaken, lest it might become too large for the safety of the region bordering upon bayou Tensas and Black river. Under any circumstances, it would be an injury, rather than a benefit, to the country below Red-river landing (see discussion of flood of 1851), and in the event of coincident floods in the Mississippi and Red rivers, it would be disastrous to the lower part of the Tensas and to the Black river country.

Cross-section and mode of construction of levees.

With reference to the proper cross-section of the levees, and the mode of constructing them, it may be remarked that the dimensions adopted by the State of Mississippi appear to be excessive, except where the soil has but little cohesion and is very permeable. The area of the cross-section of these levees is from one-half to one-third greater than the area of cross-section of the dikes of Europe* in soil of the same consistency and permeability. (See plate XVIII.) Experience has proved the latter to be sufficiently strong. The dikes of Europe, in localities where the soil is loose and sandy, have about the same area of cross-section as the levees of the State of Mississippi. The additional cost resulting from these excessive dimensions becomes important when the height is great; and except where the soil is very porous and sandy, they may be reduced, and proportions adopted similar to the following, that is—the width at top equal to the height—the outer slope 3 to 1—and the inner slope 2 to 1. These dimensions being used, the cost will be diminished about one-fourth.

The mode of constructing the levees of the State of Mississippi (see Chapter II) is admirable. Many good hints upon this subject may also be found in a treatise upon levees† published by Mr. W. Hewson in 1860.

Approximate estimate of the cost

Although no precise estimate of the cost of perfecting the levee system can be made until exact surveys are extended throughout the entire alluvial region, an approximation will be attempted in order to show that the

* The French dikes on the Rhine in that part of its course lying between the Black Forest and the Vosges mountains, where the height is 7 feet, have a width of 10 feet, the slope toward the river being 2 to 1, and toward the land 1.5 to 1. When the height exceeds 7 feet, the width is increased by a banquette on each side. The area of cross-section of this dike, 7 feet high, is 154 square feet; the area of cross-section of a levee of the State of Mississippi, of that height, is 252 square feet.

The dikes of the Rhine in Holland, when near the river bank and when used for the road, have a width of 20 feet on top, when 16 feet high, a slope of 3 to 1 on the river side and a slope of 1.5 to 1 on the land side. The outer slope, when exposed to running ice, is protected by a revetement of brick or fascines. When the dike is not near the river bank and is not used as a road, the width is only 6.5 feet. The area of cross-section of the first dike is 900 square feet; of the second, 640 square feet; a levee of the State of Mississippi, of the same height, would have an area of cross-section of 1230 square feet.

The dikes on the Po (those of the Adige have similar dimensions) are 2.5 feet above the highest flood mark; usually the width is equal to the height, and the slope of the sides is 2 to 1. When the soil is permeable, they are reënforced at the height of the mean floods (10 feet below the top of the dike) by a banquette, whose width is 20 feet when the height is 20 feet or over. The area of cross-section of this dike is 1400 square feet; a levee of the State of Mississippi, of the same height, would have an area of cross-section of 1800 square feet. Where the soil is very sandy and has but little cohesion, the dikes of the Po, when 20 feet high and over, have a width at top of 26 feet, two banquettes of 20 feet width, an outside slope of 3 to 1 and an inside slope of 2 to 1. The area of cross-section of this dike, 20 feet high, is 1840 square feet; a levee of the State of Mississippi, of the same height, would have an area of cross-section of 1800 square feet. The river roads are usually upon the levee or the banquette.

The average height of the dikes on the Vistula is 20 feet. The top of the dike is from 2 to 3 feet above the highest flood; the thickness at top is 15 feet, or three-fourths of the height, and the slopes 3 to 1 and 2 to 1. The area of cross-section of such a dike is 1300 square feet; a levee of the State of Mississippi, of the same height, would have an area of cross-section of 1800 square feet.

The highest dike on the Vistula is 28 feet in height. It has a width at top of 18 feet, and an area of cross-section of 2460 square feet. A levee of the State of Mississippi, of the same height, would have an area of cross-section of 2660 square feet.

The dimensions and forms of the cross-sections of these dikes are shown on plate XVIII.

† Principles and Practice of Embanking Land from River Floods as applied to Levees of the Mississippi. New York, 1860.

of a perfected levee system.

expense of securing this country against inundation is not large, in comparison with the interests to be protected and the advantages to be gained by the execution of the work.

The dimensions of cross-section just proposed for levees, and the rules of construction adopted by the State of Mississippi, will be taken as the basis of this estimate. Experience has shown that 105 miles of this levee—including about 4,000,000 cubic yards of new embankment (after allowing one-sixth for settling), 500 acres of ploughing and clearing, and the salaries of the engineers—can be perfected in six months at a cost of 20.35 cents per cubic yard. (Report of State Engineer, June 18, 1860.) This accords with the reported prices in other States, and the sum of 20 cents per cubic yard will therefore be adopted. The high water of 1858 will be assumed to be 4 feet above the level of the natural bank from the Ohio to Red river, and 3.5 feet above it below the latter point. The height of the present levees, assumed to be continuous, will be taken at 4.5 feet, except on the front of Yazoo bottom, where the new State levees will be supposed to be completed to the proposed height (about 10 feet). The cross-section of the present levees above Red river (except the Yazoo-bottom levees) will be assumed to be the same as that measured between Red river and Carrollton (Chapter II), or 38 square feet.

It will first be supposed that no levees exist, and the cost of constructing them with the proper dimensions to secure the country against inundation will be computed. The cubical contents of the present levees under the conditions above assumed will then be given. What *ought* to be their cubical contents with their present heights will next be presented. In each of these cases, the levees will be supposed to extend from the mouth of the Ohio to the head of Yazoo bottom on the right bank; thence to the mouth of Yazoo river on both banks; thence to Red-river landing on the right bank, and in detached portions equivalent to half this distance on the left bank; thence to Baton Rouge on the right bank; thence to Fort St. Philip on both banks. To perfect the system of protection, levees must be extended up the swamp rivers, but the information necessary for the determination of their extent and cost has not been obtained.

Estimated cost of levee system.

Locality.	Distance.	Proposed levee (supposed to be entirely new).						Present levee.						
		Mean height.	Cross-section.	Cost per mile.	Cost.			Approximate cubical contents as existing.			Proper cubical contents with present height.			Cost of perfecting existing levees to present height.
					Right bank.	Left bank.	Total.	Right bank.	Left bank.	Total.	Right bank.	Left bank.	Total.	
	Miles	*Feet*	*S. ft.*	$	$	$	$	*Cu. yds.*	*Cu. yds.*	*Cu. yds.*	*Cu. yds.*	*Cu. yds.*	*Cu. yds.*	$
Cairo to Osceola	149	9.0	283	11,068	1,649,000	0	1,649,000	1,107,000	0	1,107,000	2,069,000	0	2,069,000	192,000
Osceola to head of Yazoo bottom	87	11.0	424	16,583	1,443,000	0	1,443,000	647,000	0	647,000	1,208,000	0	1,208,000	112,000
Head of Yazoo bottom to Island 71	137	12.0	504	19,712	2,701,000	2,701,000	5,402,000	1,018,000	12,726,000	13,744,000	1,902,000	9,377,000	11,279,000	177,000
Island 71 to Napoleon	35	13.0	591	23,114	809,000	809,000	1,618,000	260,000	3,251,000	3,511,000	486,000	2,396,000	2,882,000	45,000
Napoleon to Lake Providence	132	13.5	638	24,952	3,294,000	3,294,000	6,588,000	981,000	12,261,000	13,242,000	1,833,000	9,038,000	10,871,000	170,000
Lake Providence to mouth of Yazoo	60	12.5	547	21,394	1,284,000	1,284,000	2,568,000	446,000	5,573,000	6,019,000	833,000	4,107,000	4,940,000	77,000
Mouth of Yazoo to Red river	181	10.0	350	13,689	2,478,000	1,239,000	3,717,000	1,345,000	672,000	2,017,000	2,513,000	1,257,000	3,770,000	351,000
Red river to Baton Rouge	70	7.5	197	7,705	539,000		539,000	520,000		520,000	972,000		972,000	90,000
Baton Rouge to Fort St. Philip	208	6.5	148	5,788	1,204,000	1,204,000	2,408,000	1,546,000	1,546,000	3,092,000	2,888,000	2,888,000	5,776,000	537,000
Total							25,932,000			43,899,000				1,751,000

This table shows that the additional sum which ought to have been expended upon the existing levees, in order to give them a proper cross-section with their present height, is about two millions of dollars. Every engineer who has written upon the subject declares that the embankments are entirely too weak, and this opinion is fully sustained both by theory and by experience. Whenever the river rises 3 feet above the level of the natural bank, disastrous crevasses occur.

The table further shows that the total cost of protecting the alluvial region against inundation, *provided there were no levees in existence,* would be about twenty-six millions of dollars, and that the cost of bringing the present levees from their assumed dimensions to this state of perfection would be about seventeen millions of dollars. It is probable that this sum does not largely exceed the amount which has actually been spent in abortive attempts to solve practically the great problem of protection against overflow.

Advantages of a levee system.

It may be well to exhibit, in connection with this approximate estimate of the cost of leveeing the alluvial region, the extent and probable value of the lands which, thus protected from overflow, will be rendered available for cultivation. The area of those lands from Cape Girardeau to Red river is 19,450 square miles. It may be assumed that one-half of this area will be rendered cultivable, and as its value per acre may be set down at 25 dollars, the total will amount to 160,000,000 dollars. The area of the alluvial land under cultivation below the mouth of Red river is not less than 1,000,000 acres, which, at 100 dollars per acre (by no means an extravagant estimate), gives 100,000,000 dollars for the value of the plantations in that section, making a total value of 260,000,000 dollars for the land that will be rendered perpetually cultivable by the expenditure of 17,000,000 of dollars.

There is another aspect under which this part of the subject may be presented. The number of acres thus protected is 7,000,000. Each acre of alluvial land will produce one bale of cotton, worth, on the average, 45 dollars. We thus have, for the value of the annual product of the alluvial lands, 315,000,000 dollars. The loss in the Tensas bottom, from the flood of 1850, furnishes an instance of the injuries resulting from inundation. It was estimated that the loss thus occasioned exceeded five millions of dollars.

Practical importance of a continued and careful system of observations.

In concluding these recommendations, it may be added that the importance of preserving accurate registers of all the oscillations of the river, and especially of securing careful records of all facts respecting the great floods, cannot be too strongly urged upon engineers charged with the construction of these works. By the aid of the tables already given and the principles laid down, such records, if sufficiently extensive, may be made to test the correctness of the practical conclusions announced in this report respecting the levee system as applied to the alluvial region of the Mississippi.

CHAPTER VII.

DELTA OF THE MISSISSIPPI.

Boundaries of the delta.—Its area and character.—Outlet bayous.—Dimensions and discharge of bayou La Fourche —Its levees and their increasing height.—This phenomenon never yet explained.—True explanation.—Proper height to be given to the levees.—Speculations as to the original character of the outlet bayous.—Characteristics of an original outlet illustrated by bayou Teche.—Two suppositions to explain the present character of the outlet bayous.—Speculative geology of the delta.—Hills.—Mounds, ancient and modern.—Shell mounds and strata.—Prolongation of the mouth of the Mississippi.—The original mouth was probably near Plaquemine.—Ancient depth of the gulf in this vicinity.—Probable age of the delta.—Future advance.—Changes which may have occurred in the condition of the Mississippi river.—Separation of branches may be effected by storms, by waves, and by drift.—Ancient geography of the delta.—Bayou Atchafalaya was never the prolongation of Red river.—The Mississippi extends its delta along the deepest part of the great marine valley.

Definition and boundaries of the delta.

ACCORDING to the usual acceptation of the term, the delta of the Mississippi begins where it first sends off a branch to the sea. This point is the head of bayou Atchafalaya, which is therefore adopted as the northern limit of the delta, although it is not believed that the mouth of the river ever occupied that position.

BOUNDARIES AND AREA.

This region is naturally subdivided into four parts.

1. The Atchafalaya basin, which, beginning at the mouth of bayou Teche, follows the meanderings of that stream to a point southeast of the town of Opelousas; thence to the town of Opelousas; thence in a northerly direction through Ville Platte and Chicotville to the dividing ridge between the source of bayous Bœuf and Rapides; thence north to bayou Rapides; thence down that bayou to Red river; thence down Red river to the southeast corner of T. 2 N., R. 2 E.; thence easterly to bayou de Glaize, excluding the Avoyelles prairie; thence with bayou de Glaize to northeast corner of T. 1 N., R. 6 E.; thence to upper mouth of the Atchafalaya; thence with Old river to the Mississippi river; thence with the meanderings of that river to the upper mouth of bayou La Fourche; thence down bayou La Fourche to the town of Thibodeaux; thence to a point on bayou Black, west of the town of Houma; thence down that bayou to bayou Bœuf; thence down the Bœuf to the Atchafalaya; thence up the Atchafalaya to the mouth of the Teche, the initial point.

2. The Terre Bonne district, which, beginning at the town of Thibodeaux, follows down the bayou La Fourche to the gulf of Mexico; thence westwardly along the coasts of the gulf, bays, inlets, etc., to the mouth of bayou Petite Anse (a bayou emptying into Vermilion bay); thence in a northeasterly direction to the town of New Iberia on the Teche; thence down the Teche to its mouth; thence down the Atchafalaya to the

mouth of bayou Bœuf; thence up the Bœuf to bayou Black; thence up that bayou to a point east of the town of Houma; thence to the town of Thibodeaux, the initial point.

3. The La Fourche district, which, beginning at the town of Donaldsonville, follows the meanderings of the Mississippi river to the gulf of Mexico; thence westwardly with the coast of the gulf to the lower mouth of bayou La Fourche; thence up that bayou to the town of Donaldsonville, the initial point.

4. The lake Pontchartrain district, which, beginning at the old mouth of the bayou Manchac, follows that bayou to the Amite river; thence down that river to lake Maurepas; thence with the southern coast of that lake to pass-Manchac light-house; thence along the southern coast of lake Pontchartrain to Fort Pike; thence with the pass of the Rigolets to lake Borgne; thence with the southern coast of that lake to the gulf of Mexico; thence with the coasts of the gulf, bays, inlets, etc., to the mouth of the Mississippi river; thence up that river to the old mouth of bayou Manchac, the initial point.

Its area and character.

The area of these subdivisions, measured with care on La Tourrette's State map of Louisiana, is as follows:—

	Square miles.
Atchafalaya basin	4,610
La Fourche district	2,420
Terre Bonne district	2,930
Lake Pontchartrain district	2,340
Total	12,300

The soil of the first division lies above the level of the gulf. Of the three other divisions, about 4000 square miles, or one-half the total area, is composed of sea marsh.

The cross-sections on plate IV exhibit the characteristic slopes of this region, the entire surface of which is below the level of the river floods, and composed of alluvial or fluviatile matter. It contains several lakes, and is traversed by many bayous, three of which, the Atchafalaya, the Plaquemine, and the La Fourche, are connected with the Mississippi river. It is important for several reasons to ascertain the real nature of these bayous; and with this object, one, the La Fourche, will be selected for examination in detail.

OUTLET BAYOUS.

General character.

Bayou La Fourche, the last of the outlets of the Mississippi, in many respects resembles an artificial canal. Its current does not exceed 3 feet per second. Its bends are few in number and gentle in curvature. There are no boils, whirls, or eddies, nor are the banks abraded to any perceptible extent.

Width.

Dimensions and discharging capacity.—Its width between the natural banks averages about 230 feet and undergoes but little variation. Thus, at Donaldsonville, it is 210 feet; at Pain Court, 210 feet; at Thibodeaux, 230 feet; and at Lockport, 240 feet. There are, however, a few narrow places above Lockport. The width at extreme low water is, at Donaldsonville, 80 feet; at Pain Court, 90 feet; at Thibodeaux, 110 feet; and at Lockport, 120 feet.

At the head of the bayou, where the range is about 24 feet, the greatest depth in

Depth. extreme low water is 3 feet, the gulf being at the mean level. A great depression of the surface of the gulf may leave the bed dry or nearly so. The greatest depth at extreme low water between Pain Court and Lockport, the gulf being at its mean level, is from 8 to 10 feet. Below Lockport the depth is greater. On the bar in the gulf the depth at mean tide is 7 feet.

Slope. The levels of the Survey show that the natural bank is at Donaldsonville 23 feet, and at Lockport 8 feet, above the mean level of the gulf. That is, on the bayou in its natural state, the slope in the upper half was nearly twice as great as in the lower half, an instructive fact to which attention will be drawn hereafter.

Area of cross-section within natural banks. The area of cross-section with the water at the level of the natural banks also diminishes rapidly below the head of the bayou. Thus by the measurements of the Survey made in 1851, and repeated with the same result in 1859, this area is at Donaldsonville 3500 square feet, at Thibodeaux 2600 square feet, and at Lockport 2000 square feet. According to the measurements of Captain G. W. Hughes, Topographical Engineers, made in 1842, this area in the lower part of the bayou, below the levees, was 2000 square feet. These facts are also important, and their bearing will be discussed in connection with the levees.

Discharge. The maximum discharge at the head of the bayou is 11,500 cubic feet per second, the mean velocity being 3.0 feet per second. The mean annual discharge at the same place is about 2000 cubic feet per second, the mean velocity being about 1.0 foot per second. This subject for each of the three outlet bayous has already been fully treated in Chapter IV, under the head, "*Interpolation of daily discharge at velocity stations.*"*

The earlier records show that the bayou formerly had about its present dimensions. So far as we have documentary evidence, these general dimensions of the bayou have undergone no change during the present century. Thus in Major Stoddard's Louisiana, published in 1812, it is stated: "*The bed* of this outlet [at low water] *is about* 90 *feet in width*, and usually dry in the summer season for a few miles from its head, when the water makes its appearance." Darby, in his Geographical Description of Louisiana, published in 1817, says: "The La Fourche, when leaving the Mississippi [at high water] *is not more than* 80 *yards wide*, and [the bottom] very little below the ordinary autumnal level of that stream. In some extraordinary seasons, the La Fourche has been dried at its efflux; it is fordable nearly every year in October and November." The measurements of this Survey show that no change, either in width or depth, took place above Lockport between 1851 and 1858.†

---

* For bayou Plaquemine the maximum discharge is 35,000 cubic feet per second, the mean velocity being 6.0 feet per second. The mean annual discharge is about 5000 cubic feet per second, the corresponding velocity being 1.5 feet per second.

For bayou Atchafalaya these four quantities are 130,000 cubic feet, 5.0 feet, 50,000 cubic feet, and 5.0 feet respectively.

† The measurements upon bayou Plaquemine, at its efflux from the Mississippi, made by the Delta Survey in 1851 and 1859 (see Appendix C and plate III) show no changes in depth or width, between those dates. Those upon the Atchafalaya at its efflux (see plate III) denote an increase of cross-section between those years. The reports of the engineers of the State of Louisiana, detailing measurements made there at different periods in the last thirty-five years, also indicate that the channel is constantly increasing. The mean annual velocity of the Atchafalaya, it will be remembered, is 5.0 feet per second; while that of the Plaquemine is but 1.5 feet per second, and that of the La Fourche 1.0 foot per second.

Levee system of bayou La Fourche.—Levees were commenced at an early day, and were extended rapidly down one-half the length of the bayou. It is stated in the Abstract of Documents of the State and Treasury Departments, 1802–05, that "on both banks of this creek there are settlements one plantation deep for near 15 leagues." In 1842 the levees terminated at or a short distance below Lockport, 56 miles below Donaldsonville, and 54 miles from the gulf. In 1859 they nominally extended 27 miles below Lockport, although, it is stated, they were not more than 3 feet high, 12 miles below the town.

Levees.

The levees are of the same height on both banks, and increase in elevation from Donaldsonville, where they are 3.5 feet high, to Lockport, where they were 8 feet high in 1858. They may exceed 8 feet at some localities between those points. At the head of the bayou, the levees have not been raised, their height being determined by the sensibly constant level of the Mississippi floods. On the bayou below, however, the high-water level has constantly risen, and the levees have been as constantly increased in height. Thus it is stated that, when the levees were first thrown up at Thibodeaux, in 1823, they were only a foot or two high. In December, 1851, they were 5 feet, and in January, 1859, 7 feet in height at this locality. A comparison of exact high-water marks at Lockport for the years 1851, 1852, 1853, and 1858, shows that the mark of 1852 was 0.3 of a foot above that of 1851; and the mark of 1853, 0.3 of a foot above that of 1852; and the mark of 1858, 1.4 feet above that of 1853; making a total rise of 2.0 feet in seven years.* It becomes, then, an important practical problem to determine what additional height should be given to the levees, in order to enable the bayou to discharge, without overflowing them, the maximum amount it receives from the Mississippi; and also to decide whether, if raised to that height, it will hereafter become necessary to raise them still higher.

Their increasing height.

The explanation usually offered to account for the necessity of constantly raising the levees in the lower part of the bayou is understood to be as follows: The levees of the La Fourche were commenced at the head, and were rapidly continued down stream to a point about 50 miles above the mouth, beyond which they were not extended for a period of thirty years, and where to all useful purpose they now end. Where the levees terminated, the waters of the bayou overflowed the banks and raised them by deposit. The current in the bayou being diminished by this escape of water, a deposit was also made in its channel. This deposit contracted the water-way and increased the lateral overflow, and thus accelerated the elevation of the natural bank, which has been in this way raised materially since the levees were first built. (By some this elevation has been estimated at 10 or 12 feet.) This has had the effect of backing up the bayou above, and thus of raising the flood level. To this explanation has been added the opinion that the turbid water of the Missis-

Usual explanation of this phenomenon.

* Mr. Morse, State Engineer of Louisiana, placed a permanent bench at Lockport, in 1852, with a view of accurately determining the relative heights of former and future floods. This bench is a cast-iron bar, with a rectangular head (wider than the body) measuring about 4 by 8 inches, and having a projecting shoulder on one side. It is placed on the left bank of the bayou, on the upper (northern) side of the lock, distant 71 feet from the rear corner of the abutment of the front (bayou) gate, and 52 feet from the front corner of the abutment of the back gate. Arcs of circles described from these points with these radii will intersect at the bench, which is buried about a foot below the surface of the ground. The high-water marks of 1852, 1853, and 1858 are 6.605, 6.87, and 8.29 feet, respectively, above this bench.

sippi, flowing in the bayou with less velocity than in the river, is unable to hold the same quantity of matter in suspension, and accordingly must raise the bed of the bayou by deposit, even where the levees have been built.*

They are erroneous.

Let us see whether these explanations are consistent with the facts ascertained by measurements in different years, by parties of the Delta Survey.

The banks below the levees have not been materially raised.

The natural bank at Lockport is 8 feet above the mean level of the gulf. It is stated on good authority at Lockport, that, in 1858, the crevasse-water of the Bell and La Branche crevasses ran over the levees into the bayou at a point 12 miles below the town, where the levees were 3 feet high. The mark of this crevasse-water at Lockport was 7.5 feet above the mean yearly level of the gulf; 12 miles below Lockport, its level could not have exceeded this elevation. Consequently, the levees there being 3 feet high, and the crevasse-water passing over them, the natural bank could not have exceeded an elevation of 4 feet above the gulf. A few miles farther down, it is probable that the natural banks are but little, if any, above the gulf. The conclusion that in the last thirty or forty years the natural bank below the leveed part of the La Fourche has been materially elevated above its original height cannot therefore be adopted.

There has been no deposit in the bed.

Neither can it be admitted that the current of the bayou, at points where there are no levees, is necessarily so much less than where there are levees, as to cause a deposit, and thus contract the channel-way. At flood, the current of the bayou where leveed is 3 feet per second; where not leveed, 2 feet per second. What proof have we that, where the first velocity exists, the bayou is either holding in suspension or pushing forward at the bottom a quantity of earthy matter which a velocity of 2 feet per second is insufficient to transport? On the contrary, the results of the investigation at Carrollton, fully detailed in Chapter II and discussed in Chapter VI, justify the assumption that the velocity in the unleveed portion of the bayou at flood is quite equal to transporting all such material. This inference becomes almost a certainty when the source is considered from which bayou La Fourche draws its supply. All the river-water that is to enter that bayou at flood passes within 200 feet of the river bank, where its mean velocity does not exceed, if it equals, 2 feet per second. This water, after entering the bayou, moves with an increased velocity of about 3 feet per second as long as the levees continue, and is only reduced to its original velocity of 2 feet per second when they cease. Neither the power of suspension nor that of transportation is therefore decreased, and no deposit in any part of the channel can be made.

Actual measurements lead to the same conclusion. Thus, so far as can be ascer-

* It has also been suggested, as an additional cause of the rising of the high-water level, that the bayou below Lockport is choked up with rafts and tow-heads. This is a question of fact which can be easily investigated, although not attempted by the Delta Survey. Lieutenant Henry L. Smith, Corps of Engineers, who examined the obstructions below Lockport in 1853, with a view to their removal, states that they begin about 5 miles below Lockport, and consist of a great number of snags, which project above low water, and for the distance of 18 miles almost entirely prevent the passage of steamboats during the low water of the summer and autumn. Such obstructions must, of course, retard the flow of the water, and to some slight extent raise the flood level for a limited distance above them, but they are evidently inadequate to aid materially in producing the constant increase of the floods throughout nearly the whole bayou.

tained by a comparison of the soundings at Lockport in 1842 (Military Reconnoissance —Approaches to New Orleans, Captain G. W. Hughes, Topographical Engineers, United States Army) and those of the Delta Survey in 1851 and 1858, there is no reason to conclude that any deposit has been made in the bed of the bayou in that vicinity. There is a difficulty in making an exact comparison of the more recent measurements with those of Captain Hughes, because he did not make a permanent bench-mark, or even record the relative level of the surface of the bayou and the natural bank. The levees terminated at Lockport in 1842; and it is probable, as the soundings were made in the spring, that the surface of the bayou was nearly even with the natural bank. If so, the bottom has certainly not been excavated since that date, although the levees have been considerably prolonged. The careful measurements made by the Delta Survey in 1851 and 1858 give more definite results. They show that although the area of cross-section of the bayou has been enlarged by the additions made to it in giving increased height to the levees, yet neither excavation nor deposit has been made in the bed, which has remained at the same absolute level. The following table exhibits the numerical results of the measurements. (For further details see Appendix C.)

Area of cross-section of bayou La Fourche.

Locality.	Area with water at the level of the natural banks.	High-water area.		Width of bayou (between levees).	Flood level above natural banks.	
		Flood of 1851 (measured in succeeding low water).	Flood of 1858 (measured in succeeding low water).		1851.	1858.
	Square feet.	*Square feet.*	*Square feet.*	*Feet.*	*Feet.*	*Feet.*
Donaldsonville	3500	3990	3980	230	2.5	2.2
Pain Court		3580	4080	280		
Thibodeaux	2600	3595	3970	230	4.0	6.0
Lockport	1700	3000	3500	240	5.5	7.5

A comparison of these independent measurements, by the aid of the last three columns of the table, will make it evident that they are all consistent with each other, and that the change in area is solely due to the change in flood level.

Real cause of the increasing floods.

This table, while thus disproving the theory usually advanced to account for the increased height of the floods, furnishes a clue to the true solution of the problem.

Natural diminution of cross-section and discharge, as the gulf is approached.

The table, and Captain Hughes' measurements already mentioned, show that the area of cross-section between Lockport and the gulf, before levees were made, did not exceed 2000 square feet. The corresponding fall of the natural bank, and hence of the water surface, as already seen, was only 8 feet. Applying equation (40) to these numbers, we find that the discharge could not have exceeded 4000 cubic feet per second. But the quantity which entered the bayou from the Mississippi could not have differed materially from what it is at present (11,500 cubic feet per second); an inference confirmed by applying the formula to the known cross-section and slope. Hence, between 7000 and 8000 cubic feet per second, or about two-thirds of the total flood volume received from the Mississippi, must formerly have escaped, above Lockport, over the natural banks. This would only require a lateral overflow 2 inches deep moving with a velocity of 1 inch per second, numbers by no means improbable.

The levees have never yet been made high enough to correct for this natural deficiency of cross-section.

It is now evident how the banks of the La Fourche can be protected against overflow. Its channel must be enlarged so that the water which formerly escaped over the natural banks may be carried by the bayou to the gulf. At Lockport, and points below, a discharge fully three times as great as before levees were built must be provided for. At that point and for many miles above, the levees have never yet been raised sufficiently high to give a cross-section competent to discharge all the water that enters the bayou in a flood. The embankments are very narrow, scarcely wide enough for a foot-path at top. When the water rises to within a few inches of the top, they give way; and so diminutive is the discharge of the bayou that a crevasse of small dimensions will lower the surface 2 or 3 feet. In the next season the levees are raised a little. The high water of the following year rises sufficiently again to break them and thus relieve the overcharged channel. Again they are raised still higher, and again they are broken; and this operation must continue until the dimensions of cross-section throughout the bayou are sufficient to carry off the water which enters from the Mississippi. If the levees had been built at first of such a height as to make the capacity of discharge throughout the bayou equal to that at the head, these annual crevasses and overflows and annually rising high-water level would never have occurred.*

The annual extension of the levees has increased the difficulty.

There is a second general cause which has contributed to increase the heights of the floods of this bayou, namely, the yearly extension of the levees. At the point where levees terminate, the natural banks are overflowed, and the effect of this lateral discharge, in lowering the surface in the bayou above, is evidently similar to that of a great crevasse. It is not necessary to determine the exact distance on the La Fourche to which this effect extends, but it is certainly as great as 20 or 30 miles. Between the crevasse and that point, the depression is nearly inversely proportional to the distance from the crevasse. The future extension of levees below Lockport must therefore constantly tend to elevate the surface of the bayou there, until after they have been perfected to a point some thirty miles below the town.

Proper dimensions to be given to the levees.

The practical conclusions to be drawn from the preceding discussion are the following: The discharging capacity of the bayou throughout must be made equal to that at its head. This must be accomplished by artificially enlarging the cross-section; for the experience of from seven to sixteen years at Lockport indicates that the waters of the bayou, even when retained by levees from 6 to 8 feet high, do not appreciably excavate the bed. The cross-section may be enlarged either by raising the levees or by excavating the

* The facts collected respecting the flood of 1858 illustrate this action perfectly. Thus, on April 11, the river at Donaldsonville was 2 feet below the high-water mark of 1851. On the same day, at Lockport, the La Fourche was 2 feet above the high-water mark of 1851, and within 6 inches of the top of the levees. The occurrence of a crevasse a mile above Lockport, which remained open until the autumn, not only prevented the water from rising higher, but depressed it to such an extent that, at the time of high water at Donaldsonville, which was 1.7 feet above its stand on April 11, the bayou at Lockport stood 3 feet below the mark of that date. The crevasse when largest had a width of only about 300 feet, but it abraded the bank so that its bottom was 9 feet below the top of the levee.

channel. The first is the readier and more economical mode. If the levees at Lockport are raised so as to permit the surface of the bayou to rise 2 feet above the high water of 1858, the area of cross-section there will be 4000 square feet, the same as at the head of the bayou; and the fall between the two places (7.9 feet) will be sufficient to carry off the greatest quantity of water that—with the present height of the Mississippi floods—can enter the bayou, provided that the area of cross-section between the two places is not less than 4000 square feet. If it be found by survey that the area of cross-section will be anywhere less than 4000 square feet (as it may be at certain narrow places), the channel must be enlarged to that size. Above Lockport, a proportional increase of height must be given to the levees as far as Thibodeaux (and perhaps somewhat above that town), so that the total height of the levees between those places shall gradually decrease from 10.5 to 8.0 feet. As far as the levees are extended below Lockport, they must be about 10.5 feet high, in order to insure a cross-section of 4000 square feet.

The extraordinary diminution of the area of cross-section and of the slope in the lower part of the course, the chief cause of the difficulty in restraining the floods of the La Fourche, is not peculiar to that bayou. It is a characteristic feature of the three outlet bayous of the Mississippi. Thus on the Atchafalaya, the fall in the first half of its length is two-thirds of the whole fall to the gulf. On the Plaquemine, the same proportion of the total fall is consumed in the first 8 miles; below that point, its banks are not cultivated. Difficulties, similar to those that have arisen on the La Fourche, will therefore be certain to occur on these two bayous when their levees are sufficiently extended.

The outlet bayous are not original mouths of the river.

Speculations as to the original character of the three outlet bayous.—An important deduction from the observed facts on bayous Atchafalaya, Plaquemine, and La Fourche is that *either they are not delta streams, whose beds are formed in their own deposits*, or the dogma heretofore received by hydraulic engineers, that in delta rivers the slope must be inversely as the quantity discharged, is erroneous; for, as already fully explained, the fall in the upper half of the La Fourche is twice as great as in the lower half, while the discharges are as three to one, and similar conditions exist on the other two bayous. In Chapter II, where the geological age of the hard clay which composes the beds of the Atchafalaya and Plaquemine is investigated, the opinion is expressed that it is not an alluvial deposit, and hence that these bayous are not original outlets, but merely drains that have been connected with the Mississippi by the erosion of the river banks. The clay bed of the La Fourche has a similar tenacity, although it may not be of the same geological age. It will be presently shown that this bayou was probably a marsh drain, changed to a Mississippi outlet by the erosion of the river banks. It was perhaps the first so connected, the Atchafalaya the second, and the Plaquemine the last, and in comparatively recent times. The facts which demonstrate this in respect to the Plaquemine are made known by Mr. Bayley in a pamphlet upon the closure of that bayou, published in Baton Rouge, 1858.* In reality

* "But few, very brief, and unsatisfactory allusions are to be found in the early histories of Louisiana relative to bayou Plaquemine. Upon some of the early maps it is shown by a mere line; upon others it is not at all represented. The waters of Grand river, at this point, approach within 8 or 10 miles of the Mississippi; and at low water the ebb and flow of the tides was quite perceptible, before the various channels connecting with Grand lake were choked up with raft and detritus. It is probable that one of the numerous overflow coulés, which existed in every bend before

the only parts of the Mississippi that are true delta streams are the passes. Their beds are formed in the deposit (not homogeneous however) made by the river-water in the gulf; those of the greatest length discharge the largest volumes; the slopes are in the inverse order of the volumes.

Characteristics of an original outlet.

The bayou Teche, which forms a portion of the southwest border of the delta, presents features directly the opposite of the Atchafalaya, Plaquemine, and La Fourche, and may be taken as a type of another class of bayous, those that *have* been gradually separated from the main stream. As now existing, the Teche may be described as a small stream that rises in the gray soil of the pine lands west of Washington. Its length from that town to its mouth in

the construction of levees, connected—whether directly or indirectly does not appear—the Mississippi river with this eastern bend of Grand river; and such coulé, however much obstructed by growing cypress-trees in its channel, would be used, as affording the nearest approach to the Mississippi, by the small keel-boats used in the interior navigation of Louisiana a century ago. Such use would associate it with the route to the early Attakapas settlements, and lead to its mention in such connection by the early historians. Du Pratz, in his history of Louisiana [1757], does so mention it; and after describing the Iberville (or Manchac) and the La Fourche, expressly says that the Plaquemine is but 'a bayou,' and unworthy the name of '*rivière*.' The 'river Iberville' is described by Pittman, in 1770, as being but 50 feet wide, and 'obstructed by wood' (raft) for 6 miles from its head.

"The old bed of the Manchac, for several miles from the Mississippi, averages less than 50 feet wide now, as stated in the Report of the State Engineer to the legislature in 1852, in answer to a proposition to reopen the Manchac in that year.

"How insignificant, then, must have been the Plaquemine if, as compared with a 'river' but 50 feet wide, it was particularly noticed as being but '*a bayou*,' and unworthy the name of '*rivière*'!

"If the Plaquemine—however insignificant according to Du Pratz, who did not place it on his maps—really had, even at high water, any connection with the Mississippi river, then, like the Iberville, it must have been filled up with 'wood,' or raft, and not navigable *from* the river. A 'portage' must necessarily have existed between the Mississippi and the Plaquemine, or more probably the bayou Jacob, as is uniformly said to have been the case, by all the aged inhabitants of Iberville and Attakapas, as testified to very recently by Judge Baker, of St. Mary, formerly a member of the old Board of Public Works, and for forty-five years a resident of Attakapas.

"Judge Baker at the same time assured us that both the Plaquemine and Jacob were but overflowed coulés, and entirely covered by a forest of cypress-trees, which trees were cut down, and the stumps recut down several times (as the bottom was washed away from around their stumps), by the inhabitants and Navigation Company of Attakapas.

"Captain Mayo (as he himself informed me), under the orders of the old Board of Public Works, with the State hands, superintended the cutting down of said stumps in more than one instance. Cypress-trees could not grow in the *bed* of an original 'pass' of the Mississippi river. * * * * * * *

"According to measurements made by the Senate Committee on Levees, in the year 1850 (Doc. No. 2), the width of the Plaquemine, 1000 feet below its head, was 264 feet; while the *average* width in 1857, according to a series of measurements by the Commissioner of the Second Swamp Land District, was 400 feet, with an occasional width of 420 to 430 feet; thus showing an increase in seven years, with only one very high water (that of 1851) since, of *nearly one hundred and fifty feet*. According to the United States Land-office maps before referred to, this width in 1842 was about 175 feet, possibly 200 feet in places, while in 1829, by same maps, it was from 50 to 75 feet wide, as nearly as the same can be ascertained by the scale upon which said maps are projected. * * *

"The cutting of a road through the canebrakes and forest, and the digging of a small ditch or canal therein leading from the Mississippi into either the head of the Plaquemine or Jacob, as alleged to have been done in the year 1770, * * * by Joseph Sorrell, appears to be well substantiated; and indeed it is rendered probable by what must have been the circumstances of the case. Judge Joshua Baker recently corroborated what has been stated by John C. Marsh with regard thereto."

In the list of maps given in Appendix C of Mr. R. Thomassy's Géologie Pratique de la Louisiane, mention is made of a map of the Mississippi from the Survey of le Sieur Diron, in 1719, in which the Plaquemine is called "river," and the La Fourche "the little river of the Chetimakas." Also of one prepared by the Chevalier de Noyan (Lieutenant French Navy), in 1769, on which the Plaquemine as well as the La Fourche is styled "river." The Atchafalaya is called "bayou." The Manchac was always called "river." Another mentioned in the list is a map of Florida and Louisiana, published in 1778, by order of the French Minister of the Navy Department, M. de Sartine, on which the Atchafalaya is for the first time called "river"—not "Atchafalaya river," but "Vermilion river." The principal branch of the Atchafalaya is now called Grand river, in accordance with the supposed meaning of its Indian name, "Atchafalaya," *Great-water*—though others have translated it *Lost-water*.

Grand lake is 140 miles. A mile and a half below Washington, the bayou Courtableau, upon which that town is situated, sends off the bayou Carron, 100 feet wide, to the Teche. Six miles below it sends off Little bayou, 15 or 20 feet wide, which likewise joins the Teche. The banks of these bayous are composed of the red alluvial soil characteristic of Red river, and the banks of the Teche, from the junction of these bayous to its mouth in Grand lake, consist of the same soil.

The present bayou is evidently flowing through a partially deserted channel, having double banks throughout the greater part of its course, the shelf between the two being flat, or gently rising. A cross-section of the higher bank presents the characteristic feature of alluvial formation, a slope from the stream. Above St. Martinsville the sides of the ancient channel-way are often covered with a growth of large trees, such as do not flourish in wet soil. Below St. Martinsville the same fact is noticeable at one or two points. Twenty miles below Washington the cross-section of the remains of the old channel has a width between banks of 300 feet, and a greatest depth of 25 feet. At St. Martinsville, 35 miles farther, it has a width not less than 500 feet, and an extreme depth of at least 30 feet. From that town to the mouth, a distance of 85 miles, the width between the old banks gradually increases from 600 to 1000 or 1200 feet, the corresponding depth being not less than 15 feet. The dimensions of the channel occupied by the present flood discharge of the Teche are much smaller. At the mouth the width of water-way is usually about 500 feet. At St. Martinsville the high-water width scarcely equals 300 feet, and 35 miles above that town, scarcely 200 feet.

The slope of the old bank of the Teche, from its efflux from the Courtableau to its mouth in Grand lake, is 0.3 of a foot per mile and nearly uniform throughout.

Thus it is perceived that the Teche must at one time have discharged a much larger volume than now; and, as indicated in another part of this chapter, it was probably a principal branch, if not the main stem, of the Red river. Thus viewed, the characteristic features of such bayous are a gradually increasing area of cross-section, from the point of total or partial separation to the mouth; an inability to occupy this cross-section fully at any point; and the consequent growth, upon the unoccupied part, of large trees, such as thrive only in soil not periodically covered with water. These conditions, directly the reverse of those existing in the outlet bayous of the Mississippi, strengthen the opinion that the latter are not the remains of original branches or "passes" of that river.

Assuming, then, that the three outlet bayous are not original outlets of the Mississippi, and that on an original outlet the slope of the natural bank, like that of the river, must be nearly uniform from the head to the gulf, let us endeavor to understand how bayou La Fourche (taken as a type) acquired its present peculiarity with respect to slope, etc. Various suppositions are plausible.

First supposition to explain the present character of the three outlet bayous.

Thus let it be assumed that when the river bank at Donaldsonville had an elevation of 16 feet above the gulf (which would make the fall of the upper half of the bayou equal to that of the natural bank as it now exists), the La Fourche was an outlet of about its present length. Next let it be supposed that, by the lodging of drift and accumulation of mud, the bayou was cut off from the river, and only reconnected with it at a comparatively recent period by the erosion of the Mississippi bank. The new alluvial bank, which would be formed along the La Fourche, would first be made near the head, because the water would chiefly escape there; but it would gradually extend to the gulf. Thus the slope of the bank, greater at first near the head than midway, would by degrees become nearly uniform, a condition which it had not attained when the levees were built at Lockport.

Second supposition.

Another supposition, which is consistent with all the known facts, appears to be still more probable. It is, that the La Fourche was originally one of many bayous that ran through the sea-marsh, like those west of the Atchafalaya, and between the La Fourche and the Mississippi, connecting the various lakes and bays. These bayous are generally deep, but when within the boundary of river deposit are shoaled. In this manner, the upper portion of the La Fourche may have been filled in by the Mississippi overflows. A connection with the river may have been made by the caving of the banks. The alluvial soil would be cut through down to the clay bed. The bayou would become a delta-making stream and gradually extend its banks toward the gulf. At first the banks would extend only a few miles, and the slope would be rapid; but each year, as they were protruded, the slope would become less; and, finally, a uniform slope to the gulf would result. When the banks were occupied and levees were built, that condition was not attained. It is not improbable that the Terre Bonne and Black, also, were originally salt-marsh bayous, which, partly filled in by Mississippi water from the La Fourche, were next converted into delta streams by the latter, and finally separated from it by the lodging of drift and consequent accumulation of deposit. Strips of high ground, which were undoubtedly the banks of small outlets from the La Fourche, project into the marsh or prairie on either side of that bayou, at intervals in its course.

Probable confirmation of this supposition.

It would give probability to this supposition if it could be shown that the delta bank of the La Fourche does not extend to the gulf. There are reasonable grounds for this conclusion. The facts mentioned in connection with the Bell and La Branche crevasse-water in 1858 indicate that the natural bank of the La Fourche at a point 12 miles below Lockport is 4 feet above the gulf, and thus show that its rate of fall is the same below as above Lockport. This affords reason to conclude that the same rate of fall continues throughout the remaining part of the bayou that possesses a delta bank,—which would bring the natural bank to the level of the gulf about midway between Lockport and the gulf.

Reason for entering upon these speculations.

These suppositions are introduced to show that there is no difficulty in explaining the present condition of these three bayous, without regarding them as original outlets or mouths of the main river, and hence that they do not necessarily prove that the mouth of the Mississippi was ever situated in the vicinity of their present effluxes. In other words, they do not in the least determine the extent of the advance of the mouth of the Mississippi into the gulf.

GEOLOGY OF THE DELTA.

Scope of the present discussion.

The facts that the alluvial soil throughout the greater part of this region is only a few feet in thickness, and that it is underlain by strata belonging to a geological epoch antecedent to the present, have been so fully discussed in Chapter II that they require no further notice here. They comprise the most important parts of the practical geology of the delta. There are, however, other facts and certain speculations respecting the changes that have occurred and are now occurring in this region, which are interesting, and will therefore be given.

Hills.

Hills, mounds, etc.—A description of the hills of Belle Isle, Cote Blanche, Grande Cote, and Petite Anse, which rise from the sea-marsh south of the bayou Teche (plate II) will be found in Mr. R. Thomassy's Practical Geology of Louisiana. He ascribes their origin to volcanic action, and classes with them a great mud lump, 25 feet high, near the mouth of the Southwest pass.

Ancient mounds or hills.

Darby, in his Geographical Description of the State of Louisiana, says that he discovered in the lowest and dreariest part of a cypress swamp in the Atchafalaya basin, between the Courtableau and the Teche, six or seven mounds, the tops of which were 7 or 8 feet above the marks of highest overflow [and probably more than 20 feet above the gulf]; that their soil was not alluvial; and bore trees and vegetation entirely different from those in the swamp; and such as never grow on lands subjected to inundation; that there was no spot within several miles of the mounds where an Indian village could have existed. Mounds of a similar character are found in the same region north of the Courtableau. The plausibility of the supposition that these mounds may be the last hill-tops of the older formation, not yet covered by alluvion, cannot be tested by Darby's account of them, which contains no other details than those just given. The Toltecs, it is stated, were the mound builders, and arrived in Mexico from the north in the seventh century of the Christian era; though it is considered by other archæologists that that race migrated northward. According to Squier, mounds are not found on the last terrace of the Ohio, but exist on all the three older terraces.

Mounds above Red river.

The character of the mounds above the mouth of Red river has been sufficiently explained in Chapter I, in treating of the St. Francis and Yazoo swamps.

Modern mounds of the delta.

Upon the high and gently undulating banks of bayou Grosse Tête, there are ten or twelve earthen mounds, evidently artificial works and of comparatively modern date. They are mostly in groups of two or three, and, according to vague Indian traditions, were built to commemorate treaties of peace entered into by different tribes,—each tribe being represented by a mound. The largest of these piles of earth is at the mouth of bayou Fordoche. It is described as being of a conical shape, rising to a height of some 25 feet. Traces of the hollow from which the earth was taken may still be seen.

Two of the mounds upon the bayou Grosse Tête were visited by a party of this Survey. They were situated about 800 feet apart, near Mr. Erwin's house, on the north bank of the bayou, about 2 miles above Rosedale. Both were of the same dimensions, having the form of a square truncated pyramid 12 feet in height, the slope of the sides being about 2.5 upon 1, and the length of each side, on the top, being about 50 feet. The western mound had a ramp on its eastern side, with a slope of about 3.5 upon 1. Both mounds were composed of the alluvial soil which surrounds them, and traces of the hollows from which the earth had been taken were plainly visible.

Great numbers of mounds, composed entirely of *gnathodon* shells, are found along

Shell mounds and strata near the gulf.

the bayous in the delta of the Mississippi, near the gulf shore. It is stated in Nott and Gliddon's Types of Mankind that along Mobile river and bay, the shellfish *unio* and *paludina* exist where the water is perfectly fresh; and that the *gnathodon* flourishes in brackish water alone; that the *gnathodon* is now rarely if ever found above Choctaw point, 1 mile below Mobile, although immense beds of its shells exist for 50 miles above that point as well as along the gulf coast; that some of these beds contain marks of fire, fish-bones, and fragments of Indian pottery and of human bones; that other beds are covered 2 feet thick with vegetable mould, on which the largest forest trees are growing; that the *gnathodon* was once a living species in the Chesapeake bay, but is now only found there in a fossil state. Major Ranney and others state that the *gnathodon* exists in large quantities in lake Pontchartrain; it is also stated that it exists in lake Palourde but not in Grand lake. A thin bed of its shells is observable in the banks of the Teche a few miles from the mouth, at about the level of the gulf.

Prolongation of the mouths of the Mississippi.—From the fact that a wide strip of alluvial land borders the Mississippi river from the gulf of Mexico to the mouth of the Ohio, some writers have supposed that an arm of the gulf once extended to that vicinity, and that the Mississippi river, entering near the head of this sound, has gradually filled it by the deposition of sedimentary matter.

The mouth of the Mississippi was never near that of the Ohio.

These hypotheses are untenable; for were they correct, the alluvial deposit near Cairo would be not less than 300 feet thick; whereas the investigations of this Survey prove it to be but 20 or 25 feet thick on the river bank along the St. Francis swamp, about 35 feet thick along the Yazoo swamp, and of a thickness not varying materially from the latter as far down as Baton Rouge. The borings of the artesian well at New Orleans show that it does not there extend farther down than 40 feet below the level of the gulf. The tough clay bar that projects obliquely across the efflux of the Atchafalaya from Old river is 35 feet below the bank, and about 15 feet above the level of the gulf. An artesian boring upon General Welles' plantation in the Atchafalaya basin, 10 or 15 miles south of Alexandria, shows that the alluvial soil there is 30 feet thick, the surface of the older formation being about 50 feet above the gulf.

Neither could this long line of swamps have been a chain of lakes; since in the Yazoo, for example, this would require the alluvial soil at the head of the swamp to be about 100 feet thick, which is contrary to the fact.*

* Probably they were originally swamps, overflowed to a much greater depth, but to a less width, than at present, which have been gradually raised by the deposits of the annual overflow; the alluvial soil, like that of the Nile above its delta, extending each year farther from the river. This elevation of the banks is not necessarily connected with, or partly in consequence of, the prolongation of the mouth of the river in the gulf, although in the lower part of the river's course, as at the mouth of Red river, for instance, the elevation of the banks may be due in part to the prolongation of the river. The area of this tract of alluvial land from Cape Girardeau to the head of the assumed delta, as given by previous writers, is too great. By careful measurements upon the most authentic maps it is as follows:—

	Square miles.
The St. Francis bottom	6,900
The Yazoo bottom	7,110
The Tensas bottom	4,440
Small swamps on the east bank from Cairo to Baton Rouge	1,000
Total area	19,450

Considering the position and direction of the general coast line (not of alluvial formation) east and west of the Mississippi river, with relation to those of the shores of lakes Pontchartrain and Maurepas and Grand lake; observing the direction of the line of surface junction of the alluvial and older soils; and remembering that near the efflux of bayou Plaquemine the alluvial soil does not extend much if any below the level of the gulf; we are led to conclude that the original mouth of the Mississippi was situated not very far from that locality, and, hence, that its prolongation into the gulf has been 220 miles.

Originally, it was probably situated near Plaquemine.

The slope of the bottom of the gulf, upon which this advance has been made, can be approximately estimated. Thus, as before stated, at the locality of New Orleans it is 40 feet below the surface of the gulf. That depth of water is found in the gulf off the coast of Mississippi and Alabama (where there is no fluviatile deposit, or, at least, none of the present geological age) at about 20 miles from the shore, the same distance that separates New Orleans from the north shore of lake Pontchartrain. According to the deep-sea soundings of the Coast Survey (see plate XIX), the old gulf bottom is 100 feet below the gulf level at the head of the passes. Beyond this point, the slope must have been much greater; since a depth of 900 feet is found 11 miles from the bar of the Southwest pass, or 28 miles from the head of the passes.

Ancient level of the bottom of the gulf in this region.

If it be assumed that the rate of progress has been uniform to the present day—and there are some considerations, connected with the manner in which the river pushes the bar into the gulf each year, which tend to establish the correctness of that opinion—the number of years which have elapsed since the river began to advance into the gulf can be computed. The present rate of progress of the mouth may be obtained by a careful comparison of the progress of all the mouths of the river, as shown by the maps of Captain Talcott, U. S. Engineers, 1838, and of the U. S. Coast Survey in 1851—the only maps that admit of such a comparison. They give 262 feet for the mean yearly advance of all the passes.*

Probable age of the delta.

This mean advance of all the passes represents correctly the advance of the river, because in the changes that take place, each pass in succession may become the main or chief pass. Adopting this rate of progress (262 feet per annum), four thousand four hundred years have elapsed since the river began to advance into the gulf.

The practical importance of this yearly progress into the gulf consists in its probable effect in raising the surface of the river. This cannot be predicted with absolute certainty, but it appears to be hardly probable that, in the future changes, the depth of the river below Fort St. Philip will be less than it is now; for the thick clay stratum in which the bed

Effect of future advance upon the surface level of the river.

* The following are the yearly rates for the different passes:—

Southwest pass, Talcott and Coast Survey	338 feet.
South pass, Talcott and Coast Survey	280 "
Northeast and Southeast passes, Talcott and Coast Survey	130 "
Pass à l'Outre, Talcott and Coast Survey	302 "
Mean annual advance of the passes	262 "

By comparing the maps of de Serigny, 1720, and de la Tour, 1722, with the map of Captain Talcott, surveyed in 1838, Mr. Thomassy finds that the mean annual advance, between those periods, of pass à l'Outre, the Northeast pass, and the Southeast pass, was 328 feet (101 metres).

lies will be found, at points farther in the gulf, to be at a greater depth than it is at Fort St. Philip. Applying then the new formulæ to the existing dimensions of the river below Donaldsonville, we find that a prolongation of the river 25 miles into the gulf will be required, in order to elevate its surface 1 foot at Fort St. Philip. Even at the present rate of progress of the delta, this extension would not be accomplished in less than five centuries. It is certain that the progress of the mouths of the river into the gulf will never be *more* rapid than it is now, although from the great depth of the gulf 10 miles seaward of their present position, it may be *less* rapid. It is shown in Chapter II that when the swamp lands are perfectly protected from overflow, the sedimentary depositions in the gulf will not be increased more than one-eighteenth.

How much the progress of the river into the gulf has raised the surface of the river at points above Plaquemine, and how far up the river this effect has been felt, are in a great degree matters of mere speculation, and, however interesting as speculations, are without practical value.

The Mississippi was once a comparatively clear stream.

Changes which may have occurred in the condition of the Mississippi river.—The age of the delta has been estimated at four thousand four hundred years, upon the assumption that the Mississippi river was of equal magnitude during the whole period of its delta-forming condition. This assumption implies that the Mississippi was suddenly brought into existence with its present condition, or was suddenly converted to that condition. The rapid, simultaneous upheaval of the whole basin of the Mississippi would have brought that river suddenly into existence with very much the same characteristics that it now possesses; but geologists do not admit the probability of such a rapid upheaval. If it had been a delta-forming river during the gradual upheaval of the basin, which at Baton Rouge has exceeded 100 feet, some part of its ancient alluvion would now be found at a greater elevation than the corresponding part of the river; but, as it is all below the high-water surface of the river, the Mississippi must have been in past times a comparatively clear stream, not subject to floods.

How it may have changed this character.

Its transformation from a clear into a muddy river may have been the result of changes which have perhaps taken place in its basin. It will be recollected that midway between St. Louis and Cairo, the Mississippi passes through the northeastern extremity of the Ozark mountains, having, apparently, cut its way through the rocks, which rise perpendicularly from the surface on both banks to the height of 300 feet. This range probably unites with the crest of the plateau in which the tributaries on the right bank of the Ohio rise, or with the high ground which separates the hilly from the prairie region. The similarity of this part of the river to the Niagara below the falls, and to the Rhine below Bingen, suggests that, like those two rivers, the Mississippi has worn a channel through a portion of the range of hills or mountains that crosses it, and that the process has been accompanied by a constantly receding fall. If so, the beds of the Missouri and Mississippi must have been at a much greater elevation than they are now, a supposition which their present character renders highly probable; and an immense lake may have extended from the falls, or their vicinity, northward, nearly to Prairie du Chien, and over a large portion of the prairie of Illinois, and perhaps of Indiana, and, uniting with lake Michigan and lake Huron, may have covered a great part of the State of Michigan. Similar lakes may have existed on the Missouri and Upper Mississippi. The summit of the cliffs mentioned is somewhat more than 600 feet above the sea. The surface of lake Michigan is 576 feet above the sea. The crest of the low divide between the sources of the Illinois river and the southern extremity of lake Michigan is from 20 to 25 feet above the lake. There is a horizontal line, apparently a water-mark, on the cliffs at Mackinac, between 150 and 200 feet above the surface of the lake, which perhaps marks the elevation of the surface of the lake when the falls of Niagara were near Queenstown, at which time it is estimated that their crest was from 150 to 200 feet higher than it is now. According to the estimate that has been made by Sir Charles Lyell, of the rate at which the Niagara falls recede (the level of the upper lakes being supposed to subside with the crest of the falls), the surface of lake Michigan was, some five thousand years ago, just even with the lowest part of the crest now dividing it from the Mississippi river.

The effect of a great lake, such as that just indicated, upon the Mississippi river below the falls would have been twofold. First, the river-water would have been clear; and, second, its rise and fall would have been inconsiderable. There are several terraces on the Ohio river, indicating that its surface occupied greater elevations formerly than now, probably caused by the dams nature had thrown across its course. Thus portions of the prairies and plateaux of that region, and of the valleys of the tributary streams (where similar obstructions must have existed), were formed into lakes, the effects of which upon the turbidness of the waters of the Ohio, and upon its rise and fall, must have been similar to those of the supposed great lake upon the Mississippi. Conditions of the same character probably existed upon the other great tributaries of the Mississippi or their chief feeders.

Thus it appears that the lower Mississippi may once have been, somewhat like the St. Lawrence, a clear stream, having but little rise or fall, and pushing forward on its bed so small a quantity of earthy matter that no bar could be formed at its mouth. The change from this condition to that of a muddy, delta-forming river, having great floods, and pushing along its bed a large quantity of earthy matter, was probably gradual. As the surface of the Ohio river sank, from the wearing away of the natural dams upon its course, the lakes in its basin were drained. The character of its lower course was consequently altered, and this produced a corresponding change in the Mississippi. As the surface of the great lake was lowered by the retrograde movement of the fall, the nature of the Mississippi was still further modified, until it finally assumed the characteristics it now possesses.

This supposition of the gradual transformation of the Mississippi requires an addition to be made to the age of the delta, as computed upon the supposition of a uniform condition during its delta-forming state, but does not afford the means of ascertaining the amount of that increase. All this, however, is mere speculation, indulged in to afford a possible solution of a speculative difficulty that has no practical bearing upon the present or future condition of the Mississippi river.

Separation of branches of the Mississippi.

How branches of the Mississippi may become disconnected.—Some indication of the manner in which the branches of the Mississippi may be disconnected from the main stem seems to be appropriate to this chapter, although, to be perfectly understood, a reference to the next chapter may be required. The following general principles will there be fully established.

The passes, and the bayous leading from them and from the river, have two bars;

Preliminary remarks.

one at the mouth in the gulf, the other at the point of separation from the river or pass. There are two great river periods; the flood stage, which lasts usually six months, and the low-water period, which lasts usually four months, the transitions from one to the other occupying on the average about one month. During the flood stage, a large quantity of river-water is discharged through all the bayous with a velocity varying from 2 to 3 feet per second, and the bars at their mouths in the gulf are formed and pushed forward. In the low-water period, on the contrary, when very little river-water is discharged through the bayous, this bar formation takes place at the point where the bayou is separated from the river. During the transition from high to low or from low to high water, the deposit takes place at every point of the bayou between the two bars, a deposit which is removed in part or wholly when the river rises. In the ordinary low-water condition of the river, the short bayous discharge salt-water into the river, when the gulf level is higher than the river at the point of junction.

A separation of branches near the mouth may be effected by storms.

A separation may be effected by storms, if the banks of the bayou at the point of leaving the river are not materially above the level of the gulf; as for instance, at the head of the passes, where the banks are but little more than 2 feet above its mean level; or at Fort St. Philip, where they are less than 5 feet above it.

Let us suppose, toward the close of a great flood, which has been protracted into the summer, and when the water is beginning to subside, a great southeast storm or hurricane takes place, which elevates the surface of the gulf 6 or 7 feet above its mean level in the lakes and bays on the eastern side of the river, where it must be higher than in the lakes and bays on the western shore. One of the effects upon the great passes will be to cause a less discharge through those debouching toward the east, and a greater discharge through those debouching toward the west. The effect upon the bayous of the east bank will probably be to drive the fresh water entirely out of those whose banks at the point of leaving the river and passes are below the raised surface of the gulf, and to make dead-water in those whose banks at the points of leaving the river are on the same level as the raised surface of the gulf. An eddy must be formed at the head of the last class of bayous; and the consequent deposit might possibly reach nearly as high as their banks, their depths being usually but 6 or 8 feet at that point. Upon the subsidence of the storm, the bayous would be thus cut off from the parent stream; and, the river being in a falling condition, the newly formed bar would be exposed several months to the air, and would become firm. Should the following year, like 1855 for instance, be one of low water in the river, when there is little or no flood state, the bar would be covered in the spring and summer with willows, grass, and other vegetation; and the permanent disconnection of the bayou would thus be secured. The deposit from subsequent overflows of the river would only increase the bank separating the river and bayou, and fill up somewhat the bed of the latter.

Or by waves.

Another process by which bayous and branches of the Mississippi may be separated from the river, when the point of divergence is but slightly elevated above the gulf, is the following. The waves of the gulf constantly tend to close the mouths of rivers and the entrances of all bays, sounds, inlets, etc., and to stretch along them a bank or narrow strip of land, thrown up from the bottom of the gulf. The variations in the level of the gulf, whether caused by winds or tides, tend to open and keep open channels through the bank thus formed by the waves. During a low stage of the river, the effect produced by a long-continued series of storms from the southeast, upon a branch discharging toward the east or southeast, might be to raise the bar so as to diminish materially the capacity of that branch for discharge, while at the same time it increased the discharge through those branches debouching toward the west, owing to the less elevation of the gulf on that side. The return of high water of the river would not necessarily restore the former condition of the branch and its bar. Another series of storms might still further diminish the capacity of the branch or pass, so that its bed would diminish, and the bar at the point of separation increase. Finally, by a continuation of such action its mouth might be entirely closed, and a bar at its head, formed by eddies, would soon afterward cut off all communication with the river. An operation like this is observable in bayou Moreau, once the east branch of the La Fourche; whose mouth is entirely closed, and whose bed at the point of divergence is nearly filled up by the accumulation of drift-wood. It may be, however, that the drift-wood first partially closed the east branch, and that the closure of the mouth followed, instead of preceding, the partial separation of the branch from the main stem.

At considerable distances from the mouth separation can only be caused by drift.

When the rise and fall at the head of a bayou is 15 or 25 feet, its separation from the river cannot be accounted for without the introduction of other causes than those named. Let us take the bayou La Fourche as an example.

The surface of the river, at the point where that bayou separates from it, is, in dead low water, only 1.5 feet above the mean level of the gulf; but any deposit formed near the head, during the period of low water, must be spread over a considerable extent, since the river sometimes rises 6 or 8 feet at Donaldsonville, and fluctuates between that height and the low-water stand until the great rise begins. The transition period from high to low water being on the average only about a month, and the length of the bayou being 110 miles, the deposit of any day must be spread over a space of 2 or 3 miles, and must, therefore, be exceedingly slight. Any deposit made in the bayou must then be so small as to be removed by the high-water discharge.

The fact observed at Donaldsonville, that the river in hurricanes like those of 1860 rises much more rapidly than the bayou, and discharges into it, shows that no such accumulation can be formed in the La Fourche as occurs at the point of separation of bayous at the mouths of the passes.

Under the ordinary conditions, then, it is not easy to perceive why the bottom of the bayou at the head, or point of divergence, should not always remain at least a foot below the low-water level of the river, unless closed by drift-wood. Many bayous at the mouths of the Mississippi are now in process of closure in this way, and bayous connected with the Atchafalaya and emptying into Grand lake are also undergoing a similar process. The lodging of drift-wood upon the shoal at the entrance of La Fourche, in conjunction with the earthy matter that must accumulate around it, may therefore in a few years effectually dam up the entrance and entirely disconnect the bayou from the river.

In general, then, we may conclude that in a delta river like the Mississippi below

General conclusions.

the mouth of the La Fourche, the relations existing between the main stem and the branches continue permanent unless disturbed by some extraneous force. These relations are, however, liable to be disturbed, since the velocity and momentum in these branches are less than those in the main stem, and are therefore more affected by storms. Some branches are exposed to the prevalent winds, and for that additional cause are liable to be closed. Drift-wood, which sooner or later must lodge in the smaller branch streams at the points of separation, where the depths are always less than in the main stem, must produce still greater disturbance. From these causes, the branches are separated from the main stream as it advances into the gulf, and the head of the delta proper is thus carried forward with the mouth of the river.

Ancient shore lines and river courses.

Ancient geography of the delta.—Some few ideas respecting the original position and direction of the gulf shore lines and the river courses will be added, since they may prove interesting as indications of the changes that have taken place. The northern shore of the gulf, or an arm of the gulf like the Mississippi sound, as already intimated, probably passed near where Plaquemine now is, and extended westward until it met the high ground west of Grand lake. It will be noticed that the line of intersection of alluvial and ancient soil in this region is parallel to the general direction of the west shore of that lake. The Avoyelles prairie is probably the remains of an ancient ridge running parallel to the Mississippi as far as the northern shore of the sound, and perhaps separating the Mississippi and Red rivers. The Atchafalaya was probably the drain in the lowest part of the valley between this ridge and the bank of the Mississippi, but not connected with that river. Red river may have emptied into the ancient sound by a course along what is now bayou Bœuf or perhaps by Choctaw bayou and part of bayou Teche,—the latter having evidently been a much larger river than it is now. The fall of Red river at Alexandria is 0.42 of a foot per mile; of the bayous Bœuf and Teche, 0.3 of a foot per mile; slopes not inconsistent with the supposition of their having once been parts of the same stream. Black river probably ran to the Mississippi along what is now the channel of Red river. The elevations caused by alluvial depositions west of the Avoyelles prairie were probably more rapidly formed than those east of it; and the banks of Red river being thus elevated, that stream may have overflowed the depression in Avoyelles prairie, where Red river now runs. On the east side of this depression, it must have found a channel partly prepared by drainage into Black river. This by degrees became a branch of Red river, and finally the main stream.

Bayou Atchafalaya was not the prolongation of Red river.

The opinion has been frequently expressed that Red river was not originally united to the Mississippi, but flowed to the sea separately in the channel now called the Atchafalaya, from which it was disconnected by the changes in the course of the Mississippi. This opinion is believed to be erroneous, because the area of the greatest cross-section of the Atchafalaya, at the efflux from the Mississippi, is but little more than half that of Red river below the junction of Black river, and because the Atchafalaya has not the capacity to discharge much more than half the volume discharged by Red river in flood. If the Atchafalaya had been the channel of Red river, its subsequent connection with the

Mississippi could not have diminished its discharge or capacity, since the floods of the Mississippi are of much longer duration than those of Red river, and it is evident, from the very small slope of Red river above its mouth, that its rise and fall at that point could not have been decreased by a junction with the Mississippi.

The fall per mile of Red river at Alexandria is 0.42 of a foot, and below the junction of Black river only 0.14 of a foot, while the fall of the Atchafalaya in the first half of its course is 0.64 of a foot per mile.

It therefore appears more probable that the Atchafalaya was a mere valley drain, discharging clear water, until the Mississippi, by eroding its own bank, converted it into a waste-weir, when, becoming a muddy stream of increasing discharge, the Atchafalaya began to raise its banks. As already seen, Mr. Bayley appears to have established by his researches that such changes have taken place in the Plaquemine.

The point of ancient land that now terminates near New Iberia on the Teche, doubtless extends much farther toward the southeast, though now covered by alluvion. If the shore line of the present Mississippi sound be prolonged, it will pass near Berwick's bay, and it is probable that on this line there existed a chain of sand islands, or *cordon littoral*, forming the southern shore of the ancient sound. Nearly parallel to this line is the chain formed now by the sand islands called the Chandeleur, Breton, Timbalier, Last Island, etc., etc.

The Mississippi extends its delta along the deepest part of the great marine valley.

Off Last Island and the coast in that vicinity, the bottom of the gulf is composed of sand, not of the sedimentary matter of the river. The depth increases gradually with the distance from the shore, 50 feet water being obtained at a distance of 24 miles from land. On the contrary, 11 miles off the mouth of the Southwest pass, the gulf is 900 feet deep. If the general course of the Mississippi from Baton Rouge to its mouth be prolonged (see plate XIX), it will be found to pass along the line of deepest water in the gulf, and lead to the entrance of the Florida straits.* The greatest depth on this line, about midway between the mouths of the Mississippi and the entrance of the straits, exceeds 6000 feet. Thus the course of the Mississippi in the gulf conforms to the lowest line of the great marine valley, as, in like manner, above the ancient gulf coast, its course follows the lowest line of the valleys, converting them, by the sedimentary depositions of annual overflow, into fertile alluvial plains.

* This fact may appear to be somewhat in conflict with the imputed influence of the southeasterly winds upon the directions of the passes (see next chapter), but in reality it is the necessary result of the manner in which the bar is formed. If it were formed upon a plane inclined across the river current, the rate of advance would be least, the depth on the crest and the velocity of current greatest on the side toward the deepest water, and the prolongation would be made on a curved line turned toward the deepest water, which the bar would finally reach and advance upon until turned away again by the southeasterly winds—again to return. The prolongation must therefore be made on curved lines

CHAPTER VIII.

MOUTHS OF THE MISSISSIPPI.

Description of the mouths.—Classification of river stages with reference to the formation of the bars.—Form and dimensions of the mouth of the Southwest pass.—Observations at this pass.—Actual conditions existing there at the different states of the river and gulf.—Experimental theory of the formation of the bars.—It is confirmed by measurements.—It explains the differences in depth on the various bars.—Modifying influence of waves.—Effect of changes in the level of the gulf surface.—Tidal currents.—Winds at the mouths of the Mississippi.—Their influence upon the form of the delta; upon the level of the gulf; and upon the bars.—Eddy currents have no governing agency in the formation of the bars.—Mud lumps.—Actual deepening operations upon the bars of the Mississippi.—Classification of plans for improvement.—Recommendations.

The mouth of the Mississippi.

BETWEEN bayou La Fourche (the last of the outlets) and Fort St. Philip, the Mississippi river flows through a tolerably uniform channel, averaging at high water 199,000 square feet in cross-section, 2470 feet in width, and 129 feet in depth in the deepest part. In the low-water stage, these dimensions are 163,000 square feet, 2250 feet, and 114 feet, respectively. Twenty miles below Fort St. Philip (plate XIX) a great change takes place. The river becomes 7000 or 8000 feet wide, with a maximum depth of about 40 feet, and an area of cross-section of about 250,000 square feet. It then separates into three principal branches, called, from the directions they take, the Southwest pass, the South pass, and the Northeast pass,—the last sending off a branch called pass à l'Outre. The dimensions of these passes are shown by the following table. It will be noted that the lengths follow the same order as the volumes.

Dimensions of the main passes of the Mississippi.

Name.	Length to outer crest of bar.	Mean width.	Mean depth.	Mean maximum depth.	Mean area of cross-section.	Proportional discharge; that of the Mississippi being unity.
	Miles.	*Feet.*	*Feet.*	*Feet.*	*Square feet.*	
Southwest pass	17	1200	58.5	70	70,000	0.34
South pass	14	700	34		24,000	0.08
Northeast pass	16	2500	37		92,000	0.225
Pass à l'Outre	15	1300	36		47,000	0.234
Remainder (mainly through Southeast pass)						0.121

A bar is formed at the mouth of each of these passes, where the river meets the gulf; and as the conditions existing there vary with the stages of the river, a classification of these stages should be made.

The low-water period usually continues about four months, varying from two to seven and a half months. (In the latter case, an extraordinary one, it lasted from August 10, 1854, to March 23, 1855.) The mean discharge during this period is 300,000 cubic feet per second.

Classification of the river stages with reference to the formation of the bars.

The flood period is considered to include the time during which the river is discharging not less than 800,000 cubic feet per second. It usually continues for six months, varying between four and eight months. (In 1855 there was no flood period, the maximum discharge not having exceeded 700,000 cubic feet per second. No other instance of the kind has been recorded.) The mean discharge is nearly 1,000,000 cubic feet per second.

The transition periods are both brief. That from low-water to flood usually lasts thirty-one days, varying between twenty and sixty days; and that from flood to low-water, thirty-three days, varying between twenty and fifty days. The former usually occurs between the last of December and the early part of March, and the latter between the first of July and the middle of September.

BARS AT THE MOUTHS OF THE MISSISSIPPI.

Before proceeding to detail and discuss the measurements made to ascertain the law governing the formation of the bars, a brief description of the mouth of the Southwest pass, where the observations were chiefly conducted, will be given. It is compiled from the surveys made by Captain Talcott, Corps Engineers, United States Army, in 1838.*

Form and dimensions of the mouth of the Southwest pass.

Mouth of Southwest pass.—The mean dimensions throughout this pass have been given in the preceding table. They are preserved with but little variation (see plate XIX) to a point 7.3 miles from the outer crest of the bar. Here the mouth begins, the pass gradually widening until on the crest it has a width of 11,500 feet, a mean depth of 11.5 feet, and a cross-section of 132,000 square feet.

The following numbers (see figure 1, plate XX) indicate the mean fall per 1000 feet on the bar toward the river:—

From outer crest for 1000 feet	nearly horizontal,
In the next 3000 feet	0.5 of a foot,
In the next 17,000 feet	1.0 foot,
In the next 5000 feet	2.0 feet,
In the next 9000 feet	7.0 feet.

The bottom is then horizontal.

The outer slope of the bar is comparatively abrupt. Thus the mean fall per 1000 feet is—

From outer crest for 1000 feet	10 feet,
In the next 3700 feet	20 feet,
In the next 38,300 feet	5 feet,
In the next 14,000 feet	43 feet.

* Neither the reports nor the maps of these surveys were published. The latter (partially represented on plate XIX) were constructed upon a very large scale, and a careful compilation was made from them in the Bureau of Topographical Engineers, War Department, and published by authority in 1839. The reports have never been printed. They contain much valuable information, and have therefore been added, by permission, to this report, as Appendix A.

That is, at 1000 feet outside the bar, the gulf is about 22 feet deep; at 4700 feet, 100 feet deep; at 43,000 feet, 300 feet deep; and at 57,000 feet, 900 feet deep. In the deep water the bottom is composed of the soft mud brought to the gulf by the river.

Discharge through the Southwest pass.

The following table exhibits the volumes of water entering the Southwest pass.

Discharge per second at the head of the Southwest pass.

River stage.	Usual		Minimum	
	Discharge.	Mean velocity.	Discharge.	Mean velocity.
	Cubic feet.	*Feet.*	*Cubic feet.*	*Feet.*
Flood	840,000	4.9	272,000	3.9
Low-water	102,000	1.4	75,000	1.1

This description being premised, we may pass to the results of the observations which were made to determine the conditions actually existing at the passes in the different stages of the river.

Observations at the mouths.—In order to determine the conditions existing at the mouths of the Mississippi in the high-water and low-water stages of the river, and the circumstances under which the bars are formed, it was proposed at a very early period of the Survey to make a series of experiments in each of those stages, and to carry each series through all the variations to which the gulf is subject from tides and winds. From a variety of circumstances, the execution of this plan was postponed from time to time, and indeed it was never fully carried out. Enough, however, was ascertained to make apparent the law under which the bars are formed.

Observations upon the bars in 1851.

In execution of the plan of operations, Professor Forshey made some experiments at the flood and low-water stages of the river in 1851.

Observations in 1859–60.

In the winter of 1858–59, Mr. C. A. Fuller, civil engineer, having charge (under the direction of Lieutenant-Colonel S. H. Long, Topographical Engineers) of the deepening of the bar of the Southwest pass, undertook the completion of the experiments. The first made by him were amateur observations, but subsequently he was furnished with all the apparatus required to conduct them with accuracy. These latter experiments were made during two weeks in May, 1859 (flood stage of river), and in the following August, September, and October (low-water stage), and with less elaboration on various occasions from that time to June, 1860. They were made on the crest of the bar; at depths of 20, 30, and 40 feet outside the bar; and extended to 18 feet water inside the bar. All these experiments are fully detailed in Appendix G, and some of the most characteristic are represented upon plate XX. Figure 2 of this plate has been prepared to afford the means of locating the observations exactly, with the aid of the notes in the Appendix.

Results of the observations as to the conditions actually existing at the bars.

After a very elaborate examination of the observations, the following conclusions have been reached. They may easily be verified by examining the observations themselves in Appendix G.

During the period of flood, the water in contact with the bar, as far as the outer crest, is fresh, and moves seaward with a comparatively rapid current. Beyond the outer crest and below the stratum of fresh-water, salt-water is found in contact with the outer slope of the bar, moving seaward with a velocity varying between 0.3 and 2.5 feet per second, the mean being about 0.5 of a foot per second. The direction of this motion, however, is not parallel to that of the river-water, the angle between them being often as great as 20 degrees. On one occasion, during a strong southerly wind, a little salt-water began to make its appearance below the fresh on the inner slope of the bar.

During the low-water period, the water in contact with the bar is always salt; moving sometimes outward and sometimes inward—but always with a gentle current—and remaining sometimes at rest. At the outer crest of the bar, when the tides are greatest and rising, there is an inward current of salt-water at the bottom, increasing in strength with the rise in the tide. When the tide turns, the current changes its direction and moves outward. In this stage of the river, the surface water is usually brackish to the head of the passes, and sometimes as far up as Fort St. Philip. During extraordinary gales, the gulf-water has been known to fill the channels of the passes with an up-stream current.

During at least half of the two transition periods, any of the current conditions found at the low-water period may exist.

Such are the conditions existing at the mouths of the Mississippi. The laws in accordance with which the bars are formed are now to be deduced from them.

Experimental theory of the formation of the bars.—Let us suppose the mouth of the Southwest pass to be removed up to the point where it begins to widen (7.3 miles above the outer crest of the bar), and the gulf to occupy its place, having a mean depth equal to that of the pass (58.5 feet). Further, let it be supposed that the river is at the flood stage, and that it meets for the first time the waters of the gulf, which, to simplify the problem, we will at first assume to remain at a constant level, without currents or other motion.

Conditions assumed to illustrate the action of the forces.

The force that would resist the entrance of the river into the gulf at the depth of 58.5 feet is greater than the force at half that depth (29.25 feet) by the difference between the weight of a column of salt-water and a column of fresh-water 29.25 feet high, and the resistance decreases in this proportion to the surface, where it is least. As a consequence, the fresh-water as it enters the gulf will rise upon the salt-water at an angle inversely as the strength of the current. This lifting force of the salt-water must widen the river current. Since the resistance of the banks of salt-water to the pressure of the river upon them is less than that of its earthen banks, this spreading will be further increased. The difference in the specific gravities of fresh-water and salt-water will also tend to produce the same result.

The fresh-water will rise and spread over the salt-water.

The conditions existing in a vertical direction, where the river-water meets the salt-water and rises upon it, are somewhat similar to those existing in a horizontal direction, where the river makes a sudden turn and forms a horizontal eddy, or where a sudden deepening in the bed occurs, and, as shown by Venturi's experiments, gives rise to a vertical eddy. In other words, there

It will thus produce vertical eddies.

must be a dead angle, where the river-water meets and rises upon the salt-water and thus forms vertical eddies.

The material pushed along upon the bottom will be left behind, and will thus form a bar.

Now, as already explained in Chapter II, experiments upon the river at various points of its course, at high water and at low water, when the river was rising and when it was falling, established the fact that earthy matter is always rolling along upon the bottom. It consists of clay, earth, sand, etc.; that is, of the material of which the delta is formed. Mr. George G. Meade (now Captain United States Topographical Engineers), when making a survey of the Southwest pass under the direction of Captain Talcott, Corps of Engineers, in 1838, also found similar material in motion along the bottom on the bar of the Southwest pass, the river being about two-thirds flood at New Orleans.

The current in the Southwest pass is quite equal to pushing this material along the bottom, but when the river-water begins to ascend upon the salt-water of the gulf, the rolling material is not carried with it, but is left upon the bottom in the dead angle of salt-water. A deposit is thus formed, whose surface is along or near the line upon which the fresh-water rises on the salt-water as it enters the gulf. *This action produces the bar.* What modifying effect the vertical eddy has upon this deposit, observation can hardly determine, for there are other and more powerful forces at work, which nearly or quite obscure its action.

Modification of this action in the succeeding low-water stage of the river.

At the low-water stage of the river, the earthy matter pushed along at the bottom will also be deposited in the dead angle formed by the fresh-water rising upon the salt-water as the river enters the gulf. There will, however, be one important difference. The velocity with which the river enters the gulf being in extreme low water about one-fourth, and in mean low water about one-third that at flood, the angles at which the fresh-water will rise upon the salt-water will be greater and probably in about those proportions. The spreading force also will be less than at the flood stage, and salt-water will be found at the sides, where at that period there was fresh-water.

We must then conclude that, as there are two great epochs of discharge in this first river year, so there will be two great periods of deposit: one at high water, when the deposit may be considered as made exteriorly; and one at low water, when it is made interiorly; the deposits during the changes from high to low water and from low to high water being made between those two, or on what is ordinarily termed the bar.

Effects of subsequent floods.

Now let us trace the effect of subsequent floods upon the new-made bar. When the velocity begins to increase, the current, at the point where the channel begins to widen and lessen its depth, will not be deflected upward by the lifting power of the salt-water, but by coming in contact with the deposit of the preceding river year, which it will erode until a channel-way is formed equal to that of the normal channel of the pass. This erosion will take place chiefly at the angle where the current is deflected upward; the wearing upon other portions of the deposit being comparatively slight. The new earthy matter pushed along at the bottom will thus be rolled over the bar and dropped in advance of the high-water deposit of the previous year. This will cause an annual advance of the bar into the gulf.

In proportion as the cross-section of discharge on the outer crest of the deposit widens, its progress into the gulf will become slower, and the depth of water upon it will constantly decrease, since the surface of the deposit will always coincide with the inclined plane along which the fresh-water rises upon the salt-water. Finally, when the yearly advance of this outer crest becomes equal to that of the excavation on the inner side of the deposit, an equilibrium will be established, and the depth and width of the crest of the bar will remain essentially permanent, so far as affected by the great controlling causes of its formation. The duration and discharge of the flood, low-water, and transition stages all varying, and the quantity of earthy matter pushed along at the bottom also varying, there will be, of course, some yearly irregularities in the form and extent of the deposit or bar. Other disturbing forces, to be presently noted, will also affect its condition; but although the changes thus brought about may seriously affect navigation, the form and progress of the bar, so far as its great dimensions are considered, must soon become permanent. Let us now see how these views respecting the general permanency of the bar are borne out by observation.

Law governing the advance of the bar.

In 1838 a thorough survey was made of the mouths of the Mississippi; of the adjacent gulf; of the passes; and of the river, as far as Forts Jackson and St. Philip. The surveys previous to that date were not of a sufficiently minute character to admit of a nice comparison.* Since that time, surveys have been limited to the bars and extended but a short distance inside of the inner crest. There is no means, therefore, of ascertaining how far the normal cross-section of the Southwest pass has advanced since 1838. We may, however, determine with much nicety the relative and absolute advance of the inner and outer crests since that date.

This law confirmed by measurements.

By Talcott's survey, the distance across the bar, from 18 feet water inside to 18

---

* This opinion was formed after a careful examination of all the maps of the mouths of the Mississippi in the archives of the Bureau of Topographical Engineers, War Department. Among them is a copy of the map of D'Anville, prepared in 1732, published in 1752. It has marked upon it "Passe à la Loutre," "Passe à Sauvol" (called now Pass à Cheval), "Passe de l'Est," "La Balise, Entrée pour les Vaisseaux," "Passe du Sud," "Passe du Sud Ouest." The Southeast pass is omitted. The river is called "Saint Louis."

On an old map with no date, signed by Osgood Carleton, it is stated that there is 18 feet water into the Balise, 12 feet over the bar, 45 feet within, and 50, 60, and 100 fathoms afterward. Yet on the large-scale plot of the entrances, the Southeast channel has a depth of only 12 feet, and the Northeast channel only 11½ feet. Fort Balise and the upper part of Balise bayou are marked on the map, and at the inner end of the bayou it is noted "Here large ships land their cargoes to lighten in order to go over the bar." This remark conforms to a manuscript tracing, likewise in the Bureau of Topographical Engineers, with the title "Carte des Embouchures du Mississippi sur les Manuscrits du Dépôt des Cartes et Plans de la Marine, 1744," on which a bar is marked at the junction of the Balise bayou and the river, and is called "La Barre;" the bayou is called "Chenal pour les Vaisseaux," and the mouth "Embouchures par ou les Vaisseaux entrent." The only passes marked and named on the map are "Passe Sauvolle" and "Passe de l'Est." It appears to be hardly probable that there was a depth of 18 feet at the entrance of this bayou from the sea, and 12 feet over the bar at its junction with the river, yet it is so implied.

French, in his historical records of Louisiana, gives Coxe's account of the expeditions sent by him to Louisiana in 169–. According to these expeditions, there were then seven mouths to the Mississippi. The greatest depth of water found was 14 feet. Three mouths were deep enough for ships to enter.

Mr. R. Thomassy, in an appendix to his Géologie Pratique de la Louisiane, gives a brief account of the maps of Louisiana and the Mississippi river, that have been prepared from the time of its discovery to the present day. This account he proposes to enlarge in the American edition of his work. The maps of Messrs. de Serigny, de Lisle, de la Tour, de Pauger, and others, and of Captain Talcott, and the Coast Survey, which accompany the work, illustrate the subject of the changes that have taken place at the mouths of the river.

feet water outside, was 7500 feet. By the survey of Lieutenant-Colonel Long, in 1857, the distance between these two curves is 7900 feet, showing a nearly equal advance into the gulf (338 feet annually) of erosion and deposit. The Coast-Survey chart of 1851 of pass à l'Outre shows in the south channel an equal advance of the inside and outside curves of equal depth. In the other channels the advance of the inner curves is not quite so rapid as that of the outer. These surveys also prove that the mean depth on the bar of the Southwest pass has remained unchanged.

These facts confirm the correctness of the explanation given of the manner in which the bars advance into the gulf, and the mode by which their form and the depth of water upon them are maintained practically the same.

These measurements establish the numerical relations existing between the power of erosion and the depositing action.

Taken in connection with the fact developed by the surveys, that the outer crest of the bar of the Southwest pass advances into the gulf 338 feet over a width of 11,500 feet annually, they also show that the erosive power of the current is only about one-tenth of its depositing action; since the river opens a channel 1200 feet wide and 338 feet long to the mean depth of the pass, while it forms a deposit about 11,500 feet wide and 338 feet long to at least the same depth.

This theory of bar formation explains the difference in depth on the different bars.

The preceding theory of the formation of the bars also explains the relation that exists between the depth on the bar and the amount of discharge over it. The quantities of matter transported along the bottom in the different passes are in proportion to their discharges; the planes of ascent upon the salt-water are inversely as their velocities. These conditions tend to produce equal depths upon all the bars. But the width and cross-section of the Southwest pass are relatively smaller than those of the other passes, and its relative velocity is consequently greater than those of the other passes. The erosive power of each of the other passes, as compared with its depositing action, is therefore relatively less than that of the Southwest pass. The advance of the deposit of any one of these passes into the gulf, before the equilibrium between the erosive power and depositing action was established, must have been relatively greater than that of the Southwest pass. But the yearly progress into the gulf, after the equilibrium was established, must have been less than that of the Southwest pass. The greatest depth of water should therefore be found upon the bar of the Southwest pass, a conclusion in accordance with the fact.

Volume of earthy matter annually pushed into the gulf.

The rate at which the bar of the Southwest pass advances, furnishes the means of computing the yearly amount pushed into the gulf along the bottom of the river. The depth of the gulf where the bar is now formed being 100 feet, and the bar advancing 338 feet each year, its profile and other dimensions give for the difference between the cubical contents of yearly deposit and erosion, 255,000,000 cubic feet, or a mass 1 mile square and 9 feet thick, which is the volume of earthy matter pushed into the gulf each year by the Southwest pass. The quantities of earthy matter pushed along by the passes being in proportion to their volumes of discharge, the whole amount thus carried yearly to the gulf is 750,000,000 cubic feet, or a mass 1 mile square and 27 feet thick. As the cubical contents of the whole mass of the bar of the Southwest pass is equal to a solid 1 mile square and 490 feet thick, it would require fifty-five years to form the bar as it now exists, or, in other words, to establish the equilibrium between the advancing rates of erosion and deposit.

Influence of gulf oscillations and currents upon the bars.—The gulf has hitherto been supposed to remain invariably at the same level and to be at rest. The modifying effects of its motions will now be considered.

Besides waves, we may expect to find tidal currents, and currents occasioned by changes of level due to winds. From the great depth of the gulf near the mouths of the river, it is also possible that the gulf-stream or its eddy may be felt at certain seasons.

Modifying influence of waves.

The oscillating motion of waves, when meeting the bottom, is changed into a motion of translation, and thus tends to arrange the deposit made by the river into the same gentle slope at which it disposes similar material at corresponding depths along the shores. These motions of wave oscillation and translation also tend to destroy a portion of the velocity of the current of the river-water, and thus induce a deposit of sediment.*

Effect of changes in the level of the gulf surface.

A rise in the level of the gulf will diminish the discharge of the river, and increase the slope of its rise upon the salt-water until the river has accumulated sufficient power to restore the former condition. The opposite effect will result from a fall in the surface. These effects will be greater for the same amount of change of level of the gulf in proportion as the discharge of the river is less. Indeed we might from these causes anticipate inward and outward movements of salt-water over the river deposit, and that they will be greatest during low water.

Tidal currents.

As already explained in Chapter II, the tides of the gulf at the mouths of the Mississippi are of the diurnal or single-day type, being, when the moon's declination is least, scarcely perceptible, and, when greatest, about 1.5 feet.

The investigations of the Coast Survey have also shown that the tidal wave approaches the mouths of the Mississippi from a southeasterly direction. With this tidal wave there is, near the coast, a tidal current in the same general direction. The tidal wave lifts up the river current in the gulf, and the tidal current passes under it, though checking it to some extent in so doing. The direction of this tidal current is modified by its contact with the river current, and to a greater degree by its contact with the outer slope of the bar deposit. In the case of the Southwest pass, a flood-tide brings a current from the southeast, which is changed to a southwesterly direction, more westerly than that of the river current, by the bar deposit along the eastern side of the mouth of the pass. The ebb-tide is accompanied by a current from the opposite direction, which is similarly diverted by the deposit on the western side of the mouth of the pass, the direction being more southerly than the current of the river. Winds may change the direction and force of these currents, which, in mid-river current, at a depth of 40 feet, are shown by the observations to vary from 0.3 of a foot to 2.5 feet per second, the mean being about 0.5 of a foot. As a velocity of 0.5 of a foot per second is sufficient to transport the material of which the bar is formed, the action of

* In flood the river-water is distinguishable in the gulf at the distance of 20 or 25 miles from the bar; in low water, at the distance of 5 or 10 miles.

gulf currents in carrying into deeper water the material pushed by the river into the gulf is evident.

In the flood stage the river current has sufficient volume and force to keep the gulf water and tidal currents outside of the outer crest of the bar, and there is therefore no tidal current into the mouth of the pass. In the low stage, when the volume and force of the river current is greatly reduced, the gulf virtually occupies the mouth of the pass, and the tidal currents move over the bar.

Winds at the mouths of the Mississippi. The winds are a great disturbing agency, since, by changing the level of the gulf and creating currents, they produce anomalous effects at the mouths of the river. Their general character becomes then an important subject of investigation.

Diagrams of the winds have been plotted from the "Army Meteorological Observations" for five years at Key West, from 1850 to 1854, and also for the year from June, 1851, to June, 1852, at the same place. Similar diagrams have been made from the wind observations of the Mississippi Delta Survey, at Fort St. Philip and at Carrollton.

The great resemblance between the winds at Key West and those near the mouths of the Mississippi is apparent when these diagrams are compared. Both have in part the characteristics of the northeast trade-winds. Blowing chiefly between northeast and southeast, they veer toward the south as the summer approaches, and continue to blow from that quarter and from the east during the summer and early part of the autumn; changing toward the north upon the approach of winter, they blow principally from that direction during the winter months. It is not intended, however, to decide upon the character of these winds, and to class them definitely among the trades. The topographical features and physical condition of the basin of the Mississippi, and its position relative to the great bodies of water lying south of it, must modify the character of the great normal winds described by Professor Henry, in his papers upon Meteorology, and perhaps produce along this portion of the gulf a resemblance to the trade-winds.

The influence of these winds upon the form of the delta is apparent. Thus, for several months in the year, the wind off the mouths of the Mississippi blows from the southeast, and it will be observed that the chief discharge of the Mississippi is made by mouths in directions nearly at right angles to this; the South and Southeast passes—the exceptions—discharging only one-fifth of the river water. The general direction of the shore line for 40 miles on either side of the Mississippi is also perpendicular to the direction of these prevalent winds—all pointing to a powerful modifying effect on the delta formation.

Their effect upon the form of the delta.

But the action of the winds is not confined to so general results. Thus, in the report of the Superintendent of the Coast Survey for 1853, it is shown in a paper upon the tides at Key West, Florida, based upon observations made there from June 1, 1851, to May 31, 1852, that the mean level of the water in that harbor increases in height regularly from January, when it is lowest, until September, when it is highest, at which time it begins to descend and falls until January. The difference of elevation is 0.8 of a foot. This change of level is attributed to the trade-winds, which for six months in the year tend to elevate the water in the harbor, and for the remaining six months to depress it.

Their effect upon the level of the gulf.

A similar case exists at Aransas bay, Texas, where, as stated by Mr. A. M. Lea, it has been noticed that an island, which is never covered by water during the winter, has always a depth of about one foot upon certain portions of it during the summer.

The observations made by this Survey upon the level of the lakes and gulf, detailed in Chapter II and Appendix B, fully accord with these facts. They show that during the winter of 1851, when the winds were northerly, the gulf was nearly a foot lower than during the succeeding summer and autumn, when the winds were chiefly southerly and easterly. It should, however, be added that the level of the gulf at the mouths of the Mississippi is doubtless affected by winds at a distance, which may not entirely correspond in direction and force with those in that immediate locality. Indeed, it is noticeable in the observations, that a change of level in the gulf does not immediately follow a change of direction in the wind, and it may not occur at all if the change of direction is of brief duration.

The effect of these periodical changes of level, is important in an economical point of view; for they occur with sufficient regularity to justify the statement that the least depth of water will be found upon the bars at the mouths of the Mississippi at the time when the greatest number of vessels is obliged to pass over them, the active business season of New Orleans being from the middle of November to the middle of April.*

Their effect upon the bars.

The effect of the gulf currents created by these wind oscillations, in abrading the bars at the mouths of the Mississippi, is, of course, similar to that induced by the tidal currents. Indeed it is the more powerful, as already indicated in describing the latter.

The eddy currents have no governing agency in the formation of the bars.

It is now easily perceived how, with these various and powerful forces at work, the eddy current at the meeting of the fresh-water and salt-water is partly, sometimes entirely, effaced. During the river flood, its existence can only be detected when there is no tide, and when the air and sea are calm. During the low-water stage of the river, the principal movements over the surface of the bar are those of the gulf currents, which thus obscure the eddy current. Even in the short transition periods, when the river discharge is large, but not sufficient to remove the salt-water from the surface of the bar, the tidal or wind currents passing over the bar, into and out of the river, increase or diminish the eddy current so that it may appear to be much greater than it really is, or may be entirely effaced. In this condition of the river the eddy current is probably stronger than at any other time, because, the velocity of the river current being considerable and the depth of salt-water on the bar being small, the vertical extent of the eddy is very limited and its velocity proportionally great.

---

* To these oscillations, it is thought, should be attributed the extraordinary shoaling of the bars at the mouths of the Mississippi that is said to have taken place in the early part of the winter of 1858–9. Upon examining the gauge observations at Carrollton—the nearest point to the mouth at which observations were made—it will be found that the wind there blew almost incessantly from the northward during the latter part of December, 1858, and during January and the first part of February, 1859; and it appears to be probable that from this cause the depths upon the bars of the Mississippi were materially less than they were during the preceding summer and early fall. During the months of December, 1857, and January and February, 1858, there was much calm weather and the proportion of northerly winds to the whole number was not nearly so great as during the winter of 1858–9. As a consequence, the depth of water upon the bar was greater.

These observed facts expose the fallacy of the theory recently advanced (in 1851) by an American engineer, that eddy currents are the governing agency in the formation of the bars at the mouths of the Mississippi.*

Facts respecting mud lumps.

Mud lumps.—All the changes and modifications that the bars undergo have now been enumerated except one, which, so far as it affects navigation, is of great importance. This change is the sudden rising, upon or near the crests of the bars, of masses of tough clay, varying in size from "mere protuberances looking like logs sticking out of the water," to islands several acres in extent. They attain heights varying from 3 to 10 (in one instance 18) feet above the surface of the gulf. Salt springs are found upon them, which emit inflammable gas.† After the lapse of a considerable time, many of these springs cease emitting gas and water, and the lump is worn away by the currents of the river and gulf. The origin of these mud lumps has been the subject of much speculation. By some their source is supposed to lie at a great distance inland; by others, in the river itself; the communication between the lumps and their source being maintained by permeable strata. Others have concluded that their origin was due to the generation of carburetted hydrogen gas in the vegetable matter which forms a part of the sedimentary material brought down by the river and deposited in the gulf. This gas constantly increases in quantity, and being covered by the tenacious, clayey mud of the bar (which the investigations of Lieutenant-Colonel Long, Topographical Engineers, show to be rendered peculiarly tough by contact with salt-water) forms constantly expanding reservoirs. These extend until the increase of size and escape of gas adjust themselves to the supply of the latter. After a time the material for the generation of gas begins to fail, and the activity of the mud lump to diminish. In the operations of the contractors for the removal of obstructions to navigation in 1858, some of these lumps upon the bar of the Southwest pass, which had not yet reached the surface of the gulf, were broken by explosions of gunpowder. A strong ebullition of gas over a wide space continued for more than twenty minutes after the explosion; and the surface of the bar, within an area 100 feet in diameter, was found to have sunk, and to have assumed the shape of the crater of an extinct volcano. This fact favors the views of those who have attributed the origin of the mud lumps to the material existing in the bar.

---

* The report of M. A. Surrell, upon the Improvement of the Mouths of the Rhone, published in 1847, contains the same theory, although not endorsed by that engineer. He attributes it to M. Aimé. The theory is briefly enunciated in the following literal translation of the language used in the report: "The river current, in gliding upon the sea, produced a counter current beneath it, in the form of an eddy, which, rubbing against the bottom, carried back into the river the earthy matter that had fallen from its waters to the bottom of the sea." It may be added that the construction of parallel jetties at the principal mouth of the Rhone, as recommended by M. Surrell, deepened the channel over the bar, and thus practically demonstrated the fallacy of the eddy theory.

† Major A. H. Bowman, United States Corps of Engineers, who made a survey of the Southwest pass in 1828, states that he burned the gas collected from these mud lumps. Mr. W. H. Sidell, one of the principal assistants in the Survey of Captain Talcott, states specifically that the gas escaping from them was inflammable. Sir Charles Lyell notes, on the authority of Mr. Bringier, that during the excavation of the new canal, inflammable gas escaped from the disturbed earth.

PLANS FOR INCREASING THE DEPTH ON THE BARS.

Before making any recommendations upon this subject, a brief resumé of what has already been done to improve the navigation at the mouths of the Mississippi will be given.

Outline of the history of operations upon the bars of the Mississippi.

Operations upon the bars of the Mississippi.—The bars at the mouths of the Mississippi river are always forming, and a perpetual annual expenditure must be incurred to increase permanently the depth of water upon them. In this all engineers who have written upon the subject agree. The appropriations made by Congress for that object, however, have been given irregularly and at intervals of several years; so that the deepening of the channels effected by one appropriation has been filled in long before the passage of the next. To be of practical benefit to navigation, the depth of the channels must be permanently increased,—a condition that could never be attained under the system of appropriations heretofore followed.

First appropriation.

When the first appropriation for improving the navigation at the mouths of the Mississippi was passed, in 1837, an extended and elaborate survey of the passes, mouths, and approaches was made by Captain A. Talcott, United States Corps of Engineers, under the direction of the Board of Engineers, and the plan of deepening by dredging with buckets was recommended. This plan was approved by the Board of Engineers, sanctioned by the War Department, and carried into effect as far as the appropriation admitted. The plan was based upon the supposition that a work thus begun would be continued by further appropriations, but no other was made until 1852, when the sum of $75,000 was appropriated, embarrassed, however, with the requirement that the work should be done by contract.

A Board of officers was then appointed, by direction of the War Department, to report a plan of operations. The Board recommended :—

Second appropriation.

1st. That the process of stirring up the bottom by suitable machinery should be tried.

2d. If this failed, that dredging by buckets should be tried.

3d. If both these modes failed, that parallel jetties should be constructed, 5 miles in length at the mouth of the Southwest pass, to be extended into the gulf annually, as experience should show to be necessary.

4th. Should it be then needed, that the lateral outlets should be closed.

Finally, should all these fail, a ship canal might be resorted to.

The recommendation of the Board to dredge by stirring up the bottom was approved by the War Department, and a contract was accordingly entered into for deepening the Southwest pass to 18 feet. The contract was successfully executed, and a depth of 18 feet obtained in 1853. No further appropriation was made until 1856, and, as anticipated, no trace of the deepening was left in 1855.

Third and last appropriation.

In 1856 $330,000 were appropriated for opening and keeping open, by contract, ship channels through the bars at the mouths of the Southwest pass and pass à l'Outre.

Upon the passage of this appropriation act, that Bureau of the War Department having charge of the work invited proposals for its execution by contract, in accordance with the terms of the act, and a Board of Engineers was convened to take into consideration the offers received.

The Board recommended that the proposals of the New Orleans Towboat Association to open and keep open the Southwest pass, by stirring up the bottom, should be accepted, there being no question of the practicability and efficiency of the mode proposed to execute the work; and that the bid of Messrs. Craig and Rightor for opening and keeping open the pass à l'Outre for five years should be accepted, *for the purpose, as stated, of enabling the bidders, by actual experiment, to prove the practicability and efficiency of the modes by which they proposed to do this work.* Their plan was that of closing minor passes and of constructing parallel or converging jetties on the bars. The Board stated it had great doubts of the practicability of the constructions proposed; and of the efficiency of the plan, should the work be constructed; but that an important point would be ascertained by its failure or success. Upon the report of this Board, the Secretary of War made the following decision:—

"If the mode proposed by the Messrs. Craig and Rightor to open and keep open the passes of the Mississippi is sufficiently feasible to justify a contract with them for the pass à l'Outre, as recommended by the Board, it is not perceived upon what ground their bid for the Southwest pass should be rejected, since they propose likewise to open and keep open that pass for a less sum than any other bidder. Should their plan be successful, the appropriation will suffice, on the terms they propose, to secure for five years a depth of 20 feet in both channels. If their plan should prove impracticable, the experience of five or six months will probably demonstrate that fact, and if it should then be necessary to resort to other methods by new contracts, the delay could not be very injurious to the commerce of New Orleans, as the period, December 1, 1857, at which the preferred bidder for the Southwest pass proposed to complete the channel of 18 feet depth, is so remote, and occurs so late in the season of trade at New Orleans, that the character of vessels destined for that port would scarcely be changed before the succeeding season. Neither is it believed, should it be necessary to make new contracts, that any loss would be sustained by inviting new bids, as those now presented for the execution of the work by tried means are not sufficient, by any combination which can be made of them, to open the passes and keep them open for one year.

"The bid of Messrs. Craig and Rightor will, therefore, be accepted for both passes, due care being taken, by the terms of the contract, to insure the prompt commencement and steady progress of the work, and sufficient guarantees will be required that the channels will be kept open for the whole period of five years."

Contracts with Messrs. Craig and Rightor were accordingly entered into by the Bureau, for opening both channels 20 feet deep, and maintaining that depth in them four and a half years.

The duty of the officer of the War Department connected with this operation was limited to marking out the channel to be deepened, and ascertaining, upon notice from the contractors, whether the contract had been fulfilled; that is, whether the required depth had been obtained and subsequently maintained.

The contractors began (see figure 2, plate XX) by building on the east side of the Southwest pass a jetty about a mile long, composed of a single row of pile planks, strengthened at intervals by piles. Portions of this jetty were carried away by storms;

and the contractors abandoned the plan, convinced that they could not, with their means, effect the desired result in that way.* With the sanction of the Department, they then resorted to stirring up the bottom with harrows and scrapers, dredging with buckets in some places, and blasting the mud lumps. By these methods they succeeded by June and September, 1858, in opening the two channels to a depth of 18 feet, their contract having been modified that year, in respect to the depth; and as long as the process of stirring up the bottom was continued by them, the channels preserved the requisite depth.

But in the latter part of 1858 those parties refused to comply further with their contracts to maintain the depth of 18 feet in the channels for a period of four and a half years; and, in consequence of their failure, the winter of 1858–9 passed without any work being done upon the bars. A new contract was entered into with other parties for deepening the Southwest pass, but they, likewise, failed to execute it.

The Department, in compliance with the appropriation law, having thus opened the work to competition in respect to plans and methods to be used, as well as cost, and having thus failed to secure a continuation of the work, was forced to resort to a contract for the use of steam dredges and machinery, to be employed under the direction of its officers, who, for the first time since 1839, with a remnant ($70,000) of the appropriation of 1856, conducted the operation of deepening the channels. The plan used was that of dragging harrows and scrapers along the bottom of the channel seaward, thus aiding the river flood in carrying the stirred-up matter to deep water. In the low stage that material was transported chiefly by the machinery itself. The plan proved to be successful; and a depth of 18 feet was maintained upon the bar for the period of one year at a cost of $60,000.

Classification of plans of improvement.

Recommendations for improving the navigation at the mouths.—The development of the laws which govern the formation of the bars has removed all uncertainty as to the principles which should guide an attempt to deepen the channels over them. The erosive or excavating power of the current must be increased relatively to the depositing action. This may be done either by increasing the absolute velocity of the current over the bar, or by artificially aiding its action. To the first class of works belong jetties and the closure of lateral outlets; to the latter, stirring up the bottom by suitable machinery, blasting, dragging the material seaward, and dredging by buckets. These plans are all correct in theory, and the selection from them should be governed by economical considerations.

Plan of jetties.

If the excavating power and depositing action of the Southwest pass had been equal, when the yearly advance of the bar was 700 feet instead of 338 feet, the least depth upon it would have been 21 feet. This increase of excavating power may be obtained by constructing two converging jetties, beginning where the depth of 22 feet is found, and extended to that depth outside the crest of the

* Attention should here be directed to the fact that the plan of jetties has not really been tried at the mouth of the Mississippi, as the contractors merely built one insecure jetty, of a single row of pile planks, about a mile long, whereas the Board of 1852 recommended jetties 5 miles long on each side of the channel, each 14½ feet wide, composed of piles 2 feet apart. The plan has been tried, however, at the principal mouth of the Rhone, a delta river like the Mississippi, and has effected the desired increase of depth. The plan was adopted by the French Government, after a full discussion of the whole subject by the engineer in charge of the work.

bar, which would give them a length of about 2.5 miles. The experience gained in the progress of the work should determine where the convergence should cease and the parallelism begin. The erosive action should be aided at first by dragging and scraping the hard portions of the bar. The depth of 21 feet thus obtained must be maintained by the annual extension of the jetties 700 feet into the gulf, and the reduction of the mud lumps by suitable machinery whenever they begin to appear. This rapid extension of the mouth of the pass into the gulf would tend to increase the volumes of the shorter passes at the expense of its own, and it would eventually be necessary to resort to another pass for the continuation of the plan.

Plan recommended.

The plan of stirring up the bottom by dragging harrows or scrapers over the bar is, no doubt, the most economical and the least objectionable. As already shown, during the low-water stage and part of each transition stage, there is often dead water or a refluent current on the bar. The operation should therefore be limited to the flood stage, during which there is an outward current on the bar. This stage, it will be remembered, usually continues about six months in the year, but its exact duration in any season may be readily determined by observing the oscillation of the river at Carrollton, where its commencement reads about 11.0 feet on the Delta Survey gauge. (For bench-mark see Appendix B.) After the remarks upon the frequent variations in the mean level of the gulf, it need hardly be added, that no exact estimate of the progress of the work can be formed without careful daily gauge observations at the pass itself.

Importance of a permanent fund.

In conclusion, it should be stated that no plan whatever will prove of any material benefit to navigation, unless a permanent fund be provided, untrammelled by restriction as to the mode of expenditure, from which a sufficient sum annually can be relied upon for the continuous prosecution of the work, after as well as before the channel has been opened to the desired depth. The bar is constantly forming, and must therefore be constantly removed.

APPENDICES.

APPENDIX A.

SURVEY OF THE MOUTHS OF THE MISSISSIPPI BY CAPTAIN TALCOTT, IN 1838.

No. 1.—EXTRACTS FROM THE REPORT OF CAPTAIN A. TALCOTT TO COLONEL J. G. TOTTEN, CHIEF ENGINEER.

New Brighton, 30th January, 1839.

Sir:—

* * * * * * * * * * * *

17. To the reports of my assistants and the maps, as referred to in the 1st, 2d, 3d, and 4th paragraphs, I must ask your attention for information in detail, as required by paragraphs 2, 3, 5, 6, and 7 of your memorandum.

18. My research for records of astronomical observations, made near the debouché of the passes, has been unsuccessful, except in a single instance. In the spring of 1801, Don José J. Ferrer made observations for the latitude of the bar of the Southwest pass. He places it in 28° 56′, and states that the observations were made on shore with a repeating circle and artificial horizon. (See 6th vol. *Trans. Am. Phil. Soc.*)

I had expected to find the bar of this pass something farther south at the present time, but, so far from it, the most southern point of the curve of 3 fathoms is now found to be in lat. 28° 56′ 22″, and what would be considered "the bar," is something farther north.

19. Such old charts as I have been able to collect are also submitted. On one we find it recorded that the latitude of old Fort Balize, from astronomical observations, is 29° 06′. The old magazine, which is still standing (see sketch), is found to be in 29° 05′ 58″.59, a very near coincidence. The same old chart presents a very different appearance of the Northeast and Southeast passes and Balize bayou to those furnished at the present date.

20. The only chart of the passes that appears to have been projected from actual survey is that by Gould, from his surveys, carried on from 1764 to 1771, in the gulf of Mexico. Could projections of this survey be obtained, on a scale sufficiently large for comparison, I have no doubt it would afford correct data from which could be ascertained the changes wrought in the lapse of seventy years. All the copies of the chart that I have seen are on a scale too small to be of any value as a medium of comparison for that object. (See title of the chart annexed; also, Sailing Directions for Entering the Mississippi, translated from a Spanish work.)

21. At the suggestion of Major Chase, the line of a ship canal, as projected by him in report of the 9th February, 1837, was embraced in the survey. It resulted in showing a fine ship channel leading up to where he proposed it should debouch, and the perforation of the ground to a depth of 40 feet indicated a firm bottom of sand mixed with mud, tenacious of water, and altogether such as would be considered favorable for excavating, and on which there would be no difficulty in securing a foundation for locks or structures of any kind. The difference of level between the high water of the river and low water in the bay is ordinarily 3.8 feet, but when the level of the bay is very much

depressed by a northwest wind, it may be as great, and I am informed has been 4.8 feet at the canal, a few miles below. The canal just referred to is about 9 miles below Fort Jackson, and affords a communication between the river and West bay for small vessels. It is furnished with a lock, for locking down from the river to the bay. The proprietor informed me that, during the low stage of the river, it was no uncommon occurrence for the water to run from the bay into the river, when the wind was favorable for elevating the water in the bay.

During hurricanes, the waters of the bays are elevated to a great height above the river level, and sometimes above its banks, over which it rushes with destructive violence to buildings and improvements on this part of the delta.

I was informed by the ordnance sergeant stationed at Fort Jackson, that during a severe hurricane, in 1830, the water rose to the spring of the arches of the embrasures. Captain Davis, of the steam tow-boat Porpoise, who was ascending the river at the time, and some distance above Fort Jackson, informed me that, when the bay water broke over the river banks, it was full 4 feet above that of the river.

22. The surveys above the point of divergence were not commenced until about the end of July, when a sub-brigade of four assistants, organized for that purpose, commenced the field labors, which were continued until the middle of August. The result of these is exhibited on Map No. 2, on a scale of $\frac{1}{30000}$.

23. The irruptions of mud, which are constantly occurring at the mouths of most of the passes, is an interesting feature, and one which must have an influence in projecting any plan for improving the natural entrance. As to the immediate cause of these irruptions, I must confess ignorance; nor is it important to the success of the improvements that it should be known, as there is little hope that it could be removed or counteracted.

The effect of these irruptions is to obstruct, and frequently to change, the channel. Their tenacity is such that it requires a long time for the current of the river to remove them, although its velocity is generally very great.

All of which is respectfully submitted by

Your obedient servant, A. TALCOTT.

Sailing Directions for Entering the Mississippi, Translated from a Spanish Work.

The true delta of the Mississippi is called the *Passes*, where the river is divided into four parts or branches, formed by low, swampy lands. Their mouths form nearly a circle. The first pass runs to the southwest, the second to the south, the third to the east, the fourth to the northeast. All these passes take their names from the directions in which they run, and the last named, or Northeast, is also called, à l'Outre.

Of all these passes, that most frequented, because of the greater depth of water on its bar, is the East, where there is a look-out to make signals and to advise mariners of their situation; and here also pilots can be obtained to take vessels into the river.

The entrance to this pass, as to all the rest, is so barren of landmarks, that it could not be known but for the flagstaff, where a large flag is hoisted when a vessel is seen in the offing. This flagstaff can be seen 3 leagues at sea, at which distance there is 40 fathoms water; mud, a sticky clay, in some places mixed with fine sand. The flagstaff is situated east and west with the entrance. Get the flagstaff to bear west, and run for it until you get 8 or 10 fathoms, which will be 1 mile from the bar, when it is best to anchor. The flagstaff bearing west, it will be better to have it bear to the south of west, than to the north, in order that you may be to windward of the entrance of the bar. At high tide there is generally from 12 to 13 feet water, and in extraordinary cases from 15 to 16. Its length is 1 league, counting from the entrance to La Fourche or the forks (as is likewise called the place where it joins the principal trunk of the river), where there is from 4 to 5 fathoms. The depth increases as you proceed up the river, which is navigable to the very banks, until you arrive at New Orleans, which is situated on the east bank, when you moor to the bank with a plank to the land.

The entrance of the river is found by those who are acquainted, and does not require a pilot; but it is advisable that strangers should procure one. The soundings of all the passes is muddy bottom, and at 6 leagues out you find 50 or 60 fathoms. (*Derrotero de las Islas Antillas, de las Costas de Tierra firme.* Madrid, 1810. Page 431.)

No. 2.—REPORT OF ASSISTANT W. H. SIDELL TO CAPTAIN TALCOTT.

SIR:—

The following is submitted as a report of the operations of the first brigade of engineers acting under my orders, and employed in the examinations and surveys deemed necessary in forming a project of improvement of the entrance of the Mississippi river.

The nature of the duties required are thus explained in a memorandum, of which a copy was furnished me. I give the substance.

The work believed to be necessary, previous to forming any plan for the improvement of the navigation of the mouth of the Mississippi river, is—

1st. Exact surveys of the branches from the point of divergence to the mouth, with the shoals at the mouth, and of the gulf out to —— fathoms at least. The latitude of one of the mouths to be fixed, and, by a great triangulation, the actual latitude and relative longitude of the other mouths to be ascertained.

2d. The actual slopes of the surface of the river from the point of divergence to the mouth, at the time of freshets, and at other times, to be known.

3d. The actual velocity of the river, and far out into the gulf, to be determined.

4th. The quantity of earthy matter held in suspension by the water at different seasons of the year and at different places, to be ascertained.

5th. The specific gravity of the fluid, within and without the bar, to be determined.

6th. Observations to be taken to ascertain the existence of a littoral current, if it exists, and its effects.

7th. Observations to be made to determine the changes that have occurred during the time employed in the survey, and to learn if these depend on an alteration of the bottom or the surface of the river, when they occur in the shoals at the mouth. Also to determine, if practicable, what changes have occurred in the gulf in the lapse of years.

The operations of the first brigade bearing on each of these points will be stated in the same order as they are above set forth.

The country in which these operations were performed may be thus described:—

The Mississippi river, at its debouché, divides into several channels, called "passes." At the highest or main point of divergence there are three of these passes, to wit, the Northeast, South, and Southwest passes. They are from 18 to 23 miles in length. The Northeast pass more nearly resembles a continuation of the river than the others, from its capacity and the fact that other passes diverge *from it.* The South pass lies more in the direction of the stem of the river, while the Southwest pass is the longest of the three. Following the course of the Northeast pass about 3½ miles, another pass diverges to the left, called pass à l'Outre, from which again, near its head, still another pass branches off to the left, called pass Cheval. This is known on Captain Delafield's map by the name of Flaherty's bayou. Pass à l'Outre and pass Cheval throw off to the right and left many bayous before they reach the gulf. Following again the course of the Northeast pass, below pass à l'Outre, we come, at about 5 miles distance, to a pass or large bayou on the right, called bayou Balize, on the banks of which, near its head, is the pilots' settlement, called "the Balize." This was once the main channel. Two miles below this the Northeast pass divides into two branches, that on the left retaining the name of Northeast pass, while that on the right is called the Southeast pass. Besides the main divergence of these three branches, there are other channels between the Northeast and Southeast pass, the banks of the latter being by no means well defined.

The banks of the lower part of the river, the passes, and bayous appear to have been formed by the alluvion; for they are no more than long strips of land, half overflowed and covered with reeds. The firmest or dryest parts are near the water's edge. Between the peninsulas thus formed by the passes, there will of course be large bays, and the same remark applies with respect to those formed by the bayous.

The names given to these bays are as follows: that between the South pass and Northeast pass and bayou Balize is known as Garden-island bay; between bayou Balize and the Southeast pass there is no well-defined bay, because so many bayous empty there that it is nearly all formed into land; nor between the Southeast and lower point of the Northeast passes, because they are so near to each other, and there are so many communications between them. Between the Northeast pass and pass à l'Outre lies Blind bay. There is also a pond near the point of divergence which is separated from Blind bay only by a group of grassy islands. It appears to have once formed a part of Blind bay, and these islands, which are still growing, appear to have accumulated gradually till the separation. Between pass à l'Outre and pass Cheval, the bay has no name. Outside of pass Cheval is the gulf of Mexico; but the appearance of the numerous islands gives reason to the belief that there was at one time another pass or large bayou to the north of pass Cheval, which, ceasing to flow by becoming choked, or other cause, was finally washed away by the waves of the gulf, leaving these islands as the only evidence of its former existence. Tradition supports this belief. This sweep of coast is called bay Ronde, said to have been so called from its shape when enclosed. Now that part of the delta lying to the north and east of a line passing through the middle of Garden-island bay, which includes the land above described, was assigned to this brigade, and to it the statements of this report are applied. It is called, for distinction, the first division.

For the survey the method of triangulation was adopted. A base of about 2 miles was measured on a sand reef near the mouth of the South pass. (See Sub-Report B.) The greatest care was observed to obtain it with precision. From this a great triangulation was spread over the part of the delta above described. A smaller triangulation was connected with it, and from the two a still smaller triangulation traced the passes and principal bayous. The filling up of the shores, etc. of the bays was effected by means of the plane-table, which work was also made to depend on the well-established points of primary and secondary triangulation. The form of the bottom of the points covered with water was obtained by sounding, and the means used to obtain the place to which each sounding belonged may be thus described: In the bays where there was no current, where the bottom was uniform, and where moreover it was a matter of comparatively small importance to obtain very accurate knowledge, soundings were taken between established points, the boat rowing uniformly, and the distance divided into intervals nearly equal, being modified by the circumstances of the wind, etc. In one of the bays, however—Blind bay—the method was more accurate.

In the passes, *not* near their mouths, the places of the soundings were obtained by rowing the boat from one known point on the bank to another on the opposite bank, an observer with an instrument being placed at a third point, who took observations to the boat at every even minute, at which time also the soundings were taken. The intersection of the lines of these observations with the line of the course of the boat would give the places of the corresponding soundings.

For the soundings of the bars, the outside soundings generally, and the part of the passes near the bars, a plan was pursued which deserves particular notice, because it is new, and, for accuracy, convenience, and quickness of execution, surpasses any previously known method.

It is due to Mr. H. A. Norris, an assistant engineer of this brigade. It is thus: At two points on shore, fixed by the triangulation, observers are placed with theodolites. One of them is supplied with a chronometer, or other accurate time-keeper, and several signal-flags; he has also an attendant, to manage them. The other observer has also an attendant, whose duty it is to watch the signal-flags of the first observer and communicate them to his principal. The object of this arrangement is to get simultaneous observations on the boat at given intervals of time, which is effected thus: A few seconds before the given time a signal-flag is hoisted, at which each observer directs the telescope of his instrument at the boat, and continues to follow its motion by means of the tangent-screw. At the given instant the signal-flag is jerked down, and the instruments left to be read in their last position. The engineer in the boat has also a chronometer, and his soundings are taken and entered in his book at the corresponding times.

On return from the field, the observations for that time are copied from the books of the observers, opposite the proper soundings, and the places of the soundings on the plat are by this means fixed with trigonometrical accuracy.

There are several signals to provide against delays, adjust time-keepers, give notice of derangement of instruments, cessation of work, etc., which cannot be detailed here. Mr. Norris himself presents an account of it in Memoir B.

One of the advantages of this method is the great rapidity and ease of its execution; but those which render it peculiarly advantageous on *this work* are—1st, the absolute correctness of its results; 2d, the facility with which it traced the sinuosity of the shores and bayous, and noted the accidents of the bottom; and 3d, the ease with which the same localities may be resumed and sounded after a lapse of time, merely by preserving the places of the observers on the shore. Every other method has a degree of looseness which would be inapplicable to a survey with the objects of the present; and this consideration may be sufficient to justify me in giving so much space to its exposition.

Having thus explained the manner of conducting the survey, I refer to the maps for the results. There are two principal maps, which embrace the whole of the work of this brigade, viz.: a map marked A, containing as much of the stem of the river as was surveyed by the first brigade, part of the Northeast pass, to the head of pass à l'Outre, pass à l'Outre itself, pass Cheval, parts of Garden-island bay and Blind bay, with bayous, etc.; and a map marked B, containing the remainder. Both these are on a scale of one ten-thousandth. Map C, giving the Northeast bar, and so much of the pass as is necessary to show the whole formation of the mouth of that pass. Map marked D, showing the whole of the Southeast pass, and map marked E, showing the bar, etc. of pass à l'Outre. Maps "C," "D," and "E" are on a scale of double the size of "A" and "B," or one five-thousandth.

The latitude and longitude of a point having been accurately fixed, the triangulation of this brigade connected this point with other points of the survey, and proper marks were left at these points, which may be referred to hereafter.

Respecting the second requirement, "the actual slopes of the surface of the river from its divergence," etc., this slope was found, from a point about 2 miles below the head of the passes, to be 2 feet. It was obtained by levelling across the land from the Northeast pass to bay Ronde. The time allotted to the survey did not allow of its being taken many times.

The actual velocity of the current in the river passes, and bayous of the first division was taken at surface, mid-depth, and near bottom, with the following results for the passes:—

MEAN VELOCITY OF CURRENT.

In stem of river	3.7	feet	per second.
In Northeast pass above pass à l'Outre	3.9	"	"
" " between pass à l'Outre and Balize bayou	3.0	"	"
" " below Southeast pass	3.9	"	"
In Southeast pass	2.7	"	"
" pass à l'Outre below pass Cheval	3.9	"	"
" pass Cheval	2.15	"	"
Balize bayou	3.07	"	"

Over the bar of the Northeast pass, the velocity at the surface and at eight feet in depth was determined by observations from two instruments, continued for several hours, with these results:—

SURFACE FLOAT.	Ft. per sec.		EIGHT FEET DEEP.	Ft. per sec.	
First observed	3.06,	½ mile out.	First observed	2.43,	in channel.
Middle observation	2.94,	1 " "	Middle observation	1.61,	⅔ mile out.*
Last observed	2.85,	2½ " "	Last observed	2.13,	⅓ " "

The above is the result of many observations, and the velocities stated are the mean of the surface, mid-depth, and bottom velocities. The mid-depth velocity, or mean, does not conform to that obtained by the ordinary formula showing the relation between the surface and mean velocities.

It will be observed that these velocities are good for the day only on which they were observed; to be extensively useful, they should be taken at short intervals throughout the year, so as to take into account the fluctuations to which the river is subject.

To ascertain the quantity of earthy matter, a number of experiments were performed, which resulted in showing 0.58 of a grain in 1000 grains of the river-water, or a little more than $\frac{1}{2000}$. Of this, much was sand. This latter fact was shown by causing the current of the river to pass through an apparatus for diminishing velocity. The heavier particles of the ~~water~~ fell to the bottom of the apparatus, and were collected in abundance.

Another experiment, in which 6000 grains of water were left to settle in a vessel an inch and a half in diameter for an hour, showed that one-eighth of all the terrene matter in the 6000 grains of water fell in that time, and of this nearly the whole was sand. In fact, there is abundance of sand, of the same character with that found above, in all parts of the passes and on the bars.

These experiments should be carried on through the year, but of this our time did not admit. Having determined the velocities of the several streams, and the quantity of earthy matter held in suspension, it added but little to the labor to ascertain the quantity of water, and, of consequence, of terrene matter discharged by the passes, as well as over the main bars. For this, cross-sections of the streams were made at the places where velocities were determined. Both at the places of starting and arrival of the floats, the mean of these was taken as the mean section of the stream to which the corresponding velocity was due. The results for the large stream are as follows:—

Main trunk of the river discharges		809,565	cubic feet per second.
Northeast pass.	Above pass à l'Outre	467,571	" "
	Between pass à l'Outre and Balize bayou	275,260	" "
	Below Southeast pass	182,142	" "
	Loss by bayous below this point	6,117	" "
Pass à l'Outre.	Below pass Cheval discharges	189,214	" "
	Loss by bayous, etc	18,687	" "
Southeast pass discharges		78,914	" "
Balize bayou		14,612	" "
Pass Cheval (sum of branches)		6,541	" "

The present and former channels of the Northeast bar are included between two mud islands, a little less than a mile apart; and through this space about nine-tenths of the water finds its way to the gulf. Nine-tenths of the gauge below the Southeast pass, bayous deducted, is 158,423 cubic feet; this is the quantity of water that passes through the space in a second.

The specific gravity of the river-water was found, as we shall show hereafter, to be 1.00033. Now, there are 359,081.6 grains of this fluid in a cubic foot, and as in each thousand grains there is 0.58 of a grain of sediment, the whole quantity of earthy matter passing in *a day* is equal to 221,014 tons.

---

* At two-thirds of a mile out, the littoral current (pro tempore) takes and changes its direction nearly at right angles. The second velocity is taken at the turning-point.

We have seen that 189,214 cubic feet per second is the quantity of water which is thrown into pass à l'Outre: 18,687 cubic feet per second is lost before passing the bar; leaving 170,527 cubic feet per second for the quantity discharged over the bar. But this passes through two channels, and also over a shoal. The approximate quantity discharged from each is here shown :—

Northern channel,	97,800	cubic feet	of water	per second	gives	136,389	tons of	earthy	matter	per diem.
Southern channel,	52,812	"	"	"	"	73,631	"	"	"	"
Over shoal,	19,915	"	"	"	"	27,775	"	"	"	"
Total,	170,527					237,795				

By the same means we find that there passes over the Southeast bar 110,083 tons of earth per day.

The two channels of pass à l'Outre correspond, as was before remarked, or will correspond, with the Southeast and lower part of the Northeast passes.

These results apply to the time of the experiments only, though the river then appeared to be about its average state.

The specific gravity of the fluid, within and without the bar, was also found by a series of experiments. Those within the bar gave, as an average, 1.00033, distilled water being 1.000000. Without the bar no experiments could give definite results, excepting those in the clear salt-water of the gulf, which was found to be 1.0245. The other experiments give a variety of results, depending on the state of the mixture. It is to be remarked, that the state of the mixture is different at times, according to the then and previous state of the weather. For instance, when the river is high and the weather calm for several days in succession, the river-water, spreading itself on the surface of the gulf-water, extends directly out to a great distance, without mingling with the salt-water below. In rough weather, on the contrary, the agitation of the waves serves to mingle the waters, and when the river is low, the salt-water has been known to extend beyond the point of divergence of the passes.

The observations taken for a littoral current were such as to induce the belief that none exists, at least within the range of our experiments. An inspection of the courses of the *passes* may lead to the same conclusion, for their degree of divergence appears to be equal in all directions, which would not be the case if there were a current to carry the earthy matter, which forms their banks, to the one side or the other.

Temporary causes may produce a current for the time, running in the one or the other direction, according to the influencing cause. Thus, when the wind has been blowing for a long time in one direction, it banks up the water of the gulf, bays, and streams that lie in that direction; this produces a return current when the wind lulls. The southerly winds, I believe, prevail, though at the time we were there they were mostly from the north and east.

The observations taken to ascertain changes of the shores, etc., during the progress of the work, could not be very extensive, but, by inquiry and observation, much information was elicited respecting changes that had occurred in times past and those now in progress. Nevertheless, changes of importance, though not of great extent, occurred during the time of the work. The one most worthy of notice was this: The boat *passed over* a certain place on the Northeast bar, at the commencement of operations, on which there was about 2 feet water. Before their termination a lump at this place projected 2 or 3 feet above water; a change which, by comparison with other known points, was shown to proceed from a *rise* of the *bottom.*

This phenomenon is not uncommon, but, on the contrary, occurs frequently. A channel of entrance may be destroyed by this means, and, until another channel is formed, the bar will be impassable. The pilots and captains of tow-boats give innumerable instances of it. Ballast stones and anchors, which have been thrown overboard or lost, have been brought to the surface. The lumps appear to be forced *through* the ordinary bottom by some power acting from below, but what may be the cause which produces effects so wonderful, future researches must determine.

As a knowledge of this subject has an important bearing on some of the projects of improvement, a surmise will be offered, after a fuller statement of facts. These lumps have a peculiar appearance. In entering the mouth of the river they may be taken for rocks, from their height, the steepness of their sides, their compactness, and the appearance of stratification produced by the cracks. In some cases they rise 8 or 10 feet nearly perpendicularly, and at one place there is a mound in the form of a truncated cone, ascertained to be at least 18 feet high. It is nearly inaccessible, through the marsh or flat that surrounds it. By looking at the map of the Northeast bar it will be found on the north bank near the cape. The material of the lumps is a clay, so fine-grained as to take the impression of a seal and receive a polish from the hand. When tried by a blow-pipe it first decrepitates, throwing off scales with considerable violence. By continuing the heat it bakes like other clay, and finally vitrifies, probably by the agency of the salt, of which it contains a sufficient quantity to give it a strong saline taste. On many of these lumps are found springs of salt-water. The water issues through a well-defined crater, as firm on the sides as a chimney, generally about 6 inches in diameter, and, as the salt-water comes up through soft mud, it brings up some of that material with it, in the form of a very flat cone, about the crater. This mud appears to be the same material as that of which the lumps are composed. The surface of the lumps is so hard as to be penetrated with difficulty with a spade, and the mud brought up by the springs bakes in the sun to the same consistency. There is an ebullition of the water of the springs at considerable intervals, and inflammable gas escapes, probably light carburetted hydrogen. An attempt was made to sound these springs, but there was so much soft mud that the lead could not be made to go far without difficulty in withdrawing it. The greatest depth to which the lead was sunk was about 4 fathoms. Universal testimony goes to show that no means have been employed sufficient to reach a definite bottom. It is believed that they extend to the original bottom of the gulf. It is to be noted, that the water stands in the springs from 2 to 3 feet *higher* than the surrounding water of the river, though that is fresh, and the water of the springs has a greater density than the gulf-water. This latter fact, however, may be attributed to the circumstance, that the spring-water on which the experiments were tried had been standing in pools for some time, and subject to concentration by evaporation. There was found amongst the mud of one of the springs a few grains of sand, white, and much larger than the sand of the river. These lumps vary in size, from mere protuberances, looking like logs sticking out of the water, to islands of several acres in extent. Pass island, at the mouth of the Balize bayou, is one of a cluster of three large islands, which, from their general appearance and the existence of salt springs in them, are known to have been upraised. This island has been for many years inhabited, and cultivated with success; in fact, when vegetation commences on the lumps, it assumes at once a more luxuriant character than the growth of the ordinary land of the delta, which is no more than marsh, producing reeds and coarse grass, with a few trees far up the passes.

Another curious circumstance relative to these lumps and salt springs is, that they are only formed in the immediate vicinity of the bars or next to the gulf. The only instance noted in which a spring came up through the marsh, was at a place near the bayou running past the northeast lighthouse; and at the mouth of this same bayou is a lump about 10 or 12 feet high, around which the marsh is forming. With this exception, and that of those lying near the mouth of the Balize bayou (which, by-the-by, was once the main pass), the lumps and salt springs are all found near the mouths of the *principal passes*. It is also curious that none of these formations exist at the mouth of the South pass; nor does that pass appear to be making out to any extent, at least so it is stated; but the South pass is within the limits of the second division.

The lumps are sometimes swept away by the attrition of the water, and sometimes become the nucleus of shoals, which may in time define the banks of the pass in which they are formed. Rains have also their effect in reducing them to their general level. Hurricanes have been known to sweep away particular lumps at once, and the ebb and flow of the tide of salt-water, when the river is low, wears them away more rapidly than the ordinary flow of the river. To this latter circumstance may be attributed the fact that the water on the bar is deeper when the water of the gulf sweeps over it, that is, when the river is low, than when the place of the clear salt-water is supplied by water holding much matter in suspension and ready to be deposited on coming in contact with the water of the gulf.

It is perhaps proper to mention in this place some experiments that were made to determine if the deposit of sediment were owing solely to the check of velocity of the current on meeting the outside waters. The conclusion was that the effect was not owing solely to this cause. Proper vessels had been provided for the experiments, and in these as many fit substances as were at hand were dissolved in a mixture with the water, each in a separate vessel. These substances were common salt, epsom salt, alum, sea-water, brine from the salt springs, and sulphuric acid. The river-water alone took from ten to fourteen days to settle, while the solutions became perfectly limpid in from fourteen to eighteen hours, or from one-fifteenth to one-eighteenth part of the time. I know not to what cause to attribute the effect, unless it be action of these substances on the vegetable matter contained in the water, which aids in the suspension of the earthy matter. Boiling the water, or even keeping it in a bottle for a long time, will so change its nature as to cause it to settle very soon after agitation. Wishing to know if soluble compounds were formed by the sea-water and sediment, 65½ grains of the latter were washed with a solution of 120 grains of salt in 1000 of pure water. After drying and washing anew with pure water, about 4 grains were found wanting; but this was attributed to the want of delicacy in the performance of the experiment; and the opinion is that no soluble compounds, material in quantity, are formed.

However, from these experiments we may conclude that the earthy matter is deposited more suddenly than would be the case if it depended on the check of velocity alone; that the bars will be formed just at the debouchés, or where the salt-water is first met; and that the greater the quantity of water brought down, the sooner, on account of the sudden precipitation, will the bars be formed at the debouchés.

Recurring to the mud lumps and their mode of formation, we have seen that they form at the bars only, or where the process of formation of land by deposit is still in progress; that they rise with considerable rapidity, and acquiring their maximum elevation in a short time, so remain until destroyed by foreign causes, resembling the effect that would be produced by a strong force acting for a limited time. That this force cannot be the pressure of the surrounding water of the river, or even the waters of the gulf brought through chasms from a distance, is evident; for they rise far above the surface of the surrounding water, and being themselves more dense, bring with them, besides, brine of greater specific gravity than the waters of either the river or gulf, or at least as great as the latter. We see, moreover, that they must come from *above* the original bottom of the gulf, for that we know the nature of, and the nature of these is not the same; that they come from great depths, for the salt springs on them are of great depth, and the shells found in them give other evidence of it; that gases are formed below them, for we see it escaping in quantity; that this gas is such as is formed from the decomposition of vegetable matter in similar situations, viz., light carburetted hydrogen; and lastly, that the composition of the lumps is of the firmest material.

From these data we proceed. In the outward flow of the river, the finest material is carried farthest, and is the first stratum on the bottom of the gulf; coarser strata are deposited over these in the inverse order of their specific gravity. These finer particles probably consisted of vegetable matter, or were much mingled with it; this the experiments went to show. The decomposition of this vegetable matter generates a gas, exerting a great elastic pressure on the plastic and compressed matter next above, causing it to rise, as we perceive in the lumps, bringing with it brine from the depths where the sea-water may be supposed to exist. The operation is aided by the pressure of the heavier material deposited above.

It is not our object, in this suggestion, to say that the lumps would sink again into the abyss, for the space at first occupied by the gas is not left an absolute vacuity, but the chasm is refilled by water and soft mud, in which case the force required to retain them in their position is only the difference of specific gravities; and the material of the lumps may take a position of equilibrium even with the chasm, for it approximates to the form of the arch. There is no proof that some of them do not subside. They disappear, and it may be in some cases that this disappearance is caused by a subsidence. It is probable that for centuries back these lumps have been generated at the then existing mouth of the river, and yet we now see none of them except at the present bars. Is it possible that, notwithstanding the vegetation which might serve to protect them, no traces of their former existence should be discovered, if their disappearance depended simply on the ordinary causes?

If this theory be correct, it offers another objection to the method of improvements by increasing the velocity by means of levees, for the lumps would form with great rapidity just opposite the end of the works.

From all this it would appear (if no other objections exist) that, to prevent the passage of part of the river-water over the bar and admit the gulf-water to supply its place, would be likely to be more effectual than the works intended to produce the contrary effect. A work to produce effect might be constructed in the form of a "redan," with its gorge toward the sea, and open at its salient angle, which will be located at the commencement of deep water within the bar. The effect may be aided by leading off some of the water by artificial bayous.

Here it may be stated, that the bayous, even the smallest, when they lead off from the passes and empty in places where they meet the action of the salt-water, are miniature passes, and present all the phenomena of the larger streams, excepting the mud lumps and salt springs. These last do not appear, for obvious reasons. The bayous must, therefore, be made the subject of experiments, and the results, if the bayous be judiciously chosen, will apply directly to the case of the passes. It was a matter of regret that the time spent in the field was so limited and burdened with other duties, as not to admit this course of experiments.

I will now leave the subject, and proceed to state the other changes that came under my notice. They are very few, and connect the information derived from others with personal information.

Where the northeast lighthouse now stands is said to be a quarter of a mile farther from the bar than it was four or five years since. The marsh surrounding the building is less frequently submerged than formerly. Boats could, at times, come close up to the little elevation on which the lighthouse stands. A wharf or landing for boats still extends from that elevation to the marsh; of course it is useless.

There is a pond between the Northeast pass and pass à l'Outre. This has the appearance of having been part of Blind bay, but is now separated from it by many grassy islands, which are increasing in firmness, and perhaps in number, so as to render it probable that the pond, in course of time, will be entirely filled.

The Balize bayou was formerly the passage for ships, and its bar was at the place where it diverged from the Northeast pass. At this point the place was defined. Now the bar is at the *mouth* of the bayou. It has but 3 feet water on it, and 15 may be carried over the place of divergence from the Northeast pass. It was mentioned before that there are three large mud islands at the mouth, besides several smaller. I am not aware of the time of the rise of these islands, but, if subsequently to the time when the bayou was practicable, it would go to show that the bar, at the place of divergence from the Northeast pass, was reduced on account of a smaller volume of water being drawn over it than formerly; but, whatever may be the time of their rise, one conclusion may be drawn from the fact of their existence and the shoalness of the bar in their vicinity, which is, that it is not a narrow and straight channel only, which is a panacea for all the disorders of the river, for the Balize bayou is narrow and straight, and formerly discharged a large quantity of water; nevertheless (or more probably in consequence of it) we see three high mud islands, besides several smaller, and a *bar immediately* at its mouth, so shoal as to be practicable for boats only.

On the north shore of Garden-island bay, not far from the south bank of the Balize bayou, is to be seen the ruins of a building, probably an old magazine. It is called by the pilots the old Spanish Magazine (no doubt correctly). It was about 20 feet square, with an arched roof, and brick walls about 4 feet thick, supported by buttresses. The roof has been intentionally broken through. In other respects the building is in good order. It is now almost inaccessible, it being difficult to get even a flat-bottomed skiff near it, and there is no bayou within a reasonable distance. It is also sunken, having a kind of ditch around it; and within, as seen through the roof, there is nothing but mud and water. It was probably once high and accessible. Some idea of the changes in this country may hence be obtained. Its situation was accurately determined by connecting it with the triangulation, and its latitude found to correspond with that given in Bowditch's Navigator as the latitude of the Balize.

Bay Ronde, as is called the sweep of coast exterior to the delta on the north and east, appears as if once enclosed like the bays between the passes. It is said by the old residents to have been so, and from its circular form, when so enclosed, took its name. It is very possible that a pass or large bayou might have diverged to the east, above the present head of the passes, and, as the general rule is for the streams to form their own banks, its southern bank, as formed, would have been the northern shore of bay Ronde. When, from becoming choked or other causes, the stream dwindled away, the surge from the gulf, in time of storms, swept away the evidences of its existence, except the few islands that remain. This, however, is only conjecture; proper information might be obtained by consulting the old maps.

By inspecting the map of pass à l'Outre, it will be perceived that there is a wide shoal or middle ground at its mouth, with channels nearly equal on both sides. It is probable that this shoal will accumulate till it projects above the water, thus forming two passes, resembling very nearly the Southeast pass and lower part of the Northeast.

This appears to depend on some cause peculiar to the passes of the first division.

One of the changes which has occurred within the memory of man is the complete formation of an island in the Northeast pass, just below pass à l'Outre. It is about three-quarters of a mile long, and is still increasing. It has trees along its shore, but its interior is marshy. This alluvial island differs in every respect from the islands of irruption on the bar. It should have been mentioned that these latter islands had their relative heights determined by levelling, and stakes left on them for purposes of future reference.

This completes the account of the duties performed by the first brigade, and the conclusion to which these duties led. There was delay in obtaining proper facilities, so that active operations were carried on only about four months, and the brigade was not fully efficient for a longer time than two months and a half. The distance from a market, and the difficulties of communication from point to point, together with the submerged condition of the land, rendered it altogether one of the most difficult countries in which to operate that could be imagined; nevertheless, a survey extending over more than 200 square miles was made with accuracy and minuteness; between 20,000 and 30,000 soundings were taken, most of which were fixed with trigonometrical precision, which it is believed is not the case in any other work. This could be effected only by great assiduity on the part of the gentlemen attached to the brigade, and this credit is due to them.

The names of these gentlemen, and the duties assigned to them, are as follows:—

H. A. Norris, H. Selden, and R. N. Isaacs constituted the sounding party.

J. W. Elass executed plane-table work, gauged bayous, and attended to other duties.

A. Hotchkiss, part of the primary and secondary triangulation, survey of pass à l'Outre, and other duties.

J. E. Cropsey and F. Schroeder, survey soundings of the Northeast pass and part of the stem of the river; also of pass Cheval, and gauging the passes.

C. King, Jr., who was attached to the astronomical brigade shortly after the beginning of operations.

The office duties which have occupied the brigade, have been:—

1st. Calculations of primary, secondary, and tertiary triangulation.

2d. Protraction of the shores by the results, and extending the soundings of passes and bays.

3d. Protraction of soundings of three bars on a double scale.

4th. Calculations and plotting relating to the regimen of the river, and digesting the chemical and other observations.

5th. Calculations of terrestrial graduation; their object was to project the work on a cone drawn secant to the earth and concentric with the tangent cone at the middle of the country surveyed; the secant cone so drawn that the part of the element between the extreme northern and southern limits of the work should be equal to the part of the meridian between the same limits; the cone then to be developed.

The latter portion of the work was begun on the 10th August, and completed on the 31st December, 1838, excepting the labors of draughtsmen, who were then employed to finish the maps.

The brigade was discharged at the latter date.

The pilots at the Balize were always ready to render all the assistance and information in their power.

Much is due to Captain Taylor, United States Revenue Officer at the Balize, whose liberal assistance on many occasions, and information derived from knowledge of the locality and general intelligence, contributed in a considerable degree to the advancement of the work.

I am, Sir, with great respect, your obedient servant,

WM. H. SIDELL,
Principal Asst. Engineer First Brig. Engrs., Miss. Survey.

Office Impt. Miss. river, BROOKLYN, 25th January, 1839.

No. 3.—REPORT OF ASSISTANT G. G. MEADE TO CAPTAIN TALCOTT.

SIR:—

I have the honor to submit for your consideration, and that of the special board of engineers, the enclosed maps, projected from the surveys made at the suggestion of that board, and by order of the Engineer Department, dated Nov. 25th, 1837, with a view to ascertain the practicability of improving the navigation of the entrance of the Mississippi river, and the following report of the mode of operations and their results, as pursued in the execution of the surveys of that part of the Mississippi delta projected upon these maps, and the charge of which was assigned to me by your letter, dated Dec. 8th, 1837.

Sheet No. B 1 represents the projection of the survey of the Southwest pass, South pass, Grand bayou, intermediate bay, and adjacent coasts, upon the scale of $\frac{1}{10000}$, and is the map of assemblage of the whole work executed by the second brigade of engineers.

Sheets No. B 2 and B 3 are the projections of the Southwest and South bars respectively, on the scale of $\frac{1}{5000}$.

Sheet No. B 4, the cross-sections made to determine the quantity of discharge of the different outlets; and sheets B 5, B 6, and B 7, the projections of the curves of the currents at the heads of the passes and over the bars.

Mode of operations.—In the mode of operations, reference was had, as far as time and circumstances would permit, to the suggestions contained in the memoir of Colonel J. G. Totten, president of the special board, enclosed to me in your letter of Dec. 8th, 1837.

The work was commenced by the measurement of a base line on "Steer's reef" (see sheet No. 1), 10,650.6 feet in length—this being the most practicable ground for measurement on the delta. Nine points were then established, extending over the whole ground, and determined from the base, constituting the primary triangulation. These points are noted on the maps by a double triangle, the lines connecting them being in red ink. Their latitude and difference in longitude from the astronomical station, Northeast Balize, have been deduced from the observations of the astronomical brigade, and a table containing them placed on sheet B 1, marked "Table No. 1." Intermediate points, constituting the secondary triangulation, were established on all the principal points of the passes and bars, and determined from the primary triangulation. The passes were then filled up by a minor triangulation, having the points on their shores, and the coasts of the bays were traced out by the plane-table. The lines of the minor triangulation in the passes and of the stations in the bays were then sounded out. The bars were sounded out with great accuracy, having the position of the boat determined at each sounding. Finally, observations were made on the tides, quantity of discharge, specific gravity of water, relative height of the passes and bays, and the level of the salt-spring formations.

Southwest pass.—This pass is 15.2 miles long, being 2800 feet broad at its head, from where it diminishes to 1200 feet, the width at station "Willow" (sheet B), thence gradually increasing to 9436 feet—the width of the extreme points of land on the bar.

It has a bar at its head, over which 48 feet can be carried. The average depth of the pass is 70 feet, the greatest being 102 feet. The bottom is soft mud, with spots of sand.

The velocity of the pass about a mile below its head (the point at which the observations were made) is 4.876 feet per second; the quantity of water discharged at this point, 342,692.5 cubic feet per second. There are 15 bayous, exclusive of the 9-feet channel, through which the discharge is 12,510 cubic feet per second—the 9-feet channel discharging 26,734.5 cubic feet per second.

South pass is 11.28 miles in length, and 4.94 miles to the head of Grand bayou. It is 2400 feet in breadth at its head, but soon narrows to 700 feet, which is the mean width until it reaches the bar, where it increases to 3200 feet. Nineteen feet water can be carried over its head. The greatest depth in the pass is 53 feet; which, with 24 feet, are the limits of the water in the channel between the bars. The bottom is generally *sand*, interspersed with spots of *soft mud*. Sixteen feet can be carried into Grand bayou, and 7 feet over the shoal at its mouth. It is about 6 miles in length, and is neither so broad nor so deep as the South pass.

At the head of the South pass the velocity is 3.319 feet per second, and the discharge 80,761.39 cubic feet per second.

There are three bayous, exclusive of Grand bayou, flowing from the South pass, of which the whole discharge is 7745 cubic feet per second—Grand bayou having a velocity of 3.342 feet per second, and discharging 15,314.07 cubic feet per second.

In the South pass there are fewer bayous, the banks are firmer and higher, and the trees of older growth than in the Southwest pass—indicating its prior formation.

Bayous, bays, etc.—The bayous flowing from the Southwest and South passes have generally from 6 to 8 feet water in them, with bars at their heads and mouths. Most of them are choked up at their heads with rafts of drift-logs, and are sensibly filling up.

There are traces in both the passes of former bayous, which have been completely filled up at their heads, and in the mouths of which the water of the bay rises and falls with the tide. By an examination of the sheet No. B 4, it will be seen, from the cross-sections of the passes and bayous, that the banks are precipitous—in some instances almost perpendicular. Immediately on the river they are firm, and a few inches above the ordinary high-water mark, but have a fall of 2 feet to the bay, and become *soft* and miry in proportion as you recede from the river. The growth on them is salt-marsh in the bays, with high reeds and canes on the shores of the passes.

The bay to the west of the Southwest pass is very shoal, the 1-fathom curve being 4 miles from the shore at the mouth of Steer's bayou (sheet No. B 1). In East bay this curve runs up about 7 miles. The other curves, for want of time, were not run out the whole distance from Southwest bar to South bar, but they keep very nearly a parallel direction to the 1-fathom.

The bottom of the bays is *soft mud* at their heads, having a greater proportion of sand mixed with it in the deeper water.

Southwest bar.—For the examination of the details of this bar, the map upon the scale of $\frac{1}{5000}$ is submitted. The soundings are reduced to the plane of mean low water, marked "plane of reference" on the tide scale.

The dimensions of the bar are 7500 feet from 18 feet within to 18 feet without, along the channel; 3500 feet from 15 feet within to 15 feet without; 5000 feet greatest distance between points of 2-fathom curves; 9436 feet, distance between extreme points of land.

The channel, having an average width of 1200 feet, is straight in a southwest and northeast line, and lies on the west of the bar. Thirteen feet can be carried over at low water, and 14.5 feet at high water; though the mud in the channel is of so soft a nature that vessels are easily drawn through an additional foot.

The bar is composed of mud and sand, the matter held in suspension by the river-water, and deposited on the diminution of its velocity caused by the resistance of the sea. Within and without the shoal the bottom is soft mud, of a *bluish* and yellow tint, having a large proportion of alumine. Immediately on the shoal the bottom is harder, and has a greater proportion of sand. The formation of this shoal is regular, having on it 9, 10, and 11 feet. The greatest irregularities are three lumps, delineated upon the map, which are uncovered about 2 feet at low water, having diameters of 4 feet. These lumps are the result of a cause, the facts relating to which are more fully detailed hereafter.

The water is constantly undergoing changes, both in the level of the surface and in the bottom; the former from the winds affecting the tides and from the freshets, the latter by the action of the salt springs, and the continual deposit and carrying off of the particles, resulting from the different velocities with which the water discharges itself. The channel also changes its position, dependent on the winds giving direction to the main current washing it out.

The water, previous to reaching the bar, discharges itself over two shoals, one on each side of the pass. Between the last points of marsh and the extreme mud lumps, the boundaries of these shoals are shown by the mud lumps, within which there is from 1 to 2 feet water. Eleven feet can be carried into the 9-feet channel, and 9 feet out of it. It is, however, so narrow as to be at present unused.

A cross-section of the bar made along the line joining the extreme points of land is shown on sheet No. B 4.

Salt springs.—The islands on the shoals and the lumps on the bar are formed by upheaving of the mud of the bottom, and are of various heights above the surface of the water—from 10 to 3 feet. On the surface of most of them are found springs of salt-water, holding in suspension a large quantity of mud. These springs are a few inches in diameter, having their sides hard, and are of various depths, one being 18 feet, situated on the lump "Final" (sheet No. B 2). The whole of the surface of the lumps is broken into fissures. These, together with the strata formed by the deposit of the mud from the springs, have every inclination to the horizon, and present the appearance of the exertion of a strong force in a vertical direction from below. Around some of the springs the ground was discolored from the presence of some chemical compound, being of a *lead*, a *pink*, and a *reddish-brown hue*. *Inflammable gas* was constantly evolved from the most active. The soil of which the lumps are composed is principally clay, though some have the chief proportion of sand. Specimens of the nature of the soil of the principal ones are submitted for the consideration of the special board. When first taken from the ground they were quite salt to the taste, as are the weeds which grow on the islands. The surface of many is covered with white pure salt, evaporated from the deposit of the springs. The water from the springs, when filtered, was clear, very salt, and weighed 1025.5 grains, the same phial filled with rain-water weighing 996.5.

Of the cause of the formation of these islands I am unable to give any opinion. It would appear to be *chemical* rather than mechanical action, as has been presumed. They are not formed, nor could any traces of their previous existence be found, in the passes or at the South bar. Their broken and distorted appearance, and their being able to withstand the whole current of the river, show the force to be of great intensity. In some the action appears to have ceased. The springs are dried up and the surface become comparatively smooth. Such is the case with the one on which station Pilot (sheet B 2) is located, and which is now used as a place of residence. In others, as the one marked Lands-end, the action is very strong, there being nine springs on it. Those immediately in the vicinity of the bar appear to be more active than the farther removed.

Care has been taken to determine the exact position of these islands. They were made points of secondary triangulation, chained and compassed, and their height above the plane of mean low water obtained. The profiles of the principal ones are contained in sheet B 2.

South bar.—The dimensions of this bar, shown on B 3, are—

6500	feet from	18	feet within to	18	feet without,	along the channel.
5000	"	15	"	15	"	"
3000	"	12	"	12	"	"
2000	"	9	"	9	"	"

There are two channels, the middle ground between having on it at the time of the survey 2 and 3 feet water. Eight feet water can be carried over the west and principal channel—6 feet in the east. The west channel, lying about north and south, has an average width of 1500 feet. The bottom of the bar is principally fine gray sand, mixed with a small proportion of mud. Without the shoal the soft yellow and blue mud of the passes is found. The character of the bar is sand (as it is of the passes and of the adjacent shoals), there being two reefs of sand extending from each extremity of the South pass, in a north and west direction. These spits of sand, together with the bar, are constantly washing away and reforming from the effects of the wind and action of the sea. It will be seen that the reef to the west of the bar has made more than a mile since Captain Delafield's survey in 1829.

Although no traces could be found of the salt springs in this part of the delta, the changes are almost as rapid as when subjected to their control. The middle ground, which in March had the water on it represented by the soundings, had by the middle of June so much increased that it was visible at high, and had a large portion of it uncovered at low water; it was composed of *sand*, very firm and hard, as if cemented by the small portion of clay that was in it. The precipitous nature of the bar renders the sea very heavy and the navigation dangerous. There is also a shoal bearing southeast from south lighthouse, which was not determined for want of time.

Tides.—Observations were made upon the rise and fall of the water during the day at the head of Grand bayou in South pass, from 1st to 31st of March; also during the period of sounding out the South bar. Observations were then made upon the tides, and from the 1st to the 31st May, the highest and lowest water, as well as the rise and fall for every half hour during the day, was noted at the Southwest bar.

The projections of the curves of high and low water at these two places are shown by the two scales on sheet B 1 and the scale on sheet B 4. From an examination of these it will be perceived that the influence of the tide is very slight in affecting the water on the bar, the mean difference between the high and low water on the Southwest bar (see table No. 1) being only 1.22 feet. There is usually one tide a day, or during the twenty-four hours, governed by the wind as to its height, and dependent on the position of the moon as to the time of high and low water; the water being lower during a north, and higher during a south wind, than under ordinary circumstances. During the summer months, when the quantity of river-water discharged is very much diminished, the influence of the tide is greater, and there is then an under-current of salt-water up the pass, which has been known to flow up as high as Fort Jackson; but, during the period of our observations there, was no influx of the sea, but merely a diminution of the velocity and a backing of the waters of the river.

The effect on the tides by freshets is shown by the curves of high and low water during the days of the 17th and 18th and 19th May (sheet B 2), when much drift-wood, indicative of a rise, was observed to float down the stream. The curves approach each other, the high water preserving its level, but the low water is much higher than usual, resulting from the increased body of water diminishing the effect of the sea and swelling the river.

The rise and fall is nearly the same in the pass as at the bar. The difference can be seen by a comparison of the scale on sheet B 4, with those on sheet B 1.

Specific gravity of the water.—The difference between the specific gravity of the water of the river and of rain-water was so slight as to be almost imperceptible with a delicate pair of French scales, although the experiments were made in all parts of the delta, as will be seen by the annexed table (table No. 2).

The weight of a phial filled with rain-water being 1219.25, the mean of the experiments on the waters of the surface was 1219.75 grains; of those below the surface, 1220.26; giving, in the one case, 0.5 of a grain, and in the other, 1.01 in 996.5 grains—the phial weighing 222.75 grains.

The weight of the water on the bar constantly changes—dependent on the discharge of the river and the force and direction of the winds. During a calm day and large discharge, river-water can be obtained for many miles outside the bar on the surface, and to a depth below equal to the mean depth of the bar; but if the discharge was not great, the tide high, or the wind strong from one direction, blowing the current toward the other, salt-water, or water mixed with salt, and weighing the same, could be obtained on the outside portions of the bar. During the months of April and May, fresh water, and only fresh, was taken from within the bar, and on the line joining the extreme points of land. Beyond this, and when the depth was greater than 11 feet (the mean depth of the bar), a mixture of fresh and salt water would be brought up, salt in proportion to the depth.

Amount of deposit.—Having weighed the water in the phial, it was filtered through a piece of filtering-paper, the weight of which was determined before and after the filtration, the difference of measurement giving the amount of deposit.

In the water of the surface, there is 0.632 of a grain, and below the surface, 0.955 of a grain in 996.25 grains (table 2).

The alluvion brought down by the river is composed of fine sand mixed with clay; it is greater in volume than in weight.

Experiments were made on the nature and quantity of the sand, by sinking a closed box, pierced on opposite sides with holes of unequal diameter, the larger orifices being placed up stream. The water, in passing through, had its velocity diminished, and deposited the coarser particles held in suspension. In this manner the sand of the bottom and surface currents was obtained in different parts of the delta, specimens of which are submitted for the consideration of the special board. The sand of the bottom is a little coarser than that from the surface.

In allowing the water to settle, it was found that in twenty-four hours it became quite clear. This time was very much diminished when a mixture of salt and fresh water was subjected to the influence of rest.

Force and direction of currents.—In the passes, the current generally coincided with the axis of the pass.

In the Southwest pass, at its head, the velocity is 4.8 feet per second, and at the bar about 3 feet per second (see sheets B 5 and B 6). The bottom velocity is nearly the same as the surface; and if there is any wind opposed to the current, the difference will be inappreciable. At the Southwest bar many observations were made to determine the existence of a littoral current. A piece of drift-wood on the surface and a box with a specific gravity sufficient to sink it to the required depth were allowed to float over the bar, and a boat was left alongside of them, to which angles were taken at regular intervals. During or succeeding a calm, the current of the axis of the pass continues in its direction till its force is expended by the resistance of the sea. The current of the east or west side has an inclination to the east or west, resulting from the spreading out of the waters, or their being released from confinement to a channel.

The velocity is increased when the tide is falling, and diminished when it is rising. If there is any wind, the current will obey the impulse given to it by its direction. If from the east, the set of the current will be to the west, more or less inclined to the axis of the pass, as the force of the wind is greater or less. So, if the wind is from the west, the same circumstances will be perceptible with regard to the set of the current to the east. The bottom velocity is slightly less than that of the surface, and is affected in the same way, though not in so great a degree, and is much sooner neutralized by the resistance of the sea.

The prevailing winds being from the east, and the axis of the pass southwest, the general set of the current is to the west; hence may have arisen the idea of a "*westerly littoral current.*" Care was taken to make the observations under all circumstances of wind and tide, and no traces of the existence of such a current is shown within 7 miles of the land—the extreme point to which the observations were carried.

There are no regular currents in the bays, but such as depend on the *wind* and *tides.*

Slopes of the surface.—It was impossible, from the great breadth of the river, and nature of the growth on its banks, to level the surface of the water from the head to the mouth of the pass; but, in order to arrive at some idea of the slope of the surface, the Southwest pass was levelled with East and West bays, at its head and mouth; and, presuming the water in the bay to maintain its level, the inclination may be deduced.

Table No. 4 contains these observations: the mean height of the pass above East bay, 2.2325 feet; and at its mouth, 0.350 feet; giving an inclination of 1.75 feet in 12 miles—the distance between the points of observation. The inclination is, however, varied by the winds, tides, and freshets—the Southwest pass, during a freshet in June, having overflowed its banks at its head by a *foot* at *high water.*

I also enclose you the journal of the observations of the survey, kept in obedience to the directions contained in your letter of Dec. 8th, 1837, and remain, sir,

With much respect, your ob't servant,

GEO. G. MEADE,

Civil Engineer, in charge Second Brigade.

NEW YORK, Jan. 22, 1839.

TABLE No. 1.

Containing the amount of rise and fall of the water at Southwest bar during the month of May, 1838, as shown by the tide scale on sheet B 2.

Date.	Amount the tide rose.	Amount the tide fell.	Time of high water.	Time of low water.	Remarks.
1838.	*Feet and tenths.*	*Feet and tenths.*	*h. m.*	*h. m.*	
May 11	1.57	1.57	9 00 A.M.	6 05 P.M.	
" 12	1.59	1.53	8 00 "	7 50 "	
" 13	1.52	1.52	8 00 "	9 20 "	
" 14	1.44	1.48	10 00 "	10 03 "	
" 15	1.47	1.41	M.	11 40 "	
" 16	1.31		M.		The low tide occurred next day (see scale).
" 17	0.98	1.07	1 00 P.M.	0 35 A.M.	
" 18	0.52	0.70	1 00 "	0 20 "	
" 19	0.23	0.27	8 00 A.M.	1 00 "	
		0.36		6 14 P.M.	Second low water (see scale).
" 20	0.58	1.30	6 12 A.M.	9 00 "	
" 21	1.51	0.95	7 00 "	5 00 "	
" 22	0.95	1.32	7 00 "	8 00 "	
" 23	1.46	1.72	8 00 "	6 45 "	
" 24	1.62	1.51	8 00 "	8 00 "	
" 25	1.52	1.55	9 00 "	8 00 "	
" 26	1.55	1.50	9 00 "	8 30 "	
" 27	1.45	1.27	11 00 "	9 30 "	
" 28	1.08	1.00	11 00 "	10 20 "	
" 29	1.07	0.94	11 00 "	11 00 "	
" 30	0.84	0.78	M. "	11 40 "	
Mean	1.22	1.23			

Mean difference between high and low water, 1.225 feet.

TABLE No. 2.

Containing observations made to determine specific gravity of, and amount of deposit in, the water.

Phial filled with rain-water weighed........1219.25 grains. } Giving weight of rain-water 996.5 grains,
Phial empty weighed........ 222.75 grains. } assumed as the unit.

Date.	Location of the observation.	Depth from which water was taken.	Weight of the phial.	Difference in weight of paper before and after filtration.	Remarks.
1838.					
April 3	Head of the Southwest pass	Surface.	1218.75	0.75	
May 2	Southwest pass, Stn. Willow	do.	1220.00	0.75	
" 1	Do. Head 9 feet channel	do.	1221.50	1.00	
" 16	Do. off 9 feet channel	do.	1220.50	0.50	
" 16	Do. do.	do.	1219.50	0.50	
" 17	Do. Stn. Willow	do.	1219.25	0.50	
" 18	Do. off 9 feet channel	do.	1220.00	1.00	
" 19	Do. do.	do.	1221.25	0.75	
" 18	Do. do.	do.	1219.25	0.50	
" 20	Do. off East bayou	do.	1221.25	1.00	
" 24	Do. 9 feet channel	do.	1218.25	0.75	
" 21	Do. Stn. Willow	do.	1223.25	0.25	
" 21	Head Southwest pass	do.	1218.25	0.50	
" 26	Southwest pass, off 9 ft. chan.	do.	1220 00	0.25	
" 29	Do. do.	do.	1220.00	0.75	
June 4	Head of Southwest pass	do.	1219.25	0.75	
April	S. Pass, off head Grand bayou.	do.	1218.25	1.00	
May 2	Southwest pass, 9 ft. channel	do.	1224.00	1.00	
	Mean		1220.15	0.635	in 996.5 grains.

TABLE No. 2.—Continued.

BELOW THE SURFACE.

Date.	Location of the observation.	Depth from which water was taken.	Weight of the phial.	Diff. in wt. of paper before and after filtration.	Remarks.
1838.					
April 20.....	S.W. pass, off Stn. Willow...	12 feet.	1219.00	0.75	
" 20.....	Do. do............	14 feet.	1219.00	0.60	
" 4.....	S. pass, off head G. bayou...	Bottom; 18 feet.	1219.25	1.00	
May 19.....	S.W. pass, off 9 ft. channel...	Do. 10 feet.	1221.25	1.25	
" 20.....	Do. do............	Do. 10 feet.	1221.00	1.25	
" 24.....	Do. do............	Do. 12 feet.	1220.00	1.00	
" 26.....	Do. do............	Do. 12 feet.	1220.00	0.75	
June 4.....	Head S.W. pass, E. side......	Do. 5 fathoms.	1221.25	1.00	
" 6.....	Head South pass, centre......	Do. 3 do.	1221.75	1.00	
	Mean................	....	1220.26	0.955	
		SOUTH BAR.			
March 31.....	South bar	Surface.	1219.25	0.50	
" 31.....	Do.	6 feet; at bottom.	1219.25	0.75	
" 31.....	Do.	Surface.	1219.75	0.80	
" 31.....	Do.	Do.	1219.50	0.50	
April 1.....	Do.	12 feet.	1222.00	1.00	
	Mean................	....	1219.95	0.710	
		SURFACE OF SOUTHWEST BAR.			
May 16.....	Southwest bar..................	Surface.	1219.25	0.50	
" 17.....	Do.	Do.	1219.00	1.00	
" 17.....	Do.	Do. 4 fath. curve.	1218.50	1.25	
" 20.....	Do.	Do. outside do.	1219.25	0.25	
" 20.....	Do.	Do. inside do.	1220.25	0 50	
" 21.....	Do.	Do. 6 fath. do.	1219.25	0.50	
" 27.....	Do.	Do. 15 do. do.	1221.25	0.75	
" 27.....	Do.	Do. inside do.	1220.25	0.75	
" 27.....	Do.	Do. 8 fath. do.	1218.75	0.50	
" 27.....	Do.	Do. 10 do. do.	1218.75	0.75	
	Mean................	....	1219.859	0.629	
		BELOW THE SURFACE ON SOUTHWEST BAR.			
May 16.....	Southwest bar..................	12 ft. on 4 fath. curve.	1238.00	0.75	Water salt.
" 16.....	Do.	Bottom on 6 do. do.	1241.25	0.00	Water salt, quite clear, a few grains of sand.
" 16.....	Do.	Do. on 6 do. do.	1239.30	0,00	Water salt and clear.
" 17.....	Do.	Do. on 8 do. do.	1244.00	0.45	Water salt and discolored.
" 17.....	Off do. at sea..................	11 fath., bottom 12 fath.	1241.25	0.00	Salt and clear.
" 20.....	Southwest bar..................	Bottom 3 fath. curve.	1242.00	1.00	Salt and turbid.
" 20.....	Do. on shoal........	Do. 10 feet.	1219.50	0.50	Fresh river-water.
" 21.....	Southwest bar..................	Do. 6 fath. curve.	1245.50	0.75	Salt and turbid.
" 27.....	Off do. at sea...........	2 fath., bottom 15 fath.	1236.00	1.00	Salt and turbid.
" 27.....	Southwest bar..................	Bottom 5 fath. curve.	1236.00	0.00	Salt, slightly discolored.
" 27.....	Do.	Do. 2 fath. do.	1219.75	1.25	River-water.
" 29.....	Do. on shoal........	Do. 10 feet.	1220.00	0.75	River-water.
	Mean................	....	1240.355	0.438	[Excepting fresh water.]
Filtered water from salt spring on Final island (sheet B 2).....			1243.25		
	Recapitulation.				
	Mean of water from surface of river........................		1220.15	0.635	
	Mean of water from below surface of river		1220.26	0.955	
	South bar, unmixed with salt water........................		1219.95	0.710	
	S.W. bar, surface unmixed with salt........................		1219.35	0.629	
	Do. below surface unmixed with salt water........		1219.75	0.833	
	Do. do. mixed with salt water..........		1240.35	0.438	
	Filtered water from salt spring..............................		1243.25		

TABLE No. 4.

Containing observations made to determine the relative height of Southwest pass with East and West bays, at its head and mouth.

Date.	Height above East bay.	Height above West bay.	Location of the observations.	Remarks.
1838.				
April 15	2.985 feet.	2.202 feet.	Head of Southwest pass.	Wind east.
June 4	2.265 "	2.135 "	Do. do.	Wind east.
" 6	2.085 "	1.958 "	Do. do.	
" 7	1.530 "	1.820 "	Do. do.	
Mean	2.2325 feet.	2.0575 feet.		
May 29	0.400 feet.	0.835 feet.	Mouth of Southwest pass.	
" 30	0.870 "	0.275 "	Do. do.	
" 31	0.810 "	0.400 "	Do. do.	
June 1	0.320 "	0.000 "	Do. do.	
Mean	0.350 feet.	0.336 feet.		

Inclination of the surface, from observations on East bay, is 1.8825

Inclination of surface, from observations taken on West bay 1.7215

Mean 1.8020

Distance between points of observation 12 miles.

APPENDIX B.

DAILY GAUGE REGISTERS.

No. 1.—RECORDS OF THE DAILY STAND OF THE MISSISSIPPI RIVER.

THE following is the list of bench-marks for future reference:—

At Cairo, the zero of the gauge is at the Cairo City company's "mean low-water mark," which is 43.54 feet below their bench on Stevens & Williams' store on the levee.

At Columbus, the gauge was situated at the foot of Dabney street. Bench-mark No. 1, left bank (near velocity base), on oak-tree, reads 46.85 feet on gauge. No. 2, left bank, on poplar-tree near northwest corner of Dabney and Front streets, reads 47.718 feet on gauge. No. 3, left bank, top of northwest corner of brick foundation-pillar at southwest corner of Methodist church, reads 45.395 feet on gauge. No. 4, right bank, on oak-tree at station 29, transit line, reads 46.621 feet on gauge. No. 5, right bank, on sycamore-tree at station 32, transit line, reads 42.403 feet on gauge.

At Memphis, the gauge was situated in Wolf river, near the northern boundary of navy yard. Bench-mark, top of the southeast corner of the water-table of rope-walk, navy yard, reads 46.26 feet on gauge.

At Napoleon, the gauge was situated in the mouth of Arkansas river, north side. Bench-mark No. 1, on southeast corner of water-table of Marine hospital, reads on gauge 49.43 feet. No. 2, at Prentiss, on sill of the middle door on the north side of the jail, reads on Napoleon gauge 47.74 feet.

At Lake Providence, the gauge was situated near wharf-boat landing. Bench-mark No. 1, top of pedestal of east column of Methodist church, reads on gauge 44.10 feet.

At Vicksburg, the gauge was situated at foot of Crawford street. Bench-mark No. 1, on curb-stone at northwest corner of Prentiss House, reads on gauge 48.40 feet. No. 5, on northwest corner of window-sill, depot Southern railroad, reads on gauge 150.56 feet. No. 6, on top of third step of Catholic church, reads on gauge 178.70 feet. No. 7, on projection near door of Catholic church, reads on gauge 183.44 feet. No. 8, on angle projecting a few inches from wall, east of main door of Catholic church, reads on gauge 184.94 feet.

At New Carthage, the gauge was situated in front of the town, and the only bench-mark was made on a tree, which, in 1859, had caved into the river.

At Natchez, the gauge was situated on Mr. Brown's breakwater. Bench-mark No. 1, on hackberry-tree about 150 yards from the breakwater. The tree is in Mr. Brown's garden. Two or three spikes form the bench, which reads on gauge 47.00 feet.

At Red-river landing, the gauge was situated at the wharf-boat landing, below Mr. Torras' house. Bench-mark No. 1, on north side of locust-tree in Mr. Torras' lane, reads on gauge 45.36 feet.

At Baton Rouge, the gauge was situated in front of Mr. Brown's mill, above the arsenal.

Bench-mark No. 1, upon a post supporting the log-way inside of the mill, is marked 36. It reads 36.3 feet on gauge.

At Donaldsonville, the gauge was nailed to piling of wharf. Bench-mark No. 1, top of pedestal of column of Land-office, northwest corner, reads on gauge 28.18 feet. No. 2, on water-table of court-house, northeast corner, reads on gauge 28.82 feet.

At Carrollton, the gauge was situated a short distance above the depot. Bench-mark No. 1 (a large railroad spike), on the northwest corner of the machine-shop of the New Orleans and Carrollton railroad, reads 7.92 feet on the gauge.

At Fort St. Philip, the gauge was situated in front of Fort St. Philip. Bench of the fort (a block of granite on prolongation of face No. 1) reads 6.0 feet on the gauge.

NOTE.—Throughout these Appendices, all "old style figures" indicate interpolation.

Records for 1843.

St. Louis Arsenal.—Observer, CAPTAIN T. J. CRAM, Topographical Engineers.

Date.	January.		February.		March.		April.		May.		June.		July.		August.		September.		October.		November.		December.	
1843.	*G'ge*	*Wind.*	*G'ge*	*Wind.*	*G'ge*	*Wind.*	*G'ge*	*Wind.*	*G'ge*	*Wind.*	*G'ge*	*Wind.*	*G'ge*	*Wind.*	*G'ge*	*Wind.*	*G'ge*	*Wind.*	*G'ge*	*Wind.*	*G'ge*	*Wind.*	*G'ge*	*Wind.*
1									24.3		19.3		18.2		12.0		6.1		4.3		4.2		2.4	
2									24.7		19.3		18.2		11.8		5.9		5.3		3.9		2.4	
3									24.7		19.6		18.2		11.5		5.9		5.3		3.8		2.2	
4									24.6		19.5		18.4		11.3		5.7		5.1		3.6		2.3	
5									24.4		19.7		18.4		10.7		5.6		5.0		3.2		2.2	
6									23.6		20.0		18.4		10.6		5.4		4.7		3.2		2.2	
7									22.4		20.9		18.4		10.5		5.1		5.2		3.1		2.1	
8									21.4				17.7		10.2		4.9		5.6		2.9		1.8	
9									20.9				17.2		9.9		4.7		6.7		2.6		1.6	
10									20.4				17.1		9.9		4.5		8.1		2.6		1.3	
11									20.1		20.1		16.9		9.9		4.3		8.4		2.5		1.0	
12									19.8		20.1		16.6		9.8		4.3		7.9		2.5		0.0	
13									19.6		20.6		16.6		9.8		4.2		7.2		2.5		0.0	
14									19.1		21.6		16.7		9.8		4.1		7.0		2.3		0.0	
15									19.1		21.8		16.1		9.8		4.1		6.6		2.1		0.0	
16									19.8		22.1		15.9		9.8		4.1		6.4		2.1		0.0	
17									20.8		21.9		15.6		9.8		4.1		6.1		2.1		0.0	
18									21.3		22.1		15.4		9.8		4.0		6.0		2.1		0.0	
19									21.6		22.1		15.1		9.7		4.3		5.9		1.9		0.0	
20									21.8		22.5		14.9		9.6		5.8		5.6		1.8		0.0	
21									21.9		22.3		14.2		9.6		6.4		5.5		1.7		0.0	
22									22.1		22.3		14.5		9.5		6.5		5.5		1.7		0.0	
23									22.1		22.1		14.5		9.3		5.6		5.6		1.7		0.2	
24									21.8		21.3		14.2		9.1		5.1		5.6		1.7		0.5	
25									21.1		20.0		13.3		8.9		4.6		5.6		1.7		0.6	
26									20.2		18.7		13.7		8.3		4.3		5.6		1.8		0.8	
27									19.0		18.4		13.2		7.9		4.1		5.6		2.0		0.8	
28									17.8		18.1		13.1		7.3		4.0		5.6		2.1		0.8	
29									18.1		17.9		12.9		6.9		4.0		5.3		2.2		0.8	
30									19.2		18.1		12.6		6.6		3.8		5.0		2.2		0.8	
31									19.1				12.3		6.3				4.2				0.8	

Records for 1844.

St. Louis Arsenal.—Observer, CAPTAIN T. J. CRAM, Topographical Engineers.

Date.	January.		February.		March.		April.		May.		June.		July.		August.		September.		October.		November.		December.	
1844.	*G'ge*	*Wind.*	*G'ge*	*Wind.*	*G'ge*	*Wind.*	*G'ge*	*Wind.*	*G'ge*	*Wind.*	*G'ge*	*Wind.*	*G'ge*	*Wind.*	*G'ge*	*Wind.*	*G'ge*	*Wind.*	*G'ge*	*Wind.*	*G'ge*	*Wind.*	*G'ge*	*Wind.*
1	0.9		2.6		7.9		15.2		24.5		28.6		36.7		23.3		12.1		8.5		6.0		5.7	
2	1.1		2.6		8.9		15.3		24.4		28.6		35.9		24.1		12.0		8.3		6.0		5.6	
3	1.3		2.6		11.6		15.1		24.7		28.5		34.9		24.1		12.0		8.3		5.3		5.5	
4	1.5		2.6		12.7		14.0		24.1		28.3		34.2		23.4		11.8		8.1		6.0		5.4	
5	1.5		4.6		13.9		14.4		23.6		28.3		33.4		22.5		11.8		8.1		6.1		5.4	
6	1.2		4.3		14.6		14.1		22.9		28.3		32.8		21.5		12.0		8.0		6.1		5.3	
7	2.0		4.3		15.9		13.0		22.3		28.2		32.3		20.5		12.1		8.0		6.1		5.3	
8	2.9		4.7		16.6		13.0		22.2		27.9		32.2		19.3		11.8		7.9		6.1		5.3	
9	4.0		4.3		16.1		13.6		22.6		27.5		32.3		18.5		11.7		7.9		6.1		5.3	
10	4.0		4.1		16.2		13.4		21.7		26.7		32.3		17.9		11.6		7.8		6.0		5.2	
11	4.0		4.1		15.1		13.3		21.9		26.5		32.1		17.1		11.5		7.8		5.3		5.2	
12	4.1		3.9		14.7		13.2		22.1		26.8		32.0		16.6		11.3		7.8		6.5		5.3	
13	4.0		3.9		14.7		13.1		22.2		27.3		31.2		16.3		11.3		7.7		6.4		5.3	
14	4.0		3.7		14.4		13.1		24.1		27.9		31.1		16.0		11.2		7.6		6.4		5.3	
15	4.0		3.6		15.0		13.2		25.0		28.7		30.4		15.8		11.1		7.7		6.3		5.3	
16	3.9		3.6		15.7		13.2		26.4		28.6		29.4		15.5		11.0		7.7		6.2		5.3	
17	3.5		3.2		16.1		13.4		27.6		30.6		28.2		15.2		10.7		7.6		6.2		5.3	
18	3.5		4.1		16.6		13.6		28.2		31.3		27.3		14.6		10.6		7.6		6.2		5.2	
19	3.5		5.3		16.9		14.0		28.7		32.3		26.1		14.3		10.4		7.5		6.2		5.2	
20	3.5		6.1		17.2		14.4		29.2		33.0		25.2		13.9		10.1		7.3		6.0		5.1	
21	3.4		5.9		17.4		14.6		29.9		34.2		25.0		13.5		10.0		7.1		6.0		5.0	
22	3.4		6.1		17.1		14.9		30.4		35.7		25.3		13.1		9.6		7.0		6.0		5.0	
23	3.4		6.2		16.6		15.4		30.2		37.1		25.3		13.1		9.5		6.9		6.0		4.9	
24	3.3		6.5		15.9		16.2		29.8		38.1		24.9		13.0		9.2		6.7		6.0		4.8	
25	3.2		6.5		15.5		16.7		29.2		38.5		24.5		12.6		9.1		6.6		6.0		4.8	
26	3.1		6.3		15.1		17.7		28.4		38.7		26.1		12.5		9.0		6.5		6.0		4.8	
27	3.0		6.6		14.7		19.4		28.0		38.8		23.7		12.5		8.9		6.5		5.9		4.8	
28	2.9		6.6		14.9		21.8		27.9		38.7		22.5		12.2		8.6		6.3		5.9		4.8	
29	2.7		7.1		14.8		23.1		27.6		38.3		24.0		12.1		8.6		6.3		5.9		4.7	
30	2.6				14.9		23.9		28.0		37.6		24.1		12.1		8.5		6.2		5.8		4.8	
31	2.6				14.8				28.2				24.0		12.3				6.1				4.8	

Records for 1845.

St. Louis Arsenal.—Observer, CAPTAIN T. J. CRAM, Topographical Engineers.

Date.	January.		February.		March.		April.		May.		June.		July.		August.		September.		October.		November.		December.	
1845.	*G'ge*	*Wind.*	*G'ge*	*Wind.*	*G'ge*	*Wind.*	*G'ge*	*Wind.*	*G'ge*	*Wind.*	*G'ge*	*Wind.*	*G'ge*	*Wind.*	*G'ge*	*Wind.*	*G'ge*	*Wind.*	*G'ge*	*Wind.*	*G'ge*	*Wind.*	*G'ge*	*Wind.*
1	5.1		8.1		11.4		10.6																	
2	5.5		8.0		11.6		10.4																	
3	5.5		7.9		11.8		10.3																	
4	5.6		7.6		12.0		10.2																	
5	5.9		7.6		12.1		10.2																	
6	6.2		7.2		12.1		10.1																	
7	6.4		7.0		12.2		10.2																	
8	6.5		6.9		12.3		10.4																	
9	6.4		6.7		12.6		10.4																	
10	6.3		6.6		12.7		12.1																	
11	6.2		6.6		12.6		12.8																	
12	6.2		6.9		12.6		13.0																	
13	6.1		7.1		12.4		13.1																	
14	6.1		7.2		12.3		13.1																	
15	6.0		7.2		12.2		13.0																	
16	6.0		7.3		12.2		12.9																	
17	6.1		7.3		12.2		12.8																	
18	6.1		7.4		12.6		13.0																	
19	6.2		7.6		12.0		13.1																	
20	6.5		7.6		12.0		13.1																	
21	6.3		7.9		11.9		13.3																	
22	7.8		8.3		11.8		13.5																	
23	8.4		8.8		11.6		13.8																	
24	8.8		8.4		11.5		14.3																	
25	9.0		9.8		11.2		14.3																	
26	9.1		10.1		11.2		14.5																	
27	8.9		10.5		11.2		14.7																	
28	8.7		11.1		11.1		15.3																	
29	8.6				11.1		16.0																	
30	8.5				10.8		16.7																	
31	8.3				10.7																			

Records for 1848.

Memphis.—From records of Navy Yard.

Date.	January.		February.		March.		April.		May.		June.		July.		August.		September.		October.		November.		December.	
1848.	*G'ge*	*Wind.*	*G'ge*	*Wind.*	*G'ge*	*Wind.*	*G'ge*	*Wind.*	*G'ge*	*Wind.*	*G'ge*	*Wind.*	*G'ge*	*Wind.*	*G'ge*	*Wind.*	*G'ge*	*Wind.*	*G'ge*	*Wind.*	*G'ge*	*Wind.*	*G'ge*	*Wind.*
1																	10.3	NW.	4.2	NE.	2.6	NW.	6.7	N.
2																			4.2	"	2.5	E.	6.7	"
3																	11.5	"	4.1	SW.	2.5	SE.	6.6	SE.
4																	11.5	W.	4.1	E.	2.6	"	7.2	"
5															12.8	N.		N.	4.0	SE.			8.1	"
6															13.1	"	11.8	"		"			9.2	N.
7															13.3	"		E.	3.7	E.				
8															13.4	"		"	3.6	NE.				
9															13.7	"	9.5	"		"				
10															13.6	NW.	9.2	SW.	3.2	"	3.4	"		
11															13.7	"	8.5	"	3.1	E.	3.7	"		
12															13.4	SW.	7.9	S.	3.0	NE.	4.2	"		
13															13.0	NE.	7.7	"	3.0	"	4.5	NE.		
14															12.3	"	6.9	W.	3.0	"	4.7	"		
15															11.4	SW.	6.8	"	3.1	W.	4.9	"		
16															10.7	NW.	6.2	"	3.2	"	5.6	NW.		
17															10.0	"	5.2	SE.	3.4		6.0	N.	27.2	SW.
18															9.3	"	5.5	"			6.1	"	26.7	"
19															8.9	"	5.2	S.	4.0	"	7.3	"	26.2	"
20															8.5	SW.	5.2	W.	3.7	"	7.7	NE.	25.9	NW.
21															7.9	N.	5.0	E.	3.5	SW.	7.7	N.		
22															7.4	"	4.8	"	3.2	"	7.9	NW.	24.7	W.
23															6.9	"		"	3.2	"	8.0	SE.	24.0	E.
24															7.5	SE.			3.0	W.	7.9	W.	23.2	W.
25															7.6	SW.			2.9	NE.	7.7	"	22.7	N.
26															8.7	SE.	4.6	NE.	2.9	SE.	7.7	"	22.0	"
27															8.9	SW.	4.6	NW.			7.3	SE.	21.7	NW.
28															9.1	"	4.6	S.			7.0	S.	21.6	E.
29																	4.5	NW.	2.5	NW.	7.2	"	22.2	N.
30															9.4	W.	4.4	N.			6.7	NW.	22.9	W.
31																							23.7	"

Records for 1848—Continued.

Carrollton.—Observer, Professor C. G. Forshey.

Date.	January.		February.		March.		April.		May.		June.		July.		August.		September.		October.		November.		December.	
1848.	*G'ge*	*Wind.*	*G'ge*	*Wind.*	*G'ge*	*Wind.*	*G'ge*	*Wind.*	*G'ge*	*Wind.*	*G'ge*	*Wind.*	*G'ge*	*Wind.*	*G'ge*	*Wind.*	*G'ge*	*Wind.*	*G'ge*	*Wind.*	*G'ge*	*Wind.*	*G'ge*	*Wind.*
1																			0.6		1.2		5.9	
2																			0.4		1.3		6.1	
3																			0.4		1.4		6.3	
4																			0.4		1.5		6.4	
5																			0.3		1.6		6.6	
6																			0.3		1.6		6.6	
7																			0.3		1.7		6.7	
8																			0.2		1.8		6.9	
9																			0.2		1.9		7.1	
10																			0.2		2.1		7.4	
11																			0.2		2.2		7.7	
12																			0.2		2.4		7.9	
13																			0.2		2.6		8.1	
14																			0.1		2.7		8.3	
15																			0.1		2.9		8.5	
16																			0.1		3.0		8.6	
17																			0.1		3.1		8.7	
18																			0.2		3.2		8.9	
19																			0.2		3.4		9.1	
20																			0.2		3.6		9.4	
21																			0.2		3.9		9.7	
22																			0.2		4.1		9.9	
23																			0.3		4.3		10.1	
24																			0.4		4.4		10.3	
25																			0.5		4.6		10.5	
26																			0.6		4.8		10.7	
27																			0.7		4.9		10.9	
28																			0.8		5.1		11.0	
29																			0.9		5.4		11.2	
30																			1.1		5.6		11.5	
31																			1.2				11.6	

Records for 1849.

Memphis.—From records of Navy Yard.

Date.	January.		February.		March.		April.		May.		June.		July.		August.		September.		October.		November.		December.	
1849.	*G'ge*	*Wind.*	*G'ge*	*Wind.*	*G'ge*	*Wind.*	*G'ge*	*Wind.*	*G'ge*	*Wind.*	*G'ge*	*Wind.*	*G'ge*	*Wind.*	*G'ge*	*Wind.*	*G'ge*	*Wind.*	*G'ge*	*Wind.*	*G'ge*	*Wind.*	*G'ge*	*Wind.*
1	24.5	E.	31.0	NW.	14.3	NE.	31.8	NE.	18.6	NW.	21.7	S.	20.1	SW.	16.3	NE.	14.2	SW.	6.3	SW.	10.6	W.	12.6	NE.
2	25.2	NE.	31.3	"	15.1	SW.	31.8	E.	18.4	"	21.0	"	19.5	"	16.8	"	13.1	E.	6.6	E.	10.2	SSW.	15.0	NW.
3	25.9	"	31.4	"	16.5	"	31.7	S.	18.4	"	20.6	NE.	18.5	E.	16.8	SW.	12.9	NW.	6.5	NW.	9.5	SW.	15.5	SW.
4	26.6	NW.	31.6	"	18.2	"	31.8	SW.	18.4	SE.	20.1	NW.	19.5	SE.	16.8	"	12.7	E.	6.4	E.	9.0	SE.	15.6	"
5	27.2	"	31.7	"	18.8	"	31.8	E.	18.6	SW.	19.6	NE.	18.8	SW.	16.8	"	12.4	"	6.5	"	8.7	"	15.5	W.
6	27.7	"	31.8	SW.	19.8	"	31.7	S.	18.7	"	19.2	SE.	18.9	SE.	16.5	SE.	12.0	NW.	6.7	N.	8.2	"	15.1	ENE.
7	28.4	S.	31.9	N.	21.7	N.	31.7	"	19.1	"	19.2	"	19.0	"	16.0	"	11.1	"	6.9	NW.	7.9	SW.	15.0	"
8	28.5	N.	32.0	SE.	22.5	SE.	31.6	"	19.2	SE.	19.2	"	19.2	"	15.7	S.	11.0	"	7.1	"	7.9	NW.	15.2	S.
9	28.7	"	31.8	"	23.8	SW.	31.4	SW.	19.7	"	19.2	NE.	19.7	"	15.4	SW.	10.5	W.	7.2	NE.	7.9	SE.	15.4	"
10	28.5	NE.	31.7	NE.	25.3	"	31.2	NW.	20.1	N.	19.0	W.	20.4	"	15.1		9.8	NW.	7.4	W.	7.4	"	15.5	NW.
11	28.0		31.5	SW.	26.6	"	30.7	W.	20.4	E.	19.1	E.	20.4	SW.	14.7	SE.	9.2	SW.	7.5	SSW.	7.0	E.	15.9	ENE.
12	27.5	E.	31.6	NW.	27.4	W.	29.8	SE.	20.6	S.	19.3	SE.	20.8	SE.	14.7	S.	8.5	NE.	7.6	NE.	6.6	NE.	16.2	NE.
13	24.6	SW.	31.8	SE.	28.6	E.	29.0	NE.	20.9	NW.	19.9	NE.	21.1	E.	14.3	"	7.9	N.	7.6	SE.	6.7	"	16.4	S.
14	23.5	"	31.8	NW.	29.3	SW.	28.3	"	21.2	"	21.2	S.	21.1	"	13.8	"	7.3	SE.	7.6	"	6.8	W.	16.5	ENE.
15	22.5	W.	31.8	"	29.8	N.	27.9	SE.	21.7	"	22.7	E.	21.9	NW.	13.3	NE.	6.7	"	7.5	"	6.9	E.	16.5	SE.
16	21.9	"	32.0	"	30.2	"	27.6	"	22.1	"	23.6	SW.	21.4	"	12.8	SW.	6.4	NW.	7.4	NW.	7.2	SE.	16.7	N.
17	20.6	N.	31.9	"	30.6	W.	27.5	S.	24.2	NE.	23.6	"	21.4	"	12.7	"	6.1	W.	7.0	W.	7.4	E.	16.8	E.
18	21.2	"	31.8	"	30.8	"	27.5	"	25.3	"	24.0	"	21.5	SE.	12.6	"	5.6	"	6.7	NE.	7.2	W.	17.0	NE.
19	24.2	"	31.2	SE.	30.9	N.	27.2	"	26.2	"	24.0	E.	21.6	"	12.6	"	5.5	N.	6.3'	"	7.0	E.	17.2	S.
20	26.2	"	30.4	"	31.1	S.	29.2	N.	27.0	"	24.0	NE.	21.7	"	12.0	"	5.5	NE.	6.0	N.	7.0	SW.	17.8	E.
21	27.3	W.	29.9	"	31.3	SW.	27.0	SW.	27.5	S.	24.2	E.	21.8	NW.	12.0	NE.	5.0	W.	6.0	NW.	7.4	S.	18.1	W.
22	28.1	NW.	27.3	"	31.4	"	26.5	"	28.0	"	24.6	SW.	20.6	NE.	12.0	SSW.	4.7	SW.	6.4	SW.	8.3	SE.	19.0	"
23	29.0	"	25.0	E.	31.4	"	25.5	S.	28.5	SE.	24.7	SSW.	19.4	"	11.8	SW.	4.6	NE.	7.2	W.	9.1	E.	20.2	S.
24	29.5	SE.	22.3		31.6	SE.	24.8	NE.	28.5	NE.	24.7	SW.	18.8	SE.	11.7	SE.	4.7	N.	7.9	N.	9.3	SE.	21.8	"
25	30.2	"	19.5		31.6	"	23.8	"	28.5	NW.	24.5	"	17.7	SW.	11.6	W.	5.1	NE.	8.4	"	9.4	SW.	23.2	"
26	30.5	N.	17.0		31.6	NE.	22.5	"	27.6	"	24.0	"	16.6	"	11.5	SE.	5.5	NW.	8.9	SE.	8.7	"	24.7	SE.
27	30.7	NE.	15.0	SE.	31.7	E.	21.3	SW.	27.6	"	23.5	NE.	16.1	"	11.9	W.	5.7	NE.	9.7	"	8.7		25.5	ENE.
28	30.8	SE.	14.2	"	31.8		20.2	"	26.8	"	22.7	SW.	15.8	W.	12.9	"	5.9	W.	10.3	SW.	8.6	W.	27.1	SE.
29	31.0	"			31.8	NE.	19.4	NE.	25.6	SW.	21.9	S.	15.8	SW.	13.6	NW.	6.1	SW.	10.8	"	8.4	SW.	26.8	"
30	31.0	"			31.8	N.	19.0	S.	24.3	W.	19.5	"	15.7	SE.	13.5	SE.	6.2	S.	11.0	"	9.8	"	26.2	"
31	31.0	NW.			31.8	"			22.9	S.					13.5	"			10.9	SSW.			27.6	ENE.

Records for 1849—Continued.

Carrollton.—Observer, Professor C. G. Forshey.

Date.	January.		February.		March.		April.		May.		June.		July.		August.		September.		October.		November.		December.	
1849.	*G'ge*	*Wind.*	*G'ge*	*Wind.*	*G'ge*	*Wind.*	*G'ge*	*Wind.*	*G'ge*	*Wind.*	*G'ge*	*Wind.*	*G'ge*	*Wind.*	*G'ge*	*Wind.*	*G'ge*	*Wind.*	*G'ge*	*Wind.*	*G'ge*	*Wind.*	*G'g*	*Wind.*
1	11.4		14.7		14.7		14.7		14.4		13.8		12.8		12.3		10.9		3.4		4.0		3.8	
2	11.6		14.7		14.7		14.7		14.4		13.8		12.7		12.4		10.5		3.0		4.2		3.8	
3	11.8		14.7		14.7		14.8		14.4		13.8		12.6		12.5		10.4		2.7		4.4		4.1	
4	11.9		14.7		14.7		14.8		14.4		13.8		12.6		12.6		10.5		2.3		4.6		4.5	
5	12.1		14.7		14.7		14.8		14.4		13.7		12.5		12.8		10.4		2.2		4.7		4.6	
6	12.3		14.7		14.7		14.8		14.4		13.7		12.4		12.9		10.4		2.1		4.8		4.8	
7	12.5		14.7		14.7		14.8		14.4		13.6		12.4		13.0		10.5		2.1		4.8		5.9	
8	12.8		14.7		14.8		14.7		14.4		13.5		12.3		13.0		10.5		2.2		4.8		6.4	
9	13.1		14.7		14.9		14.6		14.5		13.4		12.2		13.0		10.5		2.3		4.8		7.2	
10	13.3		14.7		15.0		14.6		14.4		13.3		12.2		13.1		10.5		2.4		4.6		7.9	
11	13.5		14.7		15.2		14.6		14.4		13.2		12.2		13.0		10.4		2.6		4.2		8.0	
12	13.6		14.7		15.2		14.6		14.4		13.2		12.2		13.1		10.4		2.6		3.8		8.4	
13	13.6		14.7		15.2		14.6		14.4		13.2		12.2		13.0		10.3		2.7		3.5		8.6	
14	13.7		14.7		15.2		14.6		14.4		13.2		12.2		13.0		10.2		2.8		3.2		9.2	
15	13.9		14.7		15.2		14.6		14.3		13.2		12.2		13.0		10.1		2.8		3.0		9.4	
16	14.1		14.7		15.0		14.6		14.2		13.2		12.1		13.0		10.0		2.9		2.7		9.5	
17	14.2		14.6		15.0		14.6		14.2		13.2		12.0		13.0		9.8		2.9		2.6		9.6	
18	14.3		14.6		15.0		14.6		14.3		13.2		12.0		12.9		9.3		2.9		2.5		9.7	
19	14.4		14.7		14.9		14.5		14.2		13.2		11.9		12.7		8.9		2.8		2.5		9.8	
20	14.5		14.7		14.7		14.5		14.2		13.2		11.8		12.6		8.2		2.8		2.5		10.0	
21	14.4		14.7		14.6		14.4		14.2		13.2		11.8		12.2		7.2		2.8		2.5		10.5	
22	14.4		14.7		14.6		14.5		14.2		13.1		11.7		12.0		6.3		2.9		2.5		10.7	
23	14.5		14.7		14.6		14.5		14.2		13.1		11.7		11.8		5.9		3.1		2.5		10.6	
24	14.6		14.7		14.6		14.5		14.2		13.1		11.7		11.7		5.6		3.1		2.4		10.5	
25	14.6		14.7		14.6		14.5		14.2		13.1		11.8		11.7		5.3		3.2		2.5		10.5	
26	14.6		14.7		14.6		14.5		14.1		13.0		11.8		11.6		4.9		3.3		2.6		10.6	
27	14.6		14.7		14.6		14.5		14.0		13.0		11.9		11.7		4.6		3.5		2.8		10.7	
28	14.6		14.7		14.6		14.5		14.0		13.0		11.9		11.7		4.4		3.6		3.0		11.0	
29	14.6				14.6		14.5		14.0		12.9		12.0		11.7		4.1		3.6		3.2		11.4	
30	14.7				14.7		14.4		14.0		12.9		12.1		11.6		3.8		3.7		3.4		11.5	
31	14.7				14.7				13.9				12.2		11.3				3.8				11.6	

Records for 1850.

Memphis.—From records of Navy Yard.

Date.	January.		February.		March.		April.		May.		June.		July.		August.		September.		October.		November.		December.	
1850.	*G'ge*	*Wind.*	*G'ge*	*Wind.*	*G'ge*	*Wind.*	*G'ge*	*Wind.*	*G'ge*	*Wind.*	*G'ge*	*Wind.*	*G'ge*	*Wind.*	*G'ge*	*Wind.*	*G'ge*	*Wind.*	*G'ge*	*Wind.*	*G'ge*	*Wind.*	*G'ge*	*Wind.*
1	27.9	N.	30.7	NE.	29.5	SW.	34.4	SE.	34.1	NE.	27.2	NW.	14.7	SW.	12.6	SW.	11.3	NW.	7.6	SE.	3.8	SE.	7.3	SE.
2	28.0	"	30.7	"	29.1	W.	34.4	"	34.2	E.	25.6		14.9	S.	12.4	WSW.	11.4	NE.	7.2	NE.	3.7	S.	7.7	"
3	27.9	E.	30.7	"	28.4	SW.	34.4	"	34.3	"	24.1	SW.	14.9	SW.	12.2	"	11.6	SE.	7.8	"	3.6	SE.	8.1	NW.
4	27.6	W.	30.7	"	27.9	N.	34.4	"	34.4	NW.	22.9	S.	14.9	"	12.2	SW.	11.8	SW.	6.6	"	3.6	"	8.6	NE.
5	27.9	ENE.	30.7	E.	27.9	"	34.3	SW.	34.5	"	21.7	SW.	14.7	S.	12.7	E.	12.1	NW.	6.4	NW.	3.7	SW.	9.2	"
6	25.9	E.	30.7	"	28.0	"	34.1	W.	34.6	"	20.7	"	14.8	SW.	12.6	NE.	12.3	"	6.3	NE.	3.7	"	9.6	NW.
7	24.9	NW.	30.7	SW.	28.4	SW.	33.8	NE.	34.6	S.	19.6	SE.	15.2	S.	13.0	SW.	12.5	"	6.1	"	3.8	N.	9.8	W.
8	24.1	"	30.7	SE.	28.8	SE.	33.4	NW.	34.6	SE.	18.6	SW.	15.7	SE.	13.3	"	12.5	SW.	6.0	"	4.0	NW.	9.8	"
9	23.2	SE.	30.8	"	29.6	"	32.9	N.	34.6	NE.	17.8	"	15.8	NW.	13.6	"	12.5	"	5.7	SE.	4.1	SW.	9.9	SW.
10	22.6	E.	30.8	"	30.3	NE.	32.0	NE.	34.6	SW.	17.6	"	16.2	SW.	14.0	"	12.5	SE.	5.6	"	4.3	"	11.8	"
11	22.2	NE.	30.6	"	30.9	"	30.5	"	34.6	N.	17.4	"	16.1	SE.	14.7	"	12.4	"	5.6	SW.	4.7	"	13.8	"
12	21.1	"	30.3	E.	31.4	"	28.8	NW.	34.6	"	17.2	NE.	16.1	SW.	14.9	"	12.2	W.	5.5	NE.	5.4	"	13.8	SE.
13	21.6	"	30.1	"	32.1	S.	27.4	SW.	34.6	E.	16.9	SE.	16.0	S.	14.7	"	11.9	SW.	5.8	"	6.1	NE.	17.2	NW.
14	21.5	"	30.1	"	32.5	SE.	26.2	NE.	34.7	N.	16.6	"	16.0	SE.	14.4	"	11.6	"	6.1	N.	6.6	"	18.7	SE.
15	21.4	SE.	30.0	"	32.9	"	25.2	"	34.7	NW.	16.3	S.	16.0	NE.	14.4	"	11.3	NW.	6.1	"	6.8	NW.	20.0	SW.
16	21.1	"	33.7	"	33.2	SW.	24.8	"	34.7	SW.	16.0	"	15.8	S.	14.6	E.	11.0	"	6.1	SW.	6.8	"	21.1	"
17	22.9	"	33.5	SW.	33.5	"	23.9	"	34.7	W.	15.8	SW.	15.5	SW.	14.6	SW.	10.7	"	6.1	NE.	6.8	SW.	21.2	N.
18	24.4	NW.	33.3	"	33.6	NW.	23.2	NW.	34.7	"	15.5	S.	15.2	NE.	14.6	"	10.7	SW.	6.1	NW.	6.6	"	21.4	SE.
19	25.2	"	33.2	W.	33.7	NE.	22.8	SW.	34.7	SW.	15.1	"	15.1	N.	14.4	"	10.7	"	6.0	SW.	6.5	NE.	21.4	NW.
20	25.6	S.	32.5	"	33.8	"	23.2	S.	34.7	"	14.9	SE.	14.9	E.	14.2	"	10.7	NE.	6.0	"	6.3	NW.	22.0	N.
21	25.9	SW.	32.2	"	34.1	"	24.7	"	34.7	E.	14.8	S.	14.6	SW.	13.8	S.	11.1	SE.	5.9	NW.	6.2	NE.	20.6	NW.
22	27.6	"	31.7	"	34.3	NW.	27.2	"	34.6	"	14.6	NW.	14.2	"	13.5	"	11.2	"	5.9	"	6.1	NW.	20.3	"
23	27.6	"	31.7	E.	34.4		30.1	N.	34.5	SW.	14.2	NE.	13.9	"	13.2	"	11.1	S.	5.3	SW.	6.0	SW.	19.8	N.
24	28.1	S.	31.7	"	34.5		31.6	S.	34.3	W.	13.9	"	13.8	NE.	13.0	W.	11.1	SW.	5.2	NW.	5.9	"	19.3	"
25	28.3	NW.	31.7	"	34.6	NE.	32.6	N.	34.1	NE.	13.7	"	13.8	"	12.7	NE.	10.6	"	5.0	"	5.8	SE.	19.5	SW.
26	29.7	"	30.9	NW.	34.5	"	33.2	S.	33.8	SW.	13.6	SW.	14.0	"	12.3	"	10.1	"	4.8	"	5.7	"	19.0	"
27	30.2	SE.	30.3	S.	34.4	"	33.6	"	33.3	S.	13.5	SE.	14.0		11.9	"	9.4	"	4.4	NE.	6.2	"	20.0	NE.
28	30.5	NW.	29.9		34.4	NW.	33.8	SW.	32.6	SW.	13.6	SW.	13.9		11.6	E.	8.6	NE.	4.2	SE.	6.5	SW.	22.1	"
29	30.5	NE.			34.5	NE.	34.1	W.	31.6	NE.	13.8	"	13.6	SW.	11.4	"	8.0	"	4.0	"	6.8	"	23.2	"
30	30.6	"			34.5	"	34.1	SW.	30.3	NW.	14.4	S.	13.2	"	11.4	"	7.8	"	3.9	"	7.1	SE.	23.7	NNE.
31	30.7	SE.			34.6	E.			28.9	NE.			12.9	"	11.4	"			3.9	SW.			24.1	"

Records for 1850—Continued.

Carrollton.—Observer, Professor C. G. Forshey.

Date.	January.		February.		March.		April.		May.		June.		July.		August.		September.		October.		November.		December.	
1850.	*G'g*	*Wind.*	*G'ge*	*Wind.*	*G'ge*	*Wind.*	*G'ge*	*Wind.*	*G'ge*	*Wind.*	*G'ge*	*Wind.*	*G'ge*	*Wind.*	*G'ge*	*Wind.*	*G'ge*	*Wind.*	*G'ge*	*Wind.*	*G'ge*	*Wind.*	*G'ge*	*Wind.*
1	11.8		13.7		12.9		12.8		12.9		12.2		11.1		5.8		2.4		2.7		0.4		1.3	
2	12.0		13.8		12.9		12.8		12.9		12.2		10.9		5.5		2.3		3.3		0.2		0.8	
3	12.2		13.5		12.9		12.9		12.9		12.2		10.7		5.2		2.3		2.8		0.1		0.7	
4	12.3		13.4		12.9		12.9		12.9		12.3		10.6		4.9		2.8		2.3		0.1		0.7	
5	12.2		13.3		13.1		12.9		12.9		12.3		10.4		4.8		2.1		1.9		0.1		0.7	
6	12.4		13.4		13.1		12.7		12.8		12.3		10.3		3.6		1.8		1.9		0.0		0.7	
7	12.4		13.4		13.1		12.7		12.7		12.1		10.3		3.3		1.6		1.3		0.0		0.8	
8	12.3		13.4		13.1		12.8		12.6		12.1		10.1		3.3		1.6		1.3		-0.1		0.3	
9	12.5		13.6		13.1		12.8		12.4		12.1		9.9		2.7		1.5		1.3		0.1		0.3	
10	12.6		13.5		13.0		12.8		12.3		12.1		9.8		2.4		1.8		1.5		0.6		0.6	
11	12.6		13.3		12.9		12.8		12.5		12.1		9.8		2.3		1.9		0.6		0.6		0.9	
12	12.7		13.3		12.9		12.8		12.6		12.1		9.5		2.4		1.9		0.7		0.2		1.0	
13	12.8		13.5		12.9		12.9		12.6		12.2		8.9		2.6		1.9		0.6		0.0		1.1	
14	12.9		13.5		12.9		12.9		12.4		12.3		8.8		2.8		2.0		0.7		0.0		1.1	
15	12.9		13.3		12.8		12.9		12.3		12.3		8.5		2.6		2.0		0.8		0.0		1.3	
16	13.2		13.0		12.8		12.8		12.0		12.3		8.3		2.8		1.3		0.9		0.0		1.8	
17	13.3		13.2		12.8		12.8		12.2		12.3		8.3		2.8		1.9		0.9		-0.4		2.3	
18	13.4		13.2		12.9		12.8		12.0		12.2		8.3		2.9		2.3		0.9		-0.5		2.6	
19	13.5		13.0		12.9		12.7		12.1		12.1		7.8		3.1		2.0		0.3		-0.3		2.6	
20	13.5		12.9		12.9		12.7		12.1		12.1		8.0		3.1		1.7		0.6		-0.1		3.9	
21	13.8		12.8		12.9		12.7		12.2		11.9		7.8		3.2		1.6		0.3		0.3		5.1	
22	13.4		12.8		12.8		12.7		12.2		12.0		7.4		2.8		1.5		0.3		0.6		6.3	
23	13.3		12.8		12.8		12.7		12.1		12.0		7.2		3.3		1.4		0.2		0.3		6.3	
24	13.3		12.9		12.8		12.7		12.1		12.0		7.2		3.8		1.3		0.1		-0.5		6.3	
25	13.4		12.9		12.8		12.7		12.0		12.0		7.3		3.3		1.3		-0.2		-0.2		6.4	
26	13.4		12.9		12.8		12.7		11.8		11.8		7.3		3.1		1.2		0.5		1.4		6.5	
27	13.6		12.9		12.8		12.8		11.8		11.8		6.8		2.7		1.3		0.5		1.8		6.7	
28	13.8		12.9		12.8		12.8		12.0		11.8		6.4		2.7		2.3		0.6		0.9		6.8	
29	13.6				12.8		12.8		12.1		11.6		6.3		2.6		2.4		0.6		0.7		6.9	
30	13.8				12.8		12.8		12.2		11.4		6.2		2.6		1.8		0.6		0.9		6.9	
31	13.7				12.8				12.2				6.1		2.6				0.5				7.0	

Records for 1851.

Memphis.—From records of NAVY YARD.

Date.	January.		February.		March.		April.		May.		June.		July.		August.		September.		October.		November.		December.	
1851.	*G'ge*	*Wind.*	*G'ge*	*Wind.*	*G'ge*	*Wind.*	*G'ge*	*Wind.*	*G'ge*	*Wind.*	*G'ge*	*Wind.*	*G'ge*	*Wind.*	*G'ge*	*Wind.*	*G'ge*	*Wind.*	*G'ge*	*Wind.*	*G'ge*	*Wind.*	*G'ge*	*Wind.*
1	24.2	E.	7.5	SE.	33.6	SW.													7.4	SE.	7.4	SW.	8.2	SE.
2	24.0	SW.	7.7	NE.	33.8	NW.													7.4	SW.	7.3	W.	8.7	SW.
3	23.5	NW.	8.0	"	34.0	"													7.4	"	7.2	NW.	8.8	NW.
4	23.0	"	7.8	NW.	34.1	SE.													7.4	NW.	7.2	SW.	8.8	"
5	22.5	SE.	7.5	SW.															7.5	E.	7.2	NW.	8.7	E.
6	21.0	SW.	6.7	W.	34.1*														7.5	SE.	7.2	NE.	8.5	SE.
7	19.7	SE.	6.8	SSE.															7.7	"	7.1	SE.	8.6	"
8	18.2	"	6.5	S.	34.2*														8.1	"	6.9	SW.	8.8	"
9	16.6	SW.	6.9	SE.															8.1	ENE.	6.8	SE.	8.8	NE.
10	14.1	"	7.5	NW.					15.2										8.3	SE.	6.7	NE.	8.7	SW.
11	13.7	"	8.7	"	34.3*														8.4	NW.	6.6	"	8.7	NE.
12	12.7	"	10.3	SE.															8.5	"	6.5	SE.	8.7	"
13	11.7	"	13.6	"	34.2*				15.4										8.6	SE.	6.5	NE.	8.7	"
14	10.8	SE.	16.7	"					15.5										8.7	NE.	6.3	NW.	8.7	"
15	10.2	SW.	19.6	NW.					16.2										9.0	"	6.2	SE.	8.7	NW.
16	9.9	"	22.4	"					16.5										9.1	SW.	6.1	NE.	8.7	"
17	9.6	N.	24.4	SE.					16.7										9.1	SE.	6.0	SW.	8.8	"
18	9.3	NE.	25.7	"	33.3*				16.5										9.1	W.	5.9	"	8.9	"
19	9.0	SE.	26.7	"					16.0		33.1*								9.1	"	5.9	NE.	8.6	SW.
20	8.8	"	28.2	SW.					15.8										9.1	SW.	5.9	SW.	8.2	NW.
21	8.7	E	29.2	·SE.					15.6		33.5*								9.2	"	5.9	W.	7.5	NE.
22	8.6	"	30.1	"															9.5	NE.	6.1	SE.	6.8	NW.
23	8.5	NE.	31.0	NW.							33.6*								9.3	"	6.4	NW.	6.4	NE.
24	8.2	SE.	32.4	SE.							33.7*								9.2	S.	6.6	"	6.0	SW.
25	7.8	"	32.1	"															9.0	SE.	6.7	SW.	5.0	"
26	7.7	"	32.6	NW.															8.8	NW.	6.7	SE.	5.1	NE.
27	7.6	"	32.9	"															8.7	NE.	6.7	"	4.6	SE.
28	7.5	"	33.4	"							34.0*								8.5	SE.	6.8	NW.	4.6	SW.
29	7.4	NW.					20.0*												8.3	SW.	7.3	NE.	4.6	SE.
30	7.2	"																	8.0	"	7.8	SW.	4.6	NW.
31	7.3	NE.																	7.7	SE.			4.6	"

* Memphis Appeal.

Records for 1851—Continued.

Lake Providence.—Observer, MR. W. J. CURRY.

Date.	January.		February.		March.		April.		May.		June.		July.		August.		September.		October.		November.		December.	
1851.	*G'ge*	*Wind.*	*G'ge*	*Wind.*	*G'ge*	*Wind.*	*G'ge*	*Wind.*	*G'ge*	*Wind.*	*G'ge*	*Wind.*	*G'ge*	*Wind.*	*G'ge*	*Wind.*	*G'ge*	*Wind.*	*G'ge*	*Wind.*	*G'ge*	*Wind.*	*G'ge*	*Wind.*
1					44.1	NW.	44.8	SE.	39.2	NW.	36.0	SE.	42.0	SW.	40.3	SW.	27 7	NE.	15.2	NE.	16.9	SE.		
2					44.3	"	44.8	NW.	38.0	NE.			42.0	NE.	39.6	SE.	27.2	"	15.1	"	16.6	NE.		
3					44.5	"	44.6	"	36.4	SW.	36.5	"	42.1	"	38.7	SW.	26.8	"	15.2	SE.	16.2	"		
4					44.7	SE.	44.5	SSE.	35.5	SSW.	36.8	SW.	42.1	"	38.2	"	26.4	"	15.3	"	15.8	"		
5					44.9	"	44.3	N.	34.5	NW.	37.0	"	42.1	"	36.9	"	26.1	"	15.4	NE.	15.4	"		
6					45.1	NW.	44.0	"	33.5	SW.	37.2	"	42.2	SW.	36.3	SE.	25.8	"	15.4	"	15.1	"		
7					45.2	W.	43.8	SE.	32.7	SE.			42.2	"	35.3	SW.	25.4	"	15.5	"	14.9	SE.		
8					45.5	SE.	43.5	W.	31.6	NW.	37.3	"	42.2	"	34.0	"	25.0	"	15.6	SE.	14.8	NE.		
9					45.5	S.	43.1	NW.	31.2	SE.	37.9	SE.	42.2	"	32.8	"	24.5	E.	15.7	"	14.6	SE.		
10					45.6	SE.	42.9	NE.	30.4	"	38.2	"	42.2	"	31.5	SE.	23.0	"	15.8	"	14.5	"		
11			17.8	E.	45.5	"	42.7	"	29.7	"	38.5	"	42.2	NW.	30.5	SW.	22.6	"	15.9	"	14.3	"		
12			18.5	SE.	45.5	E.	42.5	SW.	29.1	SW.	38.8	E.	42.2	NE.	29.9	"	22.1	"	16.4	NE.	14.3	NE.		
13			19.5	"	45.5	N.	42.5	"	28.6	"	39.2	SW.	42.2	"	29.2	"	21.5	"	16.5	"	14.2	SW.		
14			20.9	SW.	45.5	"	42.5	W.	28.4	NW.	39.5	"	42.2	"	29.0	"	20.7	NE.	16.6	"	14.1	NW.		
15			23.3	W.	45.5	"	42.6	"	28.2	SW.	39.9	"	42.2	SW.	29.4	"	20.0	"	16.8	"	14.0	SW.		
16			26.3	N.	45.4	E.	42.7	"	28.1	"	40.2	"	42.3	"	29.6	"	19.3	"	17.0	"	13.9	"		
17			29.8	NE.	45.5	"	43.0	NE.	28.1	"			42.2	"	29.7	"	18.6	"	17.1	"	13.7	NW.		
18			32.6	"	45.4	N.		"	28.3	"			42.2	"	29.9	"	18.1	"	17.4	"	13.5	"		
19			34.9	SE.	45.3	NW.	43.1	"			41.1	E.	42.1	W.	30.1	SSW.	17.6	"	17.5	"	13.4	NE.		
20			36.7	"	45.3	SE.	43.2	"	28.7	SSE.	41.2	"	42.1	NNE.	30.3	SW.	17.5	SE.	17.6	SE.	13.2	SW.		
21			38.5	NE.	45.3	"	43.2	"	28.7	S.	41.4	"	42.1	"	30.6	"	17.3	"	17.7	NE.	13.1	NW.		
22			39.7	SE.	45.3	W.	43.1	NE.	28.4	SW.	41.5	SW.	42.1	"	30.8	NNW.	16.9	E.	17.6	"	13.3	SE.		
23			40.9	"	45.3	NW.	43.1	S.	28.2	"	41.6	"	42.1	SW.	30.9	NE.	16.6	NE.	17.7	"	13.8	NW.		
24			41.7	W.	45.3	"	42.9	NW.	28.1	NNE.	41.7	NE.	42.0	"	31.1	"	16.4	SE.	17.8	"	14.1	"		
25			42.3	SE.	45.3	SE.	42.7	"	29.5	SW.	41.7	NW.	41.9	SE.	31.2	SSW.	16.2	NE.	17.9	SW.	14.4	"		
26			43.0	"	45.3	"	42.4	SW.	31.3	"	41.8	SW.			31.1	"	16.0	E.	17.9	NE.	14.5	SW.		
27			43.4	S.	45.2	"	42.1	W.	32.5	SE.	41.9	"	41.8	SW.	30.9	"	15.8	NE.	17.9	SE.	14.7	SE.		
28			43.9	NW.	45.2	"	41.5	SW.	34.0	"			41.7	"	30.3	NE.	15.7	"	17.8	"	14.9	NW.		
29					45.1	"	40.9	NW.	34.7	SW.	42.0	SE.	41.5	"	29.7	"	15.5	"	17.6	"	14.9	NE.		
30					45.0	"	40.2	"	35.3	"	42.0	"	41.4	"	29.2	"	15.3	"	17.4	SW.	14.9	"		
31					45.0	"			35.7	SE.			41.0		28.3	"			17.1	NE.				

Records for 1851—Continued.

New Carthage.—Observer, Mr. A. R. Adkins.

Date.	January.		February.		March.		April.		May.		June.		July.		August.		September.		October.		November.		December.	
1851.	*G'ge*	*Wind.*	*G'ge*	*Wind.*	*G'ge*	*Wind.*	*G'ge*	*Wind.*	*G'ge*	*Wind.*	*G'ge*	*Wind.*	*G'ge*	*Wind.*	*G'ge*	*Wind.*	*G'ge*	*Wind.*	*G'ge*	*Wind.*	*G'ge*	*Wind.*	*G'ge*	*Wind.*
1					40.1	NW.	44.0	SW.	39.4	N.	34.4	Calm.	41.1	SE.	41.1	Calm,	24.8	SE.	10.3	Calm.	11.3	Calm.	9.5	Calm.
2					40.4	"	44.0	NE.	38.7	NE.	34.6	"	41.2	Calm.	40.8	"	24.1	NE.	10.2	"	11.0	SW.	9.6	N.
3					40.7	NE.	43.9	"	37.9	SE.	34.8	SW.	41.2	SE.	40.3	SW.	23.5	S.	10.1	"	10.8	NE.	9.8	Calm.
4					41.1	SW.	43.8	SW.	36.9	SW.	35.2	"	41.2	S.	39.6	Calm.	23.0	Calm.	10.0	NE.	10.4	Calm.	10.2	NE.
5					41.4	E.	43.7	NW.	36.0	NW.	35.4	"	41.3	Calm.	38.5	"	22.5	SE.	9.9	"	10.1	NW.	10.7	Calm.
6					41.7	N.	43.6	NE.	34.9	SE.	35.6	"	41.3	SW.	37.6	SE.	22.0	"	9.9	SE.	9.8	NE.	11.1	SE.
7					42.0	"	43.5	Calm.	33.8	"	35.9	"	41.4	SE.	36.5	"	21.5	"	9.9	NE.	9.6	Calm.	11.4	"
8					42.3	NW.	43.4	N.	32.7	"	36.2	Calm.	41.4	"	35.5	Calm.	21.1	"	9.9	SW.	9.2	SE.	11.5	Calm.
9			12.2	SE.	42.5	NE.	43.3	SE.	31.8	"	36.5	N.	41.5	Calm.	34.1	"	20.6	"	9.9	SE.	9.1	"	11.5	SW.
10			14.3	NW.	42.6	"	43.1	E.	31.2	SW.	36.9	NE.	41.5	"	32.9	"	20.1	E.	10.0	"	8.9	Calm.	11.6	Calm.
11			14.9	N.	42.8	SW.	42.9	Calm.	30.8	Calm.	37.3	Calm.	41.6	"	31.5	SW.	19.6	Calm.	10.1	"	8.9	SE.	11.7	N.
12			15.3	NE.	42.9	NE.	42.7	SE.	30.3	"	37.5	"	41.6	SW.	30.3	Calm.	19.1	SE.	10.4	NW.	9.0	"	11.7	Calm.
13			15.8	SE.	43.0	"	42.5	"	29.9	"	37.7	SW.	41.7	SE.	29.4	"	18.9	"	10.6	Calm.	9.2	Calm.	11.7	N.
14			17.0	"	43.0	"	42.4	NW.	29.6	"	38.0	SE.	41.7	"	28.6	"	18.3	N.	10.6	SW.	9.2	NW.	11.7	S.
15			18.9	NW.	43.0	Calm.	42.3	"	29.2	"	38.3	Calm.	41.7	Calm.	28.0	"	17.7	SE.	10.7	NE.	8.9	SE.	11.6	N.
16			21.0	NE.	43.1	SW.	42.2	"	28.9	SW.	38.6	NW.	41.7	"	27.5	"	17.0	"	10.9	"	8.6	Calm.	11.6	"
17			23.9	SE.	43.1	NW.	42 3	"	28.5	SE.	39.0	Calm.	41.7	SW.	27.4	SE.	16.3	NE.	11.0	Calm.	8.5	"	11.5	"
18			26.8	E.	43.2	N.	42.2	NE.	28.4	"	39.3	SW.	41.8	Calm.	27.4	S.	15.6	Calm.	11.2	"	8.6	"	11.5	Calm.
19			29.5	SE.	43.2	NE.	42.2	SW.	28.4	SW.	39.6	NE.	41.8	N.	27.3	Calm.	14.8	SE.	11.3	NE.	8.4	SE.	11.5	SW.
20			31.9	NW.	43.3	NW.	42.1	NE.	28.4	S.	39.8	Calm.	41.8	"	27.4	SE.	14.0	Calm.	11.5	S.	8.2	NW.	11.6	Calm.
21			33.6	"	43.3	SW.	42.1	NW.	28.4	SW.	40.0	SE.	41.8	Calm.	27.4	SW.	13.6	SE.	11.5	Calm.	7.9	Calm.	11.6	"
22			35.0	NE.	43.4	W.	42.0	SE.	28.2	"	40.2	SW.	41.8	"	27.5	SE.	13.0	"	11.6	NE.	8.1	NW.	11.7	"
23			36.2	SW.	43.5	NW.	41.9	E.	28.0	"	40.4	SE.	41.7	SE.	27.6	NW.	12.7	Calm.	11.7	SE.	8.2	SW.	11.9	"
24			37.1	SE.	43.5	N.	41.9	SE.	27.6	NE.	40.5	Calm.	41.7	NE.	27.7	SW.	12.2	"	11.8	Calm.	8.3	NE.	12.0	"
25			38.0	S.	43.6	NE.	41.7	"	27.8	Calm.	40.6	"	41.8	SE.	27.7	Calm.	11.8	N.	12.0		8.6	SW.	11.1	SW.
26			38.4	SE.	43.7	SE.	41.6	Calm.	28.6	"	40.8	SE.	41.7	"	27.7	W.	11.5	NW.	12.0	N.	8.9	SE.	10.2	Calm.
27			38.8	S.	43.8	Calm.	41.3	SE.	30.1	SW.	40.8	S.	41.5	S.	27.5	Calm.	11.2	N.	12.0	SE.	9.0	Calm.	8.7	"
28			39.8	NE.	43.9	SE.	41.0	"	31.3	Calm.	40.9	SW.	41.6	"	27.1	SE.	10.9	SE.	12.0	"	9.3	NW.	7.7	SW.
29					43.9	NE.	40.7	SW.	32.5	"	40.8	"	41.5	"	26.7	"	10.8	SW.	11.9	SW.	9.3	NE.		
30					43.9	SE.	40.2	NW.	33.4	"	41.0	SE.	41.4	SW.	26.1	"	10.5	SE.	11.7	"	9.4	NW.		
31					44.0	"			33.9	SW.			41.3	Calm.	25.5	NE.			11.5	Calm.				

Records for 1851—Continued.

Natchez.—Observer, Mr. J. C. Brown.

Date.	January.		February.		March.		April.		May.		June.		July.		August.		September.		October.		November.		December.	
1851.	*G'ge*	*Wind.*	*G'ge*	*Wind.*	*G'ge*	*Wind.*	*G'ge*	*Wind.*	*G'ge*	*Wind.*	*G'ge*	*Wind.*	*G'ge*	*Wind.*	*G'ge*	*Wind.*	*G'ge*	*Wind.*	*G'ge*	*Wind.*	*G'ge*	*Wind.*	*G'ge*	*Wind.*
1					46.9	NW.	51.8	W.	48.3	N.	39.7	S.	45.6	NW.	45.9	NE.	31.3		12.1	NW.	13.8	S.		
2					47.1	W.	51.8	S.	47.8	SW.	40.0	"	45.7	NE.	45.8	NW.	30.6		11.9	SW.	13.4	W.		
3					47.5	N.	51.8	SW.	47.2	S.	40.2	"	45.7	S.	45.5	NE.	30.0		11.7	"	13.2	NW.		
4					47.7	S.	51.8	"	46.4	SW.	40.6	"	45.7	"	45.1	SW.	29.5		11.7	"	12.9	NE.		
5					47.8	"	51.8	W.	45.6	NW.	40.7	"	45.8	SE.	44.6	"	28.8		11.7	"	12.6	SE.		
6					48.1	NW.	51.7	NW.	44.8	"	41.0	"	45.9	S.	43.9	"	28.3		11.4	"	12.0	NW.		
7					48.6	"	51.7	S.	44.0	"	41.2	"	45.9	SE.	43.1	"	27.7		11.4	SE.	11.7	SW.		
8					48.8	N.	51.7	NW.	43.0	S.	41.4	"	45.9	S.	42.3	"	27.1		11.8	SW.	11.4	NW.		
9					48.9	NW.	51.5	W.	42.2	"	41.6	"	46.0	"	41.4	"	26.6	NE.	11.3	SE.	11.3	W.		
10					49.2	SW.	51.4	N.	41.4	"	42.0	"	46.0	SW.	40.3	"	26.6	E.	11.3	S.	12.2	S.		
11					49.4	S.	51.2	NW.	40.6	"	42.2	"	46.1	W.	39.3	"	25.5	W.	11.7	NW.	12.5	"		
12					49.6	SW.	51.0	"	39.9	"	42.6	"	46.2	"	38.3	"	25.0	S.	11.8	W.	12.8	E.		
13					49.8	S.	50.9	W.	39.0	"	42.9	"	46.2	SW.	37.3	W.	24.5	"	11.8	NW.	13.3	NE.		
14					49.9	SE.	50.7	N.	38.3	"	43.1	SW.	46.2	W.	36.3	SW.	23.9	SE.	12.0	W.	12.7	W.		
15					50.0	S.	50.6	"	37.7	"	43.3	SE.	46.2	SW.	35.4	W.	23.3	W.	12.1	"	12.5	SW.		
16					50.2	NW.	50.5	NW.	37.1	SW.	43.5	"	46.2	S.	34.6	SW.	22.6	E.	12.2	SW.	12.2	"		
17					50.4	"	50.4	SW.	36.6	S.	43.8	S.	46.3	W.	34.3	"	21.9	"	12.4	S.	11.9	S.		
18			32.9	NW.	50.5	"	50.4	S.	36.1	"	44.1	"	46.3	"	34.0	"	20.9	"	12.5	"	11.6	SW.		
19			35.5	S.	50.6	"	50.3	"	35.9	"	44.3	W.	46.4	"	33.8	"	20.2	SW.	12.7	W.	11.4	"		
20			38.1	SW.	50.7	S.	50.2	N.	35.7	SW.	44.5	"	46.4	NW.	33.8	S.	19.0	S.	13.0	"	11.1	NW.		
21			40.2	"	50.9	"	50.1	NE.	35.6	S.	44.7	NE.	46.3	"	33.7	W.	17.6	SW.	13.1	"	11.0	N.		
22			41.7	"	50.9	SW.	50.2	N.	35.3	"	44.9	W.	46.3	W.	33.7	NW.	16.0	"	13.2	NE.	10.8	SE.		
23			43.0	S.	51.0	N.	50.1	"	35.2	"	45.0	"	46.3	"	33.7	SW.	15.1	"	13.2	N.	10.7	NW.		
24			43.7	NW.	51.1	W.	50.0	NW.	34.8	"	45.1	SW.	46.3	SW.	33.8	"	14.8	S.	13.3	W.	10.8	N.		
25			44.5	SW.	51.3	"	49.8	N.	34.6	"	45.2	S.	46.3	NE.	33.8	"	14.0	SW.	13.5	"	11.1	W.		
26			45.7	"	51.4	E.	49.8	W.	34.8	"	45.3	"	46.3	SW.	33.8	E.	13.6	S.	13.5	NW.	11.4	SW.		
27			45.6	WSW.	51.4	S.	49.6	NW.	35.6	"	45.4	SW.	46.2	SE.	33.7	S.	13.3	N.	13.8	W.	11.7	SE.		
28			46.5	N.	51.5	SW.	49.4	S.	36.7	"	45.0	SE.	46.2	S.	33.4	"	12.8	"	14.1	"	11.9	N.		
29					51.7	S.	49.1	"	37.7	SW.	45.5	"	46.2	SW.	33.0	SW.	12.6	"	14.2	"	12.1	W.		
30					51.7	"	48.7	N.	38.6	S.	45.5	"	46.1	"	32.5	"	12.3	S.	14.2	S.	12.4	N.		
31					51.8	SW.			39.2	SW.			46.0	"	31.8				14.0	"				

Records for 1851—Continued.

Red-river landing.—Observer, Mr. Miguel Torras.

Date.	January.		February.		March.		April.		May.		June.		July.		August.		September.		October.		November.		December.	
1851.	*G'ge*	*Wind.*	*G'ge*	*Wind.*	*G'ge*	*Wind.*	*G'ge*	*Wind.*	*G'ge*	*Wind.*	*G'ge*	*Wind.*	*G'ge*	*Wind.*	*G'ge*	*Wind.*	*G'ge*	*Wind.*	*G'ge*	*Wind.*	*G'ge*	*Wind.*	*G'ge*	*Wind.*
1					39.2	N.	46.4	E.	43.4	N.	33.9	SW.	38.0	SE.	38.8	N.	24.7	S.	3.4	S.	5.2	N.	3.1	N.
2					40.2	“	46.4	N.	43.0	S.	34.1	SE.	38.1	S.	38.8	S.	23.8	N.	3.3	“	5.1	SW.	3.1	“
3					40.5	“	46.4	“	42.7	“	34.4	S.	38.2	SE.	38.8	W.	23.5	S.	3.2	N.	5.0	N.	3.0	“
4					40.7	S.	46.3	S.	42.5	N.	34.6	“	38.2	W.	38.6	S.	22.9	SW.	3.2	NE.	4.9	NE.	3.0	“
5					41.1	“	46.2	N.	41.9	“	34.8	SW.	38.3	SW.	38.3	“	22.4	N.	3.0	S.	4.9	NW.	3.2	S.
6					41 5	N.	46.2	“	41.5	S.	35.0	W.	38.5	“	38.0	“	20.8	SE.	2.9	N.	4.8	N.	3.6	“
7					41.7	“	46.1	S.	41.0	“			38.5	“	37.6	N.	22.1	Calm.	3.0	S.	5.4	S.	3.9	“
8					42.0	“	46.1	N.	40.4	“	35.2	NW.	38.5	N.	37.0	“	21.5	S.	3.1	Calm.	4.0	N.	4.3	“
9					42.2	“	46.1	“	39.9	“	35.4	N.	38.4	NE.	36.9	“	20.7	“	3.2	SE.	3.5	S.	4.5	“
10					42.6	NE.	45.9	S.	39.2	“	35.6	SW.	38.5	SW.	36.0	S.	20.4	SW.	3.3	S.	3.0	“	4.6	N.
11					42.9	S.	45.7	“			35.8	E.	38.5	N.	34.9	N.	20.1	S.	3.5	SE.	3.0	“		
12					43.0	“	45.6	“	38.0	“	36.0	“	38.5	“	33.3	Calm.	19.6	NE.	3.6	W.	3.2	“	4.8	“
13					43.3	N.	45.5	N.	37.3	SE.	36.2	SW.	38.6	“	32.3	NW.	19.1	SE.	3.7	N.	4.2	N.	4.9	“
14					43.5	S.	45.4	“			36.4	NE.	38.6	“	31.3	S.	18.5	N.	3.9	“	4.4	“	4.9	“
15					43.7	N.	45.3	“			36.5	N.	38.6	Calm.	29.8	“	17.0	SE.	3.9	“	4.0	“	5.7	“
16					44.0	NE.	45.2	NW.	35.0	SW.	36.5	E.	38.7	S.	29.8	SW.	15.1	W.	3.9	“	3.5	Calm.	4.6	“
17					44.1	N.	45.1	S.	34.7	“	36.6	N.	38.7	N.	28.8	SE.	12.7	S.	4.0	“	3.0	S.	4.5	NE.
18			26.3	S.	44.2	“	44.9	“	34.1	S.	36.9	SE.	38.7	Calm.	27.9	NW.	11.0	NE.	4.2	“	2.8	N.	4.4	N.
19			28.6	SW.	44.5	NE.	44.8	“	33.6	SE.	37.0	N.	38.8	“	27.5	N.	10.2	S.	4.3	S.	2.6	SE.	4.4	S.
20			30.7	S.	44.5	N.	44.8	“	33.1	S.	37.1	NW.	38.8	N.	27.3	S.	9.4	N.	4.4	“	2.4	S.	4.7	N.
21			32.7	N.	44.8	S.	44.6	N.	32.6	“	37.2	“	38.8	S.	27.0	SE.	8.5	“	4.6	“	2.4	“	4.9	S.
22					45.0	“	44.6	“	32.1	SW.	37.3	NE.	38.8	“	26.8	S.	7.5	S.	4.7	N.	2.5	N.	5.5	“
23					45.1	NW.	44.5	“	31.9	S.	37.5	Calm.	38.8	Calm.	26.7	NW.	6.7	NW.	4.7	“	2.3	“	6.2	N.
24			37.0	“	45.2	“	44.3	“	31.5	“			38.8	N.	26.6	S.	6.1	NE.	4.8	“	2.2	“	6.2	“
25			37.3	S.	45.3	N.	44.2	“	31.2	“			38.9	E.	26.5	SW.	5.5	N.	4.9	S.	2.2	S.	5.9	S.
26			38.0	“	45.5	S.	44.1	“	31.3	“			38.9	SE.	26.6	S.	4.9	W.	5.0	N.	2.3	N.	6.0	N.
27			38.5	“	45.6	“	44.0	S.	32.1	“			38.9	“	26.5	N.	4.5	N.	5.2	S.	2.5	S.	6.1	“
28			39.4	N.	45.7	“	43.9	“	32.6	“			38.9	S.	26.3	“	4.1	“	5.3	“	2.6	N.	5.6	S.
29					46.0	NE.	43.7	“	32.9	E.			38.9	SW.	26.5	S.	3.7	“	5.4	“	2.7	“	5.4	“
30					46.2	E.	43.5	“	33.3	SE.			38.9	Calm.	26.4	SE.	3.6	Calm.	5.4	SW.	3.0	“	5.4	“
31					46.3	“			33.6	E.			38.8	S.	25.2	Calm.			5.3	S.			5.4	“

Records for 1851—Continued.

Baton Rouge.—Observer, Mr. J. W. Brown.

Date.	January.		February.		March.		April.		May.		June.		July.		August.		September.		October.		November.		December.	
1851.	*G'ge*	*Wind.*	*G'ge*	*Wind.*	*G'ge*	*Wind.*	*G'ge*	*Wind.*	*G'ge*	*Wind.*	*G'ge*	*Wind.*	*G'ge*	*Wind.*	*G'ge*	*Wind.*	*G'ge*	*Wind.*	*G'ge*	*Wind.*	*G'ge*	*Wind.*	*G'ge*	*Wind.*
1			10.5	SE.	28.1	N.	33.4	Calm.	31.0	N.	23.8	S.	26.8	S.	27.6	NW.	16.7	Calm.	3.6	E.	4.8	S.	3.4	SW.
2			10.6	“	28.5	“	33.3	N.	30.8	E.	24.0	“	26.9	“	27.6	“	16.1	S.	3.6	S.	4.9	NW.	3.4	NW.
3			10.5	N.	28.8	“	33.1	NW.	30.6	S.	24.2	“	26.9	“	27.6	W.	15.8	“	3.5	“	4.4	“	3.1	“
4			10.4	“	28.9	SW.	33.1	SE.	30.4	NW.	24.3	“	26.9	“	27.4	SW.	15.2	Calm.	3.5	E.	4.1	Calm.	3.0	“
5			10.2	Calm.	29.3	Calm.	33.1	NW.	30.0	“	24.5	“	27.0	“	27.1	S.	14.7	“	3.4	NE.	3.9	NW.	3.2	E.
6			10.2	“	29.5	S.	33.1	NE.	29.6	E.	24.5	“	27.1	“	26.8	“	14.2	“	3.3	E.	3.7	“	3.4	“
7			10.1	“	29.7	NW.	33.0	S.	29.2	“	24.6	SW.	27.1	“	26.5	Calm.	13.8	NW.	3.5	“	3.6	NE.	3.8	SE.
8			10.1	S.	29.9	Calm.	33.0	N.	28.8	“	24.7	S.	27.1	“	26.2	NE.	13.2	S.	3.6	“	3.5	E.	4.1	E.
9			10.5	SE.	30.2	“	33.0	NE.	28.4	S.	24.8	“	27.1	“	25.8	“	12.8	Calm.	3.6	SE.	3.4	S.	4.2	NE.
10			11.1	W.	30.5	“	32.8	“	27.9	SE.	24 9	“	27.2	W.	25.2	SW.	12.3	E.	3.7	“	3.4	“	4.3	SE.
11			11.6	N.	30.7	“	32 8	E.	27.5	S.	25.1	“	27.2	Calm.	24.7	S.	12.0	“	3.8	E.	3.6	E.	4.5	NE.
12			12.1	E.	31.0	“	32.7	SE.	27.0	SE.	25.2	“	27.2	“	24.0	Calm.	11.6	“	4.9	N.	4.3	NW.	4.5	NW.
13			12.5	SE.	31.2	“	32.6	N.	26.5	S.	25.4	E.	27.3	NW.	23.2	NW.	11.2	“	4.0	“	4.8	N.	4.5	N.
14			12.9	S.	31.4	SE.	32.5	“	25.9	“	25.6	S.	27.4	“	22.4	“	10.7	“	4.0	“	4.0	NW.	4.5	SE.
15			13.8	NW.	31.6	“	32.5	“	25.4	Calm.	25.5	SE.	27.4	SE.	21.5	Calm.	10.3	“	3.8	NW.	3.7	Calm.	4.5	NW.
16			14.7	N.	31.8	NW.	32.3	W.	24.9	S.	25.5	“	27.4	S.	20.8	S.	10.0	“	3.7	“	3.2	S.	4.3	N.
17			15.7	NE.	31.9	N.	32.3	NW.	24.4	SE.	25.4	Calm.	27.4	Calm.	20.2	“	9.6	“	4.0	“	3.5	Calm.	4.4	NE.
18			16.9	SE.	32.1	“	32.1	S.	24.0	“	25.5	NE.	27.5	“	19.5	“	9.1	“	4.3	“	3.2	NE.	4.2	NW.
19			18.9	“	32.2	“	32.0	“	23.6	S.	25.8	E.	27.5	N.	19.1	“	8.5	“	4.3	Calm.	3.2	SE.	4.2	SW.
20			21.0	NW.	32.4	E.	32.0	NE.	23.3	“	26.0	N.	27.5	“	18.9	“	7.8	“	4.3	S.	3.2	NW.	4.2	“
21			22.9	“	32.5	SE.	32.0	“	23.0	“	26.0	“	27.5	W.	18.7	Calm.	7.3	“	4.3	“	2.7	“	4.4	S.
22			24.3	SW.	32.7	SW.	32.0	“	22.8	“	26.1	“	27.6	E.	18.6	“	6.7	“	4.2	NE.	2.5	SE.	5.3	NW.
23			25.3	S.	32.9	NW.	31.9	N.	22.5	“	26.2	Calm.	27.6	S.	18.5	NE.	6.1	“	4.2	NW.	2.7	NW.	5.1	NE.
24			25.9	NW.	32.8	N.	31.8	“	22.3	SE.	26.3	SE.	27.6	E.	18.5	W.	5.5	Calm.	4.2	“	2.4	“	5.3	Calm.
25			26.3	SE.	33.0	SW.	31.7	“	22.0	“	26.4	E.	27.7	“	18.3	“	4.8	NW.	4.3	SW.	2.6	“	5.4	SW.
26			26.8	“	33.1	SE.	31.6	“	21.8	“	26.5	S.	27.7	S.	18.2	S.	4.6	W.	4.6	N.	2.6	SE.	5.2	Calm.
27			27.3	N.	33.3	S.	31.5	SW.	21.8	S.	26.5	E.	27.6	“	18.1	W.	4.2	N.	4.6	E.	3.1	“	5.2	S.
28			27.9	“	33.3	Calm.	31.4	S.	22.0	“	26.6	S.	27.6	“	18.0	N.	4.0	NE.	4.8	SE.	3.3	NW.	5.9	“
29					33.4	“	31.3	“	22.5	SE.	26.7	“	27.5	“	17.8	Calm.	3.8	“	5.0	NW.	3.3	N.	5.6	SE.
30					33.4	S.	31.2	N.	22.9	S.	26.8	SE.	27.5	SW.	17.6	S.	3.7	E.	5.0	“	3.4	NW.	5.7	NE.
31					33.4	SE.			23.4	SW.			27.5	W.	17.2	E.			4.8	Calm.			5.7	N.

Records for 1851—Continued.

Donaldsonville.—Observer, Mr. A. Gingry.

Date.	January.		February.		March.		April.		May.		June.		July.		August.		September.		October.		November.		December.	
1851.	*G'ge*	*Wind.*	*G'ge*	*Wind.*	*G'ge*	*Wind.*	*G'ge*	*Wind.*	*G'ge*	*Wind.*	*G'ge*	*Wind.*	*G'ge*	*Wind.*	*G'ge*	*Wind.*	*G'ge*	*Wind.*	*G'ge*	*Wind.*	*G'ge*	*Wind.*	*G'ge*	*Wind.*
1			11.5	E.	26.2	N.	30.2	S.	28.3	NE.	22.2	S.	24.8	SE.	25.4	SW.	16.9	NW.	6.5	E.	7.3	E.	6.1	E.
2			11.6	S.	26.5	NW.	30.1	E.	28.1	SE.	22.5	"	24.9	E.	25.5	N.	16.4	W.	6.7	"	7.4	SW.	6.0	NW.
3			11.5	N.	26.8	"	30.0	"	27.9	"	22.7	W.	24.9	SE.	25.6	SW.	16.0	NW.	6.6	N.	7.1	"	5.8	"
4			11.4	NW.	27.0	NE.	30.0	S.	27.7	NW.	22.8	S.	25.0	"	25.4	"	15.5	E.	6.6	"	6.7	E.	5.7	NE.
5			11.3	N.	27.3	SE.	29.9	SW.	27.4	N.	22.8	"	25.0	"	25.1	"	15.1	"	6.6	"	6.6	W.	5.7	"
6			11.2	S.	27.6	SW.	29.8	E.	27.1	SE.	22.8	"	25.1	"	25.0	SE.	14.8	SE.	6.5	E.	6.3	N.	5.8	E.
7			11.2	SE.	27.6	NW.	29.8	S.	26.8	"	23.0	SW.	25.1	"	24.6	E.	14.4	"	6.6	NE.	6.2	E.	6.1	"
8			11.2	S.	27.7	"	29.8	NW.	26.4	"	23.1	"	25.0	"	24.4	SE.	14.0	"	6.7	E.	6.1	"	6.3	"
9			11.4	"	27.9	"	29.7	E.	26.1	"	23.2	E.	25.1	"	24.0	E.	13.6	"	6.8	SE.	6.1	"	6.5	"
10			12.0	NW.	28.2	E.	29.7	"	25.8	"	23.3	NE.	25.1	W.	23.6	N.	13.4	E.	6.7	"	6.2	"	6.6	S.
11			12.2	N.	28.4	"	29.6	SE.	25.4	"	23.4	SE.	25.1	NW.	23.2	"	13.1	SE.	6.8	"	6.4	"	6.7	NW.
12			12.8	E.	28.6	"	29.6	S.	25.0	"	23.5	S.	25.2	SW.	22.6	W.	12.8	"	6.9	N.	7.4	N.	6.7	"
13			13.2	"	28.3	"	29.5	NW.	24.6	W.	23.7	"	25.3	NE.	22.0	NW.	12.4	E.	6.7	"	7.4	NW.	6.5	N.
14			13.4	S.	28.9	SW.	29.4	"	24.1	NE.	23.9	"	25.3	SE.	21.3	"	12.1	SE.	6.7	"	7.8	N.	6.8	"
15			14.1	NE.	29.0	"	29.3	"	23.7	SE.	24.0	N.	25.3	NW.	20.6	"	11.8	"	6.7	E.	7.4	NW.	6.7	NW.
16			14.8	N.	29.3	W.	29.2	W.	23.1	S.	23.8	NE.	25.4	E.	20.1	"	11.6	"	6.8	NW.	7.0	E.	6.6	NE.
17			15.6	NE.	29.3	NW.	29.1	"	22.8	SE.	23.6	NW.	25.4	SW.	19.5	SW.	11.4	"	6.9	E.	6.5	"	6.6	"
18			16.7	SE.	29.4	"	29.1	SW.	22.5	"	23.6	SE.	25.4	"	19.0	N.	10.9	E.	7.1	W.	6.3	"	6.3	N.
19			18.3	"	29.5	E.	29.0	"	22.3	"	23.9	E.	25.4	W.	18.7	"	10.3	SE.	7.1	SW.	6.2	"	6.2	NW.
20			20.0	NW.	29.6	"	29.0	"	21.9	S.	24.1	"	25.5	N.	18.6	S.	9.9	"	7.1	"	6.2	NW.	6.2	SW.
21			21.6	"	29.9	S.	29.0	NE.	21.7	"	24.2	SE.	25.6	W.	18.5	NE.	9.5	NE.	7.0	"	5.6	"	6.4	S.
22			22.9	SW.	29.9	SW.	28.9	E.	21.5	SW.	24.3	NE.	25.6	NE.	18.4	"	9.2	SE.	6.9	N.	5.4	"	7.1	NW.
23			23.8	S.	30.0	NW.	28.9	N.	21.3	"	24.5	SE.	25.7	SE.	18.4	N.	8.6	"	6.8	NE.	5.7	"	7.1	N.
24			24.1	NW.	29.9	N.	28.8	"	21.1	S.	24.5	E.	25.7	E.	18.4	SW.	8.0	"	6.8	"	5.4	N.	7.1	"
25			24.6	E.	30.1	E.	28.8	"	20.9	"	24.6	S.	25.7	SE.	18.2	"	7.6	NE.	6.8	SW.	5.5	NW.	7.1	"
26			25.1	S.	30.2	SE.	28.8	"	20.7	SE.	24.6	"	25.7	SW.	18.0	NW.	7.2	"	7.0	N.	5.6	E.	7.2	S.
27			25.5	SW.	30.3	"	28.6	NW.	20.7	"	24.7	"	25.5	"	17.9	W.	6.9	N.	6.9	NE.	6.1		7.1	"
28			26.0	NW.	30.3	S.	28.5	"	20.9	S.	24.7	"	25.6	NW.	17.8	SE.	6.7	"	7.1	E.	6.2	N.	7.8	"
29					30.3	E.	28.4	SE.	21.3	"	24.7	SW.	25.5	SW.	17.7	NE.	6.5	NE.	7.5	SW.	6.2	E.	7.9	SE.
30	11.7	N.			30.3	S.	28.4	E.	21.7	SE.	24.7	W.	25.4	"	17.5	E.	6.5	E.	7.4	"	6.1	NW.	7.8	SW.
31	11.6	E.			30.3	SE.			22.1	S.			25.4	"	17.2	"			7.2	E.			7.9	"

Records for 1851—Continued.

Carrollton.—Observer, Professor C. G. Forshey.

Date.	January.		February.		March.		April.		May.		June.		July.		August.		September.		October.		November.		December.	
1851.	*G'ge*	*Wind.*	*G'ge*	*Wind.*	*G'ge*	*Wind.*	*G'ge*	*Wind.*	*G'ge*	*Wind.*	*G'ge*	*Wind.*	*G'ge*	*Wind.*	*G'ge*	*Wind.*	*G'ge*	*Wind.*	*G'ge*	*Wind.*	*G'ge*	*Wind.*	*G'ge*	*Wind.*
1	7.0		3.8	E.	13.4	N.	15.3	W.	14.3	NE.	10.9	SW.	12.2	E.	12.4	W.	7.3	Calm.	1.1	W.	1.7	S.	0.8	N.
2	7.0		4.0	SE.	13.4	"	15.3	SE.	14.3	E.	11.0	Calm.	12.3	"	12.5	"	7.0	"	1.5	E.	1.8	NE.	0.8	"
3	7.5		4.0	NW.	13.6	"	15.2	E.	14.2	SE.	11.1	SW.	12.2	NE.	12.6	N.	6.7	N.	1.5	NE.	1.5	N.	0.5	NE.
4	8.0		4.0	"	13.7	ESE.	15.2	S.	14.1	SW.	11.1	"	12.2	SE.	12.5	S.	6.5	SE.	1.5	W.	1.3	SE.	0.5	"
5	8.3		3.8	NE.	13.9	SE.	15.3	"	13.8	NE.	11.1	SE.	12.2	Calm.	12.4	Calm.	6.3	NE.	1.6	E.	1.2	W.	0.3	E.
6	8.5		3.7	"	14.2	S.	15.2	N.	13.4	SE.	11.0	SW.	12.3	SW.	12.2	"	6.1	"	1.7	SE.	1.0	N.	0.4	SE.
7	8.9		3.7	S.	14.1	N.	15.2	S.	13.4	"	11.1	NW.	12.3	"	12.1	NW.	5.7	"	1.8	E.	1.0	NE.	0.6	"
8	9.2		3.7	SW.	14.1	NE.	15.2	N.	13.2	"	11.2	"	12.3	Calm.	12.0	SE.	5.7	SW.	1.8	"	0.8	Calm.	0.6	"
9	9.4		4.2	S.	14.2	Calm.	15.0	E.	13.0	"	11.2	NE.	12.4	SW.	11.8	E.	5.4	E.	1.7	SE.	0.9	SW.	0.6	"
10	9.5		4.3	W&S.	14.3	SE.	15.1	SE.	12.8	"	11.3	Calm.	12.3	W.	11.6	Calm.	5.3	"	1.7	S.	0.9	S.	0.7	S.
11	9.3		4.1	N.	14.3	NW.	15.0	E.	12.6	"	11.3	S.	12.5	N.	11.3	"	5.1	"	1.7	"	1.1	SE.	0.8	N.
12	9.0		4.5	NE.	14.3	SE.	15.1	S.	12.4	"	11.5	Calm.	12.4	"	10.9	"	4.9	"	1.7	W.	1.9	S.	0.9	Calm.
13	8.7		5.1	SE.	14.5	"	15.0	W.	12 2	"	11.6	"	12.6	SW.	10.5	N.	4.7	"	1.3	N.	1.9	"	0.8	NE.
14	8.5		5.2	SW.	14.7	"	14.9	N.	11.8	"	11.7	"	12.5	N.	10.1	NW.	4.4	SE.	1.2	"	2.1	NW.	1.0	SE.
15	7.9		5.4	N.	14.7	"	14.8	"	11.6	NW.	11.9	N.	12.5	"	9.8	"	4.2	E.	1.2	"	1.7	N.	0.8	N.
16	7.4		5.6	"	14.9	SW.	14.8	NW.	11.3	S.	11.8	NE.	12.5	SE.	9.5	N.	4.3	"	1.3	"	1.7	NE.	0.9	NE.
17	7.2		6.3	NE.	14.9	NW.	14.8	N.	11.2	SE.	11.5	"	12.5	Calm.	9.1	Calm.	4.2	"	1.5	NE.	1.2	E.	0.8	N.
18	6.3		7.0	E.	15.0	N.	14.7	SW.	10.9	S.	11.5	E.	12.5	"	8.7	SW.	3 9	"	1.7	NW.	1.4	SE.	0.5	"
19	6.0		8.2	S.	15.0	"	14.7	NW.	10.8	"	11.7	"	12.5	NW.	8.5	NE.	3.5	"	1.7	NE.	1.2	"	0.4	SW.
20	5.8		9.0	SE.	14.9	SE.	14.6	SE.	10.7	"	11.8	NE.	12.5	NE	8.5	SE.	3.4	"	1.7	S.	1.3	NW.	0.2	W.
21	5.4		10.2	NE.	15.1	"	14.7	NE.	10.5	SW.	11.9	Calm.	12.6	Calm.	8.4	E.	3.5	"	1.7	N.	0.6	N.	0.5	SW.
22	5.1		11.0	S.	15.2	"	14.7	SE.	10.4	"	12.0	"	12.6	E.	8.5	"	3.2	"	1.4	NE.	0.4	SE.	0.7	NW.
23	4.8		11.5	"	15.3	N.	14.7	N.	10.2	"	12.2	N.	12.7	SE.	8.6	N.	2.8	Calm.	1.4	"	0.4	N.	0.6	N.
24	4.6		11.7	NE.	15.1	"	14.6	NE.	10.0	SE.	12.0	SE.	12.7	E.	8.7	SW.	2.4	"	1.4	NW.	0.2	NE.	0.7	Calm.
25	4.5		12.0	SE.	15.2	SE.	14.7	N.	9.9	"	12.1	"	12.9	SE.	8.2	"	2.5	N.	1.2	W.	0.2	N.	0.9	SE.
26	4.5		12.4	S.	15.2	"	14.6	NE.	9.9	"	12.1	Calm.	12.8	"	8.2	W.	1.8	"	1.3	N.	0.2	SE.	1.0	Calm.
27	4.3		12.7	"	15.4	"	14.6	W.	9.9	S.	12.0	NW.	12.7	"	8.0	NW.	1.5	NE.	1.2	E.	0.8	"	1.2	S.
28	4.2		13.1	NW.	15.4	"	14.5	Calm.	9.9	SE.	12.1	S.	12.7	Calm.	7.9	SE.	1.1	E.	1.3	SE.	0.8	NE.	1.5	"
29	4.1	N.			15.4	E.	14.4	SW.	10.3	E.	12.2	SW.	12.6	W.	7.9	E.	1.1	N.	1.9	S.	1.0	E.	1.7	"
30	3.9	NNE.			15.4	SE.	14.3	SE.	10.4	"	12.2	Calm.	12.4	NW.	7.7	"	1.1	NE.	1.6	N.	0.8	N.	2.0	"
31	3.7	NE.			15.3	"			10.7	Calm.			12.4	"	7.5	"			1.6	SE.			1.8	N.

Records for 1851—Continued.

Fort St. Philip.

Date.	January.		February.		March.		April.		May.		June.		July.		August.		September.		October.		November.		December.	
1851.	*G'ge*	*Wind.*	*G'ge*	*Wind.*	*G'ge*	*Wind.*	*G'ge*	*Wind.*	*G'ge*	*Wind.*	*G'ge*	*Wind.*	*G'ge*	*Wind.*	*G'ge*	*Wind.*	*G'ge*	*Wind.*	*G'ge*	*Wind.*	*G'ge*	*Wind.*	*G'ge*	*Wind.*
1			4.3	E.	7.1	NE.	8.0	NW.	7.7	N.	7.2	S.	7.5	NE.	7.3	SW.	5.5	SE.	3.4	NE.	3.7	S.		
2			4.0	SW.	7.1	NW.	7.9	NE.	7.9	E.	7.2	SE.	7.6	SE.	7.3	"	5.5	NE.	3.8	E.	3.8	NE.		
3			4.0	SE.	7.1	NE.	8.1	E.	8.0	SE.	7.3	S.	7.4	"	7.2	W.	5.4	"	3.8	"	3.5	N.		
4			4.0	NW.	7.2	"	8.1	SE.	8.0	SW.	7.2	SE.	7.3	"	7.2	SW.	5.6	"	3.8	N.	3.5	E.		
5			3.8	NE.	7.4	E.	8.2	S.	7.7	N.	7.1	SW.	7.3	"	7.1	"	5.6	E.	4.0	E.	3.7	N.		
6			3.7	W.	7.8	S.	8.1	NE.	7.7	NE.	6.9	W.	7.2	SW.	7.2	SE.	5.5	SE.	4.3	SE.	3.5	"		
7			3.8	E.	7.6	WNW	8.3	S.	7.7	E.	6.8	"	7.2	"	7.3	"	5.4	NE.	4.8	E.	3.7	NE.		
8			4.0	SE.	7.4	NE.	8.0	N.	7.6	"	6.8	"	7.1	SE.	7.3	"	5.3	S.	4.8	"	3.3	"		
9			4 4	S.	7.5	"	8.0	E.	7.5	"	6.8	NW.	7.2	"	7.3	S.	5.3	SE.	4.7	SE.	3.7	ESE.		
10			4.3	WSW.	7.6	"	7.8	NE.	7.4	SE.	7.0	NE.	7.3	NW.	7.3	"	5.7	S.	4.7	S.	3.6	"		
11			3.9	N.	7.6	E.	8.0	E.			6.9	S.	7.4	N.	7.2	"	5.6	SE.	4.7	"	3.4	"		
12			4.2	NE.	7.5	"	7.9	SE.			7.0	SW.	7.6	"	7.0	N.	5.5	E.	4.7	W.	4.4	"		
13			4.5	SE.	7.7	SE.	7.8	NW.			7.3	SE.	7.4	NW.	6.9	NE.	5.3	SE.	3.7	N.	4.3	S.		
14			4.4	S.	7.9	"	7.8	"	7.0	E.	7.3	NE.	7.5	SE.	6.8	N.	5.3	E.	3.6	"	4.3	N.		
15			4.5	NW.	7.8	S.	7.8	N.	7.1	"	7.4	SE.	7.6	"	6.8	"	5.3	"	3.5	"	3.4	"		
16			4.3	N.	7.8	SW.	7.8	NW.	7.1	SE.	7.4	"	7.4	"	6.6	E.	6.0	"	3.4	"	3.5	"		
17			4.4	NE.	7.7	NW.	7.8	N.	7.2	"	7.3	E.	7.4	"	6.5	NE.	5.8	"	3.8	NE.	3.3	NE.		
18			4.8	"	7.7	"	8.0	SW.	7.2	"	7.3	"	7.3	"	6.2	SW.	5.5	"	3.8	NW.	3.8	"		
19			5.5	SE.	7.7	NE.	7.9	"	7.2	S.	7.4	NE.	7.3	NW.	6.2	NE.	5.2	"	3.8	NE.	3.9	E.		
20			5.8	S.	7.9	E.	7.9	SE.	7.0	E.	7.3	"	7.2	N.	6.3	SE.	5.7	"	3.7	S.	4.0	SW.		
21			6.2	N.	8.1	SE.	7.9	NE.	6.8	ENE.	7.3	SE.	7.2	SE.	6.3	"	5.3	"	3.9	N.	3.4	N.		
22			6.5	SE.	8.1	SW.	8.0	"	6.8	NE.	7.3	"	7.2	"	6 4	NE.	5.8		3.8	NE.	3.4	S.	2.8	N.
23			6.6	SSE.	8.0	NE.	8.0	"	6.7	N.	7.3	"	7.3	"	6.9	N.	5.0	SW.	3.8	"	3.9	N.	2.6	NE.
24			6.5	Calm.	7.9	N.	7.8	"	6.6	NW.	7.3	"	7.6	"	6.9	SW.	4.8	NE.	3.7	NW.	2.7	NE.	2.6	"
25			6.7	NE.	7.9	E.	8.0	"	6.5	"	7.2	"	7.6	"	6.5	"	4.7	"	3.6	W.	2.6	NW.	2.7	SW.
26			6.9	SE.	7.9	SE.	7.9	S.	6.5	"	7.2	S.	7.5	"	6.5	"	4.5	SE.	3.4	N.	2.5	E.	2.8	"
27			6.9	S.	7.9	"	7.7	SW.	6.6	W.	7.3	"	7.6	"	6.4	NW.	3.8	N.	3.4	E.	3.2	SE.	3.0	S.
28			7.1	NNW.	8.0	"	7.6	"	6.8	S.	7.4	"	7.2	"	6.3	S.	3.3	E.	3.3	SE.	3.1	NE.	3.3	SW.
29					8.1	E.	7.7	S.	6.8	SW.	7.5	"	7.6	W.	6.3	SE.	3.3	"	3.5	S.	3.5	SE.	3.6	S.
30					8.0	"	7.8	SE.	6.9	S.	7.5	"	7.4	"	6.2	"	3.3	NE.	3.4	N.	3.1	NE.	3.9	"
31					8.0	SE.			6.9	SE.			7.3	NW.	5.8	"			3.6	SE.			3.6	N.

Records for 1852.

Memphis.—From records of Navy Yard.

Date.	January.		February.		March.		April.		May.		June.		July.		August.		September.		October.		November.		December.	
1852.	*G'ge*	*Wind.*	*G'ge*	*Wind.*	*G'ge*	*Wind.*	*G'ge*	*Wind.*	*G'ge*	*Wind.*	*G'ge*	*Wind.*	*G'ge*	*Wind.*	*G'ge*	*Wind.*	*G'ge*	*Wind.*	*G'ge*	*Wind.*	*G'ge*	*Wind.*	*G'ge*	*Wind.*
1	4.6	NW.	7.2	SW.	23.8	SE.	22.7	NE.	33.0	SW.														
2	4.6	"	7.2	NW.	25.0	NW.	21.1	"	32.9	"														
3	5.9	NE.	7.2	NE.	25.8	NE.	21.6	SE.	32.8	"														
4	7.9	SE.	7.8	SW.	26.7	SE.	21.4	SW.	32.8	NE.														
5	11.2	NE.	8.2	"	27.7	SW.	21.2	"	32.8	SE.														
6	14.3	NW.	10.2	"	28.9	NW.	21.4	NW.	32.9	"														
7	16.6	NE.	12.2	NW.	28.8	"	22.7	SE.	32.9	S.														
8	17.8	SW.	13.7	NE.	29.4	"	24.7	NW.																
9	18.8	NW.	15.2	"	30.1	SW.	27.2	NE.																
10	18.9	"	16.2	NW.	30.8	NE.	29.2	"																
11	19.0	"	18.2	"	32.2	SE.	31.0	SW.																
12	18.8	"	19.1	SW.	31.5	"	31.7	"																
13	18.2	"	20.0	"	31.6	"	32.2	SE.																
14	17.4	SW.	20.4	NW.	31.6	SW.	32.7	NE.																
15	16.4	"	20.8	SW.	31.6	SE.	33.0	"																
16	15.1	"	22.2	"	31.6	"	33.2	SE.																
17	14.7	SE.	21.0	NE.	31.8	NW.	33.4	SW.																
18	12.6	NW.	22.7	"	32.0	NE.	33.6	NW.	33.3*															
19	11.0	"	23.2	"	32.2	"	33.8	SE.																
20	9.6	SE.	23.2	"	32.4	"	34.0	NW.	33.3*															
21	8.7	SW.	22.8	SE.	32.5	SW.	34.1	"																
22	7.7	NE.	22.5	"	32.5	SE.	34.1	"																
23	7.7	SE.	22.2	NW.	32.2	SW.	34.1	SE.																
24	6.1	"	22.0	SW.	31.8	"	34.0	"																
25	5.4	"	21.7	NW.	31.0	NE.	33.9	SW.																
26	5.4	W.	21.4	"	30.3	SW.	33.9	"																
27	4.6	SE.	21.2	NE.	29.3	NW.	33.9	NW.																
28	4.2	SW.	22.0	W.	28.3	SE.	33.8	S.W																
29	5.2	"	22.7	SE.	27.2	S.	33.6	"																
30	6.2	"			26.2	"	33.4	"																
31	6.8	"			25.2	"																		

* Memphis Appeal.

Records for 1852—Continued.

New Carthage.—Observer, Mr. A. R. Adkins.

Date.	January.		February.		March.		April.		May.		June.		July.		August.		September.		October.		November.		December.	
1852.	*G'ge*	*Wind.*	*G'ge*	*Wind.*	*G'ge*	*Wind.*	*G'ge*	*Wind.*	*G'ge*	*Wind.*	*G'ge*	*Wind.*	*G'ge*	*Wind.*	*G'ge*	*Wind.*	*G'ge*	*Wind.*	*G'ge*	*Wind.*	*G'ge*	*Wind.*	*G'ge*	*Wind.*
1					32.9	SW.	40.7	Calm.	41.4	SE.	42.7	NE.									4.4	NE.	18.0	Calm.
2					33.2	Calm.	40.6	"	41.5	"	42.7	SE.									4.4	Calm.	18.1	SE.
3					33.6	SE.	40.4	"	41.5	SW.	42.8	Calm.									4.4	"	18.4	NW.
4					33.8	S.	40.3	SW.	41.6	"	42.8	"									4.6	SE.	18.6	Calm.
5			10.0	SW.	34.3	"	40.1	"	41.6	SE.	42.7	SW.									4.8	S.	19.2	SW.
6			10.4	"	34.8	SW.			41.6	E.	42.6	Calm.							6.9	SW.	5.1	Calm.	19.6	"
7			10.8	E.	35.3	"			41.6	SE.	42.6	"							6.5	"	5.5	NW.	20.1	NW.
8			11.2	Calm.	35.8	S.			41.7	Calm.	42.6	"							6.3	S.	6.0	Calm.	20.4	Calm.
9			11.9	NE.	36.3	Calm.			41.7	SW.	42.5	"							6.2	NE.	7.0	NE.	20.5	"
10			13.2	NW.	36.9	"			41.7	"	42.5	SE.							6.1	Calm.	8.6	"	20.4	N.
11			14.7	N.	37.3	SE.			41.7	"	42.5	Calm.							6.2	"	11.1	SE.	21.0	Calm.
12			16.4	Calm.	37.5	"			41.7	"	42.4	"							6.9	NW.	12.8	NE.	21.2	SE.
13			18.1	NW.	37.9	N.			41.7	SE.	42.3	SE.							7.4	N.	13.8	"	21.8	Calm.
14			19.8	Calm.	38.2	Calm.			41.7	Calm.	42.0	Calm.							7.6	"	14.6	N.	22.5	"
15			21.5	W.	38.5	SE.					41.8	SE.							7.4	Calm.	15.1	NE.	23.4	"
16			22.9	Calm.	38.7	"					41.5	Calm.							7.1	SE.	15.8	"	24.3	SW.
17			24.0	"	39.3	N.					41.1	"							6.8	"	16.6	NW.	25.2	N.
18			24.9	NE.	39.4	"													6.7	Calm.	17.3	N.	25.7	SE.
19			25.6	Calm.	39.8	Calm.													6.5	"	18.0	NE.	25.8	SW.
20			26.3	"	40.0	"													6.3	SE.	18.8	SE.	25.8	"
21			27.2	S.	40.2	"													6.1	Calm.	19.6	NE.	25.7	N.
22			28.2	Calm.	40.3	"													5.9	SE.	20.9	N.	25.5	NE.
23			29.0	"	40.5	N.													5.7	"	21.3	SE.	25.7	S.
24			29.8	W.	40.7	SW.													5.5	Calm.	21.2	"	24.7	SW.
25			30.8	SW.	40.6	SE.													5.3	"	20.9	N.	24.7	SE.
26			31.6	Calm.	40.5	SW.													5.2	"	20.4	"	24.8	Calm.
27			32.2	"	40.5	Calm.													5.0	SE.	19.6	NW.	25.5	NE.
28			32.5	"	40.6	SW.													4.8	Calm.	18.7	NE.	26.2	"
29			32.7	"	40.7	SE.													4.7	N.	18.0	Calm.	27.3	NW.
30					40.7	S.													4.5	Calm.	18.0	"	28.3	SW.
31					40.8	NE.													4.5	N.			30.1	"

Records for 1852—Continued.

Red-river landing.—Observer, Mr. Miguel Torras.

Date.	January.		February.		March.		April.		May.		June.		July.		August.		September.		October.		November.		December.	
1852.	*G'ge*	*Wind.*	*G'ge*	*Wind.*	*G'ge*	*Wind.*	*G'ge*	*Wind.*	*G'ge*	*Wind.*	*G'ge*	*Wind.*	*G'ge*	*Wind.*	*G'ge*	*Wind.*	*G'ge*	*Wind.*	*G'ge*	*Wind.*	*G'ge*	*Wind.*	*G'ge*	*Wind.*
1	5.7	N.	8.7						43.2	SE.	43.8	N.												
2	6.1	"	8.5						43.2	S.	43.8	NE.												
3	5.0	"	8.3						43.2	SE.	43.8	"												
4	5.5	S.	8.1						43.2	Calm.	43.8	"												
5	5.5	N.	8.1				41.8	Calm.	43.2	SE.	43.8	"												
6	5.5	"	8.2				41.7	W.	43.3	"	43.8	"												
7	5.9	"	8.3				41.5	NW.	43.3	S.	43.9	"												
8	5.9	W.	8.4				41.2	"	43.3	"	43.9	Calm.												
9	7.3	NW.	8.5				41.0	SW.	43.2	SE.	43.9	"												
10	8.2	"	8.5				40.9	SE.	43.2	"	43.9	SW.												
11	9.2	N.	8.6				41.1	"	43.2	S.	43.9	"												
12	10.2	"					41.2		43.1	Calm.	43.9	"												
13	11.7	"					41.3	"	43.1	"	43.9	NW.												
14	13.2	"					41.5	"	43.0	SW.	43.9	"												
15	14.2	"					41.8	"	43.0	"	43.8	SW.												
16	15.0	"					41.9	SW.	42.9	"	43.8	"												
17	15.4	"					42.1	NW.	42.9	W.	43.8	"												
18	15.4	"					42.1	"	43.0	"	43.7	W.												
19	15.2	"					42.2	NNE.	43.1	N.	43.5	"												
20	15.0	"					42.3	NW.	43.2	"														
21	14.1	"					42.6	"	43.2	SW.														
22	13.3	"					42.7	SE.	43.2	"														
23	12.1	Calm.					42.7	"	43.2	"														
24	11.4	"					42.7	"	43.3	"														
25	10.7						42.8	W.	43.4	"														
26	10.2						43.0	"	43.4	"														
27	9.7						43.1	NW.	43.4	"														
28	9.5						43.1	SE.	43.5	"														
29	9.3						43.1	"	43.6	"														
30	9.1						43.2	"	43.7	NE.														
31	8.9								43.8	N.														

Records for 1852—Continued.

Baton Rouge.—Observer, Mr. J. W. Brown.

Date.	January.		February.		March.		April.		May.		June.		July.		August.		September.		October.		November.		December.	
1852.	*G'ge*	*Wind.*	*G'ge*	*Wind.*	*G'ge*	*Wind.*	*G'ge*	*Wind.*	*G'ge*	*Wind.*	*G'ge*	*Wind.*	*G'ge*	*Wind.*	*G'ge*	*Wind.*	*G'ge*	*Wind.*	*G'ge*	*Wind.*	*G'ge*	*Wind.*	*G'ge*	*Wind.*
1	5.4	NW.	5.5	NW.	23.1	SW.	28.4	SW.	29.9	SE.	30.6	NE.	28.2		12.9	NW.	4.2	SE.	4.2	SE.	3.0	SW.	14.0	SE.
2	5.3	“	4.9	“	23.4	“	28.6	SE.	29.9	“	30.5		27.9		12.6	SE.	4.4	“	4.7	“	3.1	“	14.0	SW.
3	4.9	S.	4.6		23.6	“	28.6	SW.	29.9	“	30.6		27.8		11.8	SW.	4.4	NW.	4.5	“	3.1	“	14.2	W.
4	4.9	SW.	4.6	SE.	23.7	SSE.	28.7	“	29.9	“	30.6		27.5		11.2	NW.	4.4	SW.	4.5	“	3.3	“	14.2	NW.
5	5.0	NW.	4.9	S.	24.0	S.	28.7	NW.	29.9	“	30.6		27.4		10.5	“	4.3	NW.	4.4	“	3.4	“	14.3	SE.
6	4.7	“	5.1	SSW.	24.3	SW.	28.6	“	29.9	SW.	30.7		27.0		9.8	SW.	4.3	NE.	4.4	SW.	3.4	NW.	14.5	“
7	4.8	“	5.5	SE.	24.6	“	28.5	S.	29.9	SSW.	30.7		26.7		8.9	“	4.3	NW.	4.5	“	3.3	“	15.0	NW.
8	5.1	SW.	5.7	“	24.8	SE.	28.5	NW.	29.9	SW.	30.7		26.2		8.4	“	4.4	NE.	4.4	“	3.6	“	15.1	SE.
9	5.9	“	6.0	“	25.2	SW.	28.2	SE.	30.0	SE.	30.8		25.8		7.9	“	4.2	NW.	4.4	NW.	3.6	“	15.7	NW.
10	7.3	NW.	6.7	NW.	25.5	“	28.1	“	29.9	SW.	30.8		25.3		7.4	“	4.2	“	4.3	“	4.1	SE.	15.9	NE.
11	9.0	N.	7.0	“	25.8	SE.	28.2	SW.	30.0	S.	30.8		24.6		7.3	NW.	4.3	“	4.3	SW.	5.0	“	16.1	SE.
12	10.7	NE.	7.6	SW.	26.1	“	28.2	NW.	29.9	SE.	30.8		23.9		7.0	“	4.3	“	3.7	NE.	6.0	NW.	16.4	“
13	12.0	NW.	8.5	S.	26.1	SW.	28.2	SE.	29.9	“	30.9		23.4		6.4	E.	4.3	“	3.7	“	7.2	“	16.6	“
14	13.1	SE.	9.8	NW.	26.1	“	28.8	“	29.9	SW.	30.9		22.9		6.2	NW.	4.3	SE.	4.0	NW.	8.2	“	16.8	“
15	14.1	NW.	11.1	SW.	26.1	“	28.8	NW.	29.9	SSW.	30.9		22.3		6.1	NE.	4.3	“	4.4	E.	8.9	“	17.9	“
16	14.7	“	12.3	“	26.3	“	28.9	SW.	29.8	“	30.8		21.6		5.9	SW.	4.8	E.	4.4	NW.	9.7	NE.	18.8	SW.
17	15.1	S.	13.6	“	27.0	NW.	29.1	NW.	29.9	NW.	30.7		20.8		6.0	“	5.1	ESE.	4.3	“	10.4	NW.	19.5	NW.
18	15.4	SW.	14.8	S.	26.7	NE.	29.3	“	29.9	“	30.7		20.0		6.0	SE.	5.5	SE.	4.3	SW.	10.6	“	20.2	SE.
19	15.2	NW.	15.8	ESE.	26.9	NW.	29.3	NE.	29.9	“	30.6		19.2		6.0	SW.	5.5	“	3.9	SE.	11.2	“	20.6	SW.
20	14.7	SW.	16.8	SE.	27.0	NE.	29.5	NW.	29.9	NE.	30.4		18.3		5.9	SE.	5.6	“	4.1	ESE.	12.6	E.	20.8	SE.
21	14.4	NW.	17.9	“	27.1	SE.	29.3	“	29.9	“	30.4		17.6		5.8	SW.	5.3	NW.	3.8	SE.	12.9	NW.	21.1	“
22	13.8	NNW.	19.0		27.3	W.	29.3	“	30.0	SE.	30.2		16.8		5.4	SE.	5.0	SE.	3.5	NW.	13.2	“	21.1	“
23	13.0	NE.	19.6	NW.	27.5	NW.	29.6	SW.	30.1	“	30.0		16.5		5.2	NE.	4.9	“	3.3	“	13.9	SE.	21.3	“
24	12.3		20.3	SW.	28.0	SW.	29.5	SE.	30.1	“	29.9		15.9		5.2	NW.	4.5	SW.	3.1	SW.	14.5	“	21.2	SW.
25	11.4		20.9	“	27.8	“	29.7	SW.	30.1	“	29.7		15.5		5.4	“	4.1	“	3.0	“	15.3	NW.	21.1	SE.
26	10.6	“	21.5	“	28.1	“	29.8	NW.	30.2	SW.	29.5		15.3		4.9	“	3.8	NW.	3.1	SE.	15.5	“	21.1	“
27	9.7		22.1	“	28.0	“	29.7	“	30.2	“	29.3		15.0		4.6	“	3.5	“	3.1	“	15.2	SW.	21.1	“
28	8.8	S.	22.5	W.	28.2	“	29.7	SW.	30.3	SE.	28.9		14.8		4.5	“	3.6	“	4.0	“	14.9	“	21.1	NE.
29	7.8	“	22.9	SW.	28.4	“	29.8	“	30.5	NW.	28.7		14.5		4.3	SE.	3.6	“	4.2	W.	14.3	NW.	21.5	SE.
30	7.0	SE.			28.4	SE.	29.8	“	30.7	“	28.4		14.2		4.2	“	3.8	SE.	3.2	NW.	14.0	“	22.6	SW.
31	6.3	N.			28.5	NW.			30.6	“			13.7		4.2	NE.			2.8	“			23.3	SE.

Records for 1852—Continued.

Donaldsonville.—Observer, Mr. A. Gingry.

Date.	January.		February.		March.		April.		May.		June.		July.		August.		September.		October.		November.		December.	
1852.	*G'ge*	*Wind.*	*G'ge*	*Wind.*	*G'ge*	*Wind.*	*G'ge*	*Wind.*	*G'ge*	*Wind.*	*G'ge*	*Wind.*	*G'ge*	*Wind.*	*G'ge*	*Wind.*	*G'ge*	*Wind.*	*G'ge*	*Wind.*	*G'ge*	*Wind.*	*G'ge*	*Wind.*
1	7.7	NW.	7.5	NE.	22.0	SW.	26.5	NE.	27.6	S.	28.0	NE.	25.8	S.	13.9	N.	7.1	SE.	7.0	SE.	6.3	SW.	14.1	E.
2	7.3	“	7.1	NW.	22.1	S.	26.5	E.	27.6	“	27.9	E.	25.7	“	13.3	E.	7.2	“	7.5	“	6.4	W.	14.2	“
3	7.1	N.	6.8	NE.	22.3	“	26.6	S.	27.7	SW.	28.0	“	25.4	SW.	12.7	SW.	7.0	“	7.3	E.	6.6	E.	14.4	W.
4	7.0	SW.	6.8	SW.	22.4	SE.	26.7	“	27.6	S.	27.9	W.	25.2	“	12.1	W.	7.2	N.	7.2	“	6.4	S.	14.3	“
5	7.1	NW.	6.9	“	22.8	S.	26.7	W.	27.5	E.	28.0	NW.	24.9	“	11.6	NW.	7.2	E.	7.1	NW.	6.8	“	14.4	SW.
6	6.8	“	7.2	“	23.0	SW.	26.5	N.	27.5	“	28.1	E.	24.8	“	11.0	NE.	7.3	“	7.3	“	6.9	NW.	14.6	SE.
7	6.8	NE.	7.5	NE.	23.2	SE.	26.6	NE.	27.5	“	28.1	“	24.6	E.	10.5	SW.	7.2	“	7.4	E.	6.4	N.	15.0	NW.
8	7.0	W.	7.7	N.	23.5	S.	26.3	NW.	27.5	“	28.1	W.	24.1	SW.	10.0	NW.	7.4	NW.	7.5	“	6.8	E.	15.2	E.
9	7.7	SW.	7.8	NE.	23.7	SW.	26.2	E.	27.5	S.	28.2	E.	23.8	N.	9.5	SW.	7.2	N.	7.6	W.	6.5	N.	15.4	“
10	8.6	NW.	8.3	SW.	24.1	SE.	26.0	SE.	27.5	SW.	28.2	NE.	23.5	“	9.6	“	7.5	NE.	7.5	E.	6.7	SE.	15.6	N.
11	9.7	“	8.5	NW.	24.3	“	26.2	S.	27.5	S.	28.2	“	22.9	“	8.7	“	7.5	NW.	7.4	W.	7.3	E.	15.8	E.
12	11.4	NE.	8.9	NE.	24.6	“	26.1	W.	27.5	“	28.3	“	22.3	“	8.0	N.	7.1	N.	6.9	E.	7.8	NW.	15.9	S.
13	12.4	NW.	9.5	SW.	24.7	“	26.1	E.	27.5	“	28.3	“	22.0	E.	8.7	NE.	7.3	NE.	6.8	W.	8.9	N.	16.1	N.
14	13.2	S.	10.7	NE.	24.8	S.	26.4	S.	27.6	SW.	28.3	“	21.6	“	8.9	“	7.1	E.	6.8	N.	9.6	“	16.5	S.
15	14.0	“	11.6	SW.	24.7	W.	26.6	N.	27.5	S.	28.4	E.	21.2	“	8.4	E.	7.3	“	7.0	E.	10.3	E.	17.3	“
16	14.5	“	12.6	“	24.8	SW.	26.8	SW.	27.5	SW.	28.2	“	20.8	NE.	8.3	SW.	7.4	“	7.2	Calm.	11.1	“	18.4	“
17	14.8	“	13.7	“	25.1	NW.	26.9	NW.	27.5	W.	28.1	“	20.1	N.	8.2	N.	7.6	“	7.3	S.	11.7	N.	18.8	E.
18	15.0	NW.	14.6	S.	25.1	N.	27.0	“	27.5	NW.	28.1	S.	19.5	NW.	8.1	E.	8.0	“	7.0	E.	11.8	“	19.3	SE.
19	14.7	N.	15.5	E.	25.4	“	27.1	SW.	27.5	“	27.9	SW.	19.0	E.	8.2	“	8.2	S.	7.1	“	12.0	E.	19.7	S.
20	14.7	NE.	16.2	“	25.4	E.	27.1	NW.	27.5	NE.	27.8	NW.	18.3	N.	8.2	“	8.2	SE.	7.2	“	12.3	NE.	19.9	SW.
21	14.3	NW.	17.6	S.	25.5	“	27.0	“	27.5	E.	27.7	W.	17.6	E.	8.0	“	8.0	NW.	7.0	“	12.7	E.	20.1	S.
22	13.9	NE.	18.6	E.	25.6	S.	27.1	SW.	27.6	S.	27.6	SW.	17.0	“	7.9	“	7.9	“	7.0	“	13.5	NW.	20.1	E.
23	13.4	“	19.0	S.	25.8	W.	27.2	S.	27.5	E.	27.4	“	16.5	N.	7.8	“	7.8	SE.	6.7	“	14.0	E.	20.3	S.
24	12.8	E.	19.5	“	25.9	S.	27.3	“	27.5	“	27.3	“	16.1	NE.	7.8	“	7.4	“	6.5	“	14.5	S.	20.2	“
25	12.2	N.	20.0	“	26.0	“	27.6	“	27.5	“	27.2	“	15.8	NW.	8.2	NW.	6.9	S.	6.4	“	15.4	NW.	20.1	“
26	11.5	“	20.5	NE.	26.1	SW.	27.4	SW.	27.6	“	26.9	W.	15.6	“	8.0	“	6.8	NW.	6.4	SE.	15.6	N.	20.3	E.
27	10.8	W.	21.0	S.	26.2	S.	27.5	N.	27.7	S.	26.8	“	15.3	NE.	7.2	“	6.7	N.	6.6	“	15.0	SW.	20.1	S.
28	10.1	S.	21.5	“	26.3	“	27.5	E.	27.8	SW.	26.5	“	15.2	E.	7.5	E.	6.7	E.	7.2	E.	14.7	E.	20.2	N.
29	9.2	“	21.7	NE.	26.4	“	27.4	SE.	27.9	E.	26.3	S.	14.9	NE.	7.2	SE.	6.6	“	6.9	W.	14.4	“	20.4	E.
30	8.6	“			26.5	“	27.6	S.	28.1	N.	26.2	SW.	14.8	W.	7.0	E.	6.7	“	6.4	NW.	14.2	“	20.9	“
31	8.2	NW.			26.4	N.			28.0	“			14.4	N.	7.0	“			6.4	N.			21.9	W.

Records for 1852—Continued.

Carrollton.—Observer, Professor C. G. Forshey.

Date.	January.		February.		March.		April.		May.		June.		July.		August.		September.		October.		November.		December.	
1852.	*G'ge*	*Wind.*	*G'ge*	*Wind.*	*G'ge*	*Wind.*	*G'ge*	*Wind.*	*G'ge*	*Wind.*	*G'ge*	*Wind.*	*G'ge*	*Wind.*	*G'ge*	*Wind.*	*G'ge*	*Wind.*	*G'ge*	*Wind.*	*G'ge*	*Wind.*	*G'ge*	*Wind.*
1	1.6	N.	1.3	NE.	10.0	S.	12.8	E.	13.4	S.	13.7	NE.	12.5	W.	5.5	E.	2.6		2.7	S.	2.1	W.	5.9	N.
2	1.4	Calm.	0.9	N.	10.0	"	12.8	"	13.4	"	13.8	"	12.4	"	5.1	W.	2.8	Calm.	2.8	SE.	2.0		6.1	E.
3	1.1	"	0.7	Calm.	10.0	Calm.	13.0	S.	13.5	"	13.5	N.	12.2	Calm.	4.7	"	2.7	E.	2.5	"	2.4	S.	6.3	W.
4	1.0	S.	0.6	S.	10.2	E.	13.1	"	13.6	W.	13.5	W.	12.1	W.	4.1	"	2.6	"	2.5		2.6	"	6.2	
5	1.2	NW.	0.7	"	10.4	Calm.	13.2	W.	13.7	SE.	13.5	N.	11.9	Calm.	3.9	NW.	2.5	"	2.4	W.	2.9	"	6.2	S.
6	0.8	N.	1.1	"	10.7	"	12.9	N.	13.7	"	13.8	Calm.	11.9	W.	3.5		2.7	"	2.7	"	3.0	"	6.4	"
7	0.8	NE.	1.1	Calm.	10.9	"	12.9	Calm.	13.5	"	13.8		11.7	"	3.3		3.0	"	3.0	SE.	2.7	N.	6.8	NW.
8	0.8	SW.	1.8	NW.	11.2	SE.	12.8	N.	13.5	Calm.	13.8		11.4	NE.	3.1		3.0	NW.	3.2	"	2.9	E.	6.8	
9	1.3	"	1.7	Calm.	11.4	S.	12.7	E.	13.3	"	13.8		11.2	N.	2.9		2.9	NE.	3.5	NW.	2.6	N.	6.9	N.
10	1.8	NW.	2.4	SW.	11.5		12.6	S.	13.4	W.	13.8		11.1	"	2.7		3.2	E.	3.3	SE.	2.6	"	6.7	"
11	2.4	NE.	2.0	N.	11.7		12.5	Calm.	13.4	S.	13.8		10.9	S.	2.5	W.	3.6	N.	3.1		2.7		6.9	
12	3.3	"	2.1	"	11.6	"	12.5	W.	13.3	"	13.9		10.5	"	2.6	"	3.4	"	2.9	N.	2.7	"	7.0	S.
13	3.9	N.	2.4	SW.	11.8	"	12.5	S.	13.5	"	13.0	E.	10.3	E.	2.8	"	3.4	E.	2.6	NE.	3.2		7.1	
14	4.3	SW.	2.8	NE.	11.8	N.	12.9	"	13.6	"	14.1	"	10.2	"	2.9	E.	2.8		2.3	"	3.6	"	7.5	
15	4.8	"	3.5	N.	11.8	E.	12.8	N.	13.4	Calm.	14.1	"	10.0	"	2.8	"	2.7		2.4	N.	4.1	"	8.0	
16	5.0	Calm.	4.0	Calm.	11.9	Calm.	12.9	W.	13.4	S.	14.0	"	9.5	"	2.6	W.	2.5		2.3	NE.	5.0		8.9	SW.
17	5.1	SW.	4.8	"	12.0	S.	13.1	"	13.4	N.	13.8	Calm.	9.2	NW.	2.4	E.	2.7	"	2.2	SE.	5.2	W.	9.3	N.
18	5.4	"	5.3	S.	11.8	NE.	13.1	N.	13.5	Calm.	13.8	"	9.2	"	2.2	S.	3.0	SE.	2.3	NE.	5.0	N.	9.5	"
19	5.0	NE.	5.9	E.	12.1	"	13.2	E.	13.4	E.	13.7	"	8.1	E.	2.2	"	3.0	"	2.5	"	5.1		9.7	S.
20	5.0	SE.	6.3	SE.	12.2	E.	13.0	NW.	13.4	Calm.	13.7	W.	8.0	"	2.2	"	2.7	S.	2.7	SE.	5.2	"	9.9	
21	4.9	N.	7.1	"	12.4	Calm.	13.0	N.	13.5	E.	13.5	Calm.	7.7	SE.	2.2	NW.	3.0	N.	2.8	E.	5.5	E.	10.1	
22	4.7	NE.	7.7	NW.	12.3		13.2	W.	13.5		13.4	"	7.3	NE.	2.0	W.	3.2	SW.	2.9	NE.	5.9	NW.	10.0	N.
23	4.6	E.	8.2	W.	12.5	W.	13.2	"	13.5	Calm.	13.4	S.	6.9	E.	2.1	N.	3.3	S.	2.8	E.	6.0	N.	10.0	S.
24	4.2	SE.	8.4	"	12.5	SW.	13.3	S.	13.6	E.	13.2	"	6.6	W.	2.7	E.	2.9	"	2.8	SW.	6.4	S.	10.0	"
25	3.9	Calm.	8.7	SW.	12.5	W.	13.2	"	13.5	S.	13.2	W.	6.5	"	4.0	N.	2.6	W.	2.8	"	6.9	"	10.0	"
26	3.7	N.	8.9	NW.	12.5	S.	13.3	Calm.	13.6	W.	13.1	Calm.	6.3	"	3.4	NW.	2.5	N.	2.7	S.	6.9	N.	10.1	"
27	3.3	Calm.	9.3	S.	12.6	"	13.2	N.	13.6	SW.	13.0	"	6.1	"	3.7	"	2.4	W.	2.9	"	6.6		10.1	"
28	2.8	"	9.8	W.	12.6	"	13.3	E.	13.7	W.	12.8	W.	5.9	N.	3.4	E.	2.3	NE.	3.2	"	6.3	E.	10.0	N.
29	2.4	SW.	9.8	NE.	12.8	SE.	13.2	SE.	13.8	SE.	12.8	S.	6.2	"	3.0	SE.	2.2	"	2.9	W.	5.9		10.3	"
30	2.1	SE.			12.9	"	13.4	S.	14.1	Calm.	12.7	Calm.	6.1	"	3.0	"	2.3	E.	2.3	NW.	5.9		10.7	"
31	1.8	Calm.			12.5	N.			13.9	NW.			5.9	"	2.5	E.			2.2	NE.			11.2	SW.

Records for 1853.

New Carthage.—Observer, Mr. A. R. Adkins.

Date.	January.		February.		March.		April.		May.		June.		July.		August.		September.		October.		November.		December.	
1853.	*G'ge*	*Wind.*	*G'ge*	*Wind.*	*G'ge*	*Wind.*	*G'ge*	*Wind.*	*G'ge*	*Wind.*	*G'ge*	*Wind.*	*G'ge*	*Wind.*	*G'ge*	*Wind.*	*G'ge*	*Wind.*	*G'ge*	*Wind.*	*G'ge*	*Wind.*	*G'ge*	*Wind.*
1	31.4	NE.	39.6	Calm.	40.3	Calm.																		
2	32.7	Calm.	38.8	"	40.4	"																		
3	33.9	NW.	37.4	"	40.4	"																		
4	34.7	Calm.	36.0	"	40.4	"																		
5	35.3	"	35.0	N.	40.4	NW.																		
6	35.8	"	33.9	"	40.3	Calm.																		
7	36.3	"	32.8	"	40.2	"																		
8	36.4	"	31.3	"	40.2	SE.																		
9	36.5	"	30.0	Calm.	40.3	N.																		
10	37.0	"	29.1	"	40.3	Calm.																		
11			28.8	"	40.4	"																		
12			28.7	"	40.5	"																		
13			28.4	"	40.5	N.																		
14			28.4	NE.	40.7	"																		
15			29.6	Calm.	40.7	Calm.																		
16			32.0	NW.	40.7	"																		
17			33.7	Calm.	40.8	"																		
18			34.8	"	40.9	NW.																		
19			35.7	NW.	40.9	Calm.																		
20			36.6	Calm.	40.9	"																		
21			37.1	N.	41.2	"																		
22	40.8	NW.	37.8	NE.	41.5	N.																		
23	41.0	N.	38.6	N.	41.5	Calm.																		
24	41.0	"	39.0	Calm.	41.4	"																		
25	41.1	Calm.	39.3	"	41.2	"																		
26	41.1	NE.	39.5	"	40.9	SW.																		
27	41.0	"	39.6	"	40.4	Calm.																		
28	40.9	Calm.	40.1	NW.	40.0	"																		
29	40.6	"			39.6	"																		
30	40.4	"			39.0	"																		
31	40.2	"			38.4	"																		

Records for 1853—Continued.

Baton Rouge.—Observer, Mr. J. W. Brown.

Date.	January.		February.		March.		April.		May.		June.		July.		August.		September.		October.		November.		December.	
1853.	G'ge	Wind.	G'ge	Wind.	G'ge	Wind.	G'ge	Wind.	G'ge	Wind.	G'ge	Wind.	G'ge	Wind.	G'ge	Wind.	G'ge	Wind.	G'ge	Wind.	G'ge	Wind.	G'ge	Wind.
1	24.5	NW.	28.4	SE.																				
2	25.5	SW.	28.2	"																				
3	26.0	NW.	27.9	"																				
4	26.1	"	27.7	SW.																				
5	26.3	"	27.5	NW.																				
6	26.4	"	27.9	"																				
7	26.5	SE.	26.5	"																				
8	26.7	"	25.9	"																				
9	27.0	"	25.1	"																				
10	27.2	"	24.4	"																				
11	27.3	"	23.8	SW.																				
12	27.5	NW.	23.0	"																				
13	27.5	"	22.6	NW.																				
14	27.7	NE.	22.3	E.																				
15	27.7	"	22.5	SW.																				
16	28 0	NW.	23.1	NW.																				
17	28.1	"	24.0	SE.																				
18	28.1	"	24.9	E.																				
19	28.2	"	25.5	NW.																				
20	28.2	"	26.0	"																				
21	28.3	NE.	26.4	SE.																				
22	28.3	NW.	27.0	NW.																				
23	28.3	"	27.1	"																				
24	28.4	"	27.2	"																				
25	28.4	SE.	27.4	SW.																				
26	28.6	NW.	27.8	SE.																				
27	28.7	"	28.0	SW.																				
28	28.5	NE.	28.5	"																				
29	28.5	"																						
30	28.5	"																						
31	28.5	"																						

Records for 1853—Continued.

Donaldsonville.—Observer, Mr. A. Gingry.

Date.	January.		February.		March.		April.		May.		June.		July.		August.		September.		October.		November.		December.	
1853.	G'ge	Wind.	G'ge	Wind.	G'ge	Wind.	G'ge	Wind.	G'ge	Wind.	G'ge	Wind.	G'ge	Wind.	G'ge	Wind.	G'ge	Wind.	G'ge	Wind.	G'ge	Wind.	G'ge	Wind.
1	21.8	E.	26.1	SW.	26.4	NW.	27.4	SW.	26.1	S.	27.9	S.	22.4	S.	15.0	S.	8.7	E.	8.8	E.	5.1	E.	6.4	E.
2	23.6	S.	26.0	W.	26.4	W.	27.4	S.	26.1	SE.	27.9	"	21.9	"	14.8	"	8.5	"	8.4	N.	5.4	"	7.9	W.
3	24.1	N.	25.7	S.	26.4	"	27.3	"	26.4	"	27.9	E.	21.4	"	14.5	"	8.2	NE.	8.4	"	5.4	NW.	7.1	E.
4	24.4	"	25.7	"	26.4	N.	27.1	NW.	26.4	"	27.9	"	20.8	W.	14.4	SW.	8.0	"	8.0	"	5.4	"	7.3	"
5	24.5	NW.	25.4	NW.	26.5	W.	26.9	S.	26.4	"	27.9	"	20.4	E.	14.2	W.	7.8	E.	8.2	"	5.5	E.	7.5	"
6	24.5	E.	24.7	N.	26.5	NW.	26.8	W.	26.5	"	27.8	Calm.	19.9	S.	14.0	"	8.0	"	8.0	E.	5.5	N.	7.5	"
7	24.7	S.	24.4	"	26.5	E.	26.6	"	26.5	"	27.8	S.	19.7	"	14.0	E.	8.1	"	7.7	"	5.7	E.	7.4	SE.
8	24.9	E.	24.0	E.	26.6	"	26.5	S.	26.7	NW.	27.7	N.	19.7	E.	13.9	"	8.0	"	7.7	"	6.0	"	6.8	N.
9	25.2	"	23.4	N.	26.7	NW.	26.3	"	26.6	E.	27.6	NE.	19.2	"	13.7	"	8.2	NE.	7.6	"	5.7	N.	6.7	NW.
10	25.4	S.	22.9	W.	26.7	E.	26.2	N.	26.7	"	27.4	S.	19.0	S.	13.4	S.	8.5	E.	7.5	"	5.7	E.	6.4	E.
11	25.3	Calm.	22.4	SE.	26.9	NW.	26.0	E.	26.7	"	27.4	E.	18.9	W.	13.1	N.	8.1	"	7.1	"	5.8	"	6.3	NW.
12	25.4	NW.	21.9	S.	26.9	S.	25.8	"	26.7	"	27.2	SE.	19.2	S.	12.7	NW.	7.9	SE.	7.2	"	6.0	"	6.2	W.
13	25.6	SE.	21.6	NE.	26.9	"	25.7	S.	26.9	"	27.0	E.	19.8	W.	12.3	E.	7.4	S.	7.1	"	5.6	NE.	6.2	E.
14	25.7	E.	21.3	E.	26.9	N.	25.5	Calm.	27.0	SE.	26.9	"	19.7	SW.	11.9	"	7.1	"	7.2	"	5.6	"	6.5	W.
15	25.8	NE.	21.4	S.	26.8	"	25.4	S.	27.0	"	26.7	"	19.6	"	11.5	NW.	6.8	"	6.9	"	6.0	S.	6.0	"
16	26.0	N.	21.8	W.	26.8	E.	25.3	SW.	27.2	"	26.6	"	19.5	W.	11.1	W.	6.8	"	6.7	"	5.8	E.	6.5	E.
17	25.9	"	22.5	N.	27.0	S.	25.1	N.	27.2	"	26.5	NE.	19.5	"	10.9	"	6.8	SW.	6.4	"	6.0	SE.	6.8	NW.
18	26.1	E.	23.2	E.	26.8	NW.	25.3	E.	27.4	"	26.4	NW.	19.3	N.	10.7	"	6.9	"	6.3	N.	6.1	E.	6.2	W.
19	26.1	NE.	23.7	NW.	26.9	E.	25.3	S.	27.4	NW.	26.3	S.	19.0	NW.	10.6	NW.	7.0	N.	6.2	"	6.6	"	6.3	NW.
20	26.1	N.	24.2	E.	27.0	"	25.4	"	27.5	N.	26.0	E.	19.0	W.	10.3	"	7.1	NE.	6.3	W.	6.5	SE.	6.0	W.
21	26.2	SE.	24.4	"	27.3	"	25.6	"	27.6	"	25.8	SW.	18.9	NW.	9.6	"	7.4	"	6.1	"	6.3	NW.	6.0	E.
22	26.1	NW.	25.0	W.	27.7	W.	25.8	"	27.6	S.	25.6	S.	18.8	S.	9.5	N.	7.5	N.	6.0	NW.	6.1	W.	6.0	W.
23	26.1	"	25.1	NW.	27.6	"	25.9	"	27.6	SE.	25.3	"	18.6	"	9.4	E.	7.6	NE.	6.0	N.	5.8	E.	6.2	N.
24	26.1	"	25.2	E.	27.6	"	25.9	"	27.7	S.	25.0	N.	18.5	W.	8.8	"	7.9	"	5.5	"	5.8	N.	6.1	"
25	26.2	N.	25.3	W.	27.7	E.	26.0	N.	27.6	NE.	24.6	"	18.2	"	8.7	"	8.2	"	5.0	E.	5.9	"	6.0	NE.
26	26.5	NW.	25.6	E.	27.6	NW.	25.9	"	27.6	E.	24.3	E.	17.8	W.	8.7	"	8.4	E.	5.0	"	6.2	NE.	5.8	NW.
27	26.5	NE.	25.8	S.	27.7	"	26.0	"	27.7	"	23.9	S.	17.6	E.	8.7	SE.	8.7	"	6.7	"	6.4	E.	5.7	S.
28	26.5	E.	26.1	"	27.7	E.	26.0	E.	27.9	"	23.6	E.	17.1	N.	8.7	E.	8.9	SE.	6.0	N.	6.6	S.	5.6	NW.
29	26.4	Calm.			27.7	"	26.0	S.	27.9	S.	23.2	"	16.6	"	8.7	"	8.9	E.	6.7	"	6.7	NW.	5.2	S.
30	26.5	W.			27.6	"	26.1	E.	27.9	"	22.8	"	16.0	E.	8.6	"	8.9	"	5.5	"	6.5	E.	6.0	W.
31	26.3	Calm.			27.5	S.			27.9	E.			15.4	"	8.6	"			5.3	"			5.3	NW.

Records for 1853—Continued.

Carrollton.—Observer, Professor C. G. Forshey. Records only approximately exact.

Date.	January.		February.		March.		April.		May.		June.		July.		August.		September.		October.		November.		December.	
1853.	*G'ge*	*Wind.*	*G'ge*	*Wind.*	*G'ge*	*Wind.*	*G'ge*	*Wind.*	*G'ge*	*Wind.*	*G'ge*	*Wind.*	*G'ge*	*Wind.*	*G'ge*	*Wind.*	*G'ge*	*Wind.*	*G'ge*	*Wind.*	*G'ge*	*Wind.*	*G'ge*	*Wind.*
1	11.9	N.	14.0		14.0		14.6	SW.	13.8	SE.	14.8	S.	11.6	S.	7.2	S.	3.4	E.	3.4	E.	1.4	E.	2.2	NE.
2	12.5		13.9		14.0		14.5	S.	13.9	"	15.0	"	11.4	"	7.1	"	3.4	NE.	3.2	N.	1.6	"	2.6	W.
3	12.8	"	13.6		13.9		14.5	"	14.0	"	15.0	Calm.	11.0	"	6.9	SW.	3.3	"	3.2	"	1.6	N.	2.4	E.
4	13.0	"	13.5		13.9		14.4	N.	14.0	"	14.9	E.	10.7	W.	6.8	W.	3.0	"	3.0	"	1.6	NW.	2.4	SE.
5	13.3	"	13.5		13.9		14.4	S.	14.0	"	14.9	"	10.4	E.	6.7	SW.	2.9	E.	3.1	"	1.6	E.	2.6	E.
6	13.3	"	12.9	N.	13.9		14.3	W.	14.1	"	14.9	Calm.	10.1	SE.	6.7	W.	3.0	"	3.0	E.	1.7	N.	2.6	"
7	13.2	"	12.7	"	13.9		14.0	"	14.1	"	14.9	S.	10.0	S.	6.6	E.	3.1	"	2.9	"	1.7	E.	2.7	"
8	13.4	"	12.4	"	14.0		14.0	S.	14.2	"	14.8	W.	10.0	E.	6.6	NE.	3.0	"	2.8	"	1.7	"	2.4	N.
9	13.5		12.2	"	14.1		13.9	"	14.2	N.	14.7	NE.	9.7	"	6.4	E.	3.1	NE.	2.8	S.	1.8	N.	2.0	"
10	13.5		11.8	"	14.2		13.9	NW.	14.2	E.	14.6	SE.	9.7	S.	6.3	S.	3.3	E.	2.7	E.	1.7	E.	2.0	E.
11	13.6		11.6	Calm.	14.3		13.8	E.	14.2	"	14.6	E.	9.5	W.	6.2	E.	3.1	"	2.5	"	1.8	"	2.1	NW.
12	13.7	"	11.3	S.	14.2		13.7	"	14.2	"	14.5	SE.	9.7	SE.	6.0	NW.	3.0	SE.	2.5	"	1.8	"	1.9	W.
13	13.8	"	11.1	N.	14.3		13.6	S.	14.3	"	14.4	E.	10.1	W.	5.6	NE.	2.7	S.	2.4	"	1.7	"	1.9	SE.
14	13.9	"	11.0	Calm.	14.3		13.5	Calm.	14.4	SE.	14.3	"	10.0	SW.	5.4	E.	2.5	"	2.4	"	1.6	NE.	1.9	W.
15	13.9	"	11.1		14.2		13.4	SE.	14.4	"	14.2	"	9.9	"	5.1	NW.	2.3	"	2.4	"	1.6	S.	2.1	SW.
16	14.3	"	11.2	N.	14.2		13.4	SW.	14.4	"	14.2	"	9.9	NW.	4.8	W.	2.2	SE.	2.2	"	1.8	SE.	2.0	E.
17	14.0	"	11.3		14.2		13.2	N.	14.5	"	14.1	NE.	9.9	W.	4.7	NW.	2.2	SW.	2.1	"	1.7	E.	2.2	N.
18	14.0	"	11.6		14.3		13.2	E.	14.6	"	14.1	NW.	9.7	N.	4.6	E.	2.3	"	2.0	"	1.8	"	2.4	W.
19	13.9	"	12.3		14.1		13.2	S.	14.6	NW.	14.0	S.	9.6	NW.	4.5	NW.	2.4	N.	1.9	N.	2.0	"	2.2	NW.
20	14.0	"	12.2		14.3		13.4	"	14.7	N.	13.8	E.	9.6	W.	4.3	"	2.4	"	2.0	W.	2.0	N.	1.9	N.
21	14.0		12.6		14.4		13.5	Calm.	14.7	"	13.7	SW.	9.6	NW.	4.0	"	2.6	NE.	1.8	"	2.1	NW.	1.8	E.
22	14.0	"	13.1		14.9		13.7	S.	14.7	S.	13.6	SE.	9.5	S.	3.9	N.	2.7	N.	1.8	SW.	2.0	E.	1.8	SW.
23	13.9	"	13.4		14.8		13.8	"	14.7	SE.	13.4	S.	9.4	"	3.8	E.	2.8	NE.	1.8	N.	1.7	N.	1.8	N.
24	13.8	NW.	13.3		14.8		13.8	SE.	14.8	S.	13.2	N.	9.3	W.	3.5	SE.	2.9	"	1.5	"	1.7	"	1.8	"
25	13.9	Calm.	13.6		14.8		13.8	N.	14.7	N.	13.0	"	9.1	NW.	3.5	"	3.1	E.	1.2	E.	1.7	"	1.9	NE.
26	14.0	"	13.7		14.8		13.8	"	14.7	NE.	12.9	E.	8.9	W.	3.5	E.	3.2	"	1.2	"	1.8	NE.	1.7	N.
27	13.9	N.	13.7		14.7		13.8	E.	14.8	E.	12.5	S.	8.7	NE.	3.5	SE.	3.4	"	2.1	SE.	1.8	E.	1.7	SW.
28	14.0	E.	13.9		14.7		13.8	"	14.9	"	12.3	SE.	8.5	N.	3.4	E.	3.4	SE.	1.8	N.	2.2	S.	1.6	NW.
29	14.0	Calm.			14.6		13.8	S.	14.9	S.	12.1	E.	8.2	"	3.4	"	3.5	"	2.3	"	2.3	NW.	1.6	S.
30	14.0	NW.			14.5		13.9	E.	15.0	"	11.9	"	7.8	E.	3.3	"	3.5	E.	1.5	"	2.2	E.	1.8	W.
31	14.0	E.			14.4				15.0	E.			7.5	"	3.3	"			1.3	S.			1.5	NW.

Records for 1854.

Donaldsonville.—Observer, Mr. A. Gingry.

Date.	January.		February.		March.		April.		May.		June.		July.		August.		September.		October.		November.		December.	
1854.	*G'ge*	*Wind.*	*G'ge*	*Wind.*	*G'ge*	*Wind.*	*G'ge*	*Wind.*	*G'ge*	*Wind.*	*G'ge*	*Wind.*	*G'ge*	*Wind.*	*G'ge*	*Wind.*	*G'ge*	*Wind.*	*G'ge*	*Wind.*	*G'ge*	*Wind.*	*G'ge*	*Wind.*
1	5.5	NW.	14.9	S.	16.4	E.	26.0	N.	23.8	E.	25.5	E.	25.0	E.	11.0	S.	6.5	E.	7.1	E.	4.8	NE.	4.3	E.
2	5.1	S.	16.2	"	16.4	S.	26.1	"	23.7	"	25.7	"	24.7	"	10.5	NE.	6.9	"	7.1	N.	4.5	E.	4.2	SW.
3	5.1	E.	17.2	N.	16.7	E.	26.2	E.	23.9	"	25.7	NW.	24.6	"	10.0	"	6.5	W.	7.4	"	4.3	"	5.0	N.
4	5.6	"	18.2	E.	17.0	NW.	26.3	"	24.0	SE.	26.0	E.	24.4	"	9.5	W.	6.9	S.	6.9	"	5.0	"	4.5	"
5	5.8	"	18.8	"	17.2	E.	26.4	"	24.3	"	26.1	"	24.1	"	9.0	NW.	6.4	E.	6.5	NE.	5.0	NE.	4.6	"
6	5.7	N.	19.5	"	17.7	"	26.5	"	24.6	W.	26.2	NW.	23.4	"	8.5	W.	6.5	NE.	6.5	E.	5.4	N.	4.0	"
7	5.5	"	20.0	S.	18.2	S.	26.7	"	24.5	"	26.2	"	22.8	"	8.0	NW.	5.8	N.	6.4	"	5.5	S.	5.0	NW.
8	5.0	"	20.5	"	18.5	"	26.8	"	24.4	NE.	26.3	SW.	22.4	NE.	7.5	W.	5.8	W.	6.5	"	5.5	E.	4.5	NE.
9	5.2	E.	20.8	E.	18.9	"	26.9	"	24.4	S.	26.3	SE.	21.7	W.	7.3	"	5.5	"	6.9	"	5.8	"	5.1	E.
10	5.4	"	21.1	"	19.1	NW.	26.8	NW.	24.3	E.	26.4	W.	21.3	N.	7.2	"	5.5	"	6.6	"	6.2	SW.	5.0	"
11	6.0	SW.	21.5	S.	19.1	E.	26.8	E.	24.5	"	26.4	"	21.0	S.	7.1	SE.	5.6	E.	6.8	"	5.8	W.	5.0	N.
12	5.3	"	21.8	"	19.5	"	26.9	"	24.5	SE.	26.3	NE.	20.5	"	7.1	E.	5.0	SW.	6.8	"	6.0	"	4.5	"
13	5.1	"	22.2	"	20.1	"	26.8	"	24.5	S.	26.5	SE.	20.0	SE.	7.1	N.	5.5	N.	6.7	"	4.3	NW.	4.0	E.
14	4.8	E.	22.5	"	20.8	N.	27.6	"	24.4	NW.	26.6	S.	19.4	S.	7.2	NE.	5.4	S.	6.6	"	5.0	S.	4.0	"
15	4.5	S.	22.9	N.	21.6	S.	27.3	W.	24.4	S.	26.6	"	18.7	E.	7.4	E.	5.5	N.	6.5	N.	5.2	SW.	4.0	S.
16	5.0	"	22.9	"	22.3	"	26.9	NW.	24.3	"	26.7	"	17.8	"	7.5	"	6.0	E.	6.3	"	4.0	N.	4.0	W.
17	5.4	SW.	23.0	NE.	22.9	"	26.7	W.	24.3	NW.	26.7	"	17.0	"	7.5	SW.	6.8	"	6.2	E.	4.8	SW.	4.0	S.
18	5.3	W.	23.0	"	23.5	"	26.6	E.	24.2	NE.	26.7	N.	16.5	Calm.	7.2	W.	7.5	"	5.8	"	4.6	NW.	3.5	N.
19	5.3	S.	22.8	E.	23.9	E.	26.4	S.	24.1	E.	26.7	W.	15.7	E.	7.3	"	6.1	"	5.4	"	4.0	"	4.0	W.
20	5.6	SW.	22.5	SW.	23.9	"	26.3	E.	24.0	"	26.7	NW.	15.4	"	7.2	N.	6.6	S.	5.0	"	4.0	E.	3.4	N.
21	5.4	N.	21.9	NW.	24.2	SE.	26.0	SE.	23.9	S.	26.7	W.	15.0	S.	7.3	S.	6.3	E.	4.6	"	5.0	S.	4.5	Calm.
22	5.0	"	21.2	S.	24.6	NW.	25.8	S.	23.8	E.	26.6	"	14.5	E.	7.2	NE.	6.7	"	5.0	"	5.5	E.	4.5	E.
23	5.0	"	20.5	N.	24.6	"	25.7	SE.	23.8	SE.	26.5	E.	14.0	W.	7.2	"	7.4	"	5.0	W.	6.0	S.	5.0	"
24	5.2	E.	19.5	E.	24.8	SW.	25.5	"	23.9	"	26.3	"	13.6	"	7.1	E.	7.5	W.	5.4	"	5.5	SW.	5.0	"
25	5.6	"	19.2	"	25.0	S.	25.2	"	24.4	"	26.1	"	13.0	E.	7.0	SE.	7.5	E.	6.0	E.	5.5	NW.	5.0	"
26	5.8	S.	18.6	NW.	25.3	NE.	25.0	S.	24.4	"	26.0	"	13.7	"	7.0	E.	7.3	"	6.7	"	5.0	W.	4.8	W.
27	6.2	N.	17.2	E.	25.5	E.	24.6	E.	24.6	"	25.9	"	13.4	"	6.7	"	7.1	SE.	6.0	NE.	4.5	NW.	4.8	E.
28	7.4	NE.	16.6	"	25.5	"	24.4	N.	24.8	S.	25.5	"	13.0	"	6.5	N.	7.1	E.	6.4	E.	4.3	"	4.8	SW.
29	9.2	NW.			25.6	S.	24.2	"	25.0	"	25.3	NE.	12.6	"	6.3	S.	6.7	"	6.3	W.	4.0	SW.	3.0	N.
30	11.5	E.			25.8	E.	23.9	NE.	25.2	"	25.2	E.	12.2	"	7.0	E.	7.0	"	5.6	"	4.0	S.	4.2	S.
31	13.3	N.			26.0	S.			25.4	"			11.6	S.	6.7	"			5.0	E.			4.0	"

Records for 1854—Continued.

Carrollton.—Observer, PROFESSOR C. G. FORSHEY. Record only approximately exact.

Date.	January.		February.		March.		April.		May.		June.		July.		August.		September.		October.		November.		December.	
1854.	G'ge	Wind.	G'ge	Wind.	G'ge	Wind.	G'ge	Wind.	G'ge	Wind.	G'ge	Wind.	G'ge	Wind.	G'ge	Wind.	G'ge	Wind.	G'ge	Wind.	G'ge	Wind.	G'ge	Wind.
1	1.5	N.	7.1	S.	8.1	S.	13.8	N.	12.5	E.	13.5	E.	13.2	E.	4.8	E.	2.1	E.	2.4	E.	1.0	NE.	0.9	E.
2	1.3	"	7.9	"	8.1	"	13.9	"	12.5	"	13.6	"	12.9	"	4.5	NE.	2.3	"	2.5	"	1.0	E.	0.8	SW.
3	1.3	E.	8.5	N.	8.2	E.	13.9	E.	12.6	"	13.6	NW.	12.8	"	3.6	E.	2.1	W.	2.6	"	0.8	"	1.3	N.
4	1.6	"	9.1	E.	8.4	"	14.0	"	12.6	SE.	13.8	E.	12.7	"	3.3	W.	2.3	S.	2.3	"	1.3	"	1.0	E.
5	1.7	SW.	9.5	"	8.5	SE.	14.0	"	12.7	"	13.9	NW.	12.6	"	3.6	NW.	2.1	E.	2.1	"	1.3	NE.	1.1	"
6	1.7	"	9.9	"	8.7	NW.	14.1	"	12.9	W.	13.9	"	12.3	"	3.3	W.	2.1	NE.	2.1	"	1.5	N.	0.7	"
7	1.5	"	10.2	S.	9.1	"	14.2	NW.	12.9	"	13.9	"	11.8	"	3.0	NW.	1.7	N.	2.0	N.	1.6	S.	1.3	NW.
8	1.3	E.	10.4	"	9.3	SW.	14.3	E.	12.8	NE.	14.0	SW.	11.7	NE.	2.7	W.	1.7	"	2.1	"	1.6	E.	1.0	NE.
9	1.4	W.	10.5	E.	9.5	S.	14.3	"	12.8	E.	14.0	SE.	11.3	W.	2.6	"	1.5	W.	2.3	E.	1.7	"	1.3	E.
10	1.5	"	10.8	"	9.6	NE.	14.3	SW.	12.7	"	14.1	W.	11.0	N.	2.5	"	1.5	"	2.2	"	1.9	SW.	1.3	"
11	1.8	SW.	11.1	S.	9.7	E.	14.3	E.	12.9	"	14.1	"	10.8	S.	2.4	SW.	1.3	E.	2.3	"	1.7	W.	1.3	N.
12	1.4	W.	11.2	"	9.8	"	14.3	"	12.9	SE.	14.0	NE.	10.5	W.	2.4	E.	1.3	SW.	2.3	"	1.8	N.	1.0	"
13	1.3	S.	11.5	"	10.2	S.	14.2	"	12.9	S.	14.1	SE.	10.2	SE.	2.4	N.	1.6	N.	2.2	"	0.8	NW.	0.7	E.
14	1.0	SW.	12.1	"	10.6	E.	14.7	"	12.8	NW.	14.2	S.	9.9	S.	2.5	NE.	1.5	S.	2.1	"	1.3	S.	0.7	"
15	1.0	N.	12.3	N.	11.1	S.	14.6	W.	12.7	S.	14.2	"	9.5	E.	2.6	E.	1.5	N.	2.1	W.	1.4	SW.	0.7	S.
16	1.3	"	12.5	"	11.6	N.	14.1	NW.	12.7	NW.	14.3	"	8.9	"	2.7	"	1.8	E.	1.9	N.	0.7	N.	0.7	W.
17	1.4	"	12.5	E.	11.9	"	14.1	N.	12.7	"	14.3	"	8.4	"	2.7	SW.	2.2	"	1.9	"	0.9	Calm.	0.7	S.
18	1.4	NE.	13.2	NE.	12.3	E.	14.0	E.	12.6	NE.	14.3	N.	8.1	Calm.	2.5	W.	2.7	"	1.7	E.	0.9	NW.	0.3	N.
19	1.4	S.	13.4	E.	12.5	"	13.9	"	12.6	E.	14.3	W.	7.6	E.	2.6	"	1.9	"	1.5	NE.	0.7	"	0.7	W.
20	1.5	"	11.7	SW.	12.5	"	13.8	"	12.6	S.	14.3	NW.	7.5	"	2.5	N.	2.1	S.	1.3	E.	0.7	E.	0.3	N.
21	1.4	N.	11.4	NW.	12.7	"	13.6	SE.	12.5	"	14.3	W.	7.3	S.	2.6	S.	2.0	E.	1.0	W.	1.3	S.	1.0	Calm.
22	1.3	NE.	11.0	S.	12.9	"	13.6	S.	12.4	E.	14.2	"	6.9	E.	2.5	NE.	2.3	"	1.3	"	1.6	E.	1.0	E.
23	1.3	NW.	10.5	N.	12.9	"	13.5	SE.	12.3	SE.	14.1	E.	6.6	W.	2.5	"	2.6	"	1.3	E.	1.8	S.	1.3	"
24	1.4	E.	9.9	E.	13.0	"	13.4	"	12.5	"	14.0	"	6.3	"	2.4	E.	2.7	W.	1.6	"	1.6	SW.	1.6	"
25	1.5	N.	9.7	W.	13.2	NW.	13.3	"	12.9	"	14.0	"	6.0	E.	2.4	SE.	2.7	E.	1.8	"	1.6	NW.	1.3	"
26	1.6	S.	9.3	NW.	13.4	W.	13.2	S.	12.9	"	13.8	"	6.5	"	2.4	E.	2.5	"	1.8	"	1.3	W.	1.1	W.
27	1.9	"	8.5	E.	13.5	S.	12.9	E.	13.0	"	13.7	"	6.3	"	2.2	"	2.4	SE.	1.8	W.	1.0	NW.	1.1	E.
28	2.5	N.	8.1	"	13.5	SW.	12.8	N.	13.1	S.	13.5	"	6.0	"	2.1	N.	2.4	E.	1.8	NW.	0.9	"	1.0	SW.
29	3.7	E.			13.5	E.	12.7	"	13.2	"	13.4	NE.	5.7	"	2.0	S.	2.2	"	2.0	E.	0.7	SW.	1.1	N.
30	5.1	"			13.6	N.	12.5	NE.	13.3	"	13.3	N.	5.5	"	2.4	E.	2.4	"	2.0	"	0.7	S.	0.0	S.
31	6.2	N.			13.8	S.			13.4	"			5.1	S.	2.2	"			1.6	NW.			0.8	"

Records for 1855.

Donaldsonville.—Observer, MR. A. GINGRY.

Date.	January.		February.		March.		April.		May.		June.		July.		August.		September.		October.		November.		December.	
1855.	G'ge	Wind.	G'ge	Wind.	G'ge	Wind.	G'ge	Wind.	G'ge	Wind.	G'ge	Wind.	G'ge	Wind.	G'ge	Wind.	G'ge	Wind.	G'ge	Wind.	G'ge	Wind.	G'ge	Wind.
1	4.2	E.	8.2	N.	4.3	NE.	16.5	S.	12.1	S.	9.7	W.	11.0	E.	7.9	S.	11.7	E.	10.2	W.	9.5	S.	13.6	W.
2	5.0	"	8.2	"	5.0	S.	16.5	"	11.8	W.	9.1	NW.	10.5	N.	8.1	NE.	11.0	"	9.9	N.	9.2	"	13.8	NW.
3	5.0	"	8.4	NW.	6.0	"	16.8		11.5	SW.	9.0	NE.	10.0	"	8.3	"	11.7	N.	9.5	"	9.0	"	14.0	E.
4	4.8	"	8.3	S.	6.2	E.	17.0	E.	11.4	W.	8.8	S.	10.0	E.	8.4	E.	10.5	E.	9.2	E.	8.7	"	14.2	N.
5	5.0	"	8.1	SW.	6.4	"	17.4	S.	11.2	N.	8.7	"	10.5	SW.	8.4	NW.	10.3	"	9.9	NW.	8.5	"	14.0	"
6	5.5	SE.	7.8	"	6.4	S.	18.5	N.	10.9	S.	8.7	"	10.5	"	8.5	W.	10.0	S.	9.5	N.	9.8	NW.	14.4	E.
7	5.2	N.	7.7	S.	6.0	"	18.8	W.	10.9	W.	8.8	SW.	10.6	N.	8.1	S.	9.7	E.	9.0	"	10.5	N.	14.1	"
8	5.0	"	7.5	NW.	6.4	"	18.6	S.	10.5	"	9.1	E.	10.9	E.	7.7	"	9.6	"	8.8	E.	9.5	"	14.1	"
9	5.2	NE.	6.9	N.	6.0	E.	18.0	"	10.5	NE.	9.3	"	11.2	N.	7.6	SW.	9.9	"	8.7	S.	9.2	"	14.0	NW.
10	4.8	E.	6.7	E.	5.8	"	17.8	"	10.3	"	9.8	N.	11.5	NW.	7.4	S.	10.0	"	8.7	E.	9.0	E.	13.7	"
11	4.8	"	6.0	S.	6.0	S.	16.4	E.	10.0	N.	10.5	E.	11.8	N.	7.5	"	9.9	"	8.8	NE.	9.0	NE.	13.6	E.
12	5.5	S.	6.2	"	6.1	"	14.6	"	10.2	SE.	10.8	"	12.0	W.	7.5	"	9.8	"	8.9	"	8.8	N.	12.9	"
13	5.5	"	6.4	W.	6.1	SW.	14.4	S.	10.4	E.	11.0	"	12.0	S.	7.9	E.	9.5	"	9.5	"	8.5	E.	12.6	"
14	5.8	N.	5.8	N.	6.0	S.	13.0	SE.	10.0	"	10.5	"	11.7	"	8.2	"	9.2	N.	9.5	"	8.5	"	12.3	S.
15	6.0	E.	5.8	NW.	6.0	"	12.4	S.	10.0	"	11.1	"	11.2	E.	8.5	W.	9.4	NE.	9.5	E.	9.0	"	12.0	Calm.
16	6.5	"	6.0	N.	6.0	"	11.8	"	10.5	"	11.5	"	10.8	S.	8.7	N.	10.3	W.	9.9	"	9.5	"	11.6	E.
17	7.2	Calm.	5.5	E.	6.3	N.	11.4	"	10.3	NW.	11.5	S.	10.3	E.	9.0	E.	10.0	S.	9.9	"	10.0	N.	11.0	N.
18	8.0	"	6.0	"	5.8	"	11.2	SW.	10.2	SW.	11.8	E.	10.0	"	9.3	S.	9.5	W.	10.3	"	10.2	"	10.6	E.
19	8.8	S.	6.7	N.	5.5	E.	11.2	S.	10.0	W.	12.0	N.	9.8	"	9.5	N.	9.0	E.	10.5	"	10.8	"	10.0	N.
20	9.5	"	6.0	E.	5.5	"	10.8	W.	10.0	S.	12.2	S.	9.6	S.	10.0	E.	9.5	N.	10.5	"	11.6	"	9.5	E.
21	9.9	NW.	5.0	"	6.0	"	10.8	E.	10.0	"	12.2	NW.	9.3	E.	10.4	"	9.1	Calm.	10.7	NW.	11.8	"	9.7	"
22	9.3	N.	5.0	"	6.0	W.	10.7	N.	10.0	NW.	12.5	S.	9.2	"	10.4	W.	9.5	E.	10.8	N.	12.0	E.	10.0	SW.
23	9.4	S.	5.0	SW.	6.4	"	11.2	E.	10.3	E.	12.5	"	9.0	"	10.2	S.	9.5	"	10.6	"	12.1	"	10.0	W.
24	9.2	SW.	4.8	N.	8.0	"	11.2	"	10.2	SW.	12.3	W.	8.8	S.	10.3	E.	10.0	"	10.3	NE.	12.2	"	11.5	N.
25	9.2	"	5.0	"	9.8	E.	11.5	"	10.1	"	12.1	SW.	8.5	E.	10.9	S.	10.3	"	10.1	"	12.6	"	12.1	"
26	9.2	N.	4.3	"	12.0	S.	11.7	N.	10.2	W.	11.9	E.	8.9	"	10.7	"	10.3	S.	10.2	E.	12.9	NE.	12.9	NE.
27	9.0	S.	5.0	E.	13.2	N.	11.9	E.	10.0	"	11.7	S.	8.8	"	11.4	E.	10.7	N.	10.0	"	13.0	N.	13.5	"
28	9.0	W.	4.5	N.	14.2	NE.	12.0	"	9.8	S.	11.5	E.	8.8	S.	11.6	S.	10.3	"	10.1	N.	13.0	NW.	15.6	"
29	8.6	N.			15.1	"	12.1	S.	9.6	"	11.2	"	8.3	"	11.5	E.	10.5	S.	9.6	E.	13.0	S.	16.6	NW.
30	8.4	"			16.0	E.	12.1	SE.	9.5	"	11.0	"	8.2	W.	11.5	NW.	10.5	N.	9.8	"	13.2	E.	16.6	N.
31	8.5	"			16.7	N.			9.5	N.			7.8	"	11.7	E.			9.8	"			17.2	"

Records for 1855—Continued.

Carrollton.—Observer, PROFESSOR C. G. FORSHEY. Records only approximately correct.

Date.	January.		February.		March.		April.		May.		June.		July.		August.		September.		October.		November.		December.	
1855.	*G'ge*	*Wind.*	*G'ge*	*Wind.*	*G'ge*	*Wind.*	*G'ge*	*Wind.*	*G'ge*	*Wind.*	*G'ge*	*Wind.*	*G'ge*	*Wind.*	*G'ge*	*Wind.*	*G'ge*	*Wind.*	*G'ge*	*Wind.*	*G'ge*	*Wind.*	*G'ge*	*Wind.*
1	0.8	E.	3.2	N.	1.0	NE.	8.1	S.	5.5	S.	4.0	W.												
2	1.3	"	3.2	"	1.3	S.	8.1	"	5.3	W.	3.6	NW.												
3	1.3	"	3.3	NW.	1.8	"	8.3	"	5.1	SW.	3.6	NE.												
4	1.1	"	3.2	S.	1.9	E.	8.4	E.	5.0	W.	3.4	"												
5	1.3	"	3.0	SW.	2.1	"	8.7	S.	4.9	N.	3.4	"												
6	1.6	SE.	2.9	"	2.1	S.	9.3	N.	4.7	S.	3.4	"												
7	1.4	N.	2.8	S.	2.1	"	9.5	W.	4.7	W.	3.4	SW.												
8	1.3	"	2.5	NW.	2.1	"	9.3	S.	4.4	"	3.6	E.												
9	1.7	NE.	2.3	N.	1.8	E.	9.0	"	4.5	NE.	3.7	"												
10	1.1	E.	2.2	E.	1.7	"	8.9	E.	4.3	"	4.0	N.												
11	1.1	"	1.8	S.	1.8	S.	8.1	"	4.2	N.	4.5	E.												
12	1.7	S.	1.9	"	1.9	"	6.9	"	4.3	SE.	4.6	"												
13	1.5	"	2.0	W.	2.1	SW.	6.8	S.	4.4	E.	4.8	"												
14	1.5	N.	2.3	NW.	1.8	S.	6.0	SE.	4.2	"	4.5	"												
15	1.8	E.	1.8	N.	1.8	"	5.7	S.	4.2	"	4.9	"												
16	2.1	"	1.6	E.	1.8	"	5.3	"	4.5	"	5.1	"												
17	2.5	Calm.	1.8	"	1.9	N.	5.0	"	4.3	NW.	5.1	S.												
18	3.0	"	2.2	N.	1.7	"	4.9	SW.	4.2	SW.	5.2	E.												
19	3.5	S.	1.8	E.	1.5	E.	4.9	S.	4.2	W.	5.4	N.												
20	3.9	Calm.	1.3	"	1.5	"	4.7	W.	4.2	S.	5.5	S.												
21	4.0	NW.	1.3	"	1.8	"	4.7	E.	4.2	"	5.5	NW.												
22	3.7	N.	1.3	SW.	1.8	W.	4.6	N.	4.2	NW.	5.7	S.												
23	3.8	S.	1.1	N.	2.0	"	4.9	E.	4.3	E.	5.7	"												
24	3.7	SW.	1.3	"	3.0	"	4.9	"	4.3	SW.	5.6	W.												
25	3.7	Calm.	0.8	"	4.1	E.	5.1	"	4.2	"	5.5	SW.												
26	3.7	N.	1.3	E.	5.4	S.	5.3	N.	4.3	W.	5.3	E.												
27	3.6	S.	1.0	N.	6.1	N.	5.3	E.	4.2	"	5.2	S.												
28	3.6	W.	1.0	"	6.8	NE.	5.4	"	4.0	S.	5.1	E.												
29	3.3	N.			7.3	"	5.4	S.	3.9	"	5.1	"												
30	3.2	"			7.8	E.	5.5	SE.	3.9	"	4.8	"												
31	3.3	"			8.3	N.			3.9	N.														

Records for 1856.

Donaldsonville.—Observer, MR. A. GINGRY.

Date.	January.		February.		March.		April.		May.		June.		July.		August.		September.		October.		November.		December.	
1856.	*G'ge*	*Wind.*	*G'g*	*Wind.*	*G'ge*	*Wind.*	*G'ge*	*Wind.*	*G'ge*	*Wind.*	*G'ge*	*Wind.*	*G'ge*	*Wind.*	*G'ge*	*Wind.*	*G'ge*	*Wind.*	*G'ge*	*Wind.*	*G'ge*	*Wind.*	*G'ge*	*Wind.*
1	17.8	N.	5.0	SW.	15.1	S.	21.0	E.	21.3	S.	26.0	NW.	13.5	SE.	6.0	SE.	5.5	NE.	3.5	NE.	3.5	NE.	5.5	SE.
2	18.2	E.	4.8	N.	16.0	NW.	20.7	S.	21.5	E.	26.0	E.	13.6	E.	5.8	SW.	5.0	E.	4.0	"	4.0	SE.	6.2	S.
3	19.2	N.	5.0	"	16.5	N.	20.0	E.	21.0	SW.	25.9	"	13.2	W.	5.5	S.	5.0	S.	4.0	E.	4.0	"	5.0	N.
4	19.6	"	4.8	SW.	17.1	S.	19.5	W.	20.5	SE.	25.9	"	12.6	"	5.5	W.	5.4	E.	4.5	"	5.0	N.	5.0	NE.
5	19.5	"	4.7	E.	17.7	Calm.	19.0	NE.	20.0	S.	25.8	N.	12.2	"	5.4	E.	5.4	SE.	4.5	"	3.5	NE.	5.0	N.
6	19.2	"	5.0	"	18.3	"	18.8	S.	19.8	N.	25.8	"	12.0	S.	5.0	"	6.0	"	4.5	"	3.8	SE.	5.0	"
7	19.0	E.	5.0	N.	19.2	E.	18.7	NW.	21.1	E.	25.5	S.	11.0	W.	5.0	W.	6.2	"	5.0	"	4.5	"	5.0	"
8	18.5	"	5.5	"	20.2	NE.	19.0	N.	21.3	NW.	25.3	W.	10.5	"	5.5	E.	6.2	E.	5.5	"	4.5	N.	6.2	"
9	18.0	N.	6.0	"	21.9	NW.	20.8	SE.	21.7	E.	24.9	S.	9.5	"	6.0	"	6.0	"	6.0	"	3.2	"	7.0	E.
10	17.3		6.0	"	22.6	NE.	21.2	W.	22.0	"	24.7	"	8.6	"	7.0	"	6.2	"	5.5	S.	3.5	NE.	8.0	S.
11	16.5		6.0	NW.	23.2	"	21.8	S.	22.5	"	24.5	W.	8.4	NW.	8.0	S.	5.5	"	5.0	SE.	3.5	E.	9.5	SE.
12	15.8		5.5	"	23.8	"	22.3	"	23.3	"	23.8	"	8.2	"	8.0	"	5.5	"	4.0	"	3.8	"	10.2	S.
13	15.0		5.0	"	24.5	N.	22.4	SE.	23.8	"	23.5	SW.	8.0	"	8.2	"	5.0	"	4.0	S.	3.5	"	12.5	"
14	14.5	"	4.8	E.	24.4	S.	22.5	S.	24.1	W.	22.8	"	7.5	S.	7.0	"	4.8	"	3.2	NW.	3.4	"	13.2	NW.
15	13.5	NW.	4.8	S.	24.4	"	22.6	"	24.3	E.	22.1	E.	7.0	NW.	5.5	"	4.5	"	3.0	"	4.0	NW.	13.6	"
16	12.8	"	4.8	SW.	24.7	E.	22.5	"	24.6	"	21.4	"	6.8	W.	5.2	"	4.8	"	3.0	"	4.0	"	14.0	"
17	12.0	N.	5.0	N.	25.0	"	21.8	"	24.8	N.	20.5	NW.	6.6	E.	5.0	W.	4.8	"	3.2	"	4.5	N.	14.6	E.
18	11.5	NE.	5.5	NE.	25.2	NW.	21.2	E.	24.9	"	20.0	NE.	6.8	W.	5.0	SW.	5.0	"	3.0	"	4.0	"	14.6	"
19	11.1	N.	5.8	E.	25.3	"	20.8	W.	25.1	"	19.5	W.	6.5	"	4.8	"	5.0	"	4.0	E.	4.0	NE.	15.0	"
20	10.9	"	6.3	SW.	25.3	S.	20.4	N.	25.2	"	18.2	E.	6.4	"	4.5	SW.	4.5	"	4.8	"	4.0	E.	15.0	N.
21	9.5	"	7.0	NW.	25.3	NW.	20.0	S.	25.5	"	17.8	S.	6.2	N.	4.0	S.	4.3	"	5.0	"	5.0	N.	15.2	"
22	8.0	NE.	7.5	S.	25.3	N.	19.6	"	25.7	W.	17.0	E.	6.0	E.	4.2	W.	4.5	N.	5.0	"	4.5	"	15.3	"
23	8.0	"	7.8	"	25.0	E.	19.2	"	25.7	E.	16.5	"	6.6	"	4.5	"	4.5	"	4.8	"	4.8	S.	16.0	"
24	7.5	"	8.2	N.	24.8	SW.	19.0	SE.	25.7	"	16.0	W.	7.0	"	5.2	"	4.5	E.	4.5	"	4.8	"	17.0	"
25	7.0	E.	8.8	"	24.5	S.	18.7	"	25.9	S.	15.5	"	7.2	W.	5.2	N.	4.0	"	4.8	"	4.8	"	18.0	S.
26	7.2	SW.	9.2	E.	24.3	W.	18.5	S.	26.2	N.	15.0	"	7.2	S.	5.5	E.	3.8	NE.	4.4	"	4.8	"	18.5	Calm.
27	6.5	W.	12.0	S.	23.3	NE.	18.2	E.	26.0	E.	14.7	N.	7.0	E.	5.5	N.	3.8	"	4.0	SE.	4.8	"	19.0	"
28	6.0	NW.	14.1	"	23.2	"	18.8	S.	26.0	NW.	14.5	S.	7.3	S.	5.2	E.	3.5	NW.	3.2	NW.	5.0	"	19.2	N.
29	5.5	N.	14.2		22.8	S.	19.0	"	26.2	"	14.0	E.	7.2	E.	5.5	"	4.0	"	3.2	NE.	5.5	N.	19.2	S.
30	5.0	"			22.2	"	19.2	E.	26.1	"	13.8	N.	7.0	W.	6.0	NE.	3.5	"	3.2	"	5.2	NE.	18.2	N.
31	5.0	E.			21.5	NW.			26.1	"			6.6	SW.	6.0	NW.			3.2	N.			17.2	S.

Records for 1857.

Columbus.—Observer, MR. J. M. MOORE.

Date.	January.		February.		March.		April.		May.		June.		July.		August.		September.		October.		November.		December.	
1857.	G'ge	Wind.	G'ge	Wind.	G'ge	Wind.	G'ge	Wind.	G'ge	Wind.	G'ge	Wind.	G'ge	Wind.	G'ge	Wind.	G'ge	Wind.	G'ge	Wind.	G'ge	Wind.	G'ge	Wind.
1																							8.0	
2																							7.5	
3																							7.0	
4																							7.5	
5																							8.0	
6																							9.0	
7																							10.0	
8																							12.0	
9																							14.0	
10																							16.9	SW.
11																							20.1	Calm.
12																							23.2	"
13																							25.8	"
14																							27.6	"
15																							29.0	"
16																							30.0	"
17																							30.8	"
18																							31.5	S.
19																							32.0	SW.
20																							32.2	NW.
21																							32.3	SE.
22																							32.0	NW.
23																							31.2	SE.
24																							29.9	"
25																							28.1	SW.
26																							26.0	N.
27																							24.0	SW.
28																							22.4	Calm.
29																							21.0	"
30																							20.3	"
31																							20.3	SW.

Records for 1857—Continued.

Donaldsonville.—Observer, MR. A. GINGRY.

Date.	January.		February.		March.		April.		May.		June.		July.		August.		September.		October.		November.		December.	
1857.	G'ge	Wind.	G'ge	Wind.	G'ge	Wind.	G'ge	Wind.	G'ge	Wind.	G'ge	Wind.	G'ge	Wind.	G'ge	Wind.	G'ge	Wind.	G'ge	Wind.	G'ge	Wind.	G'ge	Wind.
1	16.4	S.	7.8	N.	24.2	N.	19.0	N.	20.5	S.	23.0	NW.	17.0	W.	9.0	S.	5.5	E.	3.4	NE.	3.5	SE.	8.5	E.
2	16.2	"	7.5	"	24.3	"	18.5	"	20.6	N.	23.0	"	18.0	"	8.3	"	5.2	"	3.5	E.	3.5	S.	8.0	N.
3	15.5	N.	7.5	S.	24.4	"	17.5	E.	20.5	"	22.8	Calm.	18.8	SW.	8.2	"	5.0	"	3.4	"	3.4	E.	7.0	E.
4	15.4	"	7.5	"	24.6	S.	17.0	S.	20.0	NW.	22.7	S.	19.0	N.	8.0	W.	5.6	"	3.4	"	3.2	"	7.0	"
5	14.0	S.	7.8	"	25.0	E.	16.5	"	19.5	S.	22.5	W.	19.1	E.	8.0	"	6.5	"	3.4	"	3.5	"	7.0	SE.
6	13.8	NE.	8.0	"	25.3	N.	16.0	N.	19.3	SW.	22.0	SW.	19.5	"	7.8	SW.	6.5	"	3.4	"	3.8	"	7.0	S.
7	13.5	N.	9.0	"	25.5	E.	16.2	E.	19.0	S.	21.8	S.	19.8	"	7.5	E.	6.2	"	4.0	"	4.5	"	7.0	"
8	12.2	NE.	9.2	N.	25.6	"	17.8	"	19.0	E.	21.5	"	19.5	"	7.4	"	6.5	"	3.8	"	5.5	N.	8.0	SE.
9	12.0	"	9.5	"	25.7	N.	18.0	N.	19.0	S.	21.3	"	18.5	"	7.0	"	6.8	"	4.0	"	5.5	NW.	8.5	NW.
10	11.7	N.	10.0	"	25.7	E.	18.5	S.	18.8	"	21.0	"	17.2	"	7.0	"	6.8	"	4.0	"	5.0	NE.	9.0	N.
11	11.0	"	10.5	E.	25.3	N.	18.5	"	18.8	"	20.8	SW.	17.0	"	7.5	"	5.8	"	4.0	"	5.0	E.	9.5	SE.
12	10.8	"	11.3	"	26.3	"	18.5	N.	18.8	"	20.7	S.	16.5	"	7.5	"	5.8	S.	3.6	"	4.0	"	9.6	E.
13	10.0	W.	12.0	"	26.4	NW.	18.8	"	18.5	"	20.4	"	16.0	S.	7.5	"	5.0	"	3.6	"	3.5	"	9·5	"
14	10.1	E.	12.7	"	26.4	SW.	19.2	"	18.7	"	20.0	SE.	15.5	"	7.0	"	4.8	"	3.5	N.	3.5	N.	10.2	"
15	10.0	"	13.7	S.	26.4	NW.	20.0	E.	19.0	"	20.0	"	15.0	W.	6.8	"	4.5	W.	3.5	"	3.4	E.	10.5	"
16	9.8	"	14.8	"	26.0	Calm.	20.2	W.	19.6	"	19.8	"	14.5	N.	6.3	"	4.3	"	3.4	"	4.0	N.	11.3	NW.
17	9.5	SW.	15.5	"	26.5	SW.	20.3	SW.	20.5	N.	19.3	W.	14.0	E.	6.0		4.0	S.	3.4	E.	4.4	NW.	13.5	"
18	9.0	NW.	17.0	"	26.6	NW.	20.0	"	21.5	"	19.0	NW.	13.5	"	6.5	S.	4.0	E.	3.4	"	4.5	"	15.5	W.
19	8.5	NE.	18.5	"	26.5	Calm.	20.0	N.	21.5	NW.	18.8	"	13.0	S.	7.0	"	4.0	"	4.0	NE.	4.5	W.	18.0	E.
20	8.2	"	20.5	"	26.4	SW.	20.0	"	21.9	"	18.5	S.	12.5	"	7.0	"	4.0	N.	4.5	NW.	4.2	NW.	19.0	"
21	8.0	N.	21.4	NW.	25.9	S.	20.0	"	22.2	"	18.2	"	12.0	"	7.0	W.	3.8	"	5.0	E.	4.5	S.	20.0	W.
22	8.0	"	22.0	Calm.	25.7	"	20.0	"	22.5	W.	18.0	"	11.5	W.	7.2	E.	4.0	NW.	4.2	"	5.0	"	21.0	N.
23	8.0	E.	22.5	E.	25.2	E.	20.2	"	22.5	SW.	16.5	E.	11.0	S.	7.5	"	4.0	N.	4.2	W.	6.0	N.	21.5	E.
24	7.0	SE.	22.9	S.	24.6	"	20.3	"	22.7	"	16.0	"	11.0	"	7.2	"	4.5	W.	5.2	N.	6.5	NE.	22.0	NW.
25	7.0	E.	23.3	"	24.2	S.	20.3	E.	22.7	S.	15.8	S.	10.8	E.	7.2	"	4.0	E.	5.2	"	7.6	"	22.5	"
26	7.0	"	23.6	"	23.4	"	20.0	S.	23.0	"	15.8	"	10.5	"	7.2	W.	3.8	"	5.4	E.	8.7	E.	23.0	"
27	7.0	SW.	23.7	Calm.	22.7	"	20.1	NW.	23.0	N.	16.5	"	10.2	S.	7.2	S.	3.8	"	5.2	"	9.6	"	23.0	E.
28	7.0	Calm.	24.0	N.	21.9	N.	20.1	"	23.0	S.	16.5	W.	10.0	E.	7.0	"	3.8	"	4.8	N.	9.4	"	23.3	S.
29	6.5	"			20.9	"	20.1	S.	23.0	"	17.0	"	10.0	S.	6.5	"	3.5	NE.	3.5	E.	9.4	SE.	23.9	W.
30	7.0	NW.			20.0	E.	20.0	E.	23.0	"	17.0	"	10.0	"	6.3	N.	3.4	"	3.8	N.	9.0	NW.	24.0	NW.
31	7·2	"			19.5	S.			23.0	W.			10.0	"	6.0	E.			3.5	NW.			24.4	W.

Records for 1857—Continued.

Carrollton.—Observer, Mr. W. H. Williams.

Date.	January.		February.		March.		April.		May.		June.		July.		August.		September.		October.		November.		December.	
1857.	*G'ge*	*Wind.*	*G'ge*	*Wind.*	*G'ge*	*Wind.*	*G'ge*	*Wind.*	*G'ge*	*Wind.*	*G'ge*	*Wind.*	*G'ge*	*Wind.*	*G'ge*	*Wind.*	*G'ge*	*Wind.*	*G'ge*	*Wind.*	*G'ge*	*Wind.*	*G'ge*	*Wind.*
1																							3.0	SE.
2																							2.6	N.
3																							2.5	E.
4																					0.2	SE.	2.3	SE.
5																					0.5	SW.	2.2	S.
6																					0.9	"	2.6	W.
7																					1.5	S.	2.7	SW.
8																					1.6	N.	3.1	S.
9																					1.1	NW.	3.6	N.
10																					1.1	NE.	3.7	"
11																					1.0	E.	3.8	NE.
12																					0.7	S.	3.7	"
13																					0.4	NW.	3.7	"
14																					0.4	NE.	3.8	N.
15																					0.4	Calm.	3.9	E.
16																					0.9	NW.	4.4	"
17																					0.7	N.	5.1	W.
18																					0.5	W.	6.1	NE.
19																					0.6	NW.	6.9	E.
20																					0.3	N.	7.9	"
21																					0.4	SW.	8.8	NW.
22																					0.7	"	9.0	NE.
23																					1.6	"	9.6	E.
24																					1.1	E.	10.3	N.
25																					1.2	SE.	10.2	W.
26																					2.7	E.	10.5	"
27																					3.1	SE.	10.9	SE.
28																					3.6	"	11.0	S.
29																					3.8	NE.	11.4	N.
30																					3.4	"	11.5	"
31																							11.8	SW.

Records for 1858.

Cairo.—Observer, Mr. Arnold Syberg.

Date.	January.		February.		March.		April.		May.		June.		July.		August.		September.		October.		November.		December.	
1858.	*G'ge*	*Wind.*	*G'ge*	*Wind.*	*G'ge*	*Wind.*	*G'ge*	*Wind.*	*G'ge*	*Wind.*	*G'ge*	*Wind.*	*G'ge*	*Wind.*	*G'ge*	*Wind.*	*G'ge*	*Wind.*	*G'ge*	*Wind.*	*G'ge*	*Wind.*	*G'ge*	*Wind.*
1	18.8		14.0		10.4		31.0		32.1		33.8		29.3		19.1									
2	19.0		13.5		10.7		29.2		30.4		33.9		26.6		18.1									
3	19.2		13.5		11.6		27.2		28.3		34.2		24.2		17.1									
4	19.6		13.0		12.4		24.7		26.3		34.5		22.6		16.4									
5	20.5		12.9		15.7		22.6		25.0		34.9		21.3		15.9									
6	21.4		12.7		15.2		20.2		23.5		35.3		20.0		15.6									
7	22.3		12.5		15.6		18.1		23.0		35.6		18.8											
8	22.8		12.2		15.3		16.6		23.1		36.2		18.1											
9	22.9		12.0		15.1		15.4		24.4		36.6		17.2											
10	22.8		12.0		15.0		15.0		24.7		37.0		16.7											
11	22.0		11.2		15.0		15.0		26.3		37.4		16.1											
12	21.0		10.6		15.0		15.2		28.0		37.8		15.5											
13	20.0		10.1		15.3		18.2		28.7		38.2		15.5											
14	19.2		9.4		16.1		19.0		29.5		38.8		15.4											
15	18.0		9.2		16.4		22.2		30.2		39.4		15.3											
16	17.0		9.7		16.6		24.4		30.4		39.7		14.9											
17	17.4		10.7		16.4		25.3		30.4		39.8		14.6											
18	17.8		11.3		17.1		27.0		30.3		40.1		14.9											
19	18.5		11.5		18.2		28.0		30.3		40.2		15.0											
20	19.0		11.5		19.7		28.8		30.1		40.3		15.9											
21	18.9		11.3		22.7		30.6		30.1		40.4		17.7											
22	18.0		11.0		26.7		32.3		30.1		40.4		18.9											
23	17.5		10.0		28.6		33.7		30.1		40.1		19.8											
24	17.2		9.3		30.0		34.8		30.2		39.7		20.9								5.1			
25	16.9		9.3		31.2		35.5		31.7		39.2		21.5											
26	16.8		8.6		31.7		35.8		33.0		38.1		21.8											
27	16.3		9.2		32.3		35.8		33.3		37.4		21.8											
28	16.1		9.6		32.5		35.4		33.7		35.7		21.8											
29	15.8				32.4		34.8		33.8		33.9		21.6											
30	15.4				32.2		33.8		33.8		31.7		21.0											
31	14.1				31.7				33.8				20.3											

Records for 1858—Continued.

Columbus.—Observers, Mr. H. C. Fillebrown, Mr. J. M. Moore.

Date.	January.		February.		March.		April.		May.		June.		July.		August.		September.		October.		November.		December.	
1858.	*G'ge*	*Wind.*	*G'ge*	*Wind.*	*G'ge*	*Wind.*	*G'ge*	*Wind.*	*G'ge*	*Wind.*	*G'ge*	*Wind.*	*G'ge*	*Wind.*	*G'ge*	*Wind.*	*G'ge*	*Wind.*	*G'ge*	*Wind.*	*G'ge*	*Wind.*	*G'ge*	*Wind.*
1	21.0	SW.	17.8	N.	15.3	NW.	33.3	NW.	34.9	SE.	36.4	NE.	33.3	S.	23.4	S.	13.1	NE.	6.3	N.	6.0	NE.	7.0	S.
2	21.9	N.	17.5	SW.	16.1	W.	32.0	NE.	33.4	NE.	36.4	E.	30.8	"	22.4	"	12.7	SE.	6.1	SE.	7.0	"	7 2	"
3	22.7	"	17.3	NE.	16.9	NW.	30.2	SE.	31.5	E.	36.6	SE.	28.8	SE.	21.8	SE.	12.3	"	5.9	"	8.0	"	8.2	SE.
4	23.5	SE.	17.2	NW.	17.6	E.	28.1	NW.	29.5	S.	36.9	"	27.2	N.	21.2	"	11.9	SW.	5.7	SW.	9.3	SW.	9.8	E.
5	24.0	S.	17.0	SW.	18.8	NE.	26.0	SW.	28.0	NW.	37.3	"	26.0	NE.	20.7	S.	11.3	"	5.5	NE.	11.8	NW.	11.2	S.
6	24.9	Calm.	16.6	"	18.6	SW.	23.8	NE.	26.8	"	37.6	"	24.8	E.	20.5	SE.	10.9	SE.	5.3	SE.	14.7	SW.	12.6	"
7	25.6	NE.	16.5	"	18.7	NE.	21.9	E.	26.3	SW.	37.9	"	23.7	SE.	20.3	N.	10.4	"	5.1	NW.	15.9	NE.	14.0	"
8	26.1	Calm.	16.4	"	18.6	NW.	20.8	"	26.4	SE.	38.1	SW.	22.9	NE.	20.5	SE.	9.9	"	4.8	SW.	16.0	NW.	15.4	N.
9	26.0	S.	16.3	NE.	18.3	WSW.	19.3	SE.	26.9	NE.	38.4	SE.	22.2	SE.	20.9	N.	9.5	"	4.7	N.	15.9	SW.	16.9	SW.
10	25.5	"	16.1	N.	18.0	SE.	18.7	NE.	27.5	"	38.6	"	21.6	"	21.1	E.	9.2	W.	4.4	NE.	15.6	SE.	17.7	S.
11	25.0	SW.	15.8	E.	18.0	N.	18.7	SE.	29.4	SW.	38.9	NE.	20.9	SW.	20.9	SW.	9.0	NE.	4.2	W.	15.4	NE.	18.8	"
12	24.0	E.	15.3	"	18.3	"	20.0	"	31.0	SE.	39.1	NW.	20.6	NW.	20.7	NE.	8.8	N.	4.0	SE.	15.0	SE.	19.7	"
13	22.6	N.	14.9	SW.	18.8	E.	21.3	SW.	31.6	E.	39.5	N.	20.4	SE.	20.2	N.	9.1	NE.	3.9	S.	14.5	NW.	20.7	"
14	21.5	NE.	14.4	"	19.2	S.	23.2	"	32.2	SE.	39.8	NE.	20.4	"	19.8	NE.	10.4	N.	3.8	N.	14.0	SE.	22.0	"
15	20.7	Calm.	14.2	NE.	19.5	"	25.5	"	32.6	NW.	40.1	SE.	20.2	"	19.4	N.	11.4	SE.	3.6	SE.	13.5	NE.	24.5	N.
16	20.6	NW.	14.5	"	19.7	SE,	27.1	NE.	32.9	"	40.3	"	19.9	"	18.9	NW.	11.6	W.	3.5	"	13.0	"	26.0	S.
17	20.8	Calm.	15.5	N.	19.7	"	28.1	"	33.0	SW.	40.5	S.	19.6	"	18.6	"	11.5	NW.	3.4	"	12.5	"	26.7	"
18	21.2	NE.	16.0	E.	20.3	E.	29.3	"	33.0	N.	40.7	"	19.5	"	18.3	SW.	11.2	SE.	3.3	"	12.1	NW.	27.2	"
19	21.9	S.	16.4	NW.	21.5	"	30.4	SE.	32.9	S.	40.7	SE.	19.9	N.	17.9	N.	11.0	"	3.2	N.	11.7	"	27.7	"
20	22.3	E.	16.3	E.	23.4	SE.	31.2	"	32.8	N.	40.8	"	20.7	SW.	17.5	SW.	10.7	S.	3.1	SE.	11.4	W.	28.1	"
21	22.3	"	16.3	N.	26.3	S.	32.8	"	32.7	"	40.8	"	22.3	SE.	16.9	"	10.3	N.	3.1	N.	11.1		28.7	N.
22	21.8	"	15.8	NW.	29.1	NE.	34.4	"	32.7	"	40.9	"	23.7	SW.	16.5	N.	9.9	NE.	3.2	"	10.8		28.0	S.
23	21.0	SE.	14.9	NE.	30.9	"	35.7	N.	32.8	S.	40.8	"	24.2	"	15.9	NE.	9.4	S.	3.2	NW.	10.1	"	28.2	"
24	20.1	E.	14.3	S.	32.2	"	36.7	NW.	33.1	"	40.7	"	24.8	NE.	15.3	"	8.8	SE.	3.2	NE.	9.7	SW.	28.5	N.
25	19.3	SE.	13.9	NE.	33.2	E.	37.2	N.	34.2	SE.	40.2	"	25.4	SE.	14.7	"	8.3	N.	3.4	SE.	9.2	N.	28.9	S.
26	18.7	SW	13.6	SE.	34.0	SE.	37.4	"	35.4	"	39.8	"	25.9	SW.	13.9	SE.	7.8	"	3.5	"	8.7	E.	29.2	"
27	18.0	"	13.9	W.	34.4	"	37.3	S.	35.9	"	39.1	"	26.2	S.	13.7	"	7.3	SE.	3.6	NE.	8.1	S.	29.5	NW.
28	17.3	"	14.6	NW.	34.7	NE.	37.2	"	36.2	"	38.0	N.	26.2	SE.	13.4	NE.	7.0	S.	3.7	SE.	8.0	"	29.5	S.
29	17.3	NW.			34.7	"	36.8	"	36.3	"	36.7	NE.	25.9	"	13.0	"	6.8	SE.	3.9	"	7.4	W.	29.2	"
30	17.7	"			34.5	"	36.1	"	36.3	"	35.0	S.	25.4	S.	12.9	"	6.5	"	4.1	"	7.1	N.	28.6	"
31	17.8	"			34.1	"			36.3	"			24.3	"	13.3	"			4.9	"			27.8	"

Records for 1858*—Continued.

Memphis.—Observer, Mr. Michael Conway.

Date.	January.		February.		March.		April.		May.		June.		July.		August.		September.		October.		November.		December.	
1858.	*G'ge*	*Wind.*	*G'ge*	*Wind.*	*G'ge*	*Wind.*	*G'ge*	*Wind.*	*G'ge*	*Wind.*	*G'ge*	*Wind.*	*G'ge*	*Wind.*	*G'ge*	*Wind.*	*G'ge*	*Wind.*	*G'ge*	*Wind.*	*G'ge*	*Wind.*	*G'ge*	*Wind.*
1	21.6	SW.	17.6	NE.	14.1	NE.	33.4	NW.	34.5	NW.	34.1	SE.	35.0	SW.	26.3	SW.	13.3	SW.	7.3	SW.	4.5	NE.	7.2	SE.
2	20.9	NE.	17.9	NW.	14.6	NW.	33.5	SW.	34.7	SW.	34.3	"	34.9	"	26.0	NW.	13.2	SE.	7.1	"	4.9	SW.	7.1	SW.
3	20.9	"	17.7	NE.	14.8	SW.	32.8	"	34.6	"	34.3	SW.	34.7	NE.	25.8	"	13.0	NW.	6.9	"	5.6	"	7.0	"
4	21.4	NW.	17.6	NW.	15.9	"	32.6	"	34.4	"	34.4	SE.	34.5	"	25.3	SE.	13.0	SW.	6.8	"	5.9	NW.	6.9	"
5	22.1	SW.	17.4	"	17.6	NW.	31.8	NE.	34.1	NW.	34.6	NW.	34.9	"	24.4	SW.	12.8	SE.	6.6	NE.	6.4	NE.	6.7	NE.
6	22.9	NE.	17.1	SW.	18.5	"	30.4	"	33.5	"	34.7	SW.	33.2	"	22.8	SE.	12.5	SW.	6.3	SW.	6.8	"	6.5	NW.
7	23.5	SW.	16.9	NW.	19.6	"	28.2	SW.	32.8	"	34.7	"	32.0	SE.	21.0	SW.	12.0	SE.	6.3	"	7.0	NW.	6.3	SW.
8	24.3	"	16.7	SW.	19.4	NE.	26.0	"	31.7	SE.	34.7	SE.	30.6	NW.	20.7	NW.	11.6	NW.	6.1	"	9.1	NE.	7.7	"
9	24.9	"	16.4	NE.	19.1	"	24.0	SE.	30.7	SW.	34.8	SW.	28.8	NE.	20.9	SW.	11.0	SW.	5.9	"	10.3	NW.	8.5	NE.
10	25.5	"	16.2	SW.	19.0	SW.	22.8	"	30.1	NW.	34.9	"	27.5	SE.	21.0	SE.	10.2	NW.	5.8	SE.	11.6	SW.	8.0	NW.
11	25.9	"	16.0	NE.	18.7	"	21.5	"	29.8	SW.	35.1	NW.	26.3	NE.	21.2	SW.	9.9	SE.	5.6	SW.	12.4	NE.	9.8	"
12	25.8	"	15.9	"	18.5	NE.	20.8	"	29.9	"	35.1	"	25.0	"	21.4	"	9.3	NE.	5.4	"	12.6	"	10.4	NE.
13	25.6	NW.	15.5	NW.	18.4	SW.	21.0	SW.	30.3	"	35.2	"	23.9	SE.	21.2	NE.	9.5	SW.	5.2	SE.	13.6	SW.	11.2	SE.
14	24.9	SW.	15.3	"	18.6	"	21.8	SE.	30.8	"	35.2	"	23.1	"	21.0	NW.	9.0	NW.	5.1	NW.	13.4	"	12.6	SW.
15	23.7	"	15.1	NE.	18.9	"	23.2	NE.	31.2	NW.	35.2	SW.	22.5	"	20.8	SE.	9.2	"	5.0	SW.	12.9	NE.	13.3	"
16	23.1	"	14.7	SE.	19.3	SE.	24.9	"	31.7	SW.	35.1	SE.	22.1	SW.	20.5	NE.	9.9	"	4.9	SE.	12.6	SW.	14.7	NE.
17	22.3	NE.	14.3	NE.	19.6	SW.	26.5	SW.	32.0	NW	35.0	"	21.6	NE.	20.4	SW.	10.3	NE.	4.8	SW.	11.8	"	15.0	NW.
18	22.0	NW.	14.6	SW.	19.9	"	27.7	SE.	32.2	NE.	35.0	"	21.1	"	20.3	SE.	11.0	S.	4.7	"	11.5	NE.	15.9	SW.
19	22.0	"	14.9	NW.	20.3	"	28.8	"	32.4	NW.	35.1	"	20.8	"	20.0	NW.	11.5	"	4.6	NE.	11.1	"	16.7	SE.
20	22.2	"	15.4	NE.	20.9	SE.	29.7	SW.	32.6	"	35.2	NW.	20.5	NW.	19.5	NE.	12 2	"	4.4	SW.	10.9	NW.	17.5	NE.
21	22.4	SW.	15.7	"	22.6	"	30.5	"	32.6	"	35.2	"	21.0	"	19.0	SE.	11.5	NW.	4.3	NW.	10.7	SW.	19.0	NW.
22	22.6	"	15.9	NW.	24.9	NE.	31.4	NW.	32.6	SE.	35.2	"	21.6	SW.	18.6	SW.	10.9	NE.	4.2	SE.	10.5	"	19.9	SW.
23	22.5	NE.	16.1	"	26.4	SW.	32.2	"	32.6	SW.	35.3	SE.	22.8	NW.	18.0	SE.	10.5	SE.	4.1	NW.	10.2	SE.	20.8	"
24	22.1	"	15.8	SW.	28.4	"	32.8	SW.	32.7	NE.	35.2	SW.	23.8	SW.	17.5	NW.	9.9	SW.	4.0	SW.	9.9	NE.	22.6	SE.
25	21.7	"	15.2	"	29.7	"	33.2	NW.	32.8	SE.	35.2	"	24.9	"	16.0	"	9.6	NE.	4.0	SE.	9.7	NW.	22.8	NE.
26	20.3	SW.	14.8	"	30.8	"	33.5	NE.	32.9	"	35.2	SE.	25.2	"	15.6	NE.	9.2	"	4.0	NE.	9.5	"	24.6	NW
27	19.8	NE.	14.2	NE.	31.6	"	33.8	NW.	33.3	NW.	35.2	"	25.6	SE.	15.0	SW.	8.8	NW.	4.0	NW.	8.7	SE.	25.4	"
28	19.1	NW.	14.2	NW.	32.2	"	34.1	SE.	33.5	NE.	35.2	"	26.2	SW.	14.3	NE.	8.4	SE.	4.1	SW.	8.3	NW.	26.0	SE.
29	18.7	NE.			32.7	"	34.3	SW.	33.7	SE.	35.1	NW.	26.4	NE.	14.0	SW.	7.9	"	4.2	NW.	7.8	SW.	27.1	SW.
30	18.1	SE.			32.9	NE.	34.5	"	33.9	SW.	35.0	NE.	26.6	SW.	13.9	NW.	7.6	"	4.4	SE.	7.4	SE.	28.0	NW.
31	17.7	NE.			33.2	"			34.1	"			26.5	NE.	13.5	SE.			4.3	NW.			29.2	SW.
*1857																								
22																							30.7	
23																							31.1	
24																							31.2	NE.
25																							31.1	SW.
26																							30.6	SE.
27																							29.7	NW.
28																							28.8	SW.
29																							26.6	"
30																							25.5	NE.
31																							22.9	SW.

Records for 1858—Continued.

Helena.

Date.	January.		February.		March.		April.		May.		June.		July.		August.		September.		October.		November.		December.	
1858.	G'ge	Wind.	G'ge	Wind.	G'ge	Wind.	G'ge	Wind.	G'ge	Wind.	G'ge	Wind.	G'ge	Wind.	G'ge	Wind.	G'ge	Wind.	G'ge	Wind.	G'ge	Wind.	G'ge	Wind.
1	38.8						40.9		41.3		40.3		44.9											
2							41.0		41.4		40.4		45.0											
3							41.0		41.5		40.4		45.0											
4							40.9		41.5		40.5		45.0											
5							40.5		41.5		40.6		45.0											
6							40.0		41.3		40.8		45.0											
7							39.4		41.0		40.9		44.9											
8							38.6		40.6		41.0		44.8											
9							37.8		40.4		41.1		44.5											
10							37.0		40.2		41.2		44.2											
11							35.5		39.8		41.3		43.7											
12							34.5		39.7		41.4		43.0											
13							33.0		39.6		41.5		42.2											
14							31.7		39.5		41.6		41.3											
15							31.0		39.5		41.8		40.5											
16							31.0		39.5		42.0		39.6											
17							31.5		39.5		42.1		39.0											
18							32.3		39.5		42.2		38.3											
19							33.5		39.5		42.4		37.6											
20							34.5		39.6		42.6		37.0											
21					29.5		36.0		39.6		42.8													
22					31.0		37.0		39.7		42.9													
23					32.5		38.0		39.7		43.1													
24					34.0		39.0		39.8		43.3													
25					35.5		39.5		39.8		43.5													
26			21.7		37.0		40.0		39.9		43.7													
27					38.0		40.5		40.0		44.0													
28					38.6		40.8		40.0		44.2													
29					39.5		41.0		4 ·.1		44.5													
30					40.0		41.2		40.2		44.7													
31					40.5				40.3															

Records for 1858*—Continued.

Napoleon.—Observer, Mr. A. A. Edington.

Date.	January.		February.		March.		April.		May.		June.		July.		August.		September.		October.		November.		December.	
1858.	G'ge	Wind.	G'ge	Wind.	G'ge	Wind.	G'ge	Wind.	G'ge	Wind.	G'ge	Wind.	G'ge	Wind.	G'ge	Wind.	G'ge	Wind.	G'ge	Wind.	G'ge	Wind.	G'ge	Wind.
1	36.0	Calm.	33.6	NW.	25.0	NW.	44.5	S.	43.4	Calm.	44.4	Calm.	44.7	SE.	37.8	S.	18.9	S.	12.5	S.	5.2	N.	5.5	NW.
2	34.9	N.	33.2	N.	24.6	"	45.0	Calm.	43.7	"	44.4	S.	44.6	S.	37.3	"	18.4	"	12.1	"	5.1	"	6.1	W.
3	33.6	NW.	33.1	NW.	24.4	N.	45.1	"	43.7	SW.	44.4	"	44.7	SW.	35.9	SE.	18.1	N.	11.7	"	5.0	"	7.0	"
4	32.9	NE.	32.8	"	24.6	NE.	45.2	"	43.9	"	44.5	"	44.7	"	35.5	S.	17.9	S.	11.3	"	4.6	"	8.4	SW.
5	32.2	NW.	32.5	N.	24.8	E.	45.3	"	43.9	W.	44.6	SE.	44.7	"	34.8	E.	17.8	"	11.0	Calm.	5.1	"	9.9	S.
6	31.9	S.	32.0	S.	25.5	"	45.4	"	44.1	Calm.	44.7	SW.	44.8	NW.	34.1	SW.	17.7	"	10.5	"	6.1	"	12.1	"
7	31.9	NW.	31.6	N.	26.4	"	45.4	"	44.1	"	44.8	S.	44.8	NE.	33.6	"	17.2	"	10.1	"	7.6	"	14.0	"
8	32.0	E.	30.8	S.	27.2	N.	45.1	"	44.1	"	45.0	Calm.	44.7	Calm.	32.2	SE.	16.7	"	10.0	N.	8.9	"	15.5	W.
9	32.2	W.	30.3	SW.	27.8	W.	44.8	E.	44.1	"	45.1	S.	44.7	SW.	31.8	SW.	16.1	"	9.7	"	10.1	NW.	17.1	"
10	32.3	S.	30.0	N.	29.3	S.	44.4	"	44.1	"	45.2	"	44.6	SE.	31.3	"	15.6	"	9.4	"	11.1	W.	18.1	"
11	32.2	SW.	30.0	SE.	30.0	"	44.0	"	44.1	W.	45.2	"	44.5	SW.	30.8	"	15.1	"	9.1	"	12.1	S.	19.7	NE.
12	32.7	W.	29.6	N.	30.1	"	43.2	S.	43.9	S.	45.2	NW.	44.0	N.	29.6	S.	14.6	"	8.9	"	13.4	"	20.1	"
13	33.5	SW.	29.4	E.	30.3	"	42.2	W.	43.8	"	45.2	"	43.8	Calm.	29.1	"	14.1	"	8.7	NW.	14.1	E.	22.4	"
14	34.2	"	29.1	SE.	30.6	"	41.2	"	43.8	"	45.3	Calm.	43.6	"	28.8	NW.	13.6	NW.	8.5	"	14.5	"	24.1	"
15	34.8	Calm.	28.8	S.	30.7	"	40.2	S.	43.9	"	45.3	"	43.3	"	28.1	N.	13.3	"	8.3	"	14.7	NE.	25.9	W.
16	35.3	"	28.4	"	30.8	"	39.9	"	43.9	"	45.3	S.	42.8	"	27.6	E.	13.2	"	8.1	S.	14.8	"	27.8	SW.
17	35.0	"	28.0	"	30.9	"	39.5	"	43.9	"	45.3	SW.	42.1	"	27.1	SE.	13.1	NE.	7.9	"	14.9	E.	30.0	S.
18	34.8	"	27.5	"	31.0	"	39.5	"	43.9	N.	45.3	"	41.4	"	26.8	S.	13.5	Calm.	7.7	"	15.1	SE.	31.7	"
19	34.4	"	27.1	N.	31.3	SE.	40.0	"	44.2	W.	45.3	S.	41.0	"	26.6	N.	14.1	"	7.5	SW.	14.8	N.	33.6	"
20	33.9	"	27.0	"	32.4	"	40.2	"	44.2	N.	45.2	Calm,	40.6	"	26.1	Calm.	14.6	"	7.3	"	14.3	"	35.3	"
21	33.7	"	27.0	"	33.5	S.	40.5	"	44.2	"	45.2	"	39.4	"	25.6	"	15.1	"	7.1	SE.	13.5	"	36.1	"
22	33.5	"	27.2	E	34.9	"	40.7	"	44.2	SE.	45.1	S.	38.1	S.	25.1	SW.	15.6	"	7.0	E.	12.3	"	36.5	SE.
23	33.4	SW.	27.4	S.	35.9	"	41.1	"	44.2	S.	45.1	SE.	38.2	NE.	24.8	"	16.2	"	6.9	N.	11.1	W.	36.7	"
24	33.4	"	27.3	"	37.2	"	41.3	W.	44.1	SE.	45.0	S.	38.2	"	24.4	S.	16.7	"	6.7	NW.	9.7	SW.	36.5	E.
25	33.2	Calm.	27.2	Calm.	38.4	"	41.7	Calm.	44.2	"	45.0	SE.	38.2	N.	23.9	"	16.6	"	6.5	W.	8.3	S.	36.1	NE.
26	33.1	"	26.8	"	39.8	"	42.1	N.	44.3	SW.	45.0	S.	38.1	Calm.	23.4	W.	16.1	S.	6.3	NW.	7.5	E.	35.8	"
27	33.5	"	26.2	N.	40.5	"	42.4	SE.	44.2	SE.	45.0	"	38.1	"	22.8	N.	15.5	SE.	6.1	S.	6.1	NE.	35.4	"
28	33.9	W.	25.6	"	41.4	"	42.8	"	44.1	SW.	44.9	"	38.1	S.	22.4	"	15.1	SW.	5.9	SW.	5.6	N.	35.1	W.
29	34.0	NW.			42.5	"	43.2	S.	44.2	S.	44.8	N.	38.1	SW.	21.6	"	14.3	S.	5.7	W.	5.1	"	34.6	SW.
30	34.1	N.			43.4	"	43.3	"	44.3	"	44.7	Calm.	38.1	S.	20.8	"	13.1	"	5.5	NW.	5.1	"	34.1	S.
31	33.7	NW.			44.1	"			44.3	SW.			38.1	Calm.	19.7	S.			5.3	N.			33.4	"
*1857																								
26																							37.7	
27																							38.0	
28																							38.2	
29																							38.0	
30																							37.7	
31																							36.9	SW.

Records for 1858—Continued.

Lake Providence.

Date.	January.		February.		March.		April.		May.		June.		July.		August.		September.		October.		November.		December.	
1858.	*G'ge*	*Wind.*	*G'ge*	*Wind.*	*G'ge*	*Wind.*	*G'ge*	*Wind.*	*G'ge*	*Wind.*	*G'ge*	*Wind.*	*G'ge*	*Wind.*	*G'ge*	*Wind.*	*G'ge*	*Wind.*	*G'ge*	*Wind.*	*G'ge*	*Wind.*	*G'ge*	*Wind.*
1							45.6		47.1		45.9		45.8		43.5									
2							46.2		47.1		45.9		45.8		43.1									
3							46.7		47.1		45.9		45.8		42.1									
4							47.1		47.0		45.9		45.8		42.3									
5							47.3		47.0		45.9		45.8		41.8									
6							47.4		46.9		45.9		45.8		41.4									
7							47.5		46.8		45.9		45.8		40.8									
8							47.6		46.7		45.9		45.8		40.3									
9							47.5		46.6		45.9		45.8		39.8									
10							47.3		46.6		45.9		45.8		39.4									
11							46.9		46.5		45.9		45.8		38.8									
12							46.5		46.5		45.9		45.8		38.1									
13							46.1		46.4		45.9		45.8		37.5									
14							45.6		46.3		45.9		45.8		36.9									
15							45.2		46.2		45.9		45.8		36.0									
16							44.8		46.2		45.9		45.8		35.6									
17							44.6		46.2		45.9		45.8		35.1									
18							44.7		46.2		45.9		45.8		34.5									
19							44.8		46.1		45.9		45.8		34.0									
20					37.6		44.9		46.1		45.8		45.8		33.5									
21					38.4		45.1		46.1		45.8		45.8		33.0									
22	43.7				39.1		45.3		46.1		45.8		45.8											
23					40.3		45.6		46.1		45.8		45.8											
24			32.1		40.9		45.9		46.0		45.8		45.8											
25					41.1		46.1		46.0		45.8		45.6											
26					42.1		46.3		46.0		45.8		45.4											
27					43.1		46.5		46.0		45.8		45.1											
28					43.9		46.8		45.9		45.8		44.8											
29					44.6		47.0		45.9		45.8		44.6											
30					45.1		47.1		45.9		45.8		44.2											
31					45.3				45.9				43.8											

Records for 1858—Continued.

Vicksburg.—Observers, Lieutenant H. S. Putnam, Mr. H. A. Pattison, Mr. J. J. Conway.

Date.	January.		February.		March.		April.		May.		June.		July.		August.		September.		October.		November.		December.	
1858.	*G'ge*	*Wind.*	*G'ge*	*Wind.*	*G'ge*	*Wind.*	*G'ge*	*Wind.*	*G'ge*	*Wind.*	*G'ge*	*Wind.*	*G'ge*	*Wind.*	*G'ge*	*Wind.*	*G'ge*	*Wind.*	*G'ge*	*Wind.*	*G'ge*	*Wind.*	*G'ge*	*Wind.*
1					31.3	NE.	44.4	NE.	46.9	SE.	47.6	SW.	48.1	SW.	46.2	SW.	26.7	SW.	16.2	SW.	8.7	SW. & W.	17.0	NE.
2					30.5	NW.	44.9	"	47.0		4[illegible].6	"	48.1	"	46.0	"	25.8	"	15.6	"	8.7	W.	16.5	E.
3					30.0	"	45.4	SE.	47.2		47.7	"	48.1	"	45.9	"	24.8	NE.	15.1	"	8.7	N&W.	15.9	SE.
4					29.5	S.	45.7	"	47.2	"	47.8	"	48.1	"	45.7	"	24.0	SW.	14.5	"	9.0	NW.	15.4	NE.
5					29.2	SW.	45.8	"	47.3	"	47.8	"	48.1	"	45.4	E.	23.5	E. & SW.	14.2	"	9.7	"	15.1	E.
6					29.1	"	46.0	"	47.3	"	47.8	"	48.0	"	45.0	NW.	23.1	SW.	13.9	SE.	10.7	"	14.6	"
7					29.2	N.	46.1	"	47.3	NE.	47.9	"	48.1	NE.	44.6	"	22.8	"	13.4	"	12.5	"	14.8	
8					29.7	NW.	46.3	"	47.3	"	47.9	"	48.1	"	44.3	"	22.4	"	13.0	"	15.1	"	15.3	NW.
9					30.2	SW.	46.4	"	47.4	SE.	47.9	SE.	48.1	SW.	43.7	"	21.9	"	12.6	SW.	16.9	"	15.9	N.
10					30.9	"	46.5	"	47.5	"	47.9	"	48.1	"	43.0	SW.	21.4	SW. & N.	12.3		19.7	SE.	17.0	E.
11					31.5	"	46.6	NW.	47.5	"	48.0	SW.	48.1	"	42.4	SE. & SW.	20.8	NE.	12.1		21.8	NW.	18.6	
12					32.0	NE.	46.6	"	47.5	Calm.	48.1	"	48.1	NW.	42.0	SW.	20.1	"	11.8	W.	23.4	"	20.5	SE.
13					32.5	S.	46.6	SW.	47.4	SE.	48.1	"	48.1	NE.	41.3	NW.	19.5	"	11.5	Calm.	24.7	"	22.6	SW.
14					33.2	SW.	46.4	"	47.4	"	48.1	Calm.	48.1	E.	40.8	N.	18.9	"	11.2	N.	25.2	SE.	24.8	"
15					33.6	SE.	46.2	SE.	47.4	"	48.1	"	48.1	"	40.0	NW.	18.3	NW.	10.9	NE.	25.5	NW.	26.3	NW.
16					33.8	S.	45.9	SSE.	47.3	"	48.1	NE.	48.1	"	39.7	N.	17.8	"	10.6	SE.	25.3	NE.	27.4	NE.
17			34.5	Calm.	34.0	Calm.	45.7	"	47.3	"	48.1	E.	48.1	SW.	39.3	E. & NW.	17.3	"	10.3		25.1	"	28.9	Calm.
18			34.1		34.2	SW.	45.6	SE.	47.4	NW.	48.1	"	48.1	NW.	38.8	NW.	17.0	NE.	10.1		24.5	N.	30.2	"
19			33.7		34.3	S.	45.4	"	47.4	"	48.1	SE.	48.0	"	38.3	"	17.0	NW.	9.8		24.0	NE.	31.7	S.
20			33.4		34.5	SE.	45.8	SW.	47.5	SE.	48.1	SW.	48.0	E.	37.5	"	17.3	"	9.6		23.5	W.	33.1	Calm.
21			33.1	S.	35.3	SW.	45.7	SE.	47.5	"	48.1	"	47.8	SW.	36.6	"	17.8	"	9.4		22.8	NW.	34.6	W.
22			32.9	NW.	36.0	NE.	45.8	"	47.5	"	48.2	"	47.7	"	36.1	"	18.4	"	9.2		22.2	W.	35.7	SW.
23			32.8	"	37.0	NW.	45.9	NE.	47.5	SW.	48.2	"	47.6	"	35.6		18.5	"	9.1	SW.	21.6	"	36.7	N.
24			32.6	"	37.9	"	46.0	"	47.5	SE.	48.2	"	47.5	NW.	34.8	"	18.6	"	8.9	"	20.9	NE.	37.3	NE.
25			32.5	Calm.	38.9	S.	46.1	SE.	47.5	"	48.2	"	47.3	"	34.4	"	18.5	"	8.8	"	20.3	"	38.0	"
26			32.2	NW.	39.9	"	46.3	NW.	47.5	NW.	48.3	"	47 1	NE.	33.4	"	18.4	"	8.6	SE.	19.7	Calm.	38.7	N.
27			32.0	S.	40.8	"	46.4	SE.	47.6	SW.	48.3	"	47.0	E.	33.0	SW.	18.1	"	8.9	"	19.1	SE.	39.2	"
28			37.7	"	41.7	"	46.5	"	47.6	"	48.2	"	46.8	SW.	31.8	NW.	17.7	NE. & NW.	8.8	SW.	18.6	"	39.7	S.
29					42.3	SE.	46.7	"	47.6	"	48.2	"	46.7	"	30.2	"	17.3	NE. & SW.	8.7	"	18.1	NE.	40.0	"
30					42.9	"	46.9	"	47.6	"	48.2	"	46.6	"	29.0	"	16.8	SW.	8.6	Calm.	17.6	NW.	40.5	"
31					43.7	NE.			47.6	"			46.4	"	2.97	"			8.6	SW.			40.7	N.

Records for 1858—Continued.

Natchez.—Observers, Lieutenant H. S. Putnam, Mr. R. F. Learned.

Date.	January.		February.		March.		April.		May.		June.		July.		August.		September.		October.		November.		December.	
1858.	*G'ge*	*Wind.*	*G'ge*	*Wind.*	*G'ge*	*Wind.*	*G'ge*	*Wind.*	*G'ge*	*Wind.*	*G'ge*	*Wind.*	*G'ge*	*Wind.*	*G'ge*	*Wind.*	*G'ge*	*Wind.*	*G'ge*	*Wind.*	*G'ge*	*Wind.*	*G'ge*	*Wind.*
1	43.8		44.6	SSW.	37.7	N.	47.4	NW.	51.3	SE.	51.9	SW.	52.5	S.	50.8	SW.	32.6	SW.	18.7	SW.	10.5	SW.	20.4	S.
2	44.1		44.6	SW.	37.4	SW.	48.0	SW.	51.4	"	51.9	"	52.4	"	50.7	"	31.5	"	18.2	"	10.4	"	19.9	"
3	44.2		44.6	NE.	36.9	NW.	48.4	"	51.7	SW.	51.9	"	52.4	"	50.5	"	30.2	"	17.7	"	10.4	NW.	19.2	"
4	44.1		44.6	"	36.4	Calm.	48.7	S.	51.8	S.	52.0	S.	52.3	SW.	50.4	"	29.4	"	17.2	"	10.4	W.	18.7	"
5	43.8	S.	44.5	NW.	35.9	S.	49.1	SW.	51.9	"	52.0	"	52.2	"	50.2	SE.	28.3	"	16.6	"	10.7	NW.	18.2	SW.
6	43.4	Calm.	44.1	E.	35.5	"	49.3	S.	51.9	"	52.0	"	52.2	"	50.0	S.	27.4	S.	16.1	"	11.3	"	17.6	"
7	42.9	N.	43.7	NE.	35.5	NE.	49.5	"	51.9	W.	52.1	"	52.2	"	49.7	E.	26.8	SE.	15.6	NW.	12.5	"	17.3	S.
8	42.6	Calm.	43.4	SW.	35.5	N.	49.7	"	51.9	S.	52.1	SW	52.2	W.	49.4	SE.	26.3	W.	15.1	"	14.0	"	17.4	NW.
9	42.2	SE.	43.0	"	35.8	SW.	49.9	"	51.9	SE.	52.2	"	52.2	S.	49.0	S.	25.8	S.	14.7	W.	16.0	"	17.6	"
10	42.1	"	42.6	NE.	36.1	"	50.1	"	52.0	SW.	52.2	"	52.2	"	48.6	SW.	25.2	SW.	14.4	S.	18.8	SW.	18.4	"
11	42.1	NW.	42.3	"	36.6	S.	50.3	SW.	52.0	"	52.2	"	52.2	"	47.8	"	24.8	NW.	13.9	NW.	20.5	N.	19.4	SE.
12	42.2	SE.	42.1	"	37.1	N.	50.3	W.	52.0	W.	52.4	W.	52.2	NW.	47.3	NW.	24.0	"	13.9	"	23.6	W.	20.6	"
13	42.9	NE.	42.3	NW.	37.6	S.	50.4	SW.	52.0	SW.	52.5	NW.	52.2	"	46.9	W.	23.2	"	13.6	"	25.3	"	21.8	"
14	43.2	Calm.	42.3	"	38.2	SE.	50.3	"	51.9	"	52.4	"	52.3	"	46.4	NW.	22.4	"	13.3	"	26.4	SE.	25.0	S.
15	44.4	SE.	42.0	"	38.7	S.	50.3	S.	51.9	S.	52.4	"	52.2	"	45.9	"	21.6	W.	13.0	"	27.3	NW.	27.0	NW.
16	44.8	NW.	41.6	SW.	39.1	"	50.3	"	51.8	"	52.5	"	52.2	"	45.3	"	20.9	NW.	12.7	W.	27.6	"	29.0	"
17	45.0	"	41.4	Calm.	39.3	"	50.2	SW.	51.8	"	52.5	S.	52.2	"	44.9	"	20.3	"	12.4	SE.	27.7	"	30.7	"
18	45.3	NE.	41.0	SE.	39.5	"	50.1	SE.	51.7	"	52.4	"	52.1	N.	44.5	"	19.7	"	12.2	E.	27.5	"	32.0	W.
19	45.2	"	40.4	NW.	39.6	"	50.1	"	51.7	W.	52.4	NW.	52.1	NW.	44.0	SW.	19.3	"	11.9	NE.	27.2	"	33.3	SE.
20	45.1	NNW.	40.3	SE.	39.7	"	50.4	W.	51.8	"	52.4	SW.	52.1	S.	43.4	W.	19.1	N.	11.6	N.	26.8	W.	35.0	"
21	45.0	W.	40.0	S.	39.9	N.	50.4	"	51.8	"	52.4	W.	52.1	"	42.7	SW.	19.3	NW.	11.4	NW.	26.2	E.	36.7	NE.
22	44.8	ENE.	39.7	N.	40.4	S.	50.3	S.	51.8	SW.	52.4	S.	52.0	SW.	42.2	W.	19.6	"	11.2	"	25.7	W.	37.8	S.
23	44.6	SE.	39.4	"	41.1	NW.	50.3	N.	51.8	S.	52.4	"	51.9	"	41.4	N.	20.0	"	11.0	SW.	25.2	NW.	38.9	W.
24	44.6	NE.	39.2	NW.	41.9	"	50.3	SW.	51.8	"	52.4	SE.	51.8	W.	40.7	"	20.3	SW.	11.0	"	24.5	"	39.9	N.
25	44.6	NW.	39.0	"	42.7	"	50.4	"	51.8	"	52.5	"	51.7	NW.	40.0	"	20.4	"	10.8	"	23.7	W.	40.6	E.
26	44.5	NE.	38.8	W.	43.5	SW.	50.6	N.	51.9	SW.	52.5	W.	51.6	N.	39.1	S.	20.4	NW.	10.7	S.	23.2	SW.	41.7	N.
27	44.5	NW.	38.6	S.	44.2	S.	50.8	NW.	51.9	"	52.5	E.	51.4	E.	38.3	W.	20.3	"	10.9	"	22.6	"	42.2	NW.
28	44.3	"	38.3	"	45.1	"	50.8	SW.	51.9	S.	52.5	"	51.3	S.	37.1	NW.	20.0	"	11.0	SW.	21.9	S.	42.6	"
29	44.3	NNW.			45.8	"	50.9	"	51.9	SW.	52.5	SE.	51.2	"	36.1	"	19.6	W.	10.8	"	21.5	NW.	43.1	S.
30	44.3	SE.			46.2	"	51.1	"	51.8	S.	52.5	S.	51.1	SW.	34.9	"	19.2	S.	10.6	"	21.0	"	43.4	SW.
31	44.4	"			47.0	NW.			51.9	SW.			51.0	"	33.8	"			10.5	"			43.5	NW.

Records for 1858—Continued.

Red-river landing.—Observer, Mr. Miguel Torras.

Date.	January.		February.		March.		April.		May.		June.		July.		August.		September.		October.		November.		December.	
1858.	*G'ge*	*Wind.*	*G'ge*	*Wind.*	*G'ge*	*Wind.*	*G'ge*	*Wind.*	*G'ge*	*Wind.*	*G'ge*	*Wind.*	*G'ge*	*Wind.*	*G'ge*	*Wind.*	*G'ge*	*Wind.*	*G'ge*	*Wind.*	*G'ge*	*Wind.*	*G'ge*	*Wind.*
1			39.0	NW.	34.8	N.	39.7	NW.	44.4	S.	45.2	S.	45.4	S.	44.8	Calm.	30.0	N.	12.9	S.	6.3	NW.	15.5	N.
2			39.0	"	34.6	"	40.1	Calm.	44.5	"	45.2	"	45.4	"	44.7	"	28.8	S.	12.4	"	6.2	N.	15.0	S.
3			39.0	NE.	34.2	"	40.5	S.	44.9	"	45.2	"	45.4	"	44.6	S.	27.5	"	11.9	"	6.1	"	14.5	"
4			39.0	N.	33.8	Calm.	40.8	SE.	45.0	"	45.2	"	45.4	"	44.5	"	26.5	SE.	11.5	"	6.1	"	14.1	"
5			39.0	"	33.5	S.	41.1	Calm.	45.1	"	45.2	SW.	45.4	"	44.4	Calm.	25.1	S.	11.0	"	6.2	NW.	13.7	"
6			38.8	E.	33.2	"	41.4	"	45.2	"	45.3	N.	45.5	"	44.3	N.	23.8	"	10.6	"	6.5	N.	13.3	"
7			38.7	N.	33.0	N.	41.7	S.	45.2	"	45.3	S.	45.6	"	44.1	W.	22.8	"	10.2	N.		"	12.8	"
8			38.6	Calm.	32.9	"	41.9	"	45.3	"	45.3	"	45.6	"	43.9	E.	21.9	"	9.8	"		"	12.6	W.
9			38.3	S.	32.8	S.	42.2	"	45.3	"	45.3	"	45.6	"	43.7	Calm.	21.1	"	9.2	"		"	12.6	N.
10			38.1	N.	32.9	"	42.4	"	45.5	SW.	45.3	"	45.6	"	43.5	S.	20.3	"	9.2	"	11.3	SW.	13.0	"
11			37.8	"	33.1	"	42.7	N.	45.5	N.	45.3	"	45.6	"	43.3	"	19.3	N.	9.1	"	12.9	N.	13.7	S.
12			37.6	"	33.3	"	42.8	W.	45.5	"	45.4	N.	45.6	N.	42.9	"	18.7	"	8.8	E.	15.2	SW.	14.6	"
13			37.7	Calm.	33.6	"	42.9	"	45.5	S.	45.4	"	45.7	"	42.6	N.	17.8	"	8.6	"	16.9	S.	15.8	"
14			37.6	N.	33.9	"	43.0	N.	45.5	"	45.4	"	45.6	"	42.2	"	16.9	"	8.3	N.	18.4	SE.	17.4	"
15			37.5	Calm.	34.2	"	43.0	S.	45.5	"	45.4	"	45.6	S.	42.2	S.	16.1	"	8.0	"	19.2	N.	21.0	N.
16			37.3	"	34.5	"	43.1	"	45.4	"	45.4	"	45.6	"	42.1	N.	16.3	"	7.8	"	20.2	"	22.7	"
17			37.1	"	34.9	N.	43.2	"	45.4	"	45.4	S.	45.6	"	42.0	"	15.6	"	7.7	S.	20.5	"	23.2	SW.
18			36.9	S.	34.8	Calm.	43.2	"	45.4	SW.	45.4	"	45.6	"	41.9	"	14.9	"	7.6	"	20.5	"	24.2	"
19			36.7	N.	34.8	S.	43.3	"	45.4	N.	45.4	"	45.6	"	41.4	"	13.3	"	7.3	"	20.4	SW.	25.5	S.
20			36.5	S.	34.8	"	43.5	N.	45.4	"	45.4	"	45.6	"	40.9	S.	13.0	"	7.0	N.	20.1	N.	26.9	"
21			36.3	"	34.8	"	43.6	"	45.4	S.	45.4	"	45.5	"	40.4	"	12.9	"	6.8	"	19.8	"	28.6	NW.
22			36.1	N.	35.0	"	43.6	"	45.3	"	45.4	"	45.5	"	39.8	"	13.2	S.	6.6	"	19.5	"	29.7	N.
23			35.8	"	35.3	N.	43.7	S.	45.2	"	45.4	"	45.5	"	39.2	N.	13.5	"	6.6	S.	19.1	"	30.8	S.
24			35.7	"	35.6	"	43.7	"	45.2	"	45.4	"	45.4	"	38.6	S.	13.5	"	6.6	"	18.5	SW.	31.5	"
25	39.3		35.6	"	36.1	Calm.	43.8	Calm.	45.2	"	45.4	"	45.3	"	37.9	"	13.8	"	6.4	"	17.9	S.	32.6	E.
26	39.3		35.4	"	36.6	S.	43.9	N.	45.2	"	45.4	"	45.3	"	37.0	Calm.	13.9	"	6.4	"	17.4	"	33.4	N.
27	39.3		35.2	S.	37.4	Calm.	43.9	"	45.3	"	45.4	"	45.3	"	35.4	"	13.8	N.	6.5	N.	16.7	"	34.0	Calm.
28	39.3		35.0	"	38.0	"	44.0	"	45.3	"	45.4	"	45.2		34.5	E.	13.7	"	6.8	"	16.2	"	34.7	N.
29	39.2				38.5	"	44.1	S.	45.3	"	45.4	"	45.1		33.5	N.	13.6	S.	6.6	W.	16.0	SW.	34.9	Calm
30	39.1				39.0	SE.	44.2	"	45.3	"	45.4	"	45.0		32.3	"	13.2	"	6.4	Calm.	15.9	NW.	35.2	
31	39.0				39.3	NW.			45.2	"			44.9		31.3	"			6.3	S.			35.6	N.

Records for 1858—Continued.

Donaldsonville.—Observer, Mr. A. Gingry.

Date.	January.		February.		March.		April.		May.		June.		July.		August.		September.		October.		November.		December.	
1858.	*G'ge*	*Wind.*	*G'ge*	*Wind.*	*G'ge*	*Wind.*	*G'ge*	*Wind.*	*G'ge*	*Wind.*	*G'ge*	*Wind.*	*G'ge*	*Wind.*	*G'ge*	*Wind.*	*G'ge*	*Wind.*	*G'ge*	*Wind.*	*G'ge*	*Wind.*	*G'ge*	*Wind.*
1	24.8	SE.	25.5	NW.	23.3	N.	26.0	NW.	29.0	SE.	29.0	SE.	29.0	S.	28.5	W.	20.3	S.	8.7	E.	5.0	S.	7.0	E.
2	24.8	"	25.5	W.	23.3	"	26.2	"	29.1	E.	29.0	"	29.0	"	28.4	SW.	20.0	"	8.5	"	4.5	W.	6.8	"
3	24.9	N.	25.5	E.	23.0	W.	26.5	S.	29.5	NW.	29.0	"	29.0	E.	28.3	"	19.5	"	8.0		4.2	NW.	6.8	"
4	24.8	E.	25.5	N.	23.0	E.	26.8	"	29.4	"	29.0	"	29.0	"	28.2	W.	19.0	W.	7.5	SE.	4.0	"	7.2	"
5	25.0	NW.	25.2	"	22.5	"	27.3	W.	29.5	"	29.0	S.	29.0	S.	28.0	NE.	18.5	E.	7.3	"	4.0	"	7.2	NW.
6	24.7	"	25.0	E.	22.0	S.	27.5	S.	29.6	W.	29.0	W.	29.0	W.	27.8	"	18.0	"	7.3	"	4.0	NE.	7.2	S.
7	24.3	E.	24.8	NE.	22.0	W.	27.7	"	29.8	E.	29.1	E.	29.0	"	27.8	W.	17.5	"	7.3	NW.	4.2	S.	7.0	"
8	24.0	"	24.5	"	22.0	NW.	27.8	"	29.9	SE.	29.1	"	29.1	"	27.5	E.	17.0	E.	7.0	W.	4.5	NW.	7.0	N.
9	24.0	"	24.2	S.	22.2	W.	28.0	"	29.9	"	29.1	S.	29.0	SW.	27.4	W.	16.5	"	7.0	E.	5.0	W.	7.0	"
10	23.8	S.	24.2	N.	22.2	SW.	28.1	"	30.0	S.	29.1	SE.	29.0	"	27.2	NE.	16.0	"	7.0	SE.	5.2	SE.	7.0	NE.
11	24.0	NW.	24.0	E.	22.2	S.	28.4	NW.	30.0	W.	29.2	S.	29.0	"	27.1	W.	14.5	N.	7.0	E.	5.5	NW.	7.2	"
12	24.2	E.	24.0	S.	22.2	"	28.2	SW.	29.8	"	29.4	W.	29.0	"	27.0	"	14.0	"	7.0		6.2	S.	8.0	E.
13	24.5	N.	24.0	W.	22.6	SE.	28.2	W.	29.9	E.	29.3	N.	29.0	W.	26.9		13.5	NE.	7.4	NE.	7.0	N.	9.0	S.
14	24.8	S.	24.0	"	23.0	"	28.2	"	29.7	SE.	29.4	NE.	29.0	S.	26.8		12.0	E.	7.4	N.	8.0	E.	9.6	"
15	25.0	E.	24.0	E.	23.5	"	28.3	S.	29.6	Calm.	29.4	Calm.	29.0	"	26.7		11.1	NE.	7.4	E.	8.5	N.	10.2	N.
16	25.2	NW.	24.0	"	23.7	S.	28.6	"	29.5	S.	29.3	SW.	29.0	W.	26.6		9.8	N.	7.2	"	8.8	"	10.8	"
17	25.5	N.	24.0	S.	23.8	W.	28.5	"	29.4	"	29.2	SE.	29.0	"	26.5		9.0	E.	7.4	"	9.0	E.	11.0	"
18	25.5	"	23.8	"	24.0	SE.	28.5	"	29.4	NW.	29.1	"	28.9	"	26.4		9.0	"	7.6	"	9.0	"	11.5	"
19	25.5	E.	23.5	NW.	24.0	"	28.6	"	29.3	"	29.1	E.	29.0	S.	26.2		8.5	"	7.2	"	9.0	"	13.0	S.
20	25.7	"	23.4	E.	24.0	"	28.7	"	29.3	E.	29.1	"	20.0	N.	26.0		8.2	"	6.8	N.	9.0	NW.	14.5	N.
21	25.8	NW.	23.4	S.	23.8	S.	28.8	W.	29.3	"	29.0	"	29.0	E.	25.7		7.9	"	6.5	E.	8.2	E.	15.2	E.
22	25.8	E.	23.3	N.	23.8	"	28.8	SW.	29.2	"	29.0	"	29.0	S.	25.4		7.8	"	6.0	"	8.0	NW.	17.0	"
23	25.8	SE.	23.0	"	24.0	E.	28.8	NW.	29.2	SE.	20.0	"	29.0	"	25.1		7.8	"	5.5	"	8.0	"	18.5	"
24	25.8	"	23.0	"	24.2	"	28.8	E.	29.2	S.	29.1	S.	28.9	W.	24.8		8.0	"	5.8	S.	7.6	"	19.0	"
25	25.8	SW.	23.0	W.	24.5	"	29.0	S.	29.2	"	29.1	"	28.8	SW.	24.4		8.7	"	6.3	Calm.	7.5	E.	20.0	"
26	25.8	"	23.0	SW.	24.8	"	29.1	NW.	29.2	"	29.1	E.	28.7	N.	23.9		9.0	W.	6.8	E.	7.4	"	21.0	"
27	25.8	NW.	23.0	S.	25.2	"	29.3	E.	29.2	SW.	29.1	"	28.7	E.	23.4		9.3	"	7.2	S.	7.0	"	21.5	"
28	25.8	"	23.2	"	25.5	SW.	29.2	SE.	29.1	S.	29.0	S.	28.7	S.	22.9		9.3	E.	7.0	NW.	7.0	"	21.6	NE.
29	25.5	W.			25.8	SE.	29.0	S.	29.1	"	29.1	W.	28.6	"	22.2		9.3	"	6.5	"	7.0	"	22.5	E.
30	25.5	E.			26.0	E.	29.0	"	29.1	"	29.0	S.	28.6	"	21.5	NE.	9.0	"	6.0	S.	7.2	N.	23.0	S.
31	25.5	"			26.0	NW.			29.1	"			28.6	W.	20.7	NW.			5.5	NE.			23.8	N.

Records for 1858—Continued.

Carrollton.—Observer, Mr. W. H. Williams.

Date.	January.		February.		March.		April.		May.		June.		July.		August.		September.		October.		November.		December.	
1858.	*G'ge*	*Wind.*	*G'ge*	*Wind.*	*G'ge*	*Wind.*	*G'ge*	*Wind.*	*G'ge*	*Wind.*	*G'ge*	*Wind.*	*G'ge*	*Wind.*	*G'ge*	*Wind.*	*G'ge*	*Wind.*	*G'ge*	*Wind.*	*G'ge*	*Wind.*	*G'ge*	*Wind.*
1	11.9	SE.	13.3	NW.	11.7	N.	13.5	N.	14.7	SE.	14.3	Calm.	13.9	SW.	13.2	W.	8.8	SW.	2.2	W.	1.3	W.	2.5	NE.
2	12.3	"	13.1	Calm.	11.5	NW.	13.6	NW.	14.8	"	14.4	"	13.9	E.	13.2	S.	8.4	S.	2.1	"	1.1	NW.	2.2	E.
3	12.4	NE.	13.2	NE.	11.4	Calm.	13.6	Calm.	15.0	"	14.3	"	13.8	S.	13.2	"	8.1	"	2.0	S.	0.7	N.	2.6	S.
4	12.5	NW.	13.2	N.	11.3	"	13.7	"	14.8	NW.	14.3	SE.	13.8	SW.	13.2	W.	7.7	W.	2.0	"	0.5	"	2.2	"
5	12.6	SE.	13.2	"	11.2	SE.	13.8	"	14.8	W.	14.3	SW.	13.8	W.	13.2	N.	7.4	S.	1.9	E.	0.4	"	2.1	"
6	12.4	Calm.	13.0	E.	11.1	S.	13.9	"	14.8	Calm.	14.4	Calm.	13.8	SW.	13.1	"	6.9	E.	1.6	S.	0.5	W.	1.9	"
7	12.3	"	12.9	Calm.	11.3	W.	13.9	S.	14.8	"	14.4	"	13.8	N.	13.1	E.	6.4	"	1.3	N.	0.4	E.	2.0	"
8	12.2	SW.	12.9	NE.	10.6	NW.	14.0	"	14.9	"	14.3	NW.	14.0	SW.	13.0	S.	6.0	N.	1.0	"	0.4	N.	1.8	N.
9	12.2	SE.	12.9	SE.	10.5	SW.	14.3	"	14.9	SE.	14.3	S.	14.0	W.	13.0	NE.	5.6	NW.	1.0	E.	0.4	"	1.6	"
10	12.1	SW.	12.8	N.	10.5	S.	14.3	SE.	15.1	SW.	14.4	"	13.8	"	12.9	S.	4.8	E.	1.1	S.	0.8	E.	1.6	NE.
11	12.1	Calm.	12.8	NE.	10.6	"	14.8	NW.	15.0	Calm.	14.4	"	13.8	"	12.7	W.	4.6	W.	1.2	E.	1.4	N.	2.0	N.
12	12.1	SW.	12.8	SW.	10.8	Calm.	14.3	SW.	15.1	"	14.3	NW.	13.8	"	12.7	NW.	4.2	N.	1.1	N.	2.2	SE.	2.4	S.
13	12.3	Calm.	12.9	Calm.	10.9	NE.	14.3	W.	15.0	"	14.2	NE.	13.7	N.	12.5	NE.	3.8	"	1.2	"	2.7	N.	2.9	"
14	12.4	SW.	12.8	SE.	11.3	SE.	14.5	SW.	14.7	S.	14.3	Calm.	13.7	"	12.5		3.4	W.	1.2	"	3.5	S.	3.3	"
15	12.5	W.	12.7	NE.	11.5	"	14.5	S.	14.8	SE.	14.2	"	13.6	NE.	12.4		3.5	"	1.3	NE.	3.9	N.	3.7	N.
16	12.7	N.	12.7	N.	11.9	"	14.5	"	14.7	S.	14.2	NW.	13.6	"	12.3		3.0	N.	1.3	E.	4.0	"	4.2	NW.
17	12.8	"	12.6	Calm.	12.0	S.	14.4	"	14.7	"	14.1	NE.	13.6	"	12.2		2.5	W.	1.9	"	4.2	E.	4.7	N.
18	13.0	E.	12.7	SW.	12.1	Calm.	14.5	"	14.8	Calm.	14.2	"	13.7	SW.	12.1		2.2	NE.	1.8	"	3.9	"	5.2	NE.
19	13.2	NE.	12.6	NW.	12.0	SE.	14.4	"	14.7	N.	14.1	Calm.	14.0	SE.	12.0		2.2	"	1.4	NE.	3.7	N.	5.9	S.
20	13.3	"	12.4	Calm.	11.9	S.	14.4	SW.	14.6	Calm.	14.1	"	13.7	SW.	11.8		2.1	"	1.1	"	3.7	NW.	6.3	"
21	13.4	"	12.1	S.	11.9	SW.	14.2	Calm.	14.6	NE.	14.1	"	13.7	"	11.6		2.2	N.	1.1	"	3.6	"	7.0	NW.
22	13.4	SE.	12.2	NW.	11.9	Calm.	14.4	SW.	14.6	SE.	14.1	NE.	13.6	"	11.5	SW.	1.9	"	0.8	N.	3.4	N.	7.6	NE.
23	13.4	"	11.9	"	11.8	N.	14.4	N.	14.6	"	14.1	Calm.	13.6	"	11.3	S.	1.8	"	0.7	W.	3.0	"	8.1	N.
24	13.5	"	11.8	N.	12.0	NW.	14.4	Calm.	14.6	Calm.	14.1	NE.	13.5	W.	11.2	NW.	1.7	SW.	0.8	S.	2.7	"	8.8	"
25	13.6	"	11.7	Calm.	12.2	SW.	14.5	S.	14.6	S.	14.2	S.	13.5	NW.	11.0	E.	1.8	N.	0.5	W.	2.6	NE.	9.6	"
26	13.4	Calm.	11.7	"	12.4	NE.	14.5	NW.	14.6	SW.	14.2	N.	13.4	E.	10.8	S.	2.0	NW.	0.6	SE.	2.6	S.	10.0	"
27	13.2	"	11.6	S.	12.6	Calm.	14.6	NE.	14.5	Calm.	14.1	S.	13.5	"	10.5	N.	1.7	N.	2.0	S.	2.7	"	10.2	"
28	13.3	NW.	11.8	SW.	12.9	"	14.6	S.	14.5	S.	14.1	"	13.5	S.	10.2	NE.	1.9	E.	1.6	E.	2.7	SW.	10.4	NE.
29	13.1	"			13.1	SE.	14.6	"	14.4	"	14.1	Calm.	13.4	"	9.8	N.	2.0	S.	1.4	W.	2.7	E.	10.5	S.
30	13.1	NE.			13.5	N.	14.5	SE.	14.4	"	14.0	"	13.3	W.	9.5	NW.	2.0	N.	1.5	E.	2.7	NE.	10.8	"
31	13.2	"			13.3	W.			14.4	Calm.			13.3	SW.	9.1	"			1.6	NE.			10.8	NW.

Records for 1859.

Columbus.—Observer, Mr. J. M. Moore.

Date.	January.		February.		March.		April.		May.		June.		July.		August.		September.		October.		November.		December.	
1859.	*G'ge*	*Wind.*	*G'ge*	*Wind.*	*G'ge*	*Wind.*	*G'ge*	*Wind.*	*G'ge*	*Wind.*	*G'ge*	*Wind.*	*G'ge*	*Wind.*	*G'ge*	*Wind.*	*G'ge*	*Wind.*	*G'ge*	*Wind.*	*G'ge*	*Wind.*	*G'ge*	*Wind.*
1	26.9	N.	20.1	S.	37.2	S.	37.4	S.	36.5	S.	26.0	S.	22.9	S.	13.0	N.								
2	25.5	S.	20.0	W.	37.5	"	37.3	"	37.0	"	25.7	N.	22.2	"	12.8	"								
3	24.1	"	19.1	"	37.7	"	37.1	"	37.4	"	25.4	"	21.8	NE.	12.3	S.								
4	24.3	"	19.0	NW.	37.8	"	36.7	N.	37.9	"	24.8	"	21.1	N.	12.0	"								
5	23.8	"	18.0	S.	37.8	"	36.6	"	38.2	"	23.9	NE.	20.5	"	11.8	N.								
6	23.4	"	18.0	N.	37.9	"	36.4	SW.	38.4	"	23.1	S.	20.2	S.	11.7	NE.								
7	23.2	N.	17.1	"	38.0	"	36.1	"	38.6	"	22.3	"	20.4	"	12.0	N.								
8	23.4	SE.	17.2	S.	37.9	N.	35.9	N.	38.8	SW.	21.6	NE.	20.2	N.	12.7	"								
9	23.4	S.	17.0	N.	37.7	S.	35.7	SW.	38.6	E.	21.0	"	19.5	"	13.0	SE.								
10	23.3	"	17.0	"	37.5	"	35.4	S.	38.2	N.	20.4	"	19.1	"	12.9	N.								
11	23.0	"	17.0	S.	37.4	"	35.3	"	37.5	S.	20.1	"	18.5	E.	12.5	S.								
12	22.3	SW.	18.0	N.	37.0	"	34.9	"	36.5	"	19.8	S.	17.8	N.	11.9	SW.								
13	21.2	N.	18.1	S.	36.4	"	34.5	"	35.1	N.	19.5	"	17.1	"	11.3	N.								
14	20.9	S.	18.1	"	35.8	"	34.2	"	33.1	"	19.3	"	16.6	"	10.9	NE.								
15	18.6	SW.	18.0	"	35.1	N.	34.1	N.	30.9	S.	18.9	"	16.1	"	10.6	N.								
16	17.8	S.	19.0	"	34.5	S.	34.1	"	30.3	"	18.6	"	15.8	S.	10.5	"								
17	17.6	W.	20.0	"	34.2	"	34.1	"	30.1	"	18.6	N.	15.4	N.	10.4	"								
18	18.1	"	21.1	"	34.1	N.	34.0	S.	29.9	"	18.5	E.	15.1	SW.	10.1	"								
19	18.6	S.	24.1	"	33.9	S.	33.9	"	30.0	N.	18.5	SW.	14.9	W.	9.9	NW.								
20	19.1	"	27.1	"	33.7	"	33.7	"	30.0	SW.	19.1	W.	14.7	S.	9.8	N.								
21	19.3	NW.	30.0	"	33.7	"	33.6	"	30.2	S.	19.8	N.	14.4	W.	9.4	S.								
22	19.3	"	31.1	"	34.0	"	33.5	N.	30.6	N.	20.6	"	14.0	S.	9.0	SW.								
23	19.3	S.	33.0	"	34.8	"	33.6	"	30.8	SW.	21.8	SW.	13.8	"	8.8	N.								
24	19.5	"	33.1	"	35.5	"	33.5	"	30.9	S.	23.1	N.	13.6	"	8.4	"								
25	20.2	"	34.1	"	36.0	N.	33.4	S.	30.9	"	23.6	S.	13.6	N.	8.1	S.								
26	20.8	E.	35.0	"	36.5	S.	33.7	"	30.6	"	23.8	"	13.3	"	7.9	"								
27	21.1	S.	36.0	"	36.9	"	34.1	N.	29.8	N.	23.7	"	13.1	"	7.7	"								
28	21.5	N.	36.1	N.	37.1	"	34.7	"	28.9	S.	23.7	"	13.2	"	8.1	N.								
29	21.6	"			37.2	N.	35.4	"	27.9	"	23.6	"	13.4	"	8.2	"								
30	21.7	"			37.3	"	35.9	"	27.1	"	23.3	N.	13.3	S.	8.1	"								
31	21.4	S.			37.3	NW.			26.5	N.			13.2	N.	7.9	"								

Records for 1859—Continued.

Memphis.—Observer, Mr. Michael Conway.

Date.	January.		February.		March.		April.		May.		June.		July.		August.		September.		October.		November.		December.	
1859.	*G'ge*	*Wind.*	*G'ge*	*Wind.*	*G'ge*	*Wind.*	*G'ge*	*Wind.*	*G'ge*	*Wind.*	*G'ge*	*Wind.*	*G'ge*	*Wind.*	*G'ge*	*Wind.*	*G'ge*	*Wind.*	*G'ge*	*Wind.*	*G'ge*	*Wind.*	*G'ge*	*Wind.*
1	30.8	SW.	22.3	SW.	34.1	NW.	34.8	SW.	34.1	SW.	29.8	SW.	24.7	SW.	13.8	SW.								
2	30.6	"	22.1	NE.	34.4	NE.	34.9	"	34.2	SE.	29.1	NE.	24.5	SE.	14.1	"								
3	30.2	NE.	21.7	NW.	34.5	SW.	34.9	NW.	34.2	SW.	28.7	"	24.0	NE.	14.1	"								
4	29.7	"	21.3	SW.	34.7	"	34.9	NE.	34.3	"	28.0	SW.	23.8	SW.	14.0	"								
5	29.3	NW.	20.8	NE.	34.7	NW.	34.9	NW.	34.4	NW.	27.3	"	23.4	NE.	14.0	"								
6	28.6	SE.	20.5	"	34.8	NE.	35.0	"	34.5	SW.	26.5	"	22.3	SW.	13.7	SE.								
7	28.0	NW.	19.9	SW.	34.9	"	35.0	"	34.6	SE.	25.8	NE.	22.1	"	13.3	NE.								
8	27.6	"	19.5	"	34.8	SW.	34.9	SE.	34.7	SW.	25.4	SE.	21.7	NE.	13.0	"								
9	27.1	SW.	18.8	NE.	34.8	"	34.8	SW.	34.8	"	24.7	"	21.2	NW.	12.8	SW.								
10	26.7	SE.	18.3	"	34.8	"	34.8	"	34.9	SE.	24.0	SW.	20.7	SE.	13.2	"								
11	26.2	NE.	17.7	SW.	34.9	NE.	34.8	NW.	35.1	NE.	23.3	NW.	20.5	SW.	13.5	"								
12	25.8	SW.	17.9	"	34.8	SE.	34.7	SW.	35.2	SW.	22.5	SE.	20.1	NW.	13.7	NE.								
13	25.1	"	18.6	"	34.8	NW.	34.7	SE.	35.2	"	21.4	SW.	19.8	SE.	14.0	"								
14	24.4	"	18.7	NE.	34.9	"	34.9	NE.	35.1	"	20.7	"	18.6	SW.	13.9	"								
15	23.5	NE.	19.5	SW.	34.9	NE.	35.0	NW.	34.9	"	20.2	"	18.0	NE.	13.7	"								
16	22.1	SW.	20.7	"	34.9	"	35.1	NE.	34.8	"	19.8	SE.	17.6	"	13.4	"								
17	21.3	SE.	21.2	"	34.9	SW.	34.9	"	34.6	"	19.3	NW.	17.1	"	12.1	"								
18	20.0	SW.	22.6	NE.	34.8	NE.	34.8	SE.	34.4	NE.	18.9	SW.	16.6	"	11.8	"					5.1			
19	19.4	"	23.8	NW.	34.8	"	34.7	SW.	34.0	NW.	18.7	"	16.0	SW.	11.5	SW.								
20	19.0	NE.	24.5	SW.	34.7	SW.	34.7	"	33.5	SW.	18.8	"	15.9	"	11.1	"								
21	20.7	NW.	26.0	"	34.6	"	34.7	"	33.1	NE.	19.4	NE.	15.7	"	10.8	"								
22	21.9	NE.	28.4	"	34.5	NE.	34.6	NE.	32.7	NW.	20.2	SW.	15.4	NE.	10.3	"								
23	21.7	SW.	30.8	NW.	34.5	SW.	34.5	SW.	32.8	SW.	20.9	"	15.1	SE.	9.8	SE.								
24	22.8	"	32.1	SW.	34.5	"	34.4	"	32.6	"	21.8	"	14.8	SW.	9.4	"								
25	22.6	SE.	33.2	NE.	34.7	NE.	34.4	SE.	32.6	"	22.6	"	14.6	"	9.1	NW.								
26	22.5	NW.	33.4	NW.	34.8	"	34.3	SW.	32.6	NE.	23.0	"	14.4	"	8.8	SW.								
27	23.3	"	33.7	SW.	34.8	SW.	34.3	SE.	32.5	NW.	23.7	NE.	14.5	NE.	8.3	"			6.8					
28	23.2	SW.	33.9	"	34.8	NW.	34.2	SW.	32.3	SW.	24.2	SW.	14.6	"	7.9	NE.								
29	22.9	NW.			34.8	NE.	34.1	NE.	32.0	"	24.9	"	14.3	NW.	7.4	"								
30	22.7	NE.			34.7	"	33.9	NW.	31.3	"	24.8	SE.	14.0	SW.	7.0	"								
31	22.4	SW.			34.6	"			30.7	"			13.9	"	6.6	"								

Records for 1859—Continued.

Napoleon.—Observer, Mr. A. A. Edington.

Date.	January.		February.		March.		April.		May.		June.		July.		August.		September.		October.		November.		December.	
1859.	*G'ge*	*Wind.*	*G'ge*	*Wind.*	*G'ge*	*Wind.*	*G'ge*	*Wind.*	*G'ge*	*Wind.*	*G'ge*	*Wind.*	*G'ge*	*Wind.*	*G'ge*	*Wind.*	*G'ge*	*Wind.*	*G'ge*	*Wind.*	*G'ge*	*Wind.*	*G'ge*	*Wind.*
1	32.8	N.																						
2	33.3	NW.																						
3	31.6	W.																						
4	30.9	"																						
5	30.1	S.																						
6	29.3	"																						
7	28.6	"																						
8	27.5	E.																						
9	26.8	"																						
10	26.1	NE.																						
11																								
12																								
13																								
14																								
15																								
16																								
17																								
18																								
19																								
20																								
21																								
22																								
23																								
24																								
25																								
26																								
27																								
28																								
29																								
30																								
31																								

Records for 1859—Continued.

Vicksburg.—Observer, Mr. A. Y. Nolley.

Date.	January.		February.		March.		April.		May.		June.		July.		August.		September.		October.		November.		December.	
1859.	*G'ge*	*Wind.*	*G'ge*	*Wind.*	*G'ge*	*Wind.*	*G'ge*	*Wind.*	*G'ge*	*Wind.*	*G'ge*	*Wind.*	*G'ge*	*Wind.*	*G'ge*	*Wind.*	*G'ge*	*Wind.*	*G'ge*	*Wind.*	*G'ge*	*Wind.*	*G'ge*	*Wind.*
1	41.1	Calm.	32.7	S.	41.3	Calm.	48.5	SE.	49.5	Calm.	48.7	S.	41.2	S.	21.4	SW.	14.4	N.						
2	41.2	S.	33.0	W.	41.9	S.	48.7	Calm.	49.5	E.	48.7	"	41.3	N.	21.2	SE.	14.1	"						
3	41.3	"	33.3	N.	42.5	SW.	48.8	N.	49.5	"	48.7	N.	41.3	S.	21.0	S.	13.9	S.						
4	41.5	"	33.3	"	42.9	Calm.	48.6	Calm.	49.5	"	48.6	"	41.1	N.	20.9	SE.	13.7	E.						
5	41.6	"	33.2	S.	43.3	S.	48.7	N.	49.5	"	48.5	NE.	40.9	"	20.8	"	13.7	N.						
6	41.6	"	33.1	N.	43.8	"	48.8	"	49.4	"	48.4	SW.	40.6	E.	20.7	"	13.7	"						
7	41.6	NW.	32.8	E.	44.0	SW.	48.9	Calm.	49.4	"	48.3	SE.	40.1	N.	20.6	Calm.	13.8	"						
8	41.5	SW.	32.5	S.	44.4	NW.	48.9	"	49.4	Calm.	48.2	N.	39.6	"	20.4	E.	14.0	NE.						
9	41.3	"	32.1	N.	44.7	S.	49.0	S.	49.4	SE.	48.1	NW.	39.0	NE.	20.1	SW.	14.3	"						
10	41.1	"	31.5	S.	45.0	"	49.0	SE.	49.4	N.	47.9	"	38.2	"	19.6	N.	14.7	SE.						
11	40.6	Calm.	30.9	"	45.3	NW.	49.0	S.	49.4	Calm.	47.7	N.	37.4	"	19.2	NW.	14.8	SW.						
12	40.4	"	30.4	N.	45.6	E.	49.0	"	49.3	"	47.5	E.	36.5	S.	19.1	W.	14.7	N.						
13	40.1	E.	30.0	F.	45.9	S.	49.2	"	49.3	"	47.2	Calm.	35.6	Calm.	19.1	SW.								
14	39.8	SW.	29.2	SE.	46.2	"	49.2	N.	49.3	"	46.9	S.	34.5	"	19.2	"								
15	39.4	N.	29.4	S.	46.5	N.	49.3	Calm.	49.3	"	46.7	"	35.5	S.	19.6	Calm.								
16	39.0	S.	20.4	SE.	46.8	E.	49.4	NE.	49.2	SW.	46.4	"	32.5	"	19.8	E.								
17	38.6	N.	29.6	S.	46.9	Calm.	49.4	NW.	49.2	S.	45.9	"	31.4	E.	19.6									
18	38.0	"	30.0	"	47.1	W.	49.4	Calm.	49.2	"	44.4	E.	29.9	"	19.6	N.								
19	37.2	S.	30.6	"	47.2	Calm.	49.4	S.	49.2	Calm.	44.0	NE.	29.0	N.	19.0	"								
20	36.3	"	31.3	N.	47.2	S.	49.5	"	49.1	"	43.8	S.	28.0	S.	18.5	W.								
21	35.4	N.	31.9	Calm.	47.3	Calm.	49.6	"	49.1	N.	43.1	N.	27.0	"	18.0	N.								
22	34.3	"	32.9	S.	47.4	S.	49.6	N.	49.0	"	42.5	"	26.5	"	17.6	Calm.								
23	33.3	Calm.	34.1	SW.	47.5	"	49.6	"	49.0	SE.	41.9	W.	25.6	"	17.3	N.								
24	32.8	"	36.0	S	47.6	Calm.	49.6	S.	48.9	S.	41.4	Calm.	24.9	"	17.0	"								
25	32.5	"	37.6	"	47.7	N.	49.6	SE.	48.9	Calm.	41.0	E.	24.4	"	16.7	NW.								
26	32.3	E.	38.8	E.	47.7	S.	49.6	S.	48.9	S.	40.8	"	23.9	"	16.5	E.								
27	32.2	Calm.	39.7	S.	47.9	"	49.6	Calm.	48.9	N.	40.8	"	23.4	N.	16.1	S.								
28	32.2	S.	40.7	N.	48.1	"	49.6	NE.	48.9	SW.	40.8	S.	22.9	"	15.7	"								
29	32.3	N.			48.3	N.	49.6	SW.	48.8	E.	41.0	Calm.	22.5	"	15.4	W.								
30	32.3	"			48.3	Calm	49.6	Calm.	48.8	S.	41.1	S.	22.1	NW.	15.0	N.								
31	32.4	E.			48.9	N.			48.7	SE.			21.8	Calm.	14.6	"								

Records for 1859—Continued.

Natchez.—Observer, MR. R. F. LEARNED.

Date.	January.		February.		March.		April.		May.		June.		July.		August.		September.		October.		November.		December.	
1859.	*G'ge*	*Wind.*	*G'ge*	*Wind.*	*G'ge*	*Wind.*	*G'ge*	*Wind.*	*G'ge*	*Wind.*	*G'ge*	*Wind.*	*G'ge*	*Wind.*	*G'ge*	*Wind.*	*G'ge*	*Wind.*	*G'ge*	*Wind.*	*G'ge*	*Wind.*	*G'ge*	*Wind.*
1	43.6	NW.																						
2	44.0	"																						
3	44.2	"																						
4	44.3	SW.																						
5	44.5	S.																						
6	44.6	"																						
7	44.7	NW.																						
8	44.6	W.																						
9	44.5	SW.																						
10	44.4	W.																						
11	44.2	"																						
12	44.0	NW.																						
13	43.9	W.																						
14	43.8	SW.																						
15	43.4	NW.																						
16	43.2	SW.																						
17	42.7	NW.																						
18	41.9	SW.																						
19	41.0	"																						
20	40.5	W.																						
21	40.0	NW.																						
22	39.6	"																						
23	38.8	"																						
24	37.8	SW.																						
25	37.2	"																						
26	36.7	W.																						
27	36.5	SW.																						
28	36.9	S.																						
29	36.8	W.																						
30	36.8	NW.																						
31	36.7	"																						

Records for 1859—Continued.

Red-river landing.—Observer, MR. MIGUEL TORRAS.

Date.	January.		February.		March.		April.		May.		June.		July.		August.		September.		October.		November.		December.	
1859.	*G'ge*	*Wind.*	*G'ge*	*Wind.*	*G'ge*	*Wind.*	*G'ge*	*Wind.*	*G'ge*	*Wind.*	*G'ge*	*Wind.*	*G'ge*	*Wind.*	*G'ge*	*Wind.*	*G'ge*	*Wind.*	*G'ge*	*Wind.*	*G'ge*	*Wind.*	*G'ge*	*Wind.*
1	35.8	N.																						
2	36.1	"																						
3	36.3	"																						
4	36.6	"																						
5	36.6	S.																						
6	36.7	"																						
7	36.8	N.																						
8	36.8	NW.																						
9	36.8	"																						
10	36.8	W.																						
11	36.7	SE.																						
12	36.7	S.																						
13	36.6	"																						
14	36.6	"																						
15	36.4	N.																						
16	36.1	S.																						
17	36.0	N.																						
18	35.7	"																						
19	35.3	Calm.																						
20	34.9	S.																						
21	34.4	"																						
22	34.0	N.																						
23	33.4	"																						
24	32.7	"																						
25	32.4	S.																						
26	32.0	SE.																						
27	31.4	"																						
28	31.6	"																						
29	31.4	Calm.																						
30	31.4	"																						
31	31.3	"																						

Records for 1859—Continued.

Donaldsonville.—Observer, Mr. A. Gingry.

Date.	January.		February.		March.		April.		May.		June.		July.		August.		September.		October.		November.		December.	
1859.	G'ge	Wind.	G'ge	Wind.	G'ge	Wind.	G'ge	Wind.	G'ge	Wind.	G'ge	Wind.	G'ge	Wind.	G'ge	Wind.	G'ge	Wind.	G'ge	Wind.	G'ge	Wind.	G'ge	Wind.
1	23.9		20.6	E.	24.3	NE.	28.3	E.	30.0	E.	28.2	S.	25.3	E.	11.4	E.	4.5	W.	4.4	N.	4.5	N.	5.5	SE.
2	24.0		20.4	W.	24.6	S.	28.5	SE.	30.1	"	28.1	W.	25.2	SE.	11.1	S.	4.0	"	4.2	"	4.8	E.	5.6	S.
3	24.1		20.4	"	25.0	NW.	28.8	NE.	30.1	"	28.1	NW.	25.0	SW.	11.0	"	4.0	S.	5.0	"	4.8	"	6.2	N.
4	24.2		20.5	NW.	25.2	SW.	28.8	N.	30.1	"	28.0	E.	24.3	"	10.8	"	3.6	"	5.0	E.	5.0	"	6.3	"
5	24.3		20.7	"	25.5	SE.	28.8	"	30.2	"	28.0	"	24.0	E.	10.7	SW.	3.5	W.	5.0	"	5.2	"	7.2	E.
6	24.4		21.4	N.	26.0	E.	28.9	E.	30.5	"	28.0	S.	23.8	"	10.5	"	3.5	NW.	5.4	"	5.2	NE.	7.5	"
7	24.5	NW.	21.5	SE.	26.0	SW.	28.8	NE.	30.2	S.	27.9	SE.	23.7	"	10.5	W.	3.5	E.	5.7	SE.	5.0	E.	8.6	N.
8	24.0	N.	21.5	"	26.0	W.	28.9	E.	30.2	E.	27.9	"	23.7	W.	10.2	SW.	3.5	"	5.8	W.	5.0	"	8.4	"
9	24.2	W.	21.6	NW.	26.2	E.	28.8	S.	29.7	SW.	27.9	S.	23.7	E.	10.0	NW.	3.5	"	6.0	NW.	5.0	"	9.0	"
10	24.5	S.	21.4	SE.	26.4	"	28.8	"	29.7	NW.	27.8	"	23.7	"	9.8	SE.	3.5	"	6.2	E.	4.5	NW.	9.8	"
11	24.5	E.	21.0	"	26.6	NW.	28.3	"	29.6	"	27.7	SE.	23.5	"	10.3	"	3.5	"	6.0	"	4.5	S.	10.0	NW.
12	24.8	"	20.5	N.	26.7	NE.	28.3	"	29.4	SW.	27.6	"	23.2	SE.	9.0	"	3.5	W.	6.2	"	4.5	"	10.5	"
13	24.7	"	20.2	E.	26.8	SE.	28.2	"	29.4	SE.	27.5	"	22.5	SW.	8.7	"	3.6	E.	6.5	"	4.0	N.	11.5	"
14	24.6	W.	20.0	"	26.9	NW.	28.8	N.	29.5	"	27.4	E.	22.0	SE.	8.5	S.	4.5	"	7.0	"	4.0	"	12.5	S.
15	24.2	NW.	19.8	S.	26.7	"	28.8	NE.	29.5	"	27.4	"	21.5	"	8.0	SW.	5.0	NE.	6.8	"	4.0	NE.	13.3	"
16	24.0	S.	19.5	E.	26.9	NE.	29.0	NW.	29.4	SW.	27.4	W.	21.4	"	7.5	"	5.2	NW.	6.8	"	4.0	SE.	14.6	W.
17	24.0	W.	19.4	"	27.1	S.	29.0	N.	29.4	S.	27.2	S.	20.6	S.	7.0	SE.	4.5	W.	7.0	"	4.2	E.	15.8	NW.
18	23.0	E.	19.4	S.	27.3	NW.	29.1	E.	29.1	"	27.0	SW.	20.0	"	7.0	E.	4.6	SE.	6.8	N.	4.3	W.	17.0	E.
19	23.0	"	19.4	"	27.4	SW.	29.1	"	28.8	SE.	26.9	S.	19.7	W.	7.1	NE.	4.5	SW.	6.8	NW.	4.0	SW.	17.5	N.
20	23.0	"	19.6	NW.	27.3	SE.	29.2	S.	28.9	S.	26.7	NW.	19.0	S.	7.0	N.	4.3	W.	6.4	NE.	3.5	S.	18.3	NW.
21	22.8	NW.	19.2	NE.	27.3	S.	29.3	"	28.8	"	26.5	NE.	18.0	SW.	6.8	NW.	4.0	N.	6.0	"	4.0	W.	19.0	NE.
22	22.8	N.	19.0	E.	27.7	"	29.3	NW.	28.7	N.	26.2	NW.	16.5	S.	6.7	SE.	3.8	NE.	6.0	E.	4.0	SE.	19.5	N.
23	22.5	"	19.4	S.	27.8	"	29.3	"	28.5	NE.	26.1	NE.	16.0	"	6.5	W.	3.7	E.	5.8	"	4.2	"	19.8	"
24	22.0	E.	20.0	"	27.8	"	29.3	S.	28.5	SE.	25.9	"	15.5	"	6.4	"	3.5	"	5.6	"	3.5	"	20.0	"
25	21.7	"	20.2	"	27.9	N.	29.3	SE.	28.4	"	25.5	E.	15.0	"	6.0	SW.	3.5	"	5.4	"	4.0	"	20.2	S.
26	21.6	"	21.5	E.	28.0	SE.	29.6	"	28.3	"	25.5	"	14.5	SW.	6.0	E.	3.5	"	5.4	NE.	4.2	S.	20.3	"
27	21.6	S.	22.0	"	28.3	E.	29.8	E.	28.1	NW.	25.5	"	13.9	"	5.5	S.	3.7	"	5.4	N.	3.8	"	20.5	"
28	21.7	"	23.5	N.	28.3	S.	29.8	"	28.1	E.	25.5	NE.	13.4	"	5.2	N.	3.7	"	5.2	"	4.2	W.	20.5	"
29	21.4	N.			28.3	"	29.9	W.	28.2	SE.	25.5	S.	12.4	W.	5.0	SW.	3.7	"	5.0	"	4.7	SE.	20.1	"
30	21.0	NE.			28.3	NW.	30.0	"	28.2	"	25.4	E.	12.2	NW.	5.0	NW.	4.3	"	4.5	E.	5.0	"	19.7	N.
31	20.8	E.			28.3	E.			28.2	W.			11.8	S.	5.0	NE.			3.8	N.			19.6	NE.

Records for 1859—Continued.

Carrollton.—Observer, Mr. W. H. Williams.

Date.	January.		February.		March.		April.		May.		June.		July.		August.		September.		October.		November.		December.	
1859.	G'ge	Wind.	G'ge	Wind.	G'ge	Wind.	G'ge	Wind.	G'ge	Wind.	G'ge	Wind.	G'ge	Wind.	G'ge	Wind.	G'ge	Wind.	G'ge	Wind.	G'ge	Wind.	G'ge	Wind.
1	10.7	N.	9.5	E.	11.2	N.	13.8	E.	15.5	SE.	13.6	NW.	11.4	S.	4.1	SW.	1.8	NW.	1.0	N.	0.8	N.		
2	10.7	"	9.6	NW.	11.5	S.	14.2	SW.	15.6	E.	13.4	W.	11.6	NW.	3.9	W.	1.7	"	1.7	"	0.7	"	2.0	
3	10.9	NW.	9.5	"	11.9	W.	14.3	S.	15.5	"	13.4	SW.	11.3	S.	3.7	S.	1.6	W.	1.7	"	0.8	"	2.1	
4	11.1	"	9.7	SW.	12.0	NE.	14.2	N.	15.6	"	13.4	NE.	11.2	"	3.5	NW.	1.7	"	1.7	"	1.2	"	2.2	
5	11.2	NE.	9.7	S.	12.1	E.	14.2	"	15.5	"	13.3	N.	11.1	NE.	3.5	S.	1.8	N.	1.8	NW.	1.4	NE.	2.4	
6	11.8	SE.	9.8	N.	12.4	"	14.3	E.	15.6	"	13.1	NW.	11.2	N.	3.4	E.	1.8	NW.	1.5	NE.	1.4	N.	2.5	
7	11.7	NW.	9.8	E.	12.4	NW.	14.3	NE.	15.3	"	13.2	N.	11.0	E.	3.5	W.	2.0	N.	2.0	N.	1.3	E.	2.8	
8	11.1	N.	9.9	S.	12.4	N.	14 4	E.	15.2	"	13.2	NE.	10.9	NW.	3.6	SW.	2.2	SE.	1.6	NW.	1.3	N.	2.9	
9	11.5	SW.	9.8	NW.	12.4	W.	14.4	S.	15.0	SW.	13.2	N.	11.0	E.	3.6	"	2.4	"	1.8	N.	1.0	S.	3.2	
10	11.5	E.	9.5	NE.	12.5	E.	14.5	"	14.8	NW.	13.2	W.	10.8	NW.	3.4	"	2.4	NE.	1.8	"	0.7	NW.	3.4	
11	11.7	NE.	9.4	"	12.7	NE.	14.6	"	14.7	"	13.2	NW.	10.7	SW.	3.7	"	2.2	SE.	1.8	"	0.7	S.	3.9	
12	11.8	"	9.2	N.	12.7	N.	14.6	"	14.6	E.	13.1	E.	10.5	NE.	3.7	E.	2.1	NW.	1.9	"	0.7	SW.	4.6	
13	11.8	SE.	9.1	NE.	12.9	S.	14.8	"	14.5	"	13.2	"	10.3	NW.	3.6	SE.	2.0	SE.	2.0	"	-0.4	NW.	4.9	
14	11.7	W.	8.9	S.	13.0	NW.	14.8	N.	14.5	"	13.1	W.	10.2	SW.	3.6	NW.	2.1	E.	1.8	S.	0.1	N.		
15	11.3	NW.	8.8	"	12.8	N.	14.8	"	14.5	NW.	13.2	SE.	9.9	"	3.2	W.	2.4	NE.	1.6	N.	0.1	NW.	5.6	
16	11.3	S.	8.7	"	12.9	NE.	14.9	"	14.5	"	13.0	W.	9.7	"	3.1	N.	1.8	N.	1.4	SE.	0.4	N.	6.3	
17	11.1	NW.	8.7	"	13.3	SW.	15.0	NW.	14.3	S.	12.9	S.	9.3	N.	3.1	NE.	1.7	E.	2.2	S.	1.0	E.	6.9	
18	11.0	N.	8.7	"	13.2	NW.	15.0	E.	14.3	SW.	12.7	SE.	9.0	E.	3.2	"	1.4	SW.	2.2	NE.	0.9	NW.	7.2	
19	11.1	"	8.7	"	13.1	W.	15.0	S.	14.1	NW.	12.6	SW.	8.6	S.	3.3	N.	1.5	SE.	2.1	N.	0.8	"	8.0	
20	11.2	E.	8.7	N.	13.2	S.	14.9	"	14.1	SE.	12.5	NW.	8.2	"	3.2	W.	1.5	NW.	2.0	"	0.6	E.	8.3	
21	11.4	NW.	8.6	E.	13.3	SE.	14.9	"	14.0	NW.	12.5	W.	7.8	W.	3.0	NW.	1.7	N.	2.0	"	1.0	W.	8.8	
22	10.8	N.	8.6	"	13.5	W.	14.9	NW.	14.0	N.	12.4	N.	7.3	"	3.0	SW.	1.5	"	2.1	NE.	0.8	N.	9.1	
23	10.4	"	8.8	S.	13.4	S.	14.9	N.	14.0	NW.	12.2	"	6.9	"	3.0	S.	1.8	NW.	1.8	E.	0.3	"	9.4	
24	10.3	"	8.9	"	13.5	"	14.9	S.	13.9	S.	12.2	E.	6.5	"	3.1	NW.	1.6	N.	1.7	N.	0.1	E.	9.4	
25	10.0	NE.	9.6	"	13.5	N.	15.0	"	13.9	E.	12.1	SE.	6.0	"	3.3	"	1.6	"	1.5	"	0.3	SW.	9.8	
26	9.9	"	9.9	E.	13.6	S.	15.1	"	13.8	"	12.0	"	5.8	"	3.0	SW.	1.3	SW.	1.2	"	0.5	"	9.9	
27	9.9	SW.	10.4	"	13.7	E.	15.3	N.	13.8	NW.	11.9	"	5.4	"	2.9	E.	1.2	N.	1.2	"	0.6	"	9.9	
28	9.9	"	10.7	NW.	13.7	SW.	15.2	E.	13.6	E.	11.6	E.	4.8	E.	2.5	SW.	1.0	SE.	1.1	"	0.7	W.	9.9	
29	9.8	N.			13.8	S.	15.4	S.	13.6	SW.	11.5	SE.	4.8	NW.	2.3	NW.	0.9	"	0.7	"	0.9	NE.	9.8	
30	9.6	E.			13.7	N.	15.5	N.	13.4	S.	11.6	"	4.3	S.	2.4	"	0.8	"	0.7	"	1.2	SW.	9.8	
31	9.6	NE.			13.6	E.			13.5	SW.			4.3	NE.	2.1	N.			0.4	"			9.7	

Records for 1860.

Donaldsonville.—Observer, Mr. A. Gingry.

Date.	January.		February.		March.		April.		May.		June.		July.		August.		September.		October.		November.		December.	
1860.	*G'ge*	*Wind.*	*G'ge*	*Wind.*	*G'ge*	*Wind.*	*G'ge*	*Wind.*	*G'ge*	*Wind.*	*G'ge*	*Wind.*	*G'ge*	*Wind.*	*G'ge*	*Wind.*	*G'ge*	*Wind.*	*G'ge*	*Wind.*	*G'ge*	*Wind.*	*G'ge*	*Wind.*
1	19.2	N.	26.5	N.	24.2	E.																		
2	18.5	NW.	26.4	SW.	24.2	"																		
3	18.0	"	26.5	"	24.2	"																		
4	17.8	E.	26.5	SE.	24.8	"																		
5	17.7	"	26.9	S.	24.8	"																		
6	17.6	"	27.0	N.	25.0	"																		
7	17.5	NW.	27.1	"	25.6	S.																		
8	17.6	SW.	26.0	SW.	25.7	"																		
9	17.5	SE.	26.0	"	25.7	N.																		
10	17.9	"	25.5	SE.	25.6	"																		
11	18.4	"	25.0	NW.	25.6	E.																		
12	18.8	NW.	24.5	SE.	25.6	W.																		
13	19.2	E.	24.2	"	25.6	NE.																		
14	19.5	NW.	23.5	S.	25.6	E.																		
15	19.5	"	23.0	SW.	25.6	"																		
16	19.5	SW.	22.3	SE.	25.7	"																		
17	19.6	NW.	22.0	S.																				
18	19.9	W.	21.5	NW.																				
19	20.1	"	21.5	"																				
20	20.5	E.	21.5	SE.																				
21	20.8	"	21.5	S.																				
22	21.1	SE.	21.6	"																				
23	22.0	E.	21.8	NW.																				
24	23.6	"	21.8	"																				
25	24.3	"	22.0	W.																				
26	24.8	SW.	22.5	E.																				
27	25.0	N.	23.0	"																				
28	25.4	NE.	23.5	"																				
29	25.6	E.	23.8	W.																				
30	26.0	S.																						
31	26.4	"																						

Records for 1860—Continued.

Carrollton.—Observer, Mr. W. H. Williams.

Date.	January.		February.		March.		April.		May.		June.		July.		August.		September.		October.		November.		December.	
1860.	*G'ge*	*Wind.*	*G'ge*	*Wind.*	*G'ge*	*Wind.*	*G'ge*	*Wind.*	*G'ge*	*Wind.*	*G'ge*	*Wind.*	*G'ge*	*Wind.*	*G'ge*	*Wind.*	*G'ge*	*Wind.*	*G'ge*	*Wind.*	*G'ge*	*Wind.*	*G'ge*	*Wind.*
1	9.3		12.6		12.2		11.5		9.4		3.4				1.8		0.9		1.2		0.1		2.4	
2	8.8				12.2		11.5		10.1		4.0				1.6		0.6		4.0	Gale.	0.0		2.2	
3	8.6		12.7		12.5		10.9		10.5		4.1				1.5		0.6		1.6		0.0		2.5	
4	8.2		12.8		12.5		10.7		10.7		4.0				1.4		0.5		0.9		-0.2		2.0	
5	7.9		13.2		12.7		10.3		10.7		4.1				1.4		0.6		0.7				1.9	
6	7.9		13.4		12.9		9.8		10.6						1.2		0.7		0.5		0.0		1.7	
7	8.0		13.2		13.0		9.6		10.6		4.0				1.0		1.0		0.5		0.3		1.7	
8	8.0				13.1		9.2		10.4		4.0		3.0		0.8		0.9		0.3		0.4		1.5	
9	8.0		12.8		13.1		8.3		10.3		4.1		2.7		1.1		1.2		0.6		0.1		1.5	
10	8.3		12.5		12.9		7.5		10.5		4.2		3.0		2.2		1.2		0.8		0.1		1.6	
11	8.6		12.3		12.8		6.3		9.7		4.4		2.5		6.0	Gale.	1.4		0.5		-0.2		1.6	
12	8.7		12.0		12.8				9.3		4.4		2.5		1.5		1.9		0.2		-0.2		1.8	
13	8.9		11.8		12.8				8.8		4.5		2.3		0.8		1.7		0.2		0.6		2.1	
14	8.9		11.6		12.7		6.1		8.3		4.5		2.5		1.7		1.0		-0.4		0.7		2.5	
15	9.1		11.5		12.8		5.7		7.3		4.5		2.3		1.6		3.6	Gale.	0.1		0.1		2.7	
16	9.2		11.2		12.9		5.6		7.1		4.4		2.6		1.7		1.2		0.0		0.4		2.9	
17	9.3		11.3		13.1		5.6		7.1		4.4		2.4		1.3		0.2		-0.3		1.0		2.8	
18	9.4		11.4		13.2		5.8		5.6		4.2		2.5		1.4		0.8		-0.7		1.0		3.0	
19	9.5		11.3		13.1		5.5		5.5		4.0		2.2		0.6		0.9		-0.5		1.8		3.1	
20	9.7		11.3		13.0		5.5		5.1		4.1		2.0		0.5		0.9		0.0		1.6		2.7	
21	10.2		11.4		13.0		5.4		4.6		3.8		1.8		0.5		0.3		-0.3		1.7		2.5	
22	10.7		11.6		13.0		5.3		4.2		3.8		1.4		0.7		1.3		0.0		2.0		2.0	
23	11.7		11.6		12.9		5.3		3.9		3.9		1.6		0.7		2.0		0.1		2.0		1.6	
24	11.4		11.4		12.9				3.6		4.1		1.5		0.9		1.4		0.0		1.8		1.6	
25	11.9		11.3		12.9		6.0		3.5				1.5		0.8		1.2		0.2		1.7		1.3	
26	12.3		11.2		12.8		6.5		3.2				1.3		0.9		1.0		-0.2		2.0		1.4	
27	12.5		11.3		12.7		6.9		3.1		4.7		1.6		1.0		0.9		0.0		2.8		1.5	
28	12.6		11.7		12.4		7.5		3.2		4.4		1.4		1.0		0.9		0.0		3.5		2.2	
29	12.4		12.3		12.3		8.5		3.4		4.4		1.5		1.0		1.1		-0.3		2.9		2.1	
30	12.6				12.0		8.8		3.5		4.4		1.8		0.9		1.2		-0.4		2.6		2.5	
31	12.9				11.7				3.6				1.8		0.9				-0.1				2.6	

Records for 1861.

Carrollton.—Observer, Mr. W. H. Williams.

Date.	January.		February.		March.		April.		May.		June.		July.		August.		September.		October.		November.		December.	
1861.	*G'ge*	*Wind.*	*G'ge*	*Wind.*	*G'ge*	*Wind.*	*G'ge*	*Wind.*	*G'ge*	*Wind.*	*G'ge*	*Wind.*	*G'ge*	*Wind.*	*G'ge*	*Wind.*	*G'ge*	*Wind.*	*G'ge*	*Wind.*	*G'ge*	*Wind.*	*G'ge*	*Wind.*
1	2.8		9.5		11.1		9.7																	
2	2.9		9.9		11.2		9.6																	
3	2.9		9.6		11.2		9.4																	
4	2.9		9.5		11.0		9.3																	
5	2.7		9.6		11.0		9.4																	
6	2.7		9.7		11.1		9.7																	
7	2.7		9.9		11.0		9.7																	
8	2.5		10.0		11.1		9.7																	
9	2.5		10.0		11.2		9.7																	
10	2.5		10.6		11.2		9.8																	
11	2.4		10.1		11.1		10.2																	
12	2.3		10.0		11.0		10.5																	
13	2.4		10.0		11.1		10.6																	
14	2.5		9.7		11.1		10.9																	
15	3.1		9.5		10.9		11.2																	
16	2.7		9.4		10.8		11.0																	
17	3.1		9.6		10.6		11.2																	
18	3.5		9.3		10.5		11.3																	
19	3.5		9.5		10.3		11.4																	
20	3.6		9.7		10.2		11.7																	
21	3.9		9.8		10.3		11.9																	
22	4.0		10.0		10.2		12.1																	
23	4.3		10.2		9.2		12.3																	
24	4.2		10.7		10.4		12.4																	
25	4.7		10.4		10.6		12.5																	
26	5.4		10.8		10.6		12.6																	
27	6.1		10.9		10.6		12.8																	
28	6.9		11.0		10.5		12.8																	
29	7.5				10.4		12.9																	
30	8.2				10.3		12.8																	
31	8.6				10.1																			

No. 2.—RECORDS OF DAILY STAND OF TRIBUTARIES AND BAYOUS.

Observations upon the Ohio river.

Observations on the "Pier-mark" at **Pittsburg,** during the years 1858–59. Compiled from THE LOUISVILLE COURIER.

Date.	Jan.	Feb.	Mar.	Apr.	May.	June.	July.	Aug.	Sept.	Oct.	Nov.	Dec.	Date.	Jan.	Feb.	Mar.	Apr.	May.	June.	July.	Aug.	Sept.	Oct.	Nov.	Dec.
1858.	G'ge.	G'ge.	G'ge.	G'ge.	G'ge.	G'ge.	G'ge.	G'ge.	G'ge.	G'ge.	G'ge.	G'ge.	1859.	G'ge.	G'ge.	G'ge.	G'ge.	G'ge.	G'ge.	G'ge.	G'ge.	G'ge.	G'ge.	G'ge.	G'ge.
1	13.3	5.7	3.6	6.0	6.5	15.0	4.1	2.2	2.0	1.6	2.5	8.8	1	9.0	8.1	11.2	8.1	11.0	3.4	5.1	1.6	1.7	4.2	2.0	4.8
2	11.1	5.3	3.6	6.0		16.5	4.0	4.0	2.0	2.5	2.5	6.2	2	9.0	8.0	10.3	7.7	9.8	3.3	6.0	1.6	2.8	4.3	2.0	5.0
3	9.0	5.0	7.0	5.5	7.0	12.9	4.0	4.0	2.0	3.5	2.6	5.4	3	9.0	6.9	9.5	7.2	8.5	3.5	5.8	1.5	1.6	4.5	2.3	8.2
4	8.5	5.0	6.0	6.5	7.0	10.8	4.0	4.0	2.0	4.3	2.6	7.3	4	8.1	6.8	8.8	6.5	7.7	3.8	6.6	1.7	1.6	4.2	2.3	9.6
5	8.0	5.0	5.5	5.1	7.0	11.0	4.0	4.0	2.0	4.1	2.8	9.3	5	7.1	6.7	8.7	6.1	7.0	3.7	7.4	3.0	1.6	4.2	2.3	11.0
6	7.5	4.6	5.5	4.7	6.5	12.5	4.0	3.9	1.6	3.7	4.2	11.4	6	6.8	6.5	8.7	6.1	6.5	3.6	6.8	4.8	1.3	4.0	2.1	11.0
7	7.0	4.3	5.0	4.5	9.3	13.5	3.8	3.7	1.6	3.0	4.0	12.0	7	6.5	6.1	8.7	5.8	5.8	3.4	6.0	6.4	1.2	3.5	2.0	14.5
8	6.6	4.0	4.0	5.1	10.5	12.5	3.7	3.5	1.6	3.3	5.0	10.8	8	6.1	5.2	10.0	5.4	5.5	3.2	5.1	5.0	1.1	2.6	2.0	16.6
9	6.2	4.0	4.0	5.0	9.5	10.5	3.5	3.3	1.6	3.5	5.6	12.0	9	6.1	5.3	11.5	9.0	5.2	3.2	4.7	4.0	1.0	2.3	2.0	14.0
10	5.8	5.1	4.0	4.9	8.5	10.9	3.1	3.0	1.5	3.7	5.7	11.1	10	6.0	5.3	12.2	9.7	4.9	4.4	4.3	2.9	1.0	2.7	2.0	11.0
11	6.0	4.9	4.0	6.2	8.0	11.3	3.0	2.6	1.5	4.0	5.8	8.1	11	5.2	5.4	10.8	10.2	4.8	4.5	4.0	2.4	1.0	2.2	2.0	9.5
12	6.0	3.7	5.5	8.0	11.0	11.5	3.4	2.6	1.5	4.3	5.3	7.6	12	5.5	5.3	10.0	10.7	4.6	4.1	3.6	2.2	1.0	2.2	3.5	8.0
13	6.0	3.7	10.0	13.0	12.3	12.0	4.1	2.6	1.5	4.0	4.9	6.9	13	6.0	5.2	10.7	13.0	4.5	3.6	3.7	2.1	1.0	2.1	5.2	7.5
14	7.3	3.6	15.0	14.0	11.0	12.5	7.0	2.6	1.5	3.7	4.5	10.2	14	6.6	5.0	10.8	11.2	4.4	3.8	3.5	4.0	0.9	2.2	6.5	7.0
15	8.2	3.6	18.5	18.3	10.1	12.8	7.0	2.4	1.5	3.6	4.0	13.0	15	6.4	5.9	10.0	12.0	4.2	4.3	3.4	6.0	3.2	2.2	7.0	6.2
16	8.8	3.6	12.0	12.3	10.1	10.5	6.2	2.3	1.5	3.5	4.0	20.2	16	6.8	6.8	9.5	11.0	4.0	5.8	3.4	5.0	5.5	1.9	7.0	5.8
17	9.4	3.6	13.3	10.8	10.2	9.3	5.6	2.2	1.5	3.4	4.0	16.5	17	8.1	14.2	9.5	10.0	4.1	8.2	3.6	4.7	7.7	2.0	6.6	5.8
18	9.2	3.6	14.6	9.5	11.4	8.0	5.0	2.0	1.5	3.1	4.0	12.8	18	7.6	14.5	9.0	9.3	3.8	7.5		4.2	9.6	2.0	4.8	5.8
19	9.2	3.6	16.0	8.5	11.5	7.3	4.5	2.0	1.5	3.1	4.0	10.7	19	7.1	15.3	11.0	8.3	3.6	7.3	3.9	4.0	9.0	2.1	5.0	5.8
20	8.3	3.6	14.3	11.3	10.0	6.5	4.0	2.0	1.5	3.0	3.9	8.8	20	6.7	16.0	12.3	7.8	3.5	7.2	3.6	3.6	7.0	2.2	6.1	5.9
21	7.3	3.6	13.5	10.3	9.5	5.8	4.0	1.9	1.1	2.7	3.7	8.5	21	6.2	16.7	13.5	7.8	4.0	7.2	4.1	3.2	5.2	2.8	7.2	5.5
22	6.4	3.6	12.5	12.5	8.7	5.3	3.5	1.9	1.1	2.6	3.6	10.0	22	7.2	17.5	11.5	7.5	3.6	5.8	4.0	2.6	4.5	2.7	7.5	6.0
23	6.1	3.6	11.5	12.5	8.0	5.0	3.2	1.8	1.1	2.5	3.5	10.8	23	8.1	12.8	11.0	13.0	4.0	5.6	4.0	2.5	5.3	2.7	8.0	5.8
24	6.0	3.6	10.0	12.5	7.2	4.7	3.1	1.6	1.4	3.3	3.5	11.5	24	9.0	10.3	10.5	19.5	3.8	5.3	3.5	2.2	5.0	2.6	7.4	4.6
25	5.9	3.6	9.5	10.5	7.0	4.3	3.0	1.5	1.4	4.2	3.6	10.0	25	7.0	9.5	11.0	16.5	4.0	6.0	3.6	2.0	4.7	2.6	6.8	4.8
26	5.7	3.6	8.8	8.0	22.0	5.0	2.7	1.6	1.4	4.0	3.7	8.7	26	6.8	10.3	11.3	17.5	3.6	6.0	3.3	1.7	4.4	2.6	6.3	5.2
27	5.5	3.6	8.5	7.8	23.2	5.4	2.7	1.5	1.5	4.0	3.8	7.0	27	6.7	11.2	12.0	18.5	3.5	6.0	3.0	2.0	4.2	2.8	5.8	5.5
28	5.3	3.6	7.8	6.9	19.3	5.5	2.6	1.5	1.6	3.2	3.9	7.5	28	6.6	12.0	9.8	22.5	3.4	5.8	2.7	1.9	4.2	2.8	5.5	5.8
29	7.0		7.2	6.4	15.5	5.0	2.5	1.7	1.6	3.2	4.0	8.3	29	8.0		9.0	19.0	3.3	5.5	2.3	2.0	4.5		5.3	5.8
30	6.8		6.5	6.0	14.3	4.5	2.2	1.7	1.6	2.8	11.0	8.6	30	9.2		8.8	15.6	3.3	5.0	2.0	2.1	5.0		5.0	5.5
31	6.3		6.3		13.0		2.2	1.8		2.6		8.8	31	9.1		8.6		3.4		1.8	2.1				5.4

Observations upon the Ohio river—Continued.

Observations on the "Canal-mark" at **Louisville,** in 1858–59. Compiled from THE LOUISVILLE COURIER.

Date.	Jan.	Feb.	Mar.	Apr.	May.	June.	July.	Aug.	Sept.	Oct.	Nov.	Dec.	Date.	Jan.	Feb.	Mar.	Apr.	May.	June.	July.	Aug.	Sept.	Oct.	Nov.	Dec.
1858.	G'ge.	G'ge.	G'ge.	G'ge.	G'ge.	G'ge.	G'ge.	G'ge.	G'ge.	G'ge.	G'ge.	G'ge.	1859.	G'ge.	G'ge.	G'ge.	G'ge.	G'ge.	G'ge.	G'ge.	G'ge.	G'ge.	G'ge.	G'ge.	G'ge.
1	9.0	6.5	7.2	8.0	9.0	14.0	5.2	3.6	2.5	2.0	3.0	5.1	1	8.9	7.3	18.0	9.0	27.0	4.2	4.7	3.0	3.5	5.1	3.1	6.1
2	9.2	6.5	7.6	7.0	8.5	12.0	5.0	3.5	2.4	1.8	3.2	5.0	2	8.0	7.3	18.0	9.0	29.0	4.1	4.6	3.0	3.3	5.0	3.1	7.0
3	10.8	7.0	7.5	6.7	8.0	11.6	5.0	4.4	2.6	1.7	3.5	5.5	3	9.1	7.6	18.0	8.0	27.8	4.1	4.6	3.0	3.2	4.8	3.0	7.3
4	11.3	7.0	7.6	6.5	8.5	11.0	5.0	4.3	2.5	1.7	3.2	5.6	4	9.5	7.8	18.0	8.6	25.3	3.9	4.5	2.8	3.1	4.6	2.9	6.8
5	12.0	7.2	8.0	7.5	9.0	11.0	5.0	4.2	2.5	2.0	3.1	5.7	5	9.5	8.0	15.2	8.8	22.3	3.7	4.5	2.8	3.1	4.6	2.9	6.8
6	13.0	6.7	7.0	7.3	9.0	11.0	5.0	4.2	2.5	2.1	3.0	7.0	6	9.3	8.0	12.0	9.0	13.0	3.6	4.3	2.9	3.0	4.6	2.8	8.0
7	14.0	6.6	7.0	6.7	9.0	12.5	4.8	3.9	2.5	2.1	3.0	7.0	7	9.2	8.0	9.0	9.7	11.0	3.6	4.3	3.1	2.9	4.4	2.8	10.5
8	13.5	6.5	7.0	6.8	9.2	13.0	4.7	3.7	2.5	2.1	3.2	7.0	8	8.9	7.8	8.7	9.0	9.0	3.6	4.1	2.9	2.2	4.5	2.7	12.0
9	11.8	6.5	6.5	6.0	9.5	12.0	4.7	4.0	2.4	2.1	3.6	7.7	9	8.6	7.7	8.5	8.3	8.0	3.7	4.1	2.8	2.7	4.6	2.7	13.5
10	10.0	6.3	6.1	6.7	11.0	10.5	4.6	4.0	2.4	2.1	3.7	8.7	10	8.0	7.7	8.5	7.7	7.5	3.7	4.1	2.7	2.6	4.5	2.6	13.0
11	7.8	6.1	6.0	7.5	11.7	11.0	4.6	4.0	2.3	2.1	3.7	9.2	11	7.4	7.7	8.5	7.3	7.0	3.6	4.4	2.8	2.6	4.4	2.6	12.5
12	8.0	5.6	6.0	9.0	12.5	14.0	4.6	4.1	2.2	2.1	3.7	9.7	12	7.0	8.0	8.5	7.0	6.5	3.6	4.5	2.8	2.6	4.2	3.1	12.0
13	8.0	5.8	7.0	9.7	11.0	17.0	4.7	4.2	2.0	2.0	3.7	9.5	13	6.6	8.1	8.6	9.0	6.1	3.5	4.6	3.1	2.6	4.1	3.7	11.5
14	8.0	5.7	8.1	9.5	10.7	17.0	4.7	4.1	2.0	2.0	4.0	9.6	14	6.5	8.2	8.7	11.0	6.0	3.7	4.4	3.4	2.5	3.9	4.5	11.0
15	7.0	5.6	7.0	9.5	10.8	17.0	5.0	4.0	2.0	2.4	4.0	14.0	15	6.6	9.6	9.0	12.0	5.7	4.0	4.2	3.7	2.4	3.7	4.1	9.5
16	7.5	5.5	7.5	10.0	11.0	18.0	5.0	3.8	2.0	2.7	4.0	18.0	16	6.8	11.0	9.0	11.4	5.5	4.1	4.1	3.7	2.4	3.5	3.6	8.5
17	8.0	5.5	6.5	10.5	12.5	17.5	5.2	3.5	1.9	3.0	4.0	18.0	17	7.0	11.0	9.0	10.7	5.2	4.1	4.0	3.6	2.3	3.4	4.0	8.2
18	7.5	5.3	6.0	11.0	13.0	17.0	5.5	3.3	1.9	3.0	4.0	17.7	18	6.7	17.0	8.7	10.0	5.0	4.5	3.6	3.5	2.3	3.5	4.5	8.0
19	7.6	5.3	8.0	11.0	12.5	14.2	5.7	3.2	1.8	3.0	4.0	17.5	19	6.6	23.0	9.8	8.0	5.0	5.0	3.5	3.5	2.3	3.4	5.5	8.3
20	7.8	5.4	9.5	11.0	12.0	11.5	6.0	3.0	1.8	3.0	3.8	17.3	20	6.5	20.0	11.0	10.0	5.0	5.3	3.3	3.8	2.3	3.3	6.5	8.7
21	8.0	5.4	11.0	11.0	11.2	9.0	6.2	3.0	1.8	3.2	3.7	17.2	21	7.0	32.0	13.0	10.0	5.0	5.6	3.2	3.8	2.3	3.2	6.5	8.6
22	8.0	5.5	10.7	11.0	10.3	9.0	6.0	3.0	1.7	3.2	3.7	17.0	22	7.5	33.5	15.0	11.0	5.0	6.3	3.0	4.1	6.0	3.1	6.5	8.2
23	8.0	5.5	10.5	11.0	9.5	8.0	5.8	3.0	1.7	3.2	3.6	14.3	23	8.1	33.7	14.0	12.0	5.0	6.7	3.0	4.6	6.3	3.1	6.5	7.7
24	7.4	5.8	10.5	10.5	9.0	7.0	5.4	2.6	1.7	3.2	3.6	11.7	24	8.3	34.0	14.5	13.0	5.0	6.5	3.1	4.6	6.4	3.1	6.6	7.4
25	7.4	6.0	10.5	10.0	11.0	7.0	5.1	2.6	1.7	3.1	3.5	12.2	25	9.0	33.2	14.5	11.5	4.8	6.0	3.1	4.5	6.5	3.0	6.7	7.1
26	7.0	6.2	10.5	10.0	13.0	6.7	4.6	2.6	1.7	3.0	3.5	12.7	26	9.2	29.0	13.2	14.5	4.8	5.9	3.1	4.3	6.6	2.9	6.8	7.1
27	7.0	6.4	9.7	11.0	13.5	6.5	4.2	2.5	1.7	2.8	3.4	10.5	27	8.7	23.5	12.0	16.0	4.7	5.7	3.0	4.1	6.6	2.9	7.0	7.2
28	7.0	6.7	9.2	10.3	14.0	5.7	4.1	2.5	1.7	3.0	3.3	10.1	28	8.2	18.0	14.0	21.0	4.7	5.5	3.0	3.8	6.2	2.9	6.8	7.5
29	7.0		8.5	10.0	14.0	5.5	4.0	2.5	1.8	3.0	3.5	9.5	29	7.9		12.0	23.0	4.7	5.2	3.0	4.0	5.6	3.0	6.6	7.5
30	6.5		8.0	9.5	14.0	5.4	3.8	2.5	1.9	3.0	4.0	9.0	30	7.6		10.4	25.0	4.6	5.0	3.0	3.9	5.3	3.1	6.4	7.1
31	6.5		7.5		14.0		3.7	2.5		3.0		8.6	31	7.5		9.5		4.5		3.1	3.7		3.2		7.0

Observations upon bayou Tensas at crossing of Vidalia and Harrisonburg road.

Flood of 1844.			Flood of 1849.			Flood of 1850.					Flood of 1858.			Remarks.
Date.	Ga'ge.	Remarks.	Date.	Ga'ge.	Remarks.	Date.	Ga'ge.	Date.	Ga'ge.	Remarks.	Date.	Ga'ge.	Remarks.	
1844.	*Feet.*		1849.	*Feet.*		1850.	*Feet.*	1850.	*Feet.*		1858.	*Feet.*		
June 7	45.3		Apr. 25	44.4		Jan. 22	40.0	Mch. 13	48.7	Previous to the 18th of January the bayou had been rising about one foot per day.	April 9	38.7		These records were presented to the Survey by MR. H. D. MANDEVILLE, by whom they were kept. They have been reduced to the same absolute zero as the gauge kept at Natchez, by means of the level survey in charge of MR. PATTISON, made in 1859.
8	45.5		26	44.5		23	40.3	14	48.8		May 27	43.5		
13	45.6		27	44.5		24	40.7	15	48.9		31	43.5		
21	46.1		28	44.7		25	41.0	16	48.9		June 6	43.6		
July 2	46.4		29	44.8		26	41.3	17	49.0		12	43.7		
3	46.7		30	44.9		27	41.4	18	49.1		15	43.6		
4	46.9		May 1	45.0		28	41.6	19	48.9		16	43.6		
5	47.0		2	45.2		29	41.8	20	48.8		17	43.6		
6	47.2		3	45.4		30	42.0	21	48.6		18	43.7		
7	47.4		4	45.6		31	42.1	22	48.6		19	43.9		
8	47.5		5	45.8		Feb. 1	42.3	23	48.3		20	43.9		
9	47.6		6	46.0		3	42.4	24	48.3		21	43.9		
10	47.7		7	46.2		4	42.6	25	48.0		22	44.0		
11	47.8		8	46.4		5	42.7	26	47.7		23	43.9		
12	47.8		9	46.6		6	42.8	27	47.4		24	43.9		
13	47.9		10	46.7		7	42.9	28	47.0		25	43.9		
14	48.0		11	46.6		8	43.1	30	46.5		26	43.9		
15	48.0		12	46.5		9	43.1	31	46.0		27	43.9		
16	48.1		13	46.4		10	43.3	April 2	46.2		28	44.0		
18	48.1		14	46.3		11	43.4	5	46.0		29	44.1		
19	48.1		15	46.1		12	43.8	6	46.0		30	44.1		
20	48.1		21	45.7	From the 21st of May fell rapidly to low water. Was very high in December, 1849.	13	44.1	7	46.0		July 1	44.2		
21	48.1					14	44.3	9	46.0		2	44.2		
22	48.1					15	44.5	17	48.2		3	44.2		
23	48.0					16	44.6	18	48.3		4	44.3		
24	48.0					17	44.8	19	48.3		5	44.4		
25	47.9					18	45.0	21	48.4		6	44.5		
26	47.8					19	45.1	25	48.4		7	44.6		
27	47.7					20	45.2	27	48.5		8	44.7		
28	47.7					21	45.5	28	48.5		9	44.9		
29	47.5					22	45.8	29	48.5		10	45.1		
30	47.5					23	45.9	30	48.6		11	45.1		
31	47.3					24	46.1	May 9	49.7		12	45.2		
Aug. 1	47.2					26	46.4	13	49.7		13	45.4		
3	47.2					27	46.7	14	49.7		14	45.5		
						Mch. 2	46.9	June 16	49.1		15	45.7		
						5	47.2	18	48.7		16	45.8		
						6	47.2	19	48.1		17	45.9		
						7	47.5	22	47.6		Aug. 5	46.7	Fell from this date to low-water mark.	
						8	47.6	23	47.1					
						9	47.7	24	47.0					
						10	48.1	27	46.8					
						11	48.3	July 1	44.1					
						12	48.5							

No. 3.—TIDAL OBSERVATIONS WITH SIMPLE GAUGE-RODS.

These observations are so numerous that a synopsis of the most important results is prefixed. It is presented in the following table, which exhibits the gauge-readings corresponding to the several headings:—

Date.	Lake Pontchartrain.				Lake Borgne.				Bayou St. Philip.			
	Mean high tide.	Mean low tide.	Mean tidal oscillation.	Mean level of lake.	Mean high tide.	Mean low tide.	Mean tidal oscillation.	Mean level of lake.	Mean high tide.	Mean low tide.	Mean tidal oscillation.	Mean level of lake.
	Feet.	*Feet.*	*Feet.*	*Feet.*	*Feet.*	*Feet.*	*Feet.*	*Feet.*	*Feet.*	*Feet.*	*Feet.*	*Feet.*
February, 1851	8.3	7.7	0.5	8.0					3.3	2.2	1.1	2.8
March, "	8.0	7.6	0.4	7.8					3.3	2.7	0.6	3.0
April, "	8.2	7.9	0.3	8.0					3.5	2.7	0.8	3.1
May, "	8.4	8.1	0.3	8.2	4.2	3.0	1.2	3.6	3.7	2.4	1.3	3.0
June, "	8.2	7.8	0.4	8.0	4.1	3.0	1.1	3.5	3.7	2.2	1.5	2.9
July, "	8.1	7.8	0.3	7.9	4.1	2.9	1.2	3.5	3.7	2.2	1.5	2.9
August, "	8.2	7.8	0.4	8.0	4.3	3.1	1.2	3.7	3.7	2.6	1.1	3.1
September, "	8.9	8.6	0.3	8.7	4.9	3.7	1.2	4.3	4.2	3.3	0.9	3.7
October, "	8.4	8.1	0.3	8.2	4.3	3.2	1.1	3.7	3.9	2.7	1.2	3.3
November, "					4.0	2.9	1.1	3.4	3.7	2.4	1.3	3.0
December, "									3.4	1.8	1.6	2.6
January, 1852									3.8	1.5	1.3	2.1
Mean	8.30	7.90	0.40	8.10	4.28	3.11	1.16	3.69	3.62	2.38	1.20	3.00

The detailed observations from which the above mean results are derived will be found in the following pages.

Date.	Lake Pontchartrain.				Lake Borgne.						Bayou St. Philip.						
	Time.	Gauge (zero at bottom of canal).	Wind.		Time.	Gauge.		Tidal oscillation.	Wind.		Time.	Gauge. Bench of fort reads 6.0.			Tidal oscillation.	Wind.	
			Direction.	Force.		High tide.	Low tide.		Direction.	Force.		High tide.	Low tide.	Mean reading.		Direction.	Force.
1851.	*h. m.*	*Feet.*			*h. m.*	*Feet.*	*Feet.*	*Feet.*			*h. m.*	*Feet.*	*Feet.*	*Feet.*	*Feet.*		
Jan. 30	6 25 a.m.	7.6															
"	5 35 p.m.	7.2															
31	M.	7.5															
"	5 40 p.m.	7.3															
Feb. 1	7 00 a.m.	7.7	NE.	3							10 00 p.m.	4.04				E.	4
"	9 00 p.m.	8.5	"	3													
2	9 00 a.m.	9.0	SE.	1							0 15 p.m.		2.45	3.2	1.59	S.	1
"	9 00 p.m.	8.6	"	1													
3	6 00 a.m.	8.5	NE.	1							1 00 a.m.	3.50				Calm.	0
"	9 00 p.m.	8.1	NW.	1							10 30 a.m.		2.29	2.9	1.21	SE.	1
"											10 08 p.m.	3.33				NNW.	2
4	9 00 a.m.	8.2	"	1							0 30 p.m.		2.37	2.8	0.96	N.	2
"	9 00 p.m.	7.8	"	2							11 40 p.m.	3.29				"	1
5	6 30 a.m.	7.6	N.	1							11 30 a.m.		2.29	2.8	1.00	NNE.	2
"	9 00 p.m.	7.2	NW.	1							10 40 p.m.	3.25				W.	2
6	6 20 a.m.	7.1	W.	1							9 00 a.m.		1.79	2.5	1.46	"	1
"	6 00 p.m.	6.9	SW.	1							4 30 p.m.	2.25				Calm.	0
"											11 10 p.m.		1.75	2.0	0.50	"	0
7	9 00 a.m.	7.0	SE.	1							5 07 a.m.	2.33				"	0
"	12 00 p.m.	7.2	"	1							8 30 a.m.		2.20	2.2	0.13	E.	1
"											5 00 p.m.	2.58				"	1
8	6 30 a.m.	7.1	"	1							4 00 a.m.		2.00	2.3	0.58	Calm.	0
"	12 00 p.m.	7.2	"	2							7 10 p.m.	2.79				SE.	1
9	9 00 a.m.	7.2	"	3							M.		2.08	2.4	0.71	"	5
"	9 00 p.m.	7.7	S.	3							7 00 p.m.	3.16				SW.	1
10	0 30 a.m.	8.0	W.	2							8 50 a.m.		1.83	2.5	1.33	"	4
"	M.	7.8	N.	2							7 00 p.m.	3.00				NW.	4
"	12 00 p.m.	7.4	NE.	3							6 10 a.m.		2.25	2.6	0.75	N.	4
11	3 00 p.m.	7.1	NW.	2							9 07 p.m.	3.75				"	2
12	6 20 a.m.	7.6	NE.	2							8 10 a.m.		2.71	3.2	1.04	NE.	4
"	6 00 p.m.	7.5	"	2							9 40 p.m.	4.00				E.	6
13	6 30 a.m.	8.2	E.	3							5 30 a.m.		2.54	3.2	1.46	"	4
"	6 00 p.m.	8.9	SE.	2							11 20 p.m.	4.16				Calm.	0
14	6 30 a.m.	9.4	S.	1							9 30 a.m.		2.29	3.2	1.87	S.	1
"	12 00 p.m.	8.7	"	1							11 40 p.m.	3.83				SW.	4

Tidal Observations—Continued.

Date.	Lake Pontchartrain.				Lake Borgne.						Bayou St. Philip.						
	Time.	Gauge (zero at bottom of canal).	Wind.		Time.	Gauge.		Tidal oscillation.	Wind.		Time.	Gauge. Bench of fort reads 6.0.			Tidal oscillation.	Wind.	
			Direction.	Force.		High tide.	Low tide.		Direction.	Force.		High tide.	Low tide.	Mean reading.		Direction.	Force.
1851.	*h. m.*	*Feet.*			*h. m.*	*Feet.*	*Feet.*	*Feet.*			*h. m.*	*Feet.*	*Feet.*	*Feet.*	*Feet.*		
Feb. 15	9 00 a.m.	9.1	NW.	3							10 00 a.m.		1.66	2.7	2.17	W.	4
"	9 00 p.m.	8.4	"	2													
16	9 00 a.m.	8.5	N.	2							0 50 a.m.	3.83				N.	4
"	9 00 p.m.	8.0	"	2							10 40 a.m.		2.54	3.1	1.29	"	4
17	9 00 a.m.	8.2	NE.	3							1 35 a.m.	3.91				"	2
"	M.	7.8	E.	1							0 45 p.m.		2.41	3.1	1.50	NE.	4
18	10 00 a.m.	8.0	NE.	2							2 10 a.m.	3.33				"	3
"	6 00 p.m.	7.7	E.	1							1 10 p.m.		2.75	3.0	0.58	"	1
19	6 30 a.m.	7.6	"	2							4 00 a.m.	3.08				Calm.	0
"	9 00 p.m.	8.2	"	2							9 20 a.m.		2.41	2.7	0.67	SE.	5
"											7 10 p.m.	3.33				S.	2
20	2 00 p.m.	8.3	SE.	1							2 08 a.m.		2.83	3.0	0.50	SE.	3
"	6 00 p.m.	8.1	N.	1							5 00 a.m.	3.08				"	2
"											10 07 a.m.		2.58	2.8	0.50	"	2
"											5 00 p.m.	2.87				"	1
"											9 10 p.m.		2.63	2.7	0.24	NE.	1
21	6 00 p.m.	8.0	NW.	1							3 14 a.m.	3.25				"	1
"	9 00 p.m.	7.9	"	1							7 20 a.m.		3.04	3.1	0.21	N.	2
"											5 10 p.m.	3.33				"	1
22	11 30 a.m.	7.6	SE.	1							4 20 a.m.		2.29	2.8	1.04	Calm.	0
"	12 00 p.m.	8.1	"	1							5 10 p.m.	3.45				SE.	1
23	6 30 a.m.	7.7	S.	2							5 10 a.m.		2.25	2.9	1.20	E.	1
"	M.	8.0	"	1							6 30 p.m.	3.21				SE.	1
24	9 00 a.m.	8.2	NW.	3							6 15 a.m.		2.00	2.6	1.21	Calm.	0
"	9 00 p.m.	7.7	NE.	1							5 30 p.m.	3.29				NE.	1
25	M.	7.8	E.	2							5 45 a.m.		1.91	2.6	1.38	"	1
"	12 00 p.m.	7.6	SE.	1							5 45 p.m.	3.50				"	2
26	6 00 a.m.	8.1	"	1							4 20 a.m.		1.96	2.7	1.54	ENE.	1
"	6 00 p.m.	7.8	"	2							7 10 p.m.	3.37				SE.	2
27	6 30 a.m.	8.2	S.	1							8 30 a.m.		1.96	2.6	1.41	SSE.	2
"	6 00 p.m.	7.8	"	1							9 15 p.m.	3.37				S.	2
28	9 00 a.m.	8.7	NW.	6							9 25 a.m.		1.95	2.6	1.42	SW.	2
"	12 00 p.m.	8.1	"	3							10 22 p.m.	3.58				NNW.	6
March 1	6 30 a.m.	7.8	"	2							10 35 a.m.		2.66	3.1	0.92	N.	3
"	6 00 p.m.	7.6	N.	2							10 45 p.m.	3.33				WNW.	2
2	6 30 a.m.	7.8	"	2							11 15 a.m.		2.41	2.8	0.92	NNW.	2
"	6 00 p.m.	7.5	"	2							11 20 p.m.	3.37				N.	3
3	6 30 a.m.	7.6	SW.	2							11 05 a.m.		2.37	2.8	1.00	NE.	2
"	6 00 p.m.	7.2	"	1							3 30 p.m.	2.45				"	1
"											7 35 p.m.		2.29	2.3	0.16	Calm.	0
4	6 30 a.m.	7.2	"	1							0 10 a.m.	2.45				"	0
"	6 00 p.m.	7.2	SE.	1							8 20 a.m.		1.96	2.2	0.47	"	0
"											10 10 p.m.	2.75				"	0
5	6 30 a.m.	7.5	"	1							1 15 a.m.		2.50	2.6	0.25	"	0
"	12 00 p.m.	7.9	"	2							4 17 a.m.	2.83				"	0
"											7 20 a.m.		2.54	2.6	0.29	NE.	1
"											7 15 p.m.	3.25				SE.	2
"											10 45 p.m.		3.00	3.1	0.25	Calm.	0
6	6 30 a.m.	8.0	S.	1							4 18 a.m.	3.50				SE.	2
"	6 00 p.m.	8.5	NW.	3							0 10 p.m.		2.75	3.1	0.75	S.	3
"											4 10 p.m.	2.95				SW.	2
"											8 17 p.m.		2.75	2.8	0.20	WNW.	3
7	6 40 a.m.	8.0	W.	3							2 15 a.m.	3.12				"	3
"	9 00 p.m.	7.5	NW.	2							11 35 a.m.		2.25	2.6	0.87	"	3
"											5 10 p.m.	2.58				NW.	2
"											10 45 p.m.		1.91	2.2	0.67	N.	2
8	7 00 a.m.	7.2	N.	2							10 15 a.m.	2.95				NNE.	2
"	10 40 a.m.	7.1	SE.	1							M.		2.85	2.9	0.10	NE.	3
"											5 30 p.m.	2.95				Calm.	0
9	M.	7.2	N.	2							3 20 a.m.		2.00	2.4	0.95	NE.	1
"	12 00 p.m.	7.6	S.	1							3 30 p.m.	3.08				"	1
10	M.	7.2	NE.	2							4 15 a.m.		1.91	2.4	1.17	Calm.	0
"	12 00 p.m.	7.6	"	1							3 35 p.m.	3.29				ENE.	2
11	M.	7.3	N.	1							5 45 a.m.		1.75	2.5	1.54	Calm.	0
"	12 00 p.m.	7.5	S.	1							5 45 p.m.	3.20				SE.	2
12	6 30 a.m.	7.5	SE.	1							6 10 a.m.		1.70	2.4	1.50	"	1
"	6 15 p.m.	7.2	"	1							5 30 p.m.	3.16				"	1
13	M.	7.4	E.	2							5 15 a.m.		2.16	2.6	1.00	ESE.	1
"	12 00 p.m.	7.8	SE.	3							5 45 p.m.	3.87				NNE.	3
14	M.	8.1	"	2							6 50 a.m.		2.87	3.3	1.00	E by S.	2
"	12 00 p.m.	8.5	"	1							8 30 p.m.	4.12				ESE.	2
15	8 00 a.m.	8.7	"	2							0 30 a.m.		3.50	3.8	0.60	S.	3
"	6 00 p.m.	8.3	S.	2													
16	6 00 a.m.	8.5	"	1							2 15 a.m.	4.25				SW.	2
"	6 00 p.m.	8.1	NW.	1							2 40 p.m.		3.66	3.9	0.59	SSW.	3
17	6 00 a.m.	8.2	"	3							3 12 a.m.	3.95				N.	3
"	12 00 p.m.	7.6	"	3							9 00 p.m.		2.83	3.3	1.12	Calm.	0
18	9 00 a.m.	7.6	NNW.	2							9 45 a.m.	3.33				NNW.	3
"	6 00 p.m.	7.2	N.	2							10 15 p.m.		2.75	3.0	0.48	"	1
19	6 00 a.m.	7.2	NE.	3							10 30 a.m.	3.04				NE.	1
"	3 00 p.m.	7.1	W.	1							11 05 p.m.		2.16	2.6	0.88	S.	1
20	6 00 a.m.	7.1	SW.	1							2 35 p.m.	3.12				E.	2
"	12 00 p.m.	7.5	SE.	1													
21	6 15 a.m.	7.4	"	1							3 10 a.m.		1.95	2.5	1.17	"	1
"	M.	7.9	"	2							2 30 p.m.	3.37				S.	3
22	M.	7.6	SW.	1							3 40 a.m.		2.66	3.0	0.71	Calm.	0
"	12 00 p.m.	7.9	NW.	1							3 37 p.m.	3.29				WSW.	2
23	6 00 a.m.	7.8	"	2							3 45 a.m.		2.79	3.0	0.50	SW.	1

Tidal Observations—Continued.

Date.	Lake Pontchartrain. Time.	Lake Pontchartrain. Gauge (zero at bottom of canal).	Lake Pontchartrain. Wind. Direction.	Lake Pontchartrain. Wind. Force.	Lake Borgne. Time.	Lake Borgne. Gauge. High tide.	Lake Borgne. Gauge. Low tide.	Lake Borgne. Tidal oscillation.	Lake Borgne. Wind. Direction.	Lake Borgne. Wind. Force.	Bayou St. Philip. Time.	Bayou St. Philip. Gauge. Bench of fort reads 6.0. High tide.	Bayou St. Philip. Gauge. Low tide.	Bayou St. Philip. Gauge. Mean reading.	Bayou St. Philip. Tidal oscillation.	Bayou St. Philip. Wind. Direction.	Bayou St. Philip. Wind. Force.
1851.	*h. m.*	*Feet.*			*h. m.*	*Feet.*	*Feet.*	*Feet.*			*h. m.*	*Feet.*	*Feet.*	*Feet.*	*Feet.*		
M'rch 23	3 00 p.m.	7.4	NW.	2							4 40 p.m.	3.66				E.	1
24	6 00 a.m.	7.7	"	3							5 50 a.m.		3.00	3.3	0.66	NW.	3
"	M.	7.8	NE.	3							5 30 p.m.	3.45				Calm.	0
25	6 00 a.m.	7.7	"	2							6 50 a.m.		2.70	3.0	0.75	"	0
"	12 00 p.m.	7.3	SE.	1							5 15 p.m.	3.20				"	0
26	3 00 p.m.	7.3	"	2							6 10 a.m.		2.87	2.7	0.83	"	0
"	12 00 p.m.	7.5	"	2							5 35 p.m.	3.79				ESE.	5
27	3 00 p.m.	7.9	"	2							7 45 a.m.		2.91	3.3	0.88	"	2
"	6 00 p.m.	8.2	W.	2							7 35 p.m.	3.66				NW.	3
28	6 45 a.m.	8.5	SE.	1							7 30 a.m.		3.41	3.5	0.25	ESE.	1
"	3 00 p.m.	8.2	"	1							8 45 p.m.	3.83				Calm.	0
29	M.	8.4	E.	2							8 15 a.m.		3.50	3.6	0.33	E.	2
"	12 00 p.m.	8.9	SE.	1							9 30 p.m.	4.12				"	1
30	6 00 a.m.	8.9	NE.	0							9 15 a.m.		3.70	3.9	0.42	E by S.	2
"	6 00 p.m.	8.6	SE.	2							10 10 p.m.	4.00				ESE.	3
31	M.	8.8	E.	2							10 30 a.m.		3.91	4.0	0.09	"	3
"	9 00 p.m.	9.0	S.	1							8 17 p.m.	4.08				SE.	1
April 1	6 00 a.m.	8.8	"	2	6 00 a.m.						11 15 a.m.		3.37	3.7	0.71	NW.	1
"	M.	8.3	NE.	2	6 00 p.m.	4.3					2 20 p.m.	3.54				SW.	3
2	6 00 a.m.	8.2	"	1							3 45 a.m.		2.95	3.2	0.59	E.	2
"	5 00 p.m.	8.1	"	1							2 05 p.m.	3.66				NE.	2
3	9 00 a.m.	8.0	"	2							1 30 a.m.		2.70	3.2	0.96	"	1
"	9 00 p.m.	8.2	E.	1							2 10 p.m.	3.62				E.	1
4	9 00 a.m.	8.0	"	1							2 07 a.m.		2.95	3.2	0.67	"	1
"	9 00 p.m.	8.3	SE.	2							2 35 p.m.	3.62				SSE.	1
5	6 30 a.m.	8.1	S.	1							2 25 a.m.		2.83	3.2	0.79	S.	2
"	10 00 a.m.	7.8	NE.	2							0 20 p.m.	3.66				"	1
6	1 30 p.m.	8.1	"	2							1 12 a.m.		2.75	3.2	0.91	SW.	3
"	12 00 p.m.	8.7	E.	2	6 00 p.m.	4.3					3 28 p.m.	4.33				NE.	2
7	9 00 a.m.	8.2	S.	3	6 00 a.m.		2.9				3 47 a.m.		3.04	3.6	1.29	S.	3
"	9 00 p.m.	8.6	SW.	3	M.	3.4					4 35 p.m.	4.87				"	5
8	6 00 a.m.	8.7	NW.	3	6 00 a.m.		3.0				5 05 a.m.		3.16	3.5	0.71	NNW.	3
"	6 00 p.m.	8.2	N.	3	6 00 p.m.	4.5					5 00 p.m.	4.12				N.	2
9	M.	8.3	ENE.	2	6 00 a.m.		3.0				4 18 a.m.		3.50	3.8	0.72	NE.	5
"	12 00 p.m.	8.7	E.	1	6 00 p.m.	4.2					4 35 p.m.	4.20				N.	2
10	6 00 a.m.	8.2	NE.	2	6 00 a.m.		3.0				5 35 a.m.		2.95	3.5	1.25	ENE.	1
"	12 00 p.m.	8.5	SE.	1	6 00 p.m.	3.8					4 40 p.m.	3.87				"	2
11	M.	8.1	NE.	3	6 00 a.m.		3.0				6 50 a.m.		2.75	3.3	1.12	E.	1
"	12 00 p.m.	8.6	E.	2	6 00 p.m.	4.9					7 30 p.m.	4.25				"	3
12	M.	8.6	"	1	6 00 a.m.	3.5					8 15 a.m.		3.16	3.7	1.09	ESE.	3
"	12 00 p.m.	8.8	SE.	1	M.		3.3				8 37 p.m.	4.25				"	2
13	6 00 a.m.	8.6	W.	2	6 00 a.m.	3.5					8 40 a.m.		2.75	3.5	1.50	NW.	2
"	9 00 p.m.	8.2	SW.	1	6 00 p.m.		3.2	0.3	W.	1	9 45 p.m.	3.12				SW.	2
14	6 00 a.m.	8.0	NW.	3	6 00 a.m.	3.7			"	1	7 35 a.m.		2.54	2.8	0.58	NNW	5
"	12 00 p.m.	7.7	"	3	6 00 p.m.		3.2	0.5	NW.	1	1 20 p.m.	3.04				WNW.	3
"											7 17 p.m.		2.70	2.8	0.34	N.	5
"											10 20 p.m.	3.04				"	2
15	6 00 a.m.	7.7	"	3	6 00 a.m.	3.4			N.	1	4 90 a.m.		2.66	2.6	0.38	"	3
"	12 00 p.m.	7.4	"	3							0 20 p.m.	3.33				NW.	3
"					6 00 p.m.		3.0	0.4	SW.	0	7 10 p.m.		2.50	2.9	0.83	Calm.	0
16	6 00 a.m.	7.3	S.	2	6 00 a.m.	3.1			"	1	0 30 a.m.	3.04				"	0
"	3 00 p.m.	7.5	"	1	6 00 p.m.		2.7	0.4	W.	1	6 00 a.m.		2.75	2.8	0.29	"	0
"											11 25 a.m.	3.08				NW.	1
17	9 00 a.m.	7.2	NE.	1	6 00 a.m.		2.4		N.	1	0 05 a.m.		1.66	2.3	1.42	SW.	3
"	9 00 p.m.	7.5	SW.	1	6 00 p.m.	3.3			W.	1	0 20 p.m.	3.25				N.	2
"											10 40 p.m.		1.62	2.4	1.68	SW.	1
18	9 00 a.m.	7.2	S.	1	6 00 a.m.		2.4	0.9	E.	1	11 30 a.m.	3.29				"	1
"	9 00 p.m.	7.7	SW.	1	6 00 p.m.	3.8			SW.	1	10 40 p.m.		1.54	2.4	1.75	"	1
19	6 00 a.m.	7.5	W.	2	6 00 a.m.		1.9	1.9	"	2	9 50 a.m.	2.95				W.	3
"	3 00 p.m.	7.2	NW.	1	6 00 p.m.	3.4			"	1	11 30 a.m.		2.87	2.9	0.08	SW.	2
"											0 35 p.m.	2.95				"	2
20	9 00 a.m.	7.2	E.	2	6 00 a.m.		2.1	1.3	W.	0	0 10 a.m.		1.58	2.2	1.37	"	1
"	M.	8.0	NE.	2	6 00 p.m.	4.5			N.	2	11 25 a.m.	3.79				ESE.	2
21	9 00 a.m.	8.1	"	2	6 00 a.m.		3.2	1.3	"	2	0 35 a.m.		2.04	2.9	1.75	SW.	2
"	12 00 p.m.	8.5	"	3	6 00 p.m.	4.3			NE.	2	3 30 p.m.	4.16				NE.	3
22	9 00 a.m.	8.4	E.	2	6 00 a.m.		3.6	0.7	"	2	3 10 a.m.		3.25	3.7	0.91	"	2
"	9 00 p.m.	8.9	NE.	4	6 00 p.m.	5.0			"	5	6 20 p.m.	4.70				ENE.	5
23	3 00 p.m.	8.7	N.	3	6 00 a.m.		3.5	1.5	E.	1	8 00 a.m.		4.08	4.3	0.62	NE.	3
"	12 00 p.m.	9.1	NE.	2	6 00 p.m.	5.0			"	1	7 45 p.m.	4.50				NNE.	2
24	6 00 a.m.	8.8	"	3	6 00 a.m.		3.8	1.2	"	1	7 30 a.m.		3.62	4.0	0.88	"	2
"	6 20 p.m.	8.5	SW.	1	6 00 p.m.	4.8			"	1	6 08 p.m.	4.16				Calm.	0
25	6 00 a.m.	8.9	NE.	3	6 00 a.m.		3.5	1.3	NE.	1	7 10 a.m.		3.58	3.8	0.58	NNE.	2
"	5 30 p.m.	8.4	NW.	2	6 00 p.m.	4.3			NW.	1	5 25 p.m.	3.95				NW.	3
26	6 00 a.m.	8.4	"	1	6 00 a.m.		3.3	1.0	"	1	6 50 a.m.		3.04	3.4	0.91	NE.	1
"	6 20 p.m.	8.0	SW.	1	6 00 p.m.	3.4			"	1	0 10 p.m.	3.41				S.	1
27	6 00 a.m.	7.8	"	1	6 00 a.m.		2.5	1.1	SW.	1	6 50 a.m.		2.16	2.7	1.25	SW.	1
"	9 00 p.m.	7.5	"	1	6 00 p.m.	2.9			N.	1	0 17 p.m.	2.65				"	1
"											7 07 p.m.		2.25	2.4	0.40	"	1
28	6 00 a.m.	7.4	"	1	6 00 a.m.		2.5	0.4	W.		1 25 a.m.	2.58				"	1
"	3 00 p.m.	7.3	N.	1	6 00 p.m.	2.9			"		7 30 p.m.		2.16	2.3	0.42	"	1
"											0 20 p.m.	2.70				"	1
29	M.	7.4	"	1	6 00 a.m.		2.8	0.1	"		0 25 a.m.		2.00	2.3	0.70	Calm.	0
"	12 00 p.m.	7.6	SE.	1	6 00 p.m.	3.1			S.	1	0 35 p.m.	2.91				S.	1
30	3 00 p.m.	7.9	"	1	6 00 a.m.		3.4		SE.	1	0 15 a.m.		1.96	2.4	0.95	ESE.	1
"	6 20 p.m.	8.0	W.	1	6 00 p.m.	3.8			"	1	0 20 p.m.	3.41				"	2
"											9 10 p.m.		3.00	3.2	0.41	SE.	1
May 1	9 00 a.m.	8.1	N.	2	6 00 a.m.		3.1	0.7	SE.	1	1 15 p.m.	4.04				N.	3
"	9 00 p.m.	8.4	NE.	3	4 00 p.m.	4.0			NE.	1	11 50 p.m.		2.75	3.3	1.29	NE.	1

Tidal Observations—Continued.

Date.	Lake Pontchartrain. Time.	Gauge (zero at bottom of canal).	Wind. Direction.	Wind. Force.	Lake Borgne. Time.	Gauge. High tide.	Gauge. Low tide.	Tidal oscillation.	Wind. Direction.	Wind. Force.	Bayou St. Philip. Time.	Gauge. Bench of fort reads 6.0. High tide.	Low tide.	Mean reading.	Tidal oscillation.	Wind. Direction.	Wind. Force.
1851.	h. m.	Feet.			h. m.	Feet.	Feet.	Feet.			h. m.	Feet.	Feet.	Feet.	Feet.		
May 2	5 30 a.m.	8.2	NE.	4	5 00 a.m.		3.7	0.3	E.	2	11 20 a.m.	4.16				E.	3
"	6 30 p.m.	8.6	SE.	2	6 00 p.m.	4.2			"	1	11 30 p.m.		2.50	3.3	1.66	"	1
3	5 30 a.m.	8.2	"	2	7 00 a.m.		3.1	1.1	"	1	11 00 a.m.	3.79				SE.	5
"	4 00 p.m.	9.2	NW.	1	3 00 p.m.	4.8			S.	2	10 10 p.m.		1.83	2.8	1.96	S.	2
4	1 00 a.m.	9.1	W.	2	6 00 a.m.		3.0	1.8	SW.	3	9 30 a.m.	3.50				SSW.	3
"	M.	8.5	"	2	5 00 p.m.	4.2			NW.	3	1 10 p.m.		3.16	3.3	0.34	W.	3
"											3 30 p.m.	3.58				"	5
"											9 25 p.m.		2.16	2.8	1.42	NNW.	5
5	M.	8.0	N.	1	7 00 a.m.		3.5	0.7	"	3	11 40 a.m.	4.08				N.	3
"	12 00 p.m.	8.4	NE.	3	6 00 p.m.	4.3			"	3							
6	9 00 a.m.	8.1	E.	2	5 00 a.m.		3.0	1.3	NE.	2	0 20 a.m.		2.00	3.0	2.08	Calm.	0
"	9 00 p.m.	9.4	SE.	1	6 00 p.m.	4.4			"	2	1 15 p.m.	3.91				NE.	2
7	M.	8.1	ESE.	3	7 00 a.m.		2.6	1.8	SE.	1	2 00 a.m.		2.16	3.0	1.75	Calm.	0
"	12 00 p.m.	8.6	E.	2	6 00 p.m.	4.4			"	1	3 40 p.m.	4.04				E.	5
8	M.	8.5	"	1	6 00 a.m.		3.1	1.3	"	1	3 10 a.m.		2.20	3.1	1.84	"	1
"	12 00 p.m.	8.7	NE.	1	5 00 p.m.	4.4			"	1	3 30 p.m.	3.91				"	2
9	M.	8.5	E.	1	7 00 a.m.		3.2	1.2	"	1	4 05 a.m.		2.58	3.2	1.33	"	1
"	12 00 p.m.	9.0	SE.	1	4 00 p.m.	4.2			"	1	5 10 p.m.	3.83				"	2
10	9 00 a.m.	8.7	S.	2	6 00 a.m.		3.5	0.7	"	1	5 50 a.m.		2.21	3.0	1.62	SE.	2
"	12 00 p.m.	8.9	SE.	1	5 00 p.m.	4.3			"	1	5 15 p.m.	3.71				ESE.	2
11	5 30 a.m.	8.8	"	1	6 00 a.m.		3.5	0.8	"	1	5 20 a.m.		2.87	3.2	0.84	E.	1
"	3 00 p.m.	8.6	S.	1	3 00 p.m.	4.2			"	1							
12	5 30 a.m.	8.5	"	1													
"	3 00 p.m.	8.3	E.	2													
13	5 30 a.m.	8.2	SE.	1													
"	6 30 p.m.	8.6	"	2													
14	5 30 a.m.	8.3	W.	2													
"	3 00 p.m.	8.1	N.	1													
15	9 00 a.m.	7.8	NW.	1	6 00 a.m.		3.0		Calm.	0	1 15 a.m.		1.96			E.	2
"	9 00 p.m.	8.1	S.	1	2 00 p.m.	4.2			NW.	1	M.	3.66				"	3
"											10 00 p.m.		1.79	2.7	1.87	Calm.	0
16	9 00 a.m.	7.7	NE.	1	5 00 a.m.		2.9	1.3	Calm.	0	1 15 p.m.	3.58				ESE.	1
"	9 00 p.m.	8.1	SE.	1	2 00 p.m.	4.1			N.	1	9 00 p.m.		2.00	2.8	1.58	"	3
17	9 00 a.m.	7.8	S.	1	6 00 a.m.		2.8	1.3	Calm.	0	10 00 a.m.	3.87				Calm.	0
"	9 00 p.m.	8.2	SE.	1	2 00 p.m.	4.3			N.	1	10 25 p.m.		2.00	2.9	1.87	SE.	1
18	9 00 a.m.	7.9	S.	2	5 00 a.m.		2.8	1.5	Calm.	0	1 00 p.m.	3.95				"	3
"	12 00 p.m.	8.5	SE.	1	2 00 p.m.	4.2			SE.	1	10 45 p.m.		2.16	3.0	1.79	"	3
19	9 00 a.m.	8.2	"	2	5 00 a.m.		2.3	1.9	"	1	10 30 a.m.	3.83				S.	2
"	9 00 p.m.	8.6	"	2	3 00 p.m.	4.3			NW.	2	9 30 p.m.		2.33	3.0	1.50	"	1
20	M.	8.3	S.	1	7 00 a.m.		3.1	1.2	E.	1	M.	3.75				E.	2
"	9 00 p.m.	8.5	"	1	3 00 p.m.	4.3			NW.	2	11 00 p.m.		2.25	3.0	1.50	"	3
21	M.	8.2	"	2	5 00 a.m.		2.7	1.6	Calm.	0	1 00 p.m.	3.70				ENE.	0
"	12 00 p.m.	8.3	"	2	2 00 p.m.	4.2			SE.	1							
22	5 30 a.m.	8.2	"	1	5 00 a.m.		2.9	1.3	Calm.	0	1 00 a.m.		2.50	3.1	1.20	"	1
"	6 30 p.m.	8.1	"	2	3 00 p.m.	4.0			SW.	1	1 00 p.m.	3.33				Calm.	0
23	5 30 a.m.	8.0	"	1	5 00 a.m.		2.7	1.3	Calm.	0	1 45 a.m.		2.37	2.8	0.96	N.	2
"	3 00 p.m.	7.9	NE.	2	3 00 p.m.	3.9			SE.	1	1 00 p.m.	3.37				"	3
24	5 30 a.m.	8.0	S.	1	6 00 a.m.		2.6	1.3	Calm.	0	1 40 a.m.		2.45	2.9	0.92	Calm.	0
"	3 00 p.m.	7.8	SE.	1	3 00 p.m.	3.8			SE.	1	2 00 p.m.	3.16				NNW.	3
25	M.	7.7	NE.	1	5 00 a.m.		2.9	0.9	"	1	1 30 a.m.		2.33	2.7	0.83	NW.	2
"	12 00 p.m.	7.9	S.	1	2 00 p.m.	4.2			"	1	M.	3.58				"	2
"											11 30 p.m.		3.00	3.2	0.58	"	3
26	5 30 a.m.	8.1	SE.	1	5 00 a.m.		2.9	1.3	"	1	8 30 a.m.	3.50				"	3
"	12 00 p.m.	8.4	E.	1	2 00 p.m.	4.2			"	1	7 00 p.m.		3.00	3.2	0.50	W.	1
27	5 30 a.m.	8.3	"	1	6 00 a.m.		2.6	1.6	"	1	6 30 a.m.	3.58				"	2
"	6 30 p.m.	8.7	Calm.	0	2 00 p.m.	4.1			"	1	7 30 p.m.		2.91	3.2	0.67	Calm.	0
28	5 30 a.m.	8.2	S.	1	5 00 a.m.		2.9	1.2	Calm.	0	11 00 a.m.	3.91				S.	1
"	6 30 p.m.	8.5	SE.	1	1 00 p.m.	4.3			SE.	1	9 00 p.m.		2.66	3.2	1.25	"	1
29	9 00 a.m.	8.3	NE.	1	5 00 a.m.		3.1	1.2	"	1	10 30 a.m.	3.87				SW.	2
"	9 00 p.m.	8.5	S.	1	2 00 p.m.	4.1			"	1	8 30 p.m.		2.41	3.1	1.46	"	2
30	5 30 a.m.	8.2	"	1	6 00 a.m.		3.0	1.1	"	1	10 00 a.m.	3.83				S.	1
"	6 30 p.m.	8.3	"	1	2 00 p.m.	4.2			"	1	9 00 p.m.		2.83	3.3	1.00	"	1
31	9 00 a.m.	7.9	W.	1	5 00 a.m.		2.8	1.4	"	1	9 30 a.m.	3.83				SE.	3
"	6 30 p.m.	8.1	SW.	1	4 00 p.m.	4.0			SW.	1	8 30 p.m.		2.83	3.3	1.00	"	1
June 1	9 00 a.m.	7.7	W.	1	5 00 a.m.		2.6	1.4	Calm.	0	11 00 a.m.	3.91				S.	3
"	9 00 p.m.	7.9	SW.	1	2 00 p.m.	4.1			N.	1	10 00 p.m.		1.75	2.8	2.16	"	3
2	9 00 a.m.	7.6	W.	1	5 00 a.m.		2.6	1.5	Calm.	0	11 30 a.m.	3.91				SE.	3
"	9 00 p.m.	7.8	S.	1	2 00 p.m.	4.2			N.	2	11 00 p.m.		2.00	2.9	1.91	"	3
3	9 00 a.m.	7.7	SW.	1	5 00 a.m.		2.5	1.7	Calm.	0	M.	3.87				S.	3
"	9 00 p.m.	8.0	S.	1	3 00 p.m.	4.1			SE.	3	11 40 p.m.		1.91	2.8	1.86	"	3
4	M.	7.7	NE.	2	5 00 a.m.		2.5	1.6	Calm.	0	M.	3.91				SE.	3
"	12 00 p.m.	8.1	SE.	1	2 00 p.m.	4.1			SE.	1							
5	M.	7.9	W.	1	5 00 a.m.		2.9	1.2	"	1	1 00 a.m.		2.00	2.9	1.91	"	3
"	12 00 p.m.	8.1	SE.	1	6 00 p.m.	4.0			"	1							
"											1 00 p.m.	3.29				SW.	3
6	5 30 a.m.	8.0	S.	1	5 00 a.m.		2.3	1.7	SW.	1	1 30 a.m.		2.08	2.6	1.21	"	3
"	3 00 p.m.	7.7	SW.	2	6 00 p.m.	3.5			"	1	1 00 p.m.	3.66				W.	3
7	1 30 p.m.	8.0	NW.	4	5 00 a.m.		2.4	1.1	"	1	2 00 a.m.		2.16	2.9	1.50	"	3
"	12 00 p.m.	7.4	"	3	2 00 p.m.	3.9			N.	1	3 00 p.m.	3.25				"	3
8	9 00 a.m.	7.1	W.	3	5 00 a.m.		2.5	1.4	E.	1	1 30 p.m.		2.00	2.6	1.25	"	3
"	9 00 p.m.	7.3	SE.	2	2 00 p.m.	3.5			SW.	1	10 00 p.m.	3.75				"	3
9	5 40 a.m.	7.1	NW.	3	5 00 a.m.		2.9	0.6	Calm.	0	6 00 p.m.		2.00	2.8	1.75	NW.	3
"	9 00 p.m.	5.4	SE.	1	1 00 p.m.	3.9			SE.	1							
10	5 30 a.m.	7.4	NE.	3	5 00 a.m.		2.8	1.1	N.	1	9 00 a.m.	3.50				NE.	3
"	6 30 p.m.	7.7	"	1	1 00 p.m.	3.9			"	1	7 00 p.m.		2.00	2.7	1.50	SE.	3
11	9 00 a.m.	7.4	SW.	1	4 00 a.m.		2.9	1.0	SW.	1	8 00 a.m.	3.33				S.	2
"	9 00 p.m.	7.7	"	2	2 00 p.m.	3.9			SE.	1	7 30 p.m.		1.75	2.5	1.58	"	2
12	5 30 a.m.	7.4	"	1	5 00 a.m.		2.5	1.4	N.	1	7 30 a.m.	3.45				Calm.	0

Tidal Observations—Continued.

Date.	Lake Pontchartrain. Time.	Lake Pontchartrain. Gauge (zero at bottom of canal).	Lake Pontchartrain. Wind. Direction.	Lake Pontchartrain. Wind. Force.	Lake Borgne. Time.	Lake Borgne. Gauge. High tide.	Lake Borgne. Gauge. Low tide.	Lake Borgne. Tidal oscillation.	Lake Borgne. Wind. Direction.	Lake Borgne. Wind. Force.	Bayou St. Philip. Time.	Bayou St. Philip. Gauge. Bench of fort reads 6.0. High tide.	Bayou St. Philip. Gauge. Low tide.	Bayou St. Philip. Gauge. Mean reading.	Bayou St. Philip. Tidal oscillation.	Bayou St. Philip. Wind. Direction.	Bayou St. Philip. Wind. Force.
1851.	*h. m.*	*Feet.*			*h. m.*	*Feet.*	*Feet.*	*Feet.*			*h. m.*	*Feet.*	*Feet.*	*Feet.*	*Feet.*		
June 12	6 30 p.m.	7.7	NE.	1	1 00 p.m.	3.9			SE.	1	8 00 p.m.		1.75	2.6	1.70	Calm.	0
13	5 30 a.m.	7.4	SW.	1	4 00 a.m.		2.8	1.1	SW.	1	9 40 a.m.	3.95				SE.	3
"	9 00 p.m.	7.9	S.	1	2 00 p.m.	4.2			N.	1	8 30 p.m.		2.08	3.0	1.87	"	3
14	9 00 a.m.	7.6	NE.	1	4 00 a.m.		2.6	1.6	Calm.	0	9 40 a.m.	3.83				NE.	3
"	9 00 p.m.	7.9	E.	1	1 00 p.m.	4.2			N.	3	10 45 p.m.		1.79	2.8	2.04	"	3
15	3 00 p.m.	7.3	NW.	1	5 00 a.m.		2.5	1.7	Calm.	0	10 40 a.m.	3.83				SE.	2
"	6 00 p.m.	8.2	SE.	2	2 00 p.m.	3.9			N.	1	11 40 p.m.		1.91	2.8	1.92	"	2
16	9 00 a.m.	7.7	NW.	1	5 00 a.m.		2.5	1.4	Calm.	0	M.	3.75				"	0
"	9 00 p.m.	7.9	S.	1	M.	4.0			NE.	1							
17	5 30 a.m.	7.5	W.	1	5 00 a.m.		3.3	0.7	Calm.	0	0 30 a.m.		2.00	2.8	1.75	"	3
"	3 20 p.m.	8.3	NE.	2	3 00 p.m.	4.4			SE.	1	0 30 p.m.	3.91				E.	3
18	5 30 a.m.	7.9	E.	2	5 00 a.m.		3.5	0.9	NE.	1	1 00 a.m.		2.25	3.0	1.66	"	3
"	12 00 p.m.	8.7	"	3	2 00 p.m.	5.0			"	3	1 00 p.m.	4.33				"	5
19	5 30 a.m.	8.7	NE.	3	5 00 a.m.		3.9	1.1	SE.	3	3 00 a.m.		3.83	4.0	0.50	"	5
"	12 00 p.m.	9.1	SE.	1	1 00 p.m.	4.5			"	3	3 30 p.m.	4.75				NE.	5
20	5 30 a.m.	8.8	NE.	3	5 00 a.m.		3.9	0.6	"	1	12 00 p.m.		3.33	4.0	1.42	"	5
"	12 00 p.m.	8.9	SE.	1	2 00 p.m.	4.5			"	1							
21	9 00 a.m.	8.7	NE.	1	5 00 a.m.		3.9	0.6	"	1	11 30 a.m.	3.91				Calm.	0
"	9 00 p.m.	8.8	SE.	1	3 00 p.m.	4.5			NE.	1	11 45 p.m.		3.00	3.4	0.91	"	0
22	5 30 a.m.	8.6	"	1	5 00 a.m.		3.4	1.1	Calm.	0	10 20 a.m.	3.66				SE.	3
"	6 30 p.m.	8.5	S.	1	1 00 p.m.	4.0			SE.	1	8 20 p.m.		3.00	3.3	0.66	"	3
23	M.	8.5	N.	1	5 00 a.m.		3.2	0.8	SW.	1	9 30 a.m.	3.87				"	3
"	12 00 p.m.	8.2	S.	1	2 00 p.m.	4.2			SE.	1	7 20 p.m.		2.83	3.3	1.04	"	3
24	9 00 a.m.	8.1	SW.	2	M.	4.1			"	1	8 00 a.m.	3.58				S.	2
"	9 00 p.m.	8.2	S.	1	6 00 p.m.		3.0	1.1	"	1	7 20 p.m.		2.58	3.0	1.00	"	2
25	5 30 a.m.	8.0	SE.	1	1 00 p.m.	3.9			"	1	8 40 a.m.	3.58				SW.	3
"	6 30 p.m.	8.2	E.	1	7 00 p.m.		3.1	0.8	Calm.	0	7 30 p.m.		2.25	2.9	1.83	"	3
26	5 30 a.m.	7.9	S.	1	M.	4.0			SE.	1	7 50 a.m.	3.62				S.	3
"	6 30 p.m.	8.2	SW.	1	7 00 p.m.		3.0	1.0	Calm.	0	5 45 p.m.		2.00	2.8	1.62	"	3
27	5 30 a.m.	7.7	"	2	6 00 a.m.		3.0		SW.	1	7 20 a.m.	3.66				"	3
"	4 30 p.m.	8.1	SE.	1	2 00 p.m.	4.2			"	1	8 00 p.m.		1.83	2.7	1.83	"	3
28	6 00 a.m.	7.7	S.	1	5 00 a.m.		3.0	1.2	SE.	1	7 20 a.m.	3.66				"	3
"	6 30 p.m.	8.0	SE.	1	2 00 p.m.	4.1			"	1	8 15 p.m.		1.66	2.6	2.00	"	3
29	5 30 a.m.	7.7	S.	1	5 00 a.m.		3.0	1.1	"	1	8 45 a.m.	3.75				"	3
"	6 30 p.m.	8.2	E.	1	1 00 p.m.	4.2			SW.	3	9 20 p.m.		1.75	2.7	2.00	"	3
30	9 00 a.m.	7.9	N.	1	5 00 a.m.		3.0	1.2	Calm.	0	11 30 a.m.	3.95				"	2
"	12 00 p.m.	8.7	E.	3	2 00 p.m.	4.3			SE.	1	11 20 p.m.		1.91	2.9	2.04	"	2
July 1	9 00 a.m.	8.0	NE.	2	5 00 a.m.		3.0	1.3	Calm.	0	1 45 p.m.	4.12				NE.	3
"	9 00 p.m.	8.3	SE.	1	2 00 p.m.	4.5			NE.	3							
2	M.	8.1	E.	2	5 00 a.m.		2.9	1.6	SE.	1	1 20 a.m.		2.16	3.1	1.96	"	3
"	12 00 p.m.	8.5	SE.	1	2 00 p.m.	4.5			NE.	3	2 00 p.m.	4.00				SE.	3
3	9 00 a.m.	8.4	NE.	2	5 00 a.m.		2.9	1.6	Calm.	0	2 30 a.m.		2.41	3.2	1.59	"	3
"	9 00 p.m.	8.4	SE.	1	3 00 p.m.	4.2			SE.	1	1 40 p.m.	3.58				"	3
4	5 30 a.m.	8.2	SW.	1	5 00 a.m.		2.9	1.3	"	1	2 30 a.m.		2.25	2.9	1.33	"	3
"	3 00 p.m.	8.0	N.	1	2 00 p.m.	4.1			"	1	1 40 p.m.	3.58				"	2
5	5 30 a.m.	8.0	SW.	1	5 00 a.m.		2.8	1.3	"	1	3 15 a.m.		2.33	2.9	1.25	"	2
"	5 00 p.m.	7.8	NW.	1	2 00 p.m.	3.5			"	1	1 30 p.m.	3.29				"	2
6	9 00 a.m.	7.7	SW.	1	5 00 a.m.		2.6	0.9	"	1	1 45 a.m.		2.33	2.8	0.96	"	2
"	9 00 p.m.	7.8	S.	1	2 00 p.m.	3.9			"	1	11 50 a.m.	3.25				SW.	3
"									"	1	9 40 p.m.		2.25	2.7	1.00	"	3
7	5 30 a.m.	7.7	SW.	1	5 00 a.m.		3.0	0.9	Calm.	0	8 20 a.m.	3.41				S.	3
"	6 30 p.m.	7.8	"	1	3 00 p.m.	4.1			SE.	1	7 00 p.m.		2.16	2.7	1.25	"	3
8	5 30 a.m.	7.6	"	1	M.	3.9			"	1	6 40 a.m.	3.50				SE.	3
"	6 30 p.m.	7.7	S.	1	7 00 p.m.		2.8	1.3	"	1	5 30 p.m.		2.00	2.7	1.50	"	3
9	M.	7.7	"	1	M.	3.6			"	1	6 40 a.m.	3.62				"	2
"	12 00 p.m.	7.5	SW.	1	7 00 p.m.		2.5	1.1	"	1	6 30 p.m.		1.58	2.6	2.04	"	2
10	9 00 a.m.	7.4	W.	2	11 00 a.m.	3.6			"	1	7 00 a.m.	3.45				WSW.	2
"	12 00 p.m.	7.5	NE.	3	6 00 p.m.		2.5	1.1	"	1	7 00 p.m.		1.58	2.5	1.87	"	2
11	5 10 a.m.	7.3	SW.	1	M.	3.7			"	1	8 20 a.m.	3.83				SE.	2
"	9 00 p.m.	7.	"	1	7 00 p.m.		2.4	1.3	"	1	7 00 p.m.		1.83	2.8	2.00	"	2
12	5 40 a.m.	7.5	"	1	1 00 p.m.	4.8			NE.	1	8 10 a.m.	3.83				N.	2
"	6 30 p.m.	7.9	SE.	1	7 00 p.m.		3.5		"	1	8 15 p.m.		2.16	2.9	1.67	"	2
13	5 30 a.m.	7.8	E.	1	M.	4.9			"	2	8 45 a.m.	3.83				NW.	2
"	6 30 p.m.	8.3	SE.	1	7 00 p.m.		3.0		Calm.	0	9 45 p.m.		2.00	2.9	1.83	"	2
14	5 30 a.m.	8.0	NW.	1	5 00 a.m.		2.9		"	0	11 30 a.m.	3.91				SE.	3
"	6 30 p.m.	8.3	S.	1	3 00 p.m.	3.8			N.	1	0 25 p.m.		2.08	2.9	1.83	"	3
15	9 00 a.m.	7.8	W.	1	5 00 a.m.		2.9		"	1	0 25 a.m.	3.83				"	3
"	9 00 p.m.	8.0	N.	1	3 00 p.m.	4.2			"	1							
16	9 00 a.m.	7.8	NE.	1	5 00 a.m.		2.9		Calm.	0	1 00 a.m.		2.08	2.9	1.75	"	3
"	9 00 p.m.	8.0	S.	1	2 00 p.m.	4.2			E.	1	1 20 p.m.	3.75				"	3
17	9 00 a.m.	7.8	SW.	1	5 00 a.m.		2.9		Calm.	0	1 50 a.m.		2.25	3.0	1.50	"	3
"	9 00 p.m.	8.0	S.	1	3 00 p.m.	4.9			N.	1	2 30 p.m.	3.58				"	3
18	5 30 a.m.	7.8	"	1	5 00 a.m.		2.6		SE.	1	2 10 a.m.		2.33	2.9	1.25	"	3
"	6 30 p.m.	7.7	SW.	1	3 00 p.m.	4.2			N.	1	1 30 p.m.	3.33				"	2
19	5 30 a.m.	7.7	"	1	5 00 a.m.		2.7		Calm.	0	1 45 a.m.		2.41	2.8	0.92	"	2
"	6 30 p.m.	7.4	"	1	3 00 p.m.	3.9			S.	1	2 00 p.m.	3.25				NW.	3
20	9 00 a.m.	7.5	NW.	1	5 00 a.m.		3.0		Calm.	0	3 00 a.m.		2.41	2.8	0.84	"	3
"	9 00 p.m.	7.7	SW.	1	3 00 p.m.	3.6			N.	1	1 30 p.m.	3.33				SE.	2
21	5 30 a.m.	7.7	S.	1	5 00 a.m.		3.1		NE.	1	1 45 a.m.		2.33	2.8	1.00	"	2
"	6 30 p.m.	7.9	E.	1	3 00 p.m.	3.8			N.	1	9 50 a.m.	3.33				"	2
"											8 40 p.m.		2.41	2.8	0.92	"	3
22	5 30 a.m.	7.8	Calm.	0	2 00 p.m.	3.8			E.	1	7 00 a.m.	3.45				S.	2
"	5 00 p.m.	8.1	SE.	1	7 00 p.m.		2.7		Calm.	0	5 15 p.m.		2.50	2.9	0.95	"	2
23	5 30 a.m.	8.0	"	1	2 00 p.m.	4.9			NE.	3	7 25 a.m.	3.83				SE.	3
"	6 30 p.m.	8.3	"	1	7 00 p.m.		3.4		"	1	5 35 p.m.		2.66	3.2	1.17	"	3
24	11 30 a.m.	8.2	NE.	3	2 00 p.m.	4.8			"	1	9 00 a.m.	4.16				"	3
"	M.	8.9	E.	2	7 00 p.m.		3.5		"	1	8 25 p.m.		3.75	3.9	0.41	"	3
25	5 30 a.m.	8.9	"	2	2 00 p.m.	5.2			"	2	10 35 a.m.	4.50				"	3

Tidal Observations—Continued.

Date.	Lake Pontchartrain. Time.	Lake Pontchartrain. Gauge (zero at bottom of canal).	Lake Pontchartrain. Wind. Direction.	Lake Pontchartrain. Wind. Force.	Lake Borgne. Time.	Lake Borgne. Gauge. High tide.	Lake Borgne. Gauge. Low tide.	Lake Borgne. Tidal oscillation.	Lake Borgne. Wind. Direction.	Lake Borgne. Wind. Force.	Bayou St. Philip. Time.	Bayou St. Philip. Gauge. Bench of fort reads 6.0. High tide.	Bayou St. Philip. Gauge. Low tide.	Bayou St. Philip. Gauge. Mean reading.	Bayou St. Philip. Tidal oscillation.	Bayou St. Philip. Wind. Direction.	Bayou St. Philip. Wind. Force.
1851.	*h. m.*	*Feet.*			*h. m.*	*Feet.*	*Feet.*	*Feet.*			*h. m.*	*Feet.*	*Feet.*	*Feet.*	*Feet.*		
July 25	7 00 p.m.	9.6	SE.	2	7 00 p.m.		3.5		NE.	1	12 00 p.m.		3.33	3.9	1.17	SE.	3
26	9 00 a.m.	8.8	E.	1	2 00 p.m.	4.8			"	1	11 30 a.m.	4.12				"	3
"	9 00 p.m.	9.1	SE.	1	7 00 p.m.		3.6		SW.	1	10 35 p.m.		2.33	3.2	1.79	"	3
27	9 00 a.m.	8.5	S.	1	2 00 p.m.	4.7			SE.	1	11 00 a.m.	4.08				"	3
"	3 00 p.m.	8.9	N.	2	7 00 p.m.		3.2		Calm.	0	10 30 p.m.		2.00	3.0	2.08	"	3
28	5 30 a.m.	8.3	NE.	1	5 00 a.m.		3.1		SE.	1	11 35 a.m.	4.00				"	2
"	6 30 p.m.	8.5	S.	1	3 00 p.m.	4.5			NE.	1	11 55 p.m.		1.75	2.8	2.25	"	2
29	5 30 a.m.	8.2	W.	1	5 00 a.m.		3.0		"	1	10 40 a.m.	3.83				W.	2
"	3 00 p.m.	8.0	S.	1	2 00 p.m.	4.1			NW.	1	10 30 p.m.		1.50	2.6	2.33	"	2
30	5 30 a.m.	7.7	SW.	1	5 00 a.m.		2.5		"	3	M.	3.50				"	3
"	6 30 p.m.	7.6	NW.	1	3 00 p.m.	3.8			SW.	1	11 00 p.m.		1.50	2.5	2.00	"	3
31	5 30 a.m.	7.4	W.	1	5 00 a.m.		2.0		E.	1	1 30 p.m.	3.00				WNW	3
"	6 30 p.m.	6.8	S.	3	3 00 p.m.	3.1			NE.	3	11 45 p.m.		1.83	2.4	1.17	"	3
Aug. 1	9 00 a.m.	7.2	E.	3	7 00 a.m.		2.9		SW.	2	10 15 a.m.	3.33				SW.	3
"	9 00 p.m.	7.4	SE.	1													
2	5 30 a.m.	7.3	E.	2	3 00 p.m.	3.5			W.	1	1 00 a.m.		2.33	2.8	1.00	"	3
"	3 30 p.m.	7.8	SE.	1	5 00 a.m.		3.1		NE.	3	10 35 a.m.	3.00				"	3
3	1 00 p.m.	7.8	NE.	2	2 00 p.m.	3.5			SW.	3	0 45 a.m.		2.58	2.7	0.42	"	3
"	12 00 p.m.	7.4	SE.	1	7 00 p.m.		2.6		S.	1	0 35 p.m.	3.00				"	3
"											9 40 p.m.		2.33	2.6	0.67	"	3
4	5 30 a.m.	7.3	SW.	1	2 00 p.m.	3.5			SE.	1	7 20 a.m.	3.33				"	2
"	3 00 p.m.	7.7	N.	1	7 00 p.m.		2.4		"	1	7 15 p.m.		2.25	2.7	1.08	"	2
5	9 00 a.m.	7.4	SW.	1	1 00 p.m.	4.0			SW.	1	7 30 a.m.	3.50				"	2
"	M.	7.7	NW.	1	7 00 p.m.		2.9		Calm.	0	6 00 p.m.		2.33	2.9	1.17	"	2
6	5 30 a.m.	7.8	SW.	1	M.	4.2			NE.	1	7 30 a.m.	3.66				SE.	2
"	6 30 p.m.	8.1	S.	1	7 00 p.m.		2.9		SE.	1	5 50 p.m.		2.08	2.8	1.58	"	2
7	5 30 a.m.	7.9	SW.	1	11 00 a.m.	4.1			NE.	1	7 40 a.m.	3.87				"	2
"	7 00 p.m.	8.2	S.	1	7 00 p.m.		2.9		Calm.	0	6 40 p.m.		2.50	3.1	1.37	"	2
8	5 00 a.m.	8.0	SW.	1	M.	4.4			SE.	1	7 20 a.m.	3.91				"	3
"	3 00 p.m.	8.4	"	1	7 00 p.m.		2.9		Calm.	0	6 30 p.m.		2.41	3.1	1.50	"	3
9	5 30 a.m.	8.1	N.	1	11 00 a.m.	4.4			NE.	1	8 00 a.m.	3.87				S.	2
"	6 30 p.m.	8.5	SW.	1	7 00 p.m.		2.9		Calm.	0	9 15 p.m.		1.91	2.8	1.86	"	2
10	9 00 a.m.	8.1	W.	2	M.	4.2			SW.	1	10 00 a.m.	3.75				SE.	2
"	9 00 p.m.	8.3	E.	2	7 00 p.m.		3.1		Calm.	0	9 50 p.m.		1.91	2.8	1.84	"	2
11	5 30 a.m.	7.9	SW.	1	5 00 a.m.		2.9		SE.	1	11 00 a.m.	3.75				"	3
"	7 00 p.m.	8.2	"	1	2 00 p.m.	4.2			NE.	1	10 30 p.m.		1.91	2.8	1.84	"	3
12	M.	7.7	"	1	5 00 a.m.		2.6		W.	1	11 15 a.m.	3.33				NE.	3
"	12 00 p.m.	7.7	SE.	1	2 00 p.m.	3.9			NW.	1	11 55 p.m.		1.83	2.5	1.50	"	3
13	M.	7.4	E.	1	5 00 a.m.		2.5		"	1	10 30 a.m.	3.33				"	3
"	9 00 p.m.	7.5	SE.	1	2 00 p.m.	3.9			"	1							
14	7 00 a.m.	7.5	S.	1	5 00 a.m.		2.6		SW.	1	1 10 a.m.		2.00	2.6	1.33	"	3
"	3 00 p.m.	7.2	"	1	3 00 p.m.	3.6			NW.	1	1 50 p.m.	3.41				N.	3
15	5 30 a.m.	7.5	NW.	3	5 00 a.m.		3.1		SW.	2	0 30 a.m.		2.41	2.9	1.00	"	3
"	5 40 p.m.	7.9	S.	1	4 00 p.m.	4.2			NE.	2	0 35 p.m.	3.41				"	2
"											11 15 p.m.		2.66	3.0	0.75	"	2
16	5 30 a.m.	7.7	N.	1	7 00 a.m.		3.1		SW.	1	9 15 a.m.	3.33				E.	2
"	7 00 p.m.	7.8	S.	1	3 00 p.m.	3.9			NW.	1	9 50 p.m.		2.58	2.9	0.75	"	2
17	9 00 a.m.	7.8	SW.	1	2 00 a.m.	3.8			W.	2	9 40 a.m.	3.25				NE.	3
"	9 00 p.m.	7.7	S.	1	7 00 p.m.		2.0		SW.	1	8 50 p.m.		2.58	2.9	0.67	"	3
18	2 00 p.m.	8.3	"	1	2 00 p.m.	3.9			NW.	1	7 30 a.m.	3.33				ESE.	2
"	6 30 p.m.	7.7	SW.	1	6 00 p.m.		2.8		SE.	1	8 00 p.m.		2.58	2.9	0.75	"	2
19	11 00 a.m.	8.7	"	1	10 00 a.m.	3.9			N.	1	7 10 a.m.	3.66				NW.	2
"	12 00 p.m.	7.7	"	1	6 00 p.m.		2.8		Calm.	0	5 40 p.m.		2.66	3.1	1.00	"	2
20	5 30 a.m.	8.0	NW.	1	8 00 a.m.	4.9			NE.	1	6 50 a.m.	3.83				SE.	3
"	6 30 p.m.	8.2	SW.	1	6 00 p.m.		3.0		SW.	1	5 20 p.m.		2.75	3.2	1.08	"	3
21	5 30 a.m.	8.2	S.	1	8 00 a.m.	4.7			NE.	2	7 15 a.m.	4.16				"	2
"	6 30 p.m.	8.6	E.	1	6 00 p.m.		3.2		E.	1	6 10 p.m.		3.25	3.7	0.91	"	2
22	9 00 a.m.	8.6	Calm.	0	9 00 a.m.	5.0			NE.	1	9 00 a.m.	4.50				NE.	4
"	9 00 p.m.	8.9	SE.	1	6 00 p.m.		4.0		"	1	8 45 p.m.		4.16	4.3	0.34	"	4
23	5 30 a.m.	9.1	"	1	7 00 a.m.	6.2			"	1	1 00 p.m.	6.08				N.	5
"	2 45 p.m.	9.7	"	1	6 00 p.m.		5.0		"	1							
24	6 00 a.m.	9.4	NE.	3	8 00 a.m.	5.3			"	1	4 15 a.m.		5.16	5.6	0.92	"	5
"	6 30 p.m.	9.1	"	3	6 00 p.m.		3.8		"	1							
25	9 00 a.m.	8.1	E.	2	5 00 a.m.		3.6		SW.	1	1 45 a.m.		3.75			"	5
"	9 00 p.m.	8.8	SE.	2	3 00 p.m.	4.7			W.	1	0 15 p.m.	4.00				SW.	4
"											10 45 p.m.		2.33	3.1	1.67	"	3
26	9 00 a.m.	8.2	E.	1	5 00 a.m.		3.5		SW.	1	11 30 a.m.	3.95				"	3
"	3 00 p.m.	8.5	SE.	1	2 00 p.m.	4.5			"	1	11 50 p.m.		2.25	3.1	1.70	"	3
27	6 00 a.m.	8.0	S.	1	5 00 a.m.		3.5		Calm.	0	0 30 p.m.	3.75				NE.	3
"	6 00 p.m.	7.9	N.	2	2 00 p.m.	4.2			NW.	1	11 30 p.m.		2.41	3.0	1.34	"	3
28	6 00 a.m.	8.1	SW.	1	6 00 a.m.		3.9		"	1	1 00 p.m.	3.58				"	3
"	12 00 p.m.	8.7	S.	1	2 00 p.m.	4.4											
29	6 00 a.m.	8.4	W.	1	5 00 a.m.		3.9		NE.	1	0 50 a.m.		2.50	3.0	1.08	SW.	3
"	6 30 p.m.	8.9	NW.	1	3 00 p.m.	4.7			"	1	2 15 p.m.	3.91				SE.	3
30	6 00 a.m.	9.0	SW.	1	5 00 a.m.		3.1		"	1	3 30 a.m.		3.41	3.6	0.50	"	3
"	12 00 p.m.	8.7	NW.	1	2 00 p.m.	4.3											
31	9 00 a.m.	8.7	SW.	1	5 00 a.m.		2.9		SE.	1	0 30 a.m.	3.75				"	3
"	9 00 p.m.	8.3	SE.	3	2 00 p.m.	4.1			"	1	M.		3.00	3.3	0.75	"	3
Sept. 1	9 00 a.m.	8.5	NE.	2	7 00 a.m.	4.2			NW.	1	1 40 a.m.	3.83				"	3
"	12 00 p.m.	8.0	SW.	1	6 00 p.m.		2.9		SW.	1	2 00 p.m.		2.58	3.2	1.25	"	3
2	9 00 a.m.	8.2	NW.	1	6 00 a.m.	4.3			NE.	1	3 20 a.m.	3.75				"	3
"	12 00 p.m.	7.8	SW.	1	6 00 p.m.		2.8		SW.	1	2 45 p.m.		2.33	3.0	1.42	NE.	3
3	M.	8.0	NW.	1	6 00 a.m.	4.0			NE.	1	3 30 a.m.	3.58				"	3
"	12 00 p.m.	7.7	SW.	1	6 00 p.m.		2.9		SW.	1	4 40 p.m.		2.33	2.9	1.25	"	2
4	6 00 a.m.	7.8	NE.	1	8 00 a.m.	4.1			NW.	1	7 00 a.m.	3.83				"	3
"	9 00 p.m.	8.0	S.	1	6 00 p.m.		3.0		SW.	1	5 20 p.m.		2.66	3.2	1.17	E.	3
5	6 00 a.m.	8.0	"	1	8 00 a.m.	4.2			NE.	1	7 25 a.m.	3.91				"	2
"	6 30 p.m.	8.3	NE.	1	6 00 p.m.		3.5	0.7	SE.	1	6 20 p.m.		2.66	3.2	1.25	"	3

Tidal Observations—Continued.

Date.	Lake Pontchartrain.				Lake Borgne.						Bayou St. Philip.						
	Time.	Gauge (zero at bottom of canal).	Wind.		Time.	Gauge.		Tidal oscillation.	Wind.		Time.	Gauge. Bench at fort reads 6.0.			Tidal oscillation.	Wind.	
			Direction.	Force.		High tide.	Low tide.		Direction.	Force.		High tide.	Low tide.	Mean reading.		Direction.	Force.
1851.	*h. m.*	*Feet.*			*h. m.*	*Feet.*	*Feet.*	*Feet.*			*h. m.*	*Feet.*	*Feet.*	*Feet.*	*Feet.*		
Sept. 6	6 00 a.m.	8.1	W.	1	10 00 a.m.	4.4			NE.	2	8 00 a.m.	3.87				ESE.	2
"	6 30 p.m.	8.4	E.	1	6 00 p.m.		3.3	1.1	SW.	1	7 15 p.m.		2.50	3.1	1.37	"	3
7	6 00 a.m.	8.1	SW.	1	9 00 a.m.	4.0			SE.	1	8 45 a.m.	3.75				NE.	2
"	12 00 p.m.	8.2	S.	0	6 00 p.m.		3.5	0.5	SW.	1	8 00 p.m.		2.25	3.0	1.50	"	2
8	6 00 a.m.	7.8	SW.	1	5 00 a.m.		2.9		SE.	1	9 15 a.m.	3.58				S.	2
"	6 30 p.m.	8.0	SE.	1	3 00 p.m.	4.4			NE.	1	8 20 p.m.		2.33	2.9	1.25	"	2
9	11 30 a.m.	8.0	E.	1	5 00 a.m.		3.5	0.9	"	1	10 30 a.m.	3.83				SE.	2
"	12 00 p.m.	8.4	"	1	4 00 p.m.	4.5			"	1	9 00 p.m.		2.75	3.2	1.08	"	2
10	6 00 a.m.	8.5	SE.	1	5 00 a.m.		3.9	0.6	"	3	M.	4.16				S.	3
"	9 00 p.m.	9.0	E.	2	3 00 p.m.	5.2			"	3	11 30 p.m.		3.83	3.9	0.33	"	3
11	6 00 a.m.	8.8	NE.	2	5 00 a.m.		4.2	1.0	"	3	0 30 p.m.	4.16				SE.	3
"	9 00 p.m.	9.1	E.	1	2 00 p.m.	5.2			"	3							
12	3 00 p.m.	8.8	"	2	6 00 a.m.		4.1	1.1	"	3	1 30 a.m.		3.75	3.9	0.41	"	3
"	12 00 p.m.	9.1	SE.	1	2 00 p.m.	5.3			"	3	3 40 p.m.	4.33				E.	3
13	6 00 a.m.	9.1	NE.	2	5 00 a.m.	4.8			"	3	10 00 a.m.		3.91	4.1	0.42	SE.	3
"	6 30 p.m.	8.8	E.	1	2 00 p.m.		3.7	1.6	"	3	6 00 p.m.	4.16				"	3
14	6 00 a.m.	8.7	N.	2	5 00 a.m.	4.6			"	3	M.		3.75	3.9	0.41	E.	3
"	9 00 p.m.	8.9	SE.	1	2 00 p.m.		3.9	0.5	"	3	8 00 p.m.	4.03				"	3
15	9 00 a.m.	9.0	NE.	3	5 00 a.m.	4.9			"	3	1 30 p.m.		3.91	3.9	0.12	"	3
"	9 00 p.m.	9.1	E.	1	3 00 p.m.		3.8	1.1	"	3							
16	6 00 a.m.	9.5	"	3	6 00 a.m.	6.2			"	3	10 30 a.m.	5.33				"	3
"	6 30 p.m.	9.8	"	2	6 00 p.m.		4.5	1.7	"	3	8 00 p.m.		5.00	5.1	0.33	"	3
17	6 00 a.m.	9.8	NE.	3	7 00 a.m.	6.5			"	3	9 40 a.m.	5.66				"	3
"	9 00 p.m.	9.9	SE.	1	5 00 p.m.		4.6	1.9	"	3	8 20 p.m.		5.00	5.3	0.66	"	3
18	6 00 a.m.	9.9	NE.	1	6 00 a.m.	5.5			"	3							
"	6 30 p.m.	10.0	"	2	4 00 p.m.		4.3	1.2	"	3							
19	M.	9.7	E.	2	6 00 a.m.	5.6			"	3	2 20 a.m.		4.16			"	3
"	12 00 p.m.	9.4	"	1	3 00 p.m.		4.4	1.2	"	3	11 45 a.m.	4.58				"	3
"											12 00 p.m.		4.00	4.2	0.58	"	3
20	3 00 p.m.	9.7	"	2	6 00 a.m.	5.2			"	3	11 15 a.m.	4.75				"	3
"	12 00 p.m.	9.3	S.	1	3 00 p.m.		4.2	1.0	"	3	10 30 p.m.		4.16	4.4	0.59	"	3
21	6 00 a.m.	9.2	NE.	2	10 00 a.m.	5.8			"	3	11 20 a.m.	4.66				"	3
"	6 30 p.m.	9.5	E.	1	4 00 p.m.		4.1	1.7	"	3	9 10 p.m.		4.16	4.4	0.50	"	3
22	9 00 a.m.	9.3	NE.	3	9 00 a.m.	5.7			"	3	1 00 p.m.	5.16				"	3
"	9 00 p.m.	9.7	"	3	6 00 p.m.		4.9	0.8	"	3							
23	9 00 a.m.	9.5	SE.	1	11 00 a.m.	5.4			"	3	4 30 a.m.		4.41	4.7	0.75	"	3
"	12 00 p.m.	9.2	S.	1	6 00 p.m.		4.3	1.1	"	3	10 40 p.m.		3.58			"	3
24	6 00 a.m.	9.0	"	1	6 00 a.m.		3.9		NW.	1	1 00 p.m.	4.00				NE.	2
"	12 00 p.m.	8.6	SW.	1	2 00 p.m.	5.5			Calm.	0	9 25 p.m.		2.91	3.4	1.09	"	2
25	6 00 a.m.	8.6	NE.	2	6 00 a.m.		3.8	1.7	NW.	1	1 00 p.m.	4.00				"	3
"	6 30 p.m.	8.5	S.	1	3 00 p.m.	4.4											
26	6 00 a.m.	8.4	NE.	2	6 00 a.m.		4.1	0.3	"	1	3 00 a.m.		3.16	3.5	0.84	NW.	2
"	12 00 p.m.	8.7	SE.	1	4 00 p.m.	4.8			Calm.	0	4 15 p.m.	3.91				SE.	2
27	6 00 a.m.	8.9	N.	3	6 00 a.m.		3.9	0.9	NW.	1	7 45 a.m.		2.41	3.1	1.50	NW.	2
"	6 30 p.m.	8.3	"	3	3 00 p.m.	4.3			"	2	8 45 p.m.	3.83				"	2
28	9 00 a.m.	8.4	NE.	2	6 00 a.m.	4.4			NE.	1	1 00 p.m.		2.50	3.1	1.33	E.	3
"	9 00 p.m.	8.1	"	3	6 00 p.m.		3.1	1.2									
29	9 00 a.m.	8.3	"	2	7 00 a.m.	4.4			"	1	1 30 a.m.	3.91				"	3
"	9 00 p.m.	8.0	S.	1	6 00 p.m.		2.9	1.5	Calm.	0	0 30 p.m.		2.50	3.2	1.41	"	3
30	M.	8.2	NE.	2	6 00 a.m.	4.2			NE.	1	2 20 a.m.	3.66				"	3
"	12 00 p.m.	7.8	S.	1	6 00 p.m.		2.8	1.4	Calm.	0	2 00 p.m.		2.41	3.0	1.25	NE.	3
Oct. 1	M.	8.0	NE.	1	6 00 a.m.	4.2			NE.	1	3 40 a.m.	3.75				ENE.	3
"	12 00 p.m.	7.8	N.	1	6 00 p.m.		2.9	1.3	"	1	2 30 p.m.		2.33	3.0	1.52	"	3
2	6 00 a.m.	8.0	"	1	6 00 a.m.	4.0			"	1	4 35 a.m.	3.91				"	3
"	3 00 p.m.	8.2	"	1	6 00 p.m.		2.9	1.1	Calm.	0	5 00 p.m.		2.58	3.2	1.33	E.	3
3	6 00 a.m.	8.0	"	1	6 00 a.m.	3.8			NE.	1	5 30 a.m.	3.75				"	2
"	6 00 p.m.	8.1	NW.	1	5 00 p.m.		2.7	1.1	Calm.	0	5 20 p.m.		2.33	3.0	1.42	"	2
4	6 00 a.m.	7.8	"	2	6 00 a.m.	3.7			NE.	1	6 30 a.m.	3.66				N.	2
"	6 00 p.m.	7.9	S.	1	6 00 p.m.		2.6	1.1	Calm.	0	6 00 p.m.		2.50	3.0	1.16	"	2
5	6 00 a.m.	7.8	"	1	8 00 a.m.	4.2			SE.	1	7 15 a.m.	3.75				"	2
"	6 00 p.m.	8.2	SE.	1	6 00 p.m.		3.4	0.8	"	1	6 45 p.m.		2.75	3.2	1.00	E.	2
6	6 00 a.m.	8.0	E.	1	6 00 a.m.	4.2			NE.	1	8 40 a.m.	3.91				"	2
"	9 00 p.m.	8.6	NE.	1	4 00 p.m.	5.2			"	3	10 00 p.m.	4.16				"	3
7	9 00 a.m.	8.6	"	3	6 00 a.m.		4.3	0.9	"	3	6 00 p.m.	4.16				"	3
"	9 00 p.m.	9.1	SE.	1	5 00 p.m.	5.0			"	3							
8	6 00 a.m.	9.0	E.	1	6 00 a.m.		4.3	0.9	"	3	4 30 a.m.		3.75	3.9	0.41	"	3
"	6 00 p.m.	9.2	"	1	5 00 p.m.	4.9			"	3	3 00 p.m.	4.08				ESE.	3
9	9 00 a.m.	9.1	"	2	6 00 a.m.		4.4	0.5	"	3	7 15 a.m.		3.66	3.8	0.42	"	2
"	12 00 p.m.	9.3	"	2	4 00 p.m.	5.0			"	3	8 00 p.m.	4.16				"	3
10	M.	9.2	"	1	6 00 a.m.		4.4	0.6	"	3	8 50 a.m.		3.41	3.7	0.75	SE.	3
"	12 00 p.m.	9.3	"	1	5 00 p.m.	5.1			SE.	1	9 20 p.m.	4.08				"	3
11	6 00 a.m.	9.2	"	1	10 00 a.m.		3.9	1.2	NE.	3	10 00 a.m.		3.25	3.6	0.83	"	3
"	6 00 p.m.	9.0	S.	1	6 00 p.m.	4.9			"	3	9 40 p.m.	3.95				"	3
12	9 00 a.m.	9.3	NW.	3	10 00 a.m.		3.8	1.1	W.	1	10 30 a.m.		2.91	3.4	1.04	"	2
"	9 00 p.m.	9.0	"	3	6 00 p.m.	4.7			N.	3							
13	6 00 a.m.	8.9	NE.	2	10 00 a.m.		3.6	1.1	"	3	1 00 a.m.	4.16				"	3
"	9 00 p.m.	8.4	N.	1	6 00 p.m.	4.6			NW.	1	11 30 a.m.		3.33	3.7	0.83	N.	3
14	9 00 a.m.	8.6	NE.	3	6 00 a.m.	4.6			NE.	1	2 00 a.m.	4.16				"	3
"	9 00 p.m.	8.2	SW.	1	6 00 p.m.		3.2	1.4	Calm.	0	1 30 p.m.		2.75	3.4	1.41	"	3
15	6 00 a.m.	8.5	NE.	2	6 00 a.m.	4.5			NE.	1	3 45 a.m.	4.08				"	3
"	12 00 p.m.	8.1	W.	1	6 00 p.m.		3.1	1.4	"	1	2 40 p.m.		2.75	3.4	1.33	"	3
16	9 00 a.m.	8.4	N.	2	6 00 a.m.	4.4			"	1	4 00 a.m.	3.91				"	2
"	12 00 p.m.	8.0	W.	1	6 00 p.m.		2.9	1.5	E.	1	2 00 p.m.		2.41	3.1	1.50	"	2
17	M.	8.4	N.	1	6 00 a.m.	4.5			NE.	1	3 35 a.m.	4.08				"	2
"	12 00 p.m.	8.2	W.	1	6 00 p.m.		2.8	1.7	E.	1	4 20 p.m.		3.00	3.5	1.08	"	3
18	M.	8.5	S.	1	6 00 a.m.	4.6			NE.	1	4 30 a.m.	4.08				"	2
"	12 00 p.m.	8.2	N.	2	6 00 p.m.		2.9	1.7	"	1	5 00 p.m.		2.58	3.3	1.50	ESE.	2
19	M.	8.2	NE.	1	6 00 a.m.	3.9			"	1	6 00 a.m.	3.91				N.	2

Tidal Observations—Continued.

Date.	Lake Pontchartrain.				Lake Borgne.						Bayou St. Philip.						
	Time.	Gauge (zero at bottom of canal).	Wind.		Time.	Gauge.		Tidal oscillation.	Wind.		Time.	Gauge. Bench at fort reads 6.0.			Tidal oscillation.	Wind.	
			Direction.	Force.		High tide.	Low tide.		Direction.	Force.		High tide.	Low tide.	Mean reading.		Direction.	Force.
1851.	*h. m.*	*Feet.*			*h. m.*	*Feet.*	*Feet.*	*Feet.*			*h. m.*	*Feet.*	*Feet.*	*Feet.*	*Feet.*		
Oct. 19	12 00 p.m.	8.0	SW.	1	6 00 p.m.		2.6	1.3	NE.	1	5 50 p.m.		2.25	3.0	1.66	S.	2
20	6 00 a.m.	7.9	S.	1	6 00 a.m.	3.8			Calm.	0	7 00 a.m.	3.58				"	2
"	3 00 p.m.	8.1	NE.	1	6 00 p.m.		2.7	1.1	SW.	1	6 10 p.m.		2.33	2.9	1.25	"	2
21	M.	8.1	S.	1	6 00 a.m.	3.7			Calm.	0	8 00 a.m.	3.41				"	2
"	12 00 p.m.	7.9	NE.	1	6 00 p.m.		2.6	1.1	SE.	1	7 15 p.m.		2.33	2.9	1.08	"	2
22	6 00 a.m.	8.1	"	1	11 00 a.m.	4.0			NE.	1	M.	3.91				N.	3
"	6 00 p.m.	8.0	N.	2	6 00 p.m.		3.2	0.8	"	1	9 00 p.m.		3.00	3.4	0.91	"	3
23	9 00 a.m.	8.1	NE.	2	10 00 a.m.	3.9			"	1	9 20 a.m.	3.83				NE.	3
"	9 00 p.m.	8.2	"	3	6 00 p.m.		2.8	1.1	"	1	7 20 p.m.		3.33	3.5	0.50	"	3
24	6 00 a.m.	8.2	E.	2	9 00 a.m.	4.0			"	1	8 40 a.m.		2.83		1.00	ENE.	2
"	6 00 p.m.	8.0	S.	1	6 00 p.m.		2.9	1.1	"	1	6 00 p.m.	3.33				"	2
25	6 00 a.m.	8.2	"	1	6 00 a.m.	3.6			"	1	10 00 a.m.		2.16	2.7	1.17	WSW.	2
"	9 00 p.m.	7.9	SW.	1	3 00 p.m.		2.6	1.0	"	1	11 10 p.m.	3.88				"	2
26	9 00 a.m.	8.5	N.	3	8 00 a.m.	3.9			"	1	M.		2.41	3.1	1.42	N.	3
"	6 00 p.m.	8.0	NW.	3	6 00 p.m.		2.8	1.1	"	1							
27	6 00 a.m.	7.7	E.	2	6 00 a.m.	3.9			"	1	2 10 a.m.	3.91				"	3
"	6 00 p.m.	8.0	S.	1	6 00 p.m.		2.6	1.3	"	1	0 50 p.m.		2.50	3.2	1.41	E.	3
28	9 00 a.m.	8.2	SE.	1	6 00 a.m.	4.0			"	1	2 25 a.m.	3.75				"	2
"	9 00 p.m.	7.9	S.	2	6 00 p.m.		2.8	1.2	"	1	1 00 p.m.		1.91	2.8	1.84	"	3
29	M.	8.3	SW.	1	8 00 a.m.	4.3			"	1	3 00 a.m.	4.00				"	3
"	12 00 p.m.	8.0	"	1	6 00 p.m.		2.9	1.4	"	1	1 30 p.m.		2.25	3.1	1.75	S.	3
30	M.	8.4	N.	1	8 00 a.m.	4.2			"	1	3 35 a.m.	3.91				"	2
"	12 00 p.m.	7.9	SW.	1	6 00 p.m.		2.8	1.4	"	1	3 25 p.m.		2.41	3.1	1.50	NW.	2
31	M.	8.2	NW.	1	7 00 a.m.	4.1			"	1	4 00 a.m.	3.66				"	2
"	12 00 p.m.	7.9	SW.	1	6 00 p.m.		2.7	1.4	SE.	1	2 30 p.m.		2.41	3.0	1.25	ESE.	2
Nov. 1	M.	8.2	SE.	1	6 00 a.m.	4.0			NE.	1	4 45 a.m.	3.66				"	2
"	12 00 p.m.	7.9	N.	1	6 00 p.m.		2.7	1.3	SW.	1	4 15 p.m.		2.25	2.9	1.41	"	2
2	9 00 a.m.	8.1	W.	2	6 00 a.m.	4.1			NE.	2	5 10 a.m.	3.33				NW.	2
"	12 00 p.m.	7.6	NW.	2	6 00 p.m.		3.0	1.1	"	2	5 10 p.m.		2.25	2.7	1.08	"	3
3	M.	7.7	"	2	6 00 a.m.	3.6			NW.	2	7 50 a.m.	3.16				"	2
"	12 00 p.m.	7.5	N.	3	6 00 p.m.		2.5	1.1	"	2	6 20 p.m.		2.41	2.7	0.75	"	2
4	M.	7.5	NE.	1	6 00 a.m.	3.3			N.	1	7 40 a.m.	3.16				E.	2
"	12 00 p.m.	7.3	SW.	1	6 00 p.m.		2.4	0.9	SE.	1	7 00 p.m.		2.25	2.7	0.91	"	2
5	6 00 a.m.	7.4	"	1	6 00 a.m.	3.0			SW.	1	M.	2.66				N.	2
"	6 00 p.m.	7.2	W.	2	6 00 p.m.		2.3	0.7	"	1	7 30 p.m.		2.50	2.5	0.16	"	2
6	9 00 a.m.	7.3	N.	3	6 00 a.m.	3.6			N.	3	10 00 a.m.	3.25				"	3
"	9 00 p.m.	7.5	"	3	4 00 p.m.		2.3	1.3	"	3	9 00 p.m.	3.50				"	3
7	6 00 a.m.	7.6	E.	2	6 00 a.m.	3.5			NE.	3	8 30 a.m.		2.58	3.0	0.92	NE.	3
"	12 00 p.m.	7.7	SW.	1	6 00 p.m.		2.9	0.6	"	3	8 00 p.m.	3.33				"	3
8	6 00 a.m.	7.9	E.	2	M.				E.	1	6 00 a.m.		2.16	2.7	1.18	"	3
"	6 00 p.m.	7.7	"	1	6 00 p.m.	3.8			SE.	1	10 15 p.m.	3.41				"	2
9	6 00 a.m.	8.0	"	1	M.		2.7	1.1	"	1	8 45 a.m.		2.25	2.8	1.16	ESE.	2
"	5 30 p.m.	7.8	S.	2	6 00 p.m.	3.5			"	1	10 00 p.m.	3.66				"	2
10	6 30 a.m.	8.2	SE.	1	6 00 a.m.	3.8			"	1	8 15 a.m.		2.25	2.9	1.41	"	2
"	5 30 p.m.	7.9	"	1	2 00 p.m.		2.6	1.2	"								
11	6 30 a.m.	8.4	"	3	6 00 a.m.	4.5			NE.	3	1 40 a.m.	4.08				"	3
"	9 00 p.m.	8.6	E.	2	3 00 p.m.		3.1	1.3	SE.	1	M.		2.58	3.3	1.50	"	3
12	6 30 a.m.	9.0	SE.	2	M.				"	3	3 00 a.m.	4.75				"	3
"	5 30 p.m.	9.8	E.	2	4 00 p.m.	6.0			"	3	2 00 p.m.		4.08	4.3	0.67	"	3
13	6 30 a.m.	10.2	"	1	6 00 a.m.	6.5			"	3	2 50 a.m.	5.33				"	3
"	9 00 p.m.	9.9	NW.	2	2 00 p.m.		4.8	1.7	"	3	8 00 p.m.		4.33	4.8	1.00	"	3
14	9 00 a.m.	10.4	"	4	6 00 a.m.	5.5			NE.	3	8 30 a.m.	4.50				S.	3
"	12 00 p.m.	9.0	SW.	2	3 00 p.m.		4.3	1.2	"	3	6 00 p.m.		3.50	4.0	1.00	N.	2
15	6 30 a.m.	8.8	N.	2	6 00 a.m.	4.6			"	3	5 00 a.m.	3.91				"	2
"	M.	8.3	NW.	2	5 00 p.m.		3.5	1.1	NW.	3	3 10 p.m.		2.50	3.2	1.41	"	2
16	M.	8.5	N.	1	6 00 a.m.	4.5			"	3	3 35 a.m,	3.83				"	2
"	12 00 p.m.	8.2	SW.	1	6 00 p.m.		2.9	1.6	"	1	2 45 p.m.		2.16	2.9	1.67	"	2
17	M.	8.2	N.	1	6 00 a.m.	4.0			NE.	1	4 20 a.m.	3.41				"	2
"	12 00 p.m.	7.9	S.	1	6 00 p.m.		2.9	1.1	"	1	3 40 p.m.		2.33	2.8	1.08	NE.	2
18	6 30 a.m.	7.9	"	1	6 00 a.m.	3.9			"	1	4 50 a.m.	3.41				"	2
"	M.	8.4	NE.	2	4 00 p.m.		2.8	1.1	"	1	4 00 p.m.		2.75	3.0	0.66	E.	2
19	6 30 a.m.	8.3	E.	2	6 00 a.m.	4.0			"	1	8 15 a.m.	3.33				"	3
"	12 00 p.m.	8.6	"	2	5 00 p.m.		3.1	0.9	"	1	10 00 p.m.	3.75				"	2
20	6 30 a.m.	8.7	"	1	6 00 a.m.	4.1			NW.	1	8 00 a.m.		2.91	3.3	0.84	SW.	2
"	M.	8.0	NW.	2	4 00 p.m.		2.9	1.2	"	1	10 40 p.m.	3.33				NW.	2
21	6 30 a.m.	7.7	"	2	6 00 a.m.	3.8			"	2	8 30 a.m.		1.75	2.5	1.58	N.	3
"	9 00 p.m.	7.2	"	2	3 00 p.m.		2.6	1.2	"	2	10 00 p.m.	3.16				"	3
22	6 30 a.m.	7.4	E.	2	6 00 a.m.	3.5			"	2	8 45 a.m.		1.75	2.4	1.41	"	2
"	9 00 p.m.	7.6	SE.	2	2 00 p.m.		2.4	1.1	"	1	10 30 p.m.	3.50				"	3
23	6 30 a.m.	8.1	SW.	1	6 00 a.m.	3.3			SW	3	9 15 a.m.		1.33	2.4	2.17	SW.	3
"	5 30 p.m.	7.8	N.	1	3 00 p.m.		2.3	1.0	NW.	1	11 10 p.m.	3.75				"	3
24	9 00 a.m.	8.2	NE.	3	6 00 a.m.	3.2			"	3	10 00 a.m.		2.66	3.2	1.09	ENE.	3
"	9 00 p.m.	7.9	NW.	3	2 00 p.m.		2.5	0.7	"	3							
25	6 30 a.m.	8.0	"	3	6 00 a.m.	3.3			"	1	2 50 a.m.	4.25				N.	3
"	12 00 p.m.	7.2	"	1	2 00 p.m.		2.3	1.0			2 30 p.m.		1.66	2.9	2.59	NW.	2
26	6 30 a.m.	7.2	SE.	1	6 00 a.m.	3.4			"	1	2 00 a.m.	3.33				E.	2
"	12 00 p.m.	7.5	"	2	3 00 p.m.		2.1	1.3	SE.	1	M.		1.41	2.3	1.92	"	2
27	6 30 a.m.	7.7	"	2	6 00 a.m.	4.5			NE.	1	1 00 a.m.	3.91				"	3
"	12 00 p.m.	8.3	E.	2	5 00 p.m.		3.5	1.0	E.	1	11 30 a.m.		2.58	3.2	1.33	SE.	3
28	9 00 a.m.	8.6	NE.	2	6 00 a.m.	4.5			NE.	2	0 35 a.m.	3.83				"	2
"	9 00 p.m.	8.3	N.	1	5 00 p.m.		3.4	1.1	"	2	2 00 p.m.		2.41	3.1	1.42	NE.	2
29	6 30 a.m.	8.3	E.	1	6 00 a.m.	4.4			"	2	3 00 a.m.	3.83				"	2
"	5 30 p.m.	8.6	NW.	2	5 00 p.m.		3.5	0.9	"	2	3 30 p.m.		2.75	2.7	1.08	"	2
30	6 30 a.m.	8.4	"	3	6 00 a.m.	3.9			NW.	2	2 45 a.m.	3.75				ESE.	3
"	5 30 p.m.	7.9	"	1	5 00 p.m.		2.8	1.1	"	3	2 35 p.m.		1.83	2.7	1.92	N.	3
Dec. 22											9 30 a.m.		1.50			"	2
"											10 40 p.m.	3.58				"	2
23											11 20 a.m.		1.66	2.6	1.92	NE.	3

Tidal Observations—Continued.

Date.	Lake Pontchartrain.				Lake Borgne.						Bayou St. Philip.						
	Time.	Gauge (zero at bottom of canal).	Wind. Direction.	Wind. Force.	Time.	Gauge. High tide.	Gauge. Low tide.	Tidal oscillation.	Wind. Direction.	Wind. Force.	Time.	Gauge. Bench at fort reads 6.0. High tide.	Gauge. Low tide.	Gauge. Mean reading.	Tidal oscillation.	Wind. Direction.	Wind. Force.
1851.	*h. m.*	*Feet.*			*h. m.*	*Feet.*	*Feet.*	*Feet.*			*h. m.*	*Feet.*	*Feet.*	*Feet.*	*Feet.*		
Dec. 24											0 45 a.m.	3.50				NE.	2
"											0 10 p.m.		1.41	2.4	2.09	"	2
25											1 15 a.m.	3.25				"	2
"											0 50 p.m.		1.25	2.2	2.00	SW.	2
26											2 00 a.m.	3.41				"	2
"											1 30 p.m.		1.41	2.4	2.00	"	2
27											3 00 a.m.	3.16				"	2
"											1 30 p.m.		1.58	2.3	1.58	S.	3
28											2 20 a.m.	3.08				"	2
"											1 00 p.m.		1.66	2.3	1.42	"	3
29											3 40 a.m.	3.41				"	2
"											1 30 p.m.		2.50	2.9	0.91	"	3
30											2 50 a.m.	3.50				"	3
"											1 10 p.m.		2.58	3.0	0.92	"	3
"											10 30 p.m.	3.50				"	3
31											11 00 a.m.		2.58	3.0	0.92	N.	3
"											10 20 p.m.	3.41				"	3
1852.																	
Jan. 1											M.		2.41	2.9	1.00	"	2
"											10 10 p.m.	3.08				"	2
2											8 30 a.m.		2.00	2.5	1.08	"	2
"											7 50 p.m.	3.08				"	2
3											8 00 a.m.		1.58	2.3	1.50	NE.	2
"											9 00 p.m.	3.00				"	2
4											8 00 a.m.		1.25	2.1	1.75	SW.	2
"											8 40 p.m.	3.25				"	3
5											11 30 a.m.		1.16	2.2	2.09	N.	3
"											10 30 p.m.	2.66				"	3
6											8 20 a.m.		1.25	1.9	1.41	"	3
"											11 35 p.m.	3.16				"	2
7											10 00 a.m.		1.25	2.2	1.91	E.	2
"											11 55 p.m.	3.25				"	2
8											10 20 a.m.		1.25	2.2	2.00	NW.	2
9											0 15 a.m.	2.83				"	3
"											11 00 a.m.		1.16	1.9	1.67	W.	3
10											2 00 a.m.	3.00				"	2
"											M.		1.16	2.0	1.84	"	2
11											3 30 a.m.	3.00				"	2
"											1 00 p.m.		1.66	2.3	1.34	NNE.	3
12											1 40 a.m.	2.91				"	3
"											M.		2.51	2.7	0.40	E.	3
13											3 35 a.m.	3.33				"	3
"											3 20 p.m.		1.75	2.5	1.58	N.	3
14											2 00 a.m.	2.00				"	3
"											9 10 a.m.		1.58	1.7	0.42	"	2
15											1 00 a.m.		1.33			W.	2
"											8 00 p.m.	1.83				NE.	2
16											8 00 a.m.		1.25	1.5	0.58	W.	2
"											7 00 p.m.	2.25				"	2
17											6 00 a.m.		1.16	1.6	1.09	"	2
"											7 00 p.m.	2.66				"	2
18											9 00 a.m.		1.25	1.9	1.41	"	2
"											8 30 p.m.	2.90				"	2
19											8 45 a.m.		1.25	2.0	1.75	N.	3
"											9 15 p.m.	3.00				"	3
20											9 00 a.m.		1.25	2.1	1.75	"	2
"											10 00 p.m.	3.00				"	2
21											8 50 a.m.		1.16	2.0	1.84	"	2
"											10 30 p.m.	2.58				"	2
22											9 15 a.m.		1.41	2.0	1.17	"	2
"											11 20 p.m.	2.66				"	3
23											10 00 a.m.		1.50	2.0	1.16	E.	2
"											11 10 p.m.	2.58				"	2
24											10 40 a.m.		1.50	2.0	1.08	N.	2
"											12 00 p.m.	2.66				"	2
25											11 20 a.m.		1.66	2.1	1.00	E.	2
26											0 15 a.m.	2.66				"	2
"											11 50 a.m.		1.75	2.2	0.91	N.	2
27											1 00 a.m.	2.58				"	2
"											M.		1.91	2.2	0.67	"	2
28											9 00 a.m.		1.66			WSW.	2
"											6 30 p.m.	2.33				"	2
29											6 00 a.m.		1.66	1.9	0.67	W.	2
"											6 45 p.m.	2.41				SW.	2
30											5 20 a.m.		1.33	1.8	1.08	S.	2
"											7 10 p.m.	2.91				"	3
31											7 30 a.m.		1.50	2.2	1.41	SW.	2
"											6 00 p.m.	2.83				SE.	2

No. 4.—TIDAL OBSERVATIONS WITH SELF-REGISTERING GAUGE.

These observations are so numerous that a synopsis of the most important results is prefixed.

It was ascertained, by corresponding observations on a tide-staff in the gulf, that there is a rise at the telegraph station, due to the river flood. The surface at this station rose 0.5 of a foot, when the river at Carrollton rose from the gauge-mark of 3 feet to that of 10 feet. To correct the "mean of tide readings" in the next table for this oscillation, the following subtractions must be made. By applying them the mean level of the gulf will be found to read 1.0 foot on the telegraph-station gauge:—

1859.	*Feet.*	1860.	*Feet.*
For May	0.7	For January	0.4
" June	0.7	" February	0.6
" July	0.4	" March	0.6
" August	0.0	" April	0.4
" September	0.0	" May	0.3
" October	0.0		
" November	0.0		
" December	0.2		

The following table exhibits the mean results of the whole series of simultaneous observations at Carrollton and at the telegraph station at the mouth of the Southwest pass:—

Date.	Telegraph station at mouth of Southwest pass, Mississippi river.						Carrollton, La.					Diff. of tidal time.
	Mean high-tide readings for lunar month.	Mean low-tide readings for lunar month.	Difference, or mean rise and fall.	Mean of tide-readings.	Mean rise and fall at full and new moon, or greatest decl.	Mean rise and fall at the moon's 1st and 2d qrs., or least decl.	Mean tidal oscillation.	Mean gauge-reading during lunation.	Mean elevation of river above gulf during lunation.	Mean rise and fall at full and new moon, or greatest decl.	Mean rise and fall at the moon's 1st and 2d qrs., or least decl.	
1859.	*Feet.*	*Feet.*	*Feet.*	*Feet.*	*Feet.*	*Feet.*	*Feet.*	*Feet.*	*Feet.*	*Feet.*	*Feet.*	*h. m.*
June 1	1.9	0.9	1.0	1.4	1.7	0.4						
" 30	2.2	0.9	1.3	1.5	2.0	0.3						
July 30	1.9	0.7	1.2	1.3	1.1	0.9						
August 28	1.7	0.4	1.3	1.0	1.3	1.3						
September 26	2.0	0.6	1.4	1.3	1.7	0.4						
October 26	1.8	0.7	1.1	1.2	1.9	0.2						
November 24	1.8	0.2	1.6	1.0	2.2	0.2		0.8	0.7	1.9		5 20
December 24	1.7	0.5	1.2	1.1	2.4	0.5	0.6	4.3	4.2	0.9	0.4	5 20
1860.												
January 23	2.0	0.8	1.2	1.4	1.8	0.6	0.4	8.9	8.4	0.6	0.3	5 58
February 22	2.2	1.2	1.0	1.7	1.4	0.6	0.4	11.9	11.1	0.6	0.2	6 36
March 22	2.0	1.1	0.9	1.5	1.4		0.4	12.5	11.9	0.4	0.2	5 40
April 21	1.7	0.9	0.8	1.3	1.6	0.6	0.3	9.5	9.1			6 01
May 20	2.0	0.8	1.2	1.4	1.7	0.4	0.4	7.8	7.3	0.5	0.3	5 48
Mean	1.9	0.7	1.2	1.3	1.7	0.5						5 49

The detailed observations from which the above mean results are derived will be found in the following pages.

Tidal Observations—Continued.

Date.	Telegraph station at mouth of Southwest pass.						Carrollton, La.						Difference of tidal time.
	Time.	Gauge.		Difference.	Wind.		Time.	Gauge.		Difference.	Wind.		
		High tide.	Low tide.		Direction.	Force.		High tide.	Low tide.		Direction.	Force.	
1859.	*h. m.*	*Feet.*	*Feet.*	*Feet.*			*h. m.*	*Feet.*	*Feet.*	*Feet.*			*h. m.*
May 11	9 00 a.m.	1.7											
"	10 30 p.m		1.4	0.3									
12	3 30 a.m.	1.8			Calm.	0							
"	4 00 p.m.		1.2	0.6	E.	1							
13	5 00 a.m	1.9			ENE.	1							
"	5 00 p.m.		1.2	0.7	"	3							
14	5 30 a.m.	2.0			E.	1							
"	6 00 p.m.		0.8	1.2	"	1							
15	6 30 a.m.	2.1			"	1							
"	7 00 p.m.		0.7	1.4	SW.	1							
16	7 00 a.m.	2.1			"	1							
"	7 30 p.m.		0.6	1.5	"	1							
17	8 00 a.m.	2.1			"	1							
"	8 00 p.m.		0.7	1.4	SSW.	1							
18	8 30 a.m.	2.2			"	1							
"	8 30 p.m.		0.8	1.4	"	2							
19	8 30 a.m.	2.1			"	1							
"	9 30 p.m.		0.6	1.5	NE.	1							
20	10 30 a.m.	2.2			S.	1							
"	10 30 p.m.		0.8	1.4	"	1							
21	11 00 a.m.	2.0			"	1							
"	11 00 p.m.		0.8	1.2	"	1							
22	M.	1.8			W.	3							
"	11 30 p.m.		1.0	0.8	NE.	1							
23	0 30 p.m.	1.8			E.	1							
"	12 00 p.m.		1.0	0.8	NE.	1							
24	1 30 p.m.	1.8			E.	1							
25	0 30 a.m.		1.1	0.7	"	1							
"	2 30 p.m.	1.5			ENE.	1							
26	1 00 a.m.		1.2	0.3	E.	2							
"	3 00 a.m.	1.5			ENE.	1							
"	2 30 p.m.		1.2	0.3	E.	1							
27	4 00 a.m.	1.7			NE.	1							
"	3 30 p.m.		1.1	0.6	SSE.	1							
28	5 00 a.m.	1.6			NE.	3							
"	5 00 p.m.		1.0	0.6	"	1							
29	5 30 a.m.	2.0			"	1							
"	6 00 p.m.		0.9	1.1	ESE.	1							
30	6 00 a.m.	2.1			"	1							
"	7 00 p.m.		0.6	1.5	"	1							
31	6 30 a.m.	2.1			SE.	1							
"	7 00 p.m.		0.5	1.6	"	1							
June 1	7 30 a.m.	2.3			NE.	1							
"	8 00 p.m.		0.5	1.8	ESE.	1							
2	8 30 a.m.	2.3			NE.	1							
"	9 00 p.m.		0.5	1.8	SE.	1							
3	9 00 a.m.	2.2			WNW.	1							
"	10 00 p.m.		0.5	1.7	NW.	3							
4	10 00 a.m.	2.2			"	3							
"	11 00 p.m.		0.6	1.6	NNE.	1							
5	11 00 a.m.	2.2			"	3							
"	11 30 p.m.		0.7	1.5	"	1							
6	11 30 a.m.	2.0			"	1							
"	12 00 p.m.		1.0	1.0	"	1							
7	M.	1.8			NE.	1							
8	0 30 a.m.		1.5	0.3	E.	3							
"	8 30 a.m.	1.6			NE.	1							
"	4 00 p.m.		1.4	0.2	E.	1							
9	4 00 a.m.	1.8			Calm.	0							
"	4 30 p.m.		1.3	0.5	SE.	1							
10	4 30 a.m.	2.1			Calm.	0							
"	4 45 p.m.		1.1	1.0	SE.	1							
11	5 00 a.m.	2.2			Calm.	0							
"	5 00 p.m.		0.8	1.4	E.	1							
12	5 30 a.m.	2.2			SE.	1							

Tidal Observations—Continued.

Date.	Telegraph station at mouth of Southwest pass.						Carrollton, La.						Difference of tidal time.
	Time.	Gauge.		Difference.	Wind.		Time.	Gauge.		Difference.	Wind.		
		High tide.	Low tide.		Direction.	Force.		High tide.	Low tide.		Direction.	Force.	
1859.	*h. m.*	*Feet.*	*Feet.*	*Feet.*			*h. m.*	*Feet.*	*Feet.*	*Feet.*			*h. m.*
June 12	5 30 p.m.		0.9	1.3	E.	3							
13	6 00 a.m.	2.5			SE.	3							
"	6 00 p.m.		0.7	1.8	"	3							
14	6 30 a.m.	2.3			"	3							
"	7 00 p.m.		0.7	1.6	"	1							
15	7 30 a.m.	2.4			"	1							
"	7 30 p.m.		0.7	1.7	NE.	1							
16	8 00 a.m.	2.3			S.	1							
"	8 00 p.m.		0.6	1.7	"	1							
17	9 00 a.m.	2.2			SSW.	3							
"	9 00 p.m.		0.8	1.4	SW.	3							
18	9 30 a.m.	2.0			"	3							
"	9 30 p.m.		0.7	1.3	S.	1							
19	10 00 a.m.	2.0			"	1							
"	10 30 p.m.		0.8	1.2	SW.	1							
20	11 00 a.m.	1.8			W.	1							
"	11 00 p.m.		1.1	0.7	S	1							
21	11 30 a.m.	1.6			SW.	1							
"	11 30 p.m.		1.2	0.4	NW.	3							
22	0 30 p.m.	1.6			W.	3							
"	12 00 p.m.		1.4	0 2	N.	1							
23	3 00 a.m.	1.7			"	3							
"	3 00 p.m.		1.5	0.2	"	1							
24	3 30 a.m.	2.0			NNE.	3							
"	4 00 p.m.		1.5	0.5	NE.	3							
25	4 00 a.m.	2.1			E.	3							
"	5 00 p.m.		1.1	1.0	NE.	1							
26	4 30 a.m.	2.3			"	3							
"	5 30 p.m.		1.1	1.2	E.	3							
27	5 30 a.m.	2.5			"	3							
"	6 30 p.m.		0.8	1.7	SE.	3							
28	6 30 a.m.	2.6			"	3							
"	7 30 p.m.		0.6	2 0	E.	3							
29	7 45 a.m.	2.6			ESE.	1							
"	8 30 p.m.		0.6	2 0	E.	1							
30	8 30 a.m.	2.6			"	0							
"	9 30 p.m.		0.6	2.0	SE.	1							
July 1	9 30 a.m.	2.5			SSE.	1							
"	9 30 p.m.		0.6	1.9	E.	1							
2	10 30 a.m.	2.3			SSW.	1							
"	10 00 p.m.		0.6	1.7	S.	1							
3	11 00 a.m.	2.1			N.	1							
"	10 30 p.m.		0.8	1.3	SSW.	1							
4	11 30 a.m.	2.8			NW.	1							
"	11 00 p.m.		1.1	1.7	S.	1							
5	M.	1.7			ESE.	2							
"	11 30 p.m.		1.3	0.4	ENE.	2							
6	2 00 a.m.	1.7			"	2							
"	3 00 p.m.		1.5	0.2	E.	1							
7	3 00 a.m.	2.0			"	1							
"	3 30 p.m.		1.1	0.9	SE.	1							
8	3 30 a.m.	2.0			NW.	1							
"	4 15 p.m.		1.0	1.0	SW.	1							
9	4 00 a.m.	2.1			NE.	2							
"	4 30 p.m.		1.0	1.1	"	1							
10	4 45 a.m.	2.4			E.	1							
"	4 30 p.m.		0.8	1.6	"	1							
11	4 45 a.m.	2.4			SW.	3							
"	5 30 p.m.		0.7	1.7	E.	1							
12	5 30 a.m.	2.2			SE.	1							
"	6 00 p.m.		0.5	1.7	S.	1							
13	6 00 a.m.	2.0			NW.	2							
"	6 40 p.m.		0.6	1.4	W.	1							
14	9 15 a.m.	2.1			Calm.	0							

Tidal Observations—Continued.

Date.	Telegraph station at mouth of Southwest pass. Time.	Gauge. High tide.	Gauge. Low tide.	Difference.	Wind. Direction.	Wind. Force.	Carrollton, La. Time.	Gauge. High tide.	Gauge. Low tide.	Difference.	Wind. Direction.	Wind. Force.	Difference of tidal time.
1859.	*h m.*	*Feet.*	*Feet.*	*Feet.*			*h. m.*	*Feet.*	*Feet.*	*Feet.*			*h. m.*
July 14	7 20 p.m.		0.6	1.5	E.	1							
15	9 20 a.m.	2.1			"	1							
"	8 20 p.m.		0.7	1.4	SSE.	1							
16	10 20 a.m.	1.8			S.	1							
"	8 45 p.m.		0.8	1.0	SSW.	1							
17	10 20 a.m.	1.8			W.	1							
"	8 25 p.m.		0.8	1.0	"	1							
18	9 45 a.m.	1.7			WNW.	1							
"	9 40 p.m.		0.8	0.9	SW.	1							
19	11 20 a.m.	1.5			"	1							
"	8 40 p.m.		1.0	0.5	SSW.	1							
20	5 45 a.m.	1.1			SW.	1							
"	6 30 p.m.		1.0	0.1	WSW.	1							
21	5 00 a.m.	1.2			"	2							
"	4 10 p.m.		1.0	0.2	SW.	2							
22	2 10 a.m.	1.2			"	2							
"	11 00 a.m.		0.6	0.6	"	2							
23	1 45 a.m.	1.2			"	2							
"	2 40 p.m.		0.3	0.9	"	2							
24	3 20 a.m.	1.4			WSW.	1							
"	2 15 p.m.		—0.1	1.5	SW.	2							
25	3 15 a.m.	1.4			NW.	2							
"	2 45 p.m.		—0.1	1.5	SW.	2							
26	4 25 a m.	1.5			W.	2							
"	3 45 p.m.		—0.2	1.7	SW.	1							
27	6 00 a.m.	1.8			W.	2							
"	4 30 p.m.		—0.3	2.1	SW.	1							
28	6 45 a.m.	2.4			NW.	1							
"	5 55 p.m.		0.4	2.0	SW.	1							
29	6 50 a.m.	2.5			NNW.	1							
"	7 50 p.m.		0.2	2.3	SW.	1							
30	5 30 a.m.	2.1			W.	1							
"	7 20 p.m.		0.3	1.8	SSW.	1							
31	10 30 a.m.	1.8			W.	1							
"	8 30 p.m.		0.5	1.3	SSW.	1							
August 1	1 30 p.m.	1.2			"	1							
"	6 15 p.m.		1.0	0.2	"	1							
2	1 30 a.m.	1.2			SW.	1							
"	6 30 p m.		1.0	0.2	SSE.	1							
3	2 30 a.m.	1.1			"	1							
"	8 15 p.m.		0.7	0.4	S.	1							
4	1 45 a.m.	1.2			E.	1							
"	1 30 p.m.		0.5	0.7	SE.	1							
5	2 35 a.m.	1.5			"	1							
"	2 20 p.m.		0.2	1.3	W.	1							
6	2 10 a m.	1.5			NW.	1							
"	0 35 p.m.		0.1	1.4	SW.	4							
7	2 50 a.m.	2.0			NW.	1							
"	3 30 p.m.		0.2	1.8	SSW.	1							
8	4 50 a.m.	2.0			W.	1							
"	3 45 p.m.		0.1	1.9	SE.	1							
9	4 50 a.m.	2.1			SSE.	1							
"	5 25 p.m.		0.3	1.8	SE.	3							
10	6 00 a.m.	2.2			ESE.	2							
"	6 10 p.m.		0.5	1.7	E.	2							
11	7 05 a.m.	2.3			ESE.	2							
"	6 15 p.m.		0.5	1.8	NW.	1							
12	7 25 a.m.	2.3			S.	2							
"	6 45 p.m.		0.6	1.7	SE.	2							
13	8 40 a.m.	2.2			"	1							
"	8 05 p.m.		0.6	1.6	SSE.	1							
14	9 30 a.m.	1.9			SW.	2							
"	6 30 p.m.		0.6	1.3	"	1							
15	11 00 a.m.	1.7			WSW.	1							

Tidal Observations—Continued.

Date.	Telegraph station at mouth of Southwest pass.						Carrollton, La.						Difference of tidal time.
	Time.	Gauge.		Difference.	Wind.		Time.	Gauge.		Difference.	Wind.		
		High tide.	Low tide.		Direction.	Force.		High tide.	Low tide.		Direction.	Force.	
1859.	*h. m.*	*Feet.*	*Feet.*	*Feet.*			*h. m.*	*Feet.*	*Feet.*	*Feet.*			*h. m.*
August 15	10 00 p.m.		0.7	1.0	WSW.	1							
16	11 00 a.m.	1.2			"	2							
"	10 30 p.m.		0.7	0.5	"	1							
17	11 00 a.m.	1.2			NW.	2							
"	7 00 p.m.		1.0	0.2	NE.	2							
18	11 45 a.m.	1.4			ENE.	2							
"	3 00 p.m.		1.2	0.2	NE.	2							
19	0 30 a.m.	1.8			"	2							
"	M.		1.0	0.8	"	2							
20	0 05 a.m.	1.9			NW.	1							
"	1 15 p.m.		0.6	1.3	SW.	1							
21	0 45 a.m.	2.0			NW.	1							
"	0 45 p.m.		0.2	1.8	SE.	1							
22	1 30 a.m.	2.0			NW.	1							
"	1 45 p.m.		0.2	1.8	NE.	2							
23	3 30 a.m.	2.5			WSW.	1							
"	2 45 p.m.		0.4	2.1	NE.	1							
24	4 15 a.m.	2.6			NW.	1							
"	4 10 p.m.		0.4	2.2	NE.	1							
25	4 45 a.m.	2.6			"	1							
"	4 45 p.m.		0.1	2.5	SE.	1							
26	6 50 a.m.	2.8			"	1							
"	6 00 p.m.		0.3	2.0	ESE.	1							
27	8 00 a.m.	2.3			NNE.	1							
"	7 15 p.m.		0.5	1.8	E.	1							
28	9 15 a.m.	2.0			SW.	1							
"	8 30 p.m.		0.7	1.3	W.	1							
29	10 30 a.m.	1.5			SW.	1							
"	11 00 p.m.		0.7	0.8	W.	1							
30					"	1							
"	M.	1.6			NNW.	1							
31	10 30 a.m.		1.0	0.6	NNE.	1							
"	11 30 p.m.	1.6			N.	1							
Sept. 1	M.		0.5	1.1	NE.	1							
"	12 00 p.m.	1.5			"	1							
2	M.		0.3	1.2	NNE.	1							
"					"	1							
3	0 15 a.m.	1.7			Calm.	0							
"	1 20 p.m.		0.0	1.7	SW.	1							
4	1 30 a.m.	1.7			NW.	1							
"	2 20 p.m.		—0.1	1.8	SW.	1							
5	2 45 a.m.	1.6			NW.	1							
"	3 00 p.m.		0.0	1.6	NE.	1							
6	4 15 a.m.	1.6			NNE.	1							
"	3 25 p.m.		0.2	1.4	NE.	2							
7	4 30 a.m.	1.8			NNW.	1							
"	4 10 p.m.		0.3	1.5	NE.	1							
8	5 45 a.m.	2.0			ENE.	2							
"	4 15 p.m.		0.6	1.4	E.	3							
9	6 30 a.m.	2.0			"	2							
"	6 00 p.m.		0.8	1.2	"	3							
10	7 50 a.m.	2.1			"	2							
"	6 30 p.m.		1.0	1.1	"	3							
11	8 30 a.m.	1.8			NE.	1							
"	7 00 p.m.		1.0	0.8	"	1							
12	9 30 a.m.	1.7			NW.	1							
"	4 30 p.m.		1.4	0.3	S.	1							
13	M.	1.4			SW.	1							
"					"	1							
14	4 00 a.m.		1.2	0.2	NE.	1							
"	11 30 p.m.	2.1			"	2							
15	7 00 a.m.		1.5	0.6	NNE.	7							
"	7 45 p.m.	2.5			W.	7							
16	10 00 a.m.		1.1	1.4	NW.	2							

Tidal Observations—Continued.

Date.	Telegraph station at mouth of Southwest pass.						Carrollton, La.						Difference of tidal time.
	Time.	Gauge.		Difference.	Wind.		Time.	Gauge.		Difference.	Wind.		
		High tide.	Low tide.		Direction.	Force.		High tide.	Low tide.		Direction.	Force.	
1859.	*h. m.*	*Feet.*	*Feet.*	*Feet.*			*h. m.*	*Feet.*	*Feet.*	*Feet.*			*h. m.*
Sept. 16	10 00 p.m.	2.2			W.	1							
17	10 30 a.m.		0.6	1.6	SW.	1							
"	10 30 p.m.	2 0			E.	1							
18	11 00 a.m.		0.4	1.6	"	1							
19	1 00 a.m.	2.2			SSW.	2							
"	M		0.6	1.6	SW.	3							
20	0 30 a.m.	1.7			NW.	2							
"	1 30 p.m.		—0.1	1.8	"	2							
21	2 45 a.m.	2.0			"	2							
"	3 00 p.m.		0.1	1.9	"	2							
22	5 00 a.m.	1.8			N.	1							
"	4 00 p.m.		0.2	1.6	E.	1							
23	5 20 a.m.	1.8			NE.	1							
"	5 00 p.m		0.1	1.7	"	1							
24	6 15 a.m.	1.8			"	1							
"	5 20 p.m.		0.5	1.3	"	1							
25	9 15 a.m.	1.5			NNW.	1							
"	6 00 p.m.		0.8	0.7	NE.	1							
26	Clock				NNE.	1							
"	stopped.				N.	1							
27	8 30 p.m.	1.7			NE.	1							
28	8 30 a.m.		0.4	1.3	"	1							
"	8 15 p.m.	2.0			E.	1							
29	9 30 a.m.		0.3	1.7	SE.	1							
"	9 45 p.m.	1.8			NNE.	1							
30	9 30 a.m.		0.3	1.5	ENE.	1							
"	10 15 p.m.	2.0			NNE.	1							
Oct. 1	11 30 a.m.		0.2	1.8	ENE.	2							
"	11 45 p.m.	1.8			NW.	2							
2	0 30 p.m.		0.4	1.4	NE.	2							
"					"	2							
3	1 00 a.m.	1.9			"	2							
"	1 20 p.m.		0.5	1.4	N.	2							
4	1 45 a.m.	2.0			ENE.	2							
"	2 20 p.m.		0.5	1.5	NE.	1							
5	3 20 a.m.	2.0			ENE.	1							
"	4 00 p.m.		0.6	1.4	NE.	1							
6	3 30 a.m.	1.5			"	1							
"	3 30 p.m.		0.4	1.1	"	1							
7	6 00 a.m.	1.6			ENE.	1							
"	4 15 p.m.		0.7	0.9	"	1							
8	8 30 a.m.	1.5			W.	1							
"	4 30 p.m.		1.2	0.3	SW.	1							
9	10 30 a.m.	1.3			NW.	1							
"	2 30 p.m.		1.1	0.2	"	1							
10	9 15 p.m.	1.2			NE.	1							
11	2 45 a.m.		1.0	0.2	"	1							
"	8 40 p.m.	1.2			"	2							
12	4 00 a.m.		0.6	0.6	"	3							
"					SE.	2							
"	10 00 p.m.	2.0			"	2							
13	6 20 a.m.		0.9	1.1	"	3							
"	7 45 p.m.	2.2			"	1							
14	8 10 a.m.		0.3	1.9	"	1							
"	9 45 p.m.	2.1			"	1							
15	10 00 a.m.		0.3	1.8	NE.	1							
"	10 30 p.m.	2.3			N.	1							
16	10 30 a.m.		0.6	1.7	ESE.	2							
"	10 50 p.m.	2.6			"	2							
17	11 10 a.m.		0.7	1.9	SE.	2							
"					"	2							
18	0 15 a.m.	2.5			NE.	2							
"	11 45 a.m.		0.4	2.1	"	2							

Tidal Observations—Continued.

Date.	Telegraph station at mouth of Southwest pass.						Carrollton, La.						Difference of tidal time.
	Time.	Gauge.		Difference.	Wind.		Time.	Gauge.		Difference.	Wind.		
		High tide.	Low tide.		Direction.	Force.		High tide.	Low tide.		Direction.	Force.	
1859.	*h. m.*	*Feet.*	*Feet.*	*Feet.*			*h. m.*	*Feet.*	*Feet.*	*Feet.*			*h. m.*
Oct. 19	0 45 a.m.	2.20			NW.	2							
“	1 00 p m.		0.50	1.70	N.	2							
20	2 30 a.m.	2.30			ENE.	2							
“	2 30 p.m.		0.60	1.70	“	2							
21	5 00 a m.	2.00			NE.	2							
“	1 40 p.m.		1.00	1.00	“	2							
22	7 30 a.m.	1.80			“	2							
“	1 40 p.m.		1.20	0.60	“	2							
23					ENE.	2							
“					“	2							
24	3 00 a.m.				NE.	3							
“	7 00 p.m.	2.30			“	2							
25	5 30 a.m.		1.00	1.30	N.	3							
“	6 45 p.m.	2.30			“	3							
26	6 45 a.m.		0.70	1.60	“	3							
“	7 40 p.m.	2.60			“	3							
27	6 40 a.m.		0.60	2.00	NW.	3							
“	7 45 p.m.	2.40			“	1							
28	8 45 a.m.		0.50	1.90	“	1							
29	10 45 p.m.	2.00			“	1							
30	11 30 a.m.		—0.10	2.10	“	1							
“	10 45 p.m.	1.50			“	1							
31	10 45 a.m.		0.20	1.30	“	1							
“	11 50 p.m.	1.63			“	1							
Nov. 1	0 30 p.m.		0.10	1.53	NNW.	1							
“					“	1							
2	0 10 a.m.	1.58			“	1							
“	1 30 p.m.		0.30	1.28	“	1							
3	1 40 a.m.	1.00			N.	1							
“	1 00 p.m.		0.50	0.50	ENE.	2							
4	1 40 a.m.	1.16			E.	2							
“	1 00 p.m.		0.83	0.33	“	2							
5	2 50 a.m.	1.42			NE.	2							
“	1 00 p.m.		1.16	0.26	“	2							
6					“	1							
“					“	1							
7	5 50 a.m.				“	1							
“	7 45 p.m.	1.83			ENE.	1							
8	4 50 a.m.		0.91	0.92	“	2							
“	7 00 p.m.	2.10			“	2							
9	5 40 a.m		0.67	1.43	E.	1							
“	6 30 p.m.	2.25			ESE.	1							
10	6 50 a.m.		0.25	2.00	SE.	1							
“	6 40 p.m.	2.16			SSE.	1	12 00 p.m.	2.60					5 20
11	6 40 a.m.		0.20	1.96	“	1	M.		1.15	1.45			5 20
“	8 10 p.m.	2.91			“	1	12 00 p.m.	2.70					3 50
12	8 00 a.m.		0.67	2.24	SE.	1	1 00 p.m.		1.20	1.50			5 00
“	8 20 p.m.	2.67			SW.	1							
13	8 10 a.m.		—0.25	2.92	NW.	7	1 30 a.m.	2.75					5 10
“	8 45 p.m.	2.00			“	7	3 10 p.m.		0.20	2.55			7 00
14	9 30 a.m.		—0.25	2.25	N.	3	2 15 a.m.	1.85					5 30
“	10 45 p.m.				“	3	3 00 p.m.		0.50	1.35			5 30
15					NW.	3							
“					“	3							
16	1 10 a.m.	1.25			ESE.	3							
“	M.		0.00	1.25	“	3							
17					E.	3	7 00 a.m.	1.85					
“					ESE.	3	7 00 p.m.		1.10				
18					W.	3							
“					“	3							
19					N.	1							
“					SW.	1							
20					SE.	1							
“					“	1							

Tidal Observations—Continued.

Date.	Telegraph station at mouth of Southwest pass.						Carrollton, La.						Difference of tidal time.
	Time.	Gauge.		Difference.	Wind.		Time.	Gauge.		Difference.	Wind.		
		High tide.	Low tide.		Direction.	Force.		High tide.	Low tide.		Direction.	Force.	
1859.	h. m.	Feet.	Feet.	Feet.			h. m.	Feet.	Feet.	Feet.			h. m.
Nov. 23					NE.	1							
“	7 00 p.m.	1.75			ENE.	3							
24	6 40 a.m.		—0.20	1.95	“	3							
“	6 50 p.m.	2.25			E.	3							
25	7 40 a.m.		0.00	2.25	“	1							
“	8 40 p.m.	2.25			“	1							
26	8 20 a.m.		0.16	2.09	SE.	1							
“	8 50 p.m.	2.25			S.	1							
27	9 40 a.m.		0.20	2.05	“	1							
“					“	1							
28					SW.	1	2 15 a.m.	2.40					
“					“	1	3 00 p.m.		1.02	1.38			
29					SE.	1	3 20 a.m.	2.24					
“	10 50 p.m.	1.83			NW.	1	3 30 p.m.		1.30	0.94			
30	10 30 a.m.		0.67	1.16	ESE.	1	4 05 a.m.	2.30					5 15
“	10 40 p.m.	1.58			“	1	3 45 p.m.		1.58	0.72			5 15
Dec. 1	10 30 a.m.		0.60	0.98	E.	1							
“	11 10 p.m.	1.50			“	1							
2	11 10 a.m		1.00	0.50	SE.	1							
“	9 30 p.m.	1.50			NW.	1	11 30 a.m.						
3	10 00 a.m.		1.10	0.40	S.	2	1 30 a.m.	2.35					4 00
“	7 00 p.m.	1.58			N.	1	2 00 p.m.		2.15	0.30			4 00
4	4 45 a.m.		0.91	0.67	“	2	0 15 a.m.	2.32					5 15
“	6 20 p.m.	1.67			“	1	10 15 a.m.		2.08	0.24			
“							12 00 p.m.	2.65					5 40
5	5 10 a.m.		1.10	0.57	NNE.	1	9 00 a.m		2.35	0.30			3 50
“	4 40 p.m.	1.91			SE.	1	10 00 p.m.	3.05					
6	3 40 a.m.		0.58	1.33	“	1	9 30 a.m.		2.40	0.65			5 50
“	5 20 p.m.	2.38			S.	1	10 30 p.m.	3.65					5 10
7	5 50 a.m.		0.20	2.18	NW.	3	11 00 a.m.		2.65	1.00			5 10
“	5 40 p.m.	1.91			NNW.	3	11 45 p.m.	3.55					6 05
8	5 20 a.m.		0.10	1.81	“	3	10 30 a.m.		2.70	0.85			5 10
“	7 00 p.m.	2.00			“	3							
9	6 30 a.m.		—0.10	2.10	“	3	0 30 a.m.	3.90					5 30
“	7 10 p.m.	1.83			N.	1	11 30 a.m.		3.00	0.90			5 00
10	6 15 a.m.		—0.33	2.16	“	2							
“	8 50 p.m.	2.16			“	1							
11	7 10 a.m		—0.10	2.26	NNW.	1							
“	9 15 p.m.	2.33			“	1							
12	9 15 a.m.		0.10	2.23	N.	1	3 00 a.m.	4.80					
“	10 20 p.m.	2.10			“	1	3 00 p.m.		4.10	0.70			5 45
13	10 10 a.m.		0.33	1.77	WSW.	1	4 00 a.m.	5.00					5 40
“	10 00 p.m.	1.91			SW.	1	3 00 p.m.		4.55	0.45			4 50
14	10 40 a.m.		0.42	1.49	NNW.	1	4 30 a.m.	5.25					6 30
“	11 40 p.m.	1.67			“	1	3 30 p.m.		4.90	0.35			
15	11 30 a.m.		0.83	0.84	“	1							
“					NE.	1							
16					NW.	1							
“					SW.	2							
17					NW.	1							
“	3 40 p.m.	1.50			SW.	2							
18	3 50 a.m.		0.91	0.59	NNE.	1							
“	6 15 p.m.	1.51			ESE.	1							
19	3 20 a.m.		0.91	0.60	N.	1							
“	5 20 p.m.	2.25			SW.	1	11 00 p.m.	8.60					5 40
20	5 10 a.m.		0.67	1.58	NW.	2	10 00 a.m.		8.20	0.40			4 50
“	5 20 p.m.	1.91			NNW.	1							
21							1 00 a.m.	9.00					7 40
“	5 20 a.m.		0.58	1.33	“	2	10 30 a.m.		8.75	0.25			5 10
“	7 00 p.m.	2.10			NE.	1	11 05 p.m.	9.25					4 05
22	6 30 a.m.		0.50	1.60	N.	3	11 45 a.m.		8.90	0.35			5 15
“	7 20 p.m.	2.16			“	2							
23	7 00 a.m.		0.50	1.66	NW.	3	2 00 a.m.						6 40
“	8 10 p.m.	2.00			W.	2							
24	7 20 a.m.		0.42	1.58	N.	1							

Tidal Observations—Continued.

Date.	Telegraph station at mouth of Southwest pass.						Carrollton, La.						Difference of tidal time.
	Time.	Gauge.		Difference.	Wind.		Time.	Gauge.		Difference.	Wind.		
		High tide.	Low tide.		Direction.	Force.		High tide.	Low tide.		Direction.	Force.	
1859.	*h. m.*	*Feet.*	*Feet.*	*Feet.*			*h. m.*	*Feet.*	*Feet.*	*Feet.*			*h. m*
Dec. 24	9 20 p.m.	1.91			E.	1							
25	9 00 a.m.		0.67	1.24	SE.	1	3 00 a.m.	9.92					5 40
"	8 50 p.m.	1.83			SSE.	1	2 30 p.m.		9.55	0.37			5 30
26	8 40 a.m.		0.75	1.08	"	1	4 00 a.m.	10.00					7 10
"	10 00 p.m.	1.91			"	1	3 30 p.m.		9.75	0.25			6 50
27	10 00 a.m.		0.83	1.08	"	1	4 30 a.m.	10.05					6 30
"	11 40 p.m.	1.83			SE.	1	5 00 p.m.		9.70	0.35			7 00
28	11 30 a.m.		0.91	0.92	S.	1	5 30 a.m.	9.95					5 50
"	10 30 p.m.				ESE.	1			9.65	0.30			
29					S.	1							
"					"	1							
30					NE.	1							
"					N.	3		9.80					
31					S.	7	4 00 p.m.		9.58	0.22			
"					"	7							
1860.													
Jan. 1					NW.	3	10 00 a.m.	9.20					
"	4 20 p.m.	1.58			N.	3							
2	4 20 a.m.		1.00	0.58	NNW.	3	2 30 p.m.		8.75	0.45			
"	5 00 p.m.	1.42			N.	3	7 00 p.m.	8.80					
3	4 30 a.m.		0.66	0.76	"	2	3 00 p.m.		8.42	0.38			
"	4 20 p.m.	1.42			"	2	11 00 p.m.	8.55					6 40
4	5 00 a.m.		0.50	0.92	"	2	11 30 a.m.		8.12	0.43			6 30
"	5 00 p.m.	1.75			NE.	1	11 30 p.m.	8.40					6 30
5	5 00 a.m.		0.50	1.25	N.	1			7.75	0.65			
"	7 15 p.m.	2.16			"	1		8.12					
6	6 00 a.m.		0.67	1.49	ENE.	1			7.80	0.32			
"	6 45 p.m.	2.75			ESE.	3		8.40					
7	6 20 a.m.		0.83	1.92	WSW.	1			7.70	0.70			
"	7 30 p.m.	2.58			SE.	1							
8	7 30 a.m.		0.67	1.91	NE.	1	1 00 a.m.	8.10					5 30
"	9 20 p.m.	2.33			E.	1	7 00 p.m.		7.90	0.20			
9	9 30 a.m.		0.75	1.58	"	1	3 00 a.m.	8.28					5 40
"	9 15 p.m.	2.33			"	1							
10	9 25 a.m.		0.75	1.58	ESE.	2							
"	10 40 p.m.	2.33			"	1	3 30 p.m.		7.95				6 05
11	10 20 a.m.		0.91	1.42	E.	1	5 20 a.m.	8.58					6 40
"					"	1	3 30 p.m.		8.25	0.33			5 10
12	1 00 a.m.	2.00			ESE.	1	7 30 a.m.	8.70					6 30
"	11 20 a.m.		1.25	0.75	SW.	1	4 30 p.m.		8.60	0.10			4 50
13	0 30 a.m.	1.50			E.	1	7 00 a.m.	8.95					6 30
"	7 45 a.m.		1.33	0.17	S.	1							
"	3 45 p.m.	1.83			"	1							
14	6 40 a.m.		1.33	0.50	"	1							
"	3 45 p.m.	1.58			WSW.	2							
15	2 10 a.m.		1.10	0.48	NNW.	1	7 00 a.m.						4 50
"	4 00 p.m.	1.83			NW.	1	10 30 p.m.	9.35					6 30
16	3 50 a.m.		0.83	1.00	N.	1	9 00 a.m.		9.14	0.21			5 10
"	3 45 p.m.	1.91			SE.	1	12 00 p.m.	9.65					8 15
17	5 30 a.m.		0.67	1.24	NNW.	2	10 00 a.m.		9.20	0.45			4 30
"	6 45 p.m.	2.00			N.	1							
18	5 40 a.m.		0.67	1.33	NW.	1	0 30 a.m.	9.70					5 45
"	6 00 p.m.	1.91			WSW.	2	11 00 a.m.		9.30	0.40			5 20
"							12 00 p.m.	9.75					6 00
19	6 00 a.m.		0.83	1.58	NNW.	1	11 30 a.m.		9.30	0.45			5 30
"	8 00 p.m.	1.83			W.	1							
20	7 00 a.m.		0.50	1.33	NNE.	1	2 00 a.m.	9.95					6 00
"	8 00 p.m.	2.00			"	1	0 45 p.m.		9.60	0.35			5 45
21	6 30 a.m.		0.83	1.17	NE.	1	3 00 a.m.	10.30					7 00
"	8 30 p.m.	2.00			"	1	11 30 a.m.		10.10	0.20			5 00
22	8 00 a.m.		0.75	1.25	"	1	3 00 a.m.	10.85					6 30
"	9 00 p.m.	2.10			"	1	2 00 p.m.		10.55	0.30			6 00
23	9 10 a.m.		0.83	1.27	"	1		11.40					
"	9 30 p.m.	2.10			"	1	1 00 p.m.		11.10	0.30			3 50

Tidal Observations—Continued.

Date.	Telegraph station at mouth of Southwest pass.						Carrollton, La.						Difference of tidal time.
	Time.	Gauge.		Difference.	Wind.		Time.	Gauge.		Difference.	Wind.		
		High tide.	Low tide.		Direction.	Force.		High tide.	Low tide.		Direction.	Force.	
1860.	*h. m.*	*Feet.*	*Feet.*	*Feet.*			*h. m.*	*Feet.*	*Feet.*	*Feet.*			*h. m.*
Jan. 24	9 45 a.m.		1.10	1.00	E.	1	3 30 a.m.	11.85					6 00
“	10 10 p.m.	1.91			ENE.	1	3 30 p.m.		11.45	0.40			5 45
25	10 00 a.m.		1.16	0.75	NE.	1	6 30 a.m.	11.90					8 20
“					“	1	M.		11.75	0.15			
26	0 30 a.m.	1.91			E.	1	7 00 a.m.	12.30					6 30
“	M.		1.50	0.41	ENE.	1	0 30 p.m.		12.20	0.10			
27					NW.	4	6 00 a.m.	12.60					
“					“	4	5 30 p.m.		12.40	0.20			
28					N.	1	5 30 a.m.	12.60					
“	3 00 p.m.	1.75			NW.	1	0 30 p.m.		12.50	0.10			
“							5 45 p.m.	12.60					
29	4 00 a.m.		1.33	0.42	N.	1	11 00 a.m.		12.40	0.20			7 00
“	4 45 p.m.	1.83			NNW.	1							
30	1 20 a.m.		1 42	0.41	ENE.	1							
“	3 30 p.m.	2.10			E.	1	10 00 p.m.	13.00					6 30
31	1 10 a.m.		1.42	0.68	SE.	1	6 30 a.m.		12.90	0.10			5 20
“	2 45 p.m.	2.33			SW.	1	9 30 p.m.	13.35					6 45
Feb. 1	6 20 a.m.		0.91	1.42	NNW.	3	9 00 a.m.		12.65	0.70			
“	5 10 p.m.	2.00			“	3							
2	4 30 a.m.		0.91	1.09	NNE.	2	M.						7 30
“	5 30 p.m.	2.25			N.	2							
3	5 00 a.m.		0.83	1.42	“	2							
“	7 00 p.m.	2.33			NNE.	2							
4	5 15 a.m.		0.91	1.42	E.	1	0 30 a.m.	13.12					5 30
“	8 15 p.m.	3.10			ESE.	3	M.		12.75	0.37			6 45
5	6 30 a.m.		1.33	1.77	SE.	3	1 45 a.m.	13.53					5 30
“	8 20 p.m.	2.91			SSE.	2	11 30 a.m.		12.95	0.58			5 00
6	7 30 a.m.		1.42	1.49	N.	3	3 00 a.m.	13.65					6 40
“	8 00 p.m.	3.00			“	2	3 00 p.m.		13.06	0.59			7 30
7	8 45 a.m.		1.58	1.42	NW.	2							
“					W.	3							
8					NW.	3							
“					SW.	1							
9					NW.	1							
“					SW.	1							
10					NW.	1							
“					NE.	1							
11	10 50 a.m.	2.10			WSW.	1							
“					NW.	1							
12	0 30 a.m.		1.10	1.00	NE.	2	9 30 p.m.	12.20					8 45
“	0 45 p.m.	2.16			ENE.	2	8 00 a.m.		11.75	0.45			7 00
13	1 00 a.m.		1.25	0.91	SW.	1							
“	1 40 p.m.	2.33			SE.	1							
14	3 20 a.m.		1.10	1.23	“	1							
“	3 20 p.m.	2.16			S.	1							
15	4 00 a.m.		1.16	1.00	SW.	1							
“	3 00 p.m.	2.33			“	1							
16	5 00 a.m.		0.83	1.50	SSW.	1							
“	6 10 p.m.	2.33			E.	1							
17	5 30 a.m.		1.33	1.00	SE.	1							
“	6 00 p.m.	2.50			SSE.	1							
18	8 40 a.m.		1.25	1.25	NW.	3							
“	6 40 p.m.	2.50			SW.	2							
19	6 00 a.m.		1.25	1.25	N.	1							
“	6 10 p.m.	2.50			NNE.	1							
20	7 45 a.m.		1.25	1.25	“	1							
“	10 15 p.m.	2.16			SE.	3							
21	7 30 a.m.		1.67	0.49	SSW.	1							
“	5 00 p.m.	2.75			SSE.	1							
22	7 45 a.m.		1.50	1.25	“	1							
“	11 45 p.m.	2.10			SSW.	1							
23	4 20 a.m.		1.25	0.85	NNW.	2							
“					ENE.	1							
24	M.	1.67			NW.	1							

Tidal Observations—Continued.

Date.	Telegraph station at mouth of Southwest pass. Time.	Gauge. High tide.	Gauge. Low tide.	Difference.	Wind. Direction.	Wind. Force.	Carrollton, La. Time.	Gauge. High tide.	Gauge. Low tide.	Difference.	Wind. Direction.	Wind. Force.	Difference of tidal time.
1860.	*h. m.*	*Feet.*	*Feet.*	*Feet.*			*h. m.*	*Feet.*	*Feet.*	*Feet.*			*h. m.*
Feb. 24	10 20 p.m.		1.25	0.42	ENE.	1							
25					NE.	2							
"					ENE.	1							
26	0 30 p.m.	1.50			E.	2							
"	10 00 p.m.		1.10	0.40	"	2							
27	1 45 p.m.	1.75			"	2							
"					"	2							
28	0 10 a.m.		1.10	0.65	"	2							
"	1 45 p.m.	2.20			"	2							
29	2 30 a.m.		1.33	0.87	SE.	1							
"	1 20 p.m.	2.33			SW.	2							
March 1	3 30 a.m.		0.91	1.42	NNE.	1	8 00 a.m.						4 30
"	2 30 p.m.	2.33			E.	1	9 00 p.m.	12.68					6 30
2	4 10 a.m.		0.83	1.50	NNE.	1	9 30 a.m.		12.20	0.48			5 20
"	4 20 p.m.	2.42			E.	1	10 30 p.m.	12.80					6 10
3	4 00 a.m.		1.10	1.32	SE.	1	0 30 p.m.		12.35	0.45			8 30
"	5 30 p.m.	2.25			E.	1	12 00 p.m.	12.82					6 30
4	5 40 a.m.		0.91	1.34	NE.	1	10 30 a.m.		12.30	0.52			4 50
"	7 30 p.m.	2.10			E.	1	12 00 p.m.	12.98					4 30
5	5 15 a.m.		1.10	1.00	"	1	10 00 a.m.		12.65	0.33			4 45
"	7 45 p.m.	2.33			SE.	1							
6	7 20 a.m.		1.25	1.08	"	1	1 30 a.m.	13.06					5 45
"	9 45 p.m.	2.25			SSE.	1	0 15 p.m.		12.78	0.28			4 55
7	7 20 a.m		1.75	0.50	"	1	4 00 a.m.	13.10					6 15
"		1.60			"	1	M.		12.95	0.15			4 40
8			1.60	0.00	"	1							
"		1.60			SW.	1							
9			1.60	0.00	N.	2							
"					NW.	2							
10	M.	2.00			"	1							
"	11 45 p.m.		1.10	0.90	WSW.	1	5 30 p.m.	13.40					5 30
11	0 30 p.m.	2.00			NE.	2	4 00 a.m.		12.75	0.05			4 15
"	12 00 p.m.		1.16	0.84	"	1	5 30 p.m.	13.12					5 00
12	11 30 a.m.	2.16			SW.	1	7 00 a.m.		12.85	0.27			7 00
"					"	1	7 00 p.m.	13.10					7 30
13	0 45 a.m.		1.10	1.06	NNE.	2	6 30 a.m.		12.76	0.34			5 45
"	2 00 p.m.	2.33			NE.	2							
14	2 30 a.m.		1.16	1.17	"	1							
"	3 00 p.m.	2.33			"	1	9 30 p.m.	13.08					6 30
15	3 30 a.m.		1.25	1.08	E.	1	9 30 a.m.		12.80	0.28			6 00
"	5 00 p.m.	2.42			NE.	1	10 45 p.m.	13.15					5 45
16	4 30 a.m.		1.42	1.00	"	3	9 00 a.m.		12.85	0.30			4 30
"	3 30 p.m.	2.58			"	3							
17	3 35 a.m.		1.67	0.91	NNW.	3							
"	5 30 p.m.	2.75			"	3							
18	6 40 a.m.		1.70	1.05	"	1							
"	6 45 p.m.	2.40			N.	1							
19	7 00 a.m.		1.50	0.90	SW.	1	1 00 a.m.	13.20					6 15
"	8 50 p.m.	1.90			W.	1	1 00 p.m.		13.00	0.20			6 00
20	6 00 a.m.		1.50	0.40	NNE.	1	3 00 a.m.	13.08					6 10
"	9 30 p.m.	2.10			NE.	2	9 45 a.m.		12.94	0.14			3 45
21	5 10 a.m.		1.83	0.27	E.	2							
"	12 00 p.m.	2.00			"	1							
22					SE.	1							
"	4 00 p.m.		1.50	0.50	"	1							
23	9 30 a.m.	2.08			SSE.	1							
"	7 00 p.m.		1.50	0.58	SW.	1	5 30 p.m.	13.10					8 00
24	9 50 a.m.	2.25			W.	1	2 30 a.m.		12.85	0.25			7 30
"	7 30 p.m.		1.50	0.75	N.	2	1 30 p.m.	13.10					3 40
"							12 00 p.m.		12.82	0.28			4 30
25	10 30 a.m.	2.25			NE.	1							
"	9 20 p.m.		1.50	0.75	E.	2	3 30 p.m.	13.10					5 00
26	9 50 a.m.	2.33			ENE.	1	4 00 a.m.		12.76	0.34			6 40
"	10 20 p.m.		1.25	1.08	N.	1	4 00 p.m.	13.05					6 10
27	11 00 a.m.	2.42			"	2	4 45 a.m.		12.63	0.42			6 25

Tidal Observations—Continued.

Date.	Telegraph station at mouth of Southwest pass. Time.	Gauge. High tide.	Gauge. Low tide.	Difference.	Wind. Direction.	Wind. Force.	Carrollton, La. Time.	Gauge. High tide.	Gauge. Low tide.	Difference.	Wind. Direction.	Wind. Force.	Difference of tidal time.
1860.	*h. m.*	*Feet.*	*Feet.*	*Feet.*			*h. m.*	*Feet.*	*Feet.*	*Feet.*			*h. m.*
March 27	11 50 p.m.		1.08	1.34	NNW.	1	5 00 p.m.	12.95					6 00
28	M.	2.50			NNE.	2	7 00 a.m.		12.45	0.50			7 10
"					"	1	5 30 p.m.	12.80					5 30
29	1 15 a.m.		1.25	1.25	SW.	1	7 00 a.m.		12.38	0.42			5 45
"	1 00 p.m.	2.25			"	1	7 00 p.m.	12.50					6 00
30	1 45 a.m.		1.00	1.25	NE.	1	10 00 a.m.		11.98	0.52			8 15
"	3 00 p.m.	2.10			ENE.	1	7 45 p.m.	12.23					4 45
31	2 30 a.m.		1.16	0.94	SE.	2							
"	4 45 p.m.	2.33			"	2	9 45 p.m.	12.10					5 00
April 1	3 45 a.m.		1.16	1.17	SW.	2							
"	4 05 p.m.	2.10			WNW.	1							
2	4 30 a.m.		1.10	1.00	N.	1							
"	7 25 p.m.	2.00			S.	1							
3	4 40 a.m.		1.50	0.50	SSW.	1							
"		1.50			S.	1							
4			1.50	0.00	SSW.	1							
"		1.50			SSE.	1							
5					SW.	1							
"			1.50	0.00	SSE.	1							
6	8 00 a.m.	1.90			NE.	1							
"	8 45 p.m.		0.90	1.00	ENE.	1							
7	9 45 a.m.	2.10			SSE.	1							
"	10 00 p.m.		0.70	1.40	"	1							
8	10 00 a.m.	2.00			SE.	1							
"	10 15 p.m.		0.70	1.30	"	1							
9	10 10 a.m.	2.16			"	1							
"	11 40 p.m.		0.67	1.49	"	2							
10	11 20 a.m.	2.00			"	1							
"					"	2							
11	1 00 a.m.		0.58	1.42	SW.	1							
"	0 45 p.m.	1.83			"	1							
12	1 45 a.m.		0.58	1.25	N.	1							
"	1 15 p.m.	1.58			NE.	1							
13	2 00 a.m.		0.58	1.00	NNE.	1							
"	3 15 p.m.	1.67			N.	1							
14	3 10 a.m.		1.00	0.67	E.	1							
"	3 30 p.m.	1.42			ESE.	1							
15	2 45 a.m.		0.91	0.51	SSE.	1							
"	4 15 p.m.	1.42			"	1							
16	1 30 a.m.		1.00	0.42	SE.	2							
"		1.20			"	1							
17			1.20	0.00	"	3							
"		1.20			SW.	3							
18			1.20	0.00	S.	1							
"		1.20			SE.	2							
"			1.20	0.00									
19	9 30 a.m.	1.50			"	2							
"	5 20 p.m.		0.91	0.59	ESE.	2							
20	7 20 a.m.	1.75			"	2							
"	7 20 p.m.		0.67	1.08	E.	1							
21	7 30 a.m.	1.96			ESE.	2							
"	7 45 p.m.		0.50	1.46	S.	1							
22					SE.	1							
"					"	1							
23	8 20 a.m.	2.42			SSE.	1							
"	7 10 p.m.		0.50	1.92	"	1							
24	9 00 a.m.	2.25			NNE.	1							
"	9 30 p.m.		0.58	1.67	"	1							
25	10 00 a.m.	2.16			"	2							
"	9 30 p.m.		0.50	1.66	NNW.	2	5 00 p.m.	6.56					7 00
26	11 30 a.m.	2.25			NNE.	2	1 45 a.m.		6.30	0.26			4 15
"	12 00 p.m.		0.67	1.58	"	2	7 00 p.m.	7.22					7 30
27	M.	2.16			"	2	4 30 a.m.		6.95	0.27			4 30
"					"	1	6 00 p.m.	7.80					6 00

Tidal Observations—Continued.

Date.	Telegraph station at mouth of Southwest pass.						Carrollton, La.						Difference of tidal time.
	Time.	Gauge.		Difference.	Wind.		Time.	Gauge.		Difference.	Wind.		
		High tide.	Low tide.		Direction.	Force.		High tide.	Low tide.		Direction.	Force.	
1860.	*h. m.*	*Feet.*	*Feet.*	*Feet.*			*h. m.*	*Feet.*	*Feet.*	*Feet.*			*h. m.*
April 28	0 30 a.m.		0.58	1.58	NNW.	1	5 30 a.m.		7.50	0.30			5 00
"	2 30 p.m.	2.00			"	3							
29	2 00 a.m.		1.30	0.70	"	1							
"	1 30 p.m.	1.60			SE.	1							
30	3 30 a.m.		1.00	0.60	SSE.	1							
May 1					N.	4							
"					NE.	1							
2	7 30 a.m.	1.67			NNE.	1	1 00 p.m.	10.32					5 30
"	5 00 p.m.		1.10	0.57	S.	1	10 00 p.m.		10.25	0.07			5 00
3	6 45 a.m.	1.75			NW.	1	1 30 p.m.	10.65					6 45
"	5 15 p.m.		0.90	0.85	SSW.	1	10 45 p.m.		10.47	0.18			5 30
4	6 15 a.m.	2.16			WNW.	1	0 30 p.m.	10.93					6 15
"	7 15 p.m.		0.83	1.33	SE.	1	12 00 p.m.		10.43	0.50			4 45
5	7 45 a.m.	2.33			SSE.	1	2 15 p.m.	10.93					6 30
"	8 00 p.m.		0.75	1.58	SE.	1							
6	8 00 a.m.	2.33			"	1	2 00 a.m.		10.45	0.48			6 00
"	9 00 p.m.		0.75	1.58	ESE.	2	1 30 p.m.	10.94					5 30
7	9 15 a.m.	2.42			SE.	1	2 15 a.m.		10.42	0.52			5 15
"	10 15 p.m.		0.83	1.59	"	2	3 30 p.m.	11.00					6 15
8	9 45 a.m.	2.50			"	2	3 30 a.m.		10.35	0.65			5 15
"	11 15 p.m.		1.00	1.50	SSE.	2	4 00 p.m.	10.90					6 15
9	9 45 a.m.	2.42			N.	3	7 00 a.m.		10.35	0.55			7 45
"					NW.	2	3 30 p.m.	10.55					5 45
10	2 00 a.m.		1.00	1.42	NNW.	1	7 00 a.m.		10.05	0.50			5 00
"	11 30 a.m.	2.16			SW.	2	5 30 p.m.	10.33					6 00
11	1 30 a.m.		1.10	1.06	W.	2	8 00 a.m.		9.75	0.58			6 30
"	M.	1.91			SW.	2	5 00 p.m.	9.83					5 00
12	1 30 a.m.		1.10	0.81	SSW.	1	M.		9.30	0.53			
"	1 00 p.m.	1.58			SE.	1							
13	2 00 a.m.		1.16	0.42	"	1							
"		1.50			"	1							
14			1.50	0.00	"	1							
"		1.50			SW.	1							
15			1.50	0.00	NW.	1							
"					SW.	1							
16	5 45 a.m.	1.42			W.	1							
"	6 45 p.m.		0.75	0.67	SSE.	1							
17	7 00 a.m.	1.50			SE.	1							
"	6 15 p.m.		0.58	0.92	SSW.	1							
18	5 45 a.m.	1.50			"	1							
"	6 00 p.m.		0.42	1.08	SW.	2							
19	6 30 a.m.	1.67			W.	1							
"	7 30 p.m.		0.33	1.34	NW.	1							
20	8 30 a.m.	1.10			SSW.	1							
"	10 00 p.m.		0.33	0.77	"	1							
21	8 30 a.m.	2.00			S.	2							
"	9 15 p.m.		0.00	2.00	"	2							
22	8 20 a.m.	2.33			ESE.	2	2 45 a.m.						5 30
"	10 15 p.m.		0.25	2.08	SE.	1	1 45 p.m.	4.53					5 25
23	8 30 a.m.	2.00			SSE.	1	3 30 a.m.		3.85	0.68			5 15
"	9 30 p.m.		−0.16	2.16	"	1	3 00 p.m.	4.38					6 30
24	10 00 a.m.	2.08			SW.	1	7 00 a.m.		3.65	0.73			9 30
"	10 45 p.m.		0.16	1.92	"	1	3 30 p.m.						5 30
25	11 00 a.m.	1.75			"	1							
"	10 00 p.m.		0.20	1.55	"	1	5 30 p.m.	3.85					6 30
26	11 00 a.m.	1.67			"	2	7 00 a.m.		3.20	0.65			9 00
"	10 45 p.m.		0.33	1.34	SSW.	2	7 00 p.m.	3.72					8 00
27	M.	1.25			"	2	7 00 a.m.		3.10	0.62			8 15
"	10 30 p.m.		0.58	0.67	"	2	4 30 p.m.	3.60					4 30
28	M.	1.08			"	2	6 00 a.m.		3.20	0.40			7 30
"	9 00 p.m.		0.91	0.17	S.	2	4 30 p.m.	3.40					4 30
29	6 00 a.m.	1.35			SSW.	2	4 00 a.m.		3.28	0.12			7 00
"	5 00 p.m.		0.66	0.69	S.	1	11 30 a.m.	3.60					5 30
"							11 30 p.m.		3.30	0.30			6 30

Tidal Observations—Continued.

Date.	Telegraph station at mouth of Southwest pass.						Carrollton, La.						Difference of tidal time.
	Time.	Gauge.		Difference.	Wind.		Time.	Gauge.		Difference.	Wind.		
		High tide.	Low tide.		Direction.	Force.		High tide.	Low tide.		Direction.	Force.	
1860.	*h. m.*	*Feet.*	*Feet.*	*Feet.*			*h. m.*	*Feet.*	*Feet.*	*Feet.*			*h. m.*
May 30	6 30 a.m.	1.30			S.	1	M.	3.70					5 30
"	4 30 p.m.		0.16	1.14	NE.	1	10 30 p.m.		3.25	0.45			6 00
31	4 15 a.m.	1.55			WSW.	1	M.	3.70					7 45
"	5 00 p.m.		0.00	1.55	S.	1	8 00 p.m.		3.20	0.50			
June 1	5 40 a.m.	1.83					M.	3.40					
"	5 00 p.m.		0.00	1.83									
2	6 15 a.m.	2.00					1 00 p.m.	4.30					
"	6 45 p.m.		—0.08	2.08			12 00 p.m.		3.60				
3	6 30 a.m.	2.00					1 00 p.m.	4.40					
"	6 45 p.m.		—0.08	2.08									
4	7 45 a.m.	2.16											
"	8 00 p.m.		0.00	2.16			2 00 p.m.	4.50					
5	9 00 a.m.	2.00					2 00 a.m.		3.80				
"							2 00 p.m.	4.50					
6													
"													
7							2 00 p.m.	4.50					
"													
8							3 00 a.m.		3.90				
"							3 00 p.m.	4.50					

APPENDIX C.

CROSS-SECTIONS OF THE MISSISSIPPI AND OF ITS BRANCHES.

No. 1.—SOUNDINGS* IN THE MISSISSIPPI RIVER.

Section No. 1.

Distance from base-line on left bank.	Depth at high water. 1858.	Remarks.
Feet.	*Feet.*	
16	—0.5	
33	13	
68	22	
76	22	
112	42	
124	43	
139	46	
146	51	
176	57	
183	59	
198	59	
220	65	
273	77	Blue clay.
331	79	
365	89	
390	97	
450	87	
538	99	
634	92	
667	99	
745	95	
875	91	
906	89	
940	90	
961	94	
1159	84	
1186	93	
1196	87	
1204	81	
1386	77	
1392	82	
1464	78	
1532	78	
1595	74	
1659	72	
1775	69	
1886	64	
1897	62	
1944	60	
2041	48	
2070	40	
2190	24	
2195	8	
2205	4	
2250	3	
2260	0	

Section No. 2.

Distance from base-line on left bank.	Depth at high water. 1858.	Remarks.
Feet.	*Feet.*	
0	—0.5	
12	—0.5	
18	8	
46	19	
58	20	
85	30	
152	58	
167	59	
185	59	
203	58	
230	57	
263	61	
302	62	
304	68	
326	77	
355	82	
368	84	
376	85	
399	83	
419	87	
449	89	
472	90	
528	91	
578	92	
598	92	
623	92	
665	92	
735	93	
776	94	
798	94	
857	94	
917	94	
946	94	
997	94	
1068	92	
1191	85	
1204	84	
1243	88	
1313	88	
1376	87	
1430	85	
1510	82	
1536	80	
1606	79	
1611	78	
1659	76	
1700	74	
1715	73	
1751	72	
1778	71	
1831	67	
1836	68	
1873	66	
1888	64	
1894	63	
1913	59	
1965	58	
1993	56	
2008	55	
2008	53	
2022	51	
2026	50	
2047	51	
2063	47	
2075	44	
2083	45	
2145	37	
2165	30	
2175	24	
2206	19	
2212	11	
2221	7	
2241	3	

Section No. 3.

Distance from base-line on left bank.	Depth at high water. 1858.	Remarks.
Feet.	*Feet.*	
0	—0.6	
12	—0.6	
27	13	
27	15	
45	15	
45	20	
99	43	
160	53	
209	60	
280	72	
343	82	
441	91	
504	89	
666	98	Gravel.
708	98	
750	96	
814	95	
920	91	
946	91	
986	89	
1073	86	Yellow clay.
1106	81	
1194	84	
1351	80	
1381	78	
1506	77	
1563	74	
1591	76	
1777	70	
1805	68	
1900	66	
1926	63	
2030	61	
2048	55	
2105	51	
2156	45	
2220	24	
2220	8	
2258	2	
2300	4	
2320	0	

Section No. 4.

Distance from base-line on left bank.	Depth at high water. 1858.	Remarks.
Feet.	*Feet.*	
0	0	
10	0	
12	5	
24	10	
26	12	
33	17	
40	18	
52	30	
80	40	
88	43	
98	46	
108	46	
110	46	
137	45	
140	46	
178	53	
232	62	
252	65	
286	71	
313	73	
331	77	
380	80	
395	85	
437	87	
461	88	
509	91	
558	92	
600	92	
635	91	
719	92	
765	92	
826	92	
857	93	
956	94	
988	94	
1019	93	
1063	92	
1124	91	
1173	91	
1245	90	
1276	90	
1369	90	
1423	86	
1480	86	
1608	85	
1666	80	
1711	81	
1829	72	
1865	64	
1944	67	
2099	52	
2225	41	
2235	37	
2250	29	
2275	20	
2283	16	
2284	12	
2298	4	

Section No. 5.

Distance from base-line on right bank.	Depth at high water. Date?	Remarks.
Feet.	*Feet.*	
0	3	
40	28	
53	33	
60	35	Clay.
93	38	
127	56	
133	62	
155	64	
177	64	
223	74	
251	78	
275	83	
334	89	
360	90	
433	85	
609	93	
910	94	
1000	88	
1010	91	
1109	89	
1223	78	
1372	72	
1505	66	
1616	54	
1721	51	
1803	48	
1871	37	
1907	24	
1940	17	
2540	16	
2833	12	
3440	14	
3940	11	
4190	10	
5240	9	
5980	4	
6790	11	
6883	—1	

* Full information respecting the localities, dates of sounding, computed high-water and low-water areas, widths, etc. of these sections, and the names of the assistants or engineers by whom they were measured, will be found in No. 3 of this Appendix.

Soundings in the Mississippi river—Continued.

Section No. 6.

Distance from base-line on right bank.	Depth at high water. Date?	Remarks.
Feet.	*Feet.*	
0	2	
10	5	
1065	1	
1075	1	
1099	18	
1110	23	
1140	23	
1178	43	
1208	59	
1269	70	
1410	76	
1657	87	
1890	83	
2064	73	
2208	64	
2365	56	
2471	46	
2562	39	
2661	31	
2727	32	
2749	36	
2784	39	
2850	28	
2955	31	
3050	31	
3248	31	
3498	33	
3712	32	
4012	33	
4262	38	
4505	36	
4658	35	
4813	30	
4940	24	
5000	21	Sand.
5012	18	"
5462	13	"
5562	11	"
5662	16	"
5812	15	"
6362	18	"
6812	12	"
6912	17	"
7012	15	"
7062	18	"
7079	18	"
7112	10	"
7157	1	"

Section No. 7.

Distance from base-line on right bank.	Depth at high water. Date?	Remarks.
Feet.	*Feet.*	
0	—2	
160	20	
171	22	
195	25	
253	27	
296	29	
340	31	
417	34	
509	37	
662	42	
831	49	
1036	50	
1217	56	
1470	61	
1627	63	Light clay and sand.
1901	68	
1906	70	
1994	71	
2026	73	
2113	76	
2134	78	
2242	82	
2309	92	
2354	95	
2460	105	
2514	112	
2526	109	
2535	116	
2597	117	
2644	117	
2652	106	
2661	108	
2666	97	Fine light clay.
2696	83	"
2710	75	
2740	65	
2746	48	"
2752	21	
2781	23	
2800	0	

Section No. 8.

Distance from base-line on right bank.	Depth at high water. 1858.	Remarks.
Feet.	*Feet.*	
0	2.5	
16	13	
34	24	
66	34	
101	45	
128	47	Blue clay.
165	52	
187	56	
235	71	
294	71	
423	71	Blue clay and sand.
577	63	
597	64	
748	62	
753	63	
854	59	
1040	51	
1215	50	
1368	50	
1538	52	
1716	48	
1882	48	
1983	39	
2028	35	
2150	36	
2303	37	
2465	40	
2606	43	
2710	48	
2855	52	
3101	58	
3285	61	
3422	59	
3511	55	
3680	53	
3831	51	
3879	50	Blue clay and sand.
3994	36	
4006	29	
4019	24	
4051	7	
4084	4	

Section No. 9.

Distance from base-line on right bank.	Depth at high water. 1858.	Remarks.
Feet.	*Feet.*	
0	0	
22	3	
202	6	
260	3	
378	8	
480	45	
511	56	
538	60	
580	64	
615	62	
645	66	
748	83	
579	83	
823	86	
907	85	Fine white gravel.
913	87	
983	88	
1159	75	White gravel
1225	66	
1291	81	
1325	73	
1378	88	
1400	68	
1453	73	
1507	61	Fine black sand.
1652	62	
1692	84	
1972	86	
2213	58	Yellow and white gravel.
2239	61	
2264	69	
2335	71	
2388	61	
2395	60	
2406	60	
2548	61	
2619	61	
2683	61	Yellow gravel.
2783	62	
2985	59	
2972	59	"
3089	54	
3096	53	
3151	55	"
3163	56	
3167	58	
3285	52	
3413	48	"
3456	37	"
3567	39	
3594	20	"
3600	10	
3600	4	
3660	1	

Section No. 10.

Distance from base-line on right bank.	Depth at high water. 1851.	Remarks.
Feet.	*Feet.*	
0	—1	
5	3	
100	3	
157	54	
265	77	
358	79	
403	77	
776	77	
1395	62	
1550	57	
1832	54	
2044	55	
2316	40	
2732	23	
2843	24	
3082	18	
3469	21	
3605	16	
3645	0	

Soundings in the Mississippi river—Continued.

Section No. 11.		
Distance from base-line on right bank.	Depth at high water. 1858.	Remarks.
Feet.	*Feet.*	
0	—1	
20	6	
53	15	
73	25	
105	46	
156	76	
197	86	
224	87	
250	87	
299	86	
363	84	
429	86	
441	83	
549	77	
606	72	
644	78	
693	72	
725	75	
778	68	
942	69	
965	64	
1001	65	
1100	65	
1408	67	
1564	68	
1766	75	
1971	65	
2172	58	
2214	51	
2287	43	
2452	43	
2554	44	
2680	45	
2806	45	
2850	40	
2888	43	
2911	40	
3004	36	
3034	35	
3096	32	
3130	30	
3202	28	
3279	27	
3329	26	
3436	25	
3460	24	
3575	22	
3589	17	
3600	15	
3625	8	
3720	2	
3735	2	

Section No. 12.		
Distance from base-line on right bank.	Depth at high water. 1858.	Remarks.
Feet.	*Feet.*	
0	—1	
60	5	
86	5	
102	5	
126	57	Clay.
193	57	Black mud.
207	55	
250	56	"
298	61	Sand.
380	62	
385	62	
456	61	
484	65	
510	63	
574	71	
832	85	
1026	83	
1404	105	
1665	133	
1839	152	
1868	123	
2015	115	
2163	122	Blue clay.
2175	59	"
2269	70	Rock.
2357	39	
2395	18	
2446	0	

Section No. 13.		
Distance from base-line on right bank.	Depth at high water. 1858.	Remarks.
Feet.	*Feet.*	
0	—1	
25	7	
345	1	
353	4	
383	4	
421	31	
448	42	Mud.
510	52	"
559	53	
599	55	
804	55	
878	57	
1068	53	
1157	58	
1278	64	
1548	70	
1773	76	
2099	84	
2189	80	
2418	101	
2572	95	
2708	92	
2801	54	
2868	38	
2922	27	
2942	18	
2992	14	
3056	5	

Section No. 14.		
Distance from base-line on right bank.	Depth at high water. 1858.	Remarks.
Feet.	*Feet.*	
0	—1	
6	—1	
25	6	
334	2	
353	11	
373	18	
393	23	
408	25	
425	38	Yellow clay.
345	48	"
470	62	Sand.
475	58	"
558	54	"
584	58	"
672	57	"
690	55	"
799	54	"
808	55	"
928	54	"
935	55	"
1016	58	"
1144	62	"
1167	67	"
1286	67	"
1384	70	"
1429	72	"
1527	71	"
1672	79	Yellow clay.
1773	77	Sand.
2165	78	"
2248	78	"
2405	85	Yellow clay.
2424	92	"
2490	92	"
2583	100	Rock and blue clay.
2635	100	"
2643	100	"
2707	87	"
2741	78	"
2766	67	"
2784	68	Rock.
2889	27	
2900	21	
2930	12	
2960	6	
2990	5	
3020	3	
3050	2	

Section No. 15.		
Distance from base-line on right bank.	Depth at high water. 1858.	Remarks.
Feet.	*Feet.*	
0	—1	
6	—1	
25	7	
345	1	
347	4	
353	4	
365	4	
425	43	
447	43	
470	50	
504	54	
552	54	
595	55	
658	58	
734	59	
878	62	
1022	61	
1102	60	
1227	63	
1555	68	
1672	73	
1923	79	
1932	76	
2096	80	
2346	86	
2493	94	
2629	93	
2692	96	
2732	75	Blue clay.
2820	44	"
2879	27	"
2909	20	
2920	16	
2944	14	
2994	5	
3109	0	

Section No. 16.		
0	—1	
25	7	
334	1	
334	3	
353	11	
424	49	Blue mud.
444	55	"
508	56	
563	57	Sand.
664	55	"
701	54	"
845	57	"
912	57	"
1019	61	"
1206	67	"
1263	68	"
1336	70	Yellow clay.
1558	74	Sand.
1575	73	"
1808	74	"
1905	78	"
2145	91	"
2267	94	Yellow clay.
2404	96	"
2538	99.	Rock and blue clay.
2691	84	Blue clay.
2758	79	"
2809	51	Yellow clay.
2829	26	
2849	23	
2879	17	
2909	9	
2939	3	
2969	3	
2999	1	
3034	0	

Section No. 17.		
Left b'nk		
0	2	
30	10	
42	20	Blue clay.
71	25	"
73	25	"
129	46	"
133	46	"
148	68	Clay.
255	83	Blue clay.
281	73	"
299	81	"
354	73	"
400	83	"
431	78	Clay.
538	88	"
581	98	Blue clay.
655	85	"
884	90	Clay.
941	94	"
1140	68	"
1162	68	"
1604	64	"
1644	61	Sand and clay.
2109	58	"
2122	56	"
2415	53	Blue mud.
2560	36	"
2610	15	
2618	13	
2620	2	
2830	2	
2840	—2	

Section No. 18.		
Left b'nk		
0	—2	
20	2	
30	12	
50	26	Sand and clay.
83	35	Sand.
108	37	"
120	48	"
149	55	
220	79	Blue clay.
260	88	"
339	79	Clay.
443	75	"
618	78	"
675	63	"
823	83	"
923	83	"
931	71	"
1053	73	"
1468	63	Sand and clay.
1872	62	"
2078	62	"
2169	65	"
2321	63	"
2376	62	"
2500	55	"
2561	52	"
2599	52	"
2680	36	"
2742	12	
2745	3	
2762	3	
2770	—1	

Section No. 19.		
Left b'nk		
0	—2	
5	2	
143	2	
153	12	
183	31	Clay.
201	33	
207	32	Blue clay.
298	51	"
320	59	"
325	57	"
375	77	Clay.
405	76	Blue clay.
433	77	Clay.
436	77	Blue clay.
543	73	Clay.
562	72	"
691	72	"
727	72	"
1050	65	"
1111	67	"
1282	62	Sand and clay.
1789	59	"
2006	62	"
2268	58	"
2494	55	"
2604	56	"
2774	47	"
2825	40	"
2855	12	
2860	2	
2870	2	
2885	—2	

Section No. 20.		
	1851.	
0	3	
50	49	
120	94	
518	97	
787	69	
1164	60	
1492	52	
1861	51	
2142	45	
2650	34	
3066	33	
3432	30	
3712	13	
4300	3	

Soundings in the Mississippi river—Continued.

Section No. 21.			Section No. 22.			Section No. 23.			Section No. 24.			Section No. 25.		
Distance from base-line on right bank.	Depth at high water. 1858.	Remarks.	Distance from base-line on left bank.	Depth at high water. 1858.	Remarks.	Distance from base-line on left bank.	Depth at high water. 1858.	Remarks.	Distance from base-line on right bank.	Depth at high water. 1851.	Remarks.	Distance from base-line on right bank.	Depth at high water. 1851.	Remarks.
Feet.	*Feet.*		*Feet.*	*Feet.*		*Feet.*	*Feet.*		*Feet.*	*Feet.*		*Feet.*	*Feet.*	
0	—2		0	—2		0	—1		0	—1		0	—1	
30	7		5	—1		5	0		62	16		6	5	
1140	4		120	1		110	2		110	28		50	7	
1158	13		285	3		260	1		195	38		70	24	
1192	29		315	3		290	1		300	55		115	39	
1228	48		385	31		358	13		390	58		125	44	
1258	50	Clay.	410	36		415	31		550	63		220	59	
1340	56	"	465	58		453	41		700	69		260	71	
1382	73		520	66		463	45		950	67		295	61	
1473	104		530	68		471	45		1170	76		345	73	
1580	111	Gravel.	600	68		537	46		1225	78	Sand.	490	79	
1670	102		630	81		551	48	Mud.	1340	84	"	500	87	
1840	92		665	82	Clay.	614	76	Clay.	1400	81	"	535	83	
2098	79		765	83		622	84	"	1440	79	"	645	86	
2403	69		770	91		727	99		1650	76	Hard sand.	730	93	
2829	56		795	107		728	100		1680	81	Sand.	755	93	
3000	52		845	108	"	732	107		1720	79	"	795	95	
3234	49		930	95	"	741	112	"	1980	78	Hard sand.	810	94	
3374	49		1015	113		795	116		2040	79	Sand.	875	101	
3536	46	Sand.	1042	111	"	834	107	"	2240	74	"	960	109	
3760	44	Clay.	1060	119		865	102		2320	72	"	1125	108	
3942	39		1065	118		909	109		2450	68	"	1210	105	
4108	35		1090	116	Sand.	921	106	"	2640	61	"	1425	101	
4223	33		1125	119	Clay.	964	103		2810	44	Soft sand.	1695	128	
4292	35		1177	109		988	81	"	2890	37		1705	121	
4301	32		1400	92		1019	96		3010	30		1860	119	
4407	37		1485	74		1050	109		3100	23		1915	110	
4612	32		1670	54		1054	118		3180	14		2335	71	
4671	31		1905	54		1121	116		3380	5		2525	48	
4731	26		1920	47		1164	118		3525	10		2595	47	
4762	24		2005	45		1295	100		3875	3		2945	42	
4805	16		2128	45		1305	97		4070	1		3065	38	
4847	15		2205	55		1325	99		4075	—1		3280	20	
4872	14		2280	49		1352	90					3290	24	
4897	15		2465	47		1393	69					3480	12	
4922	17		2650	45		1455	61					3555	9	
4991	19		2690	43		1608	69					3645	8	
5017	20		2740	43		1663	66					3715	0	
5025	20		2965	41		1720	46							
5078	18		2980	43		1740	43							
5406	13		3070	41		1829	39							
5439	4		3200	41		1878	43							
5516	0		3390	39		1940	31							
5526	—1		3415	38		1955	46							
			3640	37		2015	46							
			3655	39		2120	50							
			3800	37		2150	45							
			3915	34		2159	46							
			4090	36		2280	47							
			4150	33		2580	46							
			4330	29		2650	44							
			4345	30		2800	43							
			4430	21		3120	40							
			4510	23		3328	37							
			4560	20		3468	35							
			4690	15		3795	35							
			4715	16		3840	32							
			4800	13		4020	31							
			4815	13		4305	28							
			4830	12		4385	22							
			4880	4		4440	19							
			4935	1		4505	15							
			5035	4		4545	13							
			5050	—3		4650	13							
						4690	10							
						4740	2							
						4795	2							
						4860	4							
						4890	—2							

Soundings in the Mississippi river—Continued.

Section No. 26.

Distance from base-line on right bank.	Depth at high water. 1851.	Remarks.
Feet.	*Feet.*	
0	—1	
5	5	
80	7	
110	23	
160	42	
200	61	
245	74	
360	93	
380	88	
560	90	
590	89	
640	95	
750	102	
910	103	
925	102	
950	106	
1155	110	
1175	110	
1420	113	
1550	122	
1575	121	
1790	86	
1870	93	
2110	64	
2120	75	
2340	51	
2505	43	
2600	41	
2820	33	
2965	29	
3055	25	
3210	20	
3385	14	
3440	15	
3570	7	
3595	7	
3700	0	

Section No. 27.

Distance from base-line on right bank.	Depth at high water. 1851.	Remarks.
Feet.	*Feet.*	
0	4	
25	4	
50	26	
125	51	
185	65	
335	91	
575	106	
1030	100	
1505	83	
1845	79	
2020	62	
2090	41	
2280	4	

Section No. 28.

Distance from base-line on right bank.	Depth at high water. 1851.	Remarks.
Feet.	*Feet.*	
0	4	
40	4	
110	27	
160	49	
230	75	
340	95	
450	106	
785	104	
1300	86	
1570	79	
1710	76	
1920	69	
2075	63	
2230	60	
2315	43	
2430	4	

Section No. 29.

Distance from base-line on right bank.	Depth at high water. 1851.	Remarks.
Feet.	*Feet.*	
0	—1	
5	3	
208	3	
335	44	
415	63	
535	101	
725	102	
942	96	
1105	80	
1345	77	
1545	69	
1790	65	
1995	62	
2078	60	
2147	59	
2325	59	
2525	59	
2615	59	
2670	60	
2790	53	
2825	39	
3165	0	

Section No. 30.

Distance from base-line on right bank.	Depth at high water. 1851.	Remarks.
Feet.	*Feet.*	
0	—1	
5	3	
208	3	
365	41	
460	71	
578	99	
753	113	
905	101	
1125	84	
1322	72	
1522	72	
1785	65	
1995	63	
2060	62	
2145	59	
2322	59	
2515	59	
2594	59	
2653	60	
2765	57	
2850	35	
3155	0	

Section No. 31.

Left b'nk		
0	0	
400	53	
560	59	
785	60	
1098	63	
1190	68	
1470	66	
1665	70	
1903	75	
2113	75	
2365	80	
2575	86	
2805	93	
2943	107	
3085	107	
3246	56	
3320	38	
3535	0	

Section No. 32.

Left b'nk		
0	0	
220	39	
320	56	
415	62	
562	68	
664	71	
790	70	
925	72	
1072	74	
1197	74	
1345	76	
1500	80	
1660	80	
1805	84	
1963	92	
2130	101	
2355	104	
2595	108	
2740	86	
2908	37	
3030	0	

Section No. 33.

Left b'nk	1858.	
0	—1	
44	2	
44	4	
72	13	
102	17	
141	29	
196	39	
227	53	
258	68	Blue clay.
299	73	
386	59	
445	71	
471	70	
583	67	
698	66	
710	67	
914	71	
1049	79	
1053	74	
1136	84	
1290	90	Clay.
1480	92	
1486	95	
1514	94	
1745	91	
1789	92	
1826	94	
1950	87	
2031	85	
2050	81	
2220	84	
2231	84	Blue clay.
2361	63	
2366	65	
2386	43	
2416	28	
2433	21	
2458	14	
2468	12	
2481	11	
2486	4	
2496	1	
2533	1	
2541	—2	

Section No. 34.

Left b'nk		
0	—1	
5	3	
20	4	
125	41	
208	63	
285	81	
380	104	
580	113	
795	107	
1095	104	
1332	105	
1552	89	
1835	90	
1920	84	
2055	41	
2215	3	
2265	3	
2270	—1	

Section No. 35.

Left b'nk		
0	—1	
10	3	
83	4	
200	44	
265	64	
335	74	
455	122	
635	119	
880	113	
1125	107	
1355	104	
1615	95	
1865	85	
2020	83	
2115	39	
2280	4	
2360	3	
2365	—1	

Soundings in the Mississippi river—Continued.

Section No. 36.

Distance from base-line on right bank.	Depth at high water. 1858.	Remarks.
Feet.	*Feet.*	
0	0	
10	3	
38	3	
73	7	
102	14	
133	18	
147	19	
208	49	Clay.
263	73	
275	75	
303	78	
330	78	Yellow clay.
340	80	
358	98	"
363	94	Blue clay.
400	112	"
458	109	"
498	149	Blue and yellow clay.
537	111	Blue clay.
611	160	Blue and yellow clay.
652	154	
698	160	
785	171	
822	169	
924	144	
962	176	
1126	135	
1182	180	
1288	124	
1330	146	
1392	117	
1436	112	
1461	139	
1581	89	
1714	56	
1745	18	
1806	18	
1848	13	
1878	8	
1908	8	
1931	0	
1956	—1	

Section No. 37.

Distance from base-line on left bank.	Depth at high water. 1851.	Remarks.
Feet.	*Feet.*	
0	0	
270	4	
390	51	Soft mud.
445	56	"
475	62	"
550	66	"
610	71	
770	83	Fine sand.
780	80	"
820	84	"
1050	89	Clay.
1219	89	"
1240	87	"
1270	90	Hard clay.
1430	96	"
1600	116	
1685	121	
1990	122	
2095	118	Fine sand.
2350	88	"
2440	72	Coarse sand.
2630	73	"
2895	75	"
3165	68	"
3255	68	Soft mud.
3290	47	"
3350	4	

Section No. 38.

Distance from base-line on left bank.	Depth at high water. 1851.	Remarks.
Feet.	*Feet.*	
0	0	
130	4	
160	13	Hard clay.
300	68	"
395	76	"
440	79	"
515	82	
545	85	Soft clay.
570	85	Hard clay.
590	83	"
770	87	"
905	87	"
1030	89	"
1070	93	"
1320	91	"
1600	110	
1635	118	
1835	113	Sand.
2160	73	"
2230	66	"
2370	61	"
2515	54	"
2840	40	"
3125	32	Mud and sand.
3180	20	"
3230	4	

Section No. 39.

Distance from base-line on left bank.	Depth at high water. 1851.	Remarks.
Feet.	*Feet.*	
0	0	
160	42	Hard clay.
239	70	"
400	79	Hard clay and shells.
535	81	Hard clay.
610	86	"
810	87	"
830	81	"
930	87	"
980	84	"
1185	91	"
1225	91	"
1408	94	Fine sand.
1435	96	"
1550	97	"
1710	104	"
1925	88	"
1935	84	"
2195	56	"
2255	50	"
2380	45	"
2605	35	"
2840	28	"
3040	21	"

Section No. 40.

Distance from base-line on left bank.	Depth at high water. 1858.	Remarks.
Feet.	*Feet.*	
0	—1	
3	1	
47	3	
70	6	
95	13	Blue clay.
125	22	"
143	20	"
180	40	"
197	49	"
265	67	
294	71	
327	75	Yellow clay.
440	76	"
595	86	"
687	82	"
739	90	"
886	89	Blue clay.
927	84	"
932	89	Yellow clay.
1142	92	"
1307	93	Blue clay.
1352	91	Sand.
1574	99	Blue clay.
1986	80	Sand.
2204	62	"
4541	43	"
2789	34	"
2984	19	"
2997	18	"
3010	6	
3050	6	
3470	1	
3480	—2	

Section No. 41.

Left b'nk	1851.	
0	—1	
400	49	Hard sand.
510	57	"
610	74	"
760	77	"
782	79	"
980	81	
1200	74	Hard clay.
1355	75	"
1610	80	"
1700	80	"
2000	66	Fine sand.
2095	55	"
2290	45	"
2400	42	"
2440	37	"
2480	31	"
2620	31	"
2755	26	"
2860	22	"
2970	20	"
3090	20	"
3200	16	"
3240	14	"
3380	1	

Section No. 42.

	1858.	
0	—1	
15	4	
115	6	
158	17	
204	27	
249	47	Blue clay.
324	69	"
330	68	"
438	78	Yellow clay.
533	75	"
545	77	"
791	77	"
1108	79	Blue clay.
1292	80	
1806	55	Sand.
1890	48	"
2012	43	"
2042	44	"
2115	45	"
2184	39	"
2249	37	"
2293	37	"
2324	34	"
2357	30	"
2389	29	"
2466	23	"
2547	16	"
2687	9	"
3128	6	Willow batture.
3328	1	"
3600	1	"
3800	1	"
4200	2	"
4400	2	"
4820	1	
4828	—1	

Section No. 43.

0	—1	
190	17	Hard clay.
300	52	"
335	67	"
410	75	"
590	79	"
630	74	"
810	74	"
1040	75	"
1445	75	"
1710	69	"
1845	61	"
2030	49	"
2280	40	"
2360	37	Hard sand.
2450	32	"
2590	27	"
2730	23	"
2830	20	"
2950	19	"
2985	15	"
3145	1	

Section No. 44.

0	—1	
50	4	
260	40	Hard clay.
335	51	"
530	77	"
550	78	"
680	80	"
775	77	"
1080	76	"
1100	75	"
1180	73	"
1200	77	"
1460	81	"
1535	79	"
1740	70	Hard sand.
1770	67	"
1915	58	"
2060	51	"
2240	41	"
2380	33	"
2490	31	"
2540	28	"
2725	23	"
2820	19	"
2960	15	"
3000	14	"
3215	1	

Section No. 45.

	1851.	
0	—1	
240	74	Hard clay.
260	76	"
380	80	"
480	79	"
770	88	"
930	82	"
980	83	"
1150	82	"
1300	81	Hard sand.
1330	79	Hard clay.
1583	75	"
1695	64	"
1770	64	"
2010	55	Hard sand.
2045	55	"
2230	47	"
2365	58	"
2405	67	"
2595	49	"
2705	28	"
2750	30	"
2950	1	

Soundings in the Mississippi river—Continued.

Section No. 46.			Section No. 47.			Section No. 48.			Section No. 49.			Section No. 50.		
Distance from base-line on left bank.	Depth at high water. 1851.	Remarks.	Distance from base-line on left bank.	Depth at high water. 1851.	Remarks.	Distance from base-line on left bank.	Depth at high water. 1851.	Remarks.	Distance from base-line on left bank.	Depth at high water. 1851.	Remarks.	Distance from base-line on left bank.	Depth at high water. 1851.	Remarks.
Feet.	*Feet.*		*Feet.*	*Feet.*		*Feet.*	*Feet.*		*Feet.*	*Feet.*		*Feet.*	*Feet.*	
0	—1		0	—1		0	0		0	0		0	0	
26	14		3	4		240	10		490	67		380	34	Mud.
46	42		30	15		420	45		615	96		395	39	"
95	57		108	22		690	105		748	94		565	94	
136	66		138	28		760	85		855	114		770	117	
173	81		175	45		790	121		995	112		872	118	
225	117		224	72		800	122		1150	108		1021	123	Hard mud.
318	138		314	93		940	115		1248	102		1040	123	"
408	138		452	88		995	113		1352	94		1050	125	
524	129		561	91		1052	115		1462	90		1065	121	
680	121		682	87		1175	97		1556	88		1145	111	
852	111		811	85		1305	96		1695	84		1170	112	
1020	96		934	84		1415	99		1808	81		1430	106	
1168	78		1104	90		1535	92		1920	78		1445	104	
1349	72		1246	102		1710	83		2050	74		1482	100	
1577	55		1354	107		1725	80		2138	75		1682	89	
1776	48		1435	117		1865	73		2272	67		1852	71	
1960	37		1495	117		2010	66		2460	66		1983	72	
2073	81		1583	122		2153	72		2592	66		2136	69	
2165	14		1677	117		2264	72		2800	64		2175	70	
2250	—1		1826	93		2310	71		2925	60		2578	62	
			1941	88		2440	70		2965	45		2658	62	
			1980	66		2540	66		3040	0		2855	50	
			2040	36		2595	68					2865	53	Mud.
			2232	—1		2690	64					2965	42	"
						2718	63					3025	17	"
						2812	62					3160	0	
						2924	59							
						3005	18							
						3028	6							
						3040	0							

Section No. 51.			Section No. 52.			Section No. 53.			Section No. 54.			Section No. 55.		
0	0		0	0		0	0		0	0		0	0	
360	35	Hard mud.	310	57	Hard clay.	190	24		410	139		20	7	Hard sand.
453	51	"	350	73		275	36		547	158		60	13	Soft mud.
525	93	"	375	71	Hard blue clay.	358	70		755	136	Hard sand.	100	54	Hard sand.
675	121	"				428	90		762	130		172	122	Hard mud.
715	123	"	395	78	Soft clay.	495	106		955	180	Blue clay.	322	161	"
735	136	"	512	121	Sand and clay.	582	129		965	127	Hard sand.	368	153	Hard sand.
815	132	"				702	124		1000	127	"	380	168	Hard mud.
830	130	"	627	144	Yellow clay.	749	124		1105	110	Hard clay.	647	166	"
990	128	"	980	135		805	124		1222	108	Hard sand.	753	143	Hard sand.
1200	113	Hard sand.	1042	133	Fine sand.	1000	123		1282	104	Blue clay.	765	145	"
1270	103	"	1230	117	"	1142	115		1482	94	Fine sand.	997	127	"
1412	97	"	1435	105	"	1260	114		1783	60	Coarse sand.	1125	120	"
1635	92	"	1585	93	"	1425	103		1960	55	"	1235	109	"
1800	80	"	1755	86	"	1597	91		2036	53	"	1465	75	
1918	78	"	2247	72	Coarse sand.	1740	82		2242	52	"	1552	80	"
1945	79	"	2433	67	"	1960	70		2445	67	Blue clay.	1775	51	"
2020	77	"	2775	60	"	2055	57		2545	37	"	1860	50	"
2140	74	"	3095	55	Soft mud.	2227	57		2955	0		1945	51	"
2218	67	"	3155	49	Soft clay.	2328	60					2120	47	
2235	68	Sand.	3267	15		2400	57					2240	48	Soft mud.
2380	62	Mud.	3377	0		2720	52					2290	31	"
2392	63	Sand.				2900	33					2360	47	"
2520	60	Mud.				3130	0					2470	19	
2660	57	Sand.										2608	0	
2726	60	"												
2813	53	Hard mud.												
2840	55	"												
3005	13	Mud.												
3048	7	"												
3143	0													

Soundings in the Mississippi river—Continued.

Section No. 56.

Distance from base-line on left bank.	Depth at high water. 1851.	Remarks.
Feet.	*Feet.*	
0	0	
65	64	
105	83	
182	124	
290	163	
430	165	
550	156	
645	156	
720	153	
815	141	
890	138	
1000	132	
1140	111	
1253	99	
1390	82	
1570	70	
1675	52	
1822	48	
1965	46	
2075	45	
2178	36	
2260	24	
2608	0	

Section No. 57.

Distance from base-line on left bank.	Depth at high water. 1851.	Remarks.
Feet.	*Feet.*	
0	0	
141	59	Hard mud.
210	134	"
260	137	"
355	163	"
455	165	"
520	153	"
532	154	Hard sand.
678	151	"
800	146	Hard mud.
826	153	Hard sand.
865	142	"
882	131	"
1038	128	"
1078	125	"
1292	107	"
1455	91	"
1765	61	"
1883	55	"
1972	41	Soft mud.
2040	29	"
2075	19	"
2460	0	"

Section No. 58.

Distance from base-line on left bank.	Depth at high water. 1851.	Remarks.
Feet.	*Feet.*	
0	0	
95	40	
120	52	
168	93	
187	109	
256	138	
320	162	
395	168	
472	168	
575	162	
672	159	
800	150	
905	142	
1030	133	
1147	129	
1238	113	
1383	105	
1505	93	
1620	79	
1735	54	
1783	51	
2015	40	
2105	25	
2460	0	

Section No. 59.

Distance from base-line on left bank.	Depth at high water. 1851.	Remarks.
Feet.	*Feet.*	
0	0	
120	31	
130	35	
150	42	
185	59	
222	80	
262	114	
360	149	
440	152	
538	155	
627	155	
740	158	
825	152	
935	141	
1025	134	
1115	129	
1220	122	
1320	107	
1425	99	
1500	99	
1585	101	
1687	93	
1775	86	
1850	74	
1918	31	
1982	29	
2460	0	

Section No. 60.

Distance from base-line on left bank.	Depth at high water. 1851.	Remarks.
Feet.	*Feet.*	
0	0	
225	121	Hard clay.
485	176	Sand and shells.
540	186	
595	181	Sand.
767	168	
862	158	
973	151	Coarse sand.
1090	144	"
1268	136	"
1490	122	Fine sand.
1683	82	
1960	54	Sand and mud.
2175	46	"
2272	27	"
2990	0	

Section No. 61.

Distance from base-line on left bank.	Depth at high water. 1851.	Remarks.
0	0	
235	38	
255	53	
275	65	
305	74	
345	101	
385	122	
510	134	
637	143	
815	152	
970	152	
1083	149	
1210	140	
1335	130	
1450	119	
1586	113	
1635	110	
1790	102	
1908	96	
2008	89	
2070	80	
2150	71	
2235	56	
2300	41	
2345	20	
2950	0	

Section No. 62.

Distance from base-line on left bank.	Depth at high water. 1851.	Remarks.
0	0	
440	108	Blue clay.
500	113	Soft clay.
690	134	Hard clay.
712	130	
930	148	Clay.
1082	136	
1175	126	Coarse sand.
1270	122	
1303	117	"
1490	103	
1605	102	
1660	92	Fine sand.
1742	87	"
1760	87	
1815	80	"
1915	73	"
1925	68	"
2150	49	
2275	41	
2352	27	"
2940	0	

Section No. 63.

Distance from base-line on left bank.	Depth at high water. 1851.	Remarks.
0	0	
285	30	
400	84	
550	93	
680	112	
815	122	
1005	23	
1145	121	
1260	122	
1400	114	
1515	105	
1630	102	
1750	108	
1865	78	
1968	78	
2065	75	
2170	54	
2230	39	
2295	24	
2360	6	
2940	0	

Section No. 64.

Distance from base-line on left bank.	Depth at high water. 1851.	Remarks.
0	0	
160	42	Mud and sand.
250	100	"
325	112	Mud.
520	127	
680	144	Blue clay.
685	146	
962	139	
1175	122	Coarse sand.
1190	121	"
1235	115	
1400	106	Fine sand.
1470	95	Hard sand.
1785	71	
1935	60	"
2042	50	"
2050	52	"
2175	39	"
2235	34	Fine sand.
2338	19	
2765	0	

Section No. 65.

Distance from base-line on left bank.	Depth at high water. 1851.	Remarks.
0	0	
115	66	
190	97	
295	118	
435	130	
565	138	
713	150	
835	151	
982	130	
1145	118	
1318	99	
1450	86	
1598	76	
1720	73	
1848	70	
1972	60	
2115	54	
2142	43	
2165	33	
2205	27	
2240	20	
2765	0	

Soundings in the Mississippi river—Continued.

Section No. 66.

Distance from base-line on left bank.	Depth at high water. 1851.	Remarks.
Feet.	*Feet.*	
0	0	
60	45	
168	88	
338	103	
490	159	
632	159	
782	141	
923	127	
1075	117	
1174	106	
1308	97	
1433	84	
1528	72	
1655	64	
1715	63	
1815	60	
1910	57	
1983	52	
2173	45	
2245	27	
2275	21	
2770	0	

Section No. 67.

Distance from base-line on left bank.	Depth at high water. 1851.	Remarks.
Feet.	*Feet.*	
0	0	
130	64	Clay.
220	93	Sand and clay.
275	100	
385	133	Clay.
475	162	"
562	164	
730	151	Sand and shells.
745	149	"
853	133	Sand.
948	122	"
1145	104	"
1235	102	
1365	93	Sand.
1495	88	"
1530	79	
1692	58	
1695	59	
1895	51	
2040	38	Sand and mud.
2667	0	

Section No. 68.

Distance from base-line on left bank.	Depth at high water. 1851.	Remarks.
Feet.	*Feet.*	
0	—1	
5	—1	
10	3	
80	3	
90	12	
120	35	
142	43	
172	52	
210	80	
235	85	
278	97	
325	103	
380	110	
480	156	
525	157	
585	154	
655	154	
775	134	
880	129	
905	125	
1065	112	
1165	102	
1237	96	
1280	92	
1425	72	
1505	67	
1575	58	
1613	57	
1645	52	
1737	47	
1755	46	
1885	40	
1912	88	
2003	36	
2080	33	
2142	29	
2180	20	
2212	24	
2285	18	
2340	14	
2385	12	
2575	3	
2580	—1	

Section No. 69.

Distance from base-line on left bank.	Depth at high water. 1851.	Remarks.
Feet.	*Feet.*	
0	0	
115	28	
135	35	
155	48	
183	56	
202	74	
235	95	
297	104	
368	123	
445	149	
505	140	
575	147	
655	146	
714	143	
765	143	
832	137	
1020	126	
1038	116	
1135	108	
1288	102	
1442	93	
1515	95	
1585	86	
1715	75	
1750	72	
1845	65	
1955	59	
2055	51	
2152	39	
2243	29	
2280	26	
2325	20	
2383	14	
2440	5	
2497	2	
2582	1	

Section No. 70.

Distance from base-line on left bank.	Depth at high water. 1851.	Remarks.
Feet.	*Feet.*	
0	—1	
5	—1	
10	3	
30	3	
40	12	
72	35	Hard sand.
155	57	"
170	57	"
210	75	"
230	87	"
310	97	Soft mud.
362	109	"
450	158	"
538	155	"
604	147	"
632	140	"
813	134	Hard sand.
837	134	"
905	126	"
957	121	"
1108	110	"
1128	108	"
1266	92	"
1275	92	"
1395	75	"
1517	63	"
1558	62	"
1655	57	"
1712	48	"
1722	50	"
1820	42	"
1835	42	"
1940	36	"
1952	37	"
2015	27	"
2085	30	"
2115	20	"
2193	25	"
2245	20	"
2285	19	"
2360	12	"
2542	3	"
2548	—1	"

Section No. 71.

Distance from base-line on left bank.	Depth at high water. 1851.	Remarks.
0	0	
75	28	
88	36	
100	45	
125	54	
162	56	
200	78	
246	95	
311	103	
382	134	
465	152	
545	148	
630	142	
740	134	
855	128	
958	121	
1050	118	
1092	107	
1175	98	
1255	93	
1330	89	
1448	88	
1525	86	
1600	79	
1642	76	
1730	70	
1797	65	
1893	61	
1945	53	
2010	46	
2120	38	
2285	29	
2325	20	
2360	14	
2380	8	
2400	5	
2440	3	
2550	1	

Section No. 72.

Distance from base-line on left bank.	Depth at high water. 1851.	Remarks.
0	—1	
5	—1	
10	3	
50	3	
60	12	
110	47	Hard sand.
135	45	"
177	77	
230	91	
246	96	Hard sand.
332	130	Soft mud.
350	129	"
418	156	"
475	155	"
572	145	"
600	150	"
735	131	"
803	127	"
935	124	"
955	121	"
1115	106	Hard sand.
1135	104	"
1204	97	"
1317	86	"
1330	87	"
1470	67	"
1576	59	"
1582	58	"
1635	53	"
1706	48	"
1775	44	"
1825	42	"
1882	39	"
1905	37	"
1944	35	"
2015	32	"
2020	33	"
2136	27	"
2183	24	"
2222	21	"
2287	16	"
2298	14	"
2335	14	"
2518	3	"
2530	—1	"

Section No. 73.

Distance from base-line on left bank.	Depth at high water. 1851.	Remarks.
0	0	
75	26	
94	35	
100	35	
125	53	
178	92	
235	95	
295	104	
375	137	
425	149	
505	149	
548	147	
610	144	
655	144	
678	146	
750	140	
935	129	
962	119	
1065	110	
1188	101	
1275	98	
1308	80	
1442	84	
1543	80	
1625	78	
1703	74	
1800	68	
1885	65	
2042	56	
2118	46	
2215	35	
2312	27	
2330	14	
2335	7	
2355	6	
2415	2	
2530	1	

Section No. 74.

Distance from base-line on left bank.	Depth at high water. 1851.	Remarks.
0	—1	
5	—1	
8	3	
48	3	
63	12	
105	32	Fine hard sand.
125	44	"
178	71	"
230	87	"
290	100	
395	139	Soft mud.
445	139	"
558	140	"
611	132	"
653	129	"
724	128	"
932	117	Hard sand.
955	116	"
1068	106	"
1105	107	"
1252	94	"
1328	88	"
1372	83	"
1440	76	"
1452	75	"
1513	67	"
1567	62	"
1615	58	"
1657	54	"
1730	48	"
1740	46	"
1835	42	"
1878	39	"
1890	38	"
2000	33	"
2095	28	"
2120	27	"
2193	23	"
2205	23	"
2255	20	"
2275	17	"
2370	12	"
2495	3	"
2520	—1	"

Section No. 75.

Distance from base-line on left bank.	Depth at high water. 1851.	Remarks.
0	0	
70	25	
90	40	
140	61	
200	94	
292	103	
395	136	
475	139	
585	142	
695	139	
828	127	
905	121	
990	116	
1120	103	
1205	94	
1320	85	
1420	82	
1510	76	
1570	73	
1670	70	
1750	67	
1840	61	
2000	50	
2122	31	
2200	26	
2340	14	
2350	13	
2355	7	
2370	5	
2430	2	
2530	1	

Soundings in the Mississippi river—Continued.

Section No. 76.

Distance from base-line on left bank.	Depth at high water. 1858.	Remarks.
Feet.	*Feet.*	
0	—1.9	
18	3	
143	3	
153	5	
205	19	
221	29	
247	39	
258	40	
296	51	Blue clay.
384	94	"
390	91	Yellow clay.
478	100	Blue clay.
538	113	Yellow clay.
629	123	Blue clay.
748	118	Yellow clay.
768	125	Blue clay.
859	122	Yellow clay.
893	117	Sand.
1028	120	"
1256	102	"
1351	90	"
1427	98	"
1539	87	"
1733	67	"
1745	67	"
1797	59	"
2045	52	"
2117	44	"
2232	31	"
2258	34	"
2297	24	"
2369	17	"
2436	18	"
2524	9	"
2575	5	"
2705	2	"
2710	—1	

Section No. 77.

Distance from base-line on left bank.	Depth at high water. 1851.	Remarks.
Feet.	*Feet.*	
0	—1	
5	—1	
10	3	
50	3	
62	12	
82	32	Hard sand.
120	50	"
130	53	"
190	89	"
285	97	"
300	105	"
370	107	
435	103	
575	110	
595	107	
662	105	Soft mud.
745	110	
793	102	"
895	103	
1045	99	
1100	99	"
1205	99	
1214	98	Hard sand.
1340	89	"
1[illegible]54	87	"
1447	77	"
1547	68	"
1558	68	"
1632	57	"
1687	55	"
1780	46	"
18[illegible]0	47	"
1906	37	"
1956	35	"
2024	31	"
2074	29	"
21[illegible]5	27	"
2182	24	"
2204	23	"
2270	18	"
2278	15	"
2310	12	"
2515	8	"
2530	—1	"

Section No. 78.

Distance from base-line on left bank.	Depth at high water. 1851.	Remarks.
Feet.	*Feet.*	
0	0	
60	19	
72	28	
90	49	
148	79	
210	100	
280	108	
355	109	
450	109	
580	111	
720	109	
810	112	
945	115	
1070	108	
1162	108	
1250	97	
1340	84	
1497	76	
1585	69	
1715	67	
1808	64	
1955	55	
2045	43	
2172	22	
2290	13	
2300	13	
2310	7	
2335	5	
2385	2	
2530	1	

Section No. 79.

Distance from base-line on left bank.	Depth at high water. 1858.	Remarks.
Feet.	*Feet.*	
0	—1.4	
26	4	
131	3	
156	5	
246	50	Blue clay.
349	83	"
379	93	"
408	98	
519	95	
570	103	
619	102	Yellow clay.
720	102	Blue clay.
785	108	Sand.
800	105	"
820	103	"
837	104	
879	103	Yellow clay.
846	103	"
980	102	"
989	102	"
1011	102	Sand.
1251	99	"
1393	96	"
1447	95	"
1626	75	"
1707	61	"
1800	60	"
1824	58	"
1971	50	"
2044	44	"
2233	33	"
2260	32	"
2364	19	"
2424	18	"
2463	12	"
2546	5	
2666	2	
2671	—1	

Section No. 80.

Distance from base-line on left bank.	Depth at high water. 1851.	Remarks.
Feet.	*Feet.*	
0	—1	
5	—1	
10	3	
50	3	
60	12	
72	33	Sand.
108	41	"
124	50	"
184	89	"
216	85	"
290	97	"
308	96	
380	101	
497	102	
623	104	
630	106	Clay.
714	101	"
754	109	"
870	104	
953	102	
998	105	Soft clay.
1165	98	
1174	98	Hard sand.
1284	90	"
1332	92	"
1408	80	"
1431	77	"
1524	70	"
1633	61	"
1655	60	"
1752	51	"
1805	46	"
1863	41	"
1925	37	"
1985	33	"
2035	31	"
2113	28	"
2132	27	"
2211	23	"
2242	20	"
2275	17	"
2325	12	"
2538	3	"
2545	—1	"

Section No. 81.

	1851.	
0	0	
60	20	
80	39	
105	51	
150	77	
215	101	
300	107	
408	107	
505	107	
580	107	
690	120	
820	111	
940	110	
1050	113	
1170	102	
1272	96	
1310	93	
1430	81	
1530	71	
1605	69	
1650	68	
1740	66	
1830	62	
1912	54	
2000	50	
2150	32	
2228	29	
2285	20	
2295	14	
2305	12	
2320	8	
2330	6	
2380	3	
2540	2	

Section No. 82.

0	0	
65	29	
75	29	
85	35	
112	50	
147	62	
175	83	
230	98	
290	103	
370	105	
440	106	
540	104	
658	107	
770	114	
855	118	
972	112	
1122	103	
1252	93	
1392	70	
1490	73	
1600	65	
1740	60	
1870	52	
1953	52	
2065	42	
2155	31	
2225	24	
2270	20	
2330	14	
2345	11	
2352	9	
2380	5	
2430	3	
2560	2	

Section No. 83.

0	0	
100	30	Sand.
165	74	"
240	105	Mud and sand.
335	150	"
427	155	"
435	155	Sand.
515	149	"
680	145	"
752	143	"
815	134	"
995	102	Hard sand.
1015	101	"
1120	94	
1397	87	
1610	74	
1662	75	
1820	62	Sand.
1820	59	Mud and sand.
1950	52	Hard sand.
2000	46	"
2010	46	"
2110	42	"
2120	41	Sand.
2160	38	"
2270	22	Mud.
2600	0	

Section No. 84.

	1851.	
0	0	
100	23	
135	54	
197	78	
265	117	
346	152	
487	149	
580	137	
680	129	
777	123	
862	119	
972	93	
1115	84	
1240	77	
1397	71	
1510	63	
1652	63	
1758	60	
1895	48	
1988	39	
2090	30	
2142	27	
2200	24	
2600	0	

Section No. 85.

0	0	
130	34	Mud.
175	85	Clay.
280	122	Mud.
295	122	Clay.
423	154	Sand.
480	157	"
518	158	"
650	136	"
670	135	"
815	119	"
905	117	"
1135	92	"
1210	88	"
1412	76	"
1507	77	"
1695	69	"
1827	57	"
1927	49	"
2130	46	"
2190	43	"
2230	39	Mud.
2650	0	

Soundings in the Mississippi river—Continued.

Section No. 86.

Distance from base-line on left bank.	Depth at high water. 1851.	Remarks.
Feet.	*Feet.*	
0	0	
125	30	
182	72	
238	102	
325	131	
438	162	
528	156	
610	144	
760	134	
880	119	
1032	104	
1188	90	
1305	83	
1390	78	
1552	71	
1742	65	
1880	59	
1984	53	
2105	42	
2190	41	
2285	38	
2325	27	
2355	23	
2650	0	

Section No. 87.

Distance from base-line on left bank.	Depth at high water. 1851.	Remarks.
Feet.	*Feet.*	
0	0	
285	33	Sand.
415	88	"
455	96	Clay.
510	104	Sand.
605	100	Clay.
615	92	
720	115	Hard sand.
860	113	"
872	111	"
1052	105	"
1127	112	Sand.
1282	97	"
1500	87	"
1510	102	"
1780	76	"
1795	87	Hard sand.
2040	59	Sand.
2292	51	"
2345	52	"
2603	43	"
2630	42	Mud.
2677	27	
3165	0	
3175	0	

Section No. 88.

Distance from base-line on left bank.	Depth at high water. 1851.	Remarks.
Feet.	*Feet.*	
0	1	
27	19	Sand.
83	40	Hard clay.
130	81	"
262	103	"
340	104	"
365	104	Clay and sand.
465	110	Sand.
560	112	"
612	110	"
828	101	"
945	91	"
1060	88	"
1325	76	"
1572	72	"
1675	66	"
1753	60	"
1867	61	"
2042	51	"
2070	51	
2242	34	
2337	43	
2375	24	
2750	3	
2760	0	

Section No. 89.

Distance from base-line on left bank.	Depth at high water. 1851.	Remarks.
Feet.	*Feet.*	
0	1	
75	38	
175	88	Clay.
195	87	Clay and sand.
200	93	
257	101	Clay and sand.
305	112	"
365	116	"
495	112	Sand.
507	111	"
552	111	"
630	107	"
795	99	"
842	98	"
1008	91	
1113	86	"
1180	82	"
1303	79	"
1600	68	"
1660	63	"
1880	63	"
2055	54	"
2070	50	"
2200	44	
2405	42	"
2485	35	
2625	31	
2750	3	
2760	0	

Section No. 90.

Distance from base-line on left bank.	Depth at high water. 1851.	Remarks.
Feet.	*Feet.*	
0	0	
475	72	Hard clay.
505	84	"
615	106	Coarse sand and shells.
765	104	"
837	104	"
959	103	Sand and mud.
969	104	Fine sand.
1104	101	"
1134	97	"
1249	92	"
1344	87	"
1429	82	"
1484	77	"
1589	74	"
1594	79	Hard sand.
1749	70	"
1839	68	Fine sand.
2039	65	Hard sand.
2079	62	
2244	58	Fine sand.
2320	49	Hard sand.
2389	52	Fine sand.
2500	59	"
2700	50	"
3010	0	

Section No. 91.

Distance from base-line on left bank.	Depth at high water. 1851.	Remarks.
0	0	
235	9	Soft mud.
275	15	
440	60	Fine sand and clay.
615	68	Fine sand.
835	76	Coarse sand.
885	82	Hard sand.
965	77	Fine sand.
1035	76	Hard fine sand.
1255	80	Coarse sand.
1285	82	Fine sand.
1540	87	"
1595	92	"
1745	98	
1760	102	"
1875	109	
1885	118	"
1895	118	
2055	128	
2095	131	
2175	135	
2255	133	
2375	103	
2500	86	Clay.
2510	79	
2530	96	Hard clay.
2555	52	"
2565	44	"
2780	0	

Section No. 92.

Distance from base-line on left bank.	Depth at high water. 1851.	Remarks.
0	0	
270	28	Sticky.
310	35	"
345	38	"
485	50	"
635	64	Hard sand.
700	67	Fine sand.
790	66	Coarse sand and shells.
975	71	Coarse sand.
1085	78	Hard sand.
1145	78	Hard fine sand.
1300	96	"
1445	101	"
1500	109	"
1605	121	"
1725	134	"
1770	139	"
1940	139	"
2075	134	"
2115	142	"
2120	136	"
2170	135	"
2320	58	Hard clay.
2355	36	"
2505	0	
2515	0	

Section No. 93.

Distance	1858.	Remarks	Distance	1858.	Remarks	Distance	1858.	Remarks
0	1		899	150	Blue clay.	1920	91	
70	4		917	149	"	2014	89	
133	6		948	151		2054	86	
176	24		1009	145	"	2056	86	
223	46		1019	149	"	2114	86	
257	56		1060	130		2182	83	
286	68		1163	127		2199	82	
336	74		1197	123		2254	82	
397	87		1320	122		2259	88	
410	87		1320	122	"	2329	80	
423	91		1394	101		2384	69	Mud.
586	112	Dark sand.	1467	101		2421	47	
596	123	Dark clay.	1628	102	Sand and clay.	2420	47	
604	125					2462	19	
630	120	Blue clay.	1655	100		2488	7	
700	131		1878	99		2494	2	
707	133		1898	91				

No. 2.—SOUNDINGS* IN TRIBUTARIES AND BAYOUS.

Section No. 1.			Section No. 2.			Section No. 3.			Section No. 4.			Section No. 5.		
Distance from base-line on left bank.	Depth at high water. 1858.	Remarks.	Distance from base-line on left bank.	Depth at high water. 1858.	Remarks.	Distance from base-line on left bank.	Depth at high water. Date?	Remarks.	Distance from base-line on right bank.	Depth at high water. 1858.	Remarks.	Distance from base-line on right bank.	Depth at high water. 1858.	Remarks.
Feet.	*Feet.*		*Feet.*	*Feet.*		*Feet.*	*Feet.*		*Feet.*	*Feet.*		*Feet.*	*Feet.*	
0	4		0	6		0	0		0	—1		0	4	
25	7		20	8		34	0		13	2		17	4	
125	27		155	28		58	10		83	2		17	12	
400	31		575	37		91	19		93	4		52	31	
570	37		635	39		96	22		127	26		68	30	
632	39		642	38		113	29		139	30		82	31	
715	44		680	40		118	36		152	34		105	32	
778	46		733	42		131	37		162	37		117	33	
858	51		760	44		140	38		186	48		155	37	
935	53		828	47		154	39	Clay.	194	51		164	36	
942	50		876	50		178	36	"	201	51		190	39	
1017	56		954	52		180	38	"	209	53		208	40	
1050	60		1042	54		194	39		228	56		235	46	
1092	58		1060	58	Fine gravel.	207	41		265	65		267	47	
1102	63		1177	62	"	224	40		296	63		337	56	
1125	64		1190	63		233	39		308	63		352	57	
1268	71		1353	69		249	38	Blue clay.	350	63		385	57	
1355	67		1373	69		256	32		394	58		420	57	
1360	72		1455	71		267	25		446	57		525	57	
1410	71		1657	69		277	23		484	57		538	56	
1565	74		1675	76		287	19		517	56		600	47	
1605	79		1725	78		304	12		527	55		625	48	Mud.
1657	77		1792	77		387	2		558	54		630	48	
1722	79		1850	85					608	53		678	47	
1778	80		1905	84					651	51		707	37	
1802	81		2043	88					695	49		732	34	
2039	88		2082	88					732	48		777	26	
2057	89		2092	90					754	45		805	21	
2110	92		2233	89					771	39		890	9	
2165	75	Fine gravel.	2258	83					787	34				
2195	72	Mud.	2416	77					797	31				
2285	72	Gravel.	2467	76					813	26				
2515	71		2542	63					832	15				
2583	63		2598	63					900	3				
2625	61		2690	64										
2732	62		2740	57										
2808	44		2777	48										
2912	22		2800	36										
2972	8		2857	23										
3015	—1		2870	28										
			3002	—2										

* Full information respecting the localities, dates of sounding, computed high-water and low-water areas, widths, etc. of these sections, and the names of the assistants or engineers by whom they were measured, will be found in No. 4 of this Appendix

Soundings in tributaries and bayous—Continued.

Section No. 6.

Distance from base-line	Depth at high water. 1858.	Remarks.
Feet.	*Feet.*	
0	7	
15	9	
15	12	
20	19	
22	22	
32	26	
45	33	
47	34	
75	50	
77	54	
100	66	
150	68	
150	68	
193	58	
237	56	
297	46	
322	38	
344	41	
358	35	
405	38	
408	37	
430	36	
450	34	
468	33	
482	33	
493	33	
507	36	
517	28	
522	21	
560	9	

Section No. 7.

Distance from base-line on right bank.	Depth at high water. 1858.	Remarks.
Feet.	*Feet.*	
0	—1	
20	7	
75	5	
125	8	
175	7	
275	3	
375	3	
449	8	
464	9	
481	9	
495	9	
507	9	
566	9	
589	9	
610	10	
642	17	
672	20	
717	24	
760	27	
800	31	
849	35	
909	44	
970	52	
988	53	
1031	57	
1147	69	Yellow mud and gravel.
1195	65	
1259	53	
1272	53	
1296	34	
1372	46	
1375	23	
1403	6	
1493	7	
1400	5	
1425	4	

Section No. 8.

Distance from base-line on right bank.	Depth at high water. 1858.	Remarks.
Feet.	*Feet.*	
0	—1	
20	7	
75	5	
125	8	
175	7	
275	3	
375	3	
452	8	
466	8	
489	9	
503	9	
523	8	
543	9	
566	10	
578	11	
603	14	
615	16	
652	20	
707	28	
747	28	
787	31	
825	35	
880	42	
925	48	
995	52	
1041	57	
1104	64	Yellow clay.
1175	63	
1213	60	"
1273	38	"
1335	20	Yellow mud.
1345	15	
1365	7	
1380	3	
1395	2	
1445	3	

Section No. 9.

Distance from base-line on left bank.	Depth at high water. 1858.	Remarks.
Feet.	*Feet.*	
0	—1	
60	14	Blue sand.
90	27	"
120	25	Sand.
150	24	"
180	25	"
210	24	"
240	25	"
270	24	"
300	23	"
320	14	
350	—1	

Section No. 10.

Distance from base-line on left bank.	Depth at high water. 1858.	Remarks.
Feet.	*Feet.*	
0	2	Yellow clay.
15	35	"
25	40	"
55	49	Sand.
85	51	"
115	55	"
145	54	Sand and gravel.
175	54	Sand.
195	53	"
225	50	"
255	41	"
265	35	"
355	4	"

Section No. 11.

Left b'nk		
0	1	
150	8	Clay.
202	18	"
240	27	"
280	36	"
298	42	"
320	47	Sand.
340	48	"
360	48	"
380	49	"
397	49	"
420	49	"
440	49	"
458	49	"
480	48	"
500	44	Blue clay.
520	36	Clay.
550	25	"
598	15	"
700	1	"

Section No. 12.

Left b'nk		
0	0	
20	9	
45	18	
57	23	
79	31	Sand.
102	36	"
118	41	"
130	43	
158	53	
175	57	Blue clay.
235	67	"
268	72	"
329	80	"
353	82	"
410	86	"
414	86	Mud.
433	86	"
467	87	"
498	87	"
548	86	"
586	74	Yellow and blue clay.
596	63	
646	55	
676	52	
704	40	
726	37	
747	33	
770	31	
792	25	
802	22	
841	19	
868	20	
882	20	
915	15	
930	9	

Section No. 13.

Left b'nk		
0	4	
40	19	
60	23	
80	41	Blue clay.
100	42	
190	45	Sand.
250	44	
270	41	
280	37	
320	31	
360	22	
400	22	
410	21	
450	18	
480	17	
560	1	

Section No. 14.

0	8	
45	11	
50	25	
77	32	
85	33	
100	41	
115	46	
155	43	Yellow clay.
185	55	
205	51	Sand.
255	62	
275	58	
340	61	
373	63	
420	49	
450	54	Blue clay.
510	30	
540	27	
590	20	
615	7	
630	0	
635	—3	

Section No. 15.

	1850.	
0	3	
10	3	
10	8	
16	12	
28	19	
60	31	
101	35	
134	40	
102	57	
168	57	
174	58	
210	62	
220	62	
271	63	
384	63	
456	56	
493	51	
537	46	
568	37	
588	34	
608	31	Willow batture.
625	25	"
634	25	"
653	27	"
668	28	"
697	25	"
715	23	"
756	23	"
760	21	"
780	18	"
800	21	"

Soundings in tributaries and bayous—Continued.

Section No. 16.

Distance from base-line on right bank.	Depth at high water. 1858.	Remarks.
Feet.	*Feet.*	
0	—4	
22	1	
79	6	
90	17	
115	29	
143	37	
152	42	Red and blue clay.
198	49	"
256	52	Red clay.
333	49	
340	49	
390	48	
401	47	
464	42	
466	44	
541	39	
599	40	
630	32	
676	29	
738	24	
748	21	
773	12	
788	6	
794	—1	

Section No. 17.

Distance from base-line on left bank.	Depth at high water. 1850.	Remarks.
Feet.	*Feet.*	
0	3	
36	3	
36	9	
52	16	
77	34	
109	44	
145	64	
211	60	
228	62	
318	59	
362	60	
466	59	
601	59	
612	58	
701	48	
712	40	
748	31	
766	27	
787	21	
798	19	
810	17	
820	9	
820	4	

Section No. 18.

Distance from base-line on left bank.	Depth at high water. 1851.	Remarks.
Feet.	*Feet.*	
0	0	
10	27	
45	32	
80	35	
140	37	
180	40	
260	43	
380	49	
485	55	
505	55	
615	60	
765	61	
725	60	
870	58	
975	56	
1065	54	
1210	52	
1255	52	
1265	48	
1335	42	
1400	37	
1450	35	
1475	27	
1525	26	
1540	27	
1610	21	
1675	24	
1705	25	
1735	25	

Section No. 19.

Distance from base-line on left bank.	Depth at high water. 1851.	Remarks.
Feet.	*Feet.*	
0	0	
35	23	
85	28	
185	45	
230	46	
320	49	
340	54	
475	56	
535	61	
605	61	
735	58	
770	57	
905	57	
915	57	
1030	54	
1085	52	
1165	50	
1230	49	
1320	44	
1355	41	
1465	33	
1495	31	
1540	27	
1590	24	
1615	25	
1690	26	
1755	27	
1785	26	
1840	25	

Section No. 20.

Distance from base-line on left bank.	Depth at high water. 1851.	Remarks.
Feet.	*Feet.*	
0	0	
35	24	
85	31	
175	54	
305	56	
380	60	
485	59	
575	58	
685	59	
760	59	
990	57	
1210	57	
1275	55	
1405	51	
1490	46	
1565	43	
1765	33	
1910	37	
2005	41	
2040	35	
2185	32	
2195	34	
2280	29	
2335	27	

Section No. 21.

Left b'nk	1851.	
0	0	
0	13	
75	13	
95	13	
110	13	
185	28	
280	49	
425	53	
435	62	
535	63	
600	63	
660	63	
680	62	
760	60	
780	62	
865	61	
890	78	
940	73	
1015	62	
1040	79	
1140	62	
1175	42	
1230	50	
1340	21	
1350	14	
1450	14	
1555	24	
1560	25	
1655	29	
1670	29	
1760	25	
1805	21	
1860	16	

Section No. 22.

	1851.	
0	10	
35	33	
65	52	
80	32	
145	71	
165	72	
270	74	
310	68	
375	81	
490	98	
510	98	
560	93	
565	92	
665	84	
700	80	
775	70	
780	76	
850	50	
900	26	
920	33	
1010	23	
1030	17	
1080	16	
1115	19	
1165	17	

Section No. 23.

Rt. bank	1858.	
0	—1.5	
36	8	
78	15	
109	20	
128	22	
150	25	
181	31	
222	35	
254	40	
306	45	
347	46	
377	50	
452	53	
500	51	
565	49	
630	44	
702	44	
758	42	
805	42	
834	42	
866	40	
889	41	
923	38	
952	34	
977	33	
1000	31	
1023	30	
1062	28	Willow batture.
1090	27	"
1100	26	"
1118	24	"
1126	24	"
1149	23	"
1173	22	"
1204	22	"
1226	22	"
1249	22	"
1273	23	"
1294	23	"

Section No. 24.

Rt. bank		
0	0	
20	10	
55	20	
95	22	
195	30	
300	36	
390	40	
420	42	
485	46	
535	51	
585	51	
695	52	
790	52	
855	52	
895	50	
1015	46	
1070	39	
1200	38	
1245	37	
1290	38	
1380	40	
1425	40	
1530	40	
1600	41	
1635	43	
1720	43	
1815	48	
1925	43	
1995	41	
2045	38	
2075	36	
2160	23	
2175	22	
2335	10	
2535	0	
2575	—2	

Section No. 25.

Rt. bank		
0	0	
30	10	
50	19	
90	21	
115	23	
230	32	
275	34	
335	37	
405	41	
475	44	
535	48	
650	52	
780	52	
885	51	
955	51	
1010	47	
1120	39	
1175	41	
1235	38	
1345	38	
1450	40	
1540	43	
1625	44	
1720	45	
1830	44	
1875	44	
1940	36	
1960	40	
2030	36	
2095	38	
2110	30	
2220	28	
2285	24	
2415	10	
2615	0	
2635	—2	

Soundings in tributaries and bayous—Continued.

Section No. 26.			Section No. 27.			Section No. 28.			Section No. 29.			Section No. 30.		
Distance from base-line on right bank.	Depth at high water. 1851.	Remarks.	Distance from base-line on right bank.	Depth at high water. 1851.	Remarks.	Distance from base-line on right bank.	Depth at high water. 1851.	Remarks.	Distance from base-line on right bank.	Depth at high water. 1851.	Remarks.	Distance from base-line on right bank.	Depth at high water. 1851.	Remarks.
Feet.	*Feet.*		*Feet.*	*Feet.*		*Feet.*	*Feet.*		*Feet.*	*Feet.*		*Feet.*	*Feet.*	
0	0		0	0		0	0		0	0		0	0	
20	10		50	18		50	23		125	22		90	26	Hard.
60	24		130	28		180	32		180	37		170	49	"
125	29		205	39		320	54		345	62		320	74	Sticky.
145	28		295	47		495	52		400	62		425	68	Hard.
255	32		395	45		690	47		475	53		600	59	"
340	37		485	44		965	39		615	51		700	46	"
360	39		605	43		1115	35		775	42		850	35	"
425	41		700	40		1300	31		900	38		1020	29	"
515	45		825	38		1445	30		1010	34		1180	39	"
565	47		975	36		1680	31		1120	30		1340	33	Sticky.
720	53		1100	35		1880	35		1230	28		1465	36	"
835	52		1190	34		2110	38		1340	29		1590	38	Hard.
875	52		1290	35		2335	43		1395	31		1820	34	Sticky.
995	50		1395	36		2585	49		1435	31		2005	36	"
1125	41		1515	35		2725	44		1520	34		2130	37	"
1280	40		1675	40		2845	27		1605	36		2395	41	
1320	40		1805	44		2920	13		1660	36		2555	45	
1415	42		1940	46					1710	37		2725	45	
1465	43		1990	48					1785	37		2825	38	Soft.
1565	43		2055	52					1895	36		2935	33	"
1615	45		2185	55					1980	37		3015	16	"
1705	47		2265	53					2160	38				
1735	47		2330	45					2285	40				
1830	46		2425	28					2375	45				
1880	45		2505	18					2530	47				
1960	43								2645	45				
2020	39								2740	40				
2055	37								2810	33				
2150	29								2860	31				
2160	27													
2255	19													
2295	16													
2550	10													
2650	0													
2660	—2													

Section No. 31.			Section No. 32.			Section No. 33.			Section No. 34.			Section No. 35.		
0	0		0	0		0	0		0	0		0	0	
105	30	Sticky.	110	30	Hard.	70	21		115	28		30	12	
190	56	"	135	37	"	235	51		180	41		115	17	
310	80	Soft mud.	265	49	"	335	64		285	54		200	21	
405	74	"	365	74		480	70		385	71		320	26	
530	64	Sticky.	505	78		600	66		565	73		420	29	
665	45	"	685	57		685	55		680	65		580	28	
815	28	Hard.	820	36		795	46		850	34		705	29	
940	25	"	980	30		940	35		930	34		975	39	
1050	28	"	1100	29		1080	32		1015	34		1200	46	
1160	37	"	1275	30		1185	31		1185	36		1370	43	
1345	38	"	1420	36		1350	34		1340	39		1565	40	
1495	37	"	1615	39		1485	39		1470	41		1655	39	
1670	37	"	1800	37		1720	40		1725	42		1850	41	
1805	36	"	2000	36		1900	38		1905	41		1950	43	
1890	35	"	2195	37		2060	38		2065	39		2110	45	
2060	36	"	2385	39		2240	38		2225	40		2300	46	
2240	39	"	2545	40		2375	39		2410	40		2480	47	
2380	41	"	2695	45		2505	39		2520	41		2690	45	
2540	44	"	2900	41		2650	39		2720	41		2920	44	
2695	45	"	3000	37	Soft mud.	2735	42		2855	41		3170	46	
2855	38	"	3005	33	"	2940	43		3035	43		3335	46	
2945	29	Sticky.	3155	25	Hard.	2980	43		3220	40		3490	44	
2980	18	"				3015	44		3340	36		3605	39	
						3100	42		3400	22		3740	27	
						3235	36							
						3240	34							
						3305	30							
						3405	24							

Soundings in tributaries and bayous—Continued.

Section No. 36.

Distance from base-line on right bank.	Depth at high water. 1851.	Remarks.
Feet.	*Feet.*	
0	0	
60	11	
70	10	
125	16	
165	18	
215	23	
270	29	
285	30	
340	37	
430	47	
505	47	
555	48	
585	44	
670	40	
770	39	
815	37	
895	37	
1040	40	
1165	36	
1210	43	
1280	45	
1395	35	
1530	43	
1540	45	
1650	51	
1755	50	
1905	51	
2000	51	
2065	52	
2225	54	
2335	54	
2360	55	
2490	62	
2645	60	
2780	52	
2825	53	
2985	51	
3090	63	
3275	65	
3455	62	
3540	58	
3630	60	
3690	55	
3780	28	
3820	22	

Section No. 37.

Distance from base-line on left bank.	Depth at high water. 1851.	Remarks.
Feet.	*Feet.*	
0	0	
50	14	
65	17	
110	20	
210	38	
255	45	
295	47	
445	61	
500	59	
560	57	
655	52	
805	52	
895	43	
1090	58	
1120	55	
1305	59	
1505	67	
1545	68	
1630	68	
1900	67	
2040	69	
2215	70	
2305	67	
2420	53	
2565	44	
2630	43	
2815	31	
2925	31	
3010	26	

Section No. 38.

Distance from base-line on left bank.	Depth at high water. 1851.	Remarks.
Feet.	*Feet.*	
0	0	
325	57	
595	91	
685	87	
735	87	
870	77	
955	74	
1035	71	
1150	69	
1345	79	
1415	86	
1565	95	
1670	92	
1910	79	
1955	78	
2005	74	
2150	72	
2270	72	
2415	53	
2475	40	
2545	31	
2580	23	
2670	14	
2685	0	

Section No. 39.

Distance from base-line on left bank.	Depth at high water. 1851.	Remarks.
Feet.	*Feet.*	
0	0	
55	15	
85	13	
100	16	
170	24	
195	24	
235	25	
390	40	
405	42	
485	86	
535	92	
610	96	
780	106	
815	103	
980	99	
1050	98	
1125	90	
1165	85	
1285	77	
1390	75	
1540	82	
1655	85	
1800	78	
1850	78	
2075	71	
2180	66	
2305	63	
2410	62	
2530	57	
2545	54	
2620	39	
2675	34	
2700	23	
2780	0	

Section No. 40.

Distance from base-line on right bank.	Depth at high water. 1851.	Remarks.
Feet.	*Feet.*	
0	—1	
36	4	
52	12	
180	28	
216	38	
236	48	
280	53	
350	64	
418	70	
484	78	
590	89	
706	94	
840	99	
984	96	
1090	89	
1166	83	
1286	78	
1396	75	
1588	70	
1758	65	
1906	53	
2150	42	
2354	35	
2636	24	
2800	24	
3032	21	
3370	12	
3630	10	

Section No. 41.

Distance	Depth	Remarks.
0	1	
40	4	
104	12	
150	28	
172	40	
236	40	
274	60	
380	87	
440	95	
540	99	
666	104	
784	99	
934	91	
1076	87	
1230	82	
1366	74	
1510	64	
1598	58	
1770	46	
1910	34	
2046	27	
2270	23	
2470	16	
2800	10	

Section No. 42.

Distance	Depth	Remarks.
Rt. bank		
0	0	
5	4	
78	17	
101	26	
155	36	
170	40	
220	60	
237	52	
393	47	
448	48	
515	47	
540	47	
583	41	
620	40	
645	34	
686	33	
730	21	
770	11	
805	4	
847	0	

Section No. 43.

Distance	Depth	Remarks.
0	—1	
5	0	
50	0	
55	4	
99	14	
128	18	
135	18	
158	21	
193	28	
230	43	
245	47	
289	46	
325	43	
330	41	
370	46	
377	48	
445	47	
455	48	
485	51	
495	51	
532	48	
545	50	
576	44	
637	46	
661	37	
682	33	
730	14	
760	3	
806	2	
830	—1	

Section No. 44.

Distance	Depth	Remarks.
0	—1	
5	0	
35	4	
70	13	
105	17	
165	23	
207	40	
227	41	
275	33	
288	40	
354	42	
367	41	
388	45	
410	45	
430	47	
435	46	
468	46	
515	48	
528	46	
552	48	
568	46	
505	45	
667	18	
743	4	
770	4	
780	7	
800	0	

Section No. 45.

Distance	Depth	Remarks.
Left b'nk		
0	—1	
5	0	
25	0	
65	5	
125	22	
155	19	
175	33	
180	37	
210	43	
218	43	
260	42	
285	50	
340	64	
357	53	
400	54	
415	48	
436	47	
487	48	
519	50	
532	50	
591	42	
610	35	
633	29	
700	5	
800	0	

Soundings in tributaries and bayous—Continued.

Section No. 46.

Distance from base-line on left bank.	Depth at high water. 1858.	Remarks.
Feet.	*Feet.*	
0	—4	
4	—2	
53	—1	
76	10	
93	10	Red clay.
118	14	"
145	17	"
166	20	"
209	23	"
221	35	"
251	35	"
303	52	Red clay and shells.
333	59	Red clay.
353	64	"
357	61	"
385	62	"
466	54	"
529	53	Blue clay and sand.
612	51	"
663	41	Red clay.
705	28	"
736	17	"
756	13	"
767	7	
817	2	
890	1	
890	6	
910	0	

Section No. 47.

Distance from base-line on left bank.	Depth at high water. 1851.	Remarks.
Feet.	*Feet.*	
0	—1	
10	0	
55	0	
75	5	
175	28	
215	33	
260	50	
280	56	
310	48	
332	34	
380	49	
420	46	
425	46	
472	49	
479	50	
501	52	
550	49	
565	45	
578	42	
613	39	
655	27	
684	19	
705	4	
760	0	

Section No. 48.

Distance from base-line on left bank.	Depth at high water. 1851.	Remarks.
Feet.	*Feet.*	
0	—2	
5	4	
30	4	
46	18	
55	17	
63	22	
76	23	
83	25	
90	27	
107	28	
109	28	
125	30	
145	31	
165	31	
167	30	
189	28	
193	29	
195	29	
227	24	
232	24	
239	21	
265	20	
305	2	

Section No. 49.

Distance from base-line on left bank.	Depth at high water. 1858.	Remarks.
Feet.	*Feet.*	
0	—2	
17	2	
54	4	
58	6	
68	11	Clay.
70	14	"
83	19	"
92	25	"
94	21	"
104	24	Blue clay.
122	23	Clay.
126	24	"
155	26	"
163	28	"
173	28	"
204	27	"
210	27	"
218	23	Sand.
260	21	"
274	24	"
277	22	"
290	20	Clay.
312	16	Sand.
318	14	"
332	10	"
338	6	
362	14	
367	14	
381	—2.4	

Section No. 50.

Distance from base-line on left bank.	Depth at high water. 1851.	Remarks.
Feet.	*Feet.*	
0	—2	
5	5	
43	11	
46	22	
50	22	
55	24	
57	24	
66	25	
68	26	
75	26	
85	26	
87	26	
98	27	
104	29	
127	30	
142	31	
148	28	
169	30	
174	29	
179	28	
182	30	
193	28	
205	25	
208	25	
225	24	
227	22	
230	21	
239	19	
262	12	
307	2	

Section No. 51.

0	—2.5	
11	1	
35	2	
47	6	
47	2	
61	10	Sand.
64	11	"
76	16	"
85	22	"
95	23	"
103	24	
111	25	Clay.
116	25	"
121	26	"
132	26	"
135	27	"
149	27	"
155	29	"
176	27	"
183	26	"
189	27	"
196	29	"
217	28	"
245	24	"
254	26	"
267	21	"
287	15	Sand.
289	15	"
293	10	"
305	6	
305	2	
335	1	
340	—2.5	

Section No. 52.

0	—1	
5	2	
23	3	
30	13	
45	20	
59	24	
78	28	
85	31	
88	32	
102	32	
122	31	
137	33	
145	31	
156	30	
158	29	
174	30	
188	26	
200	26	
203	27	
204	25	
208	25	
218	24	
230	16	
290	2	

Section No. 53.

	1858.	
0	—3.2	
12	1	
38	4	
63	6	
71	15	Clay.
75	18	"
76	17	"
88	22	"
94	22	Blue clay.
110	25	"
116	26	"
120	28	"
128	30	"
137	29	"
142	29	"
153	30	"
179	27	Clay.
204	26	Blue clay.
213	26	"
234	24	"
258	22	Sand.
262	21	"
267	19	"
291	9	"
301	6	
313	2	
327	1	
338	—3	

Section No. 54.

0	—2	
7	2	
25	2	
33	6	
52	11	Sand.
64	16	Clay and sand.
64	16	Clay.
72	18	"
113	23	"
117	23	"
129	24	"
140	25	"
152	27	"
182	29	"
195	29	Sand and clay.
206	27	"
216	27	"
236	27	Blue clay.
237	27	"
238	27	"
263	26	"
273	20	Sand.
282	23	"
302	13	"
323	6	
328	1	
428	1	
433	—2	

Section No. 55.

Rt. bank		
0	—1	
5	4	
10	6	
18	11	
37	17	
42	19	
46	21	
51	22	
61	26	
70	28	
72	29	
79	31	
82	31	
86	29	
97	30	
101	29	
112	29	
120	28	
123	28	
139	24	
141	22	
151	20	
160	18	
177	12	
183	8	
186	7	
210	5	
212	—1	

Soundings in tributaries and bayous—Continued.

Section No. 56.

Distance from base-line on right bank.	Depth at high water. 1858,	Remarks.
Feet.	*Feet.*	
0	—1	
10	7	
20	10	
30	11	
38	18	
47	27	
63	27	
89	29	
95	30	Blue clay.
108	29	Sand.
111	30	"
128	26	Clay.
133	22	Sand.
153	18	
163	14	
169	12	
190	7	
210	1	
215	—2	

Section No. 57.

Distance from base-line on right bank.	Depth at high water. 1851.	Remarks.
Feet.	*Feet.*	
0	—1	
5	5	
25	5	
36	7	
48	12	
61	21	
65	23	
75	23	
83	26	
87	25	
100	26	
110	28	
114	28	
121	28	
124	29	
131	28	
135	28	
142	29	
145	28	
155	26	
168	21	
175	20	
185	19	
187	18	
200	14	
212	9	
219	6	
224	5	
228	—1	

Section No. 58.

Distance from base-line on right bank.	Depth at high water. 1858.	Remarks.
Feet.	*Feet.*	
0	—1	
3	1	
33	1	
36	7	
50	14	
54	19	Quicksand.
70	24	"
84	29	
112	28	Sand.
125	28	"
136	28	"
160	23	"
170	19	
185	21	
193	14	
205	10	
215	7	
225	2	
235	1	
238	—1	

Section No. 59.

Distance from base-line on right bank.	Depth at high water. 1851.	Remarks.
Feet.	*Feet.*	
0	—1	
5	5	
42	5	
55	11	
58	14	
71	20	
85	24	
91	25	
103	25	
114	26	
116	28	
124	29	
135	29	
137	29	
142	29	
140	29	
168	25	
170	23	
192	18	
198	18	
208	17	
218	14	
232	9	
240	7	
252	5	
250	—1	

Section No. 60.

Distance from base-line on right bank.	Depth at high water. 1858.	Remarks.
Feet.	*Feet.*	
0	—1	
3	0	
46	0	
46	7	
57	14	Clay and sand.
66	19	"
78	23	
87	28	Quicksand.
121	29	Sand.
134	28	"
160	26	
195	17	Blue clay.
189	18	"
207	14	"
215	11	
231	7	
251	1	
256	0	
259	—1	

Section No. 61.

Left b'nk	1851.	
0	—1	
5	0	
25	7	
45	12	
65	16	
85	20	
105	24	
125	24	
145	23	
165	20	
185	15	
205	10	
225	6	
245	4	
245	0	
255	—1	

Section No. 62.

	1858.	
0	—1.5	
2	0	
10	0	
22	6	
49	11	
62	16	
67	20	
78	21	Quicksand.
104	30	"
112	32	
118	32	
144	29	
146	30	Clay and sand.
160	27	"
167	25	"
195	12	"
200	11	"
223	6	
228	—1	

Section No. 63.

	1851.	
0	—1	
5	0	
45	16	
80	21	
102	22	
125	24	
150	23	
185	17	
195	15	
225	10	
232	0	
237	—1	

Section No. 64.

	1858.	
0	—1	
10	4	
23	7	
30	9	
38	12	Sand.
43	13	"
60	19	
67	20	"
103	26	
105	25	Blue clay.
107	25	"
108	27	"
109	28	
141	25	Sand.
149	24	"
155	24	"
188	25	Sand and clay.
223	9	
228	4	
234	—2	

Section No. 65.

0	—0.5	
4	6	
20	12	
45	19	
65	24	
85	24	
105	24	
125	24	
145	17	
165	12	
190	7	
230	3	
236	—0.5	

Soundings in tributaries and bayous—Continued.

Section No. 66.			Section No. 67.			Section No. 68.			Section No. 69.			Section No. 70.		
Distance from base-line on right bank.	Depth at high water. 1851.	Remarks.	Distance from base-line on right bank.	Depth at high water. 1858.	Remarks.	Distance from base-line on right bank.	Depth at high water. 1851.	Remarks.	Distance from base-line on right bank.	Depth at high water. 1851.	Remarks.	Distance from base-line on right bank.	Depth at high water. 1851.	Remarks.
Feet.	*Feet.*		*Feet.*	*Feet.*		*Feet.*	*Feet.*		*Feet.*	*Feet.*		*Feet.*	*Feet.*	
0	—2		0	0.5		0	0		0	—6		0	—6	
10	5		3	4		20	6		10	—6		10	—6	
35	7		11	4		44	13		15	0		15	0	
55	8		22	11	Sand and clay.	80	17		102	8		52	11	
65	10		38	17	Sand.	114	16		142	19		68	19	
90	14		48	20	Clay.	162	18		191	20		114	20	
105	19		51	20	Sand and clay.	180	18		336	46		152	40	
120	22		74	26	"	205	19		509	98		168	43	
140	21		76	26	"	248	19		528	104		206	47	
160	22		89	25	"	285	19		671	119		266	49	
180	19		104	21	Clay.	324	19		786	125		308	53	
200	14		120	25		340	19		887	127		400	54	
205	14		141	23	"	372	18		1011	119		406	60	
225	7		151	19	"	442	16		1094	112		518	61	
232	0		160	17	Sand.	550	15		1221	101		638	66	
237	—5		174	13	"	570	6		1257	103		666	68	
			183	11	"	620	3		1536	31		724	69	
			207	7	"	640	0		1572	4		858	72	
			256	6	"				1735	0		865	72	
			260	4					1745	—6		975	72	
												1018	76	
												1034	75	
												1164	78	
												1242	80	
												1310	77	
												1430	66	
												1518	54	
												1574	60	
												1662	40	
												1694	37	
												1700	26	
												1710	20	
												1738	40	
												1750	40	
												1782	0	
												1786	—6	

Section No. 71.												Section No. 72.		
	1828.			1828.			1828.			1828.			1828.	
0	1		355	55	Yellow clay.	931	57		1460	68		0	1	
15	1		388	56		990	63		1484	70		60	38	
40	10		419	57		1025	64		1584	62		225	68	
58	17		507	58		1094	61		1615	54		430	68	
68	20		532	57		1096	64		1673	43		570	56	
95	35		600	57		1154	65		1687	30	Clay.	800	62	
109	37		670	59		1231	66		1730	11		1000	62	
142	45	Blue gravel.	694	59		1256	66		1740	9		1220	62	
196	50	"	756	60		1282	68	Blue and black clay.	1760	7		1425	56	
202	51		800	65					1760	4		1640	50	
278	55		876	60		1368	69		1820	0		1680	29	
285	55	Black clay.	889	63		1413	69					1733	4	

No. 3.—COMPUTED DIMENSIONS OF CROSS-SECTIONS OF THE MISSISSIPPI RIVER.

No. of section.	Locality.	Measurements.		High-water dimensions.						Low-water dimensions.			
		Party of—	Date.	Year.	Area.		Width.		Perimeter between levees.	Year.	Area.	Width	Perimeter.
					Between banks.	Between levees.	Between banks.	Between levees.					
					Sq. feet.	*Sq. feet.*	*Feet.*	*Feet.*	*Feet.*		*Sq. feet.*	*Feet.*	*Feet.*
1	Columbus, Ky. (foot of Dabney st.)	Lieut. Abbot.	Dec. 1857.	1858	161,248	161,419	2190	2260	2308	1855	64,274	1905	1920
2	" " " "	Mr. Fillebrown.	Oct. 1858.	"	164,292	164,350	2230	2260	2295	"	65,585	1955	1965
3	" " 200 feet below Dabney street	Lieut. Abbot.	Dec. 1857.	"	164,393	164,568	2240	2320	2376	"	64,286	2020	2034
4	The same as No. 3	Mr. Fillebrown.	Oct. 1858.	"	175,225	175,345	2290	2320	2350	"	72,604	2025	2030
5	New Madrid, Mo. (¼ mile above)	Lieut. Abbot	Mar. 1858.	Date?	195,844	No levees.	6880	No levees.	6920	1858(?)	83,290	1840	1855
6	Osceola, Ark. (2 miles above)	"	" "	Date?	184,717	214,537	6080	7157	7179	"	52,600	2300	2311
7	Randolph, Tenn. (½ mile below)	"	" "	Date?	165,649	No levees.	2800	No levees.	2876	"	73,950	2310	2365
8	Helena, Ark.	"	" "	1858	205,846	"	4080	"	4124	1840(?)	23,944	2940	2960
9	Napoleon, Ark.	Lieut. Putnam.	Dec. "	"	211,674	213,462	3220	3660	3740	1858	82,700	2980	3002
10	Lake Providence, La.	Prof. Forshey.	Sept. 1851.	1851	173,630	175,490	3545	3725	3760	1851	71,910	2630	2642
11	" " (Washington st.)	Lieut. Abbot.	Feb. 1858.	1858	201,739	201,996	3580	3735	3815	1851	34,730	2980	3005
12	Vicksburg, Miss. (mouth of Glass bayou)	Mr. Pattison.	Dec. "	"	207,455	207,632	2345	2445	2510	1855	166,100	2200	2235
13	Vicksburg, Miss. (200 feet above foot of Crawford st.)	Lieut. Abbot.	Feb. "	"	176,890	178,648	2720	3056	3072	"	55,399	2340	2348
14	The same as No. 13	Mr. Pattison.	Sept. "	"	176,693	178,450	2710	3050	3080	"	55,800	2385	2398
15	Vicksburg, Miss. (foot Crawford st.)	Lieut. Abbot.	Feb. "	"	175,732	177,392	2710	3040	3080	"	55,003	2335	2346
16	" " " "	Mr. Pattison.	Sept. "	"	180,151	181,800	2695	3034	3069	"	59,865	2395	2400
17	" " (Ferry landing)	"	Dec. "	"	171,932	172,471	2630	2840	2902	"	50,610	2320	2350
18	" " (½ mile below Ferry landing)	"	" "	"	177,163	177,311	2750	2790	2840	"	47,869	2500	2515
19	Vicksburg, Miss. (1 mile below Ferry landing)	"	" "	"	162,187	162,720	2710	2880	2919	"	34,507	2450	2460
20	New Carthage, La.	Prof. Forshey.	Sept. 1851.	1851	203,000	210,000	4300	5500	5540	1852	54,200	2260	2272
21	" " "	Lieut. Abbot.	Feb. 1858.	1858	219,652	226,147	4300	5526	5640	"	87,700	2600	2611
22	Natchez, Miss. (250 feet above breakwater)	"	Jan. "	"	231,973	232,811	4600	5050	5086	1853	44,270	1450	1470
23	Natchez, Miss. (50 feet above breakwater)	"	" "	"	222,297	222,842	4485	4890	4949	"	43,990	1135	1180
24	Routh's point, near Red-river landing	Mr. G. C. Smith.	Mar. 1851.	1851	203,530	203,900	3880	4075	4087	1851	77,700	2650	2655
25	Red-river landing (in front of post-office)	"	" "	"	270,208	270,500	3646	3700	3745	"	139,920	2836	2866
26	Red-river landing (in front of post-office)	"	" "	"	260,784	261,300	3586	3700	3732	"	130,340	2456	2466
27	Raccourci cut-off (upper end)	"	" "	"	186,510	No levees.	2250	No levees.	2290	"	101,080	2000	2013
28	" " (500 feet below No. 27)	"	" "	"	182,000	"	2400	"	2434	"	90,100	2170	2180
29	Baton Rouge, La. (above barracks)	Prof. Forshey.	Oct. "	"	190,630	196,946	2800	3160	3180	"	107,670	2600	2617
30	Baton Rouge, La. (200 feet below No. 29)	"	" "	"	191,390	197,694	2800	3150	3175	"	108,880	2580	2597
31	Baton Rouge, La. (from No. 29 to Ferry landing)	"	" "	"	180,010*	185,590*	2720*	2790*	2806*	"	103,290*	2520*	2535*
32	Baton Rouge, La. (from Ferry landing to Convention street)	"	" "	"	182,890*	188,293*	2490*	2700*	2715*	"	110,020*	2350*	2364*
33	Baton Rouge, La. (600 feet below State-house)	Lieut. Abbot.	Feb. 1858.	1858	180,250	180,300	2460	2541	2597	"	107,000	2250	2284
34	Baton Rouge, La. (1 mile below State-house)	Prof. Forshey.	Oct. 1851.	1851	186,000	190,439	2190	2220	2255	"	125,180	1990	2015
35	Baton Rouge, La. (200 feet below No. 34)	"	" "	"	192,300	196,939	2190	2320	2350	"	129,820	2010	2035
36	22 miles below Bonnet Carré church	Lieut. Abbot.	Jan. 1858.	1858	202,051	202,191	1900	1956	2126	"	167,880	1650	1818
37	Bonnet Carré, 700 feet above No. 38	Mr. G. C. Smith.	June, 1851.	1851	261,700	263,000	3080	3500	3540	"	204,240	3000	3029
38	" " 300 feet above No. 39	"	" "	"	235,400	237,000	3100	3500	3530	"	177,750	3000	3015
39	Upper end of Bonnet Carré crevasse, 1850	"	" "	"	207,540	208,100	3085	3480	3510	"	150,610	2940	2955
40	Upper end of Bonnet Carré crevasse, 1850	Mr. Pattison.	Feb. 1859.	1858	207,490	207,822	3050	3480	3504	"	151,950	2890	2906
41	Bonnet Carré, 650 feet above No. 42	Mr. G. C. Smith.	June, 1851.	1851	166,900	168,000	3380	4800	4818	"	132,770	2940	2945
42	Lower end of Bonnet Carré crevasse, 1850	Mr. Pattison.	Feb. 1859.	1858	151,244	154,084	3200	4828	4850	"	99,000	2470	2482
43	Lower end of Bonnet Carré crevasse, 1850	Mr. G. C. Smith.	June, 1851.	1851	163,046	163,500	3145	4830	4853	"	108,390	2670	2683
44	Bonnet Carré, 300 feet below No. 43	"	" "	"	162,222	162,700	3170	4800	4824	"	107,800	2620	2625
45	Bonnet Carré, 1000 feet below No. 44	"	" "	"	179,500	182,000	2950	4600	4621	"	125,830	2760	2780
46	At Sauvé crevasse (17 miles above New Orleans)	Prof. Forshey.	Oct. "	"	174,400	174,700	2200	2250	2296	"	139,000	2130	2168
47	Below Fortier crevasse (15 miles above New Orleans)	"	" "	"	181,200	181,500	2200	2230	2280	"	147,040	2070	2102
48	Carrollton, La. (18,400 feet above Barataria-canal locks)	Mr. G. C. Smith.	June, "	"	206,540	215,643	3020	3035	3075	"	172,330	2740	2775
49	Carrollton, La. (18,400 feet above Barataria-canal locks)	Prof. Forshey.	Nov. "	"	206,700	215,806	3020	3035	3060	"	172,493	2740	2760

* Corrected for obliquity of section-line.

Computed dimensions of cross-sections of the Mississippi—Continued.

No. of section.	Locality.	Measurements.		High-water dimensions.						Low-water dimensions.			
		Party of—	Date.	Year.	Area.		Width.		Perimeter between levees.	Year.	Area.	Width	Perimeter.
					Between banks.	Between levees.	Between banks.	Between levees.					
					Sq. feet.	*Sq. feet.*	*Feet.*	*Feet.*	*Feet.*		*Sq. feet.*	*Feet.*	*Feet.*
50	Carrollton (18,050 feet above locks).	Mr. G.C. Smith.	June, 1851.	1851	216,610	226,088	3055	3160	3185	1851	211,113	2830	2855
51	" 17,550 " "	"	" "	"	220,570	229,989	3000	3140	3170	"	185,614	2825	2845
52	" 16,550 " "	"	" "		Section-	line not	perpen	dicular to	the	banks.			
53	" 16,550 " "	Prof. Forshey.	Nov. "	"	221,870	231,255	2975	3130	3155	1851	186,067	2895	2915
54	" 15,600 " "	Mr. G.C. Smith.	June, "	"	226,330	235,180	2860	2950	2985	"	192,767	2705	2730
55	" 14,650 " "	"	" "	"	227,630	235,450	2485	2605	2685	"	197,837	2410	2485
56	" 14,650 " "	Prof. Forshey.	Nov. "	"	218,450	226,267	2485	2605	2665	"	188,805	2390	2450
57	" 14,250 " "	Mr. G.C. Smith.	June, "	"	212,000	219,381	2350	2460	2520	"	184,731	2160	2220
58	" 14,250 " "	Prof. Forshey.	Nov. "	"	220,080	227,458	2350	2460	2510	"	192,808	2160	2210
59	" 13,250 " "	"	" "	"	215,210	222,594	2220	2460	2505	"	189,144	2000	2035
60	" 12,850 " "	Mr. G.C. Smith.	June, "		Section-	line not	perpen	dicular to	the	banks.			
61	" 12,300 " "	Prof. Forshey.	Oct. "	"	242,100	250,930	2425	2945	2985	1851	212,155	2225	2260
62	" 11,600 " "	Mr. G.C. Smith.	June, "	"	209,600	218,393	2510	2930	2960	"	178,980	2325	2340
63	" 11,600 " "	Prof. Forshey.	Nov. "	"	227,280	236,069	2510	2930	2960	"	196,656	2325	2340
64	" 10,580 " "	Mr. G.C. Smith.	June, "	"	199,860	208,141	2575	2760	2790	"	170,041	2320	2345
65	" 10,580 " "	Prof. Forshey.	Nov. "	"	213,760	222,036	2575	2760	2800	"	183,673	2355	2390
66	" 9,700 " "	"	" "	"	205,690	213,986	2520	2765	2805	"	175,811	2325	2350
67	" 9,500 " "	Mr. G.C. Smith.	June, "	"	202,830	210,809	2475	2660	2700	"	173,346	2335	2360
68	" 8,800 " "	"	" "	"	182,350	190,080	2375	2575	2620	"	154,630	2245	2285
69	" 8,800 " "	Prof. Forshey.	Oct. "	"	201,520	209,241	2375	2575	2615	"	172,941	2265	2305
70	" 8,600 " "	Mr. G.C. Smith.	Feb. "	"	182,890	190,538	2375	2550	2600	"	154,990	2275	2315
71	" 8,600 " "	Prof. Forshey.	Sept. "	"	203,880	211,530	2375	2550	2590	"	175,305	2280	2320
72	" 8,400 " "	Mr. G.C. Smith.	Feb. "	"	183,730	191,320	2330	2530	2585	"	156,410	2240	2245
73	" 8,400 " "	Prof. Forshey.	Sept. "	"	203,350	210,937	2330	2530	2585	"	176,012	2260	2315
74	" 8,200 " "	Mr. G.C. Smith.	Feb. "	"	177,740	185,312	2335	2525	2565	"	149,361	2223	2355
75	" 8,200 " "	Prof. Forshey.	Sept. "	"	193,870	201,446	2335	2525	2560	"	165,495	2238	2270
76	" 8,200 " "	Mr. Pattison.	Feb. 1859.	1858	184,990	185,338	2425	2705	2740	"	150,030	2260	2290
77	" 8,000 " "	Mr. G.C. Smith.	" 1851.	1851	163,690	171,278	2340	2530	2565	"	135,327	2219	2240
78	" 8,000 " "	Prof. Forshey.	Sept. "	"	181,540	189,128	2340	2530	2570	"	153,177	2259	2295
79	" 8,000 " "	Mr. Pattison.	Feb. 1859.	1858	172,610	173,014	2390	2670	2700	"	138,200	2220	2244
80	" 7,800 " "	Mr. G.C. Smith.	" 1851.	1851	162,480	170,096	2350	2540	2575	"	135,000	2230	2265
81	" 7,800 " "	Prof. Forshey.	Sept. "	"	178,710	186,333	2350	2540	2575	"	150,520	2235	2270
82	" 7,600 " "	"	Oct. "	"	169,990	177,656	2340	2555	2590	"	141,468	2270	2305
83	" 7,050 " "	Mr. G.C. Smith.	June, "	"	184,950	192,746	2375	2600	2645	"	156,033	2295	2335
84	" 7,050 " "	Prof. Forshey.	Dec. "	"	177,290	185,092	2375	2600	2645	"	148,342	2300	2340
85	" 6,250 " "	Mr. G.C. Smith.	June, "	"	196,680	204,627	2400	2650	2695	"	167,164	2345	2390
86	" 6,250 " "	Prof. Forshey.	Dec. "	"	196,400	204,348	2400	2650	2690	"	166,885	2345	2385
87	" 5,200 " "	Mr. G.C. Smith.	June, "	"	195,950	205,427	2750	3160	3195	"	161,889	2645	2680
88	" 4,200 " "	"	" "	"	175,800	184,574	2600	2925	2960	"	145,200	2500	2535
89	" 3,800 " "	"	" "	"	180,420	189,268	2640	2950	2980	"	149,010	2595	2625
90	" 2,800 " "	"	" "	"	176,490	185,490	2600	3000	3030	"	143,977	2535	2560
91	" (at canal locks)...............	"	" "	"	211,910	220,246	2585	2780	2830	"	180,000	2460	2505
92	" (at canal locks)...............	"	" "	"	194,430	202,228	2450	2600	2640	"	164,115	2355	2390
93	Fort St. Philip (50 feet below boat-shed)......................................	Lieut. Abbot.	Jan. 1858.	1858	231,300	231,360	2360	2494	2576	"	212,500	2335	2387

No. 4.—COMPUTED DIMENSIONS OF CROSS-SECTIONS OF TRIBUTARIES AND BAYOUS.

No. of section.	Locality.	Measurements.		High-water dimensions.						Low-water dimensions.				Range below adopted high water.
		Party of—	Date.	Year.	Area.		Width.		Perimeter between levees.	Year.	Area.	Width	Perimeter.	
					Between banks.	Between levees.	Between banks.	Between levees.						
					Sq. feet.	*Sq. feet.*	*Feet.*	*Feet.*	*Feet.*		*Sq. feet.*	*Feet.*	*Feet.*	*Feet.*
1	Ohio river, at Cairo, Ill......	Lieut. Abbot.	Dec. 1857.	1858	168,150	No levees.	2992	No levees.	3013	1858	54,000	2110	2126	42
2	“ “ “	“	“ “	“	166,010	“	2925	“	2947	“	54,300	2025	2040	42
3	Hatchee river, at crossing of Fulton road..............	“	Mar. 1858.	Date?	8,157	“	353	“	376	Date?	700	145	152	32
4	St. Francis river, 0.7 of a mile above mouth..........	“	Feb. “	1858	37,053	37,250	805	900	924	1859	8,200	595	602	41
5	White river, ⅛ of a mile below cut-off..................	“	Jan. “	“	36,343	No levees.	890	No levees.	920	1858	4,300	490	494	41
6	Cut-off between Arkansas and White rivers...........	“	“ “	“	24,500	“	560	“	607	“	4,100	250	265	41
7	Arkansas river, in front of Marine hospital.........	Lieut. Putnam.	Dec. 1857.	“	34,900	37,000	1050	1450	1472	“	6,700	400	406	41
8	“ “ “	“	“ “	“	33,100	35,200	1020	1400	1422	“	5,900	410	415	41
9	Bogue Falaya, at Hallam's ferry............................	Mr. Pattison.	“ 1858.	“	7,365	No levees.	345	No levees.	356	“	2,300	290	297	15
10	Sunflower river, at Dougherty's ferry..................	“	Nov. “	“	14,515	“	355	“	395	“	3,440	245	258	36
11	Yazoo river, at Beck's ferry, near Greenwood............	“	“ “	“	17,270	“	700	“	712	“	2,330	240	245	37
12	Yazoo river, 500 feet below Steele's bayou...............	Lieut. Abbot.	Feb. “	“	49,850	“	930	“	959	“	18,430	580	602	40
13	Bayou Tensas, at Mandeville's ferry..................	Mr. Pattison.	Jan. 1859.	“	15,690	“	560	“	580	1850	190	130	131	43
14	Washita river, ferry landing, Harrisonburg.........	“	“ “	“	26,220	“	635	“	673	“	4,100	375	380	43
15	Black river, 1000 feet above mouth.........................	Lieut. Abbot.	Feb. 1858.	1850	34,850	“	790	“	835	“	4,900	405	409	46
16	Red river, at Alexandria...	“	“ “	1858	27,347	27,450	715	794	822	1855	1,330	280	282	44
17	Red river, ¼ mile below mouth Black river........	“	“ “	1850	40,400	No levees.	785	No levees.	830	1850	7,500	610	618	46
18	Red river, 750 feet above mouth..........................	Mr. G. C. Smith.	Mar. 1851.	1851	79,700	“	1745	“	1795	1851	11,300	1045	1048	44
19	Red river, at mouth..........	“	“ “	“	82,965	“	1840	“	1890	“	11,600	1140	1143	44
20	“ “ “	“	“ “		Section-	line too	oblique	for correc	tion.					
21	Mouth of Old river, above Red-river landing.........	“	“ “	“	78,600	No levees.	1750	No levees.	1810	“	16,300	975	995	44
22	Mouth of Old river, 475 feet north of No. 21.............	“	“ “	“	70,090	“	1165	“	1245	“	26,100	780	810	44
23	Mouth of Old river, about 3 miles above Red-river landing.........................	Lieut. Abbot.	Feb. 1858.	1858	42,200	“	1150	“	1185	1858	3,300	645	647	40
24	Old river, about 4 miles above Red-river landing.	Mr. G. C. Smith.	“ 1851.	1851	91,570	“	2535	“	2545	1851	3,900	740	743	44
25	Old river, 900 feet NW. of No. 24.........................	“	“ “	“	94,770	“	2615	“	2632	“	3,500	640	643	44
26	Old river, 1200 feet NW. of No. 24.........................	“	“ “	“	96,925	“	2650	“	2660	“	3,700	917	920	44
27	Old river, 6225 feet from mouth Red river to the east.............................	“	Mar. “	“	99,415	“	2505	“	2535	“	3,100	840	841	44
28	Old river, 1425 feet west of No. 27.........................	“	“ “	“	99,124*	“	2565*	“	2591*	“	3,200*	790*	791*	44
29	Old river, 800 feet west of No. 28.........................	“	“ “	“	106,915*	“	2750*	“	2786*	“	4,600*	670*	672*	44
30	Old river, 600 feet west of No. 29.........................	“	“ “	“	114,982*	“	2810*	“	2847*	“	8,900*	710*	712*	44
31	Old river, 550 feet west of No. 30.........................	“	“ “	“	114,576*	“	2800*	“	2831*	“	8,500*	635*	637*	44
32	Old river, 300 feet west of No. 31.........................	“	“ “	“	115,224*	“	2825*	“	2860*	“	10,000*	600*	602*	44
33	Old river, 500 feet west of No. 32.........................	“	“ “	“	112,010*	“	2865*	“	2894*	“	8,100*	540*	542*	44
34	Old river, 550 feet west of No. 33.........................	“	“ “	“	122,430*	“	2890*	“	2924*	“	10,200*	510*	512*	44
35	Old river, 1050 feet west of No. 34.........................	“	“ “		Section-	line too	oblique	for correc	tion.					
36	Old river, 450 feet west of No. 35.........................	“	“ “		Section-	line too	oblique	for correc	tion.					
37	Old river, just below mouth of Red river to the west.............................	“	“ “	“	149,560*	No levees.	2795*	No levees.	2830*	“	19,800*	2280*	2284*	44
38	Old river, 900 feet west of No. 37.........................	“	“ “	“	181,870*	“	2685*	“	2708*	“	72,900*	2200*	2215*	44
39	Old river, 1200 feet west of No. 38.........................	“	“ “	“	184,885*	“	2710*	“	2737*	“	76,700*	2125*	2140*	44

* Corrected for obliquity of section-line.

Computed dimensions of cross-sections of tributaries and bayous—Continued.

No. of section.	Locality.	Measurements.		High-water dimensions.						Low-water dimensions.				Range below adopted high water.
		Party of—	Date.	Year.	Area.		Width.		Perimeter between levees.	Year.	Area.	Width	Perimeter.	
					Between banks.	Between levees.	Between banks.	Between levees.						
					Sq. feet.	*Sq. feet.*	*Feet.*	*Feet.*	*Feet.*		*Sq. feet.*	*Feet.*	*Feet.*	*Feet.*
40	Old river, at mouth of and above bayou Atchafalaya	Mr. G. C. Smith.	Mar. 1851.	1851	183,000	No levees.	3600	No levees.	3630	1851	59,000	1910	1930	44
41	Old river, at mouth of and below bayou Atchafalaya	"	" "	"	150,500	"	2775	"	2805	"	57,000	1550	1570	44
42	Bayou Atchafalaya, at mouth	"	" "	"	29,500	29,800	847	920	940	"	1,860	380	385	44
43	Bayou Atchafalaya, 300 ft. below No. 42	"	" "	"	26,590	26,900	760	830	857	"	1,400	410	414	44
44	Bayou Atchafalaya, 300 ft. below No. 43	"	" "	"	24,050	24,300	760	820	844	"	550	220	223	44
45	Bayou Atchafalaya, 300 ft. below No. 44	"	" "	"	25,430	26,000	750	880	910	"	2,300	314	322	44
46	Bayou Atchafalaya, 180 ft. below No. 45	Lieut. Abbot.	Feb. 1858.	1858	28,700	28,700	830	910	938	1858	5,300	400	407	40
47	Bayou Atchafalaya, 600 ft. below No. 45	Mr. G. C. Smith.	Mar. 1851.	1851	23,950	24,400	730	840	864	1851	1,500	280	289	44
48	Bayou Plaquemine, centre of Greaud St	"	April, "	"	6,340	6,450	300	370	382	"	0	0	0	31
49	The same as No. 48	Mr. Pattison.	Jan. 1859.	1858	6,225	6,375	305	375	388	"	0	0	0	31
50	Bayou Plaquemine, 200 ft. below No. 49	Mr. G. C. Smith.	April, 1851.	1851	6,050	6,120	280	340	353	"	0	0	0	31
51	The same as No. 50	Mr. Pattison.	Jan. 1859.	1858	5,850	5,942	275	335	351	"	0	0	0	31
52	Bayou Plaquemine, 400 ft. below No. 49	Mr. G. C. Smith.	April, 1851.	1851	5,860	5,950	300	340	354	"	0	0	0	31
53	The same as No. 52	Mr. Pattison.	Jan. 1859.	1858	5,900	5,931	295	335	349	"	0	0	0	31
54	Bayou Plaquemine, 600 ft. above bayou Jacob	"	" "	"	6,030*	6,190*	287*	405*	418*	"	0	0	0	31
55	Bayou La Fourche, upper mouth, 1000 feet below drawbridge	Mr. G. C. Smith.	April, 1851.	1851	4,160	4,180	210	212	238	"	190	73	75	26
56	The same as No. 55	Mr. Pattison.	Jan. 1859.	1858	3,872	3,872	210	210	226	"	180	82	84	26
57	Bayou La Fourche, upper mouth, 1200 feet below drawbridge	Mr. G. C. Smith.	April, 1851.	1851	3,880	3,910	198	225	243	"	110	58	59	26
58	Bayou La Fourche, upper mouth, 1150 feet below drawbridge	Mr. Pattison.	Jan. 1859.	1858	3,970	3,990	198	231	250	"	150	72	74	26
59	Bayou La Fourche, upper mouth, 1400 feet below drawbridge	Mr. G. C. Smith.	April, 1851.	1851	3,830	3,880	210	245	261	"	100	54	56	26
60	The same as No. 59	Mr. Pattison.	Jan. 1859.	1858	4,090	4,090	209	255	272	"	150	73	74	26
61	Bayou La Fourche, Pain Court	Prof. Forshey.	Dec. 1851.	1851	3,520	3,530	230	240	257	1858	200	80	81	20
62	The same as No. 61	Mr. Pattison.	Jan. 1859.	1858	4,080	4,080	210	220	238	"	500	87	91	23
63	Bayou La Fourche, Thibodeaux ferry-landing	Prof. Forshey.	Dec. 1851.	1851	3,595	3,595	228	228	240	"	580	120	122	16
64	The same as No. 63	Mr. Pattison.	Jan. 1859.	1858	3,970	3,970	230	230	243	"	600	112	115	19
65	Bayou La Fourche, Field's mills, at steamer-landing	Mr. Williams.	Nov. 1858.	"	3,555	3,555	236	236	256	"	650	105	108	17
66†	Bayou La Fourche, Field's mills, at canal locks	Prof. Forshey.	Dec. 1851.	1851	3,500	3,500	250	250	265	"	650	115	118	15
67†	The same as No. 66	Mr. Pattison.	Jan. 1859.	1858	4,045	4,045	260	260	276	"	680	121	124	17
68	Bayou Bœuf, at Penison's ferry	Prof. Forshey.	Aug. 1851.	1828	12,575	No levees.	680	No levees.	685		5,850	535	539	11
69	Berwick's bay, at Dr. Brashear's house	"	" "	"	131,720	132,980	1560	1740	1786		115,000	1490	1535	11
70	Berwick's bay, 1000 feet below No. 69	"	" "	"	110,450	No levees.	1780	No levees.	1817		91,030	1710	1740	11
71	Berwick's bay, at steamer-landing	Lieut. Abbot.	Jan. 1858.	"	98,240	"	1750	"	1788		79,190	1690	1713	11
72‡	The same as No. 71	Mr. Bayley.	" 1853.	"	98,220	"	1725	"	1763		79,280	1720	1740	11

* Corrected for obliquity of section-line.

† These sections extend from lock to lock, and are, consequently, a little oblique. No. 65 exhibits the true area for discharge.

‡ The notes of this measurement were kindly furnished by Mr. Bayley. The water stood about 8 feet below the high-water level of 1828, and 13,800 square feet have accordingly been added to the area as sounded.

APPENDIX D.

CURRENT-MEASUREMENTS UPON THE MISSISSIPPI AND ITS BRANCHES.

No. 1.—CURRENT-MEASUREMENTS AT CARROLLTON, BY PARTY OF PROF. C. G. FORSHEY.

Station.	Date.	Gauge.	Wind.	No. of floats.	Velocity in divisions numbered— I.	II.	III.	IV.	V.	VI.	VII.	VIII.	IX.	X.	XI.	XII.	XIII.	Discharge per second.	Mean velocity of river.
	1851.	Feet.			Feet.	Feet.	Feet.	Feet.	Feet.	Feet.	Feet.	Feet.	Feet.	Feet.	Feet.	Feet.	Feet.	Cu. feet.	Feet.
Prime base.	Feb. 15	5.4	Down 2	7	2.50	2.94	3.33	3.45	3.45	3.33	3.23	3.03	2.74	2.33	1.89	1.50		506,628	3.1129
" "	17	6.3	Down 2	9	2.86	3.60	3.90	3.80	3.70	3.50	3.40	3.08	2.82	2.47	1.98	1.59		534,777	3.2578
" "	18	7.0	Up 2	16	3.20	3.70	4.00	4.00	3.90	3.70	3.50	3.10	2.67	2.27	1.82	1.46		583,715	3.5153
" "	20	9.1	Up 3	12	3.57	4.60	4.88	4.80	4.50	4.00	3.57	3.45	3.08	2.50	2.11	1.68		690,709	4.0434
" "	21	10.1	Down 2	13	4.00	4.80	4.88	4.88	4.65	4.44	4.26	4.08	3.92	3.64	2.86	2.22		766,497	4.4114
" "	22	11.0	Up 1	29	4.00	4.88	5.41	5.26	5.20	5.00	4.60	4.30	4.00	3.33	2.67	2.13		819,583	4.6643
" "	24	11.8	Down 2	21	4.00	5.50	5.60	5.50	5.40	5.30	5.20	4.70	4.44	3.57	3.23	2.50		894,401	5.0410
" "	25	12.1	Up 2	20	3.77	4.88	5.88	5.71	5.71	5.41	5.00	4.76	4.55	4.26	3.33	2.67		909,900	5.1063
" "	26	12.5	Up 2	27	4.70	5.50	5.71	5.56	5.56	5.55	5.41	5.00	4.55	4.26	3.77	2.94		938,536	5.2376
" "	March 1	13.3	Down 3	17	4.50	5.60	6.20	6.10	6.00	5.80	5.60	5.41	5.13	4.50	4.00	3.17		1,012,568	5.5724
" "	3	13.6	Down 2	24	4.35	6.06	6.25	6.20	6.00	5.80	5.50	5.30	5.00	4.50	3.70	3.00		1,019,966	5.5976
" "	4	13.7	0	27	4.08	6.06	6.45	6.45	6.06	5.90	5.70	5.41	5.00	4.76	3.85	3.08		1,042,127	5.7112
" "	5	13.9	0	26	4.35	5.88	6.25	6.25	6.06	5.88	5.71	5.71	5.41	5.00	4.76	3.13		1,050,388	5.7405
" "	6	14.2	Up 3	14	5.00	6.25	6.25	6.06	5.88	5.71	5.56	5.41	5.41	5.00	4.65	3.33		1,048,009	5.7043
" "	8	14.1	Down 2	31	4.88	5.88	6.45	6.06	6.06	6.25	5.88	5.41	5.41	5.13	4.88	3.51		1,068,464	5.8151
" "	10	14.3	0	29	4.35	5.88	6.45	6.45	5.88	5.88	5.88	5.88	5.56	5.41	5.26	4.00		1,077,416	5.8638
" "	11	14.3	Down 1	45	5.00	6.50	6.67	6.45	6.25	6.06	5.85	5.71	5.45	5.10	4.30	3.50		1,007,901	5.9753
" "	12	14.3	0	20	4.44	6.45	6.45	6.40	6.06	6.00	5.88	5.56	5.41	4.88	4.55	3.64		1,078,279	5.8685
" "	13	14.4	Down 1	21	4.55	6.25	6.90	6.25	6.25	6.25	5.88	5.71	5.56	5.00	4.00	3.23		1,004,462	5.9402
" "	14	14.6	Up 2	27	4.55	6.25	6.67	6.67	6.25	6.25	6.06	5.88	5.71	5.41	4.35	3.51		1,116,084	6.0413
" "	15	14.7	Up 3	10	4.55	6.45	6.80	6.90	6.67	6.45	6.06	5.88	5.50	4.80	4.08	3.28		1,134,955	6.1262
" "	17	14.8	Down 2	28	4.88	6.67	6.67	6.67	6.45	6.25	6.25	6.06	5.88	5.71	5.00	4.17		1,152,504	6.2209
" "	19	14.9	0	42	5.26	6.67	6.67	6.67	6.50	6.20	6.00	5.88	5.56	5.00	4.76	3.85		1,136,688	6.1270
" "	20	14.9	0	32	5.00	6.67	6.90	6.90	6.45	6.30	5.88	5.88	5.71	5.20	4.88	3.92		1,149,398	6.1956
" "	21	15.1	Up 3	21	5.00	6.25	6.80	6.70	6.60	6.40	6.06	5.88	5.56	5.13	4.50	3.90		1,139,697	6.1265
" "	22	15.2	0	20	5.26	6.25	6.67	6.45	6.25	6.25	6.25	5.88	5.56	5.13	4.17	3.33		1,122,174	6.0241
" "	24	15.1	Down 3	12	5.71	6.50	6.70	6.50	6.25	6.25	6.00	5.88	5.71	5.00	4.00	3.23		1,129,393	6.0710
" "	25	15.2	Up 1	44	5.00	6.25	6.45	6.50	6.30	6.10	5.80	5.60	5.30	5.00	4.30	3.51		1,098,804	5.8986
" "	28	15.4	0	31	5.50	6.25	6.45	6.45	6.40	6.20	5.88	5.70	5.41	5.00	4.30	3.50		1,113,133	5.9592
" "	31	15.3	0	34	4.88	6.25	6.60	6 50	6.30	6.06	5.90	5.70	5.50	5.00	4.70	3.50		1,112,766	5.9654
" "	April 2	15.3	0	20	4.88	6.40	6.60	6.60	6.25	6.06	5.90	5.70	5.50	5.00	4.70	3.50		1,117,774	5.9923
" "	3	15.2	0	19	4.76	6.25	6.45	6.50	6.30	6.06	5.80	5.60	5.40	5.00	4.30	3.50		1,107,344	5.9364
Preston base.	9	15.0	Up 2	6	4.20	5.00	5.10	5.10	5.06	5.02	4.99	4.83	4.86	4.66	3.72	2.97		1,095,014	4.8415
" "	10	15.1	Up 3	10	4.02	5.03	4.87	4.80	4.92	4.92	4.89	4.73	4.76	4.56	3.64	2.91		1,063,701	4.6980
" "	11	15.0	Up 3	18	4.00	4.65	4.80	4.76	4.95	5.13	5.00	4.88	4.70	4.40	3.40	2.72		1,047,593	4.6425
Prime base.	12	15.1	Up 2	19	4.44	5.88	6.25	6.25	6.06	5.80	5.00	5.41	5.00	4.76	4.08	3.33		1,048,345	5.6353
Preston base.	16	14.8	Up 3	9	4.04	5.30	5.16	5.16	4.97	4.70	4.50	4.40	4.30	4.10	3.74	2.99		1,071,857	4.7493
" "	18	14.7	0	8	4.08	5.11	5.08	5.06	4.76	4.67	4.44	4.44	4.44	4.45	3.56	2.84		1,056,266	4.6852
Prime base.	22	14.6	0	16	4.35	6.06	6.06	6.00	5.90	5.70	5.50	5.30	4.90	4.40	3.70	3.00		1,026,320	5.5474
" "	May 5	13.7	Down 2	48	5.00	5.71	5.56	5.56	5.56	5.26	5.00	4.76	4.44	3.70	3.20	2.70		932,442	5.1029
" "	7	13.3	Up 2	23	4.26	5.41	5.56	5.50	5.40	5.30	5.00	4.70	4.30	3.70	3.10	2.50		907,692	4.9953
" "	9	13.0	Up 2	12	4.50	5.10	5.30	5.80	5.70	4.96	4.62	4.30	4.04	3.78	3.00	2.40		883,996	4.9033
Preston base.	12	12.3	Up 2	12	3.89	4.25	4.00	4.00	3.90	3.72	3.90	3.80	3.90	3.63	2.50	2.00		849,468	3.8674
Locks base.	13	12.1	Up 1	12	2.65	3.32	4.14	4.32	4.40	4.50	4.60	4.70	4.70	4.80	4.00	3.00		839,571	4.1915
Race-course base.	15	11.5	0	12	4.02	5.02	4.91	4.91	4.72	4.53	4.65	4.49	4.33	4.17	4.01	3.20	2.56	796,729	4.5010
Prime base.	16	11.2	0	42	3.28	4.88	5.00	4.80	4.70	4.60	4.30	4.00	3.70	3.50	2.50	1.83		774,584	4.3899
" "	17	11.0	Up 1	43	3.80	4.76	4.90	4.80	4.70	4.60	4.40	4.10	3.70	3.20	2.50	1.90		768,718	4.3749
Locks base.	20	10.6	Up 1	12	2.00	2.80	3.18	3.50	3.80	4.20	4.56	4.50	4.13	4.23	3.38	2.70		718,941	3.6552
Prime base.	21	10.4	Up 2	58	3.28	4.20	4.60	4.50	4.40	4.30	4.00	3.70	3.40	2.80	2.11	1.72		700,542	4.0149
Race-course base.	23	10.1	0	12	3.55	4.48	4.37	4.20	4.10	4.00	3.68	3.74	3.60	3.50	3.85	3.08	2.46	682,092	3.9859
Prime base.	26	9.8	Up ·2	45	3.17	4.20	4.17	4.40	4.30	4.10	3.80	3.23	2.99	2.67	2.06	1.69		660,188	3.8158
" "	27	9.8	Up 1	90	3.50	4.00	4.26	4.30	4.20	3.77	3.70	3.50	3.10	2.60	1.96	1.59		652,335	3.7703
" "	28	9.9	0	45	3.13	4.10	4.50	4.40	4.30	4.10	3.80	3.50	3.10	2.70	2.30	2.20		673,378	3.8920
" "	29	10.1	0	56	3.50	4.00	4.50	4.40	4.30	4.10	3.80	3.50	3.10	2.70	2.30	2.00		676,124	3.8913
Preston base.	June 2	10.9	0	62	2.64	3.28	3.85	3.77	3.70	3.65	3.57	3.32	3.35	3.15	2.52	2.01		738,342	3.4141
Race-course base.	3	11.0	Up 2	58	3.52	4.66	4.55	4.49	4.44	4.35	4.26	4.09	3.93	3.77	3.70	2.96	2.36	730,514	4.1580
Locks base.	4	11.1	Up 2	60	2.37	2.96	3.23	3.50	3.77	3.93	4.09	4.26	4.35	4.44	3.55	2.84		720,699	3.6420
Prime base.	5	11.1	Up 1	34	3.50	4.50	4.65	4.60	4.50	4.30	4.00	3.51	3.33	3.00	2.40	2.00		719,803	4.0913
" "	6	11.1	Up 3	97	3.23	4.55	4.65	4.60	4.50	4.40	4.00	3.60	3.30	2.90	2.40	1.70		719,219	4.0932
" "	7	11.0	Down 3	64	3.23	4.17	4.65	4.60	4.35	4.20	4.00	3.60	3.30	2.80	2.30	1.63		702,529	3.9982
" "	9	11.2	Down 1	112	3.80	4.50	4.80	4.70	4.50	4.30	4.00	3.51	3.23	2.99	2.38	1.90		727,217	4.1271
" "	10	11.2	0	60	3.23	4.35	4.65	4.70	4.60	4.35	4.10	3.80	3.50	3.00	2.50	1.74		729,570	4.1348
" "	11	11.2	0	144	3.50	4.50	4.90	4.80	4.70	4.50	4.20	3.80	3.50	3.00	2.50	1.74		740,973	4.2504
" "	12	11.4	Down 1	160	4.00	4.70	5.00	4.90	4.60	4.50	4.20	3.80	3.50	3.00	2.50	1.74		761,190	4.3078
" "	13	11.5	Down 2	128	3.50	4.60	5.00	5.00	4.80	4.60	4.40	4.00	3.57	3.20	2.50	2.00		775,622	4.3772
" "	16	11.7	0	42	3.13	4.35	5.26	5.26	5.00	4.76	4.55	4.08	3.28	2.90	1.92	1.54		782,895	4.4059
" "	17	11.4	0	51	3.50	4.41	5.00	4.80	4.70	4.50	4.30	4.08	3.53	3.34	2.68	2.10		764,709	4.3279

Current-measurements at Carrollton—Continued.

Station.	Date.	Gauge.	Wind.	No. of floats.	Velocity in divisions numbered— I.	II.	III.	IV.	V.	VI.	VII.	VIII.	IX.	X.	XI.	XII.	XIII.	Discharge per second.	Mean velocity of river.
	1851.	Feet.			Feet.	Feet.	Feet.	Feet.	Feet.	Feet.	Feet.	Feet.	Feet.	Feet.	Feet.	Feet.	Feet.	Cu. feet.	Feet.
Prime base.	June 20	11.8	Down 3	63	3.70	4.69	5.06	5.00	4.94	4.80	4.64	4.32	3.71	2.82	2.20	1.80		794,060	4.4687
" "	24	12.0	Up 2	42	3.13	4.44	5.00	4.90	4.70	4.65	4.26	3.92	3.39	3.00	2.60	2.08		763,298	4.2836
" "	25	12.0	Up 2	50	3.33	4.60	4.80	4.65	4.64	4.55	4.26	3.85	3.45	3.17	2.50	2.00		754,508	4.2341
" "	26	12.0	0	40	3.33	4.65	5.00	4.76	4.76	4.65	4.26	3.85	3.45	3.13	2.50	2.00		767,127	4.3052
" "	27	12.0	Up 2	64	3.51	5.13	4.88	4.76	4.76	4.44	4.26	3.77	3.45	3.13	2.94	2.22		773,310	4.3398
" "	July 2	12.2	Up 2	80	3.77	5.00	5.10	5.00	4.88	4.76	4.17	4.08	4.00	3.45	2.78	2.22		805,444	4.5075
" "	3	12.1	Up 2	78	3.33	5.00	5.26	5.70	4.88	4.65	4.44	4.00	3.51	2.94	2.35	1.89		809,510	4.5306
" "	5	12.2	0	58	3.23	4.65	5.41	5.26	4.88	4.76	4.65	4.08	3.92	3.70	2.94	2.35		818,847	4.5825
" "	10	12.2	Down 2	60	4.00	5.26	5.26	5.26	5.00	5.00	5.00	4.44	4.17	3.70	2.94	2.35		856,448	4.7862
" "	16	12.5	0	64	3.85	5.41	5.26	5.13	5.00	5.00	4.76	4.55	4.17	3.70	2.94	2.35		854,451	4.7618
" "	18	12.5	Down 2	108	4.10	5.20	5.20	5.25	4.92	4.87	4.88	4.53	4.20	3.87	3.12	3.06		855,957	4.7701
" "	26	12.7	Up 2	64	3.92	4.65	5.26	5.26	5.13	5.00	5.00	4.76	5.00	3.92	3.13	2.50		868,854	4.8217
" "	29	12.5	Down 2	64	4.00	4.76	5.26	5.26	5.00	5.00	5.00	4.65	4.26	3.28	2.33	1.85		844,245	4.6983
" "	Aug. 2	12.5	0	64	4.00	5.13	5.13	5.13	5.00	5.00	4.88	4.76	4.44	4.00	3.17	2.38		858,907	4.7837
" "	5	12.3	0	80	3.85	5.00	5.40	5.41	5.26	5.13	4.88	4.65	4.26	3.64	3.10	2.50		868,610	4.8473
" "	7	11.9	0	64	3.70	4.88	5.41	5.13	5.13	5.13	4.65	4.26	3.77	3.57	3.13	2.50		834,958	4.6922
" "	9	11.6	0	64	3.45	4.65	5.00	4.88	4.88	4.76	4.44	4.55	4.55	3.45	2.99	2.38		804,650	4.5347
" "	11	11.1	0	80	3.85	4.88	4.88	4.88	4.55	4.44	4.26	3.85	3.64	3.57	3.13	2.50		769,648	4.3679
" "	13	10.4	Down 3	64	3.85	4.50	4.70	4.60	4.35	4.26	4.08	3.64	3.45	2.86	2.30	1.83		716,241	4.1050
" "	15	9.7	Down 3	80	3.33	4.40	4.50	4.40	4.30	4.20	3.80	3.50	3.00	2.08	1.68	1.35		669,388	3.8744
" "	19	8.5	0	48	2.99	4.00	4.17	4.20	3.85	3.77	3.45	3.23	2.99	2.63	2.11	1.68		616,090	3.6371
" "	20	8.4	Up 1	65	3.03	4.26	4.00	4.00	4.00	3.92	3.45	3.33	2.99	2.60	2.11	1.68		620,400	3.6626
" "	22	8.3	0	65	2.90	3.64	4.26	3.92	3.92	3.85	3.57	3.17	2.90	2.53	2.02	1.61		606,158	3.6375
" "	25	8.1	Up 1	64	2.86	3.64	3.92	3.70	3.57	3.45	3.39	3.28	2.78	2.47	1.98	1.60		572,388	3.3888
" "	27	8.0	0	80	2.86	3.85	3.85	3.77	3.64	3.51	3.39	3.08	2.86	2.47	1.98	1.60		576,086	3.4203
" "	29	7.9	0	72	2.86	4.00	3.85	3.57	3.45	3.45	3.39	2.90	2.78	2.44	1.96	1.57		564,238	3.3505
" "	Sept. 1	7.2	0	64	2.00	3.50	3.85	3.85	3.70	3.51	3.28	3.03	2.50	2.00	1.50	0.80		548,738	3.2953
" "	3	6.6	Down 2	86	2.70	3.28	3.70	3.57	3.33	3.28	3.17	3.03	2.78	2.53	2.00	1.60		521,458	3.1538
" "	5	6.2	0	84	2.56	3.33	3.39	3.39	3.39	3.39	3.08	2.74	2.60	2.38	2.13	1.69		518,963	3.1509
" "	8	5.5	0	64	2.35	3.13	3.40	3.30	3.08	3.00	2.90	2.70	2.50	2.27	1.82	1.46		480,136	2.9545
" "	10	5.2	0	48	2.30	3.20	3.40	3.30	3.20	3.60	2.90	2.74	2.41	2.22	1.77	1.42		481,430	2.9709
" "	11	5.2		22	2.15	3.13	3.13	3.13	3.08	2.99	2.86	2.67	2.47	2.17	1.74	1.39		488,637	3.0242
" "	12	4.9	0	80	2.22	3.13	2.94	2.90	2.90	2.78	2.70	2.63	2.22	2.04	1.64	1.33		467,511	2.9017
" "	17	4.1	0	80	2.04	2.70	2.80	2.70	2.63	2.50	2.44	2.41	2.27	2.00	1.75	1.40		401,398	2.5168
" "	18	3.7	0	80	1.89	2.56	2.56	2.56	2.56	2.56	2.44	2.30	2.08	2.00	1.60	1.28		382,792	2.4176
" "	19	3.4	0	80	1.72	2.56	2.53	2.47	2.50	2.50	2.40	2.30	1.94	1.85	1.48	1.18		371,898	2.3557
" "	22	2.9	0	40	1.60	2.40	2.40	2.40	2.25	2.25	2.17	2.11	1.87	1.57	1.31	1.05		341,529	2.1824
" "	24	2.2	Down 2	56	1.60	2.10	2.10	2.10	2.02	2.00	1.92	1.82	1.69	1.53	1.23	0.99		301,371	1.9428
" "	30	1.2	0	40	1.29	1.75	2.00	1.92	1.90	1.83	1.70	1.50	1.40	1.50	1.10	0.90		265,214	1.7402
" "	Oct. 2	1.5	Down 2	40	1.20	1.68	1.65	1.75	1.77	1.72	1.59	1.47	1.44	1.35	0.87	0.70		246,485	1.6077
" "	4	1.3	Down 2	40	1.49	1.77	1.65	1.72	1.74	1.64	1.53	1.57	1.35	1.20	0.96	0.77		245,585	1.6042
" "	7	1.7	0	40	1.16	1.90	1.90	1.77	1.70	1.64	1.64	1.43	1.29	1.16	0.92	0.74		251,502	1.6360
" "	9	1.7	0	40	1.20	2.00	2.00	1.90	1.70	1.60	1.54	1.50	1.15	1.02	0.81	0.65		254,608	1.6558
" "	11	1.8	Up 2	40	1.50	2.10	2.10	2.00	2.00	1.90	1.70	1.55	1.38	1.23	0.93	0.74		281,207	1.8288
" "	13	1.5	Down 2	56	0.70	1.32	1.70	1.90	2.00	1.90	1.80	1.70	1.60	1.10	0.80	0.50		254,147	1.6577
" "	14	1.4	Down 2	68	0.70	1.30	1.70	1.90	2.00	1.90	1.80	1.70	1.60	1.10	0.80	0.50		253,011	1.6552
" "	15	1.4	Down 1	92	0.70	1.30	1.70	1.90	2.00	1.90	1.82	1.68	1.56	1.10	0.80	0.50		253,904	1.6610
" "	17	1.6	0	40	1.32	1.85	1.92	1.77	1.68	1.74	1.74	1.48	1.05	0.96	0.77	0.62		251,030	1.6374
Preston base.	20	1.6	Up 2	40	1.04	1.32	1.40	1.49	1.54	1.50	1.45	1.40	1.43	1.23	0.90	0.72		275,217	1.4203
Locks base.	21	1.6	0	40	0.84	1.05	1.18	1.38	1.50	1.60	1.74	1.92	1.87	1.71	1.55	1.24		256,422	1.4657
Prime base.	23	1.4	Down 3	40	1.35	1.98	1.89	1.89	1.82	1.77	1.77	1.60	1.60	1.39	1.11	0.89		269,718	1.7502
" "	25	1.4	Down 1	32	1.43	1.96	2.00	1.90	1.92	1.82	1.71	1.69	1.50	1.53	1.22	0.98		275,869	1.8020
" "	Nov. 4	1.3	0	40	1.27	1.94	1.94	1.83	1.79	1.71	1.61	1.48	1.30	1.34	1.08	0.86		258,830	1.6957
" "	7	1.0	0	38	1.32	2.00	2.00	1.90	1.83	1.74	1.63	1.53	1.49	1.32	1.06	0.85		265,693	1.7458
" "	10	1.2	Up 3	40	1.24	1.90	2.04	2.00	1.90	1.80	1.65	1.45	1.36	1.27	1.02	0.82		266,721	1.7474
" "	15	1.7	0	40	1.32	1.80	2.00	2.04	1.87	1.80	1.79	1.69	1.50	1.40	1.28	1.03		275,625	1.7925
" "	18	1.3	0	40	1.25	1.69	1.69	1.74	1.82	1.64	1.49	1.49	1.39	0.93	0.71	0.62		241,199	1.5779
" "	20	1.3	Down 3	74	1.32	1.71	1.72	1.71	1.69	1.63	1.57	1.50	1.42	1.30	1.04	0.83		244,189	1.5975
" "	26	0.4	0	36	1.24	1.80	1.79	1.68	1.72	1.00	1.50	1.30	1.10	0.90	0.70	0.50		228,042	1.5114
" "	Dec. 2	0.8	Down 2	40	1.28	1.83	1.82	1.96	1.72	1.89	1.74	1.52	1.29	1.10	0.88	0.70		256,554	1.6908
" "	10	0.9	Up 2	40	1.25	1.98	2.06	2.15	2.13	2.11	2.02	1.83	1.53	1.28	1.04	0.83		293,496	1.9314
" "	19	0.5	Down 2	40	1.48	2.10	2.00	2.00	1.90	1.89	1.75	1.52	1.50	1.39	1.11	0.89		275,130	1.8236
" "	24	1.0	0	36	1.67	2.30	2.20	2.20	2.10	2.00	1.82	1.70	1.60	1.50	1.37	1.10		302,184	1.9886
" "	31	1.8	Down 3	40	1.69	2.25	2.38	2.44	2.47	2.22	1.92	1.89	1.69	1.54	1.23	0.99		330,087	2.1435
	1852.																		
" "	Jan. 6	0.9	Down 2	40	1.72	2.40	2.30	2.20	2.10	2.00	1.87	1.79	1.67	1.52	1.21	0.97		307,991	2.0298
" "	14	4.4	Up 2	37	2.35	3.51	3.64	3.64	3.50	3.39	3.23	2.78	2.67	2.44	2.06	1.65		518,971	3.2493
" "	21	5.0	Down 2	40	2.27	3.04	3.30	3.20	3.10	3.00	2.90	2.70	2.63	2.22	1.79	1.43		482,392	2.9941
" "	28	2.7	0	40	1.79	2.82	2.78	2.63	2.46	1.90	2.17	2.04	1.70	1.40	1.00	0.50		356,049	2.2785
" "	Feb. 5	1.0	Up 2	40	1.50	2.20	2.10	2.00	1.90	1.80	1.94	1.74	1.52	1.47	1.18	0.94		286,305	1.8813
" "	14	3.0	0	9	2.17	2.70	3.03	2.86	2.67	2.56	2.44	2.27	2.08	1.83	1.47	1.18		400,288	2.6541
" "	18	5.4	0	40	2.67	3.33	3.70	3.57	3.51	3.28	3.13	2.94	2.82	2.53	2.02	1.63		524,861	3.2389

No. 2.—CURRENT-MEASUREMENTS AT TEMPORARY STATIONS.

Locality.	Date.	Stage below high water. 1851.	Wind.	No. of floats.	Depth of floats.	Velocity observed in divisions numbered—																	Discharge per second.		Mean velocity.	Observations by party of—
						I.	II.	III.	IV.	V.	VI.	VII.	VIII.	IX.	X.	XI.	XII.	XIII.	XIV.	XV.	XVI.	XVII	Approx.	Corrected.		
	1851.	*Feet.*				*Feet*	*Feet*	*Feet*	*Feet.*	*Feet*	*Feet*	*Feet*	*Feet*	*Feet*	*Feet*	*Feet*	*Feet*	*Feet*	*Feet*	*Feet*	*Feet*	*Feet*	*Cu. feet.*	*Cu. feet.*	*Feet.*	
Routh's Point, near Red-river landing	Feb. 25	9.0	Up 1	22	Surface.	3.50	5.77	7.91	10.11	9.60	8.70	7.70	6.78	6.00	5.20	4.40	3.55	2.80	2.13	1.20	0.50		1,012,356	1,009,600	5.9365	Mr. G.C. Smith.
Routh's Point, near Red-river landing	Mar. 12	3.5	Up 1	8	"								(See	note	a.)									1,149,400	6.0489	"
Red-river landing	" 16	2.5	Down 2	32	"	1.87	3.39	4.65	5.26	5.71	5.88	6.06	5.88	5.71	5.88	5.56	5.56	5.56	4.88	4.08	3.08	2.50	1,225,958	1,182,200	4.9088	"
Red-river landing	" 19	2.0	0	7	"								(See	note	b.)									1,204,200	4.9650	"
Raccourci cut-off	" "	2.0	0	24	"	1.00	5.54	7.15	7.80	8.44	7.92	7.06	6.60	5.99	5.48	5.10	4.09						1,189,382	1,177,300	6.5568	"
Baton Rouge	April 1	0.0	0	33	"	3.51	4.55	5.00	5.41	5.56	5.41	6.45	8.00	8.33	8.70	8.33	6.90	4.35	3.45				1,172,819	1,160,100	5.8793	"
Baton Rouge	" 26	1.8	Down 2	39	"	3.17	3.92	4.65	5.12	5.40	5.40	6.06	6.45	7.41	8.00	8.00	7.69	6.67	4.26				1,109,745	1,071,800	5.5743	Prof. Forshey.
Baton Rouge	" 28	2.0	0	45	All depths.	3.08	4.00	4.35	4.76	5.13	5.26	5.56	6.06	6.67	7.69	8.00	7.69	6.06	4.26				1,056,108	1,056,108	5.5086	"
Baton Rouge	" 29	2.1	0	97	"	3.33	4.25	4.44	4.76	5.13	5.26	5.71	6.45	7.41	7.69	8.00	7.14	5.00	3.64				1,053,460	1,053,460	5.5022	"
Baton Rouge	Oct. 28	28.7	Up 2	40	"	1.43	2.00	2.15	2.25	2.67	2.53	2.50	2.47	2.53	2.60	2.67	2.70	2.90	2.33				272,838	272,838	2.3316	"
Above Bonnet Carré crevasse	May 20	6.2	Up 1.5	29	Surface.	2.50	3.17	3.33	3.51	3.85	4.26	4.26	4.26	4.17	4.17	4.17	4.08	4.08	3.33	2.82	2.22		728,121	728,121	3.8792	Lieut. Warren.
Below Bonnet Carré crevasse	April 28	1.5	0	38	All depths.	4.00	5.00	7.69	7.69	7.41	7.14	6.90	6.90	6.90	6.90	6.45	5.71	3.70	2.11	1.59	1.27		1,022,117	1,022,117	6.4759	Mr. G.C. Smith.

a. Mean of floats (all in divisions II, III, IV, V) is 8.505 feet. Mean in same places on February 25 is 8.347 feet.

b. Mean of floats (all in divisions I, IV, VI, VII, XI) is 2.426 feet. Mean in same places (corrected for wind) on March 16 is 2.398 feet.

No. 3.—CURRENT-MEASUREMENTS AT COLUMBUS, BY PARTY* OF MR. H. C. FILLEBROWN.

Date.		Gauge.	Wind.		No. of floats.	Velocity 5 feet below surface in divisions numbered—											Discharge per second.		Mean velocity of river.
						I.	II.	III.	IV.	V.	VI.	VII.	VIII.	IX.	X.	XI.	Approx.	Corrected.	
1857.		*Feet.*				*Feet.*	*Feet.*	*Feet.*	*Feet.*	*Feet.*	*Feet.*	*Feet.*	*Feet.*	*Feet.*	*Feet.*	*Feet.*	*Cubic feet.*	*Cubic feet.*	*Feet.*
December	11	20.1		0	10	3.45	4.65	5.88	6.90	7.40	7.40	6.80	5.80	4.70	3.40	2.20	699,893	691,630	5.7411
	12	23.1		0	24	3.70	5.56	7.69	8.33	6.66	6.66	6.90	6.65	5.41	4.11	3.91	829,140	810,110	6.4428
	14	27.6		0	34	4.65	6.06	7.69	8.33	8.33	8.33	8.70	6.90	6.06	4.76	3.36	975,337	965,380	7.0457
	15	29.0		0	75	4.44	6.67	8.33	8.70	8.70	8.33	8.33	7.69	7.14	6.67	4.87	1,071,228	1,061,480	7.5766
	16	30.0		0	58	5.26	7.41	8.70	8.70	8.70	8.70	8.70	8.33	7.69	7.14	6.06	1,148,044	1,137,600	7.9938
1858.																			
January	12	24.0		0	51	2.86	4.26	5.56	6.67	6.90	6.07	6.06	5.26	4.17	3.17	1.97	685,692	676,110	5.2380
	13	22.6	Down	3	46	3.33	4.55	5.71	6.90	6.90	6.90	6.06	5.26	4.16	3.16	1.96	684,576	656,000	5.2031
	14	21.5	Down	1	55	2.94	3.57	5.13	6.45	6.45	6.45	5.71	4.76	3.85	3.23	2.03	620,127	606,110	4.8999
	16	20.6	Down	2	88	2.86	4.08	5.13	6.06	6.25	6.25	5.71	4.76	3.77	3.13	1.93	602,424	583,180	4.7901
	18	21.2	Down	1	64	3.03	4.00	5.13	6.25	6.25	6.25	6.06	5.26	4.44	3.64	2.44	631,000	616,730	5.0122
	19	21.9	Up	1	70	3.17	4.26	5.26	6.06	6.25	6.25	5.88	5.26	4.08	3.70	2.60	641,411	639,640	5.1349
	20	22.3		0	84	3.17	4.26	5.41	6.25	6.45	6.45	6.45	5.41	4.55	3.70	2.40	669,524	660,480	5.2498
	23	21.0	Up	3	82	2.90	3.70	4.76	5.56	6.25	5.88	5.88	4.88	4.08	3.45	2.25	592,070	602,680	4.9068
	26	18.7	Up	3	84	2.68	3.51	4.08	5.13	5.56	5.56	5.41	4.76	3.77	3.13	2.17	527,666	537,700	4.4671
	27	18.0	Up	1	57	2.53	3.39	4.35	5.13	5.71	5.56	5.13	4.55	3.77	3.08	1.78	517,196	515,330	4.4384
	29	17.3	Down	2	46	2.67	3.39	4.65	5.56	5.71	5.56	5.26	4.44	3.92	3.23	1.93	525,558	506,760	4.4218
	30	17.7	Down	1	43	2.45	3.45	4.65	5.71	5.88	5.56	5.41	4.76	4.08	3.51	2.21	544,495	530,660	4.5956
February	3	17.3	Down	2	65	2.38	3.45	4.65	5.41	5.71	5.56	5.26	4.65	4.00	3.17	1.87	525,519	506,730	4.4215
	5	17.0	Up	1	88	1.99	2.99	3.92	4.88	5.41	5.26	5.13	4.44	3.57	3.08	1.78	482,251	481,020	4.2260
	6	16.6	Up	4	36	2.13	3.13	3.92	4.65	5.26	5.26	5.00	4.17	3.45	2.35	1.05	460,089	474,150	4.1919
	8	16.4	Up	1	53	2.17	3.17	4.00	4.65	5.56	5.26	5.00	4.08	3.45	2.99	1.69	480,284	478,550	4.2470
	11	15.8		0	70	2.13	3.13	4.08	4.88	5.26	5.18	4.65	4.17	3.77	3.03	2.41	468,235	460,776	4.1357
	18	16.0		0	20	2.27	3.33	3.85	4.65	5.00	5.00	4.88	4.55	3.92	3.17	1.87	468,034	460,585	4.1190
	20	16.3		0	55	2.45	3.45	4.17	4.65	5.00	5.00	4.76	4.08	3.77	2.86	1.56	462,557	455,180	4.0476
	23	14.9	Down	2	78	1.99	2.99	3.92	5.00	5.00	4.76	4.65	4.26	3.85	2.67	1.37	444,457	428,560	3.9153
	24	14.3	Up	1	75	1.99	2.99	3.57	4.35	4.65	4.44	4.17	3.85	3.45	2.60	1.23	402,744	400,800	3.7050
	25	13.9	Down	1	55	2.13	3.13	3.85	4.65	4.65	4.55	4.26	3.85	3.45	2.56	1.26	411,096	399,230	3.7201
	26	13.6	Up	2	77	1.96	2.86	3.51	4.35	4.55	4.55	4.08	3.70	3.39	2.67	1.37	393,482	396,500	3.7168
March	4	17.6		0	54	2.74	3.77	4.65	5.56	5.71	5.41	5.13	4.76	4.08	3.13	1.83	532,522	525,320	4.5582
	5	18.8	Down	3	47	3.08	4.08	5.26	6.06	6.06	6.06	5.56	5.00	4.35	3.70	2.40	596,249	568,860	4.8274
	9	18.3		0	67	2.99	4.08	4.76	5.88	5.56	5.56	5.13	4.55	3.92	2.86	1.56	540,907	533,590	4.5701
	10	18.0	Up	1	64	2.64	3.64	4.65	5.56	5.71	5.56	5.26	4.55	3.85	2.99	1.69	531,331	529,410	4.5597
	11	18.0	Down	2	53	3.08	3.92	4.76	5.71	5.71	5.71	5.56	4.88	4.26	3.28	2.33	559,025	539,080	4.6430
	13	18.8		0	71	2.82	4.17	4.88	5.56	5.71	5.71	5.41	4.76	3.92	3.33	2.03	559,583	552,030	4.6846
	16	19.7	Up	3	58	2.62	3.92	4.65	5.41	6.06	6.06	5.41	4.76	4.17	3.39	2.19	573,530	583,800	4.8732
	18	20.3		0	84	2.94	4.00	5.00	5.56	6.45	6.06	6.25	5.18	4.35	3.57	2.56	614,970	606,660	5.0097
	22	29.1	Down	1	57	4.55	5.41	6.67	8.33	9.52	8.33	8.00	6.90	6.45	5.71	4.17	999,135	981,070	6.9017
	23	30.9	Down	1	50	5.00	6.25	7.41	9.09	9.09	8.70	8.00	7.41	6.90	5.88	4.35	1,078,375	1,058,880	7.3384
	24	32.2	Down	1	70	4.88	6.25	7.41	8.70	9.52	8.70	8.33	8.00	7.14	6.25	4.26	1,118,632	1,098,400	7.4640
	25	33.2		0	40	5.26	6. 6	7.14	8.70	9.09	9.09	8.33	7.69	6.90	6.06	3.92	1,116,148	1,105,990	7.4045
	26	34.0	Up	1	52	4.44	6.25	7.69	9.09	8.70	8.70	8.00	7.69	6.67	6.45	4.55	1,131,059	1,129,800	7.4749
	29	34.7	Down	2	41	5.00	6.90	7.69	8.70	8.70	8.70	8.00	7.69	7.14	5.88	4.08	1,134,772	1,104,900	7.2356
April	1	33.3	Down	4	53	4.88	6.67	8.33	8.70	8.70	8.70	8.00	7.69	6.25	5.00	4.08	1,105,646	1,058,670	7.0772
	2	32.0	Down	2	55	4.08	5.71	6.90	8.33	8.33	8.33	8.33	6.90	6.25	4.88	4.00	1,019,102	989,850	6.8929
	3	30.2	Up	3	51	4.08	5.71	6.45	7.69	8.00	7.69	7.41	7.14	5.71	4.44	3.17	930,715	946,780	6.6324
	5	26.0	Up	4	67	3.17	4.55	5.56	6.45	7.14	7.41	6.45	5.88	4.76	3.70	3.08	757,226	777,640	5.8742
	6	23.8	Down	3	71	2.99	4.35	5.41	6.45	7.41	7.41	6.90	6.25	4.88	3.77	2.67	740,550	709,660	5.5141
	7	21.9		0	62	2.60	3.77	4.44	5.56	6.25	6.90	6.67	5.56	4.17	3.03	2.44	631,619	623,070	5.0019
	9	19.8	Up	2	64	2.60	3.45	4.26	5.26	5.71	6.06	5.71	4.88	3.57	2.56	2.18	568,583	567,810	4.7744
	14	23.2	Down	3	64	3.17	4.26	5.26	6.45	7.14	7.14	6.67	5.88	4.65	3.45	2.90	711,846	682,150	5.3548
	15	25.5	Up	2	61	3.39	4.26	5.26	7.14	8.00	8.00	7.14	6.06	4.88	4.00	3.03	793,401	799,540	6.0380
	20	31.2	Up	4	60	4.17	5.41	6.90	8.33	8.70	8.33	8.00	7.41	6.06	4.76	3.57	1,005,145	1,030,770	7.1112
	21	32.8	Up	2	65	4.76	6.06	7.41	9.09	8.70	8.33	8.00	7.41	6.45	5.41	4.00	1,077,426	1,085,620	7.3116
	22	34.4	Up	4	60	4.08	6.06	7.14	8.70	9.09	8.33	8.00	7.41	6.67	5.26	3.77	1,092,308	1,120,160	7.3675
	24	36.7	Down	3	63	5.41	6.67	9.52	10.00	9.52	9.52	9.52	8.33	7.41	6.90	3.64	1,303,330	1,260,920	8.0238
	27	37.3	Up	1	63	4.65	6.67	8.33	9.52	9.09	9.09	8.33	7.69	7.41	6.90	3.85	1,237,964	1,236,600	7.8030
	30	36.1	Up	4	53	3.92	5.71	6.45	8.70	8.70	8.70	8.00	6.90	6.67	5.00	2.82	1,085,717	1,113,390	7.1455
May	1	34.9	Up	1	64	4.08	5.56	6.90	8.33	9.09	8.33	7.69	7.14	6.06	4.44	2.60	1,051,493	1,050,000	6.8545
	4	29.5	Up	4	49	3.03	4.76	5.88	6.67	7.14	6.90	6.45	5.71	4.76	2.82	2.11	780,947	803,249	5.6888
	5	28.0		0	58	3.17	4.44	6.25	7.14	7.41	7.14	6.67	5.88	4.88	3.33	2.27	795,933	786,550	5.6907
	6	26.8	Down	3	33	3.51	4.55	6.06	6.90	8.00	7.69	7.41	5.88	5.13	3.57	2.47	812,684	778,682	5.7506
	7	26.3	Up	1	70	3.13	4.35	5.71	6.45	7.69	8.00	7.14	6.06	4.65	3.33	2.20	778,669	776,550	5.7873
	8	26.4	Up	2	47	3.28	4.55	5.41	7.14	7.69	7.41	6.90	5.88	5.00	3.39	2.22	781,208	786,570	5.8529
	11	29.4	Up	4	57	3.70	5.00	6.45	7.69	8.00	8.00	7.41	5.56	4.88	3.57	2.30	865,971	889,324	6.3082
	12	31.0	Up	1	65	3.85	5.41	6.45	8.00	8.70	8.70	7.69	6.67	5.56	4.17	2.57	956,912	955,320	6.6108
	13	31.6		0	61	4.17	5.71	6.45	7.69	8.33	8.70	8.00	7.41	5.88	4.44	2.35	980,090	970,080	6.6517
	14	32.2	Up	3	59	4.26	5.41	6.90	8.00	8.70	8.70	7.69	6.90	5.71	4.17	2.50	987,628	1,004,640	6.8271
	17	33.0	Up	3	49	4.35	6.06	7.41	8.00	8.33	8.00	7.41	6.90	5.71	4.08	2.56	993,758	1,010,900	6.8040
	18	33.0	Down	2	47	4.44	6.45	7.41	8.33	8.33	8.00	7.69	7.41	5.88	4.44	2.82	1,037,397	1,007,700	6.7665
	19	32.9	Up	2	62	4.00	5.88	7.14	8.00	8.33	8.33	7.69	6.90	5.88	4.17	2.63	997,229	1,005,000	6.7582
	21	32.7	Down	1	70	4.00	5.56	7.14	8.70	8.00	8.00	7.69	6.90	6.25	4.76	2.56	1,002,093	982,340	6.[illegible]
	25	34.2	Up	4	60	4.08	5.26	6.67	8.00	8.70	8.70	8.00	7.69	6.25	4.65	2.82	1,050,710	1,077,500	7.1081
	26	35.4	Up	1	73	4.35	5.71	7.41	8.33	9.09	9.52	8.33	7.69	6.67	4.65	2.78	1,115,206	1,114,000	7.2216
	27	35.9	Up	1	60	4.55	5.88	6.90	8.70	9.52	9.52	8.33	7.41	6.90	5.00	2.78	1,134,641	1,133,390	7.2949
	29	36.3	Up	2	69	4.00	5.88	6.90	8.70	9.52	9.52	8.70	7.41	6.90	4.65	2.00	1,131,358	1,139,880	7.2947
June	1	36.4	Down	2	69	5.00	6.45	8.00	9.09	9.09	8.70	8.33	7.69	7.14	5.71	2.86	1,174,191	1,143,300	7.3061
	2	36.4		0	29	4.44	6.06	7.14	9.52	9.52	9.09	8.33	7.41	7.14	4.55	2.67	1,162,591	1,150,720	7.3538

* The measurements in December, 1857, were made by party of Lieutenant H. L. Abbot, Corps Topographical Engineers.

O

Current-measurements at Columbus—Continued.

Date.		Gauge.	Wind.		No. of floats.	Velocity 5 feet below surface in divisions numbered— I.	II.	III.	IV.	V.	VI.	VII.	VIII.	IX.	X.	XI.	Discharge per second. Approx.	Corrected.	Mean velocity of river.
1858.		*Feet.*				*Feet.*	*Feet.*	*Feet.*	*Feet.*	*Feet.*	*Feet.*	*Feet.*	*Feet.*	*Feet.*	*Feet.*	*Feet.*	*Cubic feet.*	*Cubic feet.*	*Feet.*
June	3	36.6	Up	4	43	4.00	5.88	7.41	9.52	9.09	8.70	8.00	7.41	6.45	5.00	2.78	1,132,110	1,160,970	7.3980
	7	37.9	Up	2	61	4.35	5.88	7.41	9.52	9.52	9.09	8.70	8.00	7.14	5.26	2.56	1,199,833	1,206,170	7.5471
	8	38.1	Up	1	59	4.44	6.45	8.00	9.09	9.52	9.09	8.70	8.00	7.41	5.41	2.94	1,223,342	1,221,980	7.6251
	9	38.4	Up	3	52	4.17	6.67	7.69	9.09	10.00	9.52	8.70	7.69	6.90	5.00	2.78	1,221,109	1,241,220	7.6947
	12	39.1	Down	3	35	4.44	7.14	9.52	10.00	10.00	10.00	9.09	8.33	7.41	5.81	2.21	1,326,045	1,280,900	7.8825
	14	39.8	Down	2	69	4.88	6.67	7.69	9.52	10.53	10.00	9.52	8.33	8.00	6.90	3.77	1,348,733	1,318,300	8.0353
	15	40.1	Up	3	73	4.44	6.25	7.41	9.09	11.11	10.53	9.52	8.70	7.69	5.56	3.03	1,328,263	1,349,460	8.1915
	16	40.3	Up	2	71	4.88	6.90	8.33	10.00	10.53	10.53	9.52	8.70	7.69	6.67	2.70	1,377,465	1,387,840	8.4016
	17	40.5	Up	1	76	5.00	6.90	8.00	10.00	10.53	10.53	10.00	9.09	8.33	6.67	3.08	1,403,585	1,402,520	8.4678
	18	40.7	Up	1	80	4.76	6.90	8.33	10.53	10.53	10.53	10.00	9.09	7.69	6.45	2.63	1,404,325	1,403,400	8.4499
	19	40.7	Up	1	83	5.00	6.90	8.00	10.53	10.53	10.53	10.00	9.09	7.69	6.45	2.70	1,400,745	1,399,690	8.4278
	22	40.9	Up	1	42	5.00	6.90	8.70	10.53	10.53	10.00	9.09	8.33	7.69	6.25	3.33	1,384,124	1,383,080	8.3054
	25	40.2	Up	2	33	4.26	7.14	9.09	9.09	9.09	9.09	8.70	8.00	6.90	6.06	2.82	1,276,390	1,286,120	7.7966
	26	39.8	Up	2	69	4.55	7.41	9.52	9.09	8.70	8.70	8.70	7.69	6.67	5.41	2.47	1,249,058	1,258,540	7.6708
	28	38.0	Down	1	64	3.92	6.90	8.70	9.09	8.70	8.70	8.33	7.14	6.67	5.26	2.70	1,180,992	1,156,960	7.2292
	29	36.7	Down	2	76	4.55	6.25	8.70	9.09	8.00	8.33	8.00	7.14	6.25	4.55	2.86	1,119,500	1,090,010	6.9362
	30	35.0	Up	3	63	3.03	5.26	7.41	8.00	7.69	8.00	7.41	6.67	5.26	3.92	2.60	980,337	997,260	6.5024
July	1	33.3	Up	2	60	2.47	4.00	5.56	6.67	7.69	7.41	6.90	6.06	5.00	3.23	1.31	835,487	841,220	5.6236
	2	30.8	Up	3	62	2.02	3.64	4.88	6.45	6.90	6.45	5.88	5.26	4.17	3.92	1.23	727,386	740,420	5.1394
	3	28.8	Up	2	31	2.60	3.64	4.35	5.13	7.14	6.25	5.88	5.13	4.17	2.70	1.23	666,207	671,260	4.8063
	5	26.0	Down	2	55	2.38	3.64	5.71	6.45	6.45	5.71	5.26	4.65	3.77	2.70	1.23	641,671	618,740	4.6341
	6	24.8	Down	2	65	2.08	3.28	5.00	5.71	6.90	6.67	5.71	4.44	3.39	2.60	1.56	624,115	601,810	4.5978
	7	23.7	Up	3	57	1.96	3.33	3.85	4.88	6.45	6.45	5.41	4.35	3.03	2.25	1.05	557,883	568,500	4.4248
	8	22.9	Down	1	64	1.59	2.67	4.35	5.26	6.06	5.88	5.00	4.55	3.64	2.30	1.25	547,212	533,320	4.2074
	9	22.2	Up	2	66	1.63	2.56	3.57	4.65	5.71	5.56	5.00	4.26	2.90	2.22	0.99	495.975	499,730	3.9909
	12	20.6	Down	4	75	1.65	2.67	4.35	5.41	5.71	5.26	5.00	4.65	3.13	2.13	0.91	509,391	477,340	3.9207
	13	20.4	Up	3	70	1.72	2.67	3.64	4.26	5.26	5.00	4.55	3.92	3.08	2.17	0.94	455,733	464,400	3.8282
	14	20.4	Up	3	50	1.38	2.47	3.33	4.44	5.26	5.41	4.55	4.00	3.08	2.17	0.87	457,109	465,810	3.8308
	15	20.2	Up	2	74	1.68	2.56	3.33	4.26	5.56	5.26	4.55	4.08	2.74	2.25	1.11	456,631	460,130	3.8066
	16	19.9	Up	1	50	1.43	2.15	3.45	4.08	5.13	5.41	4.70	3.92	3.08	2.02	0.87	445,212	443,060	3.6869
	17	19.6	Up	1	50	1.26	2.22	3.13	3.85	5.26	5.13	4.35	3.92	2.82	2.15	0.95	426,583	424,530	3.5502
	19	19.9	Down	2	54	1.48	2.67	3.45	4.35	5.71	5.26	4.55	4.17	3.23	2.20	0.85	464,197	445,230	3.7082
	20	20.7	Up	2	53	1.50	2.56	3.51	4.55	6.25	6.06	5.13	4.35	3.17	2.20	1.12	488,974	492,720	4.0400
	21	22.3	Up	2	54	1.68	2.67	4.26	5.00	5.71	6.06	5.26	4.55	3.13	2.20	1.22	516,917	520,840	4.1525
	22	23.7	Up	2	50	1.79	3.28	4.88	6.25	6.90	6.25	5.56	4.55	3.45	2.44	1.10	591,867	596,350	4.6416
	24	24.8	Down	3	63	2.50	4.35	6.25	7.14	7.14	6.25	5.41	4.65	3.17	2.50	1.32	669,799	639,010	4.8821
	26	25.9	Up	1	58	2.47	3.51	5.00	6.45	7.41	6.67	6.06	5.13	3.64	2.70	1.50	666,721	664,900	4.9880
	27	26.2	Up	2	57	2.27	3.70	4.76	6.25	7.41	6.45	5.71	5.13	3.64	2.47	1.23	660,887	665,430	4.9673
	28	26.2	Up	2	64	2.22	3.70	4.88	6.45	7.14	6.25	5.88	5.13	3.70	2.33	1.17	659,770	664,310	4.9590
	29	25.9	Up	2	60	2.15	3.85	5.13	6.25	7.14	6.45	5.88	5.00	3.39	2.38	1.18	657,022	661,530	4.9628
	30	25.4	Up	2	59	2.08	3.39	4.44	5.56	6.90	6.45	5.41	4.65	3.33	2.38	1.05	608,965	613,580	4.6414
	31	24.3	Up	1	57	2.04	3.39	4.65	6.25	6.67	6.25	5.41	3.85	3.03	2.22	1.03	590,700	588,580	4.5346
August	2	22.4	Up	2	61	1.74	3.23	4.00	4.76	6.06	6.25	5.13	4.35	2.90	2.06	0.74	527,556	531,560	4.2208
	3	21.8	Up	2	58	1.59	2.78	4.00	5.13	5.71	5.56	5.00	4.26	3.17	2.11	0.92	509,873	513,730	4.1314
	4	21.2	Up	2	61	1.56	2.86	3.64	4.55	5.71	5.88	4.76	4.35	2.82	1.96	0.82	488,893	492,590	4.0033
	5	20.7	Up	2	61	1.43	2.50	3.70	4.88	5.88	5.13	4.55	4.08	2.99	2.02	1.04	476,225	479,830	3.9344
	6	20.5	Up	1	62	1.69	2.50	3.51	4.88	5.71	5.56	4.88	4.35	2.86	2.11	0.66	481,004	479,270	3.9437
	7	20.3	Down	1	58	1.41	2.90	3.77	4.65	6.06	5.56	4.88	4.35	3.08	2.15	0.99	492,610	480,110	3.9718
	9	20.9	Down	1	53	1.67	2.99	3.92	4.88	6.06	6.25	5.00	4.26	2.86	2.00	0.75	508,732	495,810	4.0508
	10	21.1		0	70	1.65	2.99	4.00	4.88	6.06	5.56	4.88	4.35	3.08	1.82	0.89	503,810	495,700	4.0458
	11	20.9	Up	1	55	1.57	2.56	3.85	5.00	5.88	5.88	4.76	4.17	2.94	2.15	0.97	497,008	495,220	4.1401
	12	20.7	Down	2	54	1.69	2.67	3.77	4.88	6.06	5.56	4.76	4.35	3.08	2.17	1.16	497,512	479,740	3.9335
	13	20.2	Down	2	51	1.57	2.60	3.70	4.35	5.71	6.25	4.88	4.26	3.13	2.04	1.16	487,985	468,060	3.8722
	14	19.8	Down	1	58	1.64	2.74	3.77	4.17	5.71	5.71	4.55	4.35	3.77	2.27	0.84	481,384	467,500	3.8955
	16	18.9	Down	2	66	1.61	2.60	3.85	4.76	5.26	4.88	4.55	4.08	3.08	1.79	0.95	450,846	432,430	3.6629
	17	18.6	Down	1	58	1.90	2.50	3.45	4.26	5.13	4.76	4.35	4.00	2.78	1.50	0.81	422,724	410,530	3.7467
	18	18.3	Up	2	55	1.35	2.38	3.28	3.85	4.44	4.55	4.26	3.70	2.47	1.45	0.77	388,515	391,310	3.3515
	19	17.9	Down	2	55	1.23	2.13	3.64	4.44	5.26	4.76	4.26	3.77	3.08	1.46	0.78	417,919	385,380	3.3254
	20	17.5	Up	1	55	1.50	2.13	3.23	3.77	4.44	4.44	4.17	3.77	2.86	1.82	0.79	385,122	383,260	3.3316
	21	16.9	Up	2	73	1.38	2.20	2.94	3.85	4.55	4.26	4.08	3.70	2.38	1.42	0.50	366,180	368,990	3.2814
	23	15.9	Down	2	58	1.46	2.25	3.08	3.85	4.65	5.00	4.08	3.51	2.82	1.57	0.90	379,047	363,560	3.2605
	24	15.3	Down	2	58	1.13	1.90	2.53	3.64	4.35	4.65	4.00	3.51	2.86	2.00	0.67	354,122	339,670	3.0790
	25	14.7	Down	2	62	1.14	1.87	2.94	3.85	4.35	4.17	3.85	3.33	2.82	1.83	0.76	346,796	332,620	3.0505
	26	13.9	Up	4	25	0.83	1.55	2.47	3.08	3.45	3.55	3.45	3.15	2.55	1.55	0.55	290,478	300,220	2.7975
	27	13.7	Up	3	65	1.30	1.80	2.33	2.60	3.45	3.70	3.39	3.13	2.56	1.67	0.83	287,873	294,380	2.7540
	30	13.0	Down	2	58	1.18	1.77	2.38	2.82	3.33	3.45	3.39	3.17	2.70	1.44	0.67	282,182	267,700	2.5460
September	2	12.7	Up	3	72	1.07	1.54	2.33	2.82	3.28	3.39	3.23	3.17	2.50	1.56	0.68	273,277	279,740	2.6703
	4	11.9	Up	2	60	0.99	1.42	1.96	2.67	2.99	3.28	3.17	2.99	2.60	1.56	0.83	255,282	257,110	2.4948
	6	10.9	Up	2	54	1.10	1.43	2.08	2.47	3.03	3.39	3.03	2.74	1.77	0.78	0.51	233,892	235,030	2.3282
	7	10.4	Up	2	58	1.14	1.41	2.02	2.60	2.74	2.82	2.94	2.70	2.25	1.07	0.45	226,681	228,260	2.2851
	8	9.9	Up	3	56	1.01	1.47	2.00	2.47	2.60	2.86	2.82	2.56	2.02	0.98	0.54	216,530	220,980	2.2396
	9	9.5	Up	3	55	0.73	1.25	2.04	2.47	2.74	2.82	2.82	2.63	1.94	1.02	0.48	214,418	219,830	2.2384
	10	9.2		0	53	0.92	1.53	1.94	2.60	3.17	3.13	2.90	2.74	2.00	1.26	0.36	228,546	222,400	2.2845
	11	9.0	Down	2	50	1.03	1.25	2.06	2.35	2.99	2.99	2.99	2.70	2.33	1.20	0.34	222,996	211,550	2.1826
	13	9.1	Down	2	64	0.87	1.33	1.96	2.35	2.78	3.28	2.82	2.50	2.17	1.21	0.39	218,586	210,590	2.1680
	14	10.4	Down	2	66	1.02	1.31	2.06	2.74	3.39	3.51	3.39	3.08	2.63	1.61	0.71	260,762	247,380	2.4766
	15	11.4	Up	2	61	0.95	1.38	2.06	2.70	3.28	3.28	3.13	2.94	2.41	1.44	0.75	254,105	255,930	2.5138
	16	11.5		0	44	1.05	1.31	2.50	3.23	3.39	3.51	3.28	3.13	2.43	1.38	0.20	271,741	266,230	2.6045
	17	11.5	Down	2	57	0.97	1.53	2.33	2.99	3.57	3.57	3.33	3.08	2.33	1.18	0.34	269,396	255,570	2.5002
	18	11.2	Up	1	54	0.99	1.48	2.38	2.90	3.17	3.45	3.13	2.94	2.20	1.20	0.26	255,804	253,730	2.4970
	20	10.7	Up	1	56	0.87	1.44	2.41	2.78	3.17	3.51	3.13	2.86	2.15	1.03	0.59	251,294	249,240	2.4793
	21	10.3	Down	1	65	1.01	1.42	2.11	2.60	3.08	3.39	3.23	2.90	2.33	1.55	0.58	247,388	238,150	2.3892
	22	9.9	Down	3	62	1.04	1.50	2.30	2.70	3.17	3.33	3.33	2.99	2.22	1.10	0.58	249,806	233,140	2.3628
	23	9.4	Up	2	58	1.12	1.41	2.00	2.38	2.86	3.03	2.99	2.60	2.04	1.08	0.49	221,005	222,590	2.2766
	24	8.8	Up	3	64	0.94	1.42	1.89	2.44	2.70	2.86	2.82	2.50	2.00	0.80	0.52	209,387	214,190	2.2194
	27	7.3	Up	3	57	0.72	1.05	1.68	2.20	2.47	2.50	2.53	2.33	1.80	0.73	0.39	180,616	184,740	1.9790
	29	6.8	Up	3	56	0.78	1.16	1.59	2.17	2.47	2.56	2.38	2.30	1.75	0.77	0.35	177,001	181,060	1.9615
	30	6.5	Up	3	54	0.83	1.18	1.77	2.02	2.20	2.41	2.33	2.13	1.71	0.92	0.42	170,174	174,070	1.8987
October	1	6.3	Down	2	53	0.79	1.23	1.85	2.22	2.50	2.70	2.60	2.50	2.00	0.92	0.51	188,556	176,840	1.9377
	2	6.1	Up	2	53	0.72	1.01	1.56	1.92	2.22	2.41	2.27	2.11	1.55	0.76	0.33	160,940	161,780	1.7808
	4	5.7	Up	3	63	0.61	1.09	1.63	2.13	2.22	2.13	2.27	2.04	1.40	0.51	0.10	155,790	159,360	1.7705

Current-measurements at Columbus—Continued.

Date.	Gauge.	Wind.	No. of floats.	Velocity 5 feet below surface in divisions numbered—											Discharge per second.		Mean velocity of river.
				I.	II.	III.	IV.	V.	VI.	VII.	VIII.	IX.	X.	XI.	Approx.	Corrected.	
1858.	*Feet.*			*Feet.*	*Feet.*	*Feet.*	*Feet.*	*Feet.*	*Feet.*	*Feet.*	*Feet.*	*Feet.*	*Feet.*	*Feet.*	*Cubic feet.*	*Cubic feet.*	*Feet.*
October 6	5.3	Up 2	55	0.63	1.05	1.46	1.74	2.00	2.08	2.17	1.94	1.48	0.77	0.39	148,302	149,070	1.6718
8	4.8	Up 2	59	0.59	0.99	1.53	1.83	2.08	2.04	2.04	1.89	1.41	0.91	0.46	145,679	146,430	1.6615
9	4.7	Down 1	58	0.83	1.07	1.53	1.94	2.17	2.33	2.17	1.87	1.49	0.86	0.56	152,997	145,930	1.6598
11	4.2	0	59	0.83	1.23	1.54	1.80	2.00	2.17	2.11	1.75	1.36	0.86	0.53	144,716	140,820	1.6209
12	4.0	Up 1	60	0.84	1.03	1.49	1.90	2.08	2.30	2.25	1.77	1.30	0.80	0.48	146,208	144,370	1.6697
13	3.9	Up 2	62	0.66	0.83	1.39	1.67	1.92	2.00	1.92	1.80	1.43	0.89	0.38	133,788	134,470	1.5591
14	3.8	Down 1	57	0.85	1.08	1.41	1.92	2.04	2.11	2.11	1.96	1.35	0.76	0.57	143,351	136,740	1.5892
15	3.6	Up 2	59	0.69	0.94	1.38	1.61	1.83	2.06	2.13	1.94	1.18	0.54	0.33	131,959	132,630	1.5490
16	3.5	Up 3	44	0.78	1.03	1.31	1.60	1.74	1.82	1.82	1.67	1.43	0.71	0.10	125,712	128,670	1.5063
18	3.3	Up 3	46	0.65	0.91	1.33	1.56	1.72	1.85	1.90	1.90	1.49	0.67	0.36	127,017	130,000	1.5614
19	3.2	Down 2	25	0.82	1.11	1.52	2.00	2.08	2.13	2.12	1.91	1.38	0.66	0.10	142,268	133,710	1.5769
20	3.1	Down 2	60	0.88	1.18	1.48	1.85	2.06	2.11	2.22	1.94	1.36	1.00	0.59	144,481	135,500	1.5991
21	3.1	Up 1	50	0.89	1.12	1.32	1.47	1.80	2.02	2.27	1.96	1.25	0.74	0.51	132,595	130,930	1.5448
22	3.2	Down 2	47	0.90	1.14	1.49	1.96	1.98	2.06	2.17	1.85	1.44	0.89	0.52	143,149	134,250	1.5833
23	3.2	Down 2	58	0.86	1.17	1.42	1.83	2.00	2.11	2.15	1.98	1.31	0.81	0.51	141,232	132,460	1.5618
25	3.4	Up 2	49	0.81	1.06	1.41	1.55	1.85	2.02	2.00	1.94	1.22	0.58	0.36	131,586	132,260	1.5522
26	3.5	Up 2	41	0.80	1.02	1.35	1.79	1.83	2.11	2.06	1.87	1.11	0.74	0.35	133,914	134,600	1.5759
28	3.7	Up 2	50	0.73	1.05	1.41	1.68	1.87	1.96	2.15	2.13	1.67	0.63	0.38	139,618	140,330	1.6350
29	3.9	Up 2	58	0.65	1.08	1.45	1.82	1.90	2.04	2.04	1.96	1.33	0.72	0.31	138,817	139,530	1.6177
30	3.9	Up 2	54	0.74	1.06	1.54	1.83	2.04	2.11	2.13	2.00	1.25	0.70	0.43	142,975	143,710	1.6662
November 3	8.0	Down 2	51	0.78	1.29	2.13	2.70	3.17	3.45	3.39	3.23	2.86	1.61	0.73	248,547	235,800	2.4869
4	9.3	Up 2	59	1.16	1.82	2.74	3.51	3.64	3.92	3.70	3.45	2.74	1.44	0.59	283,113	285,280	2.9240
5	11.8	Down 1	58	1.31	2.30	3.17	4.08	4.26	4.26	4.08	3.64	3.08	1.57	0.65	365,017	354,490	3.4467
8	16.0	Down 3	41	1.65	3.51	4.35	4.88	5.26	5.13	5.00	4.44	3.70	2.11	1.02	466,081	441,990	3.9527
9	15.9	0	59	1.01	2.06	3.17	4.88	5.13	5.00	5.00	4.55	3.77	2.63	1.43	440,773	433,760	3.8891
10	15.6	Up 2	53	1.29	2.11	3.13	4.08	4.65	5.00	4.76	4.35	3.77	2.74	1.33	417,041	420,230	3.7873
11	15.4	Down 2	58	1.65	2.67	4.26	4.55	4.88	4.88	4.76	4.17	3.45	3.25	1.26	435,147	417,370	3.7758
12	15.0	Up 2	60	1.60	2.50	3.45	4.08	4.55	4.44	4.55	3.90	3.51	2.04	1.14	396,825	399,860	3.6457
16	13.0	Down 2	54	2.28	3.13	3.51	4.08	4.26	4.17	4.00	3.64	3.39	2.13	1.05	373,506	358,250	3.3993

No. 4.—CURRENT-MEASUREMENTS AT NATCHEZ, BY PARTY OF LIEUTENANT H. S. PUTNAM.

Date.	Gauge	Wind.	No. of floats.	Velocity 5 feet below surface in divisions numbered—																						Discharge per sec.		Mean velocity of river.
				I.	II.	III.	IV.	V.	VI.	VII.	VIII.	IX.	X.	XI.	XII.	XIII.	XIV.	XV.	XVI.	XVII.	XVIII.	XIX.	XX.	XXI.	XXII	Approx.	Corrected.	
1858.	*Feet.*			*Feet*	*Feet*	*Feet*	*Feet*	*Feet*	*Feet*	*Feet*	*Feet*	*Feet*	*Feet*	*Feet*	*Feet*	*Feet*	*Feet*	*Feet*	*Feet*	*Feet*	*Feet*	*Feet*	*Feet*	*Feet*	*Feet*	*Cu. feet.*	*Cu. feet.*	*Feet.*
Jan. 8	42.6	0	13	0	3.77	5.56	5.56	6.06	5.13	4.76	4.55	4.55	4.55	4.55	4.44	4.35	4.35	4.35	4.26	4.08	4.00	3.77	3.51	3.17	1.80	858,573	844,800	4.7892
9	42.2	Up 3	33	0	2.82	3.70	5.56	6.25	6.25	5.13	4.44	4.44	4.44	4.44	4.26	4.17	4.17	4.17	4.17	4.26	4.00	3.77	3.51	3.17	1.80	823,825	836,360	4.7103
11	42.1	Down 2	61	0	3.39	4.76	5.71	6.25	5.71	5.13	4.76	4.55	4.55	4.44	4.35	4.26	4.17	4.17	4.00	4.00	3.92	3.92	3.92	3.85	2.04	856,358	825,990	4.6631
12	42.2	Up 3	53	0	2.86	3.92	5.71	6.06	5.71	5.13	4.55	4.55	4.44	4.44	4.44	4.35	4.26	4.35	4.17	4.17	4.08	3.85	3.70	3.33	1.85	827,200	839,790	4.7296
13	42.9	Down 2	78	0	4.00	5.88	6.25	6.06	5.71	5.26	4.76	4.65	4.55	4.55	4.26	4.35	4.55	4.44	4.44	4.44	4.17	4.00	3.92	4.08	3.17	913,592	879,170	4.8805
18	45.3	Down 2	47	0	3.57	5.13	6.06	6.45	5.56	5.41	5.00	4.76	4.65	4.55	4.44	4.44	4.44	4.55	4.55	4.08	4.08	4.08	4.08	4.08	2.22	948,776	915,130	4.7956
20	45.1	Down 2	90	0	4.26	4.55	6.06	6.25	5.71	5.26	4.88	4.65	4.55	4.65	4.65	4.44	4.44	4.44	4.44	4.35	4.17	3.92	3.77	3.28	1.60	933,922	900,790	4.7417
21	45.0	Down 1	82	0	2.78	5.13	5.88	6.25	5.26	5.00	4.88	4.65	4.44	4.55	4.55	4.44	4.35	4.65	5.00	4.65	4.08	3.85	3.45	3.23	1.54	912,143	888,670	4.6885
22	44.8	0	100	0	3.23	4.65	5.56	6.06	5.56	5.00	4.65	4.55	4.44	4.44	4.44	4.41	4.44	4.44	4.35	4.26	4.26	4.00	3.70	3.28	1.59	891,323	877,130	4.7237
23	44.6	Up 4	52	0	2.67	3.70	5.00	6.06	5.26	5.00	4.55	4.55	4.44	4.35	4.35	4.35	4.35	4.35	4.35	4.35	4.26	4.17	3.85	3.33	1.85	846,644	868,670	4.6247
28	44.3	Down 3	107	0	4.44	5.00	5.71	6.45	5.56	5.13	4.65	4.55	4.55	4.65	4.65	4.55	4.88	4.65	4.17	4.26	4.08	4.00	3.23	2.35	1.08	916,463	875,230	4.6917
29	44.3	Down 2	83	0	4.65	5.41	6.06	5.71	5.13	5.00	4.65	4.65	4.65	4.65	4.65	4.55	4.35	4.35	4.35	4.26	4.08	3.92	3.92	3.51	2.25	902,963	870,940	4.6687
30	44.3	Up 3	100	0	2.06	4.65	5.56	5.71	5.41	5.00	4.65	4.65	4.65	4.65	4.44	4.35	4.35	4.44	4.00	4.08	4.00	4.00	3.77	3.70	2.47	860,904	874,000	4.6852
Feb. 1	44.6	Up 2	32	0	4.55	4.88	6.06	5.56	4.88	4.76	4.55	4.44	4.35	4.44	4.55	4.55	4.44	4.17	4.26	4.35	4.17	4.17	3.70	3.33	1.85	891,309	895,450	4.7673
4	44.6	Down 1	11	0	3.85	5.13	5.88	5.71	5.00	5.13	4.88	4.65	4.35	4.44	4.55	4.55	4.44	4.17	4.26	4.35	4.35	4.26	3.70	3.33	1.85	903,902	880,650	4.6885
5	44.5	Down 1	100	0	4.08	5.00	5.56	5.71	5.26	4.76	4.65	4.35	4.44	4.55	4.44	4.35	4.44	4.44	4.35	4.08	3.92	3.92	3.85	3.57	2.74	886,820	864,000	4.6104
6	44.1	0	100	0	3.17	4.35	5.71	5.71	5.41	4.76	4.35	4.35	4.55	4.44	4.44	4.44	4.35	4.26	4.35	4.08	4.17	3.85	3.45	3.33	1.63	855,085	841,560	4.6047
8	43.4	Up 1	98	0	3.33	4.65	5.71	5.41	4.88	4.44	4.35	4.35	4.35	4.35	4.35	4.35	4.35	4.35	4.17	4.08	4.17	4.08	3.85	3.51	1.57	830,940	826,210	4.5224
9	43.0	Up 3	91	0	3.13	4.26	5.41	5.71	4.88	4.26	4.17	4.35	4.35	4.35	4.26	3.92	4.00	4.08	4.08	3.92	3.92	3.77	3.39	3.13	1.79	797,313	809,440	4.4724
10	42.6	Down 3	99	0	3.51	5.00	5.41	5.56	5.00	4.65	4.44	4.55	4.55	4.55	4.55	4.44	4.55	4.55	4.44	4.26	4.26	4.17	3.92	3.77	1.83	840,589	802,750	4.4779
11	42.3	Down 1	95	0	3.51	5.00	5.56	5.26	4.55	4.55	4.26	4.35	4.44	4.26	4.26	4.17	4.35	4.17	4.26	4.08	4.08	3.85	3.85	3.17	2.13	814,333	793,380	4.4575
13	42.3	0	87	0	3.33	5.13	5.00	5.41	4.55	4.17	4.17	4.44	4.55	4.44	4.35	4.35	4.55	4.35	4.44	4.44	4.35	3.85	4.00	3.70	2.99	807,650	794,880	4.5377
16	41.6	Up 3	100	0	2.99	4.35	5.13	5.26	4.65	4.17	4.08	4.26	4.26	4.26	4.35	4.35	4.35	4.35	4.26	4.00	4.08	3.70	3.39	2.63	1.41	759,537	771,090	4.4064
17	41.4	0	100	0	3.70	4.44	5.26	5.26	4.76	4.55	4.44	4.35	4.35	4.35	4.35	4.26	4.26	4.26	4.17	3.85	3.77	3.51	3.17	2.90	1.50	775,751	763,490	4.4549
18	41.0	Up 4	76	0	3.08	4.17	5.13	5.13	4.44	4.17	3.92	4.35	4.26	4.35	4.35	4.08	4.08	3.85	4.08	3.92	4.08	3.57	3.33	2.94	2.15	734,750	753,860	4.3721
19	40.8	Down 2	100	0	5.00	4.65	5.26	5.41	4.76	4.35	4.35	4.44	4.35	4.35	4.17	4.17	4.26	4.17	4.17	4.08	3.85	3.77	3.03	2.82	1.75	781,411	753,690	4.3929
20	40.3	Up 3	98	0	3.45	4.26	4.65	5.13	4.55	4.44	4.35	4.35	4.35	4.26	4.17	4.17	4.17	4.17	4.17	4.00	4.00	3.70	3.45	3.13	1.79	729,466	740,560	4.3712
Mean	....	....	....	0	3.53	4.72	5.57	5.77	5.17	4.79	4.52	4.49	4.46	4.46	4.41	4.34	4.36	4.32	4.29	4.18	4.09	3.90	3.64	3.32	1.93			4.6122

No. 5.—CURRENT-MEASUREMENTS AT VICKSBURG, BY PARTY* OF MR. H. A. PATTISON.

Date.	Gauge.	Wind.	No. of floats.	Velocity 5 feet below surface in divisions numbered—													Discharge per second.		Mean velocity of river.
				I.	II.	III.	IV.	V.	VI.	VII.	VIII.	IX.	X.	XI.	XII.	XIII.	Approx.	Corrected.	
1858.	Feet.			Feet.	Feet.	Feet.	Feet.	Feet.	Feet.	Feet.	Feet.	Feet.	Feet.	Feet.	Feet.	Feet.	Cubic feet.	Cubic feet.	Feet.
February 24	32.6	0	21	3.39	4.88	5.26	5.26	5.71	6.06	6.06	6.06	6.06	6.25	5.88	4.26	2.56	744,071	734,330	5.3796
25	32.5	0	69	3.03	4.65	5.03	5.41	5.56	5.88	6.06	6.06	6.06	6.45	6.06	4.26	2.74	741,502	731,300	5.3711
26	32.2	0	78	3.17	4.65	5.26	5.41	5.56	5.71	5.88	6.06	6.25	6.45	6.25	4.26	2.26	739,572	729,880	5.3871
27	32.0	Up 3	82	3.17	4.55	4.88	5.56	5.56	5.71	5.71	5.88	6.06	6.45	5.71	3.57	1.57	706,151	716,860	5.3107
March 4	29.5	Up 1	55	3.45	4.44	4.88	4.88	5.26	5.41	5.88	6.06	6.25	6.25	5.88	5.00	3.00	695,770	693,080	5.3875
5	29.2	Up 1	94	3.51	4.65	4.76	5.00	5.56	5.71	6.06	6.06	6.36	6.40	6.20	3.50	2.40	685,843	683,200	5.3422
6	29.1	Up 4	58	3.70	4.55	4.55	5.00	5.13	5.41	5.71	6.06	6.25	6.25	5.13	3.77	1.77	654,230	670,550	5.2538
8	29.7	*Down 1	77	3.77	4.88	5.00	5.26	5.88	5.88	6.25	6.06	6.06	6.67	6.45	4.76	2.76	729,262	713,090	5.5213
9	30.2	Up 3	100	3.85	4.65	4.76	5.13	5.41	5.71	6.25	6.06	6.25	6.67	6.25	4.26	2.26	715,456	726,300	5.5690
10	30.9	Up 3	90	3.39	4.76	5.00	5.26	5.57	5.88	5.88	6.06	6.45	6.67	6.25	4.65	3.00	737,012	748,200	5.6598
11	31.5	Up 2	93	3.64	4.76	5.13	5.57	5.57	6.06	6.45	6.25	6.67	6.45	6.06	4.88	2.70	759,398	763,610	5.7108
12	32.0	Down 2	96	3.93	5.13	5.41	5.71	5.88	6.06	6.45	6.25	6.90	7.14	6.45	5.00	3.00	801,707	776,810	5.7548
13	32.5	Up 3	78	3.39	5.13	5.57	5.41	5.88	6.06	6.25	6.45	6.45	6.45	5.88	4.88	2.88	775,732	787,500	5.7799
15	33.6	Up 3	75	3.92	5.13	5.71	5.71	5.88	6.25	6.25	6.45	6.25	6.67	5.88	4.38	2.38	796,311	808,400	5.8138
17	34.0	0	94	4.35	5.56	5.88	5.88	6.25	5.88	6.25	6.67	6.90	7.14	6.67	5.41	2.90	853,157	844,190	6.0209
18	34.2	Up 2	76	3.92	5.41	5.56	5.56	6.25	6.25	6.45	6.45	6.67	6.90	6.45	5.41	3.41	843,115	849,070	6.0395
19	34.3	Up 4	78	3.92	5.26	5.88	5.71	5.88	6.06	6.25	6.45	6.67	6.45	6.25	5.00	2.47	819,134	839,780	5.9626
20	34.5	0	74	3.70	5.71	5.88	5.88	6.06	6.45	6.67	6.67	7.14	7.41	6.45	4.88	2.41	850,502	841,570	5.9537
23	37.0	0	79	4.44	5.71	6.25	6.25	6.67	6.67	6.90	7.41	7.41	7.41	6.90	5.56	3.28	957,510	947,460	6.4120
24	37.9	0	74	4.00	6.06	6.25	6.45	6.67	6.67	6.90	7.41	7.41	7.41	7.14	5.26	2.76	971,059	960,860	6.4027
25	38.9	Up 1	80	4.88	6.06	6.45	6.45	6.67	6.67	7.41	7.14	7.14	7.41	6.90	5.26	2.76	989,566	990,090	6.4870
26	39.9	Up 1	80	3.92	6.25	6.45	6.67	6.90	6.90	7.14	7.41	7.41	7.41	7.14	5.41	2.70	1,019,233	1,017,480	6.5535
27	40.8	Up 1	78	4.65	6.25	6.90	6.67	6.67	6.90	6.67	7.41	7.41	7.69	7.14	5.71	2.94	1,043,946	1,042,100	6.6125
29	42.4	Down 1	76	4.88	6.45	6.90	6.90	6.90	6.90	7.41	7.69	8.00	7.69	7.30	6.25	2.86	1,114,480	1,090,800	6.7438
30	43.0	0	70	4.76	6.67	6.67	6.67	7.14	7.41	7.41	7.69	7.69	8.00	6.90	5.88	3.38	1,121,178	1,109,430	6.7940
31	43.8	Down 1	54	4.17	6.45	7.41	6.90	7.14	7.14	7.14	7.41	7.41	7.69	7.69	6.29	3.79	1,143,208	1,121,500	6.7799
April 1	44.4	0	81	4.08	5.26	7.41	7.14	7.14	7.41	7.41	7.69	7.69	8.00	7.41	5.56	3.06	1,140,800	1,128,800	6.7593
2	44.9	Down 1	90	4.00	7.14	7.14	7.14	7.14	7.41	7.41	7.41	7.69	7.41	7.14	5.88	3.08	1,152,549	1,130,700	6.7167
3	45.4	Up 2	80	4.65	6.67	6.67	6.90	7.14	7.14	7.14	7.69	7.41	7.41	7.14	5.26	2.56	1,130,973	1,139,000	6.7133
5	45.8	Down 2	120	4.08	6.67	7.14	7.14	7.14	7.14	7.41	7.69	8.00	8.00	6.67	6.25	3.08	1,176,748	1,144,300	6.7024
6	45.9	0	98	4.65	6.25	7.14	6.90	7.14	7.41	7.14	7.69	7.69	7.41	7.14	5.74	3.24	1,161,021	1,148,800	6.7185
7	46.2	Up 4	86	4.00	6.45	6.67	6.67	6.67	6.67	7.41	7.41	7.69	7.69	6.45	5.05	2.55	1,114,355	1,139,800	6.6353
8	46.3	Up 2	47	4.76	6.06	6.45	6.45	6.67	7.14	7.14	7.14	7.14	7.69	7.14	5.74	3.24	1,132,907	1,140,900	6.6247
9	46.4	0	89	4.00	6.67	6.67	6.45	6.67	6.90	7.14	7.14	7.41	7.69	7.69	6.06	3.33	1,154,942	1,142,800	6.6326
10	46.5	0	100	4.35	6.45	6.67	6.67	6.90	6.90	7.14	7.14	7.41	7.69	7.41	6.06	2.53	1,151,209	1,139,100	6.6007
12	46.6	Up 3	44	4.08	5.88	6.90	6.67	6.90	6.90	6.90	7.41	7.69	7.41	6.90	5.26	3.92	1,134,275	1,152,450	6.6677
13	46.5	Up 3	69	3.64	6.45	6.90	6.90	6.90	6.90	7.14	7.69	7.41	7.41	6.67	5.56	3.06	1,135,751	1,154,000	6.6867
14	46.3	0	87	3.45	6.06	6.67	6.67	6.67	6.90	7.41	7.69	8.00	8.33	6.25	7.41	2.27	1,166,374	1,154,100	6.7083
15	46.1	0	95	4.08	6.25	6.67	6.90	6.90	7.41	7.14	7.41	8.00	8.00	7.14	5.56	3.17	1,158,988	1,146,800	6.6864
16	45.9	0	94	3.13	5.71	6.90	7.14	7.14	7.14	7.41	7.41	7.41	8.00	7.41	5.88	2.78	1,149,728	1,137,600	6.6532
17	45.7	0	90	3.45	5.71	6.90	6.67	6.90	6.90	7.14	7.41	7.69	7.69	7.69	6.06	2.74	1,140,758	1,128,800	6.6219
20	45.7	Up 3	111	3.77	5.41	6.25	6.25	6.45	6.90	7.14	7.69	7.41	7.69	7.14	4.76	2.27	1,085,995	1,103,400	6.4739
21	45.7	0	112	3.70	5.88	6.25	6.06	6.67	7.14	7.14	7.41	7.69	7.69	6.90	5.88	2.44	1,111,143	1,099,400	6.4499
22	45.8	0	103	3.77	6.25	6.25	6.67	6.67	6.90	7.14	7.14	8.00	7.69	7.14	5.41	3.13	1,122,754	1,110,900	6.5073
23	45.9	Down 4	64	3.70	6.90	6.67	6.90	6.90	7.41	7.69	7.41	8.00	8.00	7.14	5.88	3.33	1,174,387	1,123,100	6.5679
24	46.1	0	110	3.70	5.56	6.90	6.90	6.90	7.14	7.14	7.69	7.69	8.00	7.14	5.56	2.94	1,141,995	1,130,000	6.6085
26	46.3	Down 1	67	3.64	5.71	6.90	6.90	7.14	7.41	7.69	7.69	7.69	8.00	6.90	5.56	3.64	1,165,155	1,143,500	6.6439
27	46.4	Down 1	103	4.26	6.25	6.67	6.90	7.14	7.41	7.69	7.69	8.00	7.69	6.90	5.56	2.70	1,167,681	1,145,600	6.6483
28	46.5	0	92	4.26	6.25	6.67	6.90	7.14	7.14	7.41	7.69	8.00	7.69	6.67	5.41	2.44	1,152,872	1,140,800	6.6103
29	46.7	0	90	3.70	6.45	6.67	6.90	7.14.	7.14	7.41	7.41	8.00	7.69	6.67	5.41	2.82	1,152,911	1,140,800	6.5903
30	46.8	0	79	3.85	6.45	6.67	6.67	6.67	6.90	7.69	7.69	8.00	8.00	6.90	5.26	2.30	1,154,686	1,142,600	6.5909
May 1	46.9	0	79	5.13	6.67	6.90	6.67	7.14	7.14	7.41	7.69	8.33	8.00	7.14	4.44	2.35	1,172,257	1,159,900	6.6804
3	47.1	Down 2	73	5.26	6.25	6.45	6.90	7.14	7.41	7.69	7.41	8.00	8.00	7.14	5.71	2.94	1,195,171	1,162,450	6.6743
4	47.2	0	33	4.88	6.67	6.90	7.14	6.90	7.14	7.41	7.69	7.41	7.69	7.14	5.26	2.99	1,177,338	1,164,900	6.6784
5	47.2	0	110	4.08	6.25	6.90	7.14	7.14	7.14	7.41	7.69	8.00	8.33	7.14	4.76	2.82	1,179,644	1,167,200	6.6915
6	47.2	0	90	4.08	6.25	6.67	6.90	6.90	7.41	7.41	7.69	8.00	8.00	8.00	5.00	2.99	1,190,492	1,178,000	6.7531
7	47.3	0	70	3.92	6.45	6.67	6.90	6.90	7.14	7.41	7.69	8.00	8.00	7.41	5.41	3.08	1,186,530	1,174,000	6.7204
8	47.3	Up 1	92	4.65	6.45	6.90	6.90	6.90	7.14	7.41	7.69	8.00	7.69	6.90	5.56	3.13	1,183,246	1,181,150	6.7609
10	47.4	Up 4	38	4.08	6.06	6.67	6.90	6.90	7.69	7.14	7.41	8.00	7.69	7.14	5.26	2.86	1,170,291	1,199,800	6.8573
11	47.5	Up 1	85	4.35	6.06	6.45	7.14	6.90	7.14	7.41	7.69	8.00	8.33	7.41	6.25	3.17	1,210,959	1,208,800	6.8982
12	47.4	Down 1	35	4.55	6.25	6.45	6.67	7.14	7.69	8.00	7.69	8.69	8.33	7.14	5.56	3.57	1,223,445	1,200,250	6.8598
13	47.4	Up 2	93	4.26	6.25	6.45	6.90	7.14	7.14	7.41	7.69	8.33	8.00	7.14	5.88	3.57	1,202,176	1,210,650	6.9195
14	47.3	Up 2	70	4.44	6.25	6.67	6.90	7.14	7.41	7.69	7.69	8.00	8.00	7.14	5.71	2.47	1,195,350	1,203,800	6.8905
15	47.3	Up 2	92	4.55	6.25	6.90	6.45	7.41	7.41	7.41	7.69	8.33	8.33	7.14	5.71	3.17	1,209,118	1,217,650	6.9698
17	47.3	0	79	4.65	6.06	6.67	6.67	6.67	7.14	7.41	8.00	8.33	8.00	8.33	6.25	3.64	1,235,137	1,222,800	6.9996
18	47.4	0	74	5.26	6.25	6.45	6.67	7.14	7.14	7.41	8.00	8.33	8.33	7.41	6.45	4.00	1,236,296	1,224,000	6.9957
19	47.4	0	66	5.41	6.45	6.90	6.67	6.90	7.69	8.00	8.00	8.00	8.00	7.69	6.25	3.17	1,241,082	1,230,000	7.0301
20	47.4	0	71	4.55	6.45	6.67	6.90	7.69	7.69	7.41	7.41	8.33	8.33	7.69	6.06	3.70	1,239,714	1,224,600	7.0149
21	47.4	0	8	4.90	6.50	6.90	7.14	7.69	7.69	7.69	7.80	8.10	8.00	7.30	5.90	3.40	1,284,814	1,222,500	6.9872
22	47.4	Up 2	66	4.85	6.45	6.90	7.14	7.41	7.41	8.00	8.33	8.00	8.33	6.90	5.26	3.13	1,223,627	1,232,250	7.0429
24	47.5	Up 1	55	5.56	6.67	6.90	6.90	7.41	7.41	8.33	8.33	8.33	7.69	6.45	6.06	3.33	1,237,380	1,235,200	7.0488
25	47.5	Up 1	74	4.85	6.45	6.67	6.90	7.41	7.69	8.00	8.33	8.33	8.00	7.14	5.88	2.82	1,236,780	1,234,600	7.0454
26	47.5	0	71	4.55	6.45	6.90	7.14	7.14	7.41	7.69	8.33	8.33	8.33	6.90	6.25	3.33	1,239,557	1,227,200	7.0031
27	47.5	0	60	4.65	6.67	6.90	7.41	7.41	7.69	8.00	8.00	8.33	8.00	6.90	6.25	3.03	1,239,580	1,227,200	7.0033
28	47.6	Up 2	50	5.2	6.90	6.90	6.90	7.14	7.41	7.41	8.00	8.00	8.00	7.14	6.06	3.03	1,227,752	1,236,450	7.0454
29	47.6	Up 2	90	5.07	6.67	6.67	7.14	7.41	7.69	7.69	7.69	8.33	7.41	7.14	6.	2.74	1,224,006	1,232,700	7.0238

* Prior to March 28 these measurements were made by party of Lieutenant H. S. Putnam, Topographical Engineers and subsequently to November 5, by party of Mr. J. J. Conway.

Current-measurements at Vicksburg—Continued.

Date.	Gauge.	Wind.	No. of floats.	Velocity 5 feet below surface in divisions numbered—													Discharge per second.		Mean velocity of river.
				I.	II.	III.	IV.	V.	VI.	VII.	VIII.	IX.	X.	XI.	XII.	XIII.	Approx.	Corrected.	
1858	*Feet.*			*Feet.*	*Feet.*	*Feet.*	*Feet.*	*Feet.*	*Feet.*	*Feet.*	*Feet.*	*Feet.*	*Feet.*	*Feet.*	*Feet.*	*Feet.*	*Cubic feet.*	*Cubic feet.*	*Feet.*
June 1	47.6	Up 2	61	4.76	5.88	6.67	6.90	6.90	7.69	7.69	8.33	8.33	8.00	6.90	5.41	3.51	1,223,022	1,231,700	7.0182
2	47.6	Up 2	57	5.13	6.06	7.14	7.41	7.41	7.41	7.41	8.33	8.00	8.00	7.14	6.06	2.67	1,231,926	1,240,650	7.0692
3	47.6	Up 1	67	4.65	6.67	7.14	7.41	7.41	7.41	8.00	8.00	8.33	7.41	7.14	6.06	2.82	1,234,984	1,232,800	7.0246
4	47.7	Up 2	59	4.44	6.67	6.90	7.41	6.90	7.69	8.00	8.00	8.33	7.69	6.90	6.06	3.13	1,232,201	1,240,900	7.0598
5	47.7	Up 2	29	4.44	6.90	6.67	6.90	7.41	7.41	7.69	8.00	8.33	8.00	6.90	5.88	4.00	1,233,172	1,241,900	7.0653
7	47.8	Up 2	73	4.35	6.06	6.90	6.90	7.69	7.41	8.33	8.33	8.33	7.69	7.14	5.26	3.03	1,229,288	1,238,000	7.0329
8	47.8	Up 2	70	3.92	6.06	6.45	6.45	7.14	7.41	8.00	8.70	8.33	8.00	7.14	5.56	3.23	1,218,177	1,226,800	6.9692
9	47.9	Up 3	83	4.08	5.56	6.25	6.67	7.14	7.41	8.00	8.70	8.00	7.69	6.67	5.71	2.70	1,195,255	1,214,400	6.8885
10	47.9	Up 3	84	4.26	5.56	6.25	6.45	6.90	7.69	8.00	8.00	8.33	7.69	7.14	5.71	3.03	1,201,050	1,220,300	6.9219
12	48.1	Up 2	83	4.35	5.56	6.45	6.45	6.90	7.41	7.69	8.00	8.33	8.33	7.14	6.06	3.57	1,220,367	1,228,700	6.9497
14	48.1	0	86	4.00	5.56	6.45	6.90	7.41	7.69	8.00	8.33	8.70	8.00	6.90	5.71	3.51	1,230,544	1,215,500	6.8734
15	48.1	0	80	4.17	5.13	6.45	7.14	7.41	7.69	8.00	8.33	8.70	8.00	7.14	5.88	3.13	1,231,464	1,219,200	6.8945
16	48.1	Down 1	67	3.85	5.71	6.67	7.14	7.41	7.41	8.00	8.33	8.33	8.00	7.41	5.71	3.17	1,234,998	1,211,600	6.8511
17	48.1	Down 1	83	4.08	6.25	6.67	7.41	7.41	7.69	8.00	8.33	8.70	8.00	7.14	5.41	3.28	1,241,410	1,217,800	6.8867
18	48.1	0	80	4.26	6.25	6.45	6.90	7.41	7.41	8.33	8.33	8.70	7.69	7.14	5.26	3.51	1,234,427	1,222,100	6.9110
19	48.1	0	81	4.26	6.06	6.67	6.90	7.41	7.41	7.69	8.33	8.70	8.00	7.14	5.26	3.51	1,230,053	1,217,800	6.8866
21	48.0	Up 3	71	4.44	6.06	6.90	6.90	7.41	7.69	7.41	8.33	8.33	7.69	6.67	5.41	3.08	1,211,580	1,231,000	6.9708
22	48.2	Up 2	78	4.76	5.71	6.67	7.14	7.14	7.69	7.69	8.00	8.70	8.00	7.14	5.41	3.08	1,229,468	1,238,150	6.9909
23	48.2	0	74	5.41	6.45	6.90	7.14	7.69	7.69	8.00	8.00	8.00	7.69	7.14	5.71	3.03	1,246,039	1,233,600	6.9654
24	48.2	Up 2	80	4.55	5.88	6.67	7.14	7.41	8.00	8.00	8.33	8.33	8.00	6.67	5.71	2.82	1,235,758	1,244,500	7.0267
25	48.2	Up 2	18	4.90	6.50	6.90	7.14	7.41	7.41	7.69	7.80	8.00	7.90	7.41	5.50	3.06	1,233,065	1,241,800	7.0114
26	48.3	Up 1	96	5.00	6.25	6.67	7.14	7.14	7.41	7.69	8.00	8.33	7.69	7.14	5.88	3.13	1,233,139	1,230,900	6.9397
28	48.2	Up 2	58	5.71	6.67	6.90	6.90	6.90	7.14	7.41	7.69	8.00	8.00	6.67	5.00	3.17	1,200,956	1,209,450	6.8288
29	48.2	Up 1	64	5.26	6.06	6.67	6.90	6.67	6.90	7.41	7.69	8.33	7.69	7.14	6.06	3.08	1,209,161	1,207,050	6.8151
30	48.1	Up 4	33	4.46	6.06	6.25	6.67	6.45	7.41	7.14	8.00	8.00	8.00	7.10	4.76	2.26	1,177,656	1,206,300	6.8214
July 1	48.1	Up 1	96	4.76	5.88	6.25	6.45	6.67	6.90	7.41	8.00	8.33	8.33	7.41	6.06	3.28	1,218,110	1,215,950	6.8760
2	48.1	Up 2	70	4.76	6.06	6.45	6.45	6.90	6.90	7.69	8.00	8.33	8.33	6.90	5.88	3.13	1,210,866	1,219,450	6.8958
3	48.0	Up 2	67	4.88	6.06	6.25	6.45	6.45	6.90	7.14	7.69	8.00	8.33	8.00	6.25	3.03	1,210.338	1,218,900	6.9024
6	48.0	Up 2	93	5.26	5.88	5.88	6.25	6.67	6.90	7.14	7.69	7.69	8.00	8.00	6.45	3.39	1,203,599	1,212,100	6.8639
7	48.0	Down 1	72	5.26	5.88	6.45	6.67	6.90	7.14	7.41	7.69	8.33	8.33	8.00	6.06	3.51	1,235,074	1,211,600	6.8614
8	48.0	Down 1	49	5.00	5.71	6.06	6.67	6.90	7.14	7.41	7.69	8.00	8.33	8.33	6.67	4.26	1,244,104	1,220,400	6.9110
9	48.0	Up 1	81	5.13	5.71	6.45	6.67	6.67	7.14	7.41	7.69	7.69	8.00	7.69	6.90	3.39	1,226,353	1,224,200	6.9324
10	48.0	Up 2	89	5.00	5.88	6.25	6.45	6.67	6.90	7.14	7.69	7.69	8.00	8.00	6.67	4.08	1,217,333	1,225,900	6.9425
12	48.1	Down 1	70	4.76	5.88	6.25	6.45	6.90	7.14	7.69	7.69	8.00	8.00	8.33	6.67	4.17	1,243,582	1,220,000	6.8088
13	48.1	Down 2	81	5.26	6.06	6.25	6.45	7.14	7.14	7.41	7.69	8.33	8.33	7.69	6.90	4.26	1,252,452	1,218,200	6.8886
14	48.1	Down 1	71	4.65	5.88	6.45	6.67	7.14	7.14	7.69	8.00	8.00	8.33	7.69	6.67	3.77	1,245,078	1,222,250	6.9115
15	48.1	Down 1	63	4.65	6.25	6.45	6.45	6.90	7.41	7.69	8.00	7.69	8.00	8.00	6.45	4.35	1,243,776	1,220,200	6.8997
16	48.1	Down 1	74	4.55	6.06	6.45	6.45	6.90	7.14	7.14	7.69	8.33	8.00	8.00	6.90	4.55	1,244,292	1,220,700	6.9028
17	48.1	Up 1	65	5.00	6.06	6.06	6.67	6.90	7.14	7.69	7.69	7.69	8.00	8.00	6.25	4.44	1,231,313	1,229,100	6.9505
20	47.9	0	55	4.88	6.25	6.45	6.67	6.90	7.41	7.41	7.69	8.00	8.00	7.41	6.90	3.45	1,230,510	1,218,200	6.9104
21	47.8	Up 2	58	4.28	5.88	6.06	6.45	6.67	7.14	7.69	7.69	7.69	8.33	7.69	6.25	3.77	1,207,340	1,215,900	6.9072
22	47.7	Up 3	47	4.44	6.06	6.45	6.45	6.67	7.14	7.41	8.00	8.00	8.00	7.41	5.88	3.38	1,198,189	1,217,500	6.9265
23	47.6	Up 3	63	4.44	5.71	6.06	6.45	6.90	7.14	7.41	7.69.	7.69	7.69	7.69	6.06	4.17	1,191,061	1,210,200	6.8956
24	47.4	0	30	4.76	5.88	6.06	6.45	6.25	7.41	8.00	8.00	8.33	8.00	7.14	6.07	3.57	1,201,201	1,188,600	6.7933
26	47.0	Down 1	75	4.65	6.06	6.45	6.67	7.14	7.41	7.41	7.69	8.00	7.69	6.90	6.25	4.00	1,192,123	1,169,500	6.7250
27	46.9	Down 1	67	4.88	6.06	6.06	6.45	6.90	7.14	7.41	8.00	8.00	7.41	7.14	6.06	3.77	1,177,749	1,155,400	6.6540
28	46.8	Up 2	63	4.76	5.88	6.25	6.67	6.67	6.90	7.41	7.69	7.69	7.41	6.67	5.88	3.77	1,140,907	1,158,100	6.6799
29	46.7	Up 1	63	4.35	6.25	5.88	6.25	6.45	6.90	7.41	7.69	7.69	8.00	7.41	5.56	3.17	1,156,976	1,154,800	6.6712
30	46.5	Up 1	64	4.35	5.71	6.25	6.45	6.67	6.90	7.14	7.41	8.00	8.00	7.14	5.88	3.45	1,150,405	1,148,300	6.6542
31	46.4	Up 1	66	4.76	5.88	6.06	6.45	6.67	6.90	7.14	7.69	8.00	7.69	7.14	5.56	4.00	1,149,138	1,147,100	6.6574
August 2	46.0	Up 1	61	4.08	5.71	6.25	6.25	6.67	7.14	7.41	7.69	7.41	8.00	7.41	5.71	2.94	1,137,814	1,136,800	6.6324
3	45.8	Up 1	60	4.44	5.71	6.25	6.90	6.90	7.14	7.41	7.41	7.41	8.00	7.14	4.44	2.99	1,118,951	1,117,000	6.5425
4	45.6	Up 1	66	4.76	5.88	6.25	6.25	6.45	6.67	7.14	7.41	7.69	7.14	7.14	5.71	2.94	1,106,496	1,104,500	6.4897
6	44.9	0	80	4.55	5.71	6.06	6.25	6.45	6.67	6.90	7.41	7.69	7.69	7.14	5.71	3.33	1,097,934	1,086,400	6.4538
7	44.5	0	63	4.35	5.71	5.71	6.06	6.25	6.90	6.90	7.14	7.41	7.69	7.14	5.71	3.57	1,078,166	1,066,800	6.3778
9	43.5	0	65	4.17	5.71	5.88	5.88	6.25	6.45	6.45	6.90	6.90	7.41	7.14	6.06	3.39	1,037,280	1,026,400	6.2348
11	42.2	Up 3	81	3.77	5.26	5.41	5.41	6.25	6.25	6.67	6.90	6.90	7.14	6.90	5.26	3.23	977,168	992,730	6.1573
12	41.8	0	68	4.00	5.41	5.56	5.56	5.88	5.88	6.45	6.67	7.14	6.90	7.14	5.71	3.45	975,116	982,000	6.1302
13	41.2	Down 2	64	3.92	5.13	5.26	5.71	6.06	6.25	6.45	6.90	6.90	7.14	7.14	5.13	3.28	960,847	950,760	5.9935
16	39.7	0	33	4.65	5.26	5.71	5.71	5.71	5.71	6.25	6.45	6.67	7.41	6.90	5.71	3.17	934,919	909,310	5.8766
17	39.1	0	63	4.00	5.00	5.13	5.56	5.88	6.25	6.45	6.67	6.90	6.90	6.67	5.41	3.28	913,556	903,070	5.9014
18	38.6	0	79	3.85	5.13	5.41	5.56	5.88	6.06	6.45	6.45	6.90	6.67	6.67	5.13	2.94	893,796	882,090	5.8078
19	38.1	0	63	4.00	5.13	4.88	5.56	5.88	6.06	6.25	6.45	6.90	6.90	6.67	5.13	3.23	884,929	873,340	5.7998
20	37.1	0	68	4.26	4.76	5.41	5.41	5.88	6.06	6.06	6.45	6.90	6.90	6.45	5.41	3.41	871,567	860,150	5.8110
21	36.5	Down 2	49	4.26	4.65	5.26	5.13	5.71	5.71	6.06	6.25	6.90	7.41	6.25	5.00	3.00	845,146	832,150	5.6941
23	35.5	0	72	3.77	4.65	4.76	5.00	5.26	5.71	5.88	6.06	6.45	6.67	6.90	5.56	3.17	816,560	791,190	5.4979
24	34.5	0	44	4.08	4.88	5.13	5.13	5.26	5.88	6.06	6.25	6.25	6.45	5.88	4.65	2.65	778,638	768,400	5.4363
25	34.2	0	24	3.77	4.65	4.65	5.13	5.26	5.71	5.71	5.88	6.25	6.35	6.15	4.65	2.65	759,183	749,190	5.3291
26	33.4	0	46	3.57	4.08	4.44	4.55	5.26	5.71	5.71	5.71	6.06	6.25	6.45	4.08	2.08	723,520	714,060	5.1544
28	31.1	0	41	3.17	4.17	4.00	4.55	5.00	5.56	5.88	5.71	6.06	6.06	5.71	4.35	2.30	680,803	671,880	5.0439
31	27.6	Down 2	60	2.82	4.26	4.08	4.44	4.88	5.13	4.88	5.41	5.56	5.88	5.41	3.77	3.18	596,723	575,880	4.6448
September 1	26.5	Up 4	68	2.38	3.85	3.92	4.00	4.26	4.76	5.00	5.26	5.26	5.41	4.44	3.17	1.39	528,304	540,920	4.4659
2	26.5	0	46	2.30	4.08	4.00	4.44	4.88	4.65	5.56	5.56	5.13	5.26	4.88	3.23	1.63	543,119	533,830	4.4816
3	24.7	0	51	2.78	4.44	4.17	4.17	4.44	4.76	5.26	5.56	5.56	5.56	4.65	3.39	1.80	537,325	528,240	4.5297
4	23.9	Up 2	52	2.72	3.92	3.77	4.08	4.35	4.65	4.88	5.41	5.41	5.71	4.88	3.64	1.04	518,860	520,460	4.5408
6	23.0	Up 1	10	2.63	4.00	3.77	4.00	4.08	4.88	5.00	5.30	5.40	5.60	5.00	3.40	1.80	508,246	504,700	4.4914
9	21.8	Up 2	58	2.30	3.77	3.57	3.77	4.00	4.35	4.88	5.00	4.88	5.00	4.44	2.78	1.18	451,077	452,450	4.1351
10	21.3	Down 3	49	2.38	3.70	3.57	3.92	4.08	4.55	4.76	5.00	5.13	5.41	4.76	2.94	1.85	463,806	442,740	4.0926
11	20.6	Down 3	62	2.20	3.70	3.64	3.70	4.00	4.55	4.76	5.26	5.41	5.00	4.55	3.33	1.49	456,470	435,740	4.0942
13	19.3	Down 3	60	2.82	3.45	3.23	3.77	4.26	4.65	4.76	5.00	5.13	5.00	4.55	2.74	1.50	431,921	412,300	3.9938
14	18.7	Down 3	45	2.50	3.28	3.23	3.57	4.08	4.44	4.65	4.88	5.00	5.00	4.65	3.08	2.86	424,587	405,290	3.9831
15	18.1	0	47	2.17	3.13	3.08	3.57	3.64	4.44	4.55	4.65	5.13	4.55	4.35	2.56	1.40	395,782	387,890	3.8638
16	17.7	0	33	2.20	3.08	2.99	3.23	3.85	4.08	4.55	5.00	5.00	4.55	4.26	2.82	1.60	390,366.	382,130	3.8485
17	17.2	0	56	2.35	3.02	2.90	3.28	3.92	4.00	4.44	4.76	4.88	5.00	4.35	2.94	1.70	389,364	382,790	3.9032
18	16.9	0	53	2.11	3.08	3.03	3.23	3.85	4.26	4.44	4.55	5.13	4.88	4.08	3.23	2.00	387,867	381,310	3.9175
20	17.4	0	51	1.72	3.13	3.08	3.33	3.70	4.35	4.35	4.76	5.26	5.00	4.35	2.70	1.50	391,889	385,260	3.9089
21	17.9	0	45	2 11	3.17	3.03	3.33	3.70	4.35	4.55	4.88	5.13	5.00	4.35	3.03	1.80	403,665	395,930	3.9678
22	18.4	0	50	2.30	3.23	3.17	3.39	3.77	3.92	4.35	5.13	5.26	5.00	4.44	3.28	2.10	414,441	407,440	4.0337
23	18.5	0	61	2.56	3.28	3.13	3 45	3.92	4.35	4.65	4.88	5.26	5.26	4.35	3.17	2.00	421,378	414,250	4.0911
24	18.6	0	61	2.27	3.28	3.23	3 45	3.77	4.26	4.55	4.76	5.13	5.00	4.26	3.33	2.10	414,951	407,940	4.0190
25	18.5	0	61	2.44	3.45	3.23	3 [illegible]	3.77	4.35	4.44	4.55	4.76	4.88	4.35	2.67	1.50	400,503	393,740	3.8885

Current-measurements at Vicksburg—Continued.

Date.		Gauge.	Wind.	No. of floats.	Velocity 5 feet below surface in divisions numbered—													Discharge per second.		Mean velocity of river.
					I.	II.	III.	IV.	V.	VI.	VII.	VIII.	IX.	X.	XI.	XII.	XIII.	Approx.	Corrected.	
1858.		Feet.			Feet.	Feet.	Feet.	Feet.	Feet.	Feet.	Feet.	Feet.	Feet.	Feet.	Feet.	Feet.	Feet.	Cubic feet.	Cubic feet.	Feet.
September	27	18.0	0	59	2.33	3.03	3.23	3.51	3.92	4.08	4.26	4.55	5.00	5.00	4.17	2.82	1.60	393,761	385,460	3.8539
	30	16.6	Up 1	52	2.13	2.99	2.94	3.17	3.39	4.00	4.17	4.44	4.88	4.88	4.26	2.50	1.30	364,598	360,780	3.7348
October	1	16.1	Up 1	43	2.35	2.78	2.74	2.94	3.57	3.85	4.08	4.44	4.65	4.55	3.85	2.86	1.70	351,836	348,160	3.6503
	4	14.4	0	43	2.20	2.56	2.56	2.82	3.28	3.64	4.00	4.35	4.88	4.76	3.92	2.50	1.30	330,059	323,090	3.5420
	5	14.0	Up 1	58	1.85	2.56	2.63	2.78	3.23	3.70	3.92	4.17	4.76	4.55	4.00	2.67	1.50	323,988	320,590	3.5528
	6	13.7	Up 2	51	2.11	2.38	2.41	2.67	3.23	3.51	3.85	4.00	4.55	4.55	3.77	2.38	1.20	307,975	308,080	3.4422
	7	13.2	Up 3	60	2.08	2.50	2.53	2.78	3.08	3.51	3.77	4.00	4.44	4.35	3.17	2.35	1.20	293,846	297,200	3.3666
	8	12.9	0	54	2.08	2.50	2 47	2.78	3.08	3.70	4.00	4.26	4.44	4.35	3.70	2.22	0.40	296,559	290,300	3.3157
	9	12.5	Up 2	50	1.80	2.00	2.38	2.60	3.13	3.57	3.70	3.92	4.26	4.26	3.64	2.56	1.30	289,200	289,300	3.3414
	12	11.7	Up 2	44	2.06	2.22	2.15	2.53	3.17	3.51	3.51	3.64	3.92	4.08	3.51	2.27	1.10	269,886	269,980	3.1897
	13	11.4	0	37	2.11	2.47	2.27	2.70	3.23	3.57	3.85	4.17	4.35	3.77	3.13	2.13	1.00	272,063	266,320	3.1738
	14	11.1	Down 1	35	2.13	2.20	2.08	2.60	2.99	3.45	3.64	3.85	4.17	4.08	2.94	2.50	1.30	265,137	256,810	3.0871
	15	10.8	Down 2	39	2.00	2.04	2.00	2.38	3.08	3.39	3.64	3.85	4.00	4.08	3.64	3.10	1.90	274,736	263,330	3.1935
	16	10.5	0	24	1.70	1.06	1.82	2.33	2.86	3.39	3.64	3.64	4.08	4.10	3.70	2.50	1.30	262,179	256,060	3.1400
	25	8.7	0	47	1.57	1.63	1.53	1.92	2.44	3.28	3.45	3.45	4.00	4.17	3.64	2.44	1.20	238,358	233,320	3.0160
	26	8.6	0	51	1.63	1.64	1.52	2.13	2.50	3.08	3.45	3.57	4.08	4.08	3.45	2.82	1.60	240,890	235,810	3.0577
November	5	9.7	0	10	1.80	2.00	1.90	2.27	2.80	3.20	3.50	3.80	4.00	4.00	3.40	2.30	1.10	248,318	243,080	3.0464
	6	11.2	0	11	2.00	2.22	2.11	2.50	3.33	4.00	4.00	4.00	4.20	4.20	3.60	2.50	1.30	283,729	277,740	3.3291
	8	15.3	0	28	2.00	3.17	2.56	3.28	3.85	4.17	4.44	4.76	5.13	5.00	3.77	2.60	1.40	361,458	353,830	3.7876
	9	17.7	0	37	2.86	3.64	3.33	3.85	4.26	4.65	5.13	5.26	5.41	5.00	3.92	2.30	0.70	411,525	404,570	4.0745
	10	19.4	0	42	3.57	4.08	3.92	4.08	4.44	5.00	5.71	5.88	5.71	5.56	4.65	3.00	1.40	482,300	474,150	4.5820
	11	21.4	0	46	3.23	4.26	4.17	4.35	5.00	5.41	5.56	6.06	5.71	5.71	4.76	3.45	1.76	525,683	516,800	4.7663
	13	24.7	0	34	3.70	4.88	4.55	4.65	5.00	5.56	5.71	5.88	6.00	6.10	5.50	3.90	2.30	601,709	593,830	5.0921
	16	25.4	Down 2	48	3.92	5.00	4.88	5.00	5.26	5.41	5.56	5.71	5.71	5.88	5.00	4.09	2.50	604,404	585,630	4.9474
	17	25.1	Down 2	50	4.00	4.65	4.55	4.65	5.00	5.13	5 26	5.56	5.71	6.06	4.88	3.57	2.00	576,407	555,780	4.7250
	19	24.1	Down 2	50	3.56	4.76	4.44	4.55	4.65	5.00	5.41	5.56	5.88	5.56	4.88	3.13	1.50	547,749	528,150	4.5879
	20	23.6	Up 2	50	3.51	4.65	4.44	4.44	4.55	4.55	5.00	5.13	5.26	5.26	4.44	3.64	2.00	518,910	520,500	4.5711
	23	21.6	0	48	3.00	4.17	4.08	4.26	4.44	4 55	4.76	5.13	5.41	5.56	4.88	3.33	1.70	491,874	483,560	4.4395
	24	21.1	0	49	3.45	4.44	4.08	4.00	4.08	4.55	5.00	5.26	5.00	4.76	4.35	3.13	1.50	464,968	457,100	4.2448
	25	20.2	Down 2	49	2.33	4.17	3.92	4.00	4.17	4.44	4.55	5.13	5.26	5.26	4.88	2.99	2.38	463,118	446,540	4.2342
	26	19.8	0	49	2.90	3.70	4.08	4.08	4.17	4.35	4.65	4.88	4.88	4.76	4.17	2.70	1.50	429,418	422,160	4.0409
	27	19.2	0	50	3.13	3.77	3.77	3.77	4.08	4.26	4.55	4.76	4.88	4.88	4.26	2.09	1.80	424,227	417,060	4.0496
	30	17.4	Down 3	49	2.90	3.64	3.70	3.92	4.08	4.35	4.55	5.00	5.13	5.00	4.44	3.33	1.10	418,573	397,020	4.0282
December	1	17.1	Down 2	50	2.99	3.23	3.51	3.64	3.77	4.17	4.44	4.05	4.65	4.65	4.00	2.80	1.60	383,150	367,230	3.7454
	2	16.6	Down 2	48	2.67	3.17	3.28	3.51	3.77	4.17	4.35	4.76	4.88	4.65	4.00	2.78	1.60	377,692	362,000	3.7473
	3	16.0	0	50	2.70	3.13	3.28	3.57	3.70	4.08	4.26	4.55	4.65	4.65	3.64	2.33	1.10	355,622	348,120	3.6586
	4	15.5	0	48	2.83	2.86	3.28	3.39	3.64	3.92	4.26	4.26	4.35	4.35	3.85	2.86	2.33	349,866	342,490	3.6471
	6	14.7	Down 1	43	2.74	2.93	2.99	3.23	3.64	3.92	4.35	4.35	4.35	4.44	3.77	2.60	1.40	337,861	327,260	3.5591
	8	15.2	Down 3	49	2.50	3.28	3.23	3.57	3.77	3.92	4.35	4.55	4.65	4.76	3.77	2.74	1.50	356,980	338,590	3.6342
	9	15.8	Down 3	50	2.94	3.83	3.70	3.77	3.92	4.17	4.55	4.76	4.76	4.88	3.64	2.40	1.20	369,406	350,380	3.7024
	10	16.9	Down 2	47	2.94	3.39	3.33	3.57	4.00	4.26	4.44	4.76	5.00	5.13	4.44	4.00	2.60	414,769	399,920	4.1087
	13	22.1	0	57	3.85	5.00	4.55	4.55	4.88	5.13	5.26	5.41	5.71	5.71	4.55	3.51	1.90	530,174	517,620	4.7318
	15	26.3	0	48	[illegible]	5.71	5.41	5.26	5.41	5.56	5.71	5.71	5.88	6.06	5.56	4.44	2.90	656,502	645,410	5.3507

No. 6.—CURRENT-MEASUREMENTS UPON THE ARKANSAS RIVER AT NAPOLEON, BY PARTY OF MR. A. A. EDINGTON.

Date.	Gauge.	Wind.	No. of floats.	Velocity near surface in divisions numbered—								Discharge per second.		Mean velocity of river.
				I.	II.	III.	IV.	V.	VI.	VII.	VIII.	Approx.	Corrected.	
1857.	*Feet.*			*Feet.*	*Feet.*	*Feet.*	*Feet.*	*Feet.*	*Feet.*	*Feet.*	*Feet.*	*Cubic feet.*	*Cubic feet.*	*Feet.*
December 29	38.0	0	9	1.10	1.67	2.82	3.23	3.39	3.57	2.08	1.25	61,373	65,103	2.5318
1858.														
January 1	36.0	0	20	1.25	1.71	2.53	3.08	3.45	3.39	1.82	1.09	55,329	58,637	2.4270
6	31.9	Up	10	1.11	1.40	2.00	2.80	2.94	2.78	1.67	1.00	41,625	45,221	2.1402
15	34.8	0	10	1.28	1.60	2.30	3.17	3.28	3.45	2.06	1.23	53,706	56,917	2.4336
16	35.3	0	10	1.28	1.60	2.90	3.03	3.28	3.28	1.96	1.18	54,107	57,342	2.4518
17	35.0	0	10	1.39	1.74	2.50	2.99	3.57	3.57	2.15	1.29	56,122	59,478	2.5435
18	34.8	0	10	1.28	1.60	2.04	3.08	3.57	3.33	2.00	1.20	52,915	56,079	2.3982
19	34.4	0	10	1.23	1.54	2.30	3.28	3.57	3.23	1.94	1.16	51,612	54,688	2.4177
20	32.9	0	10	1.08	1.34	1.92	3.23	3.45	3.39	2.00	1.20	49,793	52,771	2.3329
21	33.7	0	10	1.21	1.52	2.00	2.94	3.28	3.17	1.90	1.14	48,520	51,421	2.2733
22	33.5	0	10	1.18	1.48	2.22	3.08	3.33	3.08	1.85	1.11	47,375	50,208	2.2958
25	32.6	0	10	1.17	1.48	2.15	2.94	3.33	3.08	1.85	1.11	46,774	49,571	2.2667
26	33.1	0	10	1.17	1.48	2.22	3.17	3.45	3.23	1.94	1.16	48,714	51,627	2.3608
27	33.5	0	10	1.23	1.54	2.27	3.08	3.17	3.08	1.85	1.11	49,002	51,932	2.2956
February 25	27.2	0	10		1.43	1.87	2.94	3.23	3.23	1.94	1.16	39,761	42,139	2.3921
26	26.8	0	10		1.43	1.94	2.78	3.23	3.13	1.87	1.12	39,008	41,340	2.3467
March 6	25.4	Up	10		1.43	1.90	2.78	3.23	3.08	1.85	1.11	35,804	38,898	2.3869
9	27.8	Down	10		1.60	2.41	3.23	3.45	3.51	2.11	1.27	45,944	48,030	2.6254
10	28.3	Up	10		1.67	2.44	3.23	3.64	3.85	2.30	1.38	50,200	54,537	2.8728
14	30.6	Up	10		1.67	2.50	3.28	3.45	3.85	2.30	1.38	53,570	58,199	2.8526
18	31.0	Up	10		1.67	2.60	3.23	3.45	3.85	2.30	1.38	53,860	58,515	2.8681
21	33.5	Up	10	1.28	1.60	2.50	3.17	3.57	4.17	2.50	1.50	57,371	62,328	2.7554
24	37.2	Up	10	1.33	1.67	2.50	3.23	4.65	4.44	2.67	1.60	68,579	74,505	2.9863
26	39.8	Up	10	1.30	1.46	2.25	3.23	4.00	4.26	2.56	1.54	71,738	77,937	2.8220
28	41.4	Up	10	1.37	1.71	2.30	3.23	4.00	4.44	2.67	1.60	76,155	82,736	2.8953
31	44.0	Up	10	1.39	1.74	2.38	3.23	3.85	4.35	2.60	1.54	83,123	90,305	2.8627
April 2	45.0	0	10	1.33	1.67	2.44	3.28	4.00	4.26	2.56	1.54	85,816	90,948	2.7926
3	45.1	0	10	1.37	1.71	2.67	3.77	4.17	4.88	2.86	1.71	94,202	99,835	3.0654
4	45.2	0	10	1.43	1.80	2.82	3.85	4.44	4.88	2.86	1.71	96,890	102,680	3.1529
5	45.3	0	10	1.39	1.74	2.67	3.77	4.76	5.13	3.08	1.85	99,298	105,240	3.2311
6	45.4	0	10	1.39	1.74	2.70	3.77	4.17	4.88	2.86	1.71	94,528	100,180	3.0760
7	45.4	0	10	1.45	1.82	2.78	3.77	4.17	5.00	3.03	1.82	97,053	102,850	3.1590
8	45.1	0	10	1.41	1.77	2.63	3.64	4.44	5.00	3.03	1.82	96,645	102,420	3.1449
15	40.2	Up	10	1.28	1.60	2.25	2.90	3.39	3.85	2.30	1.38	65,421	71,074	2.5735
16	39.9	Up	10	1.12	1.40	2.00	2.60	3.28	3.85	2.30	1.38	61,900	67,240	2.4350
17	39.5	Up	10	1.10	1.38	1.98	2.56	3.13	3.70	2.22	1.33	60,069	65,259	2.3620
26	42.1	Down	10	2.41	3.03	4.35	4.65	5.00	5.26	3.17	1.90	80,416	84,066	2.8450
27	42.4	Up	10	1.89	2.35	3.28	4.08	4.35	4.76	2.86	1.71	93,379	101,440	3.4331
May 1	43.4	0	10	2.27	2.86	4.35	4.35	4.76	5.00	2.99	1.79	108,307	114,780	3.7580
2	43.7	0	10	2.50	3.17	3.92	4.44	4.65	4.55	2.74	1.64	108,873	115,380	3.6577
6	44.1	0	10	2.47	3.08	3.70	4.55	4.76	4.88	2.86	1.71	110,451	117,050	3.7107
7	44.1	0	10	2.50	3.17	4.26	4.44	4.65	4.88	2.86	1.71	112,264	118,970	3.7716
8	44.1	0	10	2.56	3.23	4.00	4.35	4.76	4.88	2.86	1.71	111,792	118,470	3.7557
9	44.1	0	10	2.67	3.33	3.92	4.44	4.76	4.88	2.86	1.71	112,660	119,390	3.7850
10	44.1	0	10	2.56	3.23	4.08	4.76	4.65	4.88	2.86	1.71	113,290	120,060	3.8068
11	44.1	Down	10	2.50	3.13	4.00	4.26	4.65	4.88	2.86	1.71	110,372	115,380	3.6577
12	43.9	Up	10	2.47	3.08	3.92	4.35	4.76	4.88	2.86	1.71	110,530	120,080	3.6858
13	43.8	Up	10	2.35	2.94	3.39	4.00	4.44	4.65	2.78	1.67	103,390	112,320	3.5607
16	43.9	Up	10	2.50	3.17	3.92	4.55	4.65	4.65	2.78	1.67	109,976	119,480	3.7875
17	43.9	Up	10	2.56	3.23	4.00	4.44	4.55	4.76	2.86	1.71	110,846	120,420	3.8175
19	44.2	Down	10	2.74	3.45	4.08	4.44	4.88	5.13	3.08	1.85	116,918	122,210	3.8746
23	44.2	Up	10	2.67	3.33	3.85	4.44	4.88	5.00	3.03	1.82	114,483	124,320	3.9410
27	44.2	Up	10	2.67	3.33	3.92	4.44	5.00	5.00	3.03	1.82	115,183	125,130	3.9668
29	44.2	Up	10	2.50	3.17	3.77	4.26	4.76	4.88	2.90	1.74	110,332	119,860	3.7997
30	44.3	Up	10	2.56	3.23	3.64	4.44	4.76	4.88	2.90	1.74	111,002	120,590	3.8228
June 1	44.4	0	10	2.86	3.57	5.00	5.41	5.13	5.26	3.17	1.90	127,303	134,910	4.2779
2	44.4	Up	10	2.86	3.64	5.26	5.56	5.13	5.26	3.17	1.90	129,259	140,430	4.4516
3	44.4	Up	10	2.86	3.57	4.88	5.13	5.41	5.41	3.23	1.94	127,879	138,930	4.4041
4	44.5	Up	10	2.82	3.51	5.00	5.13	5.41	5.41	3.23	1.94	132,105	143,480	4.4058
5	44.6	Up	10	3.08	3.85	5.00	5.13	5.56	5.56	3.33	2.00	136,421	148,210	4.5508
6	44.7	0	10	3.03	3.77	4.76	5.13	5.13	5.56	3.33	2.00	133,165	141,130	4.3334
8	45.0	0	10	2.86	3.57	4.88	5.13	5.41	5.71	3.45	2.06	134,630	142,680	4.3810
9	45.1	Up	10	2.86	3.64	4.76	5.13	5.41	5.56	3.33	2.00	133,082	144,580	4.4394
10	45.2	Up	10	3.03	3.77	4.76	5.26	5.41	5.41	3.23	1.94	133,570	145,110	4.4557
14	45.3	0	10	3.03	3.77	4.65	5.26	5.41	5.56	3.33	2.00	134,385	142,420	4.3731
15	45.3	0	10	2.86	3.64	4.65	5.26	5.56	5.56	3.33	2.00	133,773	141,770	4.3532
20	45.2	0	10	2.82	3.51	4.88	5.26	5.41	5.71	3.45	2.06	134,750	142,810	4.3850
21	45.2	0	10	2.86	3.64	4.76	5.26	5.26	5.56	3.33	2.00	133,000	140,950	4.3334
30	44.7	0	10	2.74	3.45	4.65	5.13	5.26	5.41	3.23	1.92	129,390	137,120	4.2105
July 8	44.7	0	10	2.99	3.70	4.88	5.41	5.56	5.71	3.45	2.08	137,518	145,740	4.4750
13	43.8	0	10	2.74	3.45	4.55	5.13	5.26	5.41	3.23	1.94	125,040	132,510	4.2008
14	43.6	0	10	2.60	3.23	4.35	4.88	5.13	5.41	3.23	1.94	121,338	128,590	4.0763
15	43.3	0	10	2.50	3.13	3.92	4.65	5.26	5.26	3.17	1.90	113,726	120,520	3.9465
16	42.8	0	10	2.22	2.78	3.51	4.55	5.13	5.26	3.17	1.90	108,900	115,380	3.7782
17	42.1	0	10	2.13	2.67	3.57	4.76	4.88	5.13	3.08	1.85	103,679	109,880	3.7184
18	41.4	0	10	2.04	2.56	3.28	4.08	4.55	4.88	2.94	1.77	93,220	98,803	3.4576
21	39.4	0	10	1.69	2.13	2.78	3.39	4.08	4.55	2.74	1.64	76,094	81,280	3.0470
26	38.1	0	10	1.60	2.00	2.67	3.23	3.92	4.26	2.56	1.54	70,105	74,297	2.8853

Current-measurements upon the Arkansas river at Napoleon—Continued.

Date.		Gauge.	Wind.	No. of floats.	Velocity near surface in divisions numbered—								Discharge per second.		Mean velocity of river.
					I.	II.	III.	IV.	V.	VI.	VII.	VIII.	Approx.	Corrected.	
1858.		*Feet.*			*Feet.*	*Feet.*	*Feet.*	*Feet.*	*Feet.*	*Feet.*	*Feet.*	*Feet.*	*Cubic feet.*	*Cubic feet.*	*Feet.*
July	27	38.1	0	10	1.55	1.94	2.63	3.23	3.92	4.26	2.56	1.54	69,623	73,786	2.8654
August	1	37.8	Up	10	1.39	1.74	2.35	2.99	3.04	4.17	2.50	1.50	66,564	72,316	2.8084
	2	37.3	Up	10	1.32	1.64	2.08	2.50	3.03	3.64	2.17	1.31	55,170	59,937	2.4024
	3	35.9	Up	10	1.23	1.54	2.00	2.41	2.90	3.45	2.06	1.23	50,798	55,188	2.2842
	5	34.8	Up	10	1.17	1.46	1.77	2.08	2.44	2.99	1.79	1.07	43,127	46,854	2.0036
	8	32.2	Up	10	0.68	0.85	1.21	1.52	2.06	2.74	1.64	0.99	30,876	33,544	1.5875
	9	31.8	0	10		0.80	1.14	1.43	1.98	2.60	1.56	0.94	31,544	33,430	1.5821
	11	30.8	0	10		0.74	1.06	1.32	1.80	2.38	1.43	0.86	27,659	29,312	1.4367
	14	28.8	Down	10		0.71	1.02	1.27	1.74	2.22	1.33	0.80	24,653	25,772	1.3575
	16	27.6	Up	10		0.73	1.05	1.31	1.80	2.20	1.32	0.79	24,044	26,121	1.4278
	17	27.1	Up	10		0.71	1.02	1.27	1.77	2.17	1.31	0.78	22,725	24,688	1.4014
	18	26.8	Up	10		0.70	1.00	1.25	1.75	2.17	1.31	0.78	22,549	24,497	1.3906
	20	26.1	0	10		0.76	1.09	1.38	1.69	2.08	1.25	0.75	21,793	23,096	1.3626
	21	25.6	0	8		0.76	1.08	1.32	1.61	1.82	1.09	0.66	20,195	21,402	1.2626
	22	25.1	Up	8		0.60	0.85	0.99	1.20	1.47	0.88	0.53	15,178	16,489	1.0079
	29	21.6	Down	5			0.35	0.43	0.64	0.83	0.50		7,925	8,284	0.5749
	30	20.8	Down	5			0.33	0.41	0.61	0.78	0.49		7,233	7,561	0.5478
	31	19.7	Down	5			0.32	0.40	0.58	0.73	0.44		6,527	6,823	0.5164
September	2	18.4	Up	5			0.31	0.39	0.57	0.71	0.43		5,815	6,317	0.5236
	4	17.9	Up	5			0.31	0.39	0.56	0.70	0.42		5,742	6,238	0.5171
	5	17.8	Up	5			0.31	0.38	0.56	0.70	0.42		5,718	6,212	0.5149
	6	17.7	Up	5			0.31	0.38	0.55	0.69	0.42		5,670	6,160	0.5106
	7	17.2	Up	5			0.30	0.38	0.55	0.69	0.41		5,363	5,826	0.5062
	10	15.6	Up	5			0.30	0.37	0.53	0.67	0.40		4,978	5,408	0.4932
	11	15.1	Up	5			0.30	0.37	0.53	0.66	0.40		4,716	5,123	0.4910
	12	14.6	Up	5			0.29	0.37	0.53	0.66	0.39		4,675	5,078	0.4867
	13	14.1	Up	5			0.29	0.36	0.52	0.65	0.39		4,382	4,761	0.4801
	15	13.3	Down	5			0.29	0.36	0.52	0.66	0.39		4,178	4,367	0.4641
	16	13.2	Down	5			0.29	0.36	0.52	0.66	0.39		4,178	4,367	0.4641
	17	13.1	0	5			0.29	0.36	0.52	0.65	0.39		4,159	4,307	0.4577
	18	13.5	0	5			0.29	0.36	0.52	0.65	0.39		4,382	4,644	0.4684
	19	14.1	0	5			0.29	0.36	0.52	0.64	0.38		4,343	4,602	0.4641
	20	14.6	0	5			0.28	0.35	0.51	0.63	0.38		4,487	4,754	0.4557
	21	15.1	0	5			0.28	0.35	0.50	0.63	0.38		4,466	4,732	0.4534
	22	15.6	0	5			0.28	0.35	0.50	0.62	0.37		4,649	4,927	0.4492
	23	16.2	0	5			0.28	0.35	0.50	0.62	0.37		4,649	4,927	0.4492
	24	16.7	0	5			0.28	0.34	0.50	0.62	0.37		4,857	5,147	0.4472
	25	16.6	0	5			0.27	0.34	0.49	0.62	0.37		4,811	5,098	0.4430
	26	16.1	Up	5			0.28	0.35	0.50	0.63	0.38		4,693	5,098	0.4649
	27	15.5	Up	5			0.29	0.36	0.51	0.64	0.38		4,781	5,193	0.4736
	28	15.1	0	5			0.29	0.36	0.53	0.67	0.36		4,612	4,887	0.4683
October	1	12.5	Up	5			0.29	0.36	0.52	0.65	0.35		4,084	4,436	0.4715
	2	12.1	Up	5			0.28	0.35	0.51	0.63	0.38		3,834	4,164	0.4671
	3	11.7	Up	5			0.28	0.35	0.51	0.63	0.38		4,725	5,133	0.5758
	4	11.3	Up	5			0.28	0.34	0.50	0.63	0.37		3,576	3,884	0.4606
	5	11.0	0	5			0.27	0.34	0.50	0.63	0.37		3,559	3,771	0.4472
	6	10.5	0	5				0.34	0.49	0.61	0.36		3,795	4,021	0.4760
	7	10.1	0	5				0.33	0.49	0.60	0.36		3,544	3,755	0.4716
	14	8.5	Down	5				0.33	0.47	0.59	0.35		3,265	3,412	0.4547
	15	8.3	Down	5				0.32	0.46	0.58	0.35		3,016	3,153	0.4469
	16	8.1	Up	5				0.32	0.46	0.58	0.35		3,016	3,276	0.4644
	17	7.9	Up	5				0.32	0.45	0.57	0.34		2,963	3,219	0.4562
	18	7.7	Up	5				0.32	0.45	0.57	0.34		2,963	3,219	0.4562
	19	7.5	0	5				0.32	0.45	0.56	0.33		2,928	3,102	0.4398
	20	7.3	Up	5				0.31	0.44	0.55	0.33		2,701	2,933	0.4427
	21	7.1	Up	5				0.31	0.44	0.55	0.33		2,701	2,933	0.4427
	22	7.0	Up	5				0.31	0.44	0.54	0.33		2,684	2,915	0.4400
	24	6.7	Down	5				0.31	0.45	0.54	0.32		2,684	2,805	0.4233
	25	6.5	Down	5				0.30	0.43	0.54	0.32		2,634	2,753	0.4155
	28	5.9	0	5				0.30	0.43	0.53	0.32		2,452	2,598	0.4186
	29	5.7	Down	5				0.30	0.42	0.53	0.32		2,436	2,546	0.4103
	30	5.5	Down	5				0.30	0.42	0.51	0.32		2,405	2,514	0.4050
	31	5.3	Down	5				0.30	0.42	0.52	0.31		2,247	2,348	0.4050
November	1	5.2	Down	5				0.30	0.42	0.52	0.31		2,247	2,348	0.4050
	2	5.1	Down	5				0.30	0.42	0.51	0.31		2,232	2,333	0.4024
	3	5.0	Down	5				0.30	0.42	0.51	0.31		2,232	2,333	0.4024
	4	4.6	Down	5				0.29	0.42	0.51	0.31		2,218	2,318	0.3998
	5	5.1	Down	5				0.30	0.43	0.53	0.32		2,290	2,394	0.4129
	6	6.1	Down	5				0.31	0.44	0.54	0.32		2,654	2,774	0.4469
	11	12.1	Up	5				0.76	0.98	1.33	0.80		7,988	8,678	0.9734
	12	13.4	Up	5				0.82	1.09	1.43	0.86		9,146	9,935	1.0560
	13	14.1	Up	5				0.88	1.20	1.52	0.91		12,929	14,040	1.4167
	14	14.5	Up	5				0.93	1.26	1.56	0.94		11,352	12,333	1.1821
	19	14.8	Down	5				0.98	1.33	1.67	1.00		12,020	12,565	1.2043
	20	14.3	Down	5				0.95	1.30	1.63	0.98		11,144	11,650	1.1750
	21	13.5	Down	5				0.91	1.23	1.54	0.91		10,530	11,007	1.1102
	22	12.3	Down	5				0.87	1.18	1.45	0.87		9,040	9,450	1.0600
	23	11.1	Down	5				0.83	1.11	1.36	0.82		8,062	8,428	0.9994
	24	9.7	0	5				0.77	1.03	1.23	0.74		6,992	7,409	0.9305
	25	8.3	Up	5				0.71	0.94	1.14	0.69		6,142	6,672	0.9451
	26	7.5	Up	5				0.65	0.85	1.03	0.62		5,560	6,040	0.8555
	27	6.1	0	5				0.60	0.74	0.87	0.52		4,236	4,489	0.7233
	28	5.6	Down	5				0.54	0.67	0.77	0.46		3,786	3,958	0.6377
	29	5.1	Down	5				0.52	0.65	0.73	0.44		3,392	3,545	0.6115
	30	5.1	Down	5				0.51	0.57	0.72	0.43		3,232	3,379	0.5828

No. 7.—CURRENT-MEASUREMENTS UPON VARIOUS TRIBUTARY STREAMS AND BAYOUS.

Locality.	Date.	Stand of water surface.		Wind.	No. of floats.	Area.	Velocity near surface in divisions numbered—											Width of division.	Discharge per second.		Mean velocity of stream.	Observations by party of—
		Below h. w. of—	Amount.				I.	II.	III.	IV.	V.	VI.	VII.	VIII.	IX.	X.	XI.		Approx.	Corrected.		
			Feet.			*Sq. feet*	*Feet*	*Feet*	*Feet*	*Feet*	*Feet*	*Feet*	*Feet*	*Feet*	*Feet*	*Feet*	*Feet*	*Feet.*	*Cu. feet.*	*Cu. feet.*	*Feet.*	
Ohio river, at Cairo	Dec. 3, 1857	1858	36.8	0	23	65,319	1.25	1.57	2.11	2.74	3.39	3.45	3.51	3.70	3.39	2.38	1.63	200	172,918	183,260	2.871	Lieut. Abbot.
" "	Dec. 7, 1857	1858	33.8	Down 1	53	72,249	1.38	2.25	3.39	3.85	3.77	3.85	4.17	4.08	3.70	2.78	2.00	200	231,324	241,830	3.347	"
Hatchee river, above forks at mouth	Mar. 3, 1858	(?)	19.5	0	10	2,933	1.59	2.38	2.50	2.44	1.69							30	6,218	6,590	2.247	"
St. Francis river, half a mile above Sterling	Feb. 27, 1858	1858	26.1	Down 1	24	17,800	0.45	1.09	1.28	1.39	1.43	1.39	0.69					100	19,632	20,523	1.153	"
St. Francis river, half a mile above Sterling	Apr. 27, 1858	1858	8.0	Up 2	16	30,727	0.30	0.77	1.16	1.16	0.83	0.56	0.37	0.26				100	20,781	22,576	0.735	"
White river, just below Arkansas cut-off	Jan. 1, 1858	1858	9.4	0	35	22,976	2.08	3.03	2.70	1.96	1.39	0.61						100	45,071	47,767	2.079	"
Yazoo river, just below Steele's bayou	Feb. 19, 1858	1858	14.7	Up 3	20	35,718	0.50	0.96	1.43	1.85	1.19	1.25	0.69					100	40,158	43,628	1.221	"
Yazoo river, just below Steele's bayou	May 4, 1858	1858	0.9	Up 2	40	46,079	1.25	1.85	2.00	2.17	2.00	1.92	1.72					100	84,983	92,326	2.004	Mr. Pattison.
Yazoo river, just below Steele's bayou	May 12, 1858	1858	0.8	Up 2	43	46,156	1.28	1.92	2.27	2.27	2.08	2.27	1.92					100	92,376	100,360	2.174	"
Yazoo river, just below Steele's bayou	June 11, 1858	1858	0.4	Up 2	32	46,541	1.39	1.85	2.94	2.94	2.78	2.63	2.00					100	109,910	119,400	2.565	"
Yazoo river, just below Steele's bayou	July 8, 1858	1858	0.3	Down 2	41	46,541	1.92	2.94	3.38	3.57	3.33	2.78	1.32					100	127,588	133,380	2.866	"
Yazoo river, just below Steele's bayou	July 24, 1858	1858	0.8	Down 2	45	46,156	2.08	3.85	4.17	3.57	2.78	2.27	1.47					100	133,159	139,210	3.016	"
Red river, at Alexandria	Feb. 1, 1858	1858	6.6	Down 3	21	22,685	2.82	3.85	4.65	4.26	3.85	2.82	1.87					100	78,166	81,715	3.602	Lieut. Abbot.
" "	Feb. 2, 1858	1858	6.3	0	20	22,900	3.39	4.88	4.44	4.17	3.64	3.13	2.33					100	84,992	90,075	3.933	"
Red river, just below Black river	Feb. 4, 1858	(?)	9.0	Down 2	16	33,333	2.63	3.57	3.70	3.85	4.35	4.55	4.17	3.33				100	125,623	131,330	3.939	"
Black river, just above mouth	Feb. 4, 1858	1850	8.4	Down 2	15	24,345	1.96	2.78	3.03	2.38	1.82	1.12						100	53,114	55,526	2.280	"
Red river, at mouth (proper)	Mar. 2, 1851	1851	6.2	Down 2	12*	68,947	0.70	1.00	1.25	1.50	1.59	1.60	1.51	1.35	1.00			200	88,120	92,119	1.336	Mr. G.C. Smith.
Red river, at mouth (proper)	Mar. 9, 1851	1851	4.2	0	12*	74,357					1.87							200	106,550	112,930	1.519	"
Atchafalaya river, at upper mouth	Mar. 8, 1851	1851	4.4	0	23	22,510	3.50	4.08	4.26	4.35	4.35	4.20						105	92,810	98,359	4.369	"
Atchafalaya river, at upper mouth	Mar. 9, 1851	1851	4.2	0	25	22,115	3.77	4.55	4.65	4.70	4.65	4.50						110	98,870	104,550	4.726	"
Atchafalaya river, at upper mouth	Feb. 11, 1858	1858	7.6	0	17	22,482	1.52	2.22	3.85	4.55	4.35	3.45	2.70					100	72,713	77,061	3.427	Lieut. Abbot.
Old river, near Red-river landing	Feb. 25, 1851	1851	9.1	Up 2			0	0	0	0	0	0	0	0	0				0	0	0	Mr. G.C. Smith.
Old river, near Red-river landing	Feb. 26, 1851	1851	8.5	Up 2			0	0	0	0	0	0	0	0	0				0	0	0	"
Old river, near Red-river landing	Mar. 9, 1851	1851	4.2	0			0	0	0	0	0	0	0	0	0				0	0	0	"
Old river, near Red-river landing	Mar. 18, 1851	1851	2.2	Down 3	6*	67,530	0.10	0.80	1.20	1.52	1.80	1.90	1.90	1.83	1.70			128	95,680	100,030	1.481	"
Old river, near Red-river landing	Mar. 20, 1851	1851	1.9	0	6*	67,996					1.81	1.91						128	96,550	102,320	1.509	"
Old river, 3.5 miles above Red-river landing	Feb. 12, 1858	1858	8.1	0	17	31,000	1.33	2.78	3.17	3.39	3.23	2.74	2.06	1.21	0.94			100	71,817	76,112	2.455	Lieut. Abbot.
Bayou Plaquemine, near upper mouth	Apr. 10, 1851	1851	0.6	0	15	5,875	5.90	6.50	6.66	6.58	6.42	5.98	5.56	5.05	4.34	3.60		25	33,430	32,990	5.669	Mr. G.C. Smith.
Bayou Plaquemine, near upper mouth	Apr. 11, 1851	1851	0.6	Down 2	9	5.875	6.10	6.70	6.96	6.81	6.50	6.22	5.82	5.30	4.60	3.80		25	34,750	33,390	5.881	"
Bayou Plaquemine, near upper mouth	Jan. 16, 1859	1858	6.2	0	27	4,190	1.00	2.94	4.35	4.87	4.65	4.36	3.40	3.57	3.08	2.35		25	15,909	16,861	4.024	Mr. Pattison.
Bayou La Fourche, near upper mouth	Apr. 18, 1851	1851	1.2	Up 0.7	20	3,630	2.58	2.98	3.20	3.10	2.90	2.68	2.34	2.00				25	10,243	10,275	2.831	Mr. G.C. Smith.
Bayou La Fourche, near upper mouth	Apr. 19, 1851	1851	1.2	0	12†	3,630	2.40	2.94	3.27	3.40	3.13	2.75	2.25	1.60				25	10,439	10,200	2.809	"
Bayou La Fourche, near upper mouth	Jan. 23, 1859	1858	7.0	0	18	2,476	1.11	1.89	2.33	2.38	2.09							35	4,853	5,143	2.077	Mr. Pattison.
Bayou La Fourche, at Thibodeaux	Jan. 28, 1859	1858	4.4	0	8	2,992	1.08	1.44	1.63	1.69	1.40	0.91						35	4,039	4,281	1.431	"
Bayou La Fourche, at Field's mills	Jan. 27, 1859	1858	4.2	Up 2	15	2,961	1.22	1.85	1.85	1.00	0.41							50	3,739	4,073	1.375	"
Berwick's bay	Jan. 20, 1858	1828	7.6	Down 1	20	84,216	1.49	2.00	2.08	2.04	2.22	2.22	1.85	1.28	0.97			200	151,116	157,980	1.876	Lieut. Abbot.

* Observations taken with a ship's log, the banks being overflowed.

† Floats 10 feet below surface.

APPENDIX E.

DAILY DISCHARGE AT VELOCITY STATIONS.

No. 1.—DAILY DISCHARGE PER SECOND, IN CUBIC FEET, OF THE MISSISSIPPI RIVER AT CARROLLTON.

Day of month.	February, 1851.	March, 1851.	April, 1851.	May, 1851.	June, 1851.	July, 1851.	August, 1851.	September, 1851.	October, 1851.	November, 1851.	December, 1851.	January, 1852.	February, 1852.
1		1,012,568	1,115,000	985,000	740,000	790,000	850,000	548,738	255,000	285,000	255,000	325,000	295,000
2		1,020,000	1,117,774	985,000	738,342	805,444	858,967	535,000	246,485	275,000	256,554	325,000	280,000
3		1,019,966	1,107,344	975,000	730,514	809,510	865,000	521,458	240,000	265,000	250,000	320,000	275,000
4		1,042,127	1,105,000	960,000	720,699	815,000	865,000	520,000	245,585	258,830	250,000	315,000	275,000
5		1,050,388	1,105,000	932,442	719,898	818,847	868,610	518,963	245,000	255,000	255,000	310,000	286,305
6		1,048,009	1,105,000	920,000	719,219	835,000	855,000	505,000	245,000	265,000	265,000	307,991	295,000
7		1,060,000	1,105,000	907,692	702,529	850,000	834,958	495,000	251,562	265,693	275,000	310,000	300,000
8		1,068,464	1,100,000	890,000	710,000	860,000	820,000	480,136	255,000	255,000	285,000	315,000	305,000
9		1,075,000	1,095,014	883,996	727,217	860,000	804,650	480,000	254,608	260,000	290,000	335,000	335,000
10		1,077,416	1,063,701	875,000	729,570	856,448	790,000	481,430	270,000	266,721	293,496	350,000	360,000
11		1,097,901	1,047,593	860,000	749,973	860,000	769,648	488,637	281,207	270,000	295,000	380,000	330,000
12		1,078,279	1,048,345	849,468	761,190	865,000	740,000	467,511	270,000	285,000	295,000	440,000	355,000
13		1,094,462	1,055,000	839,571	775,622	865,000	716,241	440,000	254,147	285,000	295,000	475,000	365,000
14		1,116,084	1,060,000	815,000	785,000	865,000	695,000	425,000	253,011	285,000	295,000	518,971	400,288
15	506,628	1,134,955	1,070,000	796,729	790,000	860,000	669,388	410,000	253,904	275,625	290,000	530,000	425,000
16	515,000	1,145,000	1,071,857	774,584	782,895	854,451	655,000	410,000	255,000	265,000	290,000	535,000	455,000
17	534,777	1,152,504	1,065,000	768,718	764,709	855,000	640,000	401,898	251,030	255,000	285,000	530,000	485,000
18	583,715	1,150,000	1,056,266	750,000	770,000	855,957	625,000	382,792	260,000	241,199	280,000	515,000	524,861
19	630,000	1,136,688	1,040,000	735,000	785,000	860,000	616,090	371,898	275,000	245,000	275,130	490,000	
20	690,769	1,149,398	1,040,000	718,941	794,060	865,000	620,409	355,000	275,217	244,189	270,000	480,000	
21	766,497	1,139,697	1,030,000	700,542	795,000	870,000	610,000	350,000	256,422	240,000	275,000	482,392	
22	819,583	1,122,174	1,026,320	690,000	790,000	875,000	606,158	341,529	260,000	235,000	285,000	465,000	
23	870,000	1,130,000	1,030,000	682,092	775,000	880,000	605,000	325,000	269,713	235,000	295,000	455,000	
24	894,491	1,129,393	1,025,000	675,000	763,298	880,000	600,000	301,371	275,000	220,000	302,184	435,000	
25	909,900	1,098,804	1,025,000	665,000	754,508	875,000	572,388	295,000	275,869	225,000	310,000	415,000	
26	938,536	1,100,000	1,025,000	660,188	767,127	868,854	575,000	290,000	280,000	228,042	315,000	400,000	
27	955,000	1,110,000	1,015,000	652,835	773,310	860,000	576,086	280,000	275,000	240,000	325,000	380,000	
28	995,000	1,113,133	1,015,000	673,878	775,000	850,000	570,000	275,000	270,000	250,000	330,000	356,049	
29		1,110,000	1,010,000	676,124	775,000	844,245	564,238	270,000	275,000	255,000	335,000	335,000	
30		1,110,000	995,000	700,000	790,000	845,000	565,000	265,214	280,000	255,000	335,000	325,000	
31		1,112,766		730,000		845,000	555,000		285,000		330,087	310,000	

No. 2.—DAILY DISCHARGE PER SECOND, IN CUBIC FEET, OF THE MISSISSIPPI RIVER AT COLUMBUS.

Day of month.	December, 1857.	January, 1858.	February, 1858.	March, 1858.	April, 1858.	May, 1858.	June, 1858.	July, 1858.	August, 1858.	September, 1858.	October, 1858.	November, 1858.
1	250,000	610,000	530,000	435,000	1,058,670	1,050,000	1,143,300	841,220	560,000	280,000	176,840	190,000
2	235,000	640,000	520,000	465,000	989,850	980,000	1,150,720	740,420	531,560	279,740	161,780	215,000
3	220,000	680,000	506,730	495.000	946,780	890,000	1,160,970	671,260	513,730	270,000	160,000	235,800
4	235,000	725,000	493,000	525,320	855,000	803,249	1,175,000	640,000	492,590	257,110	159,360	285,280
5	250,000	760,000	481,620	568,860	777,640	786,550	1,185,000	618,740	479,830	246,000	155,000	354,490
6	270,000	810,000	474,150	565,000	709,660	778,682	1,195,000	601,810	479,270	235,030	149,070	420,000
7	300,000	835,000	475,000	565,000	623,070	776,550	1,206,170	568,500	480,110	228,260	147,000	440,000
8	350,000	830,000	478,550	550,000	585,000	786,570	1,221,980	533,320	490,000	220,980	146,430	441,990
9	400,000	800,000	475,000	533,590	567,810	800,000	1,241,220	499,730	495,810	219,330	145,930	433,760
10	500,000	745,000	470,000	529,410	565,000	820,000	1,255,000	490,000	495,700	222,400	143,000	420,230
11	691,630	720,000	460,776	539,080	570,000	889,324	1,270,000	485,000	495,220	211,550	140,820	417,370
12	810,110	676,110	450,000	545,000	595,000	955,320	1,280,900	477,340	479,740	210,000	144,370	399,860
13	895,000	656,000	438,000	552,030	625,000	970,080	1,300,000	464,400	468,060	210,590	134,470	390,000
14	965,380	606,110	425,000	565,000	682,150	1,004,640	1,318,300	465,810	467,500	247,390	136,740	380,000
15	1,061,480	590,000	420,000	575,000	799,540	1,030,000	1,349,460	460,130	450,000	255,930	132,630	370,000
16	1,137,600	583,180	430,000	583,800	860,000	1,030,000	1,387,840	443,060	432,430	266,230	128,670	358,250
17	1,170,000	590,000	450,000	590,000	900,000	1,010,900	1,402,520	424,530	410,530	255,570	130,000	345,000
18	1,190,000	616,730	460,585	606,660	950,000	1,007,700	1,403,400	425,000	391,310	253,730	130,000	330,000
19	1,190,000	639,640	460,000	650,000	1,000,000	1,005,000	1,399,690	445,230	385,380	250,000	133,710	325,000
20	1,180,000	660,480	455,180	740,000	1,030,770	990,000	1,398,000	492,720	383,260	249,240	135,500	320,000
21	1,160,000	660,000	450,000	870,000	1,085,620	982,340	1,395,000	520,840	368,990	238,150	130,930	310,000
22	1,120,000	635,000	438,000	981,070	1,120,160	985,000	1,383,080	596,350	365,000	233,140	134,250	300,000
23	1,075,000	602,680	428,560	1,058,880	1,210,000	1,010,000	1,360,000	620,000	363,560	222,590	132,460	285,000
24	1,005,000	580,000	400,800	1,098.400	1,260,920	1,045,000	1,330,000	639,010	339,670	214,190	132,000	275.000
25	910,000	560,000	399,230	1,105,990	1,265,000	1,077,500	1,286,120	660,000	332,620	205,000	132,260	260,000
26	810,000	537,700	396,500	1,129,800	1,260,000	1,114,000	1,258,540	664,900	300,220	194,000	134,600	245,000
27	720,000	515,330	400,000	1,130,000	1,236,600	1,133,390	1,220,000	665,430	294,380	184,740	135,000	230,000
28	650,000	503,000	415,000	1,120,000	1,210,000	1,137,000	1,156,960	664,310	285,000	183,000	140,330	225,000
29	600,000	506,760		1,104,900	1,170,000	1,139,880	1,090,010	661,530	275,000	181,060	139,530	215.000
30	580,000	530,660		1,090,000	1,113,390	1,140,000	997,260	613,580	267,700	174,070	143,710	200,000
31	580,000	535,000		1,075,000		1,142,000		588,580	278,000		170,000	

No. 3.—DAILY DISCHARGE PER SECOND, IN CUBIC FEET, OF THE MISSISSIPPI RIVER AT VICKSBURG* OR NATCHEZ.

Day of month.	January, 1858.	February, 1858.	March, 1858.	April, 1858.	May, 1858.	June, 1858.	July, 1858.	August. 1858.	September, 1858.	October, 1858.	November, 1858.	December, 1858.
1		895,450	705,000	1,128,800	1,159,900	1,231,700	1,215,950	1,140,000	540,920	348,160	234,000	367,230
2		895,000	705,000	1,130,700	1,161,000	1,240,650	1,219,450	1,136,800	533,830	340,000	235,000	362,000
3	870,000	890,000	700,000	1,139,000	1,162,450	1,232,800	1,218,900	1,117,000	528,240	330,000	236,000	348,120
4	865,000	880,650	693,080	1,142,000	1,164,900	1,240,900	1,218,000	1,104,500	520,460	323,090	237,000	342,490
5	860,000	864,000	683,200	1,144,300	1,167,200	1,241,900	1,215,000	1,098,000	512,000	320,590	248,080	330,000
6	855,000	841,560	670,550	1,148,800	1,178,000	1,240,000	1,212,100	1,086,400	504,700	308,080	277,740	327,260
7	850,000	833,000	680,000	1,139,800	1,174,000	1,238,000	1,211,600	1,066,800	490,000	297,200	310,000	330,000
8	844,800	826,210	713,090	1,140,900	1,181,150	1,226,800	1,220,400	1,050,000	470,000	290,300	353,830	338,590
9	836,360	809,440	726,300	1,142,800	1,190,000	1,214,400	1,224,200	1,026,400	452,450	289,300	404,570	350,380
10	828,000	802,750	748,200	1,139,100	1,199,800	1,220,300	1,225,900	1,010,000	442,740	280,000	474,150	399,920
11	825,990	793,380	768,610	1,145,000	1,208,800	1,225,000	1,223,000	992,730	435,740	275,000	516,800	430,000
12	839,790	792,000	776,810	1,152,450	1,200,250	1,228,700	1,220,000	982,000	425,000	269,980	565,000	470,000
13	879,170	794,880	787,500	1,154,000	1,210,650	1,222,000	1,218,200	950,760	412,300	266,320	593,830	517,620
14	900,000	792,000	800,000	1,154,100	1,203,800	1,215,500	1,222,250	935,000	405,290	256,810	600,000	585,000
15	930,000	783,000	808,400	1,146,800	1,217,650	1,219,200	1,220,200	920,000	387,390	263,330	595,000	645,410
16	932,000	771,090	825,000	1,137,600	1,220,000	1,211,600	1,220,700	909,310	382,130	256,660	585,630	
17	928,000	763,490	844,190	1,128,800	1,222,800	1,217,800	1,229,100	903,970	382,790	252,000	555,780	
18	915,130	753,860	849,070	1,110,000	1,224,000	1,222,100	1,225,000	882,090	381,310	250,000	540,000	
19	908,000	753,690	839,780	1,105,000	1,230,000	1,217,800	1,220,000	873,340	380,000	248,000	528,150	
20	900,790	740,560	841,570	1,103,400	1,224,600	1,226,000	1,218,200	860,150	385,260	245,000	520,500	
21	888,670		870,000	1,099,400	1,222,500	1,231,000	1,215,900	832,150	395,930	243,000	505,000	
22	877,130		910,000	1,110,900	1,232,250	1,238,150	1,217,500	812,000	407,440	240,000	495,000	
23	868,670		947,460	1,123,100	1,234,000	1,233,600	1,210,200	791,190	414,250	238,000	483,560	
24	869,000	734,330	960,860	1,130,000	1,235,200	1,244,500	1,188,600	768,400	407,940	235,000	457,100	
25	877,000	731,300	990,090	1,140,000	1,234,600	1,241,800	1,180,000	749,190	393,740	233,320	446,540	
26	879,000	729,880	1,017,480	1,143,500	1,227,200	1,230,900	1,169,500	714,060	390,000	235,810	422,160	
27	879,000	716,860	1,042,100	1,145,600	1,227,200	1,220,000	1,155,400	700,000	385,460	235,000	417,060	
28	875,230	710,000	1,070,000	1,140,800	1,236,450	1,209,450	1,158,100	671,880	380,000	235,000	410,000	
29	870,940		1,090,800	1,140,800	1,232,700	1,207,050	1,154 800	640,000	370,000	234,000	400,000	
30	874,000		1,109,430	1,142,600	1,230,000	1,206,300	1,148,300	610,000	360,780	234,000	397,020	
31	885,000		1,121,500		1,230,000		1,147,100	575,380		233,000		

* Prior to February 21 these measurements were made at Natchez. Subsequently to that date they were made at Vicksburg.

No. 4.—DAILY DISCHARGE PER SECOND, IN CUBIC FEET, OF THE ARKANSAS RIVER AT NAPOLEON.

Day of month.	December, 1857.	January, 1858.	February, 1858.	March, 1858.	April, 1858.	May, 1858.	June, 1858.	July, 1858.	August, 1858.	September, 1858.	October, 1858.	November, 1858.	December, 1858.
1		58,637	52,000	39,000	77,000	63,000	65,000	67,000	72,316	6,500	4,436	2,348	4,000
2		53,000	52,000	38,000	78,000	63,000	70,000	68,000	59,937	6,317	4,164	2,333	4,000
3		48,000	51,000	38,000	79,000	63,000	69,000	69,000	55,188	6,000	5,133	2,333	5,000
4		46,000	51,000	38,000	79,000	64,000	73,000	70,000	51,000	6,238	3,884	2,318	6,000
5		45,000	50 000	38,000	80,000	64,000	78,000	71,000	46,854	6,212	3,771	2,394	8,000
6		45,221	49,000	38,898	80,000	65,000	71,000	72,000	42,000	6,160	4,021	2,774	9,000
7		45,000	48,000	41,000	80,000	67,000	72,000	74,000	36,000	5,826	3,755	4,000	
8		46,000	48,000	44,000	80,000	66,000	73,000	76,000	33,544	5,500	3,500	5,000	
9		46,000	47,000	48,030	79,000	67,000	75,000	78,000	33,430	5,500	3,500	6,000	
10	33,000	47,000	46,000	54,537	78,000	68,000	75,000	79,000	32,000	5,408	3,500	7,000	
11	36,000	48,000	45,000	56,000	77,000	63,000	75,000	80,000	29,312	5,123	3,500	8,678	
12	39,000	49,000	44,000	57,000	76,000	68,000	74,000	80,000	28,000	5,078	3,500	9,935	
13	43,000	51,000	43,000	58,000	74,000	60,000	73,000	81,000	27,000	4,761	3.500	14,040	
14	46,000	54,000	43,000	58,199	73,000	63,000	72,000	77,000	25,772	4,500	3,412	12,333	
15	48,000	56,917	42,000	58,000	71,074	66,000	72,000	86,000	26,000	4,367	3,153	13,000	
16	50,000	57,342	41,000	58,000	67,249	67,000	73,000	80,000	26,121	4,367	3,276	14,000	
17	53,000	59,478	41,000	58,000	65,259	68,000	74,000	82,000	24,688	4,307	3,219	14,000	
18	55,000	56,079	40,000	58,515	64,000	69,000	74,000	81,000	24,497	4,644	3,219	13,000	
19	57,000	54,688	40,000	59,000	64,000	70,000	74,000	81,000	24,000	4,602	3,102	12,565	
20	59,000	52,771	40,000	60,000	63,000	71,000	73,000	81,000	23,096	4,754	2,933	11,650	
21	60,000	51,421	40,000	62,328	63,000	71,000	71,000	81,280	21,402	4,782	2,933	11,007	
22	62,000	50,208	41,000	64,000	64,000	72,000	70,000	80,000	16,489	4,927	2,915	9,450	
23	63,000	49,000	42,000	66,000	64,000	72,000	69,000	79,000	14,000	4,927	3,000	8,428	
24	64,000	49,000	42,000	67,000	65,000	72,000	68,000	77,000	13,000	5,147	2,805	7,409	
25	65,000	49,571	42,139	69,000	66,000	73,000	68,000	75,000	12,000	5,098	2,753	6,672	
26	65,000	51,627	41,340	70,000	66,000	73,000	67,000	74,297	11,000	5,098	2,500	6,040	
27	66,000	51,932	40,000	71,000	66,000	73,000	67,000	73,786	10,000	5,193	2,500	4,489	
28	66,000	52,000	39,000	72,000	66,000	72,000	67,000	74,000	9,000	4,887	2,598	3,958	
29	65,193	52,000		74,000	65,000	68,000	67,000	74,000	8,284	4,500	2,546	3,545	
30	64,000	53,000		75,000	64,000	69,000	67,000	73,000	7,561	4,500	2,514	3,379	
31	62,000	53,000		76,000		66,000		73,000	6,823		2,348		

No. 5.—DAILY DISCHARGE PER SECOND, IN CUBIC FEET, OF THE YAZOO RIVER AT MOUTH.

Day of month.	December, 1857.	January, 1858.	February, 1858.	March, 1858.	April, 1858.	May, 1858.	June, 1858.	July, 1858.
1	32,000	44,000	49,000	42,000	64,000	88,000	114,000	131,000
2	32,000	45,000	48,000	42,000	65,000	90,000	115,000	131,000
3	32,000	45,000	48,000	42,000	66,000	91,000	115.000	132,000
4	32,000	46,000	48,000	42,000	67,000	92,826	116,000	132,000
5	32,000	46,000	48,000	42,000	68,000	94,000	117,000	132,000
6	32,000	47,000	48,000	42,000	69,000	95,000	117,000	133,000
7	32,000	47,000	47,000	42,000	69,000	96,000	118,000	133,000
8	33,000	47,000	47,000	43,000	70,000	97,000	118,000	133,380
9	33,000	48,000	47,000	43,000	70,000	98,000	119,000	134,000
10	33,000	48,000	47,000	43,000	71,000	99,000	119,000	134,000
11	34,000	48,000	46,000	43,000	71,000	100,000	119,400	135,000
12	34,000	49,000	46,000	43,000	71,000	100,360	120,000	135,000
13	35,000	49,000	46,000	44,000	72,000	101,000	121,000	135,000
14	35,000	49,000	45,000	44,000	72,000	102,000	122,000	136,000
15	36,000	49,000	45,000	44,000	73,000	103,000	122,000	136,000
16	36,000	49,000	45,000	44,000	73,000	103,000	123,000	137,000
17	37,000	49,000	44,000	45,000	74,000	104,000	123,000	137,000
18	37,000	50,000	44,000	45,000	75,000	105,000	124,000	137,000
19	38,000	50,000	43,628	45,000	75,000	106,000	125,000	138,000
20	38,000	50,000	43,000	46,000	76,000	106,000	125,000	138,000
21	39,000	50,000	43,000	46,000	77,000	107,000	126,000	138,000
22	39,000	50,000	43,000	47,000	78,000	108,000	126,000	139,000
23	40,000	50,000	43,000	48,000	79,000	108,000	127,000	139,000
24	40,000	50,000	43,000	49,000	80,000	109,000	127,000	139,210
25	41,000	50,000	43,000	50,000	81,000	110,000	128,000	
26	41,000	50,000	43,000	52,000	82,000	110,000	128,000	
27	42,000	50,000	43,000	54,000	83,000	111,000	129,000	
28	42,000	49,000	43,000	56,000	84,000	112,000	129,000	
29	43,000	49,000		58,000	86,000	112,000	130,000	
30	43,000	49,000		60,000	87,000	113,000	130,000	
31	44,000	49,000		62,000		113,000		

APPENDIX F.

SECTIONS OF MISSISSIPPI SWAMP LANDS.

No. 1.—SECTIONS OF ST. FRANCIS BOTTOM LANDS.

Cairo and Fulton railroad.

Locality.	Distance from the Mississippi R.	Flood of 1849. Ground below h. w. level at the Miss. R. (322 feet ab. gulf.)	Flood of 1849. Depth of overflow.
	Feet.	*Feet.*	*Feet.*
Opposite Cairo	0	2.0	2.0
	5,000	3.0	3.0
	10,000	5.0	5.0
	15,000	6.0	6.0
	20,000	2.0	2.0
	25,000	2.0	2.0
	30,000	2.0	2.0
	35,000	3.0	3.0
	40,000	5.0	5.0
	45,000	2.0	2.0
	50,000	—3.0	0.0
	55,000	—3.0	0.0
Matthew's prairie	60,000	—4.0	0.0
	65,000	—3.0	0.0
	70,000	—2.0	0.0
	75,000	1.0	0.0
	80,000	10.0	2.0
	85,000	14.0	4.0
	90,000	14.0	4.0
	95,000	13.0	3.0
	100,000	14.0	2.0
Lake St. John's	105,000	19.0	4.0
	110,000	—8.0	0.0
Big prairie	115,000	—9.0	0.0
	120,000	8.0	0.0
	125,000	12.0	0.0
	130,000	14.0	0.0
	135,000	15.0	1.0
	140,000	15.0	1.0
White-water river	145,000	16.0	2.0
	150,000	16.0	2.0
	155,000	16.0	2.0
Castor river	160,000	16.0	2.0
	165,000	14.0	0.0
	170,000	14.0	0.0
	175,000	17.0	0.0
	180,000	16.0	0.0
	185,000	16.0	0.0
	190,000	17.0	0.0
	195,000	18.0	0.0
	200,000	19.0	0.0
	205,000	20.0	0.0
	210,000	21.0	0.0
	215,000	20.0	0.0
	220,000	21.0	0.0
	225,000	22.0	0.0
	230,000	20.0	0.0
	235,000	21.0	0.0
	240,000	12.0	0.0
	245,000	0.0	0.0
	250,000	—28.0	0.0
	255,000	—40.0	0.0
Bloomfield ridge	260,000	—60.0	0.0
	265,000	—30.0	0.0
	270,000	—32.0	0.0
	275,000	—20.0	0.0
	280,000	—18.0	0.0
	285,000	—12.0	0.0
	290,000	— 4.0	0.0
	295,000	— 2.0	2.0
St. Francis river	300,000	0.0	0.0
	305,000	— 2.0	2.2
	310,000	0.0	2.0
	315,000		2.0

Military road, Memphis to St. Francis river.

Locality.	Distance from the Mississippi R.	Flood of 1828. Ground below h. w. level at the Miss. R. (221 feet ab. gulf.)	Flood of 1828. Depth of overflow.
	Miles.	*Feet.*	*Feet.*
Opposite Memphis	0	0.0	0.0
	1	2.0	2.0
	2	5.0	6.0
	3	0.0	0.0
5-mile bayou	4	0.0	0.0
	5	0.0	0.0
	6	0.0	0.0
	7	0.0	0.0
	8	0.0	0.0
	9	0.0	0.0
	10	0.0	0.0
	11	0.0	0.0
	12	0.0	0.0
	13	0.0	0.0
	14	0.0	0.0
	15	0.0	0.0
Leave bank of old lake	16	0.0	0.0
	17	5.0	1.5
	18	8.5	4.0
	19	10.5	4.5
	20	12.0	5.0
	21	13.0	5.0
	22	13.5	4.0
	23	13.0	3.0
	24	13.0	1.5
Blackfish lake	25	14.0	2.0
	26	11.0	0.0
	27	14.0	2.0
	28	17.0	5.0
Shell-lake bayou	29	14.0	2.5
	30	13.5	2.5
	31	13.5	2.5
Bevin's-lake bayou	32	12.5	2.0
	33	11.0	1.0
	34	12.0	3.0
	35	10.5	2.0
	36	9.0	1.5
St. Francis river	37	8.0	0.0
	38	8.0	0.0
	39	12.0	4.0
Foot of Crowley's ridge	39.5	0.0	0.0

Memphis and Little Rock railroad.

Locality.	Distance from the Mississippi R.	Flood of —. Ground below h. w. level at the Miss. R. (221 feet ab. gulf.)	Flood of —. Depth of overflow.
	Feet.	*Feet.*	*Feet.*
Opposite Memphis	0	5.0	5.0
	5,000	7.0	2.0
	10,000	8.0	6.0
	15,000	8.0	6.0
4-mile bayou	18,000		
Leave bank of Mississippi	20,000	2.0	0.0
	25,000	3.0	1.0
	30,000	4.5	2.0
	35,000	4.5	2.0
	40,000	3.0	0.0
	45,000	7.0	3.5
10-mile bayou	48,000		
	50,000	5.0	0.0
	55,000	9.0	1.0
	60,000	8.0	0.0
	65,000	9.0	1.0
	70,000	13.0	3.0
	75,000	13.0	3.0
	80,000	20.0	10.0
15-mile bayou	81,000		
	85,000	13.0	3.0
	90,000	13.5	3.5
	95,000	11.5	2.5
	100,000	15.0	5.0
	105,000	16.0	6.0
	110,000	17.5	7.5
	115,000	18.5	8.5
	120,000	19.5	9.5
Lost-swamp bayou	125,000	22.0	13.0
	130,000	16.0	6.0
	135,000	16.0	6.0
	140,000	16.0	6.5
	145,000	15.0	5.0
	150,000	15.0	5.0
Blackfish bayou	155,000	15.0	5.0
	160,000	17.0	7.0
	165,000	20.0	10.0
	170,000	20.5	10.5
	175,000	26.0	15.5
	180,000	21.5	11.0
	185,000	16.5	6.0
	190,000	20.0	9.5
	195,000	17.0	7.0
Snake pond	198,000		
	200,000	19.5	9.0
St. Francis river	203,700	11.5	1.0
Foot of Crowley's ridge	206,000	0.0	0.0

No. 2.—SECTION OF YAZOO BOTTOM LANDS.

Section across Yazoo bottom surveyed by party of this Survey in charge of Mr. H. A. Pattison.

Locality.	Distance from the Mississippi at Prentiss.	Flood of 1858.		Locality.	Distance from the Mississippi at Prentiss.	Flood of 1858.	
		Ground below h. w. level at the Mississippi river. (162 feet ab. gulf.)	Depth of overflow.			Ground below h. w. level at the Mississippi river. (162 feet ab. gulf.)	Depth of overflow.
	Feet.	*Feet.*	*Feet.*		*Feet.*	*Feet.*	*Feet.*
Prentiss	0	2.6	2.6		220,000	20.2	2.5
	5,000	4.8	4.8		225,000	21.5	3.0
	10,000	4.0	4.0		230,000	22.2	3.0
	15,000	4.0	4.0		235,000	22.1	2.0
	20,000	4.5	4.5		240,000	23.5	2.0
	25,000	4.5	4.5		245,000	25.5	3.2
	30,000	4.5	4.0		250,000	24.0	2.0
Melrose landing, Mississippi river	32,000				255,000	25.0	3.0
	35,000	6.5	3.5		260,000	25.7	3.0
	40,000	9.5	6.5		265,000	27.0	4.0
	45,000	11.0	8.0		270,000	28.5	5.0
	50,000	12.1	9.1		275,000	29.1	5.0
	55,000	13.0	10.0		280,000	29.0	5.0
	60,000	14.0	11.3		285,000	28.4	3.6
	65,000	17.4	1.0		290,000	29.5	4.5
Clear creek	70,000	20.0	4.5	Thompson's bayou	291,500		
	75,000	19.0	3.0		295,000	28.7	4.0
	80,000	18.3	3.0		300,000	26.8	2.5
	85,000	20.0	4.0		305,000	21.5	0.0
	90,000	21.0	5.8		310,000	19.2	0.0
Bogue Falaya	94,500				315,000	18.0	0.0
	95,000	18.0	3.0		320,000	20.7	0.0
	100,000	21.5	6.0		325,000	19.0	0.0
	105,000	23.9	7.0		330,000	21.0	1.0
	110,000	22.5	7.0		335,000	18.9	0.0
	115,000	23.0	8.2		340,000	19.0	0.0
	120,000	21.0	6.0		345,000	18.6	1.0
	125,000	18.0	3.0		350,000	17.8	0.0
	130,000	18.9	3.5		355,000	16.3	0.0
	135,000	17.5	2.0		360,000	17.8	0.0
	140,000	16.5	2.0		365,000	19.3	0.0
	145,000	22.6	8.0		370,000	13.3	3.5
	150,000	23.2	8.0		375,000	18.5	0.0
	155,000	14.3	1.0		380,000	19.0	0.0
	160,000	23.5	8.0	Yazoo river	385,000	22.8	0.0
	165,000	18.5	5.0		390,000	20.5	0.0
	170,000	15.6	2.0		395,000	19.7	0.0
	175,000	17.7	3.6		400,000	25.6	2.0
	180,000	17.5	3.6		405,000	24.5	2.5
	185,000	13.9	0.0		410,000	23.5	2.0
Horse-shoe bayou	190,000	16.5	2.0		415,000	27.3	5.0
	195,000	14.5	0.0		420,000	20.5	0.0
	200,000	18.2	3.0		425,000	21.0	0.0
Sunflower river	201,500				430,000	16.5	0.0
	205,000	14.5	0.0		435,000	8.0	0.0
	210,000	16.5	0.0		440,000	0.0	0.0
	215,000	18.0	1.0				

No. 3.—SECTIONS OF TENSAS BOTTOM LANDS.

Gaines' landing and Fulton railroad.

Locality.	Distance from the Miss. at Gaines' landing.	Flood of 1858.	
		Ground below h. w. level at the Miss. R. (149 feet ab. gulf.)	Depth of overflow.
	Feet.	*Feet.*	*Feet.*
Gaines' landing	0	2.0	2.0
	5,000	5.0	4.5
	10,000	7.5	6.5
Boggy bayou	11,000		
	15,000	9.0	8.0
	20,000	10.0	7.2
	25,000	9.0	6.0
Bayou Maçon	27,000		
	30,000	4.0	0.0
	35,000	2.0	0.0
	40,000	7.5	2.5
Black-powder bayou	45,000	6.0	1.5
	50,000	6.0	1.0
	55,000	6.5	1.0
	60,000	6.5	2.0
Big bayou	63,500		
	65,000	5.5	0.0
	70,000	0.0	0.0
	75,000	0.0	0.0
	80,000	4.5	0.0
	85,000	5.5	1.0
Bayou Bartholomew	90,000	0.0	0.0
	95,000	2.5	0.0
	100,000	7.0	1.0
	105,000	4.5	1.0
Western boundary of swamp	108,000	0.0	0.0

Along Arkansas and Louisiana boundary, surveyed by Prof. Forshey.

Locality.	Distance from the Mississippi R.	Flood of 1858.	
		Ground below h. w. level at the Miss. R. (127 feet ab. gulf.)	Depth of overflow.
	Feet.	*Feet.*	*Feet.*
Mississippi river	0	0.0	0.0
	1,000	0.0	0.0
	2,000	0.0	0.0
	3,000	2.0	2.0
	4,000	3.5	3.5
	5,000	5.5	5.5
	6,000	6.0	6.0
	7,000	6.0	6.0
	8,000	5.5	5.5
	9,000	6.0	6.0
	10,000	6.5	6.5
	11,000	7.5	7.5
	12,000	7.5	7.5
	13,000	7.5	7.5
	14,000	7.5	7.5
	15,000	7.5	7.5
	16,000	7.5	7.5
	17,000	7.0	7.0
	18,000	5.0	5.0
Bayou Maçon	18,400	3.5	3.5
	19,000	5.0	5.0
	20,000	3.0	3.0
	21,000	4.5	4.5
	22,000	6.0	6.0
Western boundary of swamp	22,800	0.0	0.0

Lake Providence and Fulton railroad.

Locality.	Distance from the Mississippi R.	Flood of —	
		Ground below h. w. level at the Miss. R. (121 feet ab. gulf.)	Depth of overflow.
	Feet.	*Feet.*	*Feet.*
Lake Providence	0	0.0	0.0
	3,000	8.0	4.0
	6,000	8.0	4.0
	9,000	8.0	2.0
Bayou Tensas	12,000	8.0	1.0
	15,000	8.0	
	18,000	15.0	
	21,000	16.0	
	24,000	12.0	
	27,000	10.0	0.0
Bayou Baxter	30,000	10.0	0.0
	33,000	13.0	0.0
	36,000	15.0	0.0
	39,000	20.0	5.0
Maçon swamp	42,000	19.0	4.0
" "	45,000	19.0	4.0
" "	48,000	22.0	7.0
" "	51,000	24.0	8.0
" "	54,000	24.0	8.0
" "	57,000	23.0	7.0
" "	60,000	23.0	7.0
" "	63,000	22.0	6.0
" "	66,000	19.0	2.0
Bayou Maçon	69,000	18.0	0.0
	72,000	6.0	0.0
	75,000	3.0	
	78,000	4.0	
	81,000	4.0	
	84,000	17.0	3.0
	87,000	20.0	5.0
	90,000	22.0	7.0
	93,000	20.0	5.0
	96,000	22.0	7.0
	99,000	25.0	10.0
	102,000	20.0	5.0
	105,000	15.0	0.0
Bayou Bonne Idée	108,000	12.0	0.0
	111,000	14.0	0.0
	114,000	11.0	0.0
	117,000	14.0	0.0
	120,000	15.0	0.0
	123,000	15.0	0.0
	126,000	20.0	0.0
	129,000	22.0	0.0
	132,000	25.0	2.0
	135,000	21.0	0.0
	138,000	19.0	0.0
	141,000	17.0	0.0
	144,000	17.0	0.0
	147,000	20.0	0.0
	150,000	21.0	0.0
	153,000	22.0	0.0
	156,000	20.0	0.0
Bastrop hills	159,000	0.0	0.0
" "	162,000	—30.0	0.0
" "	165,000	—25.0	0.0
" "	168,000	—40.0	0.0
" "	171,000	—45.0	0.0
" "	174,000	—40.0	0.0
" "	177,000	—34.0	0.0
" "	180,000	—30.0	0.0
" "	183,000	—39.0	0.0
" "	186,000	—33.0	0.0
" "	189,000	—40.0	0.0

Sections of Tensas bottom lands—Continued.

Lake Providence and Fulton railroad—continued.

Locality.	Distance from the Mississippi R.	Flood of — Ground below h. w. level at the Miss. R. (121 feet ab. gulf.)	Flood of — Depth of overflow.
	Feet.	*Feet.*	*Feet.*
Black bayou	192,000	20.0	2.0
	195,000	19.0	0.0
	198,000	20.0	0.0
	201,000	18.0	0.0
	204,000	19.0	0.0
	207,000	20.0	0.0
	210,000	23.0	0.0
	213,000	31.0	10.0
	216,000	20.0	0.0
	219,000	20.0	0.0
	222,000	22.0	0.0
	225,000	25.0	0.0
	228,000	33.0	8.0
	231,000	25.0	0.0
Bayou Bœuf	234,000	23.0	0.0
	237,000	25.0	0.0
	240,000	26.0	0.0
	243,000	24.0	0.0
Bayou Siard	246,000	22.0	0.0
	249,000	24.0	0.0
	252,000	24.0	0.0
	255,000	25.0	0.0
	258,000	24.0	0.0
	261,000	25.0	0.0
Washita river	264,000	23.0	.0.0

Vicksburg and Shreveport railroad.

Locality.	Distance from the Miss. R. at Vicksburg.	Flood of 1850. Ground below h. w. level at the Miss. R. (100 feet ab. gulf.)	Flood of 1850. Depth of overflow.
	Miles.	*Feet.*	*Feet.*
Opposite Vicksburg	0	0.0	0.0
	1	12.0	11.0
Walnut bayou	12	1.0	0.0
	13	14.0	11.0
	14	14.0	11.0
	15	14.0	10.5
	16	14.0	10.5
Grassy lake	17	14.0	10.5
	18	7.0	3.0
	19	13.0	9.0
	20	10.0	5.0
Roundaway bayou	21	6.5	1.0
	22	16.0	10.0
	23	14.0	7.0
	24	11.5	4.0
	25	21.0	13.0
	26	11.0	2.0
	27	13.5	4.0
	28	18.0	7.5
	29	15.5	4.5
	30	13.5	1.5
Tensas river	31	11.0	0.0
	32	22.0	10.5
Joe's bayou	33	11.0	0.0
	34	16.5	3.5
	35	19.0	6.0
	36	22.0	8.0
	37	23.0	9.5
Bayou Maçon	38	15.5	1.5
	39	19.0	5.0
	40	18.5	4.5
	41	17.5	3.5
	42	16.5	2.5
	43	16.0	2.0
	44	15.0	1.0
	45	14.0	0.0
	46	16.5	2.5
	47	13.0	0.0
	48	18.0	4.0
	49	17.5	3.5
	50	17.0	2.5
	51	17.0	2.7
	52	15.5	1.0
	53	13.5	0.0
	54	12.0	0.0
	55	10.5	0.0
	56	8.5	0.0
	57	22.0	
	58	22.0	
	59	21.5	
	60	21.0	
	61	24.0	
	62	24.0	
	63	31.0	
Bayou La Fourche	64	37.5	
	65	37.5	
	66	35.0	
	67	32.0	
	68	29.0	
	69	26.0	
	70	23.5	
	71	20.5	
	72	17.5	
	73	15.0	
Washita river	74	12.0	

Vidalia and Harrisonburg road, surveyed by party in charge of Mr. Pattison.

Locality.	Distance from the Miss. R. at Vidalia.	Flood of 1850. Ground below h. w. level at the Miss. R. (66 feet ab. gulf.)	Flood of 1850. Depth of overflow.
	Feet.	*Feet.*	*Feet.*
Vidalia	0	2.0	2.0
Bank of lake Concordia	5,000	2.0	2.0
" "	10,000	0.0	0.0
" "	15,000	0.0	0.0
" "	20,000	0.0	0.0
" "	25,000	0.0	0.0
" "	30,000	0.0	0.0
" "	35,000	0.0	0.0
" "	40,000	0.0	0.0
" "	45,000	0.0	0.0
" "	50,000	0.0	0.0
	55,000	8.0	6.0
	60,000	10.0	7.6
	65,000	9.0	6.6
	70,000	9.0	6.5
	75,000	9.0	6.0
	80,000	12.0	8.3
	85,000	10.0	7.0
	90,000	5.0	2.0
	95,000	6.0	3.5
	100,000	6.0	2.7
	105,000	6.0	3.0
	110,000	7.0	3.8
	115,000	11.0	8.0
Bayou Tensas	117,000		
	120,000	5.0	2.8
	125,000	11.0	8.0.
	130,000	16.0	14.0
Ben's bayou	133,000		
	135,000	16.0	14.0
	140,000	15.0	12.5
	145,000	13.0	11.0
	150,000	11.0	9.0
	155,000	9·0	6.5
	160,000	8.0	5.0
Washita river	161,000		
Harrisonburg	162,000		

No. 4.—SECTIONS OF THE DELTA OF THE MISSISSIPPI.

Morganza to Washington.

Locality.	Distance from the Mississippi at Morganza.	Flood of 1850.	
		Ground below h. w. level at the Miss. R. (44 feet ab. gulf.)	Depth of over. flow.
	Miles.	*Feet.*	
Morganza	0	5.0	
Crossing old Opelousas road	12.25	11.0	
Bank of Courtableau, opposite Washington	31.25	6.0	

Baton Rouge to Port Baré.

Locality.	Distance from the Mississippi at Baton Rouge.	Flood of 1850.	
		Ground below h. w. level at the Miss. R. (34 feet ab. gulf.)	
	Miles.	*Feet.*	
Opposite Baton Rouge	0	0.0	
	1	14.0	
	2	11.0	
	3	15.0	
	4	17.0	
	5	16.0	
	6	17.0	
	7	18.0	
	8	19.0	
	9	19.0	
	10	21.0	
	11	18.0	
	12	22.0	
	13	20.0	
	14	20.0	
	15	17.0	
Bayou Grosse Tête	16	16.0	
Bayou Alabama	26.5	17.0	
Mouth bayou Courtableau	31	17.0	
Port Baré	50.5	7.0	

New Orleans and Opelousas railroad.

Locality.	Distance from the Miss. R. opposite New Orleans.	Flood of 1858.	
		Ground below h. w. level at the Miss. R. (14 feet ab. gulf.)	Depth of overflow.
	Feet.	*Feet.*	*Feet.*
Opposite New Orleans.	0	0.0	0.0
	5,000	8.5	4.5
	10,000	11.5	7.5
	15,000	9.0	5.0
	20,000	8.0	4.0
	25,000	8.0	4.0
	30,000	8.0	4.0
	35,000	8.5	4.5
	40,000	13.5	9.5
	45,000	15.0	11.0
	50,000	15.0	11.0
	55,000	14.0	10.0
	60,000	10.0	6.0
	65,000	6.5	2.5
	70,000	9.5	5.5
	75,000	9.0	5.0
	80,000	13.0	9.0
	85,000	13.5	9.5
	90,000	13.5	9.5
	95,000	13.0	9.0
	100,000	12.0	8.0
	105,000	13.0	9.0
	110,000	12.5	8.5
Leave vicinity of Mississippi	115,000	9.0	5.0
	120,000	10.5	6.5
	125,000	10.5	6.5
	130,000	10.0	6.0
	135,000	12.5	8.5
	140,000	12.5	8.5
	145,000	14.5	10.5
	150,000	14.0	10.0
	155,000	16.5	12.5
	160,000	13.0	9.0
Bayou Des Allemands	165,000	13.0	9.0
	170,000	12.5	8.5
	175,000	14.5	10.5
	180,000	14.5	10.5
	185,000	14.0	10.0
	190,000	14.0	10.0
	195,000	14.0	10.0
	200,000	14.0	10.0
	205,000	10.0	6.0
	210,000	11.0	7.0
	215,000	13.0	9.0
	220,000	12.5	8.5
	225,000	11.0	7.0
	230,000	8.0	4.0
	235,000	13.0	9.5
	240,000	14.0	10.0
	245,000	14.0	10.0
	250,000	10.0	6.0
	255,000	10.0	6.0
	260,000	5.0	1.0
	265,000	5.0	1.0
	270,000	2.5	0.0
Bayou La Fourche	271,000	0.0	0.0
	275,000	7.0	2.0
	280,000	6.5	1.5
	285,000	6.0	1.0
Terre Bonne	290,000	0.0	0.0
	295,000	7.0	
	300,000	10.0	
	305,000	14.5	
	310,000	14.0	
	315,000	14.0	
	320,000	10.0	
	325,000	11.0	
	330,000	11.0	
	335,000	12.0	
	340,000	14.0	

New Orleans and Opelousas railroad—continued.

Locality.	Distance from the Miss. R. opposite New Orleans.	Flood of 1858.	
		Ground below h. w. level at the Miss. R. (14 feet ab. gulf.)	Depth of overflow.
	Feet.	*Feet.*	
	345,000	14.5	
Bayou Tiger	350,000	12.0	
	355,000	11.0	
	360,000	13.5	
	365,000	10.5	
	370,000	14.0	
	375,000	14.0	
	380,000	14.0	
Bayou Bœuf	385,000	7.0	
	390,000	14.0	
	395,000	13.0	
	400,000	10.0	
	405,000	8.0	
	410,000	9.5	
	415,000	9.5	
	420,000	7.5	
Berwick's bay	422, 00	7.0	

Section down bayou Atchafalaya.

Locality.	Distance from the upper mouth of the Atchafalaya.	Flood of 1850.	
		Ground below h. w. level at upper mth. of Atchaf. (50 feet ab. gulf.)	
	Miles.	*Feet.*	
Head of bayou	0	0.0	
Simmsport	3.25	2.0	
Bayou Rouge	29	13.0	
Crossing old Opelousas road	30	17.0	
Cow-head bayou	32	18.0	
Mouth bayou Alabama.	46	26.0	
Mouth bayou Courtableau	52	33.0	
Grand river	80	42.0	
Head of Grand lake	94	47.0	

APPENDIX G.

CURRENT-MEASUREMENTS AT THE SOUTHWEST PASS.

No. 1.—OBSERVATIONS IN 1851 BY THE PARTY OF PROFESSOR C. G. FORSHEY.

PROFESSOR FORSHEY employed the velocity apparatus, fully described in Chapter IV, where a detailed account is given of the method adopted for gauging the Mississippi. His first observations were made at low and at high tide (oscillation 1.33 feet) at the bar of the Southwest pass on August 8–9, the river being at its "flood" stage. He found the water both at surface and bottom flowing outward. At the surface and at 8 feet below, it was fresh; at the bottom it was brackish. His second observations were made on December 19, at mid-tide (rising), at the same locality, the river being at its "low-water" stage. He found the water at the surface flowing outward, and at the bottom at rest. It was brackish at surface and mid-depth, and salt at the bottom. The following extracts from his report furnish the details of these two sets of observations:—

August 8–9.—"The tide had a range, independent of winds, of 1.33 feet, and reached its highest point at 4 A.M., and continued to fall from about 6½ A.M. till 3 P.M., then was stationary for an hour or two. * * * * * * * * * *

"I next repaired to the bar itself for velocity observations. A pilot-schooner was anchored at the bar, just inside, and, for my accommodation, the pilots placed their vessel in the narrowest and last difficult point of the bar. I found 15 feet large as the depth at this time, low-tide, 6½ P.M., August 8th, 1851. I measured 50 feet on the deck of the schooner, established ranges, and cast out our float-kegs. The result gave a mean of—

"Surface	2.56 feet per second.
15 feet deep	2.13 " "

"I then rigged the hydrodynameter, with the steel rods screwed together, and measured four times at 7 feet, four times at 12 feet, and three at 15 feet, with the results differing a little from the above; thus, 3.3 feet, 2 feet, and 1.31 feet per second. I prefer the results given by the kegs, as the friction of the machine, and some doubts as to its real value, must be recollected in using the meter.

"Then we have a velocity *at the bottom* on the bar, full 2 miles outside of the land, of 2 feet per second.

"I then took up parcels of water from the *surface*, 8 and 15 feet deep; the former two were fresh, the last brackish, although running out. It was turbid like the others.

"In order to test these currents under circumstances the most favorable to an upward current, I resolved to remain on the bar during the night and continue experiments.

"At 2 o'clock A.M., by a bright moon, I made another set of velocity measurements with the kegs. I cast out surface and 16 feet floats, allowing one foot for rise of tide since the evening experiments. Thus:—

"At surface	2.56 feet per second.
At 16 feet	1.85 " "

"I again obtained water from surface, mid-depth, and 16 feet, and found the former fresh, and the last brackish as before, but still as turbid to the eye as the others."

"In December, 1851, I made a second survey about the mouth of the river. * * The gauge at Carrollton ranged from 0 to 1 foot, the lowest water ever known. * * * * *

"The pilots' boat lay anchored upon the bar where the channel depth was 16 feet at mean tide, having nearly one foot greater depth than when tested in August under high-water influences. Upon its deck, I established a base of 50 feet, and with range sights timed the passing keg-floats started along the channel, past the anchored boat.

VELOCITIES ON BAR.

"Set 1—Surface	1.92 feet per second.
7 feet	1.51 " "
14 feet	touched bottom and hung.
"Set 2—Surface	1.72 feet per second.
7 feet	1.39 " "
14 feet	0.41 " "

Tide rising at 0.6 of a foot above low tide when velocities were measured.

"Second series, at 300 feet east of pilot-boat, same base of 50 feet on deck, channel 17 feet deep.

"Set 1—Surface	1.39 feet per second.
7 feet	0.91 " "
15 feet	stood still, no current.
"Set 2—Surface	2.38 feet per second.
7 feet	1.51 " "
13 feet	drifted very slowly down.

"Third series, at outer verge of the bar, 15 feet water.

"Surface	2.38 feet per second.
6½ feet	0.40 " "
12 feet	Stood a minute, and in five minutes drifted 50 feet across channel eastward."

No. 2.—OBSERVATIONS IN 1859-60 BY THE PARTY OF MR. C. A. FULLER.

Prior to his elaborated measurements, Mr. Fuller made a set of amateur observations, respecting which he states:—

"The observations were made on the 13th, 14th, 15th, and 16th January, 1859. The stage of water in the river being at New Orleans about 3½ feet below high-water mark [Carrollton gauge 11.5 feet]. The tide during the four days, as above, ranging about 2 feet between high and low tide. Very little, if any, wind was blowing, and that little from N. to NNE."

"I do not feel perfectly satisfied with the results of the sub-velocities. Want of time alone prevented my making experiments on the under currents in a more satisfactory manner. The results I furnish herewith may serve as tests for other experiments I expect to make during the ensuing spring, and in making which I hope to be better prepared for ascertaining with correctness the *direction* as well as the force of the under current."

The record of these amateur observations is given to make the list complete. The velocities were obtained by noting the time of passage of the floats between two points, 100 feet apart; the upper station being designated by a buoy, while at the lower station a boat was anchored, and at the same time connected with the upper station by a line 100 feet in length.

The surface floats used were made of cypress roots, as light as or lighter than cork. The sub-velocities were obtained by means of a submerged keg, connected by a line to a surface float (made of light wood—about 8 inches diameter at base—in form of a *cone*—length of axis about 6 inches—signal flag at apex), the length of the connecting line being regulated by the depth at which the velocity was required.

Anchorage.	Tide.		Depth.		Velocity.				Water.
	Elevation above low tide.	Oscillation.	Total.	Of float.	January 13.	January 14.	January 15.	January 16.	
	Inches.	*Inches.*	*Feet.*	*Feet.*	*Feet.*	*Feet.*	*Feet.*	*Feet.*	
Outside of bar. Bottom slightly sandy.	6 (flood)	24	42	Surface.	3.33	3.57	3.12	3.33	Fresh.
				6					Brackish.
				20	2.00	2.04	2.00	1.96	Salt.
				Bottom.	2.50	2.38	2.44	2.44	"
Outside of bar. Bottom slightly sandy.	3 (flood)	24	30	Surface.	3.33	3.45	3.70	3.33	Fresh.
				6					Brackish.
				12					"
				15	2.00	2.08	1.96	2.08	
				Bottom.	2.86	3.03	2.70	2.94	Salt.
Immediately outside of bar. Bottom blue mud; little grit.	0	24	20	Surface.	3.12	3.12	3.03	3.12	Fresh.
				6					"
				12	2.22	2.17	2.22	2.27	Brackish.
				18	2.50	2.50	2.38	2.44	
				Bottom.					Salt.
Same as last.	18 (flood)	24	20	5					Fresh.
				6					Slightly brackish.
				9					Brackish.
				12					"
				18					Clear salt.
Crest of bar. Bottom sandy.	18 (flood)	24	14	Surface.	2.13	2.08	2.13	2.17	Fresh.
				6					"
				7	2.17	2.17	2.13	2.17	
				12					"
				Bottom.	2.27	2.22	2.27	2.27	Brackish.
Above bar. Bottom mud and sand.	21 (flood)	24	20	Surface.	3.03	3.23	2.86	2.94	Fresh.
				6					"
				10	2.86	2.94	2.70	2.78	
				12					"
				18	2.22	2.22	2.08	2.27	
				Bottom.	2.08	2.00	1.96	2.13	Slightly brackish.

It was directed that all Mr. Fuller's elaborated sub-surface velocity observations should be made with tin sub-floats 6 inches in diameter, and from 9 to 12 inches long, connected by a fine wire with surface floats 6 inches in diameter and from 1 to 2 inches deep. The experiments of May 12 were made with such floats; but several of the sub-floats having been suddenly broken off (probably by fish), wooden floats were substituted, whose surfaces, like those of the tin floats, were to each other as 5 to 1. They were, however, connected by a line nearly $\frac{3}{16}$ of an inch in diameter. The experiments in August, and all subsequent to that date, were made with tin floats, connected by a fine wire. At the beginning or end of each experiment the sub-float was suspended near the bottom, the wire being held in the hand. This hand experiment was directed to be made from the first, but from some misapprehension it was for a time omitted. The experiments subsequent to October were made by suspending a tin float 6 inches in diameter and 12 inches deep by a fine twine.

When the current observations at the bar of the Southwest pass, made in May, 1859, are examined, the tides of the gulf, and the direction of the winds and waves, should be considered; and it should also be borne in mind that in an experiment made by Mr. Fuller in August, when the exposed surface of the surface float was one-fifth that of the sub-float, the latter, although in still water, was carried forward by the surface float with a velocity equal to one-fifth of its own.

The observations during the flood stage show that there was at no time an inward current of salt-water at bottom, but that all the salt-water had an outward motion. Where moving slowest, it had a velocity varying from 0.3 of a foot to 1.0 foot per second, the mean being about 0.5 of a foot per second. Sometimes, where the depth was 42 feet, the salt-water at a depth of 25 feet was moving outward with a velocity of at least 2.5 feet per second. It is stated in the notes of the observer that these sub-currents were not in the same direction with the surface currents, but sometimes made an angle as large as 20 degrees with them.

The observations during August, when the river was very low, show that in that condition the bar was always covered with salt-water, sometimes still and sometimes in motion up the river; the up-stream motion apparently depending upon the wind, and not upon an eddy, for its existence and strength. This up-stream current was sometimes just perceptible; at others it was from ½ to ¾ of a mile per hour. It was stronger on the outer edge of the bar than at the inner edge, which could not have been the case, if it had been an eddy current. When there was a down-stream wind (northerly), the sub-surface refluent current was not perceptible either at the inner crest of the bar or on the bar (the water at the bottom, in the absence of tide, being still); while at the outer crest of the bar the up-stream current was just barely perceptible. After an easterly and southeasterly wind of some days' duration, this up-stream current was found to be quite strong at the outer and inner crest. In September and October, the river being then also at its "low-water" stage, and the tide rising (range about 1.5 feet), salt-water moved in at the bottom on the outer slope of the bar, the thickness of the stratum and its velocity increasing as the tide rose. When the tide fell, the salt-water moved outward.

The observations subsequent to October confirm the conclusions based upon those made previous to that time; namely, that the salt-water currents sometimes found on or in advance of the bar are chiefly due to changes in the level of the gulf, caused by wind or tide. The eddy current, although, theoretically, it must exist, was rarely detected, being usually hidden by the action of other and more powerful agencies.

It is a fact well established by the observation of pilots and other reliable persons, that in the low stage of the river, the surface water is usually brackish to the head of the passes, and sometimes as far up as Fort St. Philip, and that it has been known to extend to New Orleans. Mr. Fuller reports that in October and November, 1859, the surface water was brackish at Fort St. Philip; and that during the extraordinary gales of August, September, and October, 1860, the gulf water filled the channels of the passes with an up-stream current.

The following tables exhibit a complete record of the elaborated observations made by Mr. Fuller's party:—

Anchorage.	Hour.	Tide.			Wind.	Depth.		Velocity.	Water.	Remarks.
		High water.	Low water.	Oscillation.		Total.	Of float.			
	h. m.	*h. m.*	*h. m.*	*Inches.*		*Feet.*	*Feet.*	*Feet.*		
Outside of bar. Outer buoy NE. 400 feet. Bottom clay and fine sand.	9 30 a.m.	3 30 a.m.	4 00 p.m.	7	SE. light.	42 & 43	5	2.86	Fresh.	*May* 12, 1859. Gentle swells. Level of gulf high. High-water reading 22 inches.
							10	1.67	Brackish.	
							15	1.11	Salt.	
							20	1.11	"	
							25	1.05	"	
							30	1.14	"	
							35	1.19	"	
	11 00 a.m.						40	1.22	"	
Outside of bar. 500 feet E. by N. from outer buoy, and 500 feet N. 80° E. from outer can buoy. Bottom fine, hard sand and clay mixed.	11 30 a.m.	3 30 a.m.	4 00 p.m.	7	SE. by E. light.	30	5	3.57	Fresh.	Very gentle swells.
							10	2.22	Brackish.	
							15	1.56	½ brack. and salt.	
							20	1.67	Salt.	
							25	1.15	"	
On bar, near east edge of channel. Outer can buoy SW. Light-house N. 10° E. Bottom fine sand.	2 00 p.m.	3 30 a.m.	4 00 p.m.	7	E. by N. very light.	17	5	4.00		Water surface quiet.
							10	3.85		
							15	2.86	Fresh.	
	2 30 p.m.						5	4.17	"	
							10	3.70	"	
							15	3.33	"	
Midway on bar, and in channel. Buoy channel to W. 200 feet. Bottom fine sand with blue clay.	4 15 p.m.	3 30 a.m.	4 00 p.m.	7	E. by N. light.	13.5	5	3.85	"	Water surface smooth.
							10	3.23	"	
							5	3.70	"	
							10	3.33	"	
Upper crest of bar. 250 feet above red upper can buoy, which has been moved or dragged down some distance.	5 15 p.m.	3 30 a.m.	4 00 p.m.	7	NE. by E. very light.	18	5	3.85	"	Water surface smooth.
							10	3.70	"	
							15	3.03	"	
							5	3.85	"	
Outside of lower buoy. Same as May 12 and outside bar. Bell buoy S. 70° E. Stake island N. 25° E. Light-house N. 17° E. Bottom clay and sand.	7 00 a.m.	5 30 a.m.	6 00 p.m.	14	E. light.	42 & 43	5	2.63	Brackish and fresh	*May* 14, 1859. SE. and E. swells, forcing sea-water into lower part of bar channel.
							10	2.27	Brackish.	
							15	2.00	Brackish and salt.	
							20	1.72	Salt.	
							25	1.25	"	
							30	1.25	"	
							35	1.28	"	
							40	1.18	"	
In west part of channel, 1000 feet above outer can buoy, which bears S. 30° W. Bell-buoy S. 63° E. Bottom hard, fine sand and clay.	9 30 a.m.	5 30 a.m.	6 00 p.m.	14	E. by S. light.	30 & 32	5	2.86	Fresh.	Long swells from E. by S. and SE., less than at 7 a.m. 250 feet to the E., soundings only 17 feet. Strong salt-water at bottom.
							10	2.22	Brackish.	
							15	2.00	Brackish and salt.	
							20	1.35	" "	
							25	1.20	" "	
	10 00 a.m.						5	3.03		
							10	2.17		
							15	2.08		
							20	1.54		
							25	1.27		
On bar near west edge of channel. 2500 feet above outer can buoy. Bottom nearly all fine clay and sand with some mud.	11 00 a.m.	5 30 a.m.	6 00 p.m.	14	E. by S. very gentle.	14	5	2.78	Fresh.	Water surface smooth.
							10	2.04	"	
							12	1.92	"	
							5	2.86	"	
							10	2.18	"	
							12	2.00	"	
	12 00 a.m.						5	2.22	"	
							10	2.86	"	
							12	2.00	"	
Inside of bar. 800 feet from upper can buoy, which bears S. 5° E. Stake island S. 75° W. Bottom fine quicksand, gritty when dry. Very little clay.	10 30 a.m.	7 00 a.m.	7 30 p.m.	17.5	W. by N. light.	21	5	3.70		*May* 16, 1859.
							10	3.70		
							15	3.45		
							18	3.33	Fresh.	
							5	3.58		
							10	3.70		
							15	3.58		
							18	3.33	"	
Near upper edge of bar. 250 feet above upper can buoy. Bottom fine sand with some clay. Very gritty.	11 00 a.m.	7 00 a.m.	7 30 p.m.	17.5	W. by N. very gentle.	18	5	3.58	"	
							10	3.33		
							15	3.03		
							5	3.45		
							10	3.33		
	11 15 a.m.						15	3.16	"	

Observations in 1859–60—Continued.

Anchorage.	Hour.	Tide.			Wind.	Depth.		Velocity.	Water.	Remarks.
		High water.	Low water.	Oscillation.		Total.	Of float.			
	h. m.	*h. m.*	*h. m.*	*Inches.*		*Feet.*	*Feet.*	*Feet.*		
Near middle of bar. Same as May 12 at 4 15 p.m. Bottom sticky clay and fine sand.	11 30 a.m.	7 00 a.m.	7 30 p.m.	17.5	W. by N. very light.	14	5	3.18	Fresh.	*May* 16, 1859—continued. Water surface smooth.
							10	2.94	"	
							5	3.23		
							10	2.94		
							5	3.23		
							10	2.86	"	
Same anchorage as May 12 at 2 p.m. On bar in east part of channel. Outer buoy S. 45° W. Stake island and light-house N. 10° E. Bottom hard sand and blue clay—mostly sand.	12 30 p.m.	7 00 a.m.	7 30 p.m.	17.5	Calm.	17 & 18	5	3.70	"	
							10	3.57	"	
							15	3.18	"	
							5	3.85	"	
							10	3.85	"	
							15	3.18	"	
							5	3.85	"	
							10	3.57	"	
							15	3.23	"	
Outside of bar. Same as 9 30 a.m. May 12. Outer can buoy NE. 400 feet. Bottom clay with some fine sand.	2 30 p.m.	7 00 a.m.	7 30 p.m.	17.5	N. by W. light.	42 & 43	5	3.23		Swells considerable and increasing, from W. and SW. Open sea to NW., W., S. and E.
							10	2.78		
							15	2.86		
							20	3.03		
							25	3.33		
							30	3.33		
							35	2.50		
							40	2.22		
	3 00 p.m.				W. light.		5	3.33	Fresh.	
							10	2.78	Fresh and brackish	
							15	2.78	Brackish.	
							20	3.18	Salt.	
							25	3.18	"	
							30	2.86	"	
							35	2.27	"	
							40	2.22	"	
Outside of bar. Same as 11 30 a.m. May 12. Outer buoy S. 80° W. 500 feet. Bottom fine sand and clay.	4 00 p.m.	7 00 a.m.	7 30 p.m.	17.5	W. light.	30	5	3.33	Fresh.	W. and SW. swells. Water surface somewhat rough.
							10	2.86	"	
							15	2.22	Fresh and brackish	
							20	1.67	Brackish.	
							25	1.79	Salt.	
							5	3.33		
							10	2.70		
							15	2.39		
							20	1.72		
							25	1.82		
Inside of bar. Upper red buoy S. 25° W. 1800 feet. Light-house N. 15° W. Mud lump 100 feet to east, and soundings 13, 13.5, 14, and 15 feet. Bottom sand and clay.	7 00 a.m.	8 00 a.m.	8 00 p.m.	16.5	W. by N. very light.	18	5	2.94	Fresh and muddy.	*May* 17, 1859.
							10	2.86	" "	
							15	1.82	" "	
							5	2.86	" "	
							10	2.63	" "	
							15	1.72	" "	
							5	2.78	" "	
							10	2.86	" "	
							15	1.75	" "	
Inside of bar. Same as 10 30 a.m. May 16. Upper can buoy S. 5° E. 1000 feet. Stake island S. 75° W. Shoal water and mud lumps to east and southeast. Bottom hard, fine sand.	7 30 a.m.	8 00 a.m.	8 00 p.m.	16.5	W. by N. very light.	21	5	3.13	" "	Current bears SE.
							10	2.86	" "	
							15	2.22	" "	
							20	2.18	" "	
							5	2.86	" "	
							10	2.70	" "	
							15	2.33	" "	
							20	1.92	" "	
							5	2.94	" "	
							10	2.70	" "	
							15	2.27	" "	
					Calm.		20	2.17	" "	
On the bar. 100 feet west of upper can buoy. Bell buoy S. 23° E. Lower end dam N. 55° E. Bottom gritty, fine sand.	8 45 a.m.	8 00 a.m.	8 00 p.m.	16.5	Calm.	16.5	5	2.94	" "	Current setting to eastward; Scattered mud lumps and shoal water to E. and W.
							10	2.78	" "	
							15	2.56	" "	
							5	2.78	" "	
							10	2.50	" "	
							15	2.63	" "	
	9 00 a.m.						5	3.03	" "	
							10	2.70	" "	
							15	2.38	" "	
							5	2.94	" "	
							10	2.63	" "	
	9 15 a.m.						15	2.38	" "	
On bar and in channel near west edge, near midway between upper and lower can buoys—nearer the lower. Bottom half hard, sand and clay.	10 00 a.m.	8 00 a.m.	8 00 p.m.	16.5	Calm.	18	5	3.23	Fresh.	Gentle swells from SW., increasing so as to stop observations. Scattered mud banks and shoal water to NW. and SE. At 12 m. found water salt at bottom (18 feet) and brackish at 15 feet, 2500 feet above outer buoy.
							10	2.86	"	
							15	3.23	"	
							5	3.33	"	
							10	2.86	"	
							15	3.23	"	
							5	3.23	"	
							10	2.94	"	
							15	2.70	"	

Observations in 1859–60—Continued.

Anchorage.	Hour.	Tide.			Wind.	Depth.		Velocity.	Water.	Remarks.
		High water.	Low water.	Oscil-ation.		otal.	Of float.			
	h. m.	*h. m.*	*h. m.*	*Inches.*		*Feet.*	*Feet.*	*Feet.*		
Inside of bar. Upper can buoy S. 15° W. 1200 feet. Bottom hard sand.	6 00 a.m.	10 30 a.m.	10 30 p.m.	17.5	Calm.	19	0	2.86	Fresh.	*May* 20, 1859. Smooth and even water surface.
							5	2.94	"	
							10	2.94	"	
							15	2.94	"	
							0	2.94	"	
							5	2.94	"	
							10	2.94	"	
							15	2.78	"	
							0	3.03	"	
							5	3.03	"	
							10	2.86	"	
	6 45 a.m.						15	2.94	"	
Inside of bar, near upper crest. Upper can buoy S. 25° W. 800 feet. Bottom hard and sandy.	7 00 a.m.	10 30 a.m.	10 30 p.m.	17.5	Calm.	18.5	0	2.86	"	Calm and smooth From upper can buoy to outer can buoy is 2 miles, or 10,560 feet.
							5	2.78	"	
							10	2.18	"	
							15	2.63	"	
							0	2.70	"	
							5	2.78	"	
							10	2.33	"	
							15	2.50	"	
							0	2.63	"	
							5	2.78	"	
							10	2.38	"	
							15	2.17	"	
							0	2.63	"	
							5	2.63	"	
							10	2.33	"	
							15	2.22	"	
In channel, on upper part of bar, 100 feet W. of upper can buoy, near anchorage of 8 45 a.m. May 17. Bottom hard and sandy; very little clay.	7 45 a.m.	10 30 a.m.	10 30 p.m.	17.5	Calm.	19	0	2.70	"	Water surface smooth.
							5	2.50		
							10	2.22		
							15	1.85		
							0	2.63		
							5	2.56		
							10	2.22		
							15	2.22		
							0	2.44		
							5	2.56		
							10	2.33		
							15	2.00		
							0	2.63		
							5	2.50		
							10	2.33		
							15	2.17	"	
On bar, in channel and in line between upper and outer can buoys. 1600 feet below upper. Bottom hard sand.	9 00 a.m.	10 30 a.m.	10 30 p.m.	17.5	Calm.	18	0	2.56	"	Very gentle and even SW. swells.
							5	2.63	"	
							10	2.04		
							15	2.08	"	
							0	2.50	"	
							5	2.63	"	
							10	2.33	"	
							15	2.27	"	
							0	2.56	"	
							5	2.56	"	
							10	2.38	"	
							15	2.17	"	
Midway on bar, in channel. Stake island and light-house N. 10° E. Near anchorage of 10 a.m. May 17, 11 30 a.m. May 16, and 4 15 p.m. May 12. Bottom fine sand with very little clay.	9 30 a.m.	10 30 a.m.	10 30 p.m.	17.5	Calm.	19.5	0	2.50	"	Very gentle and even swells, called by pilots "current swells." Breakers W. by S. and SE. on mud banks and lumps. Velocities averaged show current about 1.7 miles per hour
							5	2.63	"	
							10	2.00	"	
							15	2.00	"	
							0	2.50	"	
							5	2.38	"	
							10	2.33	"	
							15	2.13	"	
							0	2.63	"	
							5	2.63	"	
							10	2.38	"	
							15	2.33	"	
On bar, near middle of channel; 1600 feet above lower can buoy. Bottom hard fine sand.	11 00 a.m.	10 30 a.m.	10 30 p.m.	17.5	Calm.	21	0	3.33		Long and even swells from SW. Mud-bank breakers to right and left.
							5	3.57		
							10	2.38	"	
							15	2.63	Salt.	
							20	2.13	"	
							0	3.45		
							5	3.45		
							10	2.50		
							15	2.38		
							20	1.96		
							0	3.57		
							5	3.70		
							10	2.33	Fresh.	
							15	2.27	Salt.	
							20	1.96	Strong salt.	

Observations in 1859–60—Continued.

Anchorage.	Hour.	Tide.			Wind.	Depth.		Velocity.	Water.	Remarks.
		High water.	Low water.	Oscillation.		Total.	Of float.			
	h. m.	*h. m.*	*h. m.*	*Inches.*		*Feet.*	*Feet.*	*Feet.*		
On bar, near middle of channel, 1600 feet above lower can buoy. Bottom hard sand.	2 15 p.m.	10 30 a.m.	10 30 p.m.	17.5	Calm.	21	0	3.70	Fresh.	*May* 20, 1859—continued. Long and even swells.
							5	4.00	"	
							10	4.00	"	
							15	3.03	Brackish.	
							20		Brackish and salt.	
							0	3.85		
							5	4.00		
							10	4.00		
							15	3.03		
							0	4.00		
							5	4.17		
							10	3.03		
							15	3.57		
							0	4.00		
							5	4.17		
							10	3.33		
							15	3.57		
In channel to west of centre, 800 feet above outer can buoy. Bottom mixed clay and sand; sticky.	3 30 p.m.	10 30 a.m.	10 30 p.m.	17.5	Calm.	30	0	4.00	Fresh.	Long and even swells. Strong salt-water at bottom.
							5	3.70	"	
							10	2.78	Brackish.	
							15	3.70	Salt.	
							20	2.27	"	
							25	2.17	"	
							0	4.17		
							5	3.85		
							10	2.86		
							15	2.94		
							20	2.63		
							25	2.04		
							0	4.35		
							5	3.57		
							10	2.78		
							15	3.23		
							20	2.70		
	4 10 p.m.						25	2.27		
Outside of bar, 400 feet sorthwest of outer can buoy. Same as at 9 30 a.m. May 12, and 7 a.m. May 14. Bottom hard, fine sand and blue clay.	4 15 p.m.	10 30 a.m.	10 30 p.m.	17.5	Calm.	42 and 43 and 45	0	4.17	Fresh.	Long and even swells. Closed observations at 5 30 p.m. Swells becoming heavy. Surface current strong, and hard to row against.
							5	3.45	Brackish.	
							10	2.85	Salt.	
							15	2.63	"	
							20	2.33	"	
							25	1.85	"	
							30	1.96	"	
							35	2.17	"	
							40	2.00	"	
							0	4.35		
							5	3.70		
							10	3.03		
							15	2.50		
							20	2.44		
							25	1.82		
							30	2.03		
							35	2.22		
							40	1.89		
	5 00 p.m.						0	4.35	Fresh.	
							5	3.57	Brackish.	
							10	3.13	Salt.	
							15	2.63	"	
							20	2.44	"	
							25	1.85	"	
							30	2.03	"	
							35	1.82	"	
	5 30 p.m.						40	1.75	"	
Near upper crest of bar, in east part of channel. Upper can buoy S. 60° W. 500 feet. Bottom sand.	6 30 a.m.	11 00 a.m.	11 00 p.m.	14	Calm.	17	0	3.33	Fresh.	*May* 21, 1859. Water surface even and smooth.
							5	3.33	"	
							10	2.78	"	
							15	3.13	"	
							0	3.33	"	
							5	2.86	"	
							10	3.13	"	
							15	2.63	"	
							0	3.23	"	
							5	3.13	"	
							10	2.94	"	
							15	2.86	"	
							0	3.23	"	
							5	3.13	"	
							10	3.03	"	
							15	2.78	"	

Observations in 1859–60—Continued.

Anchorage.	Hour.	Tide.			Wind.	Depth.		Velocity.	Water.	Remarks.
		High water.	Low water.	Oscillation.		Total.	Of float.			
	h. m.	*h. m.*	*h. m.*	*Inches.*		*Feet.*	*Feet.*	*Feet.*		
On bar, in east part of channel, about 400 feet below upper buoy, and 400 or 500 feet to east of line between upper and lower can buoys. Bottom hard sand; very little clay.	7 00 a.m.	11 00 a.m.	11 00 p.m.	14	Calm.	13	0	2.94	Fresh.	*May* 21, 1859—continued. Water surface smooth.
							5	2.86	"	
							10	2.17	"	
							0	2.86	"	
							5	2.86	"	
							10	2.08	"	
							0	2.94	"	
							5	2.86	"	
							10	2.38	"	
							0	2.94	"	
							5	2.63	"	
							10	2.17	"	
On bar, east of channel centre, 700 feet below last anchorage. Stake island (staff-post) N. 30° W. Bottom hard, fine sand.	8 00 a.m.	11 00 a.m.	11 00 p.m.	14	Calm.	15	0	2.70	"	Even water surface.
							5	2.70	"	
							10	2.27	"	
							0	2.56	"	
							5	2.56	"	
							10	2.22	"	
							0	2.63	"	
							5	2.50	"	
							10	2.27	"	
							0	2.70	"	
							5	2.56	"	
	8 30 a.m.						10	2.22	"	
On bar, east of line of buoys 400 or 500 feet, 1800 feet below upper can buoy. Stake island signal-post N. 8° W. Bell buoy S. 38° E. Bottom hard, fine sand and clay.	8 45 a.m.	11 00 a.m.	11 00 p.m.	14	Calm.	15	0	2.70	"	Quiet surface. Scattered mud lumps and shoal mud banks to SE. and NW.
							5	2.78	"	
							10	2.44	"	
							0	2.70	"	
							5	2.78	"	
							10	2.50	"	
							0	2.70	"	
							5	2.70	"	
							10	2.38	"	
On bar, east of channel centre, midway between upper and lower can buoys. Bottom equal parts fine sand and clay.	10 10 a.m.	11 00 a.m.	11 00 p.m.	14	Calm.	13	0	2.70	"	
							5	2.70	"	
							10	2.27	"	
					SE. light.		0	2.50	"	
							5	2.44	"	
							10	2.22	"	
In east part of channel, 70 feet east of east spar buoy. Lower can buoy S. 60° W. about 2500 feet. Bottom mixed clay and fine sand.	11 00 a.m.	11 00 a.m.	11 00 p.m.	14	SE. light.	24	0	3.23		Swells from S. and SE. East spar or breaker buoy is near east edge of channel, 2500 feet nearly NE. from outer can buoy.
							5	3.45	Fresh.	
							10	2.70	Brackish.	
							15	2.50	Salt.	
							20	2.00	"	
							0	3.33		
							5	3.45		
							10	2.38		
							15	2.27		
							20	1.96		
							0	3.45		
							5	3.23		
							10	2.38		
							15	2.38		
							20	1.75		
							5	3.23		
							20	1.72		
Same anchorage as last, near east spar buoy, 1600 feet above outer can buoy. Bottom clay and sand.	2 00 p.m.	11 00 a.m.	11 00 p.m.	14	Calm.	24	0	3.13		Very gentle, easy swells from SE. Mud lumps and mud-bank breakers 1500 to 1800 feet to E.
							5	3.57		
							10	2.63		
							15	2.86		
							20	1.92		
							0	3.70		
							5	3.45		
							10	2.56		
							15	2.50		
							20	1.96		
							0	3.70		
							5	3.57	Fresh.	
							10	2.70	Brackish.	
							15	2.50	Salt.	
							20	2.22	"	
Outside of bar, east of channel mouth, 800 feet NE. by E. from outer can buoy. Bottom fine, hard sand.	2 45 p.m.	11 00 a.m.	11 00 p.m.	14	Calm.	30	0	3.57		Long, dead swells from SE. Open sea to right and left. Current and tide meeting cause some irregularities in deep floats.
							5	3.03	Fresh.	
							10	2.04	Salt.	
							15	2.08	"	
							20	1.79	"	
							25	1.47	"	
	3 00 p.m.						0	3.57		
							5	2.94		
							10	2.04		
							15	2.17		
							20	1.72		
							25	1.33		
	3 15 p.m.						0	3.70		
							5	2.94		
							10	1.75		
							15	2.17		
							20	1.59		
	3 30 p.m.						25	1.32		

Observations in 1859–60—Continued.

Anchorage.	Hour.	Tide.			Wind.	Depth.		Velocity.	Water.	Remarks.
		High water.	Low water.	Oscillation.		Total.	Of float.			
	h. m.	*h. m.*	*h. m.*	*Inches.*		*Feet.*	*Feet.*	*Feet.*		
Outside of bar. Outer can buoy NW. by W. 800 feet. Bottom fine sand with some clay.	3 40 p.m.	11 00 a.m.	11 00 p.m.	11	Calm.	45 & 50	0	3.57		*May* 21, 1859—continued. Strong SE. swells; becoming by 4 30 p.m. too strong for further trials outside. Observations at 35 feet not reliable; rejected.
							5	2.94	Brackish.	
							10	2.17	Salt.	
							15	2.22	"	
							20	1.67	"	
							25	1.45	"	
							30	1.47	"	
							40	1.43	"	
							0	3.57	Fresh.	
							5	2.70	Brackish.	
							10	2.17	Salt.	
							15	2.22	"	
							20	1.79	"	
							25	1.59	"	
							30	1.47	"	
	4 30 p.m.						40	1.49	"	
Inside bar, near upper crest, 800 feet above upper can buoy. Bottom fine sand with some clay.	6 45 a.m.	1 30 p.m.	0 30 a.m. (May 25.)	9	Calm.	17	0	3.23	Fresh.	*May* 24, 1859. Even water surface. First four observations taken with Saxton's meter.
							0	3.33	"	
							0	3.23	"	
							0	3.33	"	
	7 00 a.m.						0	3.23	"	
							5	3.03	"	
							10	2.70	"	
							15	2.78	"	
					E. light.		0	3.13	"	
							5	2.94	"	
							10	2.50	"	
							15	2.44	"	
							0	3.03	"	
							5	2.78	"	
							10	2.44	"	
	7 45 a.m.						15	2.50	"	
100 feet west of upper can buoy. Bottom blue clay, sand and mud.	8 00 a.m.	1 30 p.m.	0 30 a.m. (May 25.)	9	Calm.	16	0	3.03	"	
							5	2.56	"	
							10	2.50	"	
							15	2.38	"	
	8 15 a.m.				E. light.		0	2.78	"	
							5	2.44	"	
							10	2.17	"	
							15	1.96	"	
							0	2.63	"	
							5	2.63	"	
							10	2.17	"	
							15	2.04	"	
							0	2.78	"	} Velocities measured with Saxton's meter.
							0	2.63	"	
							0	2.56	"	
	9 00 a.m.						0	2.56	"	
On bar in west part of channel, 2500 feet below upper can buoy. Bottom clay and fine sand.	10 30 a.m.	1 30 p.m.	0 30 a.m. (May 25.)	9	E. by S. gentle. (160 feet in 30 sec. by meter.)	17	5	2.56	"	Ripply surface.
							10	2.70	"	
							15	2.38	"	
250 feet to east of last anchorage. Bottom clay and sand.	10 40 a.m.	1 30 p.m.	0 30 a.m. (May 25.)	9	E. by S. gentle. (160 feet in 30 sec.)	17	5	2.78	"	Ripply surface.
							10	2.56	"	
							15	2.56	"	
							5	2.94	"	
							10	2.56	"	
	11 00 a.m.						15	2.63	"	
100 feet east of east breaker spar buoy; nearly same as 11 00 a.m. May 21. Bottom fine sand.	11 15 a.m.	1 30 p.m.	0 30 a.m. (May 25.)	9	E. by S.	33	5	2.78		Very lumpy bottom, with soundings at and around buoy from 14 to 33 feet. Open sea to WNW., and round S. to lower mud lumps to E. Rough river.
							10	2.50	"	
							15	2.17	Brackish.	
							20	1.19	Salt.	
							25	1.05	"	
							5	2.63		
					E. by S. fresh.		10	2.56		
							15	2.22		
							20	2.32		
							25	1.04		
							20	1.22		
	M.						25	1.01		
In east side of channel, 600 feet above east spar buoy. Bottom sandy.	2 15 p.m.	1 30 p.m.	0 30 a.m. (May 25.)	9	E. by N. light.	15	5	2.78	Fresh.	Water rough.
							10	2.78	"	
At east breaker buoy. Same as 11 15 a.m. Bell buoy bears S. 65° E. Outer mud lump S. 80° E. Bottom fine sand.	2 30 p.m.	1 30 p.m.	0 30 a.m. (May 25.)	9	E. by N.	33	5	2.38		Water rough.
							10	2.04	"	
							15	2.00	Brackish.	
							20	1.27	Salt.	
					E. by N.		5	2.44		SE. swells, increasing with wind.
							10	1.82		
							15	1.72		
							20	1.03		
					E. by N. fresh.		5	2.44		Wind by meter 400 feet in 30 seconds.
							10	2.04	Fresh.	
							15	1.85	Brackish.	
	3 30 p.m.						20	1.33	Salt.	

Observations in 1859–60—Continued.

Anchorage.	Hour.	Tide.			Wind.	Depth.		Velocity.	Water.	Remarks.
		High water.	Low water.	Oscillation.		Total.	Of float.			
	h. m.	*h. m.*	*h. m.*	*Inches.*		*Feet.*	*Feet.*	*Feet.*		
Near outer can buoy, outside of bar. Bottom fine sand and clay.	4 15 p.m.	1 30 p.m.	0 30 a.m. (May 25.)	9	E. by N.	35	5	2.17	Fresh.	*May* 24, 1859—continued. Long and even SE. swells.
							10	1.69	Brackish.	
							15	1.72	Salt.	
							20	1.47	"	
							25	1.25	"	
					E. fresh.		5	2.38		Wind and swells too strong for trial outside the buoy.
							10	1.82		
							15	1.79		
							20	1.49		
							25	1.30		
In river, 1000 feet above upper can buoy. Lower end pile-dam bears N. 73° E. Light-house N. 12° W. Stake island post, S. 70° W. Bottom hard, fine sand.	6 15 a.m.	3 00 a.m.	2 30 p.m.	4.5	E. light.	17	0	2.94	Fresh.	*May* 26, 1859.
							5	2.78	"	
							10	2.44	"	
							15	2.44	"	
							0	2.86	"	
							5	2.70	"	
							10	2.44	"	
							15	2.50	"	
							0	2.70	"	Velocities measured with Saxton's meter.
							0	2.70	"	
							0	2.78	"	
	7 00 a.m.						0	2.78	"	
800 feet northwest of upper can buoy. Bottom clean, fine sand.	7 15 a.m.	3 00 a.m.	2 30 p.m.	4.5	E. light.	17 & 18	0	2.94	"	
							5	2.70	"	
							10	2.86	"	
							15	2.78	"	
							5	2.94	"	
							10	3.03	"	
							15	2.63	"	
							0	2.86	"	Velocities measured with Saxton's meter.
							0	2.86	"	
							0	2.78	"	
							0	2.78	"	
On bar, in channel, 800 feet below upper can buoy. Bottom hard, fine sand.	7 45 a.m.	3 00 a.m.	2 30 p.m.	4.5	E. light.	17 & 18	5	3.13	"	Current meter works well, when it can be used or held in its place.
							10	3.13	"	
							15	3.23	"	
							5	3.33	"	
							10	3.18	"	
							15	2.94	"	
	8 00 a.m.						0	3.45	"	Velocities measured with Saxton's meter.
							0	3.28	"	
							0	3.33	"	
							0	3.23	"	
On bar, in channel, 2000 feet below upper can buoy. Bottom fine sand, with very little clay.	8 15 a.m.	3 00 a.m.	2 30 p.m.	4.5	E. light, increasing to fresh.	18	5	3.57	"	
							10	3.45	"	
							15	3.57	"	
							5	3.57	"	
							10	3.33	"	
							15	3.70	"	
							5	3.57	"	
							10	3.83	"	
							15	3.45	"	
							0	3.45	"	Velocities measured with Saxton's meter.
							0	3.33	"	
							0	3.70	"	
On bar and in channel, 2800 feet below upper can buoy. Bottom hard, fine sand, with some clay.	9 00 a.m.	3 00 a.m.	2 30 p.m.	4.5	E. fresh.	17	5	3.70	"	Wind 600 feet to one minute. Smooth water.
							10	3.57	"	
							15	3.57	"	
							5	3.70		
							10	3.45		
							15	3.57	"	
							0	3.70		Velocities measured with Saxton's meter.
							0	3.70		
							0	3.70		
	9 30 a.m.						0	3.70		
On bar and in channel, near midway between upper and outer buoys. Bottom clean, fine sand.	9 45 a.m.	3 00 a.m.	2 30 p.m.	4.5	E. fresh.	18	5	3.70	"	Water surface slightly rough. Breeze 600 feet to one minute.
							10	3.57		
							15	3.85		
							5	3.85		
							10	3.70		
							15	4.00		
							0	4.00		Velocities measured with Saxton's meter.
							0	4.00		
							0	4.00		
							0	4.00		

Observations in 1859–60—Continued.

Anchorage.	Hour.	Tide. High water.	Tide. Low water.	Tide. Oscillation.	Wind.	Depth. Total.	Depth. Of float.	Velocity.	Water.	Remarks.
	h. m.	*h. m.*	*h. m.*	*Inches.*		*Feet.*	*Feet.*	*Feet.*		
On bar, in channel, near basket buoy. Bottom hard and fine sand.	10 30 a.m.	3 00 a.m.	2 30 p.m.	4.5	E. fresh.	19	5	3.57	Fresh.	*May* 26, 1859—continued. Ripply surface, but no swells.
							10	3.33	"	
							15	3.45	"	
							5	3.33		
							10	3.70		
							15	3.57	"	
							0	3.45		Velocities measured with Saxton's meter.
							0	3.85		
							0	3.70		
	11 00 a.m.						0	3.70		
On bar, in west part of channel, 1200 feet above outer can buoy. Bottom fine, hard sand, with slimy clay and mud.	3 00 p.m.	3 00 a.m.	2 30 p.m.	4.5	SE. by E. light.	30	5	3.45	"	SE. swells, even. Bottom lumpy, giving soundings 15, 17, 20, 25, and 30 feet. New spar barrel buoy placed here.
							10	2.78	Brackish.	
							15	2.63	Strong salt.	
							5	3.57		
							10	2.94		
							15	2.50		
							0	3.85		Velocities measured with Saxton's meter.
							0	3.85		
							0	3.85		
	3 30 p.m.						0	3.70		
Outside of bar at mouth of channel, 400 feet northwest of buoy. Bottom fine sand, with some clay.	3 45 p.m.	3 00 a.m.	2 30 p.m.	4.5	Calm.	32	5	3.23	Strong brackish.	Even SE. swells, increasing. Too rough below outer buoy for floats.
							10	2.70	Salt.	
							15	2.33	Strong salt.	
							20	2.00	" "	
							25	1.39	" "	
	4 00 p.m.						5	3.13		
							10	2.33		
							15	2.22		
							20	1.67		
							25	1.33		
							30	1.49		
At new bush buoy, in west part of channel, near 1200 feet above (N. 5° E. from) east breaker buoy. Bottom hard sand, with some clay.	7 00 a.m.	4 00 a.m.	3 30 p.m.	8	Calm.	18 & 19	5	3.33	Fresh.	*May* 27, 1859. Smooth surface. Old basket buoy is about midway between this lower bush buoy and the east breaker buoy.
							10	3.13	"	
							15	2.63	"	
							5	3.45	"	
							10	2.94	"	
							15	2.86	"	
							0	3.33	"	Velocities measured with Saxton's meter.
							0	3.23	"	
							0	3.33	"	
							0	3.33	"	
Outside of bar, 400 feet southwest of outer can buoy. Same as May 12 and 14. Bottom fine sand and clay.	7 45 a.m.	4 00 a.m.	3 30 p.m.	8	N. by W. light.	45	5	2.70	Brackish.	Smooth water.
							10	2.04	Salt.	
							15	1.75	"	
							20	1.43	"	
							25	1.39	"	
							5	2.78		
							10	2.08		
							15	1.85		
							20	1.67		
							25	1.35		
							35	2.25		
					200 feet per minute by meter.		0	3.13	Fresh.	Velocities measured with Saxton's meter.
							0	3.23	"	
							0	3.45	"	
	8 30 a.m.						0	3.57	"	
Outside of bar, west of channel mouth. Outer buoy S. 15° E. 700 feet. Bottom hard, fine sand, with very little clay.	8 45 a.m.	4 00 a.m.	3 30 p.m.	8	N. by W. gentle.	32	5	2.56	Brackish.	Smooth water.
							10	2.04	Salt.	
							15	1.79	"	
							20	1.61	"	
							25	1.32	"	
							5	2.70		
							10	2.00		
							15	1.75		
							20	1.32		
							25	1.27		
							5	2.38		
							30	1.23		
							0	3.33	Fresh.	Velocities measured with Saxton's meter.
							0	3.45	"	
							0	3.33	"	
	9 30 a.m.						0	3.33	"	

Observations in 1859–60—Continued.

Anchorage.	Hour.	Tide.			Wind.	Depth.		Velocity.	Water.	Remarks.
		High water.	Low water.	Oscillation.		Total.	Of float.			
	h. m.	*h. m.*	*h. m.*	*Inches.*		*Feet.*	*Feet.*	*Feet.*		
Outside of bar, 1200 feet east from outer can buoy. Bottom hard and fine sand, with some clay.	9 45 a.m.	4 00 a.m.	3 30 p.m.	8	Calm.	35	5	2.70	Brackish.	*May* 27, 1859—continued. Rapid surface current.
							10	1.89	Salt.	
							15	1.79	"	
							20	1.59	"	
							25	1.27	"	
							5	2.78	Brackish.	
							10	2.00	Salt.	
							15	1.89	"	
							20	1.49	"	
							25	1.20	"	
	10 15 a.m.						5	2.78	Brackish.	
							30	1.32	Salt.	
							0	3.45	Fresh.	Velocities measured with Saxton's meter.
							0	3.70	"	
							0	3.70	"	
							0	3.85	"	
On bar at east breaker buoy (east spar buoy). Same as 11 a.m. May 25. Bottom lumpy and soft.	11 00 a.m.	4 00 a.m.	3 30 p.m.	8	Calm.	15	5	3.13	Fresh.	Sounding 19 feet at lower boat. 15 feet float touched bottom. At this east spar buoy there was a mud lump, said to have disappeared soon after great gale of August, 1856.
							10	2.44	Brackish.	
							15		Salt.	
							5	2.78		
							10	2.33		
							14	1.75		
							0	2.63		Velocities measured with Saxton's meter.
							0	2.78		
	M.						0	2.70		
Near lower bush buoy; in west part of channel. Bottom sand and clay.	4 30 p.m.	4 00 a.m.	3 30 p.m.	8	Calm.	18	5	4.00	Fresh.	Smooth water.
							10	3.85	"	
							15	3.85	"	
							5	4.00	"	
							10	3.85	"	
							15	3.70	"	
In centre of channel, 400 feet south of basket buoy. Bottom hard sand.	4 45 p.m.	4 00 a.m.	3 30 p.m.	8	Calm.	18	5	3.70	"	Smooth water.
							10	3.45	"	
							15	3.23	"	
							5	3.70	"	
							10	3.57	"	
							15	3.33	"	

It is shown by an experiment made on the 17th August, that when the exposed surface of the surface float was one-fifth that of the sub-surface float, and the surface current was 2 feet per second, and the sub-surface float was in still water, the latter was dragged by the former about 0.4 of a foot per second.

Anchorage.	Hour.	Tide.			Wind.	Depth.		Velocity.	Water.	Remarks.
		High water.	Low water.	Oscillation.		Total.	Of float.			
	h. m.	*h. m.*	*h. m.*	*Inches.*		*Feet.*	*Feet.*	*Feet.*		
At upper can buoy.	10 00 a.m.	8 30 a.m.	8 30 p.m.	19.5	S. and E.	19	0	2.20	Fresh.	*August* 13, 1859. Wind from S. and E. during this and several previous days. High tide at 8 30 a.m. reads 26.5 inches. Up-stream current beginning at 15 feet and increasing to bottom, float being suspended by twine held in hand.
							5		Brackish.	
							10		Salt.	
							14	0.00	"	
							Bottom.	—0.80	"	

Observations in 1859–60—Continued.

Anchorage.	Hour.	Tide.			Wind.	Depth.		Velocity.	Water.	Remarks.
		High water.	Low water.	Oscillation.		Total.	Of float.			
	h. m.	*h. m.*	*h. m.*	*Inches.*		*Feet.*	*Feet.*	*Feet.*		
At lower bush buoy; on outer crest of bar.	11 00 a.m.	8 30 a.m.	8 30 p.m.	19.5	S. and E.	20.0	0 5 12 Bottom.	 0.00 —1.00	Brackish. Salt. " "	*August* 13, 1859—continued. Up-stream current at 12 feet, increasing to bottom; rather stronger than at can buoy. Depth and velocity of salt-water moving up stream are greater here than at inner end of bar, yet velocity of upper stratum of fresh-water is much less; in fact it is nearly all checked and dispersed. If the refluent sub-surface current were due to an eddy force generated by the river-water, the reverse would be the case. It is probable that a mass of salt-water, forced up for several days, is pouring out; and it is possible that at this position, on outer crest of bar, part of the up-stream current at bottom is an eddy current, occasioned by the salt-water pouring out over the bar and coming in contact with the still water of the gulf.
Near upper can buoy.	M.	8 30 a.m.	8 30 p.m.	19.5	S. and E.	19.0	5 10 16 Bottom.		Brackish. Salt. " "	Up-stream current at 16 feet, increasing to bottom.
At upper can buoy.	11 00 a.m.	11 00 a.m.	10 30 p.m.	8.0	SSW. fresh.	18.5	0 5 10 12.5 15 Bottom.	2.37 2.24 1.90 1.00	Fresh. " Little brackish. Salt. " "	*August* 16, 1859. Below 15 feet, water nearly stationary; slight up-stream motion, which could not be measured. No eddy, but actual outpouring of salt-water. It may be that the water is still, below 15 feet, because the tide is just ceasing to run up.
On board pilot-schooner, on bar. Near upper can buoy.	3 00 p.m.	11 00 a.m.	10 30 p.m.	8.0	SSW.	16.0	0 5 10 15 Bottom.	2.37 1.74 0.85 0.48	Fresh. " Salt. " "	Below 15 feet, slight up-stream current. Outpouring of salt-water evidently not from vertical eddy, for there is no corresponding inward movement to maintain the supply.
Near upper can buoy.	7 30 a.m.	11 00 a.m.	4 00 p.m.	1.0	W. light.	19.0	0 5 10 15 18 Bottom.	3.17 2.71 1.73 1.27 0.76	Fresh. " Brackish. Salt. " "	*August* 17, 1859. No refluent sub-surface current. Salt-water evidently carried seaward by fresh-water. Very little tide. Slight oscillations in level of gulf.

Observations in 1859–60—Continued.

Anchorage.	Hour.	Tide.			Wind.	Depth.		Velocity.	Water.	Remarks.
		High water.	Low water.	Oscillation.		Total.	Of floats.			
	h. m.	*h. m.*	*h. m.*	*Inches.*		*Feet.*	*Feet.*	*Feet.*		
On outer crest of bar.	9 00 a.m.	11 00 a.m.	4 00 p.m.	1	Calm.	16.5	0 5 10 13 Bottom.	2.11 1.27 0.53 0.18	Fresh. " Brackish. Salt. "	*August* 17, 1859—continued. Float at 13 feet stopped several times for 4 or 5 seconds. In subsequent hand-experiment, no current at 12 feet. Refluent current increasing thence to bottom. That is, a stratum of salt-water 2 feet thick (from 8 to 10 feet depth) moves outward with a mean velocity of 0.3 of a foot per second, and a stratum of salt-water 4 feet thick at bottom should move in to supply it at a mean velocity of 0.15 of a foot per second, but it is evident from the remarks of the observer that the velocity was greater than this, and it appears that much more salt-water was passing in than out. But if there is a vertical eddy, that portion of velocity at the bottom due to it could not have exceeded 0.3 of a foot per second, and we have a surface velocity of 2 feet per second, giving the first particles of still salt-water with which it is in contact, a velocity of 0.6 of a foot per second, creating an eddy, the greatest velocity of which, along the bottom, could not have exceeded 0.3 of a foot per second.
On outer crest of bar.	2 00 p.m.		1 00 p.m.	18	NNE. and E.	16	0 5 10 15		Fresh. Brackish. Salt. "	*September* 2, 1859. No refluent sub-surface current perceptible at any depth.
	3 00 p.m.						0 5 10 15		Fresh. Brackish. Salt. "	
Same anchorage.	4 00 p.m.		1 00 p.m.	18	ESE.	16.5	0 5 10 15		Fresh. Salt. " "	Slight refluent sub-surface current from 15 to 16½ feet; effect of wind and tide.
Same anchorage.	5 00 p.m.		1 00 p.m.	18		17	0 5 10 15 17		Fresh. Salt. " " "	Refluent sub-surface current from 12 to 17 feet. Increases in strength as the tide does.
Outer crest of bar; westerly edge of channel.	7 30 a.m.	0 30 a.m	2 00 p.m.	21	S. light.	16.5	0 5 10 15 16	2.00 1.54 0.86 0.71	Fresh. Brackish. Salt. "	*September* 3, 1859. No perceptible refluent sub-surface current at any depth. At surface, current sets to SSW.; at 10 feet, to southward.
Same anchorage.	9 00 a.m	0 30 a.m.	2 00 p.m.	21	S. light.	16	0 5 10 15 16	2.31 1.58 0.86 0.81	Fresh. Brackish. Salt. "	No perceptible refluent sub-surface current, yet if the eddy theory were correct, it would have been found. The salt-water moving seaward is evidently the pouring back by fall of tide, of what the river received from rise of tide. Now here is evidently an outward current on the bottom greater than that of any refluent sub-surface current yet measured, at the very time when, by the eddy theory, the eddy current should be found to the upper end of the bar.

Observations in 1859–60—Continued.

Anchorage.	Hour.	Tide.			Wind.	Depth.		Velocity.	Water.	Remarks.
		High water.	Low water.	Oscillation.		Total.	Of float.			
	h. m.	*h. m.*	*h. m.*	*Inches.*		*Feet.*	*Feet.*	*Feet.*		
Outside of bar.	10 00 a.m.	2 00 a.m.	3 30 p.m.	20	NW. light.	24	0 5 10 15 20 22 24	3.16 2.31 1.22 1.11 0.92 	Fresh. Salt. " " " " "	*September* 5, 1859. No perceptible refluent sub-surface current.
Outside of bar (same as last).	2 45 p.m.	2 00 a.m.	3 30 p.m.	20	NNE. fresh.	24	0 5 10 15 20 22 24	3.33 2.40 1.20 1.02 0.90 	Fresh. Brackish. Salt. " " " "	No perceptible refluent sub-surface current. If such current be the effect of wind and tide, we ought not to expect one under the above circumstances. If the effect of an eddy, it ought to have been found.
On outer crest of bar.	7 35 a.m.	3 30 a.m.	4 30 p.m.	20	NE. fresh.	16.5	0 5 10 15		Fresh. Brackish. Salt. "	*September* 6, 1859. No perceptible refluent current at any depth. Water too rough for velocity experiments.
										September 7, 8, and 9, 1859. Northeasterly storm.
On outer crest of bar in east edge of channel.	10 00 a.m.	7 30 a.m.	7 00 p.m.	15	ENE. fresh.	18	0 5 10 16 18		Fresh. Brackish. Salt. " "	*September* 10, 1859.
On crest of bar, in east edge of channel.	M.	7 30 a.m.	7 00 p.m.	15	ENE. fresh.	16	0 5 10 12 15 16	2.69 1.50 0.57 0.63 	Fresh. Brackish. Salt. " " "	No perceptible refluent current at any depth. At surface, current sets SW.; at 10 feet, to eastward.

On November 10, 1859, Mr. Fuller writes: "I can only say that I have repeatedly made the experiment (between the 1st June and the present time) with the large sub-float, suspended by a fine twine, the end held in the hand; but that, until the 13th August, I was unable to detect a decided refluent sub-current, which current I am satisfied increases as the river falls."

Observations of December 15, 1859, at half flood. Tide 8 inches. Wind northerly and light. Gauge at Carrollton 5.6 feet. A great tide two or three days before.

At upper can buoy; depth 18 feet. Water fresh from surface to bottom. Current at bottom not nearly as strong as at the surface; about the same difference as in previous experiments, viz.: from 0.5 of a foot to 1 foot per second.

At upper bush buoy; depth 18.5 feet. Water fresh from surface to bottom.

Outside of bar; depth 20 feet. Water fresh from surface to 5 feet; brackish at 10 feet; salt from 15 feet to bottom.

No refluent sub-surface current at any place. Strong surface current running out.

Observations of January 5, 1860, at half flood; the sub-surface current being sought for as usual by means of a tin sub-surface float suspended from the hand by a small twine. Tide 22 inches. Northerly breeze. Gauge at Carrollton 8.0 feet.

Outside of bar; depth 30 feet. Water at surface fresh; brackish at 4 feet; salt from 5 feet to bottom. No refluent sub-surface current.

Outside of bar; depth 20 feet. Water fresh at surface; brackish at 5 feet; salt from 10 feet to bottom. No current at bottom; at 5 feet above, slightly outward.

On crest of bar; depth 14.5 feet. Water fresh at surface; brackish at 5 feet; salt from 10 feet to bottom. A very slight refluent current at bottom.

Inside of bar; depth 18 feet. Water fresh from surface to 10 feet; brackish from 15 feet to bottom. No refluent sub-surface current. Current at bottom not nearly as strong as at the surface; about the same difference as in previous experiments, viz.: from 0.5 of a foot to 1 foot per second.

Observations of February 3, 1860, at two-thirds flood. Tide 18 inches. Wind northerly and fresh. Gauge at Carrollton 12.7 feet.

Inside of bar; depth 18 feet. Water fresh from surface to bottom. No refluent sub-surface current. Slow current running out at and near bottom.

On bar, at middle bush buoy; depth 17 feet. Observations same as above.

On bar, at outer edge; depth 15 feet. Observations same as above.

Outside of bar; depth 30 feet. Water fresh at surface; brackish at 5 feet; salt from 10 feet to bottom. Strong refluent sub-surface current.

Observations of February 4, 1860, at high tide. Tide 26 inches. Wind east, light. Gauge at Carrollton, 12.8 feet.

Inside of bar; depth 18 feet. Water fresh from surface to bottom. No refluent sub-surface current. Slow current running out at and near bottom.

On bar, at middle bush buoy; depth 17.5 feet. Observations same as above.

On bar, at outer edge; depth 16 feet. Observations same as above.

Outside of bar; depth 30 feet. Water brackish at 5 feet; salt from 7 feet to bottom. Slow refluent sub-surface current.

Observations of February 6, 1860, at half flood. Tide 19 inches. Wind northerly and fresh. Gauge at Carrollton 13.4 feet.

Inside of bar; depth 18 feet. Water fresh from surface to bottom. No refluent sub-surface current.

On bar, at middle bush buoy; depth 17 feet. Observations same as preceding.

On bar, at outer edge; depth 16 feet. Observations same as preceding.

Outside of bar; depth 31 feet. Water brackish at 4 feet; salt from 7 feet to bottom. Very slight refluent sub-surface current.

Observations of February 8, 1860, at half flood. Tide not recorded, as the gauge was out of order. Being a neap tide, it was small. Wind westerly and light.

At outer edge of bar; depth 14 feet. No salt-water. No refluent sub-surface current.

Observations of February 9, 1860, at low tide. Tide not recorded, as the gauge was out of order. Being a neap tide, it was small. Wind westerly and light. Gauge at Carrollton 12.8 feet.

Inside of bar; depth 18 feet. No salt-water. No refluent sub-surface current.

On bar, at middle bush buoy; depth 16.5 feet. Observations same as above.

On bar, at outer edge; depth 15 feet. Observations same as above.

Outside of bar; depth 30 feet. Water brackish at 4 feet; salt from 6 feet to bottom. No refluent sub-surface current perceptible.

Observations of February 10, 1860, at high tide. Tide not recorded, as the gauge was out of order. Being near the neap tide, it was less than a foot. Wind northerly and light. Gauge at Carrollton 12.6 feet.

On bar; depth 16 feet. No salt-water. No refluent sub-surface current.

Outside of bar; depth 30 feet. Water brackish at 4 feet; salt from 5 feet to bottom. Slight refluent sub-surface current.

Observations of March 3, 1860, at three-fourths flood-tide. Tide 14 inches. Wind easterly and light. Gauge at Carrollton 12.5 feet.

On crest of bar; depth 14.5 feet. No salt-water. No refluent sub-surface current. Surface current 4.03 feet per second.

Observations of March 5, 1860, at half flood-tide. Tide 15 inches. Wind southeast, light. Gauge at Carrollton 12.7 feet.

On outer crest of bar; depth 14 feet. No salt-water. No refluent sub-surface current. Surface velocity 3.99 feet per second.

Outside of bar; depth 20 feet. Water fresh from surface to 15 feet; salt at 18 feet. No refluent sub-surface current perceptible.

Outside of bar; depth 30 feet. Water fresh at surface; brackish at 7 feet; salt from 10 feet to bottom. Slight refluent sub-surface current.

Observations of March 8, 1860. No perceptible tide. Wind southerly and light. Gauge at Carrollton 13.1 feet.

Inside of bar; depth 18 feet. No salt-water. No refluent sub-surface current.

On outer crest of bar; depth 15 feet. No salt-water. No refluent sub-surface current.

Outside of bar; depth 20 feet. Water fresh from surface to 12 feet; brackish at 14 feet; salt from 16 feet to bottom. Refluent sub-surface current just perceptible.

Outside of bar; depth 30 feet. Water fresh from surface to 10 feet; brackish at 12 feet; salt from 15 feet to bottom. Slight refluent sub-surface current.

In all cases, the current near the bottom, when not refluent, was sluggish; more so, however, on the bar and outside than inside, although in the latter cases it was invariably much slower than at the surface.

Observations of March 18, 1860, at half flood-tide. Tide 8 inches. No swell or wind. Gauge at Carrollton 13.2 feet.

Outside of bar; depth 20 feet. Water fresh from surface to 5 feet; brackish at 7 feet; salt from 10 feet to bottom. No current at bottom either way.

Outside of bar; depth 30 feet. Water fresh from surface to 4 feet; brackish at 5 feet; salt from 6 feet to bottom. No current at bottom.

Within and near outer edge of bar; depth 17 feet. Water fresh from surface to 10 feet; brackish at 12 feet; salt from 13 feet to bottom. Very slow outward current at bottom. Surface current 3.08 feet per second.

Inside of bar, at upper can buoy; depth 18 feet. Water fresh, with outward current, from surface to bottom.

Observations of March 24, 1860, at half flood-tide. Tide 9 inches. Wind westerly and light. Gauge at Carrollton 12.9 feet.

Outside of bar; depth 20 feet. Water fresh from surface to 5 feet; brackish at 6 feet; salt from 7 feet to bottom. Slow refluent current at bottom.

Outside of bar; depth 30 feet. Water fresh from surface to 4 feet; brackish at 5 feet; salt from 6 feet to bottom. Very slow refluent current at bottom.

Outer edge of bar; depth 16.5 feet. Water fresh from surface to 10 feet; brackish at 11 feet; salt from 13 feet to bottom. No current either way at bottom.

Inside of bar, at upper can buoy; depth 18 feet. Water fresh, with outward current, from surface to bottom.

Observations of March 26, 1860, at three-fourths flood-tide. Tide 10 inches. Wind northeasterly and light. Gauge at Carrollton 12.8 feet.

Outside of bar; depth 22 feet. Water salt from 6 feet to bottom. Slow refluent current at bottom.

Outside of bar; depth 30 feet. Water salt from 4 feet to bottom. Slow refluent current at bottom.

Observations of March 29, 1860, at three-fourths flood-tide. Tide 12 inches. Wind westerly and light. Gauge at Carrollton 12.3 feet.

Outside of bar; depth 20 feet. Water fresh from surface to 6 feet; brackish at 7 feet; salt from 8 feet to bottom. Slow refluent current at bottom.

Outside of bar; depth 30 feet. Water brackish at 4 feet; salt from 5 feet to bottom. Strong refluent sub-surface current.

On bar; depth 16.5 feet. Water fresh from surface to 10 feet; brackish at 12 feet; salt from 14 feet to bottom. No current either way at bottom.

Inside of bar, at upper can buoy; depth 18 feet. Water fresh, with outward current from surface to bottom. Current at bottom about half that at the surface, say 1.47 feet per second.

Observations of April 6, 1860, at one-fourth ebb-tide. Tide 12 inches. Wind northeasterly and light. Gauge at Carrollton 9.8 feet.

On outer crest of bar; depth 15 feet. Water fresh from surface to 10 feet; brackish at 12 feet; salt from 14 feet to bottom. No current at bottom.

Observations of April 7, 1860, at one-fourth ebb-tide. Tide 17 inches. Wind SSE., light. Gauge at Carrollton 9.6 feet.

On outer crest of bar; depth 15 feet. Water fresh from surface to 10 feet; brackish at 12 feet; salt from 14 feet to bottom. No current at bottom.

Observations of April 12, 1860, at one-half ebb-tide. Tide 12 inches. Wind northerly and light.

Outside of bar; depth 20 feet. Water fresh at surface; brackish at 7 feet; salt from 12 feet to bottom. Slight refluent current at bottom.

Outside of bar; depth 30 feet. Water fresh at surface; brackish at 3 feet; salt from 8 feet to bottom. Slight refluent sub-surface current.

On outer crest of bar; depth 16 feet. Water fresh at surface; brackish at 5 feet; salt from 10 feet to bottom. Slight refluent sub-surface current.

Inside of bar, at upper can buoy; depth 18 feet. Water fresh from surface to bottom. No refluent sub-surface current.

Observations of April 18, 1860. No perceptible tide. Wind fresh from southeast. Heavy swell outside of bar. Gauge at Carrollton 5.8 feet.

On outer crest of bar; depth 16 feet. Water fresh at surface; brackish at 6 feet; salt from 8 feet to bottom. Strong refluent sub-surface current.

Observations of April 19, 1860, at one-half ebb-tide. Tide 7 inches. Wind fresh from southeast. Heavy swell outside of bar. Gauge at Carrollton 5.5 feet.

On outer crest of bar; depth 16 feet. Water fresh from surface to 10 feet; brackish at 11 feet; salt from 13 feet to bottom. Very slight refluent current at bottom, scarcely perceptible.

Inside of bar, at upper can buoy; depth 18 feet. Water fresh from surface to 16 feet; brackish from 17 feet to bottom. Slight outward current at bottom.

Observations of April 21, 1860, at three-fourths ebb-tide. Tide 18 inches. Wind fresh from southeast. Heavy sea outside of bar. Gauge at Carrollton 5.4 feet.

On outer crest of bar; depth 16 feet. Water fresh from surface to 8 feet; brackish at 10 feet; salt from 11 feet to bottom. Slight outward current at bottom, increasing to surface.

Inside of bar, at upper can buoy; depth 18 feet. Water fresh from surface to 17 feet; slightly brackish thence to bottom. Slow outward current at bottom.

Observations of April 23, 1860; begun at one-fourth ebb-tide, concluded at one-half ebb. Tide 23 inches. Calm. Gauge at Carrollton 5.3 feet.

Inside of bar, near upper can buoy; depth 19 feet. Water fresh from surface to 10 feet; brackish at 15 feet; salt at bottom. Surface current 1.93 feet per second; slow outward current at 15 feet; slow refluent current from 18 feet to bottom.

Three-fourths of a mile above outer edge of bar, a little west of channel; depth 15 feet. Water fresh from surface to 10 feet; brackish at 12 feet; salt at bottom. No current either way at bottom. Slow outward current thence to surface.

Half a mile above outer edge of bar, east of channel; depth 17 feet. Water fresh from surface to 10 feet; brackish at 11 feet; salt from 12 feet to bottom. Slight refluent current at bottom. Surface current 1.92 feet per second.

Near outer crest of bar; depth 16 feet. Water fresh from surface to 9 feet; brackish at 10 feet; salt from 11 feet to bottom. Slight refluent current at bottom. Surface current 1.77 feet per second.

Outside of bar; depth 20 feet. Water fresh from surface to 5 feet; brackish at 6 feet; salt from 7 feet to bottom. Slow refluent current at bottom.

Outside of bar; depth 30 feet. Water fresh from surface to 5 feet; brackish at 6 feet; salt at 7 feet. Very slow refluent current at bottom.

Observations of April 27, 1860, at one-half ebb-tide. Tide 19 inches. Wind northeasterly and light. Gauge at Carrollton 7.0 feet.

Near outer crest of bar; depth 16 feet. Water fresh at surface; brackish at 5 feet; salt from 7 feet to bottom. Slight refluent current at bottom.

Observations of April 28, 1860, at three-fourths ebb-tide. Tide 8 inches. Wind light from NNW. Gauge at Carrollton 7.5 feet.

Near outer crest of bar, a little to the eastward of the channel; depth 15 feet. Water fresh at surface; brackish at 4 feet; salt from 7 feet to bottom. Slight refluent current at 10 feet; strong at 15 feet.

Observations of April 30, 1860, at one-half ebb-tide. Tide 6 inches. Wind southeasterly and light. Gauge at Carrollton 8.8 feet.

Near outer crest of bar; depth 16 feet. Water fresh from surface to 5 feet; brackish at 7 feet; salt from 10 feet to bottom. Slight refluent current at bottom.

Observations of May 1, 1860, at one-half ebb-tide. Tide 6 inches. Wind northerly; stiff breeze. Gauge at Carrollton 9.4 feet.

Near outer crest of bar; depth 16 feet. Water fresh from surface to 5 feet; brackish at 9 feet; salt from 11 feet to bottom; slight refluent current at bottom.

Observations of May 4, 1860, at three-fourths ebb-tide. Tide 16 inches. Wind northerly, light. Gauge at Carrollton 10.7 feet. River rising at Carrollton at the rate of 1 foot in two days.

Near outer crest of bar; depth 16.5 feet. Water fresh from surface to 10 feet; brackish at 11 feet; salt from 12 feet to bottom. Strong outward current at bottom.

Observations of May 16, 1860, at one-half ebb-tide. Tide 8 inches. Wind southerly, light. Gauge at Carrollton 7.1 feet.

On outer crest of bar; depth 16.5 feet. Water fresh at surface; brackish at 7 feet; salt at 10 feet. Outward current to 14 feet; thence to bottom slight refluent current.

Observations of May 18, 1860, at one-half ebb-tide. Tide 13 inches. Wind light from SSW. Gauge at Carrollton 5.6 feet.

On outer crest of bar; depth 16.5 feet. Water fresh at surface; brackish at 8 feet; salt at 10 feet. Outward current from surface to bottom.

Observations of May 23, 1860, at one-fourth ebb-tide. Tide 26 inches. Wind south, light. Gauge at Carrollton 3.9 feet.

On outer crest of bar; depth 16.5 feet. Water fresh at surface; brackish at 5 feet; salt at 7 feet. Outward current from surface to 14 feet; slight refluent current at bottom.

Observations of May 25, 1860, at young ebb-tide. Tide 19 inches. Wind fresh from southwest. Gauge at Carrollton 3.5 feet.

On outer crest of bar; depth 17 feet. Water fresh at surface; brackish at 5 feet; salt from 8 feet to bottom. Slow refluent current at bottom.

Observations of May 31, 1860, at low tide. Tide 19 inches. Light breeze from WSW. Gauge at Carrollton 3.6 feet.

On outer crest of bar; depth 16 feet. Water fresh at surface; brackish at 7 feet; salt from 8 feet to bottom. No current either way at bottom.

Observations of June 1, 1860, at one-fourth ebb-tide. Tide 22 inches. Light breeze from SSW. Gauge at Carrollton 3.4 feet.

On outer crest of bar; depth 16 feet. Water fresh at surface; brackish at 5 feet; salt from 6 feet to bottom. Under current commences running in slowly at 9 feet, and increases to strong refluent current at bottom.

Observations of June 2, 1860, at young ebb-tide (one hour). Tide 25 inches. Light breeze from south. Gauge at Carrollton 4.0 feet.

On outer crest of bar; depth 16 feet. Water fresh at surface; brackish at 3 feet; salt from 5 feet to bottom. Refluent current begins at 8 feet, and increases in velocity to bottom.

ERRATA—PLATE II.

Lake St. Mary, west of New Madrid, the name of which is omitted on the Map, should be colored *blue*.

Big Prairie, on the eastern border of this lake, is erroneously colored *brown;* it is above overflow, and should be *white*. Part of the continuation of the same ridge on the east bank of the river is also erroneously colored *brown*.

On the Atchafalaya, near the word Bayou, a *white* space erroneously indicates land above overflow; the space should be colored *brown*.

There are spots of *white* at the head of Grand Lake, in that lake, and on Bayou Terre-Bonne, all of which should be colored *brown*.

There are two small lakes in the marsh southeast of New Orleans, which should be colored *blue*.

www.ingramcontent.com/pod-product-compliance
Lightning Source LLC
LaVergne TN
LVHW021104110826
845150LV00001B/162